Twentieth-Century Literary Criticism

Guide to Gale Literary Criticism Series

When you need to review criticism of literary works, these are the Gale series to use:

If the author's death date is:

You should turn to:

After Dec. 31, 1959
(or author is still living)

CONTEMPORARY LITERARY CRITICISM

for example: Jorge Luis Borges, Anthony Burgess,
William Faulkner, Mary Gordon,
Ernest Hemingway, Iris Murdoch

1900 through 1959

TWENTIETH-CENTURY LITERARY CRITICISM

for example: Willa Cather, F. Scott Fitzgerald,
Henry James, Mark Twain, Virginia Woolf

1800 through 1899

NINETEENTH-CENTURY LITERATURE CRITICISM

for example: Fyodor Dostoevsky, Nathaniel Hawthorne,
George Sand, William Wordsworth

1400 through 1799

LITERATURE CRITICISM FROM 1400 TO 1800
(excluding Shakespeare)

for example: Anne Bradstreet, Daniel Defoe,
Alexander Pope, François Rabelais,
Jonathan Swift, Phillis Wheatley

SHAKESPEAREAN CRITICISM

Shakespeare's plays and poetry

Antiquity through 1399

CLASSICAL AND MEDIEVAL LITERATURE CRITICISM

for example: Dante, Homer, Plato, Sophocles, Vergil,
the Beowulf Poet

Gale also publishes related criticism series:

CHILDREN'S LITERATURE REVIEW

This series covers authors of all eras who have written for
the preschool through high school audience.

SHORT STORY CRITICISM

This series covers the major short fiction writers of all nationalities
and periods of literary history.

POETRY CRITICISM

This series covers poets of all nationalities, movements, and periods of
literary history.

ISSN 0276-8178

R

Volume 32

Twentieth-Century Literary Criticism

**Excerpts from Criticism of the
Works of Novelists, Poets, Playwrights,
Short Story Writers, and Other Creative Writers
Who Died between 1900 and 1960,
from the First Published Critical Appraisals
to Current Evaluations**

**Paula Kepos
Dennis Poupard
Editors**

**Marie Lazzari
Thomas Ligotti
Joann Prosyniuk
Associate Editors**

 Gale Research Inc. · *DETROIT* · *LONDON*

STAFF

Paula Kepos, Dennis Poupard, *Editors*

Marie Lazzari, Thomas Ligotti, Joann Prosyniuk, *Associate Editors*

Keith E. Schooley, Laurie A. Sherman, *Senior Assistant Editors*

Sandra Liddell, Timothy Veeser, *Assistant Editors*

Thomas J. Votteler, *Contributing Editor*

Susan Miller Harig, Melissa Reiff Hug, Debra A. Wells, *Contributing Assistant Editors*

Jeanne A. Gough, *Permissions & Production Manager*
Linda M. Pugliese, *Production Supervisor*
Christine A. Galbraith, David G. Oblender, Suzanne Powers, Linda M. Ross,
Lee Ann Welsh, *Editorial Assistants*
Maureen A. Puhl, *Senior Manuscript Assistant*
Donna Craft, Jennifer E. Gale, *Manuscript Assistants*

Victoria B. Cariappa, *Research Supervisor*
Maureen R. Richards, *Research Coordinator*
Mary D. Wise, *Senior Research Assistant*
Rogene M. Fisher, Kevin B. Hillstrom, Karen D. Kaus, Eric Priehs,
Filomena Sgambati, *Research Assistants*

Janice M. Mach, *Text Permissions Supervisor*
Kathy Grell, Mabel E. Gurney, Josephine M. Keene, *Permissions Coordinators*
Kimberly F. Smilay, *Senior Permissions Assistant*
H. Diane Cooper, *Permissions Assistant*
Melissa A. Brantley, Denise M. Singleton, Sharon D. Valentine,
Lisa M. Lantz, *Permissions Clerks*

Patricia A. Seefelt, *Picture Permissions Supervisor*
Margaret A. Chamberlain, *Picture Permissions Coordinator*
Pamela A. Hayes, Lillian Quickley, *Permissions Clerks*

Mary Beth Trimper, *Production Manager*
Laura McKay, *External Production Associate*

Arthur Chartow, *Art Director*
Linda A. Davis, *External Production Assistant*

Laura Bryant, *Production Supervisor*
Louise Gagné, *Internal Production Associate*
Shelly Andrews, Sharana Wier, *Internal Production Assistants*

The paper used in this publication meets the minimum requirements
of American National Standard for Information Sciences—Permanence
Paper for Printed Library Materials, ANSI Z39.48-1984.

Library of Congress Catalog Card Number 76-46132
ISBN 0-8103-2414-8
ISSN 0276-8178

Printed in the United States of America.

Published simultaneously in the United Kingdom
by Gale Research International Limited
(An affiliated company of Gale Research Inc.)

Contents

Preface   vii

Preface

It is impossible to overvalue the importance of literature in the intellectual, emotional, and spiritual evolution of humanity. Literature is that which both lifts us out of everyday life and helps us to better understand it. Through the fictive lives of such characters as Anna Karenina, Jay Gatsby, or Leopold Bloom, our perceptions of the human condition are enlarged, and we are enriched.

Literary criticism can also give us insight into the human condition, as well as into the specific moral and intellectual atmosphere of an era, for the criteria by which a work of art is judged reflect contemporary philosophical and social attitudes. Literary criticism takes many forms: the traditional essay, the book or play review, even the parodic poem. Criticism can also be of several types: normative, descriptive, interpretive, textual, appreciative, generic. Collectively, the range of critical response helps us to understand a work of art, an author, an era.

Scope of the Series

Twentieth-Century Literary Criticism (TCLC) is designed to serve as an introduction for the student of twentieth-century literature to the authors of the period 1900 to 1960 and to the most significant commentators on these authors. The great poets, novelists, short story writers, playwrights, and philosophers of this period are by far the most popular writers for study in high school and college literature courses. Since a vast amount of relevant critical material confronts the student, *TCLC* presents significant passages from the most important published criticism to aid students in the location and selection of commentaries on authors who died between 1900 and 1960.

The need for *TCLC* was suggested by the usefulness of the Gale series *Contemporary Literary Criticism (CLC),* which excerpts criticism on current writing. Because of the difference in time span under consideration *(CLC* considers authors who were still living after 1959), there is no duplication of material between *CLC* and *TCLC.* For further information about *CLC* and Gale's other criticism series, users should consult the Guide to Gale Literary Criticism Series preceding the title page in this volume.

Each volume of *TCLC* is carefully compiled to include authors who represent a variety of genres and nationalities and who are currently regarded as the most important writers of this era. In addition to major authors, *TCLC* also presents criticism on lesser-known writers whose significant contributions to literary history are important to the study of twentieth-century literature.

Each author entry in *TCLC* is intended to provide an overview of major criticism on an author. Therefore, the editors include fourteen to sixteen authors in each 650-page volume (compared with approximately thirty-five authors in a *CLC* volume of similar size) so that more attention may be given to an author. Each author entry represents a historical survey of the critical response to that author's work: some early criticism is presented to indicate initial reactions, later criticism is selected to represent any rise or decline in the author's reputation, and current retrospective analyses provide students with a modern view. The length of an author entry is intended to reflect the amount of critical attention the author has received from critics writing in English, and from foreign criticism in translation. Critical articles and books that have not been translated into English are excluded. Every attempt has been made to identify and include excerpts from the seminal essays on each author's work.

An author may appear more than once in the series because of the great quantity of critical material available, or because of a resurgence of criticism generated by events such as an author's centennial or anniversary celebration, the republication or posthumous publication of an author's works, or the publication of a newly translated work. Generally, a few author entries in each volume of *TCLC* feature criticism on single works by major authors who have appeared previously in the series. Only those individual works that have been the subjects of vast amounts of criticism and are widely studied in literature classes are selected for this in-depth treatment. Thomas Hardy's *Mayor of Casterbridge* and Stephen Crane's *Red Badge of Courage* are examples of such entries in *TCLC,* Volume 32.

Organization of the Book

An author entry consists of the following elements: author heading, biographical and critical introduction, list of principal works, excerpts of criticism (each preceded by explanatory notes and followed by a bibliographic citation), and a bibliography of additional reading.

- The *author heading* consists of the author's full name, followed by birth and death dates. The unbracketed portion of the name denotes the form under which the author most commonly wrote. If an author wrote consistently under a pseudonym, the pseudonym will be listed in the author heading and the real name given in parentheses on the first line of the biographical and critical introduction. Also located at the beginning of the introduction to the author entry are any name variations under which an author wrote, including transliterated forms for authors whose languages use nonroman alphabets. Uncertainty as to a birth or death date is indicated by a question mark.

- The *biographical and critical introduction* contains background information designed to introduce the reader to an author and to the critical debate surrounding his or her work. References are provided to past volumes of *TCLC* and to other biographical and critical reference series published by Gale, including *Children's Literature Review, Contemporary Authors, Dictionary of Literary Biography,* and *Something about the Author.*

- Most *TCLC* entries include *portraits* of the author. Many entries also contain reproductions of materials pertinent to an author's career, including manuscript pages, title pages, dust jackets, letters, and drawings, as well as photographs of important people, places, and events in an author's life.

- The *list of principal works* is chronological by date of first book publication and identifies the genre of each work. In the case of foreign authors with both foreign-language publications and English translations, the title and date of the first English-language edition are given in brackets. Unless otherwise indicated, dramas are dated by first performance, not first publication.

- *Criticism* is arranged chronologically in each author entry to provide a perspective on changes in critical evaluation over the years. All titles of works by the author featured in the entry are printed in boldface type to enable the user to easily locate discussion of particular works. Also for purposes of easier identification, the critic's name and the publication date of the essay are given at the beginning of each piece of criticism. Unsigned criticism is preceded by the title of the journal in which it appeared. Many of the excerpts in *TCLC* also contain translated material to aid users. Unless otherwise noted, translations in brackets are by the editors; translations in parentheses or continuous with the text are by the critic. Publication information (such as publisher names and book prices) and parenthetical numerical references (such as footnotes or page and line references to specific editions of works) have been deleted at the editors' discretion to provide smoother reading of the text.

- Critical excerpts are prefaced by *explanatory notes* providing the reader with information about both the critic and the criticism that follows. Included are the critic's reputation, individual approach to literary criticism, and particular expertise in an author's works. Also noted are the relative importance of a work of criticism, the scope of the excerpt, and the growth of critical controversy or changes in critical trends regarding an author. In some cases, these notes cross-reference excerpts by critics who discuss each other's commentary.

- A complete *bibliographic citation* designed to facilitate location of the original essay or book by the interested reader follows each piece of criticism.

- The *additional bibliography* appearing at the end of each author entry suggests further reading on the author. In some cases it includes essays for which the editors could not obtain reprint rights.

An acknowledgments section lists the copyright holders who have granted us permission to reprint material in this volume of *TCLC*. It does not, however, list every book or periodical reprinted or consulted in the preparation of the volume.

Cumulative Indexes

Each volume of *TCLC* includes a cumulative index listing all the authors who have appeared in *Contemporary Literary Criticism, Twentieth-Century Literary Criticism, Nineteenth-Century Literature Criticism, Literature Criticism from 1400 to 1800, Classical and Medieval Literature Criticism,* and *Short Story Criticism,* along with cross-references to the Gale series *Children's Literature Review, Authors in the News, Contemporary Authors, Contemporary Authors Autobiography Series, Dictionary of Literary Biography, Concise Dictionary of American Literary Biography, Something about the Author, Something about the Author Autobiography Series,* and *Yesterday's Authors of Books for Children.* Useful for locating an author within the various series, this index is particularly valuable for those authors who are identified with a certain period but who, because of their death dates, are placed in another, or for those authors whose careers span two periods. For example, F. Scott Fitzgerald is found in *TCLC,* yet a writer often associated with him, Ernest Hemingway, is found in *CLC.*

Each volume of *TCLC* also includes a cumulative nationality index, in which authors' names are arranged alphabetically under their respective nationalities.

Title Index

TCLC also includes an index listing the titles of all literary works discussed in the series since its inception. Foreign language titles that have been translated are followed by the titles of the translations—for example, *Voina i mir (War and Peace)*. Page numbers following these translated titles refer to all pages on which any form of the titles, either foreign language or translated, appear. Titles of novels, dramas, nonfiction books, and poetry, short story, or essay collections are printed in italics, while all individual poems, short stories, and essays are printed in roman type within quotation marks. In cases where the same title is used by different authors, the author's surname is given in parentheses after the title, for example, *Collected Poems* (Housman) and *Collected Poems* (Yeats).

Acknowledgments

No work of this scope can be accomplished without the cooperation of many people. The editors especially wish to thank the copyright holders of the excerpted criticism included in this volume, the permissions managers of many book and magazine publishing companies for assisting us in securing reprint rights, and Anthony Bogucki for assistance with copyright research. We are also grateful to the staffs of the Detroit Public Library, the Library of Congress, the University of Detroit Library, the University of Michigan Library, and the Wayne State University Library for making their resources available to us.

Suggestions Are Welcome

In response to suggestions, several features have been added to *TCLC* since the series began, including explanatory notes to excerpted criticism, a cumulative index to authors in all Gale literary criticism series, entries devoted to a single work by a major author, more extensive illustrations, and a title index listing all literary works discussed in the series since its inception.

Readers who wish to suggest authors to appear in future volumes, or who have other suggestions, are cordially invited to write the editors.

Authors to Be Featured in Forthcoming Volumes

Black Elk (Native American autobiographer)—The life story of Black Elk, published as *Black Elk Speaks,* is considered one of the most authentic accounts of the experience of the Plains Indians during the nineteenth century. In the twentieth century, this book has played a crucial role in encouraging the expression of native American heritage and consciousness.

Samuel Butler (English novelist and essayist)—Butler is best known for *The Way of All Flesh,* an autobiographical novel that is both a classic account of the conflict between father and son and an indictment of Victorian society.

Theodore Dreiser (American novelist)—A prominent American exponent of literary Naturalism and one of America's foremost novelists, Dreiser was the author of works commended for their powerful characterizations and strong ideological convictions.

Ivor Gurney (English poet)—One of the most gifted English poets of the First World War, Gurney focused in his work on the experiences of the common soldier during the war.

Vyacheslav Ivanov (Russian poet and philosopher)—Ivanov was among the principal theorists and poets of Russian Symbolism, the dominant literary movement in Russia during the first decades of the twentieth century. His strong spiritual values were influential in leading the movement away from its early focus on aesthetics and toward the development of a worldview that synthesized art and religion.

Nikos Kazantzakis (Greek novelist)—Kazantzakis was the author of works embodying Nietzschean and Bergsonian philosophical ideas in vividly portrayed characters, the most famous of which was the protagonist of *Zorba the Greek.*

D. H. Lawrence (English novelist)—Controversial during his lifetime for the explicit sexuality of his works, Lawrence is today considered one of the most important novelists of the twentieth century for his innovative explorations of human psychology. *TCLC* will devote an entry to his highly esteemed novel *Women in Love.*

Thomas Mann (German novelist)—Mann is credited with reclaiming for the German novel an international stature it had not enjoyed since the time of the Romantics. *TCLC* will devote an entry to his novel *Buddenbrooks,* a masterpiece of Realism which depicts the rise and fall of a wealthy Hanseatic family.

Zsigmond Móricz (Hungarian novelist)—Móricz was the first writer to introduce the themes and techniques of literary Realism into Hungarian literature. His coarse, often sordid portrayals of village life are credited with revitalizing Hungarian literature during the first half of the twentieth century.

Marcel Proust (French novelist)—Proust's multivolume *A la recherche du temps perdu (Remembrance of Things Past)* is among literature's works of highest genius. Combining a social historian's chronicle of turn-of-the-century Paris society, a philosopher's reflections on the nature of time and consciousness, and a psychologist's insight into a tangled network of personalities, the novel is acclaimed for conveying a profound view of all human existence.

Charles-Ferdinand Ramuz (Swiss novelist)—A central figure in francophone Swiss literature during the early twentieth century, Ramuz surmounted the dominance of French literary style in Swiss letters to produce works that more faithfully represented life in Switzerland.

Alfonso Reyes (Mexican essayist, poet, and fiction writer)—One of the finest Spanish-American writers of the twentieth century, Reyes has been especially praised for the humanist values expressed in his diverse and impressive body of works.

Joseph Roth (Austrian novelist)—A chronicler of the last years of the Austro-Hungarian Empire, Roth is best known for his novels *Radetzky March, Job,* and *Flight without End.*

Umberto Saba (Italian poet)—Saba is ranked among the most important Italian poets of the twentieth century; his major work, *Il canzoniere,* is a poetic document reflecting his often tormented life.

Italo Svevo (Italian novelist)—Svevo's novels, which characteristically demonstrate the influence of the psychoanalytic theories of Sigmund Freud, earned him a reputation as one of the most original and influential authors in modern Italian literature.

Mark Twain (American novelist)—Considered the father of modern American literature, Twain combined moral and social satire, adventure, and frontier humor to create such perenially popular books as *The Adventures of Tom Sawyer, The Adventures of Huckleberry Finn,* and *A Connecticut Yankee in King Arthur's Court.*

Paul Van Ostaijen (Belgian poet)—Influenced by the Dada and Expressionist movements, Van Ostaijen is best known for experimental poetry expressing the nihilistic sensibility of the post-World War I generation of writers and artists.

Additional Authors to Appear
in Future Volumes

Abbey, Henry 1842-1911
Abercrombie, Lascelles 1881-1938
Adamic, Louis 1898-1951
Ade, George 1866-1944
Agustini, Delmira 1886-1914
Akers, Elizabeth Chase 1832-1911
Aldrich, Thomas Bailey 1836-1907
Aliyu, Dan Sidi 1902-1920
Allen, Hervey 1889-1949
Archer, William 1856-1924
Austin, Alfred 1835-1913
Bahr, Hermann 1863-1934
Bailey, Philip James 1816-1902
Barbour, Ralph Henry 1870-1944
Benjamin, Walter 1892-1940
Bennett, James Gordon, Jr. 1841-1918
Berdyaev, Nikolai Aleksandrovich
    1874-1948
Beresford, J(ohn) D(avys) 1873-1947
Binyon, Laurence 1869-1943
Bishop, John Peale 1892-1944
Blake, Lillie Devereux 1835-1913
Blum, Léon 1872-1950
Bodenheim, Maxwell 1892-1954
Bowen, Marjorie 1886-1952
Byrne, Donn 1889-1928
Caine, Hall 1853-1931
Cannan, Gilbert 1884-1955
Carswell, Catherine 1879-1946
Churchill, Winston 1871-1947
Corelli, Marie 1855-1924
Croce, Benedetto 1866-1952
Crofts, Freeman Wills 1879-1957
Cruze, James (Jens Cruz Bosen) 1884-
    1942
Curros, Enríquez Manuel 1851-1908
Dall, Caroline Wells (Healy) 1822-1912
Daudet, Léon 1867-1942
Delafield, E.M. (Edme Elizabeth Monica
    de la Pasture) 1890-1943
Deneson, Jacob 1836-1919
Douglas, (George) Norman 1868-1952
Douglas, Lloyd C(assel) 1877-1951
Dovzhenko, Alexander 1894-1956
Drinkwater, John 1882-1937
Durkheim, Emile 1858-1917
Duun, Olav 1876-1939
Eaton, Walter Prichard 1878-1957
Eggleston, Edward 1837-1902
Erskine, John 1879-1951
Fadeyev, Alexander 1901-1956
Ferland, Albert 1872-1943
Field, Rachel 1894-1924
Fogazzaro, Antonio 1842-1911
Francos, Karl Emil 1848-1904
Frank, Bruno 1886-1945

Freud, Sigmund 1853-1939
Fröding, Gustaf 1860-1911
Fuller, Henry Blake 1857-1929
Futabatei Shimei 1864-1909
Gamboa, Federico 1864-1939
Glaspell, Susan 1876-1948
Glyn, Elinor 1864-1943
Golding, Louis 1895-1958
Gould, Gerald 1885-1936
Guest, Edgar 1881-1959
Gumilyov, Nikolay 1886-1921
Gyulai, Pal 1826-1909
Hale, Edward Everett 1822-1909
Hernández, Miguel 1910-1942
Hewlett, Maurice 1861-1923
Heyward, DuBose 1885-1940
Hope, Anthony 1863-1933
Ilyas, Abu Shabaka 1903-1947
Imbs, Bravig 1904-1946
Jammes, Francis 1868-1938
Johnston, Mary 1870-1936
Jorgensen, Johannes 1866-1956
King, Grace 1851-1932
Kirby, William 1817-1906
Kline, Otis Albert 1891-1946
Kohut, Adolph 1848-1916
Kuzmin, Mikhail Alexseyevich 1875-
    1936
Lamm, Martin 1880-1950
Leipoldt, C. Louis 1880-1947
Lima, Jorge De 1895-1953
Locke, Alain 1886-1954
López Portillo y Rojas, José 1850-1903
Louys, Pierre 1870-1925
Lucas, E(dward) V(errall) 1868-1938
Machar, Josef Svatopluk 1864-1945
Maragall, Joan 1860-1911
Marais, Eugene 1871-1936
Masaryk, Tomas 1850-1939
Mayor, Flora Macdonald 1872-1932
McClellan, George Marion 1860-1934
Mirbeau, Octave 1850-1917
Mistral, Frédéric 1830-1914
Monro, Harold 1879-1932
Moore, Thomas Sturge 1870-1944
Morley, Christopher 1890-1957
Morley, S. Griswold 1883-1948
Murray, (George) Gilbert 1866-1957
Nansen, Peter 1861-1918
Nobre, Antonio 1867-1900
O'Dowd, Bernard 1866-1959
Ophuls, Max 1902-1957
Orczy, Baroness 1865-1947
Oskison, John M. 1874-1947
Owen, Seaman 1861-1936
Page, Thomas Nelson 1853-1922

Parrington, Vernon L. 1871-1929
Peck, George W. 1840-1916
Phillips, Ulrich B. 1877-1934
Powys, T. F. 1875-1953
Prévost, Marcel 1862-1941
Quiller-Couch, Arthur 1863-1944
Randall, James G. 1881-1953
Rappoport, Solomon 1863-1944
Read, Opie 1852-1939
Reisen (Reizen), Abraham 1875-1953
Remington, Frederic 1861-1909
Riley, James Whitcomb 1849-1916
Rinehart, Mary Roberts 1876-1958
Ring, Max 1817-1901
Rozanov, Vasily Vasilyevich 1856-1919
Saar, Ferdinand von 1833-1906
Sabatini, Rafael 1875-1950
Sakutaro, Hagiwara 1886-1942
Sanborn, Franklin Benjamin 1831-1917
Sánchez, Florencio 1875-1910
Santayana, George 1863-1952
Sardou, Victorien 1831-1908
Schickele, René 1885-1940
Seabrook, William 1886-1945
Shestov, Lev 1866-1938
Shiels, George 1886-1949
Solovyov, Vladimir 1853-1900
Sorel, Georges 1847-1922
Spector, Mordechai 1859-1922
Squire, J(ohn) C(ollings) 1884-1958
Stavenhagen, Fritz 1876-1906
Stockton, Frank R. 1834-1902
Subrahmanya Bharati, C. 1882-1921
Thoma, Ludwig 1867-1927
Tomlinson, Henry Major 1873-1958
Totovents, Vahan 1889-1937
Tuchmann, Jules 1830-1901
Turner, W(alter) J(ames) R(edfern)
    1889-1946
Upward, Allen 1863-1926
Vachell, Horace Annesley 1861-1955
Van Dyke, Henry 1852-1933
Villaespesa, Francisco 1877-1936
Wallace, Lewis 1827-1905
Walsh, Ernest 1895-1926
Webster, Jean 1876-1916
Whitlock, Brand 1869-1927
Wilson, Harry Leon 1867-1939
Wolf, Emma 1865-1932
Wood, Clement 1888-1950
Wren, P(ercival) C(hristopher) 1885-
    1941
Yonge, Charlotte Mary 1823-1901
Yosano Akiko 1878-1942
Zecca, Ferdinand 1864-1947
Zeromski, Stefan 1864-1925

Henri Bergson

1859-1941

French philosopher.

Bergson's reputation as one of the most brilliant and influential philosophers of the twentieth century is based upon his formulation of a complex metaphysical doctrine that directly contradicted the materialist theories favored in the late nineteenth century. Believing that materialists, in regarding the universe as composed solely of the predictable actions of matter, had failed to either account for or disprove the existence of free will, Bergson proposed the existence of a purely subjective level of reality not governed by the laws that control matter. He further suggested that the materialists' error stemmed from their reliance upon pure intellect, when in fact the true nature of reality is comprehensible only by combining logical inquiry, which is the proper domain of the intellect, with a nonrational process he termed "intuition." Bergson's assertions concerning the limitations of the intellect drew harsh criticism, particularly from England, where the tradition of rationalism had been firmly entrenched since the seventeenth century, yet his affirmation of the possibility of free, unpredetermined human action carried wide appeal and brought him enormous popularity among those who found the materialist view inadequate.

Bergson was born in Paris, the son of a successful, cosmopolitan Polish composer. By all accounts a brilliant youth, he attended the prestigious Lycée Condorcet, excelling in his studies of English, Latin, Greek, philosophy, and mathematics; he received his secondary education at the Ecole Normale Supérieure, graduating in 1881 with a degree in philosophy. Shortly afterward, Bergson accepted a professorship at the Lycée Angers in western France, and he taught at a succession of provincial schools throughout much of the following decade. In 1888, he returned to Paris to teach at the Lycée Henri Quatre; one year later he published his doctoral thesis, entitled *Essai sur les données immédiates de la conscience* (*Time and Free Will*).

During his studies of philosophy at the Ecole Normale, Bergson had been exposed to two diametrically opposed schools of thought: the metaphysical idealism that had originated in the ancient tradition of mysticism and had been reawakened by Immanuel Kant's *Critique of Pure Reason* (1781), and materialism, which drew corroboration from the rapidly increasing body of scientific knowledge. Bergson was initially inclined more toward a materialist conceptualization of reality. However, as he prepared his doctoral thesis, which was originally planned as an exploration of the philosophical implications of Newtonian physics, he began to perceive what he considered grave flaws in the essentially mathematical nature of the materialist interpretation of time. After wrestling with his doubts at length, he proposed an alternate view in *Time and Free Will,* suggesting a qualitative difference between time and space. Despite Bergson's profoundly original assertions in *Time and Free Will,* the essay attracted little attention at the time of its publication, but as he continued to extrapolate his theory in subsequent volumes, most notably *Matière et mémoire* (*Matter and Memory*) and *L'évolution créatrice* (*Creative Evolution*), his reputation increased. In addition to his many French followers, who crowded by the hundreds into his lectures at the

Ecole Normale and later at the Collège de France, Bergson drew positive reactions from English philosophers T. E. Hulme, H. Wildon Carr, and Alfred North Whitehead, and from the dean of American philosophers, William James. However, his growing influence also elicited a strongly negative response from materialist thinkers, who issued a flood of studies denigrating his work. More damning still were the denunciations of eminent philosophers George Santayana, Bertrand Russell, and Wyndham Lewis. Nevertheless, he remained a highly revered figure throughout the first three decades of the twentieth century; following World War I he was asked to participate in the formation of the League of Nations, and in 1927 he was awarded a Nobel Prize in literature.

After the 1932 publication of his essay *Les deux sources de la morale et de la réligion* (*The Two Sources of Morality and Religion*), Bergson's name began to fade from the public memory, supplanted in part by the more temporal concerns of worldwide economic depression and approaching war. Forced by severe arthritis to retire from teaching, he spent the final decade of his life in virtual seclusion. Contemporaries report that Bergson became increasingly concerned with the kinds of moral questions raised in *The Two Sources of Morality and Religion* and considered converting from his native Judaism to Catholicism during this period, but refused to do so while his fellow Jews were suffering persecution at the hands of Adolf Hitler's

Third Reich. It is further reported that he refused the offer of special treatment extended by the Nazi occupation government and insisted upon wearing the yellow arm band used by the Nazis to identify Jews. In sympathy with Bergson's strong personal convictions, his friends and colleagues protested the Nazi occupation by refusing to stage official ceremonies to mark his death in January of 1941.

Bergson wrote: "Any summary of my views will deform them as a whole and will, by that very fact, expose them to a host of objections, if it does not take as its starting point, and if it does not continually revert to, what I consider the very center of the doctrine: the intuition of duration." In *Time and Free Will*, the essay in which Bergson initially developed this concept, he argued that the materialists had erred in viewing time as an abstract concept that describes the successive states of matter in the same way that space describes the positions of matter. Bergson maintained that time is qualitatively different from space since it is not divisible into measurable increments; to do so would be to portray a series of static moments and so would rob time of its most essential characteristics, movement and change, which Bergson described collectively as flux. The time that can be measured in increments by a clock, he asserted, is simply a convenient fiction, while real time, which he called *la durée* (usually translated as "duration"), is a purely subjective, nonmaterial phenomenon, without discrete components and without the temporal demarcations of past, present and future. Bergson was thus able to reaffirm the possibility of free action on the part of human beings, since predetermination implies a linear temporal structure not consistent with his definition of duration. Bergson further argued that because duration is an experiential phenomenon, it can never be accessed by empirical means, which employ sensory data to draw logical conclusions about the nature of reality, but must be realized through a process of intuition. According to Bergson's theory, human intellect evolved as a capacity for receiving, organizing, and interpreting only information about matter, while intuition served to assimilate such data into a vision of the ultimate nature of reality, a function restricted by the materialists to the faculty of reason.

Bergson further developed his concept of intuition in *Matter and Memory*, contending that the materialists had failed to prove an absolute unity of brain and mind despite their studies of the impact of pathological physical states upon human consciousness; he therefore concluded that the human mind is a transcendent phenomenon indicating a plane of existence independent of the physical world. Continuing his exploration of the nature of this higher reality in *Creative Evolution*, he proposed the existence of a universal opposition between matter, which is characterized by stasis, and an *élan vital*, or vital impulse, which he described as an intangible, infinitely mutable, and ultimately unpredictable universal force. Rejecting the Darwinian view of evolution as the interaction between organisms and their environments, Bergson maintained that evolution resulted from the interaction of matter and the vital impulse. Finally, in *The Two Sources of Morality and Religion*, he argued that the most desirable moral system would both acknowledge and manifest this universal drive toward the creation of life, observing that in his own experience the Christian religion had best done so.

Critical assessments of Bergson's ideas have displayed a marked polarity. At his death, he was hailed by the noted French poet Paul Valéry as the greatest philosopher of his time, while the English critic Sir Ray Lankester pronounced his writings "worthless and unprofitable matter, causing waste of time and confusion of thought to many of those who are induced to read them." Early responses to Bergson's books were predominantly positive, and even when disagreeing with the specifics of his doctrine, critics often praised the clarity of his prose, the strength of his rhetorical powers, and, in the words of John Dewey, "the air of freedom and release" that permeated his discussions of the human condition. Analyzing the positive response to Bergson's works during the early decades of the twentieth century, a phenomenon described by one contemporary as "Bergsonitis," J. Alexander Gunn has explained that "men were growing impatient of a science claiming so much and yet admittedly unable to explain the really vital factors of existence, of which the free action of men is one of the most important." Yet it was precisely Bergson's insistence upon the reality of human free will that led George Santayana to denounce his writings as "occasional and partial, the work of an astute apologist, a party man, driven to desperate speculation by a timid attachment to prejudice." Negative appraisals of Bergson's work have also focused on his contentions regarding the limitations of the intellect, which many critics, most notably Bertrand Russell, have dismissed as mere semantic confusion.

Nevertheless, several recent commentators have discussed Bergson's thought as prophetic in view of modern discoveries in the fields of quantum physics and relativity theory, which because of their quasi-occult nature are not susceptible to the ordinary methods of empiricism. Moreover, despite his influence on such major figures as William James and Alfred North Whitehead, contemporary critics agree that Bergson's greatest impact upon twentieth-century thought has been felt not in the area of philosophy but in literature, where his concept of duration was translated into the influential stream-of-consciousness narrative technique by such authors as Marcel Proust, Virginia Woolf, Gertrude Stein, and James Joyce. Finally, many commentators contend that, in reaffirming the essential uncertainty of scientific endeavor, Bergson provided a tonic to the overly strict materialist interpretation of reality and thus established one of the central tenets of modern thought.

PRINCIPAL WORKS

Essai sur les données immédiates de la conscience   (essay) 1889
   [*Time and Free Will: An Essay on the Immediate Data of Consciousness*, 1910]
Matière et mémoire   (essay)   1896
   [*Matter and Memory*, 1911]
Le rire   (essay)   1900
   [*Laughter*, 1911]
Introduction à la métaphysique   (essay)   1903
   [*The Introduction to a New Philosophy*, 1912; also translated as *An Introduction to Metaphysics*, 1912]
L'évolution créatrice   (essay)   1907
   [*Creative Evolution*, 1911]
L'énergie spirituelle   (essays)   1919
   [*Mind-Energy*, 1920]
Durée et simultanéité   (essays)   1922
   [*Duration and Simultaneity*, 1965]
Les deux sources de la morale et de la réligion   (essay) 1932
   [*The Two Sources of Morality and Religion*, 1935]
La pensée et la mouvant   (essays)   1934
Oeuvres   (essays)   1959

WILLIAM JAMES   (lecture date 1909)

[*One of the most influential figures in modern Western thought, James was an American philosopher and the founder of the doctrine known as Pragmatism. In opposition to the tenets of scientific materialism and philosophic idealism, which had prevailed in Western philosophy throughout the eighteenth and nineteenth centuries, James attempted to comprehend and describe human life as it is actually experienced, rather than formulating abstract models of reality far removed from the passion and pain of life. Despite formidable resistance to James's ideas during his lifetime, his works have become recognized as landmarks in the development of modern thought, and the English philosopher Alfred North Whitehead has called him "one of the greatest philosophic minds of all time." In the following excerpt, James explicates Bergson's central doctrines and praises his verbal facility.*]

I have to confess that Bergson's originality is so profuse that many of his ideas baffle me entirely. I doubt whether any one understands him all over, so to speak; and I am sure that he would himself be the first to see that this must be, and to confess that things which he himself has not yet thought out clearly, had yet to be mentioned and have a tentative place assigned them in his philosophy. Many of us are profusely original, in that no man can understand us—violently peculiar ways of looking at things are no great rarity. The rarity is when great peculiarity of vision is allied with great lucidity and unusual command of all the classic expository apparatus. Bergson's resources in the way of erudition are remarkable, and in the way of expression they are simply phenomenal. This is why in France, where *l'art de bien dire* ["the art of speaking well"] counts for so much and is so sure of appreciation, he has immediately taken so eminent a place in public esteem. Old-fashioned professors, whom his ideas quite fail to satisfy, nevertheless speak of his talent almost with bated breath, while the youngsters flock to him as to a master.

If anything can make hard things easy to follow, it is a style like Bergson's. A "straightforward" style, an American reviewer lately called it; failing to see that such straightforwardness means a flexibility of verbal resource that follows the thought without a crease or wrinkle, as elastic silk underclothing follows the movements of one's body. The lucidity of Bergson's way of putting things is what all readers are first struck by. It seduces you and bribes you in advance to become his disciple. It is a miracle, and he a real magician. (pp. 226-27)

The ruling tradition in philosophy has always been the platonic and aristotelian belief that fixity is a nobler and worthier thing than change. Reality must be one and unalterable. Concepts, being themselves fixities, agree best with this fixed nature of truth, so that for any knowledge of ours to be quite true it must be knowledge by universal concepts rather than by particular experiences, for these notoriously are mutable and corruptible. This is the tradition known as rationalism in philosophy.... In spite of sceptics and empiricists, in spite of Protagoras, Hume, and James Mill, rationalism has never been seriously questioned, for its sharpest critics have always had a tender place in their hearts for it, and have obeyed some of its mandates. They have not been consistent; they have played fast and loose with the enemy; and Bergson alone has been radical. (pp. 237-38)

Thought deals . . . solely with surfaces. It can name the thickness of reality, but it cannot fathom it, and its insufficiency here is essential and permanent, not temporary.

The only way in which to apprehend reality's thickness is either to experience it directly by being a part of reality one's self, or to evoke it in imagination by sympathetically divining some one else's inner life. But what we thus immediately experience or concretely divine is very limited in duration, whereas abstractly we are able to conceive eternities. Could we feel a million years concretely as we now feel a passing minute, we should have very little employment for our conceptual faculty. We should know the whole period fully at every moment of its passage, whereas we must now construct it laboriously by means of concepts which we project. Direct acquaintance and conceptual knowledge are thus complementary of each other; each remedies the other's defects. If what we care most about be the synoptic treatment of phenomena, the vision of the far and the gathering of the scattered like, we must follow the conceptual method. But if, as metaphysicians, we are more curious about the inner nature of reality or about what really makes it go, we must turn our backs upon our winged concepts altogether, and bury ourselves in the thickness of those passing moments over the surface of which they fly, and on particular points of which they occasionally rest and perch.

Professor Bergson thus inverts the traditional platonic doctrine absolutely. Instead of intellectual knowledge being the profounder, he calls it the more superficial. Instead of being the only adequate knowledge, it is grossly inadequate, and its only superiority is the practical one of enabling us to make short cuts through experience and thereby to save time. The one thing it cannot do is to reveal the nature of things—which last remark, if not clear already, will become clearer as I proceed. Dive back into the flux itself, then, Bergson tells us, if you wish to *know* reality, that flux which Platonism, in its strange belief that only the immutable is excellent, has always spurned; turn your face toward sensation, that fleshbound thing which rationalism has always loaded with abuse.—This, you see, is exactly the opposite remedy from that of looking forward into the absolute, which our idealistic contemporaries prescribe. It violates our mental habits, being a kind of passive and receptive listening quite contrary to that effort to react noisily and verbally on everything, which is our usual intellectual pose.

What, then, are the peculiar features in the perceptual flux which the conceptual translation so fatally leaves out?

The essence of life is its continuously changing character; but our concepts are all discontinuous and fixed, and the only mode of making them coincide with life is by arbitrarily supposing positions of arrest therein. With such arrests our concepts may be made congruent. But these concepts are not *parts* of reality, not real positions taken by it, but *suppositions* rather, notes taken by ourselves, and you can no more dip up the substance of reality with them than you can dip up water with a net, however finely meshed.

When we conceptualize, we cut out and fix, and exclude everything but what we have fixed. A concept means a *that-and-no-other*. Conceptually, time excludes space; motion and rest exclude each other; approach excludes contact; presence excludes absence, unity excludes plurality; independence excludes relativity; "mine" excludes "yours"; this connexion excludes that connexion—and so on indefinitely; whereas in the real concrete sensible flux of life experiences compenetrate each other so that it is not easy to know just what is excluded and what not. Past and future, for example, conceptually separated by the cut to which we give the name of present, and defined as being the opposite sides of that cut, are to some extent, however brief, co-present with each other throughout experience. The literally present moment is a purely verbal supposition, not a position; the only present ever realized concretely being the "passing moment" in which the dying rearward of time and its dawning future forever mix their lights. Say "now" and it *was* even while you say it. (pp. 250-54)

We are so inveterately wedded to the conceptual decomposition of life that I know that this will seem to you like putting muddiest confusion in place of clearest thought, and relapsing into a molluscoid state of mind. Yet I ask you whether the absolute superiority of our higher though is so very clear, if all that it can find is impossibility in tasks which sense-experience so easily performs.

What makes you call real life confusion is that it presents, as if they were dissolved in one another, a lot of differents which conception breaks life's flow by keeping apart. But *are* not differents actually dissolved in one another? Hasn't every bit of experience its quality, its duration, its extension, its intensity, its urgency, its clearness, and many aspects besides, no one of which can exist in the isolation in which our verbalized logic keeps it? They exist only *durcheinander* ["in confusion"]. Reality always is, in M. Bergson's phrase, an endosmosis or conflux of the same with the different: they compenetrate and telescope. For conceptual logic, the same is nothing but the same, and all sames with a third thing are the same with each other. Not so in concrete experience. Two spots on our skin, each of which feels the same as a third spot when touched along with it, are felt as different from each other. Two tones, neither distinguishable from a third tone, are perfectly distinct from each other. The whole process of life is due to life's violation of our logical axioms. Take its continuity as an example. Terms like A and C appear to be connected by intermediaries, by B for example. Intellectualism calls this absurd, for "B-connected-with-A" is, "as such," a different term from "B-connected-with-C." But real life laughs at logic's veto. Imagine a heavy log which takes two men to carry it. First A and B take it. Then C takes hold and A drops off; then D takes hold and B drops off, so that C and D now bear it; and so on. The log meanwhile never drops, and keeps its sameness throughout the journey. Even so it is with all our experiences. Their changes are not complete annihilations followed by complete creations of something absolutely novel. There is partial decay and partial growth, and all the while a nucleus of relative constancy from which what decays drops off, and which takes into itself whatever is grafted on, until at length something wholly different has taken its place. In such a process we are as sure, in spite of intellectualist logic with its "as suches," that it *is* the same nucleus which is able now to make connexion with what goes and again with what comes, as we are sure that the same point can lie on diverse lines that intersect there. Without being one throughout, such a universe is continuous. Its members interdigitate with their next neighbors in manifold directions, and there are no clean cuts between them anywhere.

The great clash of intellectualist logic with sensible experience is where the experience is that of influence exerted. Intellectualism denies . . . that finite things can act on one another, for all things, once translated into concepts, remain shut up to themselves. To act on anything means to get into it somehow; but that would mean to get out of one's self and be one's other, which is self-contradictory, etc. Meanwhile each of us actually *is* his own other to that extent, livingly knowing how to perform the trick which logic tells us can't be done. My thoughts animate and actuate this very body which you see and hear, and thereby influence your thoughts. The dynamic current somehow does get from me to you, however numerous the intermediary conductors may have to be. Distinctions may be insulators in logic as much as they like, but in life distinct things can and do commune together every moment.

The conflict of the two ways of knowing is best summed up in the intellectualist doctrine that "the same cannot exist in many relations." This follows of course from the concepts of the two relations being so distinct that "what-is-in-the-one" means "as such" something distinct from what "what-is-in-the-other" means. It is like Mill's ironical saying, that we should not think of Newton as both an Englishman and a mathematician, because an Englishman as such is not a mathematician and a mathematician as such is not an Englishman. But the real Newton was somehow both things at once; and throughout the whole finite universe each real thing proves to be many differents without undergoing the necessity of breaking into disconnected editions of itself.

These few indications will perhaps suffice to put you at the bergsonian point of view. The immediate experience of life solves the problems which so baffle our conceptual intelligence: How can what is manifold be one? how can things get out of themselves? how be their own others? how be both distinct and connected? how can they act on one another? how be for others and yet for themselves? how be absent and present at once? The intellect asks these questions much as we might ask how anything can both separate and unite things, or how sounds can grow more alike by continuing to grow more different. If you already know space sensibly, you can answer the former question by pointing to any interval in it, long or short; if you know the musical scale, you can answer the latter by sounding an octave; but then you must first have the sensible knowledge of these realities. Similarly Bergson answers the intellectualist conundrums by pointing back to our various finite sensational experiences and saying, "Lo, even thus; even so are these other problems solved livingly."

When you have broken the reality into concepts you never can reconstruct it in its wholeness. Out of no amount of discreteness can you manufacture the concrete. But place yourself at a bound, or *d'emblée*, as M. Bergson says, inside of the living, moving, active thickness of the real, and all the abstractions and distinctions are given into your hand: you can now make the intellectualist substitutions to your heart's content. Install yourself in phenomenal movement, for example, and velocity, succession, dates, positions, and innumerable other things are given you in the bargain. But with only an abstract succession of dates and positions you can never patch up movement itself. It slips through their intervals and is lost.

So it is with every concrete thing, however complicated. Our intellectual handling of it is a retrospective patchwork, a postmortem dissection, and can follow any order we find most expedient. We can make the thing seem self-contradictory whenever we wish to. But place yourself at the point of view of the thing's interior *doing*, and all these back-looking and conflicting conceptions lie harmoniously in your hand. Get at the expanding centre of a human character, the *élan vital* of a man, as Bergson calls it, by living sympathy, and at a stroke you see how it makes those who see it from without interpret it in such diverse ways. It is something that breaks into both honesty and dishonesty, courage and cowardice, stupidity and insight, at the touch of varying circumstances, and you feel exactly why and how it does this, and never seek to identify it stably with any of these single abstractions. Only your intellectualist does that,—and you now also feel why *he* must do it to the end. (pp. 256-62)

What really *exists* is not things made but things in the making. Once made, they are dead, and an infinite number of alternative conceptual decompositions can be used in defining them. But put yourself *in the making* by a stroke of intuitive sympathy with the thing and, the whole range of possible decompositions coming at once into your possession, you are no longer troubled with the question which of them is the more absolutely true. Reality *falls* in passing into conceptual analysis; it *mounts* in living its own undivided life—it buds and bourgeons, changes and creates. Once adopt the movement of this life in any given instance and you know what Bergson calls the *devenir réel* ["'real becoming'"] by which the thing evolves and grows. Philosophy should seek this kind of living understanding of the movement of reality, not follow science in vainly patching together fragments of its dead results. (pp. 263-64)

You may say, and doubtless some of you now are saying inwardly, that [Bergson's] remanding us to sensation in this wise is only a regress, a return to that ultra-crude empiricism which your own idealists since Green have buried ten times over. I confess that it is indeed a return to empiricism, but I think that the return in such accomplished shape only proves the latter's immortal truth. What won't stay buried must have some genuine life. *Am anfang war die tat;* fact is a *first;* to which all our conceptual handling comes as an inadequate second, never its full equivalent. When I read recent transcendentalist literature—I must partly except my colleague Royce!—I get nothing but a sort of marking of time, champing of jaws, pawing of the ground, and resettling into the same attitude, like a weary horse in a stall with an empty manger. It is but turning over the same few threadbare categories, bringing the same objections, and urging the same answers and solutions, with never a new fact or a new horizon coming into sight. But open Bergson, and new horizons loom on every page you read. It is like the breath of the morning and the song of birds. It tells of reality itself, instead of merely reiterating what dusty-minded professors have written about what other previous professors have thought. Nothing in Bergson is shopworn or at second hand.

That he gives us no closed-in system will of course be fatal to him in intellectualist eyes. He only evokes and invites; but he first annuls the intellectualist veto, so that we now join step with reality with a philosophical conscience never quite set free before. As a French disciple of his well expresses it: "Bergson claims of us first of all a certain inner catastrophe, and not every one is capable of such a logical revolution. But those who have once found themselves flexible enough for the execution of such a psychological change of front, discover somehow that they can never return again to their ancient attitude of mind. They are now Bergsonians . . . and possess the principal thoughts of the master all at once. They have understood in the fashion in which one loves, they have caught the whole melody and can thereafter admire at their leisure the originality, the fecundity, and the imaginative genius with which its author develops, transposes, and varies in a thousand ways by the orchestration of his style and dialectic, the original theme." (pp. 264-66)

William James, *"Bergson and His Critique of Intellectualism,"* in his A Pluralistic Universe: Hibbert Lectures at Manchester College on the Present Situation in Philosophy, *Longmans, Green, and Co., 1909, pp. 225-73.*

WALTER B. PITKIN   (essay date 1910)

[*Pitkin was a distinguished American psychologist and journalist. In the following excerpt, he suggests that William James's inter-pretation of Bergson in* A Pluralistic Universe *(see excerpt dated 1909) is based on an essential misunderstanding of the French philosopher's ideas.*]

If there is one task more thankless and unprofitable than criticizing critics, it is reporting reporters. Yet even this seems warranted by its benefits in the case of Professor James and his recent accounts of M. Bergson. Professor James is the unchallenged veteran leader of American psychology and philosophy; M. Bergson the rising marshal of French thinkers. Each man's marching orders are taken in deadly earnest at home and abroad. So, if both speak as in agreement while differing profoundly, the unhappy rank and file, which is trained to take words at their mouth value, will be confused. That this danger is neither remote nor imaginary, can scarcely be doubted by any one who takes pains to compare James's anti-intellectualism with Bergson's, and James's report of Bergson with Bergson's report on himself. Behind one or two important common convictions, which are chiefly on questions of method, a mass of far-reaching, irreconcilable doctrines lies half-concealed. For the sake of clarity and with no approval or criticism of either philosopher's opinions, I should like to point out a few divergent tendencies and sharp oppositions which, I believe, must constitute a perpetual injunction against every attempt to identify or even to harness up the radical empiricism of Cambridge with Parisian intuitionalism. "Abridgments like this of other men's opinions are very unsatisfactory. They always work injustice," says Professor James at the close of his sketch of Bergsonism in *A Pluralistic Universe.* This is twice true of the following remarks, which are largely an abridgment of an abridgment; but their injustice weighs lightly over against their fairness.

Professor James can find much in Bergson's pages echoing his own sentiments. Like him, Bergson opposes every static view of reality, stands out for genuine freedom and continuous creation in a flowing world. Both thinkers insist that man must look inward, dive into the stream of consciousness, for the richest truths. As destructive critics of static absolutism, both stand shoulder to shoulder. But at these broader tendencies of speculation and of method agreement stops. Bergson goes the way of the older cosmologists, James stays with the subjectivistically inclined psychologists. Bergson repudiates psychophysics and nearly all experiment and hypothesis going with it, while James often unconsciously, as in his *Principles of Psychology,* embraces Fechner and all he stands for. Bergson peers through his "mental stream" and spies something underneath; but James forever lingers in the flood, saying: *"though one part of our experience may lean upon another part to make it what it is in any one of several aspects in which it may be considered, experience as a whole is self-containing and leans on nothing."* Bergson declares that the *élan vital* and its antagonistic countercurrent are each in its pure form unknowable, inasmuch as all cognition is nothing but a kind of collision between these two streams and a mixing of them: James long ago assured us that his radical empiricism "must neither admit into its constructions any element *that is not directly experienced* nor exclude from them any element *that is directly experienced.*" Where Bergson thinks of life as transcending experience, James thinks only of experience as transcending conceptual thinking. Were I to attempt an all-around account of their systems, I should certainly turn everything in them about this fundamental difference in the point of view. Hence, for Bergson, the last inwardness of every experience is quite beyond the most searching intuition; it is, however, not in the least "absolutely dumb and evanescent, the *merely ideal* limit of our minds,'' as that reality ''independent'' of human thinking appears to James. It is twofold, a tremendous creative activity and an enormously stubborn, by no means ''evanescent,'' matter. Such antitheses might be multiplied almost indefinitely, but let them pass; it is more profitable to limit ourselves to a contrast of our two philosophers' theories of the concept. For it is Bergson's critique of intellectualism, as founded on his interpretation of conceptual experience, that wins the space of a whole chapter for him in James's *A Pluralistic Universe*. And yet it is precisely on this topic that Professor James makes me suspect that he has called upon an opponent to do a friend's service. If I read both writers correctly, Professor James has sympathetically chalked up against Bergson many a costly item which the Frenchman has never entered on his books—and never will. Before accepting this statement, you should peruse the citations in their original context I shall make; the obligation is peculiarly strong because both men freely indulge in all the tropes known to the literary artist, and still more because, in many points, their theories differ no more than but just as much as an infinitesimal segment of a curve does from an infinitesimal segment of a straight line.

James thinks to find in Bergson's theory of concepts confirmation of his own view that ''the completer our definitions of ether-waves, atoms, Gods, or souls become, the less instead of the more intelligible do they appear to us. . . . Ether and molecules may be like coordinates and averages, only so many crutches by the help of which we practically perform the operation of getting about among our sensible experiences.'' But this kind of pragmatic psychology seems to me absolutely incompatible with everything Bergson is driving at. Far from pronouncing ''matter,'' ''energy,'' and like concepts mere ''extraordinarily successful hypotheses'' whose sole claim to our preferences is their superior utility for human purposes, the French intuitionalist firmly holds to the objective reality of matter. On the very first page of his introduction to *L'evolution créatrice* I read: . . . notre intelligence, au sens étroit du mot, est destinée à assurer l'insertion parfaite de notre corps dans son milieu, *à se representer les rapports des choses extérieures entre elles, enfin à penser la matière* [''our intellect in the narrow sense of the word, is intended to assure complete integration of our body into its environment *by representing to itself the relations of exterior objects to one another, in short, to think matter*''].

To think matter! Hardly a Cambridge performance, this! The external things are ''out there,'' they are tough, thick, obstinate—quite loath to evanesce or to be the mere ideal limits of thought. And in a later chapter, ''De la Signification de la Vie,'' Bergson says that science commits no sensible error in cutting up the universe into relatively independent systems, for ''la matière s'étend dans l'espace sans y être absolument étendue'' [''matter extends in space without being extended absolutely there'']. What does this mean? That the physicist's interpretation of nature carries us further from the latter as he works out his concepts more fully? Not at all. Science is always approaching an adequate description of matter, but such a description is unattainable only as 2 is the unattainable sum of the series $1 + \frac{1}{2} + \frac{1}{4} + \frac{1}{8} + \ldots$ (pp. 225-27)

Summarizing Bergson's treatment of Zeno's paradoxes and mathematical-geometrical concepts of time and space, Professor James reports the intuitionalist as teaching that, ''instead of being interpreters of reality, *concepts negate the inwardness of reality altogether*.'' Note, please, the two words I have italicized [''concepts'' and ''altogether'']. Not Zeno's con-

cepts, not yours nor mine, but concepts *as such* are guilty. And they are not simply defective or incomplete; they are *altogether* mendacious in what concerns the interpenetrating densities of cosmic action. I defy anybody to grub so much as a grain of this ore out of Bergson's mine! Here is another fragment even less amenable to Professor James's reading:

> L'entendement est chez lui dans le domaine de la matière inerte. Sur cette matière s'excerce essentiellement l'action humaine, et l'action, . . . ne saurait se mouvoir dans l'irréel. Ainsi, *pourvu que l'on ne considère de la physique que sa forme générale, et non pas le détail de sa réalisation, on peut dire qu'elle touche l'absolu.*
>
> [''Understanding is at home in the domain of inert matter. Human action exercises itself fundamentally upon this matter, and action . . . does not know how to proceed in the unreal. Hence, *provided one considers only the general form of the physical, and not the particulars of its realization, one can say that it touches the absolute.*'']

Lo! The horrid absolute rears its head even in Bergson! And it is the dead, chopped-out concept, the ''form'' of physical knowledge, which actually fingers the monster. The concept is not invented at each man's own sweet will, by breaking up the flux with the same freedom; we do not ''create the subjects of our true as well as of our false propositions,'' as James thinks.

Atoms and ether and potential energy and all the other things of physical nature are all perfectly real objects or forces in a perfectly real space. They are, indeed, so exceedingly real, so chock full of existence, that, when we encounter them in the

A youthful portrait.

sudden shock that constitutes intelligence, we simply can not take them all in; all we gather about them in discrete thought is their surfaces at the points of our collision with them and their standstill at the instant of that collision. On this score Bergson speaks beyond all equivocation. The escape from Democritus, Aristotle, Hume, and Kant, so far as the question of spirit and matter is concerned, is found in the hypothesis

> "... que ni la matière ne determine la forme de l'intelligence, ni l'intelligence n'impose sa forme à la matière, ni la matière et l'intelligence n'ont reglées l'une sur l'autre par je ne sais quelle harmonie préétablie mais que *progressivement l'intelligence et la matière se sont adaptées l'une à l'autre pour s'arrêter enfin à une forme commune.* Cette adaptation se serait d'ailleurs effectuée tout naturellement, parce que c'est la même inversion du même mouvement qui crée à la fois l'intellectualité de l'esprit et la matérialité des choses."

> ["... that neither does matter determine the form of the intellect, nor does the intellect impose its form upon matter, nor are both arranged one upon the other in some unknown preestablished harmony but that progressively intellect and matter adapted themselves one to the other to finally arrive at a common form. This adaptation, moreover, would have been performed quite naturally, because it is the same inversion of the same movement that created at the same time the intellectuality of the mind and the materiality of objects."]

(pp. 228-29)

How can Professor James report that Bergson says "concepts make things less, not more intelligible, when we use them seriously and radically?" How can he believe that Bergson thinks concepts "serve us practically more than theoretically"? That the Frenchman regards them as "throwing their map of abstract terms and relations around our present experience"? And that the author of *L'evolution créatrice* thinks that "conception, developing its subtler and more contradictory implications, comes to an end of its usefulness, . . . and runs itself into the ground," whereupon Bergson "*drops* conception"? (Professor James himself italicizes this last verb.)

The fact is, according to Bergson, that concepts alone make things intelligible; that they serve us in theory better than in practise ("action," he says, "breaks the circle of logic"); and that, far from being a map *thrown about* our present experience, they *are* our present experience itself, halted in its flight, and by the shock of stopping or "kicking back" condensing, as it were, into hard lumps—always into lumps of perfectly real, objective nature. These lumps or precipitations are not "cut out" of reality, at all, as Professor James construes Bergson. They are a phase of reality, they stay in their stream. They are neither copies nor distortions of matter in the picture-gallery of the vital force; they are intelligence itself and matter itself, each in a *special* relation to the other. What Bergson sees and James apparently does not is that things are none the less real when they are motionless and external to one another than when they shoot through one another and interpenetrate and move. James imagines that Bergson agrees with him in supposing a concept to be a convenient misrepresentation made for exclusively practical purposes. But, as I read Bergson, he clearly states that a concept is reality (a part or phase of reality) retarded and solidified, representing nothing whatever, distorting nothing whatever, but simply *being* that which we *live* it as being, a cosmic character distinct from others. In its particular setting the characteristic is distinct, but only there;

where there is no collision between the vital energy and obstructing matter, where the former runs on smoothly (and perhaps also where matter is serenely alone and uninvaded by spirit?), there all other qualities of nature shoot through it and live in it, so that it is external to them in neither space nor time. Were more quoting called for, we might reprint pages iii and iv of *L'evolution créatrice.* where Bergson—after describing all those who, like James, deem the best product of intellectual effort a symbol or pragmatic construct, as suffering from "un excès d'humilité" ["an excess of humility"]—argues that the pragmatic nature of human activity makes it most probable that conceptual thinking reaches the absolute or some feature of it. "Une intelligence tendue vers l'action qui s'accomplira et vers la réaction qui s'ensuivra, palpant son objet pour en recevoir à chaque instant l'impression mobile, est une intelligence qui touche quelque chose de l'absolu" ["An intellect extended toward the action that will occur and toward the reaction that will follow, touching its object in order to receive from it at each moment the changing impression, is an intellect that touches something of the absolute"].

These random gleanings misrepresent each philosopher, of course, for each writes a flux even as he preaches one. But I think that whoever will work out in detail some of the contrasts indicated must sooner or later come to wonder how such an acute, sympathetic, and well-seasoned reader as Professor James ever fancied he saw an exponent of his anti-intellectualism in Bergson. How could he write that Bergson and Bradley together "have broken my confidence in concepts down"? Surely, if ever a man taught that concepts are to be trusted, *in so far as we know what we are doing with them, and in so far as we use them intelligently,* that man is Bergson. For James, the lead of intellect sends us over the divide between rationalism and empiricism down into the intellectualistic valley of dry bones and into the abyss of deception. For Bergson, the intellect heads always for the living reality of things, but, finding each next advance more arduous than the last, stops always at an approximation of that last truth which one bold, keen intuition suggests but can never quite lay bare. Could two theories of the concept differ more in spirit? (pp. 229-31)

> *Walter B. Pitkin, "James and Bergson: Or, Who Is against Intellect?" in* The Journal of Philosophy, *Vol. VII, No. 9, April 28, 1910, pp. 225-31.*

THE NATION, NEW YORK   (essay date 1910)

[*In the following excerpt, the critic explicates Bergson's ideas concerning the space-time dichotomy.*]

What is called Bergsonism is not entirely a doctrine without recognizable ancestry. The germ of some of it is discernible in an important little book, *De la contingence des lois de la nature,* 1874, by Bergson's teacher at the Ecole Normale, Emile Boutroux, who has recently visited America. Some of it also may be found—combined with much else—in the philosophy of a notable French thinker, too little read outside of France, Renouvier, who exercised likewise a considerable influence upon the formation of James's metaphysical ideas. Bergson is very far from merely repeating doctrines of these older contemporaries of his; but he represents the same general tendency of French thought, and part of his work has consisted in developing further certain conceptions found in one or the other, or in disengaging these conceptions from their former contexts to recombine them with one or two other familiar motives of nineteenth-century speculation. Yet the outcome of this process has as high a degree of originality as is often found in philosophical reasonings; and the principal argument of *Time and Free Will* may be regarded as an essentially novel contribution to metaphysics.

Time, as Kant had observed, is "the form of inner experience," as space is of our perception of external objects; and this, Renouvier had contended—giving up as barren and incomprehensible Kant's supra-temporal ego behind both series of phenomena—properly means that succession and duration and becoming are of the very essence of the reality that is inwardly and directly known to us. But precisely what, Bergson asks, is the nature of our time-consciousness, and what is its relation to our spatial imagery? The subtle analysis which he brings to bear upon this question leads him to the conclusion that there is in mankind a strong disposition to think time under forms borrowed from, and properly applicable only to, space, to assimilate the idea of duration to that of extension; and this, he finds, is the source of a host of errors in philosophy, including the error of determinism. All the perplexities of the ancient puzzle of the freedom of the will "come back, without our suspecting it, to the following question: 'Can time be adequately represented by space'?" Bergson's answer is a decided "No." Time past may, indeed, be translated by subsequent reflection into categories alien to its original nature; but time in actual flow has a nature unique and irreducible. Space we think of in terms of quantity, and as having all its points simultaneous with one another and external to one another, their true relations *inter se* being unmodified by change. We can ideally pass through it in any direction, can repeat the same course, can come back to the same point. Now our ideas of causal uniformity—derived largely from our experience of physical objects in space—though they refer to temporal sequences, are yet, so to say, woven upon a spatial warp. By "the same cause" we mean a set of conditions to which we can revert, which can be reconstituted without being significantly modified by the mere lapse of time. But time itself—the pure duration of inner experience—is, says Bergson, not a homogeneous and measurable quantity at all; it is, moreover, a one-directional flow whose successive moments imperceptibly inter-penetrate, which permits no repetition and no returning, and in which every later phase, merely because it *is* later, must be different from and incommensurable with every earlier one. Thus our temporal inner life is a kind of existence to which the principle that "the same cause must always be followed by the same effect" is irrelevant, since the required "sameness" can there never be wholly realized. Future time, again, is not, to one actually involved in the temporal process, "contained in" present or past; and to say that the entire content of the future is completely preformed in the present or past, that

> With earth's first clay they did the last man knead,

is simply to treat succession as if it were simultaneity, to abandon the point of view of real temporal experience, where the future always appears as in process of production through and partly by means of the present. The easy triumph of the old determinist arguments over the old freedomist arguments was due, Bergson holds, to the failure of the freedomist to utilize this distinction between the temporal and the spatial ways of thinking reality. Both parties, for example, "pictured the deliberation preceding choice under the form of an oscillation in space, while it really consists in a dynamic process in which the self and its motives, like real living beings, are in a constant state of becoming." . . .

It may be remarked . . . that in his determination to make a complete severance between the temporal and the spatial categories, Bergson goes so far as to defeat his own purpose. To say that duration is pure quality with no quantitative aspect, and that its moments, though successive, are "without reciprocal externality," is itself a way of reducing time to simultaneity. Bergson's pages on this point at times singularly resemble the arguments by which Professor Royce has ingeniously sought to show that experience as a whole—the "Absolute Experience"—must be timeless. (p. 499)

> *A review of "Time and Free Will: An Essay on the Immediate Data of Consciousness," in* The Nation, *New York, Vol. XCI, No. 2369, November 24, 1910, pp. 499-500.*

THE NATION, NEW YORK   (essay date 1911)

[*In the following excerpt, the critic examines Bergson's concept of duration, contending that the superficial clarity of his language masks major flaws in his arguments.*]

The latest notable modern French philosopher is at one with the earliest in his conception of the proper starting-point of philosophy. Like Descartes, M. Bergson begins his metaphysical construction with "that existence of which we are most assured and which we know best—our own"; his earliest work was characteristically concerned with "the immediate data of consciousness." His whole doctrine, indeed, might not uninstructively be interpolated at a definite point in the Cartesian framework; it is in some sort an attempt at the completion of a specific task which Descartes undertook but almost immediately abandoned. That the "thinking thing" is known to us directly, and most surely to exist, the author of the *Discourse on Method* showed; that it has no attributes in common with that other kind of possible entity of which the essence is spatial extension, M. Bergson . . . heartily agrees. But *what sort* of being that inwardly certified existence is, what *its* positive essence is, Descartes only perfunctorily inquired; certainly he did not stay for an answer. Mathematician and physicist by training, he allowed his attention too quickly to become engrossed by that clear and simple external world of space wherein it was possible to geometrize.

The answer to the neglected question M. Bergson offers. The essence of the *moi qui pense* is ["self who thinks"] is change; to be conscious is, first and foremost, to experience temporal transition. If the distinctive attribute of pure matter is extension, the distinctive attribute of pure consciousness is duration. But in that inner world which has duration for its attribute, it is quite impossible to geometrize; for it is not at all a clear and simple world. So radical is the difference in nature between the two kinds of being, that all the preconceptions and habits of thought appropriate in dealing with the one must be put off by those who would understand the other; above all must the mathematician's habit of thinking in terms of quantity—of homogeneous and commensurable magnitudes—be abandoned by those desirous of apprehending the nature of the "real duration" characteristic of consciousness. The philosophy which develops seriously the Cartesian insight that reality is best known to us immediately and inwardly is, therefore, not likely to be a philosophy of "clear and distinct ideas"; probably few readers of M. Bergson, whether in French or English, will find it so. "*If*," Professor James once wrote, "anything can make hard things easy to follow, it is a style like Bergson's." The praise is deserved, but the saving clause was a wide one. M.

Bergson's talent for exposition is extraordinary, and may beguile his most superficial readers into supposing that the matters expounded are clear; but they are not so in fact, and are scarcely even meant to be so. It is one of the articles of the new doctrine that "for our intelligence to insert itself into the movement of reality, to grasp the nature of reality by means of that *intellectual sympathy* which we call intuition—*cela est d'une difficulté extrême*" ["that is extremely difficult"]. Those who do not experience the difficulty are to understand that they have not been initiated into the doctrine.

To its obscurities, no doubt, the new system owes part of its popular vogue. Of nothing does mankind talk more willingly than of the ineffable; and there is a good deal of the ineffable in M. Bergson's philosophy. There is in it—to use a much-abused word—more than a touch of mysticism; only, the object revealed to the direct mystical intuition (though hidden from the logical understanding) is not the peace "which holds quiet the centre" of things, . . . but rather the unceasing restlessness and infinite ability of the inner nature of each of us. Very curiously, however, the contrast between these two natures—the immutable One of historic mysticism and the *flux posé sur flux* ["flux on top of flux"] of the new metaphysics—tends in the course of M. Bergson's analyses to become, at several points, rather evanescent. He discovers, as he believes, in "real duration," when the idea of it is purified of all foreign elements, some surprising peculiarities. It is not a succession of discrete moments, but an indivisible unity; its parts are not "outside of" one another, but reciprocally "permeate" one another; it has, properly speaking, no quantitative attributes at all; and it appears to have the right (claimed by the Absolutes of many philosophical systems) to take some liberties with the principle of contradiction. A time-process so characterized can not easily be discriminated from the changeless and the eternal. The truth is that M. Bergson—led by certain plausible dialectical considerations—has, in spite of his best intentions, falsified the real nature of our consciousness of temporal duration; and he has consequently come perilously near to a metaphysics diametrically opposite to that at which he aimed. To think of even "subjective" time with a mind wholly purged of the category of quantity is not merely "of an extreme difficulty"; it is a psychological impossibility—just as it is a logical self-contradiction. To be aware of a transition or to feel duration without in some degree distinguishing "before" from "after," the lapsing from the incoming content of consciousness, is an inconceivable feat; internal multiplicity, "reciprocal externality," of elements is of the essence of the experience.

In one of the arguments by which M. Bergson is led into this misconception, it is possible to discern precisely the point at which his philosophy is diverted from its proper course. The argument is simply a revival of the ancient paradox of the Eleatic Zeno about the moving arrow. Change, it is argued, cannot be constituted by the serial addition of distinct and definite moments, nor is a duration produced by the mere consecutive aggregation of states. For each of the component moments, taken by itself, can only be a static mass of content; transition as such consists in the *getting from* one moment to another. Nor can this gulf be bridged by multiplying the number of units and imagining them to be very near one another. Between any two nominally successive moments there must be an interval; and it is in these ever-elusive intervals that the transition takes place. "Before the intervening movement," we are told in **L'evolution créatrice**, "you will always experience the disappointment of the child who by clapping his hands together tries to crush the smoke. The movement slips away from you through the interval." Now what M. Bergson has done here is, first, to assume that if the sequence of our states of consciousness is divisible at all, it must constitute a continuum like the mathematician's line—which is such that between any two distinct points, however near, intervening points may be taken; then, in order to rid "real duration" of the paradoxes of the continuum, M. Bergson has gone on to deny that it *is* a numerical sum of smaller "pieces" of duration. But if, instead of applying, or misapplying, this sort of dialectic to our time-experience, M. Bergson had simply examined that experience itself, he would have found his initial assumption false. "All our sensible experiences, as we get them immediately," wrote William James (in the very chapter of *A Pluralistic Universe* which was intended to be a defence of M. Bergson's philosophy), "change by discrete pulses of perception, each of which keeps us saying 'more, more, more,' or 'less, less, less,'" as the definite increments or diminutions make themselves felt. Fechner's term of the 'threshold' is only one way of naming the quantitative discreteness in the change of all our sensible experiences. They come to us in drops. Time itself comes in drops." It is, James adds, our intellect that transforms and falsifies this concrete succession of definite amounts of content by representing it as a continuum, by "insisting that in every pulse of it an infinite number of minor pulses shall be ascertainable." In so far as we are concerned only with the real changes in our perceptions, there need be "no Zenonian paradoxes or Kantian antinomies to trouble us."

Such is the report of actual psychological introspection about the consciousness of succession; it exactly reverses M. Bergson's account of the matter, according to which, in order to avoid the Zenonian paradoxes and Kantian antinomies, we must represent duration as in itself indivisible, irreducible to separate "drops," but must charge the intellect with falsely picturing duration by converting the idea of it into that of a sequence of discrete elements. This misrepresentation, moreover, M. Bergson regards as due to the intellect's unhappy habit of ascribing to time the attributes of space; whereas the truth seems to be rather in the view expressed a number of years ago by another French philosopher, M. Pillon: "Time, with its two aspects of co-existence and succession, assumes in appearance the character of *continuity* only because it borrows it from space, only by being, so to speak, exteriorised and spatialised by the imagination." In short, it seems to be M. Bergson himself who consults logic rather than introspection for his conception of the nature of duration as a phenomenon of direct experience; and it is he who "spatializes" the idea of "subjective time" by gratuitously importing into the pulse-like sequence of our conscious states, the ancient difficulties about infinite divisibility which inhere in the spatial continuum.

M. Bergson's notion of the *durée réelle* ["real duration"] is the fundamental as well as the most characteristic thing in his philosophy; the foregoing comments, therefore, touch the taproot of the system in its present form. But its present form is not the one in which the profound and germinal idea from which it springs finds its true expression. Meanwhile, there are in these volumes many other fruitful conceptions more or less dissociable from the misapprehension which has been pointed out. The most important of these, and the one most likely to gain wide popular currency and to influence the general view of things of our generation, is the doctrine of the "creative" character of the evolutionary process; the universe for M. Bergson is no block-world, no ready-made article, but a constant "becoming" of genuine novelties and of real enrichments of content. This doctrine is by no means a new one; it has been growing up for a century, though long overshadowed by mechanistic interpretations of evolution; it has, for example, been vigorously defended for above thirty years by one of our American biological vitalists, Dr. Edmund Montgomery. But it has, perhaps, never been set forth so fully, so impressively, or with so much ingenuity of argumentation as in *L'evolution créatrice.* (pp. 648-49)

"Bergson in English," in The Nation, *New York, Vol. XCII, No. 2400, June 29, 1911, pp. 648-49.*

J. M'KELLAR STEWART   (essay date 1911)

[*In the following excerpt, Stewart analyzes Bergson's concept of intuition.*]

In the *Critique of Pure Reason* Kant complains that Metaphysics has not been able to enter into the sure path of a science, and he sets himself the task of expounding a method by means of which such an entrance may be secured and progress achieved. Bergson, too, is dissatisfied with the progress hitherto made by philosophy, and also with the outlook even from the Kantian and post-Kantian point of view. He, too, has the desire to lead metaphysics into the sure path of a science capable of indefinite progress, and with this end in view he formulates his method. (p. 3)

The foundation of Bergson's philosophy is his method of intuition. "Philosophizing just consists in placing one's self, by an effort of intuition, in the interior of concrete reality." By intuition is meant "that kind of *intellectual sympathy* by means of which one transports one's self to the interior of an object so as to coincide with that which constitutes the very reality of the object, the *unique* reality, consequently inexpressible" (in concepts). Briefly, to philosophize is to feel the palpitating of the heart of reality.

When Kant was seeking a safe method for philosophy he was guided by the methods which had succeeded in scientific construction. He passed in review the sciences of formal logic, mathematics, and physics, and proceeded to extend to philosophy the method of hypothesis which had been found successful in physics. Hence his demand that objects should conform to our faculty of knowledge; hence his constant proof by reference to the possibility of experience.

Kant was influenced in his dissection of the faculty of knowledge by the state of science in his time. Mathematics, physics, and, to a less extent, chemistry, had attained to a high degree of perfection; psychology and biology were quite undeveloped. The application of Kant's critical method consisted in discovering what the nature of our mind must be, and what the constitution of nature must be, *if* the pretensions of the science of his time were justified; but of these pretensions themselves he has not made any criticism. "He accepted without discussion," says Bergson, "the idea of a single science, capable of binding with the same cogency all parts of the given, and of co-ordinating them in a system which should present in all its parts an equal stability."

Kant's categories are for him the conditions of all possible knowledge, but these categories are the general notions which form the foundation of science in one of its stages—in the mechanical stage. That this is implicit in Kant's system, though not intentionally so, we may see from one of the later developments of his thought, which issued in philosophical agnosticism, and in the elevation to an exclusive validity of the physical and mathematical sciences. Bergson's criticism of

Kant is that he did not realize, in the *Critique of Pure Reason,* that science becomes less and less objective, more and more symbolic, in proportion as it proceeds from the physical to the vital, from the vital to the psychical. Experience does not move, in his eyes, in two different and perhaps opposed directions, the one conformable to the direction of the intelligence, the other contrary to it. There is, for him, only *one* experience, and intelligence covers its whole ground. Kant expresses this by saying that all our intuitions are sensuous, or, in other words, infra-intellectual. And this would have to be admitted, in fact, if our science presented in all its parts an equal objectivity. But suppose, on the contrary, that science is less and less objective, more and more symbolic, as it proceeds from the physical to the psychical, passing through the vital: then, as it is certainly necessary to perceive a thing in some way in order to succeed in symbolizing it, there would be an intuition of the psychical, and, more generally, of the vital, which the intelligence would doubtless transpose and translate, but which would, none the less, transcend the intelligence. There would be, in other words, a supra-intellectual intuition.

Kant was landed in an opposition between understanding and reason, between categories and ideas, between phenomena and noumena, between nature and spirit. Knowledge, for him, was confined to phenomena; we may *think* God, Freedom, Immortality, as limiting or regulative "ideas," but we cannot *know* them. This limitation of knowledge to the phenomenal, and this problematic conception of noumenal reality arise from the difficulty in which Kant involved himself by taking his cue as to the nature of mind from the science of his day. . . . The nature of his categories precluded, made impossible, the *knowledge* of human freedom, for example. The framework of intelligence or understanding was such for Kant that freedom could not be fitted into it. Freedom must be relegated to the sphere of faith. "If one reads closely the *Critique of Pure Reason* one sees that Kant has criticized, not reason in general, but reason fashioned to the habits and exigencies of the Cartesian mechanical theory or of the Newtonian physics. If there be a *single* science of nature (and Kant does not seem to doubt this), if all phenomena and all objects are spread out on one and the same plane, so that our knowledge of them will be a single and continuous but entirely superficial experience (and such is the constant hypothesis of the *Critique of Pure Reason*), then there if only one sort of causality in the world; all phenomenal causality implies rigorous determination, and one must seek for liberty outside of experience."

Bergson, so far as I can see, does not quarrel with Kant's conception of the nature of the human understanding, nor does he contend for an extension of its dominion. It is true that he repudiates with decision any suggestion that intelligence-knowledge is relative, and maintains that, while it may be limited knowledge, it brings us, in a very true sense, into touch with the "absolute," if we understand by that term no than reality in some one of its windings. In other words, Bergson discards, in the first place, the distinction between noumena and phenomena, and substitutes for it the notion of two opposed movements constitutive of reality—spirituality or duration on the one hand, and materiality or matter on the other. In the second instance, he replaces the distinction between understanding in the narrow sense as the faculty of conceptions, and reason as the faculty of ideas, by the distinction between two complementary but opposed faculties of knowledge, intelligence and intuition. Bergson will have nothing to do with "things-in-themselves," either with subjects in themselves or with objects in themselves. He will not allow for a moment that we are condemned to the phantom of an incomprehensible "thing-in-itself," but insists that by means of intelligence and intuition, complementary faculties, we are introduced into the absolute. By means of that which is material in ourselves we are enabled to know matter; and by means of that which is vital and spiritual in ourselves we can come into sympathy with life and spirit. The principle here implied—that of "ontological affinity" between knower and known—seems to be an unobjectionable one. The difficulty arises when we come to analyse the nature of the knower. Kant illegitimately limited that nature, and so limited the knowable. Bergson seeks a more accurate analysis, though in a way far removed from Kant's deduction. He endeavours to establish the position that the faculty of knowledge as Kant understood it is a mere fragment of that faculty in its entirety.

It is not by increasing the number of the categories of understanding or intelligence by adding, for example, such a one as that of "purpose" that mechanical limits will be removed, and life and spirit brought within the grasp of intelligence. In virtue of its very nature it is incapable of seizing the meaning of life. Even when it makes use of teleological conceptions it merely *appears* to escape a mechanical theory of life, for the most radical finalism is only an inverted mechanical theory. In short, no multiplication of the conceptions of intelligence will ever bring us into closer touch with life and spirit, for the concept applies only to the static, the inert, the permanent, whereas life is always going, ever becoming. Intelligence is characterized by a native inability to comprehend life. Its work is to re-constitute, and to re-constitute with ready-made conceptions, so that what is *new* in each moment of a history escapes it, and still more the process itself from moment to moment is beyond its grasp. If the intelligence were capable of knowing reality in its fulness then the assumption would be necessary that reality is given, in its completeness, from all eternity. This conception of reality is fundamentally opposed to Bergson's view of life and mind; consequently he insists on the limitations of intelligence as a faculty of knowledge.

Must life and mind, then, be relegated to the sphere of unknowable realities? Is life in its creative activity incomprehensible? Must man for ever remain deprived of it secret? Must he content himself with taking a number of snap-shots of it as it glides by; pictures which show him only patches of its surface? Must he despair of entering into the sanctuary in which life shows itself in the making? Truly, if intelligence were his only faculty of knowledge, and if intelligence were such as Bergson holds it to be, the way of the knowledge of life would be closed, and its secret remain hidden from human eyes. But this is not the tragic conclusion of Bergson's philosophy. Life may stubbornly refuse to yield up its secret to intelligence, but it can be known by a second faculty, which man possesses in germ, and which he may develop—the faculty of intuition. It is vague and discontinuous—"an almost extinguished lamp, which flickers up only at intervals for a few instants." Nevertheless, by a literally superhuman effort the philosopher may transcend the point of view of intelligence, and by a stroke of sympathetic insight perceive or feel the impulsion at the heart of reality. Experience is not confined within the bounds of rational experience; thought is wider than reasoned thought. Intelligence is supplemented by intuition, and a perfect humanity would be one in which intuition and intelligence were both developed; for intelligence, as it progresses, gives us a clearer knowledge of matter, and so enables us to adapt ourselves to our material environment; and intuition, as it develops, projects a flickering and feeble light upon "our person-

ality, our freedom, the place which we occupy in the whole of nature, our origin, and perhaps also our destiny." Thus the facts which Kant has extruded from knowledge and relegated to faith are brought again by Bergson within the sphere of knowledge by means of intuition. (pp. 5-10)

Bergson has no desire to oppose intelligence to intuition with a view to the disparagement of the former faculty. In fact, he claims to rid knowledge acquired by intelligence of the relativism with which it has again and again been charged. He has no desire, at any rate, to encourage intellectual scepticism. Intelligence does tend to give us a knowledge of absolute reality, but its range is limited. Intelligence and intuition are *complementary* the one of the other, when each is confined to its own sphere. It is true that they move in directions the inverse of each other, but reality displays just such opposing movements, and, so long as intelligence is content to confine itself to following the movement towards materiality, its knowledge, though incomplete, is not relative. In fact, as we have already noted, Bergson wishes to break down the barrier raised by Kant between "phenomenal" and "metaphysical" knowledge; his aim is to bring about an agreement between science and metaphysic without compromising either. "The realities of 'metaphysical' order are not," he says, "transcendent to the world of 'phenomena.' They are internal to the phenomenal life (*i.e.* the physiological or organic life), although limited by it." Kant had illegitimately introduced an extra-intellectual element into his explanation of knowledge. As extra-intellectual, it was unknowable in itself. Now Bergson holds that reality may be extra-intellectual, that is to say, either infra-conceptual or supra-conceptual, and yet knowable. We may instal ourselves in this extra-intellectual real by an effort of intuition. If this be

A letter written by Bergson to George Guyau, secretary of the Académie française.

possible, metaphysic and science, though still two opposed ways of knowing, will be complementary of each other. The one will be increasingly dominated by the law of identity; it will proceed by means of concepts, in which space is always immanent; it will involve a distinction between the knower and the known. The other will be dynamic, by immediate intuition, in which the distinction between the knower and the known is removed or has not yet emerged; in which the act of knowledge coincides with the generative act of reality. "Science and metaphysic are re-united in the intuition. A truly intuitive philosophy would realize this so much desired union. At the same time as it constituted metaphysic a positive (*i.e.* progressive and indefinitely perfectible) science, it would lead the sciences specifically called positive to become aware of their true range, which is often greater than scientists themselves imagine."

It is just here that Bergson disclaims all alliance with or kinship to the mystics in their reaction against positive science. "The doctrine which I hold," he says, "is throughout a protest against mysticism, since it proposes to reconstruct the bridge (broken since Kant) between metaphysic and science." Nevertheless, he holds that if by mysticism one understands "a certain appeal to the inner and profound life," his philosophy is mystic, as all philosophy must needs be. But the reality to which he rises or descends in his intuitive efforts is not more abstract than that from which he sets out. It is more concrete, and intelligible reality is immanent in it.

Scientists sometimes rise above their method. Indeed in every case of great scientific advance that is just what happens. The fruitful ideas of science are due to an intuitive metaphysical effort in which the scientist or philosopher has, by a flash of genius, been able to transport himself to the heart of reality, round which he had hitherto been hovering, penetrate to its depths, and like the poet "quaff the live current." At that moment he transcends intelligence. Immediately, however, the idea is immobilized in concepts, and the attempt initiated to express the reality in fixed terms. Every science has, ultimately, its basis of intuition, which has been elaborated, in a sense degraded, by dialectic or logical process, and *the* great aim of the philosopher is to mount the slope down which science has travelled in its immobilizing, that is, its intelligizing of the moving real, and by a violent reversal of the procedure of science to instal himself once more in this reality and feel the original impulsion at its source—an extremely difficult operation, in which the mind "does violence to itself," entirely reversing the manner in which it habitually thinks. Divesting itself of all the categories which are so many nets in which to imprison, immobilize, and intelligize living reality, it will *see* reality, form, if any, "fluid" concepts which will differ for each tendency or qualitative shade exhibited by reality, and which will remain for ever inexpressible in speech or image or fixed concept. It will thus attain to disinterested, immediate knowledge—"immediate" in the sense in which Bergson uses the word in the title of his book, *The Immediate Data of Consciousness,* that is, knowledge "emptied of all which does not come from the object itself and, consequently, infallible and perfect." It is the perception of reality, "as it would perceive itself if its apperception and its existence exactly coincided." It is consciousness illuminating the throbbing heart of reality, but in no sense interfering with or influencing it. With Wordsworth we feel

> A sense sublime
> Of something far more deeply interfused,
> Whose dwelling is the light of setting suns,
> And the round ocean and the living air,

And the blue sky, and in the mind of man:
> A motion and a spirit that impels
> All thinking things, all objects of all thought,
> And rolls through all things.

Science is this metaphysical intuition in logical dress. Philosophy must remove the dress, lay bare the intuition.

All knowledge, it may be admitted, implies a species of "sympathetic insight." The scientist, for example, seeks to tune himself as much as possible into harmony with his object. He desires to eliminate, so far as he can, the subjective factor. He approximates, as nearly as is practicable, to a "mere" intelligence. Practical considerations may have influenced him in the undertaking of his task, a glow of enthusiasm appears again and again as he finds nature yielding up her secrets to him; but these are sternly put out of mind in the actual pursuit of his object, *quâ* scientist. This sympathy, however, is usually regarded as a condition, a necessary presupposition, of insight. Insight is the important thing when it is *knowledge* of the object that is in question. Bergson appears to lay the greatest stress on the effort of sympathy, the intellectual expansion which conditions the insight, the subjective functioning which, accordingly as it is at a higher or lower degree of tension, coincides with some one or other of the rhythms of the reality in which we are immersed. A first effort of dilatation or concentration of the self is necessary for an insight into each different qualitative tendency, or rhythm, of reality. This is what Bergson means when he says that we must form "fluid concepts, capable of following reality in all its sinuosities." What he has in mind is the awareness of the effort of expansion or tension necessary for sympathy with one or other of the aspects of reality. In this effort we ourselves are performing a pre-logical, if not alogical, movement which has its counterpart, and which we feel has its counterpart, in reality. Our act of spirit coincides with the creative activity in the universe. The intuition, then, is awareness of this activity of the self, *plus,* necessarily, the awareness of something which is not ourselves which has the same rhythm or movement, the same degree of tension, the same perfection of interpenetration of parts as we. Or more accurately, perhaps, there is the feeling of a movement, originally in the self, no longer, however, regarded as a movement of the self, but simply as a *real* movement. The subjective factor has disappeared; the distinction between subject and object has vanished; life, in that moment, the life of the whole in one of its movements, is felt, as it proceeds to new creation.

The position of Hegel is immediately suggested to one's mind. He, in his *Logic* reaches the conception of perfected knowledge as that in which the difference between subject and object disappears. "If we suppose cognition and volition, as finite activities, to have done their work, then the matter, which at first has the appearance of being extraneously received, will have been thoroughly intelligized and reduced to law; while on the other hand, through volition, it will have become, in all its parts, the vehicle or expression of rational ends. In that case, it may be argued, the self-conscious knower would recognise in the object nothing foreign, but only, as it were, the realization of his own personality." But while for Hegel this ideal was capable of realization through the perfect synthesis of intellectual knowledge, for Bergson, though there is much in his work which brings him into line with Hegel at this point, the intuition is attainable only by undoing what intelligence has performed. His thought, generally, exhibits a closer affinity to that of Schopenhauer, who says that all great scientific discoveries are works of "immediate apprehension by the understanding.'' Each one of them is ''an immediate intuition and, as such, the work of an instant, an *aperçu,* a flash of insight. It is not the result of a process of abstract reasoning, which only serves to make the immediate knowledge of the understanding permanent for thought by bringing it under abstract concepts, that is, it makes knowledge distinct, it puts us in a position to impart it and explain it to others.'' It may be noted, however, that while Schopenhauer lays stress on the insight, Bergson emphasizes, as we have seen, the sympathetic effort which conditions the insight. Nevertheless, both are equally emphatic in insisting that intuitive insight is not gained by a synthesis or *resumé* of conceptual knowledge; nor is it achieved by perfecting such knowledge. Bergson is never tired of reiterating that we can pass from intuition to conceptual knowledge, but not from conceptual knowledge to intuition. The metaphysical intuition which is at the basis of every science, from which, indeed, the science has arisen, must be released from the trammels of concepts. The movement of mind which was necessary in order that the scientific genius might adopt the life of that which he studied must be immediately grasped, for in that moment, he was *living* the activity of his object. The intuition is to be found, then, at the beginning, and not at the end, of the process of scientific analysis. It constitutes the basis of the science. Analysis, refraction, elimination of the qualitative, begin when the genius himself and the lesser men, his disciples, elaborate it in fixed concepts. ''The simple act which has set analysis in motion, and dissimulates itself behind analysis, emanates from a faculty quite other than that of analysis.'' In passages such as this, which are very numerous, the underlying thought is that intelligence is bare identity.

There is, however, a sense in which the intuition may be said to be arrived at *after* analysis. ''One does not obtain from reality an intuition, that is, an intellectual sympathy with its more secret parts, unless its confidence has been gained by a long comradeship with its superficial manifestations.'' But Bergson does not admit, in this metaphor, that we have just to continue the processes of logical synthesis, in order to gain an intuition. Such an admission would certainly clash with the principle that intelligence is identity. But Bergson proceeds to say: ''It is a question of disengaging the raw materiality of the known facts,'' and this is not possible except by an expansion of mind akin to that of the mind of the scientific genius who laid the foundation of the science. ''The metaphysical intuition, although one can reach it only by means of material knowledge, is quite different from the *resumé* or synthesis of such knowledge.''

The movement of mind which Bergson calls intuition is an activity prior to or subsequent to what is usually called knowledge. From one point of view it is that out of which knowledge comes, from another point of view it is that into which knowledge goes. In either case knowledge, in the ordinary sense, vanishes. Metaphysical knowledge consists in a series of actions, in which we *live* the life of the universe in its various rhythms. We *are* for the instant that which we know. Conceptual representations are the outcome of our attempt to translate this life in fixed symbols. The psychical activity which is apprehended in metaphysical knowledge is the ultimate subject of all predication, but every predication made of it is symbolic. It is itself simple and indivisible.

Finally, you do not exhaust the nature of reality in one single effort of intuition. You do not, like the mystic in his highest flight of ecstasy, gain in one flash of insight ''the eternal wisdom which abides above all.'' In each effort of intuition

the philosopher sympathizes with reality in only one of its rhythms. Then metaphysic becomes a progressive science, empirical and positive, not completed by any one thinker, however great his genius or untiring his labour. The effort demanded is extremely difficult, and it cannot be sustained for more than an instant, but it ''nevertheless pierces the obscurity of the night in which intelligence leaves us'' with regard to the subjects which have supremely vital importance to us, our personality, our freedom, our origin, and our destiny. When it has been achieved it is impossible to express it fully in concepts or in words, or even to express it at all. Any attempt to do so will result in eviscerating it of some of its meaning. Thus in Bergson's pages we shall find images piled upon images, metaphors innumerable, all the resources of a charmingly flexible literary style and a vivid, fertile imagination brought into requisition. Edward Caird wrote of Plotinus: ''The inmost experience of our being is an experience which can never be uttered. To this difficulty Plotinus returns again and again, from new points of view, as if driven by the presence of a consciousness which masters him, which, by its very nature, can never get itself uttered, but which he cannot help striving to utter. He pursues it with all the weapons of a subtle dialectic, endeavouring to find some distinction which will fix it for his readers, and he is endlessly fertile in metaphors and symbols by which he seeks to flash some new light upon it. Yet in all this struggle and almost agony of his expression he is well aware that he can never find the last conclusive word for it, and he has to fall back on the thought that it is unspeakable, and that his words can only stimulate the hearer to make the experience for himself.'' Substitute the name of Bergson for that of Plotinus in this deliverance, and we have an accurate description of his brilliant, untiring, yet futile efforts to limn for his readers the nature of the intuition. (pp. 20-8)

> *J. M'Kellar Stewart, in his* A Critical Exposition of Bergson's Philosophy, *Macmillan and Co., Limited, 1911, 304 p.*

T. E. HULME (essay date 1911)

[*An English poet and philosopher, Hulme was one of the principal theorists of the Modernist movement in art. Rejecting the tenets of European Romanticism as intellectually diffuse, he advocated classical aesthetic standards, including clarity of statement and simplicity of form, and adhered to such standards by communicating primarily through concrete imagery in his own poetry. While Hulme's poetry has been highly praised, he is nevertheless best known for his many theoretical essays, which are collected in two posthumously published volumes:* Speculations *(1924) and* Further Speculations *(1955). Despite his contempt for European Romanticism, Hulme was greatly influenced by the essentially Romantic philosophy of Bergson, serving as the Frenchman's translator, explicator, and defender in England. In the following excerpt from an essay that originally appeared in the journal* New Age *in 1911, he defends Bergson's ideas against the charge that they are unoriginal.*]

We have been treated during the last two weeks [in the correspondence columns of the two preceding issues of the *New Age*] to a number of not very profound witticisms on the subject of Bergson. It has been triumphantly demonstrated that all his conclusions are of extreme antiquity, and great play has been made, both in prose and verse, with ''the people who discovered for the first time that they had souls, being told that it was the latest thing from Paris.'' In any case, this is a fairly mechanical form of wit, because it is the kind of attack which could have been predicted beforehand. The only effective kind of sneer is the one which only your enemy could have thought of, while these things, as a matter of fact, were anticipated in detail by me in the last of my Notes [on Bergson]. I knew they would be sure to come and I defended myself in advance.

But my attitude towards the state of mind behind these attacks has become so complicated by the mixture of partial agreement and partial disagreement that I shall try to disentangle the thing out clearly.

I agree entirely with the point of view from which these jokes spring, but, at the same time, I do not see that they have any "point." Some jokes one can never appreciate because they spring from a general mental make-up which one dislikes. I don't appreciate jokes about stupid Conservative candidates, for example. But in this case I am on the same side as the people who make the jokes. Why, then, do they seem to be rather pointless?

Take first the sneer about the antiquity of Bergson's conclusions. I agree with the statement it makes. It is so true that it is merely a platitude. But if it is to have any point as an attack, behind it must lie the supposition that philosophers may, and, indeed, ought to, establish some absolutely new conclusion—if they are to be considered of any importance. This is the most vulgar of all superstitions. No new conclusions can ever be expected, for this reason, that when a philosopher arrives at his conclusions he steps right out of the field of philosophy and into that of common knowledge, where nothing new is, of course, possible. I don't mean by this that he has made a step which he ought not to have made; it is, on the contrary, a necessary and inevitable step, which is involved in the very nature of "conclusions." Every philosopher in his conclusions must pass out of his own special craft and discipline into the kind of knowledge which every man may and should have. He passes from the study to the market-place. I use market-place here something in the sense which is intended in the epitaph which I quote below. It is one which is fairly common, but I happened to see it myself first in a churchyard in Sussex. I put in the second verse just for the fun of the thing:—

> Life is a crowded town,
>   With many crooked streets.
> Death is a market place,
>   Where all men meets.
>
> If life were a thing,
>   Which money could buy,
> The rich would live
>   And the poor would die.

By the "conclusions" of a philosopher one means his views on the soul, on the relation of matter and mind and the rest of it. If, then, in the above epitaph I take the market-place not to be death itself, but "thoughts and opinions about death," I get the position accurately enough. When the philosopher makes the inevitable step into this market-place, he steps into a region of absolute constancy. Here novelty of belief would be as ridiculous as novelty in the shape of one's body. In these matters, in this market-place, "all men meets." There can be no difference between the philosopher and the ordinary man, and no difference between the men of one generation and the men of another. There is a certain set of varied types of belief which recur constantly.

In this region there could not then be any new conclusion, and expectation of any such novelty could only spring from a confusion of mind.

But though I hold this opinion, yet at the same time I cannot see anything ridiculous in the people who have suddenly discovered that they have souls. I can explain the cause of my apparent inconsistency. To make the task more difficult in appearance I assert that not only do I accept the statement that there is no novelty as a truth, but I welcome it with considerable enthusiasm as the kind of truth I like. My defence of the people who have "discovered their souls" will be the more sincere from the fact that I personally sympathise with the attitude from which they have been laughed at. I find no attraction in the idea that things must be discovered, or even re-stated, in each generation. I would prefer that they were much more continuous with the same ideas in the past even than they are. There is tremendous consolation in the idea of fixity and sameness. If the various possible ideas about the soul at the present moment are represented by certain struggling factions in the market-place, then my own opinion in this flux and varying contests seems, if I confine myself to the present, to be a very thin and fragile thing. But if I find that a certain proportion of the men of every generation of recorded history have believed in it in substantially the same form that I myself hold it, then it gains a sudden thickness and solidity. I feel myself no longer afloat on a sea in which all the support I can get depends on my own activity in swimming, but joined on by a chain of hands to the shore. The difference it produces in the atmosphere of one's beliefs is like the difference which was produced in my outlook on London in the year when I discovered by actually walking that Oxford Street does actually go to Oxford and that Piccadilly is really the Bath road.

I need not be suspected, then, of the kind of excitement about Bergson which would be caused by the delusion that in him one was for the first time in the world's history, in the presence of the truth. That would have caused my instant flight in some other direction.

Though I do not, then, admit that there can be any real novelty in his "conclusions," yet I can sympathise with the people who find their souls a novelty. I am prepared to defend these people as having instinctively seized an aspect of the truth which the traditionalists had neglected.

The traditionalist view, I take it, is this: To state the thing, I take one definite problem and state, in the terms of the market-place, a certain view of the soul which has always existed, and has always been represented by one of the factions. More than that, the objections to that view have also always existed and always been represented. What excuse is there, then, for the people who became suddenly excited at the discovery of their soul? It is not a new view of the soul that is put forward, and it has not overcome any special obstacles peculiar to this period. Why make this tremendous fuss then?

The answer to that I should put in this way: The opposing sides in this dispute, I supposed, are represented by opposing factions in the market-place—always remembering, of course, that the market-place exists in you. These factions represent not only the various views it is possible to hold, but also the force with which these views press themselves on your mind. Beliefs are not only representations, they are also forces, and it is possible for one view to compel you to accept it in spite of your preference for another. Now, while it is impossible to create a new faction, it is possible to alter the weapons with which they are armed and so to decide which shall be predominant.

This is just what has happened in the matter of the beliefs about the soul. The growth of the mechanistic theory during the last two centuries has put a weapon of such a new and powerful nature into the hands of the materialist, that in spite of oneself one is compelled to submit. It is as if one side in the faction fight had suddenly armed themselves in steel breast-plates while the other went unprotected.

It is idle to deny this. It seems to me to be the most important fact which faces the philosopher. If one examines the psychology of belief one finds that brutal forces of this kind decide the matter just as they do more external matters. A candid examination of one's own mind shows one that the mechanistic theory has an irresistible hold over one (that is, if one has been educated in a certain way).

It isn't simply a question of what you would like to win. It is a matter simply of the recognition of forces. If you are candid with yourself you find, on examining your own state of mind, that you are forcibly, as it were, carried on to the materialist side.

It is from this frank recognition of forces that comes my excitement about Bergson. I find, for the first time, this force which carries me on willy-nilly to the materialist side, balanced by a force which is, as a matter of actual fact, apart from the question of what I want, able to meet on equal terms the first force. As the materialist side became for a time triumphant, because it became, to a certain extent, artificial by putting on heavy armour (this is how the effect of the mechanistic theory appears to me), so in Bergson, in the conception of time, I find that the other side, the scattered opposition to materialism, has taken on, for its part, a, to a certain extent, artificial form which is able to meet the other side on equal terms.

It could not be said, then, of me that I had "discovered my soul." But simply that for the first time the side that I favoured was able to meet fairly without any fudging the real force which was opposed to it. It would have been sheer silliness on my part to pretend that this force did not exist, for I knew very well that it did and affected me powerfully.

The attitude behind the sneer seems then to me to be childish, because it takes no account of real conditions. To ignore what one gets in Bergson seems to me to be as silly as to take no interest in Dreadnoughts because one is convinced that one Englishman is a match for fifty Germans. I could not be said to have suddenly discovered that I was an Englishman if I exhibited some delight in a naval victory, but merely that I had some sense of the real forces which move the things. There is, then, nothing comic in the attitude of the people who suddenly discovered their souls, but merely an admirable sense of reality, a sure instinct for the forces that really exist. They had the capacity to understand "the Realpolitik" of "belief."

Summing it all up, then, there exists this constant struggle between the two attitudes we can assume about the soul. But during the last 150 years the balance between the two has been greatly disturbed. The materialist side has clothed itself in a certain armour which makes it irresistible, at least to people of a certain honesty of mind and a certain kind of education. (pp. 38-43)

T. E. Hulme, "Notes on Bergson," in his Further Speculations, *edited by Sam Hynes, University of Minnesota Press, 1955, pp. 28-63.*

IRVING BABBITT   (essay date 1912)

[*With Paul Elmer More, Babbitt was one of the founders of the New Humanism (or neo-humanism) movement which arose during the twentieth century's second decade. The New Humanists were strict moralists who adhered to traditional conservative values in reaction to an age of scientific and artistic change. In regard to literature, they believed that the aesthetic qualities of a work should be subordinate to its moral and ethical purpose. They were particularly opposed to Naturalism, which they believed accentuated the animal nature of humans, and to any literature, such as Romanticism, that broke with established classical tradition. Besides Babbitt and More, other prominent New Humanists included Norman Foerster and T. S. Eliot, although the latter's conversion to Christianity angered Babbitt, whose concept of humanism substituted faith in humanity for faith in God. The author of several books propounding his philosophy, Babbitt was more a theorist than a literary critic; most of the New Humanist criticism was written by More, Eliot, and—until the mid-1920s—Stuart P. Sherman. In the following excerpt, Babbitt suggests that Bergson's concept of* élan vital *is essentially a restatement of the philosophical doctrines of Jean-Jacques Rousseau.*]

Perhaps the two men most talked and written about internationally of late have been Rousseau and M. Bergson. The world has, to be sure, just been celebrating the bicentenary of Rousseau's birth; but quite apart from the bicentenary there has been a constant stream of books and articles for years past, nearly all designed to show that Rousseau is, in Amiel's phrase, an ancestor in all things. The *Revue de Métaphysique et de Morale* recently devoted a special double number to a symposium on this very theme. To what extent does Rousseau embrace in his universal influence M. Bergson and his philosophy? No one of the distinguished foreign and French contributors to the Paris symposium, nor, so far as I am aware, any one else, has spoken clearly on this point. Yet this relationship would seem worth establishing, even though M. Bergson may not prove to be, as one of his admirers recently asserted in the *Revue des Deux Mondes,* a more important philosophical figure than Kant, and probably as important as Socrates. Like other thinkers, M. Bergson can be understood only with reference to his background—the previous ideas that he is continuing or from which he is reacting.

In any case what he is reacting from is perfectly clear. The so-called anti-intellectualist movement of which he is the leader is a protest against the scientific dogmatism that reached its height during the second half of the nineteenth century, a sign that the world is growing weary of a certain type of naturalistic positivism and its attempt to lock up reality in its formulas. The walls of that particular prison house of the spirit are plainly crumbling. Parts of the edifice have been collapsing of late with almost dramatic suddenness. M. Bergson's attack has been directed mainly against the pretensions of pure science to impose its methods on the study of the living and the organic. But even in the field of inorganic science itself points of view are appearing that would, if accepted, be in some respects a menace to the whole structure, the foundation of which was laid by Kepler and Galileo, Newton and Descartes. The "relativists," for example (of whom the chief is, perhaps, Mach of Vienna), have been arriving at novel conclusions regarding certain underlying conceptions of physics. What has been going on among the mathematicians may be inferred from the title of a recent volume—*Mysticism in the Higher Mathematics.* The late Henri Poincaré put his emphasis on intuition rather than on intellect even in geometry (though the geometry was to be sure non-Euclidean).

There can be no doubt as to the shrewdness of some of the blows that M. Bergson has delivered at what one may term scholastic science. The danger is, of course, manifest that men may argue from the abuse of the intellect by certain pseudoscientists of the mid-nineteenth century, a Herbert Spencer, let us say, or a Taine, against its legitimate use in scientific inquiry. The scientific intellectualists, especially the Darwinians, are as a matter of fact rallying briskly to the defence of their position against M. Bergson.

I have, however, neither space nor competency to discuss the bearings of the anti-intellectualist movement on science, whether organic or inorganic. My interest is in the contention that Bergsonism and similar tendencies are on their constructive side "humanistic" or "religious"; for both epithets have been applied to them. For example, a recent writer in the *Deutsche Rundschau* entitles an article on the contemporary French philosophical movement (he enumerates more than twenty leaders, of whom M. Bergson is only the best-known internationally) "The Renascence of Idealism in France." I am going to examine M. Bergson briefly from this point of view, admitting that he does not represent the whole of the movement.

M. Bergson's aim, as he himself would define it, has been to rid philosophy of every form of the metaphysical illusion (including the scientific form) and so to make it vital—an aim that is in itself highly laudable. With the older type of metaphysician ordinary mortals felt that they had very little in common. . . . But the philosophers of late have been coming out of their chilling clouds of abstractions. If, on the one hand, they have been breaking down the barriers that separate them from science, on the other, they have been growing literary, so literary, in fact, that the time would seem to have arrived for the men of letters to return the compliment and become to the best of their ability philosophical.

The literary critic especially should be willing to meet the philosopher at least half way, if, as I believe, both are confronted at present by the same central problem. For to inquire whether the critic can judge and, if so, by what standards, is only a form of the more general inquiry whether the philosopher can discover any unifying principle to oppose to mere flux and relativity. We are told by the new school that any attempt to unify life in terms of the intellect and impose on it a scale of values, is artificial. We must oppose to this artificial unity our vivid intuitions of change, of the infinite otherwiseness of things. Now, however little we may accept the whole of this thesis, we must grant that M. Bergson—and [William] James, it seems to me, even more than M. Bergson—has rendered a service to philosophy in thus turning its attention to what Plato would have called the problem of the One and the Many. Most people, James admits, do not lose much sleep over this problem, yet he is right in thinking that all other philosophical problems are insignificant in comparison. If philosophy once gets firmly planted on this ground, it may recover a reality that it has scarcely had since the debates of Socrates and the Sophists. Instead of the intricate fence with blunted foils to which the intellectualists have too often reduced it, we may once more see the flash of the naked blade.

In his own dealings with the problem of the One and the Many M. Bergson is evidently not a new Socrates, as the writer in the *Revue des Deux Mondes* suggests, but rather a new Protagoras. But in the actual form that the philosophy of the flux assumes in him, he reminds us even less of the ancient sophists than of Rousseau. James, indeed, would have it that M. Bergson reminds us of no one. "Open Bergson," he says, "and new horizons loom on every page you read. It is like the breath of the morning and the song of birds. It tells of reality itself, instead of merely reiterating what dusty-minded professors have written about what other previous professors have thought.

Nothing in Bergson is shop-worn or at second hand." All this exaltation of M. Bergson's spontaneity has itself a highly Rousseauistic flavor. What one always finds in Rousseauism is the thirst for immediacy as compared with something that is secondary, artificial, conventional. Moreover, one gains this fresh contact with reality, not by rising above the ordinary intellectual level, but by sinking below it, though the Rousseauists have employed a thousand pseudo-mystical devices to convince themselves and us of the contrary.

Now, M. Bergson is plainly a Rousseauistic primitivist, in that he would have us get our vision of reality by looking downward and backward instead of forward and up. The opposition he establishes between concepts and percepts, between intellect and intuition, is nothing but Rousseau's old opposition between thought and feeling, the head and the heart. The good Bergsonian must come to feel like Rousseau, that his "head and heart do not seem to belong to the same individual." Anything he can attain intellectually he is to regard as artificial, secondary, conventional, to be justified not philosophically but only practically (it will be observed that M. Bergson abandons both thought and action to the utilitarians). If a man would become philosophical, he must turn his back on both the intellectual and the active life, and "intuit" the creative flux; he must twist himself around, in M. Bergson's own phrase, and peer down into the vast swirling depths of the evolutionary process. He then sees life as it is, a pure process of motion and change, no longer artificially immobilized by the intellect.

To the student of the romantic movement M. Bergson's constant insistence on intuition as opposed to intellect will seem very familiar. The whole movement from Rousseau down is filled with the preaching of the vital and the intuitive and the spontaneous, with protests against those who would, in Carlyle's phrase, convert the world "into a huge, dead, immeasurable steam-engine." The similarity here between M. Bergson and the German romanticists, between him and Schopenhauer, etc., has been pointed out. I should like to show, if I had space, that Goethe, in his warnings against the over-intellectualizing of science, also anticipated M. Bergson at his best. The pretension of the intellectualist to imprison both nature and human nature in his formulas is, as a matter of fact, intolerable. Taine offends as gravely in this respect as those earlier rationalists from whom Carlyle and the German Rousseauists were reacting. Taine would reduce man, to quote his own words, to a "problem of mechanics," to a "living geometry," whose formula may be worked out and whose future may be predicted from his present in such a way as to eliminate time as an effective factor. But we must not, says M. Bergson, thus impose the geometric upon the vital order, or, what amounts to the same thing, confound the mechanical and spatial with the temporal. For the vital and the organic "time is the very stuff of reality," accompanied as it is by a "constant gushing forth of novelties," unpredictable from the platform of intellect. M. Bergson's treatment of time and of the rôle of time is perhaps the most original part of his philosophy.

But why are we forced to get our glimpse of reality by looking backward and downward instead of forward and up? Why can we not effect our escape from intellectualism by rising above it as well as by sinking beneath it? M. Bergson replies that to grasp what is above the ordinary intellectual level would require a special order of intuitions, and that, according to Kant, no such intuitions exist. But perhaps, in a matter of this gravity, it would not be well to trust too implicitly to Kant. If it is a question of citing authorities, we have Plato and Aristotle on the other side, supported, one is tempted to add, by the immemorial wisdom of the human race. "After reading Bergson," says James, "I saw that philosophy had been on a false scent ever since the days of Socrates and Plato." On the contrary, to get back to Socrates and Plato and Aristotle might be the best way of recovering the great tradition in philosophy after many years of wandering in the romantic wilderness; for these men, instead of being mere intellectualists, as M. Bergson is constantly assuming, put their final emphasis on intuition at least as much as he does—only the intuition in which their philosophy culminates is not of the Many, but of the One. In working towards this type of intuition the soundest method may still prove to be the Socratic and Platonic method of definition. Instead of reducing the intellect to a purely utilitarian rôle, as M. Bergson does, we should employ it in multiplying sharp distinctions and then put these distinctions into the service of the character and will. These sharp distinctions are, as it were, the railings on either side that protect a man in the toilsome ascent from the lower levels of his being and keep him from being precipitated into the outer void. The very word intuition is much in need of being defined, that is, divided and subdivided, Socratically. Good sense itself, according to Dr. Johnson, is intuitive, and this is a form of intuitiveness of which we stand in special need at the present crisis, for this word would scarcely seem too strong to apply to a time when the philosophy of the flux is proclaimed so confidently and received with such applause. This naturalistic vertigo seized upon Greek society at the very height of its achievement and marked the first downward step towards the abyss. "Too many of our modern philosophers," says Plato in words that might have been written to-day, "in their search after the nature of things are always getting dizzy from constantly going round and round, and then . . . they think there is nothing stable or permanent, but only flux and motion."

M. Bergson himself admits the kinship between a philosophy of pure motion and vertigo. "In vertigo," says James in turn, "we feel that motion *is*." Perhaps that is why Rousseau, as readers of the *Confessions* will remember, deliberately courted giddiness by gazing down on a waterfall from the brink of a precipice (making sure, first, that the railing on which he leaned was good and strong). One might fairly, indeed, bring against Rousseau the charge that Aristophanes brought unjustly against Socrates—that of being a worshipper of the god Vortex. Faust himself is only a good Rousseauist, and at the same time a forerunner of the modern point of view in philosophy, when, having despaired of dealing rationally with the problem of reality, he dedicates himself to vertigo. . . .

Now, we not only can define Socratically other forms of intuition besides this giddy "intuiting" of the flux, but we can bring to the support of our definitions a wealth of concrete illustrations that was not at the command of the Greeks. When Pascal, for example, says that "the heart has reasons of which the reason knows nothing," he evidently refers to the superrational intuitions. When La Rochefoucauld, on the other hand, says that "the head is always the dupe of the heart," he no less plainly refers to the region of impulse and instinct in human nature that is below the rational level. One might again so compare Rousseau and Pascal as to show that, though both writers make everything hinge upon the "heart," they attach to the word entirely different meanings, because they use it to describe entirely different orders of intuitions.

We might deal in a similar fashion with M. Bergson's assertion that we should strive to see life not *sub specie æternitatis* ["under the aspect of eternity"], but *sub specie durationis* ["under the aspect of finitude"]. Let us cite a few examples of the opposite doctrine from the most diverse sources. "The sage is delivered from time," says Buddha. "Happy is the soul in which time no longer courses," says Michael Angelo. In "the core of God's abysm," says Emerson,

> Past, Present, Future, shoot
> Triple blossoms from one root.

And so we might go on indefinitely lengthening the list of those who have found their supreme reality not in time, but in transcending time. For M. Bergson past, present, and future also melt together, but not as a result of transcending time, but, on the contrary, of plunging into it more deeply. He would have us feel time directly in its continuous flow and forget the artificial divisions imposed upon it by our "meddling intellects." M. Bergson's "direct vision" of time is, as a matter of fact, difficult to distinguish from the revery towards which Rousseau aspired—a point that might be made clear by a comparison of his [*La perception du changement*] with the fifth "Promenade." *Il s'agit,* says M. Bergson, *d'un présent qui dure* ["it is a question of a present which persists"]. In the ordinary enjoyments of life, even the keenest, says Rousseau, "there is scarcely an instant when the heart can say to us: I would that this instant might last forever" (Cf. "Faust"). But revery is a state "in which the present lasts forever" (*où le présent dure toujours*), and in which the soul suffers from "no void that it feels the need of filling."

To attempt to transcend time is, according to both James and M. Bergson, to fall inevitably into the metaphysical illusion. In general, everything that makes for unity is, according to these philosophers, dead, inert, merely conceptual. Readers of the *Nation* will remember the paper in which James, adopting Taine's identification of the classic spirit with the spirit of abstract reasoning, concludes that the only way to be vital is to be romantic, that is, to expand from the One to the Many, or, as we may say, to fly off the centre. According to M. Bergson, the process by which one grows vital is not merely expansive, but "explosive."

The underlying assumption of M. Bergson and other recent philosophers that a man becomes vital only by expanding from the One to the Many, only by moving from the centre towards the periphery, will not, as a matter of fact, bear serious scrutiny. The process of moving towards the centre may be just as intuitive and vital and also just as "infinite." For though a man may move towards the centre, he can never within the bounds of finite experience reach it. The romanticists have been assuming for a century or more that they have a monopoly of all the imagination and intuition. They have accorded at most to the classicist the possession of reason. But if a genuine classicist should appear in our midst he would agree with Rousseau that "cold reason has never done anything illustrious." In his warfare on romanticism he would oppose enthusiasm to enthusiasm and intuition to intuition. The way is open for a swift flanking movement on the whole romantic position. A man may, however, we must admit, make the proper distinctions and do all in his power, and then, instead of attaining "theory" in the Aristotelian sense (that is, immediate vision), he may not get beyond theory in our sense, and so become a fair target for M. Bergson. We are simply forced to say, in Joubert's quaint phrase, that some men's heads have no skylights in them.

Nor do we get round this difficulty by following M. Bergson. The sum of his message is that we should be æsthetically perceptive, that we should try to see life as the great artists see it. But it is no more given to the ordinary man to be as æsthetically perceptive as Keats, let us say, than it is to be as spiritually perceptive as Emerson. The enterprise in either case is of somewhat the same order as that of adding a cubit to one's stature.

We should not, however, spend too much time brooding on what would once have been called the mystery of grace. We should rather fix our attention on the feasibility of adding something by our own efforts to both our spiritual and æsthetic perceptiveness. For æsthetic perceptiveness is a precious thing if only it be directed to some adequate end. Right here it seems to me, is the fundamental weakness of M. Bergson. We are to perceive, in his own phrase, purely for the pleasure of perceiving. It is not we who are spontaneous in this system. We are merely privileged at most to contemplate the spontaneity of nature within us and about us, its expansive or "explosive" processes, without knowing whether these processes are moving towards any goal, or, if so, whether the goal is one with which we can concur. We do not, as the saying is, know where we are going, but merely that we are on the way. One might suppose that a spontaneity more worth having would be that of the individual who reacted upon his vital "urge," and imposed upon it the yoke of a human purpose. "Life," M. Bergson replies, "can have no purpose in the human sense of the word." It is hard to see how even its admirers can claim virility for a philosophy that would have us turn away from both thought and action and seek our vision of reality in an aimless æstheticism. It is at just the opposite pole from the philosophy of Aristotle, with its emphasis on acting with a purpose, a purpose, moreover, that is linked intuitively by a series of intermediary purposes with the supreme and perfect End itself. For if the intuition of the Many makes itself felt as vital impulse (*élan vital*), the intuition of the One is felt rather as sense of direction, as inner form, as vital control (*frein vital*).

Those who exalt vital impulse and deny vital control may, as I have said, simply err from lack of light. But they may do so for another reason that is far less flattering to human nature. "Most persons," says Aristotle, in his downright fashion, "would rather live in a disorderly than in a sober manner." The ordinary man, says Goethe in a similar vein, prefers error to truth because the truth imposes limitations and error does not. But the ordinary man is not going to do anything so crude and inartistic as to admit such a preference either to himself or to others. In lieu of the reality of truth, he would like at least to have its specious semblance. Here lies the everlasting opportunity for the sophist and the pseudo-idealist. The world, as the Latin adage puts it, wishes to be deceived (*vult riundus decipi*). The idea of decorum, as worked out under Jesuitical auspices, did something to satisfy this permanent need of human nature. Perhaps the last triumph of the *genre* was Talleyrand, whom Napoleon described as "a silk stocking filled with mud." Rousseau attacked and overthrew this conception of decorum, but only to set up a still more fetching form of pseudo-idealism. "You wish to have the pleasures of vice and the honor of virtue," said Julie to Saint-Preux in a moment of unusual candor. Saint-Preux would indulge his lower impulses and at the same time pass as a noble enthusiast. He would live in a universe with the lid off, to borrow an elegant image from the pragmatist, and yet be accounted "spiritual." Rousseauism on this side may be defined as the art of throwing a pseudo-idealistic glamour over unrestraint; or, in Lasserre's phrase, as the rapturous disintegration of human nature. You remain uncurbed (to take the form of this disintegration with which we

are most familiar at present) but make up for it by clamoring furiously that curbs be put on other people. You enjoy the illusion of reforming society instead of settling down to the sober reality of reforming yourself. Lacking the substance of a thing, you at least go through the motions and flaunt your *panache* confidently in the eyes of the world.

The ancient tradition of the world is that wisdom abides with the One and not with the Many. In seeking to persuade men to the contrary, M. Bergson is holding out to them the hope that they may become wise by following the line of the least resistance, that they may grow "spiritual" by diving into the flux. Why the pathway that M. Bergson opens into "reality" should prove so alluring to the men of the present is obvious. Men are now devoting their active intellectual powers to building up a vast machinery, and then manipulating it to practical ends. The intellect is properly employed in this way, says M. Bergson reassuringly, being as it is an obstacle rather than an aid to "vision." A man, we are to believe, may devote all his mental energy to the stock market, and yet be numbered with the sages, if only he succeeds in his odd moments in immersing himself in *la durée réelle* ["real duration"] and listening, in M. Bergson's phrase, to the "continuous melody of his inner life." The romantic æsthetes and the utilitarians, the two classes of persons who have most flourished during the past century, are both flattered by this solution of the difficulty. The romantic æsthete that often co-exists with the utilitarian in the same man is flattered. The Bergsonian philosophy is indeed in its essence an ingenious *modus vivendi* between æsthetes and utilitarians. Like the kindred philosophy of James, it may be best described,

Bergson.

to borrow the title of M. René Berthelot's book on M. Bergson, as *un Romantisme utilitaire* ["a utilitarian Romanticism"].

Let me repeat that I am not attempting in this article to do justice to M. Bergson's philosophy as a reaction against scholastic science. I have not emphasized, as I might have done, its striking originality in details. I have merely tried to show that in its general emotional expansiveness it is a late birth of Rousseauistic romanticism, and as such allied with all that is violent and extreme in contemporary life from syndicalism to "futurist" painting. It would seem to encourage rather than correct the two great permanent maladies of human nature—anarchy and irrationality. In so far, instead of being humanistic or religious, it is at the opposite pole from humanism or religion. (pp. 452-55)

> Irving Babbitt, *"Bergson and Rousseau,"* in The Nation, *New York, Vol. XCV, No. 2472, November 14, 1912, pp. 452-55.*

EDWIN BJÖRKMAN (essay date 1913)

[*Björkman was a Swedish-American novelist and critic who, through his translations, introduced American readers to the works of such major Scandinavian authors as August Strindberg, Bjørnstjerne Bjørnson, and Georg Brandes. In the following discussion of Bergson's writings, he attempts to discover the reason for the enormous influence of the philosopher's ideas.*]

To make straight for the point of this article: Why should, out of an unobtrusive and unknown French scholar like Professor Henri Bergson, suddenly emerge a figure of world-wide interest and importance?

Ten years ago nobody dwelling outside the inner courts of organized knowledge paid the least attention to his sayings or doings. And to-day the whole civilized world is asking eagerly for the slightest details relating to his private or public life. His books—of which there are only four, not counting his doctor's thesis—have each reached six or seven editions in the original, and they are now being hurriedly translated into one language after another. His teachings are spreading, like flames across a sun-scorched prairie. Everywhere laymen and learned alike feel compelled to define their intellectual, moral and artistic attitudes by reference to his ideas. We find him quoted as their spiritual authority by leaders of the Syndicalist labor movement in France and by the young Tory Democrats of England, by the Modernist reformers within the Catholic Church and by those audacious iconoclasts who, as Post-Impressionists, are startling the world with a new art form.

"He has been accepted by the Symbolists as the philosopher of the new idea," writes an English journalist in regard to the latest movement in French poetry. And the same man informs us that "the intuitional philosophy of Bergson has so taken possession of Paris that the spirit of it seems to fill every place." All this superficial popularity might merely arouse suspicion as to the man's genuine power and scope as a thinker, but when we turn to the other side—to the world of expert opinion *par preference*—we meet with the same almost unanimous recognition of Bergson's place and influence. "His appearance in the field of philosophy promises to be a turning point in the history of human thought," writes a critic like G. R. T. Ross in the London *Nation*, and from innumerable other quarters the same note of unbounded enthusiasm is heard. Even when his ideas, as such, are bitterly opposed, the learning and ingenuity displayed in their presentation are ungrudgingly acknowledged.

In our search for causes capable of explaining this abrupt rise of a quiet thinker into world-circling fame it is of little use to speak of "faddisms" and "passing fashions." For in the voice of Bergson there is not one sensational note. He has taken no step to attract or hold the attention of the greater public—though he believes passionately in working and writing for nothing less than all men. In his attitude toward truth and its right of way against all selfish interests or established superstitions, he is as uncompromising as any other typical representative of his class. And in spite of his lucid prose, vivid power of illustration, and constant effort at clearness and conciseness, his writings are by no means easy reading to a mind not trained in the ways of systematic thinking. There is, in a word, every reason to assume that his position is founded on true merit, and that, whatever ebb or increasing flood his outward popularity may experience after this, his spirit will become indelibly stamped on the world's thought, so that after having passed through him that thought must for all future be different from what it was before he appeared.

To account for his extraordinary renown to-day, we must assume that his qualities and gifts and achievements are those of men like Descartes and Spinoza, Kant and Hegel, Schopenhauer and Comte, Spencer and James. In each such case, when the efforts of a single man have exercised marked effect not only on all subsequent thinking but on the conduct of the mass of his contemporaries, we have, I think, to lead the result back to three coöperating factors: first, a strong and highly magnetic personality, so that what the man *says* or *does* becomes supported and supplemented by what he *is;* secondly, a distinctly new way of seeing life and interpreting it, whereby man's timidity in front of the world-riddle becomes to some additional degree abated; and thirdly, a particular need on the part of mankind which is administered to by the wider vision of the man in question. We have in this country had a most striking example, in the person of the late William James, of such cooperation between a man's character, his creative thought, and the acute demand of the world at large. And Bergson's case is, I feel sure, another one of the same kind, though perhaps even more remarkable—for did we not hear James himself at the height of his fame apply the title of "master" to the younger and then less known Frenchman? (pp. 205-09)

Too often in the past the academic lecturer seems to have measured his accomplishments by the degree of abstruseness he managed to attain. And philosophy has equally often been nothing but an exciting game of hide and seek, with vanity for goad, and for goal alleged "truths" having little or no bearing on the "vulgar" issues of ordinary life. To this entire tendency of what has sometimes been called "mandarinism" the attitude of Bergson has from the start been frankly hostile. He seeks above everything else to make himself clear. And he does so to a large extent by constant reference of his argument to the facts of actual existence. For mere sophistries he has no use whatever. And he takes his place conspicuously with that growing group of thinkers the world over who insist that philosophy, like everything else, must be for all mankind.

What has just been said of his speaking applies with equal truth to his writing. He is a master of style, but one who always insists on making style a servant of the thought to be expressed. An English reviewer says that his written work has "the unity and flow, above all the imagination, of a poem." Nevertheless it is always "loaded"—every line betrays a vast knowledge that is never one-sided or pedantic. Thus the reviewer just quoted wonders at the fact that Bergson shows equal command of "ancient speculation" and of modern biology. Though starting as a mathematician, he has mastered the most difficult art of translating abstract thought into terms of concrete life—as when, to give only one instance, he speaks of consciousness as "a momentary spark flying up from the friction of real actions against possible actions."

So far he has, as already mentioned, produced only four volumes—the first of these in 1889, and the latest one in 1907. The third to be completed and the last to be translated into English was *Le rire* (*Laughter*), on which its author spent nearly twenty years of study and thought. It deals with laughter as a social function, the author's leading idea being contained in this sentence: "The function of laughter is to punish and to repress certain actions that appear as defects to the social consciousness." This sharp accentuation of man's social side is very characteristic of Bergson's whole attitude. It colors all his ideas and theories, and in the light of it one finds it hard to understand how some of his avowed but uninvited followers—like the anarchistically inclined Syndicalists—have been able to draw any inspiration from his teachings.

His other three volumes have been brought out here under the following titles: *Time and Free Will, Matter and Memory, Creative Evolution*. The first two deal with certain fundamental problems of consciousness and are more closely specialized than the third. Through them Bergson has endeavored to establish the reality of time—of which he says that "we do not think it, but live it, because life transcends intellect"—and the presence of an element of free choice and consequent unforeseeableness in all of man's actions. In the introduction to *Matter and Memory* occurs a passage that seems to summarize both the basis and the spirit of all that he has written. There are two principles, he says, which he has used as a clue throughout his researches:

> The first is that in psychological analysis we must never forget the utilitarian character of our mental functions, which are essentially turned toward action. The second is that the habits formed in action find their way up to the sphere of speculation, where they create fictitious problems, and that metaphysics must begin by disposing of this artificial obscurity.

From first to last, *Creative Evolution* is largely concerned with the clearing away of just such "artificial obscurities," by which reality has become overlaid in the course of man's millennial groping toward an understanding of it. Beyond all doubt it is Bergson's greatest book, as it is his latest—and the one into which he has put most not only of his system but of himself. The personality of the man—with all its rare treasures of simplicity and sincerity, of insight and of sympathy, of common sense and of fancy—shines gloriously through every one of its pages. And it is in these pages he has given that something which is at once new and fitted to meet the crying need of his time—the something, in other words, that sets him aside as a thinker of creative originality. In this work he has no longer been satisfied to deal with mere isolated phases of life, but has—in accordance with the philosopher's time-honored right—pushed on toward certain universal conclusions, shaping themselves at last into a logical totality of cosmic interpretation.

For the professional philosopher the book is rich in startling and, of course, debatable propositions, with which I shall not concern myself here. For I want to get at the very heart of the Frenchman's thought—the way in which he conceives and meets the riddle of life itself. First of all, then, he finds us using two different instruments in dealing with life, and he draws a sharp distinction between the origin, nature and function, on one side, of instinct, and, on the other, of intellect. The main thing to all philosophy so far has been thought: the main thing to Bergson is the act of living and our unformulated sense of it—that is intuition, or "instinct turned self-conscious."

"Instinct," he says, "is moulded on the very form of life. If the consciousness that slumbers in it could awake, if it were wound up into knowledge instead of being wound off into action, if we could ask and it could answer, it would give up to us the most intimate secrets of life." And he cries to us:

> Let us try to see, no longer with the eyes of the intellect alone, which grasps only the already made and which looks from the outside, but with the spirit; I mean with that faculty of seeing which is immanent in the faculty of acting and which springs up, somehow, by the twisting of the will on itself, when action is turned into knowledge, like heat, so to say, into light.

He does not scorn or spurn intellect. On the contrary, its cooperation is needed for the utterance of what is laid bare by intuition. Seen thus, "with the spirit," an essential dualism is found at the bottom of all existence—the dualism between matter and life, between unorganized and organized being. "The vision we have of the material world is that of a weight which falls," he says; "but all our analyses show us, in life, an effort to remount the incline that matter descends." Out of the effort made by life, "the reality which ascends," to overcome, or at least to suspend, the downward rush of matter, springs the tangible and visible universe.

Life proper reveals itself above all as a flux and a creation. "To exist is to change, to change is to mature, and to mature is to go on creating oneself endlessly," Bergson tells us. Back of all this creative change he finds a common impetus that he calls the *élan vital*—the life-urge. We may imagine it as "a centre from which worlds shoot out like rockets in a fire-works display." As here, so it is at work everywhere, shaping, developing, initiating. "It is probable that life goes on in other planets, in other solar systems also, under forms of which we have no idea." For life, in the eyes of Bergson, is neither an accident nor a voluntary act of some supernatural being: it is a universal necessity.

Evolution he sees not as a straight line, but as a sheaflike divergence of forms. Some lines come quickly to an end. Others stretch onward with constant offshoot of new branches. Each onward step has to be bought by the surrender of something that until then had remained common property, and which thereafter will become characteristic of a parallel form. Thus, for instance, the vegetable kingdom represents chiefly the general tendency of life to store up energy, while the animal kingdom specializes, so to speak, in the expenditure of energy.

To Bergson each form appears as a narrowly restricted delegate of the life-urge, devised for a distinct purpose, and permitted to regard this purpose as the end of all life. "Each species, each individual even, retains only a certain impetus from the universal vital impulsion and tends to use this energy in its own interest." Hence the egoism that marks each separate species as well as specimen. The principal social significance of Bergson's ideas, however, lies in his statement that "everywhere the tendency to individualize is opposed and at the same time completed by an antagonistic and complementary tendency to associate." The evolution of being in this double direction is due to the very nature of life. Thus "society, as soon as formed, tends to melt the associated individuals into a new organism, so as to become itself an individual, able in its turn to be part and parcel of a new association.'' Beyond the human mind we divine the race-mind: behind the individual will, an all-inclusive world-will.

When we have reached this point we have also reached the most comprehensive aspect of Bergson's thought—an aspect which Professor Lovejoy has indicated by his reference, in the works of more than one prominent thinker of to-day, to ''a genuinely radical evolutionism, which is at the same time of a highly romantic and religious spirit.'' It is nothing less than a new religious formulation that seems to shape itself before our rapt vision when Bergson says that God, as defined in the light of the life-urge theory, ''has nothing of the already made,'' but is ''unceasing life, action, freedom.'' Another vista of equally startling nature is opened up by his assertion that ''the whole of humanity, in space and in time, is one immense army galloping beside and before and behind each of us in an overwhelming charge, able to beat down every resistance and clear the most formidable obstacles, perhaps even death.''

A divine principle, lying ahead and not behind us; an immortality not miraculously conferred but logically attained: these appear to be some of the possibilities contained in Bergson's audacious conclusions. And it is undoubtedly through his courage in drawing out the consequences of his own thoughts thus far—and through his ability to do so without for a moment losing his firm hold on the actuality with which we are all familiar—that he has won his dominant place not only in the heads of the few but in the hearts of the many.

Like President Eliot, like the late Professor James, like all those earnest and able men who are banded together in the world-embracing Monistic Union, Bergson must feel that much of what still passes current as religion has lost its background of actual experience, while at the same time the need of man to relate himself to the unknown as well as to the known has grown no less poignant than it was in the past. And to him more that to anybody else, as I see it, has it been given to restate the truths of being in such manner that they become, not a religion in themselves, but the firm basis on which a new and more reverential conception of the great insolvable mysteries of life may be reared. (pp. 212-23)

> *Edwin Björkman, ''The New Mysticism,'' in his* Voices of To-morrow: Critical Studies of the New Spirit in Literature, *Mitchell Kennerley, 1913, pp. 154-223.*

GEORGE SANTAYANA (essay date 1913)

[*Santayana was a Spanish-born philosopher, poet, novelist, and literary critic who was for the most part educated in the United States, taking his undergraduate and graduate degrees at Harvard, where he later taught philosophy. His earliest published works were the poems of* Sonnets, and Other Verses (1894). *Although Santayana is regarded as no more than a fair poet, his facility with language is one of the distinguishing features of his later philosophical works. Written in an elegant, non-technical prose, Santayana's major philosophical work of his early career is the five-volume* Life of Reason (1905-06). *These volumes reflect their author's materialist viewpoint applied to such areas as society, religion, art, and science, and along with* Scepticism and Animal Faith (1923) *and the four-volume* Realms of Being (1927-40) *put forth the view that while reason undermines belief in anything whatever, an irrational animal faith suggests the existence of a ''realm of essences'' which leads to the human search for knowledge. Late in his life Santayana stated that ''reason and ideals arise in doing something that at bottom there is no reason for doing.'' ''Chaos,'' he wrote earlier, ''is perhaps at the bottom*

of everything.'' In the following excerpt, Santayana dismisses Bergson's philosophy, particularly his concept of the élan vital.]

The most representative and remarkable of living philosophers is M. Henri Bergson. Both the form and the substance of his works attract universal attention. His ideas are pleasing and bold, and at least in form wonderfully original; he is persuasive without argument and mystical without conventionality; he moves in the atmosphere of science and free thought, yet seems to transcend them and to be secretly religious. An undercurrent of zeal and even of prophecy seems to animate his subtle analyses and his surprising fancies. He is eloquent, and to a public rather sick of the half-education it has received and eager for some inspiriting novelty he seems more eloquent than he is. He uses the French language (and little else is French about him) in the manner of the more recent artists in words, retaining the precision of phrase and the measured judgments which are traditional in French literature, yet managing to envelop everything in a penumbra of emotional suggestion. Each expression of an idea is complete in itself; yet these expressions are often varied and constantly metaphorical, so that we are led to feel that much in that idea has remained unexpressed and is indeed inexpressible.

Studied and insinuating as M. Bergson is in his style, he is no less elaborate in his learning. In the history of philosophy, in mathematics and physics, and especially in natural history he has taken great pains to survey the ground and to assimilate the views and spirit of the most recent scholars. He might be called outright an expert in all these subjects, were it not for a certain externality and want of radical sympathy in his way of conceiving them. A genuine historian of philosophy, for instance, would love to rehearse the views of great thinkers, would feel their eternal plausibility, and in interpreting them would think of himself as little as they ever thought of him. But M. Bergson evidently regards Plato or Kant as persons who did or did not prepare the way for some Bergsonian insight. The theory of evolution, taken enthusiastically, is apt to exercise an evil influence on the moral estimation of things. First the evolutionist asserts that later things grow out of earlier, which is true of things in their causes and basis, but not in their values; as modern Greece proceeds out of ancient Greece materially but does not exactly crown it. The evolutionist, however, proceeds to assume that later things are necessarily better than what they have grown out of: and this is false altogether. This fallacy reinforces very unfortunately that inevitable esteem which people have for their own opinions, and which must always vitiate the history of philosophy when it is a philosopher that writes it. A false subordination comes to be established among systems, as if they moved in single file and all had the last, the author's system, for their secret goal. (pp. 58-9)

A good way of testing the calibre of a philosophy is to ask what it thinks of death. Philosophy, said Plato, is a meditation on death, or rather, if we would do justice to his thought, an aspiration to live disembodied; and Schopenhauer said that the spectacle of death was the first provocation to philosophy. M. Bergson has not yet treated of this subject; but we may perhaps perceive for ourselves the place that it might occupy in his system. Life, according to him, is the original and absolute force. In the beginning, however, it was only a potentiality or tendency. To become specific lives, life had to emphasise and bring exclusively to consciousness, here and there, special possibilities of living; and where these special lives have their chosen boundary (if this way of putting it is not too Fichtean) they posit or create a material environment. Matter is the view each life takes of what for it are rejected or abandoned possibilities of living. This might show how the absolute will to live, if it was to be carried out, would have to begin by evoking a sense of dead or material things about it; it would not show how death could ever overtake the will itself. If matter were merely the periphery which life has to draw round itself, in order to be a definite life, matter could never abolish any life; as the ring of a circus or the sand of the arena can never abolish the show for which they have been prepared. Life would then be fed and defined by matter, as an artist is served by the matter he needs to carry on his art.

Yet in actual life there is undeniably such a thing as danger and failure. M. Bergson even thinks that the facing of increased dangers is one proof that vital force is an absolute thing; for if life were an equilibrium, it would not displace itself and run new risks of death, by making itself more complex and ticklish, as it does in the higher organisms and the finer arts. Yet if life is the only substance, how is such a risk of death possible at all? I suppose the special life that arises about a given nucleus of feeling, by emphasising some of the relations which that feeling has in the world, might be abolished if a greater emphasis were laid on another set of its relations, starting from some other nucleus. We must remember that these selections, according to M. Bergson, are not apperceptions merely. They are creative efforts. The future constitution of the flux will vary in response to them. Each mind sucks the world, so far as it can, into its own vortex. A cross apperception will then amount to a contrary force. Two souls will not be able to dominate the same matter in peace and friendship. Being forces, they will pull that matter in different ways. Each soul will tend to devour and to direct exclusively the movement influenced by the other soul. The one that succeeds in ruling that movement will live on; the other, I suppose, will die, although M. Bergson may not like that painful word. He says the lower organisms store energy for the higher organisms to use; but when a sheep appropriates the energy stored up in grass, or a man that stored up in mutton, it looks as if the grass and the sheep had perished. Their *élan vital* is no longer theirs, for in this rough world to live is to kill. Nothing arises in nature, Lucretius says, save helped by the death of some other thing. Of course, this is no defeat for the *élan vital* in general; for according to our philosopher the whole universe from the beginning has been making for just that supreme sort of consciousness which man, who eats the mutton, now possesses. The sheep and the grass were only things by the way and scaffolding for our precious humanity. But would it not be better if some being should arise nobler than man, not requiring abstract intellect nor artificial weapons, but endowed with instinct and intuition and, let us say, the power of killing by radiating electricity? And might not men then turn out to have been mere explosives, in which energy was stored for convenient digestion by that superior creature? A shocking thought, no doubt, like the thought of death, and more distressing to our vital feelings than is the pleasing assimilation of grass and mutton in our bellies. Yet I can see no ground, except a desire to flatter oneself, for not crediting the *élan vital* with some such digestive intention. M. Bergson's system would hardly be more speculative if it entertained this possibility, and it would seem more honest.

The vital impulse is certainly immortal; for if we take it in the naturalistic exoteric sense, for a force discovered in biology, it is an independent agent coming down into matter, organising it against its will, and stirring it like the angel the pool of Bethesda. Though the ripples die down, the angel is not affected. He has merely flown away. And if we take the vital impulse mystically and esoterically, as the *only* primal force, creating matter in order to play with it, the immortality of life is even more obvious; for there is then nothing else in being that could possibly abolish it. But when we come to immortality for the individual, all grows obscure and ambiguous. The original tendency of life was certainly cosmic and not distinguished into persons: we are told it was like a wireless message sent at the creation which is being read off at last by the humanity of to-day. In the naturalistic view, the diversity of persons would seem to be due to the different material conditions under which one and the same spiritual purpose must fight its way towards realisation in different times and places. It is quite conceivable, however, that in the mystical view the very sense of the original message should comport this variety of interpretations, and that the purpose should always have been to produce diverse individuals.

The first view, as usual, is the one which M. Bergson has prevailingly in mind, and communicates most plausibly; while he holds to it he is still talking about the natural world, and so we still know what he is talking about. On this view, however, personal immortality would be impossible; it would be, if it were aimed at, a self-contradiction in the aim of life; for the diversity of persons would be due to impediments only, and souls would differ simply in so far as they mutilated the message which they were all alike trying to repeat. They would necessarily, when the spirit was victorious, be reabsorbed and identified in the universal spirit. This view also seems most consonant with M. Bergson's theory of primitive reality, as a flux of fused images, or a mind lost in matter; to this view, too, is attributable his hostility to intelligence, in that it arrests the flux, divides the fused images, and thereby murders and devitalises reality. Of course the destiny of spirit would not be to revert to that diffused materiality; for the original mind lost in matter had a very short memory; it was a sort of cosmic trepidation only, whereas the ultimate mind would remember all that, in its efforts after freedom, it had ever superadded to that trepidation or made it turn into. Even the abstract views of things taken by the practical intellect would, I fear, have to burden the universal memory to the end. We should be remembered, even if we could no longer exist.

On the other more profound view, however, might not personal immortality be secured? Suppose the original message said: Translate me into a thousand tongues! In fulfilling its duty, the universe would then continue to divide its dream into phantom individuals; as it had to insulate its parts in the beginning in order to dominate and transform them freely, so it would always continue to insulate them, so as not to lose its cross-vistas and its mobility. There is no reason, then, why individuals should not live for ever. But a condition seems to be involved which may well make belief stagger. It would be impossible for the universe to divide its images into particular minds unless it preserved the images of their particular bodies also. Particular minds arise, according to this philosophy, in the interests of practice: which means, biologically, to secure a better adjustment of the body to its environment, so that it may survive. Mystically, too, the fundamental force is a half-conscious purpose that practice, or freedom, should come to be; or rather, that an apparition or experience of practice and freedom arise; for in this philosophy appearance is all. To secure this desirable apparition of practice special tasks are set to various nuclei in felt space (such, for instance, as the task to *see*), and the image of a body (in this case that of an eye) is gradually formed, in order to execute that task; for evidently the Absolute can see only if it looks, and to look it must first choose a point of view and an optical method. This point of view and this method posit the individual; they fix him in time and space, and determine the quality and range of his passive experience: they are his body. If the Absolute, then, wishes to retain the individual not merely as one of its memories but as one of its organs of practical life, it must begin by retaining the image of his body. His body must continue to figure in that landscape of nature which the absolute life, as it pulses, keeps always composing and recomposing. Otherwise a personal mind, a sketch of things made from the point of view and in the interests of the body, cannot be preserved.

M. Bergson, accordingly, should either tell us that our bodies are going to rise again, or he should not tell us, or give us to understand, that our minds are going to endure. I suppose he cannot venture to preach the resurrection of the body to this weak-kneed generation; he is too modern and plausible for that. Yet he is too amiable to deny to our dilated nostrils some voluptuous whiffs of immortality. He asks if we are not "led to suppose" that consciousness passes through matter to be tempered like steel, to constitute distinct personalities, and prepare them for a higher existence. Other animal minds are but human minds arrested; men at last (what men, I wonder?) are "capable of remembering all and willing all and controlling their past and their future," so that "we shall have no repugnance in admitting that in man, though perhaps in man alone, consciousness pursues its path beyond this earthly life." Elsewhere he says, in a phrase already much quoted and perhaps destined to be famous, that in man the spirit can "spurn every kind of resistance and break through many an obstacle, perhaps even death." Here the tenor has ended on the inevitable high note, and the gallery is delighted. But was that the note set down for him in the music? And has he not sung it in falsetto?

The immediate knows nothing about death; it takes intelligence to conceive it; and that perhaps is why M. Bergson says so little about it, and that little so far from serious. But he talks a great deal about life, he feels he has penetrated deeply into its nature; and yet birth, together with birth, is the natural analysis of what life is. What is this creative purpose, that must wait for sun and rain to set it in motion? What is this life, that in any individual can be suddenly extinguished by a bullet? What is this *élan vital*, that a little fall in temperature would banish altogether from the universe? The study of death may be out of fashion, but it is never out of season. The omission of this, which is almost the omission of wisdom from philosophy, warns us that in M. Bergson's thought we have something occasional and partial, the work of an astute apologist, a party man, driven to desperate speculation by a timid attachment to prejudice. Like other terrified idealisms, the system of M. Bergson has neither good sense, nor rigour, nor candour, nor solidity. It is a brilliant attempt to confuse the lessons of experience by refining upon its texture, an attempt to make us halt, for the love of primitive illusions, in the path of discipline and reason. It is likely to prove a successful attempt, because it flatters the weaknesses of the moment, expresses them with emotion, and covers them with a feint at scientific speculation. It is not, however, a powerful system, like that of Hegel, capable of bewildering and obsessing many who have no natural love for shams. M. Bergson will hardly bewilder; his style is too clear, the field where his just observations lie—the immediate—is too well defined, and the mythology which results from projecting the terms of the immediate into the absolute, and turning them into powers, is too

obviously verbal. He will not long impose on any save those who enjoy being imposed upon; but for a long time he may increase their number. His doctrine is indeed alluring. Instead of telling us, as a stern and contrite philosophy would, that the truth is remote, difficult, and almost undiscoverable by human efforts, that the universe is vast and unfathomable, yet that the knowledge of its ways is precious to our better selves, if we would not live befooled, this philosophy rather tells us that nothing is truer or more precious than our rudimentary consciousness, with its vague instincts and premonitions, that everything ideal is fictitious, and that the universe, at heart, is as palpitating and irrational as ourselves. Why then strain the inquiry? Why seek to dominate passion by understanding it? Rather live on; work, it matters little at what, and grow, it matters nothing in what direction. Exert your instinctive powers of vegetation and emotion; let your philosophy itself be a frank expression of this flux, the roar of the ocean in your little sea-shell, a momentary posture of your living soul, not a stark adoration of things reputed eternal.

So the intellectual faithlessness and the material servility of the age are flattered together and taught to justify themselves theoretically. They cry joyfully, *non peccavi* ["I am not to blame"], which is the modern formula for confession. M. Bergson's philosophy itself is a confession of a certain mystical rebellion and atavism in the contemporary mind. It will remain a beautiful monument to the passing moment, a capital film for the cinematograph of history, full of psychological truth and of a kind of restrained sentimental piety. His thought has all the charm that can go without strength and all the competence that can go without mastery. This is not an age of mastery; it is confused with too much business; it has no brave simplicity. The mind has forgotten its proper function, which is to crown life by quickening it into intelligence, and thinks if it could only prove that it accelerated life, that might perhaps justify its existence; like a philosopher at sea who, to make himself useful, should blow into the sail. (pp. 100-09)

> *George Santayana, "The Philosophy of M. Henri Bergson," in his* Winds of Doctrine: Studies in Contemporary Opinion, *J. M. Dent & Sons Ltd., 1913, pp. 58-109.*

HERMANN HESSE (essay date 1916)

[*Recipient of the Nobel Prize in literature for 1946, Hesse is considered one of the most important German novelists of the twentieth century. Lyrical in style, his novels are concerned with a search on the part of their protagonists for self-knowledge and for insight into the relationship between physical and spiritual realms. Critics often look upon Hesse's works as falling into the tradition of German Romanticism, from the early bildungsroman* Peter Camenzind (1904) *to the introspective* Steppenwolf (1927) *to the mystical* Das Glasperlenspiel (1943; Magister Ludi), *his last major work.* Magister Ludi *is generally held to epitomize Hesse's achievement, delineating a complex vision which intermingles art and religion to convey a sense of harmony unifying the diverse elements of existence. This work, along with such earlier novels as* Siddhartha, *established Hesse's reputation as an author who to many readers and critics approximates the role of a modern sage. In the following excerpt, Hesse praises Bergson's "prophetic perception."*]

Bergson is very far away from all "fashions," although he understands the essential intellectual currents of our time and has expressed himself about them. Anyone who has found Nietzsche profitable can also find value in Bergson. Like Nietzsche, he is a champion of life against doctrine; he fights for new ways of perception and fights against the hallowed dogmas of the Kantian school. Bergson denies to the understanding, to the intelligence operating with concepts and logic, the ability of real perception, of true apprehension of what is alive. And so, for Kant's disciples and for intellectualists of every kind, he is ipso facto dismissed as no more than a romantic and poet. He forgoes all claim to the provability and universal validity of logicoscientific work, not because he does not understand it and has not mastered it, but because his strongly artistically inclined nature urges him along the path of intuition, of empathy, and of supralogical, prophetic perception. Let the professional philosophers decide how high they wish to rate Bergson as a thinker. For the rest of us, there is no reason to neglect Bergson's splendid books. They are so full of sagacity and liveliness, so fresh and personal, at the same time so admirably written and full of apt, lightning inspirations and similes that their reading alone must count as valuable and beneficial, even though for philosophers working scientifically they may contain dangers. After all, that's the experience we had with Nietzsche; in his time we began to read him with philosophical hunger and then, as years passed, his works became for us more and more a grandiose exception, the powerful record of a daring, noble, original mind whose wholly personal attitude toward the world was in itself enlightening and worth learning, whereas the actual philosophical conclusions no longer entered much into the question. It's possible that sometimes this will happen to us with Bergson, although his temperament is certainly less forceful than that of Nietzsche. In any case, his gifted books give us the splendid portrait of a thinker for whom all paths for apprehending the living world that have hitherto been investigated are inadequate, who with instinctive urgency but with well-trained mind is in pursuit of the riddle of life. Just as he sees in the capacity of intuition the highest of our faculties, so he sees life throughout as a spiritual phenomenon and finds in natural history a history of the soul. Thorough training in the natural sciences keeps him from becoming an ideologue, so that he stands far closer to Schelling than, say, to Hegel. He is the seeker, and, following in his steps, we find the journey itself, the walking and seeking, delightful. And the more we recognize his work as not yet completed, as needing many additions, many sequels, to just that extent we must treasure him as a source of the greatest stimulation. (pp. 364-65)

Hermann Hesse, "Henri Bergson," in his My Belief: Essays on Life and Art, *edited by Theodore Ziolkowski, translated by Denver Lindley, Farrar, Straus and Giroux, 1974, pp. 364-65.*

J. ALEXANDER GUNN   (essay date 1920)

[*In the following excerpt, Gunn discusses Bergson's abilities as a philosopher and the importance of his ideas concerning human evolution.*]

We must remember, in fairness to Bergson, that he does not profess to offer us *a system* of philosophy. In fact, if he were to do so, he would involve himself in a grave inconsistency, for his thought is not of the systematic type. He is opposed to the work of those individual thinkers who have offered "systems" to the world, rounded and professedly complete constructions, labelled, one might almost say, "the last word in Philosophy." Bergson does not claim that his thought is final. His ideal, of which he speaks in his lectures on *La perception du changement*—that excellent summary of his thought—is a progressive philosophy to which each thinker shall contribute.

If we feel disappointed that Bergson has not gone further or done more by attempting a solution of some of the fundamental problems of our human experience, upon which he has not touched, then we must recollect his own view of the philosophy he is seeking to expound. All thinking minds must contribute their quota. A philosophy such as he wishes to promote by establishing a method by his own works will not be made in a day. "Unlike the philosophical systems properly so called, each of which was the individual work of a man of genius, and sprang up as a whole to be taken or left, it will only be built up by the collective and progressive effort of many thinkers, of many observers also, completing, correcting, and improving one another." Both science and the older kind of metaphysics have kept aloof from the vital problems of our lives. In one of his curious but brilliant metaphors Bergson likens Life to a river over which the scientists have constructed an elaborate bridge, while the laborious metaphysicians have toiled to build a tunnel underneath. Neither group of workers has attempted to plunge into the flowing tide itself. In the most brilliant of his short papers: **"L'intuition philosophique,"** he makes an energetic appeal that philosophy should approach more closely to practical life. His thought aims at setting forth, not any system of knowledge, but rather a method of philosophizing; in a phrase, this method amounts to the assertion that Life is more than Logic, or, as Byron put it, "The tree of Knowledge is not the tree of Life."

It is because Bergson has much to say that is novel and opposed to older conceptions that a certain lack of proportion occasionally mars his thought; for he—naturally enough—frequently lays little emphasis on important points which he considers are sufficiently familiar, in order to give prominent place and emphasis to some more novel point. Herein lies, it would now appear, the explanation of the seeming disharmony between Intuition and Intellect which was gravely distressing to many in his earlier writing on the subject. Later works, however, make a point of restoring this harmony, but, as William James has remarked: "We are so subject to the philosophical tradition which treats *logos*, or discursive thought generally, as the sole avenue to truth, that to fall back on raw, unverbalized life, as more of a revealer, and to think of concepts as the merely practical things which Bergson calls them, comes very hard. It is putting off our proud maturity of mind and becoming again as foolish little children in the eyes of reason. But, difficult as such a revolution is, there is no other way, I believe, to the possession of reality."

Bergson's style of writing merits high praise. He is no "dry" philosopher; he is highly imaginative and picturesque; many of his passages might be styled, like those of Macaulay, "purple," for at times he rises to a high pitch of feeling and oratory. Yet this has been urged against him by some critics. The ironic remark has been repeated, in regard to Bergson, which was originally made of William James, by Dr. Schiller, that his work was "so lacking in the familiar philosophic catchwords, that it may be doubted whether any professor has quite understood it." There is in his works a beauty of style and a comparative absence of technical terms which have contributed much to his popularity. The criticism directed against his poetic style, accuses him of hypnotizing us by his fine language, of employing metaphors where we expect facts, and of substituting illustrations for proof. . . . But it does not seem a fair criticism to allege that he substitutes metaphor for proof, for we find, on examination of his numerous and striking metaphors, that they are employed in order to give relief from continuous abstract statements. He does not submit analogies as proof, but in illustration of his points. For example, when he likens the *élan vital* to a stream, he does not suggest that because the stream manifests certain characteristics, therefore the life force does so too. Certainly that would be a highly illegitimate proceeding. But he simply puts forward this to help us to grasp by our imaginative faculty what he is striving to make clear. Some critics are apt to forget the tense striving which must be involved in any highly philosophical mind dealing with deep problems, to achieve expression, to obtain a suitable vehicle for the thought—what wrestling of soul may be involved in attempting to make intuitions communicable. Metaphor is undoubtedly a help and those of Bergson are always striking and unconventional. Had Kant, in his *Critique of Pure Reason,* given more illustrations, many of his readers would have been more enlightened.

Bergson's thought, although in many respects it is strikingly original and novel, is, nevertheless, the continuation, if not the culmination, of a movement in French philosophy which we can trace back through Boutroux, Guyau, Lachelier and Ravaisson to Maine de Biran, who died in 1824. (pp. 135-38)

As a thinker, Bergson is very difficult to classify. [According to Bertrand Russell]: ''All classification of philosophies is effected, as a rule, either by their methods or by their results, 'empirical' and '*a priori*' is a classification by methods; 'realist' and 'idealist' is a classification by results. An attempt to classify Bergson's philosophy, in either of these ways, is hardly likely to be successful, since it cuts across all the recognized divisions.'' We find that Bergson cannot be put in any of the old classes or schools, or identified with any of the innumerable *isms*. He brings together, without being eclectic, action and reflection, free will and determinism, motion and rest, intellect and intuition, subjectivity and externality, idealism and realism, in a most unconventional way. His whole philosophy is destructive of a large amount of the ''vested interests'' of philosophy. ''We are watching the rise of a new agnosticism,'' remarked Dr. Bosanquet. A similar remark came from one of Bergson's own countrymen, Alfred Fouillée, who, in his work *Le mouvement idéaliste et la réaction contre la science positive,* expressed the opinion that Bergson's philosophy could but issue in *le scepticisme et le nihilisme.* Bergson runs counter to so many established views that his thought has raised very wide and animated discussions. (pp. 140-41)

In his preface to the volume on Gabriel Tarde, his predecessor in the chair of Modern Philosophy at the Collège de France, written in 1909, we find Bergson remarking: *On mesure la portée d'une doctrine philosophique à la variété des idées où elle s'épanouit et à la symplicité du principe où elle se ramasse* [''One measures the importance of a philosophical doctrine by the diversity of the ideas upon which it is premised and by the simplicity of the principle from which it springs'']. This remark may serve us as a criterion in surveying his own work. . . . Bergson is most suggestive. Moreover, no philosopher has been so steeped in the knowledge of both Mind and Matter, no thinker has been at once so ''empirical'' and so ''spiritual.'' His thought ranges from subtle psychological analyses and minute biological facts to the work of artists and poets, all-embracing in its attempt to portray Life and make manifest to us the reality of Time and of Change. His insistence on Change is directed to showing that it is the supreme reality, and on Time to demonstrating that it is the stuff of which things are made. He is right in attacking the false conception of Time, and putting before us *la durée* as more real; right, too, in attacking the notion of empty eternity. But although Change

and Development may be the fundamental feature of reality, Bergson does not convincingly show that it is literally *The* Reality, nor do we think that this can be shown. He does not admit that there is any *thing* that changes or endures; he is the modern Heraclitus; all teaching which savours of the Parmenidean ''one'' he opposes. Yet it would seem that these two old conceptions may be capable of a reconciliation and that if all reality is change, there is a complementary principle that Change implies *something* permanent.

Then, again, we feel Bergson is right in exposing the errors which the ''idea of the line,'' the trespassing of space, causes; but he comes very near to denying, in his statements regarding *durée pure,* any knowledge of the past as past; he overlooks the decisive difference between the ''no more'' and the ''not yet'' feeling of the child's consciousness, which is the germ of our clear knowledge of the past as past, and distinct from the future.

To take another of his ''pure'' distinctions, we cannot see any necessity for his formulation of what he terms ''Pure Perception.'' Not only does it obscure the relation of Sensation to Perception, but it seems to be quite unknown and unknowable and unnecessary as an hypothesis. As to his ''Pure'' Memory, there is more to be said. It stands on a different plane and seems to be the statement of a very profound truth which sheds light on many difficult problems attaching to personality and consciousness, for it is the conservation of memories which is the central point in individuality. His distinction between the habit of repeating and the ''pure'' memory is a very good and very necessary one. In his study of the relation of Soul and Body, we find some of his most meritorious work—his insistence on the uniqueness of Mind and the futility of attempts to reduce it to material terms. His treatment of this question is parallel to that of William James in the first part of his Ingersoll Lecture at Harvard in 1898, when he called attention to ''permissive'' or ''transmissive'' function of the brain. Bergson's criticisms of Parallelism are very valuable.

No less so are his refutations of both physical and psychological Determinism. Men were growing impatient of a science claiming so much and yet admittedly unable to explain the really vital factors of existence, of which the free action of men is one of the most important. The value placed on human freedom, on the creative power of human beings to mould the future, links Bergson again with James, and it is this humanism which is the supremely valuable factor in the philosophies of both thinkers. This has been pointed out in the consideration of the ethical and political implications of Bergson's Philosophy. Nevertheless, although his insistence on Freedom and Creative Evolution implies that we are to realize that by our choices and our free acts we may make or mar the issue, and that through us and by us that issue may be turned to good, the good of ourselves and of our fellows, there is an ethical lack in Bergson's philosophy which is disappointing. Then . . . there is the lack of teleology in his conception of the Universe; his denial of *any* purpose hardly seems to be in harmony with his use of the phrase ''the meaning of life.''

Much in Bergson would point to the need for the addition of a philosophy of Values. This, however, he does not give us. He shirks the deeper problems of the moral and spiritual life of man. He undervalues, indeed ignores, the influence of transcendent ideas or ideals on the life-history of mankind. The study of these might have led him to admit a teleology of some kind; for ''in the thinking consciousness the order of growth is largely determined by choice; and choice is guided by valuation. We are, in general, only partially aware of the ends that we pursue. But we are more and more seeking to attain what is good, true and beautiful, and the order of human life becomes more and more guided by the consciousness of these ends.'' Bergson, however, will not ultimately be able to evade the work of attempting some reconciliation of moral ideas and ideals with their crude and animal origins and environment, to which they are so opposed and to which they are actually offering a very strong opposition. That he himself has seen this is proved by the attention he is now giving to the problems of social Ethics.

There are four problems which confront every evolutionary theory. These concern the origin of: Matter, Life, Consciousness, and Conscience. Bergson finds it very difficult to account for the origin of Matter, and it is not clear from what he says why the original consciousness should have made Matter and then be obliged to fight against it in order to be free. Then, in speaking of the law of Thermodynamics, he says: ''Any material system which should store energy by arresting its degradation to some lower level, and produce effects by its sudden liberation, would exhibit something in the nature of Life.'' This, however, is not very precise, for this would hold true of thunder-clouds and of many machines. In regard to Instinct, it has been pointed out by several experts that Instinct is not so infallible as Bergson makes out. Of the mistakes of Instinct he says little. Dr. McDougall in his great work *Body and Mind* says, when speaking of Bergson's doctrine of Evolution: ''Its recognition of the continuity of all Life is the great merit of Professor Bergson's theory of Creative Evolution; its failure to give any intelligible account of individuality is its greatest defect. I venture to think,'' he continues, ''that the most urgent problem confronting the philosophic biologist is the construction of a theory of life which will harmonize the facts of individuality with the appearance of the continuity of all life, with the theory of progressive evolution, and with the facts of heredity and biparental reproduction.''

In the light of such criticism it is important to note that Bergson is now giving attention to the problem of personality which he made the subject of his Gifford Lectures. It is a highly important problem for humanity, and concentration on it seems the demand of the times upon those who feel the urgent need of reflection and who have the ability to philosophize. Can philosophy offer any adequate explanation of human personality, its place and purpose in the cosmos? Why should individual systems of energy, little worlds within the world, appear inside the unity of the whole, depending on their environment, physical and mental, for much, but yet capable of freedom and unforeseen actions, and of creative and progressive development? Further, why should ideals concentrate themselves as it were round such unique centres of indeterminateness as these are? On these problems of our origin and destiny, in short, on an investigation of human personality, thinkers must concentrate. Humanity will not be satisfied with systems which leave no room for the human soul. Human personality and its experience must have ample place and recognition in any philosophy put forward in these days.

Bergson's work is a magnificent attempt to show us how, in the words of George Meredith: ''Men have come out of brutishness.'' His theory of evolution is separated from Naturalism by his insistence on human freedom and on the supra-consciousness which is the origin of things; on the other hand, he is separated from the Idealists by his insistence upon the reality of *la durée*. He contrasts profoundly with Absolute Idealism.

While in Hegel, Mind is the only truth of Nature, in Bergson, Life is the only truth of Matter, or we may express it—whereas for Hegel the truth of Reality is its ideality, for Bergson the truth of Reality is its vitality.

The need for philosophical thought, as Bergson himself points out, is world-wide. Philosophy aims at bringing all discussion, even that of business affairs, on to the plane of ideas and principles. By looking at things from a truly ''general'' standpoint we are frequently helped to approach them in a really ''generous'' frame of mind, for there is an intimate connexion between the large mind and the large heart.

Bergson has rendered valuable service in calling attention to the need for man to examine carefully his own inner nature, and the deepest worth and significance of his own experiences. For the practical purposes of life, man is obliged to deal with objects in space, and to learn their relations to one another. But this does not exhaust the possibilities of his nature. He has himself the reality of his own self-consciousness, his own spiritual existence to consider. Consequently, he can never rest satisfied with any purely naturalistic interpretation of himself. The step of realizing the importance of mental constructions to interpret the impressions of the external world, and the applying them to practical needs, was a great advance. Much greater progress, however, is there in man's realization of qualities within himself which transcend the ordinary dead level of experience, the recognition of the spiritual value of his own nature, of himself as a personality, capable even amid the fluctuations of the world about him, and the illusions of sense impressions, of obtaining a foretaste of eternity by a life that has the infinite and the eternal as its inheritance; ''He hath set eternity in the heart of man.'' Man craves other values in life than the purely scientific. ''There are more things in heaven and earth than are dreamt of'' in the philosophies of the materialist or the naturalist. Bergson assures us that the future belongs to a philosophy which will take into account *the whole* of what is given. Transcending Body and Intellect is the life of the Spirit, with needs beyond either bodily satisfaction or intellectual needs craving its development, satisfaction and fuller realization. The man who seeks merely bodily satisfaction lives the life of the animal; even the man who poses as an intellectual finds himself entangled ultimately in relativity, missing the uniqueness of all things—his own life included. An intuitive philosophy introduces us to the spiritual life and makes us conscious, individually and collectively, of our capacities for development. Humanity may say: ''It doth not yet appear what we shall be,'' for man has yet ''something to cast off and something to become.'' (pp. 141-47)

> *J. Alexander Gunn, in his* Bergson and His Philosophy, *Methuen & Co. Ltd., 1920, 190 p.*

DICKINSON S. MILLER   (essay date 1921)

[*Miller was an American philosopher. In the following discussion of Bergson's ideas, he argues that while the philosopher's observations on the nature of subjective experience are a valuable contribution to modern thought, other aspects of his philosophy are seriously flawed.*]

''The greatest philosophical luminary that has risen above the horizon for a long time''; such was the verdict on M. Bergson of a very eminent American philosopher. But he went on to say that he did not profess to understand all his thought. A dozen philosophic specialists could be mentioned who have made the same confession. William James, who by generous praise gave the first great impetus to M. Bergson's fame in England, remarked: ''I have to confess that Bergson's originality is so profuse that many of his ideas baffle me entirely. I doubt whether any one understands him all over, so to speak'' [see excerpt dated 1909]. The greatest luminary does not appear to give a very clear light.

None the less in the years immediately before the war he was probably the object of a more widespread, a more nearly world-wide interest than any philosopher in history has during his life commanded. This was due in part, of course, to modern communications. But the fact remains that his impressiveness is exceptional. And since not even the specialists find him pellucid, it is obvious that he has conquered, not by clearly proving his point and compelling acceptance, but by the fascination and inherent acceptability of the ideas he propounds. The countless readers undrilled in the abc of philosophy who have found a certain thrill for the imagination in the current summaries of his philosophy, the numerous women of fashion who have listened to his lectures and derived sensations from his ideas, may be our witnesses. His volumes, crowded with arguments for these ideas, could not be called popular; but there is something in the ideas themselves which is unmistakably popular.

Can it be that the reason why the specialists do not fully understand him and the reason why the popular mind is drawn to him are connected—are consequences of one and the same fact? Can it be that the same trait makes his thought alluring to the mind's embrace and baffling to its understanding? Let us see.

Nothing makes much headway toward a full comprehension of M. Bergson but a long, plodding, minute study of his writings, the collation of passages, the persistent putting of questions about any difficulties in his meaning and the insistence upon finding the answers. Even this does not light up all the dark crannies. But it brings some interesting results. The philosophers mentioned had not bestowed this kind of labor upon him; they were busy bestowing it on the universe.

First of all, the broad features of his teaching familiar to all his readers must be recalled. He has published six volumes, all of which deal with the relation of matter to mind; each of which in one respect or another tries to show the ascendancy of mind over matter. The first book, *The Immediate Data of Consciousness,* translated under the title *Time and Free Will,* argues that mind or consciousness is not, like matter, a subject of calculation, because it is not, like matter, a thing of quantity. It is not composed of separable units whose sum may be cast up; if it has any parts they are fused into one being. We could never calculate its future acts, for there are no calculable factors. Mind is ''free.''

The second book *Matter and Memory* argues that mind is not a *product* of matter (that is, of the material brain) for matter has no power of producing mind. The nature of mind has been misconceived. In reality the brain is the point at which mind, treating the present material situation in the light of memory, can act upon matter, through an original and ripe decision. Memory is not dependent on the brain, but by its own nature retains always the whole of one's past (such is M. Bergson's bold assertion) and is merely restricted and brought to bear by the brain. Moreover matter itself turns out to be a form of mind in disguise; a lower form produced by the mind's ''running down.'' The tables are turned; matter is a product of mind.

In his third book, on *Laughter,* the theory is charmingly original. It is that we laugh only at people, not at things, and only then when people are behaving as if they were things. This book has sometimes been spoken of as though it represented an excursion quite apart from the author's philosophy and main interests, but in fact it is precisely in the line of them. It stands for the ascendancy of spirit and spontaneity over matter and necessity. The great joke is when a man, a free spirit, behaves as if he were an automaton, when he fails to *live,* with spontaneity or freedom, when he lets his habits or mannerisms or confirmed crotchets rule him, instead of making a fresh living response to a new situation.

An *Introduction to Metaphysics* (as the translation is called) deals with the proper method of philosophy. Philosophy has been impaired, M. Bergson maintains, by the encroachment of methods appropriate to matter only. Analysis, or the intellectual division of things into their parts, is a process appropriate to matter, but, as he sought to prove in his first book, not appropriate to that of living, continuous consciousness, which we are. Instead of seeking mentally to tear limb from limb, to dismember a living reality, we should rather seek to realize it as it is. This the author calls the method of intuition. It is, so to speak, the method of *being* the thing we wish to understand, so far as by imagination we can, rather than that of taking it apart and putting it together. It might also be called the method of sympathy. Living realities can indeed be approached analytically, if we desire. We do so rightly so far as we desire to take action with reference to the things studied, to foresee consequences, to calculate so far as calculation is possible. But so far as we wish really to face and see reality as it is, the external, analytic method is of no use. It merely substitutes some dead combination of units for the living, energizing thing.

The fifth and most famous book, *Creative Evolution,* maintains again the ascendancy of the mind's life over matter. It argues that living bodies, as we call them, are not a product of matter alone, but that psychic life, not dependent on body but slowly working out its will upon and through body, has developed organs that it requires and is still developing them. This effort and energy of life, which the author variously terms the ''vital push,'' the ''vital impetus,'' the ''vital current,'' and which he compares to a wave and to a wind, has been the directive principle of the whole process. There was in living beings a bent, a tendency, a set toward seeing, for instance, that steadily pushed toward the creation of an eye. Here the method of intuition and not the method of physical analysis will avail us. It is when we lend ourselves to share the instinct of life itself that we comprehend something of the process. Physical or mechanical explanation is the device of the intellect. But intellect is secondary, has only arisen for purposes of action, is useful for those purposes but cannot tell the truth about the nature of things. The intellect is intended ''to think matter.'' It ''feels at home among inanimate objects, more especially among solids, where our action finds its fulcrum and our industry its tools.'' Our author extends his vitalism to the whole universe. He carries it into metaphysics. All matter, again he urges, is a low form of life, a form in which the tension or push of life is slackened.

Lastly, . . . *L'energie spirituelle,* translated *Mind-Energy,* consists of seven occasional addresses and essays, of which the most important are the last three, on ''Recognition,'' ''Effort,'' and ''Brain and Thought.'' It maintains and extends the ideas above.

What manner of mind is it that is behind these volumes, all densely packed, except perhaps the last? What are its characteristics?

1. First of all, for the man himself we must have unfeigned respect. He is careful. He scrupulously verifies what he tells us of scientific fact, of history, of the views of past authors. Before he ventures to deal with any concrete subject, such as aphasia, localization of functions in the brain, the process of animal evolution, he fairly immerses himself in the study of its literature and traces threads with patient fidelity. His work is in the highest tradition of scientific conscience, modesty, and self-respect. And there is something else. There is a certain fineness of fibre, taking two forms: fine observation and fine feeling. These contribute greatly to his results. In examining consciousness as a psychologist he sees it afresh and for himself. He does not yield his mind to the facile customs of thought about it that have prevailed. Examples of this are the very first chapter he published, on what is called intensity in consciousness, and that chapter in creative evolution where he is discussing the process by which evolution is supposed to have taken place. The man has sharp eyes. He looks a fact in the teeth. He does not call a lawn all green when the part in shadow is dark green and the part where the sun shines is greenish yellow. This, of course, is a priceless merit in a thinker. We may put it first amongst his distinctive traits.

2. He has a taste or rather a passion for originality or freshness of thought. This is allied with what has just been mentioned, his love of seeing a fact with a fresh, acute vision. His original ideas are remarkably numerous. He evidently has a kind of conscience about *filling* his books, furnishing them amply and even densely with new thoughts. His books do not appear to be consecutively written. They are put together. They are a kind of conscientious masonwork of his best ideas only, all the rest being left out—written by one who would dislike to leave any commonplace stretches or interstices in his work. Now this love of originality in his own work is one with his desire to find originality, creative quality, fresh emanation in the world and in life, one with his rejection of mechanism, one with his distaste for the notion that the past controls the future, one with the pertinacious strain of thought through all his books according to which human will, animal life, nay, the inmost reality of things, have spontaneity and exert a certain "tension" of original effort which may bring forth undreamt-of fruit. He has a deep love of the new, of change, of intellectual adventure. In other words, by his temper of mind this philosopher is romantic, akin to what in literature was called the Romantic School. He has every mark of that school. He has, we see, its taste for the unfamiliar. He has its love of spontaneity. He has its frequent preference of intuition to reason. Like it he is fascinated by mystery and by sublimity in its wilder forms. Like it he is fascinated by personality, by the self, by its unique quality. These are deep-reaching influences in all he has produced.

3. There is another characteristic of his world. He is always telling us that the mind or soul is not made up of separate parts like matter, that its parts are fused and inseparable. He cannot accept "the association of ideas" because that makes ideas separate elements and treats the mind like matter. All that we call different thoughts, emotions and the like which the mind has at one time, really, in M. Bergson's view, "interpenetrate." This is a beloved word of his. We cannot consider first one by itself and then another by itself without doing violence to the intermingling of their natures. Now whatever may be

true of the mind this is certainly true of his writing. It is a curious trait. The parts are not rigorously divided. We never know when we have finished any subject. He will take up a problem and offer a solution; then state the problem again, introducing new difficulties, and give his solution with vital additions. Then a third version, etc. We never know but that we shall have the matter over again, with equally vital additions. We never know, therefore, that he means what he says to be taken as unqualifiedly true. His book goes forward somewhat as he says conscious life goes forward, "carrying the past with it" but not controlled by the past, and rolling up more and more of the theory as it goes.

This habit is largely due to our author's inability to see very far around him. He cannot survey his whole subject at once in clear arrangement and analytical array. What he sees at any moment is some real fact of consciousness or life or whatever. In every chapter of his books he has hold of some bit of experience, of fact, not manufactured, not spurious. Moreover, important fact. He goes deep. But he goes deep by an extremely narrow shaft. He does not remain at the moment clearly conscious of other facts, facts to the right and facts to the left, that should influence his conclusion. Only he dimly feels that what he sees is not all. He wants to survey the whole, but cannot. He feels the whole but can only see a small part; so he falls back on the idea that the part is darkly pregnant with the whole. The consequence is a peculiar helplessness. For example one is sure he would not be well able to defend his own doctrines in relentless debate. He has too little clear sense of his own bearings. He has too little clear sense of manifold relation. His eye does not take in at any one sweep the lie of the land and the several positions of the opposing forces. It does not take in at any one sweep his own philosophy. He is at times out of touch with his own base of operations. All this gradually forms in the reader a sense of the *difficulty* with which M. Bergson writes a book. It is, as has been said, carefully and most cautiously constructed. It never sweeps forward with a natural progress, an easy gait. Emphatically his writing has no élan vital.

4. He is not by nature a logician. It is the whole nature of logic to take in much at one sweeping glance. That is the sole purpose for which logic exists. Logic is able to say "either . . . or . . . ," and the whole universe of possibilities is at once marshalled in two opposite ranks. Logic classifies, by considering *all* things that have a certain quality, including things yet unborn and undreamt of perhaps, if only they have that quality—things monstrous and inconceivable in all other respects perhaps, if only they have that quality. At this one point logic has hold of them each and along the line of that resemblance runs out into the infinite. It is possible for the mind to put its eye down to one of those lines and look out along its endless course. In this he is not skilled.

M. Bergson, we saw, has delicacy of observation and delicacy of feeling. He has no intellectual delicacy. He has no sensitive avoidance of mental confusion and disorder. At some point, of course, where argument invites it, he may be logical for a brief space. But his mind soon escapes from the captivity of logic and makes its way back to the free and luxuriant forest of metaphor. The law of metaphor is that it exists for the sake of force and not for the sake of logical clearness. It may even in scientific exposition be everywhere present, but there it should be everywhere subordinate. In other words, the definitions and formulas which are the pivots upon which the whole turns should not be metaphor. But in M. Bergson's work they *are* metaphor. He seldom supplies a clear definition of anything. In this latest book ''an immense current of consciousness'' ''traverses'' matter ''to draw it towards organization.'' Yet consciousness is not a current; consciousness does not traverse anything; consciousness does not draw anything, in a literal sense; it remains to be proved that it draws things in any sense whatever. And not seldom the formulas are metaphor that involves logical confusion. He has no intellectual or logical delicacy about language. Else he could not speak of prolonging a fact into a law, an ill phrase for those who take the trouble to remember what a fact is and what a law is. Else he could not speak of prolonging the past into the present, an ill phrase indeed for those who take the trouble to remember what past means and what present means. Such confusions are innumerable. Else he could not use the term ''intuition'' as he does. The word ''intuition'' has two meanings absolutely distinct. Both are based on metaphor, but there is less of metaphor in one than in the other. In Latin the term means, of course, ''looking upon,'' ''seeing.'' In philosophy it means an immediate acquaintance with concrete fact, an acquaintance with it because it is directly present. The other meaning, wholly different from this, appears when we say colloquially that a man knows something by intuition. We mean that he knows it not by the steps of the reasoning process but by a sudden leap to a conclusion which we believe to be a sure leap. The fact is here not present, but he divines it by a single act of the mind. Now it is hardly credible, but it is true, that this word, on which so much is made to rest, is used by him in both these senses undistinguished.

M. Bergson carries ''interpenetration'' really too far. He allows logically distinct ideas to fuse. The philosophy of interpenetration becomes the philosophy of fusion—of con-fusion. The fault vitiates his work through and through. We begin to understand his very qualified regard for the logical intellect. We begin to understand how in his craving for originality he can perpetrate such an essay as that on ''Brain and Thought'' in this volume, a tour de force of sophistical ingenuity.

Now what solid contribution to philosophy comes out of his work? He tells us that the intellect demands solids. Reasoning by metaphor is contagious. Can it be that he questions the jurisdiction of the intellect because he is not going to offer us anything solid?

Broadly speaking, his work (and this is true of the present volume) may be described as a reaction against mechanical explanation in matters of life, against causal explanations in matters of human action, and against ''intellect'' in matters of conclusion and knowledge; in brief, a tilt against mechanism, a tilt against determinism, and a tilt against rationalism. The positive ideas which he possesses on these topics he carries even into the ideal of life and the conception of God.

Consider his assault on the mechanical view of the world. He assaults it with learning, with imagination, with the most accomplished ingenuity. But, rather oddly, the full import of his attack has seldom been discussed. This is because we do not consider the full nature of what he is attacking. The mechanical is the controllable. Man, beginning with primitive man, has more and more sought to find mechanics in the world in order that he might control the world, to sustain his life and to better it. And if the world proves mechanical in practice it is so far mechanical in reality. A machine is something that he has made to control for a particular purpose. He tries to find how he can control nature for his purposes. If nature is not machine-like or mechanical, just so far it is not controllable and cannot be

made to serve the deliberate purposes of man. So far as the processes of life of the organism are not mechanical they are not governable and we cannot husband and manage our health, our energy, our life, the life of society. He who prefers to feel that the doings of life are in the hands of an incalculable vital principle has a thought very striking and perhaps very inspiriting, but not applicable in any reliable manner. He has the spectacle of life, not an art of living. He admires life, but does not master it. He has a thrill in place of a satisfaction. Now this is thoroughly in the spirit of our day. Activity for its own sake is on all hands praised and celebrated. We tend to be, as a wise man has said, ''bound nowhere under full sail.'' The author himself emphasizes that mechanical analysis is practical; so far then as he limits or excludes it, he is limiting or excluding practical control.

There are a great many arguments in books of philosophy that are plausible because they are long. If they were brought down to a few words they would not impress. M. Bergson's argument about the eye, to prove that it did not owe its origin to physical causes, is exactly of this character. It is impressive because he never commits it to a few words. Caligula or Nero is understood to have said that he wished all Rome had but one neck so that he might cut its head off. Some philosophers have a species of unconscious instinct that warns them against giving all their argument on a subject one neck, lest some ill-disposed critic might cut its head off,—nay, it must in justice be said, lest they might unexpectedly find it their duty to cut it off themselves. He assumes in his argument that a psychic force could by its steady urge produce eyes concurrently in independent lines or branches of animal life that did not affect one another at all. And he assumes that the physical factors of evolution, the physical necessities of animal life, could not have produced them. His argument rests thus on a negative proposition unproved and on a positive proposition not only unproved but so vague as to be incapable of proof.

What is the real import of his own theory of evolution? It means that if we could fully see the working of an animal body we should see particles of matter moved and shaped not by other particles of matter, but by an invisible force; moved and shaped without contact. M. Bergson was one of the group of French savants who sat as investigators of Madame Eusapia Palladino and were completely mystified or deceived by her. Now what he calls the ''vital current'' irresistibly reminds one of what Eusapia used to call her current, her ''corente,'' that ''levitated'' tables and left banjos and toy-pianos, after the light was raised, standing where they ought not. The analogy in the case is completed by the fact that there is a light in this case too, which M. Bergson insists upon having turned down at the beginning of the performance. That is of course the light of the understanding. Just as Palladino used to say that there was something inimical to her sensitive and bashful current in the nature of light, and that the light had to be got out of the way before the current would flow, so it is here. There is something inimical to M. Bergson's theory in the nature of the logical intellect.

This philosopher might well be apprehensive of reason. For what he is asking us to do is simply to abandon explanation. To explain a thing is to show that it had to be as it was. The only way of doing this is to find a law and to show that the event was a case of this law. We show, for instance, that A will always be followed by B. Here was an A, so B had to follow. B is thus explained. There is no other way of explaining. So explanation involves laws of sequence. It involves distinguishing. It involves distinguishing between A and B, and distinguishing in any confused heap of facts between A and the rest of the facts. To explain we always have to analyze. Science is an effort to explain, and all science is analysis. If we stop analyzing and begin to contemplate something as a whole, just to have the feeling of it, then we have turned away from science to aesthetic appreciation or personal appreciation or religious appreciation. It is in this realm that the mystical attitude of the soul has its place, the highest place. M. Bergson's philosophy has been called mystical. Exactly! That is, it is mystical philosophy. His philosophy is mysticism standing where it ought not. No real philosophy can be mystical. No real mysticism can be philosophy. Mysticism and philosophy are both justified, but we are not talking about the same thing when we talk about a philosophy and about mysticism. All that is striking, sublime, contagious, inspiriting, in M. Bergson's contemplations, and there is much, is justly and admirably so. But that part is not philosophy. Philosophy, like science, is all analysis. It is simply the profoundest of the sciences.

The truth is that our philosopher represents a relapse to the abortive science of the Middle Ages. That attempted science would explain the behavior of some physical substance, what we should now call its chemical properties, by its alchemic essence. It knew nothing about this alchemic essence except that it was, so to speak, the actuating temperament of the substance. It was like explaining a man's actions by saying: "That is a way he has." And so the physical activities of an animal body were explained by a vital principle, or, as it was sometimes called, a vegetative soul, that dwelt within the body and simply contained in itself the secret of all the body did and was.

Now modern chemistry, for example, goes about the task in a wholly new way. It says that the rich properties of a substance are a result of the combination of simpler elements. It explains by analysis. The mediaeval idea was that if a thing had remarkable properties there must be something inside it to give it those properties, an occult cause of its properties, something that had all the richness to itself and infused it into the visible matter. This occult cause appears to be merely the relic of the idea of a spirit or ghost. It was not called a spirit or ghost any longer, but it played something of the same part in the affair. It was an "énergie spirituelle" invoked for physical explanation.

Now the professed explanations of *Creative Evolution* and the other books are almost all of this nature. The fact is concealed by the admirably conscientious acquaintance of the author with scientific details and literature. He speaks the language of modern science with an excellent accent. He entrenches himself with the utmost caution behind the facts. But all the while he is just a learned, punctiliously equipped, overpoweringly impressive spokesman of folklore. He is employing the ideas of "sympathetic magic." This is the real secret of his immense vogue. And this is also, as was suggested at the outset, a chief reason why for a workman in philosophy it requires hard labor to understand him. His thought resists analysis. He is a representative of purely popular philosophy attired in fastidiously correct academic costume. We may give up explanation and adopt our author's theory, but we could never call his theory explanation. But indeed his is not a theory we could adopt, for it is not a coherent theory at all. It is an unsubstantial compound of metaphors.

There is a quaint philosophic tragedy in the fact that this relapse to mediaeval science should be seen in a philosopher who is a compatriot of Descartes and the first French philosopher of worldwide influence after him. For Descartes it was who made the best achievements of modern philosophy possible by drawing those very distinctions which M. Bergson is determined to blur. It was Descartes who clearly and decisively brought us out of mediaeval science and it is his most celebrated French successor who would lead us back. The conception that mind, by "running down," relapses into the form of matter, is of a singular crudity. It ought to be noted, however, that M. Bergson seems hardly French. The French genius is lucid. He has caught a certain superficial lucidity of style, but in essence his thoughts are,—well, "interpenetrating," confused.

It is true, of course, that mechanical analysis has not gone to the heart of things and never can, but it is humanly advisable to push it as far as it will possibly go. It represents our practical hold on the world. Spirit exists and materialism is discredited, but that does not supersede the mechanical analysis of the physical world. So also does the case stand in regard to determinism and free will. Our actual deterministic explanation of conduct does not go all the way and never will, but it represents our practical hold on conduct. It has been an error to suppose that so far as our acts of will are undetermined by causes they are free and responsible. It may conceivably be that indeterminism is in some slight degree true, but if so, in precisely that degree, we do not control our acts, we are not free and we are not responsible. Determinism stands for the element of control, the control of the character over actions. So far from being incompatible with freedom it is the only principle that is compatible with freedom. Determination by motives is merely the process, another name for which is free choice. M. Bergson's assault on determinism has a wholly harmful tendency. William James's assault on determinism had partly a wholesome tendency, for he was practical while M. Bergson is contemplative, and James's stress was really on a certain practical philosophy of life.

So it stands too with rationalism. Everybody thinks by instinct. Rationalism really means a belief in the wisdom of using a certain collection of tests and precautions called logic to make sure that our instinctive conclusions are trustworthy. There are no subjects in which these tests and precautions are not in some degree available. Throughout his long discussion of intellect our author offers no definition and gives evidence of no clear conception of what he means by intellect.

The tendency and bearing of this author's thought is best seen when we come to his conception of God. He identifies God with the "vital impetus," which though embedded in different organisms is, he maintains, all the while numerically one. He describes this one great vital impulse as "a centre from which worlds shoot out like rockets in a display of fireworks." This centre, however, is not a person or thing, but a mere continuity of shooting out! "God is unceasing life, action, freedom." "God," thus conceived has no clear foreknowledge of His own purpose. The author expressly denies what he calls "finalism." "God" is, as it were, a continual struggle. A human organ is not designed, but the principle of life, pushing dimly in the direction of its needs, at last produces it. It is as if we thought of a near-sighted gentleman who is dimly aware of objects that concern him and without knowing just what they are or why he should look at them, by a vague, half-conscious impulse raises his eye-glass. Thus it is, according to our author, that animal life has raised the eye. Not only is deity conceived as struggle without foresight, but it is not defined with reference to the good. It unmakes as well as makes. It appears to have for the contemplative M. Bergson the very legitimate fascination of being intensely alive. The centre "from which worlds shoot out like rockets in a display of fireworks" is a picture congenial to the romantic temper. But Deity so conceived is not one with the good and offers no guidance to life.

What is the permanent importance of M. Bergson's work? On this question close examination can have in the end but one result. The only sound portions of any extent in his work are the first two chapters of his first book, *The Immediate Data of Consciousness.* They form certainly an admirable piece of work, though his thought there was less original than elsewhere. When we take up any one of the other portions of his work and examine it closely it collapses and seldom is anything but a little heap of dust left in the hand. As texts for philosophic study his volumes have permanent importance, for they are suggestive, they turn up most interesting questions, they have an important bearing upon our time. But as philosophy, that is, as an attempt to give us philosophic truth, they are not valuable. They are one more example of the unhappy waste of philosophic gifts due to the want of logical and critical education. It is not until the schools of philosophy make it their first business to supply this education, that splendid talent such as M. Bergson's will be protected against itself and enabled to give the world fruit of permanent value. (pp. 242-46)

> *Dickinson S. Miller, "M. Bergson's Theories: What Is Their Permanent Importance?" in* The New Republic, *Vol. XXVI, No. 333, April 20, 1921, pp. 242-46.*

WYNDHAM LEWIS   (essay date 1928)

[*Lewis was an English novelist who, with T. S. Eliot, Ezra Pound, and T. E. Hulme, was instrumental in establishing the anti-Romantic movement in literature during the first decades of the twentieth century. He also emerged as a leader of the Vorticist movement, founded by Pound. Although its principles are vague, critical consensus holds that Vorticism is related to Imagism in poetry and to Cubism in painting, and that one of its primary characteristics is a belief in the total impersonality of art, achieved by fragmenting and reordering the elements of experience into a new and more meaningful synthesis. Pound and Lewis established the short-lived but now-famous periodical* Blast *to give the movement a voice and a rallying point. Lewis's savage, satiric fiction has been compared to the work of Jonathan Swift and Alexander Pope. His best-known novel,* The Apes of God (1930), *is a long and aggressive satire on the cultural life of England in the 1920s. Some critics believe he will eventually be ranked with Eliot, Pound, and James Joyce as one of the most fascinating, controversial, and influential writers of the early twentieth century. In the following excerpt from his highly disparaging study of what he described as the Bergsonian "time-cult" in Western art and philosophy, Lewis presents a critique of Bergson's concepts of time and space.*]

It is Bergson who put the hyphen between Space and Time. The at that time unborn hyphen is suggested by him when he is insisting on *continuity,* as against, in Descartes, the conceptualizing of time. "Evolution," he writes, "implies a real persistence of the past in the present, a *duration which is, as it were, a hyphen, a connecting link.*" It is out of the bergsonian "durée" that the hyphenated "space-time," in philosophy, was born. His doctrine of *durée* is the hyphen. (p. 419)

First of all "Time," for Bergson, is *mental* as opposed to *physical.* Before him the mental character of Time had not been stressed in philosophy. The physical is "real" for him, in the sense that it is *dead mind,* as it were—the result of the great reverse movement in the heraclitean see-saw of his flux.

As the opposite of life, however, it is no more "unreal" than Nothing is nothing. Space and Time become for Bergson personified; and he has an ecstatic feeling of veneration at the thought of the latter. But at the thought of Space he has nothing but a sensation of disdain and hatred. So to all the pagan, "spatializing," instincts he is hostile, in the manner of Spengler. The unfolding of the fan is the *spatial* image. The closing of it is the time image. They are, respectively, extension and intensity.

In philosophy the problem of Space (not its "Reality," but whether it is isolable, as Kant thought, or not) is somewhat the same as the problem of Nothingness. For [Professor Alexander, author of *Space, Time and Deity*] the "unextended blank" that Space would be without Time to break it up into fragments, is very like the Nothing, on the face of it. The things that are contrasted in the traditional conception of Space are precisely what we mean by "something" and "nothing." Space is a paradigm, a Tussaud's, of Something and Nothing. It is Time that makes reality.

Kant's conception of Space is about identical with the popular or "common-sense" view: it is a datum we cannot get behind, installed in the very centre of our perceptive faculty. It is independent of its content. The homogeneous, empty, isolable space of Kant, is as instinctive to us as the supposed ineradicably qualitied, full, differentiated space of animals. The manner in which birds and insects find their way to their destination, sometimes covering great distances, is apparently owing to the fact that for them there is no space, as we apprehend it, but an infinitely varied, thick, highly magnetized and coloured, medium, instead. *Their world is not a world of distinct objects. It is an interpenetrating world of direct sensation.* It is, in short, Mr. Bergson's world. It is not our hated geometric world, of *one space.* It is a *mental,* as it were an *interior* world, of palpitating movement, visually indistinct, electrical; not all arranged on the principles of surfaces and lines; and it is without a "void" at all. What we have to grasp in the Bergson world of "durée," is that it is an *interior* world. And the world of animals or insects is also a mental, interior, world. The exterior world is where "Space" is, or the mere conception "external," which is the prime "spatial" one, is enough: to that concept Bergson, as Alexander, is extremely and temperamentally hostile.

Memory, again, is a thing Bergson does not like to think about very much, as memory, for the simple reason that, with it *stretched out behind us,* we have a sort of *Space.* When we cease to act, and turn to reflect or dream, immediately we "degrade duration" into a bastard Space. We make it into an old-fashioned "Time," in short. The living principle, which we illustrate and enjoy, make us one-way machines, essentially forward-moving—"go-ahead." But our consciousness, "though it does indeed move in the same direction as its principle, is continually drawn the opposite way; obliged, though it goes forward, to look behind." But what we see when we "look behind" is the artificial landscape cut out for us by the mere intellect; the "tout-fait," the already-made, the completed. We have turned away from what is *in-the-making,* from the "becoming," the world of *action,* to idle away our time in this private space of ours, provided by the machinery of memory, with its mass of images, which we can arrange at will. "Suppose we let ourselves go and instead of acting, dream . . . our past, which till then was gathered together into the indivisible impulsion it communicated to us, is broken up into a thousand recollections made external to one another. They give up interpenetrating in the degree that they become fixed. Our personality thus descends in the direction of space." This "dreaming" is to be very much reprehended. We do not *live* when we behave in this way. When we "look back" in this fashion we turn everything into a stone, as it were, in a trice, ourselves included. Everything in our minds takes on the qualities of matter and of the extended. But matter, for Bergson, is relaxation of the same sort, only *outside* our minds instead of *inside*. And since we have these deplorable habits *inside*, it is no wonder we have them *outside* as well. We feel quite *chez nous* ["at home"] when we open our eyes, look around, and notice the sleepy drove of twisted "objects," stretched untidily in front of us on a summer morning, as devoid of pep as a herd of cattle. But that might have been expected of us, by any one acquainted with our mental habits. He says: "We shall now understand why the mind feels at its ease, moves naturally in space, when matter suggests the more distinct idea of it. This space it already possessed as an implicit idea of its own eventual *detention*, that is to say, of its own possible *extension*." "Since physics is simply psychics inverted," physics comes naturally to man. That is it: man is a physical animal, his whole life one long, almost scandalous, *detention*.

How this disparaging view of Space affects Science, whose "domain is inert matter," is as follows. "For a scientific theory to be final, the mind would have to embrace the totality of things in block, and place each thing in its exact relation to every other thing. But in reality we are obliged to consider problems one by one, in terms which are, for that very reason, provisional. Science as a whole is relative to the particular order in which the problems happen to have been put." Science bears "on reality itself," but it works with intellect only. Mind, however, "overflows" the intellect. This overflowing of the intellect by the mind is "at bottom the same thing" as to say that *duration* has an absolute existence. So the business of metaphysics is clear: it is to place itself in the "mind" overflowing the intellect, or in other words in "duration"; and from that central vantage-spot it will occasionally catch very brief glimpses of the Whole. These difficult and semi-mystical exercises will give it an immediate superiority over Science.

Bergson's "main concern is with motion": but his fanatical objection to the static is satisfied once Time is radically installed in the heart of everything that otherwise might momentarily flout Time, or set up Space against it by offering to men that illusion of security and repose necessary for human creativeness, and belonging to contemplation, but which Time, with its "becoming" and never "finishing," its fidgeting or flowing away, its inability to remain in one place, is unable to provide.

Having acquainted ourselves with Bergson's "space," let us turn to "durée." "Duration" is what occurs when we completely telescope the past into the present, and make our life a fiery point "eating" like an acetylene flame into the future. "Duration" is *inside us*, not outside. There is nothing but "mathematical Time" outside us. "Duration" is the *succession* of our conscious states, but *all felt at once* and somehow caught in the act of generating the "new," as "free" as Rousseau's natural man released from conventional constraints, but with much more élan; never, at least, *dreaming*, as that personage was in the habit of doing. It is the organization of the past into a moving and changing present, into an incessantly renewed intensive quantity, which produces what Alexander calls, following the same line of thought, the "emergent quality"—also, like Bergson's, both absolutely "new" and peculiarly "free." Memory, on the other hand, unorganized, with

its succession of extended units, is that degraded *spatial-time*, as it might be called, regarded with so much hostility by the inventor of "duration." "Duration" is all the past of an individual crammed into the present; and yet this present is not the bare present that forgets its past and is unconscious of its future. This mystical condition of "pure duration" is a kind of ecstatic fishing for the Whole; the past is hauled in like a rope, and concentrated upon the present spot, gathered into unity by action. The present pervades the past, and so the past is renewed: for, for some reason, the present, concentrated in this way, and swelled out to bursting with *all* the past, is both "free" and "new." It is never *quite* free, or absolutely "new," we are told, even for the fraction of a moment. But it is quite free and new enough to provoke a great deal of rejoicing and enthusiasm, we are assured; though the delicate subject of *how* new and free is invariably dropped at the moment that our enthusiasm is supposed to be reaching boiling point, and that a discreet withdrawal seems necessary. But the main condition to be borne in mind for the achieving of "duration," is the complete *interpenetration* of all the parts of the past. The sign that it is *not* a "duration," is when you find these parts *separating* and *lying side by side*. That shows that you are not in the presence of "duration," but of its degraded, spatial, counterpart. On that you must immediately turn your back.

Musical analogy is frequently indulged in by Bergson. The separate notes or isolated sounds composing a piece of music are by themselves without meaning. Organized into a *whole*, they have meaning. This whole is like the living being. Time, as it is generally understood, is nothing but space and simultaneity—it is an exterior succession of impenetrabilities, and not an organized whole. "To say that an event will occur at the end of a time *t*, is to say that our consciousness will note meanwhile a number *t* of simultaneities of a certain order." And we must not be taken in by the term "meanwhile" (*d'ici là*), since the interval of *duration* only exists for us, because of the mutual penetration of our states of consciousness. Outside ourselves, we should find nothing but *Space*, and, consequently, *simultaneities*, of which one cannot even say that they are objectively successive, since all "succession" is arrived at by a comparison of past and present. Concrete consciousness *lives* these intervals: but, on the other hand, outside us nothing *lives*. When we surrender ourselves to Space we, too, cease to live. We convert our sort of *lived* time, or "duration," into space: or, on the other hand, we interpret our concrete, qualitied time by analogy with spatial simultaneity. We keep the past alive for Space, and hold the image in veneration of its past, and so provide it with a succession which it does not possess itself. On the other hand, we divide up our interior indivisible concreteness into mathematically-intervalled conceptual units, by reference to Space. In short, it is we who supply Space with a past, a duration. We in that sense break it up, just as it breaks us up into parts: and that is Alexander's explanation of what happens, as it is that of Bergson.

The clock is the central object of Bergson's time-philosophy, naturally, as it is the central object in einsteinian physics. It is not a clock that says, "Esto Memor! Souviens-toi!" ["Be mindful! Remember!"] but a metal object whose pendulum cuts up "mathematical time" into neat little parcels. It is quite an objective instrument; the romantic timepiece of poetry is *inside us*. The poor metal machine does not even remember its last oscillation: it possesses (without our assistance) nothing but simultaneities, and is irretrievably spatial. In watching a clock, and following its movements, you are counting simultaneities, merely. "Outside of me, in space, there is never any more than *one* position of the hand of the clock, since the past positions of the hand do not any longer exist.'' *Inside me,* however, a process of organization and penetration is going on, which is ''durée.'' ''It is because I endure in this fashion that I represent to myself what I call the past oscillation of the clock.'' Once more, then, according to Bergson, in watching the oscillations of the pendulum of the clock, I reduce my own qualitied, ''concrete,'' heterogeneous, psychologic states to a series of simultaneities, with intervals not filled with ''life'' or ''lived-time,'' but lifeless mathematical intervals. The way to interpret Time, to make it into ''durée,'' is, holding the memory of all the past oscillations of the clock, to conceive them all as ''penetrating and organizing each other like the notes of a melody, in such a way as to form what we will call *an indistinct or qualitative multiplicity,* without any resemblance at all to number.''

> The distinctive character of Time . . . is to be a succession within duration; it conceives of Time as given all at once as if it were a line. In other words, it conceives of Time as if it were precisely the same as Space. But Time in the abstract is distinct from Space in the abstract. The one is in the abstract mere coexistence; the other mere succession. Since the instants of abstract Time are homogeneous, the conclusion is drawn that in an infinite Time everything that can happen has happened. . . . But this overlooks what is essential to Time, that it is creative: that something comes into being which before was not.
>
> (pp. 419-24)

But the Time conception of Bergson seems to us entirely to misrepresent the rôle of Space, and, as it were, shuffle and transpose their respective ''realities.'' So what we seek to

Bergson in later years.

stimulate, and what we give the critical outline of, is a philosophy that will be as much a *spatial-philosophy* as Bergson's is a *time-philosophy*. As much as he enjoys the sight of things ''penetrating'' and ''merging,'' do we enjoy the opposite picture of them standing apart—the wind blowing between them, and the air circulating freely in and out of them: much as he enjoys the ''indistinct,'' the ''qualitative,'' the misty, sensational and ecstatic, very much more do we value the distinct, the geometric, the universal, non-qualitied—the clear and the light, the unsensational. To the trance of music, with its obsession of *Time*, with its inalienable emotional urgency and visceral agitation, we prefer what Bergson calls ''obsession of Space.'' If the painter's heaven of exterior forms is what above all delights you, then the philosophy of Time, with its declared enmity for ''spatializing'' mankind, will, if you understand it, please you as little as it does me. You will prefer the world of Greek philosophy, the pagan exteriority, to the world of music, or to the time-mathematics, or mathematics of events or ''durations,'' the mathematics of *motion*, which is temperamentally associated with that.

The interpretation of the ancient problems of space and time that consists in amalgamating them into space-time is for us, then, no solution. For, to start with, space-time is no more real, but if anything a little less real, in our view, than Space and Time separately. The wedding of these two abstractions results, we believe (as a triumphant feminism would result not in equality but in feminine ascendancy), in the ascendancy of Time (which also happens to be the feminine principle in this partnership) over Space: and of the two, if we have any preference, it is for Space; for Space keeps still, at least is not (ideally) occupied in incessantly slipping away, melting into the next thing, and repudiating its integrity. Regarding mind as Timeless, it is more at home, we find, with Space. And as stability is the manifest goal of all organic life, and the thing from which we all of us have most to gain, we see no use, in the first place, and in the second see no theoretic advantage, in this fusion. For the objective world most useful to us, and what may be the same thing, most ''beautiful,'' and therefore with most *meaning*, and that is further to say in a word with most *reality*, we require a Space distinct from Time.

If then, in recapitulation, Space and Time are mere appearances, as we believe, riddled with contradictions that bar them from anything but a relative reality, they are, from that standpoint, in the same case when joined to each other by a hyphen, as when standing distinct and unhyphenated. (pp. 427-29)

Space seems to us by far the greater reality of the two, and Time meaningless without it. Time as change was the ''Nothing'' of the Greek, and it is ours. *Space* is rapidly, under the guidance of a series of Bergsons, each Time-obsessed, becoming the ''Nothing'' of the modern European. (p. 429)

> *Wyndham Lewis, ''Space and Time,'' in his* Time and Western Man, *Harcourt, Brace and Company, 1928, pp. 419-29.*

JOHN DEWEY   (essay date 1935)

[*Dewey was one of the most celebrated American philosophers of the twentieth century and the leading philosopher of pragmatism after the death of William James. Like James's Pragmatism, Dewey's philosophy, which he named ''instrumentalism,'' was an action-oriented form of speculation which judged ideas by their practical results, especially in furthering human adaptation to the changing circumstances of existence. Dewey criticized the de-*

tached pursuit of truth for its own sake and advocated a philosophy with the specific aim of seeking improvements in human life. Much of Dewey's influence has been felt in the fields of education and political theory. In the following excerpt, he examines the ideas presented in The Two Sources of Morality and Religion.]

In [*The Two Sources of Morality and Religion*] M. Bergson goes back to the theme of the vital impetus (*élan vital*) that he developed in its relations to biology and philosophy in his *Creative Evolution*. In [*The Two Sources of Morality and Religion*] this conception is used to interpret the phenomena of morals and religion. To readers who are aware of the distinction M. Bergson makes between the two polar manifestations of the push of life—namely, instinct and intelligence—the reference in the title to *two* sources will already be suggestive. But M. Bergson is accustomed, in dealing with a subject, to soak himself thoroughly in all relevant literature, so that the interpretation he gives of two types of morals and two types of religion is far from being a mechanical application of pre-formed ideas.

He gives in this book (though not in the opening chapter) a resumé of his conception of life as a moving force; and a brief account of this basic conception is the best introduction to the book before us. Life is inherently a simple integral act, forever pushing onward to new forms. Its operations supply us with the key, and the only key we can command, to understanding life, mind and society. Life operates both with and against recalcitrant matter—which ultimately, though not proximately, may be traced to residua of the *past* creative action of life. Being past, this matter offers resistance to the new creative ventures of the same force that created it. It is as conservative in function as the vital impetus is radical.

Life-movement has two methods of dealing with the matter that confronts it: one is the way of instinct, the other that of intelligence. Evolution, the record of the action of life, is not a one-way process. In insect communities, life carries to virtual exhaustion the method of instinct. In the vertebrates, especially in man, the evolutionary force is itself freed, but, for the most part, in the direction of intelligence. There remains, however, a penumbra of instinct that is capable of becoming an intuition, penetrating directly into the movement of life itself. Intelligence as such is fabricative of matter through the invention and use of tools, which do for man what organic structures do for insects. Moreover, among insects, the social phase of the vital impetus is carried to such a height that the individual is completely subordinated to the group. Intelligence, on the other hand, works through initiative and invention—through, that is to say, the liberation of individuals from socially instituted organizations.

Consequently, from the standpoint of existing social organization—which is to man what the operations of social instincts are to bees and ants—intelligence threatens dissolution in some respect. Moreover, its exercise is dangerous. It brings foresight, and foresight imports inquietude, and inquietude brings in turn a slackening of attachment to life—a slackening that is harmful both individually and socially. One source of religion is a protest, coming from the depths of life itself, to this dissolvent and potentially dangerous action of individual intelligence. In behalf of its own persistence, especially upon the side of its social manifestation, the revolt creates myths, ghosts of experience. The author illustrates with some particularity from the idea of death—which is not found among animals. Intelligence perceives its inevitability. The automatic reaction of life against the uncertainty and "slackening" that result is

the building of theories about perpetuation of life in spite of death. If we generalize on this subject, we arrive at the thesis laid down by M. Bergson: "Religion is a defensive reaction of nature against the dissolvent power of intelligence."

But religions generated in this way determine one type of religion. There is another "source." A generative means of much higher type is found in the intuition, of which some individuals are capable, of the life impetus itself. Such intuitions characterize the mystic experiences that are the ground for everything the founders and prophetic renovators of religion do and say. Since these individuals penetrate the immediate ongoing of life, the ultimate reality, their experiences are as veridical as the outgivings of the other (socially useful) types of religion are mythical.

M. Bergson follows this reasoning with an interesting historical account in which the defects of all mysticism that is Greek in origin are traced to the opposition set up between contemplation and action, since true mystic contemplation is intrinsically a fountainhead of active energy. The defects of Indian mysticism are found in its pessimistic accompaniments, which made Nirvana the goal; while true mysticism, as expressed in Christian mystics, flows into "action, creation, love." The social phase of the life impetus, when it is freed from encumbrances, is expressed in love; the identification of it with life as ultimate is the meaning of God. When thus freed, it is no longer concerned with the preservation of institutional forms; while at the same time it is not attended with the danger found in the dissolving intellect, for love is a creative and constructive force. Mysticism, however, has to use the language and meanings that are current, and therefore soon assumes a diluted and adulterated form.

I have left no space to speak of the application of the leading ideas to morals, beyond saying that there also M. Bergson recognizes two modes, the closed and the open. The former is that of social pressure and conformity, corresponding to, though not identical with, the work of instinct among the insects. The latter is the morality of free individuals who have penetrated to the life-current that is below both instinct and intelligence. Incidentally, in the course of this discussion, M. Bergson makes a just and successful criticism of the notion that the source of obligation is rational, showing how, after social pressure has created it, the mind finds rational support for it.

Any adequate appraisal of the merits of M. Bergson's interpretations would involve a consideration of his basic philosophy, and that is out of the question here. I imagine, however, that ordinary readers, even cultivated readers, will not trouble themselves much about the philosophical foundations. They will be moved by the esthetic charm of the presentation, which time has not dimmed; by the air of freedom and release that permeates the discussion, and, if they are wise, by the incidental discussion of many points regarding the anthropological material of myths, magic and spirits. One who finds nothing sound in the philosophical foundations may nevertheless learn a great deal from Bergson's clear and informed discussion of these matters.

To engage briefly in adverse criticism, I should say that instinct plays such manifold roles in M. Bergson's system as to arouse suspicion. There is no difficulty in which it cannot be appealed to. There is a kind of instinct that creates social organization among insects, and something closely allied to it that creates closed morality, that reacts defensively against intellect in man—and that yet is capable of being translated into mystic as well as philosophic intuition. Now intuition and its manifestations are things not to be checked by logic; indeed by its nature intuition is opposed to intelligence and logic. When the immediate charm of M. Bergson's expression has waned, a reader is compelled to ask himself whether an organ that by definition is susceptible of no control beyond itself is a safe guide. Fundamentalists will surely protest against the antinomian tendencies inherent in the exposition of mystic religion and open morals. Others who have nothing in common with fundamentalists will wonder whether such a heavy burden has not been thrown upon "intuition" that they will have to be content to plod along with the aid of intelligence alone. (pp. 200-01)

John Dewey, "Bergson on Instinct," in The New Republic, *Vol. LXXXIII, No. 1073, June 26, 1935, pp. 200-01.*

JACQUES MARITAIN (essay date 1941)

[*A French philosopher and educator, Maritain was the foremost spokesman for the Catholic Literary Revival in France as well as a vigorous proponent of the theology of Thomas Aquinas, which affirms the validity of Aristotelian philosophy and recognizes no conflict between reason and faith. His own philosophical system, which has been described as a modified form of Thomism, emphasizes the importance of rationality in theology, thereby opposing the intense mysticism of much nineteenth-century theology. Maritain wrote a large number of essays supporting his beliefs, and his works are universally applauded for their elegant prose and logical coherence. The following excerpt is taken from the chapter "The Metaphysics of Bergson" in Maritain's study* Bergsonian Philosophy and Thomism. *This chapter originally appeared in an earlier work by Maritain,* Ransoming the Time.]

Bergson was a born metaphysician; how otherwise could he have been a great philosopher and a great renovator of the mind? But would Bergson himself have been willing to say that he undertook a metaphysical life-work or that he propounded a metaphysical system for his contemporaries? I do not think so. In this there is both an indication of Bergson's admirable modesty—not, indeed, unaware of its own quality—and an effect of that unbounded, scrupulous *conscience* and extraordinarily lucid *consciousness* (I use both words—a psychological *consciousness*, awareness, of himself and a meticulous scientific *conscience*) by reason of which he held himself strictly within the results which he believed he was justified in expecting from his method, which is an experiential or *empirical* method, utilizing indeed the most intelligent and the most refined of empiricisms, but still at root empirical.

Here we are at the very outset, before we have even made a real beginning, at the heart of the matter. The whole is in every part, especially for a philosophy of a vital-organic and, as it were, biological variety (this, be it noted in passing, makes Bergson and Aristotle neighbors): we cannot take up one problem without all the others being also present. Let us hope, despite this, that we may develop the present discussion without going into everything at the same time and not without parcelling out our ideas in some suitably ordered sequence.

In the days when I, in company with the little group associated with Charles Péguy and Georges Sorel, enthusiastically followed Bergson's lectures at the Collège de France, what we looked for was the revelation of a new metaphysics, and it was that which the lecturer himself seemed to promise us.

This was not the case, in reality. Bergson did not give us that metaphysics; he never intended to do so. And for many among us that was a very vivid disappointment; it seemed to us that a promise on which we relied had not been kept.

When we look back on all this today, distance casts a new light on things. When Bergson revived the worth and dignity of metaphysics in the minds of his listeners, minds engaged to their sorrow by agnosticism or materialism, when he said, with an unforgettable emphasis, to those minds brought up in the most depressing pseudo-scientific relativism, "it is in the *absolute* that we live and move and have our being," it was enough that he should thus awaken in them a desire for metaphysics, the metaphysical *eros:* that was accomplishment enough. And nothing is perhaps more moving than that species of detachment with which he freely let that desire, once aroused, travel its own road, in the minds of everyone, and lead some to a metaphysics which was not his metaphysics, which was even directly opposed to his metaphysics, until there should be, on deeper terms, relating not so much to philosophic conceptualization as to the spiritual directives of philosophy, new meetings of the mind.

If Bergsonian philosophy never completely avowed the metaphysics it involved, and which it could have brought forth into the light of day, if it remained much more rigidly linked to the science of phenomena, and more dependent on the latter than its lively reaction against the pseudo-metaphysics of scientism would have led one to suppose, it was because that very reaction had been managed from its outset by a radical empiricism. It is with the very weapons of anti-metaphysical science—with experience, but an *experience* incomparably more true and more searching—that Bergson sought to overcome the false cult of scientific experience, the mechanistic and determinist experimentalism which a philosophy of vulgar simplification claimed to be necessary for modern science. In this way he hoped for the possibility of a philosophic method (to use his own words) "rigorously drawn from experience (internal and external)," and which "does not allow the assertion of a conclusion that in any way whatever goes beyond the empirical considerations on which it is based." Here is a singularly bold declaration of integral empiricism.

Determined to remain rigidly faithful to the method thus defined, it would seem that Bergson was progressively drawn to foreswear the metaphysical in order more and more to fall back on the experimental. For one thing, what he expected from his philosophy was not the elaboration of a metaphysics which would be placed on a level in the scale of knowledge higher than experimental knowledge (thus, indeed, he objected when his philosophy was compared with metaphysical doctrines so elaborated and so *placed*); what he expected from his philosophy was that it make fertile the experimental sciences and that it even arouse the latter (especially the biological sciences) to certain new directions. For another thing . . . he was to move not so much in the direction of a metaphysics as in the direction of a philosophy of morals and religion, precisely because there only could he find the experiential knowledge which he needed to follow, in accordance with the method he had once and for all adopted, the upward movement of his enquiries.

Yet it is clear that there is a metaphysics implied in Bergsonism. And even if it were only in the nature of *excursuses,* of what one might call marginal trials, Bergson could not but from time to time give his explicit attention to the principles of that metaphysics. It is with that metaphysics, in an attempt to extricate it as a whole and examine its value, that we shall here be concerned.

It is well to indicate first certain elements relating to the genesis of the Bergsonian metaphysics. What is truly central and primary in that genesis is the deepening of the sense of *duration*.

Let us recall the passage where Bergson himself supplies us with important and precise indications of the history of his thought. ''In my opinion,'' he wrote to Harald Höffding, ''any summary of my views will deform them as a whole and will, by that very fact, expose them to a host of objections, if it does not take as its starting point, and if it does not continually revert to, what I consider the very center of the doctrine: the intuition of duration. The representation of a multiplicity of 'reciprocal penetration,' altogether different from numerical multiplicity—the representation of a heterogeneous, qualitative, creative duration—was my point of departure, and the point to which I have constantly returned. It requires of the mind a very great effort, the breaking of many frames of reference, something like a new way of thinking (for that which is immediate is far from being that which is the easiest to perceive); but once you have attained that representation and possessed it in its *simple* form (which must not be confused with a reconstruction by concepts), you feel obliged to shift your point of view on reality; you see that the greatest difficulties have arisen from the fact that philosophers have always put time and space on the same line: you see that the greater number of those difficulties are eased or dispelled.''

Arising above all from a close study of modern science and modern physics, and perhaps brought about—if we are prone to believe certain evidences thereof—by the examination of the arguments of the Eleatics against movement, what, in this, has been the central discovery of Bergson? I am not thinking at the moment of the Bergsonian *theory* of duration, nor of the Bergsonian *theory* of the intuition of duration. I am thinking of that kernel of *genuine intellectual intuition* which was for Bergson a discovery of duration.

In discussing the central intuition from whence proceed the great philosophical doctrines and the intermediary ''image'' between the absolute simplicity of that intuition and the complexity of its conceptual interpretations, Bergson writes: ''What first of all characterizes that image is the power of *negation* it carries in it. Confronted with currently accepted ideas, with theses which seemed self-evident, with assertions which had until then passed muster as scientific, it whispers in the philosopher's ear, *impossible!* Impossible even though data and reasoning would appear to urge you to believe that it is possible and real and sure. Impossible because a certain experience, confused perhaps but decisive, speaks to you by my voice; impossible because it is incompatible with the data that are alleged and the reasons given, and because therefore these data are wrongly observed, those reasonings false. . . . Later on [the philosopher] will be able to vary in what he affirms; he will not vary in what he denies. And if he varies in what he affirms, it will again be by virtue of the power of negation immanent in the intuition or in its image.''

Thus, according to Bergson himself, his basal intuition of duration above all carried with it a negation. And of what sort was that negation—so powerful and invincible? Real time *is not* the spatialized time of our physics; and this is true indeed, for the various times of the physicist are mathematical entities which are built up on complex patterns of spatio-temporal measurements, and which are doubtless based on real time, but are not that time. The latter is in the ontological, not the mathematical, order. And the negation in question goes much further. Not only is real time *not* the spatialized time of physico-math-

ematics; motion is *not* a scattering of positions succeeding and replacing each other; reality is *not* reducible to reconstruction worked out after the event, reality is *not* a reiteration of identical happenings, reality is *not* that concatenation of immobilities and of ready-made elements, without internal ontological substance or propensity or internal power of expansion, conceived by the mechanist.

Still there is not merely a negation, however strong, however important, however fruitful, in the intuition Bergson has had of duration. There is also a positive content in that intuition. (Herein I still do not accept that intuition in the conceptual form in which Bergson has thought it; but, by an abstractional procedure which I am well aware is not devoid of a certain presumption, I try to rediscover this intuition in so far as it has been an authentic intellectual intuition—in other words, within the very peripheries where, I believe, it evinces truth.) The positive content, then, of the experience under discussion seems to me to relate to the internal progress of the life of the psyche, or the lived movement, wherein, on a level deeper than that of consciousness our psychic states are fused in a potential multiplicity which is one nevertheless, and by which we feel that we are moving forward through time—that we endure while we change in a way which is really unfragmented, and yet which enriches us qualitatively and triumphs over the inertia of matter.

Here indeed is an experience of the concrete reality of *duration*, of *existence continuing itself* of our deep *psychic life*, in which is enfolded, implicitly present, the irreducible metaphysical value of the act of being. Let us have confidence in the light of metaphysical abstraction, let us not fear the extreme purification which abstractive or eidetic intuition involves, and which does not attenuate but rather concentrates into an absolutely crucial simplicity that which is most important in the real and that which before everything makes the real manifest. This experience of the lived duration of the soul will transfigure itself, will open out directly not only on duration, but on *existence*, or rather upon the actual *esse* in its pure consistence and its intelligible amplitude, will become the metaphysical intuition of this act: *to be*. This further step Bergson did not take. With all this intuition of psychic duration, faultless to the extent that it involved an authentic intellectual intuition, he did not himself grasp all the ontological content with which it was, and despite all would continue to be, pregnant; he did not express to himself that actuality and that generosity of being, and that creative abundance which permeates action and movement (and which indeed derives from the cause of being)—in short, everything ontological which his intuition in fact attained in the experience of psychic duration. On the contrary, he at once conceptualized his intuition in the *notion*, in the idea (to my mind equivocal and misleading) of that which it is proper to call, in an historical and systematic sense, *Bergsonian duration*.

Here we are face to face with a great—and a forbidding—mystery of intellectual life. There is no intuition *per modum cognitionis* [''by means of conceptualization''], there is no intellectual intuition without concepts and conceptualization. And yet the intuition can be true and fruitful (indeed it is, to the extent that it is truly intuition, infallibly true and fruitful) and the conceptualization in which it finds expression and in which it takes place can be mistaken and illusory.

How can this be? Let us first of all remember that the intelligence sees by and in the concepts which it, in a living way, produces from its own depths. Everything in the way of concepts and ideal constructions that the intelligence—ceaselessly leading its insatiable hunger for reality over the whole extent of exterior and interior experience, the whole extent of truths already acquired, perpetually on the *hunt for essences,* as Aristotle put it—causes to surge up in itself is only to serve that *sense of being* which is indeed the deepest thing in the intelligence, and to achieve an intuitive discernment which is the act itself of the intelligence. In those matchless moments of *intellectual discovery,* wherein we seize for the first time upon a pulsing, intelligible reality in the seemingly infinite abundance of its possibilities for expansion, and wherein we feel rising and confirming itself in our deepest beings that intellectual word which makes such reality manifest, we then know well what the intuitive power of the intelligence is, and that it is exerted by means of concepts.

True enough, but then we shape that intellectual word as the ultimate term of all the immense equipment of conceptual tools, of the universe of ideas and images already dwelling within us, which results from the years and years of the workings of knowledge to which we have yielded ourselves from the first wakening of reflection in our mind. If there is some serious lack, or if there are warpings and distortions in that universe; in other words, if the doctrinal equipment with which we are already supplied admits of errors and deficiencies, the effort of the mind through which the intelligence—by virtue of the active light which is within it—suddenly extricates from experience and from the accumulation of data and from all sensory contacts the freshness, murmuring with life, of some new countenance of the real . . . it touches that countenance, grasps it, looks upon it; the intelligence has brought it forth out of things; with it the intelligence ends its act of intellection, for it is things that that act seeks out; it does not stop at signs or statements . . . well then, the effort of the mind which achieves an authentic (and to that extent infallible) intuition will thus only reach reality by and in signs which, being produced and patterned under the ægis of a pre-existing equipment encumbered with errors and deficiencies, will ill express that intuition and will express it in statements more or less erroneous—sometimes seriously, irremediably erroneous. This will be the case as long, at least, as our general scheme of concepts has not been recast, perhaps by virtue of that very intuition and the ruptures it produces.

At the heart of every great philosophic system there is thus a very simple and yet inexhaustible insight—Bergson has singled it out in a celebrated passage—which on some occasion has overwhelmed the mind with its certitude. With every great philosopher and every great thinker there is a central intuition which in itself does not mislead. But that intuition can be conceptualized, and in fact in a great number of cases is conceptualized, in a mistaken, perhaps even pernicious, doctrine. So long as he remains bound to his own ideas, the philosopher himself cannot effectuate discernment in this matter; yet some day a proper discernment must be effectuated. How grand a dramatic spectacle is this! Here we have an intuitive certitude through which the real suddenly yields itself to the mind, through which the real and the mind suddenly enjoy a mutual ecstasy; and here is at the same time and in the same event, since all this cannot take place without a conceptualization drawn from our invested capital, the risk of deceiving oneself more or less seriously and of jeopardizing an entire, well-tested system of statements held as true by the sages. To avoid this risk, will the mind turn away from the real which offers itself, away from being for an instant overtaken by an aspect which had never before been manifest to the mind? That is impossible.

The mind knows that its first duty is not to sin against the light. It must subject to the most careful verification its conceptual equipment, but it cannot prevent itself from rushing toward being. No matter what the price. It is required of the mind not to fall into error, but first of all, it is required of the mind that it *see.*

But let us cease from this digression and return to the idea, the notion of Bergsonian duration. I have said that in my judgment it is an illusory notion.

Why and how? We were considering, a while back, the primarily *negative* signification of the intuition. Well, the Bergsonian notion denies *more* than does the intuition; it stretches that negation beyond the proper content of the intuition. The Bergsonian notion of duration does not merely say that real time is not the spatialized time of our physics, that change is not a scattering of positions succeeding each other, that movement is *non-divided, undivided,* that is to say *one* in act and of such nature that if it be divided, its own proper quality together with its unity is thereby suppressed (in this sense Aristotle went so far as to say that *6* is different from *3 plus 3*). Even more—and this is what is false—the Bergsonian idea would have movement be *non-divisible, indivisible,* and such that no parts in it can be distinguished from each other, even were they potential as in all *continua.* And it would have time not be *something* of change or of movement, *distinct* from change itself and *distinct* from the subject of change—indeed, the uninterrupted flux of the impermanence of change. Real time is that, it is this flux of impermanence, which is to say that it is that which is the least substantial in the world. And yet the Bergsonian notion of duration would not have it be that.

And what does this notion do in its *positive* aspect? It makes of time something substantial; it seems indissolubly to lump together in one same idea-image the idea of substance and the idea of time and the idea of psychic flow and multiplicity, all this making that "snowball which gets bigger as it moves forward" of which Bergson has so often spoken.

Instead of directing itself toward being and instead of opening out into the metaphysical intuition of being, as the nature of things requires, the Bergsonian experience of duration, in brief, took a wrong direction to conceptualize itself—while at the same time, in so far as it is experience, it continued, without saying so, to pulse with all the ontological content discussed above. Bergsonian experience of duration, then, has conceptually opened out into an unstable and fleeting notion of *time* as *substitute for being,* of *time* as primary stuff of the real and specificating object of metaphysics, of *time* as first object not, of course, of the intelligence, in the sense in which Aristotle said that being is the first object of the intelligence, but of that twisting of the intelligence back onto itself which would have it recover the virtualities of instinct and which is called Bergsonian intuition and which for Bergson replaces the intelligence as a power vitally apprehending the real, despite the fact that he himself momentarily considered calling it itself "intelligence."

To press the discussion further, we can note that metaphysics—the science which is wisdom, the highest sort of knowledge which human thought can attain—from its beginning constituted itself as transcending time. It was born when the intelligence of the philosophers lifted its head above the flood of succession. But from the very moment when the physico-mathematical method permitted the setting up of a science of phenomena *as such*, with the condition that concepts shall be resolved only within the *measurable* and *sensible* and the rôle of the ontological be reduced to the construction of "explanatory" ideal entities (*entia rationis*), intended to sustain a tissue of mathematical law-structures unifying phenomena, from that moment one can say that thought, coming back to the world of the senses, took up its abode in time. It required three centuries and the Kantian revolution to make men see what had happened.

What then is to become of metaphysics? If it is faithful to itself and to what is, metaphysics will transcend the science of phenomena as it transcends time, and it will at the same time recognize that that science, from the very fact that it consists in an *empiriological* or *empiriomathematical* analysis of the real, is autonomous with regard to the analyses of an ontological order to which philosophy proceeds—precisely because science does not itself contain, hidden away in it, a philosophy.

But if one denies to metaphysics that transcendence and that autonomy with regard to science and yet would wish to set up a metaphysics, one's only recourse is to seek out that metaphysics not at a level above that of the world appropriate to the mathematization of the sensible, but in its own depths. It will be necessary to seek within the physico-mathematical tissue a metaphysical substance, a stuff with which the physico-mathematical cognition of nature is unconsciously pregnant.

But where dwells this physico-mathematical cognition if not in the flux itself? What does it strive to organize through its formulas if not the relational stabilities which it isolates in the very flow of sensible becoming? Bergson's stroke of genius has been to see that if phenomenal science itself enfolds and hides, on its own level and in its formal object, a metaphysical stuff, that stuff can only be time. It is in time that we must immerse ourselves in order to find a knowledge which shall no longer have for its direct goal the necessary and the universal, but the flux itself of the singular and the contingent, pure movement considered as the very substance of things. All this presupposes, as Bergson perfectly well saw, the absolute superseding of the concept and a total inversion of the natural movement of the intelligence. In this same *time*, in which physics dwells without wishing to ponder its reality (for physics is indeed well satisfied with its mathematical substitute) and which physics translates into spatial symbols and the reality of which mechanicism suppresses, in this *time* metaphysics will fasten upon the absolute itself, which is invention and creation.

Much more basically dependent on modern physics than the immanent Cause of Spinoza, which substantialized the mechanistic explanations of a still youthful phenomenal science, Bergsonian duration achieves in metaphysics the very soul of pure empiricism or of pure experimentalism, of which modern physics has become aware as it progressed and with which it approaches reality in order to explain it. The last pages of *Creative Evolution* are supremely significant in this connection. "It seems then," writes Bergson, "that parallel to this physics [modern], a second type of knowledge should have set itself up. . . . It is to the inwardness of becoming that it would have transported us by an effort of sympathy. . . . If [this knowledge] were to succeed, it is reality itself which it would clasp in a final embrace." And again, "An experience of this type is not a non-temporal experience. It merely seeks, beyond spatialized time wherein we believe we see continual rearrangements of parts, the concrete duration wherein ceaselessly operates a radical recasting of the whole." And again, "The more one reflects upon it, the more one will find that this conception of metaphysics is that which modern science suggests." "Thus understood," he finally says, "philosophy is not only the return of the mind to itself, the coincidence of the human consciousness with the living principle from whence it emanates, an establishment of contact with the creative effort. Philosophy is the deepening of becoming in general, the true evolutionism, and hence the true continuation of science." In short, and properly speaking, metaphysics consists in "seeing in time a progressive growth of the absolute"; it is summed up in the affirmation that *time is creator*.

Such, it seems to me, considering what is most basic about it, has been the genesis of the Bergsonian metaphysics, and at the same time these considerations have already indicated a few of its essential characteristics.

It is from *this*, from this fundamental discovery (and, in truth, as we have seen, ambivalent discovery) which Bergson thought he had made concerning duration that issues as a secondary (if inevitable) characteristic the *irrationalism* of the Bergsonian philosophy. The irrationalism is secondary, not primary. It is as though involuntary; I should even say that it goes against his grain. And that creates a fundamental difference between Bergson's thought and a thought by first and deliberate intention inimical to the intelligence, like the thinking of Klages. Still the Bergsonian philosophy is an irrationalist philosophy: Irrationalism is the ransom set by the errors we discussed a few pages back in the conceptualization of the fruitful realities toward which moved, in so far as it was a genuine intellectual intuition, Bergson's original intuition.

For one thing no labour of metaphysical reflection, properly so called, had preceded this intuition and prepared the conceptual equipment which it was to use. There was no metaphysics of being nor of the intelligence, and no previously worked out critique of knowledge (the first chapter of *Matière et Mémoire* clearly shows that at that time Bergson believed he could still do without a choice between the idealist conception and the realist conception of knowledge; later on he was freely to assert that if he must choose between two *isms*, as he put it, it is realism he would choose, and with no hesitation.) . . . Bergson's original training was entirely scientific, or rather scientistic; it was from Spencer that he emanated. And that very fact renders more moving for us, and even more deserving of gratitude the work he has done for the rediscovery of the spirit. But this also explains certain deficiencies in that work.

Then again (and this is only another aspect of the same consideration, this also was a legacy of the modern philosophic tradition, unrectified by a sane metaphysics of knowledge) the one and only sure recourse to which thought might have access was in Bergson's eyes, and was exclusively to remain, *experience*. Faced with the contradiction and the fluctuations of abstract knowledge, experience alone (as though it itself were not inevitably indicated in abstract knowledge)—experience alone in his eyes had any philosophic value. Hence if experience—an experience more profound than the experience of the laboratory sciences—seems to admit me to the presence of a *creative time* and a *change which is substance* and a duration which is a kind of *pure act in becoming*, well then, let logic and the principle of identity and all the rational requirements of the intelligence perish as they must. All that is secondary from the point of view of the truth which I hold. This kind of desperate energy whereby the intelligence tears itself to pieces and prefers to deny its most vital law and its very existence rather than loosen its grip, rather than let go the truth which a deficient conceptualization causes the intelligence to hold badly, but to hold onto for dear life—we find this desperate energy in several of those philosophers who today call themselves existentialists, in Heidegger, for example, and in Berdyaev. It was for this that William James expressed his gratitude to Bergson with charming frankness, when he thanked Bergson for having helped him to liberate himself once and for all from logic. Such deliverances are scarcely more profitable than an immersion in the river of Heraclitus, in which one does not bathe twice, for one drowns the first time one tries it. For Bergsonism, the continuous duration of life escapes all logic, and cannot accommodate itself to the principle of non-contradiction; from this it follows, as has been said, that "the method made necessary by that density proper to the things of the soul can only be entirely *irrational.*"

That assertion is taken from one of the best statements yet made of Bergsonism from the point of view of Bergson, and it has the merit of leaving no doubt in the reader's mind on this point of capital importance.

One of the results of this actual irrationalism, and one of its expressions, indeed its specific and systematic expression, is the Bergsonian theory of the *intelligence,* essentially incapable of understanding life, capable only of knowing matter and making geometry, and the Bergsonian theory of *intuition.* Here we have that which in Bergsonism plays the rôle of a metaphysics of knowledge. These are well-known portions of the teaching of Bergson on which it does not seem to me that there is any need to elaborate here.

On the subject of the theory of intuition, a theory which, as Bergson wrote Höffding, occurred to him later than the theory of duration, I shall point out only one thing. An intuition which requires a kind of violent recovery, through an effort contrary to our nature, of the instinctive virtualities spaced out along the course of zoological evolution; an intuition "which prolongs, develops, and carries over into thought whatever remains of instinct in man, which buries us in concrete perception in order to deepen and broaden it, which is, thanks to the instrumentality of the will, an expansion of the perception of the senses and the consciousness, a painful effort wherein "the faculty of *seeing,* bending and twisting back on itself" should no longer be "but one with the act of *willing*"—such an intuition it seems very difficult effectively to consider as a *supraintellectual* intuition. I am nevertheless convinced that if the Bergsonian conceptualization here requires criticism, it still expresses in a deficient way views which are profoundly true on the supremely vital act of the intellect, on that which in the intellect is the most genuinely intellectual and is more valid than the reason. However questionable may be the Bergsonian intuition, as Bergson describes it, true intellection, that is to say intellectual intuition, often slips into it on the sly. It is the intelligence which gives value to all this, even though Bergson objects to the intelligence. (pp. 303-14)

If, as I have indicated at the beginning, Bergson did not desire to erect a whole system of metaphysics, his metaphysics is nevertheless one of the most profound, most penetrating, and most audacious of our time. The critical discussion thereof I have endeavoured to conduct . . . is in homage to his greatness. For the errors for which one is justified in reproaching him could only take shape as the ultimate, logical consequences of the projection, in a field of conceptualization unhappily altogether empiricist and nominalist, of intuitions and of truths which touch at the very roots of things. (p. 324)

Jacques Maritain, "The Metaphysics of Bergson," translated by Harry Lorin Binsse, in his Bergsonian Philosophy and Thomism, *translated by Mabelle L. Andison with J. Gordon Andison, Philosophical Library, 1955, pp. 303-24.*

BERTRAND RUSSELL   (essay date 1945)

[*A respected and prolific author, Russell was an English philosopher and mathematician known for his humanistic concerns. Two of his early works,* Principles of Mathematics *(1903) and* Principia Mathematica *(1910-1913), written with Alfred North Whitehead, are considered classics of mathematical logic. His philosophical approach to all his endeavors discounts idealism or emotionalism and asserts a progressive application of his "logical atomism," a process whereby individual facts are logically analyzed. Russell's humanistic beliefs often centered around support of unorthodox social concerns, including free love, undisciplined education, and the eradication of nuclear weapons. His staunch pacifism during World War I led to a six-month imprisonment and began a history of political and social activism which culminated when, at the age of eighty-nine, he was again jailed for his active participation in an unruly demonstration advocating unilateral nuclear disarmament. After the incident Russell stated: "What I want is some assurance before I die that the human race will be allowed to continue." Regarding Russell, biographer Alan Wood states: "He started by asking questions about mathematics and religion and philosophy, and went on to question accepted ideas about war and politics and sex and education, setting the minds of men on the march, so that the world could never be quite the same as if he had not lived." In recognition of his contributions in a number of literary genres, Russell was awarded the Nobel Prize in literature in 1950. In the following excerpt, Russell rejects Bergson's philosophy as logically untenable.*]

[As a rule, Bergson] does not give reasons for his opinions, but relies on their inherent attractiveness, and on the charm of an excellent style. Like advertisers, he relies upon picturesque and varied statement, and on apparent explanation of many obscure facts. Analogies and similes, especially, form a very large part of the whole process by which he recommends his views to the reader. The number of similes for life to be found in his works exceeds the number in any poet known to me. Life, he says, is like a shell bursting into fragments which are again shells. It is like a sheaf. Initially, it was "a tendency to accumulate in a reservoir, as do especially the green parts of vegetables." But the reservoir is to be filled with boiling water from which steam is issuing; "jets must be gushing out unceasingly, of which each, falling back, is a world." Again "life appears in its entirety as an immense wave which, starting from a centre, spreads outwards, and which on almost the whole of its circumference is stopped and converted into oscillation: at one single point the obstacle has been forced, the impulsion has passed freely." Then there is the great climax in which life is compared to a cavalry charge. "All organized beings, from the humblest to the highest, from the first origins of life to the time in which we are, and in all places as in all times, do but evidence a single impulsion, the inverse of the movement of matter, and in itself indivisible. All the living hold together, and all yield to the same tremendous push. The animal takes its stand on the plant, man bestrides animality, and the whole of humanity, in space and in time, is one immense army galloping beside and before and behind each of us in an overwhelming charge able to beat down every resistance and to clear many obstacles, perhaps even death."

But a cool critic, who feels himself a mere spectator, perhaps an unsympathetic spectator, of the charge in which man is mounted upon animality, may be inclined to think that calm and careful thought is hardly compatible with this form of exercise. When he is told that thought is a mere means of action, the mere impulse to avoid obstacles in the field, he may feel that such a view is becoming in a cavalry officer, but not in a philosopher, whose business, after all, is with thought: he may feel that in the passion and noise of violent motion there is no room for the fainter music of reason, no leisure for the disinterested contemplation in which greatness is sought, not by turbulence, but by the greatness of the universe which is mirrored. In that case, he may be tempted to ask whether there are any reasons for accepting such a restless view of the world. And if he asks this question, he will find, if I am not mistaken, that there is no reason whatever for accepting this view, either in the universe or in the writings of M. Bergson.

The two foundations of Bergson's philosophy, in so far as it is more than an imaginative and poetic view of the world, are his doctrines of space and time. His doctrine of space is required for his condemnation of the intellect, and if he fails in his condemnation of the intellect, the intellect will succeed in its condemnation of him, for between the two it is war to the knife. His doctrine of time is necessary for his vindication of freedom, for his escape from what William James called a "block universe," for his doctrine of a perpetual flux in which there is nothing that flows, and for his whole account of the relations between mind and matter. It will be well, therefore, in criticism, to concentrate on these two doctrines. If they are true, such minor errors and inconsistencies as no philosopher escapes would not greatly matter; while if they are false, nothing remains except an imaginative epic, to be judged on aesthetic rather than on intellectual grounds. I shall begin with the theory of space, as being the simpler of the two.

Bergson's theory of space occurs fully and explicitly in his *Time and Free Will,* and therefore belongs to the oldest parts of his philosophy. In his first chapter, he contends that *greater* and *less* imply space, since he regards the greater as essentially that which *contains* the less. He offers no arguments whatever, either good or bad, in favour of this view; he merely exclaims, as though he were giving an obvious *reductio ad absurdum:* "As if one could still speak of magnitude where there is neither multiplicity nor space!" The obvious cases to the contrary, such as pleasure and pain, afford him much difficulty, yet he never doubts or re-examines the dogma with which he starts.

In his next chapter, he maintains the same thesis as regards number. "As soon as we wish to picture *number* to ourselves," he says, "and not merely figures or words, we are compelled to have recourse to an extended image," and "every clear idea of number implies a visual image in space." These two sentences suffice to show, as I shall try to prove, that Bergson does not know what number is, and has himself no clear idea of it. This is shown also by his definition: "Number may be defined in general as a collection of units, or speaking more exactly, as the synthesis of the one and the many."

In discussing these statements, I must ask the reader's patience for a moment while I call attention to some distinctions which may at first appear pedantic, but are really vital. There are three entirely different things which are confused by Bergson in the above statements, namely: (1) number, the general concept applicable to the various particular numbers; (2) the various particular numbers; (3) the various collections to which the various particular numbers are applicable. It is this last that is defined by Bergson when he says that number is a collection of units. The twelve apostles, the twelve tribes of Israel, the

twelve months, the twelve signs of the zodiac, are all collections of units, yet no one of them is the number 12, still less is it number in general, as by the above definition it ought to be. The number 12, obviously, is something which all these collections have in common, but which they do not have in common with other collections, such as cricket elevens. Hence the number 12 is neither a collection of twelve terms, nor is it something which all collections have in common; and number in general is a property of 12 or 11 or any other number, but not of the various collections that have twelve terms or eleven terms.

Hence when, following Bergson's advice, we "have recourse to an extended image" and picture, say, twelve dots such as are obtained by throwing double sixes at dice, we have still not obtained a picture of the number 12. The number 12, in fact, is something more abstract than any picture. Before we can be said to have any understanding of the number 12, we must know what different collections of twelve units have in common, and this is something which cannot be pictured because it is abstract. Bergson only succeeds in making his theory of number plausible by confusing a particular collection with the number of its terms, and this again with number in general.

The confusion is the same as if we confused a particular young man with youth, and youth with the general concept "period of human life," and were then to argue that because a young man has two legs, youth must have two legs, and the general concept "period of human life" must have two legs. The confusion is important because, as soon as it is perceived, the theory that number or particular numbers can be pictured in space is seen to be untenable. This not only disproves Bergson's theory as to number, but also his more general theory that all abstract ideas and all logic are derived from space.

But apart from the question of numbers, shall we admit Bergson's contention that every plurality of separate units involves space? Some of the cases that appear to contradict this view are considered by him, for example successive sounds. When we hear the steps of a passer-by in the street, he says, we visualize his successive positions; when we hear the strokes of a bell, we either picture it swinging backwards and forwards, or we range the successive sounds in an ideal space. But these are mere autobiographical observations of a visualizer, and illustrate . . . that Bergson's views depend upon the predominance of the sense of sight in him. There is no logical necessity to range the strokes of a clock in an imaginary space: most people, I imagine, count them without any spatial auxiliary. Yet no reason is alleged by Bergson for the view that space is necessary. He assumes this as obvious, and proceeds at once to apply it to the case of times. Where there seem to be different times outside each other, he says, the times are pictured as spread out in space; in real time, such as is given by memory, different times interpenetrate each other, and cannot be counted because they are not separate.

The view that all separateness implies space is now supposed established, and is used deductively to prove that space is involved wherever there is obviously separateness, however little other reason there may be for suspecting such a thing. Thus abstract ideas, for example, obviously exclude each other: whiteness is different from blackness, health is different from sickness, folly is different from wisdom. Hence all abstract ideas involve space; and therefore logic, which uses abstract ideas, is an offshoot of geometry, and the whole of the intellect depends upon a supposed habit of picturing things side by side in space. This conclusion, upon which Bergson's whole condemnation of the intellect rests, is based, so far as can be discovered, entirely upon a personal idiosyncrasy mistaken for a necessity of thought, I mean the idiosyncrasy of visualizing successions as spread out on a line. The instance of numbers shows that, if Bergson were in the right, we could never have attained to the abstract ideas which are supposed to be thus impregnated with space; and conversely, the fact that we can understand abstract ideas (as opposed to particular things which exemplify them) seems sufficient to prove that he is wrong in regarding the intellect as impregnated with space.

One of the bad effects of an anti-intellectual philosophy, such as that of Bergson, is that it thrives upon the errors and confusions of the intellect. Hence it is led to prefer bad thinking to good, to declare every momentary difficulty insoluble, and to regard every foolish mistake as revealing the bankruptcy of intellect and the triumph of intuition. There are in Bergson's works many allusions to mathematics and science, and to a careless reader these allusions may seem to strengthen his philosophy greatly. As regards science, especially biology and physiology, I am not competent to criticize his interpretations. But as regards mathematics, he has deliberately preferred traditional errors in interpretation to the more modern views which have prevailed among mathematicians for the last eighty years. In this matter, he has followed the example of most philosophers. In the eighteenth and early nineteenth centuries, the infinitesimal calculus, though well developed as a method, was supported, as regards its foundations, by many fallacies and much confused thinking. Hegel and his followers seized upon these fallacies and confusions, to support them in their attempt to prove all mathematics self-contradictory. Thence the Hegelian account of these matters passed into the current thought of philosophers, where it has remained long after the mathematicians have removed all the difficulties upon which the philosophers rely. And so long as the main object of philosophers is to show that nothing can be learned by patience and detailed thinking, but that we ought rather to worship the prejudices of the ignorant under the title of ''reason'' if we are Hegelians, or of ''intuition'' if we are Bergsonians, so long philosophers will take care to remain ignorant of what mathematicians have done to remove the errors by which Hegel profited.

Apart from the question of number, which we have already considered, the chief point at which Bergson touches mathematics is his rejection of what he calls the ''cinematographic'' representation of the world. Mathematics conceives change, even continuous change, as constituted by a series of states; Bergson, on the contrary, contends that no series of states can represent what is continuous, and that in change a thing is never in any state at all. The view that change is constituted by a series of changing states he calls cinematographic; this view, he says, is natural to the intellect, but is radically vicious. True change can only be explained by true duration; it involves an interpenetration of past and present, not a mathematical succession of static states. This is what is called a ''dynamic'' instead of a ''static'' view of the world. The question is important, and in spite of its difficulty we cannot pass it by.

Bergson's position is illustrated—and what is to be said in criticism may also be aptly illustrated—by Zeno's argument of the arrow. Zeno argues that, since the arrow at each moment simply is where it is, therefore the arrow in its flight is always at rest. At first sight, this argument may not appear a very powerful one. Of course, it will be said, the arrow is where it is at one moment, but at another moment it is somewhere else,

and this is just what constitutes motion. Certain difficulties, it is true, arise out of the continuity of motion, if we insist upon assuming that motion is also discontinuous. These difficulties, thus obtained, have long been part of the stock-in-trade of philosophers. But if, with the mathematicians, we avoid the assumption that motion is also discontinuous, we shall not fall into the philosopher's difficulties. A cinematograph in which there are an infinite number of pictures, and in which there is never a *next* picture because an infinite number come between any two, will perfectly represent a continuous motion. Wherein, then, lies the force of Zeno's argument?

Zeno belonged to the Eleatic school, whose object was to prove that there could be no such thing as change. The natural view to take of the world is that there are *things* which *change;* for example, there is an arrow which is now here, now there. By bisection of this view, philosophers have developed two paradoxes. The Eleatics said that there were things but no changes; Heraclitus and Bergson said there were changes but no things. The Eleatics said there was an arrow, but no flight; Heraclitus and Bergson said there was a flight but no arrow. Each party conducted its argument by refutation of the other party. How ridiculous to say there is no arrow! say the ''static'' party. How ridiculous to say there is no flight! say the ''dynamic'' party. The unfortunate man who stands in the middle and maintains that there is both the arrow and its flight is assumed by the disputants to deny both; he is therefore pierced, like Saint Sebastian, by the arrow from one side and by its flight from the other. But we have still not discovered wherein lies the force of Zeno's argument.

Zeno assumes, tacitly, the essence of the Bergsonian theory of change. That is to say, he assumes that when a thing is in a process of continuous change, even if it is only change of position, there must be in the thing some internal *state* of change. The thing must, at each instant, be intrinsically different from what it would be if it were not changing. He then points out that at each instant the arrow simply is where it is, just as it would be if it were at rest. Hence he concludes that there can be no such thing as a *state* of motion, and therefore, adhering to the view that a state of motion is essential to motion, he infers that there can be no motion and that the arrow is always at rest.

Zeno's argument, therefore, though it does not touch the mathematical account of change, does, *prima facie*, refute a view of change which is not unlike Bergson's. How, then, does Bergson meet Zeno's argument? He meets it by denying that the arrow is ever anywhere. After stating Zeno's argument, he replies: ''Yes, if we suppose that the arrow can ever *be* in a point of its course. Yes, again, if the arrow, which is moving, ever coincides with a position, which is motionless. But the arrow never *is* in any point of its course.'' This reply to Zeno, or a closely similar one concerning Achilles and the Tortoise, occurs in all his three books. Bergson's view, plainly, is paradoxical; whether it is *possible,* is a question which demands a discussion of his view of duration. His only argument in its favor is the statement that the mathematical view of change ''implies the absurd proposition that movement is made of immobilities.'' But the apparent absurdity of this view is merely due to the verbal form in which he has stated it, and vanishes as soon as we realize that motion implies relations. A friendship, for example, is made out of people who are friends, but not out of friendships; a genealogy is made out of men, but not out of genealogies. So a motion is made out of what is moving, but not out of motions. It expresses the fact that a thing may be in different places at different times, and that the places may still be different however near together the times may be. Bergson's argument against the mathematical view of motion, therefore, reduces itself, in the last analysis, to a mere play upon words. And with this conclusion we may pass on to a criticism of his theory of duration.

Bergson's theory of duration is bound up with his theory of memory. According to this theory, things remembered survive in memory, and thus interpenetrate present things: past and present are not mutually external, but are mingled in the unity of consciousness. Action, he says, is what constitutes being; but mathematical time is a mere passive receptacle, which does nothing and therefore is nothing. The past, he says, is that which acts no longer, and the present is that which is acting. But in this statement, as indeed throughout his account of duration, Bergson is unconsciously assuming the ordinary mathematical time; without this, his statements are unmeaning. What is meant by saying "the past is essentially *that which acts no longer*" (his italics), except that the past is that of which the action is past? the words "no longer" are words expressive of the past; to a person who did not have the ordinary notion of the past as something outside the present, these words would have no meaning. Thus his definition is circular. What he says is, in effect, "the past is that of which the action is in the past." As a definition, this cannot be regarded as a happy effort. And the same applies to the present. The present, we are told, is "*that which is acting*" (his italics). But the word "is" introduces just that idea of the present which was to be defined. The present is that which *is* acting as opposed to that which *was* acting or *will be* acting. That is to say, the present is that whose action is in the present, not in the past or in the future. Again the definition is circular. An earlier passage on the same page will illustrate the fallacy further. "That which constitutes our pure perception," he says, "is our dawning action. . . . The *actuality* of our perception thus lies in its *activity,* in the movements which prolong it, and not in its greater intensity: the past is only idea, the present is ideo-motor." This passage makes it quite clear that, when Bergson speaks of the past, he does not mean the past, but our present memory of the past. The past when it existed was just as active as the present is now; if Bergson's account were correct, the present moment ought to be the only one in the whole history of the world containing any activity. In earlier times there were other perceptions, just as active, just as actual in their day, as our present perceptions; the past, in its day, was by no means only idea, but was in its intrinsic character just what the present is now. This real past, however, Bergson simply forgets; what he speaks of is the present idea of the past. The real past does not mingle with the present, since it is not part of it; but that is a very different thing.

The whole of Bergson's theory of duration and time rests throughout on the elementary confusion between the present occurrence of a recollection and the past occurrence which is recollected. But for the fact that time is so familiar to us, the vicious circle involved in his attempt to deduce the past as what is no longer active would be obvious at once. As it is, what Bergson gives is an account of the difference between perception and recollection—both *present* facts—and what he believes himself to have given is an account of the difference between the present and the past. As soon as this confusion is realized, his theory of time is seen to be simply a theory which omits time altogether.

The confusion between present remembering and the past event remembered, which seems to be at the bottom of Bergson's

theory of time, is an instance of a more general confusion which, if I am not mistaken, vitiates a great deal of his thought, and indeed a great deal of the thought of most modern philosophers—I mean the confusion between an act of knowing and that which is known. In memory, the act of knowing is in the present, whereas what is known is in the past; thus by confusing them the distinction between past and present is blurred.

Throughout *Matter and Memory,* this confusion between the act of knowing and the object known is indispensable. It is enshrined in the use of the word "image," which is explained at the very beginning of the book. He there states that, apart from philosophical theories, everything that we know consists of "images," which indeed constitute the whole universe. He says: "I call *matter* the aggregate of images, and *perception of matter* these same images referred to the eventual action of one particular image, my body." It will be observed that matter and the perception of matter, according to him, consist of the very same things. The brain, he says, is like the rest of the material universe, and is therefore an image if the universe is an image.

Since the brain, which nobody sees, is not, in the ordinary sense, an image, we are not surprised at his saying that an image can *be* without *being perceived;* but he explains later on that, as regards images, the difference between *being* and *being consciously perceived* is only one of degree. This is perhaps explained by another passage in which he says: "What can be a non-perceived material object, an image not imaged, unless it is a kind of unconscious mental state?" Finally he says: "That every reality has a kinship, an analogy, in short a relation with consciousness—this is what we concede to idealism by the very fact that we term things 'images.'" Nevertheless he attempts to allay our initial doubt by saying that he is beginning at a point before any of the assumptions of philosophers have been introduced. "We will assume," he says, "for the moment that we know nothing of theories of matter and theories of spirit, nothing of the discussions as to the reality or ideality of the external world. Here I am in the presence of images." And in the new Introduction which he wrote for the English edition he says: "By 'image' we mean a certain existence which is more than that which the idealist calls a *representation,* but less than that which the realist calls a *thing,*—an existence placed half-way between the 'thing' and the 'representation.'"

The distinction which Bergson has in mind in the above is not, I think, the distinction between the imaging as a mental occurrence and the thing imaged as an object. He is thinking of the distinction between the thing as it is and thing as it appears. The distinction between subject and object, between the mind which thinks and remembers and has images on the one hand, and the objects thought about, remembered, or imaged—this distinction, so far as I can see, is wholly absent from his philosophy. Its absence is his real debt to idealism; and a very unfortunate debt it is. In the case of "images," as we have just seen, it enables him first to speak of images as neutral between mind and matter, then to assert that the brain is an image in spite of the fact that it has never been imaged, then to suggest that matter and the perception of matter are the same thing, but that a non-perceived image (such as the brain) is an unconscious mental state; while finally, the use of the word "image," though involving no metaphysical theories whatever, nevertheless implies that every reality has "a kinship, an analogy, in short a relation" with consciousness.

All these confusions are due to the initial confusion of subjective and objective. The subject—a thought or an image or a memory—is a present fact in me; the object may be the law of gravitation or my friend Jones or the old Campanile of Venice. The subject is mental and is here and now. Therefore, if subject and object are one, the object is mental and is here and now; my friend Jones, though he believes himself to be in South America and to exist on his own account, is really in my head and exists in virtue of my thinking about him; St. Mark's Campanile, in spite of its great size and the fact that it ceased to exist forty years ago, still exists, and is to be found complete inside me. These statements are no travesty of Bergson's theories of space and time; they are merely an attempt to show what is the actual concrete meaning of those theories.

The confusion of subject and object is not peculiar to Bergson, but is common to many idealists and many materialists. Many idealists say that the object is really the subject, and many materialists say that the subject is really the object. They agree in thinking these two statements very different, while yet holding that subject and object are not different. In this respect, we may admit, Bergson has merit, for he is as ready to identify subject with object as to identify object with subject. As soon as this identification is rejected, his whole system collapses: first his theories of space and time, then his belief in real contingency, then his condemnation of intellect, and finally his account of the relations of mind and matter.

Of course a large part of Bergson's philosophy, probably the part to which most of its popularity is due, does not depend upon argument, and cannot be upset by argument. His imaginative picture of the world, regarded as a poetic effort, is in the main not capable of either proof or disproof. Shakespeare says life's but a walking shadow, Shelley says it is like a dome of many-coloured glass, Bergson says it is a shell which bursts into parts that are again shells. If you like Bergson's image better, it is just as legitimate.

The good which Bergson hopes to see realized in the world is action for the sake of action. All pure contemplation he calls "dreaming," and condemns by a whole series of uncomplimentary epithets: static, Platonic, mathematical, logical, intellectual. Those who desire some prevision of the end which action is to achieve are told that an end foreseen would be nothing new, because desire, like memory, is identified with its object. Thus we are condemned, in action, to be the blind slaves of instinct: the life-force pushes us on from behind, restlessly and unceasingly. There is no room in this philosophy for the moment of contemplative insight when, rising above the animal life, we become conscious of the greater ends that redeem man from the life of the brutes. Those to whom activity without purpose seems a sufficient good will find in Bergson's books a pleasing picture of the universe. But those to whom action, if it is to be of any value, must be inspired by some vision, by some imaginative foreshadowing of a world less painful, less unjust, less full of strife than the world of our every-day life, those, in a word, whose action is built on contemplation, will find in this philosophy nothing of what they seek, and will not regret that there is no reason to think it true. (pp. 799-810)

Bertrand Russell, "Bergson," in his A History of Western Philosophy, and Its Connection with Political and Social Circumstances from the Earliest Times to the Present Day, *Simon and Schuster, 1945, pp. 791-810.*

ENID STARKIE   (essay date 1959)

[*Starkie was an English literary critic and the author of numerous studies of nineteenth- and twentieth-century French writers. Her works include* Baudelaire *(1933),* Arthur Rimbaud *(1938),* André Gide *(1954),* From Gautier to Eliot *(1961), and a two-volume study of Gustave Flaubert. In the following excerpt, she considers Bergson's writings in the context of nineteenth- and early-twentieth-century French literature.*]

To understand Bergson's significance he should not be considered only as a philosopher. He was certainly not of the same philosophic family as—for instance—Aristotle, Descartes or Kant. It is indeed fashionable today amongst philosophers to denigrate his contribution to philosophy, and to deny him the name of philosopher at all. One must also take into account the period in which he flourished in the history of thought in France, and the feeling of liberation which he gave to many people, the feeling of hope in a better world of thought. He gave that hope with authority because he was a trained philosopher, and not merely an aesthete waffling sentimentally. He gave hope to those who were not philosophers just because he was a thinker himself who used his mind. And, by making up the quarrel between the idealists and realists, he set spiritual values again on the map, on a firm basis of intellectual experience. He considered that, in the academic teaching of his youth, intuition had been sacrificed to the intellect, and yet he believed that intuition alone could reveal the unity of life, that if a unity existed, it must be a spiritual one, that life must be wider than the intellect and the materiality which binds us. Bergson's ideas lit up the path for many other minds which had been wandering in a wilderness.

One must remember what was the state of intellectual studies in the university when Bergson began to teach, in order to appreciate the force of his message, and to give it full justice. This was the time when Hippolyte Taine's theories were the staple intellectual diet. Their main feature was a passionate and intolerant cult of positive science, so that metaphysics was considered only a deception or an empty fantasy. The dream of thinkers was the discovery of a universal science, a mathematics which would explain everything, and this was expected to fulfill all the needs of man. Everything was subjected to it and explained by it. Taine, in the introduction to his history of English literature, declared that vice and virtue did not exist as moral factors but were only two products like vitriol and sugar, neither of which was better than the other, only dissimilar to it. He even considered that the whole of art and literature could be explained rationally, by scientific investigation, through the principle of Race, Environment and Historical Moment. That is to say that it would be stated scientifically, and inevitably, what kind of art would be produced by any given people at a given moment of history, and in a given environment. This theory left completely out of account personal genius, and, like psychoanalysis, it could not be concerned with aesthetic or spiritual values.

But, after the Franco-Prussian War, especially from the eighteen-eighties onwards, there was growing dissatisfaction with rationalism and positivism, with the amoral and unspiritual attitude of Taine's teaching, and this is seen clearly in the novel by Paul Bourget, *The Disciple*, published in 1889. The hero is a young man who has always taken to heart the teaching of his Master, who, in his magnum opus, *The Anatomy of Will*, expressed the theory that all human desires follow certain inevitable laws; and that crime and virtue only exist from the social point of view but that, for the philosopher, they are meaningless.

The young man seduces a young girl who is engaged to another man, and then promises her that they will commit suicide together, but he backs out of the pact and she dies alone. He writes to his Master, in despair, for help and comfort, saying:

> I write to you *de profundis*. Answer me, dear Master, I implore you, direct me, guide me! Strengthen me in the doctrine which was, and still is, mine; in the conviction of universal necessity, which means that our worst actions—this cold plan of seduction, the suicide pact—all are part of the natural laws of the immense universe. Tell me that I'm not a monster, that there are no monsters; that you'll still be there, if I escape this terrible ordeal, and that you'll accept me again as a disciple.

The old professor is filled with horror when he discovers the results of his teaching. After the girl's fiancé kills the young man, and when he himself watches beside the bed where his young follower lies ready for burial, he is overcome with horror and remorse at the outcome of his life's work. (pp. 75-7)

In the Symbolist movement in French literature there had also been a reaction against positivism and materialism. The writers had found their theories largely in Baudelaire, who had been, during the Second Empire, the only poet in France to have spiritual aspirations and not to be wedded to positivism, but he was not understood or appreciated in his own day.

Baudelaire had seen art as an essentially spiritual activity, its main function being to get into touch with the beyond, with the ideal. For him there was a unity in art, and he dreamed of one perfect art encompassing all the rest, and appealing to all the senses in one. This could not, however, be achieved through the efforts of reason alone. Indeed the only way to reach it was to break down the tyranny of the mind by any possible means. Later Rimbaud was to say that the poet could reach the ultimate only through the "dérèglement de tous les sens" ["derangement of the senses"], by becoming a sensitive plate on which impressions could be written without his volition or effort. The poet was to become an inspired prophet or seer, through which the eternal voice found expression.

Later on, in 1934, Daniel-Rops was to declare that any action which tended to ruin the primacy of reason, to humiliate it for the part it dares to play on earth, seemed to him worthy of interest.

Bergson, who was in his middle twenties when the Symbolist movement began, is nearer in thought to these writers than to the academic philosophers of his time, and he was either influenced by them, or else the products of his mind sprang up from the same roots and needs, in the same soil. He became for them the heaven-sent thinker, who carried their theories further, who had the authority of a trained mind, and who was not merely a sentimental and emotional aesthetician, such as Villiers de L'Isle Adam and Théodore de Wyzewa. He became the link between the men of letters of the literary coteries and the men of scholarship of the learned academies. (pp. 78-9)

Bergson, in his doctoral thesis entitled *Time and Free-Will*, published in 1889—the same year as Bourget's *The Disciple*—already asserted the freedom of the mind as an experimental fact, to be realized by intuition. This was very daring at the time. He wanted, he said, to build up again the bridge between metaphysics and science, which had been demolished since Kant.

In his next book, *Matter and Memory,* Bergson showed that he believed that the mind could have some effect on matter in a mysterious way. He thought that intellectual knowledge does not give reality as it is, but transmutes it into a set of symbols which are useful for the guidance of action, but which have no metaphysical significance. By symbols here he does not mean the symbols of the Symbolists, but only such symbols as telegraphic signs. He believed that if philosophy was to become a true metaphysics it must relinquish the method of analysis for that of intuition. The mind must place itself into a living relation with its object; it must, for the time being, become the object itself, through the exercise of intellectual sympathy. Only then will it be able to follow the creative movement and to grasp its living wholeness, instead of seeing it as so many separate things and states. (pp. 85-6)

In the *Introduction to Metaphysics* he said that the absolute can only be reached and expressed through intuition, and by this he meant the spiritual sympathy by which one places oneself within an object in order to coincide with what is unique in it, and consequently inexpressible. Analysis, on the contrary, is the operation which reduces it to elements common to it and to other objects. He therefore considered that there were two types of knowledge: intellectual and intuitive—the intellectual being directed towards the already known, and the intuitive attaching itself to the unknown, the being-made. The intellect, according to him, is totally incapable of grasping time, motion, and life, while these are the unique objects of intuition.

Philosophers who are in disagreement with Bergson believe that if the intuitive method which he advocated were adopted instead of their critical method of reflection, then philosophy would be condemned to remain forever silent and inarticulate; or if philosophy sought to express itself it could do so only through Symbolism, which is literature and not philosophy. This was, however, the belief of Baudelaire and the Symbolists, that the deep reality, the absolute, which we perceive in a state of vision, can never be expressed directly in logical words, but can only be communicated through symbols. (pp. 87-8)

Bergson considered that his predecessors, when they had not despised intuition, had elevated it too far above the world, had isolated it from everything. He wanted to give it a scientific basis. He saw man as being made up of both intellect and intuition. Intellect could give only a very relative and practical idea of objects. But intuition enables us to enter into the object itself. Within all of us is a spiritual power in which we can take refuge and meditate. It is there that are found the deep roots of our personality, communicating with all nature. Like his inspirer Pascal, he believed in truth directly revealed to the heart. True intuition, he says, "by a kind of intellectual auscultation is able to feel the throbbing of its soul"; it is able to attain the absolute. That is mysticism. In *Morality and Religion,* he writes of mystic experience:

> True mystics simply open their souls to the oncoming wave. Sure of themselves, because they feel within them something better than themselves, they prove to be greater men of action, to the surprise of those for whom mysticism is nothing but visions, and raptures, and ecstasies. That which they have allowed to flow into them is a stream flowing down and seeking through them to reach their fellowmen; the necessity to spread about them what they have received affects them like the onslaught of love. A love which each one of them stamps with his own personality. A love which is in each of them an entirely new

emotion, capable of transposing human life into another tone.

Bergson thought that the divorce between science and metaphysics was the greatest evil from which modern philosophy suffers. In his *Introduction to Metaphysics,* he declared that "concepts are only symbols"—meaning only hieroglyphics—"substituted for the images which they symbolise, and which are incapable of giving more than an artificial reconstruction of the subject; they present the shadow of reality." He believed that there was something in the universe which science cannot weigh, measure, or calculate, and which it will never be able to calculate. But a true intuitive philosophy would be able to realize the much desired union between science and metaphysics.

Bergson's spiritual attitude to philosophy influenced the Catholic revival in the twentieth century, such writers as l'Abbé Brémond, Charles du Bos, Charles Péguy, Paul Claudel, Julien Green—and many others. Raïssa Maritain says that Bergson had created in them all an enthusiasm and a joyous gratitude, which was to last them for many years, even through grave philosophical differences and despite necessary and sustained criticism.

As he grew older, Bergson was moving closer to religion, to Christianity. In 1920, in his *Spiritual Energy,* he began to consider the possibility of the human soul. The consideration received fuller expression in his *Morality and Religion,* published in 1932. This effected the fusion of Christianity and philosophy, though he never became a Catholic himself—he did not wish to do so while his people, the Jews, were being persecuted. As Raïssa Maritain said: "Bergson travelled uncertainly towards God, still far off, but the light of whom had already reached him, and us through him."

No philosopher in France—with the exception of Descartes, perhaps, who must be studied in order to understand the seventeenth century—was better entitled than Bergson to be studied, amongst the men of letters, as an integral part of the literature. He was read not only by philosophers, but by all men of letters, and he spoke the kind of language which all understood. His lectures at the Collège de France were a social event. They were thronged with people from all sections and classes of the community. With philosophers, scientists, men of letters, students, priests, clergymen, rabbis, and fashionable women, holding their finger tips together, high up before him, to show that they were clapping silently, since applause at lectures was not the custom. It was very "snob" to go to hear him lecture, and he harmonized well with the literary and artistic trends of the day.

His approach to his work was literary and artistic more than intellectual—he must have inherited this creative talent from his father who had been something of a musician. Bergson saw the clearest evidence of intuition in the work of the artist. It is the same conception which we find in Baudelaire's poem, "Les Phares," where each artist is seen as a beacon shining in the surrounding darkness to light it up, and also to show God that man is there.

> They are a cry passed on by a thousand sentinels,
> An order re-echoed through a thousand megaphones;
> They are a beacon lighted on a thousand citadels,
> A call from hunters lost deep in the woods.

Genius, Bergson believed, was the power the artist possessed of seeing more than ordinary people can, of enabling him, by his superior experience and intuition, to penetrate further into reality. Writing about the philosopher Ravaisson, he said that

from the contemplation of a work of art could arise more concentrated truth than can be found in a philosophic treatise. He himself was first and foremost an artist, and a great many of his most telling efforts came from the beauty and harmony of his style. As a poet, ideas did not seem to exist for him until they had crystallized in an image. He was a poet in language—we see that in his use of metaphor. In his *Introduction to Metaphysics,* he says: "Is it astonishing that, like children trying to catch smoke by closing their hands, philosophers so often see the object they would grasp fly away before them?" This is a literary image rather than a philosophic concept. He was a poet with a beautifully modulated voice. Those with this gift of the tongue have always given the impression of visionary powers. It was thus also with Mallarmé at his Tuesday evening literary sessions at the rue de Rome. Bergson's lectures awakened in his hearers a sense of mystery through the imagination, and it seemed to reach to the core of their being, where the springs of consciousness well up. Like the Symbolist poets he managed to suggest a spiritual reality which he had perceived himself. People listened to the beauty of the style and not all paused to think whether there was any profound meaning contained in it. The passage which ends *Laughter* is very typical of such speaking—or writing:

> Such is also the truceless warfare of the waves on the surface of the sea, whilst profound peace reigns in the depths below. The billows clash and collide with each other, as they strive to find their level. A fringe of snow-white foam, feathery and frolicsome, follows their changing outlines. From time to time the receding wave leaves behind a remnant of foam on the sandy beach. The child who plays hard by, picks up a handful, and, the next moment, is astonished to find that nothing remains in his grasp but a few drops of water, water that is far more brackish, far more bitter, than that of the waves which brought it. Laughter comes into being in the self-same fashion. It indicates a slight revolt on the surface of social life. It instantly adopts the changing forms of the disturbance. It, also, is a froth with a saline base. Like froth it sparkles. It is gaiety itself. But the philosopher who gathers a handful to taste may find that the substance is scanty, and the after-taste bitter.

Bergson's eloquent and precise language held his audience enthralled, so that no distraction was possible. The attention of his listeners did not wander for a moment, nothing could break the precious thread of the discourse. It was like perfect and beautiful music, captivating the mind, just as music's richness does, allowing it no escape. The absence of heavy technical vocabulary made it all a joy to hear, and he was the least Germanic of philosophers. His words slipped out as if on silk, and the rhythm lulled the senses of his hearers so that they felt that they saw with his eyes, with the eyes of a poet. Indeed, in his *Introduction to Metaphysics* he frequently compares the philosopher and the poet. And yet he had a profound distrust of language, that is logical language, which he felt to be too abstract. Like the Symbolists he believed that there were thoughts so profound that words were powerless to express them, that abstraction created a veil which hides reality from us. Music he felt was more capable of being a satisfactory art, as it was dynamic, the very manifestation of the activity which pushes the world forward, its vibrations laden with our emotions which enable us to recover contact with life. (pp. 90-5)

Bergson led the writers of his age into the regions to which they naturally aspired, where they could breathe freely, where they began to realize that there exists a spiritual reality. Most of Proust's work is an exposition of Bergson's philosophy. Proust also forced his readers to accept the inexpressible. His theory of memory resembles that of Bergson, in seeing the difference between habit memory and pure memory—the first is physiological and the second psychological and spiritual. (pp. 97-8)

Bergson's doctrine may not have altered the course of philosophical reflection, but he did affect literary thought, and what writers call philosophy, with the result that the focus of personality was no longer intelligence, but intuition and feeling; and that the most precious intimation of experience, the immediate data of consciousness, was considered, at best, half conscious, and capable only of being revealed to the artist's probing.

Bergson's views of the problems which confront modern civilization are as true today as when he expressed them thirty years ago. He understood how, without further spiritual development, the world could not continue to live. The words which end this last work, published in 1932, *Morality and Religion,* are tragically apposite for the sixth decade of the twentieth century, in an atomic age. Those who today read Baudelaire in search for a remedy to our ills, in a desire to find something new which will lift mankind out of its rut, will find similar spiritual food in Bergson:

> But whether we go bail for small measures or great, a decision is imperative. Mankind lies groaning, half-crushed beneath the weight of its own progress. Men do not sufficiently realise that their future is in their own hands. Theirs is the task of determining first of all whether they want to go on living or not. Theirs the responsibility, then, for deciding if they want merely to live, or intend to make just the extra effort required for fulfilling, even on their refractory planet, the essential function of the universe, which is a machine for the making of gods.

(pp. 98-9)

Enid Starkie, "Bergson and Literature," in The Bergsonian Heritage, *edited by Thomas Hanna, Columbia University Press, 1962, pp. 74-99.*

ANDRE MAUROIS (essay date 1963)

[*Maurois was a French man of letters whose versatility is reflected in the broad scope of his work. However, it was as a biographer that he made his most significant contribution to literature. Following the tradition of Lytton Strachey's "new" biography, Maurois believed that a biography should adhere to historical facts regardless of their potential for tarnishing the image of the subject. Furthermore, he believed that biography should delve into the psychological aspects of personality to reveal its multiplicity, its contradictions, and its inner struggles, and that a biography should be an interpretative expression of the biographer. Most of Maurois's works have been translated into English and many of his biographies were widely read in America, including* Ariel: The Life of Shelley *(1923) and* Proust: A Biography *(1949). In the following excerpt from an essay originally published in French in 1963, Maurois presents a sympathetic critique of Bergson's philosophy.*]

[Marcel Proust's] *A la recherche du temps perdu* begins and ends on the theme of Time; it has been shown that the nature of memory was one of the problems that most interested Proust. Bergson's philosophy, which is the philosophy of *la durée* (duration) and the philosophy in which Time and Memory are the principal players in the drama of life, follows a course parallel to that of Proust's thought. The whole period was

dominated by this philosophy. In the history of ideas in France it has played a role comparable (and complementary) to that of Cartesian philosophy. It has led fine minds into religious thought. It has inspired artists, Proust and Péguy among them, and has obliged scientists to revise their conclusions. One must attempt, then, to describe at least its principal features.

Alain, the philosopher who taught me philosophy, was not a Bergsonian. He accepted Bergson but not the school. He often said, however, that nothing was more unprofitable in studying a great man's work than splitting hairs, arguing, and disproving. He believed one should do one's utmost to immerse oneself in a system, to make as good a case for it as possible, and embrace it as one's own, at least during the period one was studying it. Criticism did not seem to him justifiable unless based on thorough understanding, and no understanding is possible without some attempt at sympathy. I shall try then to set forth the elements of Bergsonism sympathetically. (p. 30)

Most men do not see reality. They spend their whole lives dealing with symbols—words—not people and things. To say that "Turkey is still (or is no longer) loyal to the British alliance" is not to reproduce a segment of reality; it is to place certain ill-defined words in a certain order. What is Turkey? If by this word one means the Turkish government, one should, before speaking, be acquainted with that government's workings, be familiar with the individuals that make it up, weigh the intensity of their feelings. If instead one means the country Turkey, one should have traveled in Turkey, have studied its various provinces and classes, have been friends with a cross-section of Turks. But such study would be too time-consuming. For life and action require rapid decisions. So we content ourselves with the label on the file-drawer and say "Turkey," hoping that others—ministers of state, ambassadors—will perhaps know what's inside the files themselves.

The human mind is above all an instrument of action and should accept the tools of language. They are imperfect but indispensable. However the mind must from time to time re-establish contact with the real. If it does not, abstract words and the concepts they represent end up at odds with one another in unreal and dangerous conflicts. An "intellectual" of the left forms a conception of a vague aggregate of relationships he calls *capitalism* and battles furiously against this monster; an intellectual of the right forms a conception of a vague aggregate of relationships he calls *socialism* and starts warning against this specter. For these two fanatics a walk-out is only a duel of abstract words. Contrarily, for the manufacturer who has grown with his plant, who knows its every cog, who has worked with his employees—and for the intelligent and well-informed worker—the factory is a living thing whose needs and failings they intuit. Both these latter arrive at proper solutions to industrial problems through an instinct based on their profound knowledge of men and machines and not through abstract reasoning.

In speaking of a woman they do not know well, men will say she's complicated, unpredictable, deceptive. They analyze her words and ponder her behavior but fail to understand. But to the man who has long loved this woman and who sees her thoughts from the inside, this whimsical personality is the most consistent and understandable one in the world. He doesn't reason; he intuits. Similarly, it is in vain that a foreigner talking about the misfortunes of France analyzes all the elements of the decisions made at the time of the 1918 Armistice. He sees nothing but confusion. He finds it impossible to explain certain reversals in policy, certain periods of inaction. But a Frenchman who loves and knows his country in depth—even if he disapproves—understands and excuses. He places himself inside French society, thinks with it, senses in his own mind the reactions of the various groups, and feels an aggregate impression taking shape within him which corresponds to the actual behavior of France—for France is made up of the same elements as he is. He does not reason; he knows.

"We know truth," says Pascal, "not by reason alone but through the heart as well; it is through the latter that we have knowledge of first principles. And it is upon these perceptions of the heart and of instinct that reason should rely and base its discourse." For example, the heart—or instinct—tells us that man is free, that the mind is distinct from the body, and that some actions are good and some bad. But it sometimes occurs that the discursive intelligence, meaning that intelligence which expresses itself in language and words, runs counter to these instinctual truths and that, by means of skillful verbal jugglings, it professes to prove that the world is all matter and that our actions are completely determined. According to Bergson, the philosopher's job is to rediscover the things concealed behind opaque and ill-defined symbols. He maintains that philosophy should be essentially a return to the real and a return to simplicity. To *discursive* knowledge, which is its principal tool, philosophy should add (and sometimes oppose) *intuitive* knowledge, which, piercing the web of symbols—lilies floating on the pond of reality—plunges into life itself. But does a form of knowledge other than discursive knowledge exist? Can we think without words? Is it possible to place oneself at the heart of things? Indeed it is. Great poets know nature through intuition, not reason. "Beneath the thousand nascent actions that give outward expression to a feeling, behind the banal, social word that expresses an individual state of soul, it is the feeling, the state of soul pure and simple they seek after. And to encourage us to exercise the same effort on ourselves, they contrive to make us see something of what they have seen: through rhythmic arrangements of words, which come to form organic groups and live a life of their own, they tell us, or rather suggest to us, things language wasn't made to express." This recalls the Valéry of *Charmes*. And like the creative poet, the painter, the man of action, the scientist is capable, too, of going beyond concepts and of merging for an instant with things themselves.

"Careful now," say opponents of Bergsonism. "If you deny the primacy of intellect, you take humanity back to the age of superstition and magic. You destroy the achievement of the eighteenth century; you endanger the accomplishments of reason, which are already so much threatened today." But Bergson never denied the role or the value of the intellect. He only said that beyond intellect, intellect itself can open the way to something superior to intellect. If the great statesman can on occasion have a sudden and brilliant intuition of what his people want, it is not because he denies the intellect; it is because, by dint of using his intellect to grasp all the details of the problem, he comes to be at one with the object of his thought.

Bergson is much too intelligent to make war on intellect, much too reasonable to make war on reason. He does make war, however, on that particular kind of intellectualism which accepts "the chaff of words for the kernel of things," on that particular kind of discourse in which reasoning has done away with reason. Descartes himself, father of rationalists, had many an intuitive prompting, and the reasonable Voltaire, in *Candide*, makes fun with good reason of the abuses of reason. The scientist and mystic, Pascal, understood that there is room for the *esprit de finesse* ["intuitive mind"] as well as the *esprit*

de géométrie ["mathematical mind"]. As for the danger of tyranny from the rule of discursive reason, one observes it when the French Revolution veered away from its original goals and fell, during the Reign of Terror, into a bloody verbalism. Bonaparte, a man of swift intuition, was able, subsequently, to see beyond the verbiage of the orators to the *facts* whose aggregate constituted the givens of the problem France. Is there anyone willing to argue that Bonaparte was not intelligent? But "he used intelligence to go beyond intelligence." "There is," says Péguy, "a great mob of men who think in ready-made ideas. There are ideas that are ready-made even while they're being conceived, just as ready-made overcoats are already ready-made while they're in the process of being made up." Bergson wants to dress reality to measure. He uses the same symbols, the same words as other philosophers, but he quickens his discourse, just as poets do, with images—often telling and beautiful ones; and he regains contact, behind the curtain of words, with living quivering nature.

And so we find ourselves in quest of a kind of knowledge lying beyond words and which we shall call intuitive—as opposed to discursive—knowledge. *Intueri* means to look within. Intuition is the mode of thought that consists of taking oneself, by means of the mind, to the center of the object being studied and of grasping its truth from within. "That's a handsome definition," says the anti-Bergsonian, "but to what reality does it correspond? How could one bring oneself by means of the mind to the center of anything? Whether a person, a country, or an object, one's only chance of grasping it lies in analysis, the description of each of its parts, as one sees them from outside, then the synthesis of all those elements. But that synthesis itself takes place in the mind. You can't get outside of yourself and enter into an exterior reality. To what, concretely, can one apply your intuitive method?" To what? replies Bergson. Why first of all to that very thought you claim we can't get outside of. When you yourself are the subject, there's no question about your being on the interior of the subject. If you should describe your interior life to another person, you would doubtless do so by using words; you would describe your visions, your dreams, your feelings, in the form of discourse. This is necessary in order to be understood. But if you carry on a conversation with yourself, if you really try to find in yourself the "*données immédiates* ["immediate data"] of consciousness," you can and should do so through pure intuition.

"Granted," says the anti-Bergsonian, "but that's a pretty sterile kind of contemplation. I concentrate on myself, I do not allow myself to use words, I listen, but I don't hear anything. If this intuition business goes on for very long, I'll fall into a kind of slumber in which I watch the transparent stream of my thought go by like a drowsy shepherd watching water flow." All of Bergson's early work is devoted to showing that we can, on the contrary, recover, by way of this simple and silent interior contemplation, infinitely precious elements of thought hitherto hidden from us by a vocabulary entirely derived from that system of knowledge which describes the exterior world.

The system of knowledge that describes the exterior world is entirely based on the notion of quantity. It requires fixed and measurable relationships, numbers, diagrams, a space that answers to mathematical laws. Interior life has nothing to do with quantity; it is the realm of quality. One grief isn't twice or ten times as intense as another. You can't square love. Feelings and sensations increase and decrease in a different way entirely, a way one can attempt to express in images but never measure. The same thing is true of perception of the *durée*. The flow of time is one of the givens, or *données,* consciousness provides to everyone. We have a clear awareness that each moment is different from the preceding one, even if none of the spatial relationships has changed in the interval. We know that this interior time is subjective and not measurable. But we are such slaves to geometrical ways of thought that the time we speak of is almost always objective time, measured by the movements in space of sand, say, or a pendulum.

"And what disadvantage do you see in not experiencing the sensation of pure *durée* and in transposing temporal data into spatial data?"

"The very serious drawback that since Time is not of the same nature as Space, we would thereby render certain problems unintelligible. Recall, for example, the problems Zeno posed to the Greek philosophers of antiquity, problems no one could solve.... 'Let us assume,' says Zeno, 'that the fastest of human beings, Achilles, tries to overtake the slowest of animals, the tortoise. I maintain that if the tortoise has the slightest head-start, Achilles will never catch up with it. For while Achilles is covering the distance separating him from the tortoise, the latter will move ahead a little. Achilles will then have to cover this new distance. But while he is doing that, the tortoise will advance again, very little, but a little nonetheless. This will go on endlessly. And thus Achilles will never catch up with the tortoise.'"

Such is the absurd conclusion Zeno's discursive, geometric thought leads us to. Intuitive understanding, which in this instance is the equivalent of common sense, knows on the contrary and beyond the shadow of a doubt that Achilles will catch up with the tortoise. Then what is wrong with Zeno's argument? The trouble is that his whole argument is falsified by the transposition of a continuous movement in time into a segment of space that can be cut up at will. Discursive thought in this instance confuses movement with the spatial trajectory that describes it. Intuition easily provides the correct answer or, to be more specific, demonstrates that the only problem is that of a misuse of words. It reinstates the factor of *durée* and the unbroken flow of time.

When Einstein's theory first came out, a thousand absurd conclusions were immediately drawn from it. A man traveling in a capsule at almost the speed of light could, it was said, come back after an interval of time that would be only two years to him but two centuries to those who stayed on the ground. He would have aged only two years and would have become a contemporary of his descendants. A man traveling at exactly the speed of light would never age, since the same light rays would always accompany him and present him with the identical view. Again, common sense balks. Bergson shows that these fabricators of hypotheses are confusing spatial time, that of signs and simultaneities, with interior, living time, the time in which one grows old. The traveler in the first capsule would, in fact, be dead long before the projectile came to earth two centuries later.

Another *donnée immédiate* of consciousness is the idea of freedom. We know we are free and responsible. A mechanistic philosopher like Taine, however, tells us that all of our thoughts and motions are as much determined as physical and chemical phenomena. "Vice and virtue are products like sugar and vitriol." And indeed, if we look for motives and explanations for our actions, we find them easily enough, and action does seem to be determined. But if we put ourselves back into the *durée* at the moment of the act, we are obliged to admit that

the decision, taken as it was in an instant and without reflection, had in most cases nothing behind it except our nature. "We all more or less resemble the poor suitor who was always late, sometimes because he had overslept, sometimes because he had missed his train, sometimes because he'd forgotten his watch—and who in the last analysis was always late because being late was part of his nature and mental make-up." Acting according to one's mental make-up, pursuing action that has no explanation other than our own nature, is precisely what Bergson and common sense call acting freely. The problem of freedom, like so many others, seems difficult only because it is badly formulated.

The implications of Bergson's method are clear. Because his thought is simple and does not allow ready-made ideas to mask actuality, he recovers that freshness of intuition and common sense shared by all great philosophers. When subjected to this intense light, many problems fade away, for they were false problems in the first place, spawned by a defective vocabulary.

In his second work, *Matière et mémoire* (*Matter and Memory*) Bergson tackles the body-mind problem. A number of his predecessors—Taine, for example—had denied the existence of the mind. To them the brain was a kind of factory in which all our thoughts are manufactured. The idealists, on the other hand, upheld the paradox of pure thought and denied the reality of the exterior world. Bergson seizes on the intuition of the real and shows that common sense is right. Common sense does not believe that a couple of pounds of gray matter can contain all the configurations of our life. Common sense believes that mind is distinct from matter but also that matter exists. All of the experiments on localization in the brain support common sense. A part of the brain can be eliminated without loss of any mental image. A lesion of the brain can cause aphasia, that is, destroy certain motor mechanisms controlling the tongue and lips, but it does not destroy memory of the images corresponding to the forgotten or lost words. The brain, says Bergson, is simply an organ of transmission between mind and the motor organs. He conceives the relationships between mind and body as follows:

All the images that at every moment bombard the senses are stored in the mind. The *entire* past is always present in the mind. The brain, however, is a sorting agent that admits only those images useful to action. These images are summoned up by a particular state of the body. In sleep, action being no longer pertinent, this evocation is free, and it may be the most distant memories and the most bizarre combinations of images that then correspond to a given state of the body. Proust speaks somewhere of the woman born of a cramped position of his thigh. Such is the realm of dream. The man who allows the realm of dream to invade the realm of action is mad. What happens to the mind if the body disappears? This is the problem of the immortality of the soul. Bergson's answer tends to the affirmative. Lacking the body to transmit and articulate thoughts in space, the mind no longer has any means of communicating with matter; however, "the life of the mind cannot be considered an effect of the life of the body.... On the contrary everything occurs as if the body were merely used by the mind, and therefore we have no reason to suppose that the mind should disappear with the body...." If we hang up the telephone, the mind of the person we were speaking to does not thereby cease to exist. And the brain is just like a telephone system. The view that the soul survives after death—which is that of most religions—seems to Bergson more likely to be true than not.

Our intellect, born of the battle of mind and matter, a weapon forged for this battle, a collection of formulae for imposing on matter the forms the mind desires, is a tool ill-equipped for understanding life. It has, moreover—in order to explain the variety and evolution of the forms of life—come up with a number of rather feeble theories. These can be divided into two groups: mechanistic and finalistic.

Mechanistic explanations maintain that the entire universe—that equally of living things and of inert matter—functions in accordance with the blind working of immutable laws. The mechanist sees life as merely one of the fortuitous properties of matter. He explains the formation of organs and the evolution of species as the accumulation of tiny, measurable changes. But this account is inadequate. First of all, experience does not show that acquired characteristics can be passed on to future generations. Furthermore, evolutionism does not explain how absolutely distinct sequences come to the same result—how, for instance, the arthropod eye has the same essential features as that of mollusks. Above all, it doesn't explain life itself, or the action of living things on their surroundings. Matter left to itself is inert; it tends toward immobility. Life, on the other hand, tends to create. Any attempt to explain life by death is doomed to failure.

Finalistic theories are no more acceptable. These would maintain that life has as its object the realization of some plan, of some particular future state of matter, a state which is already known at the present time, for otherwise it would not be possible to talk about it. But none of the facts justifies this view. If life were working according to some pre-established plan, it would in the course of history show an ever-increasing degree of harmony. "Just as a house, as the stones go up, increasingly expresses the architect's idea." But we observe nothing of the kind. Disharmony among species is increasing rather than decreasing. "There are some species which are at a standstill, others which are retrogressing." The world of living things does not correspond to any plan in process of being worked out, but rather to a creation which proceeds unceasingly by virtue of an initial motion. This motion is alone responsible for the unity of the world, "a unity of infinite variety, superior to any the intellect might invent, for the intellect is but one of its aspects, one of its products."

This then is roughly how Bergson conceives of the life process. Its basis is a simple source, a creative force which he calls the *élan vital* and which transmits itself from seed to seed. This primal force is common to all life, animal and vegetable. "Just as the wind sweeping into a crossroads breaks up into divergent currents of air which are all but one and the same gust," so the *élan vital* impels to the conquest of matter species which are but emanations of one and the same force. Harmony in nature does not lie ahead in the future as the finalists would have it; it lies behind in the past, in the original afflatus.

Then what are animal forms? They are the shape of the resistance matter sets up against the vital force. If the wind blows on the sand at a beach, that sand will take symmetrical and distinct forms; it will assume regular wavy patterns. Each of these wrinkles of sand is actually of infinite complexity; it could be broken down into millions of grains of sand, and each of those grains could again be broken down into atoms, protons, and electrons. But the simple explanation of this entire phenomenon is the wind. Similarly, the simple explanation of evolution is the creative will. Everything happens as if some superior being had sought to realize itself and could do so only by relinquishing in the process—as does the wind in blowing

over water and sand—a part of its force. Our body is the negative mold of our lack of force, the boundary separating our free will from matter.

Creation then is like a burst of force from a single center spreading out in diverse series, each of which is sooner or later arrested by the resistance of matter, just as fireworks blossom and fade. But the force of creation is continuous. Bergson calls this center of force *God*. "God so defined has nothing ready-made about him; he is life unceasing, action, freedom. Creation so conceived is not a mystery; we experience it in ourselves when we act freely."

And what is the end of this continuous creation? Asking such a question means falling back into the errors of finalism and attributing a plan to God. But Bergson's God is a poet, not a geometrician. That creation is an end in itself, and perhaps the only end, is indicated to us by nature in the joy attendant on any act of creation. "He who is certain, absolutely certain that he has produced a viable and durable work, has no further use for praise and feels beyond mere fame—because he is a creator, because he knows it, and because the joy he feels in it is a divine joy."

Among the *données* of consciousness, one finds, in nearly all men, a sense of moral obligation. We know without reflection and without coercion that certain actions in certain circumstances are wrong. We are often prepared to sacrifice personal interest in order to preserve the peace of mind and heart that only "a good conscience" can give. Where does this sense come from? Bergson's originality as an ethical thinker lies in his reply that this sense arises from two different sources, and that there are two moralities.

The first is the morality of societies. Man, like the wolf and dog, is a social animal. He can live only in groups. The size of the group varies over the course of history. Sometimes it's a family, sometimes a tribe, sometimes a religious order, sometimes a sect, sometimes a nation. But since man is not able to live without the group, he always needs its approval. Indeed, the judgment of the group, which is known instinctively, is never absent from the consciousness of any member of the group. This herd instinct can be stronger even than the instinct for self-preservation. It explains why the wolf, or the soldier, prefers death to flight. Even Robinson Crusoe, alone on his island, remains a moral man—for the isolated man believes that this abnormal situation will not last and prepares himself to face the judgment of the herd on his return.

That this social morality is bound up with the approval or disapproval of a group is clearly demonstrated in time of war or revolution. Certain of the support of the herd, ordinarily moral people are at such times prepared to commit against people opposed to the group, the most heinous and cruel kinds of acts. The fact that all men do not do this—and that some of them maintain, even in time of battle, a spirit of charity—indicates that another form of moral consciousness exists.

This second kind of morality is expressed by such words as: selflessness, giving of oneself, spirit of sacrifice, charity. But if it remained at the level of such concepts it would inspire few acts. Example is much more powerful. In order to be convincing, this higher and broader morality must be incarnated in certain exceptional individuals. Everyone has asked himself, at moments when all ordinary rules of conduct seem inadequate, what such and such a person he admires or reveres would have expected him to do in similar circumstances. "Founders and reformers of religions, mystics and saints, unsung heroes of the moral life, all are there; drawn by their example, we join with them as with an army of conquerors.'' It is never an intellectual process that leads us to imitate them. ''It is not by preaching love of one's neighbor that one achieves it. . . . One must in this case pass through heroism in order to arrive at love.'' The drastic change that leads a man to charity has all the swiftness of intuition. It is an interior *coup d'état*. ''So long as you reason over an obstacle it will remain where it is. . . . But you can dismiss the whole thing in one fell swoop by denying it.''

The first kind of morality—social morality—is the morality of repose. It has rules that are permanent, or at least valid for a given period of time. The second kind is a morality of movement. It is a thrust, a progress; it means to be, and *is*, ever more demanding. It inclines strongly to poverty and even martyrdom. Like all free creation, it gives joy. The morality of the Gospels is the best example of dynamic morality. The Sermon on the Mount, in its antitheses, sets forth social and sublime morality at one and the same time: ''Ye have heard that it was said . . . But I say unto you . . .'' Whence two methods of moral training: first, the adoption and inculcation of the customs of the country, of the group—which is the social morality taught in families; and second, the imitation of some person taken as a spiritual model, and more or less complete identification with him—which is mystical morality and that of the Christian.

Thus we arrive at Bergson's ideas about religion. In these we again encounter the two terms he opposes in all of his thought. Again, he draws a distinction between static religion and dynamic religion, the ''ready-made'' and the ''self-creating,'' the discursive and the real. Static religion externalizes, in the guise of gods or saints, those forces which should regulate our behavior from within. Mankind invents fables, and this mythmaking is a defensive reaction of nature against the dissolvent skepticism of the intelligence. ''Religion braces and disciplines. In order to perform this function, continuously repeated exercises are necessary. . . . Which means there can be no religion without rites and ceremonies. . . . These religious acts doubtless spring from belief, but they immediately react upon belief and strengthen it; if gods there be, a form of worship must be devoted to them, but the moment a form of worship exists, the gods exist . . .''

In the case of dynamic religion, the soul allows itself to be penetrated by a being immensely more potent than it is. It becomes ''love of that which is naught but love. It also gives itself to society, but to a society which is now humanity as a whole, loved through inclusion in the love of that which is its source''—i.e., loved in God. True mysticism, that total communion of the saint with God, is rare, but there is some echo of it deep down in most men. We feel there is a mysterious and infinite force within us. We are in touch with it only in rare moments of exaltation (which are nearly always moments of sacrifice and humility), but we know it exists and we reserve a place for it in our minds. Thus we arrive at a dual religion— the religion of most men—and the religion in which the antique god, the god of the myth-making function, tends to merge with the god ''who illumines and restores by his presence exceptional souls.''

And what, in Bergson's view, is the mystic quality of these exceptional souls? ''It is contact with and consequently partial union with the creative effort life manifests. This effort is *from* God, even perhaps *is* God.'' The great Christian mystics knew the ecstasy of this union with their God. Their experiences are significant to the philosopher, inasmuch as they help him in his attempt to understand the nature of God. Bergson thinks, as did Alain, that the superiority of Christianity over the religions preceding it lies in the fact that God, in order to be perceived and felt, must become man. ''Creation turns out to be an undertaking by God to create other creators, to adjoin to himself creatures worthy of his love.''

At this point the physical scientist will protest and point to the misery of man, to his insignificance as regards the infinite universe, to the naïveté of attributing so much importance to this mite. But isn't the physical scientist looking at the universe through the wrong end of the telescope? Isn't the least human being as infinitely complex as the universe itself, and doesn't that universe exist, moreover, only by virtue of being perceived by some consciousness? Isn't he who understands and conceives the world a world himself? Such a notion of man's place in the universe may seem singularly optimistic. It is confirmed, however, by the intensity of the pure joys to which great souls can rise.

One sees how much this philosophy is of a piece. It springs entirely from one swift and intense intuition. Early in life, Bergson, who was a fine geometrician, was tempted to believe in the mechanistic disciplines then in vogue. One day, just after giving his students at the University of Clermont-Ferrand a lecture on Zeno, a lecture in which he presented the problem of Achilles and the tortoise, he continued during his stroll to meditate about this intriguing, ancient enigma, and in a moment of sudden illumination hit upon the intuition of pure *durée*. Bergsonism was born.

From that moment he had his method. Rather than a method, moreover, this was ''the very line of the movement that leads thought into the density of things.'' It consists—no matter what the problem—of seeking the naked core of reality beyond the ready-made cloak of doctrines and words. Bergson's intention is to construct for facts a philosophy to measure, and to rethink one by one all of the great problems of philosophy. Does he solve them? Indeed no—as no one ever will. Like any human theory, his has its gaps and weaknesses; but ''a great philosophy,'' as Péguy so admirably put it, ''isn't one against which there is nothing to say, but one which has said something.'' (pp. 31-46)

André Maurois, ''Henri Bergson,'' translated by Carl Morse, in From Proust to Camus: Profiles of Modern French Writers *by André Maurois, translated by Carl Morse and Renaud Bruce, Doubleday & Company, 1966, pp. 30-46.*

IDELLA J. GALLAGHER (essay date 1970)

[*Gallagher is an American philosopher and critic. In the following excerpt, she discusses* The Two Sources of Morality and Religion *as the culmination of Bergson's work.*]

The full implications of Bergson's intuition of duration are brought to light in *The Two Sources of Morality and Religion* which he presented to the public after forty years of philosophical reflection on reality *sub specie durationis*. Experience had revealed to him two distinct and irreducible moralities— the closed morality which he identified with nature, instinct, social cohesion—in a word, with biological necessity; and the open morality which he identified with the direct movement of the *élan vital*, intuition, creative emotion, and universal brotherhood. All the oppositions which had been set up in his earlier works are preserved here, for the closed morality is static, routine, conservative, while the open morality is dynamic, novel and progressive.

It must be remembered, however, that Bergson did not pretend to offer a complete moral philosophy in *The Two Sources.* He made this quite clear when he announced prior to its publication that he did not intend to present *une morale,* but merely wished to trace the sources of morality and religion. There were moral facts which he was not considering because he had not yet discovered a way to submit them to an empirical investigation. He was merely interpreting the facts of social pressure and moral progress, that is, the infra-rational and supra-rational elements in morality.

In *The Two Sources,* therefore, Bergson was but continuing the philosophical method he had employed in his other works and which was the only method appropriate to philosophy as he conceived it. The philosopher's task was, he believed, to illuminate reality. But the philosopher cannot do this by erecting a formidable, rationally elucidated system in which he attempts to explain "all the possible, and sometimes even the impossible." Rather he must plunge back into real duration and try to describe reality as he experiences it there. And since the ceaseless becoming that is reality is incommensurable with rational thought and therefore can never be encompassed in concepts, he will have to have recourse to comparisons and metaphors to communicate what intuition has disclosed to him. According to Bergson, philosophical language is that of images. To many this language may seem vague, and it is in what it expresses, but it will not lack precision for those who succeed in experiencing what it suggests. Philosophy was not meant to be the manipulation of ready-made concepts and the construction of theoretical systems. It is a lived experience in which one reinserts himself into the *élan vital* in order to live again creative evolution by becoming one with it in sympathy.

Confronted by a philosophical problem, the philosopher should seek to probe it experimentally. To accomplish this he will have to undertake long, laborious research, and his solution will not always be complete. He may have to be satisfied with provisional conclusions, but, although unfinished, such a philosophy will push solid roots deep into the real. And other philosophers will come to take up the work, for philosophy, like science, is a common endeavor. True philosophy can never be enclosed in a rational system because reality is not *tout fait* ["finished"] but *se faisant* ["in the process of becoming"]. Philosophy must remain open and unfinished like the forward movement of the *élan vital* which it traces.

Bergson was more interested in establishing a method of grasping reality than in propounding a rationally contrived doctrine. The important thing is that one follow the authentic philosophical method which is that of intuition. To think intuitively is to think in duration. It is only by approaching reality in this way that we can recapture it in the very mobility which is its essence. And furthermore, philosophizing according to this method will have the effect of extending further and further the boundaries of our understanding and expanding human thought indefinitely. It was this view of the nature of philosophy with its emphasis on openness, ineffable intuition, and the use of imagery which won for Bergson the reputation of being an impressionist philosopher.

In the light of Bergson's conception of philosophy and of the philosopher's task, it would seem necessary for an appreciation of his work that one enter into it by an act of sympathy. Bergson tells us that we understand a philosophy only if we pierce through its formulations and try to live again the original intuition which is its soul. William James describes what many have felt when they have come to Bergson's philosophy in this way, "Open Bergson, and new horizons loom on every page you read. It is like the breath of the morning and the song of birds" [see excerpt dated 1909].

Bergson tells us also that each of his books was the expression of a discontent and a protest. Just as in *Time and Free Will* he opposed the determinists who made freedom seem impossible, and protested in *Creative Evolution* against the mechanistic interpretation of biological evolution, so in *The Two Sources* he opposed the sociologists who sought to reduce all morality to social facts, and the rationalists who reduced all morality to reason.

The primary aim of *The Two Sources* was to call attention to a higher morality which Bergson regarded as the complete and absolute morality, and to mystical experience which is its ultimate source. It is only the example and spiritual call of the moral heroes and mystics that can account for moral progress. Mystical experience is an undeniable fact. Philosophers must be willing to recognize it, for it is the indispensable aid without which many crucial philosophical problems must remain forever unsolved.

Bergson was ready to give the sociologists their due, for he admitted the social elements in morality and gave a brilliant exposition of closed, or social, morality. He wished to give reason its due as well, and his efforts in this direction constitute one of the most ingenious and original parts of his philosophy. But he wished above all to call attention to the supra-rational and supra-natural element in morality. He wished to demonstrate the limitations of conventional morality which he conceived to be a morality of obligation directed solely to the preservation of one society against another, by contrasting it with the morality of aspiration which calls men to universal brotherhood and union with the divine creative principle. In the language of creative evolution, Bergson wished to remind us that the creative *élan* which thrust man into matter seeks now to draw him above matter toward a higher destiny, and that his future evolution is in his own hands.

A profound distaste for the rationalistic conception of a morality based on pure reason led Bergson to turn away from the intellect and seek the source of morality elsewhere. Consequently, he did not locate the roots of morality in reason and freedom and proceed then to show the manner in which social pressure and creative emotion influence it from below and above. His view of the nature of intellect and of freedom precluded the possibility of erecting a moral philosophy this way. Rather, he rooted morality in social pressure (a direct manifestation of nature) and creative emotion (a direct manifestation of the *élan vital*), and attempted then to show the non-essential although important way in which freedom, and more particularly intellect, are related to the moral life.

In his endeavor to show the radical difference between the closed and open moral attitudes, Bergson separated the two moralities more than the moral data from which he started out would seem to justify. He gave meticulous care to his exposition of social morality and left us in Chapter I of *The Two Sources* a document full of penetrating social insights and striking images. And he surpassed himself in the inspiring description he gave of the open morality and the open soul. But the lines are so sharply drawn between social morality which, through moral obligation, binds man to his social group as the ant is bound to the ant-hill, and the morality of aspiration which is all spiritual response and creative emotion with no pressure or desire to resist, that many critics have been led to question whether a humanity that oscillates between these two moralities can be said to have any properly human nature.

Bergson's most important contribution to moral philosophy is not his doctrine of moral obligation which was conditioned by a faulty conception of the nature of intellect and of freedom and hence too narrowly conceived, but his view of an open morality in which he stresses the possibility of man's transcending the plane of conventional morality and by an effort of intuition and will rising above nature to insert himself into the spiritual *élan*. In an age dominated by materialism and mechanism Bergson created a new climate. He satisfied the yearnings of many individuals by opening up to them once again the door that had been closed on belief in spiritual values, human freedom, the existence of God, and immortality. Bergson was a dedicated and conscientious scholar, but to many of his contemporaries he was above all *une grande présence* ["a great presence"]. Étienne Gilson tells us, recalling the effect that **Creative Evolution** had in the early years of the century, "Bergson was a great metaphysician for he looked at the world and said what he saw, leaving in men's minds a renovated image. . . . One must have lived through those years to realize what a liberation the teaching of Bergson was."

The Two Sources, extending into the domain of morality and religion the findings of **Creative Evolution,** sustained this sense of liberation. Turning his back upon the moral theories of the past and appealing solely to experience in its full sense, Bergson had singled out the most fundamental and indisputable of moral facts and sought to interpret them in accordance with the method of intuition and the phenomena of evolution. Despite the limitations in his moral doctrine, to which such an approach would inevitably give rise, Bergson had once again looked at the world, said what he saw and left in men's mind a new image. His conception of open morality is of particular worth for it awards an essential role in morality to the creative power of the human spirit, and presents with remarkable eloquence and conviction a vision of the future of human evolution. (pp. 98-102)

> *Idella J. Gallagher, in her* Morality in Evolution: The Moral Philosophy of Henri Bergson, *Martinus Nijhoff, 1970, 107 p.*

ADDITIONAL BIBLIOGRAPHY

Alexander, Ian W. *Bergson: Philosopher of Reflection.* London: Bowes & Bowes, 1957, 109 p.
    Study of Bergson's philosophy in which Alexander attempts to separate Bergson's ideas from those erroneously attributed to him.

Balsillie, David. *An Examination of Professor Bergson's Philosophy.* London: Williams & Norgate, 1912, 228 p.
    Extensive, essentially sympathetic analysis of Bergson's thought.

Buber, Martin. "The Silent Question." *Judaism* I, No. 2 (April 1952): 99-105.
    Discusses Bergson and Simone Weil as examples of Jews "whose religious needs have remained unsatisfied by Judaism."

Campbell, Sue Ellen. "Equal Opposites: Wyndham Lewis, Henri Bergson, and Their Philosophies of Space and Time." *Twentieth Century Literature* 29, No. 3 (Fall 1983): 351-69.
    Examination of Lewis's *Time and Western Man* (see excerpt dated 1928). Campbell observes that, while Lewis denounced Bergson as the originator of the "time-cult" he so fervently opposed, his thought in fact resembles that of Bergson in significant respects.

Carr, H. Wildon. "'Time' and 'History' in Contemporary Philosophy: With Special Reference to Bergson and Croce." In *Proceedings of the British Academy, 1917-1918,* pp. 331-50. London: Oxford University Press, n.d.
    Argues that both Bergson and Benedetto Croce focus primarily on "the dynamic aspect of reality and [throw] the whole emphasis on the concept of activity as an interpretative principle."

——. *Henri Bergson: The Philosophy of Change.* London: T. C. & E. C. Jack, 1910, 126 p.
    Sympathetic analysis of Bergson's philosophy.

Chessick, Richard D. "The Search for the Authentic Self in Bergson and Proust." In *Psychoanalytic Approaches to Literature and Film,* edited by Maurice Charney and Joseph Reppen, pp. 19-36. Rutherford, N.J.: Fairleigh Dickinson University Press, 1987.
    Views Bergson's philosophy as the source of the modern idea of seeking one's "true" or "authentic" self, which Chessick considers a misinterpretation of the need to "heal a fragmented sense of self." Chessick uses the example of Proust's *A la recherche du temps perdu* to illustrate this confusion.

Chevalier, Jacques. *Henri Bergson.* New York: Macmillan, 1928, 351 p.
    Analysis written by a student of Bergsonism.

Cornu, Auguste. "Bergsonianism and Existentialism." In *Philosophic Thought in France and the United States,* edited by Marvin Farber, pp. 151-68. Buffalo: University of Buffalo Press, 1950.
    Views Bergson's subjective spiritualism as "the ideological expression of the decadent bourgeoisie, which feels that it is less and less master of the forces of production and so turns more and more from concrete practical activity, escaping from reality by turning in on itself."

Cunningham, Gustavus Watts. *A Study in the Philosophy of Bergson.* New York: Longmans, Green, 1916, 212 p.
    Critique in which Cunningham focuses on the historical context of Bergson's thought.

Dodson, George Rowland. *Bergson and the Modern Spirit.* Boston: American Unitarian Association, 1913, 296 p.
    Examines some implications of Bergson's philosophy.

Elliot, Hugh S. R. *Modern Science and the Illusions of Professor Bergson.* London: Longmans, Green, 1912, 257 p.
    Refutation of Bergson's ideas. This study is prefaced by Sir Ray Lankester's essay denigrating Bergson's philosophy.

Fiddian, R. W. "Unamuno-Bergson: A Reconsideration." *Modern Language Review* 69, No. 4 (October 1974): 787-95.
    Examines a number of similarities in Bergson's concept of duration and Miguel de Unamuno's concept of *intrahistoria.*

Fleischmann, Wolfgang B. "Conrad's *Chance* and Bergson's *Laughter.*" *Renascence* XIV, No. 2 (Winter 1962): 66-71.
    Contends that while Joseph Conrad has not traditionally been grouped among the many twentieth-century authors who were influenced by Bergsonism, his novel *Chance* clearly reflects Bergson's concept of the comic as set forth in *Laughter.*

Forsyth, T. M. "Bergson's and Freud's Theories of Laughter: A Comparison and a Suggestion." *South African Journal of Science* XXIII (December 1926): 987-95.
    Discusses the definitions of humor proposed by Sigmund Freud and Bergson, noting that both emphasize the "humanizing" function of laughter.

Gilson, Etienne. "The Glory of Bergson." *Thought* XXII, No. 87 (December 1947): 581-84.
    Memorial tribute. Gilson pronounces Bergson "the greatest philosopher [France] has known since Descartes."

Green, F. C. "Le Temps Retrouvé (continued)." In his *The Mind of Proust*, pp. 494-546. Cambridge: Cambridge University Press, 1949.
    Analyzes Proust's use of Bergson's concept of duration in *Remembrance of Things Past*.

Gunter, P. A. Y., ed. *Bergson and the Evolution of Modern Physics*. Knoxville: University of Tennessee Press, 1969, 348 p.
    Collection of essays concerning the relevance of Bergsonism to modern physics. Gunter notes in his preface that "the twentieth century has witnessed a striking and as yet unfinished series of revolutions in every branch of physics. It is clear in retrospect that Henri Bergson considered such conceptual revolutions in physics inevitable and, further, that he was able schematically to foresee certain of their most important theoretical consequences."

Hanna, Thomas, ed. *The Bergsonian Heritage*. New York: Columbia University Press, 1962, 170 p.
    Collection of essays concerning various aspects of Bergson's importance in modern thought, including tributes written by some of Bergson's colleagues.

Herman, Daniel J. *The Philosophy of Henri Bergson*. Washington: University Press of America, 1980, 102 p.
    Analyzes Bergson's refutation of the concept of evolutionary finality.

Hermann, E. "Henri Bergson and His Philosophy of Creative Evolution." In his *Eucken and Bergson*, pp. 127-79. Boston: Pilgrim, 1912.
    Finds Bergson's concept of *élan vital* harmonious with the doctrines of modern Christianity.

Hulme, T. E. "Bergson's Theory of Art" and "The Philosophy of Intensive Manifolds." In his *Speculations: Essays on Humanism and the Philosophy of Art*, pp. 143-69, pp. 173-214. London: Kegan Paul, Trench, Trubner & Co., 1936.
    Detailed analyses of Bergson's aesthetic theories. In "Bergson's Theory of Art," Hulme notes that "the two parts of Bergson's general philosophical position which are important in the theory of aesthetic[s] are (1) the conception of reality as a flux of interpenetrated elements unseizable by the intellect . . . ; and (2) his account of the part played in the development of the ordinary characteristics of the mind by its orientation towards action."

Kallen, Horace Meyer. *William James and Henri Bergson*. Chicago: University of Chicago Press, 1914, 248 p.
    Comparative analysis. Kallen notes: "the difference between James and Bergson has seemed to me much more than little. . . . James' theory of life seems to me to face forward, to be an expression of the age's underlying and hence vaguely felt and unformulated tendencies. Bergson's theory of life sums itself up as a consummation of the philosophic tradition, restated in the modes of thought and harmonized with the modes of feeling of the age."

Klawitter, Robert. "Henri Bergson and James Joyce's Fictional World." *Comparative Literature Studies* III, No. 4 (1966): 429-37.
    Argues that while Joyce has traditionally been viewed as "a master literary technician who unthinkingly lent his talents to Bergson's [theories]," he specifically addressed elements of Bergson's philosophy in *Finnegans Wake*.

Kumar, Shiv K. *Bergson and the Stream of Consciousness Novel*. New York: New York University Press, 1963, 174 p.
    Contends that Bergson was the single most important influence in the development of the stream of consciousness novel.

LeBrun, Phillip. "T. S. Eliot and Henri Bergson." *Review of English Studies* n.s. XVIII, Nos. 70, 71 (1967): 149-61, 278-86.
    Attempts to show that "T. S. Eliot was greatly influenced by Bergson, in particular by Bergson's accounts of time, change, and the individual consciousness; influenced to such a degree in fact that, had he not known Bergson's philosophical writings, Eliot's major formulations about poetry—about tradition, the associated sensibility of the artist, and the work of art as objective correlative—would have been quite different from what they are."

LeRoy, Edouard. *The New Philosophy of Henri Bergson*. New York: Henry Holt, 1913, 235 p.
    Introduction to Bergson's works.

Lindsay, A. D. *The Philosophy of Bergson*. New York: George H. Doran, n.d., 247 p.
    Defense of Bergson's ideas.

Lovejoy, A. O. *Bergson and Romantic Evolutionism*. Berkeley: University of California Press, 1914, 61 p.
    Relates the concept of creative evolution to Bergson's philosophy as a whole.

Luce, A. A. *Bergson's Doctrine of Intuition*. London: Society for Promoting Christian Knowledge, 1922, 122 p.
    Study described by the author as a "sympathetic presentation of the salient features of Bergson's thought."

MacWilliam, John. *Criticism of the Philosophy of Bergson*. Edinburgh: T. & T. Clark, 1928, 336 p.
    Refutation of Bergson's theories.

Perry, Ralph Barton. "Vitalism, Voluntarism, and Pragmatism." In his *Philosophy of the Recent Past*, pp. 168-96. New York: Charles Scribner's Sons, 1926.
    Explanation of Bergson's theories.

Pilkington, A. E. *Bergson and His Influence: A Reassessment*. Cambridge: Cambridge University Press, 1976, 253 p.
    Summarizes Bergson's phiosophy and examines its influence in the writings of Charles Péguy, Paul Valéry, and Julien Benda.

Poulakidas, Andreas K. "Kazantzakis and Bergson: Metaphysic Aestheticians." *Journal of Modern Literature* 2, No. 2 (1971-1972): 267-83.
    Examines the influence of Bergson on Nikos Kazantzakis's fiction. Poulakidas observes that "without the cheerful and calm philosophy of Bergson which Kazantzakis introduces into his works, the influence of Nietzsche's terrifying and turbulent philosophy could well have refrigerated Kazantzakis's warm and animate love of life."

Stephen, Karin. *The Misuse of Mind: A Study of Bergson's Attack on Intellectualism*. New York: Harcourt, Brace, 1922, 107 p.
    Defends Bergson's concept of the intellect-intuition dichotomy, contending that many commentators exaggerate Bergson's criticism of the place of intellect in human cognition.

Turquet-Milnes, G. *Some Modern French Writers*. New York: Robert M. McBride, 1921, 302 p.
    Discusses Bergson's ideas concerning intuition and duration and related concepts in the writings of Paul Bourget, Anatole France, Paul Claudel, Jules Romains, Jean Moréas, Charles Péguy, and Emile Clermont.

Valéry, Paul. "Funeral Address on Bergson." In his *Masters and Friends*, pp. 302-06. Princeton: Princeton University Press, 1968, 406 p.
    Reprint of Valéry's 1941 memorial tribute to Bergson. Valéry judges Bergson the greatest philosopher of his time and notes that he "performed an indispensable service by restoring and rehabilitating the taste for a form of meditation closer to our own essence than the purely logical elaboration of concepts that, in any case, cannot be satisfactorily defined."

Wilm, Emil Carl. *Henri Bergson: A Study in Radical Evolution*. New York: Sturgis & Walton, 1914, 193 p.
    Brief, neutral analysis of Bergson's philosophy.

Edgar Rice Burroughs

1875-1950

(Also wrote under the pseudonyms Norman Bean and John Tyler McCulloch) American novelist, short story writer, journalist, and scriptwriter.

For further discussion of Burroughs's career, see *TCLC*, Volume 2.

A prolific author of science fiction and adventure tales, Burroughs is best known as the creator of Tarzan, an orphaned English lord raised by apes in the African jungle. Published from 1914 to the mid-1960s, the Tarzan series has captivated generations of readers, making its hero among the most enduring characters in literature. Inspiring comic strips, films, and radio and television programs, these popular novels represent the cornerstone of Burroughs's work. Although not as universally recognized as the Tarzan stories, Burroughs's science fiction novels are generally regarded as a significant contribution to the early development of the genre. Chronicling episodes of heroic adventure, these stories share with the Tarzan novels a rapidly paced narrative style and exotic settings and characters.

Burroughs was born in Chicago to an upper middle-class family. Educated at both public and private schools, he excelled in reading, geography, and Latin. In 1891, before receiving a high school degree, Burroughs traveled to Idaho to work on a ranch operated by two of his older brothers. Content with this rustic environment, in which he developed a love of animals and an ability for horsemanship, Burroughs disliked the prospect of returning to school. Nonetheless, Burroughs's father, an austere man intent on seeing his son attain at least a secondary school education, sent him to Phillips Academy in Andover, Massachusetts, and later to the Michigan Military Academy. Graduated from the latter school in 1895, Burroughs accepted a position there as geography instructor. During the spring of 1896, however, he left this post and, following a brief stint with the United States Cavalry on an assignment that entailed chasing elusive Apache Indians across the Arizona Territory, he spent several years shuttling between numerous jobs. In 1900 he married a childhood sweetheart, and in 1903 he and his wife moved back to Idaho to assist Burroughs's brothers in dredging gold along the Snake River. After the failure of this undertaking, Burroughs worked at a series of occupations and engaged in several unsuccessful business ventures. While running a small enterprise devoted to the sale of pencil sharpeners, he began writing what would become his first published piece of fiction, *Under the Moons of Mars.* Later retitled *A Princess of Mars* when it was issued in book form as the initial volume in Burroughs's Mars series, this story was published serially in the magazine the *All-Story* in 1912. By 1913, Burroughs's life had been substantially transformed. Having written and sold two more books, including the original Tarzan story, *Tarzan of the Apes,* Burroughs and his family moved to California. His literary output from late 1913 to early 1914 was extraordinary—he completed seven new novels and secured book publication for *Tarzan of the Apes*—and the sales from these projects assured Burroughs's financial security. In 1919, he and his family settled on a 540-acre estate in the San Fernando Valley that he named Tarzana.

Beginning in 1923, this property was subdivided into lots for homes and eventually incorporated as the city of Tarzana.

The 1920s were years of increasing literary success for Burroughs (in 1923 he acquired the dubious distinction of being the first American writer to incorporate himself) and his achievements in other media were also noteworthy. Burroughs's involvement with Hollywood's rapidly developing motion picture industry resulted in numerous adaptations of his books, though he continually expressed disappointment with the results, and during the 1930s the Tarzan series became the basis for a radio program. Comic book versions of the Tarzan adventures also appeared and were immediately popular. In addition, many of the Tarzan books had been widely translated—seventeen languages by 1925—and royalties from foreign sales were considerable. During these years of often frantic activity, Burroughs suffered various illnesses, while his wife developed a drinking problem that proved a severe strain on their marriage. In 1934 they were divorced, and the following year Burroughs remarried. By this time, it was becoming apparent that Burroughs had squandered his wealth through extravagant living, and, with intentions of tempering their lifestyle, he and his second wife moved to Hawaii. Their difficulties persisted, however, and his wife eventually left him. Remaining in Hawaii, Burroughs witnessed the bombing of Pearl Harbor and, during the flood of media activity that followed, began to write a regular column for a Honolulu newspaper. In 1942, Burroughs became a war correspondent for United Press, and his experiences in the Pacific theater provided information for his twenty-second Tarzan novel, *Tarzan and "The Foreign Legion."* Toward the end of the war, Burroughs was seriously hampered by attacks of angina pectoris and was bedridden for several months. During the late 1940s his health continued to deteriorate, and he died in 1950.

Burroughs's immense production of fiction—more than seventy books—is readily arranged into four groups: The Mars, Pellucidar, and Venus series of science fiction novels and the series of Tarzan books. The Mars series, featuring the novels *A Princess of Mars, The Gods of Mars,* and *The Warlord of Mars,* concerns the adventures of John Carter, an earthly hero from aristocratic Southern lineage who mystically transports himself to Mars, which is known to its inhabitants as Barsoom, and encounters a decadent civilization. Carter discovers that what was once a great Martian society has devolved into hundreds of diverse cultures populated by a variety of semihuman tribes submerged in senseless, violent, and unending struggle against one another. It has become a world where savagery and science coexist. Through the sequence of eleven volumes, Carter rises to the supreme Warlordship of Barsoom, marries the beautiful, oviparous, and red-skinned Princess Dejah Thoris, becomes a father and a grandfather, travels extensively throughout Barsoom, visits one of its moons, and ultimately journeys to the planet Jupiter. A prototype of the interplanetary romance, the Mars cycle provided the model for much of Burroughs's subsequent science fiction. Burroughs's second group of novels, the Pellucidar series, comprises six books. The most important works of this series are *At the Earth's Core* and *Pellucidar,* in which a giant earth-boring machine carrying hero David Innes pierces the earth's crust and reveals the planet's hollow core. Earth's inner world is illuminated by a miniature sun and inhabited by a variety of exotic species, including primitive humans and Paleocene creatures. This series is also notable for the cross-over title *Tarzan at the Earth's Core,* which merges characters from two of Burroughs's separately created worlds. A third series of science fiction novels is set on Venus and details the adventures of Carson Napier. These novels, which Burroughs wrote late in his career, include *Pirates of Venus, Lost on Venus,* and *Carson of Venus.* While imaginative in their descriptive detail, the Venus novels are considered derivative of Burroughs's Martian cycle.

By far Burroughs's most popular books belong to the Tarzan series. This well-known story opens as John Clayton, an English lord, and his pregnant wife, Alice, are journeying to Africa on government business when they are marooned on the African coast as a result of a mutiny aboard their ship. Temporarily enduring the jungle's harsh and unfamiliar conditions, the couple dies one year after the birth of their son. The orphaned child is discovered by a distraught female ape who exchanges the corpse of her lifeless infant for the Claytons' baby, naming him Tarzan, which means "white skin" in the language of the apes. Years later, Tarzan discovers his parents' cabin and, using the books he finds there, teaches himself to read and speak English. He soon becomes king of his ape band, and eventually falls in love with Jane Porter, a young American woman whose seafaring party is coincidentally marooned in the same area as the Claytons due to a shipboard mutiny. In subsequent novels, Tarzan visits France, the United States, and other countries. In addition to these four major series, Burroughs wrote several independent adventure tales and a few attempts at realistic fiction, including *The Girl from Hollywood* and *The Efficiency Expert.*

Following decades of critical derision, Burroughs's works received serious analytical scrutiny beginning in the 1960s. While many commentators still contend that Burroughs's adventure novels are no more than diverting entertainment, others attribute higher values to these works. Erling B. Holtsmark has suggested that Burroughs's fiction derives from the classical tradition of heroic literature which includes Homer's *Iliad* and *Odyssey.* Discussing Burroughs's Martian series, Richard A. Lupoff has stated: "These stories call out to the human psyche at a largely unconscious level, they call up the suppressed urges of the primitive man to take sword in hand and confront once and for all the vexatious world around him, they manipulate the most powerful of human archetypes." Sam Moskowitz called the Tarzan saga "one of the world's great romances" and considered its eponymous hero an important twentieth-century myth figure. He also referred to Burroughs as "the major influence on the [science fiction] field through 1934." Other admirers note Burroughs's concern with social criticism, speculations on the nature of time and space, evolutionary theory, death, and eroticism. In spite of these claims, detractors and supporters alike acknowledge the problematic aspects of Burroughs's fiction: repetitiousness, abundant clichés, patchwork construction, narrative inconsistencies, and flawed characterizations. Commentators also acknowledge that much of Burroughs's fictional world reflects the pervasive attitudes of the time in which it was created. The xenophobia and racism of the period between the two World Wars is given ample expression in Burroughs's works, and his tales of adventure and romance are commonly viewed as escapist literature intended to divert readers from turbulent times. Yet, whether praised or condemned, it is widely recognized that the abiding popularity of Burroughs's works suggests that they have touched an essential stratum of the human imagination. As Holtsmark concluded: "And that is not bad for a fellow who set out to do a little entertaining and at the same time support his family."

(See also *Contemporary Authors,* Vol. 104; *Something about the Author,* Vol. 41; and *Dictionary of Literary Biography,* Vol. 8.)

PRINCIPAL WORKS

Under the Moons of Mars   (novel)   1912, published in *The All-Story;* also published as *The Princess of Mars,* 1917
Tarzan of the Apes   (novel)   1914
The Return of Tarzan   (novel)   1915
The Gods of Mars   (novel)   1918
The Warlord of Mars   (novel)   1919
Tarzan the Untamed   (novel)   1920
Thuvia, Maid of Mars   (novel)   1920
The Mucker   (novel)   1921; also published as *The Man without a Soul.* 2 vols., 1921-22
Tarzan the Terrible   (novel)   1921
At the Earth's Core   (novel)   1922
The Girl from Hollywood   (novel)   1923
Pellucidar   (novel)   1923
Tarzan and the Golden Lion   (novel)   1923
The Land That Time Forgot   (novel)   1924
Tarzan and the Ant Men   (novel)   1924
The Eternal Lover   (novel)   1925; also published as *The Eternal Savage,* 1963

The Moon Maid　(novel)　1926; also published as *The
　Moon Men* [abridged edition], 1962
The War Chief　(novel)　1927
Tarzan, Lord of the Jungle　(novel)　1928
Tarzan and the Lost Empire　(novel)　1929
Tanar of Pellucidar　(novel)　1930
Tarzan at the Earth's Core　(novel)　1930
A Fighting Man of Mars　(novel)　1931
Apache Devil　(novel)　1933
Pirates of Venus　(novel)　1934
Tarzan and the Lion Man　(novel)　1934
Lost on Venus　(novel)　1935
Tarzan and the Leopard Men　(novel)　1935
Back to the Stone Age　(novel)　1937
The Lad and the Lion　(novel)　1938
Carson of Venus　(novel)　1939
Escape on Venus　(novel)　1946
Tarzan and "The Foreign Legion"　(novel)　1947
Llana of Gathol　(novel)　1948
The Girl from Farris's　(novel)　1965
The Efficiency Expert　(novel)　1966

SAM MOSKOWITZ　(essay date 1963)

[*Moskowitz is a noted American science fiction critic and historian
whose extensive collection of memorabilia includes, he wrote, "a
copy of every science fiction and fantasy magazine ever published
in the English language, virtually every book or pamphlet on the
subject, and 200 file drawers of clippings and material related
to the subject." Named by Gerald Jones "the quintessential SF
fan and author," Moskowitz has produced several highly regarded critical studies of the genre, including* Explorers of the
Infinite: Shapers of Science Fiction *and* Strange Horizons: The
Spectrum of Science Fiction *(1976). In the following excerpt from*
Explorers of the Infinite, *Moskowitz surveys Burroughs's fiction
and literary career, identifying him as "the acknowledged master
of the scientific romance."*]

"*Tarzan, Lord of the Jungle,* is the great romance of the present
day, surpassing in its popular appeal even the *She* and *King
Solomon's Mines* of Rider Haggard's yesterday and the *Twenty
Thousand Leagues under the Sea* of Jules Verne's days before
that," wrote editors Edwin Balmer and Donald Kennicott in
the November 1927 issue of *Blue Book Magazine*.

"The touch of the great romances of tradition . . . is in *Tarzan,*" they continued. ". . . The reader feels himself also partly
the writer. He himself joins in the story-telling and calls upon
his own imagination to share in the delightful business of creating romance. And that's just about the best fun there is."

Edgar Rice Burroughs, principally as a result of his creation
of the by now almost mythical character Tarzan, far outstripped
Jules Verne, H. Rider Haggard, and H. G. Wells in catching
public favor. Some of the Tarzan novels qualify rather obviously as science fiction—*Tarzan and the Ant Men* and *Tarzan
at the Earth's Core* to name two—but the spirit of science fiction
underlies the entire series.

It is not necessary to rely upon borderline elements in the
Tarzan series to establish Burroughs' reputation in the science
fiction world. The first novel Burroughs ever wrote was an
interplanetary tale—*Dejah Thoris, Princess of Mars*. It was
literally a transcription on paper of daydreams engaged in by
the author to divorce himself from the cold failures of his

everyday life. When he coupled to this daydreaming his born
gift of storytelling, these same fantasies were to act to make
more bearable the problems of others.

Thomas Newell Metcalf, editor of *All-Story*, bought that first
novel, which he retitled **Under the Moons of Mars** and ran as
a six-part serial, beginning in the February 1912 number of
his monthly. For the only time in his life, Burroughs used a
pen name. **Under the Moons of Mars** bore the by-line "Norman
Bean," a typesetter's corruption of "Normal Bean," with which
Burroughs had intended to imply that though the story was
mad the author was not.

So we see that Edgar Rice Burroughs' earliest dreams were
centered on a world forty million miles beyond ours, Mars,
whose red disk at the turn of the century had become a favorite
topic of astronomical discussion. The impetus for this interest
was provided by Professor Percival Lowell's famous book,
Mars As an Abode of Life. In that book, Lowell advanced the
hypothesis that Mars was probably a much older world than
ours, and that at one period in the past it may have supported
a high order of civilization. That the so-called canals were
actually artifical waterways created by highly intelligent creatures, was, of course, his major premise.

Burroughs' Martian stories, ten of them novels, are framed
against the background of a planet in decadence, where the
great civilization of the past has given way to hundreds of
diverse cultures, the product of a variety of semihuman tribal
groupings, who carry on a senseless, violent, and never-ending
struggle against one another as a way of life. It is a world
where savagery and science live side by side and where the
strength of a man's swordarm counts for as much as the
achievements of science in the struggle for survival and power.

It might seem a bizarre world, if it did not bear a satiric
resemblance to the one we live in. The endless contest of
strength and cunning in Burroughs' Mars is no more pointless
and illogical than the military history of mankind, or adventures
of Ulysses. In fact, Burroughs' science fiction is a direct descendant of the travel tale typified by the *Odyssey*. It is the
traditional romance brought up to date with the addition of a
few modern scientific trimmings.

This variety of science fiction has become known as "scientific
romance." In such stories, colorful adventure of the classical
kind is seasoned with just enough science to lend wonder and
enchantment to the background and locale. Edgar Rice Burroughs was to become the acknowledged master of the scientific romance, and the rousing enthusiasm that greeted his
first novel was to usher in the golden era of escape science
fiction. (pp. 172-74)

Burroughs was a natural storyteller. His style never jarred. It
flowed along, quickly and smoothly, catching the reader up in
the spell of the story. Rarely was the reader called upon to
think. Whatever "messages" appeared in the story were essential to the narrative, there was no sermonizing, no separation
of theme, no clearly didactic pointing out of lessons to be
learned.

Burroughs had an unsurpassed sense of pace, and his ability
to keep several situations moving simultaneously, coupled with
his mastery of the flashback technique, established him as an
authentic literary craftsman.

And by far most important, Burroughs could make characters
come full-bodily alive from the page, and achieve a maximum
of reader identification. This was impressively evident in his

initial Mars novel, where first-person narration offered easy identification with John Carter, enabling the reader to share closely with him wondrously thrilling and romantic adventures. Particularly vivid is the memorable scene in the Mars air-manufacturing plant, the fate of the entire planet resting upon the telepathic ability of John Carter to open the doors and permit a Martian to crawl in and restart the stalled air machinery.

This talent for apt characterization was to provide a firm foundation for Burroughs' fame. He would have been a successful author if he had written the Mars stories alone. But the creation of the character Tarzan in *Tarzan of the Apes,* his second published novel, which appeared in the October 1912 issue of *All-Story,* elevated him to literary greatness and world renown.

According to Alva Johnson, in his article *Tarzan, or How to Become a Great Writer,* published in the July 29, 1939 issue of *The Saturday Evening Post,* Rudyard Kipling was a great fan of the Tarzan stories, believing that they were inspired by his own *Jungle Tales.*

If the influence of any writer can be strongly discerned in the theme and style of *Tarzan of the Apes,* it would seem to be that of Kipling. But Burroughs stoutly and vigorously denied this. He has been quoted as saying: ''I started my thoughts on the legend of Romulus and Remus who had been suckled by a wolf and founded Rome, but in the jungle I had my little Lord Greystoke suckled by an ape.''

Characterization in Burroughs' novels was not confined to the lead character. Read a Tarzan story and the very lions, leopards, elephants, apes, and monkeys come to life as distinct personalities in their own right. The effect is heightened by giving the jungle creatures names and identifying their peculiarities. There was the female ape who mothered Tarzan, Kala, and her mate, Tublat. They even had family quarrels over raising Tarzan. Numa was the lion and Sabor the lioness, Histah the great snake, and Tantor the elephant. Through the magic of Burroughs' pen, all come into being as three-dimensional fictional people.

Of the literature mankind has ever produced from its imagination, only Sherlock Holmes is nearly as well known as Tarzan. And *Tarzan of the Apes* is a great and fabulous adventure epic. The development of the story is inspired. The young English couple who are cast away on the shores of the Dark Continent . . . the child who is born to them in a primitive cabin . . . their deaths . . . the female ape, Kala, who finds and raises the child with all the patience and love of a human mother . . . the self-education of the ape-boy Tarzan as he grows to manhood . . . his encounters with human beings . . . his love for the American girl Jane Porter and, finally, his act of self-sacrifice when he steps aside to let William Cecil Clayton, a British nobleman, marry her, add up to one of the world's great romances. . . . (pp. 175-77)

This was no corn, no Pollyanna-ish cliché. The hero does not get the girl. The novel ends on a realistic and powerful back-to-earth note. As a concession to readers, Tarzan does get Jane at the end of the sequel, *The Return of Tarzan,* but the artistry of the first story remains unimpaired.

With *All-Story* readers of *Under the Moons of Mars* frantic about whether the atmosphere plant on Mars had been put back into operation in time to save the planet, Burroughs wrote a sequel, *Gods of Mars.* It was signed with his own name this time and ran for five monthly installments, beginning in the January 1913 issue of the magazine.

After learning that Mars had been saved, the readers sat back to revel in an even more enthralling series of adventures which culminated in a cliff-hanger of movie-serial intensity. The book ends with Dejah Thoris, queen of Helium, most beautiful woman of the planet Mars and beloved wife of John Carter, trapped in a revolving chamber with two other women, Thuvia and Phaidor.

The chamber, which revolves deep in the earth and permits entrance for only one day in a Martian year—almost twice as long as our terrestrial year—moves out of sight as Phaidor, who has developed a jealous passion for Carter, dagger in hand, lunges at Dejah Thoris. Thuvia bravely attempts to slip between them. As the chapter, and the book, ends, the chamber closes and John Carter will not know for an entire Martian year whether his beloved has died under the knife of her murderous assassin.

Burroughs' first Mars novel, published in 1912, brought him less than a third of a cent per word, or $400. His second Mars novel, published a year later and shortly after *Tarzan of the Apes,* brought many times that sum. Before the appearance of his first hard-cover book, *Tarzan of the Apes,* published by A. C. McClurg in 1914, he was earning twenty thousand a year from magazine sales alone.

Tarzan of the Apes proved a runaway best-seller, accounting for almost a million book sales under the McClurg imprint and many others when it went into A. L. Burt and Grosset & Dunlap lower-priced reprints. These rewards came to Burroughs after he had attempted a score of jobs and businesses and considered himself a complete failure. (pp. 177-78)

The fact that he did not make his mark until the age of thirty-five has been pointed to by Burroughs as proof of his ineptness in business matters. The facts do not bear him out. It is doubtful if any writer in the history of literature up to that time earned more money than Burroughs. Before his death, he admitted to having assembled an estate worth over ten million. . . .

With the publication of *Tarzan the Invincible* in 1931, he formed his own publishing company, Edgar Rice Burroughs, Inc., situated in Tarzana, California, a town named after his most famous character. Though it was begun during a period of bitter national economic depression, the venture proved well starred. (p. 179)

The Gods of Mars was followed in 1913 by *The Cave Girl,* a Jack Londonish novel in which a skinny, overprotected Bostonian is stranded on a Pacific Island where a primitive cave culture still exists. Casting off the veneer of civilization, he rebuilds himself into a Tarzan-like character, survives, and wins for his mate a beautiful cave girl. *A Man Without a Soul,* which was first published in *All-Story* in 1913 and later appeared in trade book form as *The Monster Men* (1929), deals with the creation of synthetic humans through the use of tissue-culture. It is unquestionably one of the pioneer stories of its type and Burroughs later used the theme in *The Synthetic Men of Mars,* first published in *Argosy,* January 7 to February 1, 1939, in four weekly installments.

The skillfully executed *The Eternal Lover,* a tale of a prehistoric man who falls into a state of suspended animation and wakes to find himself on Tarzan's estate in Africa, was Burroughs' first offering for 1914, and was followed a month later by *At the Earth's Core,* the novel which began the Pellucidar series. This exciting story, first published in *All-Story Weekly,* April 4 to April 25, in four weekly installments, postulated that the center of the earth was hollow, and its interior another world—

heated and lighted by the molten core of the earth which hung suspended like a sun at its center. It was an ideal setting for marvelous adventure and Burroughs was eventually to write seven sequels: *Pellucidar* (*All-Story Cavalier Weekly*, May-June, 1915), *Tanar of Pellucidar* (*Blue Book*, March-April, 1929), *Tarzan at the Earth's Core, Back to the Stone Age, The Land of Terror, The Return to Pellucidar,* and *Savage Pellucidar.* (p. 180)

[Burroughs] divorced the reader completely from problems. His background, while made acceptable by his own brand of artistry, was no more real than L. Frank Baum's Land of Oz. His aim was to provide pleasure through complete escape, and he succeeded. (p. 181)

The critics, judging Edgar Rice Burroughs by absolute literary standards, have never been kind. They have pointed out that his plots are repetitious and his prose often hasty, with an overwhelming emphasis on action and violence and a seemingly pointless procession of incidents rather than a completely co-ordinated whole. Most sternly they condemn the lack of significance for our times in the themes forming the essential framework of his efforts.

Burroughs never denied the charges and with almost a note of apology explained that it was his purpose to write for those who desired entertainment and escape, that he expected his works to be judged by that standard. He noted that his books were clean without being prudish and while he did not know if they had potentialities for good, he was sure that no one had been harmed by them. The near-farce of 1962, when a western school board banned and then reinstated the Tarzan books on the ground that Tarzan and Jane were never legally married might have amused Burroughs, though precision requires noting that he carefully had married them.

The truth is somewhat removed from either the viewpoint of the critics or Burroughs' claims. As to literary worth, it seems likely that *Tarzan of the Apes,* at least, will be printed and read long after many books "with pointed messages for our times" have been forgotten.

As food for thought: Burroughs did try to convey a message of social import on many significant subjects. *The Mucker,* published in *All-Story* in 1914, deals with the influence of environment on character. Billy Byrne was Burroughs' Studs Lonigan, raised on the rough West Side of Chicago. "There was scarce a bartender who Billy did not know by his first name . . . he knew the patrolman and plainclothesmen equally as well, but not so pleasantly."

For at least half its length *The Mucker* is a revelation of the power Burroughs was capable of commanding when dealing with grim realism instead of escape. *The Girl from Hollywood,* originally published in *Munsey's Magazine* from June to November, 1922, is a straight-from-the-shoulder exposé of drug addiction in the film capital; *The Oakdale Affair,* which first appeared in *Blue Book* for March 1918, forcefully dramatizes the author's disgust at mob violence and lynching; *The Girl from Farris's* (*All-Story Weekly,* September 23 to October 14, 1916) has as its central theme prostitution; *The Efficiency Expert,* from *Argosy-All Story,* October 8 to 29, 1921, is a prototype of the novel of behind-the-scenes-doings in big business, along lines of the much-later *Executive Suite;* and *The Outlaw of Torn* (*New Story,* January to May 1914) is as carefully researched a historical novel of the age of chivalry as you are likely to read anywhere.

All of which proves that Burroughs was far from being a writer without social conscience. It was simply that he discovered that other authors could play that role with greater impact than he. To refuse to recognize that fact and waste the great talent he possessed for entertaining millions would have been pointless.

Absolute literary standards apart, judged by their own standards, two Burroughs novels are most frequently nominated by science fiction devotees as established classics. Those two are *The Moon Maid,* a trilogy collected into a single book in 1926, and *The Land That Time Forgot,* another trilogy which appeared as a single volume in 1924.

The means of interplanetary travel in the early novels of Mars were so ill-defined as to border on the mystical, but in *The Moon Maid* the Mars of John Carter supplies earth by radio with the plans for constructing a spaceship which functions on reaction principles. Led by a renegade earthman, the people of the moon invade and devastate the earth. Primitive earth societies evolve in the wilderness and, eventually, the descendants of the Americans drive the moon men from the North American continent. Though some of the science is dated today, the scenes depicting the reconstruction of civilization are superbly conceived.

The Land That Time Forgot tells of the discovery of a giant island in the South Pacific where prehistoric creatures still survive. There are also seven species of human beings, in various stages of evolutionary development. In a single lifetime, each of these creatures evolves from a point a little higher than the ape to humanity, comparable to modern man. This concept is highly original, and most other elements of the book are as well thought out and effectively developed.

Burroughs' early Martian stories all went into hard cover. *Under the Moons of Mars* became *A Princess of Mars,* to be followed by *The Gods of Mars, The Warlord of Mars, The Chessmen of Mars,* and *Thuvia, Maid of Mars.* All were rollicking, swashbuckling scientific romances in the grand tradition. None displayed too careful a regard for scientific accuracy until the appearance of *The Master Mind of Mars.* This novel was first published complete in *Amazing Stories Annual,* 1927.

The title and the author's name were featured on the cover in larger letters than the magazine's own title. *Amazing Stories Annual* was intended to test the feasibility of publishing a companion to *Amazing Stories* and a big name was needed to help put it over. [Editor Hugo] Gernsback had previously reprinted *The Land That Time Forgot* in *Amazing Stories* and claimed that all he did to obtain *The Master Mind of Mars* was to write Burroughs asking him for a novel with some good scientific thought behind it.

Except for the opening scene, where the story's hero, Ulysses Paxton, is *wished* to Mars, the inventions and machinations of Ras Thavas, Martian scientific genius, are meticulously described. The novel also contains surprising philosophical passages. It is difficult to believe that Burroughs wrote this novel specially for Gernsback, yet it is even harder to conceive of *Argosy-All Story* or *Blue Book* rejecting it merely because it was more thoughtful than the others. Certainly not *Blue Book,* which during this very period thought nothing of giving *six* covers, one for each installment, for a serialization of an Edgar Rice Burroughs novel—which occurred not once but several times. It was in *Blue Book* that the majority of Burroughs' novels were printed in their first magazine appearance. The truth is that Burroughs had temporarily been victim of a vogue for westerns instigated by Zane Grey's bestseller popularity and the top offer he could get was from Hugo Gernsback's new science fiction markets. A few years later he would be riding the crest of magazine popularity again.

The writing of the Venus novels with Carson Napier as that watery world's heroic counterpart of John Carter came about through a literary rivalry. Otis Adelbert Kline, who had written for early issues of *Weird Tales* and *Amazing Stories,* had watched Burroughs' rise with undisguised admiration. He attempted to get on the bandwagon with a facile imitation of Burroughs' style and method in *The Planet of Peril,* a novel serialized in 1929 by *Argosy,* with Venus as its locale. Readers' raves resulted in a sequel, *The Prince of Peril,* which appeared in 1930.

Impressed by their popularity, A. C. McClurg & Co., Chicago, put the novels into hard covers immediately following magazine publication. Grosset & Dunlap issued low-priced editions soon afterward. Both of these companies had been Burroughs' traditional publishers, but he had gone to the newly formed Metropolitan Books, Inc., New York, in 1929, with *Tarzan and the Lost Empire.* Their action may have been a result of this move, or possibly, Burroughs, piqued by the scheduling of a competitive kind of novel, had withdrawn his books in retaliation.

This did not end the matter. A simulation of Tarzan by Kline appeared as *Tam, Son of the Tiger* in *Weird Tales* in 1931. So substantial was Kline's popularity at the time that the rumor prevailed that *Tam, Son of the Tiger* saved *Weird Tales,* which had gone bimonthly, from extinction and restored it to monthly publication. Adding insult to injury, Kline ran still *another* carbon copy of Tarzan, *Jan of the Jungle,* in *Argosy* the same year.

Stung into action, Burroughs launched a counter-invasion, setting his **Pirates of Venus,** his next novel, in Kline's territory, The Evening Star. It arrived at the editorial offices of *Argosy* just as they were evaluating a new Kline novel, *Buccaneers of Venus.* Caught on the horns of a dilemma, the editors of *Argosy* decided in favor of the more famous name, Edgar Rice Burroughs, especially since his Venus story, in thrills, action, and characterization, was at the top of his form.

Filled with righteous indignation, Kline, now forced to peddle his jilted Venus novel to *Weird Tales* at a lower rate, came back with a haymaker, turning out a novel of the Red Planet, *The Swordsman of Mars,* which was *Argosy*'s lead-off serial of the year. Burroughs thundered back with **Lost on Venus,** a sequel to **Pirates of Venus,** which was the equal of his first, and Kline then countered with another Mars story, *The Outlaws of Mars.*

From an entertainment standpoint there seemed little to choose between them, but from the aspect of economics, Kline was unable to get further book publication for his Venus and Mars stories, while Burroughs, who had formed his own publishing company, was parlaying every blow of the feud into profits. As far as sales were concerned, Burroughs was still the bigger draw.

The contest continued through 1935, when Kline's popularity began to fade. He was an imitator, and though he was an outstanding one, his success did not rest on solid ground. Burroughs nevertheless continued to grind out Venus stories even after Kline turned his attention away from writing to steering the destinies of other authors as head of The Otis Adelbert Kline Literary Agency.

However, relieved of the pressure of competition, the quality of Burroughs' Venus stories, after the first two, suffered seriously, and they are not among his better works. They consisted of **Carson of Venus** (*Argosy,* 1938), **Slaves of the Fish Men, Goddess of Fire, The Living Dead,** and **War on Venus,** all in *Fantastic Adventures,* the first three in 1941, the last in 1942. The last four were published in hard covers, under the title **Escape on Venus. Wizard of Venus** appeared in his **Tales of Three Planets,** 1964.

Of great interest is the serialization of **Tarzan and the Lion Man** in *Liberty Magazine,* beginning with the November 11, 1933 number. *Liberty,* then one of the three leading weekly slicks, along with *The Saturday Evening Post* and *Collier's,* solicited this story from Burroughs. The style is slick-magazine throughout. The novel is loaded with dialogue, often good dialogue. The sentences are direct and modern and crisp. The book version does not differ from the magazine's—a good bet that it was Burroughs' original.

Considering the fabulous popularity of Tarzan, why did Burroughs bother to write anything else? Of the fifty-nine books published during his lifetime, twenty-four featured Tarzan. Burroughs has been quoted as claiming thirty-five million sales for all his hard-cover books in North America alone. Of this number, he credited only fifteen million sales to Tarzan. The thirty-five other books accounted for another twenty million sales, an average of better than half a million copies per title. While we know a few to have been "lemons," we can see where his science fiction tales of Mars, Venus, and Pellucidar must have enjoyed greater popularity and profit than is generally believed.

Burroughs at the Michigan Military Academy, 1895.

During World War II, though in his sixties, Burroughs served as a war correspondent; the strain resulted in several heart attacks. Ill almost to the point of becoming a semi-invalid, he knew that he did not have long to live. In the foreword to *Llana of Gathol,* probably the best written of all the Martian books—it was published just before his death in March 1950—John Carter, the character who first brought his creator success, reappears to Burroughs. Here is the episode in the author's own words:

> ". . . I never expected to see you again."
>
> "No, I never expected to return."
>
> "Why have you? It must be something important."
>
> "Nothing of Cosmic Importance," he said, smiling, "but important to me, nevertheless. You see, I wanted to see you."
>
> "I appreciate that," I said.
>
> "You see, you are the last of my earthly kind whom I know personally. Every once in a while I feel an urge to see you and visit with you, and at long intervals I am able to satisfy that urge—as now. After you are dead, and it will not be long now, I shall have no Earthly ties—no reason to return to the scenes of my former life."
>
> "There are my children," I reminded him. "They are your blood kin."
>
> "Yes," he said, "I know; but they might be afraid of me. After all, I might be considered something of a ghost by Earth men."
>
> "Not by my children," I assured him. "They know you quite as well as I. After I am gone, see them occasionally.'
>
> He nodded. "Perhaps I shall," he half promised.
>
> (pp. 182-88)

Sam Moskowitz, "To Barsoom and Back with Edgar Rice Burroughs," in his Explorers of the Infinite: Shapers of Science Fiction, *World Publishing Co., 1963, pp. 172-88.*

JOHN HOLLOW   (essay date 1976)

[*Hollow is an American critic and educator who specializes in popular literature. In the following excerpt, he offers a reminiscence of his youthful appreciation of the Tarzan books and discusses what he considers the most valuable aspect of the series—the universality of its protagonist.*]

"I had this story," Edgar Rice Burroughs begins, "from one who had no business to tell it to me, or to any other." And I in turn had my second-hand copy of Burroughs' *Tarzan of the Apes* from one who had no business to sell it to me, or to any other child my age. I was too young even to suspect the implications of Tarzan's fight with Terkoz the bull-ape, when Jane Porter, "her lithe, young form flattened against the trunk of a great tree, her hands tight pressed against her rising and falling bosom, and her eyes wide with mingled horror, fascination, fear, and admiration—watched the primordial ape battle with the primeval man for possession of a woman—for her."

I am told that no one is that young anymore. But when I happened upon a paperback rack full of the reprints of the Tarzan series, I remembered being that young. I remembered shedding the outside world as Tarzan always shed his clothes at the edge of the jungle. I remembered taking to the trees and

swinging hand over hand through the forest branches. I even remembered that Burroughs claimed to have pieced together the story of Tarzan from a "musty manuscript," from the "dry official records of the British Colonial Office," and from "the yellow, mildewed pages of the diary of a man long dead." And I remembered buying Burroughs' book in an equally dusty place, a used-book store run by a little goblin of a man, one-eyed and missing some fingers from his right hand. (p. 83)

The rack of paperback reprints was in a bookstore which was both clean and collegiate, full of beermugs and sweatshirts, but I bought a copy of *Tarzan of the Apes* anyway—because it suddenly occurred to me that just as Tarzan taught himself to read in the jungle, so I learned to read while reading Burroughs' two dozen Tarzan books. My education, in other words, was hardly classical: for Perseus, Andromeda, and the sea-monster, I had Tarzan, Jane Porter, and Terkoz the bull-ape.

The point is, I think, worth making. We are, all of us, but especially those of us who wandered into civilization and culture instead of being brought up there, too apologetic about the youth we misspent in the bush country outside of literature.

Not everyone, of course, would agree. When I paid for my paperback copy of *Tarzan of the Apes,* the clerk, who affects the voice of an FM radio announcer, asked: "Light reading?" But since I have learned, perhaps from Tarzan himself, to tolerate the overly civilized, I kept my fingers and fangs to myself.

I took the book home and tried to recapture my youth. But Wordsworth is right: there is always a tree, of many, one, which reminds us that nothing can bring back those splendid hours. Rereading *Tarzan of the Apes,* I toppled out of that very tree against which Jane Porter pressed herself while Tarzan battled to save her from the less than honorable intentions of Terkoz. I suddenly remembered that every Burroughs book—be it about Africa, Mars, Venus, or the centre of the Earth—is about a woman fleeing from rape and also pursued by the hero whose lust for the lady is legitimized by love. And when I recalled that standard plot, the tree against which Jane Porter flattened herself—her eyes wide with mingled horror, fascination, fear, and admiration—became a phallus of enormous size; I realized that I have long since lost an innocence as difficult to regain as the one Burroughs' heroines are always ready to die to protect. I may never again be able to read a Tarzan story.

One thing, however—to continue the almost irreverent parallel with Wordsworth—does seem to remain behind. Having read again a little of Burroughs, I think he is better than generally supposed, that we were not stupid as well as young, the thousands of us who grew up reading about the ape-man. But let me use the second book of the series, *The Return of Tarzan,* as an example of what I mean. The last half of the book, which features the lost city of Opar and a white high-priestess, must have been derived from Rider Haggard; but the probable debt to Poe for an earlier chapter entitled "What Happened in the Rue Maule" is more interesting. In that chapter, Tarzan, who is exploring the back streets of Paris on his first visit to civilization, is lured to an upper room by a woman's cries for help. It is a trap, of course, the sort which always proves to Tarzan that civilization is worse than the jungle; and he is set upon by apaches. The thin veneer of civilization drops from him, Tarzan reverts to the beast, and the thugs—who expected only a routine ambush—find themselves trapped in a small room with a wild animal. When the police arrive, they find Tarzan's attackers broken in body as well as spirit and the ape-man fled, out the window, up a pole, and over the rooftops. Surely this parallel between Tarzan and the orangutan of "The Murders of the Rue Morgue" was intentional; more to the point, a writer who can use a literary echo to intensify and clarify a scene—Tarzan does not become *like* a beast, he becomes again the ape he was raised to be—such a writer may have been worth misspending a little youth on.

In the original book, when John and Alice Clayton, Lord and Lady Greystoke, the parents-to-be of Tarzan, are marooned on the wild African shore, one of the frightful sights they are forced to confront is that of a great figure standing erect and dimly silhouetted against the deeper shadows of the jungle. "Look," Lady Alice whispers, "what is it, a man?" She might well ask the same question about her son, who will be orphaned in his first year and raised by Kala the she-ape; Tarzan's mother is in fact asking a question about a future she can only glimpse and will not live to see. Burroughs is not only pulling off a nice bit of narrative foreshadowing, Lady Alice's question also seems to me an answer, an explanation of why we continued to read Tarzan books long after we discovered the pattern of the plots—long after we realized that this blow to the head had caused amnesia, that this double had tried to impersonate the hero, that even these lost cities had been found before. Like most books which endure for more than fifteen minutes, the Tarzan books are about what a thing is man, how like an angel and how like an ape.

Tarzan has to discover that he is more man than ape. He learns it from the books in his father's cabin, from the cannibal warrior who kills his foster-mother, and from Jane Porter, to whom he finally says: "I have come across the ages out of the dim and distant past from the lair of the primeval man to claim you—for your sake I have become a civilized man—for your sake I have crossed oceans and continents—for your sake I will be whatever you will me to be."

Tarzan has to come so far because his parents were forced back down the evolutionary ladder by the mutineers who deserted them on the savage African coast. "John, if it were only you and I," sobs the already pregnant Lady Alice (without, however, mussing either her subjunctive verb or her subjective pronoun), "we could endure it I know; but——" "Yes dear," he answers gently,

> but we must face it. . . . Hundreds of thousands of years ago our ancestors of the dim and distant past faced the same problems which we must face, possibly in these same primeval forests. That we are here today evidences their victory. What they did may we not do? And even better, for are we not armed with ages of superior knowledge, and have we not the means of protection, defense, and sustenance which science has given us, but of which they were totally ignorant?

"I only hope you are right, John," she answers. "I will do my best to be a brave primeval woman, a fit mate for the primeval man."

The rifles given to them by science only protect the Claytons for a while. They build a tree house and then a cabin, thus halting for a year or so the regression from civilization to savagery; but finally Lady Alice weakens and dies, leaving behind an infant and still nursing son. Clayton, grown careless with grief, is killed by the apes, one of whom then adopts Tarzan (the name given to the little Lord Greystoke by the apes). Devolution is complete: in killing his father and adopting

him, the apes seize Tarzan's identity, deny his origins, and insist upon his deeper origins.

Tarzan is raised by Kala the she-ape. "That the huge, fierce brute loved this child of another race is beyond question, and he, too, gave to the great, hairy beast all the affection that would have belonged to his fair young mother had she lived." "In a dim, vague way Kala explained to him that his father had been a strange white ape, but he did not know that Kala was not his mother."

"He was nearly ten before he commenced to realize that a great difference existed between himself and his fellows." At first Tarzan is ashamed of being hairless, of "that tiny slit of a mouth and those puny white teeth," but then he comes upon his father's cabin and the books therein. Gradually he begins to understand that he is a B-O-Y. (pp. 84-7)

As Tarzan leaves the cabin after his first chance discovery of the wonders that it holds, he is met by a huge gorilla which rises up out of the dark jungle as if to claim him. He is only able to survive the ensuing battle because "in one hand he still clutched the knife he had found in the cabin of his father, and as the brute, striking and biting, closed upon him, the boy accidentally turned the point towards the hairy breast." Using the brain, in other words, and the books and the weapons which are the legacy of his father, Tarzan begins to assert his manhood and to deny his bestiality.

That other hairy breast, at which Tarzan nursed, is also pierced—not by Tarzan, who is ever the grateful child—but by an arrow from the bow of the first man Tarzan ever sees, a cannibal warrior. . . . As Tarzan learns that he is a boy and not an ape, his foster-mother, Kala the she-ape, falls victim to the terrible inevitability of plot and theme.

Tarzan eventually wins the kingship of the apes, but he abdicates in order to seek out his own kind; it is as a man among men that Tarzan must complete his evolution from the apes. He does not hesitate to revenge the death of his foster-mother; but he finds that he is unable to eat the body of the savage, even though animals eat their kills and these savages (the only men Tarzan has ever seen) are cannibals. And when he rescues Jane Porter from the bull-ape, he refrains from the "possession" Terkoz had in mind because he wants to act as men are supposed to act. "True, it was the order of the jungle for the male to take his mate by force; but could Tarzan be guided by the laws of the beasts? Was not Tarzan a man? But what did men do? He was puzzled; for he did not know."

Which is to say that blood tells, as it always does in Burroughs. (pp. 87-8)

When Jane was frightened by the prospect of having to spend a night alone with him in the jungle:

> Tarzan of the Apes did the only thing he knew to assure Jane of her safety. He removed his hunting knife from its sheath and handed it to her hilt first, again motioning her into the bower.
>
> The girl understood, and taking the long knife she entered and lay down upon the soft grasses while Tarzan of the Apes stretched himself upon the ground across the entrance.
>
> And thus the rising sun found them in the morning.

And thus Tarzan is as natural a knight as Perceval, his sword of chastity more honest than that of Sigurd or of Tristan, and his savagery noble indeed. His final act in *Tarzan of the Apes*—

his refusal to claim his rightful title as the true Lord Greystoke because Jane Porter is engaged to the false Greystoke—is both a pretended denial of manhood ("'If it's any of my business, how the devil did you ever get into that bally jungle?' 'I was born there,' said Tarzan quietly. 'My mother was an Ape.'") and at the same time a noble gesture proving his true humanity. "Fingerprints prove you Greystoke. Congratulations," cables Tarzan's friend D'Arnot; but it does not take the imprint of four ink-begrimed little fingers in the margin of John Clayton's diary to prove Tarzan worthy of any House of Lords.

In *The Return of Tarzan* the ending of the first book is reversed—Tarzan does finally win and wed Jane—but before he does he returns to the jungle. "He told her then of his life since he had returned to the jungle—of how he had dropped like a plummet from a civilized Parisian to a savage Waziri warrior, and from there back to the brute that he had been raised." In *The Beasts of Tarzan*, the third book of the series, Tarzan is marooned by his enemies on a jungle island (which is more than a little like throwing Br'er Rabbit into the briar patch), and he again—for Jane—fights his way up the evolutionary scale, conquering the beasts and the beast in himself, and thus regaining civilization. In brief, the early Tarzan books copy the original story, of which Tarzan's victory cry, the victory cry of the bull-ape, is a miniature. When Tarzan fights he becomes again an animal, and when he wins he puts one foot upon the slain foe and throwing back his head gives the horrible scream of the victorious bull-ape. Spectators, usually those whom Tarzan has just rescued, find themselves suddenly as afraid of their protector as they had been of their attacker; but then Tarzan always calms himself and speaks to them as a rational and civilized man.

In the fourth book of the series, *The Son of Tarzan*, Tarzan's son ("Jack") is forced by the twists of the plot—chiefly two killings in self-defense—to flee from civilization and into the jungle, accompanied by an ape he met at a circus (the latter surely an embodiment of his father's past). Each time Jack tries to re-approach men, he is rebuffed, even shot at. He becomes so embittered that even the apes will have nothing to do with him, calling him "Korak the Killer," a name of no little meaning in the jungle where all are killers. Korak is redeemed, as was his father, by the love of a woman, a small girl he adopts, protects, and learns to love as she grows to womanhood.

And Korak is also saved by his father who arrives in the nick of time. "There is but one Tarzan," Korak acknowledges; "there can never be another." But if Tarzan's son knows his place, imposter Tarzans do still sometimes appear in the series—at one point Jane Clayton herself is almost fooled (a variation on Burroughs' threat-of-rape situation). Burroughs does not, however, allow false Tarzans before the real, and such machinations are always doomed by the last minute arrival of the ape-man. In fact, as the series continues, these providential appearances become Tarzan's main activity. The later books focus upon people who are either going to be saved or destroyed by Tarzan; there is usually the discovery of some lost civilization, always a likable young man and a beautiful woman, and several sub-plots which are slowly woven together. It is, in other words, highly ordered, this world of the later Tarzan books: Burroughs cuts from one set of characters to another—always at a moment of crisis—and finally Tarzan arrives, *deus ex machina*, usually back from being thought dead.

Acting like a god is, in fact, for Tarzan as for Odysseus, Hercules, or Beowulf, the hero's other temptation—other, that is, than reverting to the beast. The titles of several of the Tarzan books are suggestive in this regard: *Tarzan the Terrible; Tarzan, Lord of the Jungle; Tarzan the Invincible; Tarzan Triumphant;* and *Tarzan the Magnificent.* Like a god, like Jehovah in fact, is exactly how Tarzan does behave towards the cannibals who murdered his foster-mother. "If you ever chance to pass that far off African village," Burroughs tells us, "you will still see before a tiny thatched hut, built just without the village, a little iron pot in which is a quantity of food"—an offering ordered by the witch-doctor of the tribe to placate the terrible "evil spirit of the jungle." And like a jealous god, Tarzan is hard on other religions: he kills or defrocks a dozen witch-doctors in the course of the series. In each of Burroughs' series, for that matter, there are false gods supported by even more false priests; and two of his heroes, Tarzan and John Carter of Mars, regularly expose these whited sepulchres to the enslaved multitudes. The result—at least in the case of Tarzan—is that he, the redeemer, is always offered the chance to make a new testament, to become the new god or at least the new high priest. But like Spenser's Odysseus, "that long wandering Greek / That for his love refused deity," Tarzan always returns to Jane.

Tarzan is not, however, above taking advantage of superstition. In *Tarzan the Terrible,* both he and Korak claim to be divine, and Korak backs up their claim with the thunder and lightning of an Enfield rifle. In *Tarzan and the Leopard Men,* Tarzan, the victim of amnesia, goes so far as to forget not only who but what he is: when a savage warrior mistakes him for the ghost of an ancestor, Tarzan, lacking a better explanation of his prowess and his identity, assumes that the warrior knows what he is talking about. Typically, though, when Tarzan regains his memory, the savages respect him even more, because while they had thought to control the ghost through prayer, they have heard that no one can control Tarzan.

In *Jungle Tales of Tarzan,* a collection of short stories about Tarzan's boyhood, the ape-boy is called upon by the apes to save their god, the moon, which is apparently being devoured during an elipse. Tarzan climbs to the top of a tall tree and fires arrow after arrow into the night sky. When the moon reappears, "In all the tribe there was but one who was at all skeptical about the plausibility of Tarzan's remarkable rescue of Goro, and that one, strange as it may seem, was Tarzan of the Apes." Such self-saving doubt is his throughout the series.

If for a moment Tarzan forgets himself, he always gets his comeuppance. In *Tarzan and the Ant Men,* Tarzan grows overconfident among the little people; he is then, of course, captured by the ant men and reduced to their size. In the later books, where his function is most godlike, Tarzan is always captured at least once, and the consequent threat upon his life reminds him of his mortality. Even the immortality pills of *Tarzan's Quest* (like the long life of Burroughs' Martians and the immortality serum of his Venusians) will not protect him against the possibility of a violent death.

Not only was Tarzan's upbringing nasty and brutish, then; but his life—like ours—is always in danger of being short. Thus, by one definition at least, Tarzan's life is the life of a man. Which is to say that, as I look back on it, the first Tarzan book, *Tarzan of the Apes,* seems to present an idea so potent that Burroughs spent the rest of his life explicating it, and so complete that it is an allegory of the whole series: Tarzan discovers that he is neither the beast of the apes, nor the god of the cannibals, but the man of Jane Porter.

But before I conclude in such positive fashion, I ought to acknowledge the charge of racism that is often made against Burroughs' Tarzan stories. It is not so much that Burroughs uses on occasion the comic darky stereotype (Stepin Fetchit, after all, is a comic rebel, a protester who succeeds through cultivated incompetence); it is more that Tarzan himself, as the only Anglo-Saxon, is so much more strong, agile, and bright than the black African savages against whom he is pitted that his race has to seem superior. And neither the handsome black Waziri of the later novels, nor the good Jews and bad Jews, good Germans and bad Germans, of the series as a whole quite counter the very real sense that in Burroughs as in Conrad the question is not whether the blacks will make a god of Kurtz but whether Kurtz will allow them to. The best thing that can be said about Tarzan is that, unlike Kurtz, he restrains himself.

The question does have one slightly more complicated wrinkle, however; while it is true that Tarzan means "white-skin," Burroughs regularly reminds us that Tarzan has in fact been burnt bronze by the equatorial sun. Tarzan is more like the Apache of Burroughs' other novels about the American Southwest, or like the red race John Carter finds to be dominant on Mars, than he is like his fellow white-skins. Burroughs' racism is finally another example of that Caucasian envy Kafka so nicely called "The Wish to Be a Red Indian." "If one were only an Indian, instantly alert, and on a racing horse, leaning against the wind . . . until one shed one's spurs, for there needed no spurs, threw away the reins, for there needed no reins. . . ."

If we now know that Burroughs has all the faults of the pulps, including a racism he shares with Poe and Haggard, and a sexism he shares with all adventure writers, then we really have grown in wisdom as in age. But we were not hopelessly wrong-headed when we were young—Burroughs did have a powerful and coherent imagination. Just as the boy Tarzan trying to learn to read presents to Burroughs "a picture filled, at once, with pathos and with promise—an allegorical figure of the primordial groping through the black night of ignorance toward the light of learning"—so growing up reading Tarzan books may be seen as a groping through the jungle of adventure toward the light of literature. (pp. 88-92)

> *John Hollow, "Rereading 'Tarzan of the Apes'; or 'What Is It,' Lady Alice Whispered, 'A Man?',*" in The Dalhousie Review, *Vol. 56, No. 1, Spring, 1976, pp. 83-92.*

FREDERIK POHL   (essay date 1976)

[*An admired American science fiction author and critic, Pohl has been a significant presence in many phases of the genre since the 1920s. His best-known novel,* The Space Merchants *(1953), in which the world becomes openly dominated by advertising magnates, has been praised both as entertainment and sharp social criticism. In the following excerpt, Pohl acknowledges Burroughs's role as an inventor of space adventure and as an early practitioner of interplanetary fiction that is based on scientific possibility.*]

Burroughs, of course, is best known as the inventor of Tarzan. To the world at large that undoubtedly overshadows everything he has done in science fiction, but his contributions to science fiction, were, in fact, enormous.

To begin with he invented the whole tradition of swashbuckling swordsmanship and derring-do in space which a thousand talentless clods have lived off ever since—and which a few really talented writers, like Leigh Brackett, Andre Norton, Henry Kuttner and C. L. Moore, among others, have taken unto themselves and developed in ways that Burroughs had not anticipated. All of the Burroughs science-fiction stories assay very high to the ton in blood, guts, violence and danger, the standard ingredients of pulp fiction always.

Now, I suppose that inserting pulp values into science fiction would have been done by somebody else sooner or later if it hadn't been done by Burroughs in *A Princess of Mars* fifty-odd years ago; perhaps that is not so great a thing in itself, although clearly its effect on all science fiction that followed was immense. However, that is not in my opinion Burroughs's only claim to fame as an innovator in science fiction. The thing he did that I think is of equal importance, perhaps of vastly more importance at least in the sense that it led to new kinds of valid and substantial stories rather than mere adventure, was to write of other planets in terms of their scientific reality.

Now, I expect that there are a few people who would be disposed to challenge that statement. Burroughs is not now considered to be scientifically very accurate—his Barsoom is a very long way from the Mariner's Mars, with its total lack of drinkable water and breathable air, its craters and its apparent complete lack of life in any form whatsoever.

But we must remember that Burroughs wrote long before Mariner was launched. The planet he described was the planet the best prevailing astronomical opinion spelled out for him. These were the years of Percival Lowell, when astronomers still saw canals in their telescopes, when the Martian ice caps were taken to be glaciers, when the color changes were deemed to represent the growth of vegetation—perhaps even of crops; when some of the best minds in science were preoccupied not with the question of whether intelligence existed on Mars—they took that as given—but with the question of how best to light huge fires in geometrical designs on the Sahara desert so that they might inform that Martian intelligent life that Earth had similar life of its own. If Burroughs's Mars turned out to be scientifically wrong, it was not Burroughs who was in error, it was science. He knew that air was scant, of course; he remedied that, by inventing "atmosphere factories." He knew that water was scarce; he described the Martian plains as "dead sea bottoms."

Even in detail, his science was not bad. Maybe not *good*, but by no means hopeless. For example, his Martian atmosphere plants were described as manufacturing air from what he called the "Eighth Barsoomian ray." Is there an eighth Barsoomian ray? Well, no. But if you think of a ray as a flux of charged particles, it is only a step to say that the phenomenon we have just recently discovered called the "solar wind" might well be considered a ray of a sort, and it happens that the solar wind consists predominantly of charged hydrogen atoms, which could in fact be made to react with the oxygen locked in Martian rocks to make at least water, if not air; and perhaps one could work out some way of extending the reaction to provide the energy to blast loose breathing oxygen at the same time. I don't know that a scientist would do this, but surely any modern science-fiction writer could do it for story purposes in a short afternoon's easy work.

Another detail: in *The Master Mind of Mars,* Burroughs described organ transplants—around 1930, remember—in terms rather better than anyone else I can think of described them, in science fiction or out, until at least a decade or two later.

So it is Burroughs, I think, who first took seriously what astronomy had to say about the universe outside our own Earth, and attempted—quite seriously—to think how human beings could live there. Even Wells fudged there; when Cavor visited the Moon Wells invented air for which there was no justification at all, and caves for which there was little more. Burroughs's Barsoom was a fair shot. And so it is to Burroughs that we owe the kind of science fiction that typifies some of the best work of people like Hal Clement, Larry Niven, and Arthur C. Clarke. (pp. 44-6)

> Frederik Pohl, "The Innovators," in The Journal of
> General Education, *published by The Pennsylvania*
> *State University Press, University Park, PA, Vol.*
> *XXVIII, No. 1, Spring, 1976, pp. 43-8.*

BRIAN ATTEBERY (essay date 1980)

[*In the following excerpt, Attebery explores the nature of Burroughs's fictional universe.*]

Edgar Rice Burroughs had a career remarkably like that of L. Frank Baum. Both entered the field of literature late, after Western excursions and a number of unsuccessful business ventures. Both achieved their first fame, not in the older literary capitals of the East Coast, but in young, free-wheeling Chicago. Both eventually migrated to the warmer pastures of Southern California. Though Baum was a few years older, they knew one another. Burroughs mentions in a letter having been

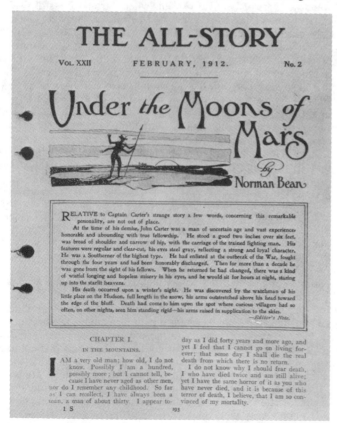

Burroughs's first novel, serialized in the magazine the All-Story *under the pseudonym Norman Bean.*

introduced to a local club by "Frank Baum, the fairy tale man." Both Baum and Burroughs wrote a great deal more than was good for their critical reputations: having had their first tastes of success through writing, the temptation was to keep on turning out the volumes and series long after inspiration had faded. Among Baum's books, only the Oz stories (and some of them by courtesy) and a few other early tales bear rereading. With Burroughs the division is not so clear between his best and his worst, but his first books, like *A Princess of Mars* and *Tarzan of the Apes,* generally outshine anything that came after. In those two stories he outlined the principles of his fictional world; all the others only fill in the chinks.

What is the nature of Burroughs' fictional world; that is, how does he stand on the first and fundamental element of fantasy? Burroughs seems to have several fantasy worlds. One is called Mars, or, by its natives, Barsoom (Burroughs' names are rarely lyrical but often memorable). Another is called Africa, and is supposedly a part of the real world. A third is the imagined hollow center of our own earth. A fourth is Venus. A fifth is displaced in time rather than space: it is Burroughs' own version of prehistoric Europe. Others appear briefly: the moon, Jupiter, a world in another galaxy. But, aside from names and certain surface phenomena, like the number of legs of the native animals or the size of the enemy warriors, all of these different places are regions of one uniform, Burroughsian universe.

Burroughs' universe is never more vividly portrayed than in its first expression, in *A Princess of Mars.* This story begins in a part of the country with a strong flavor of the exotic, the mountains of Arizona, among hostile Indians, mineral treasures, and mysterious caves and ruins. Burroughs, who was briefly in the cavalry in Arizona, takes a chapter to set the scene in proper local color/adventure style, as if he were writing, not space fantasy, but Western formula fiction. Then, with a hint of Indian or pre-Indian magic, his hero, John Carter, is seized by an unknown force, lifted out of his earthly body, and transported, in an instant, to Mars. There he finds dry, ancient-looking scenery, relieved by small flowers and succulent plants; wild animals well suited for riding; tribes of fierce fighting men; ruined cities of barbaric splendor—in other words, he finds a dream or fantasy version of the American Southwest.

The landscape of Mars is clearly analogous to that where his journey begins. Just before his translation to the Other World, Carter muses on the scene before him in magical, atmospheric terms, like those used by Irving and Hawthorne for the very different scenery of the Northeast:

> Few western wonders are more inspiring than the
> beauties of an Arizona moonlit landscape; the sil-
> vered mountains in the distance, the strange lights
> and shadows upon hogback and arroyo, and the gro-
> tesque details of the stiff, yet beautiful cacti form a
> picture at once enchanting and inspiring; as though
> one were catching for the first time a glimpse of some
> dead and forgotten world, so different is it from the
> aspect of any other spot upon our earth.

Out of this insight into the strangeness of the familiar (to Burroughs) landscape comes the overall inspiration for his conception of Mars. Other elements enter into it as well. By Burroughs' time, astronomical observations of Mars had swirled together in the popular imagination to produce an image of arid wastes, interlocking canals, and cool, fertile bands around the polar caps. Burroughs found it easy to marry his knowledge of the West to the popular conception of Mars: the poles were like glaciers, the broad expanses were plateaus and dry sea beds, and the canals were a great, tree-lined irrigation system, like those he was familiar with in Utah and Idaho. . . . Even the rocks carry the message that this new land is somehow an extension of the old; that certain of the rules (like gravitation) may be altered, but that most knowledge learned in the old world will relate to the new, and vice versa.

Burroughs had a facility for inventing fauna as required by twists of his plot; otherwise his worlds are rather empty. On Mars, there are two types of animals: those which threaten the main characters and those which get them out of scrapes. Both kinds are grotesque in appearance—Mars seems to favor extra legs, tusks, bulging eyes, and gaping, froglike mouths—but Burroughs gives the game away by assigning each monstrosity an earth analog. The *calot* is a Martian dog, the *thoat* a Martian horse, the *sorak* a Martian cat, the *banth* a Martian lion, and so on. Once we know the analog we can pretty much forget the animal's description: its character and function are set. Pat a calot and he will smile like a collie.

Of Martian flora we hear very little. There is an ubiquitous carpet of ochre moss, reminiscent of Arctic moss and appropriate to the general starkness of the Martian scene. There is a milk-producing plant that might be inspired by Southwestern succulents like cactus and agave. Mostly there are generalized trees and flowers, of interest only as shade or shelter or fodder.

The physical appearance of Burroughs' Mars, in its contours and life forms, is weird and alien but at the same time strongly reminscent of and derived from a part of the known earth. It is a consistent place. The animals, as I have said, all fit into a general mold. Burroughs is careful to keep in mind the low gravitation, thin air, and lack of water that are the prime considerations for the preservation of life on Mars. Likewise, after making one break with known reality, such as the so-called ninth ray that opposes gravitation, he is conservative in compounding the violation, so that the unknown operates within a stable, predictable framework. There are airships, yes, but they frequently break down, just like automobiles. There is telepathy, but it seems to be of limited use: primarily it helps in managing one's animals or in judging other people's reactions. This way of bounding the impossible, of keeping it within believable limits, is common to both fantasy and science fiction. Indeed, to judge from John Carter's adventures on the planet Mars alone, the Mars books might better be classed with the latter, where telepathy, antigravity, radium guns, and so on are more familiar than they are in traditional fairy tale and legend.

Nevertheless, I do think these stories at least lap over into the realm of fantasy, and that the Other World, here called Mars, is to be understood as a fantasy world; not accessible from our own through space and time and the extension of knowledge, but discontinuous with it, to be found only through some back door of the mind. The major indicator of its fantastic nature is John Carter's journey, or, rather than journey, his advent on Mars, as Burroughs calls it. The ingredients of this celestial voyage are clearly magical: a hidden cave, an ancient Indian witch, a binding spell, a compulsion from the heavens, and a threshold of cold and darkness. These are not the accouterments of a scientific space journey but of a voyage to heaven or hell or their buffer state, fairyland; and that last I believe Mars, on a symbolic and functional level, to be.

The plot that winds through Burroughs' half-scientific, half-fantastic fairyland is a rambling one that is extended and compounded through another ten books. The broad framework of

A Princess of Mars could, if one wished, be made to fit Propp's morphology of the folktale with a bit of tailoring—the essential boy-gets-girl-and-kingdom movement is there—but there is a more accurate forecast of Burroughs' tale in the popular romances of Bulwer-Lytton, Conan Doyle, and especially H. Rider Haggard. Here is an approximate "morphology" of these tales:

First function: the hero sets out from society. He is generally rich, handsome, and successful in the civilized world, but something calls him into parts unknown and wilds uncharted.

Second function: a mysterious messenger appears. He picks out the hero from among his companions and hints to him of a lost civilization to be found in the wilds of Africa, South America, or outer space.

Third function: the journey. Preferably tropical, but the arctic will do. Must be arduous.

Fourth function: capture by strange warriors. They are the outlying guards of the hidden kingdom.

Fifth function: protection of the hero by a young girl. This girl may or may not be attractive. She is not the heroine, and may even be opposed to the heroine, but she loves the hero with a doglike faithfulness and nurses, protects, and instructs him with no thought of reward.

Sixth function: appearance of the queen. This is the true heroine. She may be either good or evil, but must possess an exotic, almost divine beauty. The men of the lost kingdom worship her as a goddess. The other women of the kingdom do not count.

Seventh function: lovemaking. Usually interrupted by eighth function.

Eighth function: battle. Sometimes the lost kingdom rebels against its priestess-queen; other times it is attacked by the less civilized tribes around it. At this point the hero goes native and shows himself to be a Roman gladiator under the skin.

Ninth function: consummation. The story may end in marriage or a Wagnerian love-death. Both are equally satisfying, since both imply a complete break with the outer world. This conclusion is in contrast with the fairy tale ending, which usually involves a return to the opening milieu and a setting of it to rights.

Probably the finest story conforming to this outline, the one that determines the type, is Haggard's *She*. More writers than Burroughs have followed his example, in England and in America. Burroughs, though, was the first successful bearer of the Haggard tradition in this country, and most American lost world inventors are stamped with his influence, as well as with Haggard's.

As Burroughs develops the outline, the hero, "a Southerner of the highest type," is already on his way into the wilds of Arizona. The messenger, who is to foretell the new land, might be either the first Indian who follows the hero into the magical cave and reacts to its eeriness or, more likely, the witch-woman whose potions bring about his translation to Mars. This woman is not seen until the end of the book. After its ten-year span Carter finds only "the dead and mummified remains of a little old woman with long black hair," leaning over "a round copper vessel containing a small quantity of greenish powder." We never know if this sorceress is an Indian medicine worker or if she is somehow connected with the Indian-like red Martians. Her message is an inarticulate one—just a moan and a puff of vapor that launches John Carter on an astral journey. The inference is that Indian magic, with its smoke and its trips down the peyote road, is a link between the two worlds.

The third function, the journey, is not so tedious as a trek across a tropical desert, but it is far longer, and seems to be spiritually, if not physically, arduous. Function four, capture, is immediate upon John Carter's appearance on Mars. Function five follows not long after, when Sola, a young girl of the green Martian tribe that has captured him, feeds and shelters him and teaches him the Martian language. She is obviously a helper and not a romantic possibility: "My fair companion was about eight feet tall, having just arrived at maturity, but not yet to her full height. She was of a light olive-green color, with a smooth, glossy hide."

The green warriors also bring about function six, the appearance of the goddess-queen, by capturing Dejah Thoris, Princess of Helium. She is the standard pagan beauty, but not, interestingly enough, a lone Caucasian among the lesser breeds, as is so often the case with these chauvinistic hero tales. Dejah Thoris is a red Martian:

> Her face was oval and beautiful in the extreme, her every feature was finely chiseled and exquisite, her eyes black and lustrous and her head surmounted by a mass of coal black, waving hair, caught loosely into a strange yet becoming coiffure. Her skin was of a light reddish copper color, against which the crimson glow of her cheeks and the ruby of her beautifully molded lips shone with a strangely enhancing effect.

In this passage Burroughs plays his full hand in the matter of describing heroines. There are only so many ways to say "beautiful and strange," at least for a prosaic writer like Burroughs. His later descriptions of Dejah Thoris grow more effusive but add nothing to our conception of her, and all his other princesses of Mars and elsewhere follow the same model. By the time we have met the strangely beautiful Thuvia and the strangely beautiful Phaidor in the second volume—to say nothing of the dozens more that twine exotically through Venus and Pellucidar—we begin to feel a powerful sense of *Dejahvu*.

Lovemaking in Burroughs is always brief and usually comic. John Carter and his princess fall in love instantly, but run afoul of their differing cultural patterns. Burroughs takes delight in portraying the otherwise flawless hero as a bumbler at love. The lovers' exchanges do not bear repeating here; the humor in them is as embarrassing as the sentiment. If there is anything Burroughs is less adept at than portraying women, it is showing men and women together. Luckily, the lovemaking is soon cut short by a "duel to the death," neither the first nor by any means the last of John Carter's battles.

Battle is supposed to follow lovemaking in the morphology, and so it does here, but Burroughs has compounded and recompounded this eighth function so that it punctuates virtually every other movement in the book. Is John Carter entering a city? He fights his way in. Is he leaving? He fights his way out. Has he met a friend? He engages in combat by his side. An enemy? He bests him in battle.

The final function, consummation, takes its happier form in *A Princess of Mars*. John Carter, the interloper, rescues his heroine, weds her, and takes his place as prince of Helium, living happily with her for ten years. Burroughs always had a taste for planting the seeds of a sequel, however, so the final pages of the book find Carter transported back to earth against his will. Then, in *The Gods of Mars* and *The Warlord of Mars*, he fights his way through another series of trials to win Dejah Thoris once again and be awarded the grander title of warchieftain of all Barsoom. The plot in these two novels is a reworking of the first plot. They are really excuses for following the hero on a voyage of discovery around the new planet, literally from pole to pole.

John Carter himself is as strictly defined by the lost world mode as is the plot he fights his way through. The hero of such a novel is significantly different from that of a traditional wonder tale. The fairy tale hero commonly has a home and family, but no distinction. He is just Jack, the woodcutter's son, or at best the disinherited third son of a minor king. The hero of a Burroughsian adventure, however, must be rootless and yet, paradoxically, of the noblest lineage. Carter is a wandering orphan of indeterminate age, a combination of Melville's Ishmael and the Wandering Jew of European legend: "I am a very old man," the story begins, "how old I do not know. Possibly I am a hundred, possibly more; but I cannot tell because I have never aged as other men, nor do I remember any childhood."

Yet this ageless outsider is, at the same time, heir to the nearest thing to an aristocratic tradition in America: landed Southern wealth. Burroughs precedes the narrative with a foreword, in his own name but not his own character, in which he expands the statement on John Carter that opened the first magazine version:

> He was a splendid specimen of manhood, standing a good two inches over six feet, broad of shoulder and narrow of hip, with the carriage of the trained fighting man. His features were regular and clear cut, his hair black and closely cropped, while his eyes were of a steel gray, reflecting a strong and loyal character, filled with fire and initiative. His manners were perfect, and his courtliness was that of a typical southern gentleman of the highest type.

Throughout the books, Carter justifies his own behavior by repeating his claim of being a Virginia gentleman. Generally, whatever it is that a Virginia gentleman will or will not do turns out to be the custom on Mars as well.

Carter's Southernness is a prop. The Southerner's belief in his own gentility provides a convenient shorthand for saying that Carter is superior innately, by inheritance. Tarzan, similarly, is not just any child raised by animals, but an English lord, whose attributes shine through all barriers of circumstance. What Burroughs is proposing in these and others of his heroes is a theory of natural aristocracy coinciding exactly with social position. If Burroughs were, as he intimates in his foreword, a distant nephew of John Carter's, equally blue-blooded, we should have to call him a fearful snob. In reality, he came of ordinary Midwestern parentage and was physically undistinguished, just another mortal daydreaming of superman.

Burroughs' Martians fit into various categories. Most are essentially human—lesser versions of the hero. Among these, there is an interesting hierarchy by race. Red men, analogous, as I have said, to American Indians, are the highest in morals and prowess. Black men are next, noble but misled by a false goddess. Yellow men are a little less impressive than black, and white men are least admirable, being spiteful, treacherous, and totally bald.

Women of all four races are mysterious, unpredictable, and alien. Any of them may unexpectedly demonstrate paranormal powers, as when Thuvia exercises control over a lair of vicious "banths." It is a woman who deludes the black men of Mars into thinking her a goddess, and it is a woman who sends John Carter to Barsoom. Actually, Burroughs places Barsoomian and earth women in the same alien class. They are all half-witch, half-goddess: the only really supernatural figures in the books. Burroughs, who is uncomfortable with women characters, generally keeps them offstage, lost or in enemy hands until the final stages of the book, leaving only fightable and therefore understandable aliens to deal with.

The green men of Mars are wonderfully fightable. Savage, grotesque giants with no trace of sentiment, they are the perfect foils for a fighting hero, either as enemies or as companions. They may have folk roots; there are many giants in European tradition, even green ones. Tars Tarkas, the giant chieftain, is a variation on the Green Knight fought by Sir Gawain. The green men are appealing in their irresponsible, innocent violence. They provide relief from the gentlemanly code of Carter and the red Martians. Freudians might call them personifications of the id.

Green and red Barsoomians, who are similar in culture, may also represent the two divisions of Indians as seen by white settlers. The red are the "good Indians," who cooperated with whites, and the green are the "bad Indians," who fought back. It is the uncooperative Indians, like Sitting Bull or Cochise, whom we secretly admire, whose role we take in childhood games. That might explain why John Carter's closest friend is not a red Martian but green Tars Tarkas.

More strange creatures appear in later Burroughs books, but none rank above mankind. The Mars stories are tales of conquest, of Western man expanding his territory across another world as he has this one, though Carter plays at being a red Barsoomian. No creature may be greater or wiser than he, because that might stop his advance. That is one of the meanings of the Mars series, as expressed in the very fabric of its invention: that man—white, male, American man—is the measure of all things.

What other meanings may be inferred from Burroughs' system of fantasy? One hesitates to dig too far below the level of pure entertainment for fear of finding, as Hans Joachim Alpers claims to have found, that such stories are nothing less than Fascism in fable form, preaching a philosophy that is mystical, violent, fatalistic, power oriented, sexist, racist, imperialistic, anti-intellectual, and conducive to leader worship. Alpers ignores the difference between writing about a thing and advocating it, but he has pinpointed a fundamental limitation in Burroughs and the subgenre that springs from him: insofar as Burroughs touches on ideas he does so immaturely, in a fashion which does suggest embryonic Fascism. But Burroughs had neither the insight nor the inclination to direct his fantasy toward dogmatic ends, and so any philosophical pitfalls beneath the surface of his adventures are so deeply buried as to be of danger to no one.

Edgar Rice Burroughs was neither more nor less than a good storyteller, with as much power—and finesse—as a bulldozer. A measure of his strength is the frequency with which he is imitated. Burroughsian science fiction and fantasy filled the popular magazines, usually called pulps, of the thirties and forties. E. E. "Doc" Smith, Robert E. Howard, Abraham Merritt, and many others turned aspects of his fiction into books

and series of their own. In recent years, the Burroughsian line has hardened into a fixed formula often referred to as "swords-and-sorcery." In this case, imitation has gone beyond flattery and become a strait jacket, but some of the practitioners of swords-and-sorcery may break loose and produce fantasy that is derived from Burroughs and yet greater than its source. (pp. 110-18)

> Brian Attebery, "Fantasy and Escape," in his The Fantasy Tradition in American Literature: From Irving to Le Guin, *Indiana University Press, 1980, pp. 109-33.*

BENJAMIN S. LAWSON   (essay date 1986)

[*In the following excerpt, Lawson discusses Burroughs's Martian novels in the context of twentieth-century American culture.*]

Edgar Rice Burroughs once claimed that he was "born in Peking and raised in the Forbidden City." Actually he was from Chicago. Readers of Burroughs usually have been attracted by his exotic and fantastic "Forbidden City" elements, which seem most amenable to mythic or psychological interpretations. . . . As John Cawelti has expressed it [in his *Adventure, Mystery, and Romance: Formula Stories as Art and Popular Culture*], "Those patterns characteristic of a number of different formulas presumably reflect basic concerns and valuations that influence the way people of a particular period prefer to fantasize." American utopias are often set in America. The radical alienness imagined in more recent novels like Stanislaw Lem's *Solaris* (so completely an inscrutability that the very definition of communication cannot be applied to it) was foreign to Burroughs's brand of earth, American, and male chauvinism. Carl Sagan's comment that "Mars has become a kind of mythic arena onto which we have projected our earthly hopes and fears" is intended to indicate a liberating of the imagination, but actually implies that these projections can be after all only parochial.

In July of 1911 Burroughs was engaged in his latest attempt to earn a comfortable living—the marketing of pencil sharpeners. The attempt, which followed other careers as cowboy, salesman, and soldier, was apparently failing. Believing in the dominant capitalistic creed of the times and always willing to take risks in the hope of unexpected bonanzas, he turned at the age of 37 to a new business: writing. What he wrote can be read as his many daydreamed escapes from the frustrations of his professional failures. Although for a time he continued to work in Chicago giving business advice to the subscribers of the business journal *System,* he soon honed his newly discovered talents as an author with such great success that by 1923 he had become the first American writer to incorporate himself. (pp. 208-09)

Burroughs's self-conscious insistence on literature as a business, which might seem artistically and ideologically naive and retrograde to an elitist critic, can be understood by listing a few other key intellectual events of the year of *A Princess of Mars* (1912). Against this progressive background, Burroughs's affiliations with a Victorian code of manners, American middle-class values, and the genteel tradition are particularly striking—making his contribution seem insignificant. While Burroughs sat in his small Chicago office, Sherwood Anderson literally walked way from his Ohio factory to Chicago and a life of art; Vachel Lindsay began an odyssey from Illinois with "rhymes to be traded for bread"; Ezra Pound searched for a meaningful poetic tradition in the troubadour country of France. In what both Willard Thorp and Hugh Kenner have called an *annus mirabilis* in American poetry, Harriet Monroe founded the progressive *Poetry: A Magazine of Verse*. Dreiser's *Sister Carrie* finally made its official public appearance. Charles Beard's revisionist *The Supreme Court and the Constitution* brought a new emphasis on scientific method and economic motive. The left-wing *The Masses* began its run as one of a large number of socially aware and politically partisan magazines, and the socialists won nearly a million votes in the presidential election. W. C. Handy's "Memphis Blues" enjoyed popularity, in the era of jazz, ragtime, and Charles Ives. Controversy resulted from the production of *Afternoon of a Faun* and, during the following year, *The Rites of Spring*. Walt Kuhn and Arthur B. Davies were organizing the internationalist and generally avant-garde Armory Show of modern art, which was to have a profound impact on American art and popular preferences. An English translation of *An Interpretation of Dreams* reinforced the fascination of American intellectuals for the psychoanalytical theories of Freud; John Watson was propounding the earliest behaviorist ideas; and in his mind, Albert Einstein was remaking the physical universe.

The role of a fantasy writer in the period which culminated in World War I would appear obvious. Burroughs furnished a ready escape from and predictable formulas in uncertain and stressful times. In so doing, he was able to establish, or at least popularize, major genres of "lowbrow" literature. "Burroughs turned the entire direction of science fiction from prophecy and sociology to romantic adventure, made the major market for such work the all-fiction pulp magazines, and became *the* major influence on the field through to 1934." Soon to follow were the all-science fiction magazines of Hugo Gernsback and others.

Burroughs's mix of action, exotic setting, and love interest, with little hard science, has also had an important effect on fantasy fiction and "sword and sorcery" literature (particularly since writers and general readers have never been as preoccupied with generic distinctions as modern academicians seem to be). Critics have discovered both direct influences on Burroughs—Edwin Lester Arnold, H. Rider Haggard, even Madame Blavatsky—and, more important here, disciples of Burroughs—Charles B. Stilson and J. U. Geisy—in the period of his first books. These early works include the Martian trilogy *A Princess of Mars, The Gods of Mars,* and *The Warlord of Mars.*

In Burroughs's novels "a retreat to the primitive" and the simple, a "flight from urban culture and rational thought," comparable to Gaugin's, logically results from the threat of a congeries of forces at work early in the century: industrialization, the growth of big business and labor, urbanization, immigration, and imperialism. The American population had increased from about forty million to over ninety million between 1870 and 1910. Many new Americans—over a million a year, mainly new immigrants, during the peak years from 1900-1914—constituted a largely urban, cheap labor force that became the subject of both settlement-house reform and nativist attack (the midwestern evangelist Billy Sunday invaded American cities in 1912 to take on the devil on Satan's own immoral, foreign, liberal, clearly non-Protestant grounds). Industrial and technological change, the immigrant and his unfamiliar tenement world were strange to many Americans. Perhaps Brian Aldiss [in his *This World and Nearer Ones*] is exaggerating only a little in his conclusion that "the important thing for ERB and his devotees is a loathing of urban culture . . . and a

mystical obsession with land, purity of blood, courage, leadership, and rape," and a preference for "women dragged away by their hair, sentries being killed barehanded, endless bloodletting, and inferior races breeding like rabbits." Ironically, Burroughs could cash in on these fantasies only in a modern American capitalistic society.

In this spirit, John Carter's voyage is "a nostalgia trip to the past," to a Mars organized into tribal units, clans, or feudal monarchies. Violence is a way of life, and Carter achieves his purposes—usually the rescuing of Dejah Thoris—by killing hundreds of Martians. In *The Warlord of Mars,* he recalls fighting with his friend "through long, hot Martian days, as together we hewed down our enemies until the pile of corpses about us rose higher than a tall man's head." Only the physically fittest survive on an atavistic Mars "where bloody strife is the first and greatest consideration of individuals, nations, and races." The very flora and fauna of the planet are threatening, and Carter frequently credits his success to instincts over which his conscious mind has lost control. This reliance upon warfare as an answer to problems, this callous fascination with maiming described in the interminable and numerous battle scenes, makes the Mars series a sort of pornography of violence.

Burroughs's typical themes of love and adventure—or, with different emphasis, sex and violence—are rooted in the fantasies made possible and appropriate by his exotic worlds, and no doubt explained by Freud. [In *The Science Fiction Encyclopedia*] Peter Nicholls calls *A Princess of Mars* "a fantastic product of frustration and daydream" and [in his *Billion Year Spree*] Aldiss finds that Jung's theories "illuminate something compulsive and repetitive in Burroughs's output." Carter's playing out of sex and power fantasies does not, however, so much remove him from history as from its circumstantial trappings. Carter's desire for power takes him to Mars and, once there, makes him the "warlord" of the planet by the end of the trilogy. Had Mars not been named after the Greek god of war, the god of Carter's profession, Carter would have remained in the Arizona cave where the Apaches had cornered him, stranded in a formula Western. But he wills himself out of both the tomb-like cave and his own body to be reborn—"naked as at the minute of my birth"—on Mars, where he finds himself standing next to an incubator of Martian eggs. Mars is a world where beings have an immense longevity, where healing salves enable one to be immediately ready for the next battle. By the conclusion of *A Princess of Mars,* with the aid of the extraordinary physical powers with which he is invested by Mars' lesser gravity, John Carter becomes the savior of Mars. The Martians are more than grateful for his plans to restart the atmosphere plant: "they loved you also, and fairly worship your memory as the savior of Barsoom."

In the next volume, Carter, having appeared from another world, unseats the old gods of Mars by revealing that they are self-seeking impostors. Issus, Goddess of Death and of Life Eternal, turns out to be a repulsive old hag, "a screaming, gibbering maniac" whom Carter shakes like "a rat." He violates a sacred law of Martian religion which makes it blasphemous—as well as hazardous—to return from the precincts of the Holy Therns: "He who be once dead may not live again." Earlier an alien on Mars, Carter has so assimilated Martian culture that he would now feel an alien on Earth.

In *The Warlord of Mars,* Carter continues to disembarrass Martians from the trammels of the old faith, stopping only when he gains sovereignty of even the mysterious poles of Mars and becomes "Jeddak of Jeddaks, Warlord of Barsoom!" Carter's title inscribes the peculiar merging of violence and religion in the books; his coronation and his title give a religious sanction to libidinous energies otherwise excluded from civilized communities. Whereas Captain Ahab discovered that physical assaults upon all that thwarts one are not efficacious, Captain Jack finds that they work quite well. The early John Carter novels are escapes from social reality, but not from psychological realities such as the need for wish fulfillment. Burroughs explained the rationale for this stepping aside from history in a proposed jacket blurb for *Savage Pellucidar:* the book will take you away from "the terrors of a world gone mad with hate—to the cleaner, finer terrors of prehistoric hunting beasts and savage, primeval men."

Carter simultaneously becomes warlord of Mars and regains his wife, "a world's most beautiful woman," "whose eternal youth and undying beauty were but outward manifestations of a perfect soul." Carter's pursuit, rescue, and defense of Dejah Thoris have constituted the substance of his martial as well as his marital life (although he and Dejah had earlier settled down long enough to have an egg). His dashing exploits in her name give the books the archaic flavor of sword and sorcery. The reader's and Carter's power fantasies and sexual fantasies are both satisfied in the final possession of Dejah Thoris, for whom the violence has been perpetrated. Lupoff perceptively notes "Burroughs's fear of and annoyance with feminine dominance," so that "the appropriate Burroughs hero [must] set out to alter society so as to establish masculine domination" [see Additional Bibliography]. The fictional world must be the hero's to save, while in the real world the various women's movements were becoming increasingly conspicuous and, to some, sources of insecurity. Before the final tableau can be presented, the hero must thwart the violence planned against the heroine. "It is a basic characteristic of Burroughs's work that the erotic is developed by a tension between the hero's awareness of the heroine's physical beauty and a threat—usually explicit—to her virtue." Possible rape can be described, but sexual intercourse is never mentioned; we are presented with either a prepubertal world or with an orgy of violence. Apparently the warlike Martians, generally chaste and lacking "that brute passion which the waning demands for procreation upon their dying planet has almost stilled," can express themselves only through violence. Even for John Carter "bloodlust" can only mean the love of battle. Mars is a singularly loveless world which lacks mature sexuality, a world which suggests images of male sexism, the West, and even Eliot's Waste Land ("There is shadow under this red rock").

Miscegenation and even bestiality are among the prime menaces to Dejah Thoris. For all his high-mindedness, Carter's responses to exhibitions of the animal passion are a mixture of prurience and apprehension: the fifteen-foot tall, six-limbed, green Tal Hajas turns the "fiendish leer" of his "bestial countenance" upon Dejah, "while his enormous bulk spread itself out upon the platform where he squatted like some huge devil fish." "The thought that the devine Dejah Thoris might fall into the clutches of such an abysmal atavism started the cold sweat" on Carter, who hopes that she would prefer suicide, as did those "brave frontier women" of America "who took their own lives rather than fall into the hands of the Indian braves." The yellow Salensus Oll, who has designs on Dejah in *The Warlord of Mars,* is "a great mountain of a man—a coarse, brutal beast of a man." That these lechers are also tyrants is a measure of Burroughs's conception of male uses of power. Later, Dejah falls "into the clutches of that archfiend, Thurid, the black dator of the First Born," in the novel

completed during a time when lynching was still far too common and when licentious blacks were indiscriminately chasing white females in *The Birth of a Nation.* In Burroughs's own Tarzan ("white-skin") books the Anglo-Saxon hero was putting down miscellaneous individual or collective black insurrections—at a time when the Ku Klux Klan remained a powerful force in American life, while more and more rural Southern blacks migrated to Northern cities. In *The Gods of Mars,* Carter had even feared Dejah's being "torn and rended by the cruel fangs of the hideous white apes" only "to be served as food upon the tables of the black nobles." Prudery, the sexual and the sexist, and racism are compounded in bizarre ways, but ways which Nicholls finds typical of Burroughs.

As suggested before, America possessed its own primitive space in the West. Passages early in *A Princess of Mars* can be disorienting to first-time readers of Burroughs brought up on firm generic distinctions: "Arming myself with my two Colt revolvers and a carbine, I strapped two belts of cartridges about me and catching my saddle horse, started down the trail." Burroughs is credited as a major contributor to a new and hybrid form, the "space opera" (as opposed to "horse opera"), described as "those works which have the typical structures and plots of Westerns, but use the settings and the trappings of science fiction." John Carter, "perhaps the first important space opera character," is a "Western story figure who somehow strayed across the border into science fiction." Even after he escapes the Apaches by teleporting to Mars, Burroughs's protagonist continues to inhabit a world of familiar mythic and psychic dimensions. Burroughs's Chicago in the nineteenth century was in many ways still a frontier town, and Burroughs himself was, at one time, a soldier and a cowboy in the West. He often depicted the Indian, writes Aldiss, "directly or indirectly." [In his *Return of the Vanishing American*] Leslie Fiedler considers this presence of the native American as one of the conceptual links between the Western and science fiction. American writers imagine any new world to be "inhabited by hostile aliens" because they have imagined the West in this way. Unless extraterrestrials await us "whom we can assimilate to our old myths of the Indian, outer Space will not seem an extension of our original America, the America which shocked and changed Europe, but a second, a meta-America, which may shock and change us." Perhaps the moon or Mars "will turn out to be a true archetypal equivalent to the Way West." John Carter cannot disassociate the first warriors he sees on Mars from "those other warriors who, only the day before," had been pursuing him. He is later struck by "the startling resemblance" a bedecked group of red Martians "bore to a band of the red Indians of my own Earth." In marrying the resplendent and nearly naked Dejah Thoris, Carter plays John Smith (another Virginia soldier whose personal motto was *to conquer is to live*) to the Pocahontas of Hart Crane's *The Bridge.* Dejah is "the mythological nature-symbol chosen to represent the physical body of the continent, or the soil" [Louis D. Rubin, Blyden Jackson, et al., eds., *The History of Southern Literature*]. "Who is the woman with us in the dawn? . . . whose is the flesh our feet have moved upon?" [Hart Crane, *The Bridge*]. In 1893 Frederick Turner had announced the closing of merely the actual West, not the mythic West. Those important Wests of the mind could only be born from the death of the real one. The region has been often displaced in American science fiction, from the West and the past to other worlds and the future. Although the locale of John Carter's adventures changes from Earth to Mars, even the landscape and climate remain much the same. Carter opens his eyes upon the "strange and weird landscape" of Mars, but his last glimpse of Arizona—a state admitted to the Union in 1912—had been "of some dead and forgotten world, so different is it from the aspect of any other spot upon our earth." Burroughs's depiction of Barsoom probably owes much to Percival Lowell, whose books on Mars, its canals, and possible life forms had just appeared and whose observatory was in Arizona. This picture of a desert land has "decisively influenced" later science fiction; "when Americans land on another world, it seems they expect it to resemble the American West" [Paul A. Carter, *The Creation of Tomorrow*].

The transferral of the native American to another planet and the constant threat of miscegenation, are not the only racial fantasies enacted in Burroughs's Mars novels. In his ethnic consciousness, Burroughs is atypical of science fiction writers whose orientation toward the future has, in the main, allowed them to assume an improvement in race relations, and in whose works "the presence of unhuman races, aliens, and robots certainly makes the differences between human races seem appropriately trivial." Burroughs's cast of more or less anthropomorphic characters comes in all colors: red, green, black, white, yellow, and blue. The xenophobia and racism of 1912 has been transferred from Earth to Mars in almost a caricature of the races. The men of Okar, for example, have "skins the color of a ripe lemon." The final despot slain by Carter is the malevolent, yellow Salensus Oll, whose defeat is a redaction of the same cultural and ethnic insecurities and fears found four years later in Oswald Spengler's *The Decline of the West*. [In their study *Science Fiction: History, Science, Vision*] Scholes and Rabkin point out that in pulp science fiction, "when it was fashionable to think of the 'Yellow Peril,' the villains in series like *Flash Gordon* could be expected to have a Mongolian appearance." (In the much later *Tarzan and "The Foreign Legion"* the Japanese are directly depicted as subhuman "monkey-men.")

Burroughs's consciousness of the parallels of Mars to Earth is illustrated in Carter's statement that the black pirates of Barsoom are handsome, "odd as it may seem for a Southerner to say it." Carter is a veteran "of a state which had vanished with the hopes of the South" and "a typical southern gentleman of the highest type" whose "slaves fairly worshipped the ground he trod." John Carter makes an Anglo-Saxon stand against the encroachments of a heterogeneous lot of enemies both domestic and foreign. Burroughs plays the amateur anthropologist and popular scientist in his speculation that there has been a great declension from the ancient high civilization of a "fair-haired, laughing people." Thomas Clareson notes that this impossible "yearning for the past" stands behind the popularity of the many "lost race" novels in the H. Rider Haggard tradition [see Additional Bibliography]. The green men have lost nearly all altruism and sentiment, and now "rove the deserted cities and dead sea bottoms of Mars." Ghosts of earlier peoples haunt the land, as they do in Ray Bradbury's *The Martian Chronicles* and Zane Grey's Western novels.

At first, John Carter is a partisan in the constant warfare among the races and clans of Mars. He assists in the rebellion of the white female slaves against their black masters; he slays various villains of all six "races." But in the triumphant conclusion of *The Warlord of Mars,* all of Carter's closest friends—each the highest type of his race, whether yellow, black, white, red, or green—come to his aid in the institution of a just pan-Martian government which is to put an end to divisiveness.

This fantasy of cooperation and amalgamation is suggested earlier in the trilogy in a variety of ways. Martian telepathy,

Cover of the October 1912 issue of the All-Story, *featuring the first publication of* Tarzan of the Apes.

for instance, has lowered barriers of communication among peoples. More importantly, Burroughs informs us that the three major races of Mars, the most human in earthly terms, had been "the blacks, the whites, and a race of yellow men," and that "the present splendid race of red men" is the result of earlier intermarriage. This new race, the most advanced on the planet, has almost regained the level of the ancient "arts of the fair-haired Martians." Guilt about the vanishing native American has been expiated in the creation of a new Martian, and through the marriage of Martian Dejah Thoris to white man John Carter. Through his various disguises Carter has experienced life as a red Heliumite, a white Thern, and a yellow Okarian. Although he could never pass as a Thark,—the fifteen-foot tall, four-armed, tusked green men—his best friend is Tars Tarkas, a Thark. Fiedler found this blood-brotherhood with an alien in a frontier setting typical in American literature. Or, putting this theme into another context, a key characteristic of stories about alien states or beings is "our dream that the unknowable can be known and related to in some meaningful fashion" [Cawelti, *Adventure, Mystery, and Romance*]. So *The Warlord of Mars* ends with a vision, a tribute to Mars for the dreams it has made possible. Desires for peace (though the means has been violent), brotherhood (yet Carter also achieves the ultimate power fantasy), and love (for the time being not threatened by lust) are satisfied. Finally, the attainment of one desire means the attainment of all. . . . (pp. 209-16)

As on earth, peace is only a truce; carnage and warfare continue beyond Carter's reign and are central to the final seven or eight Mars novels. Precisely what is missing in the Martian trilogy is what H. P. Lovecraft saw as the sine qua non of interplanetary fiction: "a deep, pervasive sense of strangeness—the utter, incomprehensible strangeness of a world holding nothing in common with ours." Although formula science fiction, writes Aldiss [in *This World and Nearer Ones*], "allays anxiety by showing us that the world is what we expect," this is "the message sf should not deliver. Astonishment is everything." Edgar Rice Burroughs was indeed from the Forbidden City; however, he was also from Chicago. (p. 216)

Benjamin S. Lawson, "The Time and Place of Edgar Rice Burroughs's Early Martian Trilogy," in Extrapolation, *Vol. 27, No. 3, Fall, 1986, pp. 208-20.*

MICHAEL ORTH   (essay date 1986)

[*In the following excerpt, Orth cites elements of pastoralism, primitivism, and utopian thought in Burroughs's fiction while portraying him as a "conservative romantic" whose vision of civilization's future is one of "inevitable tragic decline."*]

Edgar Rice Burroughs wrote more than seventy books, and at least fifty of them contain elements of utopian thinking—that is, they offer more or less detailed presentations of imaginary cities, peoples, or nations which the author clearly wishes his readers either to admire or detest; and they express a conservative vision of human history and possibility. . . . Over and over again, Burroughs takes his reader to a lost valley city or to a new world and shows him a society which pretends to be perfect, but which proves to be terribly flawed; in fact most of Burroughs's fiction reveals both a desire for utopia and fear of it. The conservative vision has always been strong in utopias. For example, the most famous utopia, Sir Thomas More's, is essentially conservative, as is the most famous American utopia, Edward Bellamy's *Looking Backward*. Both were the products of men suspicious of real social change, and interested rather in the perfection of traditional modes. Some students of the history of modern consciousness have even argued that such a conservative fatalism is the fundamental structure of modern belief. . . . The desire for perfection, or at least improvement, even if only the negative improvement of escape, combined with an almost Calvinist pessimism about the possibility of positive social evolution, remains a lively element in contemporary science fiction, and a dilemma for anyone proposing social reform or writing utopian fiction in America.

In his utopian focus, Burroughs is in harmony with his times. The last decades of the nineteenth century were full of utopian tales which provided challenges to the rapid economic expansion, urbanization, and industrialization of America. . . . Burroughs experienced his greatest success just when America shifted from a rural to an urban nation, and just as Americans began to dream of fleeing their chaotic cities to the new garden suburbs to avoid the social and institutional changes taking place as urban life developed. Remembering Burroughs's desire for and suspicion of utopia helps us understand the suspicion and fear of change which still dominate conservative and populist reactions to reform, as well as to the literary acts of social imagination which science fiction so often provides. In most popular stories, as too often in history, apocalyptic destruction must precede utopian reform, so most sensible humans reject even the thought of such painful and radical changes.

Burroughs began his first book, *Dejah Thoris, Princess of Mars*, in 1911 with the hero, John Carter, going to sleep on Earth under the influence of drugs and waking up in a new and more exciting world, a Bellamite device readers of American utopian literature will recognize. The fantasy world of Mars, or "Barsoom," is the setting for a whole series of books which fascinated generations of adolescent readers, as later fantasy worlds have captivated the Trekkies and Duneites of the 1980s. While the settings and history of Barsoom are only incidental for Burroughs, part of the machinery of his story, they build into a gloomy vision of dead cities and dying civilizations that comments on the futility of Earthly hopes of progress. This attitude is fully in harmony with the theme of mutability which dominated so much nineteenth-century American metahistorical, or mythic, thinking. . . .

The next year, 1912, Burroughs created what is perhaps the most artistically powerful conservative vision of utopia as a state or condition rather than as a society, the Tarzan theme. . . . To form the Tarzan theme Burroughs adopted two ideas from romantic naturalism—cultural primitivism and beneficial atavism—and added to them two other elements: first the typical romantic insistence that if a man (or occasionally a woman) or a culture were to benefit from a return to the primitive, he must be of the finest civilized stock, and second, the sentimental irony that once the perfect man had been formed in nature, he would be forever disappointed with civilization, and yet be unable to deny his responsibilities to it.

Of course, the Tarzan theme remained a type of cultural primitivism, in the classic sense as defined by Arthur O. Lovejoy—avoiding or fleeing civilization in favor of savagery or a romantic primevalism. But most of Burroughs's stories, including those about Tarzan, are as much pastoral—they seek resolution of the conflict between nature and human life—as they are primitive, and the conservative pastoral theme is most important. In history, as in religion, a feeling of freedom arises from conscious submission to what is felt as necessity.

The escape in Burroughs's tales is flight from contemporary urban complication, from modernism, into pastoral myth. The pastoral ideal is clear throughout the Tarzan books, but we can find it in perhaps purest form at the end of the first story, when Tarzan dreams of "a patch of greensward surrounded by a matted mass of gorgeous tropical plants and flowers," of "mighty trees," of "the blue of an equatorial sky," and above all of a young woman who sat beside him as they ate "pleasant fruit and looked into each other's eyes and smiled. They were very happy and they were all alone." In his longing for escape, as in so much else, Burroughs reflected the dreams of most of his fellow Americans, and the paradox they felt in expressing their individuality within an increasingly urban community which inevitably qualified individual freedom in the interest of an ideal of justice for all. Burroughs's stories are always conservative politically and socially. Once we recognize that, what seems the subversion of escape in the Tarzan stories is really a return to superior (and largely imaginary) traditional values and to an earlier, more vital stage of the inevitable process of history.

When Tarzan, John Carter, and all the other heroes of Burroughs's fiction bring change to the lost worlds they encounter, the change is to restore a lost order, to put a rightful prince back on the throne—and once the old order is restored, the hero leaves, headed back to his own static valley or peaceful kingdom. Burroughs's heroes never question the righteousness of the political and social order they support. It is always an aristocracy of the good, of the hero's friends, and that is enough.

In later Tarzan stories, the isolated plantation of Tarzan, operated by his faithful Waziri, provides a place apart where a pastoral middle ground between savagery and civilizations may be found. As the story of Tarzan continued, Burroughs gradually purified his theme until the average Tarzan story, like the later Barsoomian books, was deliberately about a static never-never land. Tarzan's African estates, in Burroughs's romances just as in the Hollywood films, became isolated utopias of natural peace where a paternal hero keeps a barbaric people in the early and virtuous stages of civilization until various forms of civilized viciousness intrude to provide plot conflict. The idea shows renewed popularity in such recent novels as *The Clan of the Cave Bear* (1980) and *The Dance of the Tiger* (1980), and in Burroughs's stories we simply see a particularly clear form of it. The cult has several parts. First, romantic conservatives since the time of James Fenimore Cooper have assigned the pioneer past responsibility for our present desirable traits, and wilderness, at least since the 1830s, has been symbolically the source of virtue. As a corollary, the savage who dwelt in the wilderness must be as virile and vital as the wilderness which engendered him. With the addition of popular social Darwinism at the end of the nineteeth century, the hero also naturally became full of fighting spirit, capable by definition of winning the battle for survival. Thus, the wilderness makes men good, and civilization makes them wicked, because in the wilderness men (seldom women) imbibe aesthetics and ethics from contemplation of the spirit of God as revealed in the woods, ocean, or desert. And the final point identifying the cult of the primtive is that the contrast between a wholesome life in the midst of nature and the complex degeneracies of civilization frequently serve to satirize urban life, in the ancient fashion of the pastoral.

The Tarzan story is certainly Burroughs's most popular expression of a pastoral utopia, but for an understanding of the conservative myth in science fiction another of Burroughs's successful series, his inner Earth or "Pellucidar" books, is more important. Burroughs wrote these stories early in his career—the first in 1914—when he still showed an easy faith in the American model for improving the world. In 1914, after all, it was still obvious (at least in pulp fiction) not only that the American Way was the best way, but also that it would be recognized as best by every right thinking tribesman who heard of it. Though the Pellucidar stories are swashbuckling pulp adventure, they are also typical early twentieth-century conservative utopias. In the typical fashion of conservative utopias, they substitute geographical change for the temporal change characteristic of liberal visions. If America is already nearly perfect, the best hope for improvement is to translate its best or true nature to some less enlightenened spot. Our generation chose to bring democracy and development to Viet Nam, and later to Grenada and Nicaragua, but for Burroughs the imaginary valley, island, or world—not the future—is the setting for utopian development. . . .

Throughout the Pellucidar series about the lost world inside our planet, Burroughs's heroes struggle to reform the savage world they discover into a bourgeois American colony, somewhat along the lines of American efforts in the Philippines a few years earlier. In the second novel of the Pellucidar series Burroughs makes his utopian intentions clear when his hero declares, "It will not be long before Pellucidar will become as nearly a Utopia as one may expect to find this side of

heaven." . . . And by the end of the story most of the problems have been resolved, all the lost princesses have been rescued, and we are invited to feel that our heroes' plan to establish an outpost of Oak Park in Pellucidar is well under way. . . .

A further clarification in Burroughs's utopian ideas occurred in 1915; while he was grinding out his fifth Tarzan story, he stumbled on what was to be his typical utopian device. The story eventually became *Tarzan and the Jewels of Opar,* an adventure leaning heavily on H. Rider Haggard plot ideas, with Burroughs's usual unscrupulous Arab slavers, villainous European renegades, lustful bull apes, and frustrated but hopeful carnivores all revolving around the long-lost Atlantean colony of Opar. . . . The exotic civilization in the lost valley has gone downhill since its pseudo-biblical origins, and it is this feature which shows Burroughs's typical metahistorical argument clearly: all civilizations are virile and moral in their youth, but senile and degenerate in their old age. This historical fatalism is part of the secularization of deuteronomic historical ideas in the late nineteenth century, found in high culture in Brooks and Henry Adams, just as in mass culture in Edgar Rice Burroughs. The process was seen as inevitable, though liberals saw it as progress and conservatives as decline.

In Burroughs's hands this myth is a corollary of the cult of the primitive; if nature makes us whole, then civilization will take us apart. Tarzan and Burroughs's other heroes hold civilization in contempt not only because of its immorality and ambiguity, but because the course of civilization is inevitably tragic as humanity moves from the purity of nature to the decadence of Byzantium. The lost valley of Opar dramatizes the nineteenth-century myth of Robert Coles's "Course of Empire" series for the pulp readers of the twentieth century, thus reinforcing the typical conservative suspicion of reform and of utopian hopes. Reformation might be temporarily successful, but real change could come only through apocalyptic destruction and a new barbarism.

To understand Burroughs's attempts to dispel the Spenglerian gloom into which he had stumbled, we might consider in some detail three utopian stories he wrote during and shortly after the Great War. These are *Beyond Thirty, The Moon Maid,* and *The Land That Time Forgot,* each of which shows a typical version of the persistently tragic conservative vision as exemplified in Burroughs's metahistory.

Beyond Thirty, which Burroughs wrote in 1915, is not likely to ring the bells of memory, even for those who read avidly in the Burroughs canon as they grew up, but it is a typical American isolationist reaction to the opening guns of the Great War, and incidentally one of Burroughs's closest approaches to conventional science fiction. It is set some year in our future when incessant warfare and chaos have caused the Western hemisphere, under the leadership of the United States, to sever all ties, including even historical memory, with Eurasia. Burroughs does not bother to describe the utopian institutions of the United States, except to make it clear that they are idealized versions of American institutions of 1914. This lack of social imagination should be no surprise, for a conservative can hope to restore or maintain but not to improve social institutions.

Jefferson Turck, the soldier-aristocrat protagonist, is the familiar pulp hero, though without the mythic dimensions of Tarzan or even John Carter. He commands an "aero-submarine" which patrols the thirtieth parallel, the boundary against intruders from the Old World of tainted Eurasia. In a storm his ship is forced ashore in England, and there Commander Turck discovers that most of Europe has degenerated into savagery under the stress of continual war. Large parts of Eurasia are divided between two opposing forces, a Christian conservative empire based in Ethiopia and a progressive, materialist Chinese empire.

Both the Ethiopians and the Chinese are sympathetically handled, though Burroughs cannot resist playing with the sexual-threat-to-white-women theme. Neither Ethiopians nor Chinese are perfect, but Burroughs clearly prefers either of them to the savage Europe which war has produced, and he prefers the rational scientism of the progressive Chinese, whose empire seems to be modelled on the pre-World War I Japanese, to the colorful barbarism of the reactionary Ethiopians, because the Chinese support science and social development, ideals which Burroughs usually praised though seldom successfully showed in action. Naturally Jefferson Turck prefers the technological and social progressivism of the Chinese too, and Burroughs lets him help the Chinese in their triumph over the Ethiopians.

Like other conservatives, Burroughs loved apocalyptic stories, and in 1919, after the war, when Russian Revolution replaced Teutonic imperialism as the Great Satan of conservatives, he began another pessimistic response to contemporary events in a series of connected tales which were eventually published as *The Moon Maid.* The story begins as a pulp fantasy of the peripatetic lunar adventures of Julian West—a hero whom the book specifically identifies as a descendent of Bellamy's hero in *Looking Backwards.* On the moon Julian discovers a totalitarian civilization of humanoids, and the usual Burroughs capture-escape-recapture plot begins cranking along, with plenty of imperiled virgins and hand-to-hand combat. Julian undergoes in a limited way the usual course of beneficial atavism, changing from an over-intellectual civilized man into an effective savage warrior. However, his development is not sufficient to defeat the Moon Men, who invade Earth with the assistance of a warped Terran scientist. The nations of the planet have been weakened by generations of peace, and Earth falls under the heel of a Lunar dictatorship.

At this point, Burroughs welded on a second novella, beginning a generation later than the unlucky lunar exploration of the first Julian. It is the story of life in the United States under the dominion of a speciously egalitarian lunar dictatorship and of the unsuccessful rebellion of old-fashioned Americans against their foreign oppressors. A new hero, descendant of the original Julian, leads the revolt, but Americans are insufficiently purified—many still fellow-travel with the Moon Men—and after the rebellion fails, America is reduced to a pastoral fief, whose inhabitants eventually degenerate to a collection of roving savages, culturally similar to the plains Indians of pulp fiction.

This cycle turns out to be America's salvation, because under pastoral conditions character returns. In the concluding section America rises under the leadership of still another Julian, and the remnant of the Moon Men, decayed after several generations of easy supremacy, is easily driven into the Pacific. Hope for the future may be entertained because love of pleasure, pacifism, and Los Angeles have been burned out of the savage remnant nation. *The Moon Maid* argues that only in the character of an Apache warrior is there hope for humans, because only such a hero can satisfy the fantasy of beneficial atavism and take bloody revenge on twentieth-century America for Burroughs and all his 200 million readers.

Red Hawk, twenty-first Julian West and triumphant hero of *The Moon Maid,* makes his system of warrior eugenics clear

enough, but to see how it permeates Burroughs's work, this is how Tarzan, his greatest (and in some ways gentlest) hero puts it: "Show me the fat, opulent coward who ever originated a beautiful ideal. In the clash of arms, in the battle for survival, amid hunger and death and danger, in the face of God as manifested in the display of Nature's most terrific forces, is born all that is finest and best in the human heart and mind." Thus *The Moon Maid* reverses the argument for social reform which most earlier cataclysmic fiction expresses. For example, Jack London's *The Iron Heel* and Ignatius Donnelly's *Caesar's Column* show even greater emphasis than Burroughs's stories on bloodshed and disaster, but they could at least be read as cautionary tales, while in Burroughs's fantasy, the utopian future is possible only for aristocratic warriors. He argues that pacifism and a too-eager egalitarianism will destroy rather than redeem civilization.

Though *The Moon Maid* and *Beyond Thirty* show Burroughs's conservative suspicions of hopes for social improvement, a third speculative fiction Burroughs ground out shortly after World War I reveals an even gloomier vision. This is one most readers will recognize, for Burroughs's *The Land That Time Forgot,* which first appeared as a magazine serial in 1918, is one of his better-known stories. The television version uses only the first part of the story, the adventurous entry into the lost world of Caspak and the battles with primitive monsters. In its full version *The Land That Time Forgot* dramatizes the poignant intellectual dilemma of conservatives in an original form, a dilemma from which Hollywood removed Burroughs's intellectual challenge to liberal hope and his evolutionary pessimism, for the sake of melodramatic adventure.

On the lost island of Caspak evolution operates as a present and individual force, not a ponderous and abstract theory. The creatures of Caspak advance individually through all the stages of evolution from egg to complete human being. On Caspak ontogeny recapitulates phylogeny not in the womb but on the surface of the island, and the lucky few rise through all the stages of chordates, living successively as reptiles, mammals, primates, and then humans—and even beyond, which is where the dystopian element enters.

Most of the dramatic action of Burroughs's story falls in the human stages of Caspakian life, for there he can work his chase-capture-escape mechanism most easily, but the theme of the story almost succeeds in overcoming the feeble romantic mechanisms. The problem of reconciling evolutionary determinism with romantic individualism exercised the whole generation of literary naturalists who immediately preceded Burroughs, and the pervasive concern for a synthesis of threatening scientific theory and comforting romantic belief appears on every page of *The Land That Time Forgot.* In tune with Burroughs's usual theme, individual prowess in savage combat shapes noble natures, leading to development of humans of the best type.

The fully evolved humans of Caspak are the Galu, Stone Age savages of the sort romantic primitivists adore. The Galu furnish some of the necessary heroines for the story, and their village is the setting for most of the conventional adventure, but another set of beings higher on the scale than humans live on Caspak too, for evolution and change do not stop—that is the real fear of conservatives and the fictional horror of Caspak. These higher beings are the Weiroo, a species Burroughs modelled on classic devils, with ghoulish admixtures. Like any good villains, they have powerful, though unspecified, mental abilities which put them above ordinary men, at least on the microcosmic island of Caspak. All are male, ugly, and vicious, and as usual in the pulp scheme, their primary activity is abducting female humans for their harems, thus providing sexual thrills and plot material. But their real interest comes from Burroughs's suggestions that the Weiroos are the logical successors to humanity—that they, or something like them, are what we are headed for in our next evolutionary ascension. Clearly, this biological dread remains a strong element in science fiction and fantasy today.

Burroughs created similar superhuman creatures in other pulp adventure series, and while to a large degree all of them are simply conventional pulp horror creatures, Burroughs persistently presents biological advances on humans as something more than accident; the Weiroos are the result of evolutionary logic. Most of the advanced societies in Burroughs's fiction are inhuman, built by and for creatures who have gone beyond humanity into ghoulish new species. . . . Other pulp stories in general are conservative too, and post-human evolution, social or physical, is seldom imagined in anything like positive terms. Perhaps the basic dissatisfaction ordinary readers feel with the whole direction of rational, instrumental, and "progressive" civilization can be seen in the Weiroos of Caspak just as clearly as in the endless tales of Tarzan.

The next time Burroughs chose a notable utopian theme was in 1922 with *Tarzan and the Ant Men,* a rare Burroughs story in which irony is allowed a significant role. Characteristically,

the satire is aimed not only at ideas for social reform but also at hopes of utopian perfection. On the surface the plot follows the lost valley formula. Tarzan, bored with his life on his utopian plantation, takes up flying and flies off alone from his secure jungle home and his loving, and by 1923 extensive, family. He flies over a part of the jungle he has never investigated before and crashes in an inaccessible valley.

In this valley, as in most of Burroughs's lost valleys, live two sets of people. Around the periphery, where Tarzan has crashed, dwell the Alali, a race of paleolithic savages, while in the broad central plain lies the domain of the Minuni, a race of barbaric white Lilliputians. The Alali, on the periphery, are dominated by their women—huge, powerful creatures. Tarzan is captured by one of them, escapes, trains an Alali male in natural masculine dominance, watches to see that his lesson will spread, and moves on. The episode is heavy-handed satire on feminism, or at least on a popular stereotype of it, but its role in the plot is typical of many other lost valley stories. The hero usually goes through some trial in a primitive tribe living on the edge of the romantic civilization which occupies most of the lost valley, and as he passes the trial he helps reform the savage tribe into a more "natural" cultural pattern, thus often releasing the natural vigor which their primitive life has given them. Many similar episodes in other stories show that Burroughs was a member in good standing of the conservative male chauvinist faction of his day. . . .

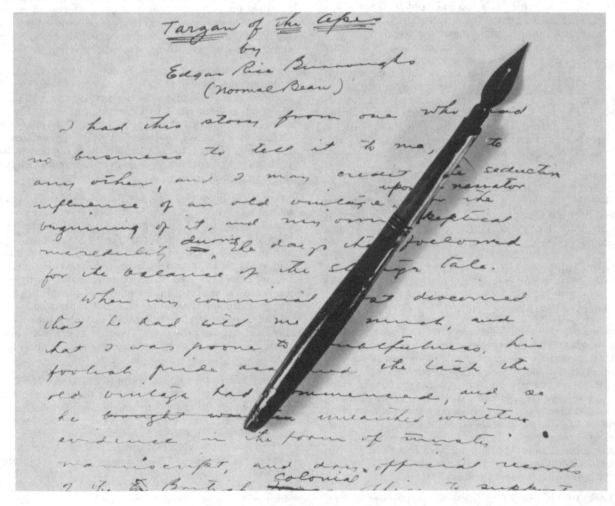

First manuscript page of Tarzan of the Apes.

Perhaps it was because Burroughs had so much fun satirizing the social absurdity of matriarchy that he also made the next component of the formula, Tarzan's adventures with the more civilized race in the center of the valley, an extensive satire on American society of his day. After serving as a cultural catalyst for the primitive but perverted Alali, Tarzan moves out in the grassy plain which fills the center of the valley. There live the Minuni, a handsome race of white midgets only seventeen inches high, who ride about the plain on small antelope. They live in domed cities, like African termites, and their culture is a rough mixture of Formican communalism and romantic feudalism. There are several cities in the lost valley, but the only two Tarzan has much to do with are Veltopismakus, which has been ruined by luxury and faulty democratic ideas, and Trohandalmakus, whose citizens work hard and efficiently. The familiar elements of Swiftian satire appear in the story, and Burroughs attacks such common conservative bugaboos as government corruption, prohibition, and the new income tax.

All this gives a political dimension to the story, and Burroughs adds more general conservative shibboleths too; for example, a policy of positive eugenics is credited with creating the moral superiority of Trohandalmakus, while indiscriminate breeding undermines both the morality and the efficiency of Veltopismakus. Unfortunately, Burroughs lacked patience for the intricate coordination of fiction and reality which satire requires, and the plot soon deteriorates into his usual capture-escape sequence. A mythic hero like Tarzan is obviously out of place in a satiric setting, so Tarzan is "scientifically" reduced to Minunian scale, opening the gate to more swashing on the buckler.

Despite its limitations as a political novel, *Tarzan and the Ant Men* emphasized Burroughs's suspicion of organized political solutions to social problems, and indeed his suspicion of any change. Veltopismakus, the good society of the story, attains its virtue by deliberate return to an aristocratic warrior ethos, while the obvious fault of the bad society of Trohandalmakus lies in its attempt to alter the forms of society from traditional patterns.

Burroughs's clearest treatment of utopian hopes appeared during the uneasy years of the 1930s, when he found his personal and professional problems echoed the national agonies of the depression years. His family, which had always been important to him, began to disintegrate and at the same time his professional life became less secure because his fiction sold less readily to magazines. Science fiction was replacing scientific romance in the pulps, and the new science fiction writers had a flair for the unusual supported by the logical beyond anything Burroughs could attempt. His two best ideas—beneficial atavism and sword-and-science Barsoom—were anachronisms in a pulp industry which had fragmented into hard-hitting mysteries, grim-lipped Westerns, and chromium-plated stories of outer space. Burroughs responded with a series full of stronger satiric and dystopian elements than he had displayed earlier. This set of stories occurs on an imaginary Venus which Burroughs calls "Amtor," a world where gigantic forests replace the sprawling deserts of the original Barsoomian series. While Burroughs did not bother to rework his plots—he still followed the old chase-capture-escape routine—the new setting allowed him to express a number of more or less good natured satires on the political and social ideas of the political left.

In the Amtorian series the conservative political function of the Burroughs hero becomes even clearer. Many of the plots—

and Burroughs's later fiction is even more profligate of plot than his earlier stories—turn on the hero leading a sort of counterrevolution in each new society he visits. The counterrevolution is aimed at restoring a responsible and aristocratic social order to the place of power it had held before the irresponsible and greedy reformers overthrew it in the name of one ideology or another. The hero either decides to fight against the current false government because of his sense of American justice or he is forced into opposition by the egregious attacks of the foolish dictators he meets. Burroughs's hero Carson Napier is always a counterrevolutionary, struggling against a corrupt ideological system, and he always restores to power a virtuous representative of the previous legitimate oligarchy.

Obvious attacks on totalitarian ideologies fill the series. In the first book, *Pirates of Venus,* a group of uglies called the Thorists are the villains. They are primitive communists who serve as a convenient vehicle through whom Burroughs can share his staunchly conservative antipathies, but they are so obviously villainous that they are even less interesting than the new varieties of that favorite Burroughs creation, the giant spider, which dangle from every branch of the enormous trees in the Amtorian forest. In the third story, *Carson of Venus,* the other end of the political spectrum, the Nazis, is parodied in a gang of clumsy totalitarians named "Zanis." The Thorists and the Zanis show Burroughs's healthy dislike of ideologies which exaggerate the inevitable restrictions civilization places on freedom in the name of a specious common good, but they make dull villains. The second book, *Lost on Venus,* is more interesting because Burroughs for the first time faces the issue of a society which honestly and intelligently attempts perfection. This is the city of Havatoo.

Burroughs tries hard to imagine Havatoo as a deliberately planned, highly technological, civilized utopia. The city is a technocracy, with merit the only source of preferment, and good behavior the only measure of virtue. It is ruled by a council of scientists who are selected on merit. The major concern of its citizens seems to be proper breeding, because Havatoo is a society of eugenicists, seeking to breed out of humanity the savagery, violence, selfishness, and passion which Burroughs's fiction had always depended on. Like many other utopias, Havatoo is presented as a reasonable, placid society, but at the same time Burroughs makes it clear that the society represents the public values of civilization he had invented Tarzan to avoid. The appeal of Havatoo, which is an island of security and peace on a planet of constant battle and danger, creates a new problem for Carson Napier, Burroughs's indecisive hero. Carson must do more than simply avoid capture or plan an escape; he must evaluate a complex social ideal and decide whether to remain in Havatoo or to continue his quest for the savage kingdom of his Amtorian princess, Duare.

Of course, in a heroic romance there is no real choice: Carson has to continue the quest for his princess. There are professional objections to utopia: once the innocence of Eden (Tarzan's youth, as presented in *Jungle Tales of Tarzan*) is reestablished in the New Jerusalem (Havatoo), history—and profitable fictional adventure—ends. But the plot explanation simply provides a device Burroughs uses to avoid admitting the appeal of his own utopian invention. Burroughs had for decades built strong eugenicist views into his stories; then in Havatoo he creates a society of thoroughgoing eugenicists, only to discover that he didn't like it, for the deliberate equality of utopia denied the freedom from social responsibility which powered all his fantasies. In order to exorcise the positive utopian appeal he had accidentally created in Havatoo, Burroughs falls back on an ancient resource of suspicious conservatives confronted by a presumed utopia, and he has his hero discover that the ideals of Havatoo are only a pious cover for its repression of the adventurous spirit so important to romantic fiction. Though the citizens of the city are content, they are not fully awake, and so not only has Havatoo failed as a utopia, but because of its parochial pride in its system it is also a danger to other societies. Burroughs's Havatoo is the perfection of civilization, a perfectly planned and scientifically operated society which does not realize that it has come to deny the human values it was originally designed to cherish. The society thus fits the definition of dystopia, "a systematic intensification of all the repressive restraints of actual civilization" [Gorman Beauchamp, "Cultural Primitivism as Norm in the Dystopian Novel"]. The "repressive restraints" of civilization are exactly what the dream of Tarzan allowed 200 million readers to escape.

This analysis may seem a heavy burden to place on pulp fiction. After all, Burroughs wrote only to entertain and to sell stories. Of his intellectual processes, he declared, "I like long silences in my own thoughts." He was always puzzled and mildly resentful about any claims for "ideas" or "meanings" which his stories might reveal, because he always claimed to write stories "which I feel would entertain me and give me mental relaxation." Yet without fully intending to, he tackled many of the issues that during the same years occupied such writers as Edward Bellamy, Austin Wright, H. G. Wells, and Samuel Butler. Burroughs wrote stories about the value of an individual in relation to society, the value of progress, the problems and possibilities of advanced technologies, humans' relation to their environment, the proper role of religion, sexual and class politics, and a hundred other typically utopian concerns. In each fictional case, what could have been the glorious beginning of a progressive new order proves instead a degenerate dead end, and utopia is clearly not worth its apocalyptic cost. It is a belief which Ernest Callenbach's *Ecotopia* and Marge Piercy's *Woman on the Edge of Time* deny, but conservative utopias like Larry Niven and Jerry Pournelle's *Oath of Fealty* accept, and a debate which continues in almost all science fiction stories that create alternative visions for human futures. For example, a recent work like William Gibson's very successful *Neuromancer* opens the old debate anew.

Burroughs's apocalyptic pessimism in his most imaginative years suggests that apocalypse and utopia are necessary psychological complements in our national fantasies—something which liberal utopians often forget. The apocalypse is necessary to destroy the power of the old faulted civilization, and while the hope of utopia is necessary to justify the horror of the apocalypse, the promise ought not to be believed, because real progress—which involves change and danger—is impossible. Cain, the founder of cities, is still cursed, and only the dream of a return to the Garden can endure. Burroughs's metahistory is entirely in the conservative spirit, an original demotic Spengler and Toynbee packaged for clerks and railroad men, dramatizing the fatalistic view that history is tragic, that any Golden Age cannot last, and that while all civilizations have grandeur, and perhaps some even a glory that can outlast them, we can see in their ruins the vanity of human wishes. Contemplation of the great drama of tragic history had served to evoke pity and awe in generations of conservative romantics before Burroughs, and he agreed with their gloomy prognosis for civilization, despite his recurrent desire for some way out of the inevitable tragic decline. He could never succeed in transcending metahistorical fatalism by a renewal of belief in the pos-

sibility of freedom and justice for all, the belief which is the core of utopian (as opposed to dystopian) vision. (pp. 221-32)

Michael Orth, "Utopia in the Pulps: The Apocalyptic Pastoralism of Edgar Rice Burroughs," in Extrapolation, *Vol. 27, No. 3, Fall, 1986, pp. 221-33.*

BRIAN W. ALDISS   (essay date 1986)

[*A British author and critic best known for his science fiction, Aldiss was a major force in science fiction's "new wave" movement during the 1960s. Like other proponents of the movement, Aldiss maintains that science fiction should not be thought of as a single mode of literature but as a varied, developing hybrid of many literary forms. Aldiss's efforts to extend the boundaries of science fiction have garnered him most of the genre's literary prizes and awards for both fiction and criticism. In the following excerpt from his study* Trillion Year Spree: The History of Science Fiction *(1986), Aldiss discusses Burroughs's fiction as a reflection of his psychological idiosyncrasies and unfavorably compares his work to that of H. G. Wells.*]

All Burroughs's novels are vaguely similar, wherever they are set, heroes and incidents being often transposable, as clips of crocodile fights were transposed from one Tarzan movie to the next. After his first burst of creativity, from 1912-14, when Barsoom, Tarzan and Pellucidar appear, Burroughs strings sequels on to these three kites. Since his characters are almost characterless—little but exotic names—they experience nothing of the difficulties of personality with which we all wrestle in real life. ERB specialized in unreal life. His novels offer to a remarkable degree every facility for identifying with the hero and daydreaming through his triumphs.

No harm in such facility, perhaps; but self-exploration is at least as important as self-indulgence, and there is always the possibility of becoming permanently drugged by such brightly coloured pipe dreams.

What, finally, are we to make of ERB, that supreme example of the dichotomy of taste, between critics who see no virtue in him, and fans who see no fault?

One peculiar feature of Burroughs's output is the frequency with which mystery surrounds birth. The lead figures in the major series all have oddities attending their infancy, except for David Innes. This is most extreme in the hero of the best series, John Carter of Mars, who could almost pass for Ayesha after a sex-change. Carter recalls no childhood, has always been adult, and remains at about the age of thirty. Other instances of children, like Tarzan, lost to or estranged from parents, are many. A comic example is the eponymous cave girl in a lesser series which begins with *The Cave Girl* . . . ; she is revealed to be the daughter of a vanished count and countess. The women of Mars, like the women of Caspak, are oviparous; in other terms, children are born away from or rejected by their mothers, rather as Tarzan is fostered by an inhuman creature.

Was there confusion as well as an attempt to glamourize his own origins in ERB's statement that "I was born in Peking at the time that my father was military adviser to the Empress of China, and lived there, in the Forbidden City, until I was ten years old.'"? (*Edgar Rice Burroughs, Fiction Writer*)

Sexual dimorphism is common in Burroughs's world. The hideous males of Opar in the Tarzan series differ markedly from the beautiful females. (Though in *Tarzan and the Ant Men* it is the females, the Alalis, who are hideous because they have achieved sexual dominance.)

Despite a considerable amount of nudity in ERB's novels, sexual intercourse is neither mentioned nor implied; we might be in a prepubertal world. This is bowing to more than the literary conventions of the times. Thuvia, maid of Mars, spends fifteen years as a "plaything and a slave" of the egregious White Martians, and runs around naked to boot, yet survives to flaunt her virginity in the very title of the novel!

Yet the *danger* of sex is always there. One industrious critic, Richard D. Mullen [see Additional Bibliography], has calculated the omnipresence of the threat of rape in Burroughs's world, and found female virtue in danger no less than an obsessive seventy-six times in the novels written between 1911 and 1915! The menaces include a marvellously miscegenously-inclined throng of apes, usurers, black sultans, Negroes, green, white, and yellow Martians, cavemen, hairy men, orangoutangs, and Japanese head-hunters. In every case, chastity is successfully preserved.

In Carl Jung's *Memories, Dreams, Reflections,* Jung recounts the vivid psychosis of one of his female patients, who believed that she had lived on the Moon. She told Jung a tale about her life there. It appears that the Moon people were threatened with extinction. A vampire lived in the high mountains of the Moon. The vampire kidnapped and killed women and children, who in consequence had taken to living underground. The patient resolved to kill the vampire but, when she and it came face to face, the vampire revealed himself as a man of unearthly beauty.

Jung makes a comment which could stand on the title page of this book: "Thereafter I regarded the sufferings of the mentally ill in a different light. For I had gained insight into the richness and importance of their inner experience." Without imputing mental illness to Burroughs, I believe that Jung provides a key to fantasy writing in general, and to the echoing of themes. He does illuminate something compulsive and repetitive in Burroughs's output.

It is idle to protest that the Burroughs books depart from facts—that an oviparous woman is a contradiction in terms, that Mars has no breathable atmosphere, that a child raised by apes would be incapable of learning human language when older, that Venus rotates and is intolerably hot, that a sun inside Earth would turn it into a nuclear bonfire, and so on. Burroughs is not interested in the facts of the external world.

As one critic has observed, by this blindness Burroughs throws away advantages—for instance, by not preserving the distinction that Lowell clearly made between old Martian sea beds and barren plateaux, thus forfeiting a sharper realization of his Barsoom. But Burroughs was reporting from his own internal Pellucidar. Burroughs's Mars, like Ray Bradbury's later Mars, reports on areas which cannot be scrutinized through any telescope.

A failure to make a simple distinction between two sorts of vision, the Wellsian and the Burroughsian, or the analytic and the fantastic, bedevils all criticism, especially SF criticism—as well it might, for the distinction is particularly hard to draw in science fiction. Lowell's Mars—in its time the latest factual study science could produce—is now itself as much a fantasy world as Barsoom.

Comparing a Wells and a Burroughs novel makes the distinction between the strategies plain. It happens both authors published novels in 1923.

In *Men Like Gods,* one of Wells's little men, a Mr. Barnstaple, drives his car into the fourth dimension, there to find a utopia of beautiful, powerful, and frequently nude people. With him is a diverse group of his contemporaries who do their best to wreck the utopia. Barnstaple defeats them with utopian aid, and eventually returns through the dimensional barrier, back to the real world.

Pellucidar, after a brief prologue intended to establish the "reality" of what follows, is the story of a world at the hollow centre of the Earth, where David Innes searches for his lady love. He is reunited with her after many strange adventures, travelling through savage country populated by monsters and primitive creatures.

Described like this, the two novels sound not dissimilar. Both are fantasies, both use people as symbols, both have their excitements. Yet their differences are many.

The fourth dimension is about as unlikely as a hollow earth, and Barnstaple's adventures no more probable than Innes's. However, Wells's fantasy device, the fourth dimension, serves merely to lead us to his utopia. The utopia is so much the thing, that the feasibility of the device which gets us there does not much matter, provided it is dealt with briefly and interestingly. On the other hand, Burroughs's Inner World is the whole story, and the narrative is largely taken up with the stones and arrows loosed there, and the fangs and claws bred there.

Burroughs's characters are exotic and bear strange and beautiful names, of which perhaps the best is Pellucidar itself. Barnstaple is allowed his handle "Mr." throughout, while the characters he is involved with are based on real politicians of the day, such as Balfour and Winston Churchill.

Action in *Men Like Gods* is leisurely. There is plenty of time for discussion, which mainly consists of contrasting our world unfavourably with utopia and airing Wells's ideas about world government. In *Pellucidar,* events move fast; one threat succeeds another, one scrape succeeds another; conversation is practically limited to threats, or to explanations of what has happened or is about to happen. Incident is all-too-frequent, but plot is non-existent.

When Barnstaple returns in his battered old car to our world, it is a recognizable dull world of hotels with waitresses serving tea, the *Daily Express, The Times,* chat about Poland, the Chinese, and sport. Our world in *Pellucidar* is represented by a telegram from Algiers, the finding of a mysterious telegraphic instrument buried in the Sahara, a call to action!

In short, Wells's is a serious tale, enlivened by a little humour. Its aim is to discuss entertainingly ways in which mankind might improve itself and its lot. Burroughs's story is fantasy adventure without structure which we do not for one minute take seriously.

The publishing history of the two novels is also interestingly in contrast. Wells's novel was published in hard-cover in 1923 and only achieved paperback publication forty-seven years later. Burroughs's novel was serialized in *All-Story Cavalier Weekly* in 1915, to appear in hard-cover in 1923, since when it has made many paperback appearances.

Which of the two is the "better" book? If the question has any meaning, my answer would be that *Pellucidar* is the better. If one's choice of company lies between a fatigued schoolmaster and an inspired anecdotalist, the better bet is the anecdotalist.

Burroughs, in this novel, writes about as well as he can write, not well but serviceably, while his fertile imagination pours out lavishly the details of his preposterous world. Wells appears constipated beside him. Wells's novel is laborious, and, whatever it was in 1923, takes an effort to read now. Burroughs still slips down easily. With Burroughs you have (moderate) fun; Wells here gives off what Kingsley Amis categorizes as "a soporific whiff of left-wing crankiness."

So why does one obstinately respect Wells the more? It must be because, whatever else his failings, Wells is trying to grapple with what he sees as the real world. Burroughs, however expertly, is dishing out daydreams.

Wells does not expect anyone to identify with his stuffy little central character; Barnstaple is just an ordinary fellow, not held up particularly for approval or ridicule. The characters who surround him are mildly satirized, though no grotesques. This may account for the reason why Wells was never a popular author as popular authors go, liable to speak of his work as "that particular brand of deathless literature of which I am guilty," as Burroughs did. All Burroughs's main characters can claim the old title "hero"—not only in the Pellucidar novels but in all the other Burroughs series, Tarzan's jungles, Napier's Venus, Carter's Mars. Burroughs wants us to identify, to sink into his dream countries and exclude the outside one.

Wells is teaching us to think. Burroughs and his lesser imitators are teaching us not to think.

Of course, Burroughs is teaching us to wonder. The sense of wonder is in essence a religious state, blanketing out criticism. Wells was always a critic, even in his most romantic and wondrous tales.

And there, I believe, the two poles of modern fantasy stand defined. At one pole wait Wells and his honourable predecessors such as Swift; at the other, Burroughs and the commercial producers, such as Otis Adelbert Kline, and the weirdies, and horror merchants such as H. P. Lovecraft, and so all the way past Tolkien to today's non-stop fantasy worlders. Mary Shelley stands somewhere at the equator of this metaphor.

At the thinking pole stand great figures, although it is easy to write badly. At the dreaming pole stand no great figures—though there are monstrous figures—and it is difficult to write well. In the eighties, the dreaming pole is in the ascendant.

Although reading is primarily for pleasure, one should try to be pleased by whatever rewards with the highest pleasure. A swimming pool is a poor place in which to swim when there is a great ocean near by. Unless, of course, you are slightly afraid of the water. . . .

Burroughs, in his proliferating series and sequels, is one of the most commercially successful authors of this century, certainly the most commercially successful science fantasy author. His sales continue. His influence has been immense, and often damaging. . . .

ERB's stories are much like Westerns, and the Chicago in which he was born still retained elements of a frontier town. The vanishing redskin was not far away in space or time. Burroughs often wrote about him, directly or indirectly; his writings are a welter of racial fantasy—even Tar-Zan means White Skin in the language of the apes.

Burroughs fits very neatly into Leslie Fiedler's synthesis of the myths which give a special character to art and life in America. Fiedler's synthesis culminates in *The Return of the Vanishing American*. The one passage in that volume which deigns to mention Burroughs is so apropos to the hordes of odd-coloured and shaped creatures which were about to descend on twentieth-century man via science fiction that it deserves quotation.

Fiedler, putting his case against the American male, shows how the image of a white girl tied naked to a stake while redskins dance howling round her appeals to both our xenophobia and a sense of horror. Often such images were used as crude magazine illustrations.

> And, indeed, this primordial image has continued to haunt pulp fiction ever since (often adorning the covers of magazines devoted to it); for it panders to that basic White male desire at once to relish and deplore, vicariously share and publicly condemn, the rape of White female innocence. To be sure, as the generations go by, the colour of her violators has changed, though that of the violated woman has remained the same: from the Red of the Indians with whom it all began, to the Yellow of such malign Chinese as Dr. Fu Manchu, the Black of those Africans who stalk so lubriciously through the pages of Edgar Rice Burroughs's Tarzan books, or the Purple or Green Martians who represent the crudest fantasy level of science fiction.

This theory does not hold water—or rather, holds more water than Fiedler thinks, for Sax Rohmer, the creator of Dr. Fu Manchu, was an Englishman, and . . . two most likely sources of Burroughs's Mars lie in *Gulliver of Mars* and *She*, both written by Englishmen. Americans are not alone in obsessional fears about sex and colour. Indeed such fears are also observed in deepest Africa. Suffice it to say that Pocahontas and Ayesha really started something. With those mother-figures, the guilts of their respective doomed continents merge. Burroughs let the spectral Red/Black/Yellow/Green men into SF, and they have been on the warpath ever since—all the way to the stars on zitidars. (pp. 160-66)

> *Brian W. Aldiss, "From Barsoom to beyond the Borderlands: Swords, Sorceries and Zitidars," in his* Trillion Year Spree: The History of Science Fiction, *Atheneum Publishers, 1986, pp. 155-74.*

STEFAN R. DZIEMIANOWICZ (essay date 1988)

[*Dziemianowicz is an American critic and editor. In the following excerpt, he provides a retrospective overview of the Tarzan series.*]

Burroughs had things he wished to say about the innate nobility of mankind and the good and bad effects wrought upon man's nature by civilization. So, in his third novel, *Tarzan of the Apes,* he took equal parts of the myths of Romulus and Remus, Kipling's *Jungle Book,* together with popular legends of the "noble savage," and distilled them into a single character. And he built a plot around this character by doing what he did best—telling a good yarn.

The story of Tarzan, the child of noble English blood who is raised to manhood by a family of apes, is so familiar that many people who have never read the book *Tarzan of the Apes* are unaware that it begins as just that, a good yarn:

> I had this story from one who had no business to tell it to me, or to any other. I may credit the seductive influence of an old vintage upon the narrator for the

beginning of it and my own skeptical incredulity during the days that followed for the balance of the strange tale.

With these two sentences, Burroughs created the perfect context for his fabulous story: on the one hand they are used to disavow any authorial responsibility for the story's truthfulness—the narrator is telling a tale got second-hand that becomes even more remote from its source when he gives Tarzan's family the pseudonym of Greystoke to protect their true identity. On the other hand, the two sentences also express concisely two complementary facets of human nature: the inescapable curiosity to listen to a story and the equally inescapable desire to tell one. Both inclinations meet head on in a moment of weakness that might be called a typical display of human nature. Questions about strengths and weaknesses of human nature, and how they set man apart from other creatures are what lie at the heart of *Tarzan of the Apes.*

Initially, it would seem that Burroughs equated savagery with strength and civility with weakness. As a child among the apes, Tarzan first perceives himself as a weakling because he does not have the brute characteristics of his ape brothers. He would like nothing more than to be an ape, not the scrawny white monkey he appears to be. Yet, as surely as the civilized moral virtues displayed by Tarzan's father, John Clayton, are what save him and his wife, Alice, during the savage mutiny at the story's beginning, so does Tarzan quickly learn to use virtues of civilization to master the savage jungle. They are, so to speak, in his blood.

To overcome his comparative physical weakness, Tarzan learns to use tools like the noose and the knife. He teaches himself the intricacies of the English language, and his ingenuity vaults him over the beasts. But it is his fundamental and ineradicable sense of right and wrong that ultimately lifts him above the level of King of the Apes to become a true "Lord" of the jungle. And when he finally meets with human beings in the second half of the book, we see that his rough primitive life has so sharpened his noble intellect and instincts that he is a human being superior to most of those whom he encounters.

The actions of "civilized" human beings are a constant source of bemusement to Tarzan, but also a source of pain, because at the same time Tarzan rightly rejects much of what he sees in other men, he realizes that unless he embraces it to some degree, he is destined to be forever alone, trapped somewhere between civilization and the jungle. The law of the jungle and the understanding that has helped man to rise above it are the two extremes which Tarzan must choose between, and, as the unexpected ending of the novel indicates, it is not an easy choice.

Regardless of the moral Burroughs instilled into his story, *Tarzan of the Apes* is first and foremost a tale of adventure. The book takes place in the jungle not only because it was the best setting for Burroughs to get across what he wished to say, but also because the jungle was wild and exotic, a source of unlimited imaginative potential for adventure writers in the early twentieth century. The jungle gave Burroughs the raw material to create his wonderful animal society, conceived along the same lines as human society. It also gave him a setting where a human could break free of the restraints of society, swing through trees like an ape, and even bellow a bloodcurdling cry after a kill.

This was the essence of the type of daydream Burroughs and other authors supplied to readers of the pulp magazines. . . . (pp. vii-ix)

Another element that pulp writers like Burroughs supplied to their fans were character types familiar to readers of the day. Such stereotypes could be identified with, laughed at, or held in contempt, but they always provided readers with a recognizable point of reference, no matter how far removed the adventure was from the everyday world. Though Burroughs has received criticism for unflattering ethnic and racial stereotypes, it should be noted that in *Tarzan of the Apes,* almost no one comes off looking completely unblemished except the title character. Burroughs distributed his scenes of savagery equally among the black cannibals and the white mutineers, and his comic views of human foibles among black domestics and no less eminent a man than Archimedes Q. Porter, Tarzan's somewhat egg-headed future father-in-law. If one considers the Tarzan stories as a single long saga, one finds that Burroughs created good guys and bad guys of every race, color, and creed. He saw conduct not as specific to a demographic category, but to a particular kind of personality.

Burroughs did not set out to write "literature." He wrote page-turners, and it does his work a disservice to single out from it caricatures that are found in much of the popular literature of the time, or to take an unflattering portrayal of a member of a minority or religious group out of its narrative context. It is more enriching and relevant to dwell on the thoughtful mind that could render the poignant scene in which Tarzan happens upon the remains of his true parents and doesn't realize it, or our final view of Tarzan as he demonstrates his humanity most fully by renouncing it altogether.

The ending of *Tarzan of the Apes* suggests that Burroughs did not intend to continue the saga, and yet acclaim was so overwhelming that he was compelled to continue for another twenty-three books. Having firmly established Tarzan's character and his hedged preference for the jungle over civilization in the first Tarzan story, Burroughs used the later novels to show how Tarzan's personality gave rise naturally to heroic adventures. (pp. ix-x)

[*The Son of Tarzan* is the fourth book in the series.] It follows *The Return of Tarzan,* in which Tarzan thwarts the sinister intentions of two Russians, Nikolas Rolkoff and Alexis Paulvitch, and finally marries Jane Porter. That leads, naturally, to the birth of the son of Tarzan, Jack Clayton, who is kidnapped by Rolkoff and Paulvitch in *The Beasts of Tarzan*, but rescued by Tarzan with the help of Akut the ape. Jack Clayton had actually appeared even earlier in one of Burrough's many non-Tarzan books, *The Eternal Lover*. . . . In that book, Burroughs made Tarzan a model of domesticity and had him fade into the background of someone else's adventure—a consequence of the civilized life, perhaps. This is the same portrait of Tarzan we see at the beginning of *The Son of Tarzan,* and his seeming normalcy is the epitome of the kind of life Jack Clayton wishes to escape.

So in *The Son of Tarzan,* Burroughs wrote *Tarzan of the Apes* in reverse. He had the English schoolboy, Jack, meet up with the ape, Akut, whom he liberates from the clutches of Paulvitch. Next, Jack masters the primitive tongue and escapes into the African jungle. He sheds his clothing and his civilized veneer to learn how to become a wise savage in the jungle, and he is finally given a name in the ape tongue—Korak, the Killer. Can anyone doubt that Jack will, like his father before him, meet the woman of his dreams, and that the story will turn on noble human impulses overcoming baser instincts to save the day?

But Jack is not quite a carbon copy of his father. If anything, the childish petulance that got him into trouble with his teachers gets him into more than one scrape that even a younger Tarzan would have avoided. Jack's jungle experience helps him to grow out of his natural adolescent wildness and shows him the importance of being a responsible adult like his father. The final chapters of the book, in which Jack and Tarzan work together to thwart Ali ben Kadin and to rescue Jack's girlfriend, Meriem, reveal *The Son of Tarzan* to be a touching treatment of an idea that predates Burroughs—and all writers for that matter: that the boy who grows up wanting to be anything *but* like his father eventually realizes his father is someone worthy of admiration. (pp. x-xii)

[As] much as the Tarzan books were masterpieces of . . . escapism, it's an inescapable fact that they were written over a period of time marked by important historical events. Between the first magazine publication of *Tarzan of the Apes* and the last Tarzan novel, *Tarzan and the Castaways,* in 1947, the globe was rocked by two world wars and other social upheavals, the consequences of which are still very much with us today. Burroughs was not oblivious to what was happening in the real world. In his last years, he personally witnessed the bombing of Pearl Harbor and was an accredited correspondent during World War II, but he had been incorporating real history into his fiction long before that.

In the seventh Tarzan book, *Tarzan the Untamed,* Jane is kidnapped by (and, of course, ultimately rescued from) German soldiers fighting in the East African campaign of World War I, and, in the sequel, *Tarzan the Terrible,* it is revealed that Jack, the son of Tarzan, fought at the battle of Argonne. (Not surprisingly, Burroughs's books were burned by the Nazis.) In *Tarzan and the Foreign Legion,* Tarzan joins the Royal Air Force and battles the Japanese occupation troops in Sumatra. Between the two world wars, Burroughs wrote the fifteenth Tarzan book, *Tarzan the Triumphant.* . . . Here we see two of the author's darkest villains, Leon Stabutch, a Stalinist cast in the mold of Rokoff and Paulvitch; and Dominic Capietro, a man so reviled that he was actually chased out of Mussolini's Italy by the Fascists.

It is not by accident that Stabutch and Capietro are lumped together on the same side of the fence as the Midianites, a culturally backward race of inbred religious zealots. Breeding and birth are dominant themes in the Tarzan books, from the early misunderstanding in *Tarzan of the Apes* that Tarzan may be the offspring of an ape and a man, through Jona's intention to kill herself in *Tarzan at the Earth's Core* if forced into a "miscegenated" match with a man from a race other than her own. In *Tarzan the Triumphant,* the Midianites stand as the terrifying opposite to the purity of Tarzan's own bloodline. Just as Tarzan stands for all that is strong and noble about man, the Midianites are the most weak and ignoble—superstitious and intolerant tyrants. In Burroughs's books, tyrants are tyrants, regardless of their race or creed, and tyrants like Stabutch and the slave raider Capietro, he seems to be saying, are little better than deformed monsters like the Midianites.

It would have been easy for Burroughs to adopt an attitude of racial superiority, but even here he holds out a chance for salvation in the character of Jezebel, a child of the Midianites who is both beautiful and innocent of their ways, and who stands as evidence that every race can produce good. This idea is reflected more comically, on a class level, in the pairing of the Runyonesque Chicago gangster Danny "Gunner" Patrick with another of Burroughs's amusing academics, Lafayette

Smith. Both separately and together, this unlikely pair learn to overcome their worst inclinations and habits and draw on resources they never imagined they had. Although *Tarzan the Triumphant* is the story of how Tarzan helps rescue Jezebel, the Gunner, Smith, and the downed flyer, Lady Barbara Collis, these other characters nearly run away with the plot. And rightly so—it's not Tarzan who needs to be shown what he could be if he just showed a little more strength of character. (pp. xiv-xvi)

Burroughs reinvented Tarzan's adventures to match the changing times he lived in, but he never had to change what was at the core of Tarzan's nature—that which was most admirable about the human species. (p. xvi)

> *Stefan R. Dziemianowicz, in an introduction to* Tarzan of the Apes: Four Volumes in One *by Edgar Rice Burroughs, edited by Claire Booss, Avenel Books, 1988, pp. vii-xvi.*

ADDITIONAL BIBLIOGRAPHY

Bleiler, E. F. "Edgar Rice Burroughs." In *Science Fiction Writers,* edited by E. F. Bleiler, pp. 59-64. New York: Charles Scribner's Sons, 1982.
    Biographical and critical essay.

Clareson, Thomas D. "Lost Lands, Lost Races: A Pagan Princess of Their Very Own." In *Many Futures, Many Worlds: Theme and Form in Science Fiction,* edited by Thomas D. Clareson, pp. 117-39. Kent, Ohio: The Kent State University Press, 1977.
    Discusses Burroughs's contribution to the form of the "lost race" novel as popularized during the late nineteenth century by British author H. Rider Haggard.

Farmer, Philip José. *Tarzan Alive: A Definitive Biography of Lord Greystoke.* Garden City, N.Y.: Doubleday, 1972, 312 p.
    A humorous biographical treatment of Burroughs's Tarzan character based loosely upon events from the Tarzan novels.

Fenton, Robert W. *The Big Swingers.* Englewood Cliffs, N.J.: Prentice-Hall, 1967, 258 p.
    An early and somewhat superficial unauthorized account of Burroughs's life and work.

Heins, Henry Hardy. *A Golden Anniversary Bibliography of Edgar Rice Burroughs.* West Kingston, R.I.: Donald M. Grant, 1964, 418 p.
    Details the publication of Burroughs's works. Heins also offers useful and interesting biographical information about Burroughs.

Holtsmark, Erling B. *Tarzan and Tradition: Classical Myth in Popular Literature.* Westport, Conn.: Greenwood Press, 1981, 196 p.
    Establishes parallels between the epic storytelling styles of Burroughs and Homer, claiming that Burroughs's novels are "conceived and to a large extent executed in a manner that speaks of a classical background and classical influences." Holtsmark rigorously explores such elements as language, technique, and theme in Burroughs's fiction as these relate to Homeric tradition.

———. *Edgar Rice Burroughs.* Boston: Twayne, 1986, 133 p.
    A biographical and critical overview of Burroughs and his fiction.

Kyle, Richard. "Out of Time's Abyss: The Martian Stories of Edgar Rice Burroughs—A Speculation." *Riverside Quarterly* 4, No. 2 (January 1970): 110-22.
    Suggests that "wholly without literary reputation, [Burroughs's] stories endure, perpetually successful, living beyond changes in literary style and content, in social behaviour, and even in scientific knowledge." Kyle focuses on Burroughs's early science fiction, stating that "Burroughs came to his Martian trilogy not as an imitator of H. Rider Haggard's ideas, but as a determined opponent of the despairing philosophy of Haggard and the Establishment of his era."

LaFleur, Laurence J. "Marvelous Voyages II: The Scientific Romances of Edgar Rice Burroughs." *Popular Astronomy* L, No. 2 (February 1942): 69-73.

> Notes Burroughs's indifference in his works to scientific accuracy and catalogs scientific improbabilities that occur in several of his novels.

Lupoff, Richard A. *Edgar Rice Burroughs: Master of Adventure*. New York: Canaveral, 1965, 294 p.

> First extensive critical analysis of Burroughs's fiction. Lupoff's study includes, "in addition to descriptions of Burroughs's books, discussions of the various characters, environments, and basic rationales he utilized. It delves into sources which Burroughs may have drawn upon, and traces to some degree the influence which he in turn exerted over later authors, and continues to exert to this day."

Mullen (the Elder), Richard D. "Edgar Rice Burroughs and the Fate Worse than Death." *Riverside Quarterly* 4, No. 3 (June 1970): 186-91.

> An extensive listing of incidents of attempted rape in Burroughs's fiction. Mullen states: "The stories of Edgar Rice Burroughs contain many lessons of great value for the attentive reader, but none more valuable than the warning that an unprotected girl is always in danger of being raped by an Arab, Negro, great ape, Green Martian, or monster of some other kind, or by a wicked white man, or sometimes even by a good white man."

———. "The Undisciplined Imagination: Edgar Rice Burroughs and Lowellian Mars." In *SF: The Other Side of Realism—Essays on Modern Fantasy and Science Fiction*, edited by Thomas D. Clareson, pp. 229-47. Bowling Green, Ohio: Bowling Green University Popular Press, 1971.

> Disputes the opinion that Burroughs derived his fictional Mars from the popular writings of turn-of-the-century author Percival Lowell, stating: "Barsoom, the Burroughsian Mars, was almost entirely the product of an undisciplined imagination—that is, Burroughs made it up as he went along and felt free to change it whenever anything he had previously written proved inconvenient for present purposes, or even when it was just hard to remember."

Mullen, Richard Dale. "The Prudish Prurience of H. Rider Haggard and Edgar Rice Burroughs: Parts I and II." *Riverside Quarterly* 6, Nos. 1 and 2 (August 1973; April 1974): 4-19, 134-46.

> Asserts: "If popular fiction is correctly defined as fiction in which the author attempts to exploit rather than examine the interests, sentiments, and prejudices of his audience, it follows that we cannot know whether Haggard and Burroughs shared the prudish prurience of their respective audiences: we can only know that each sought to exploit the abiding interest in sex without violating the taboos of his time and place."

Nesteby, James R. "The Tenuous Vine of *Tarzan of the Apes*." *Journal of Popular Culture* XIII, No. 3 (Spring 1980): 483-87.

> Examines the literary origins of Burroughs's Tarzan stories with particular attention to Rudyard Kipling's *Jungle Books*.

Opubur, Alfred E. and Ogunbi, Adebayo. "Ooga Booga: The African Image in American Films." In *Other Voices, Other Views: An International Collection of Essays from the Bicentennial*, edited by Robin W. Winks, pp. 343-75. Westport, Conn.: Greenwood Press, 1978.

> Refers to the series of Tarzan films adapted from Burroughs's novels as "probably the most notorious films in the incarnation of the jungle image." Opubur and Ogunbi posit that "there's no doubt about the fact that Tarzan films were employed to legitimize ideas about the 'superior' race, and the implied notions of the civilizing mission."

Porges, Irwin. *Edgar Rice Burroughs: The Man Who Created Tarzan*. Provo, Utah: Brigham Young University Press, 1975, 817 p.

> Described by one critic as "a milestone in the history of Burroughs scholarship." Porges's book is widely considered the definitive biography.

Topping, Gary. "The Pastoral Ideal in Popular American Literature: Zane Grey and Edgar Rice Burroughs." *Rendezvous* 12, No. 2 (Fall 1977): 11-25.

> Examines aspects of pastoralism in the Tarzan novels and compares them to the western novels of Zane Grey.

Giosuè Carducci

1835-1907

(Also wrote under the pseudonym Enotrio Romano) Italian poet and critic.

Carducci was the most important poet of the late nineteenth-century neoclassical movement in Italian literature. An ardent patriot, he deplored the extent to which the passive temper of Christianity and the anti-rational aspects of Romanticism colored nineteenth-century Italian life and literature, and he believed these influences could be best counteracted through a return to purely classical ideals. In his most controversial work, *Inno a Satana (Hymn to Satan),* Carducci extolled classical virtues, praising reason, social progress, and pagan enjoyment of nature while denouncing passion, adherence to tradition, and otherworldly asceticism; further, he adopted classical models for his verses, most notably in his three collections of *Odi barbare (The Barbarian Odes).*

Born in Val di Castello, Tuscany, Carducci was the eldest son of a country physician and his wife. His father, Michele, was a political activist whose role in the Romagnol revolt of 1831 resulted in his imprisonment. When Carducci was three years old, the family moved to the Tuscan Maremma, where Carducci gained an appreciation of nature through explorations of the countryside near their home. He was tutored in literature and history by his father, an enthusiastic admirer of the works of Romantic novelist and poet Alessandro Manzoni (1785-1873), and the elder Carducci attempted to impose on his son the same Romantic ideals and Roman Catholic morality to which he himself subscribed. Although Carducci found much to praise in the works of certain Romantic writers, including Heinrich Heine and Victor Hugo, he reacted violently to his father's dogmatic beliefs, and throughout his life blamed the weakness and disjointedness he perceived in contemporary Italian culture on the influences of Romanticism and Roman Catholicism.

Following the political unrest of 1848, in which Michele Carducci was again involved, the family relocated to Florence, where Carducci attended school for the first time. Studying classics and Italian literature he quickly distinguished himself as a scholar, and subsequently studied in Pisa to prepare himself for a teaching career. In 1856 he accepted a position as a professor of rhetoric at San Miniato al Tedesco, and while there published his first volume of poetry. Carducci also engaged in philosophical disputes in the local press over literary and political matters. His outspoken manner provoked the anger of education authorities, and as a result of this conflict he resigned his teaching position. Unable to win the necessary government approval to occupy another post, Carducci settled once again in Florence, where he tutored students privately and wrote for literary journals. With more liberal-minded officials in power in 1860, he was awarded a professorship in classical studies at the University of Bologna, and remained there until his retirement in 1904. During his long career as a university professor, Carducci published many scholarly works in addition to his collections of poetry, and in 1906 he was awarded the Nobel Prize for his contributions to literature. He died in early 1907 in Bologna.

Reflected in all Carducci's works are his three life principles: "In politics, Italy above everything; in aesthetics, classical

poetry above everything; in action, candor and strength above everything." Politically, the unification and renewal of Italy were his primary concerns; he considered Italian society listless and unimaginative in the late nineteenth century owing to the influence of Romantic ideals in literature and Christianity in public life. To combat these cultural ills, Carducci sought to reassert the glory of the ancient Roman and Greek civilizations through his poetry, and believed that his works would inspire Italians to reclaim their greatness and succeed in forging a future as distinguished as their past. Carducci declared his era the "vile little age that Christianizes," and his poetic expression of this sentiment, the controversial *Hymn to Satan,* represents his first important artistic breakthrough. Called an "intellectual orgy" by one contemporary critic, the *Hymn to Satan* celebrates pagan ideals, epitomizing Carducci's attempt to rouse his compatriots into action to remove influences of Christianity and Romanticism that he considered alien to the true national spirit of Italy. The hymn is dedicated to Satan not as the embodiment of evil, but as the lord of reason and human triumph, rejoicing in the revitalization of paganism. According to Frank Sewall, with the *Hymn to Satan* Carducci became "truly the nation's poet, in giving utterance again to those deeply hidden and long-hushed ideas and emotions which belonged anciently to the people and which no exotic influence had been able entirely to quench."

In technique, Carducci's poetry is noted for reviving classical motifs, meters, and diction. Many of his poems particularly reflect an appreciation of the works of Horace and Virgil, both of whom he celebrated in dedicatory odes. Among the most notable of his writings based on classical poetry are his *Barbarian Odes*. In these poems, Carducci adapted ancient meters based on accented syllables rather than number of syllables, the latter approach being the more common among modern Italian poets. Additionally, his vast erudition prompted many historical allusions and details in his poetry, a practice that critics have found detrimental to the impact of his works and their accessibility to a wide audience.

Unrivaled as the leading figure in Italian neoclassical literature of the late nineteenth century, Carducci enjoyed wide fame in Italy during his lifetime. However, his reputation did not extend beyond the European continent, and audiences in England and America generally greeted his works with indifference. Nevertheless, his achievement in Italian literature remains unchallenged. According to Benedetto Croce, Carducci was one of the great poets of nineteenth-century European literature, "a heroic poet, 'an ultimate pure descendant from Homer'."

PRINCIPAL WORKS

Rime (poetry) 1857
Inno a Satana [as Enotrio Romano] (poetry) 1865
*Poesie (poetry) 1871
Nuove poesie (poetry) 1873
Odi barbare (poetry) 1877
  [*The Barbarian Odes*, 1939]
Giambi ed epodi (poetry) 1879
Studii letterari (criticism) 1880
Nuove odi barbare (poetry) 1882
Rime nuove (poetry) 1887
Terze odi barbare (poetry) 1889
Poems of Giosuè Carducci (poetry) 1892
Rime e ritmi (poetry) 1899
Carducci: A Selection of His Poems (poetry) 1913
Edizione nazionale. 30 vols. (poetry and criticism)
  1935-40

*Includes the collections *Juvenilia*, *Levia gravia*, and *Decennalia*.

THE SATURDAY REVIEW, LONDON (essay date 1882)

[*In the following excerpt from a review of* Poesie, Nuove poesie, *and* Odi barbare, *the critic introduces Carducci to English readers.*]

Signor Carducci is known to students as the author of several valuable works on Italian literature. He is also known, at least by name, to a wider circle of readers as a poet. In the latter capacity his reputation, however, is much greater on the Continent than in England, where the interest felt in foreign poetry, even among educated people, is curiously languid. It is to this indifference only that we can attribute the fact that Signor Carducci's poetry stands in need of an introduction to English readers. Without being blind to obvious defects in his work, and without claiming for him merits such as would entitle him to a place among the great poets, we can safely recommend persons who are familiar with Italian to read what he has written, and particularly what he has written last, with the assurance

that they will not only enjoy what they have read, but return to it with undiminished interest and pleasure. (p. 448)

Of the earlier poems of Signor Carducci the sonnets are those which will be read with least pleasure. It may be true, as has been contended, that the sonnet has been of essential service to Italian literature (especially in its earlier stages), by restraining the rhetorical diffuseness of the national genius within strict and well-defined limits. But the method has long been universally understood, and sonneteering has become a trade. A marriage or a birth in Italy will at any time call forth a shower of sonnets, in return for which a gratuity of a couple of francs is thankfully received. The sonnets of Signor Carducci, unlike his later poems, have about them the fatal ring of commonplace; they are such as most educated Italians would find little difficulty in composing. The writer, indeed, seems to be conscious that this is not the true medium by which he can express himself; for, as we advance in his works, the sonnets become fewer and fewer; and in the last two volumes of his poems, which are incomparably the best, they disappear nearly altogether. The political poems which abound in the earlier volumes have at least the merit of passion and sincerity; but the interest of political poetry, unless it be of the highest merit, must always be fugitive; and none that Signor Carducci has written will have a chance, as it appears to us, of surviving along with that of Petrarch, Filicaja, and Leopardi. It is in the lyrical poems that he is at his best. If they often remind us of Horace and Catullus, it is not because Signor Carducci imitates these poets—for in his lyrical poems he is always and most truly himself—but because they have formed so large a part of his intellectual nourishment and have appealed so powerfully to his taste. . . . But, on the whole, Signor Carducci has succeeded in preserving his independence both of the Latin poets and of the German Romanticists, while feeling strongly the influence of both.

In the *Nuove poesie* this second influence begins to tell. But it tells chiefly through Heine, who, though a Romanticist at heart, took a malicious pleasure in deriding his own ideal. One of the best of the *Nuove poesie,* entitled **"Classicismo e romanticismo,"** reads almost like a translation from the German poet. . . . Throughout all the later poems of Signor Carducci we meet with this protest against a charm which he can only partly resist; how powerfully the charm has affected him, notwithstanding the protest, will be evident to any one who compares the poems written before he knew German with those written afterwards. Several German critics, finding in Signor Carducci affinities to their own poets which they miss in most Italian writers, have been led to assign to him a place much higher, we think, than is fairly his due. He is, in fact, more highly esteemed in Germany than in his own country. Some of his later poems have been translated into German by Dr. Mommsen. Dr. Hillebrand goes so far as to maintain that he ranks as the first poet whom Europe has produced since the death of Heine; and another critic of the same nation places him in some important respects above Heine himself. Italy and Italian things have from the time of Goethe, and even earlier, had a peculiar attraction for the imagination of Germans; and it is not surprising that a writer who combines with this attraction something of the familiar charm of their own household poets should meet in Germany with an admiration far beyond that which an impartial criticism will allow. The value of the estimate which places Signor Carducci next only to Heine may be judged of by the added remark that even Bret Harte, "the limpid Star of the West," must yield to him the palm. If in the gaiety and *verve* of some of his poems he reminds us of

Heine, his melancholy is of another kind. In that of Heine the sense of suffering is so prominent as often to affect the reader painfully. Carducci treats the ills and the inevitable close of life in the true Pagan spirit, as a fate to be accepted with a calm and dignified acquiescence. There is no cry of pain, as in Heine; and no hope overcoming suffering and death, as in Uhland: If any German writer has affected his thoughts and style on these matters, it is Goethe. Nothing that Carducci has written is more exquisitely graceful, and more characteristic of him at his best, than the verses in the *Odi barbare* entitled **"Mors,"** which were written on the occasion of an epidemic of diphtheria.... This last volume of Carducci's works, the *Odi barbare,* is the smallest in point of quantity, but decidedly the best, we think, in quality. The poet appears here in the full maturity of his powers; he has much to say; he says it with admirable grace and finish of style; and, above all, he says it briefly. The advance of years has not made him garrulous, and we can open his books without seeing before our eyes the spectre of "the impending eighty thousand lines." The longest of the *Odi barbare,* which contains just one hundred and fifty-six lines, is that addressed **"Alle fonti del Clitumno,"** and is perhaps the best of all. It is certainly the most powerful.

In one respect Signor Carducci's Radicalism has affected his poetry unfortunately. It is his mission, writes one of his admirers, "to tear the *infula* from the priests of the *venerable Imposture,*" and, generally speaking, to play the part of Capaneus to what the poet himself terms "the solitary Semitic abstraction." The sight of a church or of a clergyman acts on him as the proverbial red rag does on the bull. He identifies Christianity with Catholicism, and Catholicism with asceticism, and can see in the Church nothing but a system of aimless self-torture for the mass of mankind, cunningly invented by "priests" and maintained by them for their private advantage. This view of a great historic process is not pardonable in a man of Signor Carducci's intelligence and culture. Heine, who was as gifted with the historic sense as Signor Carducci appears to be destitute of it, never blunders in this way. He assuredly outdoes Signor Carducci in profanity, if that is what the Italian poet is aiming at; but neither in his fits of blasphemy nor in his equally profane recantation does he ever treat the great religions of the world as if they were priestly manufactures. Nor would German culture have tolerated a conception as puerile as it is obsolete. The *Hymn to Satan* is a clever and amusing *gaminerie,* with which a critic will no more find fault than with Burns's "Address to the De'il"; but Signor Carducci's anti-clerical frenzy, breaking out, as it does, at all times and places, introduces, to our mind, a discordant and offensive note into his poetry. With this qualification, it may be said to be eminently enjoyable. Especially in the later volumes there are many pieces which may be read and re-read with increasing pleasure and admiration. (pp. 448-49)

"Carducci's Poems," in The Saturday Review, *London, Vol. 54, No. 1405, September 30, 1882, pp. 448-49.*

FRANK SEWALL   (essay date 1890)

[*In the following excerpt, Sewall discusses Carducci's contribution to the reassertion of Italian nationalism in the nineteenth century through an examination of such themes in Carducci's poetry as veneration of ancient poets, adoration of nature, and disdain for the otherworldly aspects of religion.*]

It was in the year 1859, when once more the cry for Italian independence and Italian unity was raised, that the newly awakened nation found its laureate poet in the youthful writer of a battle hymn entitled **"Alla croce di Savoia"**—**"The Cross of Savoy."** Set to music, it became very popular with the army of the revolutionists, and the title is said to have led to the adoption of the present national emblem for the Italian flag. As a poem it is not remarkable, unless it be for the very conventional commingling of devout, loyal, and valorous expressions.... But six years later, in 1865, there appeared at Pistoja a poem over the signature Enotrio Romano, and dated the "year MMDCXVIII from the foundation of Rome," which revealed in a far more significant manner in what sense its author, Giosuè Carducci, then in his thirtieth year, was to become truly the nation's poet, in giving utterance again to those deeply hidden and long-hushed ideas and emotions which belonged anciently to the people, and which no exotic influence had been able entirely to quench. This poem was called a *Hymn to Satan.* The shock it gave to the popular sense of propriety is evident not only from the violence and indignation with which it was handled in the clerical and the conservative journals, one of which called it an "intellectual orgy," but from the number of explanations, more or less apologetic, which the poet and his friends found it necessary to publish. Of these one, which appeared over the signature Enotriofilo in the *Italian Athenæum* has been approvingly quoted by Carducci in his notes to the *Decennali.* We may therefore regard it as embodying ideas which are, at least, not contrary to what the author of the poem intended. From this commentary it appears that we are to look here "not for the poetry of the saints but of the sinners—of those sinners, that is, who do not steal away into the deserts to hide their own virtues so that others shall not enjoy them, who are not ashamed of human delights and human comforts, and who refuse none of the paths that lead to these. Not *laudes* or spiritual hymns, but a material hymn is what we shall here find. "Enotrio sings," says his admiring apologist,

> and I forget all the curses which the catechism dispenses to the world, the flesh, and the devil. Asceticism here finds no defender and no victim. Man no longer goes fancying among the vague aspirations of the mystics. He respects laws, and wills well, but to him the sensual delights of love and the cup are not sinful, and in these, to him, innocent pleasures Satan dwells. It was to the joys of earth that the rites of the Aryans looked; the same joys were by the Semitic religion either mocked or quenched. But the people did not forget them. As a secretly treasured national inheritance, despite both Christian church and Gothic empire, this ancient worship of nature and of the joys of the earth remains with the people. It is this spirit of nature and of natural sensuous delights, and lastly of natural science, that the poet here addresses as Satan. As Satan it appears in nature's secret powers of healing and magic, in the arts of the sorcerer and of the alchemist. The anchorites, who, drunk with paradise, deprived themselves of the joys of earth, gradually began to listen to these songs from beyond the gratings of their cells—songs of brave deeds, of fair women, and of the triumph of arms. It is Satan who sings, but as they listen they become men again, enamored of civil glory. New theories arise, new masters, new ideals of life. Genius awakes, and the cowl of the Dominican falls to earth. Now, liberty itself becomes the tempter. It is the development of human activity, of labor and struggle, that causes the increase of both bread and laughter, riches and honor, and the author of all this new activity is Satan; not

Satan bowing his head before hypocritical worshippers, but standing glorious in the sight of those who acknowledge him. This hymn is the result of two streams of inspiration, which soon are united in one, and continue to flow in a peaceful current: the goods of life and genius rebelling against slavery.

(pp. 265-66)

This poem, while excelled by many others in beauty or in interest, has nowhere, even in the poet's later verses, a rival in daring and novelty of conception, and none serves so well to typify the prominent traits of Carducci as a national poet. We see here the fetters of classic, romantic, and religious tradition thrown off, and the old national, which is in substance a pagan, soul pouring forth in all freedom the sentiments of its nature. It is no longer here the question of either Guelph or Ghibelline; Christianity, whether of the subjective Northern type, brought in by the emperors, or of the extinct formalities of Rome, is bidden to give way to the old Aryan love of nature and the worship of outward beauty and sensuous pleasure. The reaction here witnessed is essentially Hellenic in its delight in objected beauty, its bold assertion of the rightful claims of nature's instincts, its abhorrence of mysticism and of all that religion of introspection and of conscience which the poet includes under the term "Semitic." It will exchange dim cathedrals for the sky filled with joyous sunshine; it will go to nature's processes and laws for its oracles, rather than to the droning priests. While the worship of matter and its known laws, in the form of a kind of apotheosis of science, with which the poem opens and closes, may seem at first glance rather a modern than an ancient idea, it is nevertheless in substance the same conception as that which anciently took form in the myth of Prometheus, in the various Epicurean philosophies, and in the poem of Lucretius. Where, however, Carducci differs from his contemporaries and from the classicists so called is in the utter frankness of his renunciation of Christianity, and the bold bringing to the front of the old underlying Hellenic instincts of the people. That which others wrote about he feels intensely, and sings aloud as the very life of himself and of his nation. This, which the foreigner has tried for centuries to crush out, it is the mission of the nation's true poet and prophet to restore.

The sentiments underlying Carducci's writings we find to be chiefly three: a fervent and joyous veneration of the great poets of Greece and Rome; an intense love of nature, amounting to a kind of worship of sunshine and of bodily beauty and sensuous delights; and finally an abhorrence of the supernatural and spiritual elements of religion. Intermingled with the utterances of these sentiments will be found patriotic effusions mostly in the usual vein of aspirants after republican reforms, which, while of a national interest, are not peculiar to the author, and do not serve particularly to illustrate the Hellenistic motive of his writing. The same may be said of his extensive critical labors in prose, his university lectures, his scholarly annotations of the early Italian poets. How far Carducci conforms to the traditional character of the Italian poets—always with the majestic exception of the exiled Dante—in that the soft winds of court favor are a powerful source of their inspiration on national themes, may be judged from the fact that while at the beginning of his public career he was a violent republican, now that he is known to stand high in the esteem and favor of Queen Magherita his democratic utterances have become very greatly moderated, and his praise of the queen and of the bounties and blessings of her reign are most glowing and fulsome. Without a formal coronation, Carducci occupies the position of poet-laureate of Italy. A little over fifty years of age, an active student and a hard-working professor at the University of Bo-logna, where his popularity with his students in the lecture-room is equal to that which his public writings have won throughout the land, called from time to time to sojourn in the country with the court, or to lecture before the queen and her ladies at Rome, withal a man of great simplicity, even to roughness of manners, and of a cordial, genial nature—such is the writer whom the Italians with one voice call their greatest poet, and whom not a few are fain to consider the foremost living poet of Europe.

It would be interesting to trace the development of the Hellenic spirit in the successive productions of Carducci's muse, to note his emancipation from the lingering influences of romanticism, and his casting off the fetters of conventional metre in the *Odi barbare*. But as all this has been done for us far better in an autobiographical sketch which the author gives us in the preface of the *Poesie*, 1871, we will here only glance briefly at some of the more characteristic points thus presented.

After alluding to the bitterness and violence for which the Tuscans are famous in their abuse, he informs us that from the first he was charged with an idolatry of antiquity and of form, and with an aristocracy of style. The theatre critics offered to teach him grammar, and the school-masters said he was aping the Greeks. One distinguished critic said that his verse revealed "the author's absolute want of all poetic faculty." The first published series of poems was in reality a protest against the religious and intellectual bitterness which prevailed in the decade preceding 1860, "against the nothingness and vanity under whose burden the country was languishing; against the weak coquetries of liberalism which spoiled then as it still spoils our art and our thoughts, ever unsatisfactory to the spirit which will not do things by halves, and which refuses to pay tribute to cowardice." Naturally, even in literary matters, inclined to take the opposite side, Carducci felt himself in the majority like a fish out of water. In the revolutionary years 1858 and 1859 he wrote poems on the *Plébiscite* and Unity, counselling the king to throw his crown into the Po, enter Rome as its armed tribune, and there order a national vote. "These," says the poet,

> were my worst things, and fortunately were kept unpublished, and so I escaped becoming the poet-laureate of public opinion. In a republic it would have been otherwise. I would have composed the battle pieces with the usual grand words—the ranks in order, arms outstretched in command, brilliant uniforms, and finely curled mustaches. To escape all temptation of this sort I resorted to the cold bath of philosophy, the death-shrouds of learning—*lenzuolo funerario dell'erudizione*. It was pleasant amid all that grand talk of the new life to hide myself in among the cowled shadows of the fourteenth and fifteenth centuries. I journeyed along the Dead Sea of the Middle Ages, studied the movements of revolution in history and in letters: then gradually dawned upon me a fact which at once surprised and comforted me. I found that my own repugnance to the literary and philosophical reaction of 1815 was really in harmony with the experience of many illustrious thinkers and authors. My own sins of paganism had already been committed, and in manifold splendid guises, by many of the noblest minds and geniuses of Europe. This paganism, this cult of form, was naught else but the love of that noble nature from which the solitary Semitic estrangements had alienated hitherto the spirit of man in such bitter opposition. My at first feebly defined sentiment of opposition thus became confirmed conceit, reason, affirmation; the hymn to

Phœbus Apollo became the hymn to Satan. Oh, beautiful years from 1861 to 1865, passed in peaceful solitude and quiet study, in the midst of a home where the venerated mother, instead of fostering superstition; taught us to read Alfieri! But as I read the codices of the fourteenth century the ideas of the Renaissance began to appear to me in the gilded initial letters like the eyes of nymphs in the midst of flowers, and between the lines of the spiritual *laude* I detected the Satanic strophe. Meanwhile the image of Dante looked down reproachfully upon me; but I might have answered: 'Father and master, why didst thou bring learning from the cloister into the piazza, from the Latin to the vulgar tongue? Why wast thou willing that the hot breath of thine anger should sweep the heights of papal and imperial power? Thou first, O great public accuser of the Middle Ages, gavest the signal for the rebound of thought: that the alarm was sounded from the bells of a Gothic campanile mattered but little!' So my mind matured in understanding and sentiment to the *Levia gravia*, and thence more rapidly, in questions of social interest, to the *Decennali*. There are those who complain that I am not what I was twenty-four years ago:—good people, for whom to live and develop is only to feed, like the calf *qui largis invenescit herbis*. In the *Juvenilia* I was the armor-bearer of the classics. In the *Levia gravia*, I held my armed watch. In the *Decennali*, after a few uncertain preliminary strokes of the lance, I venture abroad prepared for every risk and danger. I have read that the poet must give pleasure either to all or to the few; to cater to many is a bad sign. Poetry to-day is useless from not having learned that it has nothing to do with the exigencies of the moment. The lyre of the soul should respond to the echoes of the past, the breathings of the future, the solemn rumors of ages and generations gone by. If, on the contrary, it allows itself to be swayed by the breeze of society's fans or the waving of soldiers' cockades and professors' togas, then woe to the poet! Let the poet express himself and his artistic and moral convictions with the utmost possible candor, sincerity, and courage; as for the rest, it is not his concern. And so it happens that I dare to put forth a book of verses in these days, when one group of our literati are declaring that Italy has never had a language, and another are saying that for some time past we have had no literature; that the fathers do not count for much, and that we are really only in the beginnings. There let them remain; or, as the wind changes, shift from one foreign servitude to another!

In the selection of poems for translation in this essay regard has been had not so much to the chronological order of their production as to their fitness for illustrating the three important characteristics of Carducci as a national poet which were enumerated above.

The first of these was his strong predilection for the classics, as evinced not only by his veneration for the Greek and Latin poets, but by his frequent attempts at the restoration of the ancient metres in his own verse. Of his fervent admiration for Homer and Virgil let the following two sonnets testify, both taken from the fourth book of the *Levia gravia*. Already in the *Juvenilia,* during his "classical knighthood," he had produced a poem of some length on Homer, and in the volume which contains the following there are no less than three sonnets addressed to the venerated master, entitled in succession, **"Homer," "Homer Again,"** and **"Still Homer."** The following is the second in order:

"Homer"

And from the savage Urals to the plain
  A new barbarian folk shall send alarms,
The coast of Agenorean Thebes again
  Be waked with sound of chariots and of arms;

And Rome shall fall; and Tiber's current drain
  The nameless lands of long-deserted farms:
But thou, like Hercules, shalt still remain,
  Untouched by fiery Etna's deadly charms;

And with thy youthful temples laurel-crowned
Shalt rise to the eternal Form's embrace
Whose unveiled smile all earliest was thine;

And till the Alps to gulfing sea give place,
By Latin shore or on Achæan ground,
Like heaven's sun, shalt thou, O Homer, shine!

In the following tribute to Virgil the beauty of form is only equalled by the tenderness of feeling. It shows to what extent the classic sentiment truly lived again in the writer's soul, and was not a thing of mere intellectual contemplation. In reading it we are bathed in the very air of Campania; we catch a distant glimpse of the sea glistening under the summer moon, and hear the wind sighing through the dark cypresses:

"Virgil"

As when above the heated fields the moon
  Hovers to spread its veil of summer frost,
  The brook between its narrow banks half lost
Glitters in pale light, murmuring its low tune;

The nightingale pours forth her secret boon,
  Whose strains the lonely traveller accost;
  He sees his dear one's golden tresses tossed,
And time forgets in love's entrancing swoon;

And the orphaned mother who has grieved in vain
Upon the tomb looks to the silent skies
And feels their white light on her sorrow shine;

Meanwhile the mountains laugh, and the far-off main,
And through the lofty trees a fresh wind sighs:
Such is thy verse to me, Poet divine!

Here it will be proper to notice the efforts made by Carducci not only to restore as to their native soil the long disused metres of the classic poets, but to break loose from all formal restrictions in giving utterance to the poetic impulse. (pp. 267-70)

In the preface of [*Odi barbare*] he pleads in behalf of his new metres that "it may be pardoned in him that he has endeavored to adapt to new sentiments new metres instead of conforming to the old ones, and that he has thus done for Italian letters what Klopstock did for the Germans, and what Catullus and Horace did in bringing into Latin use the forms of the Eolian lyric."

In the *Rime nuove* are three Hellenic Odes ["Eolia," "Dorica," and "Alessandrina"], under the titles **"Primavere elleniche,"** written in three of the ancient metres, the beauty of which would be lost by translation into any language less melodious and sympathetic than the Italian. (p. 270)

The second of these . . . demands translation as exhibiting perhaps more forcibly than any others we could select the boldness with which Carducci asserts the survival of the Hellenic spirit in the love of nature as well as in art and literature, despite the contrary influences of ascetic Christianity:

> The other gods may die, but those of Greece
> No setting know; they sleep in ancient woods,
> In flowers, upon the mountains, and the streams,
>   And eternal seas.
>
> In the face of Christ, in marble hard and firm,
> The pure flower of their naked beauty glows
> In songs, O Lina, and alone in songs,
>   Breathes their endless youth.

From this glance at the classic form, which is so distinct a feature in Carducci's poems, we proceed to examine the feeling and conceptions which constitute their substance, and which will be found to be no less Hellenic than the metres which clothe them. Nothing could stand in stronger contrast with the melancholy of the romantic school of poets, or with the subjective thoughtfulness and austere introspection of the Christian, than these unfettered outbursts of song in praise of the joy of living, of the delights of love and bodily pleasure, and of the sensuous worship of beautiful form.

"Sun and Love"

> Fleecy and white into the western space
> Hurry the clouds; the wet sky laughs
> Over the market and streets; and the labor of man
>   Is hailed by the sun, benign, triumphal.
>
> High in the rosy light lifts the cathedral,
> Its thousand pinnacles white and its saints of gold,
> Flashing forth its hosannas; while all around
>   Flutter the wings and the notes of the brown-
>   plumed choir.
>
> So 'tis when love and its sweet smile dispel
> The clouds which had so sorely me oppressed;
> The sun again arises in my soul
>   With all life's holiest ideals renewed
>
> And multiplied, the while each thought becomes
>   A harmony and every sense a song.

The following is from the *Nuove odi barbare:*

"All Aurora"

> Thou risest and kissest, O Goddess, with rosy breath the
>   clouds,
> Kissest the dark roofs of marble temples.
>
> The heavens bent down, a sweet blush tinged the forest and
>   the hills,
> When thou, O Goddess, didst descend.
>
> But thou descendest not; rather did Cephalus, drawn by thy
>   kiss,
> Mount through the air all alert, and, fair as a beautiful god,
>
> Mount on the amorous winds and amid the sweet odors,
> While all around were the nuptials of flowers and the marriage
>   of streams.

This has all the freshness and splendor of morning mists rising among the mountains and catching the rosy kisses of the sun. Equally beautiful but full of the tranquillity of evening is the following, from the *Odi barbare* of 1877:

"Ruit hora"

> O green and silent solitudes far from the rumors of men!
> Hither come to meet us true friends divine, O Lidia,
>   Wine and love.

> O tell me why the sea far under the flaming Hesperus
> Sends such mysterious moanings; and what songs are these, O
>   Lidia,
>   The pines are chanting?
>
> See with what longing the hills stretch their arms to the setting
>   sun!
> The shadow lengthens and holds them; they seem to be asking
>   A last kiss, O Lidia!

No one will fail to be struck with the beauty of the figure in the last stanza, nor with the picturesque force of the "green and silent solitudes" of the first, a near approach to the celebrated and boldly original conception of a *silenzio verde*, a "green silence," which forms one of the many rare and beautiful gems of Carducci's sonnet to the ox.

As an example of a purely Homeresque power of description and coloring, and at the same time of an intense sympathy with nature and exquisite responsiveness to every thrill of its life, this sonnet stands at the summit of all that Carducci has written, if indeed it has its rival anywhere in the poetry of our century. The desire to produce in English a suggestion at least of the broad and restful tone given by the metre and rhythm of the original has induced us to attempt a metrical and rhymed translation, even at the inevitable cost of a strict fidelity to the author's every word, and in such a poem to lose a word is to lose much. Nothing but the original can present the sweet, ever-fresh, and sense-reviving picture painted in this truly marvellous sonnet. The unusual and almost grotesque epithet of the opening phrase will be pardoned in view of the singular harmony and fitness of the original.

"Io t'amo pio bove."
"The Ox"

> I love thee, pious ox; a gentle feeling
> Of vigor and of peace thou giv'st my heart.
> How solemn, like a monument, thou art!
> Over wide fertile fields thy calm gaze stealing,
> Unto the yoke with grave contentment kneeling,
> To man's quick work thou dost thy strength
>   impart.
> He shouts and goads, and answering thy smart,
> Thou turn'st on him thy patient eyes appealing,
>
> From thy broad nostrils, black and wet, arise
> Thy breath's soft fumes; and on the still air swells,
> Like happy hymn, thy lowing's mellow strain.
>
> In the grave sweetness of thy tranquil eyes
> Of emerald, broad and still reflected dwells
> All the divine green silence of the plain.

We know not where else to look for such vivid examples as Carducci affords us of a purely objective and sensuous sympathy with nature, as distinguished from the romantic, reflective mood which nature awakens in the more sentimental school of poets. We feel that this strong and brilliant objectivity is something purely Greek and pagan, as contrasted with the analysis of emotions and thoughts which occupies so large a place in Christian writing. No one is better aware of the existence of this contrast than Carducci himself. For the dear love of nature—that boon of youth before the shadows of anxious care began to darken the mind, or the queryings of philosophy, the conflicts of doubt, and the stings of conscience to torment it—for this happy revelling of mere animal life in the world where the sun shines, the soul of the poet never ceases to yearn and cry out. The consciousness of the opposite, of a world of thought, of care, and of conscience ever frowning in sheer stern contrast from the strongholds of the present life and the opinions of men—this is what introduces a kind of tragic motive into many of these poems, and adds greatly to their moral, that is, their human interest. For the poetry of mere animal life, if such were poetry, however blissful the life it describes, would still not be interesting.

Something of this pathos appears in the poem **"To Phœbus Apollo,"** where the struggle of the ancient with the present sentiments of the human soul is depicted. (pp. 270-72)

There is traceable in [**"To Phœbus Apollo"**] a romantic melancholy, the faint remnant of the impression left by those writers through whom, says Carducci, "I mounted to the ancients, and dwelt with Dante and Petrarch," viz., Alfieri, Parini, Monti, Foscolo, and Leopardi. He has not yet broken entirely with subjective reflection and its gloom, and placed himself on the life which the senses realize at the present moment as the whole of human well-being. This sentiment becomes more strongly pronounced in the later poems, where not even a regret for the past is allowed to enter to distract the worship of the present, radiant with its divine splendor and bounty. The one thought that can cast a shadow is the thought of death; but this is not at all to be identified with Christian seriousness in reflecting on the world to come. The poet's fear of death is not that of a judgment, or a punishment for sins here committed, and hence it is not associated with any idea of the responsibility of the present hour, or of the amending of life and character in the present conduct. The only fear of death here depicted is a horror of the absence of life, and hence of the absence of the delights of life. It is the fear of a vast dreary vacuum, of cold, of darkness, of nothingness. The moral effect of such a fear is only that of enhancing the value of the sensual joys of the present life, the use of the body for the utmost of pleasure that can be got by means of it. (pp. 272-73)

In studying the religious or theological tendency of Carducci's Muse, it is necessary to bear in mind constantly the inherent national blindness of the Hellenic and, in equal if not greater degree, the Latin mind to what we may call a spiritual conception of life, its duties, and its destiny. But in addition to this blindness toward the spiritual elements or substance of Christianity there is felt in every renascent Hellenic instinct a violent and unrelenting hostility toward that ascetic form and practice which, although in no true sense Christian, the greater religious orders and the general discipline of the Roman Church have succeeded in compelling Christianity to wear. The mortification of nature, the condemnation of all worldly and corporeal delights, not in their abuse, but in their essential and orderly use, the dishonoring of the body in regarding its beauty as only an incentive to sin, and in making a virtue of ugliness, squalor, and physical weakness—these things have the offensiveness of deadly sins to the sensuous consciousness of minds of the Hellenic type. To spiritual Christianity Carducci is not adverse because it is spiritual—as such it is still comparatively an unknown element to Italian minds—but because it is foreign to the national instinct; because it came in with the emperors, and so it is indissolubly associated with foreign rule and oppression. It is the Gothic or Teutonic infusion in the Italian people that has kept alive whatever there is of spiritual life in the Christianity that has been imposed on them by the Roman Church. The other elements of Romanism are only a sensuous cult of beautiful and imposing forms in ritual, music, and architecture on the one hand; and on the other a stern uncompromising asceticism, which in spirit is the direct contradiction of the former. While the principle of asceticism was maintained in theory, the sincerity of its votaries gradually came to be

believed in by no one; the only phase of the church that seized hold of the sympathies and affections of the people was the pagan element in its worship and its festivals; and seeing this, the popes were wise enough to foster this spirit and cater in the most liberal measure to its indulgence, as the surest means of maintaining their hold on the popular devotion. In the ever-widening antagonism between the spirit and the flesh, between the subjective conception of Christianity on the one hand, as represented by the Teutonic race and the empire, and the sensuous and objective on the other, as represented by the Italic race and the pope, may we not discern the reason why the Italian people, in the lowest depths of their sensual corruption, were largely and powerfully Guelph in their sympathies, and why the exiled and lonely writer of the *Divina commedia* was a Ghibelline? It is at least in the antagonism of principles as essentially native *versus* foreign that we must find the explanation of the cooling of Carducci's ardor toward the revered master of his early Muse, even while the old spell of the latter is still felt to be as irresistible as ever. This double attitude of reverence and aversion we have already seen neatly portrayed in the reference Carducci makes in the autobiographical notes given above to Dante as the great "accuser of the Middle Ages who first sounded the signal for the reaction of modern thought," with the added remark that the signal being sounded from a "Gothic campanile" detracted but little from the grandeur of its imports. (pp. 273-74)

But nowhere is the contrast between the Christian sense of awe in the presence of the invisible and supernatural and the Hellenic worship of immediate beauty and sensuous pleasure displayed in so bold and majestic imagery as in the poem entitled **"In a Gothic Church."** Here, in the most abrupt and irreverent but entirely frank transition from the impression of the dim and lofty cathedral nave to the passion kindled by the step of the approaching loved one, and in the epithets of strong aversion applied to the holiest of all objects of Christian reverence, the very shock given to Christian feeling and the suddenness of the awful descent from heavenly to satyric vision tell, with the prophetic veracity and power of true poetry, what a vast chasm still unbridged exists between the ancient inherent Hellenism of the Italian people and that foreign influence, named indifferently by Carducci Semitic or Gothic, which for eighteen centuries has been imposed without itself imposing on them.

The true poet of the people lays bare the people's heart. If Carducci be, indeed, the national poet of Italy we have in this poem not only the heart but the religious sense, we had almost said the conscience, of the Italian people revealed to view. Nor is this all Bacchantic; the infusion of the Teutonic blood in the old Etruscan and Italic stock has brought the dim shadows of the cathedral and its awful, ever-present image of the penalty of sin to interrupt the free play of Italian sunshine. But just as on the canvas of the religious painters of the Renaissance angels as amorous Cupids hover about between Madonna and saints, and as in the ordinary music of an Italian church the organist plays tripping dance melodies or languishing serenades between the intoned prayers of the priests or the *canto firmo* psalms of the choir, so here we behold the sacred aisles of the cathedral suddenly invaded by the dancing satyr, who, escaping from his native woods, has wandered innocently enough into this his ancient but strangely disguised shrine.

"In a Gothic Church"

They rise aloft, marching in awful file,
The polished shafts immense of marble gray,
And in the sacred darkness seem to be
    An army of giants

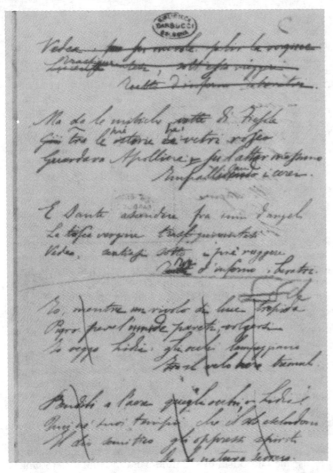
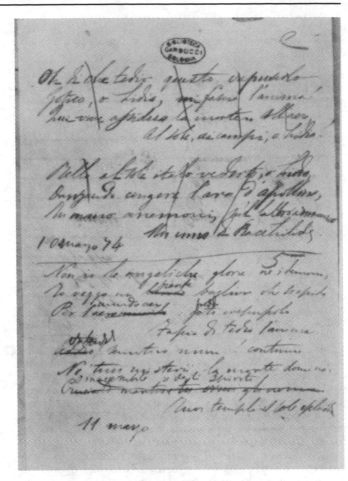

Two manuscript pages from "In una chiesa gotica."

Who wage a war with the invisible;
The silent arches soar and spring apart
In distant flight, then re-embrace again
    And droop on high.

So in the discord of unhappy men,
From out their barbarous tumult there go up
To God the sighs of solitary souls
    In Him united.

Of you I ask no God, ye marble shafts
Ye airy vaults! I tremble—but I watch
To hear a dainty well-known footstep waken
    The solemn echoes.

'Tis Lidia, and she turns, and, slowly turning,
Her tresses full of light reveal themselves,
And love is shining from a pale shy face
    Behind the veil.

The stanzas that follow describe Dante's vision of the "Tuscan Virgin" rising transfigured amid the hymns of angels. The poets, on the contrary, sees neither angels nor demons, but is conscious only of feeling

              "the cold twilight
    To be tedious to the soul,"

and then exclaims:

Farewell, Semitic God: the mistress Death
May still continue in thy solemn rites,
O far-off king of spirits, whose dim shrines
    Shut out the sun.

Crucified Martyr! Man thou crucifiest;
The very air thou darkenest with thy gloom.
Outside, the heavens shine, the fields are laughing,
    And flash with love.

The eyes of Lidia—O Lidia, I would see thee
Among the chorus of white shining virgins
That dance around the altar of Apollo
    In the rosy twilight,

Gleaming as Parian marble among the laurels,
Flinging the sweet anemones from thy hand,
Joy from thy eyes, and from thy lips the song
    Of a Bacchante!

Notwithstanding the bold assertion of the Hellenic spirit in this and in the greater part of his poems, that, nevertheless, Carducci has not been able to restore his fair god of light and beauty, the Phoebus Apollo, to the undisputed sway he held in the ancient mind is evident from the shadows of doubt, of fear, and anxious questioning which still darken here and there the poet's lines. It is here that the stern element of tragedy, the real tragedy of humanity, makes itself felt in this rhapsodist of joy and of love. It comes to tell us that to the Italian as he is to-day life has ceased to be a carnival, and that other sounds than that of the Bacchante's hymn have gained an entrance, with all their grating discord, to his ear: and to silence this intruder will the praises of Lidia and of Apollo suffice, be they sung on a lyre never so harmonious and sweet? With this sonnet, in which is depicted in wonderful imagery the ancient and awful struggle which the sensuous present life sustains with the question of an eternity lying beyond, we conclude our citations from Carducci's poems:

"Innanzi, Innanzi!"

On, on! through dusky shadows up the hill
　　Stretches the shining level of the snow,
　　Which yields and creaks each labored step I go,
My breath preceding in a vapor chill.

Now silent all. There where the clouds stand still
　　The moon leaps forth into the blank, to throw
　　An awful shadow a gaunt pine below,
Of branches crossed and bent in manner ill.

They seem like the uneasy thought of death.
O Winter vast, embrace me and quick stay
In icy hold my heart's tempestuous waves!
For yet that thought, shipwrecked, again draws breath,
And cries to heaven: O Night, O Winter, say,
What are the dead doing down there in their graves?

While our interest in Carducci is largely owing to the character he bears as the poet of the Italian people, it would be quite erroneous to consider him a popular poet. For popularity, whether with the court, the school, or the masses, he never aimed, as is evident from his satisfaction at narrowly escaping being made a political poet-laureate. Instead of writing down to the level of popular apprehension and taste, he rather places himself hopelessly aloof from the contact of the masses by his style of writing, which, simple and pure as it seems to the cultured reader, is nevertheless branded by the average Italian as learned and obscure, and not suited to the ordinary intelligence. As an innovator both in the form and in the content of his verse, he has still a tedious warfare to wage with a people so conservative as the Italians of old habits and old tastes, confirmed as these have been by the combined influence of centuries of political and ecclesiastical bondage. (pp. 274-75)

Frank Sewall, "Giosuè Carducci and the Hellenic Reaction in Italy," in Harper's New Monthly Magazine, *Vol. LXXXI, July, 1890, pp. 262-76.*

M. W. ARMS (essay date 1905)

[In the following excerpt, Arms examines elements of classicism, impressionism, and idealism in Carducci's poetry.]

Carducci the patriot, Carducci the artist, Carducci the thinker—these are fused and find their full expression in Carducci the poet. And just as all the actions of the man are seen to be regulated by a few deep-rooted convictions, so all the poet's vast work is kindled at the one torch of an enthusiastic idealism. In the title of a certain poem of the volume *Iambics and Epodes* (*Giambi ed epodi*) we discern the author's own watchword. **"Avanti! Avanti"** (**"Forward! Forward!"**)—this is the cry the changes of which he is ever ringing in our ears. As we turn the pages of his many volumes, we shall indeed become cognizant of a profound disgust sometimes underlying his singing—disgust with the pettiness, the sordidness, the intellectual and moral weakness of the age. Weariness, too, is often there, prompting rather a proud retirement into self than a struggle amidst the world's din and dust; and now and then, discouragement and doubt as to his ability and fitness so to struggle,—but ever recurrent, too strong to be resisted, is the call of the battle, drawing him away from the roses of art, from the hedged garden of an idle fancy, once more into the great field of mankind's passions, endeavors, and aspirations.

Over this field, Carducci's genius ranges with a versatility that is no less remarkable than his fearless originality. He has written satirical poetry, in which we find the follies and insincerities of men handled, as he himself says, "without gloves"—with a stinging sarcasm which might repel the reader were it not that it is never merely personal, but rather the protest against hypocrisy of a soul to whom the pursuit of truth is life's one great end. He has written patriot poetry which breathes the very spirit that brought a united Italy into being; battle-calls like **"To the Cross of Savoy"** (**"Alla Croce di Savoia"**), **"Plebiscitum"** (**"Il plebiscito"**), **"Piedmont"** (**"Piemonte"**), **"To Giuseppe Garibaldi,"** and a host of others which still stir the blood, vibrating as they do with the exultancy, the agony, the dauntless endurance and heroism that raised Italy's birth-struggle to heights of epic grandeur. He has written the most musically exquisite of lyrics—full of a fanciful and tender charm like **"Pantheism"** (**"Panteismo"**), **"Morning Song"** (**"Matinata"**), **"Serenade"** (**"Serenata"**); or a simple and haunting pathos like **"A Funeral Toast"** (**"Brindisi funebre"**); or a mediæval chivalry like **"Jaufré Rudel."** He has written lines that are as dewdrops from the purest of Greek fountains, and poems that are masterpieces of a subtile impressionism.

Notwithstanding this variety of subject and expression, certain critics, perhaps puzzled by constant and often obscure allusions to ancient history and legend, have accused Carducci of trying to resurrect a dead classicism. That the simplicity, force, dignity, and reserve of the ancient writers strongly appeal to him, and that he dislikes and condemns many phases of modern literature, is true enough and very natural. From his early youth, Carducci drank from the pure fountain of the great Latins, becoming imbued, as it were, with the very essence of their genius. They were his teachers; often, especially in the case of Horace, his models. Moreover, as Chiarini amusingly relates, the patriotism of the little band of comrades to which they both belonged in their student days led to certain odd developments. It induced, among other things, a passionate cult of the mother-tongue and the repudiation and neglect—for which Carducci, at least, has since nobly atoned—of all foreign literature and thought. The Romantic Movement had its root in other than Italian soil; hence these young minds threw themselves with avidity and conviction upon the classicism of which they could esteem themselves the natural heirs. Carducci himself, however, in his poems, **"Classicism and Romanticism"** (**"Classicismo e romanticismo"**), gives us a deeper and probably truer interpretation of his attitude. In praising classicism, typified by the benignant and life-giving sun, he is praising the large simplicity, the golden spontaneity, the primal saneness and force, of which it is the expression; in depreciating romanticism, typified by the pale moon, he is deploring the hollowness, the artificiality, and the demoralizing influence of a sickly sentimentality and a morbid Byronism. He has not tried to resurrect a dead form; he has only felt stirring in himself the spirit that made its life and that has endured through the ages, the spirit that gives immortality to the *'Iliad'* and to the *'Æneid.'* As for the objections of the critics who feel aggrieved because they fail to place "Lalage" or who have lost touch with all the beautiful nature symbolism of the ancients, their best answer is found in Carducci's own note to the **"Song of Legnano"** (**"Canzone di Legnano"**), wherein he protests against "certain theories which, in the name of truth and of liberty, would condemn poetry to the forced labor of a word for word description of everyday reality, and close to it the territories of history, of legend, of myth. To the poet it is permitted, if he wills and can, to go to Persia and to India, even as to Greece and to the Middle Ages; the ignorant and the indifferent have the right not to follow him.''

So much for Carducci's ''classicism''; no less important is the consideration of his impressionism—probably, artistically speaking, the most striking quality of his poetry. Carducci is an impressionist in the same sense that Coleridge was an impressionist; that is, he has to a supreme degree the power of creating atmosphere and conveying an impression. Take, for instance, his sonnet beginning

> Immense, profound, and solitary night,

and notice how, without detail, without drawing a specific word-picture, he succeeds in making us *feel* the immensity, the profundity, the solitude, in a word, the infinity of night. Take his more famous **"Sonnet to an Ox,"** the **"Sonnet to Virgil,"** the **"Hellenic Springs"** (**"Primavere elleniche"**), **"Egle,"** **"Midday in the Alps"** (**"Mezzogiorno alpino"**),— but most of all, take that marvellous **"Ode to Rome"** (**"Roma"**), in which the long, gravely musical lines convey, by some indefinable means, a sense of infinite majesty and significance, of subtile twilight quiet, of the ineffable sadness and poetry and peace that form as it were the very essence of Rome the Eternal.

> Rome, on thine air I cast my soul adrift
> To soar sublime; do thou, O Rome, receive
> This soul of mine and flood it with thy light.
>
> Not curiously concerned with little things
> To thee I come; who is there that would seek
> For butterflies beneath the Arch of Titus?
>
> Do thou but shed thine azure round me, Rome,
> Illumine me with sunlight; all-divine
> Are the sun's rays in thy vast azure spaces.
>
> They bless alike the dusky Vatican
> The beauteous Quirinal, and ancient there
> The Capitol, amongst all ruins holy.
>
> And from thy seven hills thou stretchest forth
> Thine arms, O Rome, to meet the love diffused,
> A radiant splendour, through the quiet air.
>
> The solitudes of the Campagna form
> That nuptial-couch; and thou, O hoar Soratte,
> Thou art the witness in eternity,
>
> Alban Mountains, smilingly sing ye now
> The Epithalamion; green Tusculum
> Sing thou; and sing, O fertile Tivoli!
>
> Whilst I from the Janiculum look down
> With wonder on the city's pictured form—
> A mighty ship, launched towards the world's dominion.
>
> O ship, whose poop rising on high attains
> The infinite, bear with thee on thy passage
> My soul unto the shores of mystery!
>
> Let me, when fall those twilights radiant
> With the white jewels of the coming night,
> Quietly linger on the Flaminian Way;
>
> Then may the supreme hour, in fleeing, brush
> With silent wing my forehead, while I pass
> Unknown through this serenity of peace,
>
> Pass to the Councils of the Shades, and see
> Once more the lofty spirits of the Fathers,
> Conversing there beside the sacred river.

Wedded to this almost magical power of seizing upon certain moments and making us see and feel what he sees and feels, we find in Carducci an imaginative penetration, a finely attuned responsiveness to every suggestion of beauty, which expresses itself through two channels. He has what one might call the passion of the past—the faculty for discerning and presenting the glamour and rich poetic suggestiveness of days gone by as they live and palpitate in grim old castle or ruined temple— and he has a remarkable love and understanding of nature, that greatest of all links betweeen past and present. Other writers have given us glowing descriptions of Italy, of her lakes, her hills, her cities; it has been left for one to interpret the very soul of her Tuscan landscape. There vibrates as it were a subtile chord between the heart of this nature and the heart of the poet who grew up in its midst. In his verse is the luminousness of the ''azure-tinted air,'' the murmur of the wind through the olive-groves, the sound of trickling streams, glimpses of the ''blond Arno'' placid between its low green banks, of the distant sapphire of the sea, of the fens with the summer sunlight glancing from their pools, and the long lines of poplars or grave cypresses fleeing towards the horizon. It is all there— all the immemorial beauty, and significance, and mystery that have made Italy the enchantress of the centuries; and it is evoked with a potency that gives it possession of the reader's imagination almost to the same degree that it has possession of the poet's.

In Italy, Carducci's fame has been well and widely established ever since the publication, in 1873, of his *New Rhymes (Rime nuove),* his previous fugitive poems and the earlier volumes of *Levia gravia* and *Iambics and Epodes* having been little noticed outside of Romagna. The interest and discussion aroused by the *Rime,* however, was as nothing to that which followed the appearance of the first volume of the *Barbarous Odes (Odi barbare)* in 1877. In these odes Carducci has established a metrical form which, if not entirely original with himself, has at least never been handled before with any degree of success. He has abandoned rhyme, and has ''reproduced, by means of combinations of Italian verses, the barbarous harmonies which we notice in Latin verses that are read according to the accent'' [Chiarini]—according, that is, to the grammatical accent of the words instead of according to the quantity which, with the Latins themselves, was given the place of first importance. The critics of Italy rose in two phalanxes, the one side approving the experiment and applauding its outcome; the other condemning the *Odes* as being indeed barbarities unfit for a civilized ear, and prophesying dire results to the whole scheme of Italian versification. For the most part this mass of criticism appears futile, as dealing much with manner and formulæ and little with substance and spirit. Whatever may be said of the literary mechanism of the *Odi barbare,* by the world at large it is the effect of the finished work that is taken into consideration—what impression it produces, what memory it leaves; and looked at from this point of view, the *Odes* will come to be recognized, I believe, as a rich addition to our poetic heritage. However the instrument was put together its notes answer with an unfailing and exquisite harmony to the poet's thought, whether they murmur of spring sunlight and beauty as in **"Cèrilo,"** or raise Garibaldi's name in a hymn of patriotism, or swell into the great symphonic dirge that commemorates the death of the third Napoleon's son.

Just what position will ultimately be assigned to Carducci in the literary annals of the world, time only can establish; but it seems to me that he stands in much the same category as Browning—in the category, that is, of those writers whose work endures because, above and beyond the charm of style it has a spiritual significance and exerts a moral force. To a century of intellectualism, Browning carried a message of emotionalism and spirituality; to a century concerned perhaps too exclusively with the material ends of life, Carducci proclaims the value of the ideal. (pp. 70-6)

M. W. Arms, "A Poet of Italy: An Appreciation of Giosue Carducci," in Poet Lore, *Vol. XVI, No. II, Summer, 1905, pp. 67-76*

GEORGE SAINTSBURY (essay date 1907)

[Saintsbury has been called the most influential English literary historian and critic of the late nineteenth and early twentieth centuries. His studies of French literature, particularly A History of the French Novel *(1917-1919), have established him as a leading authority on such writers as Guy de Maupassant and Honoré de Balzac. Saintsbury adhered to two distinct sets of critical standards: one for the novel and the other for poetry and drama. As a critic of poetry and drama, Saintsbury was a radical formalist who frequently asserted that subject is of little importance, and that "the so-called 'formal' part is of the essence." In the following excerpt, he assesses Carducci's poetry in the context of European literature of the late nineteenth century.]*

Of the positive value of the work of Giosuè Carducci—whose death followed Ibsen's with a sort of annual stroke of removal of the great ones of the last age—it is perhaps too early to judge with absolute certainty of justice. How great it is Time must decide; that it is great we are perhaps justified in deciding already. But relatively, and taking the conditions in, it may certainly be said that in no other country of Europe during the half century do we find any one—not even Hugo, not even Tennyson—occupying such a position. Like these two, Carducci has been the hardly-questioned head of the poetry of his country for a generation and more; and, like the first, but unlike the second, he has been an important figure in politics as well. But Tennyson was a poet pure and simple; and Hugo, though a grandiose novelist and dramatist, and on certain occasions no mean critic, was all abroad in any regions but these. Carducci has been critic as well as poet, historian at least of literature as well as critic, and centre, rallying-point, starting-point alike to the literary forces of his country, after a fashion thrown up no doubt by the comparative absence of others—by the very poverty of that country for the time in great men of letters, but real in itself and hardly to be parallelled elsewhere or elsewhen. Through the time when Italy, nominally freed in political matters, was least fruitful in literature,—when Manzoni had long been silent, when d'Azeglio was giving himself to politics, Carducci's poems . . . maintained the credit of pure literature in Italy as nothing else did, and as few things could have done better. Whether too much importance has or has not been assigned to the sort of literary *cénacle* which the publisher Sommaruga gathered round him about 1880, and of which Carducci was, as it were, summoned from his tent to become the leader, is again one of the questions that must be kept for Time to answer. But there is no doubt that his leadership did more or less animate many, if not most, of the young men and women of letters who have made their mark since; and no one whose attention has been drawn at all, during the last thirty years, to Continental literature can fail to have been more or less aware of the singular position—not exactly as of a light shining in darkness, but certainly that of a light both burning and shining—which this masterful writer and poet has held.

The great glory which has been assigned to him by his admirers, and which does not seem to be merely a fond imagination, is that of having not only strengthened the always graceful form of Italian poetry, but of having applied to it an austere and astringent influence which has to a great extent removed the facility and (in the original, not the offensive, sense) *lubricity* of its effect. He has really done this to some extent, perhaps to a great one; but it is a question whether the Protean slipperiness of the language has not been too much for him after all. For instance, his most famous, or at least notorious, piece, the **Hymn to Satan,** is a glorification of revolt in every form. As such we need not discuss it much, except to point out that, by its date, such a glorification was nothing new or daring, but rather a *pont aux ânes,* as Diderot said to Rousseau in days when it was the other way about. Moreover, Baudelaire had undoubtedly preceded him in his *Litanies de Satan;* and the resemblance of the two is much greater than might be thought from Carducci's rather qualified denial of acquaintance, combined as it is with a rather awkward citation of the part of Baudelaire's verse *least* like his. But this matters little. The question is whether **Satana,** though undoubtedly a fine piece of flowing declamation, does not still run too smoothly,—its little verses almost skipping as they pass. The sonnet, of course, saves him from this danger, and so do many of the longer-lined measures of the **Odi barbare**; while his Italian Sapphics are things of the greatest interest, the *lubricus vultus* being here quite attractive. Whether the Alcaics do quite as well may be questioned, yet the poem to Queen Margherita is a beautiful thing. (pp. 256-59)

George Saintsbury, "The Southern Literatures," in his The Later Nineteenth Century, *William Blackwood and Sons, 1907, pp. 253-94.*

G. L. BICKERSTETH (essay date 1913)

[In the following excerpt from his introduction to a collection of Carducci's poetry, Bickersteth presents an extensive analysis of chief themes and characteristics of Carducci's work. Translations in brackets are the critic's own.]

Carducci's importance in literature is due to the fact that he introduced a new ideal into Italian poetry. It is essential to define at the outset the nature of this ideal in order to avoid the error, committed by some critics, of blaming him for not performing something which he never set out to achieve. Carducci was one of the most outspoken of poets. He was provocatively frank both in his criticism of contemporary literature and in the statement of his own views. Caring nothing at all for public opinion, he never wrote to catch a public. "Let a poet express himself, his moral and artistic convictions, as sincerely, straightforwardly, and resolutely as he can: the rest is not then his affair." Such was his attitude, and it should not be difficult to discover what these convictions were. They are summarised distinctly enough in a letter which he wrote at a time when his disgust with contemporary literature was at its height. After a very acute analysis of the genesis and the progress of Italian Romanticism, he defines the need of the present age in the following terms:—"We must make art realistic: represent what is real, in more natural terms, with truth. We must do away with the ideal, the metaphysical, and represent man, nature, reality, reason, liberty. To that end unite study of the ancients, who are realistic and free, Homer, Aeschylus, Dante, and of the popular poetry with modern sentiment and art." . . . It is obvious that, on its negative side, Carducci's diagnosis of the literary maladies of his age was defined by [his . . . hostility to the Italian Romantics]. Because Romanticism indulged in the mystical and the vague, Carducci loved the real and the matter of fact; because the Romantic school was the school of the neo-Catholics and neo-Guelfs, Carducci stood for intellectual freedom and political independence; because Romanticism was attracted by the eccentric and abnormal, Carducci aimed at sanity of thought and strictness of form. But, on the positive side, Carducci's poetic ideal resulted quite logically from the nature of his own personal character, from his views on the relationship between poetry and politics, and from the fact that he possessed the true scholar's enthusiasm for classical literature.

His was an essentially practical nature. He was never troubled with doubts or questionings about life, nor did the great problems of modern philosophy interest him at all. He was a Hellenist who, finding this world lovely and good to live in, did not concern himself about the next. He loved life for its own sake, and if in old age he is oppressed by melancholy at the thought of death, it is not the melancholy of Leopardi's "Shepherd of Asia," questioning the moon . . . and yearning for an explanation of the secrets of the universe, but rather that of the Greek anthologist, . . . or of the cultured humanist, for whom the dark entrance to the unseen world is lit up by the calm radiance of Greek poetry:—

> A me prima che l'inverno stringa pur l'anima mia
> Il tuo riso, O sacra luce, O divina poesia!
>   Il tuo canto, O padre Omero
>   Pria che l'ombra avvolgami.

["Smile upon me ere the winter wraps my soul in melancholy Darkness; smile on me, O Poetry divine, O Radiance holy! Father Homer, hear my crying Ere the shade o'erwhelmeth me!"]

Hence he turns with relief, if not with contempt, from the barren speculations of the metaphysicians and theologians. "The lazy fool, in hazy day-dreams rapt" is no true poet, or at least not the poet for modern Italy. What the country needed were men who, far from wasting time and energy over the "questions, the broods that haunt sensation insurgent," would employ all the resources of their imagination and insight in solving the practical problems of the national life.

When a nation is coming into existence, the most pressing problems that call for solution are political. So far from divorcing politics from poetry, it seemed to Carducci that the poet had a most necessary part to play on the political stage—a part, moreover, which none but he could play, and which could not be omitted without risk of disaster to the State. The poet, he maintained, when contented to pass with the public either for a *pitocco,* the servile minion of a patron or a party, or for a *giardiniero,* the writer of pretty but shallow, and possibly vulgar, society verse, is miserably failing in the duties of his own high calling. The nature of these duties may be deduced from Carducci's ideal picture of himself as his country's poet-seer. In *Critica ed arte,* after dividing the history of poetry into clearly defined epochs, he thus describes the one at the close of which he himself was living: "And lastly there are other ages less glorious, in which, the nation being in a state of transition to new political conditions, the poets whom I will not by an archaism call true *vati* (seers), but who feel instinctively, like certain animals, a nervous uneasiness before the earthquake, begin transforming certain forms of art which are fully developed. These are the critical ages, when poets fight over their work with offensive and defensive weapons: and Alfieri writes the letter to Calsabigi, and Manzoni the letters on the dramatic unities and on Romanticism, and Victor Hugo the preface to *Cromwell.*" Here, then, he defines the poet-seer or *vate* as one who watches the times, who, by the exercise of a sense of intuition possessed by himself alone,

perceives earlier than others the direction in which events are tending, and whose duty it is to warn and guide the nation in every crisis through which it may have to pass. It is the practical value of the imaginative faculty upon which Carducci here insists. The poet's function in his capacity of *vate* is moral. Himself anchored fast to some great guiding principle—in Carducci's case the ideal of a united Italy—he must, through good report or ill report, and without respect of person or of party, perform the office of inspired prophet of his people, expressing for them in outbursts of lyrical passion the emotions they feel but cannot utter, and equally prepared with warning or reproach whenever, through ignorance or blindness or pride, they seem to his clear sight in danger of falling short of their own highest ideals. For these reasons Carducci never feared the charge of being inconsistent in politics. The poet, as he rightly considered, has no concern with political consistency. "I intend, and have always intended, to express by a process of psychological purgation, with the greatest sincerity and efficacy possible, certain fancies and passions by which my spirit is moved, and to represent them exactly with the momentary shapes and colours in which I myself feel and see them, not with the shapes of yesterday, to-morrow, or some other day, and not with the shapes and colours in which other people wish to make me believe that other people will be better pleased to see them, or in which other people may be able to see and feel something similar." The poet, in fact, must be absolutely genuine, and if true to himself preserves a fundamental consistency that remains unaffected, however many times he may change sides in the conflict of political parties.

If personal characteristics and political enthusiasm were instrumental in shaping his poetic ideal, this was no less profoundly affected by his instincts as scholar and humanist. His innate hatred of the vague and superficial, not only in thought but in the realms of art and criticism, increased yearly in proportion as the true scholar's attention to accuracy and thoroughness of workmanship grew with him into a habit. The sense of clearly defined form, the lack of which he deplored in poets of the Romantic school, seemed to him to be an absolute essential of the great poet; and he held that it could only be learnt from the Greek. It was their power of treating romantic subjects with "that great classical art which is of all time" that caused him to place Goethe and Schiller so high above the German poets of their age. He himself was never tired of applying the principles of Greek art in the composition of his own verse, with the result that probably no poet that ever lived has composed so few slipshod lines or written his own language with greater purity of diction.

But he loved the classics not only for what they taught him about beauty of form. That beauty was to him only the outward and visible sign of the life and ideals of the ancient Greek world, to which he was as passionately devoted as the mediæval humanist himself. "The ancients who are realistic and free"—by this he meant that, in contrast with the prevalent modern opinion, the old Greeks considered life to be something worth living for its own sake, not a mere vestibule of the world to come. Their thought was free because unfettered by dogmatic religions and unclouded by the vague abstractions of mysticism. Theirs was a concrete, not spiritual world, in which love was untinged by sentimentality, the virtues of the cloister unknown, and patriotic pride and manly vigour not yet superseded by the Christian qualities of resignation and humility. Into Carducci's ideal of poetry there entered, therefore, a very definitely pagan element. And herein he differs from other so-called classicists, who have earned the name merely in virtue of their allegiance to certain literary forms and conventions. Carducci wished to make the *content* of his poetry classical also, to regard both man and nature (so far as modern thought permitted) from the same point of view as the ancient Greek poets or as those Latin poets who had modelled themselves on the Greek. By so doing he hoped to knit up again a literary tradition, which the Romantic movement in Italy had interrupted, but which he believed to be as distinctively native to his country as it was sanctioned by its antiquity and eternal youth. It was for these reasons that in his earlier work he employed every device of language and literary reminiscence, not excepting even literal translation, to reproduce as far as possible both the substance and the atmosphere of the Greek, Latin, and Italian classics; while in his later poetry he resorted more and more to his country's past, both in myth and history, as being the fittest of all possible subject-matter to inspire a patriot poet.

So much having been said, it becomes easier to understand why his poetic ideal took just the form it did. We shall expect to find him as a poet banishing from his verse all intellectual vapouring, meaningless abstractions, and vague emotionalism—suppressing, in fact, the subjective element in poetry, as far as may be, altogether in order to concentrate his efforts on the objective presentation of life as it really is, in its beauty and ugliness, its joy and sorrow. If he is true to his own theories, we shall expect to find him pouring, as it were, the ancient Greek and Italian ideals into moulds of thought and language modelled, as closely as a sympathetic study of the classics can make them, upon those used by the ancient Greek and Italian poets. And, finally, we shall expect to find in him one who, by the true poet's gift of prophetic intuition, knows how to point his countrymen towards the glorious destiny that his ardent patriotism has imagined for them, while guiding, comforting, and exhorting them in their efforts to reach it.

If all this be summed up in his own words as the "representation of reality with truth," study of his poetry will reveal the fact that few men have more honestly put their own principles into practice. Carducci's conception of reality, considered from the artistic point of view, controls his treatment of all the chief themes of his poetry, as will at once become apparent if we examine any of these at all closely. Man, Nature, and Liberty, for instance—he held it incumbent upon the poets of his own time to deal mainly with these three, and they constitute accordingly a large portion of the subject-matter of his own verse. How are they treated according to the canons of Carduccian realism?

If we consider first the human element in his poems, it will be found that he eschews all abstract reasoning about mankind as such. Mankind, to Carducci, meant simply individual men and women. These men and women, moreover, are not creations of the poet's own brain, like Browning's "Cleon, Norbert, and the fifty." We find in Carducci's poetry no long reflective monologues, no dramatic lyrics, in which the inmost working of the human mind is revealed, and the hidden springs of action are traced to their source. On the contrary, it is the action itself, not the psychological dissection of the mind of the agent, which interests Carducci. Consequently the men and women that move across his pages are not there to illustrate his reading of human nature; they are not types but individuals, considered purely from the outside, objects of his respect, his hatred, or his admiration for something they have done or suffered in real life. They are, as already said, not created by his imagination at all, but contemporaries of himself or persons

famous in political or literary history. Life, as lived in his own day or in past ages, teemed with poetic figures, ready to the poet's hand: men like Carlo Alberto, "the Italian Hamlet"; Garibaldi and Napoleon III; women like Marguerite of Savoy and Elizabeth, Empress of Austria. To be realistic, according to Carducci, is to take advantage of such historical figures as these, rather than to feed the fancy on the joys and sorrows of beings whom that fancy has itself created. Nor do the demands of realism end with the selection of subject; treatment must be realistic also. At this point Carducci the historian and Carducci the opponent of Romanticism join hands. No veil of romance must be spread by the poet over the personalities with which he deals. Imagination, which tends to idealise men out of all relation to humanity as it really exists, must be strictly controlled by historical fact. Yet Carducci did not believe that a man, simply because historical, is of necessity a good subject for a poem. A man's career or character, to admit of poetic treatment, must be raised by some element of tragedy, beauty, or romance above those of the common herd. It is the duty of the poet as artist to isolate such figures in life or history as are suitable to his purpose from the *milieu* in which they occur, and then present them as graphically and truthfully as he can. For where the romantic element is a matter of historical fact, there is no need for the poet to invent it. On the other hand, it generally happens that the poet alone can disentangle that element from essentially prosaic ones by which it is obscured. Carducci therefore is realistic, because he insists that if the romance is not there the poet must not imagine it; he is an idealist, in so far as he perceives that though facts . . . be his subject-matter, his art must confine itself to those facts only which are in themselves instinct with poetry. What such facts may be it is for the poet alone to say. A poem like **"At the Station on an Autumn Morning"** shows, at any rate, that Carducci, without falling away for an instant from his own high standard of poetic form, yet lacked none of the ability—which the modern realist is apt to consider peculiarly his own—to unearth poetry in apparently altogether prosaic material.

Carducci, then, felt that the more realistic, in the sense of truer to history, a poet shows himself to be, the greater will be the appeal of his poetry, just because it *is* true. And this was a consideration which in his character of poet-seer, with a moral function to perform, he could not afford to neglect. Consequently his men and women are not only historical characters, and hence obviously *true* from one point of view, but they are drawn with realistic touches either of person or setting, which serve to bring the man or the scene very vividly before us, and by their truth to fact and locality convince our reason at the same time as they stimulate our emotion. Take, for instance, the picture of Garibaldi retreating from Mentana:

> Il dittatore, solo, a la lugubre
> Schiera d'avanti, ravvolto e tacito
> Cavalca: la terra e il cielo
> Squallidi, plumbei, freddi intorno.
>
> Del suo cavallo la pésta udivasi
> Guazzar nel fango: dietro s'udivano
> Passi in cadenza e sospiri
> De' petti eroici ne la notte.
>
> ["First of the dismal host, unaccompanied,
> Rode the Dictator silently, wrapped in thought;
> Grey, cheerless, cold, the earth and heaven
> Sullenly, gloomily round him lowered.
>
> Clear through the stillness echoed his horse's hoof
> Splashing the mud; behind him a measured tramp
> Resounds of marching feet, and stifled
> Sighs in the night of some breast heroic."]

This is realistic, and it is poetry. The poetry consists in the historical truth of the picture, both subject and treatment. Garibaldi, the hero of the nation: fighting to win Rome, the ideal of the nation: retiring defeated because unsupported by the Government of the nation! Here is no figment of the poet's brain but a tragic fact. The poem focuses and embodies for all time the storm of outraged patriotism which swept over Italy after the battle of Mentana. The realism of Carducci's descriptive touches intensifies but does not create the tragedy.

Again, to quote the last two matchless verses of the Alcaic ode on the death of the Prince Imperial:

> Sta nella notte la còrsa Niobe
> Sta sulla porta donde al battesimo
> Le usciano i figli, e le braccia
> Fiera tende su 'l selvaggio mare:
>
> E chiama, chiama, se da l'Americhe,
> Se di Britannia, se da l'arsa Africa
> Alcun di sua tragica prole
> Spinto da morte le approdi in seno.

> ["She stands by night, that Corsican Niobe,
> Stands at the threshold whence at their baptism
> Her sons went forth from her, and stretcheth
> Proudly her arms o'er the wild sea-water,
>
> And calleth, calleth, if from America,
> From England, from parched Africa e'en but one
> Of all her tragic offspring, tossed by
> Death, should find haven in her yearning bosom."]

Does not the tragedy of this wonderful picture gain immensely in effect from the fact of its *historic* truth? The mother of the Napoleons mourning for her children! How much less poignant would have been the haunting pathos of that "chiama, chiama" had Letizia never lived but in the imagination of the poet, or had her offspring been just ordinary children and not Napoleons!

If this is what Carducci means by representing reality with truth in his treatment of humanity, we shall find a still clearer instance of his application of the same principle when he deals with Nature. He loved Nature; but for him the word had no abstract signification. He constructed no religion of Nature like Wordsworth or Meredith; he made no allegories about her like Shelley; he had not the naturalist's knowledge of her that Tennyson possessed. Nature for him meant primarily the country as opposed to the artificiality of the town—the mountains, the sea, the sky, and all the beautiful and familiar scenes of country life. But he does not describe the country in general. Never having travelled abroad, he identifies Nature with the Italian landscape; nor is it even the Italian landscape in general, but limited in much of his poetry to the scenery of the Maremma and the Versilia, in the midst of which he had been brought up, and which he loved to revisit. When in later life he took to spending his holidays in the Italian Dolomites, this district also comes in for its due share of attention, though his descriptions of it lack the spontaneous charm that breathes from every verse of a poem like **"Davanti San Guido."** The point, however, to be emphasised is that the country he paints in his poetry is always *real*. It actually exists apart from his imagination. Indeed, the accuracy of the descriptions in many of his poems—**"Piemonte,"** for instance—errs not infrequently on the side of being too photographic, and at times even smacks a little of the guide-book. But Carducci felt that the natural beauty of Italy, like the poetry of such a career as Garibaldi's, needs the adornment of no romantic colouring. His principle was to use his eyes, not to read into Nature what was not there, but to describe what he saw with exactness and sympathy. . . .

He tends to become conventional, however, the moment he attempts to describe what he has not seen. Thinking of Nature always as she appears in certain localities known to himself, he could not give verisimilitude to a purely ideal landscape. What is particular and matter of fact in Nature appeals to him. He has been called Virgilian in his treatment of Nature, but he has none of Virgil's haunting sense of the mysterious power shadowed forth in natural phenomena. He is Virgilian only in his affection and reverence for simple country scenes and rustic pursuits. The figures of man and beast at work in the fields, illustrating what he so happily calls "La giustizia pia del lavoro," as opposed to the unnatural conditions under which labour is pursued in great cities, never fail to make instant appeal to his imagination. He loves, like Virgil, to sing

> Wheat and woodland,
> Tilth and vineyard, hive and horse and herd.

Over and over again his poems bear convincing testimony to the intimate sympathy he felt with all the homely details of the peasant's life. Characteristic scenes and incidents of the Italian countryside are drawn with such a sure and vivid touch that even a single line or phrase frequently contains a complete picture; while the moral symbolism of toiling cattle or changing season is expressed (as in **"Il bove"** and **"Canto di marzo"**) with a grave simplicity and power, which recall Millet in painting, but to which it would be hard to find a parallel in the whole range of modern poetry.

It is interesting, further, to observe how characteristically Carducci's attitude towards Nature is affected by his patriotism. Many of his finest descriptions of Italian scenery occur in poems dealing with historical events and personages. He does not, however, simply make use of landscape as the *cadre* or setting for the historical and literary associations which must of necessity attach themselves to almost every square yard of an ancient country like Italy, and which it was his special delight, as a historian and archæologist, to discover. His love of Nature and his love of history are really only two different manifestations of a deeper emotion still, his love of country; and patriotism enables him to combine the two in the description of a *paessaggio storico* in such a way as to give equal effect to both. Thus in the historical ode **"Cadore"** the poet's patriotism forms an emotional bond between the beauty of the mountain scenery and the heroism of Pietro Calvi's deed. Pelmo and Antelao are pictured as sympathising with the band of patriots fighting below them. For the mountains *are* Italy, and Pietro Calvi was fighting for Italy; and it is because Carducci loves Italy that not only the natural beauty but the historical associations of Cadore appeal to him so forcibly. Consequently it is in deference to no mere literary convention that Carducci is led to personify Italy. He feels that she really is his mother, and he adores her with a filial affection. . . . She is the bond that unites all the many nations that have ever called themselves Italian; all the poets who have ever sung her praises; all the patriots who "for her sake have fallen"; all those "who for her sake shall live." His love for her makes it easy and natural for him to pass from describing her beauty, as seen in mountain, stream, and sky, to reminiscence of her people and her history. He visits Sirmio, for instance, and the peninsula suggests memories of Catullus, Virgil, and Dante; they are indeed historically connected with the locality, but Carducci's interest in the place is not merely archæological. The real link between the three poets and himself is the common affection which all have cherished for "Italia bella," "Italia madre." Sirmio, with its lovely scenery, is the outward and visible object by which this common affection is symbolised, and as such has a message for the poet which the archæologist would have missed.

The best example of this intermingling of Nature-description and historical reminiscence is afforded by the **"Alle fonti del Clitumno,"** one of the most characteristically Carduccian (for this reason) of all Carducci's poems. He there exclaims:—

> A piè de i monti e de le querce a l'ombra
> Co' fiumi, O Italia, è de' tuoi carmi il fonte.

> ["On the hills, by streams, in the shade of oak-trees
> Seek the springs of Poetry, O my country!"]

Carducci believed this with his whole soul, just because his intense patriotism saw in mountains, trees, and rivers not merely beautiful natural objects but his Mother Italy; and to him they were doubly a source of poetry, since besides their own intrinsic loveliness he looked upon them as links with the Past, beings whom he could compel by sheer force of learned imagination to speak to him of all the wonderful events of which they had been witnesses.

Turning now to Carducci's treatment of Liberty, a theme which for a hundred years had more than any other inspired Italians to be poets, we shall find him as careful as ever not to lose touch with concrete reality.

Of all his earlier poetry Liberty may be said to have been the dominating theme. It never ceased to be one of his main sources of inspiration. But if we are to call him a poet of Liberty, we must use the title in a very different sense to that in which he himself conferred it upon Shelley. The author of the *Prometheus Unbound* pursues Liberty as an abstract ideal, fashioned after a pattern laid up in heaven, and only dreams of it as wholly realisable in some paradise of the poet's imagination. Such a Platonic conception as this Carducci would have speedily banished "tra le fantasmagorie di un mondo impossibile." It partook far too much of the romantic and mystical; whereas his own ideal of the free citizen in the free state presented a practical end, clearly conceived and capable of very definite statement. That practical end was neither the liberation of the human soul nor of the world in general, but the freedom of Italy. As an ideal to be fought for, it calls up visions of the battles and heroes of the Risorgimento, of Pisacane, the brothers Cairoli, and above all, Garibaldi; as an ideal to be realised, it simply means the Tricolour flying over Rome. Not until Rome is free and the Papacy overthrown does his conception of Liberty at all widen its scope; and the poet, with the history of ancient Rome in his mind, dreams of a time when the capital of united Italy shall once more become the central source of all principles of freedom and justice throughout the world. (pp. 23-36)

Enough has perhaps been said to enable the reader to grasp the chief themes of Carducci's poetry, together with the point of view from which he treats them. It was obviously impossible for him, holding the opinions he did, to be a love-poet in the ordinary sense of the term. Much of modern love-poetry is essentially romantic. It springs from the idealisation of woman. The lover endows his mistress, whether she possesses them or not, with every imaginable grace and virtue, and sets her on a pedestal, from which, like a deity, she is permitted to influence his life for good or bad. Carducci, as Professor Croce has pointed out, removes Love from this central position in life; and he does so by rehumanising woman. He brings her down from her pedestal, and transforms her again into a creature of flesh and blood. With a healthy naturalism which is never coarse, he loves, like Walt Whitman, to dwell upon the mere physical attractiveness of a beautiful woman. He does not care for ethereal types of female loveliness. The latter, to appeal to him, must be combined with health and strength, because every young girl is potentially a wife and mother, and it is in the due performance of her functions in both these capacities that Carducci finds the truest poetry of womanhood. Thus in the **"Idillio maremmano"** he plunges into no sentimental rhapsodies about "la bionda Maria," whom he had once loved, but merely gives us a realistic sketch of a young *contadina* crossing the cornfields on a summer afternoon—a girl whose vigorous personal charms, he thinks, must surely very soon have secured for her the joy of husband and children:—

> Ché il fianco baldanzoso ed il restio
> Seno a i freni del vel promettean troppa
> Gioia d'amplessi al marital desio

> Forti figli pendean da la tua poppa
> Certo, ed or baldi un tuo sguardo cercando
> Al mal domo caval saltano in groppa.

> ["Too rich in promise to a husband's pure
> Embrace was that young form, that heaving breast,
> Which its confining veil could scarce endure.

> Surely strong sons were to thy bosom pressed,
> Who now leap on their steeds of mettle keen,
> With loving glances unto thee addressed."]

Again, his poem **"La madre,"** one of the most beautiful he ever wrote, paints for us the picture of healthy human motherhood as opposed to the *disutili amori* with which Romanticism loves to coquet.

What, then, is to be said of the Lalages, Lidias, and other ladies with Greek names to whom he addresses so many of his later odes and elegies? We have only to compare any one of these with the "Maria" of the **"Idillio maremmano"** to perceive that there is in them no more substance than the literary flavour of their names is intended to suggest. They only serve, in fact, as part of the conventional furniture of poems written on classical models. The real motive to lyrical passion in these cases must be sought, not in the poet's love for Lalage or Lidia, but in Patriotism, Liberty, or the purely literary enthusiasm of an ardent Hellenist. The beautiful **"Primavere elleniche,"** for instance, addressed to Lina, are not love-poems. They only seek, like Alma Tadema's pictures, to reproduce artistically the idyllic charm of ancient Greek life. Their interest is æsthetic and literary, not personal. The same holds true of Lidia in **"In a Gothic Cathedral,"** and of Lalage in **"By the Urn of P. B. Shelley"**—in both of which lyrics the writer appears primarily as Hellenist, not lover. Even the Alcaic ode entitled **"At the Station on an Autumn Morning,"** where personal affection for Lidia seems to play a more important part, is chiefly interesting as a specimen of modern impressionism cast in an ancient classical verse form. Of love-poems proper Carducci wrote none.

This purely artistic use of women's names in his poetry suggests the consideration of Carducci as literary craftsman. From this point of view he himself invented the figure which most aptly describes him when he pictures the poet as a mighty smith, who hammers into beautiful shapes "the elements of Thought and Love, and the memories and glories of his fathers and his nation." It is as a master of style and of metrical composition that Carducci, as some believe, is destined to live longest. "Carducci," says Dr. Garnett, "has solved the problem which baffled the Renaissance, of linking strength of thought to artifice of form." The secret of his style, a secret he wrung from the great classical poets after years of loving study, consists in its restrained power and in the precision of its artistic finish. Metaphors from sculpture naturally suggest themselves to describe the massive and noble form in which all his most characteristic poems are cast. Like the statuary's, his art does not rely upon atmospheric charm or vague suggestiveness for securing its effects. He conceived some large and simple thought, and then endeavoured to achieve an equal breadth and simplicity in the form of its expression. His frequent success in accomplishing this is due partly, of course, to his stern practice of eliminating from the verse all words not absolutely essential. But strict economy in language would not in itself wholly account for the firm, smooth surface and clear-cut, definite outline attained by his best poems. These result from clearness and simplicity of thought combined with a complete mastery over his artistic medium—words. His confessed model was Horace, and there are abundant signs that he both studied and practised the precepts of the *Ars poetica*. What particularly attracted him to Horace was the inimitable and inevitable form into which the Augustan poet cast his thought. The Horatian *curiosa felicitas* is a striking characteristic of Carducci himself, and frequently defies translation. No servile imitation of his model, however, could have given him the power thus to manipulate language. It was because he shared with Horace a real love for words and their literary history that he became like him

> In verbis etiam tenuis cautusque serendis.

                                                        (pp. 37-40)

[Carducci's] profound knowledge of both ancient and modern literature naturally affects his style. He was particularly fond of insisting on the unbroken linguistic ties connecting the Latin and Italian languages. Nothing delights him more than to surprise the reader with cadences and phrases definitely recalling passages of Horace and other Latin poets; nor, if occasion demands, does he hesitate to coin words direct from the Latin in proof of the close kinship still existing between the two tongues. For a similar reason it interested him to imitate old Italian verse forms, and sometimes to reinstate words which had fallen into disuse. All this gives a distinctly literary atmosphere to his poetry, which, if it delights some readers for this very reason, will as inevitably fret others who cannot command one tithe of the vast learning which the poet himself had amassed. To quote his own simile, he hammered his verse with immense care, and very few of his best poems give the impression of having been written down hurriedly under the stress of an overmastering inspiration. The *Hymn to Satan* was indeed composed in a single night, and many of the *Iambics and Epodes* were evidently thrown off in moments of intense emotion. But for the most part, at any rate in later life, he preferred to concentrate thought and feeling into few but telling words, rather than to let them carry him away in a torrent of passionate eloquence. The elaborated intensity of his descriptive word-painting is the outward sign of the conscious art with which he worked; nor could any poet have evolved the metres of the *Barbarian Odes* without spending years of labour on problems of metrical technique. (pp. 41-2)

There have been ages which lacked their sacred bard, and there have been bards, potentially great poets, who lacked a sacred age to draw out their genius. Had Carducci been starting his career now he might perhaps have had to be included in the latter category. It is possible, or at least arguable, that Nature gave him greater powers of artistic expression than of creative imagination. If he had lived in the twentieth century he might only have ranked as one among a host of minor poets, who attain a high standard of technical ability in their art, yet fall short of true greatness for lack of a great theme. But Carducci was fortunate in the age into which he was born. No country can pass through a "springtime more holy" than that in which it is acquiring National Liberty and laying the foundations of National Unity. At such a time a nation does not need a great poet to dream great dreams for it. It dreams them of itself. It rather demands one who can express its great ideals for it and save it from forgetting them in the reaction which follows victory. To perform this double function Carducci's genius was admirably fitted. He possessed to the full the necessary sympathy which enabled him to identify himself with the national aspirations. (pp. 49-50)

And so it is that Carducci's greatness seems due not only to what he said but even more to the way in which he said it. Whatever in his poetry makes him truly representative of his age—ideas such as Country, Patriotism, Liberty—would no doubt have found poetic expression for themselves somehow, even if Carducci had never lived. Wherever he admits the intrusion of his own purely personal views—on religion or politics, for instance—the necessary limitations of a man of his particular temperament and bringing up immediately betray themselves. What gives its distinctive value and quality to his work is its form. There exists a relationship between form and substance in art which Carducci was quick to perceive, and certainly intended his own verse to illustrate, as the following lines, prefixed to his *Barbarian Odes,* prove:—

> Schlechten gestümperten Versen genügt ein geringer Gehalt schon,
> Während die edlere Form tiefe Gedanken bedarf:
> Wollte man euer Geschwätz ausprägen zur sapphischen Ode,
> Würde die Welt einsehn, dass es ein leeres Geschwätz.

>> ["A mean content is enough for bad bungling verses, whereas the nobler form needs profound thoughts. Were your idle chatter to be stamped into a Sapphic ode, the world would perceive its emptiness."]

These two couplets of Platen summarise Carducci's artistic creed, and suggest his view of the relation of poetry, as an art, to life. Nobility of form demands a corresponding nobility of content. The value of ideas may be tested in their formal expression. From the purely artistic point of view this means no more than that in all really great art form and substance must be so intimately bound up with one another as to be inseparable even in thought. But Carducci is also thinking of the relation of art to life. The life and ideals of a nation are indicated by the forms of its art. If its life be controlled by reason, so will its art be also. Similarly, by a reverse process, form will react on content, art upon life. "Es liegen," said Goethe, "in den verschiedenen poetischen Formen geheimnissvolle grosse Wirkungen." It is the privilege of the great artist to elevate, as it is in his power to debase, the ideals of his countrymen. We have already referred to the moral implication involved in the title *vate* to which Carducci aspired. Realising that the restraint of Greek art resulted from the same controlling intellect as governed Greek life, and since restraint was the note he desired to introduce not only into the poetry, but through poetry into the ideals, of his own age, he deliberately adopted classical forms into Italian verse. By so doing he hoped to introduce the classical spirit also. Idealise Liberty in an Alcaic ode, he argued, and if the art be good—that is, if form and content correspond—the idea itself will of necessity assume the severe yet majestic proportions of the verse which expresses it. On the other hand, the qualities that belong to the sensuous language and loose or rhymed metres of modern poetry envelop the thought in an enervating atmosphere highly charged with emotion, which, be it good or bad, is apt sometimes to burst in a storm of passion beyond all the bounds of reason, and in any case favours the growth of an unwholesome aestheticism, ending often in undisguised sensuality. . . . [Carducci] did not . . . try to make the present fit the past, as initiators of classical reactions have sometimes done, seeking to impose the outworn forms of "a grave old time" upon new material unfitted to receive them. On the contrary, he forced the past to acknowledge its oneness with the present by endeavouring to show that the same principles of formal beauty which had produced the *anti-chità serena* of old Greece and Rome were still those in obedience to which modern Italy could best develop and control the nascent powers wherewith her Risorgimento had endowed her. His was not, indeed, the mental *Allgemeinheit* ["universality"], which knows how to interpret man and nature in verse that appeals to all nations and all ages. But in his poetry the third Italy saw herself reflected in her purest and serenest aspect, and her ideals linked on to many, if not all, the most cherished traditions of her past. (pp. 51-3)

> *G. L. Bickersteth, in his* Carducci: A Selection of His Poems, with Verse Translations, Notes, and Three Introductory Essays, *Longmans, Green, and Co., 1913, 346 p.*

THE SATURDAY REVIEW, LONDON   (essay date 1913)

[*In the following excerpt, the critic discusses Carducci's synthesis of seemingly incongruous social and political ideas in his works.*]

English taste in foreign literature was ever eclectic; but, even so, how strange that Carducci—for most of his life a mighty influence in European letters—should have had to wait so long for his first English edition! Perhaps it is because the nineteenth century and its ideas have suddenly become very remote . . . ; but still more it is because Carducci is a difficult man to handle. He was a bundle of contradictions. Always the preacher of action, he was himself a professor and even held the same chair for nearly fifty years. Always a patriot of the third Italy, his mind was thoroughly cosmopolitan, influenced by Greek and Latin classics, by Byron, Victor Hugo, and, above all, by the great German poets. A hater of Christianity, his verse is yet full of a most Christian enthusiasm for humanity. A hater of romanticism, he was a romantic who could not describe an Italian landscape without calling up its historical atmosphere, and who could find the modern spirit of action and progress embodied in the railway locomotive. A man of passion, who could only see one side of a question at a time, he saw all its sides in time. He was an ardent Republican after 1860, but he died a Senator of the Italian Kingdom; and though he first won fame by his **Hymn to Satan**—to him a rationalist anti-Pope— he yet wrote an ode in aid of a church restoration fund. A man of the encyclopædic learning which usually produces treatises, he wrote poetry; and, the apostle of a new movement, he revived old metres and renewed the life of old words. His secret is hard indeed to discover!

Yet Carducci's contemporaries understood him. He cared as little as Browning for popular applause, and his poems are often so allusive that only a scholar can understand them; but his fame in Italy was the fame not of a Browning but of a Tennyson. His many-sidedness gave Carducci his power. The makers of the third Italy dreamed of a new state which should be the heir of all the ages, and Carducci was the answer to their dream.

His task was to blend all that was best out of older civilisations with the ideas of the new age, and in executing it he knew how to work ideas from the Classics and the German lyrists into a poem about a railway train.

He conceived it to be his special function to fuse Classical and Teutonic mythology into a common poetic tradition. There is nothing more characteristic of him than the passage in the poem on Shelley's funeral urn, where he imagines the great legendary figures of both peoples conversing in the isles of the blest. Achilles is there with Siegfried, Roland with Hector, Oedipus with Lear; the women, too, Cordelia and Antigone, Helen and Iseult, Clytemnestra and Lady Macbeth. The mere happy marshalling of names—the scholar's work—makes the proper effect. It is suggested that Latin and Teuton have devised kindred though differently-named conceptions of the same ideas. Those ideas are still living, it is implied, and Carducci invites the new Italy to develop a new treatment of them in the light of all the artistic achievement of the past. Thence the paradox that his patriotism is vested in cosmopolitanism. He is the one great Italian writer steeped in German literature, and is all the more Italian for it. He had read everything and could use everything he had read. He loved to recall a Horatian or Virgilian cadence, or to employ a phrase from Homer or Theocritus. He borrowed his metres from the troubadours and wrote sonnets as the successor of Dante, Petrarch. Tasso, Alfieri, and Ugo Foscolo. Above all, he was intensely alive to the history of every bit of Italian soil. It was impossible for him to think of Umbria without thinking of St. Francis and Perugino, and a dozen more. But with all this learning Carducci was no pedant. He knew what the past could give to the future. That is why he wrote poetry and why the best men of his time honoured him as the true Vates of the new Italy— the author of her traditions.

Let us glance at what is, perhaps, the best-known of all his poems—the sapphic ode, rendered in curious but very Carduccian English sapphics by Mr. Bickersteth [in *Carducci: A Selection of His Poems*], called "**By the Sources of Clitumnus.**" Every English lover of Italy knows the scene—the most gracious in all Umbria—with its transparent pool and dainty trees, the little Temple where Christians once worshipped, the characteristic white oxen in the fields around. Carducci describes it all, and the point of his description is that his Umbria is the Umbria of the Georgics. The first seven stanzas send the reader to his Virgil to hunt out parallel passages. Then comes a complaint. There are willow trees about the spring, melancholy trees, quite out of keeping with the poet's idea of it. Italian nature should be the setting of Italian history. There should be oaks and cypresses, emblems of strength and noble memories. To justify this idea Carducci runs through Umbrian history— the Etrurian Kingdom, the Roman conquest, the victorious march of Hannibal after Trasimene. Then, by quick transition, comes a sketch of the serene beauties of the place to-day, leading up to the doctrine that it is in her own woods and hills and streams that the new Italy should seek inspiration for her poetry. Why has this inspiration failed? Because, he insists, the curse of an ascetic monasticism has swept over the land. But now that a more human spirit rules by Tiber's banks, Italy can again become the mother of men that Virgil proclaimed her, and through the mountains and thickets and streams of green Umbria rushes the herald of new activities—the railway engine. That final touch—Virgil and the locomotive in successive stanzas—is most Carduccian, and contemporaries felt that by odes like these the poet was giving the third Italy her soul. So he was. It is a long way from Cavour to Giolitti, from the Expedition of the Thousand to the expedition to Tripoli, but modern Italy feels the progress as a continuous development, and Carducci is the key to her thought.

Put into prose, Carducci's habit of combining incongruities raises a smile. Carducci's verse raises no smile; even the foreign reader can feel that his touch is sure. This is because he took immense pains over form. He had ideas of his own about it. As Horace took the metres of the Greek lyric poets and made them express the ideas of Imperial Rome, Carducci took the Horatian metres and made them express the ideas of the new Italy. Here, again, the reader feels that for any man but Carducci—poet and scholar in one—the attempt would have been ridiculous. But Carducci combined metrical knowledge with a perfect ear. . . . The ordinary reader need only note that the odes have the sound of modern Italian. Be the metres new or old, they are right, as Swinburne's metres are right. But it is a great boon to Italian literature that Carducci should have given his successors metrical forms which submit themselves to rule. Form is the Circe that brutalises Italian poets. Just as English poetry, whose inspiration is often ethical, easily degenerates into the goody-goody, so Italian poetry, whose inspiration is largely aesthetic, easily degenerates into the pretty-pretty. Carducci is never pretty-pretty, and, besides setting a good example himself, he shows later men how pretty-prettiness may be avoided. Let them only keep the great models before their minds, and by sympathetic use of them they can write good modern poetry. It is because Carducci is at once traditional and original that he gives a message. To ask whether there is or is not a Carduccian school in Italy were quite superfluous. The truth is, all future Italian poets will be Carduccians. For Carducci has again quickened Italian artistic inspiration.

His is a new torch whose flames have been kindled from torches that the purblind thought extinguished. The flame will burn throughout the centuries, much as Dante's flame has burnt and for the same reasons. Carducci is, indeed, no Dante; but, like Dante, he has started a poetic risorgimento. (pp. 687-88)

> *"The Torch of Carducci," in* The Saturday Review, *London, Vol. 116, No. 3031, November 29, 1913, pp. 687-88.*

FRANCES SHAW   (essay date 1914)

[*In the following excerpt, Shaw praises Carducci's early poetry for its patriotic and anti-Romantic sentiments.*]

To recommend a volume of Carducci's verse to American readers is to answer the question—what has the poet to say to the present generation? He was born in 1835, and lived through all those stirring years that transformed Italy into a modern nation. To achieve this end splendid political victories had to be won. But, more important still and more fundamental, a moral change had to be wrought in the character of the whole Italian nation. Enslaved for centuries to foreign powers, the oppressed people had to be taught to walk erect and had to learn afresh the meaning of such sacred words as Liberty and Independence; and because Carducci, more successfully than any other, lit the altar-fires in their hearts they acclaimed him as their *vate,* their inspired seer. But while urging his countrymen to renew their own moral and spiritual beings as the best preparation for freedom and union, he did not fail to direct piercing shafts of hatred and contempt at every enemy of progress, and above all at the Roman Catholic Church. It is astonishing how large a part of his work is permeated with these

patriotic themes; if we note in addition that he grew up at a time when the romantic movement was at its palest and its sickliest, and that he shared the strong reaction against its tenets that set in shortly after the middle of the century, we have pretty much the compass of his work till the learned second period of his life.

It is this learned second period which, according to the present reviewer at least, spells disaster. Not unnaturally, a man whose wholesome vigor and simple sense of the realities of life turned him in his youth against the current romantic flabbiness, felt his heart go out more and more strongly to the great and self-contained literature of Greece and Rome. But misfortune would have it that to earn a livelihood the poet accepted a professorship in the University of Bologna, and in a few years alas! the transformation had been wrought and his winged Pegasus was hardly distinguishable from the average academic carthorse. Carducci took to imitating classical forms, he peopled his verse with a forgotten mythology, and although he was too great a man ever to become insincere, the stream of his inspiration grew too thin to sweep along the heavy litter of superimposed scholarship. There are many who, far from sharing this opinion, date the real Carducci from the *Odi barbare;* but, if fire and passion are the just prerogatives of verse, the reviewer submits that such early pieces as the *Hymn to Satan,* celebrating the triumph of Reason over Superstition, and **"Per Giuseppe Monti e Gaetano Tognetti,"** which blasts the Vatican into "a nameless shame," are worth more than several volumes of nobly reserved Alcaic and Sapphic stanzas. In any case the patriotic verse of the youthful Carducci has the feel of molten metal, and when, in what we will call his professorial period, his poetry acquires a sudden glow, the occasion is usually supplied by a return to the old theme of freedom and Italy.

Because the American reader is sure to feel himself nearer to the red-blooded young Carducci than to the high-minded, excessively Olympian, old man, it is to be regretted that so many of the . . . [selections in *Carducci: A Selection of His Poems*] confess the classical spirit. But even here Carducci is far from negligible, being from first to last an oak-hearted son of the Italian mother-earth, of whom it may said—and of how many poets besides?—that he never penned a line that did not express an absolute conviction. (pp. 199-201)

> *Frances Shaw, in a review of "Carducci: A Selection of His Poems, with Verse Translations, Notes, and Three Introductory Essays," in* Poetry, *Vol. IV, No. 5, August, 1914, pp. 198-201.*

JOHN BAILEY   (essay date 1926)

[*In the following excerpt from a lecture given at Oxford University, Bailey considers prominent characteristics of Carducci's work and focuses on several of his most important poems, particularly the six odes that he considers to be Carducci's finest.*]

I believe a common notion about Carducci is that he was partly a Professor making imitations of ancient poets, and partly an Italian patriot putting ephemeral politics into verse. And what sort of poetry could be less worth troubling about than a mixture of political speeches with Prize-medal echoes of the Classics?

Now that notion has some truth in it and, so far as it is true, it is fatal to Carducci. I should not recommend any one who was not making a very special study of Carducci to spend much time over the *Juvenilia* where the scholar has hardly escaped from the schoolmaster, or even from the schoolboy, stage of development. Nor should I think him wise to trouble himself much with the *Giambi ed epodi* for the reason that they mainly deal with events of passing political interest which the poet has hardly known how to lift into that atmosphere of the universal and eternal which is the atmosphere of great poetry. But what of that? To confess so much is only to confess that Carducci, like most other poets, produced a good deal of mediocre work now best ignored by the judicious reader. The accusation only becomes damaging if it can be upheld against his poetry generally. But can it? It is true that in all his work, including his finest, there is almost invariably a felt presence both of literature and politics. And there are people in whose eyes that is enough to condemn him. One of the truest poets we have in England to-day, Mr. W. H. Davies, remarks in his Preface to one of the best selections of recent poetry that in it "patriotic poetry has been purposely avoided as it is seldom enjoyed by lovers of real poetry." It is this kind of feeling which acts against Carducci. Somehow or other it is common to-day: part of the price, I suppose, which we have to pay for those seekings after a better international feeling which are among the most hopeful political signs of our time. But we ought not to pay it. Few things would appear more certain than that if we cannot be internationally-minded without ceasing to be patriotic we shall never be internationally-minded at all. (pp. 4-5)

The other attack I can hardly need to repel in this place. Here in Oxford I hope we are not very likely to think learning fatal to a poet. We know that the history of European poetry is an almost unbroken tradition, and that every poet of importance inherits a past and creates a future. And we know how much the scholarship of poetry, in hands that know how to use it, can enrich and glorify its own verse with memories and suggestions of the art and thought of older masters. (p. 6)

We are entitled, then, to reassure ourselves. Carducci may have to plead guilty to both those accusations; he may be learned and he may be political; and yet neither his learning nor his politics may be fatal to his poetry. I believe, even, that as he has used them in his happiest moments, they are both of its essence. If they are present in his failures they are also present in his triumphs. They were in fact an inseparable part of the man himself. . . . What separates his successes from his failures is not a difference of subject but a difference of quality; the presence or the absence, or the presence in a greater or a less degree, of the mood and power of poetry. . . . Poetry gives us a picture of life and the world in which the imagination sees much more than is commonly seen, the heart feels much more than is commonly felt, the mind thinks more than is commonly thought, and the tongue or the pen, whatever name you give to the power of expression, expresses much more of these feelings, thoughts, imaginations, than can be expressed at ordinary times or by ordinary persons. Well, all poets have their ordinary times; and unfortunately they sometimes write in them. And they are in part ordinary persons; and sometimes the ordinary person confuses himself with the poet and puts on the poet's mantle. That happened in Carducci as in others; and as in him the ordinary person, the person who was not a poet, was sometimes a pedant and sometimes a journalist, we have some poems published in his complete works which are exercises in pedantry and others which are outbursts of journalism. But they are not the poems with which we are concerned to-day; for they do not affect, or ought not to affect, our estimate of the poet Carducci. (pp. 6-7)

[Carducci's early poems] are chiefly interesting as showing how free Carducci was from both of the two opposite (or are they opposite?) vices of youth: its coarseness and its gushing sentimentality. In youth as in age he is muscular, sane, clean, virile in manner and thought: and, immature as these *Juvenilia* are, they already have style and are the work of a scholar and an artist. Only the three elements of scholar, artist, and patriot are not yet fused, as they presently will be, into the poet. Did I speak of three elements? There is a fourth more important than any of them. In the scholar, the artist, the patriot there is always visibly present a man. It is sometimes said that Carducci lacks heart. Even Mr. Bickersteth says of him such things as that he cannot be called a poet of the "human soul" and that "to repress all merely personal emotion was the end at which he aimed." Both these remarks, even partly qualified as they are by their context, are in my judgement serious misrepresentations of the truth. It is quite true that Carducci had little of the religious and nothing at all of the philosophic habit of mind: and therefore made no attempt at using his poetry to utter the deepest searchings of the human spirit, still less to offer a solution of the ultimate problems which confront the human mind. He was no Job, no Lucretius, no Dante, no Goethe: he was entirely without the speculative curiosity of his contemporary Browning; and though some of the poems of his old age, waiting outside the dark portal, are curiously like those which the old age of Tennyson was producing a few years earlier, yet he had in him little or nothing of that continual sense of a Mystery, unknown indeed but certainly Divine, which was never many hours absent from the mind of Tennyson. But to admit this is only to admit that he was not one of the great seers of poetry. It is not at all to admit either that he had no heart or that he did not allow it to make itself felt in his poetry. It is true that he made it his business from the first to turn utterly away from the facile and gushing emotionalism of the Romantics. He defiantly promised his critics that they should never be able to accuse him of having written poems with the object of showing what a fine fellow he was. He did not wear his heart on his sleeve. . . . But have we yet to learn that a fluent verbosity of sentiment is no proof of heart? Which moves us most in the Anthology, the few words of Simonides or the many of Meleager? Which are the great moments in Shakespeare, the bursts of exuberant rhetoric, or the brief sentences which utter a world of emotion in three or four monosyllables? So with Carducci. I do not envy the man who has read him without perceiving that he has in him more heart than a whole tribe of Rousseaus and Chateaubriands and Mussets. I say without any doubt or hesitation that few poets have gone so deep down into those secret places of the human heart where alone we realize all the meaning that there may be in such words as son and brother and father, home and country. The proof is there for all of us to see. The grave and poignant beauty of the poems about his little son Dante, whom he lost so young, is a thing unforgettable: and except the brother of Catullus I do not remember any brother whose memory lives in such verse as Carducci gave, and more than once, to his.

Let me, then, insist that beside the scholar and artist and patriot whom all can see in Carducci there is also, what has not always been seen, a man of large and tender heart, who has again and again written verse which some of us find among the most moving we know. And let me try now to show how much poetry he has left us in which those various elements escape from their insolation.

To see that we must come to his mature work. I spoke briefly of the *Juvenilia*. . . . I need say even less of the *Giambi ed epodi* which follow. They are the product of Carducci's disillusion with the kingdom of Italy and what seemed to him its compromises and cowardices. In his earlier years he had addressed poems to Victor Emmanuel, calling him the champion for whom Italy was waiting and the son of a noble father; and he was later on to return to loyal acceptance of the House of Savoy, addressing odes to Queen Margaret and making of Charles Albert the most human and moving of all his historical portraits. But poets have hardly ever understood that politics are, in the main, an art of awaiting opportunities and of accepting compromises; and Cavour, who understood that so well, was hardly dead before Carducci was clamouring for action which might easily have strangled the infant Italy in its cradle. No doubt there was plenty of field for righteous scorn and hatred in the Italian politics of those days. But Carducci's angry impatience made journalism rather than poetry: the patriot feels only the happenings of the moment which are sufficient food for the journalist but never for the poet: and after the fine prologue with its note of

> Be through my lips to unawakened earth
> The trumpet of a prophecy

we do not get much from the *Giambi* but rhetoric, invective, and epigram. (pp. 9-11)

[With] *Rime nuove,* of which the earliest are much earlier and the latest are much later than the *Giambi ed epodi,* we reach the Carducci who is one of the poets of the whole world. There are still here many more or less commonplace exercises in verse, imitations and avowed translations: and there is still a little political invective of the journalistic order. . . . But in the finest of the *Rime nuove,* all that was in Carducci, scholar, artist, historian, patriot, human being, are fused into a union in which memory and mind, heart and imagination, the sense of literature and the sense of life, all unite in something rarer than themselves, something which is great poetry. Take, first of all, the pieces in which the scholar and artist predominate. They are not all successes. I confess to finding the **"Primavere elleniche"** rather frigid: and of the three sonnets to Homer only the first seems to me quite worthy of so great a poet as Carducci. . . .

But though Carducci was always returning to the Greeks and more than once declared that Greek poetry was the supreme poetry which had no equal, yet he was a Latin in heart and mind as well as in blood, and, as it is Horace who was the chief model of his verse, so it is Virgil who moved him to the noblest of his poetic tributes. (p. 13)

Like Milton, Carducci is chiefly known by poems in which he broke away "from the troublesome and modern bondage of rhyming." But, again like the denouncer of that bondage, he used rhyme in some of his loveliest poems; and [in his **"Ode to Rhyme"**], confessing himself a heretic, he yet brings a splendid offering to the temple of rhyme. **"Alla rima"** is a thing of rushing verve and go, full at once of the learning and of the vigorous personality of Carducci. He shows how the troubadours by whom rhyme was carried all over Europe made it serve all the purposes for which they used poetry, and then how Dante called it to other tasks and made with it the first great poem of the poet-classical world. And there he leaves it, queen, as he admits, of Latin metre. . . . (p. 14)

Poetry is the union of opposites, the solution of contradictions. As the poet of *Odi barbare* pays his homage to rhyme, as the pedant is absorbed in the man, so it is curious to see that even the hater of the Romantics, the lifelong classic both by temper and education, could transcend these antitheses and write poems which are purely Romantic in temper. The four stanzas called

"Pantheism" might well have come from Heine by whom he was much influenced at this time, though a hundred things, and chiefly health and daylight, kept him from ever becoming either the cynic or the sentimentalist, each of whom was a large part of Heine. "I never uttered her name; it echoed only in my silent heart: but the stars told my secret to each other and the setting sun whispered it to the moon, and birds and trees and flowers, nay, earth and heaven themselves, murmur all round me 'She loves you, she loves you'." And, if in the poem **"Classicism and Romanticism"** he puts all his weight into the scale of the sun which is his symbol of the Classical— the sun, the giver of corn and wine and spring and light and joy—and none into that of the Romantic moon whose milky languors bring neither flowers nor fruit and only flatter idle poets and empty loves, yet in the purely Romantic **"Moon's Revenge"** which follows, he actually makes of this same "lewd and barren nun with the stupid face" the giver to his mistress of all the beauty in which he desires to drown his soul. Who, again, has written a ballad fuller of medieval romance than the rhymed stanzas of **"Jaufré Rudel,"** which are to be found in his last volume? So varied, so contradictory, so double-faced, such reconcilers of opposites, are even the most definitely doctrinal of poets; as we may see in the fact that some of the most purely Romantic lines of English verse are to be found in Milton and some of the most entirely classical in Keats. Indeed in their happiest moments, all poets, the Classical as well as the Romantic, the Romantic as well as the Classical, transcend these distinctions, or exhibit the two moods at once. . . . And if we look at the famous Sonnet, **"Il bove"**, . . . one of such extraordinary quality that it could hardly be excluded from any selection of the finest sonnets in the world, do we not find in it an almost miraculous combination of classical directness, simplicity and truth with a sentiment, a "dolcezza," to use its own word, which moves us as we are moved by the masters of Romance? So, also, the two poems about his brother and his child are as simple as a Greek epitaph or a marble stele of Athens: yet Carducci's marble, like that of Greece, can take us very close to tears, perhaps beyond them. The sonnet **"Funere mersit acerbo"** and the brief stanzas **"Pianto antico"** are very well known to every one who has ever looked into Carducci. But I lay stress on them because, even if they stood alone, they would be a complete refutation of the notion which keeps many people from making trial of him; the notion that he was never really stirred by anything more human than old books and contemporary politics. It is impossible to make a greater mistake. Carducci was a man of passionate nature and, if he put passion into his love of literature and his love of Italy, as he assuredly did, he had abundance left in him for the love of men and women and children. (pp. 15-16)

And while I am insisting on the heart of Carducci let me add that it is not only death that shows it to us. How many poets have so often written about the marriages of those whom they loved and with such evident personal feeling? Many have written *Epithalamia* for the marriages of great personages to whose hopes and fears they were entirely indifferent, and sometimes the result has been a great poem. But that was not Carducci's way. On these subjects at any rate he wrote no verses into which he did not put his heart. And what a collection of them, those poems of death and marriage and home and friendship, he has left us! If we included only the very finest the list would not be a short one: for, beside these two poems on his dead child and brother which are only the finest of several, it must at the least include the **"Ave"** of *Odi barbare* and the **"Funeral of the Alpine Guide"** in *Rime e ritmi*: while to marriage he returned again and again, always with the same grave tenderness, his heart speaking in every word, from the two fine sonnets in *Levia gravia,* "For a Marriage in Spring" and "The Marriage of a Geologist," to the two beautiful *Odi barbare* about his daughter's marriage, "Colli Toscani" and "Per le nozze di mia figlia," and the touching stanzas in *Rime e ritmi* addressed to the daughter of Crispi on her marriage. And the list would have in it more than one showing his love of children, such as the pretty little lines put at the head of *Rime e ritmi* and the poem called "Sabato santo" written for the birthday of the daughter of an old friend. And then there would be some at least of the many poems in which he returned to his home and his childhood and his first love: "Davanti San Guido" and "Idillio maremmano," if nothing else; and one or two at any rate of the poems he gave to friendship which in him had a Roman constancy and strength. Whatever else was omitted the four stanzas of "Alla mensa dell' amico" would have to be included; for, though others address particular friends with more open and personal affection, none has more of Carducci than this. All his worships are in it, not only friendship but the Sun God and the God of Wine: all his strong, and again partly Roman, feeling for the family, for him the greatest of all human institutions: and finally the grave and quiet tenderness, without fear, without revolt, without impatience, with which he always met the thought of death. (pp. 17-18)

The genius of many poets, as we know, pales in middle life. The exact reverse of this is seen in Carducci. He published little of importance before he was thirty: of the *Odi barbare,* by which he will always be chiefly remembered, the first did not appear till he was forty and the final series not till he was past fifty: and his last volume, which is as fine as *Odi barbare* and much finer than any of its predecessors, appeared in 1899 when he was sixty-two. That long scholarly life spent in a Professor's Chair at Bologna had in no way dulled his fire or dried his heart. It had made him wiser and gentler and less of a partisan: but he never loved Italy more, or showed his love more passionately, than in those later years; and his love of the great dead, who were to him so alive, his love of Nature, of Man, of all the wonder, mystery and tenderness of life, is seen at its height in his last two volumes. For any one who wishes to read a little of Carducci and has no time to attempt the whole there is no question that these two small volumes are the things to be recommended. No doubt such a reader will miss a few wonderful things, especially the Sonnets of which I have spoken. But they are not much more than a few: and whoever has read *Odi barbare* and *Rime e ritmi* knows Carducci and knowing him will probably not be content with two only of his books. There is a special reason too why these two volumes are the best to be read. The scholarship of literature is nothing if it does not teach the man who gives himself to it the gulf which separates the only perfect word from the many imperfect. Carducci was learning that all his life. In his later poems, very much more than in his earlier, one continually feels that he has not been content to let his pen touch his paper until he has found the one word which will give all he wants to give of meaning and association and music. So with the artist. Carducci loved form and he loved it more and more as he grew older. Only a few times in these last volumes—perhaps in "Bicocca di San Giacomo" perhaps in the "Ode to Ferrara"—does he allow the garrulity of age to ignore the first rule of art, that the half is greater than the whole. He had shown in his early volumes more than enough of the exuberant rhetoric of youth. Now he almost always compresses his thought and emotion into a mould of sculpturesque severity. It was no mere whim of classical scholarship that made him rewrite the Alcaics and Sapphics and Asclepiads of Horace on a system

of his own. He chose very definite forms for his verse because he thought poetry gained by strictness and was weakened by looseness of structure.... There can be no question that his later work, almost all in one or another form which resists the poet and makes his task a difficult one, is not merely finer art but richer stuff than his earlier. All his subjects have grown larger. His politics are not less Italian, less actual and contemporary: but now they are put into the presence of history without which politics cannot make literature. He is still himself in every poem. But the self that is felt in them is now, what it was not always, at once himself and all the world. He has in fact risen to the full stature of a poet; who is at once more of an individual than other men, more arresting, singular, and solitary, and also more representative of the whole of humanity, abler to think and feel for all men, abler to say what, when it has been said, they all recognize as their own.

One might roughly divide the contents of these last volumes into poems of nature, poems of politics and history, and poems of the human affections. I will say a word of each. Carducci's attitude to nature is like his attitude to life, simple and direct. He has no philosophy here or elsewhere.... His faith in Italy and her people was built partly on the memory of the great Italians of the past and partly on the two seas of Italy and the lakes, rivers and mountains among which Italians live. Such a people, he thought, with such a past and so lovely a land to inspire them, must have a future too. Wordsworth would have agreed with every word of that. But that was only a part of Wordsworth's faith: and when he said such things as

> Winds blow and waters roll
> Strength to the brave and Power and Deity

part of his meaning was a mysticism which was outside Carducci's ken. Carducci did not ask what was behind Nature. He was content with her as a visible presence of beauty and delight, and as the giver of good things to men, especially of bread, the strength of man's labour, and wine, the joy of his rest. As woman was for him, not, as for the Romantics, a dream of sensuous or sentimental beauty, but always a power of life as daughter, wife, or mother, often too as worker in the fields, so his Nature was not a vision but an energy of life, perpetually inheriting, and perpetually using its inheritance for new creation. To this conception of a working and beneficent Nature, which has its parallel in our own Meredith, he continually returns. The *Georgics* were never far away from his mind, and when he makes his salutation to Italy at the end of that "Ode to the Springs of Clitumnus" which some have thought his finest poem it is as mother of oxen and horses, corn and vines, as well as of arts and laws, that he hails her.... (pp. 18-21)

This realism of Carducci's was at once an instinct and a doctrine. "Away with metaphysics" he said: "let us poets get back to nature and reason and reality: let us return to the ancients who are at once realistic and free." But his realism was no mere utilitarianism. He saw the things of nature as they are, as few men see them: and loved the sight and could render it in verse with extra-ordinary exactness and vividness. There is more than one wonderful picture of snow in poetry: but is there any, even that of Mr. Bridges, which more makes us feel as if we were ourselves in it than the "Nevicata" of Carducci, his only and not too successful experiment in the accentual hexameter? It is done in quite a different way from "London Snow," with far less detail and with a greater insistence, natural to an Italian, on the silence and gloom of snowfall. But I find myself almost equally conscious of the snow in both poems. And everywhere Carducci's poems are sown with little pictures of particular scenes, or seasons of the year, of a wonderful clearness of beauty. One feels oneself on the Italian Alps as one reads **"Piemonte"**; when one reads **"Mezzo giorno"** one is as conscious of a southern noon as one is when reading the *Midi* stanzas of Leconte de Lisle. And though Carducci will never put a philosophy into his landscapes he will often put himself. How many poems of Spring are either lovelier or tenderer than his **"Primavera"**? It is more fanciful than he commonly is. But how well the fancy is fitted into the facts, how exactly the epithets chosen at once help out the fancy and express the facts! And, simple as all the words are, how hard it would be to change one without injuring the poem! Like all Carducci's later work these four short stanzas are a lesson in the art of expression

> Ecco: di braccio al pigro verno sciogliesi
> ed ancor trema nuda al rigid' aere
> la primavera: il sol tra le sue lacrime
> limpido brilla, o Lalage.
>
> Da lor culle di neve i fior si svegliano
> e curïosi al ciel gli occhietti levano:
> in quelli sguardi vagola una tremula
> ombra di sogno, o Lalage.
>
> Nel sonno de l'inverno sotto il candido
> lenzuolo de la neve i fior sognarono;
> sognaron l'albe roride ed i tepidi
> soli e il tuo viso, o Lalage.
>
> Ne l'addormito spirito che sognano
> i miei pensieri? A tua bellezza candida
> perchè mesta sorride tra le lacrime
> la primavera, o Lalage!

There may be some here who do not follow the Italian. I ask the pardon of those who do for adding a translation of my own:

> Behold from sluggish winter's arm
>   Spring lifts herself again:
> Naked before the steel-cold air
>   She shivers as in pain;
> Look, Lalage, is that a tear
>   In the sun's eye which yet shines clear?
>
> From beds of snow the flowers awake
>   Lifting in deep amaze
> To heaven their eager eyes: but yet
>   More in that wistful gaze
> Than wonder lies: sure trembles there
>   O Lalage, some memory fair,
>
> Some dream which 'neath the coverlet white
>   Of winter snow they dreamed,
> Some sleeping sight of dewy dawns
>   And summer suns that gleamed,
> And thy bright eyes, O Lalage;
>   Was not the dream a prophecy?
>
> To-day my spirit sleeps and dreams;
>   Where do my far thoughts fly?
> Close to thy beauty's face we stand
>   And smile, the spring and I;
> Yet, Lalage, whence come those tears?
>   Has spring, too, felt the doom of years?

These Lalages and Lydias whom Carducci occasionally introduces are of course only Horatian shadows. But he will often connect his landscapes with historical figures, Dante or Titian, the Emperor Maximilian or Charles Albert, Garibaldi or Cairoli or Calvi. And sometimes with figures belonging to his own private affections like the Maria of the **"Idillio maremmano,"** his first love whom he half enviously pictures on some farm with stalwart sons around her; like his summer hostess of the

Inn at Gaby: or again like his daughter for whom in *Colli Toscani* he prays to the beautiful hills which he once knew and loved so well to give her the happiness they had denied to him and to whisper to her no word of her near ones whom she never knew, who lived there in sorrow and died in despair, and may be greeting her, perhaps even awaiting her, in their graves. (pp. 21-4)

I have left to the last those historical and political odes which are unquestionably the most original work of Carducci. There is nothing quite like them anywhere so far as I know. The passion for history had been a feature of the Romantic movement. Carducci took history out of the hands of the Romantics and made it the chief subject of poems of classical form and classical temper. What the Romantics had often made an amusement or an embroidery or a languishing sigh over a shadowy and often imaginary past became in Carducci's hands a fountain of moral energy and political life. Hating the dilettantism which was so common among Romantics, he took care to know every inch of the ground over which he travelled; and the great figures of his historical odes have the substance and solidity of truth. But of course truth of history will not alone make poetry, and too much truth in the shape of too many facts may easily, as sometimes in Carducci himself, stifle poetry in information. But there is no mere history in the best of Carducci's Odes. The facts and personages are selected: Carducci was never one of those poets who think that all subjects are equally suitable for poetry. He knew the immense advantage with which a poet starts who has chosen for his theme, as he chose, such figures as Maximilian or Charles Albert or the mother of Napoleon. And more than that; even in these selected subjects he never confined himself to history. In his most historical poems there are always present two things which are not history, or were not then, himself and the Italy in which he lived. History was for him, in no meagre or pedantic sense, a living lesson: and as Horace when he wrote of Regulus thought of the Rome of Augustus, so when Carducci wrote of the Rock of Quarto he thought not only of Garibaldi's Thousand but of those who had so soon forgotten them and the cause for which they had set out into the unknown that wonderful night. His Odes are no page of dead history; they are chapters in the life of a poet and a nation, and both speak through every burning word of them, the poet in his own voice and as he really was, Italy, as she was not always, in the voice the poet gave her. (pp. 24-5)

There are a good many of these historical odes, as everybody who has looked at Carducci knows. It would be difficult to say which are the finest. But at least six, those **"To Rome,"** **"To the Springs of Clitumnus,"** **"On the Death of the Prince Imperial,"** **"Miramar,"** **"Piemonte,"** and **"La chiesa di Polenta,"** must certainly, I think, rank among the very finest examples in all the world of what poetry can do with history. Many would add to this list the ode to the statue of Victory at Brescia, that on the River Adda, the two Garibaldi odes, that called the Rock of Quarto and that written after Garibaldi's death, or those to Cadore and Ferrara and that called **"Bicocca di San Giacomo."** But the Garibaldi poems, marvellous as is the vividness of their pictures of the hero himself and of the scenes of his embarking at Quarto and of his retreat after Mentana, are not entirely characteristic of Carducci's manner in these odes; for the present in them hardly takes us back to the past at all. They are rather contemporary than historical. There are some again, like the **"Victory Ode,"** in which the range is much narrower than in the great odes, while in others, notably in the **"Bicocca,"** poetry tends to be drowned in a sea of obscure details of history and geography. A Carduccian will find in all of them, and in others which I have not mentioned, things to delight in, things to stop and read aloud again and again till all the pleasure of art and thought and imagination has been got out of them. But I would not advise any one to expect that reading the **"Bicocca"** and **"Ferrara"** odes will make him a Carduccian if he is not one already: for there is no doubt at all that they are long, and not much that they are in parts both obscure and tedious. (pp. 27-8)

The first of my six is the ode written in 1877 to celebrate the 2630th year of Rome. Other odes of Carducci's may have more imagination; none equals this in passionate concentration. It begins with the contrast between the Rome of Romulus looking out on wood and wilderness, and the Rome of to-day, the capital of the Italian race. It is a small point, but I always wish I could find in the first line a various reading of "redimita,' in the feminine, agreeing with Rome, instead of the "redimito" of the text, agreeing with April. It seems to me that "redimita" would make a much better point with its contrast between the hills once crowned with flowers and now, "dopo tanta forza di secoli," crowned with monuments and memories which are the greatest in all the world. However, all the editions I have seen read "redimito"; so evidently Carducci judged otherwise. The ode goes on to the opposite contrast, that between the Forum of consuls and triumphs and the silent and solitary Forum of to-day. And the poet takes the opportunity, after his wont, to work in some famous ancient words and make them no longer Latin but Italian, no more Virgil's but his own. (p. 28)

The **"Ode to the Springs of Clitumnus,"** equally Roman in spirit, is very much longer [than **"Ode to Rome"**], is in Sapphics instead of Alcaics, and is besides in rather a different poetic manner. It was conceived on the spot in 1876, a year earlier than the Roman Ode. It contains far more historical detail and begins with one of those landscape scenes, with nature and man and the animals all playing their parts, in which Carducci has few poetic rivals. Very likely it is founded on something he saw when he went there. The flocks still come to the ancient springs: and the Umbrian boy still plunges the shrinking sheep into the stream while his sunburnt and barefoot mother sits singing by her cottage door and the chubby baby at her breast throws his big brother a smile; while close by is the father, clothed in goatskin like a faun, driving his painted plough and his team of the famous oxen, strong and beautiful in all the beauty of their massive breasts, of the horned crescents above their foreheads, of their snow-white skins and those wistful eyes which the gentle Virgil loved! From this incomparable picture of the present which is also the past, he goes back to the beginning, to the past which is lost in obscurity: the original Umbria and its native gods, its woods of ilex and ivy and cypress. And so we see the Umbrian surrendering to the Etruscan and the Etruscan to the Roman, and conquerors and conquered uniting to resist the Carthaginian: the disaster of Trasimene, the victory of Spoleto, and all the crowd and noise of both, where now all is once more so silent, as the poet sits alone among the mountains, valleys and streams which he declares to be the source and life of Italian poetry. And so remembering that the oxen of Clitumnus were once the chosen victims for Roman triumphs, he laments that Rome triumphs no more since the native nymphs fled before Christian monks, who took men from their fathers and their wives and their ploughs, and made them renounce all the works of life and love. But, the ode ends, the dark days are gone: Italy is again the mother of corn and wine and human laws: and the dirges

of monks are replaced by the whistle of the engine with its promise of new conquests of the earth.

An abstract of this sort can of course give little idea of the poem. It only serves to indicate something of the ground the ode covers, and of its varying moods, at once more realistic, more sentimental (if that were a word one dare ever use of Carducci), more historical and more controversial than the **"Ode to Rome."** (pp. 29-30)

The third of my six is the **"Ode on the Death of the Prince Imperial,"** killed by Zulus in Africa in 1879. Here we get a feature of the Carduccian ode which neither of the two of which I have been speaking exhibit; and that is the contemporary or historical portrait. The ode begins with the sons of the two Napoleons, both dying so young, so far from the thrones they had been destined to fill, so far from the mothers who bore them. And then we go on to the mother of the race, Letizia Buonaparte, the "Corsican Niobe," who is the most imaginative creation, though not the most moving, in the work of Carducci. Her spirit haunts the empty home: she had never cared to wear a crown: she dwells among the old tombs and altars, and there she waits. Her children all lie far away from her: the son of fate with the eagle eyes, the daughters radiant like the dawn, the sons breathing dreams of hope; and now she stretches out her arms across the wild seas, demanding whether from America, from England, from Africa, death will yet send home to her breast any of her tragic race. Poetry, outside the greatest dramas, has not many figures of more tragic power than this of the Letizia whose name of joy has, as Carducci says, through her become for ever a name of sorrow.

The fourth ode is **"Miramar,"** and takes its name from the castle at the top of the Adriatic from which Maximilian and his wife sailed to the fatal throne of Mexico. Carducci is a moralist who never preaches and has only one doctrine, that ancient one of the connexion between sin and suffering of which the Hebrew prophets are so full, which Aeschylus, I suppose, first gave to our Graeco-Roman world. As the burden of the Napoleon ode, more felt than uttered, is that the crimes of the two Emperors find their inevitable fate in the deaths of their innocent heirs and the ruin of their house: so here, in **"Miramar,"** the old sins of the Hapsburgs, especially the crimes they and their agents committed in Mexico, are seen paying their long delayed penalty in the miserable adventure which cost Maximilian his life and his Empress her reason. The Ode begins with a sinister landscape of Miramare and the gulf of Trieste. And yet how fair it all looked that April morning. . . . Dante and Goethe, whose portraits hung in Maximilian's study, warn him in vain: he leaves the book of old stories open on his table: an evil destiny, the Sphinx of Empire, entices him across the seas to a fate out of which no tales of love or knighthood will ever be made. Dirges sound around the ship as it sails away: and the beckoning sphinx takes in turn all shapes of horror; the white face of mad Joanna, the murdered head of Marie Antoinette, the yellow cheeks and hollow eyes of Montezuma. And as they draw near the coast of Mexico the Mexican war-god is there on his pyramid, breathing flame through the dark woods of aloe, and scenting the young blood for which he has thirsted so long. "Come, heir of Charles the Fifth," he says; "thy ancestors, vile in heart, diseased in body, were not the victims for me: thee I desired, for thee I waited, thee I take, my offering to the mighty soul of Guatimozino, O flower of the race of Hapsburg, Maximilian, beautiful, and brave, and pure." (pp. 31-2)

[The] historical or biographical facts which, reshaped by imagination, form the scheme of a Carduccian ode, are of primary importance for the understanding of his mind and art. And as they lend themselves to analysis, as the components of a purely psychological or emotional poem do not, it can give us, however imperfectly done, more of Carducci than of many poets. I hope that what I have given of "**Miramar**" may have been enough to suggest at least some faint idea of its intensity of daring imagination: more than enough to show how absurd it is to think of this passionate poet, breathing fire into the dark places of human story, as a cold pedant making imitative exercises in his study.

My two last odes are to be found in *Rime e ritmi*. The first is "**Piemonte**" which begins rather heavily, or at least rather geographically, with nine stanzas of the praises of the various cities of Piedmont. It is not till we get to the tenth that Asti gives us Alfieri whose name always set Carducci on fire, being, as he once said, that of the most Italian of all Italians except Dante and Machiavelli. With him the real poem begins: Alfieri calling to Italy, Dante and Petrarch echoing his call, and the great dead arising to demand war for the deliverance of Italy. The rest of the ode is Charles Albert, . . . the Italian Hamlet, with the sword in his hand and the Christian's hair shirt on his breast. It was once said of him that he fought as a hero, lived as a monk, and died as a martyr; and he is, I think, certainly the most moving, though perhaps not the grandest, figure in Carducci's gallery of historical portraits. The poet's own memory looks back to the first victory of Italy, the fall of Peschiera, and the first cries of "Viva il re d' Italia!" The Lombard plain, that evening, was blazing in the sunset and Virgil's lake lay quivering like a bride's veil opening to the kiss of plighted love. But the pale king sat motionless on his saddle: his eyes saw the distant shadow of the Trocadero, where he had fought against freedom. And, indeed, Novara was close upon him, and abdication, and then the soon-following end at the villa far away on the Douro. Carducci never conceived anything more beautiful than the last part of this ode with its wonderful vision of the martyred heroes of Italy descending to the bedside of the dying king who had persecuted so many of them, who had sinned so against Italy, and yet had tried to serve her; who now gave a smile of pride and joy to the news of Garibaldi's defence of Rome. The spirits conduct his soul to heaven. . . . (pp. 32-3)

Carducci had praised Charles Albert in his early days and called Victor Emmanuel the Caesar who was to save Italy; but in disappointment at the first results of half-achieved unity, he had turned in bitterness against the Monarchy and the House of Savoy. Then he changed once more: the grace and kindness of Queen Margaret helped the "mitis sapientia" which crowns all healthy old age to judge the royal House more fairly: and he wrote two odes to the Queen and this noble tribute to Charles Albert, the king, as he says, of his young years, whom he once could not name without blasphemies and groans. The truth is, he was no ungenerous foe. No one, for instance, ever hated Austria more than he: but the House of Hapsburg cannot have received many tributes of sympathy more moving than his "**Miramar**" and his poem on the murder of the Empress Elizabeth.

The last of my six is "**La chiesa di Polenta**" which Carducci himself is said to have thought his finest. It was written in 1897 as his contribution to the effort made at the end of the last century to restore the little church of Polenta, not far from Ravenna, whose walls may have held Dante worshipping within

Carducci in his later years.

them, and may have looked down on his Francesca in her childhood playing outside. It begins with them and with Carducci's anti-feudal joy that what remains of the old castle of Francesca's fathers is now the home of industrious peasants. It goes on to a picture of the darker, earlier ages when the barbarians overran Italy, when Rome was forgotten and Gothic saints and devils replaced the fair forms of classical sculpture. Ruin and misery were everywhere: nothing was left to the people but the church, at once their country and their home and their tomb. And then the conquerors are converted and come there too, and the great Gregory remakes the beginning of a new Italy and a new freedom. And so the poet turns from history to salute the little church . . . and bids Italy, born once more, to give back to it the voice of prayer and to let its bell once more sound *Ave Maria* from hill to hill. And as the humble folk uncover at the sound they will not be alone: Dante and Byron and a host of spirits will be with them. . . . A call to prayer and to the *Ave Maria* issued by the writer of the **Hymn to Satan** could not but arouse surprise. There were rumours that Carducci was about to make his peace with the Church. But some stanzas of the ode itself were enough to refute that hope or fear. There had been a change. Carducci could not have written his **Satan** in his old age: he could now understand, and more than understand, he could respect and sympathize with, beliefs which he did not hold. In 1905 he wrote, for publication, a letter admitting that, even so late as in the "**Clitumnus**" ode, he had allowed himself to be carried away by the "Roman Spirit" which was so strong in him, and had been led by it to say things about Christianity which he now regretted. The "**Polenta**" ode may be said to complete him. It shows how entirely he had outgrown the poet of faction, negation, and controversy who was so large a part of him in his youth.

My object to-day has been to speak, as when speaking of poets one always ought, of what is great and permanent in the work of Carducci. I have said little or nothing of his metrical system of which so much has been written. The question of importance seems to me to be, not what its relations were to other systems, ancient or modern, but whether Carducci has been able to use it with power and make with it a living poetry, a poetry which affects our minds and imaginations as only living poetry can. I have made it clear that I think he has. No doubt much of his work, and the finest, demands a capacity for being stirred by history, and even by politics, which not everybody possesses. Nor, perhaps, will any one fully appreciate Carducci who does not take exceptional pleasure in the form of verse and in the fitness and felicity of language. But for my part, I cannot think it a small thing that it can be said of him, as Mr. Bickersteth has said, I think with truth: "probably no poet that ever lived has composed so few slipshod lines or written his own language with greater purity of diction." And it seems to me a still greater thing that, in the words of another critic, "Carducci has solved the problem which baffled the Renaissance, of linking strength of thought to artifice of form." But it has been my object to insist that strength of thought and perfection of form are far from being the whole of what he brought to his verse. He himself in the fine **"Congedo"** of *Rime nuove* compares the poet to a smith, shaping on his burning forge love as well as thought, memories and glories, past and present, and all the emotions they arouse, till he has made he knows not what; only when it is done he looks upon it and is glad and asks no more.

The smith does not always succeed nor does the poet: each is clumsy sometimes and each sometimes finds his metal too hard to shape. What I have wished to say to-day is that Carducci succeeded often, and that when he succeeded it was with such materials, so finely worked, that his place among the poets is assured and immortal. (pp. 34-6)

> *John Bailey, in his* Carducci, *Oxford at the Clarendon Press, 1926, 36 p.*

A. MICHAEL DE LUCA (essay date 1951)

[*De Luca is an American educator and critic who specializes in Italian studies. In the following excerpt, he discusses the major themes, subjects, and aims of Carducci's polemical writings.*]

Giosuè Carducci's major polemical writings, collected in the two volumes entitled *Confessioni e battaglie,* and a number of shorter combative articles known as *Ceneri e faville,* contain some of his most significant and original pages of prose. It is natural that Carducci's contentious instinct should have brought him a host of adversaries. As he spoke out against these adversaries he expressed many poignant ideas on the aesthetic, moral, and political problems of the Italy of his time. These writings are, consequently, indispensable to the biographer of Carducci and to the literary and political historian of the second half of the nineteenth century in Italy.

Carducci's penchant for difficult classical form and erudite content rendered his poetry inaccessible to the great mass of readers. His scholarship was restricted only to a professional audience. On the other hand, the impact of his polemical prose upon the Italian nation was more widespread and of greater practical importance. As a matter of fact, in his polemical writings Carducci acquired a genuinely popular quality. The reading public derived sheer enjoyment out of the familiar manner, the blunt honesty, the bold invective, and the satirical humor with which he treated his enemies. In addition to these elements of style and presentation, Carducci's readers were particularly attracted to the substance of these writings which vividly underscored Italy's national weaknesses and aspirations. They came to realize that Carducci spoke with a profound concern for the Italian people at a time when Spartan values were needed for the good of the country; that he did not consider his adversaries merely as personal enemies, but as enemies of the nation. (p. 233)

As the self-declared priest and prophet of Italy's future Carducci drew from his people much of his strength and inspiration. In **"Avanti! Avanti!"** he wrote:

> O popolo d'Italia, vita del mio pensier.

And in **"Nell'annuale della fondazione di Roma"** he described himself as

> . . . cittadino per te d'Italia,
> per te poeta, madre de i popoli.

Gradually Carducci became imbued with a sense of patriotic responsibility that led him to lash out at men whose ideas he considered detrimental to the nation. On penetrating Carducci's polemical prose, one grows progressively conscious of the poet's political, aesthetic, and moral principles, and decreasingly conscious of the men who contested them. It can be conclusively said that Carducci was more concerned with ideas than with men. In his first conflicts, between 1855 and 1860, the unfolding of his antiromanticism was of greater significance than the opposition of Pietro Fanfani and the Florentine Journals. Giuseppe Solimbergo (Kappa) and Quirico Filopanti are less important in the subsequent *Polemiche Sataniche* than the revelations of Carducci's rationalistic, anticlerical, and paganistic orientation around 1860. One may wonder why Carducci devoted the 111 pages of *Critica e arte* in answering Giuseppe Guerzoni and Bernardino Zendrini, two men who were decidedly inferior to him in critical, scholarly, and creative ability. An examination of *Critica e arte* will show, however, that this essay is not simply an invective and confutation; it is a serious critique of unobjective and incompetent criticism, and a protest against the excesses of emotionalism in the literature of the late Italian romantics. **"Moderatucoli"** is not so much an attack on Antonio Fogazzaro and the Italian Moderate Party as it is an explanation of the poet's belief in historical justice. In **"Tibulliana"** Carducci is more seriously preoccupied with the glorification of the pagan naturalism of ancient Rome than he is with correcting Rocco De Zerbi's errors in translating Tibullus. In the **"Ça ira"** essay, written in defense of his twelve sonnets on the French Revolution, Carducci was more absorbed in the importance of unbiased historical research and the debt modern society owes to the French Revolution, than in castigating Ruggero Bonghi, Marco Tabarrini and other detractors of his sonnets. This essay, composed in 1883 as the poet was approaching middle life, is characterized by frequent digressions on political problems of the times and on the scenic beauties of the Valdarno and the region of Lake Garda. The digressions point to the poet's diminishing inclination to wrangle with his enemies and an increasing propensity for the idyllic enjoyment of nature. (pp. 233-35)

There is evidence that Carducci came to regard his polemical activity as wasteful, especially when he compared it with useful physical toil. In August 1881, while visiting relatives at La

Maulina, near Lucca, he was profoundly impressed by the productive labor of the tillers of the soil. Writing about it to his friend, Giuseppe Chiarini, he could not refrain from disparaging his absorption in verbal conflict. . . .

To this sense of wastefulness must be added certain misgivings Carducci experienced on the possible damage of these conflicts on the ideal of national unity which was so sacred to him. (p. 235)

There is no denying that Carducci frequently manifested in his combative prose a certain lack of discretion and taste that produced and still produces an unfavorable impression upon many of his readers. The immoderateness displayed, particularly in such writings as "**Moralità . . . fanfullarda**," and in certain pages of "**Novissima polemica**," "**Rapisardiana**," and "**Moderatucoli**," is a decidedly detracting quality. In these the poet assumed the bullying manner of a gladiator who thoroughly enjoyed mauling an adversary. But Carducci's moral and political idealism saved him from succumbing to malicious and vindictive intentions. He was too sound, too rational, and too conscious of his patriotic mission to lose himself in acrimonious personal invective.

There were times when Carducci himself came to regret his virulence. For example: In 1875 he had been quite unrestrained in an attack on Bernardino Zendrini, a harsh critic of Carducci's *Nuove poesie*; but five years later, realizing that he had been too severe, he modified his earlier opinions and expressed considerable respect for his former critic.

It would seem that Carducci's repudiation of his polemical writings should have caused him to desist from such activity. The fact is that the poet could not help himself because he was never fully at peace with the world. No one was more conscious of his irascibility and lack of serenity than Carducci himself. In "**Davanti San Guido**" he imagined that the young cypresses of Bolgheri, a little town of his native Maremma Toscana, were chiding him for his "eternal quarrels." (p. 236)

Perhaps Carducci's greatest disappointment was his failure to convert his political passion into action. He expressed this disappointment during a conflict with Eduardo Arbib who accused the poet of being unpatriotic because he did not take up arms in the military action of the Risorgimento. Indeed, the vehemence of the invective of the patriotic *Giambi ed epodi* may be ascribed to Carducci's frustration at not having served as a soldier in this action. Circumstances forced him to limit his participation only to glorifying the national heroes in song. Much of the ardor of the *Giambi ed epodi* overflowed into the political disputes he had with Angelo Camillo De Meis, Francesco Fiorentino, Baron Franco Mistrali, and a number of adversaries of the Moderate Party. The passion with which he engaged in these political polemics was maintained at a high pitch by an intransigent political idealism that was concerned only with the greatness of Italy. Carducci was not endowed with practical political instincts, nor was he ever actively involved in the affairs of government. Had he participated in the government he would have had to compromise with certain political realities which the layman finds difficult to comprehend. It is ironical that Carducci was destined to remain permanently an outsider to the military and political action of the period he represented. In such an action he might have found an outlet for his tempestuous political rage. This being the case he had to content himself with a remote polemical outlet. . . .

In spite of Carducci's derogation of his polemical papers, there is no doubt that they exerted a notable influence upon Italian character and thinking in the latter half of the nineteenth century. Carducci realized that the accomplishment of national unification had to be accompanied by moral elements that would preserve and strengthen political unity. One of the greatest dangers to the moral strength of the nation repeatedly condemned by Carducci in these papers is the emotional sensualism of the literature of his times. (p. 237)

Carducci opposed the complexities, subtleties, emotionalism, and sensuousness of the late Italian romantics with a severe beauty of form, a rigorous self-restraint, and a devotion to ideas that would ennoble his country. At no time did his adversaries prove that the undesirable qualities of decadent Italian romanticism could have been eradicated by better ideas or attitudes than his. None of his opponents established, as Carducci did, a relationship between art and life. He did not subscribe to the idea of art for art's sake because he was convinced that the life and ideals of a nation are demonstrated in the forms of its art, and that the great artist enjoys the unique privilege of elevating the ideals of his fellow citizens. This conviction undoubtedly prompted him to write the following brazen epigram in the preface of Ettore Sanfelice's translation (1894) of Shelley's *Prometheus Unbound*:

> Alla fin fine il Manzoni trae la gente in sacrestia, il
> Byron in galera e il Leopardi all'ospedale.

Along with "**Mosche cocchiere**" this preface must be regarded as one of Carducci's strongest attacks against the inroads of contemporary French literature in Italy and against the decadent aestheticism of D'Annunzio and his followers, to whom Carducci bluntly referred in this writing as "degenerati." (p. 238)

Frequently the manner in which Carducci expressed himself in his combative writings was as important as what he said, and even more important. The outstanding quality of this manner is a priestly solemnity which derives its force from the reverence with which he beheld his country. In one of the digressions of "**Ça ira**" he spoke of the social goal toward which the nation should evolve in these terms:

> L'idealità d'una nazione, la religione cioè della patria, ha per fondamento . . . una o più realità: ciò sono una graduale trasformazione e ascensione delle classi inferiori verso il meglio; un ordinato e sano svolgimento delle forze economiche nelle classi mezzane; un'aristocrazia almeno del pensiero, della scienza, dell'arte, in una coltura superiore di genio altamente nazionale.

These are but a few of the innumerable ethical, aesthetic, and social lessons which Carducci preached to his people. They are the only worthwhile and durable elements of his combative prose. They supplement and render more intelligible his vast poetic and critical production. At the same time, they constitute the most human aspect of his work.

Carducci's polemical prose had an appreciable influence on the journalistic style of his period. All over Italy provincial politicians and newspaper men imitated his irate outbursts and impetuous manner in order to dramatize their trivial café debates and editorial polemics. It would be safe to assert, however, that none of these imitators inherited his sincerity and nobility of purpose. (pp. 239-40)

A. Michael De Luca, "An Evaluation of Carducci's Polemical Writings," in Italica, *Vol. XXVIII, No. 4, December, 1951, pp. 233-40.*

ERNEST HATCH WILKINS (essay date 1954)

[*In the following excerpt, Wilkins surveys the major collections of Carducci's poetry. Translations in brackets are the critic's own.*]

By 1899 [Carducci] had published ten volumes of poems, which in a definitive edition he rearranged in six collections: *Juvenilia* (containing poems written from 1850 to 1860), *Levia gravia, Light and Serious Verse* (poems of 1861-1871) *Giambi ed epodi, Iambics and Epodes* (poems of 1867-1879), *Rime nuove* (poems of 1861-1887), *Odi barbare, Barbarian Odes* (poems of 1873-1889), and *Rime e ritmi, Rhymes and Rhythms* (poems of 1885-1898). In the first two collections the prevailing mood and intent are classic, but the poems show familiarity not only with Greek and Latin verse but also with the whole range of Italian poetry. There is much variety in theme and in form.

Between the *Levia gravia* and the *Giambi ed epodi,* in the definitive edition, there stands, as an independent poem, the *Hymn to Satan,* an explosive manifesto of rebellion—very startling to the readers of the early 1860's—in which the repressions of traditional religion are scornfully denounced, while the natural energies of life and thought are exalted.

Most of the *Iambics and Epodes* are powerfully political and satiric: they include, in particular, bitter attacks on the still resisting Pius IX and on the insufficiencies of the Italian government. Very different from the satirical poems (though linked to them by certain references) is the **"Canto dell' amore,"** placed as the last poem of this group. As the poet stands in the *piazza* of Perugia, looking away over the Umbrian plain to the rising hills, evoking with his clear vision the centuries of struggle and endurance enacted in that scene, there comes upon him an intense consciousness that the bygone ages are joining in one brief insistent message:

> From Umbrian hamlets nestling in the vales
>   Where swift and still the darkling rivers flow,
> From summits where Etruscan citadels
>   Tower aloof and watch the world below;
>
> From fields wherein the busy plowman oft
>   Upturns the relics of a Roman day,
> From the invader's castle, perched aloft
>   Like falcon spying out the distant prey;
>
> From answering dark turrets that defy
>   The foreigner, and hold the towns in ward,
> From churches raising upward to the sky
>   Long marble arms in prayer unto the Lord . . .
>
> Amid the tender green of the ripening grain,
>   O'er terraced hillsides fragrant with the vine,
> O'er lakes and rivers silver in the plain,
>   From the distant snowy crests of Apennine;
>
> Amid the clamor of the busy mills,
>   Where open meadows in the sun rejoice,
> Rises one chant among the listening hills,
>   One hymn, in a thousandfold and mighty voice:
>
> "Greeting to you who live and toil and move
>   In the swift-passing yet eternal day!
> Too much we hated, suffering. So love!
>   Holy and fair the world shall be alway."

In the three later collections, the *Rime nuove,* the *Odi barbare,* and the *Rime e ritmi,* Carducci achieves his spiritual and poetic maturity. The earlier fire still glows, but it is under control; and negative rebelliousness is supplanted by a positive, even a serene, acceptance of all that has been and is wholesome and beautiful and good in life, and by a projection of this concept of the good life into the future. The *Rime nuove* are in familiar Italian metrical forms; the unrhymed *Odi barbare* are modeled on various types of the Horatian ode; poems of both kinds appear in the *Rime e ritmi.*

Several of the sonnets of the *Rime nuove* are among the most perfect sonnets of modern times. One of them, **"Sole e amore,"** is, like Leopardi's "La quiete dopo la tempesta," a poem suggested by calm after storm—but two poems on the same theme could hardly be more different. Carducci's reads, in translation:

> Soft and white into the distant west
> The clouds are gone; the wet sky laughs again.
> The sun, triumphant, hails the labor of men
> In busy streets astir with the daily quest.
>
> High above, in the golden radiance pressed,
> The thousand pinnacles of a mighty fane
> Intone Hosanna; and in swift-wing'd train
> The circling swallows speed from spire to nest.
>
> So shines again the sun within my soul
> When love has swept away with its sweet smile
> The heavy-lowering clouds of doubt and wrong:
>
> In luminous wonder is revealed the whole
> Ideal of life—my every thought the while
> A harmony, and every sense a song.

As Leopardi had used the word *pietade* to express his sense of the common human bond, so Carducci, in these sonnets and elsewhere, uses the adjective *pio* to express his sense of the same bond, his willing consciousness of interwoven life. Leopardi's *pietade* had been for defense: Carducci's is vigorous, positive, good for its own sake, a fellowship in everyday toil and in all forms of ennobling effort. Such phrases as *il pio travaglio* and *la giustizia pia del lavoro* recur in his poems; and in one of the most famous of his sonnets he calls the ox *pio,* as a willing sharer in man's toil.

The series of sonnets is followed by several smaller groups of poems, in which, with a completely satisfying metrical mastery, Carducci chooses for his varying moods a great many different lyric and semi-lyric forms. Among the poems of these groups are freshly imaginative love poems, a most poignant and exquisitely wrought little poem written after the death of his three-year-old son, Alpine poems, poems of autumn and winter and springtime, a serenade and an aubade, childhood reminiscences—one of these, **"Davanti San Guido," "Before (the church of) San Guido,"** is the best-loved of all Carducci's poems—and many historical and legendary evocations. Three of the springtime poems are grouped as **"Primavere elleniche," "Hellenic Springs"**: in one of these—as Leopardi had done in his "Hymn to Spring"—Carducci seeks again the beauty of the classic illusion:

> Though other gods may wane, the gods of Greece
> Live on for aye. They sleep in the maternal
> Trees, on the hills, in streams, and in the peace
>   Of seas eternal. . . .
> And if there summon them the enamour'd face
> Of a fair woman, or a poet's strain,
> They, laughing, from their sacred biding-place,
>   Flash forth again.

Historic and legendary evocation constitutes one of the most distinctive features of Carducci's art. "The present," he once wrote, "belongs to the drama, the novel, and the newspaper; the future, to God; the past, to poetry." And elsewhere:

> Great poetry aspires ceaselessly to the past and pro-
> ceeds from the past. The dead are infinitely more
> numerous than the living, and the spaces of time
> under the Triumph of Death are incomparably more
> immense and more tranquil than the brief moment
> agitated by the phenomenon of life. Hence the imag-
> ination of the poet can there freely take its flight . . .
> while the appearances of the present, in their contin-
> ual flux, do not allow the artistic faculty so to fix
> them as to be able to transform them into the ideal.

The intense sensation of the past is indeed a natural thing in
Italy. It comes with overwhelming power when one stands
high above a plain that quivers with the life of generations: at
Fiesole, looking down on Florence and the Arno; on Vesuvius,
with Herculaneum and Pompeii at one's feet; on the hill of
Tusculum, with Rome in the distance. Some such mountain
experience as this gave Carducci the phrase by which he expresses his visualization of the past: "I stand upon the mount
of centuries." From that height he directs his vision over the
immense continent of experience and imagination that lies below, discerning men and scenes that shine with some rich
human significance; and then, as creator, he evokes those men,
those scenes, for the modern world.

The "Envoi" of the *Rime nuove* is a poem called **"Congedo,"**
the best of Carducci's several poems on poetry, in which he
sings of the creative activity of the poet under the figure of
the smith at his forge—a fitting symbol for the virile strength
of Carducci's own genius. (pp. 437-40)

Carducci's "barbarian" stanzas, like those of Chiabrera, imitate the corresponding Latin strophes through the use of unrhymed lines of different lengths that are arranged according
to the pattern of the particular type of Latin strophe that is
being imitated, and follow that type of strophe also, at least
approximately, in the usual distribution of their verbal stresses.
A typical Carduccian Alcaic stanza reads thus:

> Il dittatore, solo, a la lugubre
> schiera d'avanti, ravvolto e tacito
> cavalca: la terra ed il cielo
> squallidi, plumbei, freddi intorno;

["The dictator, alone, at the head of his saddened
troop, rides on wrapped in his cloak and silent: earth
and sky squalid, leaden, cold around him."]

a typical Sapphic stanza thus:

> Solenni in vetta a Monte Mario stanno
> nel luminoso cheto aere i cipressi,
> e scorrer muto per i grigi campi
> mirano il Tebro;

["On the summit of Monte Mario the cypresses stand
solemnly in the luminous and quiet air, and watch
the Tiber flowing silently through the gray fields."]

and a typical elegiac distich thus:

> Rompendo il sole tra i nuvoli bianchi a l'azzurro
> sorride e chiama—O primavera, vieni!

["The sun breaking through the white clouds smiles
to the blue sky and calls: 'Oh springtime, come!'"]

Such stanzas appealed to Carducci as affording appropriately
classic forms for the expression of moods that he felt to be
classic, and in particular as being at a far remove from the
easy forms favored by Romantic poets. He was familiar with
poems in which Chiabrera and Campanella and other Italians
had made use of similar stanzas; and he was interested in the
somewhat similar poems of Klopstock, Goethe, and Platen.

His own consummate artistry enabled him to write in these
forms more successfully than anyone else has ever done. His
"barbarian" odes are of great dignity, and often of great strength
and beauty. He presumably derived the term "barbarian" from
Campanella's line

> Musa latina, è forza che prendi la barbara lingua.

Several of the *Odi barbare* are classic in theme as well as in
form, but Carducci is conscious simultaneously of the classic,
the medieval, and the modern worlds, and likenesses and contrasts and resulting prophecies occur to him continually. Thus
in an ode in which he celebrates the triumphs of ancient Rome—
"everything in the world that is humane, great, and august is
Roman still"—he prophesies that the future Italian triumph
will be not a triumph of kings or Caesars over other nations,
but a triumph of the Italian people, for all nations, over darkness, barbarity, and injustice. In the ode **"At the Source of
the Clitumnus"** he pictures the quiet beauty of the unvarying
peasant life that borders the gentle course of the little river,
tells in superb stanzas of the rush of Umbria to arms after
Thrasimene, condemns the servile fanaticism of the Middle
Ages, and then returns to the normal vigor of Italian life, hailing
Italy as the perennial mother of harvests, of laws, of the arts,
and of new industry. Familiar legendary figures of the ancient
and medieval worlds are brought together, like meeting like,
in the ode **"At the Urn of Percy Bysshe Shelley,"** written in
elegiac distichs. The scene is a faraway island "resplendent
with fancy":

> There, leaning on their spears, Siegfried and Achilles, tall
> and fair, wander winging along the resounding sea:
>   To the one Ophelia, escaped from her pallid lover, gives
> flowers; to the other Iphigenia comes from the sacrifice.
>   Under a green oak Roland speaks with Hector;
> Durendal flashes with gold and gems in the sun:
>   Andromache calls her boy to her bosom;
> Alde the fair in silence watches her stern lord.
>   King Lear of the flowing locks tells his sorrow to the
>   wandering Oedipus;
> with uncertain eyes Oedipus seeks ever the sphinx:
>   The loving Cordelia calls—"Ah, white Antigone, come!
> Come, O Greek sister! Let us sing of peace to our fathers."

There also Helen and Ysolde go pensively together, and Lady
Macbeth and Clytemnestra vainly dip their stained white arms
into the sea. To this island Shelley, alone among modern poets,
has been borne by Sophocles.

Modern history takes classic form in several odes, one of them
on the nemesis that overtook the Bonapartes. At the end of
this poem the mother of Napoleon vainly calls her children and
her children's children:

> Stands in the night the Corsican Niobe,
> stands at the door whence to their baptism
> her children went; and her arms,
> guiltless, she lifts to the wild sea,
>
> and calls, and calls: perchance from America,
> perchance from Britain or burning Africa,
> some one of her tragic sons,
> freed by death, may come to her breast.

In still other odes history gives way to contemporary moods
and scenes: companionship and love, a reading of Marlowe,
flights of birds, a railroad station on a rainy autumn morning,
Tuscan hills, Alpine meadows.

Many of the poems of the last collection, *Rime e ritmi*, were
written in the Alps, and many are imbued with an Alpine clarity

and breadth of vision. Some of them are purely Alpine, as for instance this rendering of noontide stillness:

> In the great circle of the Alps, over the bare gray granite, over the gleaming glaciers, noon reigns, serene, intense, infinite, in the great silence.
>
> Pines and firs, unstirred by any breath of wind, rise in the sunlight that shines through them. Only the tiny brook flowing amid the stones sings its soft lyric song.

In other poems the Alpine setting serves as Carducci's "mount of the centuries," and he brings back into a life newly interpreted noble figures of the Italian past. One of the last poems of all, the *ode barbara* (not Alpine) entitled **"La chiesa di Polenta," "The Church of Polenta,"** suggested by the restoration of a very ancient church not far from Rimini—a poem filled with medieval memories—ends in the imagined healing peace of the Ave Maria rung at sunset from the new belltower. The collection ends with this *stornello* (in which the *tricolore* refers to the three colors of the Italian flag):

> Fior tricolore,
> Tramontano le stelle in mezzo al mare
> E si spengono i canti nel mio core—
>
> ["Tricolored flower, the stars are setting in the midst of the sea, and all my songs are dying in my heart."]

In prose Carducci wrote plentifully in three fields: literary history and criticism; Italian history and patriotism; and personal reminiscence. Whatever his theme, his prose is fresh, imaginative, and vigorous. It has always a vocal quality, as though it had been spoken, and spoken with a great and yet a natural distinction.

He was often called upon to make addresses on literary occasions. Thus he spoke in Pietole on Virgil, in Rome on Dante, in Arquà on Petrarch, in Certaldo on Boccaccio, in Lecco on Manzoni, and in Recanati on Leopardi. In such addresses the distinction of his style rises often to a disciplined eloquence, and his evocations are comparable in their insight and their power to those of his poems.

In the field of Italian history and patriotism Carducci wrote occasional essays and reports, and several *discorsi*. The best of these *discorsi*, rich in content, profoundly loyal, and irresistibly impassioned in style, are among the greatest of modern orations.

At a mass meeting held in Bologna on June 4, 1882, two days after the death of Garibaldi, Carducci out of the fullness of his mind and heart delivered extemporaneously an oration hardly to be surpassed in any time or place. Every sentence is memorable, and the successive paragraphs rise to supreme heights of eloquence. When applause greeted his preliminary words he bade his hearers refrain from any further demonstration: but toward the end the audience, moved beyond control, was shouting its assent. The opening summary of the career of Garibaldi, a summary at once solemn and resplendent, begins thus:

> The revelation of glory that appeared to us in our childhood, the epic of our youth, the ideal vision of our maturity, have closed and disappeared forever. . . . That blond head with its lion's mane and its splendor as of an archangel, that head that passed along the Lombard lakes and beneath the Aurelian walls, reawakening Roman victories and spreading fear and dismay among foreigners, lies now cold and motionless . . .

Similar sentences follow for hand and eyes and voice and heart. From this summary the orator moves through a characterization that draws upon likenesses in ancient and in modern heroism, through a fiercely satirical condemnation of the partisan politics of the new Italy for which Garibaldi had given his life, and through a marvelous telling of the legend of Garibaldi as it might be told and sung by the poets of a far distant century, to a final summoning of Italy to cast all her unworthiness into the flames of the funeral pyre:

> So and only so we may hope that in the days of trial and of peril that are to come . . . the General's spirit may return to ride at the head of our armies, and to lead us again to victory and to glory.

(pp. 441-45)

Ernest Hatch Wilkins, "Carducci and Other Poets," in his A History of Italian Literature, *Cambridge, Mass.: Harvard University Press, 1954, pp. 436-47.*

NICOLAS J. PERELLA   (essay date 1979)

[*In the following excerpt from his thematic study* Midday in Italian Literature: Variations on an Archetypal Theme, *Perella discusses the various manifestations of midday in Carducci's poetry. Translations in brackets are the critic's own.*]

In considering the role of midday in Carducci, we may begin with the idyllic and nostalgic evocation of **"Idillio maremmano" ("Idyll of the Maremma")**. Here, at the center of the world-weary poet's vision of a simple and healthy life in communion with nature, which might have been his, is the figure of a young woman who strides "alta e ridente" along the furrows of fields and wheat. Carducci's "bionda Maria" . . . is clearly a pagan poet's vision of a nature goddess of health and fertility, a nostalgic but vigorous nympholepsy. The high-noon sun of mid-summer with its heat and light bathes her in glory as in an act of homage, and she moves Juno-like in it as in her natural element:

> . . . . e a te d'avante
>
> La grande estate, e intorno, fiammeggiava;
> Sparso tra'verdi rami il sol ridea
> Del melogran, che rosso scintillava.
>
> Al tuo passar, siccome a la sua dea,
> Il bel pavon l'occhiuta coda apria
> Guardando, e un rauco grido a te mettea.
>
> [" . . . and before you,
>
> And all around, the great summer blazed.
> The sun was laughing scattered through the green
> Boughs of the pomegranate tree that sparkled red.
>
> When you passed by, the beautiful peacock, as though
> Looking at its goddess, opened its eye-splendored tail
> And hailed you with a strident cry."]

An even more openly paganizing classical midday scene is at the center of the second of the three odes of **"Primavere elleniche" ("Spring in Hellas")**. In this hymn to love the poet invites his beloved to an imaginary voyage to a Theocritean Sicily "where the shepherd Daphnis sang divine songs amid the fountains." There, with the magic of his verse he will enrapture her, and in the midst of the noontide calm and leisure, at that hour when light and silence pervade all of nature, he will evoke the presence of the swift-footed sylvan nymphs:

> Ti rapirò nel verso; e tra i sereni
> Ozi de le campagne a mezzo il giorno,
> Tacendo e refulgendo in tutti i seni
> Ciel, mare, intorno,
>
> Io per te sveglierò da i colli aprichi
> Le Driadi bionde sovra il piè leggero.
>
> ["I will steal you away with my verse; and midst
> The placid indolence of the fields at noon,
> Silently shining in all breasts
> The sky and sea, around,
>
> For you I will summon from the sun-bathed hills
> The blond dryads fleet of foot."]

How emblematic of refuge into a world of calm, happiness, and harmony with nature this theme of midday nympholepsy was for Carducci is evidenced by the fact that the same invitation and evocation are at the center of what still remains his best-known poem—**"Davanti San Guido"** (**"Passing by San Guido"**). As in **"Idillio maremmano"** here too the theme is that of the pastoral opposition between the simple rural life close to nature and the active, care-filled life demanded by the city. As the poet returns by train to the city and his obligations as a man of the world, the cypress trees familiar to him from his childhood seem to invite him to stay, offering the promise of innocent pleasures and repose. It has become fashionable of late among critics to belittle this poem, but there can be no doubt that the three stanzas containing the nympholeptic evocation are among Carducci's finest poetic achievements. It is a vision of pagan bliss invoked in one sentence that carries over three quatrains, syntactically one of the most amply constructed sentences of Italian poetry in the second half of the nineteenth century:

> Rimanti; e noi, dimani, a mezzo il giorno
> Che de le grandi querce a l'ombra stan
> Ammusando i cavalli e intorno intorno
> Tutto è silenzio ne l'ardente pian,
>
> Ti canteremo noi cipressi i cori
> Che vanno eterni fra la terra e il cielo:
> Da quegli olmi le ninfe usciran fuori
> Te ventilando co 'l lor bianco velo;
>
> E Pan l'eterno che su l'erme alture
> A quell'ora e ne i pian solingo va
> Il dissidio, o mortal, de le tue cure
> Ne la diva armonia sommergerà.
>
> ["Stay, and tomorrow at noon
> When in the shade of the great oaks
> The horses stand muzzle to muzzle and all around
> Everything is silent in the burning plain,
>
> We cypresses will sing to you the chorus
> That wafts eternal between earth and sky:
> From those elms the nymphs will come forth
> Fanning you with their white veils;
>
> And Pan the Eternal who goes along the solitary heights
> At that hour and all alone over the plains,
> Will submerge the anguish of your cares,
> Oh mortal, in the divine harmony."]

First we have the evocation of the midday hour as a time of stillness and fierce heat over a vast expanse in which arcane sentiments and voices seem to float, then the sylvan nymphs who fan the poet. Finally there is Pan, not asleep at noontide and not the *daimon* causing terror, but Pan the Eternal, personification of a pantheistic concept of the universal harmony of nature that is revealed in the sacred hour of midday and into which the care-worn individual can sweetly merge.

There are other midday references in Carducci. **"Elegia del Monte Spluga"** once again evokes, as in an atmosphere between dream and reality (cf. Leopardi, Foscolo, Chenier, Mallarmé), a classically nympholeptic midday in which, however, a Nordic Lorelei also appears. And leaving the classical and paganizing world, the solemn evocation of the medieval Alpine commune in **"Il comune rustico"** (**"The Rustic Commune"**) acquires a quality of fixity and stunning intensity by virtue of the poem's final image in which we learn that the midday sun has illuminated the scene:

> A man levata il popol dicea Sì.
> E le rosse giovenche di su 'l prato
> Vedean passare il piccolo senato,
> Brillando su gli abeti il mezzodì.
>
> ["With hand raised high, the people said 'Yes.'
> And the red heifers from the meadow
> Saw the small senate pass by,
> As midday shone brightly on the fir trees."]

In **"Fuori alla certosa di Bologna"** (**"Outside the Charterhouse of Bologna"**), the sun at its zenith figures as the symbol of the joy and intensity of life in opposition to the symbols of death (as extinction of the self) represented by the tombs of the Carthusian cemetery the poet has just visited. Under that blazing midday sun flooding the earth with a "kiss" of light, the cicadas' "song" is not an irritant but a paean to summer, and even the dead, in the poet's mind, seem to invite the living to love one another. The noonday sun is here equated with the eternal splendor of love. In this vein, however, Carducci's most exalted paean to the midsummer midday sun and to the sense of a rich immersion of the self in nature at the hour of Pan occurs at the beginning of one of his best-known prose compositions, **"Le risorse di San Miniato al Tedesco"** (**"The Resources of San Miniato al Tedesco"**). And here the poet's cue is taken from the ubiquitous and (for him) much maligned cicadas whose persistent shrill filling the air is interpreted as the audible voice of the irrepressible energy and joy of all of nature, eternally young and drunk with the light and heat of the sun:

> Come strillavano le cicale giù per la china meridiana del colle di San Miniato al Tedesco nel luglio del 1857. . . . Io non ho mai capito perché i poeti di razza latina odiino e oltraggino tanto le cicale. . . . Poi tutto un gran coro [di cicale] che aumenta d'intonazione e d'intensità co 'l calore e co 'l luglio, e canta, canta, canta. . . . Nelle fiere solitudini del solleone, pare che tutta la pianura canti, e tutti i monti cantino, e tutti i boschi cantino: pare che essa la terra dalla perenne gioventù del suo seno espanda in un inno immenso il giubilo de' suoi sempre nuovi amori co 'l sole.
>
> ["How the cicadas stridulated down along the slope of the hill of San Miniato al Tedesco under the midday sun in July 1857. . . . I have never understood why poets of Latin descent so greatly hate and insult the cicada. . . . Then a whole large chorus [of cicadas] that increases in intonation and intensity with the heat of July, and sing, sing, sing. . . . In the fierce solitude of the midsummer sun it seems as though the whole plain sings, and that all the mountains sing, and all the forests sing: it seems that from the perennial youth of its bosom the very earth expands into an immense hymn the celebration of its ever new love with the sun."]

In this pantheistic nirvana—the metaphor of nirvana is Carducci's own—of light and exultation, which is in fact the sensation of an intense life, Carducci "drowns" in a willing surrender of the self's identity and its cares in order to become at one with the pulsating life of the All of nature, and the very body of the poet seems to be of the essence of the cicadas' wild song:

> A me in quel nirvana di splendori e di suoni avviene e piace di annegare la coscienza di uomo, e confondermi alla gioia della mia madre Terra: mi pare che tutte le mie fibre e tutti i miei sensi fremano, esultino, cantino in amoroso tumulto, come altrettante cicale.

> ["In that nirvana of splendor and sounds I have the pleasurable experience of drowning my human consciousness and of merging with the joy of my mother earth: I feel that all my nerves and all my senses quiver, exult, sing in an amorous tumult like so many cicadas."]

It would be difficult to find a more extreme contrast than that between the noontide vision and sensations recounted by Carducci in this passage and the *meriggio* of Leopardi's "Vita solitaria." In a strict sense, to be sure, the term *nirvana* does not apply to either noon piece, but as a metaphor it is more suited to characterize the earlier poet's experience. Leopardi . . . is released from sentiency and the consciousness of self into a metaphysical nothingness emblematized by the perfect stasis of his noonscape. On the other hand, Carducci's senses are literally thrilled and set to vibrating by an exuberance that throbs in the very heart of hot midday's fierce silence— "Nelle fiere solitudini del solleone." In a moment of Panic inebriation and expansion, Carducci is "released" precisely from the anguish of the thought of the nothingness that follows death, an anguish symbolized by the image—frequent in this writer—of the cold silence of the tomb: "Non è vero che io sia serbato ai freddi silenzi del sepolcro! io vivrò e canterò, atomo e parte della mia madre immortale" ["It is not true that I am destined for the cold silence of the tomb! I will live and sing, particle and part of my immortal mother"].

It is quite possible that Carducci's use of the metaphor of drowning to speak of the surrender of the self may be an echo from Leopardi's "L'infinito," although it is a common enough image in the writings of religious mystics. Again, however, where Leopardi drowns voluptuously in a sea of infinite silence—"E il naufragar m'è dolce in questo mare"—Carducci drowns in a sea (or "nirvana," as he puts it) of luminosity and sounds—"nirvana di splendori e suoni." These meridian "sounds" are first of all the actual chirring of the cicadas, but also, it should be noted, the metaphorical yet exultant "singing" of all of nature—fields, mountains, and forests. What may be involved here is the acoustical impression that the very absoluteness of midday's silence seems at times to arouse in an absorbed spectator. (pp. 98-104)

But the experience of the midday sun as an ambiguous and even negative demonic power of nature was not unknown to Carducci. This is most evident in the short lyric "**Davanti una cattedrale**" ("**In Front of a Cathedral**"), as sardonic a poem as any written by the *Scapigliati* (i.e., Italy's *poètes maudits*) contemporary with him. Here the images of the sun and tombs, normally used by the poet as terms of an opposition between life and extinction, appear in an ambivalent relationship:

> Trionfa il sole, e inonda
> La terra a lui devota:
> Ignea ne l'aria immota
> L'estate immensa sta.

> Laghi di fiamma sotto
> I domi azzurri inerte
> Paiono le deserte
> Piazze de la città.

> Là spunta una sudata
> Fronte, ed è orribil cosa:
> La luce vaporosa
> La ingialla di pallor.

> Dite: Fa fresco a l'ombra
> De le navate oscure,
> Ne l'urne bianche e pure,
> O teschi de i maggior?

> ["The sun triumphs, and floods
> The earth that is devoted to it:
> Afire in the motionless air
> Summer hovers immense.

> The abandoned and inert
> Squares of the city
> Seem lakes of flames
> Beneath blue domes.

> There, suddenly a sweaty
> Forehead emerges, and it is a horrible sight:
> The misty light
> Gives it a yellow pallor.

> Say: Is it cool in the shadow
> Of the dark naves,
> Within the pure white urns
> Oh skulls of our ancestors?"]

A fiercely triumphant summer sun vanquishes the earth and fixes everything in a broiling immobility. Already in the first stanza an ambiguity or irony is suggested by the attitude of devotion that the earth is said to have toward the sun, for in point of fact the earth has succumbed to the sun. The second stanza makes it clear that this is specifically an urban noonscape (itself a rarity), and the deserted squares of the city (a sure sign it is noontide) appear as lakes of motionless fire beneath a deep blue sky. In the third stanza the sense of noontide oppression is heightened by the sudden appearance of a solitary perspiring figure. We may take this figure to be the poet himself who is approaching the cathedral in the square. He is rendered grotesque and yellowish in a deathlike pallor by the light that seems to deform and disintegrate all objects. Finally, the last stanza brings a macabre twist to the motif of the midday retreat to a shady refuge. The cathedral before which the poet stands contains cool shade but also the tombs of the dead. It is a place of darkness and so, in a Carduccian view, a place where life is absent. But the derisive, Baudelairean guise in which he poses his question to the dead interred in the cathedral may also be self-mockery. For in this case, at least, the midday sun in which he stands is experienced as the destructive Gorgon.

But let us take leave of Carducci on a more truly solar note. The following Alpine midday in the poem by that title ("**Mezzogiorno alpino**") is, for all its brevity, among the most highly suggestive evocations of the special sense of timelessness that noontide seems so often to arouse:

> Nel gran cerchio de l'alpi, su 'l granito
> Squallido e scialbo, su' ghiacciai candenti,
> Regna sereno intenso ed infinito
> Nel suo grande silenzio il mezzodì.

> Pini ed abeti senza aura di venti
> Si drizzano nel sol che gli penètra.
> Sola garrisce in picciol suon di cetra
> L'acqua che tenue tra i sassi fluì.

["In the great circle of the Alps, on the granite rock
Bleak and pale, on the shining glaciers,
Serene, intense and infinite
Midday reigns in its majestic silence.

Pines and firs in the windless air
Rise in the sun that penetrates them.
Alone, like a faint sound of a lyre, chirps
The water that has flowed tenuously through the rocks."]

One must revert to the category of the sublime in considering this poem which presents the grandiose spectacle of the Alps in the absolute silence and light of midday. In part there is gray granite whose barrenness seems to be the more exposed in the totality of light, in part, the peaks and patches of ice and snow glistening with a dazzling radiance. Sole protagonist here is midday "reigning" over all things in majestic immobility, imparting a light and silence that are the same phenomenon. The adverbial adjective *intenso* refers not to the sun's heat, but to the quality of fixity and absoluteness of the light and silence, just as *sereno* bespeaks their purity while denoting a vision of a cloudless sky, and *infinito* conveys the impression of their timelessness. Below these highest regions, forests of pines and firs stand tall and motionless in the windless air and seem now to be of the substance of the luminous silence that has penetrated and possessed them. The one sound is that of a vein of water playing steadily like a musical instrument. But it is not a wild or intense sound like that of the cicadas. Significantly, the acoustic sensation suggested by *garrisce* is immediately attenuated by the qualifying notation of *in picciol suon,* and like the soft rustling of the wind through the foliage in Leopardi's "L'infinito," its effect is not to break a surrounding preternatural silence but rather to throw that silence (and the majestic setting to which it is attached) into a greater relief, to deepen it, as it were. This effect is heightened by the daring use of the past absolute tense of the important verb *fluì.* The idea or impression that this creates is that the water, even as it flows through and by the stones and rocks, seems continually to have already passed by. The flow of water is an archetypal image of the fluidity of time, and here it signifies the present moment that is continually transforming itself into the past, becoming lost or nullified in the stillness and timelessness (as opposed to never-ending time) experienced in the deep midday stasis. Here then time is recognized less in Plato's sense of a moving image of eternity than as an illusion that vainly seeks to conceal the reality of eternity.

The final word in each of the two stanzas of Carducci's poem has extraordinary value in contributing to the quality of the evocation. The key word *mezzodì* (midday) occurs precisely at the midway point of the poem, at the very end of the first stanza. The word, of course, also refers to the subject of the poem, and as the subject of the sentence occupying the whole stanza, it has been postponed to the very end by the syntactical inversion. With its strong accent on the last syllable, it creates a sense of suspension (the midday pause) and fixes the entire vision of the first part of the poem in a zone of indeterminacy, wonder, and expectation. Likewise *fluì,* the last word of the poem, echoes the acoustic effect of *mezzodì* with its accented last vowel (which creates the illusion of a rhyme) and thereby keeps us suspended in the midday impression of indeterminacy and timelessness. Thus the word *fluì* has an enormously important role in the poem. It functions on one level—the visual—to indicate motion, whereas on another level—the acoustical—it suggests immobility. Such an impression of motion in immobility, or energy in stasis, is one of the ambiguities, perhaps the most important one, that contribute to the mystery of midday. (pp. 104-07)

Nicolas J. Perella, "The Nineteenth Century," in his Midday in Italian Literature: Variations on an Archetypal Theme, *Princeton University Press, 1979, pp. 70-113.*

ADDITIONAL BIBLIOGRAPHY

Amram, Beulah B. "Swinburne and Carducci." *The Yale Review* V, No. 2 (January 1916): 365-81.
    Compares the careers of Carducci and Algernon Swinburne, noting that "both were professed pagans, exalting the spirit of man and the conquest of human thought, rebelling against Christian asceticism and aspiring towards the serene beauty of antiquity.... Both, because of their natural command over the musical resources of their native languages, augmented by their studies in prosody, exercised a profound influence over versification, giving freedom and variety in place of metrical monotony and conventionality."

Collison-Morley, Lacy. "The Decay of Romanticism: Carducci and the Classical Revival." In his *Modern Italian Literature,* pp. 267-91. Boston: Little, Brown and Co., 1912.
    Includes a biographical and critical sketch appraising Carducci's poetry and prose, and judging Carducci "the greatest poet of modern Italy."

——. "Carducci." *The Athenaeum* XXIX, No. 4757 (21 May 1921): 293-94.
    Review of *A Selection from the Poems of Giosuè Carducci,* translated by Emily A. Tribe. According to Collison-Morley: "Carducci's intense historical sense enabled him to breathe the spirit of the whole past of the peninsula into the new Italy which was struggling into being in his day, and of which he was the prophet-poet, through his art."

Croce, Benedetto. "Carducci." In his *European Literature in the Nineteenth Century,* pp. 359-69. London: Chapman & Hall, 1924.
    Praises the tone, subjects, and form of Carducci's mature verses, claiming him as one of the great poets of nineteenth-century European literature and "a poet-Vates, a heroic poet, 'an ultimate pure descendant from Homer'."

"Modern Italian Poets: Cossa and Carducci." *The Edinburgh Review* CLV, No. CCCXVII (January 1882): 27-60.
    Introduces Carducci's works to English readers through a comparison with the poetry of his contemporary Pietro Cossa.

"The Poetry of Carducci." *The Edinburgh Review,* No. 428 (April 1909): 334-62.
    Retrospective study of Carducci's life and career. According to the critic: "If it is true that [Carducci] did not see the whole of life, it is also true that to what he saw, and it is no small part, he brought the eye of a great artist, the heart and imagination of a great poet, a great man's virile and masterful sincerity and strength."

Garnett, Richard. "Contemporary Italian Literature." In his *A History of Italian Literature,* pp. 394-418. London: William Heinemann, 1911.
    Considers Carducci's career within a general survey of Italian literature. According to Garnett, Carducci combines classic and romantic elements in his works: "romantic in his revolt against convention, classic in his worship of antique form; and it is in great measure this duality which renders him so important and interesting."

Giuntoni, Julius. "The Reaction of Giosuè Carducci to Romanticism." *Italica* VIII, No. 1 (March 1931): 9-12.
    Considers Carducci Italy's foremost foe of Romanticism, citing as evidence his attacks on numerous characteristics of Romantic literature, including egoism, idealization of love, sentimentalism, rejection of reality, and exaggeration of emotion.

Gnudi, Martha Teach. "Shelley and Carducci." *Italica* XIII, No. 3 (September 1936): 79-84.

Maintains that "Carducci and Shelley frequently converge in their ideals; they have the same faith in liberty and justice; they have the same concept of love and the same hatred for tyrants and for those elements of the church which limit and hinder human progress. . . . For both, the poet is a sacred *vates*, a seer: Carducci is the 'vate italico' . . . Shelley is the *vates* of humanity."

Greene, G. A. "Giosuè Carducci." In his *Italian Lyrists of Today*, pp. 61-79. New York: Macmillan and Co., 1893, 232 p.

Includes an introductory sketch on Carducci as well as translations of several of his verses, including "Rome," "Pantheism," "To the Statue of Victory," and "Snowfall."

Haight, Elizabeth Hazelton. "Giosuè Carducci: The Italian Horace." *Studies in Philology* XLVI, No. 3 (July 1949): 387-99.

Examines the extent to which Carducci drew on Horatian phraseology, meters, themes, and subjects in his works.

Keeling, Anne E. "Giosuè Carducci: The Man and the Poet." *The London Quarterly Review* CVIII, No. VI (July 1907): 36-48.

Biographical and critical portrait based on the reminiscences of those who knew Carducci.

Kuhns, Oscar. "The Nineteenth Century." In his *The Great Poets of Italy: Together with a Brief Connecting Sketch of Italian Literature*, pp. 284-342. Boston and New York: Houghton, Mifflin and Co., 1903.

Surveys major subjects and themes of Carducci's poetry, concluding that his works comprise "a link between the older and the newer generation" in Italian literature.

Marble, Annie Russell. "Giosuè Carducci—Italian Poet (1906)." In her *The Nobel Prize Winners in Literature*, pp. 72-84. New York: D. Appleton and Co., 1925.

Appreciative, informal biography. According to Marble: "As a poet, Carducci mingled vigour and grace to an unusual degree. He was an artist both in his conceptions and his forms."

Marinoni, Antonio. "Giosuè Carducci." *The South Atlantic Quarterly* VI, No. 3 (July 1907): 236-47.

Tribute recalling Carducci's career as a poet and prose writer. According to Marinoni: "The attempt of Carducci to revive old meters was more than an attempt; it was an achievement. The poet did all that the resources of the language would permit."

Mario, J. W. "Carducci and His Critics." *The Nation* 57, No. 1,462 (6 July 1893): 7-8.

Challenges the designation of Carducci as Italy's national poet and discusses Carducci's poems on Italian cultural figures and historical events.

Paolucci, Anne. "Moments of the Creative Process in the Literary Criticism of Giosuè Carducci." *Italica* XXXIII, No. 2 (March 1956): 110-20.

Examines Carducci's critical writings, concluding that "his method [of literary criticism] was . . . not systematic; it was nothing more than the instinctive effort to explain literature by tracing or re-creating the essential moments of its genesis. He knew from his own intimate experience as a poet that the choice of subject and its elaboration in a work of art, the technical skill of the artist, his personality, and the motive force which initiates and sustains the creative process, are essential constituents of the perfected work of art."

Pepper, Mary Sifton. "Giosuè Carducci." *The Arena* XVII, No. 3 (February 1897): 430-38.

Discusses important influences on Carducci's literary development, notable achievements in his long career, and significant political, aesthetic, and moral positions he maintained.

Phelps, Ruth Shepard. "Giosuè Carducci." In her *Italian Silhouettes*, pp. 11-32. New York: Alfred A. Knopf, 1924.

Introductory biographical and critical essay.

Praz, Mario. "Giosuè Carducci as a Romantic." *The University of Toronto Quarterly* V, No. 2 (January 1936): 176-96.

Contends that Carducci was essentially Romantic, basing his conclusions on comparisons of the works of Carducci with those of Charles Baudelaire, Victor Hugo, Heinrich Heine, Théophile Gautier, and August Platen. According to Praz: "The romantic Hugo and Heine had supplied Carducci only with a store of baroque metaphors and epigrammatic conceits; but this Carducci still had a firm grip upon reality, upon the present, kept upon it a steadfast gaze in order to warn and inveigh. It was the 'classical' craftsmen, the polished Gautier and Platen, who transformed Carducci into a thorough romantic; while hammering his verse, he might well have imagined he was imitating his ancient master Horace; actually his face was turned away from reality."

Rossi, Joseph. "Scott and Carducci." *Modern Language Notes* LIII, No. 4 (April 1938): 287-90.

Draws a similarity between Carducci's "Alle fonti del Clitumno" and Walter Scott's "The Gathering Song of Donald the Black." According to Rossi: "The central thought is the same in both passages—a war call issued to the inhabitants of the countryside commanding them to leave their wonted pursuits, and to rush with their weapons—with some alterations due to the differences of time and place of the respective settings."

Scalia, S. Eugene. *Carducci: Critics and Translators in England and America, 1881-1932*. New York: S. F. Vanni, 1937, 103 p.

Discusses English-language commentary on Carducci's works and rates the strengths and weaknesses of his translators in England and the United States.

Sewall, Frank. "Giosuè Carducci and the Hellenic Reaction in Italy" and "Carducci and the Classic Realism." In *Poems of Giosuè Carducci*, translated by Frank Sewall, pp. 1-28; pp. 29-56. New York: Dodd, Mead & Co., 1892.

Reprint of Sewall's examination of classic themes in Carducci's poetry [see excerpt dated 1890] and an essay discussing the realistic aspects of his poetry and his devotion to classical forms. In the latter, Sewall maintains that it is in his "poetic power or interpretation that . . . Carducci proves himself the true realist. Whatever form he chooses, is for the time filled with its own life, and speaks from that and no other."

———. "Italy's Laureate." *New York Times Book Review* (21 December 1913): 755.

Review of Bickersteth's translations of Carducci's poems by a noted Carducci scholar.

Thayer, William Rosco. "Giosuè Carducci." In his *Italica: Studies in Italian Life and Letters*, pp. 347-63. Boston and New York: Houghton, Mifflin and Co., 1908.

Considers Carducci's career as a professor, critic, and poet. According to Thayer: "Great as he is as prose writer, critic, and leader, it is as poet that he holds the supreme place in modern Italy; it is as poet that his fame will endure, and that he will become more than a name outside of Italy."

Williams, Orlo. *Giosuè Carducci*. Boston and New York: Houghton Mifflin Co., 1914, 124 p.

Chronological study of Carducci's life and work concluding that Carducci's poetry represents an art closely akin to sculpture. According to Williams: "All temperaments are not equally responsive to the divinity of marmoreal beauty, and for them Carducci may seem lifeless and hard: but others who penetrate beneath chiselled outlines to the ever-living mystery of sculptural form can never fail to recognize in the poet of the *Odi barbare* a master of the highest order."

Emily Carr
1871-1945

Canadian painter, essayist, and autobiographer.

Known primarily for her dramatic paintings of the western Canadian wilderness, Carr was also the author of several highly praised volumes of autobiographical essays that provide insight into her artistic development. Carr's works feature in addition many accounts of her sketching trips throughout Canada and Alaska, which Peter Sanger has described as "some of the finest passages of natural description in Canadian prose."

Carr was born into a large, moderately wealthy family in Victoria, British Columbia. Educated at home by her older sisters until the age of seven, she later attended local primary and secondary schools and began taking private art lessons. Carr left high school after her first year, but she continued to attend art classes, planning to study painting in Europe if possible. Opposed in this by her eldest sister, who had taken charge of the family after the death of their parents, Carr appealed to her legal guardian and eventually obtained permission to study at the California School of Design in San Francisco.

Returning to Victoria late in 1893, Carr began teaching art classes in her home and continued to refine her own skills, making frequent sketching trips to remote areas of British Columbia. It was during this period that she first came into contact with native American Indians and developed an interest in their culture and art forms, which strongly influenced her paintings. Carr subsequently studied in England, where she suffered a nervous breakdown and spent more than a year in a sanatorium. She also studied in France before returning to Canada in 1913 and settling in Victoria. Although her work had begun to attract some attention, she was unable to support herself solely by painting, and she used what remained of her inheritance to build a small apartment building, from which she earned a meager living for the next twenty-five years.

Throughout most of her adult life, Carr concentrated her energies on painting, and it was only in the late 1930s, when her health began to fail, that she first wrote for publication. Between 1937 and her death in 1945, she prepared several manuscripts recounting various periods in her life; the first of these, published as *Klee Wyck* in 1941, was an immediate success. As a result, her publisher gladly accepted three more volumes of her reminiscences during the next year, and her journals and another collection of autoiographical writings were edited for publication by her friend Ira Dilworth.

The four collections of autobiographical writings compiled by Carr before her death are grouped according to subject matter: *Klee Wyck* contains recollections of Carr's experiences among the Indians, *The Book of Small* recounts the significant events of her early childhood, *The House of All Sorts* concerns her days as a landlord, and *Pause* comprises memories of her stay in the sanatorium during 1902 and 1903. *Growing Pains* is a collection of memoirs describing various episodes in Carr's life, while *The Heart of a Peacock* was compiled from letters to Dilworth. Although Carr's writings are drawn from the events of her life, recent biographers have uncovered significant misrepresentations and distortions in her accounts. Paula Blanchard has summarized the patterns of these distortions, noting

that Carr "consistently portrayed herself as younger than she was; she exaggerated her isolation on her trips north; she suppressed the identity of the man she loved; she submerged the encouragement of some Victorians under the hostility of most, tarring them all with the same brush; . . . she was shy of revealing the depth of her feeling for Ira Dilworth; in her bitterness over her years of 'landladying' she made herself seem more sinned against by her tenants than she actually was. And finally, the full force of her revulsion against the ordinary mass of human beings [was] understated." While some view Carr's misrepresentations as the deliberate lies of a pathological personality, others maintain that she presented the events of her life as she perceived them, but that her perceptions were distorted by her vision of herself as the quintessential Romantic artist: impatient with conventionality, misunderstood, abused, with her works unfairly neglected.

Initial response to Carr's writing was overwhelmingly positive, with critics praising her powers of description and the acuity of her perceptions. Her work was also valued for its account of the artistic development of an important painter. Revelations concerning the inaccuracies contained in these accounts have not led to revised estimations of their value in these respects, since the nature of Carr's distortions provides important information about her vision of herself, her world, and her art.

(See also *Dictionary of Literary Biography,* Vol. 68.)

PRINCIPAL WORKS

Klee Wyck (essays) 1941
The Book of Small (essays) 1942
The House of All Sorts (essays) 1944
Growing Pains (essays) 1946
The Heart of a Peacock (essays) 1953
*Pause (essays) 1953
Hundreds and Thousands: The Journals of Emily Carr
       (journals) 1966
Fresh Seeing (lectures) 1972
"Letters from Emily Carr" (letters) 1972; published in
       journal *University of Toronto Quarterly*

*This work was written in 1938.

THE NEW YORK TIMES BOOK REVIEW   (essay date 1942)

[*In the following essay, the critic offers a positive assessment of* Klee Wyck.]

The well-known Canadian painter, Emily Carr, became the friend of the West Coast Indians at the age of 15. It was then, when she was visiting at the remote mission station of Ucluelet, that she received her nickname of Klee Wyck—"Laughing One." But, as Ira Dilworth explains in his foreword to [*Klee Wyck*], she was not called "Laughing One" because she was always laughing; she didn't, actually, laugh a great deal; what was important in her laughter was its use and quality: friendly laughter that went out to meet the Indians' own moods and feelings, and became a bridge of communication even when there were no words. During all her many years as "Klee Wyck," Emily Carr has been setting down these Indian memories and sketches, without thought of publication. But she is, it seems, a natural-born writer. There is vividness and poignancy as well as spontaneity in the enlightening collection which makes this book.

One of her first memories is of pride and self-sacrifice at the mission station, when a man disobeyed rules and came to church with a flapping shirt-tail and bare legs. His wife pulled off her shawl to be laid quickly across his knees and shield him from disgrace among the white people. And thus she took disgrace upon herself. For a woman to go shawless is considered more indecent than for a man to go barelegged. The heroic gesture shamed her among her own people as she saved her husband's dignity.

That Emily Carr noticed and remembered this incident is characteristic. She always sought out and defended the Indians' native ways. She went to abandoned island settlements, difficult of access, in search of the old totem poles whose significance she respected and whose power in craftsmanship she understood. Two of her four paintings [reproduced in *Klee Wyck*] are of totems, and of one matriarchal figure she writes: "The big wooden hands holding the child were so full of tenderness they had to be distorted enormously in order to contain it all." At that village, not abandoned but vigorously primitive, she was slowly but at last strongly welcomed by people who, she later learned, had been notoriously "making trouble"; and she learned later, too, that their current village hero was thus exalted because he had been in jail!

Most of the Indian folk who people these effortless memories are, however, gentle and friendly and perhaps even too adaptable. The book is dedicated to one of the most interesting of them, the stanch, jealous, punctiliously honest Sophie, who always wanted to do as "nice ladies" did. But there is a cruel desolation in the story of Martha, who sheltered an abandoned white baby and had to give him up when he was a grown boy. In her wanderings among the Indians in search of subjects for her paint brush Miss Carr learned many of their beliefs and came upon those beliefs' strange expressions. She dared danger in treacherous coastal waters. She saw, and catches in a few words, the characteristics and atmosphere of lonely islands and wilderness settlements. And she writes with a brisk and sensitive originality, as if she were smiling, or sighing, to herself.

> *"Indian Ways," in* The New York Times Book Review, *June 7, 1942, p. 24.*

THE CANADIAN FORUM   (essay date 1942)

[*In the following review, the critic praises* The Book of Small *for its affectionate portrait of Carr's hometown and its evocative portrait of childhood.*]

Three things are true of anything Emily Carr makes, be it book or picture: she has something to tell, it is something of her own, and it is a Canadian something. In . . . *The Book of Small,* she proves this again, better than ever.

Many who aver a love of Canada in writing, give the impression they mean a love of each of its three million, seven hundred and forty-five thousand, five hundred and seventy-four square miles, though to cover this area, much of which is comparatively unknown to them, they seem obliged to spread their affection so thin that we are left approving but unstirred.

Emily Carr knows relatively few of Canada's square miles, but these she actually knows and really loves. Knows them, not only because she was born in their midst and has lived from their strength, but because she has always paid them the credit that is their due. Loves them, and the folk that people them, because all her life long she has seen and heard and smelt and touched and tasted the banquet being held all round her, instead of mistaking it for a stop-gap while yearning for far feasts she could not have. So kind is her knowledge and so keen her love that the one has no need to fear the other, and, as a result, both collaborate with such intensity that there is life, rather than recollection, on the firm canvas of *The Book of Small.*

Small, who "wanted to see NOW what was out here in our West," is Emily Carr as a little girl, a little girl who did not love anything because it reminded her of something else but because it was vivid enough to remind her of itself. "Mrs. Mitchell . . . said she loved me . . . because I was fat and rosy just like an English child. But I was not an English child and I didn't love her because she was English. I loved Mrs. Mitchell because . . . ," but read and see.

If Small is still in Emily Carr, she must object with all her sturdy soul to one detail in this book's otherwise faultless get-up. Says the distinguished dust-cover: "She writes about Victoria as English writers do about England." The marvel is, perhaps, that, from Victoria of all places, Emily Carr does not write as English writers do about England, but writes in such a way as to help hasten the time when equally well-meaning dust-jackets will doubtless say of other Smalls in other localities: "They write about *X.* as Canadian writers do about Canada."

Yet Emily Carr is not primarily concerned with writing about Canada nor even about Victoria. Her book is neither landscape nor historical tableau, except as brilliant background for a portrait, that of Small. This book is a portrait, and, for any kind of profitable comparison to be made, would have to be looked at together with a definite English counterpart, of which possibly no neater example exists than *The Small Years,* by Frank Kendon (1930). Both are contemporary portraits of children, but all they have in common is the claim that both can make: "The memories contained in this book are something which the world could not have without me," and it is this they have in common that makes them different from each other and from anything else. *The Book of Small* is indeed Small's book. It may well be Canada's book of the year. (pp. 284, 286)

> R. F., "Something of Her Own," in The Canadian Forum, *Vol. XXII, No. 263, December, 1942, pp. 284, 286.*

KATHLEEN COBURN   (essay date 1945)

[*Coburn is a distinguished Canadian critic and editor. In the following excerpt, she expresses admiration for Carr's personal courage and for the forthright style of* The House of All Sorts.]

Whether one thinks of [Emily Carr's] pictures or her books one has the sense of a strong integrity fighting for its freedom, a rich and full intuition hampered by irrelevant circumstances, an essentially reticent spirit compelled to express itself boldly. She lives and will live by her complete candor as a writer and artist, a candor at times almost brutal. . . .

The House of All Sort, refers to the period when it was necessary for her to earn, as landlady, the living the public denied her as artist. *Klee Wyck,* the first collection of personal sketches, and *The Book of Small,* will be more popular works, but *The House of All Sorts* is perhaps the best test of a reader's real appreciation of Emily Carr. Those who overlook the reticences won't care deeply for it, nor will those among the intellectuals whose snippety sounding-line is too short for this sort of thing; and, as among readers of her other volumes, there will be those afraid of vividness and intensity and bluntness. But those who come to her without these disqualifications will find in her three volumes by far the best familiar essays that have appeared in this country, and some of our strongest prose.

In [*The House of All Sorts*] one enjoys afresh her forthrightness, her sensitivity to the physical world plus her small sufferance for fools, her anger at cruelty, her acute awareness of bonds with all forms of life, except self-distorted human beings. It may be complained, in spite of the humor (here grimmer than in the other books) that she takes herself too seriously. Certainly she is not detached enough to see life as any comedy of manners, except sporadically, and she is too pagan to see it as a divine comedy. She is, indeed, violently attached to life, living in a relation almost too conscious for happiness, to all the elements, sounds and silences and space, sea and forest and wind, the seasons, flowers, persons, dogs. She fights and loves and there aren't many vegetative interspaces. Her landladyhood burned itself into her like caustic, and left scars. Some of the scars she hates—the punch in the face, for instance, from a sinister, bullying tenant.

"He was crude, enormous, coarse; his fleshy hands had fingers like bananas. You could feel their weight in the way they swung at the end of his arms."

Some of the scars she scorns, as she scorns the "Victoria smart set" and what she considers the decadent-dilettante snobs of the Island Arts and Crafts Society. "My change in thought and expression had angered them into fierce denouncement. To expose a thing deeper than its skin surface was to them an indecency. They ridiculed my striving for bigness, depth. The Club held exhibitions, affairs of tinkling teacups, tinkling conversation and little tinkling landscapes weakly executed in water colors."

Catching her baker and a coal carrier peering in her studio windows to see her pictures, she conceived the idea of a people's exhibition, strictly non-artsy-crafty, held in two of her apartments. It included a beautiful exhibit of water colors by a young Chinese boy. "Examples of my new and disliked work I would hang in the kitchens." The success of the show led to the idea of a People's Gallery, which "did not materialize."

"The everyday public were disappointed. The wealthy closed their lips and their purses. The Arts and Crafts Society smiled a high-nosed, superior smile. Lee Nam, the Chinese artist, many boys and girls and young artists were keenly disappointed. I closed the connecting door between the suites and again rented Lower East and Lower West as dwellings. The wise, painted eagles on my attic ceiling brooded—sorry for my disappointment. The Indians would say 'They made strong talk for me.' Anyway, they sent me down to the studio to forget my disappointment and to paint earnestly."

So, resilient and determined, the artist in her rebounds. When the hurts are inevitable—the departure of the dogs, for instance—she comes to terms with them. She smiles at herself, often. But the general effect of the book is of suffering, more because of what is concealed or only hinted at than what is expounded.

> Kathleen Coburn, "Emily Carr: In Memoriam," in The Canadian Forum, *Vol. XXV, No. 291, April, 1945, p. 24.*

KATHLEEN COBURN   (essay date 1947)

[*In the following essay, Coburn finds* Growing Pains *somewhat uneven, but sincere and objective in presentation.*]

> We were playing in the sitting-room. Brother Dick was in his cradle. Mother came into the room with water in her best china bowl. While she lighted the lamp my big sister caught me, dragged me to the kitchen pump and scrubbed my face to smarting. I was then given to Dr. Reid who presented me kicking furiously to God.

Had Emily Carr been writing in the eighteenth century she might have used other words. Innocence playing; enter Authority and Elegance, with their daughter Respectability to usher in Politeness and Tradition. So far she might have written. The rest is a twentieth-century tale—"Me kicking furiously to God." The old words represent what Emily kicked furiously to God about all her life. And somehow when we have read the book through from this unhappy beginning to the mellower ending we feel that God was on Emily's side. For instance when Dr. Reid manhandled her, "I would have been quite content to sit on Dr. Reid's knee but his tipping me flat like a baby infuriated me." Failure to appreciate the dignity of her personality or attempts on her integrity as a person or as an artist continued to infuriate her to the end. And God was pleased, and made her the greatest Canadian artist since Tom Thomson and one of the most finished of our prose writers.

"Whom the Lord loveth he chasteneth" is a hard saying for which Emily Carr's story provides bitter support. From childhood on she suffered a sense of rejection in her family, of both her personality and her art; this was extended in adult life by her rejection in Victoria's art circles as teacher and as artist. In turn she defied her family, their English tradition, their unimaginative conventional tastes, and came to identify herself aggressively with Canada, its vastness and terrifying grandeur as against the restricting confinement of her father's English hedges. Refusing to look with her family nostalgically into the past, she stared hard into the present and the future; scorning their conventional elegance and bourgeois manners, she took to Indians and animals with their primitive grace. Disgusted with the china painting atmosphere of Victoria she went further and further afield—San Francisco, England, France—suffering the tortures of the not-quite-damned to learn to paint as she felt she should in defiance of how they *knew* she ought.

There are very few facts in [*Growing Pains*]. Some readers may feel cheated by the omission of dates and a straight-forward narrative of events. . . . At times the most important events are brushed aside. What actually was the illness that kept her so long in a sanitarium? "Poetry was pure joy, love more than half pain. I gave my love where it was not wanted." We could willingly know more about the poetry. Whose? "Marked passages are all earth and nature." Perhaps this is all we need to know, but we should be interested to know more. And the love that was not wanted? The inquisitive will be very curious. Yet is it not more important that we should have this piece of reticence, this restraint, this delicacy, than any number of facts whatever? Do we not know more of the essential Emily Carr from this dignified closing of a private door than anything we should want to know from a recounting of the so-called facts? Artistically and personally it is wholly admirable.

Yet other readers will find the unconscious self-exposure almost too poignant to be borne, as for instance the story of the satiric sketches of San life, or the wonderful occasion of the seventieth birthday party. So innocent, so childlike, even in the very exposure itself, yet so magnificent. At that age, after all the hurts, to be still so unguardedly open to the world! If Ira Dilworth never did another tap in his life he would have justified his existence when he gave that kiss and made it "the real thing."

The writing of these essays "this summing up of a number of things" is to my eye and ear more uneven than in the earlier books, but it still leaves Emily Carr the best of our essayists. Take the five strokes that paint the family picture after her mother's death. "His office desk and chair were brought home and put into the room below Mother's bedroom. Here Father sat, staring over his garden. His stare was as empty as a pulpit without a preacher and with no congregation in front of it. We saw him there when we came from school and went stupidly wandering over the house from room to room instead of rushing straight up to Mother's bedroom. By-and-by, when we couldn't bear it any longer, we'd creep up the stairs, turn the door handle, go into emptiness, get caught there and scolded for having red eyes and no bravery."

The beautifully rounded chapter, "English Spring," typically exhibits that principle of contrast and opposites on which she worked as a painter. London *vs.* village, village sociability *vs.* the artist stranger's solitariness, song birds *vs.* church bells,

gravestones *vs.* gaiety, the real cuckoo *vs.* cuckoo clock of memory, "the shimmer of greenery that was little more than tinted light" *vs.* the "money-grabbing and grime" of London, baby daffodils and Mrs. Radcliffe's cheek "not soft nor used to being kissed." This, or the last chapter on the Clearing is powerful writing, and I suspect that those that don't like it are afraid of it as Victoria, B.C., was afraid of her pictures.

One more thing about *Growing Pains* considered as an autobiography. It is quite devoid of self-dramatization. Here is not the ego-inflated artist telling her important story for the world to behold and admire. We could wish even that she had taken herself as an artist more seriously as a public figure and told us more about her work on her pictures. But again, she would not have been Emily Carr. She says she learned something from every teacher, from one that there was sun in all shadows, from another that leaves are not plane surfaces. We see the struggles toward artistic confidence. But we get no indication of anything like an adequate self-appraisal. Emily Carr has not thought a discovery of herself very important; she has tried to describe the discovery of a Canadian art.

The publishers have counteracted her modesty by a very good choice of illustrations, at the beginning, "The Clearing" and at the end, a richly satirical comment on "Artist with Friends." The last is worth the price of the whole volume. Lady, stiff and disapproving. Gentleman, blank. From the cut of their clothes and the way her hat matches his moustache they are man and wife. Two lumpish males confused and uncomprehending. The artist, smock, cap, camp-stool, tries with her wonderfully expressive hands, to explain the unseen picture behind her. Hens, sleepy or querulous, bird popping out of its cage, the most intelligent part of the audience two dogs who alone really seem to be enjoying themselves. Is this to be the artist's summing up of the response of the Canadian public to art? (pp. 234-35)

Kathleen Coburn, "Canadian Artist," in The Canadian Forum, *Vol. XXVI, No. 312, January, 1947, pp. 234-35.*

THE TIMES LITERARY SUPPLEMENT (essay date 1954)

[*In the following excerpt, the critic praises the narrative style of* The Heart of a Peacock *as well as Carr's courage and individuality.*]

[*The Heart of a Peacock*] is a collection of short sketches and stories which [Emily Carr] left to her friend, Ira Dilworth. They are mainly autobiographical and tell of episodes concerned with wild animals and Indians, set in the landscape of British Columbia. The cumulative effect of the sketches is a picture of the writer as a girl who had a passion for wild life, great hardihood in bearing its vicissitudes, a peculiar power of taming animals and birds, and an understanding of Indians.

In writing about the relations between animals and people sentimentality easily creeps in. Emily Carr's nearest approach to it is in the name of the child who was herself—"Small." Even that is in relation to her sisters, who are called "Elder," "Middle," and "Bigger." As a teller of stories she has power; the reader is eager to know what happens next. Emotion there is in plenty, but no unassuaged grief, nothing mean or brutal or beyond human sympathy.

In the course of expeditions along the coast of British Columbia "with books, at least one dog and sketching materials" Emily Carr visited many Indian communities and painted their totems and villages. The stories that result are absorbing. One, called

"Two Women and an Infant Gull," gives in short space the essence of her quality as a person and a writer. "Grey and gentle, the dusk ran down the Skidigate Inlet," it begins, and goes on to describe how she found a young gull just hatched. "I stole it and left quickly. . . ." An Indian's wife demanded the gull. Without any sense of satire the author says: "All her babies had died. She had only her husband and a white kitten left to love." Given the gull, the woman snatched it. "Indians give and take; they don't thank. Proportions scale differently with them and with us." Explanations and humour are not this author's strong points, but storytelling is. "On my return I went to see Clara and the gull. The kitten and the gull were cuddled together under her cook-stove." When Clara went to work in a cannery she taught the bird to fly back and forth between her village and the cannery. When her mother saw the bird come "it was like a greeting from her daughter." The style is spare and simple and short extracts cannot give its quality, which is partly in a point of view.

"My father never shot living things," she tells us. "He talked often about the birds of England which he had loved in his English boyhood. Young Canada had very, very few wild song-birds when I was little." She came to England to study art and found her way to Seven Dials, where captive birds distressed her. English methods of hunting and shooting disgusted her—"deer hounded up to the royal guns; birds driven by beaters to the guns of men called sportsmen." In the Canadian, who "hunts" birds and other game through the woods, pursuing them on foot and needing them for food, the idea of standing still and waiting for the birds to arrive always arouses contempt. She first saw and heard English song-birds in Kent.

> "They don't deserve them! They don't deserve them!" was all I could say as I stood listening, drunk with delight. . . . I wish Canada, too, had song-birds. But, oh, I would not trade Canada's spacy silence—dim, tremendous—for England's warbling woods! When Canada is peopled end to end, then, perhaps . . . not now, not yet.

Emily Carr's youth was over before the cult of "popularity" which is to-day forced upon young girls in Canada had become extreme. It produces sweetness and insipidity. She would have stood outside it at any period. The delicate flavour of individuality and wild life will be enjoyed by all who have any taste for either.

"Thoughts from Canada," in The Times Literary Supplement, No. 2736, July 9, 1954, p. 436.

DAVID P. SILCOX   (essay date 1966)

[*Silcox is a Canadian art critic and author. In the following excerpt, he discusses* Hundreds and Thousands: The Journals of Emily Carr, *finding the work unsuccessful as literature.*]

Susie, Emily Carr's pet white rat, had a propensity for tearing up paper. It's a pity she never got at the manuscript [that **Hundreds and Thousands: The Journals of Emily Carr**] is based on.

The **Journals** are a collection of diary entries made during a dozen-year span near the end of the artist's life. They're so badly written or edited it's hard to believe they were ever meant for publication, or, since in the end they actually detract from our appreciation of Emily Carr as an artist, that publishing them was the momentous public service the blurb-writer suggests.

Still, here the book is and here Emily portrays herself and her doings. She emerges as a person with unusual mixtures of acerbity and kindness, of remarkable freedom and equally remarkable inhibitions, of tormenting doubt and strong resolve. She resented those who ignored or could not understand her work and she was suspicious of those who praised it. She wanted love and companionship but, like Diogenes, could never find someone honest enough to suit her. Her ally in the battle against loneliness and depression was Epsom Salts and by her own admission she loved trees better than people. Much of her affection was lavished on the four or more dogs she always had around, on the rat, the monkey and later on the chipmunks and her great quantities of birds.

Emily Carr's paintings are for the most part thinly disguised studies in sexual symbolism and straightforward affirmations of pantheism. Her *Journals,* however, while they divulge an obsession with underclothes, record her valiant and frustrating attempts to find and accept a religious faith. Influenced by Lawren Harris, she took up theosophy and consumed dollops of Ouspensky which she could not digest. Later she "hurled H. P. Blavatsky across the room" and went back to Christ and the idea that God was present in all living things and particularly in B.C. forests and, when she had it right, in her paintings. Her idea of heaven was of a place where not only race, creed and colour, but also, sex, were abolished.

What Emily knew about trees and forests she knew exceptionally well. It shows not only in her painting but in her writing, which surges with vitality and intention the moment she leaves gossip for direct description. A landscape—U.S. prairie, forest or just sea and sky—is her proper milieu and it's here that her comments about painting gain some profundity over her normal complaints about lack of appreciation, lack of sales and the extreme difficulty she had in controlling her will. She knew what her goal in painting was and when she was close to it. Her paintings had to "swing" and move with a kind of elemental strength and simplicity. She sought and expressed intense vibrant spaces, "emptiness but not vacancy." Her canvases bulge with the irrepressible "push of life" and growth. She wanted to catch "a breath that draws your breath with its breathing." And she succeeded.

But those illuminating passages are very few and are found mostly in the last hundred pages of this 332-page volume.

There are three reasons why the book as a whole fails. The first is that Emily Carr's life, according to this gospel, was dull. She was fussy, grouchy and critical. She didn't meet swinging people, she didn't do violent things, she didn't go a little mad. She was just a little eccentric and not much more so in her way than her neighbours in theirs. Secondly, she was, in considerable contrast to her painting style, a Victorian. She was for Morality and King and Empire. She was sentimental. Her literary sources were not her own generation of Eliot, Yeats and Pound, but Walt Whitman and the Hymnary. It is a startling experience to move from those muscular canvases to a prose so insipid and gutless, and so ridiculous at times that one is embarrassed to give examples: "I utter the senseless squawks of a feathered fowl. Often I wonder at the desire in me being so strong and driveling out in such feeble words and badly constructed sentences." "Oh, the lazy minds and shrinking hearts of us who shirk the digging grind!" "The fog-horn comes thickly, shouting a stomachy blare like a discontented cow." The reader also stumbles over the obstacles of such homely expressions as "Gee!" (or variant "Gee whiz!") and "shucks" or "I dunno." I had thought Sarah Binks could never find a competitor; but here she is and the more pathetic because she was in other ways so great:

> Artist, Poet, Singer, what are you
> after today—
> Blindly, dimly, dumbly trying to say?

Emily, in a Binksian moment, once put herself in the hands of the International Correspondence Criticism Service and disappointed even them. Her creative energy went first into painting and somewhat less forcefully into story-writing. She had a passion to be able to write well but her *Journals* are where she wiped her verbal brushes.

The third reason why the book is a failure is perhaps a result of the dullness and Victorianism: Emily Carr was a humourless writer and anecdotes need a light hand. We never laugh with her in her little book but only at her literary awkwardness. (pp. 54-6)

But I suppose we ought to be thankful to have anything by great people. We are certainly glad to have letters by Rubens and Van Gogh, the autobiographies of Augustus John and A. Y. Jackson and the journals of Delacroix. But the *Journals* of Emily Carr are another matter, and for me they are a fine example to support those who argue that painters should be seen but not heard. (p. 56)

> David P. Silcox, "Emily Carr's Journals," in Saturday Night, Vol. 81, No. 11, November, 1966, pp. 54-6.

DAVID WATMOUGH (essay date 1967)

[*Watmough is a prominent Canadian novelist, short story writer, and critic. In the following essay, he finds Carr's journals compelling despite obvious literary shortcomings.*]

As a painter Emily Carr can be neatly niched: lyric representationalism touched to surrealism under the influence of Lawren Harris. Sturdy work, one might say, with a persistent vision of local landscape and regional matter such as Indian totem poles and the pervasive presence of the coniferous forest. Above all, there is consistency. Rarely do the paintings and drawings tail off into mediocrity, rarely do they break through a final restriction of imaginative limitation to speak cosmically or beyond the touchstones of a familiar local context.

But her writing? It is a long time since I have experienced such a rushing, breathless exploration of the entire gamut of prose—from a rough and wiry quality that neatly nails reality, to a gushy naïveté that recalls the very worst kind of amateur lady writer who is all itchy ardour to evoke the grand solemnities of life.

Yet when all is said and done, when the last protest against the arch phrase, coy stance and self-conscious attitudinizing in anthropomorphic terms before the beauties of nature has been duly registered, there remains a down-to-earthness, a so-eminent humanity and an intimate tearing away of the veils that conceal any artist's true anguish, that there is finally only room for admiration.

In several respects *Hundreds and Thousands* recalls for me the journals of Denton Welch that appeared shortly after the Second World War. To be sure the custodian of a white rat, a monkey and a batch of little Griffon Bruxellois terriers does not for one moment display the rounded perfection of the wholly natural writer that Denton Welch does. Yet given the restrictions of this nature—the blatant anthropomorphisms, the inability or

refusal to probe the depth of introspection—*Hundreds and Thousands* yet manages to yield a great deal that is fascinating and pleasurable while largely irrelevant to the fact its author was also a painter. Denton Welch, too, of course, was a painter. But whereas, for the young and crippled Anglo-American, writing was the primary activity, with this Canadian Spinster, a diarist here in her riper years, the word-business took very much second place to her pursuit of a visual aesthetic.

What emerges, however, is that both of them *unconsciously* offer the reader a marvellous sense of period. With Welch it was wartime Britain, blackout, gasoline rationing and the problems of a sweet-tooth confronting an economic austerity.

For Victoria's Emily, the world of 1927-1941 was largely an absentee affair. Maybe there are more references to international sheenanigans than Jane Austen ever permitted to cast shadows over her œuvre. But all the same the provincial capital that lurches in and out of focus through the pages of this diary is cosy, smug, familiar, and altogether reassuring.

So for that matter are the contours of the author's life as she sets them down—whether in breathless hyperbole, bitchiness or, just occasionally, in that real strength of language that certainly betrays an exceptional imagination if not a skilled literary practitioner.

I have the impression that *Hundreds and Thousands* might well find greater favour in the United Kingdom than in Canada. For amateurism is still a fragrance in Britain whereas in North America it is observed as merely a stench. Too, Emily Carr's thoughts and arguments, whether religious, æsthetic or purely social, are essentially Anglo-Saxon in their matter. This means something parochial rather than racial, but it does necessitate, I think, a basic empathy for her between-wars kind of environment in a tucked away corner of the British Empire to feel the nuances of her anguish and to appreciate the fierce flame of determination to sustain a high doctrine of artistic pursuit in a mundane world of non-comprehension and basic uninterest in the affairs of the imagination.

Hundreds and Thousands is not a notebook of Emily Carr: artist. And because it is arbitrary in the selection of its entries, devoid of an index and bereft of any kind of accompanying essay "setting" her in her proper context, it will be of no avail to the grimmer kind of scholarship that demands such *a priori* factors in order that the machinery of criticism might run smoothly.

I do not mean to be unnecessarily perverse, however, when I suggest that because it patently cannot serve the Emily Carr Industry, it has a more honest position as a piece of literary creation. For better or for worse it has to stand on its own two feet as an evocation of person, place and period—for those of us for whom the ancillary data is lacking.

As it is, I think these journals, lopsided in style, lopsided in focus, and lopsided in chronological presentation though they may be, do in fact stand up as a fascinating literary chronicle. The woman who emerges through this literary portrait is nonetheless remarkable even though her feet were of clay, her surroundings mundane, and her vision sometimes commonplace.

Indeed, because of these things, her *sui generis* features stand out yet more badly. There is something to chuckle over legitimately in her snippety comments followed so swiftly by her *mea culpa* guilt-offerings. There is pathos, too, in her struggle to grasp the inner core of reality, after flirting with theosophy and dallying with what seems a pretty tepid and Erastian-tinged Anglicanism.

Emily Carr, this record reveals, knew herself better than most of us know ourselves, and torn between affront at her period for its (relative) modernity and an equal determination to paint herself free of straightjackets wrought from demoded idioms, she experienced a loneliness that can surely find current echo.

The ingredients are a frustrated female, surrounded by her pets, living out the artist's life in a stuffy provincial capital between the wars. The finished article is a compelling journal that manages to push sophistication to the wings and wrings genuine if containable emotions in steady succession from the reader. Emily was all kinds of painter, but as rough and ready diarist her vivid portrait declares she was also quite a girl. (pp. 72-5)

> David Watmough, "*Quite a Girl*," in Canadian Literature, *No. 33, Summer, 1967, pp. 72-5.*

K. P. STICH   (essay date 1984)

[*In the following excerpt, Stich considers Carr's writings a reflection of her search for a unified vision as a painter.*]

Emily Carr and William Kurelek lived their artistic lives primarily as painters; but their eyes and their minds' eyes have also given us impressive autobiographical narratives in which they explore and commemorate their growing up as artists in the New World. Carr's *Growing Pains* and her journals, which were published as *Hundreds and Thousands,* and Kurelek's *Someone With Me* (1973; rev. ed. 1980) . . . , owe their existence to the two painters' need for words to help them realize their calling. (p. 152)

In Carr's case, the need for words resulted partly from her struggle against states of ill health . . . and partly from her habit of wording in notebooks what she wanted to express in her paintings. Her "double approach," as she calls this striving for essentials through verbal and visual affinities, reflects a lifelong fondness for words that is evident in her occasional verse, particularly during her 1903-04 hospitalization in the East Anglia Sanatorium, and in her journals and annotated sketchbooks, in her many stories about her life, and in her fullfledged autobiography.

The word-consciousness of Carr and Kurelek strikes me as an inevitable complement to their expanding artistic impulses and intentions. When successful, such pioneering through words allows them to psychologize, to construct, or to dramatize their personal and public selves; when unsuccessful, their wordconsciousness tends to intensify their extreme sensitivity and rebelliousness as growing artists. The underlying notion of writing as therapy shapes the autobiographies of the two painters in decisive ways and provides a central motif for their verbal quests for artistic fulfillment. (pp. 152-53)

Maria Tippett has documented well how Carr's writing for book publication began about 1937 when a first heart attack and other health problems severely curtailed her activity as a painter. Carr's comments that she wrote *Klee Wyck* in the hospital to overcome the frustrations of her invalidism by reliving her past are strong evidence of writing as immediate self-therapy. At the same time, her comments underline her ongoing intentions of gaining control over her creative self through words. For this purpose she prefers to maintain a childlike persona in rebellion against the language of dogmatic, patriarchal authority and in search of voices that inspire her with awe, love,

Carr on horseback in 1904.

and encouragement for her own voice. The rebellion leads from her baptismal record and the "fat family Bible" to her own "little book," as she calls her journals begun in 1927, and from this quasi-confirmation of her voice to her first volumes of autobiographical narratives, *Klee Wyck* and *The Book of Small.* That, at least, is the framework Carr wants the reader to see in *Growing Pains,* a framework of organized words, reflecting growth and hope as much as retrospection and stability.

Growing Pains begins with Carr's account of her Presbyterian baptism. After she and her brother "were done together" at home, with her "kicking furiously to God,"

> Father sat at the table with the fat family Bible open at the page on which the names of his seven other children were written. He added ours, Richard and Emily, which as well as being ours were his own name and Mother's. The covers of the Bible banged, shutting us all in.

Whether Carr, who was four then, presents actual recollections is immaterial here; the fact that she satirizes religious convention and paternal autocracy is not. God's word seen as a denominational prison and her father seen as its keeper serve as Carr's justification for finding her own way as a creative child. Her defence against "being used as a soother" for a temperamental father who acted "as if he was God," is complicated by a mother who "was Father's reflection—smooth, liquid reflecting of definite, steel-cold reality" and whose reflection overshadowed the original in Carr's memory.

Carr's mother and father died when she was twelve and fourteen respectively. Her unmarried eldest sister, who took over the household, was "an autocrat like Father" and no doubt reinforced Carr's negative attitude towards her parents. Parental images are further complicated in her recollections: "Mother knew all about God. Father knew all about the earth.'' This reversal of traditional roles establishes her mother as the real authority of the household and helps to explain why her father rather than her mother appreciated young Carr's drawing skills. Her rebellion against her father is clearly a rebellion against unnatural, contrived, or received authority and is the beginning of her quest for true authority through art.

For this purpose she consistently adopts childlike perspectives with disregard for formal education and with emphasis on curiosity. ''I was always wondering and wondering,'' she says of her childhood self:

> Some wonders started inside you just like a stomach-ache. Some started in outside things when you saw, smelled, heard or felt them. The wonder tickled your thinking—coming from nowhere it got into your head running round and round inside until you asked a grown-up about this particular wonder and then it stopped bothering you.

She appropriately calls her child self ''Small'' and maintains that identity as one of her masks in old age, as if implying a continuous reduction to life's essentials. The relative anonymity of Small keeps alive the possibilities of experiencing wonder and joy. Her other child self, her identity as Klee Wyck or Laughing One, her name among the West Coast Indians, complements the life-affirming connotations of Small.

The importance of Small as a mask is particularly evident in the second to last chapter of *Growing Pains,* ''The Book of Small.'' Talking about the publication of her book by the same title, a portrayal of her childhood in Victoria, Carr prefers to speak simply of Small, without italics or quotation marks. Thus ''Small's flopped,'' ''Small's all right,'' and ''All who read Small . . . love her'' are phrases about herself as much as about the book. Exploiting such tension further, Carr concludes the chapter:

> dear Bill [Clarke, her publisher] and his kind little wife felt so sorry about all the doldrums I had been through because of Small. Bill's first question was, ''Is the next book ready? I plan to publish one each year.'' The script was ready, but we were deeper than ever in war. Hitler is a nuisance from every possible angle!

This incongruous combination of over and understatement is no small achievement in self-praise through the guise of verbal naïveté and with the confidence of a successful artist.

Again and again in *Growing Pains,* Carr relates her accomplishments as a painter directly to her ability to transform curiosity and intuition about life into word-consciousness, that is, the writing part of her ''double approach.'' At the San Francisco Art School, which she attended in her early twenties, her name was still ''Dummy'': ''I don't know who gave me the name or why, but 'Dummy' I was from the day I joined to the day I left.'' Whatever the other connotations of the name, to Carr it means the lack of a voice of her own, for she says:

> The type of work which I brought home from San Francisco was humdrum and unemotional—objects honestly portrayed, nothing more. As yet I had not considered what was underneath surfaces, nor had I considered the inside of myself. I was like a child printing alphabet letters. I had not begun to make words with the letters.

The progression from eyesight to seeing life through creative consciousness gains momentum in Carr's first experience of the West Coast frontier at Ucluelet: ''I loved every bit of it—

no boundaries, no beginning, no end, one continual shove of growing—edge of land meeting edge of water, with just a ribbon of sand between.'' Yet she was not yet ready to translate her instinctive awe of the primeval wilderness the way D. C. Scott, for instance, was able to do in ''The Sea by the Wood'' and ''The Wood by the Sea.'' ''Unknowingly,'' she says, ''I was storing, storing, all unconscious, my working ideas against the time when I should be ready to use this material.'' In a methodical way she tries to balance her childlike infatuation with the reality of grand nature; she begins to read poetry for its revelation of ''nature and beauty,'' underscoring passages about ''earth and nature.'' While the effect of this double vastness of nature and art stimulates and channels her intentions to be a painter, she has increasing difficulties with the correlated necessity of seeing the growing vastness within herself, knowing herself.

The difficulties intensify at the next stage of apprenticeship: attending art school in London where ''Dummy'' becomes ''Motor'' and ''Carlight.'' Unlike San Francisco, London reveals itself as an enormous prison, the source of her bourgeois shackles of law and order. The considerable self-discipline and dedication with which she attends art classes in England cannot contain the opposing pressures from her unshackled imagination as represented by the West Coast frontier and from the wastelands of cultural conformity and propriety as represented by the city of Victoria and magnified by London. Since the concept of Carr's ''double approach'' of painting and writing is central to *Growing Pains,* her mental breakdown in England implies that her apprenticeship to master painters as well as, indirectly, to master poets has not yet allowed her to either paint or speak with adequate self-knowledge to transform the threatening creative energy within her. The aesthetic, religious, and social discipline imposed from without, which may guide a nonartist or an art student, will of necessity come to fail a creative artist like Carr. Her energy as ''Motor'' and her life-long rebelliousness have given her an almost heroic drive against cultural conformity and hypocrisy. Yet to one of her placid English friends at art school, ''rebellious Carlight'' is allegedly but ''rebellious little Carlight''—in other words, a dramatized variant of Small.

As if to clarify name through deed, idea through reality, Carr carefully follows up the epithet in the ensuing chapter, ''Kicking the Regent Street Shoe-Man,'' in which Mrs. Radcliffe, one of her parental figures sparkling with middle-class respectability, takes her to an equally respectable shoe store:

> It was a very swell shop. The clerks were obsequious, oily tongues, oily hair, oily dignity and long-tail black coats like parsons. Our salesman was officious, he would persist in poking, prodding, pressing the shoe to my foot in spite of my repeated protests.

Carr eventually sends him reeling with ''a kick square amidships.'' The evidently liberating kick is also a wild gesture of a Canadian native: ''Klee Wyck!' gasped Mrs. Radcliffe.'' Carr achieves her self-defence against the tyranny of Victorian respectability not through verbal ingenuity but through naively heroic action, unhampered even by thoughts of hypocritical apologies:

> We waited for our bus, standing among all the Oxford Circus flower women on the island. The flowers were gay in their baskets, the women poked them under our noses, ''Tuppence-a'penny a bunch, lydy! Only tuppence!''
>
> ''Um, they do smell nice, don't they, Mrs. Radcliffe?''

> "Thirty years," she moaned, "I have dealt there!
> Dear me, dear me! I shall never be able to face those
> clerks again."

Though minor as one of many anecdotal sparks in *Growing Pains,* an example of "Carlight's" rebelliousness, this chapter is a skilful example of Carr's artistic spontaneity and predisposition for "fresh seeing." Yet her conclusion to the incident—"Oh, I wanted my West! I wasn't a London lady"—indicates that she wants to understand her London self in terms of the symbolic comfort of nature against the discomfort of society. Her aspiring creative self is still hampered by inadequate verbal and pictorial power. Instead, there are concomitant signs of growing depression: "I made myself into an envelope into which I could thrust my work deep, lick the flap, seal it from everybody." Only within the protective confinement of the East Anglia Sanatorium would she begin to open the envelope to let words and ideas out in order for her to grow again: "I wrote long doggerel verses and illustrated them by some thirty sketches in colour, steadily crying the while." Her aim is self-revelation through humour, irony, and satire directed at herself and at hospital life. Significantly, it is humour, irony, and satire in varying proportions that again characterize her self-therapy through personal narratives after her physical breakdowns in her sixties.

In her miniportrait, the "Author's Note" of 1903 that introduces *Pause,* her reminiscences about the sanatorium, she affirms the importance of words to her at that early time:

> The fat girl came from the far west where the forests
> are magnificent and solemn but no singing birds are
> there. The fat girl found birds in the early days of
> her sojourn in England. She heard a thrush sing. It
> was a poor prisoner in London, broken tailed and
> bedabbled, in such a dirty cage, but the pure song
> coming from its dreary prison touched the fat girl.
> By and by illness came and the fat girl subsided into
> a San with a limp and stutter. Then it was that the
> plan came to her to rear some thrushes and take home
> to her glorious silent woods. The fat girl bucked up.

The limp and stutter are evidently psychosomatic manifestations of Carr's withdrawal from social reality into a private envelope. They signal for a fundamental revival of creative will through movement and speech. "The fat girl bucked up" not only to rear some songbirds for her homeland but also to join them there, a songbird herself, a sort of hermit thrush at liberty in the grand life-giving envelope of the rain forests rather than trapped in the patriarchal prison of society. Together, the songbirds would become the voice of the silent wilderness and as such replace barren social voices of law and order. Essentially, however, Carr's intention as a "Birdmammy," though clearly a progression in her creative apprenticeship roles so far, implies merely another attempt at learning to make Canada her home through imported means. The plan failed. Yet Carr's identification with birds in an effort to capture the voice and spirit of the Canadian wilderness remains.

In "Wild Geese," the last chapter of *Growing Pains,* fused images of primeval woods, of the clearing where she did her last major painting, of spring, and of migrating geese allow her to see her life's work from a perspective that is concentrated and, at the same time, expansive—one that relies confidently on voice. Her artistic achievement is to her like a clearing already being overgrown again. Wild geese flying overhead, unlike English thrushes, represent the voice of the country—"every Canadian thrills at the sound"—and, like "a live necklace flung across the throat of heaven," draw near to the voice of God. The flight and sound of the geese give Carr in her seventies energy, courage, and will; even an "old goose would fill the bitter moment, pouring out proud, exultant honks that would weave among the clatter of the migrating flock."

The geese also draw her out from self-consciousness towards cosmic consciousness:

> God give me the brave unquestioning trust of the
> wild goose! No, being humans, we need more trust,
> our hopes are stronger than creatures' hopes. Walt
> Whitman's words come ringing—*We but level this
> lift to pass and continue beyond.*

Characteristically, Carr sees herself still as a wondering and learning child, listening for God's voice with the help of Whitman, her verbal master of growth from self to cosmic self.

The voices at the end of *Growing Pains* are but a variation of the voices at its beginning, and they are echoed throughout. Whitman is seen as her new father figure. His poetry brings together as catalysts for her creative growth the silence of her own father, the word of God, the "language" of the Group of Seven, the voices of Carr's bird selves (wild geese in her old age, a thrush in her early thirties, a sparrow at her birth), and her lack of a kind social voice ("I'm a *frost!*"). Her discipleship to Whitman (and one can add Emerson here) did not start until she was nearly sixty and was, it seems, the result of her friendship with Lawren Harris, another father figure, and Fred Housser. Whitman completes her quest for a master voice to guide her consciousness as an artist.

Although Whitman has the last word in *Growing Pains,* it is in *Hundreds and Thousands* that Carr discloses her debt to him. She quotes him numerous times and, in general, lets his psychological self-reliance and religious transcendence of self guide her will to fuse life with art and art with nature as well as religion. Whitman's exaltation of the word and of the divinity of the poet ("I speak the pass-word primeval...") would account for Carr's urgency to write about the "God quality in [her]." Yet in *Hundreds and Thousands,* as in *Growing Pains,* her autobiographical voice tends to prefer the mask of Small for her Whitmanesque optimism in a typical statement like "I claim my brotherhood to you [mountains]." Such optimism conflicts not only with her recurring despair at the uselessness of writing but also with her translation of Small into her image as a "little book," a leitmotif in her journals.

Caught between feelings of being small and a desire for being great, loving as well as hating her role of the proverbial artist who is misunderstood and shunned by society, she compares her situation to being "on the fence between yourself and yourself." One self is concentrated into Small. The other self expands ultimately into the woods, the sea, and the mountains; in other words, it grows into the vast wilderness she sees personified in the carved figure of D'Sonoqua, her "totem mother," "the 'wild woman of the woods'—wild in the sense that forest-creatures are wild—shy, untouchable." Small is, I think, essentially Carr's mask as a writer; D'Sonoqua is the maternal mask behind which she grows as a painter to achieve her response to Whitman's "free flight into the wordless." Yet for this mask to suit her, she needs to become a creative mother figure. "Have been struggling with 'D'Sonoqua,'" she writes in her journal for 11 December 1934:

> Big, strong simplicity is needed for these carvings
> and forests. I am appalled at the petty drivel I get
> down. It feels strong when I'm doing it; afterwards
> it's crude. Ugh! How does one bridge "feels" with

"words"? . . . Often I wonder at the desire in me being so strong and drivelling out in such feeble words and badly constructed sentences.

Although words are no shortcuts to final truths, Carr still believes that "writing is a splendid sorter of your good and bad feelings, better even than paint." In concrete terms, personal writing is Carr's therapy against the shortcomings of her maternal self, against her depressions, her self-centredness, and her masochistic streak. "Until people have been fathers or mothers," she maintains, "they can hardly understand the fullness of life." Obviously aware of her yearning to be a mother figure and of her need for a father, Carr seems to use the ambiguous cliché of "fullness of life" to encompass sexual as well as artistic or spiritual creativity. In fact, her fear of sexuality that manifested itself in her relationships with men and may have had its origin partly in a "traumatic experience" with her father, is a fundamental objective correlative to her roles as Small and as D'Sonoqua.

Through her writing, she imposes law and order on her creative energy and thus finds an answer to her quest for authority. Her writing also allows her to balance "on the fence between yourself and yourself" and to explore these selves. In this respect, her writings act either as necessary preludes and interludes to her paintings or as postludes like *Growing Pains* and *Klee Wyck*. Indeed, her response to the triumph of *Klee Wyck* pinpoints the function of her personal narratives as a psychological charting of her own life; it is also a kind of cultural charting of Canada because she wants all her work to be "in the big way with the feel and spirit of Canada behind it":

> in my misery I had written the book seeking escape from a hospital bed, I had transported myself back to these [West Coast] places I knew so well. They healed me.—I went on writing because I loved it and wanted to, [and] now to hear it said that my writing had helped to enrich Canada, helped to show to others even a little bit of her . . . made me almost happier than I could bear.

Her authorial self as Small, however, would be incomplete without a fatherly editor whom she found in Ira Dilworth or "Eye," as she suggestively calls him in *Growing Pains*. "My Editor," she says, "never altered my wording arbitrarily. Occasionally he suggested re-phrasing a sentence, always explaining why. He never added or omitted anything without consulting me. Sometimes he made suggestions, but he made me re-word the thought myself." Although a draft of *Growing Pains* shows that "arbitrarily" and "without consulting me" were added later and "clearly explaining" has become only "explaining," I see no cause to question Dilworth's editorial integrity. Carr's gift as a writer is undeniable, and, furthermore, somewhat reminiscent of Grove, she liked to be her own *editor* of biographical fact and fiction.

While there is no need here to examine Carr's manipulation of such facts, it is useful to consider briefly her opinion of portraits. "I hate painting portraits" she says:

> I am embarrassed at what seems to me to be an impertinence and presumption, pulling into visibility what every soul has as much right to keep private as his liver and kidneys and lungs and things which are coated over with flesh and hide. . . . The better a portrait, the more indecent and naked the sitter must feel. An artist who portrays flesh and clothes but nothing else, no matter how magnificently he does it, is quite harmless. A caricaturist who jests at his victim's expense does so to show off his (the artist's)

own powers, not to portray the subject. To paint a self-portrait should teach one something about oneself. I shall try.

This journal entry indirectly affirms the therapeutic value *and* danger of (auto)biographical narratives; it also forewarns the reader that Carr's verbal self-analyses are likely tailored to cover up the unpleasant reality she sees underneath her masks. While the voice of Small provides a persuasive excuse for self-analysis, self-pity, self-irony, and self-caricature in Carr's literary introspections, this protective filter for her mind's eye appears to be less effective in her "Portrait of Small" and her "Self-Portrait." The former, painted in brown and gray tones often associated with states of depression, shows Carr with her head tilted forward and her eyes staring slightly to the right and slightly upward. A haunted look in her eyes emphasizes the general impression of anxiety, depression, and smallness without any relief from self-irony. The latter portrait, in primarily dull and heavy tones, shows a massive Carr in something like a surgeon's gown and cap. The piercing look in her right eye and the haunted look in her left eye seem to reflect the verbal and spiritual agonies of advanced introspection or, putting it differently, of exploratory "surgery" by a creative artist. This painting suggests Carr's D'Sonoqua self.

Both self-portraits are complemented by Carr's last painting, "Woo," a portrait of her monkey. Woo had been a favorite among her numerous pets who, like the birds already mentioned, all seem to be extensions of herself. Cowering under twisting branches full of ripe applelike fruit, his hands cupping one of the fruit, Woo is staring demonlike at the viewer; his right pupil is wider than the narrow slit of his left pupil, creating a double stare comparable to Carr's in "Self-Portrait." In other words, "Woo" reveals an image of paradise and hell which Carr, as a painter, has come to see at the end of her self-centred exploration for cosmic consciousness. The devilish reality of "Woo" at the end of Carr's quest to become D'Sonoqua, after all her paintings of primeval nature, dramatizes the demoniacal side of extreme romanticism whose power Carr had experienced early in her breakdown in England. "Woo" also suggests a final failure of the quest for authority. Even the picture's self-explanatory sexual overtones are significant here. They corroborate the frequently erotic imagery of her forest scenes as well as her sexual complexes.

In this context, her inspiration by Whitman is curious because he must have played a stronger role than she discloses in either *Hundreds and Thousands* or *Growing Pains:* no one can read *Leaves of Grass* without coming to terms with Whitman's abundant metaphors of sexual energy and liberation. That Carr remains conspicuously silent on these aspects is implicit proof not only of the importance of such energy to her in her art but also of her editorial control in her personal narratives. Unlike her paintings, her words allow her to remain on the fence between the world of Small and the demonic aspects of the world of art and sexuality. Words seemed to allow her painter self to act less objectively and more playfully than did paint, without deceiving her or the reader.

As is the case in most literary autobiographies, her editorial discipline is aimed at winning the public's confidence and reverence, while maintaining just enough of a veil, as Hawthorne would say, or a sort of *trompe l'oeil* to protect her inner self from her mind's eye that can be so destructive in her paintings, and from the mind's eye of her reader. Although Carr did not paint *trompe l'oeil* in the technical sense, it is fitting to appropriate the term for her autobiographical writing. (pp. 153-64)

K. P. Stich, ''Painters' Words: Personal Narratives of Emily Carr and William Kurelek,'' in Essays on Canadian Writing, *No. 29, Summer, 1984, pp. 152-74.*

PETER SANGER   (essay date 1987)

[*In the following excerpt, Sanger views inaccuracies in Carr's accounts of her life as the result of sexual repression, and contends that the Indian legend of D'Sonoqua, which recurs throughout Carr's writings and paintings, serves as the symbol of Carr's sexuality, repressed on a personal level yet expressed in her paintings.*]

Start with D'Sonoqua, the giant wild woman of the woods in Kwakiutl mythology. She is a thief, kidnapper, liar, sometimes a cannibalistic murderess. Occasionally male, she nevertheless always has female sexual characteristics. But in spite of her strength, ruthlessness and cunning, D'Sonoqua can be killed and outwitted by one of the children she kidnaps. Those who defeat her take bear and mountain goat skins from her cave. They take furs, berries, grease, dried meat and salmon.

Emily Carr met D'Sonoqua. The first time was in 1912 at the deserted village of Guyasdoms, Gifford Island, off the northeast coast of Vancouver Island. There Carr made a watercolour study of a totem. This became the source of ''Guyasdoms' D'Sonoqua,'' an oil painting she finished in 1930.

Between 1930 and 1931, Carr also sketched or painted four more representations of figures she believed to be D'Sonoqua's, basing them upon totems seen during the late summer of 1930 at Quattiche on the northwest coast of Vancouver Island.

Her interest in D'Sonoqua continued during the next five years. On November 9, 1934, she noted in her journal that she was still thinking about . . . ''the big wooden image, the woods, the deserted villages, the wet, the sea and smells and growth, the lonesomeness and mystery, and the spirit of D'Sonoqua over it all, and what she did to me.'' She began writing an autobiographical story describing three of the totems she had seen on her painting expeditions. This story was worked, reworked and tested by being read aloud to friends between 1934 and 1936. Eventually, it became the sixth chapter of *Klee Wyck.* (pp. 211-12)

What was it the figure of D'Sonoqua ''did'' to Emily Carr in 1912? Why, nearly a quarter of a century later, did that figure still elicit such supple, attentive description? It was Carr's own ''fixed stare'' staring back at her which she saw and felt boring in, for representations of D'Sonoqua, like those of all mythological figures, are both one and many. (p. 220)

[In a simplified account of Carr's life], it is clear how courageous, active and persistent she was. But there is another, one less obviously admirable, which needs expression. It is a shadow life, not to be narrated simply. Ironically, this life is most apparent in the autobiographical books which Carr wrote largely to conceal it.

Six of these books will be used in the following discussion. *Klee Wyck* describes Carr's relationship with the Indians and adventures she had on painting expeditions among them. *The Book of Small* contains stories about Carr's childhood in Victoria. The first two-thirds of *The House of All Sorts* concern characters and events in the boarding and apartment house Carr

kept between 1913 and 1935. Its latter third is devoted to the bobtail sheepdogs she raised and sold between 1917 and 1921. *Growing Pains,* Carr's autobiography, was completed just before her death. It was followed by the publication of *Pause.* Although one of the last of her books to appear, Carr wrote it in 1938. Its subject is the stay in East Anglia Sanatorium from 1903 to 1904. Finally, there is *Hundreds and Thousands,* edited by Phyllis Inglis from the journals Carr kept between 1927 and 1941.

The qualities of *Hundreds and Thousands* set it apart from Carr's other books. It will be discussed in a later section of this essay. In contrast, the quality, effect and intent of the other five books are oddly mixed and unsettling. On the one hand, they are written with wit, concision, respect and love. They also offer some of the finest passages of natural description in Canadian prose. On the other hand, they are often disingenuous, malicious, and evasive. In the discussion that follows, these five will be called the autobiographies.

Several of those who have written about Carr recently have acknowledged the untrustworthiness of the autobiographies. Shadbolt has noted how ''the uncertain process of memory, heightened—even distorted—by her literary skill and sense of drama, has made them unreliable sources for biographical detail.'' Tippett [see Additional Bibliography] has described them as . . . ''not accurate accounts of her past. They are a mere reflection, altered and coloured by literary instinct.'' The truth is that while some of the inaccuracies and alterations at issue may have involved slips of memory, most derive from instincts that were anything but ''literary.'' A clue as to what these instincts often were appears in a letter Carr sent to Edythe Hembroff-Schleicher when at work on *The House of All Sorts.* With her ''filthy tenants,'' Carr wrote, ''I'll be even yet, using them for stories.''

The best known and most obvious of Carr's alterations involve her age. *Growing Pains,* for example, contains the sentence: ''I was twelve—when Mother died—the raw green Victoria age, twelve years old.'' Carr's mother died in 1886. Carr was 15. Later in *Growing Pains* she describes asking her guardian for permission to attend art school in San Francisco, pleading ''I am sixteen almost.'' Carr was nearly 20. Probably the most notorious alteration occurs in *Klee Wyck,* which begins with a chapter describing Carr's stay in Ucluelet in 1898. Its third sentence reads: ''Everything was big and cold and strange to me, a fifteen year old school-girl.'' Carr's real age was 26.

Even when she did not mention her age in years in the autobiographies, Carr consistently wrote them as if she were far younger than she actually was when events occurred. In *Growing Pains,* for example, she explained her failure in teaching the Ladies' Art Club of Vancouver in 1906 by saying that she was snubbed as an ''unimportant, rather shy girl.'' Carr was 35. As at least one photograph taken at the time attests, she looked anything but girlish.

Forgetfulness alone was not at work in these adjustments of age. They are too consistent and radical to be accidental. They enabled Carr to reconstruct the past in her favour. The request, for example, to study in San Francisco at ''sixteen almost'' sounds more courageous than the real request made at 20, almost. The visit to Ucluelet by a ''fifteen year old'' (in an account which never identifies the presence of Carr's sister, Elizabeth) sounds more heroic than the real visit made at 26. Less forgiveably, the adjustments of age are often worked to malign those Carr disliked. By stating, for example, that she was "twelve" when her mother died, and therefore 14 when her father died in 1888, Carr was able to make it sound plausible that her brother Richard "and I got the riding whip every day. It was a swishy whip and cut and curled around our black stockinged legs very hurtfully." This whip was supposedly used by Carr's eldest sister, Edith. According to Carr's chronology, these attacks took place between the ages of 14 and 17. However, if they did occur, it could only have been between those of 17 and 20. But at those ages, as photographs show, Emily was larger and stronger than Edith. Carr also wore the long dress usual for women of her age and class, not a little girl's short dress and stockings. Even Ira Dilworth, Carr's editor and closest friend towards the close of her life, admitted: . . . "it is quite unlikely that Emily's elder sister ever punished her with a riding whip."

Carr's lies about her age obviously have their pathos. They show what she was ashamed of and afraid to reveal: her immaturity, dependence, and the contrast between what she was and wished to become. But the vicious treatment of Edith, who died in 1919, is anything but pathetic. It can also be paralleled by other similar manoeuvres in the autobiographies.

There is, for example, consistent ignobility in the way Carr suppresses or evades acknowledging her indebtedness to other artists, with the exception of Lawren Harris. To him she dedicated *Growing Pains,* and she devoted a chapter in it to their relationship, quoting extensively from his letters of advice and encouragement. But Theodore Richardson, the American artist she met in Sitka in 1907, is not named. Unfairly and untruthfully Carr wrote that his work represented "drab little scenes which might have been painted in any place in the world. He did occasionally stick in a totem pole but only ornamentally as a cook sticks a cherry on top of a cake." Richardson, as one might guess from Carr's tone, was a more competent artist in 1907 than she. A similar instance concerns Frances Hodgkins, the New Zealand painter with whom Carr studied in Brittany in 1911. As Tippett has noted, Carr was probably Hodgkins' only student at the time. They were both unmarried women artists from the dominions who must have much in common. Hodgkins in 1911 was also an artist of reputation and achievement, just as Carr hoped to be. Carr's work during the period shows a great deal of Hodgkins' influence. Yet all Carr ever wrote about Hodgkins (without ever mentioning her name) appears in *Growing Pains* as: "I heard there was a fine water colourist (Australian) teaching at Concarneau, a place much frequented by artists. I went to Concarneau—studied under her. Change of medium, change of teacher, change of environment, refreshed me. I put in six weeks' good work under her." A third example of Carr's ingratitude involves Ambrose and Viola Patterson, the young Seattle art teachers who stayed with Carr occasionally during the 1920's and 1930's. It was they who led her to Cezanne's work and helped persuade her to begin painting and exhibiting again. Carr simply ignored them in her books. A fourth example is her treatment of Mark Tobey, the American artist who probably visited Carr for a week in 1924 and made other visits during the 1920's. In the fall of 1928, at Carr's request, he used her studio to give a three-week advanced course in painting which she attended. In the spring of 1930, at her invitation, he used her studio while she was in Toronto and New York. One memorial of their relationship is Tobey's oil, "Emily Carr's Studio," which is reproduced in Tippett's biography. It was Tobey who helped Carr discover the use of light and rhythm which are so moving in her late work. Yet he is not named in *Growing Pains.* He appears there only as an anonymous "American artist," who

"came to visit at my house," and dragged her away one morning from beds, dishes, and meals to paint in Beacon Hill Park.

Such verifiable instances of evasion and alteration make one suspect that there are others semiconcealed by the self-contradictions and apparent implausibilities which occur in the autobiographies. Consider, for example, Carr's picnic with her mother, described in the second chapter of *Growing Pains* as a moment when "I was for once Mother's oldest, youngest, her companion-child." Tippett has called this "perhaps her most sensitive autobiographical sketch." The implausibility involved is that Carr states that the picnic took place "a short while" before her mother's death. Carr's mother probably died of tuberculosis. She had been an invalid, living mainly upstairs in her bedroom, since 1875. Was she really capable of walking around Beacon Hill Park, unattended except for her 13- or 14-year-old daughter (10 or 11 by Carr's account)? Perhaps. But it is suggestive that this section of *Growing Pains* was written in Mount Douglas Park in July, 1942, during Carr's last sketching trip. Could it be that Carr, in Mount Douglas Park, rewrote the past in Beacon Hill Park so that she, as her own mother, could nurture herself, as her own child? Reading Tippett's biography and Carr's autobiography together often leads to such kinds of inference. Consider a less contestable example. In *Growing Pains,* Carr claimed that her sister Elizabeth was sent to England in 1902 because Elizabeth "was on the edge of a nervous breakdown." The Carrs in Victoria may have been capable of misjudgements, but it is doubtful if they would ever try to cure Elizabeth, "on the edge of a nervous breakdown," by sending her to look after Emily, who was having one.

In particular, there are two of Carr's narrative sequences in the autobiographies which are probably affected by suppression or reversal of fact. There is also a third sequence, involving the deepest layers of Carr's psyche, a sequence which will probably never be clarified, which needs even more careful discussion. Begin with the simplest of these three. It appears in *The House of All Sorts.* The last chapter of that book's first section, "How Long," describes what happened when a "crude, enormous, coarse" lodger, with "fleshy hands" and "fingers like bananas," a man who ground "the life out of his little third wife," a man who wore "glasses with thick lenses," caught Carr in the basement furnace room and complained about a frozen hand basin tap. Carr explained how difficult it was to get a plumber, and: "As I stooped to shovel coal his heavy fist struck across my cheek. I fell among the coal." A different version of what must be the same incident appears in the second part of the same book in a chapter entitled "Loo." Here, Carr is described as going into the basement to tend the furnace: "As I stooped to shovel coal, a man's heavy hand struck me across the face. A tenant living in one of my flats bellowed over me, 'I'll teach you to let my pipes freeze'." Carr "reeled, fell on the coal pile," got up to slam the door shut and "bolt the brute out," saw him "on the step, his hand lifted to strike me again. Quick as lightning I turned on the tap with hose attached . . . and directed icy water full into his face; it washed the spectacles from his nose." Although Tippett does not point it out, the source of both stories appears in her biography. Carr found a tenant stoking the furnace. She pulled off his glasses and trampled them into the basement floor. The tenant then pushed her into the coal bin. Other lodgers cheered.

The second sequence of adjustment, reversal and suppression is less naive. It appears in its fullest form in *Pause,* Carr's memoir about her stay in East Anglia Sanatorium between

January, 1903, and March, 1904. There she describes hand-rearing "six nests of thrushes, two of blackbirds," and, later, "two nests of black-bonneted, rose-breasted, chesty bullfinches." The birds were nestlings taken from the surrounding hedge country. In *Pause,* they are not merely decoratively whimsical. They are the book's organizing and controlling metaphor and intended to prove Carr's sanity and integrity in contrast to the obtuseness and brutality which by her account surrounded her. According to Carr, patients and staff at the sanatorium brought worms, beetles, ant eggs and slugs to feed them. Carr became known as "Mammy" or "Bird Mammy." As the birds matured, they were moved from the room "to a large cage out of doors." The birds and Carr constituted a centre of interest, affection and attention. But after "eighteen months" in the sanatorium, "losing ground," Carr was subjected to a new "special treatment" which meant she could no longer look after the birds. Anxious to save them from the suffering their tameness might lead to if they were freed, she had them chloroformed. Substantially the same story appears in *Growing Pains,* with the additional information that the birds were "nine months old" when, after "sixteen months" in the sanatorium, Carr was forced to undergo special treatment and chloroformed them. There also exists a sub-variation on both these accounts in which the bullfinches were not kept in an outside cage but . . . "put in a wicker cage in my room." One pair of bullfinches, according to this account, "got out to Canada with me," the rest having been given away, not chloroformed. The pair taken to Canada thrived for five years.

Tippett's biography offers the factual source of these narratives. On March 13, 1903, one month after entering the sanatorium, Carr stole and began to raise thrush nestlings. The birds were not kept in an outdoor cage but in one in her room. Carr's special treatment did not begin after she was "sixteen months" in the sanatorium. She only stayed there, in total, 15 months, not the 18 stated in *Growing Pains.* According to Tippett, the treatment began "a few . . . weeks" after the birds were captured. The birds were chloroformed, therefore, not at "nine months," but when little more than fledglings. The story of the bullfinches (were there ever any?) which survived to thrive in Canada is not only contradicted by *Pause* and *Growing Pains,* but also, given the range and complexity of Carr's travels after leaving the sanatorium, unbelievable. Possibly the real fate of all the birds is depicted in a chapter of *Pause* called "The Garden." There Carr describes the sanatorium's garden, "queened" over by "Miss Brown" and her "understudy, one Miss Lavinia Mole." In this garden, Carr found "a pile of little bodies, glossy black or mottled brown . . . music stilled in twisted throats—dead! Thrushes and blackbirds." The birds had been netted to protect the garden. "Miss Brown would fertilize her garden with their beautiful bodies!," while "naked fledglings waiting, waiting, in nearby nests, holding up scrawny necks till they could no longer support the gaping mouths" died. Whenever Carr's writing becomes melodramatic and self-righteous it is often suspect as truth. In the light of other projections and reversals in the autobiographies it would not be unreasonable to suppose that "Miss Brown" carries Carr's guilt.

The third of these sequences of lying and adjustment to be examined is the most complex. It concerns her father. He appears in *The Book of Small* as an authoritarian, somewhat distant, but benevolent man, to be said goodnight to with a kiss on his bald spot. In *Growing Pains,* however, Carr's feelings about her father change from respect and love to suspicion, disillusionment and, finally, contempt. Richard Carr's was a "definite, steel-cold reality. . . . Our childhood was ruled by Father's unbendable iron will, though in spite of Father's severity and his overbearing omnipotence, you had to admit the justice even in his dictatorial bluster." Carr describes in *Growing Pains* how she used to be her father's companion: "He let me snuggle under his arm and sleep during the long Presbyterian sermons. I held his hand during the walk to and from church." Then, in this version, Carr gradually saw that "I was being used as a soother for Father's tantrums . . . and began to question why Father should act as if he was God." She decided "disciplining would be good for Father and I made up my mind to cross his will sometimes." As a result, "his fury rose against me. . . . His soul was so bitter that he was even sometimes cruel to me." (It is hard to resist the suspicion, at this point, that the narrative's factual accuracy could be secured simply by substituting Emily Carr for her father, and vice versa.) The account of their relationship reaches its climax with Carr telling her mother that her father "is cross, he thinks he is as important as God." Its catastrophe appears a few pages later when Carr describes her father's depression and withdrawal after his wife's death: "His stare was as empty as a pulpit without a preacher and with no congregation in front of it."

Since the publication of Tippett's biography, this narrative is usually regarded as a screen for events and feelings which were too complex and frightening for Carr to reveal in her autobiographies. As noted in the previous section of this essay, she wrote to Ira Dilworth in 1935 that the real cause of the estrangement from her father was a "brutal telling," in which he spoiled "all the loveliness of life with that bestial brutalness of explanation filling me with horror instead of gently explaining the glorious beauty of reproduction, the holiness and joy of it." Tippett has proposed that Richard Carr may even have used physical display to illustrate his meaning.

It is true that such a "brutal telling" could explain Carr's subsequent behaviour and the symptoms which appeared during her breakdown in 1903 and 1904. And yet, there is room for speculation. Dilworth, admittedly, was Carr's closest friend and her editor during the 1940's. It would be odd if she lied to him. But she did, on the other hand, implicate him in the autobiographical adjustments noted in this essay, even to the point where he felt it needful later to excuse one. In addition, the extracts from Carr's letters to Dilworth which appear in Tippett's biography reveal her manipulative emotional use of him. She may have told him the truth about the "brutal telling," but the nature of their relationship did not stop her from deceiving him.

Other reservations are worth considering. First, we do not know when the "brutal telling" took place, but if it occurred before the wife's death, why did Richard Carr try to explain matters which were in his time (and are usually now) explained to a daughter by her mother? Second, if the explanation occurred after the death of Emily's mother, or during her final weeks of life, why was it not given by the eldest sister, Edith, or by the next eldest, Clara, who had married in 1882 when Emily was ten or eleven? Clara, incidentally, must surely have had several of her six children by the time of the "brutal telling." Third, even given the reticence and secrecy about sex in Victorian families, how could Emily Carr have grown up in a household with five other women and been as unknowing about it as she implies she was in her correspondence with Dilworth? Finally, if it was the custom for Richard Carr to give such explanations to his daughters, why after instructing Edith, Clara, Elizabeth and Alice did he blunder with his youngest daughter,

Emily? Could, therefore, the "brutal telling" Carr offered Dilworth have been as much a screen for the truth as that depiction of her father's pseudo-divine megalomania she offered the public in *Growing Pains*?

Another chapter in *Growing Pains* offers an accessory complication. It is entitled "Evil" and purports to describe what Emily discovered about vice in San Francisco. Her informant is not her father but "Mrs. Piddington," a malicious caricature of Mrs. Hayes, her guardian in San Francisco from 1891 to 1892. Mrs. Piddington (her name's allusion to "piddle" and "piddling" is obvious) told Carr that a short cut through Grant Street had taken her into San Francisco's "red light district." Naively asking, "What are prostitutes?", Carr is described as being unable to understand Mrs. Piddington's anger. On the next page, Carr recalls her bewilderment at Mrs. Piddington's explanation that a child can be born illegitimately. Outraged, saying "your sister has no right to send you into the world as green as a cabbage!", Mrs. Piddington then illuminated Carr about "Opium dens in Chinatown, drug addicts, kidnappings, murder, prostitution." Carr returned fearfully to her room and after talking to her cagebird, Dick, resolved only partly to believe and mostly to forget Mrs. Piddington's lecture.

This chapter raised one of the usual problems associated with Carr's autobiographies. According to her own chronology, she would have been 16 or 17 when the events in "Evil" occurred. At that age, the naivety she ascribed to herself is possibly credible. But her age was really 20 or 21. It is unbelievable that Carr was so naive at such an age.

The chapter also raises a second difficulty. It contradicts what Carr told Ira Dilworth. The "brutal telling" could hardly have left her as ignorant as she depicts herself being in San Francisco. Admittedly, one is left with the possibility that Mrs. Piddington has been given words actually spoken by Richard Carr. But if that is so, it undermines the main motive for the hatred (often with sexual insinuation) that Carr used in creating her caricature of Mrs. Piddington. Perhaps an explanation is concealed in Carr's resentful comment that Edith "had a deep infatuation for Mrs. Piddington."

Obviously speculations like these cannot really be drawn to a conclusion. Something central is missing from the pattern, and even the "brutal telling" does not fully provide it. Deceptions overlay deceptions in Carr's public and private accounts. Facts have been hidden, lost and perverted. Taken together, two further passages in Carr's work reveal at least one of the principles at work in this process. The first appears in *Pause,* where she describes making dolls representing her doctors in the sanatorium: "I had trouble in getting Dr. Mack's legs long enough and the right twist on Dr. Sally's neck . . . I had to borrow Cook's meat-saw, saw through the neck and glue it back twisted. I had to give Dr. Mack's legs an extra joint." The second passage is from a journal entry for 1933 in *Hundreds and Thousands.* There, Carr describes how she played with her dolls as a child. "I used to love to make mine sit with their back hair facing their laps and their hind-beforeness ridiculous. I loved to make my dolls look fools to get even with them for their coldness, particularly the wax or china ones." Dolls are mirrors. In discussing Carr's relationships with her father, with her sisters, with other people, with the facts of her life and her understanding and portrayal of them, we are involved with emotions Carr indulged, projected, struggled against, disguised from her readers and probably, on the reasoning level, often concealed from herself.

A story about these emotions appears in *Growing Pains.* Whether the story is fact or fable hardly seems to matter. It has the mythopoetic rightness possessed by so many of Carr's later paintings. It takes place in San Francisco again, in the gardens of "Last Chance," "a place behind bars where they put monstrosities, abnormalities while doctors decide if anything can be done for them." Carr tells how she went there with Alice and Mrs. Piddington for a flower-picking picnic. "Shadowy forms moved on the other side of the bars." Carr suddenly found herself "at the brink of a great hole several yards around. My foot hung over the hole." She screamed, and the hole "was filled with a slithering moil of snakes, coiling and uncoiling. Had my lifted foot taken one more step, I should have plunged headlong among the snakes and I should have gone mad!" Carr, apparently, did not take that step in San Francisco in 1892 and went mad in 1903 and 1904. Had she taken it, her autobiographies would have been very different, or she might not have been able to write them at all.

Return to D'Sonoqua, the Kwakiutl wild woman of the woods with whom this essay began. Like Carr, she is a complex figure, both creative and destructive. When Carr asked an Indian, probably during the major sketching expedition in 1928, if D'Sonoqua was "bad," he answered, "Sometimes bad . . . sometimes good," and walked away. Alone, staring up at the totem which had led her to ask the question, Carr saw a small bird, its beak full of grass or moss, fly into D'Sonoqua's circular, soundless, screaming mouth.

The Indian stories about D'Sonoqua, like the many stories about Carr, depict her ambiguity. The stories are usually a sequence of paradoxes and reversals. Most involve young children who are kidnapped by D'Sonoqua and free themselves by using their wits. In one, for example, a boy's parents threaten to call D'Sonoqua unless he stops crying. The boy runs away into the night and is caught by D'Sonoqua who drags him underground. The boy offers to pierce D'Sonoqua's ears so that she can wear ornaments. D'Sonoqua agrees, stoops for the piercing, and the boy pushes her into the fire. She is burned to death. The boy returns to his parents, tells his story, and his people go to D'Sonoqua's cave to possess her riches.

Seen as a pattern, this story consists of contradictions, whose logic is the symmetry of opposition. The boy, for example, is young and small, D'Sonoqua, primordially old and grotesquely tall. The boy lives in civilization, D'Sonoqua, in the wild. The boy's natural parents reject him, while D'Sonoqua, the alien, wants him. The boy runs away to escape, but escapes into the situation from which he is running away. The boy kills D'Sonoqua, who logically should have been able to kill him. The boy becomes the murderer of his own intending murderer, and he and his parents become predators who plunder the one who would be predatory. Does D'Sonoqua capture the child, or the child, D'Sonoqua? The answer is both.

The masked dancer who represents D'Sonoqua at Kwakiutl ceremonies and celebrations always acts as if he is asleep or near sleep. He is not a figure for ridicule, nor (within the protection of ritual) is he quite to be feared. If any one of the audience points a finger at him, he falls asleep. The masker represents both the passivity and terrifying power of the preconscious, the source of wealth, and the place of chaos. The child D'Sonoqua captures is not the sentimentalized innocent Carr tried so often to pretend she always had been and still was. She called that child by her own baby nickname, "Small." This "Small" often has the characteristics of an infant D'Sonoqua. The other child, whom D'Sonoqua could not imprison, lies buried in Carr's autobiographies.

But the child does ultimately appear in Carr's prose. He is "Drummie," the dream-child companion of her childhood, who appears in an entry in her journals, *Hundreds and Thousands.* She recalled: "I used to ride all round the garden with him on a dream horse. . . . The dream horse and the dream boy and I all talked and had a splendid time that nobody ever knew about except ourselves." Three years later, in 1936, Carr remembered "Drummie" again: . . . "that corner of the garden. I can see it so clearly and the boy 'Drummie' who came sometimes—just a felt presence, not a seen one. I so often have wondered who and why he was. I don't remember anything he did or said—only the jog trot of my own fat legs which was the jog of the two white horses."

"Drummie" was not a fantasy. He was myth. His absence from the welter of truth, half-truth and lies which takes up so much of Carr's public autobiographies is fitting. He properly appears in *Hundreds and Thousands,* where Carr stopped trying to force her experience into vindictive, self-contradictory patterns of self-exculpation.

Carr's wonder about "who and why" "Drummie" was shows that she did not consciously recognize him as some kind of Eleusinian animus. But his appearance signified the start of a process of individuation which Carr was able to carry to magnificent conclusion in her painting. About nine months after Carr first mentioned "Drummie" in her journal (July 23, 1933), she recorded this dream on April 16, 1934:

> I woke to the dream: I was in a wood with lush grass underfoot and I was searching for primroses and a little boy came. I did not see him, only his bare feet and legs among the grass and I saw my own feet among the grass also. "What are you looking for?" said the boy. "Primroses." "There are no primroses here," said the boy, "but there are daisies. Gather them." Perhaps what I want most is not for me. I am to take "daisies" instead of primroses.

Daisies, not prim roses. A month later, accompanied by her dogs and monkey, Woo, she was in her caravan [nicknamed "The Elephant"] at Esquimalt Lagoon:

> It is very Heavenly, this daisy patch. The old Elephant is sitting in millions and millions of these daisies. They are thick under the van, and growing harder so as to peep out from beneath and are even more lovely, gleaming there palely. The fellows out in the open are straddled out, exultantly staring up in the sun. The others are striving harder, aspiring, working out of the gloom. The dew is still on them though it is noon and it looks like great tears sparkling on their faces. Woo rolls among the daisies with her four hands in the air, playing with her tail. There are immense bushes of sweet briar roses that will be in bloom soon scattered all over my pasture. The sheep come to the far corner under the trees with their lambs. The dogs keep them from coming too close. A beautiful bird with a lemon yellow breast with a jet black brooch in the middle is under one of the rose bushes feeding a youngster that flaps and squawks. The air is full of bird song and the frogs were croaking right in the awning lean-to of the van, which is hemmed in by a nettle patch. From the van window beside my bed I can see the sea and the stars at night as thick as the daisies by day.

During 1934 and the six or seven years which followed, Carr's painting met the standard she had always set for it, but never before quite reached. Her work achieved the kind of self-generating energy and coherence one associates with the paintings of artists like Thomson and Borduas. She created oils and oil sketches on paper like "A Rushing Sea of Undergrowth," "Wood Interior," "Forest Edge and Sky," "Shoreline," "Sunshine and Tumult," "Overhead," "Scorned As Timber, Beloved of the Sky," and "Above the Gravel Pit." As well as these and other landscapes, she also painted "Self-Portrait," an oil on paper which shows her not as the idealized, ageless child "Small," frozen in the faked chronology of *Growing Pains,* but as a woman in her sixties, with staring, steady eyes, a thinned, slightly twisted, truculent mouth, and a thick, almost shapeless, powerful body.

One of the paradoxes of Carr's creative life is that while she was able to face herself as this woman, in one of the most self-revelatory portraits in Canadian painting, she was also writing or about to write the deceptions of the autobiographies, concealing and falsifying most of the inner life out of which such paintings grew. The paradox has to be accepted. It cannot be resolved. It can be explored.

Ultimately, its source is that snake-pit of experience, feeling, and repression already discussed in this essay. But for reasons which have been explained, we can go no further in discovering what it actually contained. Obviously Carr found its contents so dangerous to handle that the denotative qualities of language were psychologically a threat to her, whereas the connotative possibilities of painting were not. Carr once wrote revealingly in her journals: ". . . I could not write my innermost thoughts if anybody was to read them, and the innermost thoughts are the only things that count in painting." For Carr, writing was "more human than painting."

What she meant by "more human" appears in comments she made after reading D. H. Lawrence's *St. Mawr.* She wrote:

> Lawrence's book is so sexy. Everything these days is people talking of sex and psychology. I hate both. This would-be-smart psychology makes me sick: it's so impertinent, digging round inside people and saying why they did things, by what law of mind they came to such and such, and making hideous false statements, and yanking up all the sex problems, the dirty side of everything . . . dirty books, filthy cinema, muck everywhere.

The accusation of "making hideous false statements" is one, of course, Carr would level at this essay. It is also one which could be levelled at Carr herself. But using it against her tends to conceal something really more important. There is no reason why Carr should have written like Lawrence, or Joyce. Until Glassco's *Memoirs of Montparnasse* (1970) no autobiographer in Canada wrote with their realism. It would be unfairly simplistic to insist that a woman of Carr's time, place and upbringing should have written as Joyce and Lawrence did. Nor does the quote from Carr really support a case that she should always have been true to fact, no matter how "sexy." There are plenty of autobiographies that are only erratically truthful about such matters, including, perhaps, Glassco's own. What the quote from Carr does imply, however, is that she reacted to Lawrence's book not as one written within a certain stylistic convention which portrayed human experience in a way logical to that convention, but as something to be classified with an amorphous mass of "dirty books, filthy cinema, muck everywhere." Perhaps Carr reacted so aggressively and defensively because she realized that her own usual writing convention, autobiographical realism, should logically include what she found so offensive in Lawrence.

Had she tackled her writing with the same degree of technical sophistication, passion and courage that she brought to painting, she might have seen how unsuitable autobiographical realism was to her experience and the limited range of expression she was actually prepared to allow it. Many of the deceptions and adjustments in her autobiographies are occasions when she had to contradict the logic of her main convention for psychological reasons. Then the realism breaks down as it shifts clumsily into sentimental romance, with its formulas of virtue and revenge.

Had Carr seen the meanness, self-contradiction and incoherence consequent, and had she thought and known more about writing, she might have been able to contrive an alternative—a form which was true to her real psychological experience without revealing its origin, content and development realistically. The kind of form she might have considered was one resorted to in Victorian and Edwardian England by writers whose social and psychological circumstances were often similar to her own. Its greatest examples are the *Alice* books. Its most charming is *The Wind in the Willows*. Kenneth Grahame's anthropomorphic pantheism in fact very much resembles her own.

Predictably, the kind of analysis just carried out is one Carr hated. She wrote: "These critics with their rules and words and theories and influences make me very tired" and ". . . I distrust criticism. It seems to be of so little worth. People that know little talk much and folk who know halt, wondering, self conscious about their words." There are times when one feels such opinions are characteristically Canadian. But Carr's hatred of criticism was not really consistently applied. The inconsistency and its consequence were crucial. By not thinking about her writing critically in any profound sense, she compromised its value. By absorbing, seeking, accepting and practising criticism in areas concerning her painting, she brought it to the highest level she could. The world of Carr's prose, which on the surface appears to be lucid, orderly and economical, is often, underneath, really D'Sonoqua's world. The world of Carr's painting, which appears to be intuitive, chthonic, uncontrolled, is usually, underneath, the work of D'Sonoqua's child. (pp. 220-35)

Passages in the autobiographies which one re-reads are mainly ones of natural description. "Small" has not aged well. When Carr used words to describe the subjects of her paintings, however, or when she used them as critical preparation or accompaniment to painting, they still ring true. Appropriately, Lawren Harris, the main external influence upon her re-awakening as a painter, suggested that she use journal entries as a way of clarifying her artistic thoughts and procedures. In the journals, Carr's words find this kind of form in apparent formlessness: "The sallal is tough and stubborn, rose and blackberry thorny. There are the fallen logs and mossy stumps, the thousand varieties of growth and shapes and obstacles, the dips and hollows, hillocks and mounds, riverbeds, forests of young pines and spruce piercing up through the tangle to get to the quiet light diluted through the overhanging branches of great overtopping trees." Or there is this passage, preliminary to her oil, "Stumps" (1936): "A dense undergrowthy thing—two great moss-grown stumps. It must be organized chaos with the elimination of unnecessaries, massing of individuals into group movements, space swinging into space, movement meeting movement, balance, borrowing and paying back, a density and

immensity. . . ." And there is this one, written not outdoors facing the actual subject, but written in her studio while facing another critical abstraction, a painting:

> I am painting a sky. A big tree butts up into it on one side, and there is a slope in the corner with pines. These are only to give distance. The subject is sky, starting lavender beneath the trees and rising into a smoother hollow air space, greenish in tone, merging into laced clouds and then into deep, bottomless blue, not flat and smooth like the centre part of the sky, but loose, coming forward. There is to be one sweeping movement through the whole air, an ascending movement, high and fathomless. The movement must connect with each part, taking great care with the articulation. A movement floating up. It is a study in movement, designed movement—very subtle.

End with D'Sonoqua. As noted at the beginning of this essay, Carr described three totems she believed to represent D'Sonoqua in the sixth chapter of *Klee Wyck*. The hands of the first "were black, with blunt finger-tips painted a dazzling white." The second was "Sometimes bad . . . sometimes good." Into the mouth of this totem flew a nesting bird. The third D'Sonoqua is the strangest.

Carr depicted it in 1931 in the oil "D'Sonoqua of the Cat Village." *Klee Wyck*'s description reads:

> She appeared to be neither wooden nor stationary, but a singing spirit, young and fresh, passing through the jungle. No violence coarsened her; no power domineered to wither her. She was graciously feminine. Across her forehead her creator had fashioned the Sisheutl, or mythical two-headed sea-serpent. One of its heads fell to either shoulder, hiding the stuck-out ears, and framing her face from a central parting on the forehead which seemed to increase its womanliness.

Carr's words are invested with the freshness and empathy of her best prose. Characteristically, they only partly hide the projection of herself upon what she observed and loved. Characteristically also, this description is not quite about what it seems. D'Sonoqua here is not D'Sonoqua. D'Sonoqua is not draped by the "mythical two-headed sea-serpent," Sisheutl. No such totem could ever have been made. Carr's D'Sonoqua has not the pursed, circular screaming lips of the real D'Sonoqua, or her flattened eagle-headed breasts. Carr's D'Sonoqua is Sisheutl himself, a horned, scaled monster who may also appear as a salmon or a snake. As Bill Holm has noted, Sisheutl is "a warrior's creature," the sight of which can cause "convulsions and agonizing death."

But Sisheutl, like D'Sonoqua, is "Sometimes bad . . . sometimes good." His blood, rubbed into one's skin, turns it to stone, impervious to arrows. His scales can be made into arrowheads, and his eyeballs thrown as slingstones to destroy what they strike. Carr's Sisheutl offers also a gentler benevolence. In "D'Sonoqua of the Cat Village" he is shown carrying under his left arm a roughly triangular slab with the points clipped off. It is a copper, the most complex of all objects in the Indian culture of the Pacific northwest. A copper both is and represents. It is both masker and mask. A copper both is and represents wealth, status, ancestry, accomplishment, moral authority, virtue, pride. It is neither entirely material, nor entirely spiritual.

Often there is truth in error. Carr's mistaken identification of Sisheutl as D'Sonoqua reveals who she wished to be, who she often thought she was, and who sometimes she managed to be: the "singing-spirit, young and fresh, passing through the jungle," free and ageless, "wild in the sense that forest creatures are wild—shy, untouchable." But her error reveals another face, also Carr's. It is one she unsuccessfully tried to hide in her prose, the face of that "warrior's creature" whose life also had and must have a way. (pp. 235-37)

Peter Sanger, "Finding D'Sonoqua's Child: Myth, Truth and Lies in the Prose of Emily Carr," in The Antigonish Review, Nos. 69 & 70, 1987, pp. 211-39.

ADDITIONAL BIBLIOGRAPHY

Blanchard, Paula. *The Life of Emily Carr*. Seattle: University of Washington Press, 1987, 331 p.
> Biography focusing on Carr's life as a painter.

Gowers, Ruth, *Emily Carr*. Leamington Spa, Eng.: Berg, 1987, 126 p.
> Biography. Although Gowers's approach is noncritical, she frequently mentions Carr's writings.

Hembroff-Schleicher, Edythe. *Emily Carr: The Untold Story*. Seattle: Hancock House, 1978, 408 p.
> Sympathetic biography written by a friend from Carr's later years.

Pearson, Carol. *Emily Carr As I Knew Her*. Toronto: Clarke, Irwin, 1954, 162 p.
> Reminiscences by a goddaughter who lived for a time with Carr.

Plaunt, Dorothy R. Review of *Growing Pains*, by Emily Carr. *Canadian Historical Review* 28, No. 2 (June 1947): 212-14.
> Laudatory review. Plaunt notes: "With the publication of *Klee Wyck* [Carr] was established as an essayist, and now *Growing Pains* places her as possibly our most skillful writer of autobiography."

Reynolds, Lorna. Review of *The Book of Small*, by Emily Carr. *Dublin Magazine* n.s. 19, No. 3 (July-September 1944): 63-4.
> Review in which Reynolds finds *The Book of Small* uneven in quality yet "not unentertaining."

Ross, Catherine Sheldrick. "'A Singing Spirit': Female Rites of Passage in *Klee Wyck, Surfacing,* and *The Diviners*." *Atlantis* 4, No. 1 (Fall 1978): 86-94.
> Views the "D'Sonoqua" episode in *Klee Wyck* as a symbolic initiation into womanhood.

Tippett, Maria. *Emily Carr: A Biography*. Toronto: Oxford University Press, 1979, 314 p.
> Highly regarded, comprehensive biography.

Warner, Janet. "Emily Carr's Tennyson." *Canadian Literature*, Nos. 113-14 (Summer-Fall 1987): 114-26.
> Examines Carr's annotations in her copy of Alfred Lord Tennyson's poems.

Stephen Crane
1871-1900

(Also wrote under the pseudonym Johnston Smith) American novelist, short story writer, poet, and journalist.

The following entry presents criticism of Crane's novel *The Red Badge of Courage: An Episode of the American Civil War*. For a discussion of Crane's complete career, see *TCLC*, Volumes 11 and 17.

Acknowledged as Crane's masterpiece, *The Red Badge of Courage* is considered a classic of American literature for its realistic depiction of Civil War combat and its convincing evocation of the psychological complexities of battle. Through a series of vivid episodes in which a young, untried Union soldier experiences a gamut of emotions, including fear, courage, pride, and humility, Crane presented a powerful study of the nature of heroism. According to Bernard Weisberger, *The Red Badge of Courage* "paints the experience of all young men who go into battle, familiar with fright but strangers to themselves, and who come out of it touched with sin but somehow stronger."

According to biographers, Crane began *The Red Badge of Courage* in March 1893 when an acquaintance challenged him to write a better war story than Emile Zola's *La débâcle*. To accomplish this, Crane studied articles on battles and leaders of the Civil War in old volumes of *Century* magazine, but after completing a draft of the story he was distracted from the project by the sudden and unexpected critical success of his first novel, *Maggie: A Girl of the Streets*. When he subsequently returned to the story, he titled it after its protagonist: "Henry Fleming, His Various Battles." In December 1894 a condensed form of the novel, now titled *The Red Badge of Courage,* was syndicated in newspapers throughout the United States; after many delays due to Crane's extended travels as a newspaper correspondent, the novel was published in book form by D. Appleton & Company in October 1895. Largely ignored by American critics at the time, *The Red Badge of Courage* created a sensation in England, where favorable reviews stressed the realism of the novel and often erroneously identified Crane as a veteran of the war. Critics in the United States quickly conformed to the prevailing English view, and praised the novel for its narrative technique, artful characterization, and honest depiction of combat.

Since he had never been to war when he wrote *The Red Badge of Courage,* Crane claimed that his source for the description of combat was the football field; when he finally experienced battle as a war correspondent, he determined, to his satisfaction, that "the *Red Badge* is all right." Whether critics consider the work as a whole realistic or not, most have accepted the view proposed by Harold R. Hungerford that *The Red Badge of Courage* is based on a historical battle. Citing parallels of time, weather, topography, and event, Hungerford has drawn a connection between Crane's unnamed battle and the Battle of Chancellorsville, Virginia, which occurred in May 1863. Scholars have found that Crane's descriptions comprise an accurate and finely detailed rendering of the background.

Considered essentially plotless by many critics, *The Red Badge of Courage* portrays Henry Fleming's actions and impressions in his first days of combat. Fearing that he will behave as a

coward in his first battle, Fleming revels in self-satisfaction after he performs well. However, a second skirmish begins almost immediately, and when Fleming sees other soldiers retreating, he flees to a safe area at the rear of the Union sector. A series of meaningful events occurs while Fleming is behind the lines: he encounters a decaying corpse; he deserts a mortally wounded soldier, who is described only as "the tattered man"; he witnesses the death of his friend Jim Conklin from battle wounds; he receives an ironic "red badge of courage" when a frenzied, retreating Union soldier strikes him in the head with a rifle; and he journeys back to his regiment led by a mysterious, anonymous guide. With a new perspective Fleming fights heroically in the next day's battle, and seizes the flag when the regimental standard-bearer is slain.

Critics have long debated whether *The Red Badge of Courage* should be considered a product of any specific literary movement or method. Proponents of a realistic reading view the book as simply an unromanticized account of the Civil War and contend that Crane truthfully depicted Fleming's maturation from a callow recruit to an experienced soldier. Other critics consider the novel a product of Naturalist literary theory and ideology, maintaining that the youth's actions and experiences are shaped by social, biological, and psychological forces and that his development as a person is incidental to Crane's expert depiction of how these forces determine human existence on or off the battlefield. In a controversial essay published in 1951, R. W. Stallman proposed a further major reading of the novel, contending that *The Red Badge of Courage* comprises a symbolic construct laden with symbols and images of Christian theology. According to Stallman's view, the description of the sun at the time of Jim Conklin's death ("The sun was pasted in the sky like a fierce red wafer") suggests a communion wafer, and the significance of this image has become one of the most disputed issues in American literature. The appeal of such exclusive readings of *The Red Badge of Courage* has largely diminished among more recent critics, who tend to view the novel in its historical context as an innovative work in which Crane borrowed thematic and stylistic elements from several major literary trends of the late nineteenth century.

Crane's narrative point of view entails both an objective panorama of the war scene and the more subjective impressions of the young soldier, and the distance between narrator and protagonist often results in ambiguities that have provoked conflicting interpretations of the work. For example, in the ending of the novel Fleming appears to some critics to reverse his progress toward a realistic view of warfare and of himself as he retreats into a pastoral vision. Some commentators have found that consulting Crane's final manuscript version of the novel, as opposed to the first edition text, resolves these ambiguities and best illuminates his intentions for the work. The manuscript reveals that two sets of editorial changes were made just prior to publication, and some critics have concluded that Crane was persuaded by his Appleton editor, Ripley Hitchcock, to make changes that he otherwise would not have made; however, Donald Pizer, who sees the ambiguity of the novel as an important element of its composition, has suggested that the deletions may represent Crane's own unsatisfactory attempt to "supply unity by striking out those passages antithetical to the image of the novel which he formed *after the fact of having written the novel.*" According to Henry Binder, a leading advocate of the manuscript text, these deletions "confused the original irony; reduced the psychological complexity of Henry Fleming, the main character; also obscured the function of Wilson and the tattered man; and left the text incoherent at several places, in particular the final chapter." While reconstruction of the manuscript text is seen by a number of critics as a responsible method of reducing textual ambiguity in the novel, other critics remain unconvinced that the clarity imposed through reconstruction necessarily improves the narrative.

The Red Badge of Courage remains one of the best-loved books in American literature. In 1959 Eric Solomon noted: "In spite of the abundance of war novels produced by two world conflicts, *The Red Badge of Courage* is still the masterwork of war fiction. Stephen Crane's novel is the first work in English fiction of any length purely dedicated to an artistic reproduction of war, and it has rarely been approached in scope or intensity."

(See also *Contemporary Authors,* Vol. 109; *Dictionary of Literary Biography,* Vols. 12 and 54; and *Yesterday's Authors of Books for Children,* Vol. 2.)

W. D. HOWELLS   (essay date 1895)

[*Howells was the chief progenitor of American Realism and the most influential American literary critic during the late nineteenth*

Title page of the first edition of The Red Badge of Courage.

century. He successfully weaned American literature from the sentimental romanticism of its infancy, earning the popular sobriquet "the Dean of American Letters." Through Realism, a theory central to his fiction and criticism, Howells sought to disperse "the conventional acceptation by which men live on easy terms with themselves" that they might "examine the grounds of their social and moral opinions." To accomplish this, according to Howells, the writer must strive to record detailed impressions of everyday life, endowing characters with true-to-life motives and avoiding authorial comment in the narrative. In addition to his perceptive criticism of the works of his friends Henry James and Mark Twain, Howells reviewed three generations of international literature, urging Americans to read the works of Emile Zola, Bernard Shaw, Henrik Ibsen, and other important authors. In the following excerpt from a review of The Red Badge of Courage, *Howells praises the subjective point of view of the novel and the characterization of its protagonist.*]

[I] have been reading several books without finding a very fresh note except in ***The Red Badge of Courage,*** by Mr. Stephen Crane. He is the author of that story of New York tough life, ***Maggie,*** which I mentioned some time ago as so good but so impossible of general acceptance because of our conventional limitations in respect of swearing, and some other traits of the common parlance. He has now attempted to give a close at hand impression of battle as seen by a young volunteer in the civil war, and I cannot say that to my inexperience of battle he has given such a vivid sense of it as one gets from some other authors. The sense of deaf and blind turmoil he does indeed give, but we might get that from fewer pages than Mr. Crane employs to impart it. The more valuable effect of the book is subjective: the conception of character in the tawdry-minded youth whom the slight story gathers itself about, and in his comrades and superiors of all sorts. The human commonness (which we cannot shrink from without vulgarity) is potently illustrated throughout in their speech and action and motive, and the cloud of bewilderment in which they all have their being after the fighting begins, the frenzy, the insensate resentment, are graphically and probably suggested. The dialect employed does not so much convinces me; I have not heard people speak with these contractions, though perhaps they do it; and in commending the book I should dwell rather upon the skill shown in evolving from the youth's crude expectations and ambitions a quiet honesty and self-possession manlier and nobler than any heroism he had imagined. There are divinations of motive and experience which cannot fail to strike the critical reader, from time to time; and decidedly on the psychological side the book is worth while as an earnest of the greater things that we may hope from a new talent working upon a high level, not quite clearly as yet, but strenuously.

W. D. Howells, in a review of "The Red Badge of Courage," in Harper's Weekly, *Vol. XXXIX, No. 2027, October 26, 1895, p. 1013.*

THE SPECTATOR   (essay date 1896)

[*In the following excerpt from a favorable review of* The Red Badge of Courage, *the critic discusses the work as a unique psychological record of the protagonist's impressions of battle.*]

The Red Badge of Courage: An Episode of the American Civil War is a remarkable book, and has been received by English reviewers with an unanimity of praise which we are in no wise desirous that its author—a young man, as it is understood—should have been deprived of. But we believe that Mr. Stephen Crane, the author in question, has received his good marks not exactly on right grounds. His episode has been praised as a novel; we are inclined to praise it chiefly as an interesting and painful essay in pathology. The substance and "thesis" of the book, as the serious theatrical reviewers might say, consists in a presentation of the effects of physical danger, in the thousand forms which danger wears in modern warfare, upon the human nervous system. Nor is this all; the nervous system on which Mr. Crane chooses to illustrate his prelection is not a normal organism but an abnormal one,—morbid, hypersensitive, and over-conscious. Mr. Crane notes the effect upon his patient of each day and hour and minute of pained experience with a precision which would do credit to Mr. Lauder Brunton or a brother specialist. We are inclined to believe that his notes are the exact production by an extraordinary memory of moments that have been lived; yet it is believed that Mr. Crane has seen nothing of actual fighting. As an achievement in imagination, in the art of placing one's self in the situation of another—of an exceptional other in exceptional surroundings—Mr. Crane's document can hardly be praised too much. It convinces; one feels that not otherwise than as he describes did such a man fall wounded and another lie in the grasp of corruption. But when we are asked to say that a specialised record of morbid introspection and an exact description of physical horrors is good art we demur; there *is* art in ***The Red Badge of Courage***—an infelicitous title by the way—but the general effect which it leaves behind it is not artistic.

But it is time to cease generalising. The scene, to come to detail, is laid in the American Civil War, and the hero is one Henry Fleming, who is spoken of invariably as "The Youth." We may note here an adroitness of Mr. Crane's. A narrative told in the first person must have been a limited affair. The author desires primarily to show us the nervous system under fire. But "The Youth," left to tell his story, could have given us only his own blurred impression of the terrible background of war which Mr. Crane, in the interest of the truth, as he conceives it, desires to present to us. Accordingly, "The Youth's" impressions are given in the third person, and he is presented to us *totus, teres, atque rotundus* ["complete in itself"], and against the lurid background of his adventures. It is a tactful arrangement. "The Youth" then enlisted in a Northern regiment, and has been some months a soldier when we are introduced to him. He has never met the enemy, and is weary of the tedium which has succeeded the first excitement of leaving home with his regiment. He has had time to fall back on his nerves, and the problem has begun to front him: will he or will he not run away?—

> A sufficient time before he would have allowed the problem to kick its heels at the outer portals of his mind, but now he felt compelled to give serious attention to it. A little panic-fear grew in his mind. As his imagination went forward to a fight, he saw hideous possibilities. He contemplated the lurking menaces of the future and failed in an effort to see himself standing stoutly in the midst of them. He recalled his visions of broken-bladed glory, but in the shadow of the impending tumult he suspected them to be impossible pictures.

At last he finds himself face to face with danger, and Mr. Crane's descriptions of approaching conflict are wonderfully right and picturesque:—

> The sun spread disclosing rays, and one by one, regiments burst into view like armed men first born of the earth. The youth perceived that the time had come. He was about to be measured. For a moment he felt in the face of his great trial like a babe, and the flesh over his heart seemed very thin. He seized time to look after him calculatingly. But he instantly saw that it would be impossible for him to escape from the regiment. It enclosed him. And there were iron laws of tradition and law on four sides. He was in a moving box.

The recorded sensations which follow in the youth's mind are far too many and too minute to pursue. But there are conspicuous moments which may be given as examples of many. The youth, it should be said, did run away at first, his regiment, it must be understood, retiring in disorder:—

> He wondered what they would remark when later he appeared in camp. His mind heard howls of derision. Their density would not enable them to understand his sharper point of view. He began to pity himself acutely. He was ill-used. He was trodden beneath the feet of an iron injustice. He had proceeded with wisdom and from the most righteous motives under Heaven's blue, only to be frustrated by hateful circumstances.

In this key of self-pity and self-defence he stumbled on a dead man:—

> He was being looked at by a dead man, who was seated with his back against a column-like tree. The eyes, staring at the youth, had changed to the dull hue to be seen on the side of a dead fish. The mouth

was open. Its red had changed to an appalling yellow.
Over the grey skin ran little ants. One was *trundling
some sort of a bundle along the upper lip.*

Presently he came on a line of wounded men, the description
of whom is the best thing in the book. This encounter was his
salvation. He got back with them to the body of the regiment,
and the sight of his comrades, notably the heroic death of one
of them, made a beginning of the end in his egoism. After a
series of endeavours to play the man he succeeded, was the
first in a rush by the men of his regiment, and won his way
not to glory but to self-respect. . . .

A story like this is a mosaic. It is impossible to illustrate its
effect by fragments. Tolstoi and another author, whose war
stories are too little known, though it seems probable that Mr.
Crane knows them—Mr. Ambrose Bierce to wit—have given
us the aspect of war as war is seen by ordinary men; and Tolstoi,
of course, with the epic touch of a great literary artist. But as
a bundle of impressions received by a temperament especially
sensitive, *The Red Badge of Courage* is a remarkable performance, and we believe without example.

> *A review of "The Red Badge of Courage," in* The
> Spectator, *Vol. 76, No. 3548, June 27, 1896, p. 924.*

STEPHEN CRANE   (letter date 1897?)

[*In the following excerpt from a letter to John N. Hilliard, believed
by scholars to have been written in 1897, Crane reveals his intention, in writing* The Red Badge of Courage, *of presenting a
"psychological portrayal of fear."*]

[I] have only one pride—and may it be forgiven me. This single
pride is that the English edition of *The Red Badge* has been
received with praise by the English reviewers. Mr. George
Wyndham, Under Secretary for War in the British Government,
says, in an essay [excerpted in *TCLC*, Vol. 11, pp. 121-23],
that the book challenges comparison with the most vivid scenes
of Tolstoi's *War and Peace* or of Zola's *Downfall;* and the big
reviews here praise it for just what I intended it to be, a psychological portrayal of fear. They all insist that I am a veteran
of the civil war, whereas the fact is, as you know, I never
smelled even the powder of a sham battle. I know what the
psychologists say, that a fellow can't comprehend a condition
that he has never experienced, and I argued that many times
with the Professor. Of course, I have never been in a battle,
but I believe that I got my sense of the rage of conflict on the
football field, or else fighting is a hereditary instinct, and I
wrote intuitively; for the Cranes were a family of fighters in
the old days, and in the Revolution every member did his duty.
But be that as it may, I endeavored to express myself in the
simplest and most concise way. If I failed, the fault is not
mine. I have been very careful not to let any theories or pet
ideas of my own creep into my work. Preaching is fatal to art
in literature. I try to give to readers a slice out of life; and if
there is any moral or lesson in it, I do not try to point it out.
I let the reader find it for himself. The result is more satisfactory
to both the reader and myself. As Emerson said, ''There should
be a long logic beneath the story, but it should be kept carefully
out of sight.'' Before *The Red Badge of Courage* was published,
I found it difficult to make both ends meet. The book was
written during this period. It was an effort born of pain, and
I believe that it was beneficial to it as a piece of literature. It
seems a pity that this should be so—that art should be a child
of suffering; and yet such seems to be the case. Of course there
are fine writers who have good incomes and live comfortably

and contentedly; but if the conditions of their lives were harder,
I believe that their work would be better. Bret Harte is an
example. He has not done any work in recent years to compare
with those early California sketches. Personally, I like my little
book of poems, *The Black Riders,* better than I do *The Red
Badge of Courage.* The reason is, I suppose, that the former
is the more ambitious effort. In it I aim to give my ideas of
life as a whole, so far as I know it, and the latter is a mere
episode, or rather an amplification. Now that I have reached
the goal, I suppose that I ought to be contented; but I am not.
I was happier in the old days when I was always dreaming of
the thing I have now attained. I am disappointed with success,
and I am tired of abuse. (pp. 158-59)

> *Stephen Crane, in a letter to John Northern Hilliard
> in 1897(?) in* Stephen Crane: Letters, *edited by R. W.
> Stallman and Lillian Gilkes, New York University
> Press, 1960, pp. 158-59.*

JOSEPH HERGESHEIMER   (essay date 1924)

[*An American man of letters, Hergesheimer is remembered as the
author of popular and critically successful novels portraying a
mythical past of sensual beauty and aristocratic privilege. In the
following excerpt, he praises Crane's masterpiece, comparing his
own youthful enthusiasm for the novel with his mature critical
opinion.*]

It is one of the minor treacheries of time that twenty-nine years
have vanished almost—as more than a quarter of a century—
unnoticed since I first read *The Red Badge of Courage.* I was,
then, fifteen years old, and beyond all doubt a better reader
than I am now. I had an enormous enthusiasm for the books
I liked, a private and unquestioned and passionate allegiance
to them long ago diluted by my own experience and difficulties,
and by the inevitable development of considerations not always
admirable. I do not mean that I wouldn't, to-day, if I were
reading it for the first time, completely surrender myself to
Stephen Crane's young private of the Civil War; I would, of
course; for his is a created story of inescapable fineness. But
in the present I would regard it, in part at least, as a deliberate
accomplishment in composed periods; while at fifteen it was
a great and personal experience.

I read it at once upon its publication—books have a habit of
reaching their specially right readers—and I was deeply engaged even before I had opened the straw-coloured buckram,
printed in black and red and gold, of its binding. It had come
to me widely heralded, borne on the excitement, the derision
and praise and curiosity, its appearance had instantly upraised.
I have no way of knowing what, at that day, made a large sale;
it may be that the interest in *The Red Badge of Courage* was
limited to a changlessly small superior public. It may be, but
it isn't in my memory that it was; trying to recall those circumstances it seems to me that Crane's novel of battle brought
out a very general, and heated, warfare in itself.

You see, it was everywhere regarded as fantastically modern,
and one sentence in it, a paragraph, really, became particularly
celebrated:

> The red sun was pasted in the sky like a wafer.

That phrase, actually, was made into the standard, the flag—
like the flag the youth himself twisted from a dying standard-
bearer and carried forward—about which the climax of the
action revolved. It was regarded in one camp as a superb piece
of imagery, a line which invested one of the oldest of obser-

vations with a new and living freshness and vigour; and by the other as a strained and artificial figure. When I reached it I hadn't, for that single instance, an entirely virgin attention; already the struggle had given it an exaggerated importance; and I was appropriately amazed. I thought of an actual red wafer, such as druggists fixed to their bottles; it had a definite, a limited, size for me, an established clear vermilion colour.

I thought of it, for the moment, constantly, repeating it for the benefit of any who could be persuaded to listen; I was, in a minute way, part of the noise that made it notable. But there was no doubt about my opinion of such a remarkable, and modern, paragraph—I was convinced that it was marvellous. The sun itself was diminished, in the sky like a wafer, a wafer of glazed vermilion paper with a regularly serrated edge. For the rest, I felt, together with my enthusiasm, an impatience at what, then, appeared to be a large lack of story; I had no recognition of an underlying structure and ordered whole.

* * * * *

It was, however, a slight compensation for the passage of so many swift years that I could, now, grasp that: the order and progression, the singleness of purpose, were exact . . . and not entirely modern, even in 1895. It was the story of the birth, in a boy, of a knowledge of himself and of self-command; the beginning, in short, of the fixed pattern of maturity. And, as was usual in such forms, it was a birth out of a tragic agony and doubt, a success scarcely won from the edge of eternal defeat.

What, I realized, had worried me at fifteen was that *The Red Badge of Courage* was not at all the story of the practically nameless youth of whom, apparently, it was written; Crane's interest in him, as an individual, was small—he was present for what, as universally as possible, he represented. This coldness to the boy himself, this aloofness from a specific sympathy—from, in realty, sentimentality—left me, too, the implicated reader, more than a little cold. It was the true, the singular, mark of an authentic classical accomplishment; but at fifteen I wasn't aware of so much.

I was perfectly merged with the subject of the book, he was a vessel carrying me over a threatening sea; his undignified cowardice, the temporary spiritual meanness of flight, were mine; when he ran I ran, when he skulked I skulked; when, in the wavering line of the retreating wounded, he was asked where he had been hit, my acute shame was his. Even the eventual firmness and triumph did not, completely, restore me to a necessary warm glow of reassurance. I had, it seemed, been studied by an essentially wise but, where I was intimately concerned, a detached intellect. Stephen Crane might have been a doctor exploring me, to my ultimate good, with frigid and unerring fingers.

I didn't then, and then I was abjectly synonymous with what is called the reading public, want to be so justly regarded, so unsparingly valued; what I did want was to be filled with praise, to hum with a beautiful valour rewarded by all material good; I wanted to be decorated before all the files of men alive, and before the loveliest lady imaginable. This Stephen Crane would not allow; and so my enthusiasm was a little subdued; privately I was even slightly bored; yet, in spite of that, *The Red Badge of Courage* had my devoted, if youngly uncritical, support.

I was not then, naturally, separately conscious of its words, they had to be indicated to me; I discovered no pleasure in them as accomplishments and ends; but I was highly responsive

to their effects. Two novels, in that past, made clearer than all others what might, perhaps, be called scenes in nature— *The Red Badge of Courage* and *Jane Eyre*. The battle-fields and wooded hills, the ruined peace of little valleys, of the first, shrouded in the smoke of guns, were as vivid as the headlong action. The men dead and dying, their sounds and pallors and last rigidity, held a fearful reality which came from the perfection of Stephen Crane's visualization, a quality not alone optical:

He saw them emotionally, in the mystery of creative perception, and put them down in a simplicity of words that cast back, like the reflection in a clear mirror, every leaf and hurt that passed through his imagination. The transition from his conception to its formal expression was as instantaneous, as untroubled, as the flight of a bar of music to a receptive brain and heart.

* * * * *

The whole form of *The Red Badge of Courage* is amazing for, as much as anything, its directness and candour. That was not, merely, the result of an æsthetic sophistication—simplicity usually is—but the effect on the entire book of the character of the pictured youth. He is singularly candid; and all the sentences, all the pages, have an air of coming from him. Even the lyrical beauty of the objective descriptions, impossible for him to formulate, take the shape and fervour of his inherited reactions to them. When, with his fellows, he moves across a field, the field and the youth are seen together; he walks or desperately charges and the grass is beaten down by his passage; he marches over the roads in loose formation or is momentarily soothed by the peace of casual meadows . . . the shuffling tramp of feet accompanies him or he is set in a calm with idly floating butterflies.

And, through it all, the army, the soldiers, talk; they talk in a dialect which seems hopelessly arbitrary, a mere scrambling of disjointed syllables; but actually it is as easy to read, its intent is as plain, as the wording on a sign-board. It's the actual living American language, or, rather, the language that was American—the talk of multitudes of small towns and farming districts. It isn't so much a dialect as it is the flexible and successful record of what promised to be the new language of a new land. (pp. ix-xiv)

There is, too—a part of Stephen Crane's accomplishment here— a strong sense of humour behind everything said; there isn't a breath, a suspicion, of satire; the spirit of the ludicrous, ungainly like the soldiers themselves, permeates their heated or philosophical or rebellious phrases. The men are eternally complaining or arguing or predicting; they are always beginning bitter quarrels that fade into diminishing curses in turn obliterated by the roll of the cannon. It is possible that no book had ever been written with so much and such a literal transcription of general and particularized talk.

That, the humour investing the things said, was a result of the detached attitude of which, at fifteen, I was critical. Crane was not his youth, the voice of one was not the voice of the other; no, the writer was a completely understanding listener. An unfailing sense of proportion—the heart of humour—gave each uttered sound its true place in the harmony of the whole, no one was covered with decorative ribbons in the face of a silent and respectful masculine world, under the tender gaze of an appealing loveliness. (pp. xiv-xv)

The controversy over what was referred to as the extremely modern form of *The Red Badge of Courage* has, naturally and long ago, died; and what, on that plane, remains is the realization that it is neither modern nor conservative. There is literally nothing in its treatment which suggests the period that saw it produced; its underlying spirit belongs to no current fashion. Its situations and development were seen not in relation to what else was then being written—it wasn't, in that sense, a piece of the time—but as independent and unliterary facts. Being, in a very fine sense indeed, literature it wasn't concerned with literary values at all. It must have fallen into its period with the effect of a shell from a heavy mortar. The result was as final—thereafter all novels about war must be different; the old pretentious attack was for ever obliterated.

Novels such as, at fifteen, I demanded would continue to satisfy the private vanity of the public; and quite admirable they were; but they had no part in the engagement that held Stephen Crane. They came and went; but here, after twenty-nine years, I was writing a preface to a book that had survived death—the story of a boy who went to war, who fell a victim to fear, and who recovered. That pattern would not have been sufficient for the writers of current successes; in it they could not have discovered a pattern at all. No romance! Nothing prepared at the beginning and no more solved at the end. Yes, and profane . . . at the expense of God, pronounced Gawd, and the dignity of men. Where, in all *The Red Badge of Courage,* was the nobility of a cause even hinted at? Where was Lincoln bearing his benevolence like a tendered pardon to fault? Where was Grant with his half-consumed cigar? Where, above everything, was General Lee?

The truth is that they were absent for the reason that they weren't needed; they could have added nothing to Crane's narrative of the Civil War. In writing, so late, the word narrative, which is supposed to carry a different meaning from the word novel, I realize that I am inviting the patronage of the learned. A narrative is not a novel. But in such a confusion of definitions I was, at least, deliberate. *The Red Badge of Courage* is both a novel and a narrative; since the difference between realism and romance has never been defined it may, as well, be both romantic and realistic. At once, I mean. I have an idea, too, that it is poetry, lyrical as well as epic; no one, certainly, can deny that it is completely classic in its movement, its pace and return.

It is all these things, and, in addition, it is life; and it can no more be neatly fitted into a definition than can the mystery of birth. As a child it disturbed and excited and challenged me; and as a man—it would be more precise to say as a writer—it satisfies me. A tranquil countryside is torn for a little by human strife, the stillness is broken by a hideous clamour of explosions and cries, and then the quiet comes back with evening. The dead are removed, the trees are healed, the brooks are again softly audible. Wars are unimportant; individuals are unimportant—actually there are no individuals, but only connected and momentary activities, one fading into the other in a march from dark to dark. That is the burden of *The Red Badge of Courage,* it is the meaning of its title, since courage is not a means but an end. Its incentives are chimeras. (pp. xvi-xviii)

Joseph Hergesheimer, "Introduction: 'The Red Badge of Courage', 1895-1924," in The Work of Stephen Crane, Vol. I, *edited by Wilson Follett, 1925. Reprint by Russell & Russell, 1963, pp. ix-xviii.*

MAXWELL GEISMAR   (essay date 1953)

[*Geismar is a prominent American critic whose major work—a multi-volume history of the American novel from 1860 to 1940—demonstrates his fascination with the impact of external forces on literature. In the following excerpt from that study, Geismar maintains that* The Red Badge of Courage *portrays Henry Fleming's social and psychological conversion from outsider to recognized member of a clearly defined social group through his acceptance of the societal code of the military.*]

The technical achievement of the *Red Badge* was the picture of war done absolutely from the inside. It was the fragmentary consciousness of impending battle from the common soldier's point of view, with no "causes" for the action which he is to determine, no sense of direction on his part, no plan of action which he understands, not to mention the larger issues of the Civil War which are never touched upon in the entire novel. During all the preliminary marching, retreating, actions, waitings, we are hardly even conscious of the officers who are controlling this military organism. There are only the routines of camp life; the gossip, boasting, joking of these farm country types—"it ain't likely they'll lick the hull rebel army all-to-oncet the first time"; and the pageantry. "In the gloom before the break of day their uniforms glowed a deep purple hue. From across the river the red eyes were still peering. In the eastern sky there was a yellow patch like a rug laid for the feet of the coming sun; and against it, black and patternlike, loomed the gigantic figure of the colonel on a gigantic horse." And the wet grass which rustled like silk at night when the air was heavy and cold with dew, or the blue, pure sky and the sun gleaming on the trees and fields, while Nature went on "with her golden process in the midst of much devilment," remind us that this was almost the last agrarian and to some degree still individualistic war for American troops. The army sits down again "to think." The first dead soldier whom Crane's hero encounters—an "invulnerable" corpse with his ashen face and tattered shoes—announces a new theme.

Earlier, this hero had suddenly realized he was caught in the "moving box" of his regiment. "As he perceived this fact it occurred to him that he had never wished to come to the war." His conflict, of course, had been related to his own fear and panic while the battle came closer to him—the "red animal—war, the blood-swollen god." On the surface it was a highly realistic, ironic and humorous account of a young boy's struggle with cowardice in the midst of a larger and brilliantly rendered scene of battle, disorganized and incoherent: the complete opposite of standard descriptions of heroics, bravery and martial discipline. "No one seemed to be wrestling with such a terrific personal problem," Crane's hero thinks. "He was a mental outcast." When he realizes that he is in a trap from which he cannot escape, he is outraged and terrified. "He lagged, with tragic glances at the sky." When the raw troops break under the rebel attack—the shells swirling and exploding like "strange war flowers bursting into fierce bloom"—there came into the youth's eyes, Crane said, "a look that one can see in the orbs of a jaded horse." Directly "he began to speed to the rear in great leaps," and his was the work "of a master's legs." Yet his expression was that of a criminal who thinks his guilt and his punishment great, and he went far, "seeking dark and intricate places."

He went indeed from "obscurity into promises of a greater obscurity." There is that curious little scene in the religious half-light of a forest chapel where another corpse was seated with his back against a columnlike tree. "The dead man and the living man exchanged a long look,'' and the youth, receiving a subtle suggestion to touch the dead body, ''burst the bonds which had fastened him to the spot and fled, unheeding the underbrush.'' . . . This was at the center of the psychological action in *The Red Badge of Courage;* the chapel scene is perfect dream symbolism in the novel. From that point the narrative tension is based on the classic theme of sin and retribution—but a sense of sin that is in fact deeper and more mysterious in its overtones than the issue of the youth's cowardice, and a retribution that takes on a very curious aspect, too. In the first trauma of battle, had Crane's young soldier developed a ''red rage'' of impotency because his rifle could only be used against one life at a time, while he was suffocating in the smoke of death? ''He fought frantically for respite for his senses, for air, as a babe being smothered attacks the deadly blankets.''

Now he returned to the battle with an obscure but nevertheless overpowering compulsion. ''He must go close and see it produce corpses.'' And there are the famous chapters which describe ''the steady current of the maimed,'' and the ''awful machinery'' in which the men had been entangled. Crane's hero walks amid wounds, in a bleeding mob of men—

> At times he regarded the wounded soldiers in an envious way. He conceived persons with torn bodies to be peculiarly happy. He wished that he, too, had a wound, a red badge of courage.

The meaning of the title of the story becomes clear, of course. But the ''red badge''—in this context of torn bodies—almost indicates as much of a yearning for the mark of mutilation as for a sign of bravery. The chapter of the maimed is suffused with references to the stigmata of suffering. There is the remarkable portrait of the spectral soldier, Jim Conklin, walking stiffly in his death throes, ''as if he were taking infinite care not to arouse the passion of his wounds.'' And the famous tag line of this chapter: ''The red sun was pasted in the sky like a wafer''—a line which became in its time the slogan of Crane's modernism—actually referred of course to the flesh and the blood of the martyred God, or the bleeding Son.

What fascinating imagery ran through these sections of the novel, to be sure! Crane's youth desired to screech out his grief. He was stabbed, but his tongue lay dead in the tomb of his mouth. If he envies the corpses—the dead—and is lacking the red wound of courage—and virility—he is confronted by the prospect of wearing ''the sore badge of his dishonour'' through the rest of his life. ''With his heart continually assuring him that he was despicable, he could not exist without making it, through his actions, apparent to all men.'' His capacity for self-hate was multiplied, Crane added. And the simple questions of the tattered man in this parable of guilt and redemption now taking place on the battlefield of the mind were like knife thrusts to the youthful hero:

> They asserted a society that probes relentlessly at secrets until all is apparent. His late companion's chance persistency made him feel that he could not keep his crime concealed in his bosom. It was sure to be brought plain by one of those arrows which cloud the air and are constantly pricking, discovering, proclaiming those things which are willed to be for ever hidden. He admitted that he could not defend himself against this agency. It was not within the power of vigilance.

Thus the maimed body was equated with the maimed spirit in the central action of *The Red Badge of Courage*. It was Henry

Fleming's shame at his psychic wound which led him to psychological sense might also block him from the maturity—the manhood—which he sought in the area of moral values. (And it is almost the first time we are conscious that Crane's anonymous youth had a name at all.) Then in swift succession there are those happy omens of his salvation: the ''false'' wound which he suffers in his struggle with another deserter; the episode of his rescue by the man of the cheery voice and of the warm and strong hand. ''As he who had so befriended him was thus passing out of his life, it suddenly occurred to the youth that he had not once seen his face.'' There is the loud young soldier who befriends him when he returns to his regiment of war-torn veterans and is received into their community with tenderness and care,—and then the youth's deep sleep of exhaustion. ''When the youth awoke it seemed to him that he had been asleep for a thousand years, and he felt sure that he opened his eyes upon an unexpected world. Grey mists were slowly shifting before the first efforts of the sunrays. An impending splendour could be seen in the eastern sky.''

An ''unexpected'' world of tribal acceptance, of course; of security within the codes and conventions of society, of law, honor and authority—and the impending splendour of equality among men after what has been really a kind of trial by ordeal. For the ceremonies of pagan ritual were implicit beneath Crane's constant use of Christian allegory in the *Red Badge*. The controlling vision of the novel is actually mythic, animistic, primitive. The deep sleep of exhaustion, extending back a thousand years—a trauma of rebirth and moral resurrection—brings the primitive elements of the fable into focus. And the theme was stressed. ''It was revealed to him that he had been a barbarian, a beast,'' Crane said after his hero's next battle. ''He had fought like a pagan who defends his religion. Regarding it, he saw that it was fine, wild, and, in some ways, easy. . . . And he had not been aware of the process. He had slept and, awakening, found himself a knight.''

But here, for the first time, the novel faltered. Having been accepted into the tribe—after the ordeal of suffering—Crane's protagonist must accept the tribal laws and customs, even the language. One notices the touches of lingering Victorian sentiment in the descriptions of the ''quiet manhood, non-assertive, but of sturdy and strong blood'' now possessed by the battle-tested hero. There is a note of adolescent heroics in the descriptions of the seasoned troops, the veterans. ''They gazed upon them with looks of uplifted pride, feeling new trust in the grim, always confident weapons in their hands. And they were men.'' In their battle fury, too—a delirium which was heedless of despair and death, a ''mad enthusiasm'' which was incapable of checking itself before granite and brass—Crane fell, as he very seldom did, into the rhetoric of war. In those ''hoarse, howling protests'' with which the men supported a desperate attack of the regiment, or in the ''vicious, wolf-like temper'' of comrades in battle—or their ''barbaric cry of rage''— this brilliant stylist even descended to the clichés of the Social Darwinism which would mark, and to some extent disfigure, the typical literary figures of the age.

The conclusion of *The Red Badge of Courage* was an anticlimax: the true tension of the novel had disappeared. The tragic potential of the narrative had shifted at the moment of the hero's ''conversion'' and acceptance of the tribal (or military) codes. The final note was that of an ironic comedy of heroism—still, however, haunted by the furies and horrors which persisted in Crane's mind if they had been exorcized from the literary work. . . . For this was ultimately a study in social appearance—or social approval—rather than a full study of conscience. At the moment of the hero's deepest conflict, the central fact was simply that he could not keep his "crime" concealed in his bosom, and not the nature of the crime itself. The enemy was still a society which probed relentlessly at the individual's secrets and proclaimed "those things which are willed to be for ever hidden"—this quite malignant agency indeed against which Crane's youth could not defend himself. And even after his conversion and social acceptance, there were ambiguous elements in his thought. "Some arrows of scorn that had buried themselves in his heart had generated strange and unspeakable hatred. It was clear to him that his final and absolute revenge was to be achieved by his dead body lying, torn and guttering, upon the field." Ambiguous and bitter elements; familiar and desperate convictions.

For it almost appeared that Crane had sought mutilation and death quite apart from the purposes of his narrative; we shall notice also that odd communion with corpses which is a recurrent feature in his work.

The technical innovations which marked the modernism of the *Red Badge*—the narrow frame of the story which in turn led to such meticulous and beautiful treatment of every detail within the frame—had certain liabilities, too. Through the process of stripping away all notions of causes and meanings for the Civil War—or any wider interpretation of it; so that this tale could have been told equally well from either side of the conflict— Crane, while he gathered a greater realism and intensity, made the experience of war an end in itself. It was almost indeed the *only* experience. And by accepting finally the martial standards as a kind of absolute, Crane seemed here almost to revoke the elements in his work which were distinctive as a foreign and rebel intelligence.

Perhaps indeed the "false" wound which had enabled his isolated protagonist to return safely to the communal fold might turn out in the end to be the true wound of the artist's work. Or at least the psychic wound which lay still deeper in Crane's consciousness had found only a temporary catharsis. As in the episode of the screaming, terrified soldier and the godlike officer whose voice expressed a divinity—"stern, hard, with no reflection of fear in it"—there was no doubt also that the little parable of the Civil War concealed beneath its moral and social levels the same religious and oedipal conflict that had preoccupied Stephen Crane in *The Black Riders* and, though more obliquely, in *Maggie,* too.

From this source came the central tension and prevailing imagery of the military story. The rebellion of the youth against the God of Wrath, the Unjust Father, had been projected into the fable of the sinful boy and the tribal law. . . . But one wonders what "crime" had rendered it necessary, as in the ceremonial exorcisms of primitive religions, for the errant youth to offer up part of his virility in the very struggle to achieve manhood. What was the real meaning of the "torn and guttering body" toward which Crane was drawn? And were the purposes and experiences of maturity to be bounded only by that baptism of fire—that bar mitzvah of blood—which had surrounded and almost obliterated the innocent youth of his tale?

At any rate, much too much of Crane's career was spent in the attempt to validate the imaginary experience in *The Red Badge of Courage* by the test of battle itself. He was obliged, as he said, to prove (but to whom?) that his first, brilliant, immensely intuitive major work was really "all right." (pp. 82-9)

Maxwell Geismar, "Stephen Crane: Halfway House," in his Rebels and Ancestors: The American Novel, 1890-1915, Houghton Mifflin, 1953, pp. 69-138.

BERNARD WEISBERGER   (essay date 1958)

[*Weisberger is an American historian whose works include* The Life History of the United States *(1964) and* The American Heritage History of the American People *(1971). In the following excerpt, he discusses* The Red Badge of Courage *as a novel of redemption and self-discovery, and examines Crane's use of stylistic devices associated with various literary movements of the late nineteenth century.*]

The Red Badge of Courage is both realistic and modern precisely because of its masterly handling of interior action. This is the first of its claims to be ranked with the best fiction of the present. It is a story with movement and with crises, but the movements are of images within the mind, and the crises are crises of soul. For the story, taken merely as a story, is a lean one. (p. 98)

[It] is hardly a story with a sweeping focus. In form, it is compressed. Its foreground is never wider than the view taken in by the single pair of eyes belonging to the hero. Its action is not of a kind for satisfactory dispatches and six-column headlines. Yet *behind* these eyes there is continuous and detailed motion, adding up to development. The book is really a rich and complete story of a successful search for identity. It is, in fact, significant that the full name of Henry Fleming is not revealed until well along in the tale. What is most important, there are no pauses in this action, no suspended moments between charges and bombardments, or halts by the roadside. Every impression, every word, every shape, color, sound and smell is in some direct way related to the emotional experience of the boy. So tight is the construction, and so continuous the flow of impression and mental reaction, that the book could easily be re-written as a monologue by Fleming in stream-of-consciousness style.

There is no character in these pages except for the frightened soldier. Almost immediately, we are introduced to the "youthful private." Within another few paragraphs we learn of the fictitious image of himself that he created before his enlistment and during his early days of service. He saw war as a series of "large pictures extravagant in color, lurid with breathless deeds," and in the first weeks of strutting in uniform, he had "believed that he must be a hero." In the following months of drill and encampment, that original image has been lost, and he has sunk into the anonymity of the army; he is "part of a vast blue demonstration." Now, confronted by action, he is aware of himself again. In a sense the other soldiers, loud and swaggering or stubbornly refusing to speculate on the impalpable tomorrow, are personifications of the various protective attitudes which he himself has adopted. But the question abides. He can no longer find rest in military depersonalization. "Now, with the newborn question in his mind, he was compelled to sink back into his old place as part of a blue demonstration." Compelled to do what was previously voluntary, he is unsatisfied. And so he continually tries "to measure himself by his comrades."

Yet his aloneness continues to be overwhelming. As they move up towards the line he is suddenly obsessed with the idea that they are headed for a trap, and that he alone knows it. "He thought that he must break from the ranks and harangue his comrades. . . . There was but one pair of eyes in the corps. He would step forth and make a speech." But of course he does not. In the first fighting he finds temporary reassurance in being a part of the regiment, "welded into a common personality which was dominated by a single desire." But then the rage of battle sweeps around him, cutting him off from the others. He is dazed and suffocated—sensations like those of being buried alive, cut off from the living earth. The words of another soldier ring in his mind: "I didn't come here to fight the hull damned rebel army." The vision of himself alone against the gray lines is all too intense. When he finally breaks and runs, he loses his sense of direction. There is no longer any comfort in the thought of others at his side, or support troops behind. Rather, "destruction threatened him *from all points.*" He is in the direct center of the stage.

In his odyssey through the rear area, this is made even more clear. The tattered soldier whom Henry meets, wounded in the head and the arm, can easily be taken for the romantic hero parading through those large and colorful pictures of war in Henry's mind as a raw recruit. There is a hint of this in the fact that the tattered soldier is first encountered gawking, his mouth "agape in yokel fashion," at a bearded sergeant who is telling a story. This is a flashback to the wide-eyed greenhorn that Henry has been. But now this pristine and virginal personage is tattered, fouled with blood and powder stains, and, wounded in the *head* and *arm,* unable to think or act sensibly. From this ghost of himself the boy hears an insistent question that racks him with shame. "Where yeh hit, ol' boy?" The answer which he cannot give, of course, is "in his manhood."

Henry escapes from this inquisitor, and meets the wounded "tall soldier," mumbling and lurching toward his death spasm, minutes away. Jim Conklin is not described as an older man, but it is clear earlier in the book that Fleming looks up to him and leans on him for reassurance. He seems to represent the consolations and supports of those who are respected in youth—parents, elders, teachers, and ministers. Now he dies, with horrible contortions, leaving Henry with a childish desire "to screech out his grief." One more refuge is gone. The tattered soldier then reappears. This time, he has become partly identified with Conklin, since he hints that he is an older man, with children. He is visibly getting weaker from his own hurts. He begins to babble and to confuse Henry with one of his own friends, highlighting Henry's further alienation from his past and from others who have shaped him. Remorselessly, the tattered man presses his question, until Henry snaps, "Oh, don't bother me!" and leaves him. But this is a fresh crime to add to cowardice. He is deserting a wounded comrade, and further deserting both his idealized self and the standards set for him before he put on the blue.

A climax is approaching. Henry is buffeted by emotions. He wishes that the army would lose the battle and share his disgrace. Then he recoils from the idea, because his need to believe in certain success for "that mighty blue machine" is overwhelming. A man cannot hide his own failure by pulling the universe down around his ears; the will to order is too strong. Next, he wishes to die. Suddenly, he is agonized by a fantasy in which the whole regiment is discussing his cowardice. In a sense, he is going through the crisis of guilt felt by the "convicted" sinner of a revival. He is thinking of "rules for the guidance of the damned," in Crane's own phrase. And the fact is that he is about to be, in the words of a Christian, "born again."

There is going to be a rebirth, indeed, but not a supernatural one. What happens, rather, is that he meets another panicky refugee, with livid face and rolling eyes. When he tries to intercept this flying fragment of an organization, the man smashes his rifle across Henry's head. This is a turning point. For the frightened soldier is precisely what Henry was himself in the moment when he began to speed toward the rear "in great leaps." Up to now the boy has angrily turned aside the tattered man's question, refusing to recognize the reality of his act. Now he is face to face with his own image at last, and what happens? Clubbed over the skull, he has at last received a wound—a "red badge of courage." From that very moment, the direction of the story changes. The trek *back* to the front begins. The wound is a first stage in redemption, and for all practical purposes, it is self-inflicted.

The next redemptive step comes soon. Henry wanders aimlessly, deliriously thinking of home. He remember days as a schoolboy, swimming in a favorite pool. He can feel "the swash of the fragrant water upon his body." This is his baptism, and the redeemer is at hand. A cheery voice at the boy's shoulder hails him, his arm is firmly taken, and he is walked along in the darkness towards his regiment. The man with him is a tower of strength, threading the mazes of the tangled forest, avoiding guards and patrols, beating "ways and means out of sullen things," steadily guiding them both on the road back to the campfire—to light, and most of all, to companionship. All the while he is delivering a long, rambling monologue, the whole point of which is that it says nothing coherent. The core of it is in a sentence that spells out the pointlessness of battle.

> . . . By dad, I give myself up fer dead any number 'a times. There was shootin' here an' shootin' there, an' hollerin' here an' hollerin' there, in th' damn darkness, until I couldn't tell t' save m' soul which side I was on.

What a shock the Reverend J. T. Crane would have experienced, had he lived to read and understand these lines by his son. "*I couldn't tell t' save m' soul which side I was on.*" The gospel that saves Henry Fleming is no assurance of purpose and ultimate salvation in an ordered universe, where good and evil are definable. No; it is the statement of the fact that there *is* no fathomable purpose, that the souls, wandering and crying in the damned darkness, never know their own side. Here is a negation of the Christian conversion, in which one sees the light and is enrolled among the saints. Yet from this negation, the boy will take strength. A man is courageous, at last, because he must be. He has no prop but himself. But let him prove himself once, and then he can never be betrayed.

And who offers this counsel of iron? No prophet, no saint, no elder—in effect nobody. For there is one enormously important detail. Once Henry has found his old outfit, the voice disappears in the darkness. And suddenly the youth realizes that not once has he seen his benefactor's face. His journey has been one of *self*-discovery. His injury has come from his own hand. Either the cure for it has come from the same place, or else from nothingness. There is no saviour to whom he can offer a prayer of thanks, just as there was no devil to blame for his wound.

One final step remains. He hesitates about going back to the campfire, trembling at the thought of the "barbed missiles of ridicule" which will be aimed his way. But he finds that he does not need to invent a story. His friends assume that he was misplaced in action, and they make a satisfying to-do about nursing his bruise, which they assume is from a bullet-graze. So he makes a final connection. He had been alone, true. But there is compensation for the isolation. Weakness, if it goes unnoticed, makes no more of a ripple in society or the universe than unseen courage. "He had performed his mistakes in the dark, so he was still a man." At first he had created a false hero-image of himself, tailored to meet false standards. The image and the standards are now as dead as Jim Conklin. The facts of the situation are plain. There is man, and there is impersonal fate. If fate is kind, the favor is accepted gratefully. If not, a man does the best he can. In neither case is there much purpose in looking further.

> In the present, he declared to himself that it was only the doomed and the damned who roared with sincerity at circumstance. Few but they ever did it. A man with a full stomach and the respect of his fellows had no business to scold about anything that he might think to be wrong in the ways of the universe, or even with the ways of society. Let the unfortunates rail; the others may play marbles.

He does not have to worry any longer about future battles. "It was not essential that he should plan his ways in regard to them. He had been taught that many obligations of a life were easily avoided." So much for the responsibilities of the "saved." Freed from fear, he knows that the necessary evil will come when it will come. Meanwhile he can sink again into the anonymity of the company, moved aimlessly here and there, and perform heroically.

His conversion has led him to a kind of traditional religion in reverse. He can take his loss of identity in battle, because he is reconciled to his own character. If he has no control over his fate, neither has anyone else. He can be a conventional warrior, because he knows that the conventions of fictitious war do not really exist, and cannot make impossible demands. So the goal of an essentially psychological story is reached. The rest of the book is merely to prove the change in Henry.

Crane's story is one of the first robins of a literary spring, in which hundreds of bewildered young men will hunt for bearings in a world they never made and are not hopeful about mending. But there is a second seal of the contemporary age stamped into the narrative, by the very manner of its telling. Crane constructed the tale with devices which were to become the badges of several schools of modern fiction. For one thing, the careful descriptions of scenery and climate are intended to create a tone matching that of the hero's mind at any given moment. In this kind of environmental symbolism, the ideas will be implicit in the action and the setting. They will not be lifted out by the intervening hand of the writer, and examined. The communication from the invented character to the reader will be direct, but carried on through suggestions.

The very start of the book—the cold, passing "reluctantly from the earth"—immediately establishes a chill, foreboding atmosphere; a sense of 3 A.M., when the muscles are torpid, the body's juices congealed, and every prospect vile. And when, in the final sentence, a golden ray of sun bursts through "hosts of leaden rain clouds," it is almost too pat, too much of a celluloid bromide. In between, this parallel construction of mood and setting reappears again and again. When the regiment is hurrying into action, it is during the "rushing yellow of the developing day." But even as the sun "strikes mellowingly" on the earth, two columns of soldiers moving across a hill look like "two serpents crawling from the cavern of the night." Readers will not be allowed to forget that encroaching darkness. As the troops make a crossing of the river by night, a fire gives to its waters a winelike tint. But the tint of wine is also that of blood, suggesting the kind of river that

is going to run through the action of the next day. It is well to notice again the occurrence of two images from the evangelical literature of conversion—the river which must be crossed for salvation, and the blood in which the sinner must be washed. When the regiment has managed to meet the first charges bravely, the boy notices that "the sky is blue and pure, and the sun gleaming." But when he is running away, as the crisis of darkness draws on, the same sun is emitting "slanted bronze rays," and when Jim Conklin dies, it is red and "pasted in the sky like a wafer."

Another development in "new" writing at this time was the effort to break down barriers between art forms and fuse different sensory images of experience. It was especially notable in symbolist poetry, where words were used for their musical effects rather than their meaning, in some cases, and certain sounds were identified with particular colors and the emotions which they evoked. *The Red Badge of Courage* is in step with this trend because in good part it is a painting.

Crane uses colors almost compulsively. In the very first paragraph the sun rises and turns the landscape from brown to green. An amber-tinted river purls at the army's feet, and at night hostile campfires gleam like red eyes. We learn later that when Henry had his first dreams of martial glory, his mother discouraged him, throwing "a yellow light" on his ambitions. The army is a "blue demonstration." But the most effective use of color is in the scene when Henry stumbles on a decaying corpse in the woods. The overarching boughs make a little chapel of the place, entered through "green doors," with a "gentle brown carpet" of pine needles. In this cloister-like atmosphere of warm browns and greens, the boy is paralyzed with terror when he discovers a long-dead soldier. The uniform has faded to a melancholy, sick green—not the fresh hue of the grass. The eyes are the color of a dead fish. The mouth has turned yellow; black ants parade hungrily over the gray skin of the face. This abrupt precipitation into violent greens, yellows, blacks and grays burns the symbol of rejection of conventional religious supports—the "church" containing only a moldering carcass—deeply into the consciousness. Towards the end of the book, when Henry is exhilarated and bold in the final fighting, pieces of the battleground are fought over as if they were "gold thrones or pearl bedsteads"—colors again taken from the popular impression of the heavenly city—and the battle flags fly "like crimson foam," setting the triumphant tone of final salvation.

A third brand identifies *The Red Badge of Courage* with writing styles that were breaking down the conventions of the novel as the nineteenth century ended. Crane is included by critics among the "naturalists" of that period—writers who made man something of a cipher in a world ruled by a "nature" which had no respect for his purposes, and which as often as not crushed him in its blind movements. *The Red Badge of Courage* seems entitled to the label. Certainly, Henry is carried, in his personal retreat, towards the conclusion that the cosmos is not interested in him. The theme is presented most directly when he stumbles into a wood, "as if resolved to bury himself" in nature, the great consoler of some many romantics. But this is not the benign nature of Transcendentalism. As Henry forces his way along, vines cling to his legs and branches shout his secret shame. He cannot "conciliate the forest." He pushes further, looking for "dark and intricate places" and it needs no profound acquaintance with psychoanalysis to guess what they are. Suddenly there is a flash of false hope. He shies a pine cone at a squirrel, which sensibly runs away and does not remain to "die with an upward glance at the sympathetic heavens." This is cheering. Here is nature supporting his own craven action with a demonstration of instinct at work. "She re-enforced his arguments with proofs that lived where the sun shone."

But immediately he blunders into a swamp, where a small animal is observed, pouncing into some *black* water, and emerging with a fish. It is a quite conventional reminder of the cruelty of the struggle for life. The thickets get deeper, but then there is a second illusion of hope. He reaches the little chapel in the forest, with the "high, arching boughs" through which a "religious half-light" is falling. Here is another conventional scene. The groves, after all, were God's first temples. The stage is set for the formal rite of purification and prayer. And what leaps out as the branches are pulled aside? The ant-eaten corpse! The shock underlines the sardonic joke, like the grin of a skull suddenly discovered. Henry runs for his life. Nature may not take the trouble to be an enemy, but she is no friend.

Crane also hammers repeatedly on the theme of the frustration of the individual will in the collective personality of the regiment. The military units are *things*—sometimes living organisms, sometimes machines. A column of stragglers and wounded is "a flow of blood from the torn body of the brigade." After one action, the regiment lies "heaving from its hot exertions." A battle in the distance is a contest between beings who strike savagely and powerfully at each other." But on the other hand, mechanistic images are frequent. The boy imagines that the charging Confederates are "machines of steel." He never quite loses his faith in the final victory of his "mighty blue machine." His company, tired out by repeated charges, is "a machine run down." Most of these similes are pedestrian, but occasionally Crane is capable of greater polish in his imagery, as when he describes bullets which "buff" into men with "serene regularity, as if controlled by a schedule."

The soldiers sense their helplessness and frustration. "The slaves toiling in the temple of this god began to feel rebellion at his harsh tasks," Crane says in one of his more awkward and inexperienced passages. Later, he returns to his proper technique of letting feelings escape in the words and deeds of his characters. (His writing is worst when he is untrue to the style he is creating.) Rebellion simmers effectively in Henry's outburst:

> "Good Gawd," the youth grumbled, "we're always being chased around like rats! It makes me sick. Nobody seems to know where we go or why we go. We just get fired around from pillar to post and get licked here and get licked there, and nobody knows what it's done for. It makes a man feel like a damn' kitten in a bag."

This is Thomas Hardy or Omar Khayyam, flavored with the American countryside. The lieutenant gives the proper naturalistic answer. "You boys shut right up! There no need 'a your wastin' your breath in long-winded arguments about this an' that an' th' other." In the end, frustration is dominant. After a successful charge, the regiment is reproached by the commanding general, who knows it only as a number, for not having gone far enough. It is as senseless as the rebuke of God for alleged sins, committed in ignorance. And what is more, when all is over, the regiment goes back across the river, presumably to its starting point. Yet there is victory of a kind, but the victory of these veterans is in their acceptance of this real war in place of the fraudulent heroic illusion towards which

they bravely marched two days before. They are disenchanted but not beaten. And the moral is plain that man does not choose his destination. He cannot even hold on to the scarred bit of ground which he has won at the price of his youth.

A final hallmark of the book is its "realism." Here, Crane was something less of an innovator. Symbolism and naturalism were somewhat new in 1893. But the pedigree of the novel's fidelity to detail goes back to the "local color" tradition which Crane inherited from the writers who were forging their fame during his childhood—Mark Twain, George Cable, Sarah Orne Jewett, and their like. These authors differed considerably from each other, but they were all trying to re-create accurately the dialects and mannerisms of certain sections and classes of the country. Crane and others were to marry this technique to a more liverish view of life than the seventies and eighties had thought fashionable. They helped to link realism with what was, in the stock phrase, "hard-boiled," and they laid down a road which some have followed all the way to Erskine Caldwell and James T. Farrell.

However, the "ash-can" school of writing was not necessarily implicit in the "realistic" writing of Crane's day. The modern thinker recognizes many "realities." Crane and his contemporaries were after a kind of "realism" which was particular and had boundaries. Sometimes it was called "copyistic," sometimes "veritistic," and sometimes more simply, "photographic." Its aim was to copy objective surroundings as faithfully as possible, and as impersonally as a wet plate. The impact was made on the audience by making the external resemblance between fact and fiction so exact, that the original sensations of an actual event were rekindled. It did not intend to shock deliberately, but it did not flinch from whatever was necessary to complete the sensation of a genuine experience, verifiable by life. (pp. 100-13)

Crane's method of achieving this special kind of realism was to record his soldier talk in what he considered a reproduction of Eastern rural speech. It is hard to tell whether or not the longer spoken passages accomplished his mission. After a time, such words as "sech," "hull," and "dumbed," and the persistent omission of final sounds, as in "t'" and "an'" become rather stylized themselves. Stenographic accuracy has a way of dating with appalling quickness. The dialogue is a weak link.

But the language of gesture and expletive, on the other hand, is timeless. There is a sense of imminence and closeness in some of Crane's prose because of what his characters do and say in their more terse moments. When we first meet the troops, they are in an argument with the tall soldier, who has picked up a rumor of impending movement, while in the unheroic act of washing his shirt. When Henry leaves his mother to rally to freedom's starry flag, she furnishes counterpoint to his fantasies by making her parting remarks to him as she peels potatoes. When he is lying in his tent, seeing visions of a "thousand-tongued fear" that will betray him the next day, the voices of his fellows are heard in a card game.

Even these homey touches can, by themselves, fade quickly into picturesque, Norman-Rockwell-like effects. Crane avoids this by contrasting them with the crashing events around them, thus making them powerful. The thunder of battle reinforces the intensely human quality of the trivial action. The flyspeck of detail underscores the solemnity of an entire scene. We are all conscious of this contrast in life between the sublime occasion and the ridiculous human animals taking part in it. Crane digs out the full dramatic value hidden in such linked opposites as the sneeze at the funeral, the nervous banality at the scene of an accident, or the drop of perspiration on the upper lip of the great orator.

These antitheses are superbly used. When the first Confederates come charging across the fields, a soldier is seen knotting a red handkerchief about his throat, giving "exquisite attention to its position." Even better, when the second wave comes over, a cry goes up: "Here they come ag'in!" Upon this, one soldier leaps to his feet and utters a simple, single word. He says, "Gosh!" It is a conversational two-cent piece, but standing out alone, it has the impact of a shout. When Jim Conklin feels his life draining away through a side which looks as if it had been chewed by wolves, he can only murmur: "An', b'jiminey, I got shot—I got shot. Yes, b'jiminey, I got shot." To deglamorize war further, Crane has the generals, in their occasional appearances, talk in the same rural patois as the men, which is historically correct as well as artistically satisfying. And as a last example of this, one of the more potent speeches in the book is made by Henry's lieutenant when a new order for a charge is carried to the exhausted and thoroughly bloodied regiment. "Charge?" he says. "Well, b'Gawd!"

Oddly, it is this kind of detail which spells out the really remarkable feat of the boy Crane's imagination. He himself might well have undergone the central struggle of his hero to find manhood. Certainly the book's moral is a rejection of his own upbringing. The fight for emancipation needed no special setting. But it is remarkable that the imagined backdrop is so convincing. (pp. 113-15)

There is no doubt that the credit for this achievement goes to Crane's genius. It is no ordinary thing to create a small masterpiece of imagination first, and wait for experience to validate it later—a little like digesting first and eating afterwards. Even more impressive is the universality of a book by a writer of such limited attendance at the school of life. *The Red Badge of Courage* rises above the times both of Henry Fleming and Stephen Crane. It paints the experience of all young men who go into battle, familiar with fright but strangers to themselves, and who come out of it touched with sin but somehow stronger. Its baptism in war might have taken place anywhere between the Trojan plain and Pork Chop Hill. Sometimes it almost seems as if it could do altogether without the background of war. The real story is in the emotional storm which divides maturity from innocence.

Yet even if we grant the truth of this, no creative work can be sliced entirely out of its context. Crane is a writer of his times, and he did not invent symbolism, or naturalism, or copyism, however much of them he unearthed on his own. But more than this, *The Red Badge of Courage* tells a story which marks a new approach to the literary treatment of the Civil War. It is a special landmark in the history of our taste, the placement of which raises some absorbing questions. And in addition, the story of Henry Fleming is not in free flight, entirely independent of its setting in the Union army of the sixties. The book is great in part just *because* it takes place when and where it does.

The first of these points is of special interest to history. *The Red Badge of Courage* is the first novel to scrub the war of moonbeams and still find wide acceptance in the market place. It is the first widely accepted work in which a writer who sees life in its rank and primal conditions sees the war in the same light as a part of the whole of that life. (pp. 117-18)

[*The Red Badge of Courage*] is not a "debunking" book in any sense. It does not deride courage as the false coinage of a propaganda machine. Rather, it simply says that courage, like the fear which it overcomes, has animal reasons for being. Yet Crane's book is free of the conventional posturing of the war fiction then current. The reader of 1895 could not really accept the death of Jim Conklin and simultaneously believe in the fairy-tale heroes in blue who expired with eyes heavenward and a dying message to Mother on their lips. Crane had made a small breach in the wall of myth surrounding the war.

The question is, Why could readers of 1895 accept even that breach? Was it merely because nothing central in the myth was sacrificed? Or did the war already seem safely remote from anything in which they were concerned—a fight between Greeks and Trojans, in which bones could splinter and bowels spill without impropriety? Had the legend done enough work in the politics of justifying the *status quo* to be safely trimmed at the edges? Or was the world of Hanna and McKinley simply too busy to care one way or another? For that matter, why does our own age still enshrine the era of Lee and Grant with legend, when it has learned long since that the years of 1861 to 1865 were as bloody, brutal and stupid as any other war years?

These questions are merely variations on a basic inquiry—what is the effect of culture on literature? The fact remains that a fundamental national experience such as war itself is translated into different kinds of art under different conditions. What circumstances must be ripe to produce "real" wars, and "useless" wars and "noble" wars in fiction? In the case of *The Red Badge of Courage,* it took twenty-eight years for a popular market to be ready for a work which said that the Civil War could be, for the common soldier, a cruel and purposeless war at times. The timing of the book gives it the status of a special problem in the sociology of art. (pp. 120-21)

Bernard Weisberger, "'The Red Badge of Courage'," in Twelve Original Essays on Great American Novels, *edited by Charles Shapiro, Wayne State University Press, 1958, pp. 96-123.*

JAMES TRAMMELL COX (essay date 1959)

[*In the following excerpt, Cox presents a detailed examination of imagery in* The Red Badge of Courage.]

"The red sun . . . pasted in the sky like a wafer" of Stephen Crane's *The Red Badge of Courage* continues to generate more critical heat than light. Since the publication in 1951 of R. W. Stallman's much-debated introduction [excerpted in *TCLC*, Vol. 11, pp. 137-39] to the Modern Library edition of the novel and his later expansions of this reading, contemporary criticism has been sharply divided on at least three issues: the significance of the religious imagery, the closely related problem of Henry Fleming's development or lack of it, and the question of Crane's fictional method, naturalist or symbolist. Seldom however are these fundamental points of disagreement recognized as such; all too frequently they are obscured or simply avoided in a dispute over critical method. (p. 209)

[Of the critical work that] has been done, the best on the significance of the religious imagery is Bernard Weisberger's recent suggestion [see excerpt above] that "There is going to be rebirth, indeed, but not a supernatural one. Here is a negation of the Christian conversion." This obvious obverse significance of the Christian symbolism, noted but misinterpreted by Stallman and quite consistent with Henry Fleming's naturalistic re-education, seems to have occurred to no one but Mr. Weisberger. On the problem of Henry Fleming's development, more specifically on its significance in the naturalistic universe depicted in the novel, Stanley B. Greenfield's summation [see Additional Bibliography] is thoughtful and valuable, especially to the extent that it reconciles what seems a discrepancy between Crane's determinism and the manifest value he attaches to individual insight and moral behavior:

> Crane's magnum opus shows up the nature and value of courage. The heroic ideal is not what it has been claimed to be; so largely is it the product of instinctive responses to biological and traditional forces. But man does have will, and he has the ability to reflect, and though these do not guarantee that he can effect his own destiny they do enable him to become responsible to some degree for the honesty of his personal vision.

Closer textual analysis—a method Mr. Greenfield inconsistently ridicules and utilizes at will—reveals a need for considerable qualification of the cheerful indifference of Nature and of the "decided growth in moral behavior" he finds in Henry Fleming's development. For the imagery suggests that this cheerful appearance of Nature is a part of its treacherous hostility. As Crane expresses the idea in an expunged passage from an earlier manuscript version, "It [Nature] could deck a hideous creature in enticing apparel." The imagery also insists upon the irony of Henry's discovery of unselfishness and courage through the wounded vanity of egocentrism, so that the decided growth toward moral manhood posited by Greenfield ignores this basic irony, as well as its chief philosophical implication: that man's relationship to his universe is paradoxical. He becomes least an animal when most an animal. On the question of Crane's fictional method, Stallman is still significantly right in his recognition of the extent to which "Crane puts language to poetic uses, which is to use it reflexively and symbolically." And it is past time that this fundamental question be considered apart from any given interpretation, for a full understanding and appreciation of the better works of Stephen Crane are absolutely dependent upon an awareness of this method.

What makes this awareness so very important, in particular, to a reading of *The Red Badge of Courage* is that the novel is an initiation story, the account of a young man's discovery of the nature of reality, and the definition of this reality, symbolically presented to the reader through the imagery, provides Henry Fleming's slow discovery with a pervasive dramatic irony as essential to a full appreciation of the work as, for example, a foreknowledge of Oedipus' origin is in *Oedipus Rex*.

Briefly paraphrased, the definition Crane provides us with is largely the same naturalism to be found in "**The Blue Hotel**." The earth and all life on it originated from the fierce fire of the sun, which continues ultimately to determine both life and death on the earth in the dependence of all life here upon its warmth and light for existence. It is this condition of things, further, which requires that all life—specifically man, animal, and plant, as enumerated by Crane—must alike struggle to survive. Whatever the decking or coloration for the plant or animal, whatever the disguises for man—which would include all the myths of man's mind that obscure this conception of himself and his universe, notably his pretense to honor and glory, his romantic concept of nature, and his belief in eternal life—all are engaged in an endless struggle to survive that necessitates a conflict relation to environment. For this reason

the inner nature of all life is hostile. Its battles are for existence, and the essence, in fact, of existence is a battle. This being true, all attempts either to escape or to deny this conflict are doomed to meaninglessness. For meaning, man's only recourse in such a universe is to heed the general's exhortation, "t' go in—everlastingly—like blazes—anything"; that is, to embrace life as conflict. In so doing, man achieves a paradoxical harmony with his hostile universe that allows him, like the regiment, to proceed "superior to circumstances until its blazing vitality fades." It also allows him to know, for a moment, "a temporary but sublime absence of selfishness" and the undeceived brotherhood which his nature, his condition, and his disguises otherwise preclude. And with full knowledge comes, finally, a certain dignity, nothing more.

What is of further interest in the imagery as a whole is that Crane employs here the same images for the same symbolic purposes he later uses in "**The Blue Hotel**." To symbolize life as an eternal conflict, he uses a battle in the novel as a "way that seemed eternal" and two fights in the short story, one of which is also described as "eternal to his [the Easterner's] sense." To suggest the deterministic inevitability of this conflict and its destructive power, he uses machine images in both, while its ferocity and its limited grandeur are compared to a firework display. To equate man with other forms of life in the identity of their struggle for survival, he relies heavily upon comparisons to animals. To call attention to the timelessness and also the brutality of this struggle, comparisons to primitive warriors are abundant. To make a mockery of man's chief delusion, which is Christianity with its promise of eternal life, Stephen Crane—no matter whose son he is—compares the victims of both conflicts to Jesus Christ. Inferno images abound for roughly the same purpose. To define the essence of reality as treacherous in that its facade conceals the inner hostility which emerges only when existence is threatened, Crane employs a blue exterior with a fire or simply red within in both works. To suggest that death is an inevitable consequence of this fire within, actually differing from life only as colors on the spectrum differ—in degree, not in kind—yellow is used to symbolize death in both. To represent miseducation, particularly in regard to Nature, green and brown have identical functions in both. To symbolize fear, white is used in both, though white in the novel is also linked with stoic calm or love—all three of which associations possess commonality in being opposites to the red of hostility and anger. Only black shows change: in the novel it is the equivalent of red, while in the story it is the oblivion of death, grey in the novel assuming approximately this significance. The two works, in fact, are companion pieces: studies of fear and courage and awareness in a naturalistic universe.

Consistently overlooked, even by Edward Stone [see Additional Bibliography], in the long wrangle over the wafer image is the central role of the sun, metaphorically and philosophically, in the novel as a whole. It is set up in the beginning of the novel in the account of Henry's misconceptions as a youth: "There was a portion of the world's history which he had regarded as the time of wars, but it, he *thought*, had been *long gone over the horizon* and had disappeared forever." To this Crane adds, "He had long despaired of witnessing a Greek-like struggle. Such would be no more. Men were better, or more timid. Secular and religious education had effaced the throat-grappling instinct, or else firm finance held in check the passions." . . . Consequently, it cannot be without significance and irony that the general who is in charge of the fighting that Henry has deserted on the first day of battle is described first as "much harassed" with the appearance "of a business man whose market is swinging up and down," secondly, as having in his eyes "a desire to chant a paean," and thirdly as one who "beamed upon the earth like a sun."

Here is ample evidence, indeed, manifest in the action and explained in the imagery, that the time of wars is anything but "long gone over the horizon." As a Greek, an ironically unfirm representative of firm finance, and a sun, this general as the immediate cause of the conflict that ensues is still very much on Henry Fleming's horizon. The explanation provided by the imagery is first of all that finance is neither firm nor capable of holding in check men's passions. Further, in their common identity through metaphor, the imagery also calls attention to the common relation both the general and the sun have to the conflict which follows: it is causal, the general immediate and the sun ultimate. This is again the chief significance and the chief irony in the timely reappearance of the "red sun . . . pasted in the sky like a wafer" when Henry has just observed in Jim Conklin's fall that his "side looked as if it had been chewed by wolves." The time of wars has still to go over the horizon because religious education has also failed to efface "the throat grappling instinct."

The lieutenant is thus ironically profounder than he knows when he observes, "I was willin' t' bet they'd attack as soon as th' sun got fairly up." This role of ultimate responsibility would also seem to be the implication of the abrupt appearance of the sun in this picture of the dead soldiers: "A dead soldier was stretched with his face hidden in his arm. Farther off there was a group of four or five corpses keeping mournful company. A hot sun had blazed upon the spot." Other corpses are described as "dumped out upon the ground from the sky" or as "stricken by bolts from the sky." The din of this battle is indeed, as Crane tells us, "fitted to the universe," and the sun, though capable of appearing "bright and gay in the blue, enameled sky," is ultimately red and responsible, as the "cloud of dark smoke, as from smoldering ruins," which goes up toward it, reveals like an accusing finger.

The red badge that Henry Fleming wears is seed and sign of this same sun. For in the necessity imposed by the sun on all life to struggle for survival, man retains within a fiery hostility as revealed in the description of his hut, where it is not surprising that we find a fire in a "flimsy chimney of clay and sticks [that] made endless threats to set ablaze the whole establishment." Philosophically, it is the same fire. It is the same fire that disturbed Henry when he "burned to enlist." In the heat of battle, with existence threatened, it is this fire that has now emerged upon Henry's "red and inflamed features" and upon the general's face, "aflame with excitement." The regiment itself is a "firework that, once ignited proceeds superior to circumstances until its blazing vitality fades."

Of course fiery hostility is not the only reaction Henry and the regiment show to this conflict threatening existence. Fear is common and is invariably denoted with expressions suggesting the emergence of white upon the features instead of fire or red, as when Henry "blanched" before turning to run. For fear, like hostility, is a constituent part of the make-up of the inner man as again he is defined in his quarters, with the suggestion that it is from his environment or the outside that his fear derives: "A small window shot an oblique square of whiter light upon the cluttered floor."

Confirming the determining role of the sun as overhanging or providing the conditions under which man, so defined, exists, the sun appears here too: "The sunlight, without, beating upon it [the folded tent which serves as a roof] made it glow a light yellow shade." Thus besides giving the fire necessary to existence, it demands finally as a consequence of this fire death. For yellow is consistently associated with death. The first corpse Henry sees is dressed in a suit of "yellowish brown," and the mouth of the corpse in the chapel of the trees has changed from red "to an appalling yellow." And overhanging the battle area Henry flees from exactly as it overhangs his quarters is "a yellow fog [that] lay wallowing on the treetops." Though the exterior of this hut is brown, careful readers of **"The Blue Hotel"** cannot fail to note the astonishing similarity between these quarters and the "proper temple" of the short story.

A further aspect of man's nature is symbolically revealed in this interior: his tendency, deriving from his hostility, to screen from himself his inner nature, wreathing it in constructs of belief and value which only obscure the truth, as the smoke from the fire here "at times neglected the clay chimney and wreathed into the room," obscuring this fire as the smoke of battle so often obscures the flames of the enemy guns, making it "difficult for the regiment to proceed with intelligence." A part of this tendency is laziness and ignorance, qualities frequently associated with smoke: "some lazy and ignorant smoke curled slowly. The men, hiding from the bullets, waited anxiously for it to lift and disclose the plight of the regiment." Primarily however it is the fear of death which leads man to construct his own smokescreens, as suggested in the frequent linkage of smoke with the color gray. For the face or prospect of death is gray in each of the deaths that Henry has occasion to observe closely: in the "ashen face" of the first, in "the gray skin of the face" of the corpse in the chapel of the trees, and in "the gray appalling face" of Jim Conklin. Also revealing is its identification with phantom: "Smoke clouds went slowly and insolently across the fields like observant phantoms." For both Jim Conklin and the guilt Henry feels over his desertion of Jim are repeatedly referred to as a "specter" or "somber phantom." The implication of the linkage would seem to be that the guilt Henry feels is a part of the "clogged clouds," from which Henry's brain must emerge before his eyes are opened to new ways and the old sympathies are defeated. It derives from those systems of false belief and value which only obscure from man the fiery essence of the naturalistically conceived universe finally recognized and accepted by Henry Fleming. As such, this "sin" may be put "at a distance" by Henry with somewhat less callousness.

Aside from the false concept of heroism and the emptiness of its values, honor and glory, which it is the obvious purpose of the story to expose as so much smoke obscuring the true nature of man and his conflicts, a romantic concept of Nature, as a part of Henry's secular education, must also be included in this smoke. This romanticism is especially apparent in the sentimental pantheism which leads him to see in the landscape he comes to in his flight "a religion of peace" where the arching boughs in a grove of trees "made a chapel," with the sunlight in them providing "a religious half light" and the wind "a hymn of twilight." The low branches are "green doors" to this chapel and the pine needles "a gentle brown carpet." But exactly as the sentimentality of his earlier reaction to "the gentle fabric of softened greens and browns" which "looked to be a wrong place for a battlefield" is revealed when it becomes the scene of the holocaust he flees, so here are his illusions shattered: within these green doors, resting on this gentle brown carpet is a rottening corpse, its uniform, once blue, now faded to a "melancholy shade of green." However gentle green and brown may seem to the miseducated Henry Fleming, Crane makes it shockingly clear to the reader here and elsewhere that green and brown are the colors of the earth which requires death and decay for its fertility.

In the further relation of image to incident, Crane tells us a great deal more about Nature in this particular passage. The eyes have the "dull hue to be seen on the side of a dead fish," linking the corpse to the frequently noted fish devoured previously by the small animal. The corpse, in other words, is like the fish in its failure to survive. What is not so frequently noted is that on five other occasions we are reminded of this resemblance. Henry, for example is a "Fresh fish!" and the courageous Lieutenant Hasbrouck "a whale." Also war is twice a "red animal" and more than twenty times either war or the enemy is a monster about to devour the men, whose frequent fear is "We'll git swallowed." Thus through its connection with this meal of the small animal and the corpse, the conflict that takes place on the battlefield becomes itself a symbol of the struggle for survival. And the connection is repeated, emphasizing that all life is involved in this struggle, in the detail of the ant on the lip "trundling some sort of bundle," for again through simile and metaphor Crane elsewhere identifies this bundle as the soldiers being devoured by the red animal, war: they are "Grunting bundles of blue" that drop here and there "like bundles." Henry himself is "a parcel."

Also significant in this passage is the threat of the branches "to throw him over upon it [the corpse]," symbolizing Henry's involvement in the natural order which demands ultimately a return to the earth like that of the corpse. Furthermore this involvement is carefully elaborated through the tree symbolism. Not only are Henry and the men frequently entangled in Nature's trees or her "brambles [which] formed chains and tried to hold him back," but they are repeatedly likened to a tree to reveal the identity of their mutual struggle, as in the song of the soldiers:

> A dog, a woman, an' a walnut tree,
> Th' more yeh beat 'em th' better they be

If they survive, that is. The tattered soldier, whose wounded arm dangles "like a broken bough" and Jim, whose body swings forward as he goes down "in the manner of a falling tree," can hardly be described as "better." To indicate that this bit of homely naturalism is to be taken seriously, incidentally, Crane frequently repeats the beating or thrashing imagery like this picture of Henry, who sprawls in battle "like a man who had been thrashed," and compares the soldiers also to women and dogs.

The idea of entanglement is also carried over into the machine imagery, which is used more than fifteen times to describe the battle, suggesting both the deterministic inevitability of this struggle and its destructive power. For instance, as Henry joins the column of the wounded: "The torn bodies expressed the awful machinery in which the men had been entangled." And this machinery is not only the battle but the fixed processes of the natural order demanding conflict and death: "The battle was like the grinding of an immense and terrible machine to him. Its complexities and powers, its grim processes, fascinated him. He must go close and see it produce corpses." A flood is also used on several occasions for the same symbolic purpose. The meaninglessness of this conflict, morally speaking, is apparent in Crane's mention only once of the causes over which the Civil War was fought and then as less important than "the subtle battle brotherhood" of the men, and it is symbolically stated in comparisons of the battle to a circus or carnival and to sporting events. Jim Conklin, for example, gestures toward the battle and says, "Ah, Lord, what a circus!" Over seventy comparisons of the men to animals contribute to this significance of the battle, and in this line, its immediate source is defined as the animal-like hostility of the inner man: "A dull animal-like rebellion against his fellows, war in the abstract, and fate grew within him." To suggest that man is as helpless as a babe in the grinding machinery of the natural order and his fury against it as foolish as that of a child, there are over twenty-five comparisons like these of the men to infants and children: An officer displays "infantile features black with rage" and another "the furious anger of a spoiled child," while Henry before his first battle feels "in the face of his great trial like a babe." This is Nature as it really is—hardly the "woman with a deep aversion to tragedy" Henry Fleming conceived it to be.

Nature's processes are not simply grim however. It is a part of its essence to conceal its inner violence behind a bright facade of blue or blue and gold, so that Nature on occasion parades a gleaming sun in a "blue, pure sky" even as the recruits strut in the "blue and brass" of their new uniforms. Previous to contact with that which threatens existence, man knows only this facade, and Henry on the march to the front sees the sky as a "fairy blue" and does not see "The rushing yellow of the developing day [that] went on behind their backs." Before the march the men themselves are still but a part of this facade, being referred to four times as only a "blue demonstration." And because isolation from the known breeds fear, the same linkage of blue and white is used here that appears in the short story: Wilson tells Henry, "You're getting blue, my boy. You're looking thundering peaked." But note what happens to both this fairly blue sky and this blue uniform when Jim Conklin falls: "As the flap of the blue jacket fell away from the body" it exposes Conklin's side, which "looked as if it had been chewed by wolves"—in other words a red and bloody side. And then as a repetition on the cosmic level temporally of the same exposure we have just observed spatially Crane reveals a "red sun" in what was a bright, blue sky. All nature is alike. This is its double essence—the red of violence within the blue of innocence. Innocence in the sense both of inexperience and of beguiling beauty. This spatial relation of blue and red is even preserved in the movement of the troops from their "eternal camp," where they are only a "blue demonstration." For as they prepare to move off toward the front "their uniforms glowed a deep purple," and when they arrive in the battle area "these battalions with their commotions were woven red and startling into the gentle fabric of softened greens and browns."

As a further aspect of the miseducation which obscures from Henry Fleming the fiery essence of his naturalistic universe, his religious education is also responsible. It too is a part of the "clogged clouds" and the old sympathies, as revealed not only in the imagery depicting Jim Conklin's death but also in the inferno imagery and in the imagery of the primitive warrior-worshiper. In the ironic resemblances of Conklin to Christ, Crane is perhaps naively, but clearly and powerfully saying that in this red world Jesus Christ is a grim joke. It is to this climactic conclusion that Crane builds in this crucial chapter exactly as he built up to the shattering revelation of the corpse in the trees. Only here it is the reader who gets the shock instead of Henry, for to have had Henry consciously perceive the resemblance would have been both too obvious and too implausible.

The resemblances are manifestly here however. Since Stallman has noted many of them, I would call attention only to the principal resemblance he's missed: when Jim Conklin falls, his "body seemed to bounce a little way from the earth." Here, the point of this carefully and subtly prepared resemblance to Christ, with eight preceding hints, becomes clear. We know why, as Henry rushes to the fallen body, he discovers that "the teeth showed in a laugh." It is because this death, which is all too real, makes of the other a palpable absurdity with its Ascension to the right hand of God. The only ascension here is a grotesque bounce "a little way from the earth." And when then the ultimate source and seal of this grimly naturalistic death appears in the sky in the shape—of all things—of a wafer, the irony is devastating and the significance no less: this *red* wafer symbolizes that there will be *no* miraculous transubstantiation from this mangled and meaningless corpse. Rather, it is a reminder of what we have seen of another corpse: the "red animal, war" and the ants will be the unholy communicants that devour this quite untransubstantiated and unrisen body which is left "laughing there in the grass"—laughing at the appalling joke Henry Fleming's religious education has perpetrated upon him in its promise of eternal life.

What has confused some readers in this resemblance is that Crane does the same thing with his religious imagery here that he does in the short story, where Scully is at one moment God and Satan the next. Jim Conklin is *also* compared to the imps of hell in his "hideous hornpipe," his arms flailing about "in expression of implike enthusiasm," and the "God!" that the tattered soldier exclaims upon the fall is starkly changed to "Hell—." The significance of this apparent inconsistency is simply that all of heaven and hell man will ever know is here on earth, the product of his own efforts to obscure from himself the truth of his hostile nature in a hostile universe. And inferno imagery, like this line linking Jim to these imps, abounds throughout the text: "The black forms of men, passing to and fro before the crimson rays made weird and satanic effects." They dodge "implike around the fires." War, like life, is hell.

It is in the interesting sense in which Crane uses "enthusiasm" that the religious imagery becomes most revealing, for this enthusiasm is "the daring spirit of a savage religion mad." Again it may be traced from the very beginning of the novel in the "enthusiast" who rings the church bell with news of battle. In Henry too we see it on the march where for a moment "The thrill of his enthusiasm made him . . . fiery in his belief in success." Finally, it is this religious enthusiasm of the pagan worshiper and warrior that defines the state of mind necessary for the performance of unselfish or heroic deeds:

> The men, pitching forward insanely, had burst into cheerings, moblike and barbaric. . . . It made a mad enthusiasm. . . . There was the delirium that encounters despair and death, and is heedless and blind to the odds. It is a temporary but sublime absence of selfishness.

In a sense Crane seems to be saying that the Dionysiac fury of the pagan worshiper, who at least recognized his universe as hostile, was closer to a valid view of man and his universe than the Christian is with his humanistic veneer and false promise of eternal life. If the general, who gives us the central thematic statement of the novel—"'t' go in—everlastingly—like blazes"—were to chant his paean, it would with more validity be addressed to the red sun than to the Heavenly Father.

This pattern is further revealing if we examine the source of this enthusiasm more closely. For it is in the flames of man's

Corwin Knapp Linson's portrait of Crane in 1894.

inner egotism, stirred up through wounded vanity to a pitch of hatred that is repeatedly described as "a dream," a "delirium," and a "state of frenzy," precluding the consciousness necessary to will. As Crane tells us on the occasion of Henry's first experience of it, from which he awakes a knight or hero, "he lost sense of everything but his hate, his desire to smash into pulp the glittering smile of victory which he could feel upon the faces of his enemies." And it is not only his enemies: "his greater hatred was riveted upon the man, who, not knowing him, had called him a mule driver." The friendly jeers of the veterans produce the same reaction, the praise of the lieutenant an infantile swelling of the same vanity. Before the final charge of the enemy it is again the recollection of being called mud diggers that determines the men to hold and again "some arrows of scorn" that generate "the strange and unspeakable hatred" in Henry, who desires nothing so much as "retaliation upon the officer who had said 'mule drivers' and later 'mud diggers'." To see in this childish hatred with its subsequent "enthusiasm of unselfishness" a "decided growth in moral behavior" is a misreading quite as mistaken as a Christian redemption. Both interpretations miss the point of the paradox Crane *labors* throughout the latter half of the book: that the selfless behavior of heroism paradoxically emerges only from the grossest, most infantile, animalistic, fiery hatred born of the vanity of egocentrism. Though in his non-conscious "enthusiasm" he may be temporarily a man, it is only after Henry Fleming's "eyes seemed to open to some new ways" that he feels "a quiet manhood." Awareness—the ability to perceive truthfully the nature of this symbolically revealed, hostile universe—alone confers this new quiet, this new dignity. (pp. 209-19)

James Trammell Cox, "The Imagery of 'The Red Badge of Courage'," in Modern Fiction Studies, *Vol. 5, No. 3, Autumn, 1959, pp. 209-19.*

ERIC SOLOMON (essay date 1959)

[In the following excerpt, Solomon focuses on the structure of The Red Badge of Courage, *concluding that the novel's design reveals the spiritual growth of its protagonist, Henry Fleming.]*

In spite of the abundance of war novels produced by two world conflicts, *The Red Badge of Courage* is still the masterwork of war fiction. Stephen Crane's novel is the first work in English fiction of any length purely dedicated to an artistic reproduction of war, and it has rarely been approached in scope or intensity since it was published in 1895.

Any judgment of the influence of *The Red Badge of Courage* on later war fiction would of necessity be conjectural. The circumstance that Ford Madox Ford and Ernest Hemingway worshipped at the Crane shrine does not in itself prove that *No More Parades* or *A Farewell to Arms* was directly affected by Crane's book. But the novel became part of the literary heritage of the twentieth century, and whether or not a war writer consciously recalls Crane's performance, the fact remains that *The Red Badge of Courage* is a touchstone for modern war fiction. Stephen Crane gave the war novel its classic form.

Crane, however, made no great innovation in style or subject matter. Realism, irony, detail, the emotional impact of combat—all these had appeared somewhere in earlier war fiction. The contribution of Stephen Crane to the genre of war fiction was twofold. First, he defined the form in his novel that deals with war and its effect upon the sensitive individual who is inextricably involved; war is treated as neither journalism nor autobiography nor dashing romance, but as a test of mind and spirit in a situation of great tension. Crane also constructed a book that still stands as the technical masterpiece in the field.

Crane accomplishes in the longer form of the novel what Ambrose Bierce attains in the short story. *The Red Badge of Courage* creates a single world, a unique atmosphere where war is the background and the foreground. Without resorting to the props of counter-plots dealing with romance and intrigue employed by every novelist who wrote of war from Scott to Kipling (with the possible exception of the Tolstoy of *Sevastopol*), Crane works within a tightly restricted area. Like the painters of the Italian Renaissance who conceived the *tondo,* a form that forced the artist to choose and manipulate his subject matter to fit a small, circular canvas, Crane chooses to restrict his novel to war and its impact upon his hero. There is no mention of the causes or motives of the war or of any battle; Crane's war is universal, extricated from any specific historical situation. We may gain an impression of how a literary artist makes war his *tondo* by an analysis of the structure of *The Red Badge of Courage.* For Crane approached the subject of war as an artist, picking his materials for their fictional value. He was not reliving an experience, but creating one. (pp. 220-21)

Even the most sympathetic critics have been unable to call the book a unified whole. It has usually been passed off as an impressionistic novel. Edward Garnett speaks of the book as "a series of episodic scenes . . . it was not constructed in any sense of the word" [see excerpt dated 1921, *TCLC* 11, pp. 126-29]; H. L. Mencken thinks Crane "lacked the pedestrian talent for linking one situation to another."

It is true that many of Crane's effects are gained by recourse to an impressionistic method, a technique used by previous war writers to convey the sense of a vast battle scene. His combat descriptions are swiftly shifting impressions of action. Furthermore, he shows the influence of the impressionists in his dependence on color, the contrasts of light and shade. And his characters have a certain anonymity. Although Crane shows many of the realities of war, there is not as much careful detail in his novel as in De Forest's *Miss Ravenel's Conversion*. It is possible to apply the term impressionistic to one aspect of *The Red Badge of Courage:* certainly intensity and expressiveness are stressed—but not necessarily at the expense of symmetry and neatness. For an example of a fully impressionistic war novel, we need only consider Andreief's *The Red Laugh,* where disjointed and blurred fragments of combat are joined together to give a vast vision of horror.

It is equally an oversimplification to think of Crane's book merely in terms of naturalistic fiction. There are, to be sure, certain naturalistic doctrines that Crane follows. Some details appear to be chosen for their shock effect, like the corpse Henry finds in the forest—a sight that makes the dead bodies in Bierce seem pleasant by comparison. But the presence of the corpse is not arbitrary. It fits into the youth-to-experience theme, teaching Henry to understand death as something ghastly—not noble. Henry's salvation comes from a newfound sense of dedication to life and beauty after he has understood the ugliness of death. When he finally risks his life in battle, after having viewed the disgusting corpse, he knows what death involves.

One aspect of naturalism that had already appeared in the war fiction of Bierce and Rudyard Kipling is the double process of animation of mechanical objects and depersonalization of human beings. Crane's novel is packed with parallels between the animal and human worlds. His picture of war shows the iron and steel weapons in the role of flesh-and-blood inhabitants of the combat world. Even the battle flag, normally a symbol, takes on a more human dimension here. The flag struggles to free itself from an agony and finally falls with a gesture of despair.

The machines are humanized, and an abstraction like war itself is described as a red animal. Men, for their part, become either animals or machines. It is interesting to note how consistently Crane avoids physical descriptions of his characters and uses animal imagery to tell how men look in war. The regiment seems like "one of those moving monsters" or "crawling reptiles"; men are pigs, worms, cows, rats, kittens, etc. Fear makes Henry look like "a jaded horse," "a craven loon." War seems so brutally deterministic to Crane that it robs man of the free will and intelligence that differentiate him from the animals. For this reason the use of animal imagery is fitting for the naturalistic interpretation of war. The images reflect the belief that combat is the most savage pattern of human existence.

Crane's vision is basically ironic, perhaps not as sardonic as that of Bierce, but certainly bitter. He understands war in the naturalistic sense of involving the loss of individual initiative and motivation. The fatalism of war seems for a time to crush Henry. He compares himself to a squirrel who automatically must run away from danger in order to obey the law of survival of the fittest. Nature is apparently allied with the superior, intangible force that rules the world of war. One of the most illuminating passages that Crane cut out of the final version of the novel represents war in naturalistic terminology. "From his pinnacle of wisdom, he regarded the armies as large collections of dupes. Nature's dupes who were killing each other to carry out some great scheme of life." But when Henry succeeds in war, nature shines upon him benignly, and the book closes with a lyric description of the sun breaking through the clouds. Neither impressionism nor naturalism is the dominant mode for dealing with the world of war. We shall see that Henry's actions are those of a free individual.

Perhaps *The Red Badge of Courage* should be called an impressionistic-naturalistic novel—or vice-versa. Certainly Crane uses both manners throughout. The combination of a vivid, swift montage of combat impressions with a harsh, overwhelming, naturalistic picture of the individuals trapped in the war machine is Crane's method of fitting the combat world into fiction. The seminal quality of Crane's novel is more evident when one considers that Barbusse and Remarque, in writing of the incredible butchery of World War I, turn to a similar joining of impressionism for the overall battle picture and naturalism for the detail and characterization.

Robert Wooster Stallman comes closest to understanding the nature of the novel's structure. He describes *The Red Badge of Courage* [in his essay "Stephen Crane: A Revaluation"] as a series of fluctuations between hope and despair, a group of withdrawals and engagements. This is accurate, and we shall notice how Crane follows war's own pattern in his alterations between action and inaction.

There is evidence of much tighter control in Crane's war novel, however. Like the careful symmetry of *The Scarlet Letter*—which has scenes on the scaffold in chapters one, twelve, and twenty-four—so in the twenty-four chapters of *The Red Badge of Courage* there is a careful unfolding of plot; in the latter work there is a triple development.

The first section of the novel shows the dilemma of the youthful hero who feels, and then actually becomes, isolated from the group in war. Crane portrays the psychological journey of Henry Fleming from a foolish romantic pride, through the depths of fear, the first qualms of conscience, and a realization of his place in the military scheme—marked by his return to the regiment following the climactic wound he received in Chapter Twelve.

The same cycle is repeated, once he has rejoined his comrades. Now he interacts with the group as the regiment undergoes *its* test of fear and the recapture of confidence in combat. Finally, the regiment and Henry act as veterans in a successful skirmish. The *Bildungsroman* ends, on the scaffold, as it were, with the young man from the provinces altered and matured by war but still an ambiguous figure who has come to terms with the realities of the world through which he has made his picaresque way to knowledge. Like a lesser Melville, Crane deals with the ambiguities of character, and the battlefield, instead of a ship, is his world.

Henry Fleming's progression, on the most obvious level, is from fear to courage. Crane also extends the meaning of war and its impact upon the hero to a more involved moral nexus. Before he joins the army, Henry is a romantic dreamer, inspired by visions of a chivalric type of warfare in which he becomes a mighty hero. The immediate shock of training destroys any Homeric view of war, but Crane shows, in the book's only flashback out of the immediate war situation, the pre-war dreams of the youth. Like the child in Bierce's "Chickamauga," Henry has been brought up on books and pictures of battle. Crane fixes the pattern of the esthetic young man off to the wars—a figure that was to become a stereotype in the fiction of two world conflicts. Henry enlists in a haze of glorious aspiration that is undercut only by his mother's sober, sad advice. Through Henry's posturing, his ability to conjure a vague smile from a female student into an idealized vision of the girl he left behind

him, Crane establishes the character of a sensitive, highly imaginative youth. As Herman Melville wrote, "All wars are boyish and are fought by boys." It is to be expected that Henry's illusions will die hard.

When the rumor of impending action reaches the waiting army, Henry withdraws to worry about the necessity of proving his courage, since he knows nothing about himself as far as war is concerned. He must prove himself in the heat of combat, in the destructive element. Just before the first engagement, Henry gives way to pure hysteria, believing that he is in a trap and being led to certain death. His feeling of persecution is replaced by a wild, animal rage, once the actual combat commences; when the first lull comes, Henry believes he has passed his test. The mercurial youth is in an ecstasy of self-satisfaction. "So it was all over at last! The supreme trial had been passed. The red, formidable difficulties of war had been vanquished."

The author, however, equates war to life, and the reality of battle is made to parallel the reality of human existence where the mere passing of one test does not remove the possibility of other tests being imposed. In war the process is speeded up. Under the shock of the enemy's second attack, Henry protests, gives in to panic, and finally flees in fear. He reaches his low point of cowardice here. From this point on his emotional movement is forward, to a rebirth of courage.

After his communion with nature in the forest, Henry starts back towards the holocaust, fully realizing the irony involved in such a return to danger. He still retains his vague dreams of leading heroic charges, but once he has come back to his regiment—half way through the novel—the fear motif of *The Red Badge of Courage* is completed. For the remainder of the book the hero is sure of himself, even over-confident; and by the end of the story he has become a war devil, exulting in action, capturing a flag, and receiving praise from his superiors. Taken as simply [in Crane's words] a "psychological portrayal of fear," the novel is not only ironic, it is amoral. The successful hero has only learned that he is not particularly cowardly. Incisive as his probing of the hero's neurotic fright is, Stephen Crane has much more to say about the influence of combat upon the inexperienced participant.

The essential quality of Crane's novel cannot be derived from the study of one man's response to war. War has presented, among other things, a highly developed social problem ever since the days of individual combat were over. The gradation of the army system and its rigid chain of command combine with the massive troop movements of modern warfare to make combat a reflection of a special society with its own precise rules of conformity. And as Mark Schorer has pointed out, any novel must find a form that will encompass both the individual and social experiences.

It may not be immediately obvious that *The Red Badge of Courage* is more than the story of the young soldier who is Crane's hero and point-of-view character. The author does not try to describe his individuals fully. We do not even know the youth's whole name until Chapter Twelve. Taking Crane's novel on its own terms, we need not expect rounded figures, logically described, having past histories; neither should we overlook Henry Fleming's comrades in the war situation.

Henry comes into close contact with five other soldiers in his passage from apprenticeship to mastery. Of these, the tall soldier, Jim Conklin, is most important. Henry identifies with Conklin's calm attitude when faced with combat and attempts to accept his steadying advice. The death of Conklin has particular meaning to the hero; just as in Crane's story, **"The Open Boat,"** the stronger personality does not survive the test. The loud soldier, Wilson, a foil to Henry's fears at the start, undergoes a similar, and even more rapid, growth to manhood through the ordeal. The attitude of the somewhat anonymous lieutenant, Hasbrouck, reflects the hero's place in the military society. When Henry is a coward, the officer strikes at him with a sword, but when the youth is fighting well, he and the lieutenant are filled with mutual admiration.

Two more figures, shadowy ones to be sure, but still vividly realized, provide a commentary on the soldier's progress. Direct opposites, the tattered soldier whom Henry leaves wandering blindly in a field, and the cheery stranger who guides Henry back to his regiment, signify respectively betrayal and comradeship. The interaction of the hero with these five characters and the regiment as a whole furnishes the fundamental theme of *The Red Badge of Courage.* The standards by which Henry's development is measured are those of group loyalty rather than fear and courage. Although the secondary characters are typed, and meant to be so, and not sharply individualized, they are still effectively presented.

The novel opens on the large picture of the entire fighting force. "The cold passed reluctantly from the earth and the retiring fogs revealed an army stretched out on the hills, resting." As in a motion-picture opening, the scene gradually focuses on a particular group of soldiers—Conklin doing his washing, Wilson arguing violently, and then on Henry in a solitude of self-mistrust.

The key to Henry's development, and the essential meaning of war for him, comes in the flashback to his farewell from his mother. The importance of this scene is not in his mother's adjuration to do his duty bravely, nor in the general anti-romantic atmosphere of cows and socks, but in her words that remind the youth of his own insignificance in the larger scheme. "Yer jest one little feller amongst a hull lot of others, and yeh've got to keep quiet an' do what they tell yeh. I know how you are, Henry." She knows, but he must learn in battle what kind of a man he is.

Henry's vanity does not allow him to be a little fellow among a whole lot of others except in the rare moments of rationalization when he comforts himself with the consideration that he is part of a vast blue demonstration. Because abstract judgment fails him in his fear, he is isolated. Crane stresses Henry's feeling of solitude. He has no one with whom to compare suspicions; he is different, "alone in space," "a mental outcast." Both the calm competence of the tall soldier and the brash assurance of the loud soldier convince Henry that his is a unique weakness.

When the regiment advances for its baptism of fire, Henry is a part of the group, albeit unwillingly. He feels himself carried along by a mob. The image Crane uses to signify Henry's attitude of helplessness is important. ". . . there were iron laws of tradition and law [sic] on four sides. He was in a moving box." He is doing exactly what his mother warned him against, considering himself an important individual. He hates the lieutenant and believes that only he, Henry, knows that the entire regiment is being betrayed. In other words, the youth revolts against the iron laws of the war world, the traditions of obedience and humility in the ranks. Crane plays off Henry's condition of rage against Jim Conklin's faithful acceptance of the new environment. The other soldiers are shadowy figures in Henry's mind, since his ego has denied him the comforts of military friendships. He is too wrapped up in himself to realize that others are in the same condition of doubt and fear.

A sudden shift in emphasis takes place when the battle starts, as Henry rapidly adjusts to reality. Losing concern with himself for the moment, he becomes "not a man but a member," a part of a "common personality," a "mysterious fraternity." Whereas in his isolation and doubt he was trapped in a moving box, now, by sinking his personality into the larger personality of the group, he regains control of himself. Crane describes Henry's combat activity with the same box image as before, but there is one important difference. Henry is now in charge. "He was like a carpenter who has made many boxes, making still another box. . . ."

Crane transfers the point of view from Henry to the regiment at this juncture. In the impressionistic battle scene, the focus is on "the men," "they," "a soldier" while the regiment goes about its grim business. An integral part of Henry's development is the realization that even the regiment is not the only important participant in the battle. He understands that the fighting involves many regiments and momentarily grasps the idea of his own relative unimportance. But Crane is too acute a psychologist to conceive such a rapid character change and have Henry learn the soldier's hardest lesson easily. When the break in the combat comes, Henry reverts to his pride and considers his rather petty action to have been magnificent. He must undergo a more serious test before he can reap the full benefits of his war experience.

The second attack is too much for him. Henry cannot comprehend the rules of war that are so irrational as to impose another test so soon. He deserts the group, and by this act he breaks all the rigid rules of war. The sight of the lieutenant, angrily dabbing at him with his sword, symbolizes for Henry his new role as an outcast. The youth is no longer, in the Conradian sense, one of them. He asks himself, "What manner of men were they anyhow?", those fools who stayed behind to meet certain death.

The novel is not merely a portrait of fear; it is the portrait of a mind that learns to come to terms with itself and to live down an act of cowardice. Henry Fleming must become a man according to the rules war sets forth. Therefore, he must cast off the egoism that made him run, and gain a true perspective on his importance.

The book is often ironic, since his growth is neither particularly moral nor is it without fluctuations. Henry's failures and successes in war are those of a hero *manqué*, if we are to measure them by the usual Christian ethic. But *The Red Badge of Courage* is a war novel, and Henry Fleming should be judged by the ideals of a war world. The lesson Henry has to learn is basic to combat. The individual cannot depend on his personal reasoning powers. Henry's mind has seen the danger and he has fled, while his stupid comrades have stayed and shown courage. The beginning of wisdom comes with the comprehension that his own judgment is insufficient. He is in the position of a criminal because of his enlightened intellect. Henry feels the bitterness and rage of an outcast, a sensitive dreamer who, trapped between romance and reality, can make the best of neither world. Caught in a box of his own making, Henry faces the age-old problem of the individual at odds with society. He has not only indulged in an act of self-betrayal, he has thrown over his responsibilities to and for the others. He does not yet understand that his own salvation (physical and spiritual) must be the product of his dedication to universal salvation. Henry's story is not tragic, because, unlike Lord Jim, the young soldier manages to compensate for his anti-social action and work his way back to the fellowship of men which, in the world of war, is represented by the regiment. But the road back is not easy.

After his dark night of the soul passed in the forest where nature appears to second war's cruelty, Henry commences his return to the battle—to life or death. The physical isolation of the youth ends when he meets a line of wounded soldiers staggering towards the rear, soldiers coming out of the active world from which Henry had fled. Henry joins the crowd, but he remains an outsider, for he has no wound. Crane reverses the symbolism of Hawthorne's *The Scarlet Letter* or ''The Minister's Black Veil.'' Henry is distinguished by his *lack* of any mark. ''He was continually casting sidelong glances to see if the men were contemplating the letters of guilt he felt burned into his brow. . . . He wished that he, too, had a wound, a red badge of courage.'' Ironically enough, he desires to be marked by the red death he had feared. Honor, or the appearance of honor, is his new goal.

As if to emphasize his sin, Henry remains with the denizens of the strange world of wounded. He meets the tattered man, one of Crane's most brilliant portraits of a nameless figure. We know nothing about the tattered man except that he is wounded, and that he is a rather naïve and gentle soul. He is the antithesis of the young soldier in every way. The tattered man has been hit; he talks proudly of his regiment and its performance; he is humble and loves the army. In other words, he stands for the simple man who has done his duty and received his mark of honor. The tattered man represents society, and to the conscience-stricken Henry the wounded solider is a reminder of guilt. Henry cannot remain with the tattered man when he asks the probing question, ''Where yeh hit, ol' boy?'', that emphasizes the youth's isolation.

A greater shock is in store for Henry Fleming. After he leaves his tattered companion behind, he meets the spectral soldier—the tall soldier, Jim Conklin—transformed by a fatal wound. Henry's feeble wish for a little wound pales into the realm of bathos in comparison to Conklin's passion. The dying man's expression of sympathy and concern for Henry adds to the acute discomfort of the youth's position. In his walk through the valley of the shadow of death at Conklin's side, Henry's education advances. Conklin's death brings home to Henry the true nature of war, brutal and forbidding, more than the sight of an unknown corpse in the forest could do. The body of his friend stretched out before him, Henry curses the universe that allows such things to be. He shakes his fist at the battlefield and swears, but his insignificance in the larger scheme is indicated by Crane's most famous line, ''The red sun was pasted in the sky like a wafer.''

Despite his genuine grief at Conklin's death, Henry is unable to accept responsibility for the tattered man, who has returned to pry at Henry's guilty secret, the crime ''concealed in his bosom.'' He deserts the tattered man a second time, and in denying him the young soldier commits his real sin. He breaks both a Christian and a military ethical rule (''Greater love hath no man. . . .''). Like his original act of cowardice, this desertion goes unpunished. If we are to read the novel as a study in irony, there is no confusion; Henry is a sinner who succeeds in war without ever changing his ways. Crane's attitude towards his hero is ambiguous throughout the novel, however, and the betrayal of the tattered man is essential to Henry's growth to maturity. Although the tattered man himself says

that ''a man's first allegiance is to number one,'' Henry realizes what he has done. His later heroism is a successful attempt to wipe out his cowardice. While he eventually rationalizes his betrayal, the memory of the tattered man blocks any real return to the egocentric immaturity that marked his character at the outset of the novel.

He heads back to the ''furnace'' of combat, since the heat of that purgatory is clearly more desirable than the icy chill of solitude. His progress is halting. Henry is unable to throw off his romantic visions; he imagines his new self in a picturesque and sublime role as a leader of lurid charges. Once again the reality of war breaks his dreams apart, reality in the forms of physical exhaustion, thirst, and the memory of his cowardice. No longer a visionary, Henry can now make his way through the war world.

Crane's bitterness comes to the surface in this part of the novel. Henry is really worried about appearance. How can he pretend to be something he is not—a hero? It is when the self-centered youth is concerned with the difficulty of fabricating a lie effective enough to account for his disappearance that his full name is given for the first time by the author. The young soldier mentions it in apprehension of the name, ''Henry Fleming,'' becoming a synonym for coward. Names and appearances are his only concern.

Henry Fleming's actions must be judged by the standards of war. While he is planning his lie (a sin, from a normal ethical viewpoint), fate, in the form of a hysterical soldier who clubs Henry out of the way, provides the wound that not only preserves the appearance of his integrity but also opens the way for his attainment of genuine honor. It is ironic, even cynical, for war to help Henry after he has broken the rules, and for the coward to pass as a hero. Two other points must be kept in mind, however. Crane constantly refers to his hero as ''the youth,'' and despite his transgressions, Henry is still an innocent fumbling for the correct path, not a hardened sinner. Furthermore, he does not receive his wound in flight, but in the performance of an act of courage! Henry is struck down (by a coward) while inarticulately striving ''to make a rallying speech, to sing a battle hymn.'' He is in a position to suffer such a wound because he has originally fled from his regiment, but he is going against the current of retreating infantry, *towards* the battle, when he gains the red badge. The wound, then, may be seen as the result of heroism, not cowardice, and the irony is vitiated. Henry has escaped from his nightmare of weakness before he is wounded. His own efforts have proved him not completely unworthy of the saving grace granted him by the fate of war.

The wounded Henry is again part of the fellowship of armed men. ''The owner of the cheery voice,'' who plays Mr. Strongheart in Henry's progress, guides the dazed youth through the forest wasteland back to the regiment. The gratuitous support of the cheery man is in direct contrast to Henry's earlier refusal to accompany the tattered man. The first twelve chapters of the novel come to an end with Henry outlined in the reflection of his regiment's campfires. The return to the company, which in war fiction has stood for homecoming from Kipling's ''The Man Who Was'' to Jones's *From Here to Eternity,* marks the completion of Henry Fleming's isolation and the start of the conquest of glory for himself and the regiment.

The hero of Crane's war novel has not yet learned what the author is in a later story to call ''virtue in war.'' His relief at the arrival back into the ''low-arched hall'' of the forest (a suggestion perhaps of the mead hall of the Old English epics, the symbol of the fellowship of strong warriors) is intense. He views the sleeping company with complacency because to all appearances he is one of them, since he performed his mistakes in the dark. In the second part of the novel Henry will come to understand war and his own nature. For the present, it is enough to go to sleep with his fellows. "He gave a long sigh, snuggled down into his blanket, and in a moment was like his comrades."

Only Joseph Conrad, of the multitude of Crane's critics, grasps the essential duality of *The Red Badge of Courage.* Conrad seems to realize that Henry Fleming *and* the regiment are in the same position. "In order that the revelation should be complete, the young soldier has to be deprived of the moral support which he would have found in a tried body of men matured in achievement to the consciousness of its worth." Conrad pinpoints the idea that the maturation process does not affect the hero alone. "Apart from the imaginative analysis of his own temperament tried by the emotions of a battlefield, Stephen Crane dealt in his book with the psychology of the mass . . .". The remainder of the novel treats the group that Henry has rejoined.

Although Crane's narrative technique still enforces the use of Henry as the point-of-view character, the youth is attentive to others as well as himself. Wilson, the former loud soldier, has been altered by his day of combat from a blatant, self-confident boy to a calm, quietly self-reliant soldier who is proud of the regiment. In order to perfect his relationship with Wilson and the other soldiers, Henry must try to understand their sources of fear and courage.

When the regiment goes into action on the second day, Crane focuses on the whole body, giving equal space to anonymous soldiers' complaints, the lieutenant's anger, and the serious determination of Wilson and Henry. The young soldier sinks himself completely into the business of battle and transfers his doubts and dreams into a savage hate of the enemy. If Crane indicated the importance of Henry's wound by giving his full name for the first time, here he emphasizes the youth's continuing growth as a human being by describing him physically. As Henry thinks less of himself, he becomes more of an individual in the pages of the novel. He fights well in this battle and becomes a hero in the eyes of his regiment.

The personal insignificance that Henry discovered applied to himself in the first section of the novel, now appears to fit the regiment which Crane describes in terms similar to those he earlier utilized for the young soldier. "The world was fully interested in other matters. Apparently, the regiment had its small affair to itself."

Henry and the regiment undergo another severe exposure to fire in their first charge. Crane describes the mass movement brilliantly, transferring the attention from the youth to the men, and back. The crucial episode is the same for all of them, "a temporary but sublime absence of selfishness."

The regiment falters in the confusion of the attack; the men go through Henry's former mental turmoil. "Here, crouching and cowering behind some trees, the men clung with desperation . . . the whole affair seemed incomprehensible to many of them." The advance is saved by the courage and leadership of three men: the lieutenant, Wilson, and Henry. They lead the regiment forward, and symbolically Henry takes over as flag-bearer, participating in the combat in the absolute center of the group, the one position that more than any other rep-

resents the mass spirit. When the regiment is forced to retreat, Henry feels *their* shame as acutely as he felt *his* earlier. (Formerly he was selfish enough to pray for the army's defeat so his cowardice might go unnoticed.) He harangues his comrades, striving to save the regiment's reputation.

The regiment turns and drives the enemy back; it passes its test. Henry is free from doubt and fear because he has committed himself to the larger unit. By losing himself in the mass, he has found himself. To the same extent, the regiment has conquered its panic and irresolution. "The impetus of enthusiasm was theirs again. They gazed about them with looks of uplifted pride, feeling new trust in the grim, always confident, weapons in their hands. And they were men."

The final stage of development in war for Henry and the regiment involves the learning of the veterans' virtues—calmness and workmanlike efficiency. The young soldier is an observer in the last attack, a tiny player in a huge, impressionistic drama. Before, as a coward, he was the god-like center of a tiny stage; now, as a good soldier, he is absorbed into the regimental chorus. Henry loses all sense of individuality. "He did not know that he breathed; that the flag hung silently over him, so absorbed was he."

Crane makes much of the fact that when the regiment is pinned down by enemy fire, Henry—the veteran—knows that the only thing to do is to return to the attack. To hang back would mean annihilation; to retreat would build up the enemy's spirit. Henry has assimilated the rules of war. Now his thoughts and emotional responses are the proper ones, forgetful of self in the face of duty. His companions, too, respond automatically to the necessities of battle, the facts of military life. The climax of *The Red Badge of Courage* comes as the regiment and its flag-bearer, without regard to vanities, charge once more and victoriously overrun the enemy's position. They have all passed the test.

The last chapter of the novel is an artfully contrived anticlimax. The regiment marches on; the author's attention is again directed to his hero. Henry has proved his courage; he has even been singled out for praise by the colonel. "He had dwelt in a land of strange, squalling upheavals and had come forth. He had been where there was red of blood and black of passion, and he was escaped." Were the novel to end here on this note of rejoicing and pride, an ironic reading of the book would be justified. Henry would be a mock hero, a Jonathan Wild. Henry cannot forget the tattered soldier, however, whom Crane characterizes in lyrically sentimental language, ". . . he who, gored by bullets and faint for blood, had fretted concerning an imagined wound in another . . . he who, blind with weariness and pain, had been deserted in the field." Again Henry considers himself a moral leper. He is filled with concern lest his comrades realize his secret sin.

Crane cancelled the passage that explains Henry's final rationalization of the betrayal, but these omitted words help to explain the moral construction of the book. "At last, he concluded that he saw in it quaint uses. He exclaimed that its importance in the aftertime would be great to him if it even succeeded in hindering the workings of his egotism. . . . He would have upon him often the consciousness of a great mistake. And he would be taught to deal gently and with care. He would be a man."

These last words, a repetition of those applied earlier to the regiment, show that Henry has matured as an individual and a member of society. Henry has learned the nature of fear and battle. "He had been to touch the great death, and found that, after all, it was but the great death." More important, he has learned the essence of man's duty to man, as well as the fact that life (like war) is not a romantic dream but a matter of compromises. Perhaps there is an element of irony, since he has not become a "good" man, but he has done a "good" act—in the terms of the war world—by displaying courage and self-abnegation in the final skirmish. At least war has shown the young soldier his real self, and the acquisition of self-knowledge is no small accomplishment. Henry has become a new man who views life in a fresh framework, aimed not towards glory but a job to be done. Glory is pleasant but irrelevant. In the final scenes of *The Red Badge of Courage,* Henry takes full responsibility for his life; he is no longer an automaton. His properly disciplined ego comprehends the nature of obedience and action. And the development of his inner life is paralleled by that of the regiment.

The novel ends with a sweeping peroration, hailing Henry as a part of the procession of weary soldiers, a part of the regiment that has proved itself worthy of the army just as he has proved himself an individual worthy of inclusion in the group. They have all succeeded in the war which telescopes such a tremendous amount of experience into a brief moment. "Over the river a golden ray of sun came through the hosts of leaden rain clouds." (pp. 221-34)

> Eric Solomon, "The Structure of 'The Red Badge of Courage'," in Modern Fiction Studies, Vol. 5, No. 3, Autumn, 1959, pp. 220-34.

HAROLD R. HUNGERFORD (essay date 1963)

[*Hungerford is an American educator. In the following excerpt, he locates the historical basis of* The Red Badge of Courage *in the Battle of Chancellorsville, Va., May 2-3, 1863.*]

The name of the battle in which Henry Fleming achieved his manhood is never given in *The Red Badge of Courage.* Scholars have not agreed that the battle even ought to have a name; some have implied that it is a potpourri of episodes from a number of battles. Yet an examination of the evidence leads to the conclusion that the battle does have a name—Chancellorsville. (p. 520)

Evidence of two sorts makes the initial hypothesis that Crane used Chancellorsville probable. In the first place, Crane said so in his short story **"The Veteran,"** which was published less than a year after *The Red Badge.* In this story he represented an elderly Henry Fleming as telling about his fear and flight in his first battle. "That was at Chancellorsville," Henry said. His brief account is consistent in every respect with the more extended account in *The Red Badge;* old Henry's motives for flight were those of the young Henry, and he referred to Jim Conklin in a way which made it clear that Jim was long since dead.

This brief reference in **"The Veteran"** is, so far as I know, the only direct indication Crane ever gave that the battle in *The Red Badge* was Chancellorsville. He appears never to have mentioned the matter in his letters, and his biographers recount no references to it. (pp. 520-21)

No one questions that *The Red Badge* is about the Civil War; the references to Yanks and Johnnies, to blue uniforms on one side and to gray and butternut on the other clearly establish this fact. If we turn now to military history, we find that the evidence of place and time points directly to Chancellorsville.

Only three actual place-names are used in the book: Washington, Richmond, and the Rappahannock River. Henry Fleming and his fellow-soldiers had come through Washington to their winter quarters near the Rappahannock River, and their army was close enough to Richmond that cavalry could move against that city. Such a combination points to northern Virginia, through which the Rappahannock flows, to which Union soldiers would come through Washington, and from which Richmond would be readily accessible. Chancellorsville was fought in northern Virginia.

Furthermore, the battle was the first major engagement of the year, occurring when the spring rains were nearly over. The year cannot be 1861; the war began in April, and soldiers would not have spent the winter in camp. Nor can it be 1862; the first eastern battle of 1862, part of McClellan's Peninsular Campaign, in no way resembled that in the book and was far removed from the Rappahannock. It cannot be 1864; the Battle of the Wilderness was fought near the Rappahannock but did not end in a Union defeat. Its strategy was in any case significantly different from that of the battle in *The Red Badge.* Finally, 1865 is ruled out; Lee had surrendered by the time the spring rains ended.

If we are to select any actual conflict at all, a *reductio ad absurdum* indicates the first eastern battle of 1863, and that battle was Chancellorsville. Moreover, 1863 marked the turning-point in the Union fortunes; before Gettysburg the South had, as Wilson remarked in *The Red Badge,* licked the North "about every clip." After Gettysburg no Union soldier would have been likely to make such a statement; and Gettysburg was the next major battle after Chancellorsville. (pp. 521-22)

The events preceding the battle occupy the first two chapters and part of the third. The opening chapter establishes the situation of the Union army. As winter passed into spring, that army was resting in winter camp across a river from a Confederate army. It had been there for some time—long enough for soldiers to build huts with chimneys, long enough for a new recruit to have been encamped for some months without seeing action. ". . . there had come months of monotonous life in a camp. . . . since his regiment had come to the field the army had done little but sit still and try to keep warm." Such was the situation of the Army of the Potomac in April, 1863; it had spent a cold, wet winter encamped at Falmouth, Virginia, on the north bank of the Rappahannock River opposite the Confederate army. The army had been inactive since mid-December; its men had dug themselves into just such huts, covered with folded tents and furnished with clay chimneys, as Crane describes. Furthermore, the arrival of a new Union commander, General Joseph Hooker, had meant hour after hour of drill and review for the soldiers; and Henry was "drilled and drilled and reviewed, and drilled and drilled and reviewed."

To this monotony the "tall soldier"—Jim Conklin—brought the news that "The cavalry started this morning. . . . They say there ain't hardly any cavalry left in camp. They're going to Richmond, or some place, while we fight all the Johnnies. It's some dodge like that." He had earlier announced, "We're goin' t' move t'-morrah—sure. . . . We're goin' 'way up th' river, cut across, an' come around in behint 'em." Of course Jim was "the fast-flying messenger of a mistake," but the mistake was solely one of dates; the infantry did not move at once. Many soldiers at Falmouth jumped to Jim's conclusion when eleven thousand cavalrymen left camp April 13 for a raid on the Confederate railroad lines near Richmond. No one in the book denied that the cavalry had left; and Jim's analysis

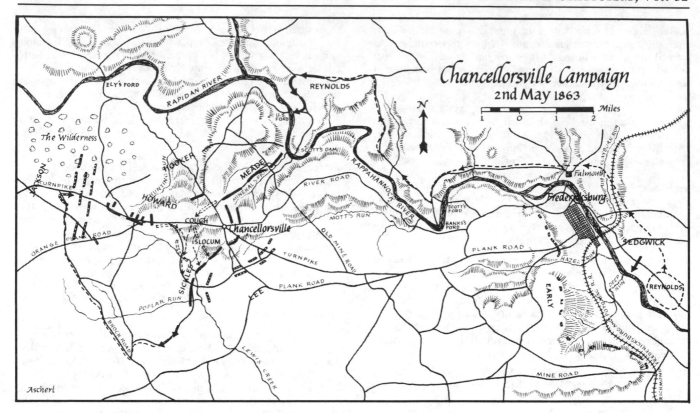

The Battle of Chancellorsville, May 2, 1863: Jackson's troops attack Howard's XI Corps (left). According to scholars, this encounter served as the model for the rout witnessed by Henry Fleming in Chapter Twelve of The Red Badge of Courage.

of the flank movement was to be confirmed at the end of the book when another soldier said, ''Didn't I tell yeh we'd come aroun' in behint 'em? Didn't I tell yeh so?'' The strategy Jim had predicted was precisely that of Chancellorsville.

The Union army at Falmouth did not leave camp for two weeks after the departure of the cavalry, and such a period accords with the time represented in the book; ''for days'' after the cavalry left, Henry fretted about whether or not he would run.

Finally Henry's regiment, the 304th New York, was assembled, and it began to march before dawn. When the sun rose, ''the river was not in view.'' Since the rising sun was at the backs of the marching men, they were going west. The eager soldiers ''expressed commiseration for that part of the army which had been left upon the river bank.'' That night the regiment encamped; tents were pitched and fires lighted. ''When another night came,'' the men crossed a river on *two* pontoon bridges and continued unmolested to a camping place.

This description fits aptly the march of the Second Corps. Many of its regiments were mustered before dawn on April 28, and then marched west and away from the Rappahannock. The Second, unlike the other corps marching to Chancellorsville, was ordered not to make any special secret of its whereabouts and was allowed fires when it camped. The Second crossed the Rappahannock on *two* pontoon bridges the evening of April 30 and camped safely near Chancellorsville that night; all the other corps had to ford at least one river, without the convenience of bridges. Furthermore, by no means all of the army moved at once; two full corps and one division of the Second Corps were left behind at Falmouth to conduct a holding action against Lee.

It is clear from the text that at least one day intervened between the evening on which Henry's regiment crossed the bridges and the morning of its first day of fighting. If Crane was following the chronology of Chancellorsville, this intervening day of pensive rest was May 1, on which only the Fifth and Twelfth Corps saw fighting.

Action began early for Henry's regiment the next day, the events of which parallel those at Chancellorsville on May 2. The statements about what Henry and his regiment did are clear enough. He was rudely awakened at dawn, ran down a wood road, and crossed a little stream. His regiment was moved three times before the noon meal, and then moved again; one of these movements took Henry and his companions back, for in the afternoon they proceeded over the same ground they had taken that morning and then into new territory. By early afternoon, then, Henry had seen no fighting. At last a brigade ahead of them went into action; it was routed and fled, leaving the reserves, of which Henry's regiment was a part, to withstand the enemy. The regiment successfully resisted the first charge, but when the enemy reattacked, Henry fled.

It might seem that tracing the path of Henry and his regiment before his flight would not be impossible, but it has proved to be so. The regimental movements which Crane describes loosely parallel the movements of many regiments at Chancellorsville; they directly parallel the movements of none. Nevertheless, broad parallels do exist. Many regiments of the Second Corps moved southeast from Chancellorsville on May 2; many of them first encountered the enemy in midafternoon.

Furthermore, it can be demonstrated that the 304th, like the regiments of the Second Corps, was near the center of the

Union line. In the first place, the "cheery man" tells Henry, and us, so. His testimony deserves some credence; anyone who can so unerringly find a regiment in the dark should know what he is talking about. Moreover, the conversation of the soldiers before the assault makes it clear that they were not facing the rebel right, which would have been opposite the Union left. Nor were they far to the Union right, as I shall show later.

The evidence given us by the terrain Henry crossed also points to a position at about the center of the Union line. During the morning and early afternoon he crossed several streams and passed into and out of cleared fields and dense woods. The land was gently rolling; there were occasional fences and now and then a house. Such topographical features, in 1863, characterized the area south and east of Chancellorsville itself. Further east, in the area held by the Union left, the terrain opened up and the dense second-growth forest thinned out; further west the forest was very thick indeed, with few fields or other open areas. But southeast of Chancellorsville, where the Union center was located, the land was cultivated to a degree; fields had been cleared and cut off from the forest by fences. Topography so conditioned action at Chancellorsville that every historian of the battle perforce described the terrain; if Crane knew the battle as well as I suggest he did, he must have known its topography.

Topography also gives us our only clue to the untraceable path of Henry's flight. At one point he "found himself almost into a swamp. He was obliged to walk upon bog tufts, and watch his feet to keep from the oil water." A man fleeing west from the center of the Union line would have encountered swamps after a few miles of flight. The detail is perhaps minor, but it corroborates the path Henry had to follow to reach the place where he received his "red badge of courage." He went west, toward the Union right held by the Eleventh Corps.

Henry's flight led him to the path of the retreating wounded soldiers, among them Jim Conklin. The scene of Jim's death contains no localizing evidence, for Crane was concentrating upon the men, not their surroundings. Nevertheless, it is appropriate to Chancellorsville; the roads leading to the river were clogged with retreating Union wounded in the late afternoon of May 2. There were no ambulances near the battle lines, and many wounded men died as they walked.

By contrast, the scene of Henry's wound can be readily fixed. He received it in the middle of the most-discussed single action of the battle, an action which cost Stonewall Jackson his life and a major general his command, almost surely won the battle for Lee, and generated thirty-five years of acrimonious debate. Even today, to mention Chancellorsville is inevitably to bring up the rout of the Eleventh Corps.

About sunset on May 2, 1863, Stonewall Jackson's crack troops attacked the predominantly German Eleventh Corps. The Eleventh, which was on the extreme right of the Union line and far from the fighting, was taken wholly by surprise, and many soldiers turned and ran in terrified disorder. The result was near-catastrophe for the Union; now that Jackson's men had turned the flank, the path lay open for an assault on the entire unprotected rear of the Union army.

Appropriately enough for such a battle, Jackson's men were halted by one of history's more extraordinary military maneuvers. For in a battle in which hardly any cavalry were used, a small detachment of cavalrymen held Jackson's corps off long enough to enable artillery to be dragged into place and charged with canister. The cavalrymen could do so because the dense woods confined Jackson's men to the road. The small detachment was the Eighth Pennsylvania Cavalry; the time was between 6:30 and 7 P.M. Theirs was the only cavalry charge at Chancellorsville, and it became famous not only because it had saved the Union army—perhaps even the Union—but also because no two observers could agree on its details; any historian is therefore obliged to give the charge considerable attention.

All these elements fit the time and place of Henry's wounding. Night was falling fast after his long afternoon of flight; "landmarks had vanished into the gathered gloom." All about Henry "very burly men" were fleeing from the enemy. "They sometimes gabbled insanely. One huge man was asking of the sky, 'Say, where de plank road? Where de plank road?'" A popular stereotype holds that all Germans are burly, and an unsympathetic listener could regard rapidly-spoken German as "gabbling." Certainly the replacement of *th* by *d* fits the pattern of Germans; Crane's Swede in **"The Veteran"** also lacks *th*. These might be vulgar errors, but they identified a German pretty readily in the heyday of dialect stories. Furthermore, plank roads were rare in northern Virginia; but a plank road ran through the Union lines toward the Rappahannock.

One of these fleeing Germans hit Henry on the head; and after he received his wound, whle he was still dazed, Henry saw the arrival of the cavalry and of the artillery:

> Around him he could hear the grumble of jolted cannon as the scurrying horses were lashed toward the front. . . . He turned and watched the mass of guns, men, and horses sweeping in a wide curve toward a gap in a fence. . . . Into the unspeakable jumble in the roadway rode a squadron of cavalry. The faded yellow of their facings shone bravely. There was a mighty altercation.

As Henry fled the scene, he could hear the guns fire and the opposing infantry fire back. "There seemed to be a great ruck of men and munitions spread about in the forest and in the fields."

Every element of the scene is consistent with contemporary descriptions of the rout of the Eleventh Corps. The time is appropriate; May 2 was the first real day of battle at Chancellorsville as it was the first day for Henry. The place is appropriate; if Henry had begun the day in the Union center and then had fled west through the swamps, he would have come toward the right of the Union line, where the men of the Eleventh Corps were fleeing in rout. The conclusion is unavoidable: Crane's use of the factual framework of Chancellorsville led him to place his hero in the middle of that battle's most important single action.

The first day of battle in *The Red Badge* ended at last when the cheery man found Henry, dazed and wandering, and led him back to his regiment by complicated and untraceable paths.

The second day of battle, like the first, began early. Henry's regiment was sent out "to relieve a command that had lain long in some damp trenches." From these trenches could be heard the noise of skirmishers in the woods to the front and left, and the din of battle to the right was tremendous. Again, such a location fits well enough the notion of a center regiment; the din on the right, in the small hours of May 3, would have come from Jackson's men trying to re-establish their connection with the main body of Lee's army.

Soon, however, Henry's regiment was withdrawn and began to retreat from an exultant enemy; Hooker began such a withdrawal about 7:30 A.M. on May 3. Finally the retreat stopped and almost immediately thereafter Henry's regiment was sent on a suicidal charge designed to prevent the enemy from breaking the Union lines. This charge significantly resembles that of the 124th New York, a regiment raised principally in the county which contains Port Jervis, Crane's hometown; and the time of this charge of the 124th—about 8:30 A.M.—fits the time-scheme of *The Red Badge* perfectly.

The next episode can be very precisely located; Crane's description is almost photographically accurate. Henry was about a quarter of a mile south of Fairview, the "slope on the left" from which the "long row of guns, gruff and maddened, denounc[ed] the enemy." Moreover, "in the rear of this row of guns stood a house, calm and white, amid bursting shells. A congregation of horses, tied to a railing, were tugging frenziedly at their bridles. Men were running hither and thither." This is a good impression of the Chancellor House, which was used as the commanding general's headquarters and which alone, in a battle at which almost no cavalry were present, had many horses belonging to the officers and orderlies tied near it.

The second charge of the 304th, just before the general retreat was ordered, is as untraceable as the first. It has, however, its parallel at Chancellorsville: several regiments of the Second Corps were ordered to charge the enemy about 10 A.M. on May 3 to give the main body of the army time to withdraw the artillery and to begin its retreat.

The two days of battle came to an end for Henry Fleming when his regiment was ordered to "retrace its way" and rejoined first its brigade and then its division on the way back toward the river. Such a retreat, in good order and relatively free from harassment by an exhausted enemy, began at Chancellorsville about 10 A.M. on May 3. Heavy rains again were beginning to make the roads into bogs; these rains prevented the Union soldiers from actually recrossing the river for two days, for the water was up to the level of several of the bridges. "It rained" in the penultimate paragraph of *The Red Badge;* and the battle was over for Henry Fleming as for thousands of Union soldiers at Chancellorsville. (pp. 522-29)

Two questions remain unanswered. First, why did Crane not identify the battle in *The Red Badge* as he did in **"The Veteran"**? One answer is fairly simple: no one called the battle Chancellorsville in the book because no one would have known it was Chancellorsville. No impression is more powerful to the reader of Civil War reports and memoirs than that officers and men seldom knew where they were. They did not know the names of hills, of streams, or even of villages. Probably not more than a few hundred of the 130,000 Union men at Chancellorsville knew until long afterwards the name of the four corners around which the battle raged. A private soldier knew his own experiences, but not names or strategy; we have been able to reconstruct the strategy and the name because Crane used a factual framework for his novel; and the anonymity of the battle is the result of that framework.

Of course the anonymity is part of Crane's artistic technique as well. We do not learn Henry Fleming's full name until Chapter II; we never learn Wilson's first name. Crane sought to give only so much detail as was necessary to the integrity of the book. He was not, like Zola and Tolstoi, concerned with the panorama of history and the fate of nations, but with the mind and actions of a youth unaccustomed to war. For such purposes, the name of the battle, like the names of men, did not matter; in fact, if Crane had named the battle he might

have evoked in the minds of his readers reactions irrelevant to his purpose, reactions which might have set the battle in its larger social and historical framework. It would have been a loss of control.

Why, with the whole Civil War available, should Crane have chosen Chancellorsville? Surely, in the first place, because he knew a good deal about it. Perhaps he had learned from his brother, [whom Thomas Beer has called] "an expert in the strategy of Gettysburg and Chancellorsville." More probably he had heard old soldiers talk about their war experiences while he was growing up. Many middle-aged men in Port Jervis had served in the 124th New York; Chancellorsville had been their first battle, and first impressions are likely to be the most vivid. It is hard to believe that men in an isolated small town could have resisted telling a hero-worshiping small boy about a great adventure in their lives.

Moreover, Chancellorsville surely appealed to Crane's sense of the ironic and the colorful. The battle's great charges, its moments of heroism, went only to salvage a losing cause; the South lost the war and gained only time from Chancellorsville; the North, through an incredible series of blunders, lost a battle it had no business losing. The dead, as always, lost the most. And when the battle ended, North and South were just where they had been when it began. There is a tragic futility about Chancellorsville just as there is a tragic futility to *The Red Badge*.

Finally, Chancellorsville served Crane's artistic purposes. It was the first battle of the year and the first battle for many regiments. It was therefore an appropriate introduction to war for a green soldier in an untried regiment.

The evidence of this study surely indicates that Crane was not merely a dreamer spinning fantasies out of his imagination; on the contrary, he was capable of using real events for his own fictional purposes with controlled sureness. Knowledge of the ways in which he did so is, I should think, useful to criticism. For various cogent reasons, Crane chose Chancellorsville as a factual framework within which to represent the dilemma of young Henry Fleming. Many details of the novel are clearly drawn from that battle; none are inconsistent with it. Old Henry Fleming was a truthful man: "that was at Chancellorsville." (pp. 529-31)

Harold R. Hungerford, " 'That Was at Chancellorsville': The Factual Framework of 'The Red Badge of Courage'," in American Literature, *Vol. XXXIV, No. 4, January, 1963, pp. 520-31.*

DONALD B. GIBSON (essay date 1968)

[*An American educator and critic, Gibson is the author of* The Fiction of Stephen Crane. *In the following excerpt from that study, he disputes a purely deterministic reading of* The Red Badge of Courage, *analyzing Henry Fleming's psychological development in order to demonstrate that the character transcends baser aspects of his nature through a conscious act of will.*]

We cannot easily rest with the conclusion that Henry has achieved nothing by the end of [*The Red Badge of Courage*], for there is too much in the novel itself which contradicts such a view. There is for instance the fact of Henry's change from one who flees danger to one who faces it squarely. In spite of the implications that he reverts to primitive subhuman response in acting heroically though in a totally nonconscious fashion, there are evidences of willed acts of heroism. In Chapter XVIII, when Henry and a friend go to seek water, they encounter the general of their division whom they overhear giving orders to a lower-ranking officer. Asked which troops he can spare to serve as cannon fodder in an effort to stop the enemy at a crucial point, the lower-ranking officer replies that he can best spare Henry's division because they are poor fighters. "I don't believe many of your mule drivers will get back," says the general. The conversation leads Henry and his friend to believe that their chances of surviving the coming action are extremely slight, still they return to their group, merely reporting that the regiment is going to charge the enemy, but omitting the information that a death trap awaits them.

> It was an ironical secret. Still, they saw no hesitation in each other's faces, and they nodded a mute and unprotesting assent when a shaggy man near them said in a meek voice, "We'll git swallowed."

Henry's decision to go into that battle indicates a conscious choice to risk the possibility of his own annihilation. Here is the conscious act of heroism.

Other evidence suggesting that Henry undergoes meaningful change is contained in one of the sections expunged by Crane in his manuscript, but reprinted in several recent editions of the novel. Of course it must be considered external evidence. However, it clearly shows Crane's unsuccessful effort to unify the disparate themes of his novel, and it supports the contention that Henry achieves significant growth during the tale because it stands in support of so much that has gone before. The tone of the passage seems straightforward, void of the irony pervading so much of the book.

> And then he regarded it [his guilt about his treatment of the tattered man in Chapters VIII-X] with what he thought to be great calmness. At last he concluded that he saw in it quaint uses. He exclaimed that its importance in the aftertime would be great to him if it even succeeded in hindering the workings of his egotism. It would make a sobering balance. It would become a good part of him. He would have upon him the consciousness of a great mistake. And he would be taught to deal gently and with care. He would be a man.

It would seem quite odd that Crane would include such a passage in the first place unless something preceding it in the novel had allowed him to consider such sentiments. He would hardly alter the meaning of his novel in one of the final paragraphs; there must have been a number of things which went before, pointing to the possibility of such a conclusion as that quoted above.

In his first engagement after receiving his "red badge" the youth fights courageously, but he seems to have no conscious awareness of what he is about. Thus his courage seems rather meaningless. But later, especially after the color-bearer is killed and Henry takes his place, the youth seems capable of exercising conscious self-control during battle.

> The youth, upon hearing the shouts, began to study the distance between him and the enemy. He made vague calculations. He saw that to be firm soldiers they must go forward. It would be death to stay in the present place, and with all the circumstances to go backward would exalt too many others. Their hope was to push the galling foes away from the fence.

Though Henry does not have a gun and must as color-bearer stand exposed to the fire of the enemy, he does not cringe in action, and is more aware of his surroundings during battle than ever before. His reactions here should be compared with those elicited by his exposure to danger in the preceding battle. The reactions exhibited indicate a third level of response to the possibility of his own annihilation. Fitst he runs from danger and possible death. Next he fights, but in an automatic, somnambulistic way. Finally he acts in a highly conscious manner, though in truth there are scattered references to the men as animals and some suggestions that Henry is not entirely aware of his motions. Yet doubtlessly he is a different person from the one who fought in the preceding battles.

Turning once again to the end of the novel, we note another passage, one which Crane left in the novel, which again suggests that Henry had undergone a meaningful change in character.

> And at last his eyes seemed to be opened to some new ways. He found that he could look back upon the brass and bombast of his earlier gospels and see them truly. He was gleeful when he discovered that he now despised them.

> With this conviction came a store of assurance. He felt a quiet manhood, nonassertive but of sturdy and strong blood. He knew that he would no more quail before his guides wherever they should point. He had been to touch the great death, and found that, after all, it was but the great death. He was a man.

> So it came to pass that as he trudged from the place of blood and wrath his soul changed.

If we consider that the central problem of the tale is defined at the point in the novel at which Henry runs from battle, then considering the material presented above, we can easily substantiate the claim that Henry is no longer a coward. It would appear that he has indeed undergone a change in character sufficient to allow him to repsond more adequately to the life situation.

Nevertheless the position supported by evidence like the above, the position declaring that Henry has achieved moral or spiritual rejuvenation, or at least has improved his lot as a human being, is not wholly satisfactory. Legislating against this position is the strong implication, so strong that few critics seem to have missed it, that in the universe of *The Red Badge* man is "nothing but" an animal determined by mechanistic forces over which he exercises no control. There is strong evidence in the novel that Crane intended this inference to be drawn, especially in Chapter XVII where Henry is about to engage in the first battle after having received his "red badge." This is the reading that many who have desired to place Crane firmly in the naturalistic camp have made. Certainly in such a world Henry could not have transcended the limits imposed by nature through conscious effort of will.

Passages deleted by Crane at the end of the manuscript are again relevant here. And again it is of significance that he saw fit to expunge them. They obviously run counter to an effect he wishes to produce *after the fact* of the writing of the novel.

> Fate had in truth been kind to him; she had stabbed him with benign purpose and diligently cudgelled him for his own sake. In his rebellion, he had been very portentous, no doubt, and sincere, and anxious for humanity, but now that he stood safe, with no lack of blood, it was suddenly clear to him that he had been wrong not to kiss the knife and bow to the cudgel. He had foolishly squirmed.

> With his new eyes, he could see that the secret and open blows which were being dealt about the world with such heavenly lavishness were in truth bless-

ings. It was a deity laying about him with the bludgeon of correction.

The irony in these passages seems unmistakable to me. The implication of them is one of Crane's recurring themes, that man is an alien in an alien universe, and all the works of his days and hands come to naught. Thus when Henry felt that "he was tiny but not inconsequent to the sun," that "in the spacewide whirl of events no grain like him would be lost," he is deluding himself in the same manner he so often deluded himself before. Only a fool would have "turned now with a lover's thirst to images of tranquil skies, fresh meadows, cool brooks—an existence of soft and eternal peace," as Henry does in the next to last sentence of the novel as Crane published it. No one leads or ever has led "an existence of soft and eternal peace."

Equally devastating to the position defending meaningful growth on the part of the hero is the last line of the novel, "Over the river a golden ray of sun came through the hosts of leaden rain clouds." If Henry has learned anything, he should know that he cannot trust any such sign from nature, that though nature might be beautiful and appealing it has no messages for men, especially messages presaging good fortune. Certainly after having been tricked so many times by nature, he would not be taken in again if he had the least bit of sense. Even if the last sentence should represent the point of view of the author rather than Henry, it yet raises problems of consistency. It has been Crane's view all along that nature is alien to man. Having read the novel up to the last page, no sensitive reader is going to accept signs from nature as meaningful.

In one sentence near the end of the novel, a sentence Crane left in his final version, he again implies that Henry's acts through the course of the novel are insignificant because Henry's perspective is just as distorted as it has been earlier in the story. "He saw that he was good." Does this short sentence call anything to mind, its structure, its diction, its rhythm? Recall Genesis 1:10, "And God called the dry land Earth; and the gathering together of the waters called the Seas: and God *saw that it was good.*" Henry's pride at the end of the novel is so overweening, his view of himself so distorted, that he equates himself with God. Evidence of this kind is ignored by those who wish to show that Henry has achieved moral or spiritual rejuvenation or that he has at least by the end of the novel become better able to function in the world.

The irony of *The Red Badge* serves Crane's intentions well only if he intended to convince the reader that Henry's seemingly heroic gestures were futile, and it of course seems doubtful that this is an adequate description of his total intention. As in *Maggie,* the irony creates an unbreachable gap between author and character and between reader and character. As late in the action as Chapter XV Crane subjects Henry to the most devastating and sustained irony appearing anywhere in the book. In this section occurs the episode in which Henry's friend Wilson asks him to return a packet of letters which he, fearing that he would not survive the battle during which Henry runs, had entrusted to him. Henry, forgetting that he ran from the battle while Wilson stayed and fought, assumes an extremely patronizing air, feeling derision for one who had been foolish enough to reveal weakness. He considers the letters a weapon "with which he could prostrate his comrade at the first signs of a cross examination." Only a person who was not very worthwhile could take such an attitude. Henry also feels superior to other soldiers who like him had run from battle. If Crane intends to show by the end of the novel that Henry

performs meaningful, heroic action, then it will be necessary to repair the disruption of affection between reader and character. Otherwise, we are likely to believe that one capable of deluding himself to such an extreme degree is not likely to change his character over the short period of time between this chapter and the end of the book.

It is relevant that Crane removed much of the irony from this chapter before publishing it, though a great deal . . . yet remains. Had he removed all the irony, nothing would have remained of the chapter. Were we to compare the sections expunged here with those taken out near the end of the book, we would note a great similarity, especially if we have in mind Henry's notions of his own role in the cosmic scheme, and more particularly of his relation to nature. . . . But the greater support for the case against the meaningfulness of Henry's actions lies in comparing what Crane left in Chapter XV with what Crane left in the final chapter.

The foregoing discussion should suggest something of the difficulty involved in attempting to reconcile the antithetical themes of *The Red Badge* by reference to any kind of duality of vision. We would be closer to the truth of the matter by recognizing that Crane has written two books in *The Red Badge,* each of which has its own theme, and the two themes are mutually exclusive. The novel does not "show up the nature and value of courage." On the contrary it asks whether courage is meaningful in the world, then it asks what is the nature of the world. Is nature, is the cosmic structure of the world, meaningful? If so, then a heroic ideal is possible; if not, then no action that man could perform could be significant beyond his own delusions. Because Crane could not answer the latter question, he could not answer the former. Hence, a rupture in the author's view of his materials; hence a rupture in the final meaning of the book. Had the novel manifested a duality of view, then we might assume that the author believed simultaneously in the possibility of a meaningful courage and in a world in which courage was meaningless because all actions and attitudes of men were ultimately meaningless. There is a difference between believing both of these equally and seeing the two as alternatives, but trusting the validity of neither.

The two major strains running through *The Red Badge* . . . [were] developed in Crane's earlier fiction. The one strain, which sees the value and necessity of heroism, of ability to act freely, unconstrained by the limitations imposed upon action by fear, was explored in *The Sullivan County Sketches. George's Mother* presented the same problem, but in a different way. That novel dealt with the limitations on free action resulting from the imposition of external authority by the parent, a situation which thwarts the development of the individual and requires exertion of will to overcome. *Maggie,* the most naturalistic piece of Crane's writing so far discussed, embodies the other strain. In this novel man is depicted as completely determined by his heredity and his environment, powerless to perform any action willfully, incapable of contributing to the development of his own character. In a certain sense *The Red Badge* is a culmination, a record of the direction of Crane's thought up to about 1895, its date of publication. Never again was Crane to write from the assumption that man had no responsibility in the determination of his own fate. From this point in his fiction man is often the victim of circumstances, but never completely out of control of his fate.

It is fortunate that we have the manuscript of *The Red Badge of Courage,* for it solves the problem of Crane's intention in the novel. The deletions in the manuscript point toward one conclusion: Crane saw that his novel lacked unity; consequently he attempted to supply unity by striking out those passages antithetical to the image of the novel which he formed *after the fact of having written the novel*. For this reason we are able to distinguish between the novel Crane actually wrote and the one he *wished* to present to the public. Clearly they are not the same.

It is significant that Crane was not able to disguise the disparity existing between the two themes of the novel by striking out certain passages. Had he been able to do this, then the controversy surrounding the meaning of the novel would not exist. But deleting entirely the evidence suggesting that Henry Fleming has accomplished nothing meaningful by the end of the novel would have destroyed the novel and required a complete rewriting job. Again, this points to the fact that the very conception of the novel led to the birth of twins, fraternal, not identical.

We will never know exactly why Crane chose to make public the one novel but not the other. There are a multitude of possibilities, but all of them are purely speculative. In any case it is clear that only one of these novels was sufficiently developed to allow publication without complete rewriting. This suggests the direction of Crane's emphasis. It suggests that of the two novels one was foremost in his mind, and that *one* is the traditional story of the hero, beset by great odds, who through fortitude and endurance is able to achieve his ends. Let us examine that novel.

Henry Fleming is a composite of the little man of *The Sullivan County Sketches* and George of *George's Mother*. Like these two, he has as his central problem the strengthening of his consciousness to the extent that he will be able to act freely, unconstrained by fear, in the world. But, unlike his predecessors, Henry Fleming is eventually strong enough to face the possibility of the actual extinction of his own ego. (pp. 60-9)

We learn in the first chapter that Henry has a firm attachment to his mother. We infer this from the amount of time it takes him to decide he is going to join the army in spite of her wishes. He does finally make "firm rebellion" against her, but when the time comes to depart, his excitement and expectancy only *almost* defeat "the glow of regret for the home bonds." Taking leave of his mother, Henry does not feel the elation he must have expected to feel from having fulfilled a long-standing wish. Seeing "her brown face, upraised, stained with tears, and her spare form quivering," he bows his head, "feeling suddenly ashamed of his purposes." Several times during the course of the novel's action, he indicates that his break with his former identity is not complete, wishing he were back at home, absolved of the responsibility of free action, and safe from the threat of extinction by the opposing army. His attempt to bury himself during the forest chapel scene suggests this same hesitancy and doubt about his own ability to survive alone in the world.

It would be quite unusual for one Henry's age to know the nature of his psychic situation as thoroughly as he does at the beginning of the novel. But because of the youth's particular situation, being a soldier in wartime, he is immediately in a position demanding the testing of his strengths and limitations. In ordinary life, one would probably not find himself faced with the immediate and acute necessity of coming to grips with the problem of identity. But this is one way in which the war background of the novel serves Crane's ends well. Here it allows him to telescope a phenomenon which might have taken months or years, suggesting the limited sense in which this is a war novel.

Henry knows that his next move after leaving home must be toward discovering who and what he is, and eventually toward discovering his relation to the universe at large; later in the novel he becomes aware that the two questions are intimately linked. Chapter I reveals his concern with discovering a new definition of himself through knowledge of his strengths and limitations. . . . Like a child lost, he seeks to learn how others feel about the impending trial, asking one and then the other in a mannner calculated to mask his own trepidation. Eventually, he discovers that he is alone, "separated from the others," as of course each person who attempts to know himself is alone. Such journeys within allow for no companions. At first Henry cannot bear his isolation from his fellows; he is not yet sufficiently strong. On an evening shortly after the time of the actual beginning of the novel, Henry withdraws from his companions—companions with whom he feels little accord—wandering into the evening gloom.

> He lay down in the grass. The blades pressed tenderly against his cheek. The moon had been lighted and was hung in a treetop. The liquid stillness of the night enveloping him made him feel vast pity for himself. There was a caress in the soft winds; and the whole mood of the darkness, he thought, was one of sympathy for himself in his distress.

This is one of the key passages in the novel. For the first time Henry feels that nature is actively sympathetic toward him and toward his particular ends. So powerfully does he feel nature's compassion for him that he imagines she "envelopes" him, protecting him from any antagonistic forces without. He imagines himself momentarily in a womb where he is protected, nourished, sustained, where there are no problems to be met, no dragons to be encountered. The grass lovingly presses "tenderly against his cheek" and the soft wind caresses him. This very same sensation, this very escape, is what Henry seeks when he burrows into the woods in the forest chapel scene later on in Chapter VII.

The paragraph immediately following this gives us a clue to the interpretation of the preceding passage as well as of the forest chapel scene. What follows but the youth's firm wish that he were home again, "He wished, without reserve, that he was at home again making the endless rounds from the house to the barn, from the barn to the fields, from the fields to the barn, from the barn to the house." He associates a constellation of ideas that he sees in nature with a constellation of ideas associated with home. In wishing to return home, it is not simply that Henry wishes to return to the womb; rather he wants to return to his situation prior to joining the army. He wants to return to his mother who defined for him who and what he was, who differentiated right from wrong, who provided for him a knowledge of the way things are. This is one of the instances in which Henry's feeble consciousness wishes to regress to a former state. Eventually he will become strong enough to forego indulgence in such meaningless fantasies, but not before a number of womb-shattering experiences. Meanwhile he wishes from time to time that he didn't have such monstrously large problems to solve.

The first four chapters describe Henry's attempts to prepare himself psychologically for the conflict occurring in Chapter V. In spite of the fact that Henry decides as early as Chapter II that intellectualization will not lead him to a conclusion about what his reactions in battle will be, that the only way of knowing his responses is to "have blaze, blood, and danger, even as a chemist requires this, that and the other," he continues to speculate up to the time of the battle about how he will react. We can in part trace Henry's difficulties to an overactive imagination, to his too great willingness to decide conclusively the outcome of his encounter with opposition, but his imagination accounts only in part for his difficulties.

During his first battle (Chapter V) the youth does indeed suspend the functioning of his imagination; he suspends indeed nearly all conscious functioning, all but a dim animal awareness that his situation is uncomfortable and that his fighting has something to do with alleviating the discomfort of the situation: "He developed the acute exasperation of a pestered animal, a well-meaning cow worried by dogs." He also has dim awareness of a "subtle battle brotherhood . . . a mysterious fraternity born of the smoke and danger of death." But throughout the scene, the youth is described as being in a "battle sleep." He fights "for respite of his senses, for air, as a babe being smothered attacks the deadly blankets." At the beginning of Chapter VI, "the youth awakened slowly. He came gradually back to a position from which he could regard himself." Here the youth has been able to disregard the question of his survival, to suspend the activity of his imagination and thus function in what is to him a desirable fashion.

But to Crane this is not enough. Henry's ability to suspend the functioning of his imagination during the first encounter by no means insures his having achieved courage. At the next encounter Henry becomes acutely conscious of himself and his situation, tumbling once more into the trap formed by his imagination. . . . [He] begins to think about the enemy and about the power of the enemy, exaggerating "the endurance, the skill, and the valor of those who were coming." Here the youth's own feelings, coupled with his observance of those of his fellow soldiers who are likewise victims of their imaginations, result in his complete loss of control of himself and his situation. Up to this point Crane has apparently shown that cowardice results from the inability to suspend the functioning of the imagination. "Directly he began to speed toward the rear in great leaps. . . . On his face was all the horror of those things which he imagined."

After his flight his fortunes are and continue to be at lowest ebb from Chapter VII to Chapter XIII in which he returns to his regiment. The experiences he undergoes during the central portion of the book allow him to act as he does during the final battles. This withdrawal from the scene of battle, from a situation in which his own extinction is imminent, seems necessary if he is to recoup his internal forces sufficiently to allow him once again to expose himself to the possibility of death.

Significantly enough, the first act after his flight is to retreat into the forest, "as if resolved to bury himself." Previously Henry has wished to bury himself, in the third chapter, where, feeling unjustly accused of lagging behind his group, he thinks "he must look to the grave for comprehension." His journey into the forest is an enactment of the fantasy he has in chapter two where he imagines that he is enveloped by "the liquid stillness of the night." Here in Chapter VII he seeks to bring the feelings generated by his fantasy into conjunction with the real world. In the past he has only *wished* to return home, to his mother, to the safety of his rural past. In this case he acts out his deepest desires to retreat from the world to the safety of an existence where he will be free from fear, where he will be protected and sustained, out of sight of the world and sheltered from its harsh judgments, where, in short, he will be

required to exercise none of the functions of consciousness. He goes far into the wood, "seeking dark and intricate places." If he goes far enough, he believes he will escape extinction putting behind him, as he does, "the rumble of death."

Henry feels closer to nature here than anywhere else in the novel. He has the impression that nature not only will comfort and succor him in the time of need, but that she will actively reveal to him ethical truth. The squirrel in the forest, running when Henry throws a pine cone at it, justifies to Henry his own conduct in running when threatened by danger. "Nature had given him a sign." But Henry fails to interpret properly the scene he sees immediately afterward. A small animal dives into a pool of water and emerges with a fish. This should have told Henry that his feeling that there was only benevolence in nature needed correction. Had he seen the significance of this event, he would have been closer to discovering his true relationship to nature. But obviously Henry is seeing only what he wants to see, creating the external world again, not as it is, but as he would have it be.

Deeper and deeper Henry burrows into the forest, "going from obscurity to promises of greater obscurity." Eventually he reaches a seemingly enclosed area, a place where he might hope to be enveloped in "liquid stillness." Pushing aside the green doors, he steps into a region where pine needles form a gentle, brown carpet and where a religious half-light overspreads the whole. If he is to find peace anywhere in nature it should be here; here should be the place where nature will take him to her bosom if she ever will. But such is not Henry's fate, nor is such the character of nature. In the very heart of the forest Henry finds not safety, escape from death, comfort, succor, peace, but death, death at the very center of nature. It would be difficult to imagine a more horrible spectacle than that which the youth sees. The descriptive details indicate a most appalling, terrifying scene. It is fitting that Henry should be met with such a sight, since he must be disabused of his faith in a sympathetic nature.

Henry meets death in the womb. Having gone as far as he has in his psychic development, he cannot turn back. He is no longer free to escape from the world without a kind of death occurring, the death of that facet of his character which finds itself dissatisfied with his failure to meet the world squarely, to deal with the life situation in order to exercise some control over it. Death is in the womb as well as without. There is no choice but to come to terms with the possibility of his own destruction. (pp. 69-75)

Since we are dealing with two novels in *The Red Badge,* each of which has a different theme, it is impossible to say in a simple sentence what the final outcome of this scene is. The primary novel, the one in which Crane seems to have had most faith and the one which he tried to create by deleting the antithetical elements, tells us that Henry was reborn as a result of his forest-chapel experience; that he learns that nature is not the least sympathetic toward man's hopes and aspirations. After his experience in the forest the youth is in a position to achieve the goal of his quest by having in large measure severed his ties with nature, becoming dependent upon his own resources. Had this scene not occurred, Henry would not have been able to return to his regiment, and subsequently be capable of heroic action. His experience is a learning experience. (pp. 75-6)

From Chapter VIII to the end of Chapter XII Henry assimilates the knowledge gained from his experience in the forest chapel. His movement from Chapter VI to the end of Chapter VII (the forest-chapel scene) has been away from battle. A reversal occurs in the latter chapter, sending Henry back toward his regiment. But before he returns, he undergoes several experiences which reinforce the implications to him of his experience in the wilderness. All that he experiences during this time tells him that he is not nature's darling, that nature does not involve herself in the affairs of men.

As he "obstinately" proceeds from the heart of the forest "on his forward way," he comes upon a battlefield deserted except for corpses lying amidst clothes and guns. He is apprehensive, yet he experiences nothing of the horror called forth by his previous confrontation with the dead. Here he notices that nature has had nothing to do with the facts before him. She has neither cared nor not cared. "A hot sun had [?] blazed upon the spot."

Throughout the succeeding chapters the youth feels increasingly guilty for having run away from battle. The tattered man whom he meets in the procession of wounded soldiers moving toward the rear seems to objectify the feelings of guilt stirring within the youth. Dogging his steps like some specter from his conscience, the tattered man, "fouled with dust, blood and powder," is a constant reminder to Henry of his cowardice. "Where yeh hit, ol' boy?" he asks.

Meeting Jim Conklin, the youth feels even more guilt-ridden than before, for Jim Conklin is someone he knows. This encounter is important in the experience of Henry Fleming, but it is important only in light of what has preceded. Death becomes more meaningful to Henry than it has ever been before as he watches his comrade Jim Conklin in the throes of death. Prior to this episode, he had been awed more by the idea of death than by death itself. Here death becomes an actuality. "The youth had watched, spellbound, this ceremony at the place of meeting. His face had been twisted into an expression of every agony he had imagined for his friend." And finally, "The red sun was pasted in the sky like a wafer." The lesson that the youth learned earlier in the forest chapel is repeated: neither caring nor not caring, nature moves on her way, oblivious to the fortunes of men.

No longer does the youth have the desire to seek "dark and intricate places," but instead "A certain mothlike quality keeps him in the vicinity of the battle." The fact of his lingering about the battle suggests that his receiving his "red badge" is not so much a fortuitous circumstance as has been heretofore supposed by practically everyone who has written about the novel. At the time he receives it, he is in the midst of an army in wild retreat. Seeing the routed army charging "down upon him like terrified buffaloes," Henry forgets "his mental pamphlets on the philosophy of the retreated and rules for the guidance of the damned." And in a line deleted by Crane from the published text, "He lost concern for himself." In spite of the obvious fact that this army is about "to be swallowed" by "war, the blood-swollen god," Henry stands his ground, not wishing to run, but "to make a rallying speech, to sing a battle hymn." Because he does not involve himself in the hysteria of the crowd, he is rewarded with "a little red badge of courage."

Afterward, the youth shows himself worthy of his reward, for he shows an increasing ability to perform consciously in opposition to his animal self, which urges him to follow the dictates of his body. The inclination of his body is to do nothing, to remain motionless, to sink down overcome by the mindless forces of nature. But instead "He fought an intense battle with his body." From its beginning this scene indicates that

Henry is finally beginning to achieve the necessary control of his actions.

But his development from that central episode occurring during the forest-chapel scene is not linear in its movement. He regresses from that initial level of strength and self-confidence which allowed him to leave home to join the army; he regresses from the level of conscious development he has attained through introspection following his act of cowardice. Immediately after his wound he becomes frightened, doubting the whole value of his progression toward the achievement of individuality. As might be expected, he turns his thoughts toward home, yearning for the comfort, security, protection and nourishment afforded by a situation in which he has neither the need nor the desire to be an independent individual, responsible for his own well-being in the world, and subject to the consequences of his own judgments.

> He bethought him of certain meals his mother had cooked at home.... The pine walls of the kitchen were glowing in the warm light from the stove. Too, he remembered how he and his companions used to go from the schoolhouse to the bank of a shaded pool.... He felt the swash of the fragrant water upon his body. The leaves of the overhanging maple rustled with melody in the wind of youthful summer.

The constellation of ideas associated by Henry with the undeveloped consciousness, with the state of being antithetical to that which he feels the driving need to attain, occurs here explicitly: home, mother, warmth, nourishment. Further, nonconsciousness is again revealed to be a state characteristic of the realm of nature. In being in the water he is immersed in nature, confined comfortably by the water below and by the overhanging maple above. This passage sheds light on the forest-chapel scene, revealing the relationship which Henry feels between nature and his state prior to joining the army. It shows that when Henry retreats from the apparent security of nature, he is retreating not only from nature, but from a complex set of earlier ties.

Significantly enough, after Henry has thought about his previous life he is overcome "by a dragging weariness." No longer does he walk "tall soldier fashion" as he had after receiving his wound, but now his head hangs forward, his shoulders are stooped, his feet shuffle along the ground. Like the song of the sirens, the call of nature attempts to lull him back into nature's domains.

Here when the youth's fortunes are again at low ebb, a series of events is initiated which in the context of the novel seems quite bizarre. Out of nowhere a stranger appears, "the man of the cheery voice." He takes Henry firmly by the arm, at a time when he is in great need of support, saying, "I'm going your way," though, there is nothing in the context to suggest that he has any natural means of knowing which way the youth is going. The man of the cheery voice asks which regiment he belongs to, and, being told, he undertakes to lead Henry there. "They're 'way over in the center," he says. "It'll be a miracle if we find our reg'ments t'-night," he says during the course of his continual chatter, Henry remaining quiet all the while. And it seems that this man does perform a miracle. He seems a wizard in his resourcefulness, in his ability to find his way in the darkness of night and the confusion of war. Leading the youth "without mistakes," the stranger eventually points out a campfire in the distance, directing the youth toward it. He clasps Henry's hand, wishes him good luck, and strides away, whistling audaciously and cheerfully. Suddenly Henry becomes aware "that he had not once seen his face." (pp. 77-80)

This mysterious man is comparable to the figure who in myth and legend gives aid to the hero faced with tasks beyond the limits of his capacities. Such figures are Ariadne, who tells Theseus how to find his way out of the labyrinth; Athene, who stands by Ulysses, aiding him throughout the course of his adventures in *The Odyssey;* the Cumaean Sibyl, whose directions allow Aeneas to enter and return from the underworld; Virgil, who leads Dante through the underworld; and the innumerable figures in fairy tales who tell the hero how he must go about achieving his task, warn him against dangers which he must overcome or encourage him toward his goal. At the time Henry meets the man of the cheery voice the youth is not heading toward any specific place, nor has he even made the decision to return to his regiment. The strange man leads Henry back, which suggests that he has a supernatural awareness of Henry's deepest needs at the particular time when he meets him. Supporting the youth both physically and morally, presenting to him an example of strength and resourcefulness, the man of the cheery voice, not Henry himself, puts the youth in the position of being able once again to encounter the forces which threaten him but with which he must come to terms.

This man, whose abilities seem to Henry to be magical, presents a striking contrast to other figures in the book because he seems to be on a different plane of existence. It is odd to meet a wizard in an apparently realistic context. But the man of the cheery voice is not such an enigma after all if we take into account the matter of point of view here, nor is it strange that a fairy-tale motif should underlie the plot of a novel which means to be primarily realistic. Since the point of view of *The Red Badge* is the third person restricted view, we are seeing events as they are interpreted by Henry, suggesting that what Henry sees or feels and what Crane sees and feels are not necessarily the same things. In the episode involving the man of the cheery voice, however, the tone indicates that Henry's interpretation of the events occurring there is not at odds with Crane's attitudes. There is none of that irony that occurs when Henry distorts his view of himself or his surroundings. We might conclude thereby that Crane feels that Henry's view of his total situation as being analogous to the situation of the hero of myth and legend is a not inadequate means of description. The point of view allows this magical man to appear without imposing on Crane the necessity of committing himself by implication to the proposition that the world is so constituted that the supernatural does in fact intervene in the affairs of men.

Chapters XIII to XVI inclusive involve Henry's preparation for his renewed encounter with the enemy force. These chapters allow a reader to believe in the possibility of a change in Henry sufficiently great to allow him to perform as he does in the next battle. In Chapter XIII the youth discovers that he is not scorned by his companions, that they in fact believe he has participated bravely in the preceding battle. Chapter XIV reveals the youth's awareness of the great change which has taken place in the loud soldier, suggesting to him by comparison (Henry often evaluates himself in terms of others) that he too could acquire the self-reliance, the inward confidence radiating from the other. Chapter XV, the section contributing most to the book's failure to maintain adequate unity of tone and theme, shows Henry become ridiculously overconfident of his own strengths and perceptions. Nevertheless it would seem that his distorted self-image contributes to his eventual

ability to perform well on the battlefield in much the same way that Christy Mahon's fantasy about killing his "da" determines what Christy becomes through the course of the action of Synge's *Playboy of the Western World.* Henry distorts reality in seeing himself as superior to his fellows, in achieving "a mighty scorn for such a snivelling race," yet he in fact grows into the image of himself projected in this chapter. His feeling that "he had been out among the dragons . . . and assured himself that they were not so hideous as he had imagined," seems ludicrous here, but when he later makes the statement it seems a natural outgrowth of the experiences he has undergone (unless of course the outcome is read as ironic). Chapter XVI corrects the impression of the preceding chapter by showing us Henry's wariness prior to the coming encounter. No longer is he the proud, arrogant swaggerer we saw a short time before. At the same time, his imagination seems in good control; he is living in the moment without thinking about his own fate.

As I suggested earlier, the ability to suspend the functioning of the imagination, to live only in the present moment, is for Crane not enough. The last three encounters of the novel (there are five in all) show Henry growing beyond that requirement. In the very first battle in the book the youth is able to accomplish this function. Still the question remains, why continue the novel beyond the point at which he fights fiercely, where he feels "the supreme trial had been passed. The red, formidable difficulties of war had been vanquished"? That is, why has Henry not achieved his goal at the end of the first encounter? There should be a reason above and beyond the fact that Crane simply wanted to continue the action. In fact there are at least two such reasons. One is that Henry has not really acted courageously, for to Crane courageous action must be conscious action. In this first encounter Henry has no consciousness of what he is about. He works at his weapon "like an automatic affair"; he tries "to rally his faltering intellect so that he might recollect the moment when he had loaded, but he could not"; he is in a "battle sleep" which after the battle he awakes from. It is during this battle and the next that Henry and his comrades are most frequently compared to animals.

The other reason Crane continued the plot beyond Henry's first battle is that Henry's ability to remain in the battle lines at that point is entirely dependent upon his identification with something larger than himself, "a regiment, an army, a cause, or a country." He does not feel at that time the personal involvement necessary for the achievement of his own individuality. He is "welded into a common personality which is dominated by a single desire." The struggle which he is really engaged in, the struggle within himself, must be dealt with alone if he is to resolve it meaningfully. Since "for some moments he could not flee any more than a little finger can commit revolution from a hand," he is not involved in an act of personal courage. Consequently, because he has not vanquished the dragons threatening the extinction of his own being, it is not surprising that the action continues, and it is not less surprising that he runs away during the next battle. (pp. 81-4)

Henry's third encounter is fought much like the first, though close observation of what goes on there will reveal that since his flight from the preceding battle, Henry has made some progress toward his ultimate goal. During the first engagement Henry "developed the acute exasperation of a pestered animal, a well-meaning cow worried by dogs." In this battle his feelings are very much the same: "He was not going to be badgered all of his life, like a kitten chased by boys, he said. It was not well to drive men into final corners; at those moments they could all develop teeth and claws.'' Again his actions are described by means of metaphors relating to animals. ''He crouched behind a little tree, with his eyes burning hatefully, and his teeth set in a cur-like snarl.'' And again, ''When the enemy seemed falling back before him and his fellows, he went instantly forward, like a dog. . . .'' After the encounter, the youth reflecting on what has gone before, feels ''that he had been a barbarian, a beast.'' The implication of such descriptions is that still the youth is acting instinctively, not exhibiting true courage. (pp. 85-6)

Henry enters the fourth engagement with the firm realization that his chances for survival are slight. He has overheard the general of his division tell one of his regimental officers that Henry's regiment will probably be destroyed. Still Henry goes into battle having no conscious concern about his own personal fate. For the first time in the novel, he is able, in full awareness, to face the probability of his own destruction.

During this encounter the youth is not unconscious of his surroundings as he has always been heretofore. No longer is it necessary that he go into a battle sleep; on the contrary his awareness seems even heightened: ''It seemed to the youth that he saw everything. Each blade of the green grass was bold and clear. He thought that he was aware of every change in the thin transparent vapor that floated idly in sheets.''

When the color sergeant of his regiment is killed, Henry gains possession of the flag. As color-bearer he appears to act even more heroically since he must stand in the fore, unarmed, and an obvious target for opposing riflemen. His new role also finds him being a leader rather than a follower, a manipulator rather than manipulated. Contrary to his way in the second battle and elsewhere in the book, he does not now take his cues for thought and action from those around him. When his companions lag, when they turn from the battle fearful and dismayed, when others hide, ''curled into depressions,'' Henry exhorts them to fight, no longer feeling the fear which had so controlled his actions before. All through the battle he is acutely aware of his surroundings, his new inner strength being sufficiently great to allow him to hold his ground in spite of impending death.

The fifth and final encounter confirms the implications of the fourth and asserts the efficacy of consciously controlled action in the world. When told that his regiment must charge the enemy, Henry ''began to study the distance between him and the enemy. He made vague calculations. He saw that to be firm soldiers they must go forward.'' He leads the charge, urging his companions onward, unmindful of the danger around him. We should contrast the youth here to the youth whom we saw in the first three encounters. Here he is no longer simply an animal, reacting instinctively to a stimulus, but a man through whom Crane asserts the meaningfulness of human endeavor, by which he means conscious endeavor. As we might expect, throughout the course of Henry's development there are fewer and fewer comparisons of men with animals. During the fifth battle there are only two, neither of them degrading.

The fifth battle is Henry's only victorious encounter. Had he remained in the lines at the second battle, he would have participated in the victory accomplished by his regiment, but in terms of the over-all structure of the novel this would not have served Crane's ends. The victory achieved in the last battle becomes a kind of celebration of Henry's whole accomplishment, a culmination revealing that the direction of Henry's whole movement has some meaningful end. The resolution of his inward struggle has an effect on the outside world.

The other novel within *The Red Badge,* the one which has as its theme that the nature of the universe is such that man can perform no meaningful action, is dependent upon the same external events as the one whose development we have been following, but its theme relies upon tone for its expression. The events of the novel, in other words, will not in themselves reveal the theme. Consequently that novel cannot be explored in the same way in which I have examined the novel having positive implications. Yet I believe that I have exhibited earlier ample evidence of its existence.

I believe that the problem of the ending of this novel came about essentially for two reasons. The first reason I admit to be speculative, not subject to ''proof'' in the same way that other opinions about literature can be ''proved.'' It is my guess that Crane did not entirely approve of Henry's development into an individual capable of exercising the prerogatives, fulfilling the functions of an autonomous being. In *George's Mother* Crane reveals tremendous guilt feelings about his relationship with his own mother, and consequently George is the least sympathetic of the two characters. The death of Mrs. Kelcey at the end of the novel serves as a kind of *deus ex machina* allowing George to pursue his attempt to discover an identity unhampered by feelings of guilt toward a parent whom he must in a sense kill in the same way that the hero must kill the dragon which threatens at once to devour him and to put an end to his aspirations toward individual existence. The death of Mrs. Kelcey at the end of that novel is a means of circumventing the problem which Henry deals with in *The Red Badge* by simply leaving home. But Crane would not allow Henry's problem to be solved so easily. Crane was not at all sure that the development of the individual at the price of in some sense destroying the parent was worthwhile. Thus he was not at all sure that what Henry had to do to Mrs. Fleming was justified by the gain of being able to face the possibility of his own destruction. (pp. 86-8)

The other reason for the problem of the novel, the one which I feel is more objectively demonstrable, amounts simply to considering the matter on a different level. There is a direct line of development in Crane's thought from *The Sullivan County Sketches,* through *Maggie,* to this novel. In the sketches we observed that Crane assumed man to be potentially free, though limited not by external forces, but by his own psychic being which until freed by conscious activity from the dominance of nature cannot exercise freedom of will. *Maggie,* on the other hand, is written from the premise that man is a determined creature having no control over what he is or what he does. The universe is such, Crane here assumes, that certain physical laws govern all phenomena; that essentially a decision made by a person is not different from the changing of the seasons. Crane was unable to relate these two ideas in such a way as to formulate them into a coherent view, a shortcoming resulting in tonal inconsistency so great as to prevent critics over the years from agreeing on what *The Red Badge* is about even in the most basic terms. (p. 89)

> *Donald B. Gibson, in his* The Fiction of Stephen Crane, *Southern Illinois University Press, 1968, 169 p.*

MARSTON LaFRANCE (essay date 1971)

[*LaFrance is a Canadian educator and critic. In the following excerpt, he discusses* The Red Badge of Courage *as an expression of Crane's ironic vision rather than as a work that is either naturalist or symbolist.*]

[The continuing popularity of **The Red Badge of Courage**] has all but buried the novel beneath layer upon layer of commentary which has been accumulating steadily since 1894. Fortunately, the thickest layers of this criticism are easily identified by a generally apologetic argument: the novel is wrenched out of its proper context among Crane's other writings, a different context—either historical or critical—is assumed by the critic, and the argument is developed in order to force the novel to conform to this new mould into which it most stubbornly refuses to fit. The two most popular contexts to be found in this apologetic criticism are the naturalistic and the symbolic, and a brief look at these two critical party lines as they have been applied to **The Red Badge** should help clear the way for a common-sense reading of the novel.

At its most obvious level of error, the assumption of a naturalistic context for **The Red Badge** has led to several studies of "sources" or "influences." This is the literary historian's attempt to identify Crane's literary ancestors as Zola, Tolstoy, Stendhal, or, if the argument is for historical realism and American sources, Bierce and DeForest (source hunters never bother to consider Howells): **The Red Badge** is literary naturalism; so young and ill-educated a man as Crane could hardly have created a major work of literary naturalism intuitively; therefore, he studied authors A, B, or C, and the novel is obviously derivative. But **The Red Badge,** of course, is not literary naturalism at all, and thus Crane had no real need to read any of these authors. He may well have read all of them, among others—most young writers read established practitioners while trying to attain a distinctive style—but Crane's works, even without **"Why Did the Young Clerk Swear?"**, strongly imply that specifically naturalistic fiction must have bored him. Henry Fleming seems even less affected, let alone determined, by his environment than Crane's Bowery characters are, largely because he is more intelligent. He obviously possesses a will of his own, a sense of responsibility as a soldier, and a conscience which he is unable to ignore; and thus endowed he is remarkably ill-fitted for philosophic determinism. In fact Henry's relations with his environment are often just the reverse of what naturalism assumes they ought to be; instead of the environment determining Henry, Henry's "weak mental machinery" usually determines his environment, so far as his own view of it is concerned—a matter which can be verified by anyone who reads the chapters in which Henry wanders about in the forest. The better naturalistic critics, who assume the context for purposes of criticism rather than source-hunting, rest their interpretation of the novel largely upon three claims: the prevalence of animal imagery, the "moving box" episode (and the similar one in which Fleming throws a pine-cone at a squirrel), and the belief that Henry undergoes no change of character and shows no moral development in the course of the action. Each of these claims is easily refuted once the novel is returned to its rightful context. For the moment let us merely have faith that **The Red Badge** was written by an important ironist, not by a Zola or a Dreiser.

But to see Crane as primarily an ironist is in itself a challenge to the literary historian's basic assumptions of historical context and literary antecedents as effective means of approach to such a writer. The ironic vision itself can in no way be explained by a particular historical context (which merely provides the necessary grist for the ironist's mill) or by literary antecedents (which help to account for an individual style). And if we assume that the recurring psychological progression to awareness [that can be traced in Crane's earlier works] is the basic structure by which his ironic vision expresses itself in fiction, that this pattern is in fact the "one trump" he mentioned to Willa Cather, then the essential *subject* of his important work comes straight from his ironic perception of the human situation, not from the sort of sources or influences a literary historian can use most effectively in explicating a writer—Emerson, for example—who is not primarily an ironist. Crane's view of the human situation, set forth more clearly in **The Red Badge** than in his earlier work, is that man is born into an amoral universe which is merely the external setting in which human moral life is lived, and that if moral values are to exist and man's life is to be meaningful, morality must be the creation of man's weak mental machinery alone; but even the best of men, the most personally honest, is prone to error and thus liable to bring misery upon himself and others because the mental machinery often distorts that reality which he must perceive correctly if his personal honesty is to result in morally significant commitment. Thus, Crane's essential subject, in **The Red Badge** as in the **Sullivan County Sketches, Maggie,** and the **"Experiment in Misery,"** is man's weak mental machinery as it labours under the stress of some emotion, usually fear, to perceive correctly an area of reality which is not yet within the compass of the perceiver's experience. And if so, **The Red Badge** does have an obvious source which is available to anyone who wishes to investigate it; but the assumption of a naturalistic, a factually realistic, or a specifically literary context leads in the wrong direction. The real source of this novel and any other important Crane work seems to me simply the ironist's incredible awareness of human nature. Our amazement should not be directed at Crane's mastery of the techniques of naturalism, or knowledge of the Civil War, or Jamesian grasp of Western literature, but at so young a man's ability to create so superb a psychological portrayal as Henry Fleming.

The attempt to impose a symbolic context upon **The Red Badge,** which apparently originates in the urge to account for Crane's obvious artistry without tampering with the naturalistic interpretation, still lures innocent converts; otherwise it would today be gratuitous to argue against it. The symbolist critic seizes upon those images which provide the key to the conundrum the novel presents in the guise of a story. Once these key "symbols" are extracted, the rest of the novel—and anything Crane said about it, all Crane's other work (including **"The Veteran"**), and everything known of Crane the man—is largely discarded as useless and misleading. This approach can easily be avoided if one merely remembers that "symbols exist, and exist only, *in context*" [Rudolph Van Abele and Walter Havighurst, "Symbolism and the Student"]. When Crane's red sun is considered in context its wafer-like appearance should not imply the wafer of the Mass. Crane never mentions any dogma, religious ritual, or god external to man except in terms of ironic attack or contempt; and his poems, like **Maggie** and **George's Mother,** do not suggest he was even a Christian, let alone a Catholic. At least five chapters in this novel end with a reference to the sun, as Edward Stone has noted [see Additional Bibliography]. This fact alone implies—not to Stone, unfortunately—that the sun is used throughout as a general image of external nature, and that one should be extremely wary of making a specific mention bear a symbolic burden which the other examples cannot assume. The mention of this enigmatic sun at the scene of Conklin's death and Fleming's futile rage and grief most obviously suggests the complete separation of man from externals, the total indifference of the heavens to death, war, heroism, blasphemy, and whatever else man may say or do. Given this rather obvious meaning (which is strongly reinforced by the rest of the novel, by Crane's other writings, and by the life of a man who apparently subjected Christianity along with everything else to his own ironic vision), the use of "wafer" and "pasted" implies the seal at the end of a legal document and thus suggests completion, finality: the separation of man from externals is absolute, just as death is, and nothing can be done by Fleming to change it.

Similarly Jim Conklin, in spite of his initials and his wound in the side, can hardly be a Christ figure. Initials in American literature can be devil's advocates: for every Joe Christmas there is a Jason Compson, for every Jim Casy a John Claggart. And Conklin received his wound in the side from dramatic necessity: he has to die slowly, remain in his right mind, and retain full use of both arms and legs—that is, he has to wander back from the front, recognize Henry, and dance the hideous hornpipe to make his death so grotesque that it will particularly horrify Henry. Given all these requirements during America's mauve decade when no one would dare be wounded in the groin, the side is really about the only spot available. Throughout his entire canon, Crane inevitably condemns the qualities which Conklin embodies: Conklin is a rumour-monger, a vain, pompous, loud-mouthed, brawling, cursing lout whose greatest joy in life is eating sandwiches, who apparently possesses the one virtue of patience in the face of impending danger. And, in view of his other qualities, even this virtue has to be attributed less to calm courage than to mere mindlessness; he is not afraid simply because he does not have enough imagination to frighten himself with. He is one of several Crane characters who "have merely a stomach and no soul." If the thought of creating a Christ figure had occurred to Crane he surely could have done better than this.

However, the symbolist approach to *The Red Badge* should immediately be stopped by a consideration of Crane's other work. Nothing in either the earlier or the later work implies a mind which conceives its fiction in terms of conceptual patterns of symbols.... Crane's work obviously abounds with emblematic imagery—the saloon in the Bowery novels, darkness and light in the portrayal of the assassin, the cash register in **"The Blue Hotel,"** the wounded soldier on the altar in **"War Memories,"** the fire in **"The Monster"**—but all these symbolic images arise out of the process of writing a story *after* it has been imaginatively conceived in terms of a specifically structural plot which in no way depends upon any particular imagery. Hence, Crane's vivid images, in *The Red Badge* as in his other work, result from an artistic labour of craftsmanship, not primarily from the conceiving imagination; and any pattern they may offer will function as an artistic embellishment of an independent plot structure.

Crane's early news articles, the *Sullivan County Sketches,* and *Maggie* provide the only context in which *The Red Badge* may be placed with certainty. And we should add *The Black Riders,* which came immediately after this novel was completed, and *George's Mother,* begun before *The Red Badge* and finished after it. These works surround the novel in the chronology of Crane's development; and a careful reading of them provides the best available approach to an understanding of *The Red Badge* because this novel does not greatly differ from these other works in its essential plot, situation, protagonist, and philosophy—even though it differs radically in its technique and resolution.

The little man of the sketches, Maggie Johnson, George Kelcey, and Henry Fleming are all cut from the same bolt: all are young, naïve, untried, subject to fear, troubled by a sense of being unique, given to silly illusions, the environment or society in which they find themselves seems hostile to the ideals they posit for their own lives, and all four protagonists struggle to bridge the gap between their romantically impossible daydreams and harsh realities. We seldom have much idea of the physical appearance of these characters. None of them can reasonably be called heroic in any traditional sense of the word. Each comes alive only through Crane's acute awareness of human imperfections—vanity, anger, fear, laziness, the capacity for whining self-pity, self-delusion, rationalization—the human limitations which are common to all mankind. Certainly none of these weaknesses is lacking in Henry Fleming. It was the coincidence of this typical Crane protagonist and a war setting that produced the prototype of the modern, anti-romantic treatment of war. Henry Fleming, Dos Passos, three soldiers, Frederic Henry, Robert Jordan, Yossarian possess [according to Sophus K. Winter] only "the common virtues of the ordinary man; their vices [are] those which experience teaches all people to recognize as typical. The significant thing about this modern hero of war literature is that his limitations constitute the essence of his reality."

Fleming is distinguished from the earlier protagonists only because he is endowed with two new qualities which make the conquest of oneself at least possible. He is given an imagination worthy of Macbeth, and hence he is aware to a degree of sensitivity far beyond that of Maggie or the little man; and he is given a strong conscience, a quality which in Crane's work is inextricably fused with awareness. If awareness permits a man to see what is actually in front of his eyes to be seen, the conscience provides for the sense of personal honesty through self-criticism. Without awareness a Crane character—such as the militant dogmatists of the poems, who would impose their will upon others by any means—remains unable to acquire the restraint and humility which signify a healthy conscience. However, if a man does have these two qualities, and the strength of will to utilize them, then a knowledge of himself and his place in the world—the only "salvation" that Crane ever offers—is possible. (No example of such a character can be drawn from Crane's earlier work because Fleming is the first one; examples in his later work are the correspondent in **"The Open Boat,"** the lieutenant of **"An Episode of War,"** Manolo Prat, and Dr. Trescott.)

As *The Red Badge* depends so entirely upon the characterization of Henry Fleming, any qualities which Crane introduced for this protagonist should provide the basis for whatever distinctions from his earlier work this novel reveals. The most distinctive innovations in *The Red Badge* are, quite obviously, the technical feats attained through the use of the third-person limited point of view, and the fact that Fleming emerges from his experience with self-knowledge and moral growth. Henry's vivid awareness makes possible the use of the third-person limited narrative technique; the story is tense and exciting only so far as Henry's imagination reacts intensely under the terrific pressures of fear, pride, and the conscience. Actually, in view of the narrative technique used throughout, this awareness of Henry's is *itself* the "action," the life and force of the entire novel. And the new ending of the story, Henry's success rather than failure, may be attributed to his conscience, that force which makes him turn his awareness upon his own actions, judge them, and thereby learn self-knowledge. The little man of the sketches never does this at all; Maggie tries, but is not intelligent or aware enough to judge properly; George Kelcey has both the conscience and sufficient awareness to judge, but—as with the professional tramps of the Bowery sketches—he lacks the force of will to face and accept his own judgement. Henry Fleming has all three qualities: awareness, conscience, and—more obviously in the latter part of the novel—the necessary strength of will.

However, to call the ending of the novel an innovation is merely to point out that in *The Red Badge,* for the first time in Crane's career, the psychological progression to awareness that [can be] . . . traced through his earlier work is completed: Henry Fleming does recall his earlier fears and illusions after he experiences the unknown, this remembrance does make him ashamed of his own weaknesses, and the result is his new understanding of himself and his real place in an amoral universe. Otherwise, the structure of the novel is, again, Crane's "one trump" pattern, this time superbly expanded from short-story to novel length by Crane's excellent method of delaying his protagonist's experience of the feared unknown until the nineteenth chapter; hence, the bulk of the novel is concerned with the first part of the pattern, with what the protagonist reveals of himself during the period of mounting tension until his climactic deflation by actual experience. This structural pattern in itself denies both the naturalistic and the symbolic contexts. Naturalism is rejected because Crane's man always fights his essential battles within himself, and externalities are ultimately of little importance; in *The Red Badge,* as in Crane's other important work, the significant action always takes place within the mind of the protagonist. And any symbols which Crane wrote into this particular rendering of his pattern remain artistic embellishments, wonderfully functional but still separate from the essential plot; as such, they are neither conceptual nor, so far as I can determine, can they legitimately be withdrawn from the story and fitted into any relationship expressive of a "meaning" which conflicts with Crane's structural psychological progression to awareness.

The novel opens with that sense of uncertainty which plagues Fleming until the last two or three pages. He hears Conklin's rumour that the regiment is about to engage in combat, and immediately withdraws to his hut to think about his own problems—and not at all about Conklin's rumour, by the way; he merely assumes the rumour will prove true (as it does not) and gives his whole attention to worrying about how he will act during his first battle. Thus, Fleming's intensely active imagination is presented at once: the really significant battles in this novel are already raging in full career within Henry's mind long before the first shot is fired in any external skirmish. He had dreamed of "bloody conflicts that had thrilled him with their sweep and fire"; and, like George Kelcey, his dreams feature great visions of personal glory in which he imagines "peoples secure in the shadow of his eagle-eyed prowess." Henry had enlisted, had voluntarily fled his dull farm life, because of these vainglorious desires set in the impossibly romantic picture of war which his imagination has evoked from village gossip and luridly distorted news reports.

The flashback to the farewell scene can serve almost as a structural précis of the novel. Henry had "primed himself for a beautiful scene. He had prepared certain sentences which he thought could be used with touching effect." But his mother merely peels potatoes and talks tediously of shirts and socks. The result is Crane's usual deflation of vanity, comic here because of Henry's romantic and sentimental foolishness. Nevertheless, buried in his mother's prosaic commonplaces is precisely the view of himself and his duty to which Henry has to inch his way in painful experience throughout the remainder

of the novel: "Yer jest one little feller amongst a hull lot of others, and yeh've got to keep quiet an' do what they tell yeh. . . . Never do no shirking, child, on my account. If so be a time comes when yeh have to be kilt or do a mean thing, why, Henry, don't think of anything 'cept what's right." Fleming is not the undiscovered Achilles of his grand illusions; he is just another lad who has to learn to be a man. And to be a man in Crane's world is to perceive the human situation as it is, accept it, and remain personally honest in fulfilling the commitments such a perception demands of the individual. The fact that Henry has to suffer the experiences of the whole novel even to approach this simple truth merely reveals, again, the most bitterly ironic aspect of Crane's psychological pattern: as in *Maggie* and the Sullivan County tales, the protagonist of *The Red Badge* also has to undergo all his suffering in order to perceive, to "see," a constant reality which is present and available to him before his progression through experience to the perception of it even begins.

Henry's weak mental machinery is at this point so busy with visions of glory and he is so impatient to leave that he hardly hears his mother's advice; but his shame, when he turns to see her praying and weeping among the potato parings, distinguishes him from Crane's earlier protagonists, and implies that eventually he will learn the truth of what he has just been told—that the real hero, in such a world as this, is the quiet, nameless man who can discern what is right and do it, simply because it is right and because he is a man.

Henry's education has already begun before the reader first encounters him. He has experienced the dreariness, boredom, filth, and part of the misery of a soldier's life. The prolonged inaction has left his imagination free to concentrate on that part of his problem which experience has not yet clarified for him, and thus he is first seen lying in his bunk trying "to mathematically prove to himself that he would not run from a battle." He contemplates the "lurking menaces of the future," in the only way he can, as these menaces exist within his own mind; and given Henry's imagination, it is no wonder that his thoughts scare him. When Conklin's rumour proves false and still more waiting has to be endured, Henry's tension becomes almost unbearable; and his imagination evokes two illusions which Crane exploits throughout the novel: the notion that moral qualities exist in external nature—"The liquid stillness of the night enveloping him made him feel vast pity for himself. There was a caress in the soft winds; and the whole mood of the darkness, he thought, was one of sympathy for himself in his distress"—and the belief that he is unique, separated (at this point by fear) from the other men in the regiment. After timidly broaching the hint of fear to Wilson only to have the conversation end in an abrupt quarrel, Henry "felt alone in space. . . . No one seemed to be wrestling with such a terrific personal problem." Henry is wrong, of course. The other men are also afraid; but without Henry's imagination they fear only the *fact* of combat, and hence they can play poker while he suffers. Henry no longer fears the actual fact: "In the darkness he saw vision of a thousand-tongued fear that would babble at his back and cause him to flee, while others were going coolly about their country's business. He admitted that he would not be able to cope with this monster." Such is Henry's state of mind when he is suddenly awakened one morning and sent running towards his first skirmish.

Crane introduces the "moving box" episode with the flat statement that Henry "was bewildered." Barely awake and intensely excited, he has to use "all his faculties" to keep from falling and being trampled by those running behind him. The passage in question constitutes Henry's *first* reaction to this situation:

> he instantly saw that it would be impossible for him to escape from the regiment. It inclosed him. And there were iron laws of tradition and law on four sides. He was in a moving box.
>
> As he perceived this fact it occurred to him that he had never wished to come to the war. He had not enlisted of his free will. He had been dragged by the merciless government. And now they were taking him out to be slaughtered.

This passage is pure rationalization without a hint of naturalism in it. The "iron laws of tradition and law" are made by men and changed by men. And Henry did enlist of his own free will; he was not dragged to this commitment by any force except his own wish to go to war. All that this passage really reveals is that Henry is so badly frightened he is considering flight even before a shot is fired.

When Henry's curiosity leads him to charge over a rise only to be confronted with still more inaction, Crane unambiguously presents his basic trouble: "If an intense scene had caught him with its wild swing as he came to the top of the bank, he might have gone roaring on. This advance upon Nature was too calm. He had opportunity to reflect. He had time in which to wonder about himself and to attempt to probe his sensations." Hence, a house acquires an "ominous look," shadows in a wood are "formidable," and Henry feels he should advise the generals because "there was but one pair of eyes" in the regiment. In the afternoon he tells Conklin the truth when he says, "I can't stand this much longer." Henry's inner turmoil again obscures his perception: he no more grasps the significance of Wilson giving him the packet than he had heard his mother's advice. He soon witnesses the rout of some troops who run blindly back through his own regimental line, and he intends to wait only long enough to see the "composite monster" which has frightened these men. But when the charge finally comes, he does not run; he stays and fights.

This episode must have taken considerable thought, for Crane had to find a means of letting Henry engage in battle, an incident to which the four previous chapters have pointed, and still not undergo the unknown experience he fears. In other words, Crane's treatment at this point would commit him one way or the other: if Henry experienced the unknown here the result would be a short story; if this experience could be further delayed the result would be a novel. Crane solved his problem by having Henry fight this skirmish in a trance, a "battle sleep" induced by fatigue and rage; and because of this Henry later does not accept this combat as that attainment of the experience he has been anticipating.

Thus, Crane in this episode is able to repeat the irony of Henry's farewell scene. When the fight begins, Crane allows Henry to attain the real bearing of responsible manhood at war—for a few moments:

> He suddenly lost concern for himself, and forgot to look at a menacing fate. . . . He felt that something of which he was a part—a regiment, an army, or a country—was in a crisis. He was welded into a common personality which was dominated by a single desire. . . .
>
> There was a consciousness always of the presence of his comrades about him. He felt the subtle battle brotherhood more potent even than the cause for which

> they were fighting. It was a mysterious fraternity born of the smoke and danger of death.
>
> He was at a task.

This is a quiet statement, without any irony, of the ideal which Crane was to honour repeatedly in his writings about the Spanish-American War. But at this point Henry enters his battle sleep. Then, after the charge has been repulsed, and before Henry emerges from his trance, he feels "a flash of astonishment at the blue, pure sky and the sun gleamings on the trees and fields. It was surprising that Nature had gone tranquilly on with her golden process in the midst of so much devilment." And this statement implies the mature man's unsentimental view of nature as an amoral external mechanism. But then, when Henry emerges from his trance, his old weaknesses reassert themselves, and he is entirely unable to recall either the achievement or the perception which came to him at either edge of his battle sleep. Once again the reality he is seeking lies within his grasp; and once again his mental turmoil prevents his awareness of it.

This episode also contains some of Crane's famous animal imagery; and, provided it is read correctly, Crane's *use* of this very imagery argues against naturalism. Crane does not use animal images until Henry begins to slip into his battle sleep; before this, there is only a single animal image in the three pages of this chapter: "the colonel . . . began to scold like a wet parrot." And, more important, there is no hint of such imagery in the above description of Henry's moment of manhood before his trance begins. But as Henry descends from full consciousness and becomes something less than a man he abruptly begins to perceive in terms of non-human images; he feels "the acute exasperation of a pestered animal, a well-meaning cow worried by dogs"; he rages like a "driven beast"; men "snarl" and "howl"; a coward's eyes are "sheeplike . . . animal-like." And this sort of imagery ends when Henry regains full consciousness. This *use* of imagery is fairly consistent throughout the novel. Hence, the demands of dramatic propriety are as insistent here as they are in the flophouse scene in the **"Experiment in Misery,"** and for the same reason: the primary function of the imagery in *The Red Badge* is . . . to represent the protagonist's agitated mind as it struggles from lurid distortions to an understanding that reality is, after all, but reality. The imagery in the novel always becomes most vivid when Henry's perception is most distorted, and such a state of mind is the extreme of the condition which Henry labours to transcend by applying his awareness, conscience, and force of will to his experience. Crane's use of such imagery in this novel, in short, strongly implies that he is a humanist, not a naturalist.

When Henry awakens from his battle sleep to find that the charge has been withstood, he becomes vain in complacent admiration of his part in this success; and all his self-congratulation is illusory. Nothing is "over" for him; no trial has been passed. He uncritically admires actions which were done in a trance; and no Crane character ever feels such pompous self-satisfaction, even for real accomplishment, unless he is a vain fool. Complacency is a delusion in a world where nothing but death is final, where no ideal can ever be possessed because man has to reckon with externalities beyond his control, a stoic's world in which a continuous present poses a continuous demand upon man's moral and physical endurance. The attack is immediately renewed; and this time, after having seen so many others flee that he believes he will be left alone, Henry runs away. One must insist that he runs only nominally from the advancing enemy; what he really runs from is his own imagination. Crane's statement could hardly be more bluntly unambiguous: "On his face was all the horror of those things which he imagined." Even as he flees, his busy mind rationalizes his flight in terms of his previous feeling of uniqueness, and thus he loiters in the rear long enough to learn that the line held and repulsed the charge a second time. Then, miserably ashamed, cringing "as if discovered in a crime," he moves into the forest.

Henry's journey through this forest, like Marlow's journey up the river into the heart of darkness, charts a pilgrimage within the mind. This moral forest clearly suggests the "direful thicket" through which the brave man of the poems has to plunge to find truth, and its "singular knives"—fear, guilt, shame, hatred of those who remained and fought, vanity, self-pity, rage, his suffering as he sympathetically experiences Conklin's death, the self-loathing evoked by the tattered man—slash at Henry's ego just as the brush and vines entangle his legs. This section of the novel probably required more virtuosity and sheer craftsmanship than any other because, in terms of Crane's structural pattern, no further progress can occur until Henry returns to face his commitment: the unknown experience is thus beautifully delayed while the protagonist undergoes an intense struggle within himself, the outcome of which merely returns him to the position from which he had fled when this section began. (pp. 96-111)

His terrible journey through this forest can be divided into four parallel scenes or episodes—the craftsman's device of *Maggie* used here with much greater subtlety—which are easily identified: each begins with a specific illusion, a direction of Henry's thought which is followed until the pathway becomes blocked; when the illusion is destroyed, or when the barricade is encountered and Henry has to seek a new direction, the episode ends and the next one begins.

His first illusion arises directly from his attempts to rationalize his cowardice. It begins when he attempts to draw illusory justification from sentimentalized nature, and it expands to include an equally sentimental religious feeling. The "landscape gave him assurance. A fair field holding life. It was the religion of peace. It would die if its timid eyes were compelled to see blood. He conceived Nature to be a woman with a deep aversion to tragedy." He throws a pine-cone at a squirrel, and the squirrel, to Henry's immense satisfaction, runs away: "There was the law, he said [conveniently forgetting that a man is not a squirrel]. Nature had given him a sign." Although he then observes a "small animal" pounce into black water and "emerge directly with a gleaming fish," Henry needs stronger medicine and, moving "from obscurity into promises of a greater obscurity," he soon gets it. He blunders into the forest "chapel" with its "gentle brown carpet," its "religious half light"; and the way in which he perceives this mere hole in the woods should recall his earlier view of death as a means of getting "to some place where he would be understood." This sentimental religious feeling is thus equated with Henry's sentimental view of nature, and both illusions are brutally shattered when he finds a rotting corpse in the "chapel" where one would expect to find the altar. This putrid matter being eaten by ants does not suggest that death is any gateway to understanding, that nature has any aversion whatsoever to such tragedies, or that some sort of Christian doctrine is the theme of the novel. Rationalization which overrides one's personal honesty can only lead to moral death (as George Kelcey also demonstrates); death literally blocks Henry's way at this point, and he has to find a new direction.

His new direction comes when out of curiosity he runs towards a great roar of battle. This first tentative step towards emerging from the forest is consciously determined, and Henry is aware that it is "an ironical thing for him to be running thus toward that which he had been at such pains to avoid"; but he now wants "to come to the edge of the forest that he might peer out." However, Henry then meets the tattered man—one of Crane's finest characters—whose question, "Where yeh hit, ol' boy?" causes him to panic; and his guilt and sense of isolation immediately lead him to another illusion: "he regarded the wounded soldiers in an envious way. He conceived persons with torn bodies to be peculiarly happy. He wished that he, too, had a wound." To reveal to Henry the real absurdity of such thoughts, to puncture this insane illusion, Crane lets him witness the appalling death of Jim Conklin. And if this seems too slight an accomplishment for so intensely written a scene, one should remember that this whole section of the novel is, after all, a virtuoso performance in prolonging the delay of Henry's actual experience of combat. Also, Conklin's death is as necessary to Henry's education as his parallel encounter with the corpse was. In its presentation of human suffering considered specifically against the infinite back-drop of the amoral universe this scene is a young author's first attempt at coping with a theme that immensely interested him; hence, as only [O. W. Fryckstedt] has noted, there is absolutely no irony in the portrayal of Henry in this passage. "Although Fleming cuts a rather pitiful figure under the towering sky, Crane's intention is not satirical. In fact this is one point in the book where the author seems to identify himself wholly with his character." Henry rebels against the universe at this grotesque and meaningless death of a man he has known since boyhood, and his rebellion is simultaneously as futile, as absurd, and as understandable as the belief of the men in an open boat who think that fate will not drown them because they have worked so hard to get within sight of shore. The implicit truth behind the destruction of Henry's illusion is that man's position in this world is bleak enough as it is without wishing for any wounds to make it worse. Finally, it must be stated that the text offers no evidence of Conklin's death accomplishing anything else. Shortly thereafter, Henry commits his greatest sin: he deliberately deserts the tattered man who selflessly worries about others even when he is himself at the edge of the grave.

Because of the importance of the tattered man in Henry's journey to awareness, this episode can reasonably be considered a parallel scene comparable to the two just examined. That is, the desertion of this dying man is in itself Henry's illusion. His bitter and immediate self-loathing—"he now thought that he wished he was dead"—foreshadows what Crane makes explicit in the final chapter: the tattered man will always haunt Henry, not because of anything he does to Henry, but because of what Henry does to him. This desertion is the limit of Henry's penetration into the direful thicket of cowardice, selfishness, and immaturity; and as he can go no further, he must once more seek a new direction—metaphorically the only one left to him—a way out of the "forest" and back to his original commitment. (pp. 111-14)

Henry begins a debate with himself: he wants to go forward, his fear invents excuses, and his reason overcomes these excuses one by one as they are raised. This debate ends in defeat only because Henry believes there is absolutely no way in which he can return to his regiment with self-respect. And this belief, of course, turns out to be the illusion which forms the basis of his final episode in the forest.

However, Henry's mental debate itself accomplishes two important results: it enables Henry to transcend by an effort of will his most absurd selfishness—his wish for the defeat of his own army—and it sufficiently calms his mind for him to realize, for the first time since his original flight, that his physical condition—hunger, thirst, extreme fatigue—suggests he is actually "jest one little feller," ordinary, weak, fallible. His inner debate ends when he sees the very men with whom he had lately identified himself flee back through the woods in terror. He leaps into the midst of these panic-stricken men *in an attempt to rally them,* and receives his red badge of courage when one of them clubs him in the head with a rifle butt.

Crane probably seized upon this incident for his final title because of the complex ironies woven into it, because of its centrality to a story about courage and various sorts of wounds, and because Henry has to win his way to manhood by struggle as one wins a badge.... He has already revealed his intent, his desire to return. The external fact of the wound changes nothing whatsoever within Henry's mind. Chance merely provides the means for which he has already been searching, the means of returning to his regiment secure from outward ridicule. He is guided back by the cheery-voiced soldier, a man who helps others without vanity or even a wish for thanks, exactly as Henry should have helped the tattered man. Henry tells his lie—which ironically proves unnecessary—is nursed by Wilson and, being both physically and emotionally exhausted, is put to bed in his friend's blankets.

In terms of Crane's structural pattern, Henry is now back in his original position and again about to confront the unknown, still untried in battle—so he believes—still afraid. Nevertheless, the short story has become a novel, and within Henry's mind a major battle has been fought and won. Although he still does not know how he will act when he confronts the unknown, the bitter experience of this fantastic day's journey through the moral forest has brought Henry to a secure knowledge of what he can *not* do when the time for this confrontation comes, for him, on the morrow.

His actions the next morning, however, are not reassuring. His vanity returns with his sense of security, he complains loudly, and he treats Wilson quite shabbily. This reassertion of the old Henry is demanded by dramatic necessity (if growth of character is contingent upon awareness Crane cannot very well make much of a change in Henry before he experiences actual combat), and Crane justifies it with great care by making it serve at least three functions. Henry's undesirable traits first provide a necessary contrast in order to emphasize the change which has occurred in Wilson, who has already had his baptism of fire:

> He seemed no more to be continually regarding the proportions of his personal prowess.... He was no more a loud young soldier. There was about him now a fine reliance. He showed a quiet belief in his purposes and his abilities.... And the youth saw that ever after it would be easier to live in his friend's neighborhood.

Given Crane's technique of the parallel scene, this passage has to foreshadow the change which Henry will also undergo once he successfully faces up to his own commitment; it can have no other function. Henry's vain foolishness at this point is also important as a contrast with his yesterday's view of himself— yesterday he had seen himself lower than all other men, and mocked by nature; today, like George Kelcey, he imagines himself "a fine creation ... the chosen of some gods," and

he considers nature "a fine thing moving with a magnificent justice"—and because these absurdities allow Crane to show that Henry is now capable of perceiving the falseness of his position. His "pompous and veteranlike" thoughts are just as foolish, of course, as those he revealed during his flight; and neither passage presents Crane's own view of the universe and man's place in it. But no one has noticed that these silly illusions form a carefully wrought sequence in themselves which begins with Henry's smug sense of power over Wilson because of the packet, rises to a climax of loud complaint, and ends suddenly when this swelling pomposity is "pierced" by a fellow soldier's lazy comment: "Mebbe yeh think yeh fit th' hull battle yesterday, Fleming." Henry is *inwardly* "reduced to an abject pulp by these chance words." Henry, in short, has assumed a vain pose and has been acting out his role as if the external view of himself were all that mattered; the laconic comment pierces this pose by abruptly awakening Henry's conscience, and the whole external pose collapses before this inner voice's inflexible command that Henry view himself as he really is. This whole sequence, finally, helps Henry prepare psychologically to face up to the coming fight.

When the battle comes, Henry turns his reawakened self-loathing and self-hatred upon the enemy, and he chooses to stay and fight rather than run again into that terrible forest: "He had taken up a first position behind the little tree, with a direct determination to hold it against the world." After making this willed commitment, Henry slips again into the trance of battle sleep, fights like a regular "war devil," and after the skirmish he emerges from his trance with the praise of his comrades ringing in his ears. (pp. 114-17)

Henry has thus successfully *passed through* the unknown, the feared experience, and *this* time because he has not run he accepts the fact, even though, again because of battle sleep, he has not actually *experienced* the unknown itself. Hence, he has a great deal to ponder about. The excellent irony of this crucial episode is *not* that Henry has become a hero in his battle sleep—Crane never offers the reader such an absurd definition of heroism—but that during this sleep Henry has successfully passed through the very experience upon which his imagination and fear have been intensely centred since the beginning of the novel: the monumental irony is that Henry has endured all his suffering, all the tortures of his imagination, over an action which is so easily done that one can do it superbly while in a trance. The implications which follow from this ironic deflation should be clear to the reader, even if Henry is not yet capable of sorting them out: if the feared unknown, the hideous dragon of war, can be successfully encountered while one is in a trance, then Henry's former imaginings, fears, concepts of knightly heroism, all such feverish activity of his weak mental machinery, stand revealed as absurd. Henry, in other words, for the first time since the novel began, is now in a position to learn authentic self-knowledge, to perceive the reality which is actually before his eyes to be seen, and to acquire the humility which Wilson has already attained.

Henry's subsequent actions immensely favour this conclusion. He accepts his own insignificance when he overhears his regiment of "mule drivers" ordered into an action from which few are expected to emerge alive. And, even though he knows the danger of the coming battle, there is no hesitation in Henry, no thought of flight. Hence, it follows reasonably from this deliberate courage that Henry should finally be able to experience actual combat in full possession of all his faculties. In fact, Crane insists upon Henry's awareness, both of the external and the inner reality, during this charge: "It seemed to the youth that he saw everything. Each blade of the green grass was bold and clear . . . all were comprehended. His mind took a mechanical but firm impression, so that afterward everything was pictured and explained to him, *save why he himself was there*" (my italics). The final phrase simply points to Henry's remembrance of his past failures. The frenzy of this charge, not a blind rage of battle sleep, is described as a "temporary but sublime absence of selfishness. And because it was of this order was the reason, perhaps, why the youth wondered, afterward, what reasons he could have had for being there." Henry, like the other men, still shows anger, pride, wild excitement; but such qualities are good ones for a soldier to have because they help him stand and fight, they could hardly be omitted from any realistic presentation of men at war, they do not make these men less than human, and Henry never again loses his grip on his consciousness because of them. These men reveal anger and pride in this situation precisely because they are men who hold themselves responsible for their own actions and seek the good opinion of their fellow men. Henry has yet to learn that if a man satisfies his own sense of personal honesty, this is enough; the opinions of others, just one more externality, will vary with the several views which others take of one's actions. Chapter 21 prepares Henry for this stoic lesson.

The elated regiment returns from their charge, only to be taunted by veterans who observe how little ground was covered. Henry soon accepts the view that the extent of the charge was comparatively "trivial," even though he feels "a considerable joy in musing upon his performances during the charge" (a joy which is not unreasonable when we recall that only yesterday Henry had fled in panic from this same situation). When a general states yet another point of view—that the charge was a military failure, and the "mule drivers" now seem to him to be "mud diggers"—the lieutenant's defence of his own men implies that a military failure is in itself no criterion of the performance of the men doing the fighting. And the chapter ends with Wilson and Fleming being told of the praise they have received from the lieutenant and colonel of their own regiment. Wilson and Fleming have every right to feel pleased at this praise; and the fact that they "speedily forgot many things," that for them "the past held no pictures of error and disappointment," does not indicate that they are mere automatons at the mercy of external circumstance: it indicates that in their first flush of pleasure they have not yet assimilated and considered this praise in the total perspective which is specifically demanded by the several points of view presented in this very chapter. There is no time for assimilation of anything at this point because the novel immediately roars on into yet another battle, a final skirmish in which Henry's actions confirm the self-control he has recently acquired. During this fight all the men act like veterans by tending strictly to business and Wilson even captures an enemy flag; after the battle he holds this prize "with vanity" as he and Henry, both still caught up in the excitement of the moment, congratulate each other. The time for reflection and assimilation comes only with the final chapter when Henry walks away from the battle-field and is again free to probe into his own mind.

The endless critical squabbles which have arisen over this final chapter hinge upon a single question: does Fleming achieve any moral growth or development of character? Yet any Crane student should be able to answer this question almost without consulting this chapter at all—without reading Crane's description of Henry's change of soul which requires at least two pages in most editions. To claim that Fleming does *not* achieve

any growth or development is to ignore many quite obvious statements of his gradual moral progress that are scattered throughout the novel, the entire function of Wilson's role, and the fact that Crane must have had some reason for endowing Henry—unlike the earlier protagonists—with awareness and a conscience. It is also well to remember that Crane is trying to be psychologically realistic: this is the *first* time Henry has full opportunity to reflect upon all the experiences which have crowded the past two days of his life, he is still a young lad not yet even twenty-four hours removed from the very nadir of self-abasement, and, like Wilson whose development preceded his own, Henry is still "capable of vanity. Even in the final chapter of the novel, Crane still writes as of a process that is going on. Fleming's mind, he says, 'was under-going a subtle change'; nevertheless, the final paragraphs describe that change in detail, and the unmistakable traits of genuine maturity . . . are present."

Crane devotes the first two pages, over a fourth of the chapter, to a careful preparation for the important matters which follow. The battle is over for the day, and, as the regiment ironically marches back over the same ground they had taken at great cost, the reader is taken direcly into Henry's mind. He begins by rejoicing that he has come forth, escaped, from "a land of strange, squalling upheavals." The deliberately ambiguous language here should suggest *all* of Private Fleming's various battles, with the enemy, the "arrayed forces of the universe," and his own weaknesses. Then Henry attempts to consider all that has happened to him from the point of view of the new perspective he has attained by living through these past two days. And here Crane is again explicit, neither ironic nor ambiguous:

> he began to study his deeds, [both] his failures, and his achievements. Thus, fresh from scenes where many of his usual machines of reflection had been idle . . . he struggled to marshal all his acts.
>
> At last they marched before him clearly. From this present view point he was enabled to look at them in spectator fashion and to criticize them with some correctness, for his new condition had already defeated certain sympathies.

Henry's "procession of memory" begins with the most recent events, his public deeds which are recalled with delight because they tell him "he was good." This recollection seems reasonable, so far as it goes; these public deeds, after all, have been good. But the next sentence reveals Henry's error a few moments before he himself corrects it: "He recalled with a thrill of joy the respectful comments of his fellows upon his conduct." Henry, in short, begins with his old error of judging himself by the opinion of others, by his external reputation. The entire remaining portion of his self-analysis consists of the assaults made upon this public image by the shameful recollections of his private deeds until, finally, an equilibrium is attained in which both public and private views of the self take permanent position in a realistic, balanced judgement. (pp. 117-21)

Once he attains this balanced view of himself, he is able to foresee "some new ways" of life for him in the future: "He found that he could look back upon the brass and bombast of his earlier gospels and see them truly. He was gleeful when he discovered that he now despised them. Henry's weak mental machinery, in short, has undergone considerable readjustment. His eyes have finally opened, and he is now able to begin perceiving correctly the reality which has been before him and largely unchanged since the novel began. Henry's personal honesty can now assert itself in morally significant action, and he is ready to begin the difficult practice of manhood in an amoral universe.

> *With this conviction* [my italics] came a store of assurance. He felt a quiet manhood, nonassertive but of sturdy and strong blood. He knew that he would no more quail before his guides wherever they should point. He had been to touch the great death, and found that, after all, it was but the great death. He was a man.

I am unable to find much irony in the closing paragraphs of the novel. Henry is exhausted from all his battles and gratefully marching to a rest. Only the most romantically obtuse reader at this point could believe in the actuality of "an existence of soft and eternal peace," but the image aptly describes how inviting the coming rest must seem to a weary young soldier. Certainly Henry is not fooling himself; his quiet confidence that he will "no more quail before his guides wherever they should point" would be meaningless if he really anticipated an existence of soft and eternal peace. And the final image seems to me merely an emblem of what has just happened to Henry. He has attained authentic self-knowledge and a sense of manhood after long and fierce battles with his own moral weaknesses; hence it seems entirely appropriate that Crane should end this tale with the image of a golden ray of sunlight appearing through hosts of leaden rain clouds. Irony has its function earlier in Crane's pattern, before the protagonist becomes aware of the reality he struggles to perceive correctly. (pp. 123-24)

> *Marston LaFrance, in his* A Reading of Stephen Crane, *Oxford at the Clarendon Press, 1971, 272 p.*

MICHAEL J. HOFFMAN (essay date 1972)

[*Hoffman is an American educator and critic. In the following excerpt, he discusses* The Red Badge of Courage *as a work signaling the transition in American literature from Realism to Naturalism.*]

The Red Badge of Courage, although not quite a purely "Naturalistic" novel, nonetheless demonstrates the transition from Realism to Naturalism as well as any American book. Through the instrument of the Realistic style the author presents a vision of man as a creature his existence in and meaningful interaction with the world. The Naturalistic novel increasingly sees the individual consciousness, not as whose reality stems more from his primitive consciousness than from interacting with a society, but as swept along by the inchoate forces that control both the social order in which he is a citizen and the cosmic order in which he is a cipher. The **Red Badge of Courage** sees man as a physiological mote swept willy-nilly by the winds of circumstance.

Stephen Crane's semicomic Everyman, Henry Fleming, is an intentionally unheroic, undistinguished individual, who lacks the social standing of either Captain Ahab or Reverend Dimmesdale and the intuitive moral vision of Huckleberry Finn. He exists on a primitive level of consciousness in which his rationalizations—his distinguishing psychological characteristic—are a direct indication of his limited moral sense, rather than a comic device, as in *Huck Finn*. As an individual, Henry is nothing at all, a cipher of no significance who may be struck down at any moment by a bullet or a rifle butt; and as a social being he is a lowly private, without any standing whatever in

the military hierarchy. Throughout most of the book he is nameless, called by his author "the youth," just as his companion Wilson is "the friend." By reducing Henry Fleming to namelessness, Crane denigrates him to the level of a simple consciousness who, in the midst of circumstances that sweep him away, rationalizes all his contradictory actions with continuous illogic.

Crane has been described as a literary impressionist who tries with verbal pigmentation to create the impression of a landscape emerging through hazy light. But this is merely a technique which embodies a much deeper urge in his writing. Here is the opening paragraph of the novel:

> The cold passed reluctantly from the earth, and the retiring fogs revealed an army stretched out on the hills, resting. As the landscape changed from brown to green, the army awakened, and began to tremble with eagerness at the noise of rumors. It cast its eyes upon the roads, which were growing from long troughs of liquid mud to proper thoroughfares. A river, amber-tinted in the shadow of its banks, purled at the army's feet; and at night, when the stream had become of a sorrowful blackness, one could see across it the red, eyelike gleam of hostile camp-fires set in the low brows of distant hills.

By personifying the landscape with an almost mystic quality of emergence, especially when his human characters are emerging from sleep into consciousness, Crane attempts to embody a world that seethes with energies beyond man's control. He does not try to show a spiritual correspondence between man and nature in the manner of Transcendentalism; Crane creates a world that is full of its own kind of life and men that are full of theirs, though the two kinds of energies cannot possibly work together.

In Henry Fleming's universe the old traditions no longer obtain. Although in the beginning Henry sees the great war with the eyes of a boy—

> He had, of course, dreamed of battles all his life—of vague and bloody conflicts that had thrilled him with their sweep and fire. In visions he had seen himself in many struggles.

—in his sober, more rational moments he understands that these youthful fantasies are no longer valid:

> From his home his youthful eyes had looked upon the war in his own country with distrust. It must be some sort of a play affair. He had long despaired of witnessing a Greeklike struggle. Such would be no more, he had said. Men were better, or more timid. Secular and religious education had effaced the throat-grappling instinct, or else firm finance held in check the passions.

His reasoning follows a curiously contradictory line of thought that brings together both biological and economic determinism. For Crane, men's choices are determined by a combination of animal instincts and social institutions.

The society to which Henry submits himself—that of an army at war—is a hierarchy in which he has no function other than to obey orders. The private is asked to live on a minimal level of consciousness and moral responsibility, subject to the control of others and to forces that are larger than anything he could possibly be conscious of fighting for. There are no issues at stake in the war that Crane recreates in **The Red Badge;** there is only movement, frustration, and death. At night Union and Confederate soldiers talk to one another when on guard, but during the day the same people kill one another, because that is the way one behaves in wartime; they shoot when shot at, they run when frightened, they are heroic by accident, and they are cowardly in the same way. Crane presents scene, action, and character through a highly controlled point of view that allows almost no authorial comment and judgment, a style that corresponds in its cold objectivity to the world in which the characters find themselves.

Because value exists in neither society nor situation, and because Crane posits nothing transcendent except natural energies, the only source of human identity lies within the individual consciousness. But this consciousness is not an autonomous unit that reflects either a consistent moral system or a coherent point of view. It reacts to situations, and the judgments it passes on its own actions are nothing more than rationalizations. However, rationalizations are a necessary defense. The environment is a continuous threat to the very existence of every human being, and because the individual can locate no value outside himself, he finds it humanly necessary to justify all he does by its role in perpetuating his sense of identity. When Henry runs, he composes in his head the following justification:

> He had fled, he told himself, because annihilation approached. He had done a good part in saving himself, who was a little piece of the army. He had considered the time, he said, to be one in which it was the duty of every little piece to rescue itself if possible. Later the officers could fit the little pieces together again, and make a battle front. If none of the little pieces were wise enough to save themselves from the flurry of death at such a time, why, then, where would be the army? It was all plain that he had proceeded according to very correct and commendable rules. His actions had been sagacious things. They had been full of strategy. They were the work of a master's legs.

The substitution of "legs" for the expected "mind" is a clever ironic touch. But except for that, Crane lets Henry's rationalizations speak without any comment by the author; for Henry's rationalizations are his only source of personal value.

Crane as an incipient Naturalist sees two primary causes for human action: an external force—nameless, inchoate, but fully felt as a presence even if but partially understood—that sweeps the individual along its inexorable path; and the unconscious reactions that control most of the individual's responses and all his rationalizations, but which are themselves almost completely controlled by the external forces. When Henry experiences his first battle,

> He was bewildered. As he ran with his comrades he strenuously tried to think, but all he knew was that if he fell down those coming behind would tread upon him. All his faculties seemed to be needed to guide him over and past obstructions. He felt carried along by a mob.

He does not choose his reactions; he simply becomes part of a mob that has an individual will but no room for the responses of individuals. He feels that the "iron laws of tradition and law" are closing in on him, and when he later begins to fire his weapon, he feels this unspoken force determining all his actions:

> He suddenly lost concern for himself, and forgot to look at a menacing fate. He became not a man but a member. He felt that something of which he was a part—a regiment, an army, a cause, or a country—

was in a crisis. He was welded into a common personality which was dominated by a single desire. For some moments he could not flee no more than a little finger can commit a revolution from a hand.

He tries to define the "something" that controls his actions, and he uses a number of different words to isolate it; but he can know only how he responds to that "something" because it is, in truth, indefinable.

The image of the finger on the hand completes the metaphor begun earlier when he felt "not a man but a member." Still later, when he is trying to find his way back to his regiment, he attempts to state his feelings of impotence more philosophically:

> He searched about in his mind for an adequate malediction for the indefinite cause, the thing upon which men turn the words of final blame. It—whatever it was—was responsible for him, he said. There lay the fault.

There has always been something comic in blaming the stars rather than ourselves for our failings, but I think that Crane takes Henry's torment with some seriousness. When one has ceased to believe in a source of value outside the self, it is still difficult to believe that blame should be placed inside, especially when it is unclear whether or not such blame is deserved. Henry's alternatives are so limited by his situation that the idea of moral praise or castigation is quite irrelevant. In such situations moral values become, as Emerson noted in "Self-Reliance," merely names.

Early in the book, when Henry discusses whether or not he will run in battle, he unintentionally insults his companion. When the loud soldier leaves indignantly, Henry feels "alone in space" like "a mental outcast." He stretches out on his blanket and "In the darkness he saw visions of a thousand-tongued fear that would babble at his back and cause him to flee, while others were going coolly about their country's business." And it is, of course, fear that causes him to run during his first action—fear and the mob psychology that causes everyone else to panic at the same time. He yells "with fright" and becomes as disoriented as a "proverbial chicken"; then he runs. And yet the fear that turns him irrational is no different from the emotion he feels later on when his acts are "heroic."

> Within him, as he hurled himself forward, was born a love, a despairing fondness for this flag which was near him. It was a creation of beauty and invulnerability. It was a goddess, radiant, that bended its form with an imperious gesture to him. It was a woman, red and white, hating and loving, that called him with the voice of his hopes. Because no harm could come to it he endowed it with power. He kept near, as if it could be a saver of lives, and an imploring cry went from his mind.

His irrational flood of emotions—now that the momentum of battle is going his way—can be turned into an outward act of bravery rather than an inward panic; but they are two sides of the same emotion. Circumstance determines action.

Throughout everything the natural world is personified as permanent and indifferent:

> As he gazed around him the youth felt a flash of astonishment at the blue, pure sky and the sun-gleamings on the trees and fields. It was surprising that Nature had gone tranquilly on with her golden process in the midst of so much devilment.

Nature, although she has her own life force, is not involved with the lives of men, except indirectly. Even at the end of the book when Henry has achieved a false sense of equanimity Crane once more emphasizes nature's indifference:

> But the sky would forget. It was true, he admitted, that in the world it was the habit to cry devil at persons who refused to trust what they could not trust, but he thought that perhaps the stars dealt differently. The imperturbable sun shines on insult and worship.

Man cannot turn to the stars for solace, and his attempts to blame the universe for his plight are comic.

But an even more pointed key to Crane's attitudes can be found in his imagery. Consistent with the view of man projected by such Darwinists as Spencer and Huxley, Crane's imagery presents man as an animal subject paradoxically to mechanical forces. (pp. 130-36)

[Men] are always animals, and the mere fact that they have a more sophisticated consciousness than dogs and horses does not change the fact that in a universe totally indifferent to human beings an individual can demand nothing more than to be at the arbitrary whim of fate and circumstance. The movement from Emerson's vision seems almost complete.

The other half of Crane's world view envisions a mechanistic universe that runs continuously with the animal metaphor. Men at war are cogs in a great machine. When Henry watches the gunners fire enthusiastically at the enemy while he himself is running, he thinks of them as "Methodical idiots! Machinelike fools!". And when his panic is over, he becomes curious once more about the state of the battle:

> Presently he proceeded again on his forward way. The battle was like the grinding of an immense and terrible machine to him. Its complexities and powers, its grim processes, fascinated him. He must go close and see it produce corpses.

This view of the war as an immense machine that produces commodities continues in his feelings about the Union army:

> His education had been that success for that mighty blue machine was certain; that it would make victories as a contrivance turns out buttons.

Later, when things go less well for a moment, he thinks that "the regiment was a machine run down." Still later, when the battle begins to go better for his side, the martial sounds take on cosmic connotations:

> To those in the midst of it it became a din fitted to the universe. It was the whirring and thumping of gigantic machinery, complications among the smaller stars.

The universal war machine obeys the laws of mechanics. Once again the images can be multiplied.

This concatenated imagery presents two major impulses of what have come to be called Naturalism; man as animal and the universe as machine. These ideas develop side by side throughout the book, giving the impression that mechanical laws govern a biological world in which not necessarily the fittest, but certainly the luckiest, survive. Both the laws of the universe and the interests of man are autonomous, and although both exist in the same space-time, they do not interact with reciprocity. Neither the universe nor the individual has any significance; they just are.

Henry Fleming seems in some way to have learned that Naturalistic lesson. The reader is told that "He had been to touch the great death, and found that, after all, it was but the great death. If one believes that man's life has no cosmic significance, that man is not here for any purpose other than to exist in a meaningless universe, then death is no longer the great mystery, for it opens up nothing on the other side. Not even as mysterious as Ahab's "pasteboard mask," it is just that event that lies at the end of the future. But some caution must be applied to the conclusions Henry draws about himself. Throughout *The Red Badge* he rationalizes every one of his actions, showing thereby that the human capacity for self-justification is unlimited. And now, at the end of the book we are told:

> He had been an animal blistered and sweating in the heat and pain of war. He turned now with a lover's thirst to images of tranquil skies, fresh meadows, cool brooks—an existence of soft and eternal peace.
>
> Over the river a golden ray of sun came through the hosts of leaden rain clouds.

Taken at face value, these words are too idyllic to fit credibly with the rest of the book. Crane shows Henry making a final ironic rationalization in order to complete the cycle of his self-delusion. Perhaps he has achieved a certain humility, but he has certainly not become "a man" in so short a time. Who knows how he will respond in the next battle? Even more, what difference does it make? He could be struck down by an arbitrary bullet the following day, and all his moral transformation would mean exactly nothing in any context larger than that of his own life—which is all that it has meant anyway. What solidifies this reading of the end of the book is the last sentence, which is given a place all by itself. It is the kind of easy emotion common in cheap fiction and the movies, in which moral transformations always seem to be symbolized by sudden changes in the weather. But cheap emotion has been a subject of irony throughout *The Red Badge.* There are no easy transformations. Crane has stated only two pages earlier that "The imperturbable sun shines on insult and worship," stressing, as always, the permanence and indifference of nature. To present a sun that suddenly smiles with meaning on Henry Fleming at the end of the book would be to violate everything that has gone before. The last lines must be read ironically if the reader is to continue to take the book with final seriousness on its own terms. Man remains an insignificant creature at the whim of forces in a universe he cannot control; and in reaction to uncontrollable circumstances he can do nothing more than rationalize.

Stephen Crane, although viscerally deterministic, is not a Naturalist in the full sense of Jack London, Frank Norris, and Theodore Dreiser. These writers believed in an *ideology* of determinism that grew out of their various readings in Marx, Darwin, Huxley, Spencer, Zola, and Nietzsche, mixed with temperaments that no doubt found these thinkers' ideas congenial. Crane, however, seems to have come upon his deterministic world view largely through his direct response to the world, examined without a mediating vision in the classic Realist manner. He dramatizes man's lack of free will without simply trying to demonstrate it as a philosophical point, and the lesson of Henry Fleming is thus more vivid than that, say, of one of Jack London's dogs. This is not to say that all Naturalistic fiction is merely thesis-ridden. The best of it, such as *Sister Carrie,* does transcend its ideology to present characters with experiences just as vivid as Henry Fleming's. And it is, after all, just this dramatic vividness of experience that constitutes much of what is considered valuable in fiction. (pp. 136-39)

Michael J. Hoffman, "From Realism to Naturalism," in his The Subversive Vision: American Romanticism in Literature, Kennikat Press, 1972, pp. 129-53.

HENRY BINDER   (essay date 1978)

[*In the following excerpt, Binder traces what he believes were Crane's original intentions for* The Red Badge of Courage *through an analysis of the numerous points of variance in the last chapter of the novel in Crane's manuscript version and the text of the Appleton first edition. For a contrasting view of Binder's conclusions, see the excerpt by Donald Pizer (1985).*]

This essay celebrates an unknown novel by Stephen Crane entitled *The Red Badge of Courage,* a novel that only a few of Crane's friends and early editors ever had a chance to read, a *Red Badge of Courage* that existed only in Crane's manuscript, not in any published version of the story. In the manuscript, the novel is longer and much different from the *Red Badge* that was first issued as a book by D. Appleton & Co. of New York in October, 1895. The Appleton edition pleased the contemporary audience and has become a classic of American literature, but it is not what Crane conceived the story to be. Most contemporary readers found the Appleton *Red Badge* to be an account of a young man's growth from confused youth to resolute manhood; but ever since the first close readings appeared in the 1940s, modern critics have argued inconclusively as to whether or not this growth takes place; and still others have said that *Red Badge* is a flawed work which cannot be satisfactorily explicated. What happened is that Crane wrote an ironic story in the manuscript, a story in which the central character does not undergo any positive growth; and then apparently in response to editorial suggestions at Appleton, made or allowed two series of deletions in the novel just prior to publication. These deletions confused the original irony; reduced the psychological complexity of Henry Fleming, the main character; also obscured the function of Wilson and the tattered man; and left the text incoherent at several places, in particular the final chapter. The critical disagreements about *Red Badge* arise mainly because of the problematic state of the text Appleton published, a text which, owing to the cuts, no longer embodied Crane's intentions.

As things stand now, Crane's masterpiece is an unread work. And because some pages are missing from the manuscript as a result of the deletions, certain details of the original *Red Badge* may never be known, and we may never be able to read the story in its full richness. Nevertheless, by restoring passages legible in manuscript but not included in the Appleton edition, and by using passages from Crane's early draft to supply closely equivalent text for some of the missing pages, the manuscript can be reconstructed to provide a satisfactory reading text, one in which the author's original conception is available in all essentials. (pp. 9-10)

The basic interpretive disagreements about *Red Badge* in modern criticism arise mainly over the final chapter which Crane originally intended as a quiet but sharply ironic coda demonstrating Henry Fleming's continuing proclivity for vainglorious egotism and self-delusion. Since in the Appleton edition the final chapter was left especially confusing and incoherent by the second-stage deletions, it is natural that critics have found that chapter difficult or impossible to explicate. A recent essay

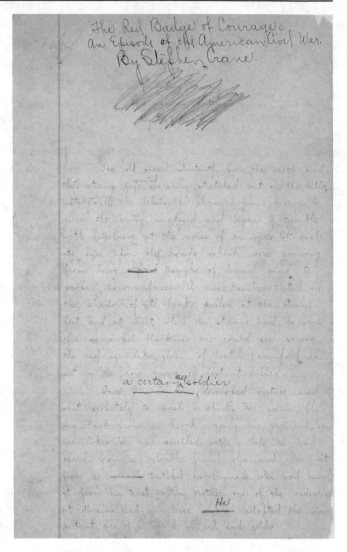

The first manuscript page of The Red Badge of Courage.

(1974) by Robert Rechnitz [see Additional Bibliography] opens with the observation that, "Studies of *The Red Badge of Courage* continue to question whether the intention of the novel's final paragraphs is literal or ironic"; Rechnitz himself concludes that "it is impossible to take the final four paragraphs as either intentionally straightforward or ironic in tone"; and he agrees with Richard Chase that, ultimately, "these paragraphs reflect Crane's embarrassment 'about the necessity of pointing a moral.'" Rechnitz is correct in observing that the final paragraphs of the Appleton text are obscure. But Chase's hypothesis proceeds from the assumption that the Appleton version of the final chapter represents Crane's intentions for ending the novel. Even if Crane was "embarrassed" about moralizing, this would have no bearing on the textual problems in the final chapter, for they exist solely because of the excisions. To agree with Chase and others who have said that Crane failed as an artist, that he could not write a satisfactory final chapter to *Red Badge,* is to deny the existence of the chapter he *did* write, the one which ends *Red Badge* in the manuscript.

In fact, the final chapter of the Appleton edition was so altered that it was left problematic in much more than the last four paragraphs, and much more than the "tone" was rendered ambiguous. By offering . . . a demonstration of why the Appleton text does *not* make sense, followed by an interpretive reading of the same chapter as it stands in the manuscript, I hope to show how different these two versions of the ending are; and as a by-product of this demonstration, make clear why critics have had such difficulty in explicating the story.

Crane's original design in the final chapter was to have Henry Fleming recall from the first day of battle those experiences about which he is still ashamed, and then have him contrive justifications and excuses to resolve his shame. The experiences in question are his flight from battle (which lost most of its sting after his success on the second day), his denunciations of the cosmos, and his desertion of the tattered man. But in the Appleton edition Henry could not reflect on his rebellions against the heavens because they had already been deleted in the manuscript. Nor could he offer his highly questionable "plan for the utilization of a sin" to justify his desertion of the tattered man if he was to be pushed toward the character of a morally changed hero. In the Appleton final chapter, Henry's guilt over these experiences is still evoked, but only shreds of the original justifications appear. With these justifications deleted along with other material, the chapter is erratic and confusing and terminates on an inappropriate note, the bright promise of "Over the river a golden ray of sun came through the hosts of leaden rain clouds." In short, the ambiguity in the final Appleton paragraphs that Rechnitz and others have noted exists for one reason: *because things are missing.*

About midway in the Appleton chapter Henry has his first guilty thoughts: "Nevertheless, the ghost of his flight from the first engagement appeared to him and danced. There were small shoutings in his brain about these matters." The Appleton text reads "these matters," but there is only one "matter" present, because the appropriate revision was not made at the time of the excision of the other matter which appeared after "danced" ("Echoes of his terrible combat with the arrayed forces of the universe came to his ears"). In the Appleton edition, Henry has a passing response to "these matters": "For a moment he blushed, and the light of his soul flickered with shame"; but it is passing indeed, for the next paragraphs which contained Henry's "explanation" and "apology" for his rebellions were cut. The following paragraph in the Appleton text opens with Henry's immediate conjuring of a different problem from the previous day: "A specter of reproach came to him. There loomed the dogging memory of the tattered soldier." Henry's thoughts about his desertion of the tattered man continue, interrupted at one point by a snatch of dialogue from the soldiers near him, until the matter is closed by a sentence that begins the fifth-to-last paragraph: "Yet gradually he mustered force to put the sin at a distance." But the reader never learns about the nature of Henry's "force" or what kind of "distance" is involved, because—except for this sentence—the Appleton edition deleted all of a two-paragraph description of how Henry transforms his "sin" into a usable voice in his moral conscience. The sentence beginning "Yet gradually" originally served to introduce this description; in the Appleton text, however, the sentence was spliced onto the paragraph that *followed* Henry's rationalizing process. A short phrase—"And at last"—was added at the beginning of the next sentence to imply the duration of the excised process of distancing and ease the transition to Henry's final thoughts on his rebellions: "Yet gradually he mustered force to put the sin at a distance. And at last his eyes seemed to open to some new ways. He found that he could look back upon the brass and bombast of his earlier gospels and see them truly. He was gleeful when he discovered

that he now despised them." Henry may well be both gleeful and despising here all at once, but the careful reader of the Appleton text can only be confused, wondering if he has not forgotten something, namely the "earlier gospels." None of their brass and bombast was any longer in the story.

Having the apparent notion that either glee or despisal or both taken together are convictive, the narrator seems to proceed positively and unhesitatingly in the next Appleton paragraph: "With this conviction came a store of assurance. He felt a quiet manhood, nonassertive but of sturdy and strong blood. He knew that he would no more quail before his guides wherever they should point. He had been to touch the great death, and found that, after all, it was but the great death. He was a man." The reader, however, has reason to be less than convinced by Henry's "store of assurance," for there is no "conviction" left: deletion of the two paragraphs which originally preceded its mention having removed the "conviction" on which Henry's assurance is founded—his sense that he is "tiny but not inconsequent to the sun." The reader of the Appleton text is also left to wonder who Henry's "guides" might be in this paragraph, since they were lost as a consequence of the excisions.

The next, third-to-last, paragraph in the Appleton edition begins, as it does in the manuscript, in high biblical style: "So it came to pass that as he trudged from the place of blood and wrath his soul changed." Then there is a paraphrase of Henry's thoughts which includes a biblical allusion: "He came from hot plowshares to prospects of clover tranquilly, and it was as if hot plowshares were not. Scars faded as flowers." The ironic tone of this allusion to Isaiah 11:4 ("They shall beat their swords into ploughshares") is clear in the manuscript when preceding it in one of the deleted passages appears the sentence, "It had been necessary for him to swallow swords that he might have a better throat for grapes"—a highly ironic echo of Revelation 19:15. But without this foregoing irony, Henry's transposition from hot ploughshares to clover seems intended literally and in concert with "his soul changed." And the two final Appleton paragraphs seem to support the idea that Henry has changed as he turns "with a lover's thirst to images of tranquil skies, fresh meadows, cool brooks—an existence of soft and eternal peace"; finally, nature herself smiles overhead, dramatically parting the clouds at just the right moment.

The heavy-handed cutting that went into the preparation of *Red Badge* for Appleton publication concerned itself only with the removal of certain pieces of the story, not at all with recasting what remained into an intelligible form. As a consequence, the final and, in some ways, most important chapter was rendered incoherent; and critics like Rechnitz and Chase have been left with the job of explicating an impossible text.

In the final chapter as it appears in the manuscript. Henry moves through a series of moods: self-congratulation, lingering shame, whimsical ratiocination, guilty fear, utter self-delusion, and finally dreamy tranquility. As already mentioned, several parallels exist between this chapter and chapter sixteen in the manuscript; but in the final chapter, Henry turns over new leaves of self-delusion and moves even deeper into the empty regress of his vanity. He awakens from his battle-sleep to "study his deeds—his failures and his achievements," and by exonerating himself of the former and exulting in the latter he can conclude that he is "not inconsequent to the sun." Henry's most delusive thought follows from this, that death is "for others," but equally crucial to his final portrayal is Crane's use of Wilson's response to the report of Jimmie Rogers's death which closes a sequence of incidents that begins in chapter fifteen.

As if Crane were inviting us to think that the youth will learn by the example of his friend, it is Henry who in chapter fifteen notes the "remarkable change" in Wilson: "He seemed no more to be continually regarding the proportions of his personal prowess. . . . There was about him now a fine reliance. He showed a quiet belief in his purposes and his abilities. And this inward confidence evidently enabled him to be indifferent to little words of other men aimed at him." Shortly after this recognition, Wilson, in his new character, interferes when three soldiers of his company, including one Jimmie Rogers, seem about to fight among themselves. Wilson prevents the fight, but reports an unexpected consequence to Henry: "'Jimmie Rogers ses I'll have t' fight him after th' battle t'-day,' announced the friend as he again seated himself. 'He's [sic] ses he don't allow no interferin' in his business. I hate t' see th' boys fightin' 'mong themselves'." Rogers is next mentioned at the opening of chapter nineteen, after the first fighting of the day has taken place; this time he is badly wounded, "thrashing about in the grass, twisting his shuddering body into many strange postures." Again in his new character, Wilson volunteers help: "The youth's friend had a geographical illusion concerning a stream and he obtained permission to go for some water. Immediately, canteens were showered upon him. 'Fill mine, will yeh?' 'Bring me some, too.' 'And me, too.' He departed, ladened. The youth went with his friend, feeling a desire to throw his heated body into the stream and, soaking there, drink quarts." No water is found, but we can see that Wilson is thinking and acting with compassion; the other soldiers only want their canteens filled; and Henry is dreaming of a soak in the cool water.

These two brief mentions of Rogers are designed to build toward a climactic scene in the final chapter in which his death comes as an unexpected report. (Since the culminating scene did not appear in the Appleton text, the other mentions were left dangling.) Coming to the final chapter, the reader has good reason to think that Henry and Wilson are equals by virtue of their similar heroism in the regimental charge. But when Rogers's death is told, their disparate responses show them to be much different. As they walk along together after the battle, Henry begins "to study his deeds," but is temporarily interrupted:

> His friend, too, seemed engaged with some retrospection for he suddenly gestured and said: "Good Lord!"
>
> "What?" asked the youth.
>
> "Good Lord!" repeated his friend. "Yeh know Jimmie Rogers? Well, he—gosh, when he was hurt I started t' git some water fer 'im an', thunder, I aint seen 'im from that time 'til this. I clean forgot what I—say, has anybody seen Jimmie Rogers?"
>
> "Seem 'im? No! He's dead," they told him.
>
> His friend swore.
>
> But the youth, regarding his procession of memory, felt gleeful and unregretting, for, in it, his public deeds were paraded in great and shining prominence. Those performances which had been witnessed by his fellows marched now in wide purple and gold, hiding various deflections. They went gaily, with music. It was pleasure to watch these things. He spent delightful minutes viewing the gilded images of memory.

Crane makes an obtrusive show of Henry's self-congratulation with all of the narrative irony balanced neatly on the "But" which follows "His friend swore." Unlike Wilson, Henry has not exchanged his youthful egotism for a mature humility and regard for his fellow man. This is the second of the moments in **Red Badge** in which Wilson is informed that another soldier has been killed; the first is when he learns of Jim Conklin's death from Henry in chapter fifteen and is regretful. In both cases there is the poignancy that these soldiers have been Wilson's antagonists, although under different circumstances— Conklin before Wilson's change in character when he is still an argumentative "loud soldier" and Rogers after Wilson has changed and attempts to be a peacemaker among the men.

Crane seems to have contrived Henry's thoughts in the next paragraph just as ironically in relation to another earlier scene: "He said to himself again the sentence of the insane lieutenant: 'If I had ten thousand wild-cats like you, I could tear th' stomach outa this war in less'n a week.' It was a little coronation." The lieutenant makes this remark in chapter eighteen after Henry has continued to fire at the battlefield without noticing that the enemy has retreated and his fellows have stopped firing. Much more of a "coronation" for Henry to recall would be the reported statement of the colonel in chapter twenty-two that Henry and Wilson "deserve t' be major-generals" for their part in the charge. But in his vanity Henry imagines a scene in which only he has been congratulated.

Henry's train of egotistical reflection halts when he remembers "his flight from the first engagement" and "his terrible combat with the arrayed forces of the universe." It remains, at this point, to be seen whether his proclivity for self-justification has abated. Obviously it has not, for his explanation and apology for his flight and rebellions are that

> those tempestuous moments were of the wild mistakes and ravings of a novice who did not comprehend. . . . It had been necessary for him to swallow swords that he might have a better throat for grapes. Fate had in truth, been kind to him; she had stabbed him with benign purpose and diligently cudgeled him for his own sake. . . . now that he stood safe, with no lack of blood, it was suddenly clear to him that he had been wrong not to kiss the knife and bow to the cudgel.

This is not far from the reflective conclusion that Henry arrives at in chapter sixteen when he feels certain his cowardice will not be discovered: "in all his red speeches he had been ridiculously mistaken. Nature was a fine thing moving with a magnificent justice." Crane never intended that Henry's concept of the heavens be of serious philosophical importance; the importance lies in his characterization of Henry as repeatedly extending his feelings to a vision of his "place" in the universe relative to a deterministic and judicial supernatural power.

As soon as Henry is able to explain away his rebellions, "the dogging memory of the tattered soldier" looms before him. Henry's cowardice is of much less concern now that he has fought well on the second day of battle, but his betrayal of the tattered man haunts him as a sin more serious than his violation of conventional codes of heroism. His guilt is severe enough to make him withdraw into silence as he thinks, for a moment, that his error may "stand before him all of his life." But he improvises an ingenious escape:

> Yet gradually he mustered force to put the sin at a distance. And then he regarded it with what he thought to be great calmness. At last, he concluded that he

saw in it quaint uses. He exclaimed that it's importance in the aftertime would be great to him if it even
succeeded in hindering the workings of his egotism.
It would make a sobering balance. It would become
a good part of him. He would have upon him often
the consciousness of a great mistake. And he would
be taught to deal gently and with care. He would be
a man.

Henry has the correct formula for manhood here, as that formula has been defined by Jim Conklin, by the cheery-voiced
stranger who returns Henry to his regiment in chapter thirteen,
and by the changed Wilson. But the narrator's ironic labeling
of Henry's scheme as a "plan for the utilization of a sin"
which Henry must combine with "his successes, or public
deeds" before he is fully content, suggests that Crane was
showing, in Henry, the same psychological irony described by
one of Pascal's *Pensées:* "When someone realizes that he has
said or done something silly, he always thinks it will be the
last time. Far from concluding that he will do many more silly
things, he concludes that this one will prevent him from doing
so." That is, we are being given a highly ironic indication that
"the workings of his egotism" are not lessened and that, unlike
Wilson, Henry has not been changed by experience.

After this "plan for the utilization of a sin" restores Henry's
composure to some extent, he once again becomes an amateur
theologian with a generous new conception of the cosmos and
his own modest but not unremarked place in it:

> He was emerged from his struggles, with a large
> sympathy for the machinery of the universe. With
> his new eyes, he could see that the secret and open
> blows which were being dealt about the world with
> such heavenly lavishness were in truth blessings. It
> was a deity laying about him with the bludgeon of
> correction.
>
> His loud mouth against these things had been lost as
> the storm ceased. He would no more stand upon
> places high and false, and denounce the distant planets.
> He beheld that he was tiny but not inconsequent to
> the sun. In the space-wide whirl of events no grain
> like him would be lost.

These two paragraphs are those which contain the "conviction" that brings Henry's "store of assurance" in the next
paragraph. Here, as in chapter sixteen, when he is self-satisfied
Henry concludes, with cosmic vanity, that he is noticed by the
heavens (thinking of himself as if he were considering a universal state of affairs); in the earlier "rebellious" passages,
when he feels guilty he concludes, with the same vanity inverted, that a universal law, blind to his individual situation,
is entirely responsible.

His conviction concerning his place in the universe leads, in
the following paragraph, to the notion that "He had been to
touch the great death and found that, after all, it was but the
great death and was for others." As Mordecai Marcus has
observed, the last four words of this sentence—which were
deleted in the Appleton text—reveal "a Henry who completely
misses the most important thing he could have learned."

The chapter ends quietly. Henry is self-satisfied and thinks,
much as he did in the opening of chapter six after he has stood
and fought in his first engagement, that war is somehow behind
him: "He had rid himself of the red sickness of battle." And
so he turns "with a lover's thirst, to images of tranquil skies,
fresh meadows, cool brooks; an existence of soft and eternal
peace." None of which, from a literal point of view, he will
find on the next day; none of which, from Crane's point of
view, he has earned on this day. (pp. 24-31)

In the final chapter Henry reflects on his experiences during
both days of battle with the intention to appraise himself. As
many critics have pointed out, Henry, from the beginning of
the story, goes to war in search of a mature identity, to discover
what kind of man he might be. He has had the usual youth's
abiding faith in his destiny, "never challenging his belief in
ultimate success and bothering little about means and roads."
Aroused in the first chapter by Jim Conklin's rumor of an
impending engagement, he becomes introspective and discovers that "as far as war was concerned he knew nothing of
himself." The Henry who sets off to war looks forward to
becoming a "man of traditional courage." But after he runs
from the first battle, he needs, more desperately, a reassurance
of dignity, even a false one, and pursues this not by examining
his own thoughts and motives but in raging against the "universe." Conklin's death compounds his despair; and when he
deserts the tattered soldier, he moves into an even more dangerous sidetrack of psychological and social cowardice by betraying a seriously wounded man. In the twelfth chapter, he
expends himself in a waste of illusions about world-reconstruc-
tion. But for all this, "fate" rewards him with the kindness
and help of the cheery-voiced soldier and the friendship of
Wilson. In the next chapters, his traditional manhood is established in the eyes of all, and it seems his earlier cowardice
will not be discovered; but in the concluding scenes, he has
no fleeting thought for the dead Jimmie Rogers; and, never
seeming to comprehend the man at his shoulder—a "duty"
more fundamental and more difficult than heroism or friendship—his "interpretation" of battle is that "death is for others."

*The **Red Badge of Courage*** as Stephen Crane wrote it is the
story of an episode in the life of Henry Fleming. The final
mystery of heroism in this episode is that Henry finds no real
identity or selfhood in battle; and his notions of "fate" remain
justifications for his own errors, reinforcements for his youthful
vanity. The intricacies of each character's thoughts and feelings
in the continuum of the war press along their own paths, perhaps breaching final walls, perhaps not. Conklin is a man
before he goes to battle; Wilson becomes one; Henry does not
change. From the first, we sense the advancing edge of Henry's
expectations for himself; but as the story proceeds, in the no-
man's land between his wavering self-image and his intermittent scorn and eagerness concerning bravery, there is no footing
for a real change to prevail, never an awakening in him to what
manhood is, only the confusion of his delusive explanations.
(pp. 40-1)

> *Henry Binder, "The 'Red Badge of Courage' Nobody
> Knows," in* Studies in the Novel, *Vol. X, No. 1,
> Spring, 1978, pp. 9-47.*

CHESTER L. WOLFORD   (essay date 1983)

[*In the following excerpt, Wolford examines the relationship of*
The Red Badge of Courage *to the tradition of epic narrative
represented by such authors as Homer, Virgil, and Milton.*]

The Red Badge of Courage establishes Stephen Crane as a writer
formally and solidly within the great tradition established and
fostered by Homer, Virgil, Milton, and others. (p. 37)

Although the reputations of Virgil and Milton as epic poets
rest in part upon how well they compare aesthetically with
Homer, nonliterary factors such as cultural and religious values

also claim the attention of these men. The most important of these values for the epic is the different ideal of heroism held by each poet, particularly regarding the object of man's duty. The Homeric epics may be termed "individual" because they tend to glorify the individual man. Virgil's is a "group" epic because it glorifies Rome and defines the state as a more worthy object of duty than the individual. Milton attempts, among other things, to glorify a Puritan God and to justify worthiness in his sight as the object of man's duty. To the degree that Milton saw man's task as an attempt to reproduce God's kingdom in the self and community of Christians, *Paradise Lost* and *Paradise Regained* become "group" epics. (pp. 37-8)

Each of these views finds an embodiment in a great epic poet's notion of heroism, for heroism consists of fulfilling the demands of duty. The Homeric hero ascribes to the code of *areté*, which demands that he strive ceaselessly for the first prize. The driving force behind all the hero's actions, *areté* often connotes values different from Roman and Christian virtue. Virtues lauded over the last fifteen hundred years and more—loyalty, honesty, charity, fair play—are simply not part of the code of *areté;* Achilles deserted the field and his friends and spent much of the war in an adolescent funk and Odysseus was a liar and a cheat, but both were great warriors and so have the highest *areté*.

What distinguishes Virgil's Aeneas from Homeric heroes is not the greatness of his deeds but the reasons for performing them. Virgil's epithet for Aeneas is "pius," a term denoting more than "pious" for Aeneas is also "dutiful." (p. 38)

[Like Virgil, later] Christian epic poets such as Tasso, Camoens, Dante, and Ariosto also despise *areté*—which they saw as almost identical to *hubris*—and show their contempt by assigning it as a quality belonging to their heroes' enemies. Milton's Satan belongs to this type, and in spite of his attractiveness as a Homeric or Shelleyan hero, he is nevertheless a personification of evil. Milton's concept of heroism and duty is as complex as his use of the epic medium, but it is also clear that genuine heroism lies in "true patience and heroic martyrdom." The real Christian hero seeks glory by following the New Testament and dedicates his deeds *ad majoram gloriam Dei*. How one plays the game determines whether one wins or loses.

When Crane includes these notions of heroism and duty in *The Red Badge,* he undertakes a task crucial to writing epics. Because these concepts of heroism and duty are among the most influential in Western history, when Crane denigrates and replaces them, he rewrites, in a very real sense, the cultural history of the West.

The first chapter of *The Red Badge* presents heroic ideals in the mind of Henry Fleming, a "youth" inclined by instinct toward *areté*, but checked by "religious and secular education" so that he feels himself to be a part of something much larger than himself. (pp. 39-40)

Throughout the first half of *The Red Badge,* the competition between the individualism of Henry's *areté* and the collectivism of *pietas* and "heroic martyrdom" swings between extremes. In his first engagement, Henry seems finally to give in to the standards of the group: "He suddenly lost concern for himself and forgot to look at a menacing fate. He became not a man but a member. He felt that something of which he was a part— a regiment, an army, a cause, or a country—was in crisis. He was welded into a common personality which was dominated by a single desire." Soon, the group becomes even more im-

portant to him than the causes: "He felt the subtle battle brotherhood more potent even than the cause for which they were fighting. It was a mysterious fraternity."

Much has been made of Henry's joining the subtle brotherhood, but few remember that when the enemy makes a second charge against the regiment, the mysterious fraternity dissolves under an individuality revived by Henry's sense of self-preservation. He turns tail and runs. Although Achilles has more grace and style, the effect is the same in either case: both Henry and Achilles desert their friends in the field. To say, as many do, that Henry should be damned for his desertion is to speak from an historically narrow perspective; from an Homeric standpoint, one cannot be so quick to judge. In fact, no moral judgements necessarily result from Henry's flight. If Henry can get away with it (he does), if no one finds out about it (no one does), and if later he can perform "great deeds" (he does), then that is all that matters. By the end of the sixth chapter, Henry's individualism, his Homeric sense, seems to have won a limited victory—victory because Henry has escaped being subsumed by the group, limited because his sense of shame dogs him throughout the novel.

In the novel's first half the battle for Henry's allegiance to Homeric or Christian-group values occurs in Henry's mind. In the first six chapters, Henry's conflicting feelings need little prodding; in the second six, the action of the novel intensifies, as do attacks on his individualism. In this quarter of the novel, Henry enters the "forest chapel," sees Jim Conklin die in a Christ-like way, and is mentally and verbally assaulted by the "tattered man." Here, too, he receives his "red badge of courage."

It should not be surprising in light of the epic structure that this section of *The Red Badge* is filled with religious imagery. Much critical ink has been spilt in a controversy over whether or not Crane, given his naturalistic bent and nihilist vision, intends Jim Conklin, for example, to represent Christ, or the tattered man to represent the Christian-group ideal; many feel that Crane himself was confused about it and that the novel fails because he fails to resolve the problem. From the standpoint of examining the traditional epic qualities of the book, there is no problem. These chapters mark what ultimately becomes a failure of the Christian-group value system—with two thousand years of indoctrination behind it—to make Henry Fleming return to the fold. It is not Crane's intent to have the reader see things in a religious way, but to see Henry succumb to the pathetic fallacy of Christian-colored glasses. (pp. 41-2)

Stallman's original reading of Conklin as Christ [see *TCLC*, Vol. 11] is fundamentally correct if one understands that it is Henry and not Crane who sees Conklin as Christ. Few figures in American literature have a better claim to the trappings of Christ's Passion than does Jim Conklin. His initials are J. C., he is wounded in the side, he dies on a hill, he is a "devotee of a mad religion," and his death stirs "thoughts of a solemn ceremony." Those who deny that Conklin is a Christ-figure usually do so by pointing out that Conklin is a loud, cracker-crunching, rumormonger. Such evidence is specious, since these qualities are part of Jim only before he became "not a man but a member" by staying on the line during the battle. Some also forget that Crane's intent is to show that Henry sees Conklin in this way, not that Conklin is that way.

One way to place the various episodes of the first half into a perspective of the moral and social competition between Christian-group values and the Homeric ideal of individualism *(areté)* may be to describe that epic competition as a representation of the psychology of Christian conversion from an egocentric individualism to an altruistic membership in the flock. The pattern is familiar; as a moral being, man in Christian process moves from the commission of sin to guilt, to alienation, to a desire for expiation, to confession, and finally to redemption. In the end, the process fails to redeem Henry for Christianity, but it does give him a rough time of it, and it organizes the epic competition and psychology of the novel's first half.

Three particular episodes are representative of this psychological movement. The episodes with Mrs. Fleming, Jim Conklin, and the tattered man each appear to bring Henry steadily closer to rejecting his Homeric individuality while ultimately functioning ironically to force his acceptance of *areté*. By the time he is hit on the head and receives his "red badge of courage," Henry has sloughed off the Christian-group concept of heroism. His red badge is, however, not ironical in that he receives it for an act of cowardice; rather it is an outward sign—what the Greeks called *geras*—of his accomplishment in rejecting two thousand years of social and religious indoctrination. An epic feat.

Occurring in the first chapter, the "Mrs. Fleming" episode serves to increase Henry's feelings of sin and guilt over his Homeric sense of selfish individuality which encompasses egoism, insensitivity, and the pursuit of personal glory at all costs—*areté*. (pp. 43-5)

The Jim Conklin episode carries Henry a step further in the process by adding to sin and guilt the anguish of alienation and the desire for expiation through good works. (p. 46)

Henry's Christian-group consciousness is pushed to its limits in the "tattered man" episode. There are two "sins" here: one is Henry's refusal to confess his earlier desertion of the regiment, and the other is his desertion of the tattered man, an act which redoubles his guilt. When Henry meets the tattered man, the latter repeatedly asks him, "Where yeh hit?" This question, asked over and over again, causes Henry to feel the "letters of guilt" burned, Dimmesdale-like, into his forehead. Instead of causing Henry to repent, however, the letters merely force him to desert the wounded tattered man and leave him to wander off into the fields to die. Immediately after deserting the tattered man, Henry's guilt reaches almost unbearable proportions: "The simple questions of the tattered man had been knife thrusts to him. They asserted a society that probes pitilessly at secrets until all is apparent. . . . He could not keep his crime concealed in his bosom. . . . He admitted that he could not defend himself." Believing that "he envied those men whose bodies lay strewn" on the field, he explicitly wants to be redeemed: "A moral vindication was regarded by the youth as a very important thing."

Confused, guilt-ridden, and afraid that the group may discover his "sin," Henry's mind goes through, as in the first chapter, the same metronomic movement between the demands of the group and the desires of the individual, but with more pain. Henry's anguish remains severe throughout the eleventh chapter. In the twelfth chapter, however, this changes.

Chapter 12 is the last chapter of the first half of *The Red Badge*. Like the end of the first half of the *Iliad*, the *Odyssey*, the *Aeneid, Paradise Lost*, and other epics, it includes both a culmination of the first half and a preparation for the second. . . . Henry completes his epic of return by sloughing off his Christian-group conscience: he accepts his individuality, and he is then prepared to battle the group in the second half.

Henry is "reborn" after being hit on the head in chapter 12. The language of the episode is carefully, even poetically, rendered to represent rebirth. After watching a group of retreating soldiers, Henry runs down from a rise, grabs one of the soldiers, and is clouted for his trouble:

> [The other soldier] adroitly and fiercely swung his rifle. It crushed upon the youth's head. The man ran on.
>
> The youth's fingers had turned to paste upon the other's arm. The energy was smitten from his muscles. He saw the flaming wings of lightning flash before his vision. There was a deafening rumble of thunder within his head.
>
> Suddenly his legs seemed to die. He sank writhing to the ground. He tried to arise. In his efforts against the numbing pain he was like a man wrestling with a creature of the air.
>
> There was a sinister struggle.
>
> Sometimes he would achieve a position half erect, battle with the air for a moment, and then fall again, grabbing at the grass. His face was of a clammy pallor. Deep groans were wrenched from him.
>
> At last, with a twisting movement, he got upon his hands and knees, and from thence, like a babe trying to walk, to his feet. . . . he went lurching over the grass.
>
> He fought an intense battle with his body. His dulled senses wished him to swoon and he opposed them stubbornly, his mind portraying unknown dangers and mutilations if he should fall upon the field. He went tall soldier fashion.

Structurally, the passages focuses first on the falling away of the old in a metaphorical death. Henry loses his sight, his hearing, and then his ability to stand erect. In the middle is a five-word, one-sentence paragraph describing a "sinister struggle" between life and death. From there, the reborn Henry gets up on his hands and knees "like a babe," and finally is able to walk. In spite of the almost allegorical nature of the passage, its essence remains one of a very physical, almost literal, and, most important, quite individual rebirth.

One cannot help but think that the anthropological cast of the passage is intentional. At least, it demonstrates that Crane, however unconsciously, was aware of the consequences for thought of the Darwinian revolution. For Henry, as for mankind, the traditional past could no longer provide solace. Indeed, as the second half of *The Red Badge* shows, the traditional past had to be rolled up and replaced by naturalism and impressionism. These terms, given Holton's appraisal of elements shared by definitions of the former and Nagel's definition of impressionism, can be seen in some lights as nearly synonymous and as twin effects of *Origin of the Species* and of the dissemination of other scientific discoveries.

The action reported in this passage is unlike anything else in the book. Except for a later instance when he pushes another fellow, it is Henry's only hostile physical encounter in the novel. Certainly this is not Christian-group combat; it is especially unusual for those engaged in modern warfare. Prior to this point all battles have been described as remote from the individual. Cannons roar at each other, and men shoot at "vague forms" shifting and running through the smoke of many rifles. Always the action has been described in terms of one group charging toward or retreating from another. Moreover, his adversary fights under the same flag as Henry.

Here, for the first time, is a representation of a "Greeklike struggle" that once had been merely a part of Henry's dreams. It has not developed as Henry had expected, and may not be distinctly Homeric, but it is close to primitive hand-to-hand combat, and bears little resemblance to the "mighty blue machine" of the group. For the first time, Henry struggles with another man. Further, Henry's wound is unusual for participants in a modern, group war. Henry's wound is not from a bullet, but from the butt end of a modern weapon used as the most ancient of weapons; as one fellow observes, "It's raised a queer lump as if some feller lammed yeh on the head with a club."

Henry's wandering off "tall soldier fashion" after receiving the blow on the head does not mean that Henry has been converted to a group view of things. To see Jim as a Christian-group figure is to make the same mistake Henry made. Strip away the dramatic symbolism of Henry's former vision of Conklin and one is left with a man dying, alone, unwilling to be helped, and as afraid of mutilation as any Homeric hero. Speech and action are "real"; Henry's interpretation of them may not be. When Henry thus goes "tall soldier fashion," it is not necessarily as a Christ-figure. Henry is in no shape at this point to interpret events; in this instance, the information comes directly from the narrator. The dying Jim Conklin and the wounded Henry Fleming are linked, or seem to be linked, only by a desire to escape the group.

Wandering in the gathering darkness, Henry is finally given direction by an epic guide. Like the role of the captain in **"The Reluctant Voyagers,"** the function of the "cheery man" is traditional to the machinery of epic. As Ariadne helps Theseus, Thetis comforts Achilles, Athena aids Odysseus, Venus supports and guides Aeneas, and Virgil leads Dante, so the cheery man helps Henry to gain self-control, and, as Gibson points out, places him in a position to confront those forces which he otherwise would have little power to oppose but which he must overcome in order to complete his epic task. The cheery man leads Henry back to the regiment.

Unlike the two men in **"The Reluctant Voyagers,"** Henry appreciates, albeit somewhat after the fact, the cheery man's help. And well he should, for as he staggers towards the campfires of his regiment in the beginning of the second half of *The Red Badge,* he has nearly done the impossible. In a sense, he has performed more courageously than Achilles. Peliades had only to reach his goal of *areté,* while Fleming had first to throw off his sense of sin and alienation. On one level, he has suffered all the slings and "arrows of scorn" that can be shot at an individual by the archers of conscience, guilt, and alienation from the group. On another level, Henry has forced his way back through two millennia of nationalism and Christianity. Such an act is impossible for an ordinary man. To oppose and overcome, even to a limited degree, the teachings of secular and religious culture is an almost incredible, even epic, feat.

Yet the battle is only half won. As the first twelve chapters are concerned with Henry's struggle to gain individuality of mind, the second half of *The Red Badge* concerns Henry's conflict with the same forces in the externalized, "outside" world. In terms of the epic of consciousness, the first half concerns Henry's escape from the cave, his coming to consciousness, and his gaining self-control, that is coming to terms with alienation from the other—the group and the rest of the material world—and the fact of death. Having come to terms internally in the first half, he is ready to confront the other externally in the second half. Here, as in the *Aeneid,* the hero is confronted with a competition between his new-found values and an externalized embodiment and proponent of the value system he has recently overcome internally. In the second half of the *Aeneid,* Aeneas must confront, battle, and finally defeat the Roman version of the Homeric ideal of *areté* embodied in Turnus. In the last half of *The Red Badge,* Henry must confront, engage, and overcome Wilson, who has not only been "converted" and initiated into the group, but also has become the embodiment of Christian-group consciousness and its value system.

When Henry returns to confront the group, to enter into the midst of the "subtle brotherhood," he manages to resist its attempts to "initiate" him into membership. Henry seems aware at this point of the nature of this confrontation, because "there was a sudden sinking of his forces. He thought he must hasten to produce his tale to protect him from the missiles already at the lips of his redoubtable comrades." The "information" is a baldfaced lie: "Yes, yes. I've—I've had an awful time. I've been all over. Way over on the right. . . . I got separated from the regiment. Over on the right, I got shot. In the head. I never saw such fighting." The lie works, and Henry seems to become the lost sheep returned to the fold.

Wilson, the sentinel who recognizes Henry staggering into camp, seems remarkably changed. Henry now views Wilson much as he had viewed the tattered man, only with colder eyes. In the first chapter, Wilson acted the part of a *miles gloriosus,* a parody of Achilles. In that chapter, which mirrors the first book of the *Iliad,* Wilson engaged Jim Conklin in an argument. Like Achilles and Agamemnon, "they came near to fighting over" their differences. Wilson also spent much time bragging about his prowess in battle. Now, however, Wilson seems to embody Christian-group values. When first seen in chapter 13, he is standing guard over the regiment. Upon recognizing Henry, he lowers his rifle and welcomes the youth back: "There was husky emotion in his voice." Later, while dressing Henry's wound, Wilson acts out the feminine role of the soothing and clucking mother hen who welcomes one of her lost chicks back to the coop: "He had the bustling ways of an amateur nurse. He fussed around." When Wilson puts his cloth on Henry's head, it feels to the youth "like a tender woman's hand."

Because he didn't run, Wilson was subsumed by that "regiment, army, cause," or country; he joined the "subtle brotherhood," the "mysterious fraternity born of the smoke and danger of death." At the beginning of the battle neither Henry nor Wilson had gained a genuine sense of individuality; both at that point were vulnerable to the group. Because he ran, Henry was excluded from the ego-annihilating forces which Wilson joined.

As a result, Henry and Wilson are now two very different kinds of men. Wilson, who had earlier jumped at any chance to get into an argument or a fight, now stops a fight between two men; he explains to Henry, "I hate t' see th' boys fightin' 'mong themselves." Henry, however, feels no such obligation to become a peacemaker; he laughs and reminds Wilson of an earlier fight the formerly loud soldier had had with "that Irish feller." Certain that he would be killed, Wilson had given Henry a packet of letters before the first battle with instructions that they be sent home after his "imminent" death. The contrast between Wilson's new-found humility and Henry's arrogance appears when Wilson asks for the letters back. Wilson flushes and fidgets, "suffering great shame." When Henry gives them back, he tries "to invent a remarkable comment upon the affair. He could conjure up nothing of sufficient point.

He was compelled to allow his friend to escape unmolested with his packet. And for this he took unto himself considerable credit. It was a generous thing. . . . The youth felt his heart grow more strong and stout. He had never been compelled to blush in such a manner for his acts; he was an individual of extraordinary virtues.'' There is a double irony here. On one level, the passage mocks Henry, but on another, Henry is essentially correct. He has not been ''compelled'' to undergo the humility of confession. He has overcome in large measure the need for communal redemption of guilt and shame. He does, indeed, have extraordinary ''virtues,'' but they are the ''virtues'' of *areté*, pride, and individualism.

As they begin the second day of battle, Henry and Wilson are very soon recognized by the group as entirely different kinds of heroes. First, Henry is transfigured by *menos*, the animallike battle-rage of Homeric heroes: ''Once, he, in his intent hate, was almost alone and was firing when all those near him ceased. He was so engrossed in his occupation that he was not aware of a lull.'' One man derides him for not stopping when the others had, but the lieutenant (whose ''voice'' had been described as expressing a ''divinity'') praises Henry in animistic terms: ''By heavens, if I had ten thousand wild-cats like you I could tear th' stomach outa this war in less'n a week!'' Finally, Henry receives the recognition from the group that Homeric heroes seek. He is viewed as someone separate, distinct, and most important, superior: ''They now looked upon him as a war-devil,'' they are ''awe-struck.''

Wilson is a hero of a different age. Henry does not incite the group to action; his only concern is for his own heroism. Wilson, the hero of the group, serves this purpose: ''The friend of the youth aroused. Lurching suddenly forward and dropping to his knees, he fired an angry shot at the persistent woods. This action awakened the men. They huddled no more like sheep . . . they began to move forward.''

Wlson has become the leader of his flock, and Henry has become an Homeric ''war devil.'' (pp. 47-55)

The crucial confrontation between the two heroes is a face-to-face physical encounter on the battlefield. It occurs, fittingly, in a contest to determine who will carry the flag across the field in the charge. For Wilson, the traditional approach to the flag as a symbol of a group is most appropriate. Possession of the flag would mean that Wilson had reached the goal of all group epic heroes: to become the idealized symbol of the group. For Henry, the flag is also a symbol of the group. But Homeric heroes strive after *geras*, the prize, the symbol by which they are acknowledged by the group as superior. Possession of the flag would mean that he had fulfilled the aspect of *areté* that demands that he achieve supremacy over the group. Consequently, the flag becomes for Henry ''a goddess, radiant, that bent its form with an imperious gesture to him. It was a woman . . . that called to him with the voice of his hopes.''

Since the flag is a symbol both for the group and for the superior individual, it is natural, when the bearer is shot, that both Henry and Wilson should go after the flag. It is also inevitable, although slightly contrived, that they should reach it at the same time: ''He [Henry] made a spring and a clutch at the pole. At the same instant, his friend grabbed it from the other side.''

Neither Henry nor Wilson relinquishes the flagpole and a ''small scuffle'' ensues. For Henry, however, possession of the flag means so much in terms of dominance over his peers that he has no compunctions about using force against his comrade: ''The youth roughly pushed his friend way.''

In gaining the flag, Henry has defeated his Christian-group rival and the value system Wilson champions. Henry has gained supremacy over his peers, achieving his *areté*. Yet the victory is not complete: there is still the enemy's flag. Were Henry to claim that flag as well, he would be proven superior not only to his peers, but also to the collective body. Henry fails. Although there is much heroism in becoming individual, one is never completely freed from the group. Its influences, physical and mental, remain forever. Although Henry has equaled or surpassed the deeds of Achilles and Odysseus, although he has overcome in large measure the long stony sleep of Christian-group culture and heritage, he fails to gain a complete victory. It is as if Henry knows what its possession would mean: ''The youth had centered the gaze of his soul upon that other flag. Its possession would be high pride.'' But Wilson, that champion of the group, had dogged Henry across the battlefield and beat Henry to it by springing like Christ the Panther: ''The youth's friend . . . sprang at the flag as a panther at prey. He pulled at it, and wrenching it free, swung up its red brilliancy with a mad cry of exultation.''

In terms of the epic tradition, Henry's possessing the other flag could have meant possibly a complete victory for the Homeric epic over the social epic after two thousand years. It might also have meant a winning back of the heroic, individual ''soul'' after two millennia of suppression by Christian-group value systems, both political and spiritual. But, as the later Scratchy Wilson of **''The Bride Comes to Yellow Sky''** and the Swede of **''The Blue Hotel''** discover, such a victory is fleeting at best and always illusory. Wilson may have lost an individual encounter with Henry, but he has also proven that the group cannot be completely defeated by the individual.

The epic tradition demands that a writer replace former concepts of epic heroism with his own if he wishes to be more than a mere imitator. In nearly all of Crane's best work, his idea of heroism is his ideal of personal honesty. Repeatedly, Crane measures his characters against this standard; Henry Fleming measures as well as any.

More than any other sort of writer, one whose work has epic dimensions lends to his fictional heroes his own supreme ambition; so much is this so, in fact, that the poet himself may be considered the ultimate hero of his own epic, and is sometimes difficult to separate from the fictional hero. For millennia the epic poet has been set apart from his fellows by his abilities, but especially by the intensity of his vision and by the degree to which he believes in it. For Crane, keeping close to his vision, in terms both of apprehension and of comprehension, is the standard not only of honesty but of heroism as well.

The desire to see clearly runs through *The Red Badge of Courage*. Henry in particular seeks continually to perceive with his own eyes. There are more than two hundred references in *The Red Badge* to Henry seeing, not seeing, or trying to see. However, his sight tends always to be obscured either by the group, which limits what the individual can see, or by a kind of Homeric hero complex in which Henry feels that an individual can see everything. Each is a form of blindness and each corresponds to one of the two epic value systems. There is an implication throughout most of the novel (the implication becomes explicit in the last chapter) that history is little more than an individual interpretation of events raised to a level of cultural reporting and collective interpreting. Both as individual and as representative man, Henry makes his own specific interpretations of events. On the other hand, those interpretations are also colored by epic concepts. If the individual's interpretation is deluded, so is the epic's, and vice-versa.

Since Crane uses "vision" as a metaphor for his own particular notion of heroism, former notions of epic heroism are first debased and then replaced by the use of images and references to seeing. One of the value systems attacked in *The Red Badge* is the Christian-group view, which obscures and distorts the attempts of the individual to "see." The group, in the form of the army or the brigade or the regiment, is constantly associated with smoke or fog. (pp. 56-9)

[Henry's] desire to see is constantly getting in the way of his assimilation into the group, but he can never get an unobstructed view and his other senses are stifled, almost annihilated by the physical and metaphorical "smoke" of the group. Against this smoke Henry directs more of his anger than against a charging enemy: "Buried in the smoke of many rifles his anger was directed not so much against the men whom he knew were rushing toward him as against the swirling battle phantoms which were choking him, stuffing their smoke robes down his parched throat."

The group has the ability to hide reality from the individual. The group takes away the individual's unobstructed use of his senses—the only means he has of perceiving the world around him. While surrounded by "smoke," a man cannot "see," and will behave in the way the group wants him to behave. Shortly before Henry becomes "not a man but a member," for example, he and the regiment are moving rapidly forward to a "struggle in the smoke": "In this rush they were apparently all deaf and blind."

After he has run, been hit on the head, and returned to the group, Henry sees the regiment in a more sinister aspect. After spending the night in sleep Henry awakes and it seems to him "that he had been asleep for a thousand years." This "sleep," of course, takes him back in time, not forward, and so he sees "gray mists," and around him "men in corpse-like hues" with "limbs . . . pulseless and dead." If every epic hero must visit hell, then, for Henry, being in the middle of the group is just that: he sees "the hall of the forest as a charnel place. He believed for an instant that he was in the house of the dead."

If the group influence which Henry has resisted and over which he has gained some dominance causes the individual to see less than he is able, the Homeric view of man purports to allow the individual to "see" more than he actually can. Crane renders the Homeric view meaningless by showing that it too is clouded. That is, if Wilson, the group hero, is given "new eyes" and now apparently sees himself as a "wee thing," then Henry, the Homeric hero, becomes so caught up in his individual desires that his eyes are reduced to "a glazed vacancy." He becomes a "barbarian, a beast." He sees himself as a "pagan who defends his religion," and he sees his battle-rage as "fine, wild, and, in some ways, easy. He had been a tremendous figure, no doubt. By this struggle he had overcome obstacles which he had admitted to be mountains. They had fallen like paper peaks, and he was now what he called a hero."

The whole of chapter 17 describes Henry as being in the grip of the blind battle-rage of Homeric heroes. He forgets that he is merely a private engaged in a small charge on one day of one battle. He thinks of himself as colossal in size and of the other soldiers as "flies sucking insolently at his blood." Although his neck is "bronzed" and he fires his rifle with a fierce grunt as if he were "dealing a blow of the fist with all his strength," he is essentially what one soldier calls this "war devil": "Yeh infernal fool." Heroic Henry certainly is, even in a traditional way, but a bit foolish as well.

Henry soon gains a truer vision. Going with Wilson to get some water, Henry, as well as his image of himself as a Homeric hero, is deflated by a "jangling general" who refers to Henry's regiment, and implicitly to Henry himself, as a lot of "mule drivers." Henry, who had earlier viewed nature as a sympathetic goddess in language filled with Virgilian pathetic fallacy and Christian symbolism (the forest-chapel, for example), and later as a capricious, sometimes malevolent beast much as Homer saw it, now has "new eyes" and sees himself as "very insignificant." This is not necessarily a Christian sense of insignificance, nor even a completely naturalistic one, but simply a realization that compared with more powerful forces, including the regiment, he is powerless. (pp. 60-2)

After discovering his insignificance, Henry is in a position to receive a new heroism, a new vision, a "real" vision. In his charge across the field on the second day of battle, it "seemed to the youth that he saw everything":

> Each blade of the green grass was bold and clear. He thought that he was aware of every change in the thin, transparent vapor that floated idly in sheets. The brown or gray trunks of the trees showed each roughness of their surfaces. And the men of the regiment, with their starting eyes and sweating faces, running madly, or falling, as if thrown headlong, to queer, heaped up corpses—all were comprehended. His mind took a mechanical but firm impression, so that afterward everything was pictured and explained to him, save why he himself was there.

A "mechanical" impression of some blades of grass, tree trunks, and sweating, frightened, dying men: that is all one can ever hope to see. The process of epic has been reversed. Virgil had expanded Homer's view of ten or twenty years of glory on the plains before a small town in Asia Minor to include a long-lived empire encompassing the known world. Similarly, the Christian epics of Charlemagne and the crusades are described as world wars. Milton extended the epic beyond human time and farther out than human space. Crane doubled back upon the epic tradition, gradually narrowing space until the epic vision includes only a minute perception and compressing time until that perception exists only for a fleeting instant. It is epical in its achievement and heroic only because Crane has shown it to be the only vision possible for man that remains "bold and clear."

Tiny but unobscured by the smoke of the group or the blinding *menos* of *areté*, Henry's vision has made him Crane's version of the best epic hero. Trying to "observe everything" in his first battle, but failing to "avoid trees and branches," Henry now sees only *something*. Gone is the Roman vision of national destiny and the Miltonic perception of a Puritan God's universe. Heroism is defined in *The Red Badge* as one man's limited but perhaps illusionless vision: grass blades, tree trunks, dying men.

This vision has dominated the literature of the twentieth century and has allowed writers who followed Crane to make the first tentative steps toward a new supreme fiction based upon consciousness of a materialistic universe while discarding the old fictions based upon the imagination. (pp. 62-3)

The epic of consciousness in *The Red Badge* is clearly set forth. Henry begins the novel in his hut, emblem of the enclosed violence of his mind. In this enclosure, cluttered by cracker boxes, clothing, and utensils, he gives vent to his cluttered and conflicting fears and anxieties. "Convicted by himself of many shameful crimes against the gods of tradition" and feeling "alone in space," he has "visions of a thousand tongued fear," and admits that "he would not be able to cope with this monster." When he first goes into combat, he sees "that it would be impossible for him to escape from the regiment. It enclosed him. And there were iron laws of tradition and laws on four sides. He was in a moving box." After escaping from the regimental enclosure, he enters a succession of archetypes for the unconscious—the forest, a swamp, "deep thickets"—each enclosing those which follow, until he reaches "a place where the high, arching boughs made a chapel." Here is a different sort of cave, for this is not at first the enclosure of unconscious fears, nor an enclosure of transcendence, but rather a false cave, like the den of Error (book 1, canto 1) and the cave of Mammon (book 2, canto 7) in the *Faerie Queene*, where the hero is lured toward a false transcendence. In Henry's case the promise comes in the form of religious transcendentalism. While the insects are praying and the trees are whispering, Henry pushes open the "green doors" and enters the chapel. In a paragraph or two Crane both anticipates W. W. Hudson and Edgar Rice Burroughs and parodies the Schianatulander and chapel scenes of *Parzival*, for Henry has no sooner entered and is standing "near the threshold," when "he stopped horror-stricken at the sight of the thing."

> He was being looked at by a dead man who was seated with his back against a column-like tree. The corpse was dressed in a uniform that once had been blue but now was faded to a melancholy shade of green. The eyes, staring at the youth, had changed to the dull hue to be seen on the side of a dead fish. The mouth was opened. Its red had changed to an appalling yellow. Over the grey skin of the face ran little ants. One was trundling some sort of a bundle along the upper lip.

The stark clarity of this paragraph, with its excruciatingly painful materialism, provides a perfect contrast to the "religious half-light" leading up to this description. While the description is faintly reminiscent of Thoreau's mock epic paragraphs on ants in *Walden*, its main purpose seems to be to pose starkly the problem that Henry and other epic heroes must face. Somehow, the pathetic fallacy, the religious rose-colored glasses, must be removed, and Henry must still be able to face the "thing"—the fact of death. At this early stage, the contrast is too great for Henry and he responds by screaming and fleeing from the enclosure, which promised transcendence but delivered only death. Another way of saying it is that he was lulled by the imagination and then confronted by pure consciousness. He heads back to the regiment. Only later, after facing death in the field, does Henry accept a classical, almost Lucretian materialism with respect to mortality. This seems to be what Henry learns: "He knew that he would no more quail before his guides wherever they should point. He had been to touch the great death and found that, after all, it was but the great death." (pp. 63-5)

The final chapter of *The Red Badge* presents perhaps the greatest critical problem in the Crane canon. Many of the critical reservations about Crane's importance and abilities rest in the complexities and supposed inconsistencies (even inanities) of this chapter.

The last chapter is both complete and consistent. It is a deliberate reversal of all that has gone before. Throughout the largest portion of *The Red Badge,* Henry is in the process of sloughing off both the Christian-group "walking-sticks" of Stallman's interpretation and the Homeric "creeds" of this reading. If the final chapter of *The Red Badge* is naturalistic, it is so only within the context of Crane's conception of the epic.

That a man may learn and then forget, as Holton says, pervades Crane's writings; in terms of the epic nature of *The Red Badge,* a man may forget and then remember. In the first twenty-three chapters, Henry proceeds to "forget" all previous cultural notions and epic concepts about the way life is. Having "forgotten," he finally achieves an impressionistic vision of the individual man unencumbered by epic and cultural trappings. In the final chapter, however, Henry "remembers"; his former epic value systems sweep back over him, and he is left at the end dreaming dreams he had dreamt in the beginning.

Throughout twenty-three chapters of the novel the major concern is to discover the true nature of heroism. In the final chapter, however, all epic values are specifically refuted. Because he forgets the vision that he has found, and the limited heroism he has discovered, Henry becomes a nonhero. *The Red Badge,* too, is negated, a nonepic. Unlike Milton, Virgil, and Homer, Crane does not wait for his particular notion of heroism to be satirized by others; he mocks it himself.

The Red Badge of Courage ends by mocking the epic genre and its heroic ideals. But the novel, so saturated with epic tradition, cannot be exiled from the epic province. Its exploitation of epic conventions attests to the lingering vitality of the genre, but its annihilation of heroism—Homeric, Virgilian, Catholic, or Miltonic—at the same time exposes the genre's vulnerability. The novel marks a transition from the formal epic tradition to all that is Homerically nonepic in modern fiction: triumphant chaos and successful deceit.

The last chapter is an ironic recapitulation of each epic value system present in the remainder of the book. Homeric *areté* is savagely mocked, as is Christian-group heroism. The primary target, however, is that final concept of heroism, Crane's own, which Henry has achieved earlier: that concept based only on the individual's ability to peer into the pit of reality with a gaze unclouded by cultural and epic notions of what the world is like. Throughout this final chapter, Henry's (and Crane's) perception-based, impressionistic heroism is mocked by means of an ironic significance attached to images of and references to the sense of sight. Henry enters the chapter a cleareyed hero; he exits blind and deluded. (pp. 67-9)

Henry's progression toward heroism during the first twenty-three chapters reverses and inverts itself in the last chapter, for Henry's vision is a distortion that destroys his notion of Homeric bravery and of *areté*. Henry's semi-sin of leaving the tattered man haunts him. Crane here employs a parody of nineteenth-century Protestant tracts, much as he has described Henry's Homeric deeds in the language traditionally used to depict the victory marches of great warriors: "A specter of reproach came to him. There loomed the dogging memory of the tattered soldier—he who gored by bullets and faint for blood, had fretted concerning an imagined wound in another; he who had loaned his last of strength and intellect for the tall soldier; he who, blind with weariness and pain, had been deserted in the field." Henry is then "followed" by a "vision of cruelty" which clings "near to him always" and darkens "his view of these deeds in purple and gold." This "somber phantom" heightens Henry's guilt; he becomes "afraid it would stand before him all his life." Thus, "he saw his vivid error."

After recognizing that he had sinned, Henry receives partial expiation in the form of partial forgetfulness: "Yet he gradually mustered force to put the sin at a distance. And at last his eyes seemed to open to some new ways. He found that he could now look back upon the brass and bombast of his earlier gospels and see them truly. He was gleeful when he discovered that he now despised them." Henry here exchanges one false view of himself for another. The Homeric vision has given way to a Christian-group one. Crane, with beautiful, lyric irony, moves Henry away from the war and from the battle in his mind: "So it came to pass that as he trudged from the place of blood and wrath his soul changed." Henry now believes that "the world was a world for him," as a Christian-group hero should.

There is yet another way, however, in which Crane sets about to destroy the epic. By ironically disparaging the epic view of man's history, Crane ridicules the concept that readers have of the epic genre. The epic has long been one of the more revered forms of historical interpretation and cultural expression. Through epic poetry Homer presents man as a godlike animal struggling to gain a measure of immortality through the public recognition of great deeds. But the Homeric man was like Lear in the storm—alone, naked, and "unaccommodated"—and this is probably why Crane preferred this view more than other traditional views: it was closer to his notion, expressed in **"The Blue Hotel,"** that "conceit is the very engine of life." Virgil gave man more hope by giving him the opportunity to identify and merge with the immortality of a national group. By interpreting history in terms of a great empire, he was also in some measure espousing a kind of immortality. Medieval and Renaissance epic, including *The Song of Roland* and Tasso's *Gerusalemme liberata*, glorified the church militant, ordained to victory. Milton went even farther. He regarded man as completely unworthy of immortality, but acknowledged man's hope in a merciful God's love; man's earthly history spans the interval between creation and final redemption.

Crane felt that these interpretations of history were, to one degree or another, part of a giant hoax willfully perpetrated on man by man. At times he could be downright Aeschylean: "Hope," as Berryman quotes him, "is the most vacuous emotion of mankind."

The Red Badge is a denial of the epic view of history, which Crane felt creates an absurd, illusory, and vacuous emotion.

In the first twenty-three chapters of *The Red Badge* an epic fable is presented which carries the reader back through history. Henry begins *in medias res,* confused and torn between the two major epic views of history, and between two epic value systems as they have filtered through the epic into and out of culture. One of Henry's great accomplishments is his success in throwing off, if only for a short time, the Christian-group view that has dominated the long history of the social epic—indeed of all intellectual life in the West. Next, Henry rejects the rest of history, as recorded by the individual epic, by sloughing off the hope of being an immortal, Homeric "war devil." Finally, past all Christian doctrine, beyond the emotional slither of patriotism and breast-beating brass and bombast, this young man finds a vision in some blades of grass and the grooved bark of a few trees. He is, for an instant, free as few have ever been free; he is loosed from the illusions of history. Perhaps, because it is so limited in duration, Crane is mocking his own illusion, and that of Americans from Franklin to Ginsberg, that man can indeed throw off the process of history and the illusions it etches into the brain.

However, those twenty-three chapters may not be a fairytale epic. Crane may have felt that through catalytic and catastrophic experiences like war, man can scrape the scales of history from his eyes. Perhaps all the teachings of history are reduced to absurdity in the midst of the immense experience, if one tries hard enough to see for himself. Perhaps one can universalize Crane's statement that "a man is only responsible for the personal quality of his honesty" of vision. "A man is sure to fail at it," he said, "but there is something in the failure." Although the paucity of the vision may make it ironic, there is some heroism involved in the sheer ability to perceive reality. In either case, however, the last chapter of the novel indicates that Crane felt heroism to be impossible beyond the immediacy of experience.

This aspect of the last chapter functions by way of a metaphorical equation: memory is to the individual as history is to the species. As Henry moves away from the immediate experience, his memory creates lies and delusions about that experience. The ironic laughter from Crane results from his belief that man cannot really learn from experience, even when he can reach an illusionless view of reality through that experience. Once it is over, once one is no longer staring at the face of red death, then memory, or history, distorts that experience all out of any recognizable proportion.

In the last chapter, history becomes what memory becomes— a mechanism for man to build his self-image. Through the two main thrusts of the history of Western civilization, as expressed by the epic genre, man is deluded into believing himself to be either more or less than he actually is. In the end, Henry is led by his memory to believe with conviction all the mad, distorted hopes of epic history. Ironically, "at last his eyes opened on some new ways." These are new ways only for Henry; they are as old as history. Darwin mounted on Mather.

These "new ways" are a collation of Homeric and Christian-group values. There is still much pride in Henry, but also much humility. Together, they form a paradoxically proud humility: "He felt a quiet man-hood, non-assertive but of sturdy and strong blood." The sum of Henry's wisdom, apparently gained from these seemingly "new" ways, and required of epic heroes, is expressed in what becomes, upon close examination, a meaningless platitude worthy of the climax of a dime-novel adventure: "He had been to touch the great death, and found that, after all, it was but the great death. He was a man."

The final delusion of history and memory Crane repudiated is that of "hope." Part of the reason that Virgil and Milton wrote epics was to give men hope. Beautifully parodic, and powerfully ironic, the last paragraphs of *The Red Badge* express the hopes of Aeneas and Adam, of Columbus and Hiawatha, and of people at all times and in all places, hot to cool, hard to soft, pain to pleasure, hell to heaven. . . . (pp. 71-4)

Chester L. Wolford, in his The Anger of Stephen Crane: Fiction and the Epic Tradition, *University of Nebraska Press, 1983, 169 p.*

DONALD PIZER   (essay date 1985)

[*An American educator and critic, Pizer is the author of several studies on nineteenth- and twentieth-century American literature. In the following excerpt, he counters the arguments of those who maintain that the ambiguity of the Appleton text of* The Red Badge of Courage *was unintentional, asserting that ambiguity and ambivalence are essential to the novel. For opposing views, see the excerpt by Henry Binder (1978) and the essays by Hershel Parker and Steven Mailloux in the Additional Bibliography.]*

During the last several years, Hershel Parker and his former student Henry Binder have argued vigorously that *The Red Badge of Courage* which we have been reading since 1895 is a defective text. Crane, they believe, was forced by his editor Ripley Hitchcock to eliminate from the version accepted by D Appleton & Co. an entire chapter as well as a number of important passages—particularly from the close of the novel—in which he underlined with biting irony the fatuousness and wrong-headedness of Henry Fleming. It is therefore the original and uncut version rather than the censored version of *The Red Badge,* Parker and Binder maintain, which we should be reading. In response to this contention Parker arranged for the uncut version of *The Red Badge* to be included in the prestigious, widely used, and in general textually responsible *Norton Anthology of American Literature* and Binder has published the version in a separate volume.

This effort to rescue Crane's uncut draft of *The Red Badge* from exclusively scholarly use (the omitted portions of the novel have been known and available since the early 1950s) would have little significance except for the coincidence of Parker's editorial involvement in the Norton anthology and thus its presence in that widely circulated form. For there is no direct external evidence that Crane cut *The Red Badge* under pressure from Hitchcock. There are only inferences and assumptions derived from long-known collateral external evidence and from the critical belief that the uncut novel is the superior work of art—the novel which presents Crane in the form of his initially more honest and powerful intentions rather than in the emasculated and muddled form of these intentions in the first edition. The Appleton text, Parker, Binder, and yet another Parker student Steven Mailloux argue, is hopelessly flawed because of the unintentional ambivalences created in its themes and form by Crane's destruction, through his omissions, of his previously consistent and clearly evident contemptuous attitude toward Henry. Thus, if we wish to read "the *Red Badge* that Crane wrote" rather than the one forced upon him by Hitchcock's desire for a less negative portrait of a Civil War recruit, we must read it in the form available to us in the *Norton Anthology* and Binder's edition.

I have already discussed elsewhere the weaknesses in the argument from external evidence that Crane was forced by Hitchcock to cut *The Red Badge* [see Additional Bibliography]. I would now like to tackle the more problematical but equally vital issue of the argument from internal evidence that the ambivalences and ambiguities in the 1895 Appleton text constitute proof that Crane was forced to warp the themes of the novel through his revision and that the more immediately clear and consistent uncut draft is thereby the superior text. I have found it best in undertaking this task to concentrate . . . on a portion of the novel which Crane wrote early in his composition of the work and which he left uncut and unrevised in its printed version—the first two paragraphs of *The Red Badge.* By demonstrating the purposeful and thematically functional ambivalences in this passage and then in the revised novel as a whole I wish of course to demonstrate that Crane's intent from the first was toward the expression of the ambivalent nature of Henry's maturation under fire and that his revision and cutting were toward the refinement of this intent. (pp. 302-03)

The opening paragraph of the novel describes the coming of spring to an army which has been in camp for the winter. One major stream of imagery in the paragraph is that of awakening—awakening both after the cold of night and the fogs of dawn and after the brown of winter. The army awakens eagerly and expectantly—life is more than the cold and darkness of sleep, and in daylight and warmth passage can be made (the roads now "proper" rather than liquid mud) in the direction of one's destiny. The setting and its images are those of the beginning of a journey in which the emotional cast or coloration of the moment is largely positive; something is going to happen, and this something is better than the death in life of coldness, darkness, and immobility. The opening of the novel thus suggests that we are to be engaged by an initiation story, since both the initial situation and its images are in the archetypal form of an awakening to experience. Out of the blankness and emptiness of innocence, youth advances through experience to maturity and manhood.

Of course, the journey will have its difficulties. Indeed, without these it would not be an initiation journey. One is of those others in life who have aims different from ours and who therefore appear before us as the contradictory, belligerent principle in experience. So there is in the first paragraph the image of a mysterious and potentially dangerous enemy whom one sees in the night. But perhaps the greater difficulty will be in knowing in truth both the nature of the journey as it occurs and its full meaning at its conclusion. This difficulty is anticipated in the first paragraph by three references to the difficulty of knowing which are expressed through images of seeing and hearing. Fogs often obscure the landscape, the army hears only rumors, and the river is in shadow. The only unequivocally clear image of knowing is that the immediate avenue of movement—the roads—are now passable. Moreover, both the awakening and opposing forces are given an animal cast (the army "stretched out on the hills"; the "low brows" of the distant hills where lies the enemy), which suggests the limited rational equipment of those seeking to know.

The first paragraph of *The Red Badge of Courage* reveals Crane in a typically complex interweaving of images. Although the images in the paragraph imply that Henry's adventures may shape themselves into an initiation story, they also suggest that Henry himself will be an inept and inadequate interpreter of what has happened to him, that he will be unable to see and know with clarity and insight. And since the narrator will choose to tell the story through Henry's sense of its nature and importance rather than with a clear authorial underlining of meaning, we as readers will be left in a permanent state of ambivalence or ambiguity. Are we to respond to Henry's experiences principally in their symbolic character as milestones in the archetype of initiation, or are we to respond to them, because of Henry's limited understanding, as fog-ridden, shadowy, and misunderstood markers on a dimly perceived road?

The second paragraph reinforces and extends the notion that we are to have difficulty fully comprehending Henry's experiences. The first paragraph rendered the distinction between a possible progressive movement through time and the difficulty of knowing what occurs in time by means of symbolic and potentially allegorical images. The second paragraph increases our sense that the conventional means of evaluating experience are not to be trusted but does so now by means of the narrator's ironic voice in his reporting of such efforts. A tall soldier goes to wash a shirt with a belief that this enterprise requires virtue and courage. (As always in Crane's narrative style, the terms describing an action—here "developed virtues" and "went resolutely"—though superficially authorial in origin are in fact projections into the third person narrative voice of the doer's own estimation of his action. It is the soldier who believes he is behaving virtuously and resolutely, not Crane.) The statement, beginning as it does with major values and ending with the minor task to which these have been applied, is couched in the classic form of ironic anticlimax. One may think that it takes virtue and courage to wash a shirt, but there is a sharp and large distinction to be made between the actual character of the act and one's estimation of it. The implication which this distinction has for the general nature of self-knowledge, for the estimation of the worth of our acts, is that we will generally both aggrandize the significance of the event and over-value our own attributes in relation to it.

The remainder of the paragraph contains two further implications for the problem of knowledge, both of which are also expressed in habitual forms of Crane's irony. The "tale" which the tall soldier has heard is rendered suspect despite the soldier's belief in its truth by Crane's account of its distant source and by his ironic repetition of the reliability, truthfulness, and trustworthiness of each of the tellers in the tangled history of its transmission. Much of what we learn about experience from our fellows is tainted by the difficulty of communicating accurately both what has occurred and what lies in store for us. Group knowledge, in short, is as suspect as personal self-evaluation.

As a further indication of the complications inherent in the acquisition and transmission of knowledge, the tall soldier—in his belief that he has something important to tell—begins to play a traditional role. He carries a banner and adopts the air of a herald. Man, when he has something to communicate, will adopt various roles to dramatize the worth both of his information and of himself. But the role will often obscure the emptiness and valuelessness of that which is being communicated. In short, Crane appears to be saying in this paragraph, the process of gaining and transmitting knowledge is warped by powerful weaknesses within both human nature and social intercourse. And the knowledge communicated by this process—that which we believe is true about ourselves and our fellows—is thus suspect.

The two opening paragraphs of *The Red Badge of Courage* constitute a paradigm for the themes and techniques of the novel as a whole. In its events and in much of its symbolism, the novel is a story of the coming of age of a young man through the initiatory experience of battle. But our principal confirmation of Henry's experiences as initiation myth is Henry himself, and Crane casts doubt—through his ironic narrative voice—on the truth and value of Henry's estimation of his adventures and himself. And so a vital ambiguity ensues.

The initiation structure of *The Red Badge* is evident both in the external action of the novel and in a good deal of the symbolism arising from event. A young untried soldier, wracked by doubts about his ability to perform well under fire, in fact does flee ignominiously during his first engagement. After a series of misadventures behind his own lines, including receiving a head wound accidentally from one of his own fellows, he returns to his unit, behaves estimably in combat, and receives the plaudits of his comrades and officers. On the level of external action, *The Red Badge* is thus a nineteenth-century development novel in compressed form. In such works, a young man (or woman) tries his mettle in a difficult world, at first believes himself weak and unworthy in the face of the enormous obstacles he encounters, but finally gains the experience necessary to cope with life and thus achieves as well a store of inner strength and conviction. Much of the symbolism in *The*

Red Badge supports a reading of the work as developmental fiction, for one major pattern of symbolism in the novel rehearses the structure of the initiation myth. Henry is at first isolated by his childlike innocence. But after acquiring a symbol of group experience and acceptance (the red badge), he is guided by a supernatural mentor (the cheery soldier) through a night journey to reunion with his fellows; and in the next day's engagement he helps gain a symbolic token of passage into manhood (the enemy's flag).

But much in the novel also casts doubt on the validity of reading the work as an initiation allegory. Chief among these sources of doubt is Crane's ironic undermining at every turn of the quality of Henry's mental equipment and therefore of the possibility that he can indeed mature. Whenever Henry believes he has gained a significant height in his accomplishments and understanding, Crane reveals—by situational and verbal irony—how shallow a momentary resting place he has indeed reached. A typical example occurs after the enemy's first charge during the initial day of battle, when Henry grandiosely overestimates the character of a minor skirmish. ("So it was over at last! The supreme trial had been passed. The red, formidable difficulties of war had been vanquished.") This ironic deflation of Henry's self-evaluation continues unrelieved throughout the novel and includes as well Henry's final summing up, when, after in effect merely having survived the opening battle in the spring of a long campaign (with Gettysburg to follow!), he concludes that "the world was a world for him, though many discovered it to be made of oaths and walking sticks."

In addition, Crane casts doubt on the depth of Henry's maturity at the close of the novel by revealing Henry's exercise in sliding-door conscience. Henry, at the end of the second day's fighting, is still troubled by two of his less estimable acts—his desertion first of his unit and later of the tattered soldier. But what troubles him most is less the intrinsic nature of these acts than that they might be discovered, and when he realizes that this is not likely, he "mustered force to put the sin[s] at a distance" and revels instead in his public accomplishments. It was this aspect of Henry's intellect—his conscience-troubled rationalizations of his behavior and his closely related fury at fate for having placed him in conscience-troubling situations—which Crane, after concluding the first draft of the novel, realized he had overdone and thus cut heavily in the interval between the draft and publication.

Crane also undermines the initiation structure of *The Red Badge* by including in the novel two major counterstructures. Initiation is essentially a mythic statement of a faith in the potential for individual growth—that the forward movement of time is meaningful and productive because through experience we acquire both the capacity to cope with experience and a useful knowledge of ourselves and the world. But *The Red Badge* also contains two major structures which imply that time is essentially meaningless, that all in life is circular repetition, that only the superficial forms of the repetition vary and thus are capable of being misunderstood as significant change and progress. One such symbolic structure is that of the rhythmic movement of troops. The novel begins with the advance to battle by Henry and his regiment, it ends with their departure from battle, and the body of the work contains a series of charges and countercharges, advances and retreats. Since these movements occur in an obscure landscape in connection with an unnamed battle, and since little meaning attends the various movements aside from their impact on Henry and his regiment, significance is attached to the fact of movement itself rather than to movement in relation to a goal or direction. One of the symbolic structures of *The Red Badge* is therefore of a flow and counterflow of men, a largely meaningless and direction-less repetition despite Henry's attribution of deep personal meaning to one of its minor phases, a moment of flow which he mistakes for a moment of significant climax.

Another such circular symbolic structure is even more con-sciously ironic in character. Henry runs on the first day of battle because of two psychic compulsions—an animal instinct of self-preservation and a social instinct to act as he believes his comrades are acting. On the next day—in a far more fully described series of combat experiences—Henry responds to battle precisely as he had on the first day, except that he now behaves "heroically" rather than "cowardly." Again an an-imal compulsion (that of the cornered animal made vicious and powerful by anger and fear at being trapped) is joined with a social one (irritation at unjust blame attached to the regiment) to produce a similar "battle sleep" of unconsciousness in ac-tion. These underlying similarities in Henry's battle perfor-mances reveal not only Crane's attack on the conventional notions of courage and cowardice but—in their role as "equal" halves in a balanced symbolic structure—his belief that life is essentially a series of similar responses to similar conditions in which only the unobservant mistake the superficially dif-ferent in these conditions and responses for a forward move-ment through time.

These two powerful drives in *The Red Badge*—the initiation plot, structure, and symbolic imagery, and the undercutting of a development myth by a variety of ironic devices which imply that the belief that man can adequately interpret the degree of his maturity is a delusion—these two drives come to a head in the final chapter of the novel. The second day's battle is over, and Henry has behaved well in his own eyes and in those of his fellows. Yet he continues as well to overvalue his ac-complishments and deny his failings. The imagery of the con-clusion reflects this ambivalence. Henry, now that the battle is over, thinks of "prospects of clover tranquility." But in fact it is raining, and "the procession of weary soldiers became a bedraggled train, despondent and muttering, marching with churning effort in a trough of liquid mud under a low, wretched sky. Yet the youth smiled, for he saw that the world was a world for him . . .". In this passage, the fatuousness of Henry's conception of what awaits him and therefore of what he has achieved is inherent in the sharp distinction between Henry's belief and the permanent condition of the group to which he belongs, of all mankind, in effect, despite his conviction that he lies outside this condition.

It might thus be argued that Crane wishes us, at this final moment, to reject completely the validity of an initiation ex-perience for Henry. Yet, in the final sentence of the novel, added after the completion of the full first draft, Crane wrote: "Over the river a golden ray of sun came through the hosts of leaden rain clouds." This flat, bald imagistic statement reaf-firms the essential ambiguity of the work as a whole, despite the possibility of reading the final chapter as a confirmation of one position or the other. For the image is not attributed to Henry; it occupies a paragraph of its own, and is the narrative voice's authoritative description of a pictorial moment rather than of Henry's suspect response to the moment. And the narrative voice wishes us to be left, as a final word, with the sense that life is truly ambivalent—that there are rain clouds and that there is the sun. The darkness and cold (and lack of vision) of the opening images of the novel are part of the human condition, but the promise of daylight and spring warmth and of vision which are also present in the opening images have in part been fulfilled by the ray of sunlight. (pp. 304-09)

> *Donald Pizer, " 'The Red Badge of Courage': Text, Theme, and Form," in South Atlantic Quarterly, Vol. 84, No. 3, Summer, 1985, pp. 302-13.*

ADDITIONAL BIBLIOGRAPHY

Allen, John Barrow. "New Novels." *The Academy* 49, No. 1241 (15 February 1896): 134-35.
  Includes a review of *The Red Badge of Courage* intended for British readers in which the critic notes: "A serio-comic effect seems to be intended throughout, and Mr. Crane is no doubt highly gifted with that grotesqueness of fancy which is peculiarly a trans-atlantic production; but the humor is scarcely of a sort to be appreciated by readers on this side."

Anderson, Warren D. "Homer and Stephen Crane." *Nineteenth-Cen-tury Fiction* 19, No. 1 (June 1964): 77-86.
  Traces parallels of subject, theme, and technique between Ho-mer's *Iliad* and *Odyssey* and *The Red Badge of Courage*. Anderson concludes that Crane's novel reaffirms ideals of Homeric heroism.

Beaver, Harold. "Models of Virtue." In his *The Great American Masquerade*, pp. 121-40. London, England, and Totowa, N. J.: Vision and Barnes & Noble, 1985.
  Sees Henry Fleming in *The Red Badge of Courage* as an example of the naturalist hero that emerged in American fiction in the late nineteenth century. According to Beaver: "Crane's theme was . . . neither the romance of heroism, nor the triumph of heroism, but the quandary of heroism in an unheroic age."

Binder, Henry. "Donald Pizer, Ripley Hitchcock, and *The Red Badge of Courage*." *Studies in the Novel* 11, No. 2 (Summer 1979): 216-23.
  Responds to criticism of his essay "The *Red Badge of Courage* Nobody Knows" [see excerpt dated 1978] in Pizer's " '*The Red Badge of Courage* Nobody Knows': A Brief Rejoinder" [see Additional Bibliography entry below.]

Bloom, Harold. Introduction to *Modern Critical Views: Stephen Crane*, edited by Harold Bloom, pp. 1-6. New York: Chelsea House Pub-lishers, 1987.
  Praises *The Red Badge of Courage* as an impressionistic novel.

"The Novels of Two Journalists." *The Bookman* (New York) 2, No. 3 (November 1895): 217-20.
  Reviews *A Daughter of the Tenements*, by Edward W. Townsend, and *The Red Badge of Courage*. According to the critic, Crane's novel may be best described as "a study in morbid emotions and distorted external impressions."

Bowers, Fredson, ed. *The Red Badge of Courage: A Facsimile Edition of the Manuscript*, 2 vols., by Stephen Crane. Washington, D. C.: NCR/Microcard Editions, 1973.
  Photographic facsimile of the final manuscript of the novel.

Bradley, Sculley, et al., eds. *The Red Badge of Courage, by Stephen Crane: An Authoritative Text, Backgrounds and Sources, Criticism*, second edition, revised by Donald Pizer. New York: W. W. Norton & Co., 1976, 364 p.
  Reprints the first edition Appleton text slightly emended, intro-ductory essays, and essays representing the major critical trends in *Red Badge* scholarship.

Breslin, Paul. "Courage and Convention: *The Red Badge of Cour-age*." *The Yale Review* 66, No. 2 (Winter 1977): 209-22.
  Discusses Crane's definition of the nature of courage and notes the lack of a typically American socio-religious context for Crane's Civil War story.

Brooks, Sydney. "Mr. Stephen Crane and His Critics." *The Dial* 20, No. 238 (16 May 1896): 297-98.

> Rebuttal to A. C. McClurg's letter to the editor of 16 April 1896 [see Additional Bibliography entry below]. Brooks defends *The Red Badge of Courage* and calls McClurg's letter "a compound of misjudged patriotism and bad criticism."

Cazemajou, Jean. "*The Red Badge of Courage:* The 'Religion of Peace' and the War Archetype." In *Stephen Crane in Transition: Centenary Essays,* edited by Joseph Katz, pp. 54-65. Dekalb: Northern Illinois University Press, 1972.

> Maintains that in *The Red Badge of Courage* "war and peace function simultaneously as factual realities and archetypal values."

Dillingham, William B. "Insensibility in *The Red Badge of Courage.*" *College English* 25, No. 3 (December 1963): 194-98.

> Maintains that Fleming is able to act courageously only when he becomes insensitive—sinking into "subhuman dullness." According to Dillingham: "The chief purpose of the novel is to objectify the nature of heroism through Henry Fleming. Through witnessing his actions and changing sensations we discover the emerging paradox of courage: human courage is by its nature subhuman; in order to be courageous, a man in time of physical strife must abandon the highest of his human facilities, reason and imagination, and act instinctively, even animalistically."

Dunn, N. E. "The Common Man's *Iliad.*" *Comparative Literature Studies* 21, No. 3 (Fall 1984): 270-81.

> Examines elements of mock epic tradition in *The Red Badge of Courage* and draws parallels between Crane's war novel and "the most dramatic war story of them all, the *Iliad.*"

Dusenbery, Robert. "The Homeric Mood in the *Red Badge of Courage.*" *Pacific Coast Philology* 3 (April 1968): 31-7.

> Draws parallels of language, religion, and scene between *The Red Badge of Courage,* which Dusenbery calls "a study in triumph, in heroism," and the *Iliad.*

Eby, Cecil D., Jr. "Stephen Crane's 'Fierce Red Wafer'." *English Language Notes* 1, No. 2 (December 1963): 128-30.

> Observes that Crane used a sequence of words paralleling the "fierce red wafer" image of his *The Red Badge of Courage* twice in his novel *Active Service* with no apparent symbolic intent. According to Eby: "[The parallel passages] show that for him the color red when placed against a sharply contrasting background suggested some fiery or 'fierce' quality. This may be idiosyncratic, but there is nothing symbolic about it."

Fraser, John. "Crime and Forgiveness: *The Red Badge of Courage* in Time of War." In his *The Name of Action: Critical Essays,* pp. 81-91. Cambridge: Cambridge University Press, 1984.

> Discusses Fleming's coming to terms with the moral complexities of battle and with himself in *The Red Badge of Courage* in an essay written during the Vietnam War era. According to Fraser: "In exploring war as a closed situation in which an intellectual cannot escape from the moral claims of events merely by willing it . . . Crane has helped to show up the fashionable nihilisms of today as the empty and arid things that they are."

Frohock, W. M. "*The Red Badge* and the Limits of Parody." *The Southern Review* n.s. 6, No. 1 (January 1970): 137-48.

> Examines Crane's use of literary stereotypes and linguistic clichés in *The Red Badge of Courage.* According to Frohock: "*The Red Badge of Courage* . . . supports the case that Crane's genius shows itself fully as much in his knowing when not to parody and when to leave stereotypes and clichés intact."

Fryckstedt, O. W. "Henry Fleming's Tupenny Fury: Cosmic Pessimism in Stephen Crane's *The Red Badge of Courage.*" *Studia Neophilologica* 33 (1961): 265-81.

> Examines Henry Fleming's revolt against the universe as it was treated in the final manuscript and in the published text of *The Red Badge of Courage.*

Gollin, Rita K. " 'Little Souls Who Thirst for Fight' in *The Red Badge of Courage.*" *Arizona Quarterly* 30, No. 2 (Summer 1974): 111-18.

> Sees *The Red Badge of Courage* as an anti-war novel and focuses on Crane's presentation of the nature of man as intrinsically quarrelsome.

Greenfield, Stanley B. "The Unmistakable Stephen Crane." *PMLA* 73, No. 5 (December 1958): 562-72.

> Discusses wide-ranging critical errors that have been made in interpreting *The Red Badge of Courage*; examines that work in combination with "The Open Boat" and "The Blue Hotel"; and analyzes Crane's ironic presentation of the nature of heroic behavior—pitting "ethical motivation and behavior versus deterministic and naturalistic actions."

Hart, John E. "*The Red Badge of Courage* as Myth and Symbol." *University of Kansas City Review* 19 (Summer 1953): 249-56.

> Demonstrates that "the construction of the story, its moral and meaning, its reliance on symbol follow in detail the traditional formula of myth." Hart concludes: "Following the general pattern of myth with peculiar individual variations, Crane has shown how the moral and spiritual strength of the individual springs from the group, and how, through the identification of self with the group, the individual can be 'reborn in identity with the whole meaning of the universe'."

Katz, Joseph. Introduction to *"The Red Badge of Courage"*: A Facsimile Reproduction of the New York "Press" Appearance of December 9, 1894, by Stephen Crane, pp. 9-42. Gainesville, Fla.: Scholars' Facsimiles & Reprints, 1967.

> Biographical and publication data concerning the syndicated "Red Badge of Courage," a work which Katz describes as "a fiction with fast pace, with less explicit introspection and with a heavier use of narrative to push the plot along."

———. "Practical Editions: Stephen Crane's *The Red Badge of Courage.*" *Proof* 2 (1972): 301-11.

> Exposes textual errors in fifteen editions of *The Red Badge of Courage,* ranging from unauthoritative additions and deletions to careless copy-editing.

Kent, Thomas L. "Epistemological Uncertainty in *The Red Badge of Courage.*" *Modern Fiction Studies* 27, No. 4 (Winter 1981-82): 621-28.

> Examines the nature of knowledge in *The Red Badge of Courage,* maintaining that through epistemological uncertainties in the text Crane defines the universe as essentially unknowable.

Knapp, Bettina L. "*The Red Badge of Courage.*" In her *Stephen Crane,* pp. 59-84. New York: Ungar, 1987.

> Examines Henry Fleming's rites of passage from youth to manhood in *The Red Badge of Courage* under the following headings: The separation, the dark night of the soul, the initiation into the patriarchal fold, the forest experience, the reintegration, the rebirth.

Lavers, Norman. "Order in *The Red Badge of Courage.*" *The University Review* 32, No. 4 (June 1966): 287-95.

> Thematic study connecting Crane's *George's Mother,* "The Open Boat," and *The Red Badge of Courage* through patterns of sin and redemption, separation and return, which the critic suggests, represent "the protagonist's, and perhaps Crane's efforts to become free of an oedipal fixation."

Lynskey, Winifred. "Crane's *The Red Badge of Courage.*" *The Explicator,* 8, No. 3 (December 1949): item #18.

> Maintains the respect awarded Fleming by his comrades at the end of the novel is undeserved, making it characteristic of the naturalistic morality prevalent in Crane's works, which sees rewards and punishments dispensed randomly.

Mailloux, Steven. "*The Red Badge of Courage* and Interpretive Conventions: Critical Response to a Maimed Text." *Studies in the Novel* 10, No. 1 (Spring 1978): 48-63.

> Recounts critical views of the Appleton text of *The Red Badge of Courage,* which the critic considers inconsistent and illogical when applied to Crane's unexpurgated manuscript of the novel.

According to Mailloux: "The maimed state of the Appleton ending necessitates critical choices in the use of interpretive conventions, choices that force critics to 'write' their own texts that they call *The Red Badge of Courage*."

Marcus, Mordecai and Marcus, Erin. "Animal Imagery in *The Red Badge of Courage*." *Modern Language Notes* 74, No. 2 (February 1959): 108-11.
   Discusses Crane's extensive use of animal imagery to describe the enlisted men and officers in the novel.

McClurg, A. C. "The Red Badge of Hysteria." *The Dial* 20, No. 236 (16 April 1896): 227-28.
   Letter to the editor written by a former Union military officer attacking the novel and those who praise it. According to the correspondent, *The Red Badge of Courage* fails both as a portrait of Civil War experience and as a piece of literature.

McDermott, John J. "Symbolism and Psychological Realism in *The Red Badge of Courage*." *Nineteenth-Century Fiction* 23, No. 3 (December 1968): 324-31.
   Examines Crane's depiction of a complicated psychological change in his protagonist, Henry Fleming. According to McDermott: "As the novel closes, Henry . . . remains a person of mixed motives and partial insights. But the fundamental thrust of his character has been set: he has discovered and developed within himself a capacity for a detached spirit of self-sacrifice based on an imperfect but nonetheless profound self-knowledge."

Mitchell, Lee Clark, ed. *New Essays on "The Red Badge of Courage."* Cambridge: Cambridge University Press, 1986, 150 p.
   Includes essays by Christine Brooke-Rose, Andrew Belbanco, Howard C. Horsford, Amy Kaplan, and Hershel Parker.

Review of *The Red Badge of Courage: An Episode of the American Civil War, Maggie: A Girl of the Streets,* and *George's Mother,* by Stephen Crane. *The Nation* 63, No. 1618 (2 July 1896): 15.
   Classifies Crane as an "animalist" writer—one who writes "a species of realism which deals with man considered as an animal." According to the critic, *The Red Badge of Courage* "is undeniably clever; its vice is over-emphasis. Mr. Crane has not learnt the secret that carnage is itself eloquent, and does not need epithets to make it so."

"A Green Private under Fire." *The New York Times* (19 October 1895): 3.
   Favorable review of *The Red Badge of Courage,* finding fault only in Crane's affectations of style.

Onderdonk, J. L. "A Red Badge of Bad English." *The Dial* 20, No. 237 (1 May 1896): 263-64.
   Letter to the editor affirming A. C. McClurg's attack on *The Red Badge of Courage* in the previous issue [see Additional Bibliography entry above]. Onderdonk disparages the work as a "literary absurdity," asserting that "amid so much that is strained and affected there is not one agreeable character, hardly one praiseworthy sentiment, and certainly no new or original thought."

Osborn, Scott C. "Stephen Crane's Imagery: 'Pasted like a Wafer'." *American Literature* 23, No. 3 (November 1951): 362.
   Maintains that in his "wafer" image Crane was "unconsciously using a figure or an impression" culled from *The Light That Failed,* by Rudyard Kipling, in which Kipling wrote: "The fog was driven apart for a moment, and the sun shone, a blood-red wafer, on the water."

Parker, Hershel. "*The Red Badge of Courage:* The Private History of a Campaign That—Succeeded?" In his *Flawed Texts and Verbal Icons: Literary Authority in American Fiction,* pp. 147-79. Evanston, Ill.: Northwestern University Press, 1984.
   Recounts Parker's interest, research, and editorial activity regarding Crane's final manuscript version of *The Red Badge of Courage.*

Payne, William Morton. "Recent Fiction." *The Dial* 20, No. 231 (1 February 1896): 76-81.
   Unfavorably reviews *The Red Badge of Courage.* According to Payne: "There is almost no story to Mr. Crane's production, but merely an account, in roughshod descriptive style, of the thoughts and feelings of a young soldier during his first days of active fighting. The author constructs for his central character a psychological history that is plausible, but hardly convincing."

Pease, Donald. "Fear, Rage, and the Mistrials of Representation in *The Red Badge of Courage*." In *American Realism: New Essays,* edited by Eric J. Sundquist, pp. 155-75. Baltimore and London: Johns Hopkins University Press, 1982.
   Maintains that *The Red Badge of Courage* was disparaged by some early critics because it represented a departure from accepted Civil War narratives, which attributed historical significance to every battle and promoted such moral principles as freedom, equality, and union.

Pelletier, Gaston. "*Red Badge* Revisited." *English Journal* 57, No. 1 (January 1968): 24-5, 99.
   Focuses on Crane's abundant use of color and sound images in *The Red Badge of Courage.* According to Pelletier: "Crane's diction is potent. So much so that it often explodes on the page. But the energy given off by the detonation often overpowers. It debilitates. It exhausts."

Pizer, Donald. "'*The Red Badge of Courage* Nobody Knows': A Brief Rejoinder." *Studies in the Novel* 11, No. 1 (Spring 1979): 77-81.
   Disputes Henry Binder's theses [see excerpt dated 1978] that Crane made revisions in *The Red Badge of Courage* only to satisfy his publisher and that the manuscript version therefore comprises the most coherent novel, closest to Crane's intention. According to Pizer: "There is not enough hard evidence that [editor Ripley Hitchcock] forced Crane to make two separate series of cuts in the *Red Badge,* and there is not enough 'soft' evidence in the critical reading of the manuscript version of the novel to warrant a belief that this version constitutes the 'true' Crane and a better novel."

Pratt, Lyndon Upson. "A Possible Source of *The Red Badge of Courage*." *American Literature* 11, No. 1 (March 1939): 1-10.
   Concludes that while the Battle of Chancellorsville "contributed the general setting and the rough plan of the novel," Henry's flight from the battlefield and the heroism of the wounded color-bearer may have been suggested by events at the Battle of Antietam, Maryland, September 1862.

Rahv, Philip. "Fiction and the Criticism of Fiction." *Kenyon Review* 18, No. 2 (Spring 1956): 276-99.
   Complains that through R. W. Stallman's allegorical reading, "*The Red Badge of Courage,* which is something of a *tour de force* as a novel and which is chiefly noted for the advance it marks in the onset of realism on the American literary scene, is transmogrified into a religious allegory."

Rechnitz, Robert M. "Depersonalization and the Dream in *The Red Badge of Courage*." *Studies in the Novel* 6, No. 1 (Spring 1974): 76-87.
   Analyzes Crane's intentions in the final four paragraphs of *The Red Badge of Courage* in terms of American traditional ideals of individuality and self-reliance versus depersonalization. According to Rechnitz: "Having dramatized the forces in modern America which were increasingly demanding the subservience of human needs to those of the machine, Crane insists at the final moment [in *The Red Badge of Courage*]—unconvincingly—that man might escape his self-imposed servitude."

Rosenfeld, Isaac. "Stephen Crane as Symbolist." *The Kenyon Review* 15, No. 2 (Spring 1953): 310, 312-14.
   Challenges R. W. Stallman's Christian interpretation of Crane's symbolism in *The Red Badge of Courage.*

Sadler, Frank. "Crane's 'Fleming': Appellation for Coward or Hero?" *American Literature* 48, No. 3 (November 1976): 372-76.
   Traces Crane's references to his protagonist's surname in *The Red Badge of Courage.* According to Sadler: "In each successive appearance of his surname Henry progresses from a fear of exposure and humiliation to a final acceptance of the consequences of his fall until, in a moment of congratulatory praise, he emerges

as a hero. After that moment his surname disappears from the novel."

Safranek, William P. "Crane's *The Red Badge of Courage*." *The Explicator* 26, No. 3 (November 1967): item #21.
Suggests parallel development in the characters of the "loud soldier" and Henry Fleming. Safranek maintains that transformations bring new insight to both characters—seeing with "new eyes," they are able to perceive their own insignificance.

Satterfield, Ben. "From Romance to Reality: The Accomplishment of Private Fleming." *CLA Journal* 24, No. 4 (June 1981): 451-64.
Views *The Red Badge of Courage* as a "consistent and unified work of art that is neither allegorical nor naturalistic, but essentially affirmative and humanistic in scope."

Sewall, R. B. "Crane's *The Red Badge of Courage*." *The Explicator* 3, No. 7 (May 1945): item #55.
Discusses the similarities and differences between *The Red Badge of Courage* and Joseph Conrad's *Lord Jim*. According to Sewall: "In each story a youth is brought to his first major test and is involved in a moral problem of conduct; he wrestles with his problem, suffers, and finally achieves peace. But the stories differ sharply in the way the resolution, in each case, is brought about."

Shroeder, John W. "Stephen Crane Embattled." *The University of Kansas City Review* 17, No. 2 (Winter 1950): 119-29.
Focuses on *The Red Badge of Courage* in one section of an essay on Crane's naturalistic thought and art.

Shulman, Robert. "*The Red Badge* and Social Violence: Crane's Myth of His America." *The Canadian Review of American Studies* 12, No. 1 (Spring 1981): 1-19.
Examines cultural and biographical influences that colored Crane's social outlook and contributed the war scenario to *The Red Badge of Courage*.

Solomon, Eric. "A Gloss on *The Red Badge of Courage*." *Modern Language Notes* 75, No. 2 (February 1960): 111-13.
Traces the character Henry Fleming through his appearances in Crane's later short stories "The Veteran" and "Lynx-Hunting." According to Solomon: " 'The Veteran' proves that even though Henry Fleming, at the end of *The Red Badge of Courage*, may seem unchanged, he has actually learned honesty and self-abnegation."

Stallman, R. W. "The Scholar's Net: Literary Sources." *College English* 17, No. 1 (October 1955): 20-7.
Considers Crane's literary inspiration in Kipling's *The Light That Failed* for the image of the sun as a "wafer," and discusses this metaphor within the contexts of the works in which it appears. According to Stallman: "In both novels the sun-wafer images appear at a moment of recognition. Crane's image is used at a crucial point in the narrative and with symbolic import, the wafer of the sun representing the wafer of the Mass."

Stone, Edward. "The Many Suns of *The Red Badge of Courage*." *American Literature* 29, No. 3 (November 1957): 322-26.
Examines the symbolic significance of the sun in *The Red Badge of Courage*.

Thomas, Donald S. "Crane's *The Red Badge of Courage*." *The Explicator* 27, No. 9 (May 1969): item #77.
Examines the passage in which troops on their way to the first battle encounter a corpse and Fleming feels the impulse to stare at the dead body hoping "to read in dead eyes the answer to the Question." According to Thomas the "question" is "What Must I Do To Be Saved?"—the title of a religious tract written by Crane's uncle. In Thomas's view: "Not only does the question in this title apply aptly to the very literary question of physical survival in the forthcoming battle, but it also has an extension to the larger symbolic question of spiritual survival that faces the youth."

Tuttleton, James W. "The Imagery of *The Red Badge of Courage*." *Modern Fiction Studies* 8, No. 4 (Winter 1962-63): 410-15.
Maintains that Crane's indictment of war in *The Red Badge of Courage* is effected through the juxtaposition of "images of pagan religion, liturgy, and ritual against images of the Christian religion."

Vanderbilt, Kermit and Weiss, Daniel. "From Rifleman to Flagbearer: Henry Fleming's Separate Peace in *The Red Badge of Courage*." *Modern Fiction Studies* 11, No. 4 (Winter 1965-66): 371-80.
Analyzes Henry Fleming's acceptance of the flagbearer's role in the final quarter of the novel.

Wasserstrom, William. "Hydraulics and Heroics: William James, Stephen Crane." In his *The Ironies of Progress: Henry Adams and the American Dream*, pp. 77-99. Carbondale and Edwardsville: Southern Illinois University Press, 1984.
Connects facets of nineteenth-century American cultural trends, values, and behavior to Crane's *The Red Badge of Courage*.

Weatherford, Richard M., ed. "*The Red Badge of Courage* (1895)." In his *Stephen Crane: The Critical Heritage*, pp. 82-170. London and Boston: Routledge & Kegan Paul, 1973.
Reprints criticism that appeared from the time of the serial publication of the novel to April 1898.

Weiss, Daniel. "The Red Badge of Courage." In his *The Critic Agonistes: Psychology, Myth, and the Art of Fiction*, pp. 57-107. Seattle and London: University of Washington Press, 1985.
Psychoanalytic explication of the novel originally published in *The Psychoanalytic Review* 52, Nos. 2 and 3 (Summer and Fall 1965).

James (George) Frazer

1854-1941

Scottish anthropologist, historian, critic, and essayist.

Frazer was a Scottish anthropologist and classical scholar who is best known as the author of *The Golden Bough,* a vast compendium of anthropological information that is generally credited with generating the enormous interest in anthropology, folklore, myth, and ritual that arose in the late nineteenth and early twentieth centuries. In addition to its impact as a scholarly document, *The Golden Bough* also had a great influence upon literature. Numerous authors have acknowledged their indebtedness to Frazer for supplying them with the background in myth and ritual that has infused much twentieth-century literature, and have embedded references to *The Golden Bough* in their own works. Frazer, who spent a lifetime examining and attempting to explain the primitive bases for human social behavior, was one of the first and most thorough of social anthropologists, and although many of the purely scientific applications of his work have been superceded by subsequent scholarship, his name is often linked with those of Charles Darwin, Karl Marx, Sigmund Freud, and Albert Einstein as central to the shaping of the modern consciousness. Herbert Weisinger has noted that "just as Darwin bound man to his physical past, Marx to his historical past, Freud to his psychological past, and Einstein to his cosmic past, so Frazer bound him to his cultural past."

Born in Glasgow to a financially secure businessman and his wife, Frazer grew up with an interest in classical studies that was encouraged by his parents, who sent him to excellent primary and secondary schools and then to Glasgow University. In 1873 he won a scholarship to Trinity College, Cambridge, where he continued to study classical Greek and Roman history, literature, and philosophy. He also took up law and eventually passed the bar exam, but he never pursued a legal practice. While at Cambridge, he read Sir Edward Taylor's *Primitive Cultures* (1871), and later said that it "marked an epoch" in his life, interesting him deeply in the study of anthropology. He was still more strongly influenced in this direction by the theologian and scholar William Robertson Smith, a professor and librarian at Cambridge. Smith, who also served as an editor of the ninth edition of the *Encyclopedia Britannica,* commissioned from Frazer articles on several topics, including "Taboo" and "Totemism." According to Robert Ackerman, the essay on totemism "grew so long that even the most sympathetic editor could print only an abridged version; the full text appeared in 1887 as Frazer's first book, *Totemism,* and immediately established him in the then thinly populated world of anthropology."

Frazer early established the habits and methods that sustained him through a lifetime of anthropological research. Among his first published works was the pamphlet *Questions on the Manners, Customs, Religions, Superstitions, &c., of Uncivilized or Semi-Civilized Peoples,* which was privately printed and distributed to missionaries, travelers, students, and field-workers embarking upon or returning from sojourns among primitive peoples. Frazer culled a vast amount of material from their responses to his questions about social behavior, habits, myths, and rituals of the "uncivilized or semi-civilized peoples" they

had observed. This remained Frazer's method: he relied exclusively upon the accounts of others in writing his massive compilations of anthropological information, most often consulting previously published texts. He did no fieldwork himself and reportedly responded with horror ("Heaven forbid!") to queries about his own direct contact with savage tribes. Frazer maintained that his approach was the soundest way to undertake the study of humankind. The field-worker, he contended, was too thoroughly immersed in a foreign culture to accurately assess the behavior of its people, and should only observe and report. He also considered the primitive practitioners of a rite or tellers of a myth unreliable sources for explication, maintaining that societies frequently lose sight of the original reasons for performing their rituals, and conceive new myths to explain them. Conclusions, he argued, are best made by the scholarly anthropologist with a trained mind. Frazer spent up to fifteen hours a day researching and writing his volumes of comparative social anthropology, and his work habits did not flag until age and failing eyesight rendered such effort impossible. With the aid of secretaries he continued to edit, expand, and reissue books on the study of humankind until a few years before his death in 1941.

In his earliest articles Frazer developed a concept that became a guiding principle for much of his subsequent work: the theory that most social systems evolve from irrational ritualistic beginnings. As a result, he viewed primitive or savage peoples as the most proper area of study for the anthropologist. He wrote: "Civilization is extremely complex; savagery is comparatively simple, and moreover it is undoubtedly the source from which all civilization has been ultimately derived by a slow process of evolution. It seemed to me therefore that if we are to understand the complex product we must begin by studying the simple elements out of which it has been gradually compounded; in other words, we must try to understand savagery before we can hope fully to comprehend civilization."

Thus, Frazer's works extrapolate from the general argument of Darwin's *Descent of Man* (1871) in its theory that all life participates in a continuous process of evolution through successively higher stages. Implicit in this approach was Frazer's assumption that the more advanced culture was superior to the primitive one. Frazer began with the theory that human development invariably entails three successive stages. The first and most primitive consists of belief in magic, and during this stage an attempt is made to control natural forces through ritual. When magic is discarded because of its demonstrable inefficacy, religion is adopted, as the developing primitive next seeks to propitiate the gods who are thought to be responsible for weather, crops, fertility, and other natural phenomena. The highest level of civilization, according to Frazer, is the scientific stage which his own era had attained. In this stage, humans still seek to control the natural world, but by experimental and objective means whose results can be measured and predicted rather than guessed at or hoped for. According to Frazer, rituals from the earliest stage frequently survive successive evolutionary stages, although often merely as social forms and habits. Maintaining that all human groups pass through the same three stages, Frazer compared rituals and social habits from widely different places, cultures, and ages in an attempt to demonstrate that societies at the same stage of development share the same systems of beliefs and behavioral patterns.

According to John B. Vickery, *The Golden Bough* is "both the most encyclopedic treatment of primitive life available to the English-speaking world and the one that lies behind the bulk of modern literary interest in myth and ritual." Frazer began *The Golden Bough* with two questions about an obscure classical account: "Why was the succession to the priesthood of Diana at Nemi in southern Italy determined by mortal combat?" and "Why must the aspirant slay his predecessor with a bough from a sacred tree?" Frazer attempted to trace the meaning of this account through the marshalled lore of hundreds of ages and places back to a common origin in a recurring figure in world mythology: the priest-king who is believed to hold godlike powers. As long as he remains strong and healthy, so too do his community and worshiper-subjects. Because the welfare of his community depends upon his vigor, he cannot be allowed to weaken, sicken, or die of natural causes while serving as ruler. Hence the transference of his office to whoever can defeat him in combat—presumably a stronger man who could be expected to flourish, and with him, his community. Frazer identified the "golden bough" as a growth of mistletoe, which remains green year-round and was considered the life or the soul of the tree.

The Golden Bough embodies many of the main currents of turn-of-the-century thought, in particular the rationalism, historicism, and evolutionary philosophy that pervaded the late Victorian consciousness. "Catching up as it does many of the scientific, philosophical, and artistic emphases of the age,"

Vickery wrote, *The Golden Bough* "is a subtly persuasive form of the loose, variegated, and often contradictory intellectual tradition that shaped the modern spirit." Numerous commentators have posited various reasons for the immediate and enduring popularity of *The Golden Bough*. Some maintain that Frazer's evolutionary theory offers a partial explanation for its enormous impact: he was in essence assuring his readers that they represented the peak of human development. Further, it has been suggested that Frazer's endless listing, categorizing, and classifying of disparate facts answered a Victorian passion for these activities. "The energetic ordering and arranging of the past," according to Sandra Siegel, assuaged Victorian uneasiness about the primitive heritage and vestigial savagery that Sigmund Freud and Charles Darwin, among other nineteenth-century scientists, had assured Victorian readers that they possessed. Frazer, though conceding that humankind shared a violent and debased past, also offered the reassurance that civilized humanity had risen far above its primordial beginnings. Other critics cite the literary quality of the work itself as a reason for its appeal to readers. It is widely regarded as a genuine literary achievement, possessing both a notable prose style and a cyclical structure that prefigured many modern literary techniques.

Frazer's methods and virtually all of his conclusions have been superseded by more modern scholarship. It has been established, for example, that his three-stage theory of human development was erroneous: even during Frazer's lifetime other anthropologists demonstrated that some very primitive tribes, whose cultures Frazer maintained were in the earliest stage of belief in magic, possessed clearly defined religious beliefs and some rudimentary scientific knowledge. More generally, Frazer's strict separation of fieldwork from evaluation and his use of the comparative method have been largely discredited. Frazer has been criticized for his avoidance of fieldwork and for basing conclusions upon unreliable accounts of rituals, ceremonies, and customs furnished by amateur or extremely biased observers, and for his lack of discrimination between information provided by the casual tourist and that proffered by the trained scientist. Most of his sources were, like Frazer himself, ignorant of native languages, and therefore even more prone to misinterpreting what they observed. Increasingly, as social anthropologists attempted to infuse their discipline with the rigorous methodology of a "hard" science, Frazer's comparative method, consisting as it did of isolating examples of human behavior for study, was discarded in favor of studying behavior as it is related to cultural context.

Perhaps the harshest criticism of Frazer since his death has come from Edmund Leach, who has assailed not only Frazer's methods and conclusions, but also the manner in which he employed his dubious sources, which were "sometimes quoted verbatim, but more often rephrased to suit the sentimental lilt which Frazer considered to be the essential quality of fine writing. Quite explicitly he thought of himself as making a contribution to literature rather than to science, and it does not seem to have occurred to him that in 'improving' his sources he might also be distorting them." Leach offers examples of such distortions by contrasting passages from Frazer's writing with the sources from which he drew his information, demonstrating that in some cases, Frazer did change the meaning of the original material.

Despite such widespread disregard for his scholarship, Frazer remains preeminent as "the father of modern anthropology." He is most highly regarded today as a popularizer of this field of study, one whose pioneering work made anthropology interesting and accessible to the general reader and a vital subject of controversy to scholars, including some who based entire careers upon opposing and disproving Frazerian anthropological methods and findings. Further, the narrative and descriptive portions of *The Golden Bough* engrossed readers, and influenced subsequent writers, by giving form and substance to the structure of myth and ritual that underlies human experience.

(See also *Contemporary Authors*, Vol. 118.)

PRINCIPAL WORKS

Questions on the Manners, Customs, Religions, Superstitions, &c., of Uncivilized or Semi-Civilized Peoples (pamphlet) 1887; revised edition, 1889
Totemism (treatise) 1887
The Golden Bough: A Study in Comparative Religion. 2 vols. (treatise) 1890; revised and enlarged edition published in 3 volumes, 1900; further revised and enlarged edition published in 12 volumes, 1911-15; abridged edition, 1922; further revised and abridged edition, 1959
Pausanias, and Other Greek Sketches (translations and history) 1900; reprinted as *Studies in Greek Scenery, Legend, and History*, 1917
Lectures on the Early History of the Kingship (lectures) 1905; reprinted as *The Magical Origin of Kings*, 1920
Adonis, Attis, Osiris: Studies in the History of Oriental Religion (treatise) 1906; revised and enlarged edition, 1907; second revised and enlarged edition, 1914
Folk-Lore in the Old Testament (essays) 1907
Questions on the Customs, Beliefs, and Languages of Savages (treatise) 1907; revised edition, 1910
The Scope of Social Anthropology (lecture) 1908
Psyche's Task: A Discourse Concerning the Influence of Superstition on the Growth of Institutions (treatise) 1909; revised and enlarged edition, 1913; revised and enlarged edition reprinted as *The Devil's Advocate*, 1927
Totemism and Exogamy: A Treatise on Certain Forms of Superstition and Society. 4 vols. (treatise) 1910
The Dying God (treatise) 1911
The Magic Art and the Evolution of Kings. 2 vols. (treatise) 1911
Taboo and the Perils of the Soul (treatise) 1911
Spirits of the Corn and of the Wild. 2 vols. (treatise) 1912
Balder the Beautiful. 2 vols. (treatise) 1913
The Scapegoat (treatise) 1913
The Belief in Immortality and the Worship of the Dead. 3 vols. (lectures) 1913-24
Jacob and the Mandrakes (treatise) 1917
Folk-Lore in the Old Testament: Studies in Comparative Religion, Legend, and Law. 3 vols. (essays) 1918; abridged edition, 1923
Sir Roger de Coverley, and Other Literary Pieces (essays) 1920
The Worship of Nature (treatise) 1926
The Gorgon's Head, and Other Literary Pieces (essays) 1927
*The Growth of Plato's Ideal Theory (essay) 1930
Myths of the Origin of Fire (essay) 1930

Garnered Sheaves (essays, lectures, and criticism) 1931
Condorcet on the Progress of the Human Mind (lecture) 1933
The Fear of the Dead in Primitive Religions. 3 vols. (lectures) 1933-36
Creation and Evolution in Primitive Cosmogonies, and Other Pieces (essays) 1935
Aftermath: A Supplement to the Golden Bough (essays) 1936
Greece and Rome (history) 1937
Totemica: A Supplement to Totemism and Exogamy (treatise) 1937

*This work was written in 1879.

THE EDINBURGH REVIEW (essay date 1890)

[*In the following excerpt, an early reviewer of* The Golden Bough *notes that Frazer's use of the comparative method to seek a common basis for much obscure folklore, ritual, superstition, and myth results in sometimes farfetched conclusions.*]

The origin of human ideas and institutions, their causes and their tendencies, their genealogy and interconnexion, have latterly been explored and examined to a degree that has profoundly influenced contemporary habits of thought. In every branch of investigation our opinions have been greatly affected by the enormous expansion of the field of enquiry and collection; by the gradual unfolding of the scattered, torn, and disfigured pages of the prehistoric record; and by observation of the various phases of primitive society still surviving in those corners of the earth that have not yet been swept out by the besom of civilisation. Out of this vast accumulation of material, out of this opening of fresh sources of knowledge, has grown up the comparative method, the most important arm of precision that has yet been invented by the science of research. Men have discovered, as they suppose, that the ideas of the world can be treated like its flora, can be gathered together, classified, and used for philosophic demonstration of some comprehensive theory of their general characteristics and growth; can be traced down to the primordial root, and upwards to their highest form of expansion and refinement. And nowhere has the doctrine of evolutionary development produced a more remarkable change than in the point of view from which recent writers have approached the study of primitive ritual and beliefs.

Mr. Frazer, in his book of *The Golden Bough,* uses the comparative method as his instrument in a peculiarly abstruse and complicated operation. He undertakes to explain a very ancient custom, which, extinct many centuries ago, is now known only through a few fragmentary descriptions and allusions that have come down to us from classical antiquity, and that have been put together by Mr. Frazer in order to give what remains of the legend and the rite. It is the story of the priest of Aricia, who dwelt by the Arician lake in a grove sacred to Diana Nemorensis, wherein was a tree of which no branch might be broken. According to the rule of this shrine, as it can be gathered from the passages to which Mr. Frazer refers his reader, the priest held office until some runaway slave could first break a bough from the tree and then slay the priest in single combat. Not before he had broken the bough could he fight the duel; and not until he had killed the priest could he succeed to the office of *Rex Nemorensis*, which he held until a stronger than he should overcome him. "Tradition averred that the fateful branch was that 'Golden Bough' which, at the Sibyl's bidding, Æneas plucked before he essayed the perilous journey to the world of the dead"; and hence the title given by Mr. Frazer to his work, although the words subjoined, "A Study in Comparative Religion," give a better indication of its true aim and character.

What is the meaning, he asks, of this strange rule, which has no parallel in the records of ancient Greece or Rome? One might reply that upon such scanty and ill-verified data it would be impossible to build any hypothesis; or that any hypothesis could be made to accord with a vague and mysterious tradition. The rationalising Euhemeristic interpreter would probably conclude that the story contained a nucleus of real incident, magnified into a rite, and perpetuated by popular imagination. He would surmise that the priest for the time being may have been once, or more than once, murdered by runaway slaves who had established themselves in his place, and who might have succeeded in convincing the people that they acted by divine command, whereby the ungodly custom hardened into an essential rite that would, nevertheless, be only acted upon occasionally. It is clear, at any rate, that the peculiarly savage nature of this rite can be accounted for by its foreign origin. The temple in the grove was dedicated to the Taurian Artemis, who had been a barbarous female divinity, worshipped with bloody rites and human sacrifice at Tauris, whence the Asiatic Greeks, identifying her with their own goddess, imported her into Europe. Strabo himself calls the custom barbarous and Scythian; and the shrine is thus very likely to have had an ill reputation. The priest might have been seen, according to Strabo, prowling round the grove with an air of wary suspicion and a drawn sword; but this kind of outward parade and dramatic representation of a traditional custom often survives as a fiction when the reality has long fallen into disuse. Under another process of interpretation, the whole story would dissolve into a solar or lunar myth, produced by a misunderstanding of the metaphors used by primitive men to describe the operations of nature. Mr. Frazer, whose reputation as a collector and analyst of folklore stands deservedly high, proposes to attain his solution of the problem by a much wider method of investigation. According to his view, the Arician rite belongs to, reflects, and illustrates certain primitive customs that have their place in all early societies; and these customs he traces back to their origin and motive in some very primary mental conceptions, some ultimate religious ideas, out of which many savage customs and barbarous institutions have been evolved, and which still survive among the rustic sports and ceremonies of European nations. So that the Arician legend chiefly serves, in this book, as a text for dissertations upon the folklore, the mythology, and the ritual of many lands and ages; upon their forms and significance, and particularly upon the connexion, transmission, and modification of different species.

Mr. Frazer's quest takes, indeed, so broad a range, and his excursions into remote times and countries lead him so far, that he is sometimes embarrassed by the necessity of keeping up communication with his starting point, and of making all his lines of inquiry converge upon the central issue. He has gathered together and collated a vast quantity of myths, legends, rituals, worships, queer ceremonies, crazy superstitions, and all the grotesque fables and fancies weaved in the brains of barbarous folk; he has arranged and combined all this miscellaneous matter with great ingenuity; he has pressed it into recognisable shape and tolerable coherency, and with this conglomerate he has built up some very curious, interesting, and

suggestive theories. If we are obliged to confess some doubt as to the solidity of some parts of his edifice, it is because we question whether any skill or industry can bind together or solidify such stuff as dreams are made of; or can fill up the gaps inevitably left in such a long-winding, many-sided, and intricate demonstration.

"Why had the priest to slay his predecessor?" and, secondly, why, before slaying him, had he to pluck the Golden Bough? Mr. Frazer begins his answer to these questions with a section headed "Primitive Man and the Supernatural," which launches him at once into the open sea of speculation and research. In the first place, why was the priest called by Suetonius King of the Wood? One would not have thought this appellation very remarkable, seeing that kingly and priestly functions and titles were so constantly combined in ancient days that at Rome the priest who performed public sacrifices was called *"Rex Sacrorum"*; and that everywhere a chief usually had some sacerdotal character, while a priest often had temporal jurisdiction within his domain or sanctuary. This is, indeed, the upshot of Mr. Frazer's explanation reached after a long and somewhat circuitous, though picturesque, excursion through diverse regions of thought and realms of superstitious fantasy. We all know that the kings of old heathen times were commonly priests and often gods; in both capacities they were expected to control the wind and the rain, to bring pressure to bear upon the barometer, and to manage the seasons; they were, in short, made as indirectly responsible as any modern ministry for everything that happened to the community under their charge. All this is in familiar accordance with the reasoning of primitive societies, who seek only to find where power resides, and with whom a great chief's authority, visible or invisible, is just what he chooses to assert. The deification or pontificate of the temporal lord soon became a principle of administrative expediency, which has had a long history under various fictions and disguises. Mr. Frazer refers, in passing, to this general conception of divinity in rulership as one way by which the idea of a man-god is reached; upon which we will only observe that the conception and the idea, as understood by very primitive minds, are identical.

> But there is another way. Side by side with the view of the world as pervaded by spiritual forces, primitive man has another conception in which we may detect a germ of the modern notion of natural law, or the view of nature as a series of events occurring in an invariable order in that human agency.

This way is, we learn, the conception of sympathetic magic, the producing an effect by imitating it, as when a man is killed by making and destroying his image, "which is, in fact, the modern conception of physical causation"; and a man-god is only an individual endowed with extraordinary magical powers over nature. Wonder-working persons and wonder-working processes abound all over the world; the vein of illustration in this department is inexhaustible. Mr. Frazer tells us of rain-gods, weather-kings; of making sunshine and making wind, of charms, tricks, and incantations; and so we are led on through the ideas of incantation, inspiration, the deification of men, possession, and all the countless varieties of demoniac or divine embodiment, up to the Dalai Lamas of Tibet, the Incas of Peru, the Chinese Emperor, and the Arsacidæ. Whence it appears that the same union of sacred functions with a royal title which meets us in the King of the Wood at Nemi is a common feature of societies at all stages from barbarism to civilisation. The phenomenon is, as we have said, perfectly well known; and, indeed, of the two ways by which Mr. Frazer reaches the idea of a man-god, the second may be thought to be little more than the reproduction, on a large scale, and with the stages marked out, of the first; since it is indubitable that kings become gods, as gods become kings, by reason of certain supernatural powers or privileges assumed and admitted to reside in them. Mr. Frazer, however, goes on to suggest that the Nemi king might have had a political origin, that his predecessors might have been a line of kings whom a republican revolution stripped of their political power, leaving them only their religious functions. But the hypothesis is too rationalistic, and it is dismissed in favour of the much more pregnant conception of the Nemi priest as a king of nature, having the wood for his special department.

Now, kings of the Rain, of Water, and of Fire have been discovered in various outlying corners of barbarism, among the African tribes, and in the backwoods of Cambodia; though, from the description of them in *The Golden Bough,* they appear to be mostly no more than ordinary conjurors or great medicine-men, who are knocked on the head if their spells fail. We are in search, however, of a King of the Wood to match the Arician priest; and in order to hit off the clue we are taken back to the extensive subject of tree worship. Here we are at once upon wide, well-trodden, and very familiar ground; we can wander at will in a jungle of primitive beliefs, for plants, trees, groves, and forests have played numberless parts on the different stages of religious evolution. Beginning with the primary and universal animism which invested motion with conscious life, we pass easily and obviously to plants and trees with mysterious attributes, to haunted woods, to trees with souls and spirits immanent, to wood nymphs, sylvan deities, and the higher notions which impersonate the vivifying powers of nature, to Diana and Dionysus. In this class of myth and ritual the connexion between ancient and modern practices is very attractive; we may be indulgent to those who see in maypoles, green bushes, Whitsuntide queens, harvest homes, Christmas trees, in the games and ceremonies of the vintage or the reaping, nothing but a survival of the quaint poetically symbolic rites by which the earliest races of men figured the spring, ripening, or decay of vegetation. Mr. Frazer conjectures that Zeus and Hera at the Bœotian festivals were the Greek equivalent of the lord and lady of the May, and "the story of Hera's quarrel with Zeus, and her sullen retirement, may perhaps, without straining, be interpreted as a mythical expression for a bad season and a failure of the crops." In the vernal pastimes of French and Russian villagers the boys and girls sometimes dress up in leaves and flowers, and one of them goes to sleep, to be awoke by the rest, or acts the part of a forsaken bride or bridegroom. "Is the sleeper," asks Mr. Frazer, "the leafless forest or the bare earth in winter? Is the girl who wakens him the fresh verdure or the genial sunshine of spring?" The evidence, he thinks, is hardly adequate, and we decidedly agree with him; for here, as throughout his book, he leans too much toward the poetic and allegorical interpretation of customs and manners that derive easily enough from the incidents and circumstances of everyday life. This inclination takes also an additional bias from the turn that he is obliged to give to all his materials in order to join in and fit them neatly into the general plan upon which he is working. After this fashion, and by various similar analogies and examples, the inference is drawn that the cult of the Arician grove was that of a tree spirit, of which spirit the king was an embodiment, and that by the plucking of the bough is signified the idea that the life of the incarnate spirit of vegetation was bound up in the tree.

To this conclusion, which Mr. Frazer reaches at the end of his first chapter, it would be illiberal to demur *in limino.* For whether the Arician priest and rite were the product of long religious evolution, the mysterious emblem of nature worship; or whether he may have been the fortuitous outcome of some such violent deed or marvellous incident as has so commonly made famous a shrine or a deity, is unknowable and really unimportant. Mr. Frazer uses the story as a starting point for a series of discussions upon the ways and thoughts of man in a state of barbarism, ignorance, or rusticity. He has made a large collection of quaint, outlandish specimens of folklore, archaic ritual, and vagrant superstitious fancies; all of which he desires to arrange so as to bring out the main lines of development and decadence, and the connexion between earlier and later forms. He wishes to do something in religious palæontology, to reconstruct the mouldering skeletons of extinct worships, and to prove the pedigrees and remote yet unbroken descent of village games or goblins from sylvan deities, and their ritual, and from the impression produced on man by the circling seasons. The study is so fascinating that much must be forgiven to him who ardently pursues it; and we can understand why Mr. Frazer delights to lead us on, like an Oriental story-teller, who ends each tale with an event or allusion that requires another one to explain it. But it must be confessed to follow him from branch to branch of his enchanting subject requires some mental agility; one has to take occasional leaps at the nearest analogy, to make clutches at slender arguments, and generally to risk what the French call *conjectures à casse-cou* ["break-neck conjectures"].

For instance—The first chapter leaves us convinced that the Nemi priest was once a tree spirit incarnate; a solution of much novelty and enterprise, with which some people might rest contented. But the next chapter opens with the Perils of the Soul; and we are immediately introduced to an old acquaintance, the Mikado, as the type of those mysterious and sacred beings who are strictly guarded and secluded, because upon their purity and preservation is supposed to depend the order of nature. This brings us to the custom of Taboo; and thence by the ever-widening stream of associated ideas we drift out into the illimitable sea of fancies, fictions, and fables regarding the soul, if by that word we may designate the principle of life or consciousness which is parted from the body temporarily in sleep and trances, permanently in death. Whither goes the soul after quitting its mortal tenement, and how does it fare? can it be lost, stolen, or strayed? does it wander about the earth until it finds another habitation in stock or stone, in beast or man? is it carried up to some heaven, or down to some Hades? does it become god or demon? can it expiate offences, be comforted by offerings, or avenge its wrongs?—all such questions mankind has been asking from time immemorial, and has caught at every sign or shadow of an answer. . . . (pp. 538-45)

Bodily death is the giving up of the ghost, which thenceforward haunts primitive man; and in his supposed relations with the innumerable phantoms that surround him for his plague or protection lie the mainspring of endless superstitions and the germ of far-reaching beliefs. Mr. Frazer has no difficulty in selecting from all parts of the world abundant examples showing that the soul, being the personal self, and identified with the visible breath, the shadow, or the reflection on water, is to the savage mind a thing incessantly surrounded by physical changes and easily damaged. Out of the precautions necessary for the safety of important souls arise, he says, the customs of royal and sacerdotal Taboo, which he further explains, very simply and sensibly, to be after all no more than a set of rules for safeguarding the life of kings or priests. Nor, indeed, need we dive very far into the depths of primeval animism to grope for and emerge with the plain observation that a chief who has to manage wild and credulous people must very soon hit upon the device of declaring himself too holy to be touched or even approached with impunity. Almost all forms and Court ceremonies were originally intended to keep intruders at arm's length; and the essence of caste rules is in the avoidance of strange, untrustworthy company, especially with regard to food, drink, or social contact. Mr. Frazer follows out this very intelligible principle into various minute and often amusing particulars, exhibiting the connexion between unlucky omens and portents, magic charms to avert dangers, taboo customs, caste prejudice, sanctity, divinity, and court etiquette. The whole subject has been examined at length in Mr. Herbert Spencer's chapters on Ceremonial Institutions, where the common origin of all these observances—religious, political, and social—is very sufficiently expounded. Mr. Frazer contributes some anecdotes that are at least amusing. When Dr. Bastian attempted to touch the skull of a Siamese prince, "in order to illustrate some medical remarks," he was warned by a threatening murmur that he was committing a breach of etiquette; and among North American Indians a young brave while under taboo is so strictly prohibited from touching his own head, that he must scratch it with a stick. Such anecdotes may illuminate an abstruse law of mental evolution, or they may be the natural outcome of circumstance, or they may be little more than random answers to satisfy curiosity. Dr. Bastian's behaviour could scarcely have passed current among civilised royalties; and if one asks an Indian why he scratches his head with a stick, he will give the first answer that occurs to him. The wild man pleads custom for everything; and a very little pressure will make him add that it is awful, ancient, and invariable. As he lives in constant terror of death, so anything odd, unaccountable, or unusual impresses him with fear and suspicion; he invents every kind of magical prophylactic, antidote, and prohibition in order to keep off or neutralise malignant influences. He forms a code of regulations which may, perhaps, be conveniently described as the practice of Taboo, being for the most part, as Mr. Frazer admits, nothing but maxims of common prudence, under the mask of mysterious laws sanctioned supernaturally. He would probably agree with us that no more recondite explanation of all these ideas and customs, taken as a class, is required; but he desires to show how they grew and were generated one from another; he wishes to lay out and assort a large and mixed repertory of folklore upon the lines of his hypothesis. Why was the Flamen Dialis not allowed to walk under a trellised vine? The answer suggested is

> that plants are considered as animate beings which bleed when cut, the red juice which exudes from some plants being regarded as the blood of the plant. The juice of the grape is therefore conceived as the blood of the vine, and since, as we have seen, the soul is often believed to be in the blood, the juice of the grape is regarded as the soul . . . of the vine. Wine is considered as a spirit, or containing a spirit, first because it is identified, as a red juice, with the blood of the plant; and second, because it intoxicates or inspires. Therefore, if the Flamen Dialis had walked under a trellised vine, the spirit of the vine, embodied in the clusters of grapes, would have been immediately over his head, and might have touched it, which, for a person like him in a state of permanent taboo, would have been highly dangerous.

We have quoted this elaborate exposition as exemplifying the defects of Mr. Frazer's method. He is not content with proving the main steps required by his general theory, such as that the early animism of tree-worship concentrated into the notion of special divinity immanent in certain particularly valuable trees, and latterly into the conception of abstract deities presiding over the vineyard or orchard. He subjects stray traditions and customs to minute analysis, yielding results that may or may not be futile. It does not seem to us probable, or even possible, that the utmost ingenuity and learning can hope to succeed in unravelling an ancient interdict of this trivial kind by stringing together a few conceptions that are so general and natural as to be applicable to almost any special case. The vine may easily have always been a sacred tree; the rare qualities and intoxicating effect of its fruit are very ample reasons not only for investing it with divinity, but also for placing any one who should touch it under a curse or ban; but in this there is nothing new, and to go farther is to strain the very slender thread of hints and imperfect indications that have come down to us. It would be easy to parody this system of interpretation by showing that the most commonplace prejudices and presages of ill luck contain the elements of savage demonolatry, or are tinged with elementary nature-worship; whereas most of them are distorted generalisations from some actual experience, as when a man who has come to harm or peril, after seeing or doing some noticeable thing, thenceforward marks off all such coincidences as uncanny and mysteriously dangerous; or else they are mere scarecrows and bugbears set up to frighten off trespassers by diabolical menace.

Mr. Frazer ends his second chapter with a passage that is earnest and sympathetic in tone, although it accepts a view of savage life that is, perhaps, too ideal and symmetrical for what is actually a very confused, unintelligent, and haphazard state of existence.

> To students of the past the life of the old kings and priests thus teems with instruction. In it was summed up all that passed for wisdom when the world was young. It was the perfect pattern after which every man strove to shape his life; a faultless model constructed with rigorous accuracy upon the lines laid down by a barbarous philosophy. Crude and false as that philosophy may seem to us, it would be unjust to deny it the merit of logical consistency. Starting from a conception of the vital principle as a tiny soul or being existing in, but distinct and separable from, the living being, it deduces for the practical guidance of life a system of rules which, in general, hangs well together, and forms a fairly complete and harmonious whole. . . .

> Contempt and ridicule, or abhorrence and denunciation, are too often the only recognition vouchsafed to the savage. Yet of the benefactors we are bound thankfully to commemorate many, perhaps most, were savages . . . and what we have in common with the savage, and deliberately retain as true and useful, we owe to our savage forefathers, who slowly acquired by experience, and transmitted to us by inheritance, those seemingly fundamental ideas which we are apt to regard as original and intuitive.

These words are imbued with a spirit of generosity—of fellow-feeling with forgotten times and vanished races—that touches the imagination and corrects the too common tendency of those who enjoy the full light and security of civilisation to ridicule and despise the struggles and blunders of primitive man. Nevertheless the tone of this passage corroborates the general impression conveyed by Mr. Frazer's book, that he discovers coherence, consistency, and orderly sequence in a confused medley of savage ways and notions, which can be sorted out into large groups according to a certain order of intellectual development, but cannot be particularly affiliated or attached, lineally or laterally, in any certain relation to each other. Natural religion and natural society follow certain well-known grooves and shapes drawn by the instinct of self-preservation and moulded by the environment; but within a very wide and elastic range of thought, and of pressure by material circumstances, these lines and forms are constantly changing, and the individual fancies of ignorant men are blown to and fro, like thistledown, with every wind of terror and delusion. There are no perfect patterns or faultless models; there is no rigorous accuracy or logical consistency; the terms have no meaning or place in application to the irrational ideas, the random guesses, the incessantly shifting practices, of superstitious barbarians. What are, in sober earnest, the true and useful ideas on such subjcts as are dealt with in *The Golden Bough,* that we owe to our savage forefathers, "whose patient thought and active exertions have largely made us what we are"? They are somewhat difficult to specify; and, even if one finds among rude tribes some glimmering of an intellectual conception, it is not easy to decide how they came by it. The note of the primitive mind is amazing inaccuracy, coupled with wonderful receptivity; the savage will adopt any new fable or ritual that strikes his fancy; he will represent a custom picked up last year as a rite of hoar antiquity; he will produce impromptu a legend or sacred ordinance to satisfy an inquirer about the origin of worship or caste rules; he borrows readily from the latest, as well as the earliest, faith or liturgy. Who shall decide what we owe to the savage, or how much the modern savage (of whom alone we know anything accurately) owes to the reflex action of the loftiest upon the lowest religious ideas, wherever there is possibility of commixture? Mr. Frazer tells us that "Buddhist animism is not a philosophical theory; it is *simply* a common savage dogma incorporated in the system of a historical religion. To suppose that the theories of animism and transmigration current among rude peoples of Asia are derived from Buddhism is to reverse the facts. Buddhism in this respect borrowed from savagery, not savagery from Buddhism." This passage exemplifies a tendency in *The Golden Bough* not only to prefer elaborate to simple explanations, but, conversely, to treat as simple and demonstrable a point which is complicated and exceedingly debateable. Does Mr. Frazer suppose that the powerfully organised religions which have spread over Asia during the last two thousand years have not influenced enormously the petty superstitions within their range, or that the savage who dreams about losing his soul is necessarily the direct intellectual ancestor of the Buddhistic teacher? This may be true in the sense of saying that the inventor of the steam locomotive is the scientific descendant of the first savage who lighted a fire; but such a genealogy is hardly worth formal announcement. In all times and countries there is constant degradation as well as evolution; the upper and nether ideas throw out fresh shoots and intertwine; they become inextricably twisted up and interfused, like the trees, brambles, and creepers of a primeval forest. A highly cultivated faith will run wild; a rough and rudimentary idea will strike root and spread, until the two become mixed and intermarried. We all know that the belief in souls, ghosts, and spirits has been universal, and has undergone transformation in various stages of physical and metaphysical speculation, and we can see that the rudimentary notion precedes the refined dogma. But any attempt to lay out distinct lines of transmission, or to determine the necessary connexion of particular customs and superstitions, is, in our opinion, a very hazardous and mostly unprofitable undertaking. (pp. 545-50)

Mr. Frazer gives us, toward the end of his book, an interesting section on Totemism (a subject upon which he has given us separately a valuable study), connecting this curious custom with the world-wide primary belief in a soul that is lost, goes and returns, transmigrates, survives the body's death, feels pain and pleasure, is feared or adored, is blest or curst. His object is to show that Totemism implies a belief in the possibility of depositing one's soul, for safe custody, in some place, animal, or plant, outside one's body; and his view is that the transfer is usually attempted at some critical moment or period, such as puberty. Now we may agree that under the word Totemism may be comprehended many of the conjuring tricks and initiatory ceremonies by which male and female adults are inducted into the tribal circle, and are guarded against the malignant influences that wage constant war against the health, virility, and bodily functions of pubescent youth; but Mr. Frazer hints at some profound and hitherto unfathomable explanation:—

> It would be easy to prove by a long array of facts that the sexual relation is associated in the primitive mind with many supernatural perils; but the exact nature of the danger apprehended is still obscure. We may hope that a more exact acquaintance with savage modes of thought will in time disclose this central mystery of primitive society, and will thereby furnish the clue, not only to the social aspect of totemism (the prohibition of sexual union between persons of the same totem), but to the origin of the marriage system.

Mr. Frazer may be right, and there may yet be in the sexual relations of savages some undiscovered element of illusion and disturbance. But for most of us it is sufficient to take account of the peculiarly capricious, mysterious, and ungovernable passion which inspires these relations, and to remember that in all ages and states of society it has provided endless employment for every species of superstition, for divinities, witches, diabolic agencies, charlatans, and quacks of every degree. It seems very unlikely that by subjecting to minute analysis the infinitely varied symptoms of this universal epidemic, we shall elicit any trustworthy addition to our knowledge of primitive ideas or institutions.

We venture to extend this observation from the particular case to Mr. Frazer's general theory. It is interesting, it is so framed as to embrace a great and valuable collection of striking and freshly gathered facts regarding primitive belief and custom; but we doubt whether the speculation enlarges our horizon beyond the solid landmarks already set up by the leading pioneers in this field of exploration. If, indeed, he had not tethered himself, so to speak, to one point, if he had not imposed on himself the task of showing how all his conclusions in regard to the main currents of primitive superstition bear upon the interpretation of one strange story—the Arician cult—he might have ranged much more freely over the ground which he has chosen, and he would have been less under the temptation of breaking down sound arguments by overriding them. We are indebted to him for a material addition to the museum of folklore, for many useful suggestions and combinations of ideas, and for some very careful excavations into the hidden bases of antique ritual. If he has not succeeded in the very arduous enterprise of co-ordinating all these customs and conceptions into a system of religious development, of proving the affinity that he detects between earliest and latest species, and of making different lines of thought meet and become embodied in the Arician cult, it is, we believe, because the trustworthy solution of such problems is impossible. The stratification of religious beliefs is like the geologic record—it attests certain great periods and vast changes, but it also reflects and is varied by innumerable lesser movements, upheavals, survivals, and catastrophes of different kinds that have marked the intellectual surface and upset the imagination of men. It represents subsidence as well as upheaval; for, although the theory of the degradation and distortion of some primeval revelation to all nations is not tenable, yet beyond doubt we find many beliefs and traditions running downward, spreading at a level much below their source; lofty symbols and doctrines become low idolatry; *hoc est corpus* becomes *hocus pocus;* the practices of high asceticism are travestied in magical quackery. The whole panorama of religious rites and images resembles, in polytheistic countries, the entangled confusion of a primeval forest, where you see trees, brambles, and creepers of all ages and sizes interlacing, supporting, and breaking down each other; with a glimpse of blue sky above the topmost branches to symbolise the infinite ideal toward which all these earthly growths are striving and shooting up. The whole forest has sprung up out of the same soil, and the same general conditions of existence; and so it may be said that all these curious religious forms have a like origin, they are generated out of the common experience and common feelings of humanity. It is possible to go further, and to register the main currents of religious tendency; but, after all, there is a great monotony and sameness in the countless and multiform vagaries of the inventive faculty among ignorant and superstitious men. The enormous accumulations now made of folklore, fairy tales, nonsensical fables, idiotic barbarous notions, legends, myths, and mumbo-jumbo ritual add little to our clear understanding of the working of the religious mind, and rather tend to render unmanageable the scientific handling of the subject. In substance all natural religion, ancient and contemporary, was—and is—Nature worship, which often had, at the same time, among the same people, different significations and methods of expression. With the vulgar it meant adoration of the marvellous and incomprehensible as embodied in things and felt in dreams and visions; in the upper classes it meant adoration of the perceptible—but, as yet, unintelligible—forces of nature as personified under more or less refined types or symbols; and with the chosen few it signified their recognition of the working, through external phenomena, of a divine and all-pervading energy. The development, upon this broad canvas, of certain persistent forms of ritual, worship, and dogma is an instructive study, as when we trace one dominant custom or cult, such as sacrifice or the worship of the dead, through a long filiation of institutions that are obviously allied. . . . It may be maintained, for example, with tolerable safety that no religious idea or rite has endured and prevailed widely that has not sprung out of some root of fact or supposed utility, or upon some primordial affection of the human mind like Fear, which means the instinct of self-preservation. But all human notions at a low intellectual level are so elastic and invertebrate, that we can get little out of collecting them in heaps beyond a general verification of the class or mental stage to which they belong; we cannot use them as data for working out the meaning or derivation of any particular rite or group of usages. And we must be cautious about going too far back in tracing the possible pedigree of such practices, lest we overrun the scent, miss the real starting-point, and fancy that we detect a veritable antique in some belief or tale that was manufactured yesterday. As for mythology, it is true that it came largely (not wholly) out of the desire to veil, obscure, and account for the real origins of religion; but for that very reason it is an unsafe guide to a clear understanding of them, and we are rather hindered than helped by those who sweep together out of many lands and libraries and discharge upon us all the mythic puzzles and whimsical nursery tales of human infancy. We know very well that in polytheistic countries it is the business of the mystery men and miracle-mongers to connect all new superstitions and fresh marvels with the older popular beliefs and traditions, to identify the latest with the antecedent divinities, to find room for strange worships and outlandish liturgies. Mr. Frazer gives many examples of the accretion of the ruder worships and legends round a superior deity or ritual; it is a familiar process in the gradual uplifting and centralisation of divine attributes; and the general connexion between successive phases of religious manners and practices is too patent to have escaped competent observers in any age. It is, moreover, quite possible to work out the modifications which a cult has undergone, in countries where, as in Italy or in India, the religious history lends itself to fairly accurate study. But it is a hazardous method to go backward over all ages, and abroad unto the uttermost parts of the earth, in search of facts, emblems, loose priestly inventions, vulgar delusions, and all the phantasmagoria of nebulous *deisidæmonia,* in order to show ground for supposing that one explanation of an obscure story, or myth, or ritual, is more probable than another. The Natural seed of religion, as Hobbes calls it, is the same all over the primitive world; but its fruits are varied infinitely by environment, by soil, climate, training, and accidental circumstance; and although the fundamental analogies can be observed everywhere, we doubt whether even the very creditable industry, ability, ingenuity, and scholarship of such students as Mr. Frazer can succeed in transmuting general resemblances into particular relations. (pp. 571-75)

A review of "The Golden Bough: A Study in Comparative Religion," in The Edinburgh Review, *Vol. CCCLII, October, 1890, pp. 538-75.*

JOURNAL OF AMERICAN FOLKLORE   (essay date 1890)

[In the following excerpt, the reviewer pronounces The Golden Bough *a remarkable book more important for the sequence of steps that Frazer takes in marshalling and explicating his garnered lore than for the conclusions he reaches.]*

In this remarkable book [*The Golden Bough*], Mr. Frazer, in order to make an extensive exploration in the domain of primitive religion, begins by propounding a riddle. Respecting the worship of Diana in the Arician grove,—the grove of Lake Nemi, represented by Turner in a famous picture,—Latin writers tell a strange story. According to their scanty allusions, the priest of the grove was a runaway slave, who had procured his office by slaying his predecessor, and might in turn himself be slain by any successor who was able, in the first place, to break off the bough of a certain tree, affirmed to be the Golden Bough plucked by Æneas before his journey to the land of the dead; hence the title of Turner's painting and of Mr. Frazer's book. What was the meaning of the strange rite, and what was the Golden Bough?

Judging by the reflected illumination furnished by the analogy of primitive religions, our author concludes that this custom was an example of the common practice of putting to death the divine king or priest who typified and embodied the generative power of the earth, a custom explained by the notion that, as this personage contained within himself the life-giving soul which was the principle of fertility, so his natural death would introduce decay and decline into the vitality of nature, and he must therefore be slain, in order that his life-giving spirit, while still in its full vigor, might be appropriated by his successor. As for the branch, he supposes this to be the mistletoe, which, being evergreen, was regarded as the life of the oak.

It is evident that such a work is not to be judged by the certainty of the result thus barely stated. Where a rite is isolated and must be interpreted through analogy, it is manifest that the chances of error are innumerable. It seems scarcely proved that the position of the priest in the Arician grove may not have been what the legend of the worship at Nemi represented it to be, namely, a survival of the custom of sacrificing strangers. In the course of time, the fugitive or wanderer may have been allowed a chance for his life; of several such visitors or captives, one may have been allowed to do battle with another, and afterwards been retained as devoted to the sanctuary. At all events, the possibilities of variation of a primitive usage are so great that one naturally doubts any single explanation.

In the present case, however, the hypothesis is not the main point of Mr. Frazer's undertaking. He proceeds in his research by a series of steps, which individually remain sound, even if the distance from one to another sometimes appear too great to surmount. His book is not only a storehouse of facts in religion and folk-lore, but exhibits those facts ingeniously gathered into sequence, and used to establish propositions, of which some are clear and indubitable, others plausible and open to controversy. It becomes clear to the reader that the study of philosophies and religions is intimately associated with folk-tale and folk-custom, that the survivals of to-day explain the dark places of past habit, and that our daily thoughts are intimately linked with those superstitions which seem rudest and crudest. (pp. 316-17)

We cannot allow this occasion to pass without a protest against our author's conception of primitive religion. He mentions four marks of such religion, as follows: (1) No special class of persons set apart for the performance of the rites; no priests. (2) No special places; no temples. (3) Spirits, not gods; names generic, not proper; no marked individuality; no accepted traditions. (4) Rites magical rather than propitiatory.

We ask, where does primitive religion exist, if this alone be primitive? What people can with certainty be affirmed to have, or any time to have had, no special places of worship, no priests, no named deities, and no oral traditions respecting these? So far as respects American races, every number of this Journal has contained records which contradict the definition of Mr. Frazer. The idea, especially, that the primitive Aryan, before the separation of the different stocks, was limited as our author implies, appears to us counter to all reasonable probability. No doubt, inferences as to the remote prehistoric state of mind of tribes concerning which no records exist, may, with more or less plausibility, be formed; but these inferences, after all, are hypotheses about on a level with those relating to the origin of language. So far as observation goes, the first glimpse we have of primitive religions of European, Asiatic, and American races exhibits a highly complicated sum of conceptions, accompanied with a literary development (if it be not a paradox to use the term as applied to literature without letters) of no mean order.

So, again, when we read that "the gods whom hunters and shepherds adore and kill are animals pure and simple," we feel constrained to ask, do these hunters and shepherds possess the conception of animals pure and simple? The animal of the savage is anything but a pure and simple being: he is, to all intents and purposes, human; he possesses the whole complex of human reason; he has a separate human form, which he may at any moment assume, in and under which he may become the hero of adventures. Is this a pure and simple conception? As primitive religion, at the earliest moment at which it presents itself to our view, is thus complicated, and as its conceptions, even in the simplest races, are already spiritualized, it is in vain to suppose that the whole system can be formulated in a small number of propositions, or summed up in a single conclusion.

But it is far from our purpose to quarrel with Mr. Frazer; we are rather grateful to him for the exhibition of materials so rich, and for the literary skill with which he has made accessible observations so important to the central ideas of our modern thought. If the pendulum of speculation in regard to mythology swings from side to side, it also beats out the progression of time; a solid basis remains established; and the interesting book before us shows how human is that basis, and how all periods, beliefs, and doctrines are connected in folk-lore. (pp. 318-19)

W.W.N., in a review of "The Golden Bough," in Journal of American Folklore, *Vol. III, No. XL, October-December, 1890, pp. 316-19.*

GILBERT MURRAY   (essay date 1923)

[*Murray was a British educator, translator, and critic whose verse translations of classic Greek drama in the early twentieth century revived the popularity of Greek drama throughout the English-speaking world. In the following essay Murray somewhat sardonically pronounces* The Golden Bough *a "dangerous" book because of the evidence Frazer advances to demonstrate that humankind has commonly employed little reason in conducting its affairs.*]

Sometime in the seventeen-nineties Mr. Pitt, when Prime Minister, was advised to institute a prosecution of Godwin's *Political Justice* as a dangerous book and likely to cause social unrest. He refused to do so, not because he approved of its doctrines or thought it safe, but because it cost three guineas. Such a price showed the author to be free from any desire of corrupting the masses. Yet, no doubt, Godwin's was an extremely dangerous book, not so much because it aimed at anarchy—it was a very polite and tolerant anarchy that it preached—but because of its unqualified faith in human reason. Godwin believed that all the ills of society were due to what he called "prejudice." Man, if allowed to follow his true nature, instinctively loved the good and hated evil. He was guided by the dictates of reason, if only you let him alone and did not confuse his mind. Life and duty, according to Godwin, are really simple things. The problems that press can be solved easily enough, if only they are looked at straight. One great key will open all the locks. Get rid of prejudice, get rid of all the unnatural, artificial, interested lies and delusions in which kings and priests and their dark associates have entangled humanity; get rid of false worships, false customs and false associations; and human nature will walk forward naturally and without hindrance on the road to its own perfection. Then will come the time when

Woman and man, in confidence and love,
Equal and free and pure, together tread
The mountain-paths of virtue, which no more
Are stained with blood from many a pilgrim's feet.

That was the promise: and on the faith of it we were to set mankind free from all restraints inward or outward, and see what happened. Obviously a dangerous doctrine.

About a century afterwards, in the year 1890 to be precise, was published Frazer's *Golden Bough,* a book equally dangerous, though almost opposite in doctrine. It also began, not quite at three guineas, but at a price almost equally inaccessible, and, what was worse, it kept increasing in size with each edition, from two volumes to three, four, ten, and eventually sixteen. But now we discover with a thrill of alarm that it is reduced to one moderate volume at a guinea, and will be let loose to do its worst. Of course, it is a long book, which is some protection, and it contains a great deal of recondite and difficult knowledge. But it is no good pretending that it will choke readers off. Quite the contrary: the style and the matter both will see to it that as soon as they begin they will be fascinated.

The danger of Godwin's doctrine was that it made people think that man was a purely reasonable being and fit to be entrusted with almost infinite freedom. The danger of Frazer is not any avowed doctrine of the author's own: he is extremely cautious in his expressions of opinion; but the tendency of the whole book is to make one think that there is no such thing as reason at all in human affairs. To rid the natural man of his prejudices would be like stripping an onion of its coats or George IV of his waistcoats; there would be nothing left. Strip off the clothings of custom and social convention, you find beneath them the clothing of previous centuries; the cowl and the mail of the Middle Ages, the blanket and the woad of the savage; and below that layer upon layer, cake upon cake, of primaeval slime, reaching back to ages before the first man stood upright on the earth. Somewhere, no doubt, in the centre of it all, a stifled heart that feels a little sympathy, and an obfuscated brain with occasional glimmerings of thought; but, in the main, an infinite complexity through which we see only rare glimpses of passions for ever unsatisfied and nerves sensitive to every extreme of pain. What seemed to Godwin simple, we now see was really only what accorded with his own prejudices; for practical purposes that is what "simple" always means. Where Godwin said that man naturally loved good and hated evil, the truth was merely that men called the things they liked by nice names and the things they disliked by nasty names. His natural state is beautifully described by a German word Urdummheit, from Ur-, which means original or primaeval, and dummheit, which is the quality of a dunderhead or a dummerer. The priests and kings whom Godwin thought to be so conventional and artificial turn out to be among the earliest facts of human society, the earliest creations, one might say, of man's natural desires. Back in the most primitive tribes we find them: priest and king, or, at the beginning, priest and king and god, undifferentiated one from another, performing, as far as one can see, much foolishness and much cruelty and nothing whatever besides, and giving apparently infinite satisfaction. "Come unto me," said Carlyle, "all ye that hunger and thirst to be bamboozled!" It seems to the reader of Frazer to be the universal desire of mankind.

Man, left to himself, uncorrupted by convention and set free to follow his own sublime instincts, did not apparently pursue virtue nor yet vice. Apart from catching his prey, at which he possessed real genius, and fighting his fellow creatures, where he showed much promise, he devoted his efforts for the most part to indescribable silliness. Of course, sometimes he was very cruel as well, in the way of sorcery and persecution and the like, but in the main he was just silly. He went and invented Totemism. He said, for no ascertainable reason, that he was a frog, whereas his neighbors were dogs or water-lilies or turnips. Then he spent ages in inventing entirely useless rules which should prevent a frog from marrying another frog, and fixing the conditions—all of them senseless—under which it might marry a dog or a turnip. He worked for generations in elaborating religious dances and ceremonies, all intended to produce results which they never produced; in devising innumerable ways of frightening and bullying the boys and women of the tribe; shutting them up, burying them alive, cutting off bits of their persons, or knocking their teeth out, all for some seriously pursued purpose which was never, never, except by accident, attained.

Godwin destroyed Christianity as an artificial invention imposed for purposes of tyranny by corrupt priests in collusion with kings. Frazer tends to destroy it by merely showing how old it is, how rooted in human nature and the Urdummheit. The most mystical Christian doctrines, like the Trinity and the Eucharist, on which have been written whole libraries of learned theology, appear as commonplaces of savage superstition, sometimes revolting, sometimes in their way sublime; for, of course, self-sacrifice and heroism are as old as human society itself. The most beautiful of Christian emblems, the picture of the mother and child, has already been traced three thousand years before the Christian era. And the central doctrine which Frazer's wonderful work illumines, the sacrifice of the divine king, thrilling and terrible as it is, is not only a tale of cruelty written in language of blood, but also a record of the eternal idealism of the human heart, which welcomes any suffering or sacrifice, if only it have about it the touch of splendor.

Of course, Reason has had a bad time of late years, not only in practice—which is normal enough—but even in profession. During the war she hardly dared to show her face in any country, and seldom spoke without being made sorry for it. Even now her appearances in public are extremely timid. The word rational has ceased to be a term of praise; logical is almost a term of abuse, perhaps because people think for obscure traditional reasons that to be logical is to be like the French. In theory, too, the new psychology has belittled the place of reason in the human mind; the religious reaction has based itself on mysticism; the psycho-analysts gravely assure us that the reasons we allege for our actions are merely protective coloring, and that most human activities are the effervescence of man's despair at finding that by the law of his religion he may not marry his grandmother. As for the behavior of nations and large masses, one is given to understand that, for practical purposes, it is entirely the result of propaganda and advertisement. Man reels upon his way through life, driven hither and thither by suggestions and complexes, much as a mindless clerk might go to his office along the advertisement-ridden streets of a great town, filled now with a suggestion that somebody's whiskey, somebody else's tobacco and the patent medicines of a crowd of other competitors form really the desire of his heart; now with the belief that two different routes to the continent are both of them the best and cheapest; now with the turbid and contradictory contents of the political headlines and posters of various newspapers. He responds automatically to the broadcasting of stentorian cries: "X. is a Jew; hit him! Y. is a capitalist; down with him! Z. is a Bolshevik; let his children starve to death!"

No doubt there is a good deal of truth in this account of mankind, enough truth to show that Godwin's rationalism was an extreme delusion. No doubt nations and parties and public adventurers who act on these assumptions have a good chance of success even in comparatively reputable societies, and a chance that steadily improves as the society becomes less reputable. In the present state of Europe it sometimes looks as if such methods might succeed altogether and accomplish not only the ruin of this or that country, not only the collapse of our present civilization, but the final failure of the great experiment which was made when our first ancestor stood up on his hind legs and began to trust in his brain rather than his arms and teeth. The poor brute would have speculated and lost!

There is a little book sold at the entrance of the Natural History Museum at South Kensington which tells of that dangerous speculation and the sacrifices that it involved. A nice well-tailed and well-furred animal, more like a lemur than an ape, he invested in an overgrown brain, lost his tail, went bald all over his body, incurred innumerable risks, diseases and even vices for the sake of one inestimable possession, the faculty of reasoning thought. And now we are taught to doubt whether it was worth the price, or whether indeed he really possesses it.

The conclusion we reach perhaps seems drab and commonplace. Truth is so often both. It is a dangerous delusion to think of man as a purely rational animal; equally dangerous and more degrading to leave his reasoning power utterly out of account. There is only a little reason in the world at the present time, little enough in each individual, and rather less apparently in nations as wholes. But what there is is like the little radium in mountains of slag, the one gem that gives value to the mass, not easy to extract, not widely scattered, but a thing leaping with light and unbroken by the shocks of mortality. (pp. 17-19)

> *Gilbert Murray, "A Dangerous Book," in* The New Republic, *Vol. XXXIV, No. 430, February 28, 1923, pp. 17-19.*

BRONISLAW MALINOWSKI　(essay date 1941)

[*Malinowski was a Polish-born British anthropologist, educator, and author. He is widely acknowledged as the father of the functional school of anthropology, which stresses the importance of scientific method over abstract theory. A proponent of the importance of original fieldwork, Malinowski is most famous for a series of monographs about his research among the Trobriand Islanders between 1914 and 1918, including* The Sexual Life of Savages in North-Western Melanesia: An Ethnographic Account of Courtship, Marriage, and Family Life among the Natives of the Trobriand Islands, British New Guinea *(1929). Although Malinowski acknowledged Frazer as a major influence and a central force in modern anthropology, the two are generally regarded as proponents of opposing schools of anthropological thought: Frazer seeking the common origin of similar myths and rituals from widely disparate cultures, Malinowski examining the interrelationship of myths and rituals with other aspects of the culture in which they appear. In the following excerpt from an essay written in 1941, Malinowski explores what he terms Frazer's paradox: "his inability to convince," which "seems to contradict his power to convert and to inspire," by discussing some of the strengths and weaknesses of Frazer's approach to anthropology.*]

Frazer was not an instructor in a narrow sense of the word; he was not able dialectically to develop clear arguments and to defend them in controversy. Few of his purely theoretical contributions can be accepted as they stand. Yet, Frazer was and is one of the world's greatest teachers and masters.

Ethnographic field-work for the last half century or so has been under the spell of Frazer's suggestions. The work of Fison and Howitt, as well as of Spencer and Gillen in Australia; the famous Cambridge Expedition to Torres Straits led by A. C. Haddon in collaboration with W.H.R. Rivers, C. G. Seligman, and C. S. Myers; the African work of Junod, Roscoe, Smith and Dale, Torday, and Rattray—to mention only a few outstanding names—were carried on under the spiritual guidance of Frazer. (p. 183)

[Sigmund Freud], turning to anthropological evidence, took it from Frazer. The first and lasting contributions of the French School under the leadership of the dominant and domineering figure of Durkheim and carried on by Hubert and Mauss, Lévy-Bruhl, Bouglé, and Van Gennep, are unthinkable without the inspiration and achievements of Frazer. In Germany, Wundt, Thurnwald, K. T. Preuss and many others have built on Frazer's foundations. In England writers like Westermarck and Crawley, Gilbert Murray and Jane Harrison, Sidney Hartland and Andrew Lang, take their cues and orientations from Frazer—whether they agree or disagree with him. The brilliant and stimulating figure of R. R. Marett of Oxford is the projection of Frazer's theories on a subtler, more analytic, but less original and comprehensive plane. Recently E. O. James still continues Frazer's tradition in his excellent contributions towards our understanding of present-day problems through anthropological analysis.

Frazer has influenced men like Anatole France, Bergson, Arnold Toynbee and O. Spengler. Frazer, more than any other writer, has made ethnographic evidence available as well as inspiring to a host of pioneer thinkers in history and psychology, in philosophy and ethics. This can be seen when the subjects with which anthropology has affected or inspired other studies are listed: taboo and totemism, magic and exogamy, forms of primitive religion and the development of political institutions. All these subjects have been first handled or most adequately treated by Frazer.

Thus in his personality, in his teaching, and in his literary achievement there is a touch of the paradoxical in the great Scottish scholar and his work. His enormous creative influence surprises sometimes even his devoted admirer when confronted by one of the naïve theoretical arguments from *The Golden Bough* or some other of his volumes. His inability to convince seems to contradict his power to convert and to inspire.

The explanation, as I see it, of Frazer's paradox lies in the specific combination of the qualities and defects of his mind. He is not a dialectician, not even perhaps an analytic thinker. He is, on the other hand, endowed with two great qualities: the artist's power to create a visionary world of his own; and the true scientist's intuitive discrimination between what is relevant and what adventitious, what fundamental and what secondary.

Out of his first virtue came his charm of style; his ability to reshape dull strings of ethnographic evidence into a dramatic narrative; his power to create visions of distant lands and of exotic cultures—which those of us who went there after reading Frazer are able best to appreciate.

Out of his scientific quality came his empirical sense. This led him—very often after he had formulated an insipid theory—to scour ethnographic literature and to extract from it evidence which often completely annihilates his own assumptions, but gives us the facts and the truths of magic or religion, of kinship or totemism in the real perspective within their relevant context, alive and palpitating with human desires, beliefs, and interests. Hence Frazer's uncanny gift of transforming crude, cumulative erudition into that wonderfully constructed architecture of evidence, where many of the theories, later put into words by others, are embodied. The long litanies of ethnographic data bore us to extinction in most writings of the classical evolutionary and comparative school. Transfigured by Frazer, they make *The Golden Bough* alive and vivid, *Totemism and Exogamy* interesting and instructive, and *Folk-lore in the Old Testament* an anthropological saga.

Frazer as a visionary lived in a very real and, to him, objective world. He molded his theories in the plastic material of evidence collected throughout the world and refashioned by him, so that without any exaggeration his facts demonstrate his true, albeit intuitive views. This explains why Frazer was always interested in field-work and seldom, if ever, in theories. He loved additions to his live world: the drama of human existence. He disliked any surgery done upon this world by theoretical criticism. Andrew Lang's satire was to Frazer not a personal insult, but a sacrilegious attack on Virbius, Osiris, and Baldur the Beautiful. Westermarck's theory of incest Frazer branded somewhat rudely as "bastard imitation of science." It irritated him, not because he, Frazer, was contradicted, but because his beloved savages, as he knew them, would have found such a tame conception of incest essentially dull and unreasonable. Frazer, somewhat prudish in his reaction to psychoanalysis, insisted that his primitives must be both promiscuous and incestuous. With an almost maternal attitude of concern, he delighted in their pranks and pleasures, while regretting their naughtiness.

There was never anything small, mean, invidious, or personal in Frazer's reactions to criticism, in his own onslaughts or dislikes. I have never known anyone so genuinely modest, so humble in his love of evidence, and completely indifferent to praise or blame. Of all his qualities, it is perhaps this genuine devotion to the subject matter of his scientific and artistic interests, his complete disregard of any personal advancement, which made him one of the greatest artists in the plastic molding of theory in the live medium of primitive human existence. (pp. 183-86)

Frazer is the representative of an epoch in anthropology which ends with his death. In all his directly theoretical contributions he is an evolutionist, interested in the "primitive," whether this refers to mankind at large, or to specific beliefs, customs and practices of contemporary "savages." He works by the comparative method, collecting and examining evidence from all parts of the world, at all levels of development, and in all cultures. The comparative method combined with the evolutionary approach implies certain general assumptions. Men are substantially similar. They develop gradually from a primitive level and pass through various stages of evolution. The common measure in their actions and their thoughts can be discovered by induction based on a vast survey of collated data. In this the concept of survival is essential to the evolutionist. It serves as the key for the understanding of continuity within transformation, and as a link between the various stages. What was a strong and flourishing belief at one level, becomes a superstition in the next higher one. Forms of marriage and kinship may become ossified into terminologies and survive as a linguistic usage, long after the practices of group marriage or promiscuity have ceased. As we move down the various levels of development we find the most primitive stage accessible, that is, the "origins" of human institutions, customs and ideas.

Frazer never developed any full theoretical statement of evolutionary principles. We cannot find in his work any precise definition of such concepts as "origins," "stage," "survival," nor yet any scheme which would allow us to assess how he imagined that evolution proceeded, or what were the driving forces of "progress." That he worked with all these concepts and constantly utilized the evolutionary as well as the comparative scheme of explanation, is obvious to the reader who has perused even a few pages in any of his works.

Frazer was essentially addicted to psychological interpretations of human belief and practice. His theory of magic, as the result of association of ideas; his three consecutive hypotheses about the origins of totemism in terms of belief in "external soul," "magical inducement of fertility," and in "animal incarnation," are essentially conceived in terms of individual psychology. Those who know his treatment of taboo, of the various aspects of totemism, of the development of magic, religion and science, will realize that, throughout, Frazer in his explicit theories is little aware of the problems of social psychology. He is, as already mentioned, fundamentally hostile to psychoanalysis, while behaviorism never enters his universe of discourse.

Although he was under the influence of Robertson Smith, the first modern anthropologist, to establish the sociological point of view in the treatment of religion, Frazer never fully faced the sociological implications in any of his theoretical arguments. This is seen in his acceptance of Morgan's theory about primitive promiscuity and the development of marriage. Frazer never became aware of the social factor in folklore and mythology. To him magic and religion are still fundamentally "philosophies of life and destiny," as these might have occurred in the mind of a primitive, a savage, a barbarian, or an ancient Greek or Roman. He hardly follows in any of his theoretical comments Robertson Smith's principle that religion is a belief carried out by an organized group of people, and that it cannot be understood unless we treat a dogmatic system as a part of organized worship and of collective tradition.

Frazer is still inclined to relate taboo to "the ambition and avarice of chiefs and priests," who would use "animistic beliefs to buttress their power and accumulate their wealth." The fact that taboo is but a small part of primitive law or custom, and that this in turn cannot be explained either as "superstition" or "political and religious trickery" is never clearly explained in any of Frazer's arguments. The treatment of economics, art, and primitive epistemology in the fourth volume of *Totemism and Exogamy* is open to similar criticism.

An entirely different Frazer comes into action as soon as his thin introductory comments are over. He appears then as the cicerone guiding our steps on the deserts of Australia, among the tropical jungles of the Amazon or the Orinoco, on the steppes of Asia, or the highlands of Africa. His actual treatment of facts is supremely contextual; the various aspects of human culture and human concerns become interrelated; the occasional comments and the collateral evidence is illuminated with real insight into human motives. It would not be difficult to show that Frazer often comes near to developing a psychoanalytic insight into the unconscious and subconscious motives of human behavior. The proof of it can be seen in the ease with which Frazer's evidence has been used by Freud, Rank, and Róheim. In his ability to interpret motive and idea through deed and performance, in his conviction that acts can be trusted while words may be discredited, Frazer is essentially a behaviorist in the sociological sense of the word. He certainly has the behavioristic tendency in documenting all psychological interpretations by forms of behavior.

Frazer's tendency to see anthropological facts as an integral part of human life in general, within the context of the whole culture and even against the background of landscape and natural environment, appears already, with beauty and clarity alike, in his commentary to the translation of *Pausanias's Description of Greece*. It comes to full fruition in *The Golden Bough*, where the somewhat unsatisfactory treatment of magic is followed by a series of pictures, in which we see the magician as chief and priestly king, the magician in his rôle of guardian of the soil, war-lord and engineer of human and natural fertility.

Read one volume after another in the long series, and you will find an encyclopædia of facts bearing upon the problems of primitive relation to nature, early political organization, taboo and other legal rules. Frazer's passion to explore not only the main road, but also the byways and perspectives opened at every step, implies and proclaims fuller and sounder theoretical interpretations than those given explicitly by the author. His discussion of the influence of sex upon vegetation contains a number of ideas which later on were formulated by psychoanalysis, but for which the facts were collected by Frazer with unerring intuition. The prohibitions and rules of conduct which he lists as "taboos" contain a large material for the study of primitive jurisprudence. Here again, following Frazer, we perceive the principle that primitive law refers to acts, interests, and claims which on the one hand refer to vital human concerns, food, sex, social position and wealth, and which, on the other hand, necessitate restrictions and delimitations since they refer to a subject matter in which man is tempted to transgress his customary rules.

The volumes concerned with agricultural ritual, the gods and goddesses of fertility, and the magical and religious interpretation of the yearly cycle, contain once more a live theory embodied in the presentation of facts. Frazer's insight in linking up ritual with the practical activities of food production tells us in so many words that religious and magical belief has always functioned as a principle of order, of integration, and of organization at primitive and at higher levels of human development. We see here magic not as a futile misconception, but rather as the crystallized optimism of hope carrying man along on his pursuits by the conviction that the desired end will be realized. We see also that sociologically the rôle of the early leader, the chief and the king, is not merely defined by his ability to exploit the commoner's superstition. Primitive leadership is seen to be the embodiment of man's conviction that the individual who is expert in the practical management of affairs can also manipulate the supernatural elements of chance and destiny. It is the pragmatic and intrinsic value of magic and religion which makes for their vitality and endurance.

Frazer's artistry, as well as his scientific sense in achieving a real synthesis from scattered and unrelated ethnographic evidence, appears at its best in his descriptive volumes on *Totemism and Exogamy*. Frazer describes totemic belief and ritual within the context of the social and political organization of each tribe. We find an outline of economics and social organization, of legal concepts and general beliefs, at times of military activities and ceremonial life. All this is prefaced, as a rule and wherever possible, by a picture of the landscape and an account of the environmental setting in which the natives live, and from which they draw their livelihood. In many ways Frazer's *Totemism and Exogamy* is about the best introductory reading for the young student of anthropology, because it gives

an easier, more attractive, and better integrated picture of a whole series of tribal cultures than any book I know. Only recently has it been paralleled by G. P. Murdock's *Our Primitive Contemporaries*, which comes near in the quality of style and presentation to Frazer's standard, and is more comprehensive as well as more precise as regards information.

The three volumes on *Folk-lore in the Old Testament* and the later works of Frazer on immortality, *The Worship of Nature*, and *The Fear of the Dead*, are perhaps less well contextualized than the descriptive chapters of *Totemism and Exogamy*. Yet even there Frazer's artistry and his love of the integral and the comprehensive make the works as instructive as they are pleasant to read.

Among the works of Sir James Frazer, the slender volume entitled *Psyche's Task* and republished later as *The Devil's Advocate*, deserves special consideration. In one way it is perhaps Frazer's most ambitious and most original contribution to the theory of human evolution. The fundamental idea hinges on the relation between magical and religious beliefs and some fundamental institutions of mankind. Taking government, private property, marriage, and respect for human life, one after the other, Frazer shows how far early "superstition" has contributed towards their establishment and development. He deals with moral concepts rather than scientific ideas. The distinctions between *good* and *bad*, between *superstition* and *rational knowledge*, occur in most arguments. We are even told "that these institutions have sometimes been built on rotten foundations."

Yet even here Frazer's common sense leads him to a caveat—and a contradiction. ". . . . There is a strong presumption that they (the institutions discussed) rest mainly on something much more solid than superstition. No institution founded wholly on superstition, that is, on falsehood, can be permanent. If it does not answer some real human need, if its foundations are not laid broad and deep in the nature of things, it must perish, and the sooner the better." The contradiction is clear. We are told in one place that these institutions sometimes rest on rotten foundations; and then, again, that their foundations have to be found somewhere broad and deep in the nature of things. The solution is indicated by Frazer himself. Such institutions as marriage, or law, or property, or government do "answer real human needs." Had Frazer inquired more fully into the nature of those needs, he might have, first and foremost, given us a correct theory of the real "origins" of human institutions and of such aspects of human culture as law, government, economics, and social organization. He would have discovered that forms of human organization which have endured from the very beginnings till our times, such as the family, kinship, the local group or municipality, and the state, correspond to definite needs of organized human life. He could then show, and show convincingly and adequately, why certain forms of magic and religion have contributed towards the permanence and the development of certain aspects of concerted human activities and of human groupings.

As it is, every one of the four chapters of *Psyche's Task*, suggestive and stimulating as it is, ends on a questionmark. After discussing the contributions of magic to government, we are told "that many peoples have regarded their rulers, whether chiefs or kings, with superstitious awe as beings of a higher order and endowed with mightier powers than common folk." Here Frazer's own evidence shows, as we have indicated, that authority, as the backbone of order and regulation, is indispensable in household, municipality, and tribe. The superstitious awe and respect given by the primitives to their chiefs is the by-product of the conviction that the leader leads in virtue of his power, his expert knowledge, and his *mana* or sanctity.

In discussing private property, we once more are told that superstitious fear operates "as a powerful motive to deter men from stealing." Yet stealing presupposes the existence of private property. Private property again, as the legally defined, exclusive right to use and to consume tools and goods respectively, is essential, and without such a principle there would occur a chronic chaos and disorganization even in the simplest activities of primitive man. Once established, private property is protected by belief and magic, as well as by secular sanctions.

Marriage and the family correspond in their origins to the cultural need of transforming physiological reproduction into an organized, legally established form of coöperative life. This is the origin of marriage. The regulation of "sexual immorality whether in the form of adultery, fornication, or incest" is then carried on by various devices, magical belief being one of them. In this chapter Frazer is involved in a complex web of contradictions. As a follower of Morgan, McLennan and Bachofen, he assumes the existence of primitive promiscuity. He does not show us how marriage develops out of this original state. Yet obviously, and this we assume, the existence of marriage and the family form the beginnings of human culture—an assumption now universally accepted by modern anthropology— and we cannot even inquire into the sanctions of early sexual morals. For under conditions of promiscuity or group marriage such morals would not exist.

Again, in the treatment of criminal law, Frazer tries to show that "the fear of ghosts, especially the ghosts of the murdered" has played an important part. Here again the modern anthropologist would insist that early criminal law was an indispensable prerequisite of the survival of primitive groups. The fear of ghosts of the murdered was the result of the sense of sin associated with murder. As such it probably fitted into the picture, but the real problem to an evolutionist is to discover how criminal law came into being. Then, and then only, can we understand all the beliefs which center around the transgression, and place them in their proper perspective.

With all this, the very problem posed by Frazer in this volume, the relation between belief and the organization of human institutions, is one of those which play a great rôle in modern anthropology. (pp. 187-95)

Bronislaw Malinowski, "Sir James George Frazer," in his A Scientific Theory of Culture and Other Essays, *The University of North Carolina Press, 1944, pp. 177-221.*

NORTHROP FRYE   (essay date 1958)

[*Frye has exerted a tremendous influence in the field of twentieth-century literary scholarship, mainly through his study* Anatomy of Criticism *(1957). In this seminal work, Frye made controversial claims for literature and literary critics, arguing that judgments are not inherent in the critical process and asserting that literary criticism can be "scientific" in its methods and results without borrowing concepts from other fields of study. Literary criticism, in Frye's view, should be an autonomous discipline in the manner of physics, biology, and chemistry. For Frye, literature is schematic because it is wholly structured by myth and symbol. The critic becomes a near-scientist, determining how symbols and myths are ordered and function in a given work. The critic need not, in Frye's view, make judgments of value about the work; a critical study is structured by the fact that the components of literature, like those of nature, are unchanging and predictable. Frye believes that literature occupies a position of extreme importance within any culture. Literature, as he sees it, is "the place where our imaginations find the ideal that they try to pass on to belief and action, where they find the vision which is the source of both the dignity and the joy of life." The literary critic serves society by studying and "translating" the structures in which that vision is encoded. In the following excerpt from an essay written in 1958 as a radio address, Frye maintains that Frazer's comparative anthropological method has more in common with literary symbolism than scientific empiricism.*]

[Frazer] was a fine classical scholar who grew up in the later Victorian period, after Darwin had changed the whole direction of science. Anthropology was a new and exciting subject, and for Frazer it threw a flood of light on his classical studies. The Greeks and Romans had been primitives once too, and many things had survived in their religion that were very like the things being reported from the African jungles and the Australian bush. The biblical scholar Robertson Smith had studied primitive Arabian tribes to discover the sort of religion that's concealed in the earliest layers of the Old Testament. He had also worked on a theory that had a great influence on Frazer: that in primitive societies ritual precedes myth: people act out their beliefs first and think up reasons for them afterward. Then again, German scholars following the Grimm brothers, especially a scholar named Mannhardt, were turning up curious customs in the German countryside that seemed to be filling in the outlines of a nature cult centuries older than Christianity. Scholars were taking much the same view of primitive man that primitive man was supposed to have taken of his own life, as a kind of dream in which everything was charged with a mysterious fascination, and they pounced eagerly on anything that had to do with "folk."

Frazer was a professor of social anthropology, yet he never to my knowledge did any real fieldwork and never came much closer than the Cambridge library to primitive societies. He certainly doesn't sound like a man who had any firsthand knowledge of primitive life, or ever wanted to have any. He speaks, for instance, of something being familiar "to the crude intelligence not only of the savage, but of ignorant and dull-witted people everywhere." *The Golden Bough* is really a work of classical scholarship that uses a very large amount of illustrative material from anthropology and folklore. In the course of his classical reading, Frazer came across a custom in Roman life that puzzled him, and as he pondered it, the work of Robertson Smith on the Bible and of Mannhardt in Germany began to suggest hundreds of parallels to it; and finally the puzzling Roman custom became the key to a vast amount of ritual, myth, folklore, superstition, and religious belief all over the world. So it was that his essay on *The Golden Bough,* which first appeared in 1890, had expanded to three volumes by 1900, and into twelve, in the usual format, by 1915—a book of about 4000 pages. The length of the book is the result of the enormous mass of material collected as evidence: if you know only the one-volume abridgment he made in 1922, you haven't really missed much of the main argument. He was a disciple of Darwin in believing that if you were going to be properly scientific, for every statement you had to choke your reader with examples and illustrations, and his text walks over a thick pile carpet of footnotes from Greek and Latin literature, from the Old Testament, which Frazer read in Hebrew, from monographs and periodicals in English, French, German, Italian, and Dutch.

Near Rome, in the time of the Caesars, there was a grove sacred to the goddess Diana, in which there was a runaway slave who was called the priest of the grove and the King of the Wood. When he got there he found his predecessor in charge, and what he had to do was to break a branch off a certain tree, then attack and kill his predecessor. Then he was King of the Wood until some other runaway slave did the same thing to him. Why was there such a custom? That was the question that started Frazer off on the twelve-volume journey that another anthropologist, Malinowski, has called "the greatest scientific Odyssey in modern humanism."

Frazer begins by explaining that magic is the belief that you can affect things either by imitating them or by getting hold of part of them. If you have an enemy, magic suggests that you imitate killing him, say by sticking pins in a wax image of him, or that you get something belonging to him, like a lock of his hair, and then injure that. Primitive tribes take a magical view of their leader or king. As long as he's strong and virile, the tribe will hold together and their food supply will be steady: if he gets old and feeble, so will the crops. So magic reasons that a king ought to be killed when his strength fails. It sounds like a funny way of preserving his strength, but the idea is to transfer it to his successor and distribute what's left over to the tribe. Magic assumes that you can get the qualities of something by eating it; so if you want the magic strength of the king, you eat his body and drink his blood.

Out of this pattern of ritual a great number of religions have developed, mostly around the Mediterranean Sea. The central figure is a god conceived in the form of a young man, who represents the fertility of the seasons in general and of the crops in particular. Hence, his body and blood become identified with the two chief products of the crops, bread and wine. At the center of this religion is a ritual representing the death and rebirth of the god, usually lasting three days. The god was called Adonis in Syria, Attis in Asia Minor, Osiris in Egypt, Dionysus in Greece, Balder in the North. There are also a great number of folk customs surviving among the European peasantry that feature similar figures, like the King and Queen of the May. Originally, Frazer thinks, these gods or mythical figures were represented by human beings who were sacrificed, and in peasant customs, even in children's games, there are many mock executions that at one time weren't mock at all.

An immense number of side issues are explored and problems solved, or at any rate fascinating guesses made, in every field of mythology and folklore. There is the "scapegoat" ritual, for instance, where an old man or woman who represents death and sterility is killed or driven away. There is the symbolism springing from the use of a temporary or mock king to serve as a substitute for the real one: he has a brief reign and is then executed, and this figure survives in all the lords of misrule and kings of the carnival in medieval Europe, besides being involved in the mockery of Jesus in the Passion. There is the connection which gives Frazer his title between the branch broken off by the King of the Wood and the golden bough Aeneas broke off before he could visit hell in Virgil's *Aeneid*. Virgil compares the golden bough to the mistletoe, and Frazer thinks it was the mistletoe, regarded as sacred in the ancient *cultus* of Europe.

Some of the side issues spill over into other books. The most important of them is the question of totemism, the identifying of a tribe with a certain animal or plant which is ceremonially eaten at stated times, and which for complicated reasons has been of great importance in developing the structure of primitive societies. Frazer's four volumes on *Totemism and Exogamy* (which means the rule that a man must marry outside his

totem clan) are still an important source book for this subject. His other books are mostly in the form of compilations. As a teacher who made hosts of readers familiar with the conceptions of anthropology, Frazer is very important; as a scholar who could apply literary and scientific knowledge to the same problem, he is equally so. But as an architect of modern thought, he has to stand or fall by *The Golden Bough.*

I am not competent to discuss *The Golden Bough* as anthropology because I'm a literary critic, and I don't know any more about anthropology than the next man. . . . *The Golden Bough* seems to be at present more a book for literary critics than for anthropologists. It is, after all, a study of comparative symbolism, and one would expect that to appeal most to artists, poets, critics, and students of certain aspects of religion. When it first appeared, *The Golden Bough* was called an example of the Covent Garden school of anthropology, meaning that it was full of vegetation, Covent Garden being a market. There doesn't seem to be much of a Covent Garden school of anthropology left. I've just checked through several textbooks on anthropology to see what they said about Frazer. They were respectful enough about him as a pioneer, but it would have taken a Geiger counter to find much influence of *The Golden Bough* in them. Of course, there's a lot of fashion in such matters, but there's also a real problem involved.

Frazer often refers to what he calls the "comparative method." In his early years, tremendous strides had been made in biology through comparative anatomy. Those were the days when there were stories about scientists who could reconstruct a whole skeleton of an unknown animal from one piece of tailbone. In the comparative study of languages, too, a fascinating new world had opened up. But to make valid comparisons you have to know what your primary categories are. If you are studying natural history, no matter how fascinated you may be by anything that has eight legs, you can't just lump together an octopus and a spider and a string quartet. Now it is the anthropologist's business, as I understand it, to study individual cultures: those are his primary categories. So when Frazer compares rituals all over the world without telling us anything about the societies they fit into, he is not doing what many anthropologists, at least at present, have much interest in doing. At the same time, he is doing precisely what the student of symbolism, looking for the recurrence of a certain symbolic theme through all the world's cultures, wants to see done.

To appreciate *The Golden Bough* for what it is we have to see it as a kind of grammar of the human imagination. Its value is in its central idea: every fact in it could be questioned or reassessed without affecting that value. We don't have to assume that once upon a time everybody everywhere used to eat their kings and then gradually evolved slightly less repulsive customs. Frazer's ritual is to be thought of as something latent in the human imagination: it may have been acted out literally sometimes, but it is fundamentally a hypothesis that explains features in rituals, not necessarily the original ritual from which all others have derived. *The Golden Bough* isn't really about what people did in a remote and savage past; it is about what the human imagination does when it tries to express itself about the greatest mysteries, the mysteries of life and death and afterlife. It is a study, in other words, of unconscious symbolism on its social side, and it corresponds to and complements the work that Freud and Jung and others have done in psychology on unconscious symbolism on its individual side, in dreams and the like. It is extraordinary how closely Frazer's patterns fit the psychological ones. Frazer's dying gods are very like the libido figures of Freudian dreams; the old men and women of Frazer's scapegoat rituals correspond to Freud's parental imagos; the temporary kings of the carnival are the social forms of what Freud has studied in the mind as the mechanism of wit.

A ritual, in magic, is done for practical purposes, to make the crops grow, to baffle enemies, to bring rain or sunshine or children. In religion, a ritual expresses certain beliefs and hopes and theories about supernatural beings. The practical results of magic don't work out; religious beliefs disappear or change in the twilight of the gods. But when deprived of both faith and works, the ritual becomes what it really is, something made by the imagination, and a potential work of art. As that, it can grow into drama or romance or fiction or symbolic poetry. Poetry, said Aristotle, is an imitation of nature, and the structures of literature grow out of the patterns that the human mind sees in or imposes on nature, of which the most important are the rhythms of recurrence, the day, the month, the four seasons of the year. Poets can get from Frazer a new sense of what their own images mean, and critics can learn more from him about how the human imagination has responded to nature than from any other modern writer.

For the student of religion, *The Golden Bough* is of immense value in showing the positive importance of myth. Up to Frazer's time, interest in religion was confined mainly to theology or to history, and myth was felt to be just something that wasn't true—something all the *other* religions had. But now we can see more clearly how religion can appeal to the imagination as well as to faith or reason. Frazer's god-eating ritual is a kind of primitive parody of Christianity and shows us how magic and superstition, even in their weirdest forms, can be seen as gropings toward a genuine religious understanding.

In Oxford, Frazer used to be referred to as "the Cambridge fellow who can write," and it is certainly true that he can write. He can take a great inert mass of evidence and with a few selective touches make it into a lively narrative that keeps you turning the pages into the small hours. Of course, people who can't write are not only apt to be jealous of people who can, but often believe quite sincerely that anybody who is readable must be superficial. That is why you get so many sniffy remarks about Frazer's "highly imaginative" or "picturesque" style in books that are a lot harder to get through than his are. But no matter what happens to the subjects he dealt with, Frazer will always be read, because he can be. There are other aspects of his style I don't care so much for. He's fond of relapsing into fine writing, and when he does, he goes in for a kind of languid elegance that reminds one of a heroine of a Victorian novel about to expire with refinement and tight corsets. But for sheer power to organize material he ranks in the first class, with Gibbon or Macaulay, and a more recent encyclopedic writer, Toynbee, has learned a lot from him.

I would not say that Frazer was a great thinker. Like Darwin, he got hold of one tremendous intuition and spent his life documenting it, but apart from that he had a rather commonplace mind. People often believe that if a man spends his time among books he will lose contact with life: actually this very seldom happens, but it is true that Frazer looks at the world through a study window. In all his work I have found only one specific expression of interest in the events of his own day, a letter urging the union of England and France, and even that was published twenty years after it was written. He gives the impression of a Victorian liberal of a somewhat vague and

sentimental kind. The theory of evolution popularized the idea that man had developed from lower forms of life, and it was easy to extend that to a theory of progress, to seeing man as still developing out of savagery into higher and higher civilization. A lot of people still think that biological evolution and historical progress are the same thing, and that one is the scientific proof of the other. Frazer thought so too, and he never doubted that man had gone steadily up an escalator from ape-man through savagery to twentieth-century Cambridge.

Now Frazer's "comparative method" is one that puts together myths from the ancient world, customs from contemporary primitive societies, and survivals of ancient beliefs in our own day. Such a method obviously hasn't anything historical about it and can hardly justify him in making any historical statements. But still, there is a historical framework to his book that is provided by his Darwinian escalator. All human societies, he believes, belong at certain points on this escalator, from the lowest, like the African bushmen, to the highest, like us. Societies that are on the same level will behave in pretty much the same way, no matter how far apart they are. This is the principle he relies on when he compares rituals that are vastly remote in time and space. In the final pages of *The Golden Bough,* Frazer ties this theory up. He suggests that there have been three ages of man: an age of magic, an age of religion, and an age of science, the last one just beginning.

Magic, Frazer says, is psychologically much the same thing as science. The magician's aim, like the scientist's, is a practical and secular aim: he believes that nature obeys fixed laws, and he tries to turn those laws to his own advantage. The difference between magic and science is not in attitude, but in the fact that magic is wrong about natural law and science right. Because the magician's notions of nature are crude, magic doesn't work, and so man turns from magic to religion, which for Frazer is a belief in mysterious external powers that man thinks he can either placate or get on his side. It is our job now to outgrow religion—Frazer isn't very explicit about this, but that is clearly what he means—and enter on an age of science, or true magic. In a series of lectures called *Psyche's Task,* he says that many of the fundamentals of civilization today, respect for government, for private property, for marriage, and for human life, grew out of primitive superstition, and all we have to do is separate the superstition in them from their rational sense.

One thinks of G. K. Chesterton's remark about the Victorians who saw the whole of human history in the form of one of their own three-volume novels, sure that they were the third volume and that history was turning out well because it was turning out with them. I imagine that not many scholars today would endorse Frazer's view that magic has always and everywhere preceded religion: it seems clear that magic and religion start off together. If there is any intermediate stage between magic and science, it isn't religion, which is quite distinct from both, but such things as alchemy and astrology. Also, there is a lot in magic—its dependence on tradition and authority, its secrecy, its emotional and dramatic elements—that make it something very different from any kind of rationalism, however crude. And if magic is just wrong science, surely primitive societies have and apply a lot of very sound knowledge of nature, which is scientific according to Frazer's definition—if they didn't they would starve to death.

As for the happy ending of his three-volume novel, outgrowing religion and becoming reasonable and scientific about everything doesn't sound like much of a program for the world in

1958. One person that Frazer seems to have had absolutely no use for was Freud, in spite of the fact that Freud based one of his books, *Totem and Taboo,* on Frazer's work. Maybe this was just prudery, but why should a man handling Frazer's kind of material be prudish? The answer seems clearly to be that Freud's discoveries about what is going on inside civilized man today makes one feel a lot more doubtful about this being an age of reason. For Frazer, it was fine for savages to be brutal and incestuous, but for well-dressed people in the nineteenth century to be full of brutal and incestuous impulses was a reflection on progress. True, Frazer often warns us that our civilization is a very thin veneer on top of what is really savagery and superstition still. But by this he appears to mean that outside the cities and universities there is a countryside full of people who want to sow their fields at the new moon and sacrifice a cat to make the crops grow. It never seems to occur to him that there might be things just as silly and more dangerous in civilization and progress themselves.

It seems a curious trick of fate that made Frazer the influence he is today. He was an old-fashioned agnostic who revolutionized our understanding of religion. He was a devotee of what he thought was a rigorous scientific method who profoundly affected the imagery of modern poetry. He was a believer in progress through reason who has told us more than any other man, except perhaps the Freud he disapproved of, about the symbolism of the unconscious. In a way he's not so much an architect of modern thought as of modern feeling and imagination. But one of the great discoveries of modern thought is that feeling and imagination are inseparably a part of thought, that logic is only one of many forms of symbolism. And that is a discovery Frazer helped to make. (pp. 85-94)

> *Northrop Frye, "Symbolism of the Unconscious,"* in his Northrop Frye on Culture and Literature: A Collection of Review Essays, *edited by Robert D. Denham, The University of Chicago Press, 1978, pp. 84-94.*

THEODOR H. GASTER   (essay date 1959)

[*Gaster is an English-born American scholar who has written extensively on comparative religion and folklore, especially of the Near East. His works include a study of ritual origins of drama, an English translation of the Dead Sea Scrolls, and a one-volume abridgement of* The Golden Bough. *In the following excerpt from his foreword to the latter work, Gaster explains the editorial principles that governed his abridgment and summarizes flaws in Frazer's conclusions and methods that have become evident in light of subsequent research. For a negative assessment of Gaster's abridgment, see the excerpt by Stanley Edgar Hyman dated 1962.*]

The Golden Bough is a classic; but classics in the field of scholarship occupy a peculiar position. For while as literature they may remain immortal and as cultural landmarks imperishable, the particular views which they expound and the particular theses which they advance tend in time to be superseded, so that they come to survive like ancient castles, venerable and imposing features of the landscape, but unsuited to habitation without extensive "changes." Or, to take a closer analogy, they suffer the fate of Frazer's own King of the Wood and are obliged in due course to yield their authority to those who pluck the golden bough from the sacred tree. All of which places the modern editor of such a classic in a singularly uncomfortable dilemma. For he is never quite sure where judicious "renovation" ends and sheer vandalism begins. On the

one hand he is supremely conscious of what Milton said about every good book being the precious life-blood, etc., and he will not wish to mutilate another man's work or to obliterate features which, however grotesque, have become familiar. On the other, he will feel it a disservice both to author and reader to compromise the permanent value and continued usefulness of a scientific product by mere pious conservation of its outmoded elements. A good fruit tree not only needs, but also deserves, periodic pruning.

The present abridgment of Frazer's masterpiece [*The New Golden Bough*] seeks to steer an even course in these treacherous waters. It offers, within reasonable compass, such a condensation of the original work as will, it is hoped, faithfully preserve its essential thesis, structure, and documentation, while at the same time omitting such subsidiary and incidental elements as more recent research has rendered obsolete or untenable. It eliminates, for example, Frazer's lengthy discussion of the relation between Magic and Religion, because the view which is there expressed that the two things stand in genealogical succession—that is, that Religion is due to a refinement of the more primitive "magical" mentality—has now been shown to be a mere product of late nineteenth-century evolutionism, without adequate basis. It likewise eliminates Frazer's identification of the sacred tree at Nemi as an *oak*—a very doubtful theory indeed, and one about which he himself was later to express misgivings.

Furthermore, this abridgment attempts, by means of extensive additional notes, to put into the hands of the readers a fairly comprehensive (though, of course, not exhaustive) guide to more recent literature on the various topics with which the work deals, and thus at the same time to orientate him towards alternative views or material (e.g., from the civilizations of the ancient Near East) which were not available when Frazer wrote, but which possess a significant bearing on his thesis.

In the several cases where Frazer's views now require to be modified in the light of subsequent research, but where mere omission or radical alteration would destroy the whole sequence of his argument, short paragraphs have been inserted in the Additional Notes, alerting the reader to the principal difficulties or objections and sometimes suggesting a different construction of the data. It may be useful here to summarize the main points on which such modification would now appear to be necessary:

(1) Frazer's interpretation of the priesthood at Aricia and of the rites which governed succession to it has been almost unanimously rejected by classical scholars. The sanctuary at that place was probably no more than an asylum for runaway slaves; and the golden bough, far from being a vessel of divine power or identical with that carried by Aeneas on his journey to the nether world, was in all likelihood simply the branch characteristically borne in antiquity by suppliants at a shrine. Accordingly, Frazer's elaborate exposition of primitive customs and their modern survivals must now be read as a treatise in its own right, and not as an illustrative commentary on the ancient Latin institutions. (Since, however, it is impossible to eliminate all reference to the latter without destroying the whole structure of the book, it has seemed best to retain it with this express warning that it must now be regarded only as an artistic and fanciful *leitmotif,* not as a factual scaffolding, and that the title, **The Golden Bough,** is in truth a misnomer.)

(2) The basic contention that in primitive cultures the king is primarily the bringer of life overlooks the fact that he is just as much the representative and epitome of those who receive

it. Accordingly, the things that he does and suffers in ritual procedures are not always, as Frazer supposes, acts performed vicariously on behalf of his people; as often as not they merely dramatize and typify what the people as a whole are doing at the same time. When, for instance, the king serves as the bridegroom in a ritual marriage, or when he undergoes periodic death and resurrection, he may really be acting *with* his people rather than *for* them, i.e., concentrating in his own person and "passion" what they themselves are doing and symbolizing concurrently in rites of sexual license, lenten abstinences and mortifications, suspensions of normal activity, and the like.

(3) In postulating "homoeopathy"—that is, the principle that "like produces like"—as one of the primary bases of Magic, Frazer cites in proof the numerous rites in which something desired is simulated in advance, e.g., rainfall by pouring water, or sunlight by kindling fire. In this, however, he overlooks the crucial distinction between *dramatized petition* and *magical procedure*. In many of the cases cited all that is really involved is a *prayer in gesture;* the performers are merely showing the gods or spirits what they want done; and, far from believing (as Frazer supposes) that their acts will be automatically effective, they usually accompany them by express invocation of those superior beings! Hence, while the general contention may be sound enough, the particular evidence adduced in support of it must be received with caution.

(4) It is now no longer accepted that the "dying and reviving" gods of ancient religions, i.e., such figures as Tammuz, Adonis, Attis, and Osiris, merely personify vegetation. (Andrew Lang called this "the Covent Garden school of mythology," in allusion to London's well-known fruit market.) Rather are they to be considered as embodiments of "providence" in general— that is, of the divine force which permeates a community or region and gives it life and increase. The myths and rituals associated with them are thus no mere allegories of sowing and reaping, but are designed rather to account for the rhythm of nature by furnishing reasons (e.g., umbrage or discomfiture) why that providence is periodically withdrawn or absent.

Moreover, in the particular case of Osiris, it has been pointed out by Egyptologists that his character as a god of vegetation is not, in fact, original, but secondary, and that he was primarily a representation of the defunct pharaoh, his entire myth and ritual being concerned with the succession to the kingship rather than with the rhythm of vegetation.

(5) The concept of a single over-all Corn-spirit or Tree-spirit— a concept which Frazer adopted from Mannhardt and then developed into one of the cardinal elements of his thesis—has been seriously challenged by more recent investigators on the grounds that it fuses into an artificial and purely schematic unity what the primitive actually recognizes as any number of distinct and disparate spirits, each personifying a different aspect, impact, or association of grain or trees.

(6) In his discussion of the widespread institution of the Scapegoat, Frazer overlooks the salient distinction between rites in which an animal serves as a mere surrogate for a human culprit and those in which it serves to remove a collective miasma which the community confesses in a blanket formula but precise responsibility for which cannot, for one reason or another, be pinned on any specific individual. The two things have different motivations and should not be confused through mere outward similarity.

(7) In the treatment of Fire-festivals, no adequate distinction is preserved between the custom of extinguishing and rekin-

dling fires at harvest or at the death of the king as a symbol of the seasonal or occasional eclipse and regeneration of corporate life—"put out the light, and then put out the light"— and that of lighting them as a magical procedure for reluming the dying sun. Here again, outward similarity of procedure does not attest identity of motive or underlying concept, and many of the practices which Frazer explains as of solar significance are not really so.

Quite apart from these specific points, more recent inquiry, with its wider coverage, its first-hand observation, and its improved techniques, has also called into question several basic aspects of Frazer's general method. Thus it has been objected that throughout his work he pays far too little regard to the necessity of *cultural stratification*, tending to place all "savage" customs and beliefs on a single vague level of "the primitive." Consequently, much of the material which he adduces as evidence of primitive or rudimentary modes of thought is in fact the product of considerable mental evolution and involution, even though it may still be far removed from our own yet higher stage of development. Moreover, in certain particular cases, what Frazer and his contemporaries commonly accepted as instances of the most primitive civilizations extant have been recognized by subsequent research to be nothing of the kind. It has been shown, for example, by Willhelm Schmidt that the Australasian Arunta, whom Frazer cites as parade exhibits of the aboriginal primitive, really represent an intrusive higher culture. Nor, even within any one or other particular area, does Frazer take into sufficient account the factor of internal evolution—that is, that even among a group of men who to us are savages all institutions and beliefs do not necessarily remain at the original primitive level. In short, he fails persistently to distinguish between the *savage* and the *primitive*, so that on closer analysis many of his examples turn out to be irrelevant or even misleading.

Equally open to criticism is Frazer's attitude toward contemporary folk customs. Rarely does he investigate their documented history, usually adopting *a priori* the principle that an explanation along historical lines is necessarily a mere later veneer, an attempt to justify or validate an older and more primitive institution. That folklore is indeed studded with such transmuted survivals no one, of course, would wish to deny; but more recent studies have suggested that a decent respect must be paid also to the factor of genuine local reminiscence and commemoration, and likewise that similarities between modern and primitive usages may often be more outward than inward. A case in point is Frazer's identification of the King of the Bean, who presides over Whitsuntide "beanfeasts" in Europe, as a survival of the ancient and primitive custom of appointing sovereigns (*qua* vessels of the spirit of fertility) on a yearly basis. This turns a deaf ear to a very simple and obvious metaphor, and overlooks the fact that in ancient Greece, for example, "king" (*basileus*) was a common title for the chairman at *any* banquet.

Lastly, there is the question of sources. All too often, it is alleged, Frazer bases his arguments on naive and amateurish accounts of native customs and local ceremonies—accounts furnished by ill-equipped tourists or biased missionaries, but now long since superseded by more disciplined observation. Moreover, even when (as usually) he cites more than one authority, these are not infrequently "much of a muchness" in their unreliability, so that the plethora of documentation merely "compounds the felony." And all too many of them were— like Frazer himself—totally ignorant of native languages, so that they are apt perforce to squeeze distinctive concepts into the molds of their own mentality and forms of expression, or to abuse native terms (e.g., *taboo*) by employing them in too wide and indeterminate a sense.

A proper recognition of its ephemeral elements should not, however, obscure appreciation of the permanent values of *The Golden Bough,* nor create the impression that it is simply a useful repository of facts. It may be said without reasonable fear of contradiction that no other work in the field of anthropology has contributed so much to the mental and artistic climate of our times. Indeed, what Freud did for the individual, Frazer did for civilization as a whole. For as Freud deepened men's insight into the behavior of individuals by uncovering the ruder world of the subconscious, from which so much of it springs, so Frazer enlarged man's understanding of the behavior of societies by laying bare the primitive concepts and modes of thought which underlie and inform so many of their institutions and which persist, as a subliminal element of their culture, in their traditional folk customs.

To be sure, Frazer was not himself the discoverer of the "facts" on which his presentation was based. They were excerpted almost entirely—in a series of notebooks carefully transcribed and indexed—from earlier compilations (notably those of Richard Andree, Alfred Bastian, and Willhelm Mannhardt) and from the reports of countless travelers and missionaries in all parts of the globe. But, apart from the fact that no one before had covered the ground so thoroughly, it was Frazer more than anyone else who first sought to classify and co-ordinate this vast body of material and to construct out of it an over-all picture of how, at the primitive level, Man in general thinks and acts, and of how that primitive mentality persists sporadically even in the more advanced stages of his development. It is in this attempt to *construe* the data in universal terms, just as much as in its unparalleled coverage of them, that the distinctive significance of *The Golden Bough* really lies; and this it is that has earned for it the status of a classic. What, in effect, Frazer did was not only to enable us to see more clearly "the rock whence we were hewn," but also to provide a broad, psychological frame of reference within which the phenomena of particular cultures, ancient and modern alike, might be more adequately interpreted and understood. And if now this King of the Wood has had to yield to his successors, it must not be forgotten that, in terms of the ancient myth, it is his own essence that they are inheriting, and that their title to kingship—until they are themselves overthrown—derives, in the first place, from their having plucked a branch from the tree which, in his time, he so jealously guarded. (pp. xv-xx)

> *Theodor H. Gaster, in a foreword to* The New Golden Bough *by Sir James George Frazer, edited by Theodor H. Gaster, Criterion Books, 1959, pp. xv-xx.*

HERBERT WEISINGER (essay date 1961)

[*Weisinger is an American critic. In the following excerpt from an address written in 1961, he ranks Frazer with Charles Darwin, Karl Marx, Sigmund Freud, and Albert Einstein as a seminal thinker whose works have been instrumental in shaping twentieth-century thought.*]

Anyone who undertakes to defend *The Golden Bough* today must concede before he can confound. He must concede that Frazer falls just short of magnitude and far short of magnanimity; he is neither embattled nor heroic nor passionate nor tragic; and the absence of these qualities shows itself in the

Sketch of Frazer by Lucien H. Monod, 1907.

magisterial blandness of his style. He must concede that Frazer never set foot in the field so far as his anthropological work is concerned, though quite the opposite is true of his classical studies; even as late as 1921, Frazer could still assert that the collection of data should be kept quite apart from the task of examining, comparing, and evaluating the evidence; should not, in fact, be entrusted to the observers in the field but is best done by others in their libraries at home or at their universities; I suppose by this he meant himself, though in all fairness we ought to remember such testimonials from fieldworkers as Malinowski's: "The letters which I received from Frazer during my sojourns in New Guinea and Melanesia helped me more by suggestion, query and comment than any other influence." He must concede that if with Darwin, Marx, Freud, and Einstein, Frazer helped shape the modern mind, he is patronising toward Darwin, McCarthyite concerning Marx, arrogant to Freud, and simply ignorant about Einstein.

Nor is this all he must concede. He must bow his head, though not so low as Raglan would demand, under such a charge as: "Frazer was a great scholar and a great writer, but, as we all are, he was a man of his age, and that age remained the Victorian. He was also emphatically a Linnaean. He spent most of his life in collecting and sorting out facts and anecdotes about the superstitions of savages. He was not very critical in his use of authorities, and since he liked adding items from old and obscure writers to his collection, he often used unreliable material when better was available. . . . In the result, the picture of the savage world which he paints is misleading in the extreme. . . . The savage of Frazer and his disciples is a creature of fiction." And he must acknowledge the force of

Frankfort's argument that there are many significant differences in the handling of the death and resurrection theme by the various peoples of the ancient Near East. Admitting the possibility of a myth of a dying god which would contain features common to the myths of Egypt, Syria, and Mesopotamia, Frankfort nevertheless asserts that Frazer's dying god is ultimately depicted as a mortal in whom the spirit of fertility is for the moment incarnate, and who dies a violent death. But such a concept, he thinks, is foreign to the myth of the dying god in the ancient Near East; he is not incarnate in a human being and is not killed but dies in the regular round of the seasons; more, there is uncertainty as to whether the dead god will be found and even more whether he will be resurrected; and the community does not passively await his resurrection but rather goes out in frantic search for him, often symbolized in the mourning and search undertaken by his wife and mother. Again, Osiris ranks below the Sun God, nor is he the child of the goddess who saves him; Adonis is not thought of as a creator; Horus does not help Osiris in the same way in which Nabu and Ninurta aid Marduk and Eulil; Osiris is not merely a dying god, he is actually a dead god who never returned, as did Tammuz, to the land of the living, and his place was taken there by Horus; there are variations in the relations of these gods to plant life, to animals, and to water; and finally, there are many disparities between the various cultic practices associated with the gods. "The gods as they confront us in the religions of the ancient Near East," Frankfort concludes, "express profoundly different mentalities."

Yet, for all this, it still cannot be denied that along with Darwin, Marx, Freud, and Einstein, Frazer does remain a major molder of the modern mind. But, when we ask ourselves how this came about, how in fact the work of such different and difficult writers was able to stir—even to inflame—the imaginations, not only of the intellectual class, which is much more open to the winds of doctrine than it likes to pretend, but also of great masses of ordinary men who are much more resistant to ideas, and especially to ideas which call out for change, then we realize that we are dealing with a much more profound problem than accounting for a mere shift in attitude through persuasion by reason, assuming this ever really does take place. For if we look at the books of these men as incitements to the imagination and provocations to passion, we are struck by the realization that if ever writing was less calculated to arouse, to excite, indeed, to convert men of all classes and conditions, it is surely their work.

Darwin writes serviceable and sturdy English, but he writes ponderously, and he was himself well aware of the inadequacies of his style. His concern is with the accumulation of detail which in the end overwhelms, but he seldom permits himself the luxury of the sweeping generalization or the flashing phrase; even his great catch-phrases lie half-hidden in the steady flow of his evidence. *The Communist Manifesto* is, to be sure, a deliberate instigation, but I strongly suspect that Engels' hand is the stronger there, for he at least writes a swift, clean, figured prose. But these qualities are certainly missing from *Das Kapital,* which is elephantine in its size, tenaciousness, and deliberation; it is faulted as a piece of prose, not by propaganda, which is at least irritating, but by a pedantry which is relentlessly dull, and never was a book less fitted to make the heart beat faster nor to set the myriad feet of millions of men to marching. Frazer's writing is carefully artful, for he was a conscious stylist who took as his models the Authorized Version—the allusions are deliberately worked in, especially in the purple passages—Addison, some Gibbon, a little Browne,

and certainly the tradition of Latinate English. The tone of his writing is majestic, calm, yet somehow artificial, like the contrived majesty and calm of Elgar's big works; he leans over backward to avoid argument and commitment; he is as chary of generalization as though he were spending it; and the carefully artful occasionally slips down into Brobdingnagian archness. Freud does write well, in a nervous—in the Latin sense—style, but his narration is often better than his exposition and there are occasions where one would willingly trade a fascinating account of a case-history for a clearer statement of a theoretical point; in addition, his thought changes and grows and deepens, so that there are many and subtle and complex Freuds with whom to contend. As to Einstein, and I am here speaking of him as a scientist and not as a citizen of the world, candor compels me to confess utter ignorance, and I must take the word of my scientific friends on his greatness. Obviously then, we cannot explain the striking effects of these men on stylistic or purely intellectual grounds alone.

I would suggest that the source of power behind the mundane prose is in each instance a vision, a way of looking at the phenomena of existence, a controlling and unifying metaphor on the grandest scale so vivid, so dramatic, so immediately convincing, both emotionally and intellectually, that we cannot help being caught up by this new sudden awareness, this startlingly fresh insight into the meaning of existence, this astounding bringing together of the disparate and lifeless fragments of experience into a pattern of order and meaning, and giving it all our most fundamental assent. And I would go on to suggest that the source of power behind the new vision is in each instance again the force of that ancient myth and ritual pattern of birth, death, and rebirth, now expressed in terms of the language, the orientation, and the needs of our own times and circumstances, and therefore once again made freshly relevant. Nor need we assume the deliberate intent on the part of these men to restate the pattern in contemporary accents; on the contrary, for too much self-consciousness would smear the pattern by imposing on it a merely artificial pseudo-relationship. Yet, without intending to, each man in his own way has been able to work his way back to the ultimate fructifying source of the Western tradition, and, as before, as in virtually every moral and intellectual crisis of the past, to re-affirm its message: that, in the face of an indifferent, even hostile, universe, man can live, and live meaningfully. (pp. 118-22)

Darwin, Marx, Freud—what, then, is Frazer's claim to a place on this roster (I must perforce omit Einstein)? Simply this, that it was Frazer who first set the myth and ritual pattern on a firm historical foundation, who traced its tortuous movements, and, above all, gave it shape and coherence. For *The Golden Bough* is not a mere conglomeration of unrelated facts, fables, and fancies, a Hearstian warehouse of myth, but a carefully structured organization of data, collected from the most heterogeneous sources, whose variety and multiplicity are poured into a single, solid form which supports the thesis that:

> we may illustrate the course which thought has hitherto run by likening it to a web of three different threads—the black thread of magic, the red thread of religion, and the white thread of science, if under science we may include those simple truths, drawn from observation of nature, of which men in all ages have possessed a store. Could we then survey the web of thought from the beginning, we should probably perceive it to be at first a chequer of black and white, a patchwork of true and false notions, hardly tinged as yet by the red thread of religion. But carry your eye further along the fabric and you will remark

that, while the black thread and white chequer still runs through it, there rests on the middle portion of the web, where religion has entered most deeply into its texture, a dark crimson stain, which shades off insensibly into a lighter tint as the white thread of science is woven more and more into the tissue. To a web thus chequered and stained, thus shot with threads of diverse hues, but gradually changing colour the farther it is unrolled, the state of modern thought, with all its divergent aims and conflicting tendencies, may be compared. Will the great movement which for centuries has been slowly altering the complexion of thought be continued in the near future? Or will a reaction set in which may arrest progress and even undo much that has been done? To keep up our parable, what will be the colour of the web which the Fates are now weaving on the humming loom of time? Will it be white or red? We cannot tell.

So, too, Freud ended his *The Future of an Illusion* on a note of gloomy apprehension, nor are Darwin and Marx simple-minded exponents of a jejune idea of progress either. Rather their tell-tale metaphors bring to mind ebb and flow, change and corruption, flowering and decay, the inter-penetration of life and death: Darwin's tangled bank, Marx's entangled net, Freud's: "The picture which life presents to us is the result of the working of Eros and the death-instinct together and against each other," and Frazer's woven web. Hyman has acutely characterized the great Tangled Bank of Life image of Darwin as ". . . disordered, democratic, and subtly interdependent as well as competitive, essentially a modern vision," and I am sure he will not object if I apply his terms to the images of the others as well.

Frazer, then, is not quite the pedant he has been made out to be, nor the naive evolutionist as some see him, nor yet the indifferent and rationalistic denigrator of the peoples he spent a lifetime studying. Frazer saw the difference between the myths of Osiris, Tammuz, Attis, and Adonis, and he indicated them, contrary to Frankfort's criticism, but he also saw more, and that more is the measure of his achievement: he saw man engaged in a most heroic attempt to work out for himself his place in a hostile universe; he sympathized with that attempt as only one who had followed it in all its bitter and frustrating detail alone could; and he evolved out of the mass of his evidence the tragic drama of man making himself over, no less. He saw it as a tragic drama because he could perceive the false starts, the wrong turns, and the bestiality and cruelty of man toward man; he could also see that in the long run the attempt was doomed to failure, not only because the methods were perhaps hopeless in the face of the problem (for reality is ultimately unknowable) but also because the aim itself was bound to be fruitless (the universe does remain indifferent); but it was a tragic drama in another sense, too, for out of the struggle he could see that man might learn what he was capable of becoming (even though, with Freud, he suspected that man would not).

Like Freud, Frazer rejoiced in the accomplishments of his discipline, calling the new comparative study of the beliefs and institutions of mankind another Renaissance; like Freud, he had the courage to face up to the fact that in the revealing light of his new science ". . . weak spots in the foundations on which modern society is built" are ruthlessly exposed, and surely he had religion in mind when he wrote that line; and like Freud, he declared as his justification: "Whatever comes of it, wherever it leads us, we must follow truth alone." It is

true, however, that Frazer occasionally used pejorative language when he wrote of primitive man; he was rather over-fond of the phrase "our rude forefathers"; but in the main he was neither insensitive nor unsympathetic and sought to understand the mental processes of primitive man within their own terms; indeed, in the second volume of *Spirits of the Born and of the Wild,* he goes so far as to declare the savage "a better reasoner than his civilised brother." In short, Frazer neither judged nor condemned: magic was the best that man could do in primitive circumstances, just as religion was the best that man could do under later circumstances, and just as science can do under present circumstances: each seeks the same goals, but along different paths, yet it is certain that neither magic nor religion nor science possesses the ultimate answers.

The foundation upon which the elaborate edifice of *The Golden Bough* is raised is the homogeneity of the human mind. In the Preface to the first volume of *Balder the Beautiful,* Frazer assessed the value of his own work: "My contribution to the history of the human mind consists of little more than a rough and purely provisional classification of facts gathered almost entirely from printed sources. If there is one general conclusion which seems to emerge from the mass of particulars, I venture to think that it is the essential similarity in the working of the less developed human mind among all races, which corresponds to the essential similarity in their bodily frame as revealed by comparative anatomy." This principle is more fully explained in his appreciation of William Robertson Smith:

> Now when, laying aside as irrelevant to the purpose in hand the question of the truth or falsehood of religious beliefs, and the question of the wisdom or folly of religious practices, we examine side by side the religions of different races and ages, we find that, while they differ from each other in many particulars, the resemblances between them are numerous and fundamental, and that they mutually illustrate and explain each other, the distinctly stated faith and circumstantial ritual of one race often clearing up ambiguities in the faith and practices of other races. Thus the comparative study of religion soon forces on us the conclusion that the course of religious evolution has been, up to a certain point, very similar among all men, and that no one religion, at all events in its earlier stages, can be fully understood without a comparison of it with many others.

Thus it would appear that Frazer is a Uniformitarian in strict opposition to the Diffusionist; you will recall Raglan's attack on Frazer on this point. However, the sentence right after the one which I just quoted from the Preface to *Balder* goes on to read: "But while this general mental similarity may, I believe, be taken as established, we must always be on guard against tracing to it a multitude of particular resemblances which may be and often are due to simple diffusion, since nothing is more certain than that the various races of men have borrowed from each other many of their arts and crafts, their ideas, customs, and institutions." Thus, sensibly and characteristically, Frazer compromised the question. . . . (pp. 125-29)

I am sure that it is no secret by now that I am not interested in Frazer the anthropologist but in Frazer the myth-maker, for it is as a myth-maker that he has succeeded in capturing the creative imagination of our time. This is not the place for a long list of names but I think I can safely say that there is hardly a writer or critic of consequence from Yeats on down who has not, to a lesser or greater degree, directly or indirectly, simply by living in the post-Frazerian climate of opinion, derived from Frazer that deep perspective in time and culture which is the particular mark of the contemporary consciousness. Just as Darwin suddenly plunged man deep into the remotest geological past, as Marx thrust him deep into the very guts of the historical process, as Freud flung him along the deep and endless corridors of the psyche, as Einstein hurled him into the fearsome deeps of a new space and a new time, so Frazer exposed the savage hidden deep in his past—and present. Frazer was right in speaking of a Renaissance, for as the first Renaissance irreparably opened the crack between microcosm and macrocosm by revealing a new earth, a new heaven, and a new man, so the second Renaissance forced the gap even more yawningly apart and the frontiers of nature and man, scarcely as yet assimilated, into even more fearsome dimensions and directions. Man was now seen as no more than a by-product casually thrown off by vast natural forces whose purposes were incomprehensible to him, if indeed there were any at all; at the mercy of forces, both within and without himself, over which he had no control, or, if he did, seemed to be used only for evil ends; the discarded plaything of nature and history alike.

So by their work, Darwin, Marx, Frazer, Freud, and Einstein forced man once again painfully to face up to the immensity, the indifference, and the evil of a universe which neither he nor his gods had made and on which, therefore, he could lay no claim. But if they left him with doubt and terror, they at the same time gave him the means of meeting that doubt and terror: they gave him the vision of man immersed in the very processes of nature and history, an integral part of them, and belonging to them, neither superior to, nor at odds with, nor inferior to, but *in* nature and history. Just as Darwin bound man to his physical past, Marx to his historical past, Freud to his psychological past, and Einstein to his cosmic past, so Frazer bound him to his cultural past; and the unity of nature, history, and man, once broken, was once more re-forged. It is this vision, bought at no small price, as we know, which accounts for the immediacy and intensity of their appeal. You have not read in *The Golden Bough* for very long when, from out of its meticulously structured sentences, so Handelian in tone and vocabulary, there emerges, vivid, exciting, arousing our fears and hopes, engaging our compassion, provoking our anger, irritating, exhilarating, degrading, ennobling, the drama of man struggling to survive, and winning that struggle. Like the dying-reborn god of his own making, he engages in conflict with the powers of darkness, death, and evil; he is defeated; he suffers; he dies; he is reborn triumphantly; and he celebrates that victory in a new vision; and then the cycle is repeated on ever higher levels of achievement. Frazer has thus created the myth of the myth. (pp. 130-31)

I like to think that what makes Darwin, Marx, Frazer, Freud, and Einstein so meaningful to us is not their science, which we must admit can now be pretty well punctured in varying degrees, but their prophecy and their poetry which are impervious to attack because they recall to us the old, harsh truth which their Epigoni would lull us into forgetting, that: "Good and evil we know in the field of this world grow up together almost inseparably.... And perhaps this is that doom which Adam fell into of knowing good and evil, that is to say, of knowing good by evil." The myth and ritual pattern tells us how and ". . . where that immortal garland is to be run for," but it tells us, too, that it must be run ". . . not without dust and heat," for ". . . that which purifies us is trial, and trial is by what is contrary." Not without dust and heat is the trial to be won—this is the meaning of the myth and ritual pattern,

and this is what Darwin, Marx, Freud, Einstein, and Frazer with them, tell us again. Raglan and Malinowski rather dismiss Frazer as the last of the Victorians and I dare say the same charge can be laid against Freud and Einstein (Toynbee, too?), but in the sense in which I am treating them, they are timeless. (pp. 131-32)

> Herbert Weisinger, *"The Branch That Grew Full Straight," in his* The Agony and the Triumph: Papers on the Use and Abuse of Myth, *Michigan State University Press, 1964, pp. 118-33.*

STANLEY EDGAR HYMAN (essay date 1962)

[*As a longtime literary critic for the* New Yorker, *Hyman rose to a prominent position in American letters during the middle decades of the twentieth century. He is noted for his belief that much of modern literary criticism should depend on knowledge from outside the field of literature; consequently, many of his best reviews and critical essays rely on his application of theories gleaned from such disciplines as cultural anthropology, psychology, and comparative religion. In the following excerpt, Hyman discusses some of Frazer's major works and assesses his lasting influence, which has shifted from anthropology to the humanities, classical scholarship, and sociology.*]

In 1910 Frazer published his first ambitious work after *The Golden Bough,* the four sizeable volumes of *Totemism and Exogamy: A Treatise on Certain Early Forms of Superstition and Society.* He explains in the preface that the subjects of his title, totemism and exogamy, are entirely unrelated. John Ferguson McLennan had discovered them both in primitive societies and had combined them; since then Spencer and Gillen in Australia and Rivers among the Melanesians had shown them to be independent. Frazer's aim in the book is no less than collecting all the evidence on both subjects, and deriving a theory of origin and function from it inductively. One theory would suffice for both origin and function, since Frazer habitually approached social institutions with the rationalist assumption that they have been originated to function as they do; thus he speaks of "those marriages of brothers with sisters and of parents with children which it was apparently the intention of exogamy to put an end to." As late as 1941, when he wrote his biographical appreciation, Malinowski took the book seriously as anthropology. He writes:

> In many ways Frazer's *Totemism and Exogamy* is about the best introductory reading for the young student of anthropology, because it gives an easier, more attractive, and better integrated picture of a whole series of tribal cultures than any book I know.

Like *Capital,* *Totemism and Exogamy* insists that it is primarily a work of science. In the preface Frazer takes account of the charges beginning to be made by anthropological critics that his method consists of wrenching traits out of their cultural contexts. He writes:

> The facts are arranged in ethnographical order, tribe by tribe, and an attempt has been made to take account of the physical environment as well as of the general social conditions of the principal tribes which are passed in review. In this way I have sought to mitigate the disadvantages incidental to the study of any institution viewed abstractedly and apart from the rest of the social organism with which it is vitally connected. Such abstract views are indeed indispensable, being imposed by the limitations of the human mind, but they are apt to throw the object out of focus, to exaggerate some of its features, and to di-

minish unduly others which may be of equal or even greater importance. These dangers cannot be wholly avoided, but they may be lessened by making our study as concrete as is compatible with the necessary degree of abstraction.

Frazer concludes the preface:

> As a plain record of a curious form of society which must soon be numbered with the past, the book may continue to possess an interest even when, with the progress of knowledge, its errors shall have been corrected and its theories perhaps superseded by others which make a nearer approach to truth. For though I have never hesitated either to frame theories which seemed to fit the facts or to throw them away when they ceased to do so, my aim in this and my other writings has not been to blow bubble hypotheses which glitter for a moment and are gone; it has been by a wide collection and an exact classification of facts to lay a broad and solid foundation for the inductive study of primitive man.

As befits a scientist, Frazer gives the negative evidence as fully as the positive. "Indeed," he writes in the middle of the second volume, "the English missionary and scholar, the Rev. Dr. R. H. Codrington, who is our best authority on Central and Southern Melanesia, doubts whether the term totemism is applicable to the beliefs and customs of the islanders with which he is acquainted." Tylor having objected to Frazer's use of the term "totemism" for the sacred animals and plants of Samoa, Frazer now writes: "I so far agree with him that I think I should not have spoken of them as totems without qualification." Frazer has a proper scientific sense of the human limitations of the field-worker. He notes:

> In all investigations of savage life the mental capacity, intelligence, tact, and sympathy of the observer are of the first importance; and as the union of these qualities is rare, so the number of first-rate observers of savages is few indeed. Where these personal qualities of head and heart are wanting, no liberal subvention of money, no costly apparatus, no elaborate machinery will supply their place.

Frazer often writes tentatively: "But this is merely a conjecture, I know of no evidence to support it"; or, "But so far as I have studied the evidence adduced to support these conclusions I have to confess that it leaves me doubtful or unconvinced." Criticizing Edward Westermarck for mechanical materialism, for his ultra-Darwinian attempt to explain the growth of institutions "too exclusively from physical and biological causes without taking into account the facts of intelligence, deliberation, and will," Frazer produces an eloquent passage against oversimplification:

> For true science reckons with all the elements of the problem which it sets itself to solve, and it remembers that these elements may differ widely with the particular nature of the subject under investigation. It does not insist on reducing the heterogeneous at all costs to the homogeneous, the multiformity of facts to the uniformity of theory. It is cautious of transferring to one study the principles and methods which are appropriate to another. In particular the science which deals with human society will not, if it is truly scientific, omit to reckon with the qualities which distinguish man from the beasts.

Sometimes Frazer is less scientific in *Totemism and Exogamy* than his principles would suggest. He carries on a curious war against phonetic symbols, "setting some of the consonants on

their feet instead of on their heads," upending them much as Marx upended Hegel. Sometimes when he encounters negative evidence he does not discard or modify his theory, but merely presents the contradiction with "It is interesting to find." When Frazer learns that the custom of the sororate, marriage to the wife's younger sister, does not exist among some peoples during the wife's lifetime, he simply assumes that things were as he would have them in the past: "In these cases we can hardly doubt that the restriction is a comparatively late modification of an older custom which allowed a man to marry the sisters of his living as well as of his deceased wife."

If the test of science, however, is discarding theories when they no longer seem to fit the facts, *Totemism and Exogamy* is probably the most scientific work in history. At times we are hip deep in discarded theories. Frazer writes in the preface:

> That my conclusions on these difficult questions are final, I am not so foolish as to pretend. I have changed my views repeatedly, and I am resolved to change them again with every change of the evidence, for like a chameleon the candid enquirer should shift his colours with the shifting colours of the ground he treads.

Frazer explains in the summary "The Origin of Totemism" in the fourth volume:

> Three different theories of the origin of totemism have at different times occurred to me as possible or probable. Two of them I have seen reason to abandon; the third I still regard as probably true.

Frazer's first theory, developed after he published *Totemism* in 1887, appears in the first edition of *The Golden Bough*. It originates totemism in a belief in the external soul. A widespread belief in external souls that must be deposited in a safe place had been announced by Edward Clodd in *Myths and Dreams*, and Frazer adopted it as an origin theory for totemism. As field studies began appearing that showed no such thing, Frazer discarded the theory. His next theory, published in "The Origin of Totemism" in the *Fortnightly Review* in 1899, and reprinted in *Totemism and Exogamy,* is that totemism is an organization for the magical increase of food. This came from the researches of Baldwin Spencer and F. J. Gillen among the Arunta of Central Australia, and their account of the *intichiuma* ceremonies, in which opossum-men or witchetty-grub-men make their totemic brothers increase. Frazer hit on the theory reading the proofs of their book *The Native Tribes of Central Australia* in 1898. About 1906, Frazer discarded this second explanation, on the grounds that "the motive which the theory assigns for the origin of the institution is too rational, and the social organization which it implies is too complex, to be primitive." Keeping the *intichiuma* idea as a functional development, Frazer soon worked out a third theory of totemic origins, based on a magical theory of conception. This was confirmed for him in 1909 by Rivers' discovery among the Melanesians of Banks Island of just the sort of belief in human fertilization by the spirit of the totem animal or plant that Frazer had decided was "absolutely primitive totemism." Since "the tap-root of totemism" was thus "the sick fancies of pregnant women," in Frazer's latest theory, "totemism may be described as a creation of the feminine rather than of the masculine mind."

Totemism and Exogamy is a hodge-podge of those three theories and others. At the same time, Frazer repeatedly chips away at his theory of the origin of exogamy as a contrivance designed to prevent incest. An article by Andrew Lang in 1906 had convinced him that primitives were not geneticists, which left him with no actual motive for incest avoidance. The Bachofen view that marriage and other ceremonies are designed to replace matriliny with patriliny comes to seem less and less likely as the book goes on. As the evidence increased, avoidance and taboo seemed to make less and less sense as incest precautions. Thus the Navajo have a strong avoidance custom between mother-in-law and son-in-law. "To avoid these embarrassments," Frazer adds, demolishing his theory, "a man will sometimes marry the mother first and then the daughter so as to make the mother-in-law also a wife, thus disarming her of her terrors." He concludes about his theory of incest-prevention:

> At least if that is not the origin of exogamy I must confess to being completely baffled, for I have no other conjectures to offer on the subject.

All of Frazer's theories evolved similarly, leaving their fossils in *Totemism and Exogamy*. The theory of myth he inherited from Mannhardt and Smith is that of ritual origin or at least association, myth as a story that accompanies, directs and sanctions a rite. That theory runs all through the book. Frazer tells a Cherokee myth of Mother Corn and relates it to the Green Corn dance. He describes Northwest Coast drama as "accompanied by a chorus of women who sing the myth which is being acted by the performers." A Kwakiutl dance "must be considered a dramatic performance of the myth." When he is in this mood, Frazer's typical entry on a myth is: "probably reflects a real custom."

In "The Golden Bough" in *The New Statesmen and Nation* in 1941, H. N. Brailsford writes of Frazer: "His interest in ritual was always slighter than his interest in myth, yet ritual is certainly the more fundamental of these two." Frazer was never content with the theory of ritual origins, as he was never content with any theory of origins; in addition some of its implications were emotionally unsettling. Frazer very much wanted a euhemerist theory that would base myths on the exploits of real men. He first got it from Haddon, who revealed to the world the warrior-hero Kwoiam in the lore of one of the peoples of the Torres Straits. Frazer writes of Kwoiam in *Totemism and Exogamy:*

> From the accounts given of him, this personage appears to have been an Australian by descent, either a pure-bred or a half-bred native of North Queensland, who so signalised himself by his prowess, that myths gathered round his memory, blurring and transfiguring the man into a cloudy being of fairyland.

Haddon had actually visited the ruins of Kwoiam's house on the island of Mabuiag, and "rescued the dusky hero and his story from oblivion." Haddon thus established that Kwoiam had been real man (since Haddon had seen the ruins of a real house) although "on his death he was raised by the people of Mabuiag to something that approached to the rank of divinity." This was fine, but not perfect, since Frazer himself hadn't seen the ruins, and the myths appeared to have been told of Kwoiam, not originated in his doings.

Sometime around 1907, exactly what Frazer wanted appeared. His friend the Rev. John Roscoe, a missionary among the Baganda of Uganda, presented to the Ethnological Museum at Cambridge the mummified jawbone, genitalia, and naval cord of Kibuka, the war god of the Baganda, which had been preserved for centuries by the Baganda and acquired from them by Roscoe. (These objects, tastefully decorated with cowrie shells, are pictured on p. 381 of Sir William Ridgeway's *The Dramas and Dramatic Dances of Non-European Races*.) Since these were unquestionably real human remains, and the Ba-

ganda assured Roscoe that they were the god's, then it followed with inexorable logic that gods had once been real men. Frazer writes in *Totemism and Exogamy:*

> It becomes highly probable that many, if not all, of the great national gods of the Baganda are simply men who have been raised to the rank of deities after their death or possibly even in their life. The inference is confirmed by the tradition that the greatest of all the Baganda gods, Musaka, was a brother of the war-god Kibuka, and that two other powerful deities, Nende and Musoke, were sons of Musaka; for if one of the divine brothers, Musaka and Kibuka, was once a man, as we know him for certain to have been, a presumption is raised that the other brother and his two sons were originally men also.

In his 1923 Frazer Lecture, Roscoe said: "I am proud to call myself a disciple of Sir James, to whose inspiration I owe my first love for this important branch of study." In a more important sense Frazer might have called himself a disciple of Roscoe, since Roscoe was instrumental in Frazer's exchanging the one indisputably sound theory of myth he ever held for a mummified scrotum.

Evolution is the only theory Frazer holds to consistently in *Totemism and Exogamy*. Since "it is now generally admitted that all the civilised races of mankind have at some time passed through the stages of savagery," a record "of the thoughts and habits of a people so low down in the scale of humanity must possess the highest scientific interest." Frazer automatically assumes that everything evolves into greater reasonableness, writing:

> In this last respect it can hardly be disputed that the central tribes have preserved the more primitive beliefs and customs, and that the gradual transition from a purely fortuitous determination of the totem to a strict inheritance of it in the paternal line marks a social and intellectual advance in culture. To imagine that the change had taken place in the opposite direction, in other words, that tribes which had once derived their totems invariably from their fathers afterwards abandoned the hereditary principle in favour of one which left the determination of their totems to the sick fancies of pregnant women—this would be a theory too preposterous to be worthy of serious attention.

At one point Frazer suggests that incest taboos develop by natural selection, tribes that do not have them suffering competitively in breeding. He concludes:

> In acting as they did, these poor savages blindly obeyed the impulse of the great evolutionary forces which in the physical world are constantly reducing higher out of lower forms of existence and in the moral world civilisation out of savagery.

At his best, Frazer believes in the sort of neo-evolutionist doctrine anthropologists have been returning to in our time, the insistence that all cultures evolve similarly, although not necessarily through the same stages. Frazer writes:

> But in the absence of proof that the Semites and the Aryans in general ever practised exogamy and counted kinship on the classificatory system we are not justified in concluding that these institutions have at one time been common to the whole human race. Nor, apart from the want of direct evidence, does there appear to be any reason in the nature of things why these institutions should be necessary stages in the social evolution of every people.

Elsewhere:

> Thus the totemism of the Baganda should serve as a warning against the supposition that totemism almost necessarily develops, first, into a worship of sacred animals and plants, and afterwards into a worship of anthropomorphic deities with sacred animals and plants for their attributes.

It was the hierarchy of evolution that Frazer never rejected. Totemism's "main interest for us lies in the glimpse which it affords into the working of the childlike mind of the savage; it is as it were a window opened up into a distant past." Frazer describes the hill tribes of Bengal: "Here, therefore, the rude children of nature could maintain their freedom and preserve their simple habits with but little change from generation to generation." He generalizes:

> Haziness is characteristic of the mental vision of the savage. Like the blind man of Bethsaida he sees men like trees and animals walking in a thick intellectual fog.

The book is studded with: "the infantine intelligence of the primitive savage"; "the inevitable haziness and confusion of savage"; "the undeveloped intelligence of the low savages." (pp. 212-18)

Frazer's influence and effect on the world has slowly shifted from anthropology to other areas. When *The Golden Bough* was first published, it was generally accepted as a work of scientific anthropology, even, as G. P. Gooch called it, "perhaps the most notable contribution of the age to our knowledge of the human race." The first generation of British anthropologists, including many of the great field ethnographers, took it as the fount of theory in their field. Malinowski, who was inspired to become an anthropologist by reading *The Golden Bough,* called Frazer "The greatest anthropologist of our age." In "Sir James George Frazer: A Biographical Appreciation," written in 1941 [see excerpt above], he lists some others influenced:

> Ethnographic field-work for the last half century or so has been under the spell of Frazer's suggestions. The work of Fison and Howitt, as well as of Spencer and Gillen in Australia; the famous Cambridge Expedition to Torres Straits led by A. C. Haddon in collaboration with W.H.R. Rivers, C. G. Seligman, and C. S. Myers; the African work of Junod, Roscoe, Smith and Dale, Torday, and Rattray—to mention only a few outstanding names—were carried on under the spiritual guidance of Frazer.

In the next generation, in England and America, a series of reactions set in against all of Frazer's assumptions. One of its leaders was Malinowski himself, who was inspired and spiritually guided by Frazer but had begun to disagree with him as early as his first published writing, on the economic aspect of Australian totemism, in 1912 ("His inability to convince seems to contradict his power to convert and to inspire," Malinowski writes in his memorial tribute). Within a short time Tylor's evolution became unfashionable and was replaced by the Ratzel-Boas history of diffusion; Smith's cross-cultural comparison gave way to Bastian's more restrained comparison within a culture area; Mannhardt's induction from a mass of amputated facts was succeeded by a new concern (led by Malinowski) with traits in their cultural context. Frazer's old-fashioned rationalist psychology, his assumption that motive and purpose are self-evident, was outmoded by the work of another man *The Golden Bough* had fundamentally influenced,

Sigmund Freud. (Frazer had always refused to read anything by Freud or his followers.) Where Frazer was not ignored, his approach was derided. Evans-Pritchard writes typically in "The Intellectualist (English) Interpretation of Magic" in 1933:

> The apparent futility of Frazer's analogy between science and magic is due to the fact that he sees both as modes of thinking and not learnt modes of technical behaviour with concomitant speech forms. If he had compared a magical rite in its entirety with a scientific performance in its entirety instead of comparing what he supposes to go on in the brain of a magician with what he supposes to go on in the brain of a scientist, he would have seen the essential difference between science and magic. [Hyman adds in a footnote: "Evans-Pritchard at least had the grace not to deliver his attacks as his Frazer Lecture. Not so Henri Frankfort, whose 1950 Frazer Lecture, 'The Problem of Similarity in Ancient Near Eastern Religions,' is a disgraceful attack on Frazer and his followers."]

In recent years, with evolutionary theory again fashionable in the form of neo-Evolutionism, and cross-cultural comparison no longer shameful, there seems to be something of a swing back. Max Gluckman, one of the newer British anthropologists, in his 1952 Frazer Lecture, "Rituals of Rebellion in South-East Africa," pays tribute to Frazer's "deep insight" into the nature and function of primitive ritual, and concludes: "But the answer to all these problems lies in comparative research, and here we must always follow in Sir James Frazer's footsteps." Although he is careful not to identify it as anthropology, M. F. Ashley Montague has acclaimed *The Golden Bough* as "one of the great books of our culture written by one of the great scholars of our time." Margaret Mead, in her introduction to the anthology *Primitive Heritage* in 1953, calls for a restoration of books like *The Golden Bough* to anthropological reading lists. It seems unlikely, for obvious reasons, that Frazer's naive assumptions will ever return to favor or that *The Golden Bough* will ever again be taken for modern scientific anthropology, but when rituals of rebellion in anthropology departments die away, there is no reason why it should not have a secure place as an early classic in the field, as magnificent and defective as the pioneering field studies.

It is in areas outside Anglo-American anthropology that Frazer's influence seems both lasting and growing. Malinowski writes:

> The first and lasting contributions of the French School under the leadership of the dominant and domineering figure of Durkheim, and carried on by Hubert and Mauss, Lévy-Bruhl, Bouglé, and Van Gennep, are unthinkable without the inspiration and achievement of Frazer. In Germany Wundt, Thurnwald, K. T. Preuss and many others have built on Frazer's foundations.

Here we are well into sociology, where Frazer has been received more sympathetically. The sociologist Donald G. MacRae, writing in *A Century of Darwin* in 1958, argues:

> The case for Frazer—who like Spencer is rather under a cloud today—is too complex and technical to be argued briefly here. His use of the comparative method on an enormous scale can be faulted, though the fascinating detail it reveals and the charm of his Augustan style ensure that he is still read. His industry was truly Darwinian, and I believe that his success in subsuming vast masses of data under a few leading ideas was considerable. Unfortunately the anti-

evolutionary reaction, largely led by Malinowski, has resulted in neglect of Frazer's achievement. Such a reaction was not surprising, for hypothetical yet untestable evolutionary theories had multiplied endlessly in the early years of the present century. In rejecting these a new freedom was gained, but, alas, much that was solid in the work of a Frazer or a Westermarck was forgotten.

The English anthropological compilers and theorists who were either Frazer's disciples, like Edward Westermarck, Ernest Crawley, and Edwin Sidney Hartland, or opponents very much influenced by him, such as R. R. Marett and Andrew Lang, are mostly recognizable now as outside the field of anthropology, as folklorists or comparative religionists. In these areas, Frazer's influence continues strong, and one such Frazerian compiler, E. O. James, is still anachronistically producing Frazerian compendia in enormous numbers. As Freud's anthropologist, Frazer is still enshrined in psychoanalysis, where a comparable anachronism, Theodor Reik, is still engaged in turning out books like *Totem and Taboo*, all heavily indebted to Sir James.

It is in his original field of classical studies, however, that Frazer may have produced his greatest effect. In *Reminiscences of a Student's Life* in 1925, Jane Harrison recalls the overwhelming effect of *The Golden Bough*. She writes:

> The happy title of that book—Sir James Frazer has a veritable genius for titles—made it arrest the attention of scholars. They saw in comparative anthropology a serious subject actually capable of elucidating a Greek or Latin text. Tylor had written and spoken; Robertson Smith, exiled for heresy, had seen the Star in the East; in vain; we classical deaf-adders stopped our ears and closed our eyes; but at the mere sound of the magical words "Golden Bough" the scales fell—we heard and understood.

In a radio address printed in *The Listener* in 1954, Gilbert Murray recalls essentially the same experience. He writes:

> I remember the shock, the combined shock of interest and perhaps of horror, with which *The Golden Bough* burst upon classical scholars like me on its first appearance in 1890. Of course it was not absolutely our first introduction to anthropology. We knew something of Tylor and Andrew Lang and perhaps Mannhardt, perhaps even of Robertson Smith's sacred camel which had to be eaten alive before sunrise. But Frazer, for one thing, overpowered us with his mass of carefully ordered facts. We had heard of "the beastly devices of the heathen" but had not realised their great number and variety, had not understood the method which underlay their madness.

There is validity in Malinowski's final judgment, that more than anything else Frazer was in the line "of great humanists and classical scholars." In the work of Murray and the Cambridge ritualists—Harrison, Francis Cornford, and A. B. Cook—the influence of Frazer permanently transformed and revitalized the field of classics, and however much it may appear to have returned to its old deaf-adder ways in recent years (and Frazer was the first to swing back from his own insights), it will never be the same again. The application of these ideas from classical to medieval and modern literature by a brilliant series of literary critics—William Troy, Francis Fergusson, Herbert Weisinger, John Speirs, C. L. Barber and others—has given Frazer an importance in literary criticism at least equal to that of Marx and Freud.

In 1959 a new one-volume abridgement of *The Golden Bough*, *The New Golden Bough*, was published under the editorship of Theodor Gaster. It is a thoroughly misguided work, attempting to rescue Frazer as up-to-date anthropology by gutting his text, translating his clear and simple terminology into Gaster's opaque terminology, dismissing his theories, and bringing his references up to date. What we need is not a face-lifting of Frazer, but a machinery for better using Frazer in his own terms. Criterion should have published, not Gaster's revision, but the *best Golden Bough*, the 1890 two-volume edition, for what it is, an 1890 book. In addition, we badly need the publication of Frazer's correspondence, an adequate biography, and a single comprehensive index of all of Frazer's books.

The Golden Bough is not primarily anthropology, if it ever was, but a great imaginative vision of the human condition. Frazer had a genuine sense of the bloodshed and horror behind the gaiety of a maypole or a London-bridge-is-falling-down game, akin to Darwin's sense of the war to the death behind the face of nature bright with gladness, or Marx's apocalyptic vision of capital reeking from every pore with blood and dirt, or Freud's consciousness of the murderous and incestuous infantile wish. The key image of *The Golden Bough*, the king who slays the slayer and must himself be slain, corresponds to some universal principle we recognize in life. It caught the imagination not only of Freud and Bergson, Spengler and Toynbee, but of T. S. Eliot, and produced *The Waste Land*. F. Beck and W. Godin explain Soviet managerial mobility in *Russian Purge and the Extraction of Confession* by "the theory of the grove of Aricia"; John McNulty in a newspaper column sees a prize ring at Madison Square Garden as the sacred wood at Nemi.

In his address on the occasion of the foundation of the Frazer Lectureship in 1921, A. E. Housman spoke of Frazer as though he were comparable to a psychoanalyst, dragging the repressed past back into consciousness. *The Golden Bough*, Housman said, has become a forest. He continues:

> There you have gathered together, for the admonition of a proud and oblivious race, the scattered and fading relics of its foolish childhood, whether withdrawn from our view among savage folk and in distant countries, or lying unnoticed at our doors.

Gaster's foreword [see excerpt dated 1959] makes the comparison directly. He writes:

> Indeed, what Freud did for the individual, Frazer did for civilization as a whole. For as Freud deepened men's insight into the behavior of individuals by uncovering the ruder world of the subconscious, from which so much of it springs, so Frazer enlarged man's understanding of the behavior of societies by laying bare the primitive concepts and modes of thought which underlie and inform so many of their institutions and which persist, as a subliminal element of their culture, in their traditional folk customs.

H. N. Brailsford, in "The Golden Bough" in the *New Statesman and Nation* in 1941, adds the other two names. He writes:

> Darwin, whose disciple and continuer Frazer felt himself to be, had traced the origins and the evolution of our physical body: he gave us the record of our mental growth. He consciously used the same comparative method, and with Marx and Freud he ranks only after the founder of modern biology among the influences which have fixed the thinking of our day.

Frazer's revolution in human thought, Downie writes hopefully as the conclusion to his biography, is "as yet scarce realized." (pp. 436-40)

Stanley Edgar Hyman, "What Do You Dance?" and "Conclusion," in his The Tangled Bank: Darwin, Marx, Frazer and Freud as Imaginative Writers, *Atheneum, 1962, pp. 212-32, 425-48.*

I. C. JARVIE (essay date 1964)

[*Jarvie is an English-born Canadian educator, critic, and anthropologist. In the following excerpt from his study* The Revolution in Anthropology, *he contends that Bronislaw Malinowski "plotted and directed" a revolution in social anthropology, instigating a shift away from speculative genetic theories of human society toward intensive, thorough fieldwork. Contending that the Malinowskian approach does not answer the interest in people and societies that first attracts social anthropologists to this field of study, Jarvie calls for a "back to Frazer" movement in social anthropology.*]

My main contention in this book [*The Revolution in Anthropology*] has been that the revolution, however many benefits it brought, went wrong. This wasn't noticed at once but began to be only when the initial post-revolutionary enthusiasm and high hopes turned stale and flat. Social anthropology only came into professional academic life with Frazer's Liverpool chair in 1908, and that was honorary. It was established in the universities on a wave of enthusiasm created by Malinowski. But although popular in the 'twenties and 'thirties in the *avant-garde* way that Freud was popular, as an academic subject for undergraduates, it did not boom until the 'fifties. In the 'twenties and 'thirties, though, the few pioneers and their students had a precious thing: a messianic intellectual enthusiasm. Like marxists and freudians they felt a great truth had been revealed to them, and their job was to carry it forth. Today, there is boundless enthusiasm for departments and journals and teachers and fieldworkers, but there is little or no intellectual progress and so little or no intellectual enthusiasm. Perhaps the messianism had to be given up to get consolidation under way. The consolidating process has been marked, however, by the most tortuous disputes as to what the aims and methods of social anthropology are. Now it is surely a very curious position that in a period of consolidation, of training students, sending them to the field, building up a substantial literature, there should be widespread doubts and calls for rethinking the subject. Curious from one point of view but not perhaps from another. The revolution in anthropology was in many ways a typical political revolution. First there came the prophet and his messianic call to salvation. Then he was joined by the first followers whose enthusiasm was so great partly because they were an *avant-garde*, perhaps even a slightly persecuted *avant-garde,* or at least an *avant-garde* not sufficiently appreciated in the academic world. Then came the success of the revolution and the accession to power and the excitement and confusion which always follows. Out of the confusion emerged a drive for consolidation; and here the trouble always begins. Messianic activity leaves little time for going into the detail and the consequences of the doctrine. But consolidation amounts precisely to going over the doctrine in detail and working out the consequences. What if, then, the detail should turn out to be shaky and the consequences unpalatable? One answer would be: rethink. Another would be: pretend to rethink while actually trying not to.

My theory is that the second answer is at present tacitly accepted by social anthropologists. It would be easy to challenge my theory and to point to attempts to rethink seriously. The best example probably being a book by [Edmund] Leach called *Rethinking Anthropology*. But J. D. Freeman, incidentally an anthropologist whose work I greatly admire, has already given, in his review of that volume in *Man,* the reply I would make. Freeman argues that Leach's rethinking has been within the structural-functional framework. But in concentrating its energies on this level of analysis social anthropology

has ceased to be "the science of man" and has become little more than the science of man's customary social behaviour. This, in my view, is a retreat from the historic task of anthropology. The time has come, I would suggest, when we ought to turn to the rethinking of even more basic issues; and, for my part, I would hope that during the decades that lie ahead there will emerge a unified science of man. . . .

In other words, Freeman wants to see anthropologists go over from rethinking inside the framework to rethinking the framework. This is what I mean when I say the anthropologists have adopted the policy of pretending to rethink while not doing so. What they are trying to do is rectify with a minimum of rethinking. Dr. Marjorie Topley has expressed this in conversation by saying that attitudes to fieldwork among some social anthropologists have come to be rather like attitudes to the belief in the existence of God among some religious people. The belief in both cases has become so integrated into the lives of these people, that the tendency is to immerse themselves deeper and deeper into the activity of worshipping God, of fieldwork, simply in order to avoid the disturbing and perhaps catastrophic question "does God exist?," "is fieldwork worthwhile?" It is preferred not to ask such questions precisely because so much turns upon them. A very understandable reaction.

But if social anthropologists are afraid of it, why do they constantly play with the fire of pseudo-rethinking or even semi-rethinking? Mightn't they accidentally do some and mightn't it be catastrophic? Why don't they leave well alone and not go near any kind of rethinking? My answer to this is that honest intellectual curiosity drives them towards the question; that is to say, they try to rethink but have not carefully distinguished rethinking within the framework from rethinking the framework. But what is their intellectual curiosity about? About, I would say, the much-lauded revolution in anthropology. In a semi-intuitive way, perhaps, they know the revolution perverted the subject so that it is no longer the true science of man. And perhaps they fully know it. Why, then, should they bother with post-revolutionary social anthropology? Why not just get on with building a new and proper science of man? I suppose they have two good reasons for not giving up post-revolutionary social anthropology entirely, even if they fully know that it has been perverted. First, it is a good rule of method not to debunk a school or a tradition because it is in error. One is only justified in debunking if one considers the error silly. Certainly I, for one, would never think of calling the revolution in anthropology silly. What, then, does this same rule prescribe for traditions in error? It is very explicit. It says: criticise the error and rescue from the doctrines everything you can. Second, because social anthropology is the only candidate for the job of the science of man, and it is nearer than it seems at first glance to being the genuine science of man. That it is nearer than it seems is my explanation for the tortuous internecine disputes on the aims and methods of social anthropology. Fearful that they have betrayed their interest in man some anthropologists repeat the malinowskian catechism of function and fieldwork, to comfort themselves. Others, bolder spirits, know that their subject is on the right lines, play with the fire of rethinking, and constantly berate the others for standing pat. (E. R. Leach's function in this respect has almost become institutionalised: he stands for the peace in the feud, as Professor Gluckman might say. His stimulus keeps everyone awake but its more positive function is unclear.) Yet almost no one dares to face the prospect of a complete revaluation of the post-revolutionary aims and methods of the subject as compared and contrasted with what it is conjectured the aims and methods of the science of man ought to be. They dare not face it because if the inquiry turns out badly their life's careers are at stake.

Such an attitude is very understandable and easy to sympathise with. My view is that it is quite unnecessary because social anthropology is *so* successful, despite its recent stagnation, that any criticism, however severe, is likely in the end to strengthen and invigorate the subject, rather than debilitate and undermine it. The whole drift of my argument in this book is that a purge of some methodological error (and, e.g. the consequences of such a purge like adopting selective fieldwork, but this is optional) will enable a new leap forward to take place. All along I have maintained that social anthropology is the Science of Man and that it is its present *impasse* which is of concern. I believe that what I have argued here is a revaluation of its aims and methods that will reaffirm the status of social anthropology as the science of man *and will change almost nothing in the organisation and teaching of the subject;* all changes will be presentational. They will be nonetheless vital for all that, because they may get social anthropology out of the structural-functional rut.

I am able to propose this "reinterpret but change almost nothing" line because it is my view that all that needs to be gone back on is the history of the subject; and in particular the history of the revolution is too much an official myth. What is needed is a new appreciation of what it is that happened in the revolution that has caused the subsequent stagnation and soul-searching confusion over aims and methods. I hope and believe I can provide that account but because it is a confused and difficult question I shall do so in two ways. First I shall present my interpretation straight, with no argument or documentation, then I shall proceed to detail it. My account will thus, I hope, be seen to be coherent, a necessary but by no means a sufficient condition of its being true. After giving my hypothetical historical reconstruction of the revolution in anthropology I shall sketch the subsequent developments we will deal with, also as coherently as I can. Where the story is more straightforward I think one should get down to cases right away; yet this is not such a case; when first I wrote this without preliminaries it was unintelligible. Therefore I unblushingly request indulgence for doing it twice.

Bronislaw Malinowski plotted and directed the revolution in social anthropology. It was a genuine revolution, aiming to overthrow the establishment of Frazer and Tylor and their ideas; but mainly it was against Frazer. Frazer committed a number of crimes and thought-crimes, the post-revolutionary literature has sensationally revealed. He had a thesis, of an evolutionary and historical character, of the development of magic (most primitive), religion (next most primitive), and science (least primitive but also liable to be superseded). This seemed to offend against the beliefs of those who believed in the unity of mankind. It was reinforced by his refusal to live among, or even to go to see, savages, and by his affection for his armchair. Frazer also enjoyed a great *avant-garde* extra-academic success—when Freud and T. S. Eliot thought about anthropology they thought about Frazer. Moreover Frazer was a classically-trained amateur scholar, refreshingly unpreoccupied with the methodological status of his studies. He was unsystematic and unscientific and relied on dubious material.

For having the burden of all these crimes, Malinowski declared Frazer's regime had to be overthrown.

One should not be misled by the curiously affectionate personal relations between Malinowski and Frazer. Admittedly Frazer wrote a nice foreword to *Argonauts* and Malinowski wrote a magnanimous tribute to Frazer after the latter's death [see excerpt dated 1941]; but this should not disguise the fact that Malinowski started a war for control and won it.

Frazer, no doubt, believed he was doing the science of man, but he was not given to going on about "science." Malinowski's revolution took terribly seriously the claim to scientific status and made it the basis of his revolution. No doubt what Malinowski intended was to preserve the science of man and make it really a science. This was why he had to overthrow Frazer and his influence. Frazer, while full of ideas, was like a man who pretended to be a scientist but who had never been inside a laboratory and who had never personally checked the results that were communicated to him. What was needed then was a methodological revolution; new ways and new standards for building the science of man.

Malinowski's new ways were fieldwork ("come down off the verandah"), and functionalism ("study the ritual, not the belief"). They were both very powerful methods; they made mincemeat of some bothersome problems and they made the intellectual theories of the evolutionists look silly. In all these ways Malinowski had provided what was called for. Unfortunately, however, action is only one category in sociology, there are also the unintended consequences of our actions. It seems as if Malinowski had pioneered a method that was too powerful, it got out of hand. I mean this quite specifically. To begin with, Malinowski intended a revolution in method, the better to achieve the aim of discussing the unity of mankind, and instituted what turned out to be a revolution of aims. But this result was more than was expected. The difference between Frazer's work and Malinowski's is not merely in methodology, as it should have been. In Malinowski's hands the science of man was twisted into an inductivist and relativist science, with no clear connections with the basic metaphysical problem of the unity of mankind at all. In all this I think the role of Radcliffe-Brown was that of a consolidator. His contribution was to strengthen the doctrine of functionalism by bringing in the element of structure; in almost all else connected with the revolution he went along with Malinowski. Although they disagreed, over basic needs, for example, he did not come to dominate the scene until Malinowski left for the States just before the war.

So much for my historical reconstruction of the revolution.

My thesis is that social anthropologists come to the subject full of interest in people and society. They are entranced by the idea that these interests can be given scientific authority. But in learning how to "scientise" their interest they actually lose or forget what their primary interests are. Something like an unconscious confidence trick is played on them. But they are left suspicious that something is missing from the science they have been taught. What about Man, they ask? "Fieldwork," is the answer they get. Yet Lévi-Strauss is the only post-radcliffe-brownian social anthropologist I know of who has written a really magnificent and humane book (his *World on the Wane*) on Man as he is seen by an anthropologist and a fieldworker. All the rest is cold, dehumanised, structuralist sociology. The early monographs of Malinowski, Firth and Schapera are full of "human interest" but their later works are less so. My plea, then, is for a "Back to Frazer" movement, or for an "Over to Lévi-Strauss" one. (pp. 170-75)

> *I. C. Jarvie, "The Aims and Methods of Social Anthropology," in his* The Revolution in Anthropology, *The Humanities Press, 1964, pp. 170-224.*

EDMUND LEACH   (essay date 1965)

[*Leach is an English educator, critic, and anthropologist. In the following excerpt, he attacks I. C. Jarvie's assessment of Frazer's and Malinowski's respective roles in contemporary anthropology (see excerpt above), denouncing in particular Frazer's scholarship, influence, literary style, and lasting importance, all of which he pronounces negligible.*]

The study of man must be central for everyone but Anthropology is just another -ology. Opinion may be about evenly divided as to whether it is the study of apes or the name of an obscure religious sect. Even so, every now and then, a professional anthropologist becomes an international "celebrity," and one wonders why. Of the living, only Margaret Mead has quite achieved this, but among the recent dead there are at least two others, Sir James Frazer, the author of *The Golden Bough,* and Bronislaw Malinowski, "who wrote something or other about sex."

Public renown need not imply professional esteem. Contemporary anthropologists for the most part consider Malinowski to be a major figure; they decry Frazer as a mere miser of facts. Anyone who doubts this need only take a look at the two latest general textbooks of the subject [*Social Anthropology*, by P. Bohannon, (1963), and *Other Cultures*, by John Beattie (1964)]. Both authors take for granted a whole set of Malinowski's concepts and build their thinking into this frame of reference; Frazer is treated as an historical figure of quite secondary significance, worth mentioning only because he was in grievous error.

But perhaps the experts are prejudiced. Dr. Jarvie, a philosopher and pupil of Karl Popper, has recently presented Malinowski as the false prophet who led British anthropologists into the wilderness of profitless fact-collecting, whereas his Frazer appears as a hero of righteousness whose vigorous and original theories clearly marked out the path of scientific virtue [see excerpt above].

It is very natural that Dr. Jarvie, as a good Popperite, should want to stimulate the thinking of his anthropological colleagues by challenging their dearest assumptions; and certainly he will be in no way abashed if I argue that his theses are false and untenable. It is just as well to get the record straight. There is a very wide discrepancy between Dr. Jarvie's account of the recent history of British anthropology and what actually happened. The living prototypes of his "Frazer" and "Malinowski" died respectively in 1941 and 1942. The myth is worth investigating.

"Frazer" is admired by Dr. Jarvie because he engaged in "comparative sociology," the comparison of similar social phenomena occurring in different contexts of time and space.

"Frazer" was a man "with lots of ideas" which is the Popperite way of saying that he was always ready to guess about causal connections linking together the facts at his disposal. The circumstance that very few of Frazer's "conjectures" seem in the least plausible and that, on the rare occasions when they can be tested, they almost invariably prove to be wrong does not worry Dr. Jarvie in the least. From his point of view, it is the method and not the truth that matters.

It seems that "comparative sociology" can help us to understand regularities in historical sequences. When investigating an exotic institution from a primitive culture we should first consider the logic of the situation as it appears to us. This will give us a theory about how the members of such a culture might be expected to behave. If we then go on to interpret our actual observations, on a comparative basis and in the light of this same ethnocentric situational logic, we shall be led to discover regularities which will enable us to predict the circumstances under which institutions of this particular kind are likely to arise and develop. Now Frazer, too, was interested in historical process and his judgments about "savages" were always based on a highly ethnocentric assessment of the logic of the savage's situation. So Frazer's "Evolutionism" must be considered sound as methodology even if it led to all the wrong conclusions.

Dr. Jarvie also greatly admires the whole ethos of the library-bound scholar of which Sir James Frazer was such a superlative example. He believes, as Frazer believed, that first-hand experience of primitive peoples is a discomfort which the more intelligent anthropologist can well afford to do without. He thinks that the best anthropologists will do their best work while cogitating about the writings of others. This mental activity will (or may) lead to useful speculations about the nature of Human Society in general. Dr. Jarvie does not claim that Frazer's own speculations were particularly illuminating, but he approves of what Frazer tried to do and of the way he tried to do it. He appreciates that this Frazerian manner may be linked with a deep-seated contempt for nine-tenths of the human race; that he is prepared to accept. He also accepts Frazer's literary style as "exhilarating"; he supposes (quite erroneously) that Frazer was an unqualified atheist; and he credits Frazer with an academic status which he never possessed.

The complementary disapproval of "Malinowski" is not so straightforward. In the Jarvie schema, "Malinowski" is the hostile antithesis of "Frazer." In the early 'twenties this aspiring and ambitious man was preoccupied with the destruction of "Frazer's" reputation: the jealous "son" had started a revolution against the all-powerful "father." This is bizarre—because the living Malinowski was the most persistent and devoted disciple of the real Frazer. In 1926 he wrote of *The Golden Bough* that:

> No sooner had I begun to read this great work than I became immersed in and enslaved by it . . . and became bound to the service of Frazerian anthropology [see Additional Bibliography].

Even sixteen years later, although he could now take an objective view of Frazer's limitations, he was still in thrall:

> His [Frazer's] enormous creative influence surprises sometimes even his devoted admirer when confronted by one of the naïve theoretical arguments from *The Golden Bough* or some other of his volumes. His inability to convince seems to contradict his power to convert and to inspire [see excerpt dated 1944].

Dr. Jarvie also disapproves of Malinowski because of the way he emphasised the value of original field work. Dr. Jarvie appears to be an anthropologist *manqué;* philosophy was his second love. He now justifies his infidelity by saying that the first lady would have been most uncomfortable.

"Frazer the Evolutionist" and "Malinowski the Functionalist" represent the contrast between a concern with how things have come to be as they are and a concern with how things, as they are, are interrelated with one another. For Dr. Jarvie, functionalist investigations are pointless because they cannot give causal explanations of historical sequences; in contrast "the evolutionists were answering different questions from those Malinowski was interested in, but theirs were satisfactory answers to the questions they had posed themselves." This is a surprising opinion for a follower of Professor Popper. What are the facts of the case?

The continuing celebrity of Sir James Frazer (Dr. Jarvie apart) is an astonishing phenomenon. There are now two quite separate one-volume abridgments of the huge thirteen volume *Golden Bough,* and both apparently have a steady sale. Who are the buyers? What do they get from their reading?

From one point of view (the evolution of his world fame), the most important single fact in the career of the historical Frazer is that in 1896, at the age of 42, he married Lily Grove, a French widow, who thereafter made the enlargment of her husband's public image her sole preoccupation. It was an outstandingly successful public relations operation, and it has contributed to the distortions of the legend. Worldly success in the form of a Knighthood, an Order of Merit, and strings of Honorary Degrees only started coming in around 1914, and it is this perhaps which has led Dr. Jarvie to imagine that in the early 1920s, when Malinowski was in the ascendant, Frazer was the securely established leader of his profession. That was not the case; Frazer's personal influence was by that time insignificant. His strictly academic reputation had begun to fade before 1900. In later years he had great renown; he maintained a voluminous correspondence; and his books were always widely reviewed. But it does not appear that his views were highly regarded. Sometimes the style of his critics suggests that they might have been his close disciples, but this too is deceptive. The leading anthropologists of his time (including Frazer himself) were all close imitators of two much more brilliant men: E. B. Tylor and W. Robertson Smith. Frazer was an outstanding representative of the anthropology of his day, but that day had ended by 1910. For the next fifteen years British historical anthropology was completely dominated by the diffusionist views of Elliot Smith and W. J. Perry; as for the sociologists, they were taking all their cues from the school of Emile Durkheim in Paris. Frazer had ceased to matter.

Frazer's original competence was in the classics and here his skill was very great indeed. Classical erudition is common enough but even so Frazer's carefully edited translations of Pausanias' *Description of Greece* and of Ovid's *Fasti* are outstanding of their kind. The source of Frazer's fame lay elsewhere; his colleagues were entranced by the novel use to which he applied the "comparative method" which he had taken over from Tylor. The first (two-volume) edition of *The Golden Bough* appeared in 1890. This was acclaimed on the quite specious ground that it revealed

> comparative anthropology [as] a serious study actually capable of elucidating a Greek or Latin text.

Classical scholars have always been frustrated by *lacunæ* in the records, and perhaps the "comparative method" could be used to make good this deficiency.

The avowed purpose of *The Golden Bough,* as expressed in the first chapter, was to investigate certain classical accounts concerning the rites associated with the worship of Diana at Nemi in southern Italy. The accounts are very incomplete, and Frazer agreed that there is not enough direct evidence to justify any particular interpretation. He proposed, however, to fill in the gaps by resorting to analogy. First he postulated that the Priest of Nemi was deemed to be the spouse of Diana; then, having cited examples of ritual theogamy from Babylon, Egypt, Athens, Eleusis, Russia, Sweden, Gaul, Peru, North America, Bengal, West and East Africa, and the Maldive Islands, he concluded:

> The evidence may, therefore, lend some countenance to the conjecture that in the sacred grove of Nemi where the powers of vegetation and of water manifested themselves in the fair forms of shady woods, tumbling cascades and glassy lake, a marriage like that of our King and Queen of May was annually celebrated between the mortal King of the Wood and the immortal Queen of the Wood, Diana. . . .

This, I may say, is a typical example of the style which admirers find so exhilarating. In fact, of course, the "evidence" is totally irrelevant to the "conjecture," and it was not very long before this irrelevance came to be fairly generally appreciated. Thereafter the interest of the professional classicists waned rather rapidly.

In the much narrower field of professional anthropology Frazer's standing was eminent and his phenomenal industry inspired awe; but his contributions to theory evoked no respect at all. Since he was a thoroughly bad public speaker, engaged in no teaching, and had no immediate pupils, his reputation rested exclusively on published work. This is bulky rather than profound, and even the bulk is deceptive.

Frazer's career as an author extended from 1884-1938. His output, excluding multiple editions of the same work, fills at least two yards of shelf space; yet in all this vast mass of print the total amount of material which represents a genuinely original contribution by Frazer himself probably adds up to only a few hundred pages. The rest consists of excerpts from the writings of others, sometimes quoted verbatim, but more often rephrased to suit the sentimental lilt which Frazer considered to be the essential quality of fine writing. Quite explicitly he thought of himself as making a contribution to literature rather than to science, and it does not seem to have occurred to him that in "improving" his sources he might also be distorting them. He was perfectly frank about his procedures. Commenting on the difference between the original quotations recorded in his notebooks and the passages which appear in his own published works, Frazer wrote:

> [The notebook extracts] are written for the most part in a plain, straightforward way, the authors contenting themselves with describing in simple language the things which they have seen or had heard reported by competent native informants. Few, if any, possess that magic charm of style which, by firing the imagination or touching the heart, can alone confer what we fondly call immortality upon a work of literature.

Frazer knew better, and how right he was! Clearly there have always been many who, like Dr. Jarvie, "find Frazer glorious and thrilling reading."

All the same the diligence is quite extraordinary. A doubtful "conjecture" does not become less doubtful by stating it twenty times over: but even the most sceptical critic finds himself yielding in fascinated incredulity as Frazer piles up his mountains of recondite "evidence." (pp. 24-7)

Frazer's strictly academic reputation seems . . . to have passed its peak before 1900. That year saw the publication of the second (3-volume) edition of *The Golden Bough* which was widely reviewed. The anthropologists were notably cool. Andrew Lang was positively insulting; Hartland and Haddon praised Frazer's zeal but were caustic about his theories. Ten years later Frazer had become a bore; at the tail of a long review of *Totemism and Exogamy* Hartland (in *Man*) drops into mock Frazerian phraseology and hints that the great man has become prematurely old.

Frazer could well afford this patronising disrespect by his professional colleagues, for he had other publics which were more rewarding and more influential. One of these came from the ranks of liberal-minded "modern churchmen" who felt a special commitment to discover the true historical origins of Christianity. For them the passages in *The Golden Bough* which draw attention to parallels between Christianity and other Middle Eastern cults were both disturbing and fascinating. This material had originally occupied less than 100 pages, but in response to special demand it was blown up into a separate volume (*Adonis, Attis, Osiris*). By 1914 this book alone took up two volumes.

Frazer's upbringing had been rigorously Presbyterian; although in later life his attitude towards established religion became increasingly cynical, his direct references to Christianity are always carefully ambiguous. As a result, *The Golden Bough* was treated as an ammunition depot by members of the Rationalist Association—and as a source book of scholarly information by professional Christians. [The critic adds in a footnote that "The widely held view that *The Golden Bough* 'explicitly sets out to discredit present-day religion' (Jarvie), derives from hostile reviews of the second edition.". . .]

When the knighthood came in 1914, Frazer's fame must still have been narrowly confined, for *The Golden Bough,* now a work of twelve volumes, was surely a daunting prospect for librarian and reader alike. It was the publication of the 1922 abridgment, timed to synchronise with a flood of public honours, which finally made this classic work the kind of fashionable book which every educated man must at least pretend to have read. Thereafter Frazer became *the* anthropologist—and the merits of the case ceased to matter. Something of this *cachet* still remains.

Just what the book is all about it is difficult to say; there is something for everybody. The motif of the sacrifice of the Divine King (with its uncomfortable association with Christianity) and the entanglement of this theme with vegetation gods and the magical preservation of fertility persists throughout; but the author's more general concern is with the worldwide irrationality of customs. Huge chunks of highly elaborate and highly valued human behaviour serve no practical purpose (judged by the standard of late 19th-century European intellectuals). Frazer could not believe that people should consciously choose to waste their time in this way. Surely the actors who devote so much effort to "ritual" must think they are doing something useful? They are mistaken, and Frazer will show us the nature of their error.

In his 'teens at Glasgow University, Frazer had studied under Sir William Thomson (Lord Kelvin) and through him had acquired a set of very simple mechanistic ideas about the nature of scientific truth. For Frazer, science is the true association of cause and effect. Magic is the corresponding false association. Primitive Man, being childish and ignorant, has much magic but little science. The modern European, being more adult and wiser, has less magic and more science. Religion, which is Frazer's third major category of action, is less precisely conceived. The notion of deity arises through an intellectual confusion. Primitive Man is groping after the definition of such abstract ideas as "power," "life," "fertility," "soul"; but he gets these ideas mixed up, and he fails to distinguish clearly between attributes of Man (*e.g.*, authority, human sexuality) and attributes of Nature (*e.g.*, vegetable fertility). Religious practices then develop out of magical techniques. When magical attempts to control the course of nature fail, the primitive mind conjures up deities, super-magicians from an unseen world, whose powers can be invoked to make good the deficiencies of mere human magic. By implication, the progress of science, which replaces magic, should make religion unnecessary. But even in the abridged edition it takes Frazer four closely printed pages to say this, and even then the argument is ambiguous. He does commit himself to the proposition that: "In short, religion, regarded as an explanation of nature, is displaced by science." Did he really suppose that religion is nothing more than "an explanation of nature"? The reader of *The Golden Bough* is left to guess.

But this much is clear enough: for Frazer, all ritual is based in fallacy, either an erroneous belief in the magical powers of men or an equally erroneous belief in the magical powers of imaginary deities. The overall effect is to represent "savages" as stupid. They have the simple-minded ignorance of children which is sharply contrasted with the sophisticated highly-trained mind of the rational European. Europeans, too, have their childish moments but, in general, the dichotomy is clear: the White man is wise; Black, Brown, and Yellow men are foolish. Frazer was writing precisely at the point when European colonial expansion had reached its peak; it must have been consoling for many liberal-minded imperialists to find that the "White Man's Burden" could be justified by such detached scholarly procedures! And this may well be an important factor in the enduring popularity of the book.

Perhaps, too, there are some who can still find pleasure in the sado-masochistic sexuality which is a prominent feature of much of Frazer's subject-matter. Frazer was so anxious not to give offence that any reference to genitalia or an act of copulation is likely to be wrapped up in a complex periphrasis which lasts for half a page. But prudery of this sort is two-sided. The devotees of Attis sometimes expressed their faith by an act of self-castration: in recording the gory details of this ritual Frazer spreads himself over thirteen pages, including long, tantalising, small-printed footnotes in the original Latin and Greek. Such drawn-out agony offers all the delights of polite pornography.

Judged by modern standards Frazer's scholarly procedures are glaringly defective. While he was scrupulous in citing his authorities, he never assessed their quality. If we trouble to check up on his footnotes we find that the most trivial observation of the most ignorant traveller is given exactly the same weight and credibility as the most careful assessment of an experienced ethnographer. Worse still, he was constantly "improving" his sources.

It is difficult to illustrate the consequences of such manipulations. Frazer started out with a number of basic assumptions: "savages are afraid of the dead," "savages have childlike imaginations," and so on. The "evidence" was put in to illustrate these principles. Since the relevance of the "evidence" to the principle is seldom obvious, Frazer helped the reader along with a liberal ration of "conjectures." Alternatively, he simply modified his source material so as to make it fit more closely with his hypothesis. The truth of the hypothesis is thus invariably demonstrated by the evidence!

Consider the following example. In the Trobriands, in Melanesia, every village holds a month-long harvest festival *(milamala)* during which the spirits of deceased ancestors *(baloma)* are supposed to return to their erstwhile homes. Malinowski's 7,000-word ethnographic account of this ritual was published in 1916, and it is one of the most penetrating and convincing records in the whole of ethnographic literature. Malinowski asserts categorically that the Trobrianders feel no fear of their spiritual guests, who are there as friends. His own summary is:

> During the *milamala* the *baloma* are present in the village. They return in a body from Tuma to their own village, where preparations are made to receive them, where special platforms are erected to accommodate them, and where customary gifts are offered to them, and whence, after the full moon is over, they are ceremonially but unceremoniously driven away.

The driving out of the spirits is a children's lark which Malinowski likens to Guy Fawkes day.

Frazer's account antedates Malinowski's. His source is a missionary, the Rev. Dr. George Brown, whose brief account is quite consistent with Malinowski's longer study:

> The dances and feasts lasted many days. When these were finished all the people gathered together, shouted, beat the posts of the houses, overturned everything where a spirit might be hiding, drove away the spirits and the feasts were over. The explanation given is that the spirits were thus made wealthy for another year. They had shared in the feasts, had seen the dances, and heard the songs. The spirits of the yams were theirs, the spirits of the property displayed were also theirs, and they were now made wealthy and fully provided for and so they were driven out.

Frazer's citation of this material comes in a section entitled "The periodic expulsion of evils." Note carefully the modifications of Dr. Brown's text (italics added):

> When the festivities were over, all the people gathered together and expelled the spirits from the village by shouting, beating the posts of the houses, and overturning everything under which *a wily spirit* might be supposed to lurk. The explanation which the people gave to the missionary was that they had entertained and feasted the spirits and provided them with riches, and it was now time for them to take their departure. Had they not seen the dances and heard the songs and *gorged themselves on the souls* of the yams, and appropriated the souls of the money and all the other fine things set out on the platform? What more could the spirits want? So out they must go. Among the Hos of Togoland in West Africa the expulsion of evils is performed annually before people eat the new yams.

By intruding emotive words like "wily" and "gorged," substituting "soul" for "spirit," and juxtaposing the "expulsion of evils" by the Hos, the kindly Trobriand ancestors are ardoitly converted into evil demons!

Such tampering with source materials seems to me indefensible. I find it quite impossible to accept Dr. Jarvie's view that Frazer's explanations, though defective, were as good as could be expected in the circumstances of the time.

During the first twenty-five years of this century, the monumental industry invested in *The Golden Bough* served to surround its author with an aura of veneration, so that he was often credited with insights which he never possessed.

Although the Divine King—also a Dying God, who is slain as his physical powers begin to wane in order that the fertility of the realm may be sustained—had been the hero of *The Golden Bough* from the very beginning, it is only in Vol. 4 of the 3rd Edition that we meet with a clear-cut example of this strange institution. All that went before had been only "conjecture." This was because it was only in 1910 that C. G. Seligman could claim to have verified that the Shilluk of the Sudan really did treat their kings just as Frazer said. This material was immediately incorporated into Frazer's new edition of *The Dying God* (this book rates as Vol. IV of the 12-volume edition of *The Golden Bough*). Likewise, Malinowski at first maintained that his studies of Trobriand garden magic fully confirmed the brilliant intuitive insights of the Master. Such retrospective confirmations of hypothesis were felt to be clear demonstrations of Frazer's genius.

But the disciples were mistaken and bemused by faith. We now feel certain that the Shilluk did *not* murder their Divine Kings, and we see quite plainly that Malinowski's view of magic is directly antithetical to that of his predecessor, for where Malinowski interpreted magic as an evocation of the mysterious, a procedure closely allied to religion, Frazer saw no more than a childishly mistaken attempt to achieve the technically impossible.

The trouble with Frazer is that he leaves no room for the imagination. A myth must always be a direct transcription of a rite and *vice versa*. If myth tells of the killing of a god-king, then the only possible origin of such a story is that an actual god-king was actually killed. The modern anthropologist, with his more immediate experience of how myth and ritual are interconnected, is much more cautious. For example, animal sacrifice is a very widespread human institution which, being irrational, must always be justified by myth. Observed *in situ*, two features of such sacrifice are easily recognised: firstly, the effect of the sacrifice is to improve the "ritual condition" (the state of purity) of the donor; secondly, there is a direct symbolic association between the donor and the animal that is killed. In a mystical sense, the donor improves the state of his own divinity by destroying a mundane part of himself. This, of course, is a thoroughly non-rational procedure, but it is fully in accord with mythological stories which tell how "in the beginning" there was a god-king who was killed (as a human being) in order that he should become an immortal god. *Some* of Frazer's "dying god stories" are accountable in this way but others may have quite a different source. If, in any particular instance, we have detailed information about a set of sacrificial rituals and the mythology that goes with them, we are certainly likely to find a structural consistency between the ritual and the mythology; but we cannot take short cuts and infer rite from myth or myth from rite in the way that Frazer tried to do. In this respect he was quite fundamentally in error.

I suppose that Dr. Jarvie might argue that it is precisely because Frazerian hypotheses have been refuted that they were worth making in the first place. No one can deny that when *The Golden Bough* first appeared in 1890 it caused a stir. It didn't actually say anything which had not been said before: but people took notice of it and started arguing: so it can be said to have advanced the subject of anthropology even if it added little to the sum of human knowledge. But Dr. Jarvie's further defence of "Frazer, the Evolutionist" against "Malinowski, the Functionalist" on the basis of the former's pre-Popperite enlightenment is pressing paradox too far.

In the first place, there is no more poverty-stricken form of historicism than late 19th-century anthropological "evolutionism." Lewis Morgan's *Ancient Society* (1877) was given the Marxist *imprimatur* by no less a figure than Friedrich Engels himself (in his *Der Ursprung der Familie* of 1884). On the other hand, the living Frazer was only a half-hearted sort of evolutionist. He tagged along with the assumptions of his predecessor, E. B. Tylor, and paid token respect to the notion that anthropology can reveal "the origins" of institutions. But this for Frazer was never a central issue, and his accumulations of ethnographic quotation might have been fitted equally well to any other frame. *Folklore in the Old Testament* is not tied to an evolutionist framework at all, and even in the earlier works the matter of time scale is irrelevant.

Frazer was concerned with what he called "mental anthropology," or the universals of individual psychology. He thought he could explain savage customs by supposing that the mental processes of the savage are those of a modern child. The much more sociological emphasis of the orthodox evolutionist with its concern for whole "stages of social development" lay quite outside Frazer's range of interests.

On the other hand, the living Malinowski was never seriously opposed to evolutionism though he was always willing to have a dig at the more preposterous form of conjectural history postulated by Lewis Morgan and Robert Briffault. Dr. Jarvie seems to imagine that Malinowski's formal adoption of a "functionalist" creed meant that thereafter he evaded all attempt to grapple with the sociological analysis of historical change. The facts are entirely otherwise. Not only in his posthumous book *Freedom and Civilization* (1947) thoroughly evolutionist in tone but nearly all the writings of the last five years of his life are concerned with problems of developmental process ("culture change").

Finally, we may note that whereas Frazer's "ideas" ("conjectures"), which Dr. Jarvie so admires, were only produced so as to force the ethnographic records into Frazer's determinist mould, Malinowski's theory of fieldwork, which Dr. Jarvie so despises, corresponds very closely to that of Professor Popper's ideal scientist. When Dr. Jarvie says "you cannot collect facts without a theory," he is quoting Malinowski verbatim. Frazer thought exactly the opposite.

This does not mean that what Malinowski said corresponds exactly to what Malinowski did; nor does it mean that either Malinowski or Professor Popper is correct about the way that scientists actually achieve their results. It is simply that by his own criteria Dr. Jarvie ought to judge Frazer's methodology deplorable. But then I am writing about Frazer and not "Frazer," and there's the rub. (pp. 28-32)

Both [Frazer and Malinowski] seem to have been more concerned with the plaudits of the gallery than with the pursuit of truth. Both made a cult of the outrageous, Frazer by cynical comments on religion, Malinowski by challenging English sexual morality. But in all other respects they at first seem notably different. Judged by what they did, what they wrote, and the way they set about propagating their views, they appear as polar types, and in the mythology of modern undergraduate anthropology (as well as in the pages of Dr. Jarvie's book) they are just that: Frazer who deals in items of custom drawn out of context from here, there, and everywhere, and takes no account at all of individuals; Malinowski who constantly emphasises the importance of the total social context, and never for a moment forgets the essential unities of time and place and *dramatis personae*. Yet in an odd way the interests of the two men were very much the same, and at their grandest, they spoke in much the same language.

For both, the field of greatest professional renown was that of magic and religion and primitive psychology. There were important technical points of disagreement. Malinowski understood the expressive nature of ritual behaviour in a way that Frazer did not, and he is inclined to merge magic with religion rather than magic with science. He did not consider it a sign of intrinsic inferiority that a man should believe in miracles. Malinowski and Frazer both accepted Robertson Smith's thesis that ritual is to be understood as a manifestation of belief (dogma, myth); but they use this insight very differently. Frazer writes as if myth and ritual were interchangeable—if he finds the record of a myth, he "conjectures" as to the nature of the corresponding ritual, and *vice versa*. Malinowski sticks firmly to the observable evidence; the myth is a "charter for social action," but only if demonstrably so: no guessing. Yet so far as the Common Reader is concerned the similarities are more striking than the differences.

Frazer was eager to outline the psychology of Primitive Man, thought of as a unity. In all Frazer's writings the immense diversity of human culture is treated as a manifestation of just a single element—the simple-minded childishness of the savage, his ignorance, his lack of understanding of cause and effect. And why not? If there is indeed "a psychic unity of mankind," Frazer was surely justified in developing a synthetic picture out of multiple parts. The parts come indifferently from all corners of the globe and have no chronological unity, but if Primitive Man is a unity then the diversity of source material cannot matter. We should be able to understand the Priest of Nemi by looking at what goes on in the Maldive Islands.

Malinowski went about things the other way round. He concentrated exclusively on one small group of "savages" and looked at them under a sociological microscope. But he too, like Frazer, postulated a psychological unity of mankind and gradually step by step found himself talking, not about the Trobrianders in their uniqueness, but about Primitive Man in his generality. And why not? Why should a Trobriand Islander be deemed any more, or less, typical of the human race than the Priest of Nemi?

And here, perhaps, we begin to see the roots of their popularity. "Typical Man" may not be a very satisfactory kind of concept from the scientific point of view, but it is surely of interest to all of us.

For the professional anthropologist, Malinowski has other virtues (and other vices) than those which I have considered here; and I need not pursue further my disagreements (and occasional agreements) with Dr. Jarvie. Malinowski made contributions to many fields which Frazer never touched—language, kinship, primitive law, and economic relations in particular. Anyone with close knowledge of the subject must concede that Malinowski has left his personal mark on contemporary anthropology in a way that Frazer has not. He was a much less trivial scholar than my cursory and biased comments might suggest. But that is not the point.

My problem at the outset was to consider why, every now and then, an eminent anthropologist should rate as a "Celebrity." What is there about a Frazer and a Malinowski (or a Margaret Mead) which gives public fame as well as professional distinction? My account suggests an answer.

Frazer and Malinowski in their different ways were both prepared to make sweeping generalisations about human nature itself. Frazer could never have seriously expected that his general reader would be terribly interested in what did or did not go on at Nemi in 200 B.C., and the reader of Malinowski can get along very well without worrying as to whether the Trobriand Islands lie North or South of the Equator or East or West of longitude 180°. Both authors are really talking about Mankind, *i.e.*, about you and me. It is because each of us can recognise in their pages the savage within us that we feel the excitement of insight, the unverifiable validity of a statement of genius.

There are many lesser, more pedantic men who in some ways can be considered much better anthropologists. But the public which has given these two a special accolade is not at fault. (pp. 35-6)

> Edmund Leach, "Frazer and Malinowski: On the 'Founding Fathers'," *in* Encounter, *Vol. XXV, No. 5, November, 1965, pp. 24-36.*

I. C. JARVIE   (essay date 1966)

[*In the following excerpt, Jarvie responds to Leach's attack upon Frazer's reputation.*]

Dr. Edmund Leach's article on Frazer and Malinowski [see excerpt above] is readable, packed with interesting and not easily accessible material on the history of anthropological studies, and I'm sure I'm not alone among *Encounter* readers in having learnt a lot from it. However, it is difficult to accept Leach's rich material just as he presents it. In fact there are flagrant contradictions in several of the main points of the article which would have to be smoothed out before it would be possible to tackle his view of Frazer and Malinowski as a possible account of "what actually happened."

Leach's view is that Frazer was "a voracious library mole," "a mere miser of facts" who took what few ideas he had from Tylor and Robertson Smith; Malinowski was a vivid and colourful writer and an inspiring teacher, but "was often careless" and

> neither Frazer nor Malinowski appears particularly laudable. Both men seem to have been more concerned with the plaudits of the gallery than with the pursuit of truth.

Why they received the "plaudits of the gallery" is no doubt a serious sociological problem, but it is not so important as their status as seekers of the truth. This especially with respect to Frazer, who gets grossly mistreated in Leach's article.

Leach and I agree that Malinowski was intellectually important and academically influential. Also, that Frazer was once academically influential and is no longer so among anthropologists. Yet we disagree sharply, it seems, in that I think Frazer was and still is intellectually important, and that he is underrated at present, especially among anthropologists; while Leach thinks he was not intellectually important and his academic influence rightly disappeared after 1910. Clearly we disagree less about the sociological facts of Frazer's reputation than about values—that is, about the true evaluation of Frazer's contribution to anthropological knowledge. And though it seems clear that this is our disagreement, I do not think it is clear to Leach, or that it becomes clear from his article.

Against my view that Malinowski ousted Frazer from the leadership of the anthropological world in a father-killing revolution, Leach holds that Frazer had ceased to be an anthropological leader by 1910 at the latest, and moreover, Malinowski thought the world of Frazer. Thus Malinowski neither needed to overthrow Frazer nor was inclined to do so.

It is true that Malinowski thought the world of Frazer: "In . . . (1923) he contributed two pieces to *Nature*. The first was a long review of . . . *The Golden Bough*. (Dr. Jarvie should study this item; Malinowski's praise of Frazer is exuberant and unqualified.)"

Such praise in no way tells against Malinowski trying to oust Frazer. The point of calling it "father-killing," of course, was that Malinowski's attitude to Frazer was ambivalent: one *loves* one's father. But all this would be unnecessary if Leach could show Frazer was not the leader of the anthropological world and so did not need ousting. In trying to argue this Leach merges the questions of the real or scientific status of a man and that of his academic influence of reputation. Indeed his arguments seem directed at both points at once. Leach discusses Frazer's ideas, but purely in terms of their reception or lack of it by the academic gallery. Perhaps Leach identifies the plaudits of the academics with the truth, but that is not clear. I shudder to think what it could do to some reputations. At any rate, it would make all discussion superfluous which aimed at showing that a man is academically underrated. What *is* clear is that nowhere in Leach's article are there any criticisms of any of Frazer's theories, or of Malinowski's theories, or of any theories whatsoever. All that is to be found is talk about Frazer inspiring awe, evoking no respect, failing to inspire enthusiasm, and becoming a bore. Now Frazer may have been a victim of the passing of *academic fashion*, which is another interesting sociological, or, if you like, anthropological problem—not necessarily connected with popular fashion—but I am sure Dr. Leach would agree that Frazer's standing as a research worker, a seeker after truth, should not be mixed up with his academic reputation. Unfortunately, Leach does not carry out such a separation in his article:

> It does not appear that his views were highly *regarded*. . . .

> Frazer propounded in all three quite different theories of the "origin" of totemism. These he prints side by side in the 1910 volumes, but no fellow anthropologist has ever expressed any marked *enthusiasm* for any of them. . . .

> [1900] saw the publication of the second . . . edition of *The Golden Bough* . . . the anthropologists were notably *cool*. Andrew Lang was positively *insulting;* Hartland and Haddon praised Frazer's zeal but were

caustic about his theories. Ten years later Frazer had become a *bore.* . . . [All my italics.]

Leach is in effect asking us to join him in decrying Frazer as a scholar and seeker after truth because his colleagues did so. But *that* they did so is less important than *why* they did so. Had they any good criticisms of his theories which showed them to be not true? A man who presents three theories side by side deserves critical discussion, not dismissal as a miser of facts, etc.

Leach frequently announces that Frazer's theories were mistaken. Again, so what? A man can be most important in the development of a subject even if all his theories were wrong, provided they stimulated others, or that he opened up new problems which were taken up by others.

Leach's suggestion that the interest of classicists "waned" after *The Golden Bough* seems on the face of it an error. Frazer certainly heavily influenced Jane Harrison and, through her, Gilbert Murray. And certainly the work of Cornford, Burnet, and Finley, not to mention Arnold Toynbee and George Sarton, owes considerable debts to the approach pioneered by Frazer. Their problems, the way they set them, and their general comparative attack on them is all Frazerian. In fact Frazer is so much part of classics now that he is no more mentioned than Boyle is at meetings of the Chemical Society.

There is also, I am afraid, a serious contradiction in Leach's account of Frazer's academic reputation among anthropologists. Leach tells us:

> Frazer's personal influence by that time [the early 20s] was insignificant. His strictly academic reputation had begun to fade before 1900. . . .

> Frazer had ceased to matter. . . . Frazer played no part in university affairs either in Cambridge or elsewhere. . . . In 1911 . . . the British Association held a major international symposium on "Totemism.". . . Frazer did not attend; his views were not represented; in the published report his name is never mentioned.

All this "evidence" is very weak, especially when set against the contradictory testimony (1926) of the leading young anthropologist of the time: B. Malinowski. Far from thinking Frazer was no good, of no importance, and a bore, *Malinowski is quoted by Leach as saying about Frazer:*

> No sooner had I begun to read this great work than I became immersed in and enslaved by it . . . and became bound to the service of Frazerian anthropology.

And later Leach cites Malinowski (1942) as speaking of Frazer's "enormous creative influence" and "power to convert and inspire." How can we reconcile Leach's view that Frazer was without influence after 1910 with Malinowski's words in 1923, 1926, and 1942?

Clearly Leach has several ways of getting out of this glaring inconsistency. Malinowski could be lying. Or, Leach could claim that Malinowski did not speak for the academic anthropologists; or that he was "mistaken and bemused by faith." Perhaps Malinowski was taken in by Lady Frazer's "outstandingly successful public relations operation"?

Whatever we conclude, Leach's account of "what actually happened" in the history of anthropology must be reckoned a non-starter; it is internally inconsistent and Leach's own evidence is inconsistent with it. A minimum requirement of an historical theory is that it is self-consistent and consistent with the known facts.

And this does not by any means exhaust the contradictions and doubtful assertions in Leach's article. Malinowski is said to hold that "you cannot collect facts without a theory" and later is said to stick "firmly to the observable evidence; the myth is a 'charter for social action,' but only if demonstrably so: no guessing." Either Leach or Malinowski (or both) doesn't know that theories are guesses. At another place I am admonished for supposing "(quite erroneously) that Frazer was an unqualified atheist"; yet later Leach says Frazer's "direct references to Christianity are always *carefully* ambiguous." Was the "careful" ambiguity intended perhaps to conceal that Frazer was a theist?

After all this discussion of contradictions and errors, I should like to end by saying something about Leach's solution to his main problem. The problem was the popularity of Frazer and Malinowski. It might be explained by publicity, as Leach mentions; or by sex, as Leach also mentions; but his main solution is the universal human appeal of their generalisations about human nature:

> here, perhaps, we begin to see the roots of their popularity. "Typical Man" may not be a very satisfactory concept from the scientific point of view, but it is surely of interest to all of us.

Now if we look at this we discover an anthropological *conjecture* about what interests "all of us," *i.e.*, "Typical Man"— unfortunately "not a very satisfactory kind of concept from the scientific point of view." In his main solution to his main problem Leach condemns himself out of his own mouth. (pp. 53-5)

> *I. C. Jarvie, "Academic Fashions & Grandfather-Killing: In Defence of Frazer," in Encounter, Vol. XXVI, No. 4, April, 1966, pp. 53-5.*

TIMOTHY HALL BREEN   (essay date 1967)

[*Breen is an American educator and critic. In the following essay, he explores the ways in which* The Golden Bough *reflects Frazer's dualistic view of humankind: although he subscribed to Enlightenment concepts of constant evolution upward from religious superstition toward rationalism, his research continually provided him with examples of human irrationality.*]

The more than fifty years since the publication of the third edition of *The Golden Bough* have in no way lessened the readability of James George Frazer's prose. The passing years have, however, deadened our appreciation of the impact which *The Golden Bough* originally made on the educated public. The reader of 1913 who followed Frazer through twelve thick volumes learned much that was startling, fresh, and exciting about primitive life. Today, *The Golden Bough* has lost much of its anthropological significance, but the massive work remains a valuable record for the intellectual historian. Frazer's book reveals much about the cultural climate of Europe at the turn of the century. In it Frazer presented two contradictory images of man. One view saw man as rational, evolving upward toward ever higher physical and mental planes; the other was more pessimistic and held that man was an irrational, often quite impulsive, being. The dualism in *The Golden Bough* clearly indicated Frazer's own confusion or indecision concerning the nature of man, but even more important, it may have also reflected a tension within the European mind itself in the two decades before World War I. To understand Frazer's position more fully, we must first examine the conflicting images in detail. We can then turn to Frazer's life, his education, and his friends, in order to place these opposing views in the proper context of European thought.

Frazer's image of rational man was related to evolutionary concepts prevalent in the late nineteenth-century flowering of Enlightenment philosophy. Like many of his contemporaries, he believed in a steady, if not inevitable, flow of social progress. Intellectually, he was much closer to eighteenth-century prophets of human amelioration, to Condorcet and Turgot, than he was to Charles Darwin. *The Golden Bough,* in fact, portrayed little of the tooth and claw combat in nature and tended to emphasize aspects of man's intellectual development. According to Frazer, the human mind had enjoyed an impressive evolution, "gradually improving from perhaps bare sensation to the comparatively high level of intelligence to which the civilized races have at present attained." Frazer's statement that "we can as little arrest the process of *moral* evolution as we can stay the sweep of the tides or the course of the stars" revealed his optimism about the future of man.

He based his anthropological findings on the "comparative method." The technique relied heavily on evolutionary theory and was itself an expression of Frazer's faith in man's progress and rationality. "The comparative method," he wrote, "applied to the human mind, enables us to trace man's intellectual and moral evolution, just as, applied to the human body, it enables us to trace his physical evolution from lower forms of animal life. For Frazer the examination of culture was more than a means for tracing man's upward trek from savagery to civilization. It was also a way to lay "bare certain weak spots in the foundations on which modern society is built." In other words, the comparative study of civilization was itself an instrument to be employed by rational minds for the improvement of society. Frazer believed that man could construct a better future from the analysis of past error. "It is inevitable," he wrote in *The Golden Bough,* "that the battery of the comparative method should breach these venerable walls [antiquated social ideas and institutions], mantled over with ivy and mosses . . . the task of building up into fairer and more enduring forms the old structures so rudely shattered is reserved for other hands, perhaps for happier eyes."

Frazer claimed that man passed through three distinct stages in his evolution out of savagery. He explained that on the most primitive level—"magic"—man thought he could regulate the entire universe. The confident savage invented elaborate magical rites to insure the return of the sun each day and to make the crops grow well. In time, the colorful witch doctor and his followers realized that nature did not co-operate with their secret spells. Men gradually began to regard their surroundings more humbly and to suspect that a being greater than themselves controlled their society. When this change of view occurred, men entered Frazer's second phase—"religion." For a time the many gods invented to explain everyday events fulfilled society's needs. As reason developed, however, a few smart individuals broke away from the accepted faith and conducted successful scientific experiments. For Frazer, this third level—"science"—was the highest which humanity had attained. "After groping about in the dark for countless ages," he explained, " man has hit upon a clue to the labyrinth, a golden key that opens many locks in the treasury of nature. It is probably not too much to say that the hope of progress—moral and intellectual as well as material—in the future is

bound up with the fortunes of science." Many thinkers who flourished in the 1880's and 1890's shared Frazer's simple, perhaps naïve, faith in science—the child of man's *rational* brain.

In his optimistic image of man Frazer emphasized human rationality. Man possessed certain fundamental desires that motivated him to act. "To live and to cause to live," wrote Frazer, "to eat food and beget children, these were the primary wants of men in the past, and they will be the primary wants of men in the future." To satisfy these drives, however, both the primitive and the civilized human reasoned about the world in which they found themselves. Frazer noted that all he knew of primitive man tended "to show that his practices, however absurd they may seem to us, originated in a definite train of thought and for a definite and very practical purpose."

With encyclopedic evidence, Frazer illustrated his belief that man generally acted in harmony with the facts of his experience. He described, for example, how savages in the age of magic invented intricate systems to explain the phenomenon of dreams. Some of the natives thought that dreams represented angry spirits, others believed them to be the visitations of departed relatives; in all cases the primitive mind reasoned about the problem before it. In another instance, Frazer noted that the oak had acquired sanctity in early religions, because our "rude forefathers" saw that lightning struck this tree more frequently than it hit any other type. Frazer had such a strong faith in human reason that it did not occur to him that crude savages might not have scientifically observed the behavior of lightning. In his optimistic image of man there was no place for violent impulse or for animal instinct. Rational self-restraint, not struggle for survival, characterized human evolution. In *The Golden Bough* Frazer defined progress as man's learning that self-control over immediate passions meant greater profits in the long run. Like Bentham, therefore, Frazer advanced a philosophy of "hedonistic calculus."

Frazer attacked Rousseau's idea of a former golden age. "The old notion," he insisted, "that the savage is the freest of mankind is the reverse of the truth." According to *The Golden Bough,* fearful demons and goblins vexed the primitive mind in its ignorance. Fortunately, in every culture, a few intelligent minds have always seen the fallacies in current social beliefs and have anticipated future stages of development. The brilliant usually have risen to power as shamans or priests, and from their positions of control have helped speed the evolutionary process by persuading their slow-witted brothers of the value of change. Reasoned ambition, therefore, has been a large factor in the upward course of humanity—driving away the hordes of haunting spirits that had made the primitive mind a hell. Man had not fallen from a Garden of Eden; quite to the contrary, he was busy creating a paradise on earth with the fruits of his scientific progress.

Frazer's treatment of religion in *The Golden Bough* revealed more about his image of rational man. He attacked the faith in higher spiritual beings with the vigor of an eighteenth-century *philosophe.* At some time in the distant past, Frazer admitted, various forms of religion may have consoled mourners or quieted man's fear of death. Religion in Western civilization, however, soon turned into a selfish concern for the afterlife, for men who were worried about the state of their souls ignored their normal civic responsibilities. What is even more important to our understanding of Frazer's optimistic image is that he condemned religious beliefs for more than their danger to political institutions. Religion was contrary to the dictates of human reason and common sense. The fanatical passions generated by worship induced people to do "things which otherwise must have filled them with horror and disgust." He cited many examples of bloody excesses brought on by crazed spiritual leaders, and Frazer noted that "cases like these verge on, if they do not cross, the wavering and uncertain line which divides the raptures of religion from insanity." Any belief that caused Russian peasants to commit mass suicide or motivated a Buddhist monk to burn himself was a sin against normal intelligent behavior. In sanguine moments, Frazer thought that behind the foolish veneer of religious ritual breathed an enlightened being—one which possessed the power to realize Condorcet's millennial dreams. If man was to attain the glories of science, however, it was mandatory that he cast off old habits of religious superstition.

Frazer's second image of man—the pessimistic one—profoundly shocked many of his readers. Educated Europeans had grown used to the glowing visions of evolutionists and they were not always ready to accept the view that man was a creature of impulse and unreason. The great classicist, Gilbert Murray, wrote that "the tendency of the whole book is to make one think that there is no such thing as reason at all in human affairs" [see essay dated 1923]. The *Listener* described how *The Golden Bough* had burst over the public. "We British," commented the editor, "were not yet fully aware of the dark depths that lie in everybody's soul. It was a surprise to learn that many still unconsciously pursued the customs of the savages." Some of Frazer's admirers were quick to see parallels between *The Golden Bough* and the works of the Vienna psychoanalysts. "I cannot refrain from noting in connection with the discoveries made by the author of *The Golden Bough*," wrote Edmund Jaloux, "that one of the peculiarities of our time has been this passionate study of the primitive human kernel, practiced by Sir James Frazer, on the one hand, and by Lévy-Bruhl and Doctors Freud and Jung, on the other." Frazer's great admirer, Bronislaw Malinowski, thought that Frazer had come very close to developing a psychoanalytic insight into the unconscious and subconscious motives of human behavior. R. R. Marett, another famous anthropologist, noted that Frazer's image of man differed sharply from that of Edward B. Tylor. In his pioneer book on anthropology, *Primitive Culture* (1871), Tylor portrayed the savage as a sort of "primitive philosopher," but in *The Golden Bough*, "Frazer's folk are frank irrationalists. They have apparently little or no use for common sense." Another reader claimed that after reading *The Golden Bough*, "it suddenly occurs to us that in spite of—perhaps because of—his claims to address only our scientific, intellectual curiosity, Frazer reaches deeper, less conscious, levels of our being, evoking and activating those primordial images and patterns which, later psychologists tell us, are the womb of our modern consciousness." T. S. Eliot was so moved by Frazer's work that he footnoted it in his own bleak poem, "The Waste Land" (1922). In general, the critics agreed that Frazer had examined more than primitive culture; he had also exposed the naked savage still lurking within civilization today.

One of the recurrent images running through Frazer's many volumes was that of civilization as a volcano:

> The smooth surface of cultured society is capped and mined by superstition. Only those whose studies have led them to investigate the subject are aware of the depth to which the ground beneath our feet is thus, as it were, honeycombed by unseen forces. We appear to be standing on a volcano which may at any moment break out in smoke and fire to spread ruin and devastation among the gardens and places of ancient culture.

Frazer here plainly denied amelioration of human society by evolution. He repudiated the very basis of his optimistic image of man.

Wherever Frazer turned he found men who refused to change, refused to climb up the three-stage ladder to earthly paradise. The inexplicable force of reaction and ignorance was not native to the dark, undeveloped continents alone. Frazer warned, "It is beneath our feet—and not very far beneath them—here in Europe at the present day." In an address delivered to the Ernest Renan Society, he noted that the study of primitive life "demonstrated that under the surface of the civilized world, a deep layer of savagery existed, a savagery not dead, but alive and aggressive, always in a state of turbulence, always about to break the thin and fragile veneer of civilization that repressed it. The danger for civilization is permanent. . . ." From time to time one could hear "a hollow murmur underground" or see "a sudden spirit of flame into the air" which indicated that the bubbling forces of unrest were biding their time. Frazer could not hide his fears about the future and agreed with a statement Renan had made while looking over the ruins of Athens, "I trembled for civilization, seeing it so limited." His constant use of the volcano image gave Frazer's appeals a sense of urgency. In the beginning of the third edition of *The Golden Bough* he wrote:

> It is not our business here to consider what the permanent existence of such a solid layer of savagery beneath the surface of society, and unaffected by the superficial changes in religion and culture, has upon the future of humanity. The dispassionate observer, whose studies have led him to plumb its depths, can hardly regard it otherwise than as a standing menace to civilization. We seem to move on a thin crust which may at any moment be rent by the subterranean forces slumbering below.

The thing that profoundly impressed Frazer about superstition, violence, irrationality, and ignorance was their persistence in a world marked by a scientific achievement. "People in Europe still believe today" was a characteristic introduction in *The Golden Bough* to a passage about crude superstition or primitive taboo. European peasants continually came under Frazer's attack, for they more than any other group represented the failure of a great body of men to progress or evolve—either mentally or morally. In Lancashire, Frazer found men chasing madly about trying to catch the soul of a departed friend in their mouths. In Norwich, he noted that a woman had recently died when she applied medicine to some rusty metal instead of to her wounded foot. A thousand similar examples of savage custom existing in modern society forced Frazer to conclude that "the domain of primitive superstition, in spite of the encroachments of science, is indeed still to a great extent a trackless wilderness."

He was also surprised to find in his research that it was the oldest and crudest superstitions which were the most tenacious. He discovered that "the ignorant and foolish multitude cling with a sullen determination" to a stationary creed that tended to thwart all efforts at human amelioration. The savage stratum of society paid outward homage to the new beliefs of an age, but inwardly it held fast to its magical superstitions. The persistent primitive elements simply could not be eradicated "so long as they have their roots deep down in the mental framework and constitution of the great majority of mankind." Frazer became discouraged when he looked at man, for he could not understand how so many people could remain completely unchanged from century to century, from millennium to millennium. "The surface of society," Frazer decided, "like that of the sea is in perpetual motion; its depths, like those of the ocean, remain almost unmoved."

The most disheartening discovery in *The Golden Bough* was not that men refused to advance themselves, but that they took real pleasure in irrational, primitive behavior. The same men that Frazer at one instant praised for their enlightened self-interest he later condemned for their joy in violence. In one example, Frazer described how the bloody, barbaric worship of Dionysus swept over Greece in the pre-Christian era. By all outward standards of judgment the mystical doctrines and extravagant rites of the new Bacchic religion "were essentially foreign to the clear intelligence and sober temperament of the Greek race." Yet the primitive cult quickly established itself in the ancient citadel of reason and logic, "appealing as it did to that love of mystery and that proneness to revert to savagery which seem to be innate in most men." If the Greeks were not immune to sudden, unexplained fits of atavistic behavior, what modern race could feel secure?

In another place Frazer explained that the early European Christians were not able to stop the pagan tribes from burning people as witches. Instead of indignantly fighting these executions, the Church continued them under the guise of a pious crusade against unbelievers. According to Frazer's three-stage theory of human development, when man passed from the realm of magic to that of religion, he evolved upward both mentally and morally. The evidence in *The Golden Bough* showed, how-

Portrait of Frazer taken in 1933.

ever, that man behaved equally badly in both stages—was equally prone to cast his innocent neighbor to the flames. The vision of rational man crumbled when Frazer concluded,

> We should deceive ourselves if we imagined that the belief in witchcraft is even now dead in the mass of the people; on the contrary there is ample evidence to show that it only hibernates under the chilling influence of rationalism, and that it would start into active life if that influence were ever seriously relaxed. The truth seems to be that to this day the peasant remains a pagan and savage at heart; his civilization is merely a thin veneer which the hard knocks of life soon abrade, exposing the solid core of paganism and savagery below.

In Frazer's pessimistic image of man, human reason was extremely weak. As he surveyed his culture, he lamented that "the circle of human knowledge, illuminated by the pale cold light of reason, is so infinitesimally small, the dark regions of human ignorance which lie beyond that luminous ring are so immeasurably vast, that imagination is fain to step up to the border line." In every culture, in every age, Frazer found proof that the clear dictates of reason were outweighed by the blind impulse of passion. "If mankind had always been logical and wise," he noted, "history would not be a long chronicle of folly and crime." For Frazer, his great work was an epic catalogue of human error.

In no place was his pessimistic view of man more clear than when he challenged the utility of science. The world of modern technology was a goal for rational men who could mold their environment to their changing needs. If men refused to progress, however, and clung to their basest animal traits, science had no special significance; in fact, used incorrectly, it could become a dangerous force of evil. When Frazer's biographer asked him what was the purpose of *The Golden Bough,* the author answered, "It is, in some measure, an epic of humanity which, starting from magic, attains to science in its ripe age, and will find there, perhaps, its death. For the monster which has created human thought to-day threatens to annihilate the very race which depends upon it for its progress and well-being." At one point at the end of the book Frazer meditated on the vast discoveries of modern physics and astronomy and concluded that while man may perfect his immediate surroundings, his "puny hands" will hardly "have strength to speed afresh our slackening planet in its orbit or rekindle the dying fire of the sun." Man became an insignificant speck, driven to an inevitable disaster by impersonal cosmic forces.

The reader who took the complete journey from the sacred grove of Nemi to the forest home of the mighty Balder might not have been struck by the two images of man which rested uneasily in *The Golden Bough,* for Frazer's detailed evidence tended to obscure the conflict. When one reflects upon the implication of Frazer's thought, however, the duality becomes clear. The clashing doctrines concerned Frazer, but he never formally attacked the problem. Instead, he made three halfhearted efforts to reconcile opposites—to unite rationality and irrationality, progress and stagnation, enlightened self-restraint and animal impulse. First, he attempted to demonstrate that all men are not equal and that either view of man could be valid depending on whom Frazer was describing. In other places, he tried to gloss over his pessimistic picture of man by pointing to the rational results often born of irrational acts. And lastly, he suggested that the movement of history was not a straight-line progression but a pendulous cycle. Civilization at times advanced; at times it receded. Depending on the direction of events, either view of man might be the correct one. For our understanding of Frazer and *The Golden Bough,* it is necessary to examine these three attempts at reconciliation in greater detail.

Frazer did not believe that all men were created equal. In a speech delivered before the Ernest Renan Society he said frankly that cultural problems were due to radical and irreducible differences between men. All men did not advance at the same rate. Some slow-witted individuals evolved less quickly than their brilliant comrades; some did not develop at all. Civilization has always been propelled by an intellectual minority that has spurred on human progress. "On the whole," wrote Frazer, "the men of the keenest intelligence and strongest characters lead the rest and shape the moulds into which, outwardly at least, society is cast. As such men are necessarily few by comparison with the multitude whom they lead, it follows that the community is really dominated by the will of an enlightened minority." Like Gabriel Tarde and some of the other early social psychologists, Frazer thought that all great ideas radiate from the outstanding minds "like shafts of light from high towers." In his view it was just and correct to speak of an intellectual elite evolving upward. The large mass of the population, unfortunately, acted as a drag on the brilliant minority. He referred contemptuously to the vast majority of men as the "common herd." The tremendous intellectual chasm between the clever elite and the "herd" led Frazer to conclude that only an absolute dictatorship could control the masses. He feared that the ignorant multitude would harm the progress of the advancing few if it were not closely regulated. By formulating two distinct levels of society, two different types of men, Frazer indicated how both of his images could logically stand together. In *The Golden Bough,* however, he did not develop this theory to the degree that it answered all the problems created by the duality.

On another level, Frazer attempted to soften the force of his pessimistic image of man by showing the many beneficial results which have developed out of apparently irrational behavior. He noted that "many men who have been least scrupulous in the acquisition of power have been the most beneficial in the use of it." From the context it is not clear if Frazer meant this statement as a parable, but throughout the book he pointed to the many moral precepts and ethical standards which have grown out of primitive savagery. In a small essay, *Psyche's Task,* he attempted to deal fully with the perplexing problem of how good ends can come from irrational, superstitious means. Frazer's admirer R. R. Marett wrote of this essay, "One sees here the rationalist who, confronted with the unreason manifest in so much of the actual policy that has swayed mankind, has to shrug his shoulders and admit that, pragmatically, such foolishness has answered well enough." Frazer did not enthusiastically expand the idea that good came from evil. No doubt he found it as difficult as did his reader to believe that any benefit could possibly emanate from the volcanic depths. He was not able to escape the problems of his duality by glossing over one of the images which he had so elaborately created.

Sometimes Frazer attempted to make his polar images of man more consistent by pointing out that history, indeed life itself, did not develop in a straight line. He suggested that the movement of events was like the path of a great pendulum, ever swinging between irreconcilable positions, but never resting at either extreme. A section of François Guizot's *Histoire de la civilisation dans l'Europe* quoted at the beginning of *Psyche's Task* indicated that Frazer did not always accept the concept of teleological evolution without qualification:

There is in all things a mixture of good and evil at once so profound and so unconquerable, that whenever you penetrate or descend to the lowest components of society or of the soul, you discover these two forces existing side by side, ever battling each other, but without victory. Human nature never ventures to extremes, neither of good or of evil; but it swings ceaselessly from one side to the other, righting itself at the second it seems nearest to disaster, faltering at the second when things seem to be going the best.

In *The Golden Bough* Frazer expressed his admiration for the philosophy of Empedocles. He thought that the pre-Socratic thinker had been prudent not to make any dogmatic affirmation of universal progress: "We may perhaps say that Empedocles was wiser than Herbert Spencer in leaving, as he apparently did, the question undecided, whether during the epoch open to human observation the force of attraction or that of repulsion has been or is predominant." Along with Empedocles, Frazer seemed to be asking whether anyone could know whether civilization was gradually evolving toward more complex forms or dissolving slowly into savagery. Who could be certain of the nature and future of man? He himself sincerely hoped that his optimistic image of a rational evolving being was the true one. He admitted, nevertheless, that man might be a stubborn, unthinking animal.

Frazer's two opposing images of man challenge the intellectual historian, for the conflict raises several difficult questions. The major problem, of course, is why Frazer held irreconcilable views. Was the clash of *The Golden Bough* the result of some personal factor in Frazer's life—some book or man that had influenced him? Or was the duality the product of a larger force—a tension within the European mind itself? Neither of these questions is capable of yielding a correct answer alone, for the man and the society do not exist in isolation. We must, therefore, examine both the author's life and his cultural environment to understand the paradox of *The Golden Bough.*

In the last decade of the nineteenth and the first decade of the twentieth centuries, Europe was beginning to feel the first tremors of an intellectual revolution that would rock every Western nation by the 1920's. Outwardly, this twenty-year period appeared to be the highest expression of the ideas of the Enlightenment. The men of this generation who had grown up in an atmosphere of materialism were proud of their achievements. More than anything else, their science made them confident. There was nothing technology could not conquer, and the men of the 1890's "talked and acted as if they shared the full rational faith of the men of the 1770's." Of the Enlightenment ideas which blossomed in this era, "probably the most characteristic and most cherished was the belief in progress, and in a progress which proceeded not along a jagged line of ups and downs with the ups only slightly exceeding the downs, but rather a straight line steeply ascending." Moreover, the theory of evolution only "bolstered the generation's optimism by rendering progress automatic."

Inwardly, the thoughtful observer could see small cracks forming in the nineteenth-century Weltanschauung. At first the dangers to the rationalist beliefs—"the lurking nemesis"—were hardly noticeable, but they were very real. Some thinkers in the two decades before World War I began to experience a "psychological *malaise*: the sense of impending doom, of old practices and institutions no longer conforming to social realities." Men of this generation investigated the human mind and were startled by their findings. "Man as an actor in society, they came to see, was seldom decisively influenced by logical considerations: supra- or infra-rational values of one sort or another usually guided his conduct.'' On another level, Max Planck and Albert Einstein countered the old certitudes in absolute, unchanging physical laws with principles of ''probability'' and ''relativity.'' In this era conservative intellectuals first called on human rationality and scientific causality to fight the new theories in a battle that few realized would bring into question the most esteemed beliefs of the Enlightenment.

Frazer could not help but be affected by the intellectual forces that were beginning to divide Western culture. The clashes in *The Golden Bough*—between rationality and irrationality, between progress and stagnation, between confidence and fear— were symptomatic of broad cultural strife on several levels. Many works in these two decades reflected the conflicting philosophies. Sigmund Freud's writings, for example, reveal a similar duality. On the one hand, Freud's ''discovery that it was man's unconscious rather than his reason that was in ultimate control'' was the highest expression of pessimism. On the other hand, the Vienna psychoanalyst was ''the greatest child of the Enlightenment which our century has known.'' In one place, Freud wrote that the persistence of the human intellect ''is one of the few points in which one may be optimistic about the future of mankind.'' Frazer's presentation of two different images of man was by no means a unique phenomenon; quite to the contrary, it must be seen as an expression of the age in which he lived.

Frazer personally was in every way a child of the Enlightenment. At Glasgow University, he received a full humanistic education. During his college years, he acquired a love of order and reason, and from Lord Kelvin's classroom he carried away ''a conception of the physical universe as regulated by exact and absolutely unvarying laws of Nature expressible in mathematical formulas.'' From Condorcet, as well as Darwin and Wallace, he took the idea of evolution and, as we have seen, applied it to the study of man. Edward Tylor and William Robertson Smith not only interested Frazer in the infant discipline of anthropology, but also reinforced his belief in reason and human development. He enjoyed Ernest Renan's attacks on Christianity, but he had no stomach for the works of Freud. Outwardly at least, Frazer appeared to be a gentle, even conservative, individual. Nothing recorded about his slow-moving life at Cambridge University revealed where or how he acquired his dark image of irrational man.

The key to the conflict of *The Golden Bough* lay not in Frazer's training or in his personal contacts with other thinkers of his generation. It should be clear that by inclination Frazer was a thorough-going optimist. Yet despite his nineteenth-century assumptions about reason and progress, he was too much of a scientist to ignore the massive evidence of irrational behavior which he discovered in his study of primitive society. He was never convinced, however, that he should drop his evolutionary faith completely, and so in *The Golden Bough* he presented both views of man—the one he wanted to find and the one he did find. (pp. 179-94)

> Timothy Hall Breen, ''The Conflict in 'The Golden Bough': Frazer's Two Images of Man,'' in South Atlantic Quarterly, Vol. LXVI, No. 2, Spring, 1967, pp. 179-94.

JOHN B. VICKERY (essay date 1973)

[*Vickery is a Canadian educator and critic who has written about the relationship between myth, ritual, and literature. In the fol-*

lowing excerpt from his study The Literary Impact of ''The Golden Bough,'' *he demonstrates technical, thematic, and generic affinities between* The Golden Bough *and numerous works of twentieth-century literature, positing both direct and indirect influence of Frazer's work on the development of modern English and American letters.*]

Why should it have been Frazer's study rather than some other work in anthropology and comparative religion that shaped modern English and American literature? Why, for instance, did not L. R. Farnell's *Cults of the Greek States* or A. B. Cook's *Zeus*, volumes equally encyclopedic and equally packed with ancient lore, acquire the same kind of status in the literary world? The content of all three is much of a piece and all were published in roughly the same decade. The explanation, then, must lie in what can be called the literary reason. Essentially, this reason has three major and interrelated aspects: the style, structure, and genre of *The Golden Bough*.

Since they stand in a diminishing order of obviousness, it is best perhaps to begin with the first. The Latinate diction, the judicious employment of periodic sentences, the eloquent peroration, the handling of sustained analogies, the apposite allusions, the leisurely development of paragraphs—all stamp *The Golden Bough* as a magnificently sustained example of the grand style and of what Sir Herbert Read has called the central tradition of English prose. And though it is obviously not the dominant style of the twentieth century, it is clearly the only appropriate rhetorical mode for that study which Frazer himself called ''an epic of humanity.'' In describing Frazer as ''a very great master of art,'' T. S. Eliot was concurring with Edmund Gosse's judgment that his volumes were among those whose ''form is as precious as their matter.'' And when we recall the elaborate word patterns of ''The Dead'' or the touching conclusion of *Finnegans Wake*, the luminous and unhurried narrative of Sir Osbert Sitwell or the bravura flourishes that heighten the travel accounts of his brother Sacheverell, it is apparent that they and *The Golden Bough* have more than a little in common. Similarly, T. S. Eliot's best prose reveals the same quality he finds in Frazer's work, a carefully adjusted combination of the tentative and the precise. Indeed, when Eliot distinguishes Frazer from Shaw and Hardy as possessing a leaner and more disillusioned sensibility whose rhythm is vibrant with the suffering of the life of the spirit, the affinities with his own work became unmistakable.

In addition, *The Golden Bough* possesses another quality that many writers in the twentieth century were to champion as a notable virtue and a cornerstone of a contemporary style. T. S. Eliot, Ezra Pound, H. D., and Ernest Hemingway—to mention only the obvious names—each in his own way stressed the importance of concreteness, of presenting the external world in all sensuous immediacy as a visual presence. They tended, by a kind of Lockean metaphor, to identify visual and intellectual clarity. (pp. 106-07)

If Frazer's style in *The Golden Bough* was a genuine literary achievement, one to be ranked with that of Gibbon, even closer connections can be found between it and the major works of modern literature. At first sight, *The Golden Bough* appears a soberly conservative narrative in the nineteenth-century manner. Yet it possesses structural properties that might well attract artists eager for experiments in form. Frazer deliberately avoided a strictly logical and systematic arrangement of his facts and chose instead ''a more artistic mould'' with which ''to attract readers.'' Hence, the priest of Nemi and his rites open the book since, though not intrinsically important, they provide a simple and easily grasped image of actions and beliefs whose mystery is gradually illuminated as the more important and complex dying gods are introduced and their functions explored. As a consequence, the form of *The Golden Bough* has been likened to that of a strict sonata.

The idea of the interrelation of the arts has been handled rather gingerly by scholars ever since Lessing, with the exception of iconographic studies of literature and art. Poets, however, have been less constrained and in particular have been consistently drawn to regard myth and music as related. From Wagner through Baudelaire and Mallarmé to Rilke and Valéry, these forms have been held to epitomize the ultimate mystery of human expression—the creation of untranslatable order, harmony, and insight that conveys more than it says. More recently, such critics as Elizabeth Sewell and Claude Lévi-Strauss have argued that thinking mythically is a species of musical thought. If they are right, then the musical form of *The Golden Bough* may possess an appositeness that extends far beyond the bounds of simple analogy. Given his subject, Frazer may have been motivated in his development of literary structure by far deeper forces than conscious determination, forces that were powerfully operative in the last half of the nineteenth century and the early years of the twentieth century. While in view of the general poetic interest in this topic, it would perhaps be futile to argue for *The Golden Bough* as a direct source, we cannot help noting the parallel here to the interest in musical form shown by T. S. Eliot in the *Four Quartets*, Conrad Aiken in *The Divine Pilgrim*, James Joyce in *Finnegans Wake* (notably Book II, section iv), Thomas Mann in *Doctor Faustus*, and Edith Sitwell in *Façade* and some of the *Bucolic Comedies*. Certainly the musical pattern of Frazer's work created a climate in which these artists could elaborate their own interests.

Bearing in mind the claims of Miss Sewell and Lévi-Strauss, we cannot help but be struck at the way in which these authors and their works betray not only affinities with music but more or less central uses of myth as well. Miss Sitwell and Aiken both struggled early in their careers with the problems of making language reflect musical properties. Miss Sitwell's technical experimentation of *Façade* was directed primarily, as her brother has remarked, on determining "the effect on rhythm, on speed and on colour of the use of rhymes, assonances and dissonances, placed outwardly, at different places in the line, in most elaborate patterns." Aiken, on the other hand, was concerned less with how closely language could be identified with music. He was more inclined to regard music and particularly the symphonic form as a suggestive analogy by which contrapuntal effects might be attained in poetry. But both launched their experiments in extending the nineteenth-century symbolist aesthetic with the aid of mythic themes, images, and metaphors.

Miss Sitwell's early poetry abounds in satyrs, centaurs, water gods, and nymphs of the caves, waters, woods, and mountains as well as references to Pan, Silenus, Midas, Apollo, Psyche, Hecate, and Thetis. While most of these seem the consequence of a classically oriented education, a few recall *The Golden Bough* and its rather special perspective on the ancient world. For instance, in "I Do Like to Be beside the Seaside," there is a sprightly hint of a humorous use of one of Frazer's key mythic figures:

> Erotis notices that she
> Will
> Steal
> The
> Wheat-king's luggage, like Babel
> Before the League of Nations grew.

The "wheat-king" hangs tantalizingly between commerce and myth. In doing so it adumbrates the comic and satiric possibilities of anthropological lore that Miss Sitwell explored more fully in *Gold Coast Customs*. In much the same way the tango rhythms of the poem mediate between grave stateliness and festive gaiety so that both myth and music conspire to reveal the serio-comic dialectic of the significant and trivial that life and human history afford.

Miss Sitwell's early work ostensibly focusses on the triviality of modern existence in order to illuminate the momentous character of human decisions and gestures. (pp. 109-12)

Of all the modern authors who have sensed the possible relations of myth and music none more thoroughly dramatizes the role of *The Golden Bough* in this perception than Ronald Bottrall. The title poem of his *Festivals of Fire* carefully integrates a deliberate emulation of the sonata form with the myth of Balder in order to mirror and diagnose the nature of the early twentieth century. In many ways it bears the impress of being modelled after *The Waste Land* and in none perhaps more than its reliance upon *The Golden Bough,* as the title, text, and notes in their several ways indicate. By giving each of the four sections of the poem representative musical directions of the sonata, Bottrall alerts us to the likelihood of the poem's possessing the structure and the effects of a musical composition. This likelihood is fully borne out by the subsections, which vary in length, rhythm, and thematic development in manners that give them the closest technical parallels to the sonata. Thus, in line, verse paragraph, and section the poem achieves a musical expression of the dramatic unfolding of the Balder myth which both crystallizes and comments on the dilemmas of modern life. (pp. 113-14)

[It is] true that Frazer himself thought of his book almost exclusively in pictorial terms. The priest at Nemi is said to be "in the forefront of the picture" while the background is crowded with priest-kings, scapegoats, dying gods, magicians, and fertility deities. Indeed, there is a sense in which Frazer, like Yeats, writes under the stimulus of an actual painting, developing its implications in his own fashion and interpreting its significance. According to Frazer, the full beauty of Turner's painting of Nemi can be felt only when Macaulay's verse account of its ritual has been explained. Thus, the frontispiece and initial epigraph of *The Golden Bough* encompass its central theme. Small wonder he should speak of his book in terms of "sinuous outline" and "its play of alternate light and shadow," or that on its very first page he should urge his readers to form "an accurate picture" of Nemi.

In his "Musée des Beaux Arts" W. H. Auden interprets the details of Brueghel's *Icarus* painting in language whose colloquial vigor and casualness verbally mimes the visual scene of the painter. Both modes function as illustrations of a general and abstract statement announced in the opening lines:

> About suffering they were never wrong,
> The Old Masters.

Yeats, on the other hand, uses particular paintings as inciters of the imagination, which thereby is encouraged to work its metamorphic powers that draw images and scenes from their visual context into the poet's elaborate and distinctive symbolism. He is less concerned to analyze the form or significance of a painting than to assimilate its relevant aspects to his own mythic iconography, as the great example of his Leda poem makes clear.

While it is impossible to argue for the direct influence of *The Golden Bough* in this regard, nevertheless some striking and significant similarities in general attitude and method are detectable. A particularly good instance occurs in the last volume where Frazer draws evidence from art and literature for his theory of the golden bough's symbolic role as a preserver of life:

> There is some reason to suppose that when Orpheus in like manner descended alive to hell to rescue the soul of his dead wife Eurydice from the shades, he carried with him a willow bough to serve as a passport on his journey to and from the land of the dead; for in the great frescoes representing the nether world, with which the master hand of Polygnotus adorned the walls of a loggia at Delphi, Orpheus was depicted sitting pensively under a willow, holding his lyre, now silent and useless, in his left hand, while with his right he grasped the drooping boughs of the tree. If the willow in the picture had indeed the significance which an ingenious scholar has attributed to it, the painter meant to represent the dead musician dreaming wistfully of the time when the willow had carried him safe back across the Stygian ferry to that bright world of love and music which he was now to see no more.

Allowing for the extreme differences in purpose between Frazer and the poets, we can still see their affinities. He adumbrates Auden in his sketching of the pictorial scenic design while basing general contentions on its evidence. Similarly he resembles Yeats, whose penchant for symbolic identifications based on the learning of others Frazer here approximates. Doubtless the same could be said of many other authors—for instance, Ruskin—but this does not alter the fact that Frazer was actually read by many modern writers. As a result he may have indirectly contributed to their burgeoning sense of the richness poetry might achieve by affecting painting's structural massing of detail and color. Pound, Eliot, and Joyce, to mention only the early giants of modern literature, were not so unsympathetic to the manner and preoccupations of the late nineteenth century that they could not find in *The Golden Bough* suggestive treatments of both figures and landscapes.

Probably the most sustained poetic effort to use poetry and painting as complementary mirrors in which the myths and classical scenes found in *The Golden Bough* are reflected is the work of Sacheverell Sitwell. In a collection such as *Canons of Giant Art*, nearly all the poems are based on or derive their inspiration from works of art such as the paintings of Poussin, Mantegna, El Greco, and Claude, the sculpture of Praxiteles and the Farnese Hercules, or classical and Indian myths. Such a collocation of sources attests not only to the diversity of Sitwell's interests but to their underlying imaginative unity that may well have found its locus in *The Golden Bough*. In addition to these poems' pictorial detail, mythic subjects, wide scholarship, and comparative perspectives, they reveal yet another feature—one not conspicuous in the work of Yeats or Auden—that aligns them with Frazer as pupils to master. That is their mastery of narrative development and pace, which makes them virtual poetic equivalents of *The Golden Bough*'s unhurried, lambent creation of scenes and actions that echo with the memories of civilization's dreams and history. (pp. 115-18)

By linking his major study to painting, in both conception and execution, Frazer provides literature with an instructive and suggestive model for a deepened exploration of novel forms of texture and perspective. Like Yeats and Auden, he plays the pictorial and the verbal off against one another and so achieves their mutual illumination; like Pound and Wyndham Lewis, he carries the visual principle of the artist into literature; and like Lawrence and Virginia Woolf, he attends to even as he creates the emotional vibrations in the object and setting. Nor in the light of this are we surprised to find the late Professor Chew likening *The Golden Bough* to the vision seen by St. Anthony and the Frazerian images and figures to the nightmarish fantasies of Brueghel or Bosch.

The musical and pictorial similarities between Frazer's study and modern poetry and fiction, though striking and suggestive, may be essentially analogies, lines of parallel development. What they indicate most sharply is the extent to which Frazer's structural techniques foreshadow those of some of the major artists of the twentieth century. Influence—if it enters at all—operates almost exclusively below the threshold of consciousness. A somewhat stronger case of influence as well as a partial explanation of the attractions of *The Golden Bough* is its nonchronological method of narration. This method results in a work whose structure is shaped by most of the devices that characterize modern literature. Consider what we may call *The Golden Bough*'s macroscopic form. Here is a work dealing with a vast subject which orders its material thematically; which juxtaposes conflicting evidence and scenes for dramatic purposes; which presents its point of view by indirect and oblique means; which sees human existence as a flow of recurring experiences; which employs repetition and restatement as both emotive and intellectual devices; which creates symbolic epitomes of human history out of apparently limited and simple actions; and which makes a unified whole out of an abundance of disparate scenes and topics by an intricate set of references backward and forward in the narrative. Without in the least denying the other contributory forces, we may legitimately suggest that *The Golden Bough* is also, in a very real measure, responsible for the form and shape of modern literature.

In *The Waste Land, The Cantos, The Bridge,* and *Paterson* the thematic ordering of material, the dissolving perspectives, the panoramic sweep, the mingling of the profound and the trivial, the poignant and the bizarre are the same techniques employed in *The Golden Bough. The Bridge*, for instance, bears such a wealth of structural and thematic resemblances to Frazer's book that it seems impossible that it did not derive from it either directly or as a representative expression of the *zeitgeist* shaped by Frazer in the years following World War I. The concern with myth, announced in the "Proem" and dramatically elaborated in the text and marginalia of "Powhatan's Daughter," is obvious. This is fortunate since it is beyond the scope of the present chapter to offer a detailed treatment of the Frazerian dimensions of *The Bridge*.

Nevertheless, we should note that these include not only controlling images, such as the Indian princess who closely resembles *The Golden Bough*'s corn-maiden, her dance of religious regeneration and fertility, the sacred river stained with the presence of the dying god, and "the mistletoe of dreams, a star," but also attitudes informed by Frazer's impact on the cultural attitudes of the times. For instance, in beseeching the bridge to descend to man and "of the curveship lend a myth to God," Crane renders his response to Frazer's disclosure of the empirical and material character of incarnation. The traditional religious language of descent is invoked here in order to utilize it as metaphor whose efficacy is not contingent on its truth. Both the deity and the stories or *mythoi* of his existence derive from man and those of his creations that project the imagination beyond its material ground. Such is the central contention of both *The Bridge* and *The Golden Bough.* Similar structural resemblances further link the two works. Both open with a voyage motif; both are engaged in an effort to relate disparate areas of experience and feeling and belief, and to circumscribe them into a single orderly synthesis; both seek to achieve this order through more or less abrupt comparisons and juxtapositions which slight the conventional categories of temporal chronology and spatial contiguity; and both organize their work loosely in a fashion that permits them to deal with the great variety of subjects that most interest them—Crane by his sequence of fifteen lyrics which taken together form a unified poem, and Frazer by what some have felt to be a series of essays gathered into book form.

Similarly, we have but to think of Joyce or, in a quite different way, William Carlos Williams, to see the extent to which contemporary literature, like Frazer, conveys its point of view through selection of details and arrangement of scenes instead of by explicit pronouncements. Joyce's work, at least through *A Portrait of the Artist as a Young Man,* orders details emblematically in accord with a rhythm that matches Frazer's in its skillful use of late-nineteenth-century models. What Joyce derived from Frazer in this regard is primarily a conspectus of rhetorical strategies for the rendering of the ironic and elegiac. The doctrine of artistic impersonality lying behind this technique and most commonly associated with Joyce and Eliot finds its discursive analogue in Frazer's calm, impartial, scholarly detachment. With it, he could survey man's entire history and find it a record of incalculable folly while contemplating the destruction of his own theories with complete equanimity.

Such personal dispassionateness was virtually the polar opposite in temperament to the late Dr. Williams, who might well be thought one of the last persons to be touched by Frazer's style and erudition. Yet the predominantly staccato rhythms of *Paterson,* alien as they are to Frazer, must be set off against its declaration:

> You also, I am sure, have read
> Frazer's Golden Bough. It does you
> Justice.

In the process of creating a poetic style to render the realities of a phenomenological America, he shattered the convention of poetry as something undefiled by prose even as he made living speech of the most vigorous and diversified sort the cornerstone of poetic language. At the same time he intensified Frazer's habit of shifting topics and focus by making the unit of organization the line rather than the chapter. As a result the process is speeded up to the point where the illusion of transitions and conventional rhetorical development can no longer be sustained, a fact which neatly crystallizes the cultural, epistemological, and verbal changes that have occurred since *The Golden Bough* first appeared.

Even more striking is the extent of modern literature's attraction to cyclical theories of life, history, and culture. *A Vision* and *Finnegans Wake* both celebrate this concept with elaborate care and a wealth of detail. So does *The Golden Bough,* which not only links the astronomical, vegetative, and human worlds in a pattern of birth, flowering, death, and revival, but also closes where it began—with the sacred grove at Nemi. In Frazer's tracing of this pattern an integral part is played by repetition of facts and restatement of hypotheses and inferences. The effect is not simply one of calling to mind points in danger of being lost sight of, but also of bringing to the reader a sense of their profound significance, of their right to a brooding and thoughtful contemplation. And though it is undoubtedly the product of a particular and individual attitude toward the actual process of writing fiction, yet just the same sort of effect is achieved by Lawrence in the almost ritualistically repetitive passages of novels such as *The Rainbow* and *The Plumed Serpent.* Lawrence, like Joyce and Eliot, also finds man's life represented symbolically in commonplace and traditional acts. For them as well as for Frazer, harvesting, love-making, bearing the sins of others, and performing the menial deeds of daily life, all reflect in different ways what is taken to be the essence of life.

Perhaps the most unequivocal instances of the ritualistic exaltation of the simplest and most fundamental acts of human survival through reliance on the patterns and behavior presented in *The Golden Bough* are to be found in the novels of Naomi Mitchison and John Cowper Powys. Miss Mitchison's *Corn King and the Spring Queen* acknowledges Frazer as one of its major sources. It also gives a cumulatively powerful rendering of the psychological states of specific primitive individuals cast in the role of fertility monarchs and deities. Where Lawrence's repetitions are substantially Frazerian-inspired ritual equivalents, Miss Mitchison's are densely concrete fictive transcriptions of Frazer's more general accounts. She follows a single individual, Tarrik, and those around him through *The Golden Bough*'s characteristic divine-king pattern so that a sense of the credibility of the underlying beliefs is conveyed to the reader. This is achieved in part through repetitive allusions to reiterated actions and convictions and through heavily detailed descriptions of avowedly crucial religious rites. The effect is both to show us how pervasively these convictions permeated the common life of the tribe and also how psychologically possible it is to perceive god and man in the same physical vehicle. (pp. 119-23)

The repetitive aspect of ritual emphasized by Miss Mitchison, Powys, Lawrence, and, in a somewhat different manner, by Joyce is balanced both in modern literature and in *The Golden Bough* by another device that similarly integrates disparate spatial and temporal orders into a coherent unity. To circumscribe the complex nature of man's changing yet somehow permanent condition, works like *The Waste Land, Ulysses, Finnegans Wake*, and *The Anathemata* rely heavily, even as does *The Golden Bough,* on a multiple series of cross-references and allusions which continually underscore the contemporaneity of all time. While Eliot, Joyce, and David Jones were all familiar with Frazer's ideas and works, it is in the main unlikely that their patterns of allusion and notes were deliberate efforts to emulate *The Golden Bough*'s habit of sustained documentation. Nevertheless, these and other writers, sought, like Frazer, workable means of controlling the modern explosion of knowledge without resorting either to exhaustive encyclopedism or deliberate abandonment of historically distant or topically recherché information. Consequently they might well have been impressed with the range and mastery of knowledge Frazer's scholarship afforded him. Certainly when we think of the training and temperament of men like Eliot, Joyce, and Pound, the extent to which the scholarly method was both congenial to, as well as a desperate bid for large-scale coherent relevance by, modern literature emerges sharply.

What makes *The Golden Bough*'s techniques of cross-reference particularly attractive and instructive to writers is their capacity to keep the focus on the author's immediate concern and to lend a status to that concern by relating it to similar ones in other times and places so that it assumes a universal or perennial character. When, for instance, Frazer documents something like the custom of secluding girls at puberty with discussions of the practice in Africa, Indonesia, the Americas, and India, a social curiosity becomes a means of insight into cultural dynamics and its symbolism. Similarly, when Frazer details items connected with magic or taboo, he suggests in a very powerful manner how commonplace and even ordinarily disgusting things can be invested with the profoundest emotional significance.

A related aspect of Frazer's scholarship that is important for modern literature is what might be called its essentially primary character. Even the most casual study of *The Golden Bough*'s footnotes convinces us that Frazer not only ransacked anthropology for his data and illustrations but went directly to other disciplines when problems in his research seemed to demand it. His view seemed to be, as R. Angus Downie has suggested, that "if, in our search for the golden bough, we might get a hint from the botanists, we must not let our ignorance of botany stand in our way, but must overcome that ignorance" [see 1940 entry in Additional Bibliography]. As a result, his notes contain a surprisingly diverse range of information all brought to bear on particular issues. Obviously such problem-solving efforts do not figure in literature, but something rather analogous does, namely, the concentration of rhetorical strategies to achieve the maximum imaginative impact. The way in which these two elements—multiple forms of knowledge and power of effect—are programmatically merged in literature is perhaps best exemplified by Ezra Pound's practice. This he summed up in the remark that readers forced to learn enough Latin or Greek or Chinese or American history to grasp certain lines in his *Cantos* were still not wasting their time because they were learning something. And as a humanistic model for modern literature's effort to attain revolutionary perspectives through a scholarly, or quasi-scholarly, use of unrelated knowledge, Pound and the others could not improve on *The Golden Bough*. (pp. 125-27)

From [the] stylistic and structural affinities between *The Golden Bough* and modern literature it is clear that even if Frazer's work had not been directly imitated, was not a consciously employed source, it would still have exercised an influence on creative artists because of its imagination and technique. With this point, the last aspect of what has been called the literary reason for *The Golden Bough*'s success comes into view. For though a sketch has been made of how and why Frazer rather than Farnell or Cook or Miss Harrison or Crawley or Hartland spearheaded the drive of comparative religion into literature, there is still the question of why *The Golden Bough* is preeminent among his works. The answer lies in its genre or literary mode, for in essence it is less a compendium of facts than a gigantic romance of quest couched in the form of objective research. It is this basically archetypal consideration that reveals *The Golden Bough*'s impact on literature to be not fortuitous but necessary and inevitable. We have but to compare its opening pages with those of *Folklore in the Old Testament*, *The Fear of the Dead in Primitive Religions,* or *Myths of the Origin of Fire* to see that in it there is much more than simply discursive writing. The latter plunge immediately and prosaically into their subject:

> Attentive readers of the Bible can hardly fail to remark a striking discrepancy between the two accounts of the creation of man recorded in the first and second chapters of Genesis. (*FOT*)

> Men commonly believe that their conscious being will not end at death, but that it will be continued for an indefinite time or for ever, long after the frail corporeal envelope which lodged it for a time has mouldered in the dust. (*FOD*)

> Of all human inventions the discovery of the method of kindling fire has probably been the most momentous and far-reaching. It must date from an extreme antiquity, since there appears to be no well-attested case of a savage tribe ignorant of the use of fire and of the mode of producing it. (*MOF*)

With *The Golden Bough,* however, rhetorical question, alliteration, allusion, metaphor, inversion, all are enlisted to create a genuine literary experience, what the Joyce of *Finnegans Wake* might have called an "anthropoetic" experience:

> Who does not know Turner's picture of the Golden Bough? The scene, suffused with the golden glow of imagination in which the divine mind of Turner steeped and transfigured even the fairest natural landscape, is a dream-like vision of the little woodland lake of Nemi—"Diana's Mirror," as it was called by the ancients. No one who has seen that calm water, lapped in a green hollow of the Alban hills, can ever forget it. The two characteristic Italian villages which slumber on its banks, and the equally Italian palace whose terraced gardens descend steeply to the lake, hardly break the stillness and even the solitariness of the scene. Diana herself might still linger by this lonely shore, still haunt these woodlands wild.

> In antiquity this sylvan landscape was the scene of a strange and recurring tragedy. In order to understand it aright we must try to form in our minds an accurate picture of the place where it happened; for, as we shall see later on, a subtle link subsisted between the natural beauty of the spot and the dark crimes which under the mask of religion were often perpetrated there, crimes which after the lapse of so many ages still lend a touch of melancholy to these quiet woods and waters, like a chill breath of autumn on one of those bright September days "while not a leaf seems faded."

Granted that *The Golden Bough* is more carefully, more imaginatively written than his other works (passages in *The Worship of Nature* and his edition of Pausanias may be exceptions), this does not in itself make the book a romance rather than the encyclopedic argument we have always thought it to be. One obvious connection between it and the traditional romance that most readers feel in some measure is suggested by the applicability to both of Ezra Pound's comment: "There are few people who can read more than a dozen or so of medieval romances, by Crestien or anyone else, without being overwearied by the continual recurrence of the same or similar incidents, told in a similar manner." Equally apparent and probably more significant is their joint development of themes out of a substratum of Nature myth and fertility ideals, their use of conflation and linking by means of central leit-motifs, their merging of incongruous materials, and their readiness to hint at possible meanings without spelling them out in detail.

And if we bear in mind that *The Golden Bough* is an instance of what Northrop Frye calls displacement, we can see certain additional features that both stamp it as a romance and account for its impact. First, like the medieval romances, it clearly deals with a quest—in this case, a quest to discover the meaning of the ritual observed by the priest of Diana, the King of the Wood, at Nemi. This fact alone almost explains Frazer's seminal role in modern literature, for the thematic quests of Eliot for redemption, Joyce for a father, Lawrence for a Golden Age, Yeats for the buried treasure or hidden mystery, and Miss

Sitwell for purification are all adumbrated in *The Golden Bough*. While Frazer announces his quest from the beginning and completes it just prior to rounding off the narrative, he does not follow the pure romance in regarding this as the major adventure led up to by a series of minor incidents and forming the climax of his story. Instead he pulls the traditional formula inside out by beginning and ending with a secondary encounter while gradually working in toward the central experiences he is dealing with, which are those of crucifixion and resurrection. The resulting effects are highly instructive for modern literature.

For one thing Frazer's de-emphasizing of plot and narrative continuity parallels much modern fiction. Nowhere is this parallel more thoroughgoing than in the tendency of both to locate their climaxes, their central, crucial experiences, in incidents of discovery or revelation almost totally devoid of action. Thus, the notion of what might be called the important unimportant situation or event, which has become a stock device of the contemporary short story, is one of the organizing principles of *The Golden Bough*.

The same reversal of the romance pattern also provides another effect central to modern literature. Thematically, it consists of the gradual accrual of meaning as the reader follows a trail of hints and artistically incomplete bits of information. Just as Frazer extends *anagnorisis* throughout the book so do *The Sound and the Fury, Absalom, Absalom!*, the major novels of Henry James, and the "Alexandria Quartet." Structurally, the reversal provides the idea of pattern by piecemeal. This is based on a dislocation of perspective which brings us too close to the scene or overwhelms us with detail so that only when we stand back and regard the whole work does the pattern emerge. Instances of this which come readily to mind are *Finnegans Wake, The Cantos*, and Dos Passos' *U. S. A.* Frazer achieves precisely the same thing, both thematically and structurally, when he forces us to follow him through a tangle of magicians' arts, species of taboo, and perils of the soul before coming upon one of his central topics—the death and resurrection of gods—in Volumes IV and V. But not even the *Adonis, Attis, Osiris* segments provide the whole core, for only in Volume VII, *The Scapegoat*, do we catch a glimpse of the earlier books' complementary theme, that of the crucifixion of gods and men.

We are told that the romance proper projects the ideals of the ruling social or intellectual class; that its quest has three stages (conflict, death, and discovery or resolution); that this threefold structure is repeated in many other features; that the quest involves two central characters (a protagonist and an antagonist); that the secondary characters are simplified and weak in outline; that the quest's most frequent goals are the slaying of a dragon and the acquisition of wealth in some form; and that the romance possesses a number of distinguishable types or phases. Not only does *The Golden Bough* have a quest motif as a dominant feature, but it also exhibits all the characteristics just mentioned, though obviously not in the same way as they appear in *Perceval*, the *Perlesvaus*, or *Sir Gawain and the Green Knight*.

Unlike the medieval romances, *The Golden Bough* does not embody the ideals of an aristocratic, feudal society, but it does convey a clear sense of the values that dominated the post-Darwinian, rationalistic ethos of late-nineteenth-century England. Reason and truth are to Frazer what mystic love was to von Strassburg, chivalric honor to Chrétien, or Christian faith to von Eschenbach. Thus, in what stands as a proem to his tale of adventure he suggests that the comparative approach has not only intrinsic intellectual significance but also social

usefulness derived from an unswerving adherence to truth. As a result, the real hero or protagonist of *The Golden Bough* proves to be the civilized mind which explores uncharted ways to uncover new facts about man's way of life, facts which may be simultaneously horrifying, engrossing, and revolutionary. In short, the hero is Frazer himself, who, like Nero Wolfe, solves the mysterious puzzles and crimes of mankind from an armchair. If this sedentary role seems to violate the notion of the quest or marvelous journey as central to the romance, we may recall that the wanderer was as frequently a book as an author. The varied and widely dispersed forms of folk tales, ballads, and romances are cases in point. (pp. 128-32)

To find the answer to the sacred kingship of Italy in Southern India is in the best tradition of the Grail knights who traveled into distant lands seeking the goal of their quest. Like them, Frazer found himself almost insensibly embarked upon his wanderings. As he says, "wider and wider prospects opened out before me; and thus step by step I was lured into far-spreading fields." The same basic image of the journey that is a quest provides the controlling frame of the entire book. In the first chapter the rational hero decides that "the survey of a wider field" may "contain in germ the solution of the problem." And like Jason, Theseus, or Odysseus, he offers his listening companions "a voyage of discovery, in which we shall visit many strange foreign lands, with strange foreign peoples, and still stranger customs. The wind is in the shrouds: we shake out our sails to it, and leave the coast of Italy behind us for a time." Eleven volumes and over a hundred chapters later, with all these predictions fulfilled, Frazer announces the end of the quest: "Our long voyage of discovery is over and our bark has drooped her weary sails in port at last." This voyage metaphor affords a powerful summation of the nineteenth century's character as an age of scientific and geographic discovery. It is the imaginative extrapolation of those voyages of discovery taken by David Livingstone, Sir Austin Layard, and Sir Richard Burton as well as the more purely intellectual ones embarked on by Darwin, Huxley and Frazer. Through it the Victorian resemblance to the Elizabethan age is thrown into sharp relief.

Within this frame of journey and incredible adventure both the quest and the central characters of *The Golden Bough* reveal their affinities with romance. Frazer's quest possesses the requisite three stages, though they are naturally blurred by his assumption that he was writing anthropology rather than literature. Secondary variations on this triple form are the book's three major subjects (magic and the sacred kingship, the principles of taboo, and the myth and ritual of the Dying God) and its three editions, the latter being equivalent perhaps to the romance hero's success on his third attempt. The stages themselves traditionally involve an extended conflict between the protagonist and his antagonist, a vital confrontation in which at least one is slain, and finally the discovery and exaltation of the hero as a dramatic resolution to the quest. In *The Golden Bough* the conflict is waged over human beliefs and customs. More particularly, two antagonistic forces try to settle whether or not there is any connection among various religious beliefs or between religious customs generally and those usually thought of as wholly secular. Frazer as the protagonist advances the cause of unaided reason and objective scientific truth against the entrenched powers of superstition whose key representative is the man of religious faith. In one sense, like the Grail legend itself *The Golden Bough* is the fruit of a crusade, though, as Robert Graves keeps reiterating, a highly discreet and covert crusade. The similarity to the romance pattern is heightened by Frazer's suggestion that his task is to help his society rid itself of afflictions and weaknesses emanating from a powerful and aged adversary who lives "in a strong tower" and who will not hesitate to tempt the hero with appeals to antiquity, expediency, and beauty.

Though the conflict of reason and faith or science and religion is perhaps endless, *The Golden Bough* imaginatively envisages the second quest stage, that of the death of one of the combatants. In this case, the defeat is dealt to the representative of tradition and faith, whom Frazer calls superstition. And while it is difficult to say just precisely at what point in the book this occurs, we would probably not be far wrong in locating the instant of fatality in the note on "The Crucifixion of Christ" appended to the ninth volume. Showing that Christ died as the annual representative of a god whose counterparts were well known all over Western Asia, Frazer intimates, "will reduce Jesus of Nazareth to the level of a multitude of other victims of a barbarous superstition, and will see in him no more than a moral teacher, whom the fortunate accident of his execution invested with the crown, not merely of a martyr, but of a god." Here Frazer joins forces with Nietzsche, for in his account of the death of a god he is slaying his antagonist who is god. As for the third stage, that of discovery, exaltation, and resolution, it occurs most unmistakably in the penultimate chapter of the entire study. Here Frazer finally discovers the link between the golden bough and the mistletoe which enables him to resolve his quest by finding a generic explanation for the exploits of Aeneas, Balder, and the Kings of the Wood at Nemi. And in so doing, he has, in effect, achieved his exaltation as a hero who completes his task and also guaranteed his recognition by his own as well as a later generation.

Traditionally the three-stage quest of the romance is directed to the slaying of a dragon and the finding of buried treasure. When we turn to *The Golden Bough,* we encounter enough dragons and treasure for scores of romances, but they don't seem to be exactly what we are after, if only because they exist in no direct, active relation to our hero, Sir James. A useful clue here is Northrop Frye's suggestion that the labyrinth is an image of the dragon or monster. To anyone who has observed *The Golden Bough*'s technique of circling around and around its particular subjects—as, say, when the identification of the mistletoe as the elusive golden bough is reached after consideration of taboos concerning the earth and sun, the seclusion of girls at puberty, fire-festivals, magic flowers, the varied locations and nature of external souls, and the myth of Balder—it is clear that here is a labyrinth of gigantic size and complexity. Pretty clearly the myth underlying *The Golden Bough*—the myth beneath the myths, as it were—is that of Theseus and the Minotaur. The monster, then, which Frazer the rational hero seeks to slay is ignorance itself, whose archetypal form is a half-human, half-animal composite of ancient myth, modern folklore, and the ritual customs of both past and present. Thus, the monster is intellectual: the puzzle created by the impingement of irrational or inadequate explanations on the rational mind rooted in common sense.

Frazer's characteristic reaction to the monster is seen at the very outset when he remarks that "it needs no elaborate demonstration to convince us that the stories told to account for Diana's worship at Nemi are unhistorical." Coupled with this is his determination to conquer his adversary by framing rational questions to be answered with the aid of his famed weapon, the comparative method. The result is his entry into the labyrinth in pursuit of the protean monster, an event dramatized by such remarks as "we must try to *probe deeper* by examining the worship as well as the legend or myth of Hippolytus." To guarantee his return he pays out behind him a slender chain of hypotheses, conjectures, and common-sense assumptions. His reward is not only the destroying (at least to his own satisfaction) of falsehood and superstition but the acquisition of the treasure buried deep in labyrinth. For the scholar such as Frazer the ideal form of wealth is knowledge ordered into a coherent form and issuing in the wisdom of revelation, in this case, of "the long march, the slow and toilsome ascent, of humanity from savagery to civilisation."

While much more could be said about *The Golden Bough* as a displaced quest romance—for instance, its complex use of pity and fear as forms of pleasure so that the appropriate romance strains of the marvellous, a thoughtful melancholy, and a tender, passive charm are pervasive—enough has been said to suggest the plausibility of the identifications. One final point still remains, however. Even if *The Golden Bough* is a quest romance, how does this account for its importance to modern literature? Obviously, important aspects in any answer would be its quest motif, religious significance, and archetypal symbolism. But modern literature has also been marked by a profoundly ironic temper which would seem at odds with the idealized world of romance. This point brings us back to the style and structure of *The Golden Bough.* Though doubtless the pure romance has little affinity with irony, it is also true that the romances closest to us in time, whether of Hawthorne or of Hudson, usually possess a considerable admixture of irony. And the same is true of *The Golden Bough.* It was not for nothing that Frazer found his prose masters in Anatole France and Ernest Renan.

One of our most sensitive critics [Harry Levin] has pointed out Joyce's use of Renan's combination of irony and pity, and the same is true too of *The Golden Bough.* It opens with "a dream-like vision" of Nemi in which descriptive charm expresses a tender pity for the human follies enacted there. From this it immediately modulates into a compound irony based on the relation of man and god, which if not central is at least typical: "In the civil war its [Nemi's] sacred treasures went to replenish the empty coffers of Octavian, who well understood the useful art of thus securing the divine assistance, if not the divine blessing, for the furtherance of his ends. But we are not told that he treated Diana on this occasion as civilly as his divine uncle Julius Caesar once treated Capitoline Jupiter himself, borrowing three thousand pounds' weight of solid gold from the god, and scrupulously paying him back with the same weight of gilt copper."

More germane to Frazer's central aim is his use of the comparative method for ironic purposes. Irony by incongruous juxtaposition undeniably reentered English literature with a heavy French accent, but we should not overlook the way in which Frazer's celebrated method frequently performed the same function on a broader range. Nor is it without significance that T. S. Eliot and Edith Sitwell, the two most assiduous students of Laforgue and Corbière, were also attentive readers of *The Golden Bough.* One version of Frazer's technique is the large-scale juxtaposition of ostensibly opposed but actually similar rites, as with the festivals of Adonis and St. John. Another is that of the sober understatement of a hypothesis such as "there is no intrinsic improbability in the view that for the sake of edification the church may have converted a real heathen festival into a nominal Christian one." Even more oblique yet pervasive is his use of terms and images that ironically expose similarities his opponent seeks to conceal, as when a worshipper of Artemis is said to pay tithes to the goddess or when it is noted that Cybele and Attis were worshipped on the site of the Vatican. And finally there is irony employed for comic purposes and directed at his own controlling concepts, like that of the dying and reviving god. Thus, in a passage such as the following we may discern the lineaments of Joyce's ironic handling of Christian rites in *Ulysses* and his more jocular chronicling of HCE's rise and fall: "in his long and chequered career this mythical personage has displayed a remarkable tenacity of life. For we can hardly doubt that the Saint Hippolytus of the Roman calendar, who was dragged by horses to death on the thirteenth of August, Diana's own day, is no other than the Greek hero of the same name, who after dying twice over as a heathen sinner has been happily resuscitated as a Christian saint."

Like that of modern literature as a whole, Frazer's irony begins in realism with a wry recognition of human folly and broadens out into a mythic treatment of men who imitate gods, are sacrificed to the needs of society, seize and hold power through unscrupulous stratagems and a shrewd knowledge of mass psychology, and abase themselves. Thus, if we take Hardy, Huxley, Lawrence, and Joyce as typifying recent modes of irony, we can see how **The Golden Bough** encompasses their moods of fatalism, anger, nostalgia, and detachment and integrates them into an encyclopedic vision of the knowledge inherent in its society: In effect, then, **The Golden Bough** became central to twentieth-century literature because it was grounded in the essential realism of anthropological research, informed with the romance's quest of an ideal, and controlled by the irony in divine myth and human custom. Together these made it the discursive archetype and hence matrix of that literature. (pp. 132-38)

> *John B. Vickery, in his* The Literary Impact of "The Golden Bough," *Princeton University Press, 1973, 435 p.*

ROBERT ACKERMAN (essay date 1978)

[*Ackerman is an American educator, critic, and anthropologist. In the following essay, he examines ironic aspects of* The Golden Bough.]

There is a real sense in which one may speak of Sir J. G. Frazer as a modern mythmaker despite himself—one who, along with Darwin, Marx, Freud, and Einstein, has supplied the underlying scientific metaphors that pervade and shape modern consciousness and permit us to think about ourselves in the world. Certainly in the English-speaking world Frazer was responsible, beyond all others and long before Freud, for the way educated persons came to see their lives as somehow problematically related to a primitive substratum of the self. The reason one finally demurs from regarding him as what the Germans call a "world-historical" figure is his insistent inability or unwillingness to see the import of his work in modern cultural terms.

It is not a question here of Frazer's not being a Frazerian. Rather, it is a question of his own extreme political conservatism and personal shyness, which led to an increasing estrangement from, and antipathy toward, the twentieth century and the modern spirit—however deeply he was investigating and bringing to light the obscure foundations of its social institutions. Although he has suffered far more from the ravages of revisionists than any of the other major figures mentioned above, there is no doubt that in his day Frazer contributed

mightily to anthropology, folklore, comparative religion, classics, and even belles lettres. Today his principal professional descendants, the anthropologists, disavow him nearly universally, or else treat him as a dinosaur whose bulk has caused him to founder in the primeval (that is, pre-Malinowskian) ooze. The title of Sir Edmund Leach's 1961 *Daedalus* essay, "Golden Bough or Gilded Twig?" [see Additional Bibliography] expresses well the current disdain. Thus it is not at all paradoxical that today Frazer is probably more of a real presence in literary criticism, to which he made no explicit contribution, than in any of the other disciplines in which he worked.

Although there have been and continue to be important exceptions, English-speaking anthropology over the last half century has been and continues to be passionately scientistic in its hopes, claims, and methods. One consequence—and it shares this trait with other sciences—is a built-in positivism and an aversion to history, both general and its own. Accordingly, when anthropologists have come to write histories of their discipline, these have tended to be rather crudely whiggish, with the historian carefully and tendentiously creating some one special tradition from the past in order to argue that the kind of anthropology in which he and his scholarly allies are now engaged represents true continuity with this privileged mainstream. Naturally, from such a profoundly ahistorical perspective, and with virtually no scholarly descendants to counterpolemicize on his behalf, Frazer has emerged as little more than an embarrassment, a horrible example of the bankruptcy of the comparative method and philosophical evolutionism. The fact that he was and still is the most widely read anthropologist who ever lived is either ignored or else adduced to illustrate the lamentable taste of the so-called educated reader. The fact that anthropology, like history, has connections with other kinds of imaginative prose, and that the literary qualities of Frazer's vision (as of Malinowski's or Lévi-Strauss's) might have something to do with his public acceptance never enters into consideration, for style and vision are scarcely quantifiable variables.

As is commonly known, the modern ethnographer, at least in the English-speaking world, works by the method of participant-observation: he first experiences the natives' reality as a modern Westerner, and then somehow imaginatively reconstructs its meaning for the natives. After a time in the field, he gains knowledge and confidence in his powers of empathy and insight, and thus increasingly internalizes the natives' consciousness until his sensibility and theirs are approximately simultaneous. Through the necessity to develop a dual consciousness, his fieldwork becomes a first-class course in ironic reflection, both personal and cross-cultural. But because so many anthropologists cherish hopes for their profession as a "hard" science, this inherently subjectivist and ironic phenomenology tends to be ignored in histories and methodological essays and appears only in diaries and informal conversations.

Accordingly, the positivist anthropological historian, who believes that social science is composed of "findings" rather than theories or ideas, scarcely has the inclination to register, much less to comment upon, the fact that leaps to the attention of the literary reader—that Frazer is a particularly ironic writer. Consequently, the nature and cause of that irony never come up.

No matter how long it has been since one last looked into **The Golden Bough**—and here I must for the moment drastically abridge Frazer by making him synonymous with his best-known work—one recalls being impressed by its author's sometimes wavering but ultimately deeply ironic sense of the way in which man, perpetually questing after knowledge, is constantly and unconsciously constrained by the unexamined primitive foundations of his social institutions, from the bonds of which he never entirely escapes. Such ultimate considerations, however, are by no means the only, or even the most frequent, irony in **The Golden Bough.** Indeed, most of the irony is much more straightforward, consisting as it does of oblique or direct potshots that Frazer takes at religious practices, institutions, and finally at religion itself, which is portrayed as fundamentally irrational and thus worthless as a guide to life.

Although psychohistorians, recalling James Mill, Philip Gosse, and Ernest Pontifex, might conclude that such a concerted, lifelong attack on religion as Frazer's *must* be construed as a kind of extended psychological protest against the father, the facts do not support such a reading. In the course of preparing to write a book about Frazer, nothing in what I have turned up about his youth leads me to believe that he was the victim of some blasting childhood trauma that marked him out and created what we might call an ironist from deepest impulse. Rather than look for a nonexistent blacking factory, I believe that his irony was not primarily caused by psychological idiosyncrasy but that it appears precisely, and not at all coincidentally, whenever Frazer adopts primitive religion as his subject.

This turning point can be dated with confidence to 1883/84. It was then that the erstwhile classicist Frazer, who had gained his Trinity College fellowship in 1879 on the strength of a dissertation on platonic epistemology, was drafted into the study of religion by his new friend, William Robertson Smith, the brilliant theologian and biblical scholar. Smith, newly arrived at Cambridge and Trinity College after having been exonerated in the last important heresy trials in Scotland, found Frazer, his fellow Scot, somewhat at a loss for direction. He immediately conscripted Frazer into writing articles on classical subjects for that great monument of late Victorian rationalism, the ninth edition of the *Encyclopaedia Britannica,* of which Smith was editor. But because the ninth edition was already well advanced in publication (in those days such works came out a volume at a time), the volumes from A through O had already appeared. Therefore all Frazer's contributions were on subjects beginning with P and subsequent letters of the alphabet: Penates, Priapus, Proserpine, and so on. And thus it was this accident of publication that caused Smith, a considerable anthropologist himself, to assign the younger man the fateful articles on Taboo and then on Totemism. This latter essay grew so long that even the most sympathetic editor could print only an abridged version; the full text appeared in 1887 as Frazer's first book, **Totemism,** and immediately established him in the then thinly populated world of anthropology.

Before going further, let me offer a sample of the famous Frazerian irony. Since, as I have said, it appeared just when he discovered his new subject, the sample I choose comes from his very first piece on primitive religion, characteristically entitled "On Certain Burial Customs as Illustrative of the Primitive Theory of the Soul." This long talk, filled with the erudition that would soon become synonymous with Frazer's name, was given to the assembled luminaries of the Anthropological Institute, including Herbert Spencer, Francis Galton, and E. B. Tylor, at a meeting in 1885. (This was fully five years before the publication of the first edition of **The Golden Bough.**) On such an occasion Frazer, always sensitive to tone and nuance, and with all the resources of a highly developed prose style at

his disposal, would have taken pains to strike the right rhetorical note with his audience of gentlemen-scholars, so they would see him as erudite but no pedant, a man of the world among other men of the world. I might add that we know the address was a success, because some of the ensuing discussion has been preserved in the minutes of the meeting.

Frazer is here talking about the treatment of illness among primitives. He argues that since the primitives believe that the soul of a sleeper wanders during sleep, and thus a sick man is in danger because some malign agency can prevent his soul's return, logic dictates that the invalid be prevented from sleeping.

> With this intention the Circassians will dance, sing, play and tell stories to a sick man by the hour. Fifteen to twenty young fellows, naturally selected for the strength of their lungs, will seat themselves around his bed, and make night hideous by singing in chorus at the top of their voices, while from time to time one of them will create an agreeable variety by banging with a hammer on a ploughshare which has been thoughtfully placed for the purpose by the sick man's bed.

Just as noteworthy as the artfully placed modifiers—"agreeable variety," "thoughtfully placed"—is Frazer's confidence that he has discerned the true motives underlying these bizarre actions, culled as they are from all quarters of the globe. To underline this, in a footnote on the first page of the printed version of his talk he announces his policy concerning his use of sources, which of course in that pre-fieldwork era were all printed texts. He says: "It is to be observed that the explanations which I give of many of the following customs are not the explanations offered by the people who practise these customs. Sometimes people give no explanation of their customs, sometimes (much oftener than not) a wrong one. The reader is therefore to understand that the authorities referred to are quoted for the fact of the customs, not for their explanations." That is, not only does Frazer use the customs as so many occasions for his ironic commentary, but he stands in adversary relationship to their very existence in the texts he employs. He consults authorities, but denies them their authoritativeness.

If one cannot trust the natives, whom, then, can one trust? A person who knows better, who can see the total spectrum of primitive religious behavior, and who also understands the laws that govern the operation of the mind and the laws that govern its evolution—Frazer himself. A caution here: The question whether an outsider can ever know better than a native the meaning of an item of behavior or an artifact is still hotly debated among ethnographers. Frazer, however, like all his British contemporaries, seems to have settled the matter in his own mind with ease. For him, there is no question that the primitive mind, less highly evolved than ours, *can* be plumbed, and without too much difficulty. Like ours, it works by association, but unlike ours it makes mistaken associations—thus it resembles most closely the minds of the children of today. The present-day failure of ethnographic nerve, generated by our sense of the complexity of culture after fifty years of field experience, is still far in the future for Frazer. By means of his simplistic assumptions, he is able to group vast masses of behavioral data under a relative handful of headings, thus making comprehensible the underpinnings of our social institutions.

These simplistic tendencies, which exaggerated the real and undeniable regularities of human behavior and institutions, enhanced the persuasiveness of Frazer's vision to a post-Darwinian, and especially a post-World War I, secularized readership.

Frazer was one of a long, noble line of scholars of grand-scale, encyclopedic inclinations for whom similarities have always been more important than differences. They were the sort who adopted some radically simple classificatory device, such as Frazer's own evolutionary lockstep movement from magic to religion to science, by which they oversimplified the confusion that human behavior, in its nearly infinite variety, presents. Certainly this scholarly predisposition is alive in our day, as witness the illustrious examples of Arnold Toynbee and Mircea Eliade.

How, then, is Frazer's tendency to work in what we might call extremely capacious and elastic categories to be connected to his irony? Along with the condescension that comes from colonialism and its attendant spirit, racism, and along with his seemingly innate rationalist temperament, another source of irony was his epistemology and its assumptions. Here he speaks, in the preface to the second edition of *The Golden Bough* (1900), about the possible future value of his work: "It has been my wish and intention to draw as sharply as possible the line of demarcation between my facts and the hypotheses by which I have attempted to colligate them. Hypotheses are necessary but often temporary bridges built to connect isloated facts. If my light bridges should sooner or later break down or be superseded by more solid structures, I hope that my book may still have its utility and its interest as a repertory of facts."

In other words, the facts stand by and for themselves. Because Frazer seems to have been unaware or unconcerned that the questions one asks largely determine the answers one gets, and because his disparagement of theory was so drastic as to permit him to dissociate theory from facts, he must have been confronted with the vast masses of data that his indefatigable industry turned up, with only a minimal explicit structure to organize them. Because he regarded the facts as representing the state of things "out there," he seems to have felt justified, in what may be the greatest example of the imitative fallacy anywhere, in offering the reader a stunning mass of data grouped in only the broadest, most general fashion and in a style permitting any number of divagations and excursions. In fact, Frazer's industry seems to have outpaced by far his capacity to absorb its results, and part of his irony may be his baffled reaction to the profusion of his data.

One example of this blind alley into which his desperate empiricism led him has to do with the central problems of the origin and meaning of myth and its relation to ritual. His own thoughts on these vexed questions had undergone great changes over the years. It seems likely that his aversion to explicit theory caused him to be unaware of the conflict, even the contradiction, between some of the explanations he embraced. Frazer went out of his way to attack Jane Harrison, Gilbert Murray, and Francis Cornford, and ritualism as well; yet it was his early advocacy of ritualism—the idea that myth is best understood as the verbal correlative of subsequently disused ritual and is a secondary elaboration of ritual—that had won them over. His ingrained rationalism must have found inimical any explanation that emphasized motor needs over those of the intellect. The words he used in his attack, in the preface to his 1921 Loeb Classical Library edition of Apollodorus's grab bag of myths called *The Library,* are revealing:

> By myths I understand mistaken explanations of phenomena, whether of human life or of external nature. Such explanations originate in that instinctive curiosity concerning the causes of things which at a more advanced stage of knowledge seeks satisfaction in philosophy and science, but being founded on ig-

norance and misapprehension they are always false, for if they were true, they would cease to be myths.

Although it may be impossible for a modern audience to suppress a smile at these words, their tone is exactly and characteristically that of the triumphant social science descendants of Bentham—those to whom we tend to offer lip service as the equal of the tribe of Coleridge, but whom literary intellectuals disparage or ignore in their reading lists and lectures. Yet this is by the way; let me return to Frazer's chastisement of the ritualists. He wrote:

> By a curious limitation of view, some modern writers would restrict the scope of myths to ritual, as if nothing but ritual were fitted to set men wondering and meditating on the causes of things. No doubt some myths have been devised to explain rites of which the true cause was forgotten; but the number of such myths is infinitesimally small, by comparison with myths which deal with other subjects and have had another origin. . . . The zealous student of myth and ritual, more intent on explaining them than on enjoying the lore of the people, is too apt to invade the garden of romance and with a sweep of his scythe to lay the flowers of fancy in the dust. He needs to be reminded occasionally that we must not look for a myth or a rite behind every tale, like a bull behind every hedge or a canker in every rose.

In the space of a paragraph, myth as the careful but mistaken efforts at science on the part of primitive man has become instead a vast field of flowers of fancy growing wild and at random in the garden of romance. Frazer's metaphors and his tone *de haut en bas* show that his epistemology has led him on a wild-goose chase, and he seems to abandon any hope of making worthwhile sense of the fantastic diversity of myth and ritual he has so successfully displayed to the reader.

Many of Frazer's most eloquent pages, and much of his undoubted visionary force, were based on what might charitably be described as a sublime indifference to theory. In a sense he was a martyr to his own empiricism and to the scientism-at-large that prevailed at the turn of the century among the social sciences. For all that, he was a seer despite himself; readers have always esteemed him for the ways in which, perhaps mainly through the considerable resources of his verbal artistry, he was able to present comprehensibly, in a phrase or an image, a compelling sight of a mysterious past that is somehow alive within us all today. (pp. 232-36)

> *Robert Ackerman, "J. G. Frazer Revisited," in* The American Scholar, *Vol. 47, No. 2, Spring, 1978, pp. 232-36.*

SANDRA SIEGEL   (essay date 1985)

[In the following excerpt, Siegel contends that Frazerian anthropology was designed to confirm late nineteenth-century convictions that Victorian civilization represented the peak of human accomplishment.]

It is questionable whether any single idea can be said to have dominated any age, as Mill thought "comparing" had dominated modernity. Darwin's *Origin* (published within two decades of Mill's essay) demonstrated considerably greater scrutiny than simple acts of comparison. We can be certain, though, that during the second half of the century classification and comparison, kindred activities, increased. Kindred, but not identical: unlike the more detached act of classifying, the act of comparing, when exercised habitually, usually elicits judgments. By 1900, the Victorians had placed nearly every act, whether social or literary, on one or another side of a great divide. No matter was too small for scrutiny. They evaluated. They took positions. And no matter was too large. While the social scientists celebrated how far contemporary civilization had advanced, social and literary critics lamented how far civilization had declined. This would not have been strange—differences have always prevailed—if attentiveness to each other's views, frequently published in the same periodicals, had led them to controversy as most other issues did. But on this issue, where one would have expected vigorous debate, there was silence.

It is worth recalling Ruskin's remark of the 1860s that "progress and decline" were "strangely mixed in the modern mind." That "mix" became stranger as the Victorians classified events according to their power to carry them forward or cast them backward in time. In the discussion that follows I want to take up two questions: how are we to account for the ease and satisfaction with which readers assimilated opposing assessments of the same facts? And how are we to account for silence where we would have expected bitter conflict? (pp. 199-200)

The writings of anthropologists, folklorists, and other antiquarians, the young James Frazer, Andrew Lang, Max Müller, for example, who contrasted modernity with antiquity, the urbane with the barbarous, were understandably self-congratulatory. Frazer's cartographies of primitive customs, beliefs, institutions, and behavior were sketched from the point of view of the superiority of the more advanced over the inferior, less advanced savage. He exalted his contemporaries. He flattered them. His vivid accounts provided readers with descriptions of what others, mostly social critics, characterized as decadent. The antiquarians' lurid accounts made available to the critics, whose muted interest in the past was equalled by their insatiable curiosity, ample imagery, abundant examples, and a powerful idiom for interpreting themselves and their contemporaries. In exchange they offered their antiquarian contemporaries animated descriptions of "decadence." They envisioned the possibility of becoming, by way of a backward movement in time, exactly like the savage—a condition that had long been likened to the natural condition of women and children. With that fear hovering over them, the social critics' descriptions intensified the anthropologists' desire to affirm progress, and, insofar as they did affirm that desire, subdued their worry that the condition of savagery might recur.

If the antiquarians took satisfaction in distinguishing "Us" from "Them," their need to preserve that difference increased as they acknowledged their fear. For as Frazer well knew, in spite of the persistence with which he affirmed how far civilization had traveled, civilization remained merely a fragile surface: savage survivals, ordinarily dormant, were a potential hazard. The social critics who were convinced that their time was "decadent" thought that they had erupted. The reciprocity the critics and antiquarians enjoyed drew them into a silent yet complicitous dependence from which both enclaves profited. To better understand their dependence as well as their silence we need to consider the unbounded optimism that characterized certain accounts of decadence—and the covert fear that prompted and sustained them.

The place of language in culture; the origin of religion; the significance of magic; the meaning of myth, ritual, and custom: on these subjects Victorian ethnographers were divided. Yet on two other issues—whether ethnography was a science, and whether it represented the newest evidence of progress—they

were in agreement. Not all antiquarians who were influenced by Darwin actually read his work, but the young Frazer, whose first articles prefigured the copious volumes he produced over the next forty years, certainly did. All Frazerian anthropology recapitulated the general argument of *The Descent of Man:* animals evolve from lower (simple) to higher (complex) forms of life; humans evolve according to stages, from a position of moral and intellectual weakness to moral and intellectual strength; and, as part of the human species, women are superior to lower forms of life, but men are intellectually, physically, and morally superior to women. Two consequences followed: Anthropology presented itself as authoritative because it studied human institutions as a "science"; second, Frazer relied on the analogy of the development of the fetus in order to interpret social arrangements. The imaginative richness of his language, which constantly likened social institutions to something else—the fetus, for example—readily deferred conclusions. Such deferral, combined with his authoritative tone, helps to explain why Victorian anthropology is as hopeful—it was scientific—as it is fearful of failure. Ethnography's typically authoritative tone replaced definitive authoritative statements even as such statements were themselves necessarily cast in metaphor. One set of observations was presented, but only to be understood in terms of yet another about something different. As Darwin, throughout his writings, but especially in *The Descent of Man,* drew frequently on the analogy between the development of the fetus and the evolution from lower to higher forms of life, so Frazer extended the analogy to the domain of "social institutions." Darwin had argued that the human embryo repeats the history of the evolution of mankind: traces of previous stages survive.

The structural derivatives of Frazer's thought, the influence Darwin exerted, and the origins of Victorian ethnography are subjects of interest that have yet to be fully explored. Here, however, I want simply to point out that Frazer's argument delineated the boundaries that separate civilization from savagery by distinguishing between the primitive past and the present. At the same time, Frazer alerted his contemporaries to traces—I shall call them embryonic survivals—the existence of which were not only essential to anthropology, but made possible the study itself. Needful as traces were in order to see how far we had come, they were also a constant reminder of the "fragile surface" of civilization. Their existence threatened to dissolve the distinction between savagery and civilization, which made preserving the concept of difference all the more important. Ethnography promised to preserve those boundaries. Survivals were visible, provided one looked at the human fetus closely, as Darwin had. *The Expression of Emotions in Animals* extended consideration of survivals to the more ambiguous domain of gesture. Following Darwin, Frazer found that rather than being lost, moments of the past, or "stages" of the past, were preserved in social life even though the species (or social life) advanced. Darwin had turned to embryology for evidence of previous stages of development. Frazer applied this method to the study of primitives. Each relied on the embryonic model, the one to map the evolution of humans from lower forms of life, the other to map the evolution of civilization from savagery. Social life passed through stages similar to those through which the embryo passed. Frazer, who was fearful that evidence for charting the development of human cultures would vanish, admonished anthropologists to study existing savages. Even if survivals were lost—if existing savages were to perish before their customs and characteristics were recorded—survivals exist in social life (social equivalents of fetal survivals): "Embryology shows that the very process of evolution, which we postulate for the past history of our race, is summarily reproduced in the life history of every man and every woman who is born into the world.'' If the life history of every man and every woman repeats the past history of the human race, then the child bears the same relation to the savage as the adult does to civilization: savagery and civilization stand in opposition to each other as the child does to the adult. The child, who represents an arrested stage of human development, provided a readily accessible embodiment of the vision of the savage in Victorian social science. Frazer described ''Social Anthropology'' as ''the embryology of human thought and institutions.'' Where savages were inaccessible one could turn to contemporary civilization: The savage past persists in the present.

Readers of *The Descent of Man* will recall that Darwin evokes the quadrumana, a half-bestial, half-human creature, so frequently, why it occupies so special a place in his account of how man came into being invites speculation. After his own laborious effort, Darwin must have been astonished by his vision of the mentally superior creature whose triumphant emergence from the animal world represented the culmination of a long process of evolution. Although the triumph of the quadrumana was no different in kind from those of other superior species, it was of considerably greater significance and interest as the essential link in the unfolding of events that led to the emergence of the fully human savage, the existing savage, and, finally, civilized man. For Darwin the quadrumana represented the end of the line. At precisely that juncture, Frazer began his inquiry. ''Well handled,'' Frazer wrote, ''the study of the evolution of beliefs may become a powerful instrument to expedite progress if it lays bare certain weak spots in the foundations of which modern society is built. At present, we are only dragging the guns into position: they have hardly yet begun to speak.'' There is more to be noticed here than Frazer's confident tone, or, even, the magnitude of the task he set for anthropology. Indeed, for Frazer the long-range effect of recovering the origin of civilization was the promise of expediting progress; but the immediate effect was to call attention to the differences that separate savagery from civilization.

Apart from the lurid pleasures of that empirical subject, really more speculative than empirical, the more fully the social scientists amplified the differences that separated ''Them'' from ''Us,'' the more readily could they congratulate themselves on the progress of civilization: Modern western man was physically, mentally, and morally superior; his social arrangements and institutions were more complex; his religion and his science were more advanced. For Frazer and others the clearest sign that civilization had indeed approached the threshold of far-reaching advance was the development of the science of anthropology, the latest example of civilization. The immediate practical gain of an otherwise recondite subject was not negligible: turning to the savage was a means of reassuring contemporary culture of how far it had advanced. The further back in time one traveled, the further civilization could be said to have progressed.

''All *existing* savages,'' Frazer wrote, ''are probably far indeed removed from the condition in which our remote ancestors were when they ceased to be bestial and began to be human.'' Our contemporary habits of thought have diverged far enough from this typically Frazerian turn of mind that it may be a little difficult to recognize the implicit analogy that Frazer is drawing here. We may need to remind ourselves that because Frazer was simply applying Darwin's theory to social life he imagined

an unrecognizably bestial, but equally unrecognizably human creature, whose successors were increasingly more advanced. Frazer admonished anthropologists not to confound the existing savage—''human documents''—as he called them, with his more remote ancestors. The existing savage differed as greatly from his ancestor as he did from civilized man. Although Frazer did not delineate the differences sharply, he brought into clear focus a world inhabited successively by bestial creatures; half-bestial, half-human creatures; fully human savages; and, finally, by civilized man who represents the present threshold beyond which, armed with the new guns of anthropology, civilization might now advance further.

It is, perhaps, merely a striking coincidence, yet interesting nevertheless, that the two pairs of oppositions—human/beast and male/female—around which Darwin organized *The Descent of Man* are also played out, but to different purposes, by the later generation of social critics in their discourse about decadence. While the first third of Darwin's *The Descent of Man* takes up the question of the differences that separate humans from lower forms of life, and accounts for the superiority of man, the balance of the book takes up the question of the differences that separate male from female, and accounts for the superiority of men over women. Although these are distinct considerations, as it turns out, the same qualities Darwin ascribes to men (as opposed to women) are also those that separate man from beast. While woman was thought to be finely wrought by nature, the formation of her skull indicated her intermediate position between the child and man. As the quadrumana gained supremacy over lower forms of life through the principle of natural selection, males gained supremacy over females through the principle of selection according to sex. Darwin not only explains the ways in which women are inferior to men; he also explains the origin of their inferiority. In the course of fighting for the possession of their women, men rivaled other men. Through the law of battle he became greater in strength and in intelligence. Those who were successful in possessing and keeping their women triumphed. Thus civilization evolved and continued to progress.

Darwin repeatedly reminds his readers that man's greater physical, mental, and moral strength is due to his inheritance from his half-human male ancestors. During the ''long ages of man's savagery'' these characters would have been preserved, or even augmented, ''by the success of the strongest and boldest men, both in the general struggle for life and in their contests for wives; a success which would have insured their leaving a more numerous progeny than their less favored brethren.'' The characteristics of primeval male progenitors—physical strength, perseverance, courage, intellectual vigor, the power of invention, and determined energy—are precisely those qualities that continue to separate male from female.

Not everyone who had opinions about Darwin read *The Descent of Man,* but echoes of Darwin are strong and clear in *The Golden Bough.* ''Even where the system of mother-kin in regard to descent and property has prevailed most fully, the actual government has generally, if not invariably, remained in the hands of men. Exceptions have no doubt occurred; women have occasionally arisen who by sheer force of character have swayed for a time the destinies of their people. But such exceptions are rare and their effect transitory; they do not affect the truth of the general rule that human society has been governed in the past, and human nature remaining the same, is likely to be governed in the future, mainly by masculine force, and masculine intelligence.'' That force and intelligence, as

Darwin plainly said, is responsible for civilization: Frazer's language and thought resemble Darwin's so closely his own voice is often indistinguishable: "In the struggle for existence progress depends mainly on competition: the more numerous the competitors the fiercer is the struggle, and the more rapid, consequently, is evolution."

The Golden Bough, twelve volumes in all, is animated by the contrast Frazer draws between the "childlike mind of the savage and his childlike interpretation of the universe" and the "forward thrust of civilization toward religion and science." Frazer substitutes the "child" for the savage more often and more vividly than he emphasizes the affinities savages and children share, ignores the differences that separate them, and uses the words "child" and "savages" interchangeably to evoke the same imaginative configuration. Whatever "They" are like, "We" are different.

By 1890, the denigrated condition of children provided familiar evidence for the analogy to function effectively. Frazer had no interest in the child as such, at least if one is to judge from his writings. In the context of his anthropological writings, however, the invocation of the child enabled him to describe the obscure, and necessarily imaginary, past of the savage as though the savage he was describing were familiar. To trace how far civilization had advanced, the figure of the child mediated access to the savage. One could, by contrast with the savage, see more clearly what was not valued within and by civilization. "We must constantly bear in mind that totemism is not a consistent philosophical system, a product of knowledge and high intelligence, rigorous in its definition and logical in its deductions from them. On the contrary it is a crude superstition, the offspring of undeveloped mind, indefinite, illogical, inconsistent." The savage, like the child, "is probably indeed much more impulsive, much more liable to be whirled about by gusts of emotion than we are."

At the turn of the century discussions of primitive man were invariably conducted from a moral point of view. That differences was neither neutral, as might be the difference between chairs and tables or circles and squares, nor was it abstract. Each time it was invoked it was recharged with meaning: unless we kept "Them" in clear focus, "We" could not understand ourselves—and vice versa. But the same difference that separates "Them" from "Us" separates the adult from child; higher from lower, vigor from pallor, strength from weakness, courage from cowardice, patience from frivolity, perseverance from capriciousness, intellect from passion, reason from emotion, idea from instinct, and science from magic. Yet some pairings, which were understood as part of a hierarchical design, originated from a more inclusive difference that distinguished men from women. The reverse was true too: discussion about the difference (of "masculine" and "feminine") preserved the validity of those oppositions, each one of which was gender marked.

The later Victorians associated the idea of culture—civilization was an interchangeable term—with "masculine force and masculine intelligence." The answers that were given to two questions—what kind of education, if any, was appropriate for women; and what women's role in political life should be—which were debated at length during the second half of the century—depended on certain presuppositions about the sexes: controversy intensified and positions became explicit as the traditional view of woman was reaffirmed more vigorously than ever before. It may seem that I am crediting Darwin with having exerted more influence than he properly deserves. While Dar-

winian science weakened biblical theology, which is well known, it strengthened the biblical view of the place of woman in the world.

In *The Descent of Man* Darwin produced evidence that supported the traditional view of the physical, mental, and moral superiority of male over female, evidence on which Frazer also relied to support his assumptions, assumptions that were so infused in the social thought of the tradition there was no need to address them unless one set out to challenge, or to meet the challenge, they posed. Rather than controvert or augment the traditional view, Darwin simply restated it and, in light of the evidence he gathered, proposed the principle of selection according to sex with fresh authority. To the degree that Darwin's thought confirmed the traditional view of gender, those who read or read about *The Descent of Man* may well have become less rather than more self-conscious about the presuppositions that justified the exclusion of women from cultural life. Although controversy over the natural equality of the sexes was vigorous by the 1880s, when cast in the metaphorical language of "separate spheres" or "woman's place," the issue inspired less controversy.

Arguments about "woman's place" had the effect of warning women—but men, too—about crossing conventional social boundaries. Women who trespassed ran the risk of becoming like men, while men ran the risk of becoming like women. Some social critics, particularly those who were fearful that such confusion was about to occur, attached the epithet "effeminate" to the time itself (and it has remained a salient figure in subsequent historiography). Although the idioms drew attention to "woman's place," there were comparable consequences for men. While the antiquarians set their sights on remote regions, yet confirmed the "masculinity" of their own civilization, others ranged over the local exotic. I will return to this subject shortly, after we observe the way the word "decadent" behaved in Victorian discussions about their own time, the fullest one of which was conducted by Max Nordau, German Hungarian physician and author. He argued, in a book that had the appearance of being scientific, that artists are insane and called them interchangeably "degenerated" or "Mattoids": persons of erratic mind, compound of genius and fool.

The first English translation of Nordau's *Degeneration* appeared in February 1895 and before the end of the year at least seven impressions had been printed. Nordau predicted that "after some centuries art and poetry will become pure atavisms and will no longer be cultivated except by the most emotional part of humanity—by women, by the mad, perhaps even by children." In his reply to *Degeneration,* George Bernard Shaw circumvented the issue of art and madness by singling out the excess that characterized *Degeneration.* He did not accuse Nordau of all the phobias and manias he had identified as signs of decadence. But he did accuse him of graphomania. With characteristic shrewdness, Shaw pointed out that in his inveterable effort to name the disease Nordau had overreached his purpose, exceeded the boundaries of rationality. He might have said that Nordau enacted his own phobia about disorder, exhibited a mania to put things in place. To enumerate all of the late Victorians' self-dramatizing acts, and to account for them, would divert us. Enough to take note of their penchant for shaping images of themselves, not as they were, but as they imagined they were (or might be), by rewriting the history of the past, and by inventing a past of their own. The idea of "comparing," whether of oneself with another or of one's own time with past times, encouraged this. Nordau's *Degeneration*, which belongs to the same genre of activity as Frazer's **Golden Bough,** provided a new idiom for discourse about decadence.

It would be foolish to describe either book as phobic or manic, although it should be kept in mind that both were guided by the same wish and motivated by the same fear. Nordau, who imagined that civilization was edging toward collapse, and who regarded much of contemporary life as threatening, scrutinized nearly every aspect of it. He searched as though with untoward acquisitiveness for phobias and manias. The need to order (according to which everything is one thing or the other, mania or phobia), was itself a sign of his fear of chaos—a phobia about chaos that quickly became a mania for ordering: he classified phobias and manias with manic excess. Although Nordau was not exemplary of the social critics who described decadence, nonetheless he represents the limiting instance of a prevailing attitude toward disorder. Pivoting on the twin ideas of restraint and manliness as the distinguishing characteristics of civilization, his argument, like the more general discussions of progress and decline, is governed by fear and lacking in restraint. (pp. 200-07)

[It] should be evident why a "falling away" from civilization was thought to be "effeminate," and why "effeminacy" was thought to represent a decline: Darwin had confirmed, and Frazer after him had reconfirmed, that civilization was a result of masculine vigor and intelligence. A man who had failed to be sufficiently masculine (or a culture that failed to be sufficiently civilized) was thought to be less than itself. A woman who falls away from herself, however, is not less than what she naturally is; she is more womanlike: more excessive, irrational, impulsive, intuitive, childlike.

Moreover, the idea of "decadence" depended upon thinking about culture as though it were identical with the organic world of plants and animals which pass through their cycle of birth, growth, deterioration, death, and decay; Darwin's (and Frazer's) conceptions depended on the analogy of the fetus; the legend of "separate spheres" depended on the language of astronomy. Yet, such "facts" as "excess," "irrationality," "effeminacy," and such likenesses as those drawn between the galaxies and social institutions, or the fetus and the evolution of social arrangements, are of a very different order of truth than, for example, that in the year 1895, Justice Wills declared Oscar Wilde had been "the centre of extensive corruption of young men of the most hideous kind"; or, that in the year 1910, King Edward died; or, that in the same year there were strikes of mine and dock workers; or, even that, in the year 1908, Arthur Balfour, in exasperation over the failed attempts to define the word "decadence," finally proposed that it "was rather like digestion: we knew it took place, but couldn't quite say how." The failure to define "decadence" did not inhibit social critics, who appeared to be innocent of the conventions their language conserved and of the fictions they shaped, from using the word. They were at least as innocent as the ethnographers who might have observed—but they too failed to take note of themselves—their own repetitive descriptions, their fascination with the lurid, their interest in Magic and Naming, in the very notion of retrieving the arcane origin of mankind in order to uncover "weak spots" in modernity. It is not difficult to see that their own ethnographic enterprise had as fragile yet complex a surface as that of the civilization they imagined. Nor is it difficult to see why, in light of their arguments, they found descriptions of decadence useful. Each discourse enacted the same ideology.

In spite of the effect Frazer's anthropology had—of confirming that we were civilized and therefore superior—the impulse to confirm, and to confirm so loudly and insistently combatted the fear that "We" were, indeed, like "Them." While the presence of savage survivals—existing "human documents"—made the "science" of anthropology imaginable, it made equally imaginable the imminent eruption of the savage self. Children, the mad, and women were constant reminders of the condition from which civilization had evolved and to which civilization could revert. Adult and manlike behavior were salient signs of progress. But the threat remained: adults could become like children; men could become like women.

The enactment of the science of anthropology was one means of confronting the threat. It would not be an exaggeration to say that the Victorian savage was an elaboration of what the Victorians feared they might too easily become if they were not "civilized." Among the many uses of nineteenth-century anthropology, it reiterated those attributes of civilization that needed to be conserved if the Victorians were not to become like savages, children, or women.

The energetic ordering and arranging of the past assuaged the uneasiness the later Victorians felt about their time and themselves: the idea of comparison enabled them to differentiate themselves from what they feared they might be or might become. The subject of primitive man, which absorbed the attention of anthropologists, led them to anticipate the consummation of their wish to establish a science that would assure them of remaining civilized, although their method required postponement of their practical ambitions. Many undoubtedly felt themselves to be on the threshold of a perpetually deferred discovery throughout their lives. Although the controversy over the priority of "language" or "will," generated by Max Müller's hypothesis, persisted into the nineties, none disputed that what needed to be understood about the world of primitive man was Magic.

The ethnographers initiated their pursuit of origins with the study of Magic because they believed Magic, particularly the magic of transformation through power of naming (and all of the accompanying rituals, customs, and habits that arise from this wish), represents the initial stage of human activity. There is more to be said about why the early ethnographers selected this aspect of primitive experience when other questions might easily have absorbed their attention. The pertinent parallel I wish to draw here is that neither the early ethnographers nor their successors noticed, perhaps because they were straining to be scientific, the affinities between their own pursuit and the activities they described, classified, and scrutinized. To name primitive man, to identify him properly, would enable them to transform modernity. Their interest in Magic, particularly in naming, is especially strong, although seeing their own ambitious enterprise as being, in itself, a Magical activity, did not occur to them. They reserved their wonder for the study of the primitive, whose history promised full knowledge of their own origins, seeking the knowledge of which obscured their own fear. The savage they imagined, more fictional than real, served to order and control the intellectual life of Victorian anthropologists: An imaginary double of their own making whose existence was mediated by accounts as lurid as the arcane world they described. The savage was a fearful version of what they suspected they might actually be. If others could be shown to be different, they could not be like those others.

Frazer's explorations into arcane origins is shrouded in astonishing excess. The study of myth and ritual that had begun earlier in the century culminated in 1889 with the publication of the first volume of *The Golden Bough.* The proliferation of articles about the subject during the second half of the century can be accounted for in a number of ways. It would be foolish to diminish the political context that nurtured the emergence of anthropology. Ethnographic and folklore studies aided colonialism even as the Celtic revival confirmed that such studies stirred national feeling. But apart from these considerations, there is something noteworthy about the individuals who devoted their sedentary lives to writing books about strange customs and beliefs, translating myths, fairytales, and epics, and finding vestiges of arcane rites in classical literatures without moving from the confines of their studies in Oxford, Cambridge, and London. Their studies are informed by a nostalgia for the past, a lament for the absence of myth and ritual from modern life, and a desire to recover something felt to be lost which science would remedy. The practical social-mindedness was oddly modulated by their pursuit of exotic excess in their most astonishingly excessive accounts. At rest in their libraries, they were buoyed by their imaginative energies to remote regions of the world. When they returned, they proceeded to prepare fastidious descriptions of cannibalism, incest, self-affliction, headhunting, nakedness, marriage customs, and much other less-forbidden but equally unfamiliar behavior. In spite of their lurid subjects, their books are often tedious exercises in repetition, books about books, more than equal in their strangeness to the customs they described so laboriously. Their convictions about the possibility of amassing enough information to arrive eventually at significant conclusions, and their ambition to find a cure, need to be seen in the context of the enchantment with which they described modes of existence different from their own. Their sedulous descriptions, which were designed to recuperate and classify the strangeness, gave them a certain authority to speak with the confidence they needed to describe still more. The unself-consciousness with which they undertook veritable descriptions separated them from their avowedly literary contemporaries and from the social critics who were describing "decadence." But the ethnographers whose lives were austere, whose descriptions were as inflated as their imaginations were vivid, flattened their exotic subjects. The titles of their books were often beguiling, but the books themselves are ponderously inclusive and tedious. Their peculiar deflation of their exotic subjects contains an excess of its own no less lurid and peculiar than the lives they described.

If the anthropologists' excessive accounts of primitive man were self-protective, the social critics' descriptions of contemporary "decadence" could only have exacerbated their fear, heightened their desire to delineate differences more sharply, and strengthened their convictions about progress. They, in turn, provided the social critics with a conceptual analogue for describing "decadence": the world of the primitive was insufficiently controlled, measured, and developed by masculine vigor and masculine intelligence; the world of the "decadents," having "fallen away" from civilization, mirrored the world of the primitive. Whether one argued the mark of the age was "progress" or "decline," each made the same claim on the imagination. Literary activity, whether of reading or of writing, inspired traffic with the lurid and, simultaneously, assigned to that activity a privileged place apart. But like all privileges, this one appears to have been in perpetual need of confirmation. Whether one was imagined to differ from or to resemble the savage, each polemical move demarcated "Them" and "Us." Savages—"They"—were repeatedly likened to women in the writings of the anthropologists. In the writings of the social critics, "We" had become like "Them." Rather than controvert each other, or engage in bitter conflict over the issue of "progess" or "decline," each confirmed for the other that civilization was "masculine." And each eschewed, with equal fear, the "feminization" of civilization.

The threat to "masculinity"—examples were found in the lives of individuals, literature, and the wider realm of the "spirit of the age"—were countered in various ways, one of which involved identifying such signs through repeated comparisons with yet other signs. Such social critics as Harrison engaged in eloquent lament, while such anthropologists as Frazer engaged in tedious affirmation: because they shared the notion that civilization was "masculine," gender mediated their discourse. As Frazer thought the savage self within culture might erupt at any time—existing savages were a constant reminder of what reversion might mean—for others, women, particularly women who moved out of their proper sphere, were a constant reminder of the possibility of what might occur if civilization reverted to barbarism, or became "effeminate."

I have argued that the legend of "separate spheres" was revived in the later part of the century as a response to anxieties about sexuality, which were acted out and intensified in discussions of "decadence" and "savagery." Both words were inseparable from political considerations. When sexuality itself became a distinct topos, men enacted their fears more boldly, yet with greater resistance to clarifying their own confusions.

Havelock Ellis and John Addington Symonds were responsible for having introduced the subject into British social thought and they, rather than Freud, or Krafft-Ebing, published the first articles about "sexual inversion," as Symonds, who borrowed the term from Italian social theory, called the phenomenon. We can fairly suppose that Ellis' studies, which recounted the details of anonymous individuals' erotic lives and habits, like the anthropologists' studies of anonymous savages, activated a dormant interest in picturing the marginal world more vividly. If fear of inversion in themselves and in those around them prompted Ellis and Symonds to describe narcissism (as Ellis was the first to call it), reading and writing about this subject could be regarded as salutary acts which, joined as they were to anthropological discourse about the "savages" and to social criticism about "decadence," contributed to the Victorian idea of civilization as a masculine invention.

Would the Victorians recognize themselves in the picture I have constructed here? We might imagine they would have chosen to present their arguments differently according to how we answer this question. More importantly, their choices would have had different consequences. (pp. 213-17)

Sandra Siegel, "Literature and Degeneration: The Representation of 'Decadence'," in Degeneration: The Dark Side of Progress, *edited by J. Edward Chamberlin and Sander L. Gilman, Columbia University Press, 1985, pp. 199-219.*

ADDITIONAL BIBLIOGRAPHY

Ackerman, Robert. "Frazer on Myth and Ritual." *Journal of the History of Ideas* XXXVI, No. 1 (January-March 1975): 115-34.
    Examines Frazer's approach to studying the relationship between ritualism and myth.

Angus-Butterworth, L. M. "Sir James Frazer (1854-1941) and *The Golden Bough*." *Contemporary Review* 230, No. 1335 (April 1977): 196-200.

　　Tribute to Frazer's life and scholarship.

Review of *The Golden Bough*, by James George Frazer. *The Athenaeum*, No. 3275 (2 August 1890): 155-58.

　　Favorable review claiming equal importance for the "method and temper" of Frazer's study as for its conclusions.

Review of *The Golden Bough* (third edition), by James George Frazer. *The Athenaeum*, No. 4497 (3 January 1914): 5-6.

　　Notes developments in Frazer's thought from the first to the third editions of *The Golden Bough*.

Bishop, John Peale. "*The Golden Bough*" (1936). In his *The Collected Essays of John Peale Bishop*, edited by Edmund Wilson, pp. 23-36. New York: Charles Scribner's Sons, 1948.

　　Contends that *The Golden Bough* appears to be structured as an attack upon Christianity, equating Christianity with earlier, discredited sects.

Campion, Sarah. "Autumn of an Anthropologist." *The New Statesman and Nation* XLI, No. 1036 (13 January 1951): 34, 36.

　　Affectionate but somewhat rueful reminiscence by a secretary employed by the Frazers when both were in their late seventies, recounting some personal quirks and foibles of both Frazers.

Cohen, Morris R. "Mythical Science." In his *The Faith of a Liberal*, pp. 420-24. New York: Henry Holt and Co., 1946.

　　Praises "the magical quality of Frazer's way of writing," which compels even a dissenting reader to complete the multiple volumes of *The Golden Bough* with pleasure. Cohen disagrees with Frazer's scientific method, calling it unhistoric and undiscriminating, and with his conclusions, which he maintains are not all supported by his evidence.

"Frazer and Malinowski: A *CA* Discourse." *Current Anthropology* 7, No. 5 (December 1966): 560-76.

　　Reprints Edmund Leach's 1965 attack upon Jarvie's view of Frazer, and Jarvie's 1966 response (both excerpted above), followed by comments on both sides of the conflict from noted anthropologists and sociologists Edwin Ardener, J. H. M. Beattie, Ernest Gellner, and K. S. Mathur. The exchange is concluded with a "Reply" from Leach.

Douglas, Mary. "Judgments on James Frazer." *Daedalus* 107, No. 4 (Fall 1978): 151-64.

　　Examines the changes in Frazer's professional reputation in the hundred years since his career began.

Downie, R. Angus. *James George Frazer: The Portrait of a Scholar*. London: Watts & Co., 1940, 141 p.

　　Biography and survey of Frazer's principal works by his longtime secretary and friend.

――――. *Frazer and the Golden Bough*. London: Victor Gollancz, 1970, 143 p.

　　Anecdotal account of Frazer's life and works, making limited use of material from Downie's earlier biography.

Feder, Lillian. "Myth and Ritual: *The Golden Bough*, Rite as Social Expression." In her *Ancient Myth in Modern Poetry*, pp. 181-85. Princeton, New Jersey: Princeton University Press, 1971.

　　Comments upon the importance of Frazer's studies of the relationship between myth and ritual, noting his contribution of poetic terminology to the scientific examination of contemporary attitudes and behavior.

Gosse, Edmund. "The Folk-Lore of the Bible." In his *Books on the Table*, pp. 91-4. New York: Charles Scribner's Sons, 1921.

　　Commends the wealth of detail that Frazer gathered in his examination of vestigial traces of superstitions and rites in the text of the Old Testament, as well as Frazer's skillful prose style, which renders his books worthy of purely literary evaluation.

――――. "Gods and Heroes." In his *More Books on the Table*, pp. 29-35. New York: Charles Scribner's Sons, 1923.

Approbatory review of Frazer's 1921 translation of and commentary on Apollodorus's *The Library*.

Hodgart, M. J. C. "In the Shade of the Golden Bough." *Twentieth Century* CLVII, No. 936 (February 1955): 111-19.

　　Credits Frazer with popularizing folklore, myth, and anthropological studies in the late nineteenth and early twentieth centuries.

Huxley, Francis. "Frazer within the Bloody Wood." *The New Statesman* LIX, No. 1518 (16 April 1960): 561-62.

　　Reassessment of the importance of *The Golden Bough*, noting some strengths and weaknesses of the work and commenting upon the areas in which it has had a pervasive and enduring effect upon modern thinking.

Kardiner, Abram, and Preble, Edward. "James Frazer: Labor Disguised in Ease." In their *They Studied Man*, pp. 78-107. Cleveland: World Publishing Co., 1961.

　　Biographical and critical sketch outlining Frazer's chief accomplishments.

Lang, Andrew. "*The Golden Bough*." *The Fortnightly Review*, No. ccccx (February 1901): 235-48.

　　Well-known and much-quoted refutation of many of the central tenets of *The Golden Bough*.

Leach, Edmund R. "Golden Bough or Gilded Twig?" *Daedalus* 90, No. 2 (Spring 1961): 371-87.

　　Negative assessment of Frazer's scholarship, impugning his originality, methods, and conclusions.

――――. "Leach's Reply." *Encounter* XXVI, No. 5 (May 1966): 92-3.

　　Response to I. C. Jarvie's 1966 defense of Frazer (excerpted above). Leach reiterates several points, including his conviction that Frazer was not highly regarded in academic circles and that his influence was never extensive.

Malinowski, Bronislaw. "Magic, Science, and Religion: Primitive Man and his Religion" and "Myth in Primitive Psychology: Dedication to Sir James Frazer." In his *Magic, Science, and Religion and Other Essays*, pp. 1-8, pp. 72-3. Boston: Beacon Press, 1948.

　　Finds that "the extended and deepened outlook of modern anthropology" is best expressed in Frazer's writings, particularly in *The Golden Bough*. According to Malinowski, Frazer supplied the field with classic definitions and was the first to identify some of its most important areas of study. In the second chapter cited Malinowski proclaims his indebtedness as an anthropologist to Frazer.

――――. "On Sir James Frazer." In his *Sex, Culture, and Myth*, pp. 268-82. New York: Harcourt, Brace & World, 1962.

　　Reprints Malinowski's reviews of the one-volume abridged edition of *The Golden Bough*, *Folk-Lore in the Old Testament*, and *Totemica*. Malinowski notes the debt all anthropologists owe to Frazer for his contributions to the field and for his popularization of anthropology. He writes: "Frazer, more than anyone else, has given the science of man wide currency among cultured people all over the world. It is largely due to the literary charm of his style and the profoundness of his insight that anthropological books are now extensively read, appreciated, and enjoyed."

Morton, A. L. Review of *Aftermath: A Supplement to the Golden Bough*, by James George Frazer. *The Criterion* XVI, No. lxiv (April 1937): 543-45.

　　Assessment of Frazer's *Aftermath*, which contains additional material pertaining to topics raised in *The Golden Bough*. Morton disagrees with Frazer's contention that belief in magic has hindered human progress, maintaining that it has often been part of a long learning process that resulted in the development of rationalism.

Review of *The Golden Bough*, by James George Frazer. *The Quarterly Review* 172, No. 343 (January 1891): 191-208.

　　Outlines some of the main points of *The Golden Bough*, with praise for Frazer's system of ordering and classifying an immense amount of material.

Trilling, Lionel. "On the Teaching of Modern Literature." In his *Beyond Culture: Essays on Literature and Learning,* pp. 3-30. New York: Viking Press, 1965.

> Extensive commentary on the value of *The Golden Bough* as a supplementary text for teaching a modern literature course. Trilling cites the work's conscious intent to contrast the primitive with the modern, and its pervasive and decisive effect on much modern literature.

Vickery, John B. "Mythopoesis and Modern Literature." In *The Shaken Realist: Essays in Modern Literature in Honor of Frederick J. Hoffman,* edited by Melvin J. Friedman and John B. Vickery, pp. 218-50. Baton Rouge: Louisiana State University Press, 1970.

> Examines some mythic perspectives provided by *The Golden Bough* that have influenced modern literature.

Wittgenstein, Ludwig. *Remarks on Frazer's "Golden Bough,"* edited by Rush Rhees, translated by A. C. Miles. Atlantic Highlands, New Jersey: Humanities Press, 1979, 18 p.

> Musings over various issues raised in *The Golden Bough*.

Martin A. Hansen

1909-1955

Danish novelist, short story writer, essayist, and cultural historian.

Considered one of the most important Danish authors of the twentieth century, Hansen was the author of works exploring the moral problems presented by the rapidly changing values of twentieth-century society. Hansen felt that an identification with tradition, and a commitment to the preservation of one's cultural heritage, provided a link between the past and the present that transcended death and resolved the existential problems posed by twentieth-century life. While his efforts to define those aspects of Danish tradition that could stabilize the chaos of modernity appealed to many Danish readers, his growing reputation outside of Denmark attests to the universality of his concerns.

Hansen was born and raised in a rural community. Descended from peasants, his parents were farmers who struggled against constant economic hardship. At the age of fourteen, Hansen was taken out of school and, according to local custom, sent to live and work on nearby farms, where he grew accustomed to the demands of farm labor. Three years later, he enrolled in Haslev Teachers' College and turned away from the conservative Christian heritage of his upbringing. Radicalized by the intellectual milieu he encountered in Haslev, he began espousing atheism and Darwinism and became sympathetic with the ideals of communism. After graduating in 1930, Hansen found a teaching job in a poor district of Copenhagen, and during his early years there began to take a serious interest in writing fiction. His first novel, *Nu opgiver han,* was acclaimed for its realistic account of a disintegrating rural society. Its sequel, *Kolonien,* described the failure of a utopian experiment in communal farming based on Marxist principles. Although both of these novels dealt with the Danish agrarian and economic crisis of the 1930s, as well as with issues of social justice, both also demonstrated that the author's main interest lay not in society but in the individual.

The German conquest of Denmark in April 1940 greatly affected Hansen's life and works. He was disappointed that his country resisted the Nazi invasion so briefly and ashamed that he did not participate in what little fighting had taken place; he also deplored the docility with which his fellow Danes accepted the German occupation. The experience prompted an even greater distaste for politics, and his next novel, *Jonatans rejse,* represented a turning point in his career. In this work Hansen abandoned the sober realism of his earlier novels in favor of a whimsical narrative style which he used to satirize dogmatic political ideologies. The form of the novel is a quest which takes its eponymous protagonist from a simple farming culture to the complex modern world, a journey that mirrors Hansen's own progression from a traditional rural to a modern urban culture. The novel expresses Hansen's belief that good and evil have become indistinguishable in the modern world, and that even those with the best intentions may end by serving evil.

As the German occupation of Denmark continued, Hansen joined the resistance movement and wrote many essays for

underground publications, encouraging others to become involved in active resistance. In his essays he compared the contemporary situation with that of medieval Europe, drawing parallels between the Nazis and the imperialistic Vikings of the pre-Christian era. According to Hansen, it was the Catholic church that had initiated democratic society based on the values of justice and the importance of the individual; however, the basis for democratic society was undermined by the trend toward secularization that began during the Renaissance, finally resulting in the resurgence of totalitarianism and the moral and existential disorientation characteristic of twentieth-century life. *Lykkelige Kristoffer (Lucky Kristoffer)*, Hansen's next novel, conveys his understanding of the problems of the modern age and his belief in individualism, coupled with an emphasis on the responsibility of the individual to society. Depicting a journey during the turbulent years of the Lutheran Reformation in the early 1500s, *Lucky Kristoffer* draws a parallel between that era and the strife-ridden years of World War II. Hansen found that no material or scientific gains could compensate for the loss of the spiritual qualities of the past. He also perceived in past ages a sense of personal and societal responsibility that governed and protected the individual and granted a meaningful life in a just society. Faith and Niels Ingwersen have written that "Hansen, who in this myth discovered his thinking and authorship's sustaining values, was to turn this mythical world into a reserve for qualities relevant to the individual who is lost in the modern world's confusion.'' The popular success of *Lucky Kristoffer* enabled Hansen to retire from teaching in order to devote all of his time to writing.

Hansen had expected that after the war a national rejuvenation would take place, but he was disillusioned by what he saw as petty bickering between factions that adhered to limiting ideologies. The postwar period was made particularly bitter for him when he learned that an essay he had written during the war, in which he had called for the slaying of informers who had betrayed other Danes to the occupation forces, had persuaded two young men to join the resistance movement and that they were subsequently caught by the Nazis and executed. The knowledge of their deaths, for which Hansen felt responsible, resulted in a brooding preoccupation with death that endured for the rest of his life. He went through a severe crisis during which he doubted that the resistance had been worthwhile and became preoccupied by the potentially destructive power of art. During this time he worked on *Kains alter,* a novel depicting the artistic process as homicidal. Hansen abandoned this project when he came to realize that literature could give meaning to death by preserving cultural heritage. Hansen came to view his profession as an ethical force and to believe that ''to be a good poet is a moral, religious destiny.''

During the last part of the war, Hansen had worked on a number of short stories that he put into final form, in the volumes *Tornebusken* and *Agerhønen,* after he abandoned the writing of *Kains alter.* Both collections mirror the crisis that Hansen experienced and convey a movement from despair to spiritual rebirth. Upon publication of these works, Hansen was acknowledged in Denmark as a major writer. In 1950 he published his last novel, *Løgneren* (*The Liar*), which describes the personal crises and spiritual transformation of its narrator, Johannes Vig. Vig suffers from the same existential malaise that Hansen saw as characteristic of twentieth-century civilization. At the end of the novel Vig resolves to find value and purpose in educational and cultural pursuits; he therefore abandons fiction in order to write an account of the nature and culture of the islands on which he lives. Significantly, Hansen wrote very little fiction after completing *The Liar,* instead devoting himself to essays on Danish culture and history and to travel essays. Prominent among these works is *Orm og tyr,* a cultural history that examines the close relationship between pagan and Christian religions in Scandinavia. This work expresses Hansen's concept of tradition and its relevance to modern times. Hansen wrote that ''when man finds himself in a purposeless and fearful world, he can be rescued by beliefs that restore harmony to his existence''; the beliefs he referred to are those of a healthy cultural tradition that give the individual the knowledge that both life and death are meaningful. Hansen died of a kidney disease in 1955, leaving many unfinished works, some of which were published posthumously.

Critics have generally considered Hansen to be the best Danish writer of his generation and among the greatest of this century. His treatment of cultural, ethical, and existential problems has appealed to a wide readership, and his ideas concerning the importance of tradition have had a significant influence on modern Danish literature. As Faith and Niels Ingwersen have stated: ''Through his works, Hansen definitely intended to bring the existential problems of his age to the fore, and if he often looked backward, it was with the purpose of recapturing the values or the sense of direction that modern man had lost.''

PRINCIPAL WORKS

Nu opgiver han   (novel)   1935
Kolonien   (novel)   1937
Jonatans rejse   (novel)   1941
Lykkelige Kristoffer   (novel)   1945
　　[*Lucky Kristoffer,* 1974]
Tornebusken   (novellas)   1946
Agerhønen   (short stories)   1947
Tanker i en skorsten   (essays)   1948
Leviathan   (essay)   1950
Løgneren   (novel)   1950
　　[*The Liar,* 1954]
Orm og tyr   (cultural history)   1952
Dansk vejr   (travel essay)   1953
Kringen   (travel essay)   1953
Paradisæblerne og andre historier   (short stories)   1953
Rejse på Island   (travel essay)   1954
Konkyljen   (short stories)   1955
Midsommerkrans   (short stories)   1956
Efterslæt   (short stories and essays)   1959
Mindeudgave. 10 vols.   (novels, short stories, and essays)
　　1961
Ved korsvejen   (essays)   1965
Against the Wind   (short stories)   1979

RICHARD B. VOWLES   (essay date 1958)

[*Vowles is an American critic and educator who specializes in Scandinavian studies. In the following excerpt, he surveys Hansen's career.*]

Surrender, Hansen's first novel, was the expression of his own revolt. It concerned the farm son Niels whose slogan is ''Away with tradition; we must specialize'' and his father Lars Jørn, a gnarled and narrow-minded free-holder who succumbs to pressure and relinquishes the farm to his son. The novel has forty characters, eleven love interests, and all the clichés dear to the *epikers* of the soil. But it also had power and promise. Its sequel, **The Colony,** which deals with the collectivist farm experiment under Niels, and its failure, is by no means so good a novel. It reveals Hansen's growing impatience with both ideology and method. Probably he would have turned to the greater latitude of fantasy whether or not the Nazi occupation had forced him to it.

Jonathan's Journey (*Jonatans Rejse*) concerns the peripatetic adventures of a smithy of good heart, who has captured the devil in a bottle and will present him to the ruler of the kingdom, and Askelad the bumptious lad who accompanies him. Though a comic realism of dialogue imbues the whole, the book is fundamentally an expression of symbolic conflict in which Jonathan represents the essential goodness of the Middle Ages and Askelad the bland amorality of modern science. The bottled devil can be read as a symbol of any perilous possession and, more specifically, a premonition of the atomic bomb. However, the book is neither social satire precisely, nor science fiction, but simply skillful narration. Yet it contains, says Sven Møller Kristensen, ''all the elements of thought that were to be deepened and extended in Hansen's later production.''

Lucky Christopher (*Lykkelige Kristoffer*) is also picaresque, but finds its setting in feudal Sweden of the Reformation. Written in an old chronicle style, constructed out of peasant idiom, the novel owes a good deal to Cervantes and Rabelais. The penniless nobleman Christopher travels from Halland, on the west coast of Sweden, to Copenhagen, experiencing all manner of human evil and indignity on the way. Riding a one-eyed giant nag, he is accompanied by an assorted crew: the wise clerk Martin, knowledgeable in medicine, and the narrator of the story; Father Matthew, representative of the cultural best of the Middle Ages; and Herr Paal, a thick-skinned old war horse of a soldier. The theme is the survival of a beautiful but irrational idealism in a world of lechery, materialism, hatred, and terror.

It is a paradox that in the spring of 1946 Hansen finally became a popular success with **The Thorn Bush (***Tornebusken***),** the most obscure of all his books. In **"Easter Bells,"** the first of three stories, Johan, a farm-hand, wins the girl; then fights a bull released by his cowardly rival; and dies a kind of ecstatic, ritualistic death. **"September Fog,"** the third story, deals with the anguish of warfare. But these two narratives are, as Thorkild Bjornvig puts it in a brilliant book about Hansen, but the transepts to the nave of the book, **"Midsummer Feast,"** a tale of "oracular ambiguity." Within the color of a festival setting, Hansen conducts a philosophic dialogue that explores the interrelation of good and evil. The book is an extraordinary *tour de force,* not only for its compactness (the three stories cover in sequence exactly twenty-four hours) but for its examination of the uses of suffering—with the thorn bush and its Christian connotations as the presiding symbol. But it seems overly ambitious compared to the books that follow.

The perfection of Hansen's short story art is best observed in **The Partridge (***Agerhønen***),** containing four stories in each of three divisions: "Legend", dealing with moments of childhood; "Revelation," with fumbling maturity; and "Myth", applying the vision of childhood to adult themes. Within this organic development, there is an interrelation of story in one group to corresponding story in another group, that gives the book a fascinating and, so far as I know, unique symmetry, a symmetry that integrates the greatest diversity of method.

"The Waiting Room" pursues the nihilistic train of thought of a woman who has bungled her emotional life and reached the end of the line. **"Sacrifice",** somewhat like Shirley Jackson's classic "The Lottery", is about the burial alive of two children by a superstitious people, in order to avert a plague. **"The Soldier and the Girl"** is a strangely diaphanous and yet comic version of the death of a soldier. But the most original is **"The Birds"** because here Hansen has, in his preoccupation with the Middle Ages, resuscitated the *fabliau,* substituting for its coarseness the most engaging naiveté.

The story is of the farm boy, Espen, who goes to work for "the foolish priest of Kyndelby," a good man who preaches dull sermons and handles his farm in a colossally inept way, albeit with a real *joie de vivre.* (pp. 34-6)

[In] spite of his brawn and skill, Espen cannot avert downfall. Debts consume profits, the priest's wife dies, and his daughter departs for a sleazy life in the city. But not before misleading Espen into thinking she will marry him. At a very funny toasting ceremony, when the priest congratulates the two, Helena breaks the news.

> "It isn't Espen, my dear. How can you think it? Espen is a lovely boy. You are Espen! But you are and remain a real farmboy. There are men who are much finer and handsomer—I happen to know."

The priest emptied his glass.

"Goodnight, children," he said, and went.

"You may kiss me," said Helena.

"But you really mustn't demand that I marry you. Can't you understand that?"

"Skaal," said Espen, and drank his raspberry juice.

Thus Hansen turns a peasant taciturnity into artistry. But it is equally his warm-hearted understanding for the imaginatively ineffectual, those with "birds" in their breasts, that gives the story its fresh charm: the priest who keeps the *Iliad* in one pocket and the *Odyssey* in the other—and of course the New Testament inside next to his heart; and Espen, the knight errant who gives a lobster claw as token to Helena, his passionate lady. Like Don Quixote and Sancho Panza they stand for the ideal and the real, two half personalities that need each other to make up a whole. The symbolism is not intrusive. In his last published work, an introduction to the first full translation of *Moby Dick* into Danish, Hansen laments the scholarly and critical preoccupation with Melville's symbols, and admires the author for rendering emotions with love and fidelity. Then and only then, symbolic values take on their true, emergent meaning, as they do in the works of Hansen himself. The story is the thing.

The Liar (*Løgneren***)** is beyond question Hansen's finest novel, and probably his finest work of any kind. It has been translated into Swedish, Norwegian, Finnish, German, French, and English; and it is our loss that it has not yet appeared in the United States. Originally intended as a radio serial, it is by no means disjointed or episodic. Instead it has a classical perfection of form that is enhanced by a rhythm of revelation. The story reveals itself gradually through the diary of the factotum on the island of Sandø, Johannes Vig, combined parish clerk and schoolmaster, an emotionally frustrated but intelligent man approaching middle age, who wavers between dignity and folly in an absorbing way. On the face of it, the narration of a schoolmaster would seem to offer little promise, but Hansen himself was no ordinary schoolmaster, and his protagonist-speaker is a humble, self-knowledgeable, human figure who ascends to a kind of greatness.

Johannes Vig is in love with the much younger Annemari, though he will scarcely admit it to himself. He anxiously argues the rights of the absent Oluf, by whom Annemari has had an illegitimate child, but she has turned cool toward him in favor of Harry, an engineer on special assignment to this bleak island to which spring is just coming—spring that "means only confusion and trouble." Oluf stands for solid peasant tradition, to which Johannes dedicates himself as friend of all that Oluf represents and as a kind of amateur archaeologist and historian, and Harry is the bland, uncomplicated interloper, the traveling salesman of technology.

When he is sure that Annemari has severed herself from Oluf, Johannes makes a vain and painful gesture for her favor, but it is too late. There might have been a time, the perfect moment, but *chronos* ["time"] has its brutal, disruptive rhythm. In desperation and somewhat in alcohol, Johannes substitutes an erotic adventure with Rigmor, the passionate and unhappy wife of the biggest landowner of Sandø, the "high-flying snipe" Frederik, as Johannes calls him. Finally the schoolmaster emerges from his neurotic upheaval and makes his private peace, as it were.

The dimensions of the novel are not immense, but they are exactly right. Sandø is documented with delightful precision; the rhythmic approach of spring is observed in a detail that is neither pedantic nor sentimental. "I noticed," observes Johannes, "that the dark spots in the sea-ice now lay almost in streaks, giving it a speckled appearance, which reminded one of the wing of an immense bird of prey." Hansen knew his birds perhaps better than anything else in nature, and he knew how the ice looked at any given moment in the cycle of things.

But nature is not the only framework. Swatches of traditional Danish poetry are woven into the texture of the story in an unobtrusive but meaningful way and give the novel an added dimension and a uniquely Danish character.

The schoolmaster is a perfect narrator for the story. If his manner is at first somewhat dry and crabbed, passion emerges in spite of restraint. Johannes is a fine observer of mores, a humane analyst of everyone's character—but his own. And therein lies the element of suspense. His introspection is always interesting and plausible. In this respect, Hansen knew exactly what he was doing. In one of his last essays he attacks Hemingway's *The Old Man and the Sea* tellingly, because Hemingway approaches the terribly isolated old fisherman at sea from the outside, as omniscient narrator and then subtly, but no less unfortunately, confuses his own dilemma as writer with that of the old man. He taps Hemingway's story and finds its hollow ring, as few critics have done; but in general he is an admirer, for "Hemingway is a prosist with tone. Not so many writers possess that." In *The Liar* Hansen, too, has his own individual tone, and his handling of the schoolmaster's angle of vision is masterly. He might have got personally involved, schoolmaster that he himself is, but he did not. He would agree with T. S. Eliot that writing is "not so much an expression of personality as an escape from it."

Johannes Vig tells his story in diary fashion to an imaginary listener, Nathanael, because, as he tells us, the Biblical Nathanael was a man without guile, whereas he, Johannes, constantly deceives himself. Hence the title *The Liar*. Did Hansen know that André Gide too wrote a novel, *Les Nourritures Terrestres,* in which the narrator addresses an imaginary Nathanael? (As Hans Ruin has pointed out). Hansen was well read and the coincidence is striking, so striking that it seems to me that Hansen's novel can only be interpreted, at least in part, as answer to Gide's book, which is, on the other hand, not so much a novel as a self-indulgent tone poem. Gide urges his young friend to exploit the senses, wipe out the line between good and evil, and find satisfaction to the hilt. Johannes creates his Nathanael out of his loneliness and ascends the last painful ramp of sensual upheaval to find quite a different answer. Spring comes and so also comes the woodcock, or Christ by symbolic transfer, and the evil spirits are driven out. Love is transient, but the world remains. Johannes will chronicle Sandø, his microcosm, for "he who takes pains to search the shadows of the past below us, can . . . more surely guess the dim curves of the future above him."

Other than *The Conch (Konkyljen),* a collection of stories and fragments issued posthumously, Hansen wrote no more fiction after *The Liar.* Like Tolstoy, he came to question the ethical validity of the esthetic act, the meaning of his work in fiction. Unlike Tolstoy, he did not throw his creative ballast overboard. Instead, through a study of Romanesque painting in Danish churches, he arrived at a new understanding of craft in the service of Christendom. But the book in which he does this is many things.

Serpent and Bull is, first of all, a kind of Scandinavian Old Testament. To Hansen the historical method of Jesus, based not on revolution but fulfillment, "surpassed in its dialectical wisdom that of the Romans and the Greeks." With this in mind, he analyzes Viking remains and legends and their cultural tendency toward Christianity. Secondly, the book is a penetrating study of death, with special attention to the peculiarly Danish myth of the serpent and the bull, according to which a serpent, which has encircled a church, is killed by a bull, nurtured by the community in preparation for this encounter. The serpent, to Hansen, stands for a barbaric concept of death, while the bull, a household animal, represents the folk Christendom that released man from his superstitious fear.

It is the folk Christendom of the Romanesque period (1000-1250 A.D.) that appealed to Hansen most, partly for a harmony of spirit reflected in the rounded arch, as opposed to the nervous and divided sensibility implicit in the Gothic arch, but even more in the uncomplicated artistry of Romanesque painting in Danish and Scanian churches. By reverting to the folk Christendom of the late Middle Ages, he was able to reconcile his belief and his art. Here Christ was a victorious, not a drawn and suffering figure. Here Christianity was as it should be, "neither religion, social science, nor ethics, but a great and fateful occurrence in man."

Yet *Serpent and Bull* is not a pretentious book. It is undeniably cultural history of a sort, supported by scholarly opinion, but it has the simplicity of everything Hansen did. I think of it as a gesture of devotion to the village church, always lovingly appraised in its natural setting, always sought as the surest way to the heart and the artistic temperament of the people.

The one thing that seems to have distressed Hansen about *Serpent and Bull* was that it did not, could not by its very nature, give free play to his instinctive story-telling persuasion. It is our complaint too. For Martin A. Hansen was and is one of the best writers of fiction of our time. He brings warmth of insight, skill of concentration, and a rare tonal quality to the story without losing sight of the truth that it is basically the story that matters. Most important of all, he was increasingly able to reveal the mystery that shimmers explosively beneath the surface of things. Working in a mode he called "metaphysical psychology," for lack of a better term, he sought "a visionary depiction of men which, to tell the truth about the human being, often must tell about something which couldn't at all happen." Not fantasy so much as a kind of luminous realism. Like Kierkegaard, he knew about the uses of the past. From the late Middle Ages he recaptured the meaning of craft, the devotion of color and form, not subservient to Christendom but Christendom itself. (pp. 36-40)

> *Richard B. Vowles, "Martin A. Hansen and the Uses of the Past," in* The American-Scandinavian Review, *Vol. XLVI, No. 1, March, 1958, pp. 33-40.*

ELIAS BREDSDORFF (essay date 1969)

[*Bredsdorff is a Danish critic and educator. In the following excerpt, he discusses Hansen's major works, focusing on* The Liar.]

Martin A. Hansen is one of Denmark's two outstanding novelists of the 1940's and 1950's—the other is H. C. Branner. Martin A. Hansen's literary output in his own lifetime (he died at the age of 45) was limited to five novels, three collections of short stories, and a number of nonfictional works, essays, cultural manifestoes, travel descriptions, and religious-historical works. Four volumes of short stories and essays have been published posthumously, and also the fragment of an unfinished novel. (p. 7)

Martin A. Hansen's first two books were novels fairly closely following the pattern of the Danish social realism of the 1930's. *Now He Gives Up (Nu opgiver han)* and its sequel *The Colony (Kolonien)* have as their background the Danish agricultural crisis of the thirties, and they describe both the dissolution of the old forms and the failure of a modern experiment in agricultural collectivism. But already in his next novel, *Jonathan's Journey (Jonatans Rejse)*, Martin A. Hansen had abandoned the social realism of his first two novels, for here his imagination had been given free rein in a grotesque folk-tale saga about Jonathan, the village blacksmith, who manages to catch the Devil in a bottle he has forged out of an old church bell and sealed with a silver cork made from an altar candlestick. Now he need only beat the bottle to make its prisoner grant him his every wish, but often his wishes—and especially the more unselfish ones—bring him into grave trouble. Accompanied by Askelad—another traditional folk-tale character, here depicted untraditionally as a clever boy with a superstitious belief in progress and reason, a kind of intellectual child prodigy—Jonathan sets out on his long journey in order to present the bottled-up Devil to the King of the country. In the end, after many complications and tribulations, the two main characters—a kind of reversed Don Quixote and Sancho Panza—arrive in the capital, a huge, contemporary city, for Jonathan's journey was really a journey in time, from ancient Danish peasant culture up to the more doubtful blessings of modern industrial civilization.

During the German occupation of Denmark Martin A. Hansen joined the Resistance, being particularly closely associated with the Danish underground press, and after the Liberation of his country he publicly defended the "liquidation of informers" carried out by the Resistance movement. His masterly novel *Lucky Christopher (Lykhelige Kristoffer)*, which has the advantage of being less obviously moralizing than *Jonathan's Journey,* is only properly understood, I think, against the background of the Occupation period, though it is set in sixteenth-century Denmark and clearly inspired by both Cervantes' *Don Quixote* and Diderot's *Jacques le fataliste*. The title character is a young penniless nobleman from Hailand, an awkward idealist who is subjected to conflicting influences in an era of internal struggles and feuds—just as chaotic as our own time. But the book is also about the problem of the creative artist, for it pretends to be the work of one of its own characters, a man named Martin, who had to put on paper the events of his time in order to understand both them and himself. Like its counterpart, Johannes V. Jensen's famous novel *The Fall of the King*, Martin A. Hansen's *Lucky Christopher* carries an important contemporary message behind its historical façade.

After the war religious and existential problems assumed an ever increasing importance in Hansen's works. *The Thornbush (Tornebusken)* is a collection of three long tales, "The Easter Bell" ("Paaskeklokken"), "The Midsummer Feast" ("Midsommerfesten"), and "September Mist" ("Septembertaagen"), all set in the present time but exploding the laws of naturalism and realism. Martin A. Hansen was a self-confessed disciple of Sören Kierkegaard—he claimed to have read Kierkegaard already as a child—and it is the Kierkegaardian concept of *angst* which lies behind these stories, in which the author gets involved in a direct discussion with his reader—incidentally like Kierkegaard's *hin enkelte* a female one.

The Partridge (Agerhönen) is another collection of short stories, twelve in all, divided into three parts with the subtitles "Legend," "Cognition," and "Myth"; the stories coming under the first two subheadings are partly about children and their unsophisticated view of the world, partly about the complexity of adult existence and the meaninglessness of death; the third group consists of a number of modern fairy tales, often told in a humorous vein, but dealing with essential problems of life and death.

Thoughts Inside a Chimney (Tanker i en Skorsten) is an important collection of artistic essays, childhood recollections, archeological and historical studies, literary appreciations, and personal confessions. The author—originally regarded by many as a disciple of Johannes V. Jensen, that rational and pagan evolutionist—had now come out clearly as a Christian mystic, a writer whose spiritual ancestors were Sören Kierkegaard and Vilhelm Grönbech, a rebel and iconoclast who warned against believing in intellectual solutions to human problems and against any cheap optimism regarding the future. Though essentially a prose writer himself Martin A. Hansen became closely associated with the young generation of Danish postwar writers, mainly lyrical poets, who gathered round the literary journal *Heretica* (1948-53), of which he himself was an editor for a time.

And it was at this time that Martin A. Hansen's last novel was published, in a way his last piece of important fiction, *The Liar (Lögneren)*. For during the last five years of his life the only volume of fiction he published was a slender collection of short stories, *Crab Apples (Paradisæblerne)*, of which most were written before 1950. All the same, he was by no means unproductive during the last five years of his life; he wrote the pessimistic politico-cultural confession entitled *Leviathan;* a poetic interpretation of the early Christian history of Denmark entitled *Serpent and Bull (Orm og Tyr);* and three volumes of sensitive Scandinavian travel impressions, *Danish Weather (Dansk Vejr), Kringen (About Norway),* and *Travel in Iceland (Rejse i Island)*. It has been suggested by Thorkild Björnvig, the leading authority on Martin A. Hansen, that during the last years of his life (after *The Liar*) Hansen deliberately turned away from creative writing because he had come to regard the creative writer as a Cain-figure—in fact the last novel Martin A. Hansen attempted, without ever finishing it, had the significant title *Cain's Altar (. . . Kains Alter)*. (pp. 8-11)

The genesis of *The Liar* is that it was commissioned by the Danish State Radio as a so-called *radioroman*—a "radio novel" to be read in installments over a period of several months. Consequently the novel appeared as a piece of "oral literature" in the spring of 1950 before being published as a book in the autumn of that year.

The entire action takes place on a small, isolated Danish island called Sandö (Sand Island), "a molehill in the sea." For the Danish edition the author drew a map of this island which is not to be found on any ordinary map of Denmark; it may be worth noticing that the contours of Sandö are almost identical with the part of Stevns which was Martin A. Hansen's home district.

The main character of the novel is a middle-aged bachelor schoolmaster, who holds also the office of a *degn* (parish clerk), which places him half-way between the laymen and the clergy; his name is Johannes Vig. But he is not only the main character (and the title character), he is also the author of the book, insofar as the story pretends to be a manuscript written by him in the form of a confidential diary, addressed to a fictional, non-existent reader, whom he chooses to call Nathanael because in the Gospel according to St. John an apostle named Nathanael is referred to as being a man without guile. The schoolmaster's own name is not without significance either, for if pronounced too quickly it sounds like "Johannes Svig," i.e. John Fraud. He is in fact the self-confessed *Liar:* every page of the twenty exercise books containing his confessions is headed with the words "The Liar" in his own handwriting. But Johannes Vig is not someone who lies for selfish reasons, or to deceive himself, or for the sheer pathological love of lying; he is neither a Tartuffe nor a Peer Gynt; to quote Göran Printz-Påhlson [see Additional Bibliography], who has written a very important essay on *The Liar,* to which reference will have to be made later on—"in a sense the point of the title is that he is no liar. His ancestry goes back to the Kierkegaardian pseudonyms for whom deceit would be a higher way of reaching the truth."

The book is divided into twelve chapters, of which the first eleven record events (as seen by Johannes Vig) which took place on the island of Sandö between Friday, March 13, and Monday, March 16—the transition period between winter and spring (marked by the breaking-up of the ice and the arrival of the woodcock). But the final chapter, which is dated April, the year after, reveals that even the diary form is a deception, for apart from the first few pages of the very first chapter everything was in fact written down by the schoolmaster twelve months after the actual events took place.

The names of the characters are at times almost as complicated—though for different reasons—as those of a Russian novel. Harry, the young engineer—a stranger on the island—is frequently referred to as Alexander—simply because Johannes sees him as a potential conqueror. At one moment the girl Annemari—a former pupil of Johannes' and engaged to the absent Oluf, another former pupil of his—may be seen by Johannes as Dido (with Harry/Alexander cast in the part of Aeneas), at other times she and Harry are being identified with Nanna and Hother, the two lovers in Johannes Ewald's eighteenth-century tragedy *The Death of Balder*—with Johannes cast in the fatal role of Balder.

The schoolmaster tries hard to conceal his love for Annemari, his former pupil, while she on the other hand does her utmost to make him understand that she reciprocates his feelings. One ingenious way of concealing his secret love is by admitting it. "Why didn't you run away with me?" Annemari asks him. "Did you never think about that?" To which Johannes replies, "I have never thought about anything else. Will you run away with me now?" But a man who speaks so flippantly cannot be serious, and she reproaches him: "You are always jesting, and about everything, Johannes." To which he replies, "As a matter of fact I never jest." Thus he lies by telling the truth. And in order to prevent Annemari from knowing that he bought a necklace for her, Johannes invents a story of having bought it a long time ago for a girl who jilted him, but he trips up on the name by calling her Birte.

"There, you see," she said, "last time you called her Betty. I do believe you have made it all up."

"That is the disadvantage of invention, my dear, one can never tell the same story twice."

For the whole point is that as long as she has not formally broken her engagement with the absent Oluf—another former pupil of Johannes Vig's—Annemari must *not* know that the

schoolmaster loves her. And when toward the end of the book Oluf has come back, and has been told everything, and has accepted breaking off the engagement, then it is too late—for by now Johannes has pushed Annemari into the arms of the young engineer, the rival he himself created, so that when Annemari is eventually free also in the formal sense of the word and Johannes runs to declare his love to her, then she has been truly conquered by the victorious Alexander. And the disappointed Don Juan, as he is now, goes to bed instead with Rigmor, a friend's wife—only to find that her love for him is so genuine that he cannot ever make her his mistress again. In the end Johannes has come to realize that even his love for Annemari was a lie: it was make-believe, playacting, a game. Rigmor was the one he loved, but he could only help her once by giving back to her her own faith in life. "But I know that she grows and will blossom into a fine humanity."

The schoolmaster gives up the kind of writing which is doomed to be lies and decides to concentrate on factual, descriptive writing, for he now takes upon himself the task of writing the history of Sandö, its topography, its legends, its folk recollections. And in the final chapter we see how the aging schoolmaster finds solace, true solace, in renunciation—not entirely unlike another Danish *degn*, the title character in Blicher's master story "The Journal of a Parish Clerk" ("Brudstykker af en Landsbydegns Dagbog," 1824), which—alongside with Harald Kidde's novel *The Hero* (*Helten*, 1912)—may well have had a considerable influence on Martin A. Hansen's novel.

But the influence of Kierkegaard is even more essential. Göran Printz-Påhlson aptly compares *The Liar* with Kierkegaard's "Guilty-Non-Guilty," the diary part of his *Stages on Life's Way:*

> There we have two series of parallel diary entries, one dated Morning and containing remembrances of happenings exactly a year before, the other dated Midnight and containing the actual diary. The diary covers a period of about half a year, leaving a dead period of another half year in between—just like the dead period of thirteen months in *The Liar.* There is no need to point out that the two works are concerned with very different psychological problems, but it is worth remembering that both are exploring the connections between guilt and deception.

Printz-Påhlson also links Martin A. Hansen's novel with Kierkegaard's concept of "indirect communication," as Hansen developed it for instance in *The Point of View for My Work as an Author;* Printz-Påhlson discusses the "logical paradox" of *The Liar* in these words:

> Johannes is lying, but the very fact that he tells that he is lying makes him tell the truth. This gives a new validity to his confession. The technical-logical paradox reinforces, through structural analogy, the series of moral paradoxes in the book. To gain happiness you have to give it up. To fight the Father of Lies man has to resort to deception himself. To reveal the shut-upness, to exorcise the demonic, requires a power that is at least partly derived from the same inner source.

Johannes Vig is a religious philosopher who calls himself a Dilettante of the Faith—"a non-believer, who believes in what he does not believe." But when Rigmor speaks of the meaninglessness of her own life and asks him how she can then believe in a God, Johannes answers: "You must! For when you reach the limits of meaninglessness, you find that all is a battleground where two forces fight, and there isn't any no man's land.'' All the same, when in his capacity of *degn* Johannes has to read the lesson about the unclean spirit and the casting out of a devil, he is fully aware that he himself has been possessed by a devil and that his hypnotic effect on the congregation is that of an evil spirit. The words from the Gospel according to St. Luke which he reads to the congregation are deeply relevant both to his own situation and to that of the age in which he lives: ''Every kingdom divided against itself is brought to desolation; and a house divided against a house falleth.'' Later on, doubts are cast on his confession that he, who was only inward emptiness, should suddenly have become the seducer himself. What is the truth? Is there in fact any truth?

> I felt like a stranger at the meeting, and then became so completely a stranger that I was like the Devil himself. Weren't you in ecstasies over it, Nathanael? Or don't you believe a word of it? What do I believe myself? Perhaps you say the same as I said to myself in the sacristy: I must be crazy to drink in the morning, on a empty stomach. Isn't that right?

But Johannes Vig is also a keen observer of nature, and accompanied by Pigro, his dog, he likes to go out shooting. The wild birds on the island play a significant part in the novel—in fact often a symbolic part. Whenever the woodcock is mentioned the reader learns to prick his ears, for in this novel it becomes a magic bird, at times clearly identified with Annemari, and by means of folk tradition it is also mysteriously linked to the particular Sunday when the lesson about the exorcism of unclean spirits is read.

The Liar is a puzzling book and in spite of its many obvious literary links a profoundly original novel. (pp. 11-17)

> *Elias Bredsdorff, in an introduction to* The Liar *by Martin A. Hansen, translated by John Jepson Egglishaw, Twayne Publishers, Inc., 1969, pp. 7-17.*

H. WAYNE SCHOW (essay date 1974)

[*In the following essay, Schow examines the philosophical themes in* The Liar *in light of the theories of Danish philosopher Søren Kierkegaard.*]

Nordic literature has a strong endemic strain of melancholy. Denmark, in particular, perhaps because of its association with Hamlet, has frequently been considered the home of despair and spiritual desolation (since the romantic movement, the German literary tradition has especially accepted and perpetuated this myth about the Danish temper). To view Danish national character and literature entirely from such narrow perspective is surely a distortion, yet the nineteenth-century Danish writers who have had the strongest impact outside their own country are Soren Kierkegaard and Jens Peter Jacobsen—both of whom revealed in their writings personal lives of tortured spiritual extremity. One an intense Christian, the other a dedicated but troubled atheist, they were ahead of their time in foreshadowing the anguished awareness of man's existential predicament basic to so much of the literature of our century.

A novel which appears likely to become a Danish classic, Martin A. Hansen's *The Liar,* is a work modern in its themes, universal in its archetypal directness, and at the same time natively Danish in its vision and values. Its spiritual forebears are Kierkegaard and, indirectly, Jacobsen. Since the dilemma at the heart of the novel was plausibly conceived in Kierkegaard's terms, recognizing the novel's Kierkegaardian overtones will illuminate our understanding by providing touchstones for the protagonist's spiritual struggle.

In the development of Hansen's thought Kierkegaard is important beyond question; indeed, his name occurs so frequently in Hansen's essays (in a variety of contexts) that the latter was clearly familiar with the Kierkegaard canon. With *The Liar,* in addition to internal implication, an interesting bit of evidence among Hansen's unpublished papers suggests that Kierkegaard was its godfather. A fragment from 1952 is entitled **"From the Idle Papers of a Confused Contemporary. Selected and with an introduction by Johannes Vig, Solitary Teacher [Enelaerer].''** Hansen never got beyond Vig's introduction, but its contents are significant because Johannes Vig is the first-person narrator of *The Liar.* Speaking of the tragic vision under which that book concludes, Vig speculates that ''in order to escape into the comic, perhaps you have as a matter of course employed great spirits far stronger than yourself, as slaves, as beasts of burden. Perhaps you have used a Kierkegaard . . . , have allowed yourself to be borne by him to the extreme point of his passionate discussion of meaning.''

Some Kierkegaardian definitions will be helpful. If the central concern of his authorship was ''How to be a Christian,'' the crux of that problem was the question of faith and how it is achieved. In his view, by far the greater part of humanity lives at what he called the esthetic and ethical levels. Esthetic life is by definition the search for sensuous gratification, whether common or highly refined. It is the ego-centric life, characterized by immediacy and finite perspective, in short, the world of the romantic. The ethical life implies responsibility beyond the self, defined in terms of infinite, eternal imperatives. Though involving limitation, it provides the security of rational, unchanging, universally sanctioned codes. It is the bastion of the establishment, the home of most who adhere to Christendom. Only few, however, cross the chasm that separates the ethical from the religious plane. In *Fear and Trembling* and the *Concluding Unscientific Postscript*, Kierkegaard delineates those who, recognizing the limits of the universal, irrationally leap to faith and, like the Biblical Abraham, establish an absolute, incommunicable relation to the absolute. In *The Sickness Unto Death* and *The Concept of Dread*, Kierkegaard analyzes the longing attempts of the soul to establish existential faith and traces the stages of despair involved in that difficult struggle. Few writers have penetrated further into the psychology of spiritual anguish.

The complexities of Hansen's vision and technique are not immediately apparent in *The Liar*'s disarmingly simple surface. Clear and direct, the language proves on closer examination to embody a rich and concentrated texture of imagery and symbolism. Similarly, the surface plot is limited in scope and apparently uncomplicated. Set on a small Danish island, the external action focuses on the relationship of Johannes Vig and an attractive young woman, Annemari. His suppressed longing for her is complicated by the presence of two younger men in her life, while simultaneously Vig is less certainly drawn toward another woman, the haunting Rigmor. The events narrated fall largely within a four-day period during which the loose ends of this amorous interplay are conclusively gathered up. In a deeper sense, the action is much larger, involving Vig's relationship to all the islanders and to the physical island itself in the perspective of past and future. Ultimately, the novel is concerned with Vig's adjustment to the human condition.

Additional complexities derive from the narrative apparatus, for the novel is more precisely an elaborate confession, written in a series of notebooks by Vig to a non-existent persona whom he calls Nathanael:

> I have come to need you, Nathanael, just to listen to me. I don't really know who you are, I only call you "Nathanael" because it is said that Nathanael was a man without guile. I fancy you are not so clever and sophisticated as I am, although I'm only as blase as the times in which I live.

As for himself, he cautions Nathanael against pronouncing his name too quickly, for Johannes Svig would be equivalent to John Fraud. Clearly, Vig's sensitivity has something to do with his titling his confessions, *The Liar*. In thus engaging in a make-believe dialogue with a guileless extension of his ego, Vig is really exposing a Kierkegaardian existential guiltiness he feels. The intuitive attempt to find himself is also perhaps a means to save himself.

The poetic advantages of locating the protagonist in the strictly circumscribed environment of Sandoe (literally, Sand Island) are considerable. Hansen makes the island not only an isolated fragment of the larger world, from which Vig has fled, but also an independent microcosm, where Vig's struggle is reduced to the lowest common human denominator—expressed, as it were, archetypally. Now in early middle age, Vig had buried himself on Sandoe in the aftermath of an affair eight years before. During that time he has assumed, in addition to his duties as schoolmaster, the roles of postmaster and parish clerk, substituting for the parish priest during the winter months when the island is ice-locked; thus, in his multiple public capacities he is symbolically almost synonomous with Sandoe. Yet ironically, his education and his poetic sensitivity, together with his alien origin, isolate him socially from the other inhabitants. No man is an island, John Donne wrote centuries earlier, but in his inner soul, Johannes Vig, in spite of himself, is something of an island. Spiritually speaking, his domicile is for him a barren place: "What do you expect to thrive in this callous sand?" he once asks. For him, Sandoe has not provided the firm foundation upon which he can rebuild his life. When he first begins to write to his imaginary Nathanael, the solitude and darkness of his inner man are externally symbolized by the foggy March weather and by the ice that still oppressively grips the island.

The sense of solitude and transience is intensified by Vig's sensitive observation of bird life on the island. With an almost religious dedication, he watches for migratory birds, whose coming conventionally symbolizes a renewal, a redemption from the dark Nordic winter. Yet the birds have for Vig another, more pronounced, significance: in them he recognizes his own rootlessness: "Have you looked into the eye of a large wild bird, . . . Nathanael? . . . If you have, you will know that she is a fugitive from your own heart." Elsewhere, he remarks that when a hunter hears the piercing shriek of a duck flying over in the dark, "he feels a great sadness, like the sadness one feels when listening to great music." Birds remind him that "man is an immigrant in his own birthplace, a passing guest in his own house, a fleeting being on earth."

Vig's character can be gaged partially by his observable behavior on the island. He is a conscientious, imaginative schoolmaster, concerned with giving his pupils values to live by. Generous and kindhearted, he understands and helps those who are misunderstood or unappreciated. Sometimes his spontaneous gestures are quite against his self interest, as when he asks Anders to fell the spruce trees he loves in order to provide the man with a much needed bit of income; as when suddenly,

without thought, he offers the pregnant, unwed Elna a job and protection under his roof. He commissioned the aged Rasmus to paint murals in the school, enabling the outmoded and forgotten man to die happy; he comforts and encourages the tubercular Kay and his poverty-stricken family.

One would think Vig a happy man with a good conscience. Alas, life for him is not quite so simple as the measure of his generous deeds. He knows he has tampered with the destinies of others because he has been in a position to do so, but he is uncertain about the purity of his motives. Has he acted as a man engaged in a definite human relationship with his fellow men, or has he acted for convenience or diversion, as a stranger? Not for nothing has he felt the contrast between himself and the guileless Nathanael. His relationship (adulterous in spirit, if not initially in fact) with Rigmor, wife of the most influential man on the island, is nihilistic and rests uneasily on his conscience. He is conscious of a calculated sin of omission in not restraining two young men from going out in a boat in terrible weather (one was Oluf, Annemari's fiance, to whom Vig felt himself a spiritual father but also recognized as a rival with a prior claim to Annemari; when the boat capsized, the other youth was drowned). Increasingly, Vig turns to alcohol for solace; the villagers ironically remark that the parish clerk is no teetotaler.

These are, however, only superficial manifestations of a more difficult dilemma. Kierkegaard's observation that "With every increase in the degree of consciousness, the intensity of despair increases" precisely describes this man, for lonely speculation and continual soul searching have brought to the surface a deep rooted *angst* in the face of existential absurdity. The swarm of profound ideas he once exulted in has been found useless in the confrontation with human suffering: "I couldn't think of a single word to say to Erik's widow, Lina [after her husband was killed by a floating mine]. So now I stick to the wisdom of nature and simple things." Recognizing the limitations of sophistry does not dispel his existential anguish. At bottom, his inability to overcome human loneliness and find a satisfactory basis for human relationships stems from his failure to find a relationship to God. In Kierkegaard's terms, Vig needs to make the arbitrary leap to faith and cannot make it. "Yes, of course," he answers when Harry, the young engineer, asks if he, the parish clerk, is a believer. But in his private moments he confesses to Nathanael that he is but a "dilettante of the faith. Maybe a non-believer who believes in what he does not believe." Desperately, he relies on alcohol and a rigid schedule to avoid plunging into the void: "it's very necessary for me to keep to my hours with almost military precision, otherwise it would spell ruin."

Hansen extends our understanding of Johannes Vig through symbolic juxtaposition with others who live on the island. On the perimeter are such characters as the dead Erik, of whom Vig says, "He was our best man on Sandoe." Brave and generous, Erik went regularly to the mainland, even in bad weather, doing numerous errands there for the islanders. He was a literal link between island and mainland and, symbolically, a genuine link between men. In one sense, he has roots, he belongs to the island; in another he has moved beyond the narrowness of himself, beyond the isolation which lies at Vig's own heart. Probably for this reason he has Vig's respect.

Other perspectives are provided by Frederik, Rigmor's husband, and Harry, the visiting engineer who is Vig's other rival for Annemari. Both of these men are doers. Perhaps they, too, have glimpses of the existential abyss on the edge of which

Vig balances, but both turn quickly away—Frederik to a life filled with political ambitions and hard work, with expensive modern products (including—ludicrously—an automobile on the tiny island), and with rakish pursuits; Harry to a life of technological achievement which he sees as the only effective means to combat mankind's suffering. They are, then, both representatives of action as opposed to Vig's contemplation. Where they avoid existential anguish through pursuit of panaceas, he allows himself no illusions.

The schoolmaster's position is most directly delineated in his relation to three women: Annemari, old Marie (Oluf's mother), and Rigmor. The first two symbolize opposite philosophic approaches to life. Though not a native, old Marie burned her boats when she married and came to the island to live, giving up her family and all reminder of her past life (save only a photograph album). Early widowed, her life is a story of stoic renunciation and perseverence. By contrast, Annemari represents a newer, less stern principle. She is "one of those modern pleasure seekers; she sought happiness, and that gave offense to Marie."

The puzzlingly cool relationship of Oluf and Annemari and Marie's almost bitter rejection of her son's fiancee are only explicable in the light of this conflict. Oluf's being caught, psychologically and symbolically, in the tension between the two women, explains his strange lassitude, his sluggish indifference to Annemari, and explains why once free from the engagement he begins to brighten up. Vig appears to be only an interested outsider in the struggle, but in fact he is centrally involved. The two young people fell in love under his school roof, with his blessing: "I practically married them," he says. Below the surface, his bringing them together suggests an attempt to solve his existential dilemma by fusing the two approaches—stoic, rooted, duty-bound acceptance of one's lot with a pursuit of pleasure and happiness not committed to anything but itself. Put in Kierkegaard's terms, he would bring together the ethical and esthetic modes of existence. Accordingly, Vig's deference in pursuing Annemari during the winter while Oluf has been on the mainland is also, on a deeper level, a reluctance to give up the possibility of symbolic fusion he longed for. Both Oluf and Annemari know that they are not right for each other, and Vig must finally realize that the solution to his personal anguish does not lie in such a tenuous philosophic alliance.

Vig's more natural affinity, as he will eventually realize, is with Rigmor rather than Annemari. "Rigmor, like me," he says, "is a stranger on the island." Like him, she has passed the bloom of young adulthood, and though beautiful, hers is the beauty of grayness, of ashen paleness. Like Vig, she is a lonely bark drifting without direction. Her wealth isolates her, she is childless, and her life seems to her a spectre of meaninglessness. She is drawn to Vig because she senses their common dilemma. If her husband's crowd "cannot romanticize," as she says, Vig apparently can. For him, this haunting woman, this "woman of the shades who breathes the sad airs of the moon," this "fairy queen" as he calls her at the pagan spring ball, this "double-tongued" temptress of a woman is subtly associated with the realm of the ethically forbidden. As object of his nihilistic attraction, she assumes connotations of the demonic.

Vig's spiritual struggle reaches the crisis stage in the period between Saturday evening and Monday morning. It is best understood when seen against the following significant external events which mark developments in the surface plot and at the same time are catalysts in Vig's spiritual ferment: the breaking of the ice which begins Saturday night; the spring ball held on Sunday evening at the Headlands, Frederik's estate; the arrival of the ship from the mainland at noon on Monday with Oluf aboard; and the coming of the woodcock late Monday afternoon. In the darkened church on Saturday evening as he prepares for the service he must conduct the following morning, Vig feels suddenly as if he is Jonah in a living whale, fleeing from God. His desolation is framed in images to which Kierkegaard's *The Sickness Unto Death* and *The Concept of Dread* are consistently relevant. Then and the following morning he contemplates a death's head so situated in the choir that it can only be seen by the priest and clerk. "Despair is the sickness unto death," says Kierkegaard, and to the fugitive schoolmaster, death all at once seems desirable, restful, undisturbed. In it, he thinks, "a man comes to belong to some place."

The text for the service is the enigmatic passage from the gospels which deals with the emptiness of the soul when the evil spirit has been driven from it. Falling upon desert places, the spirit returns, finds the soul swept and garnished but empty; whereupon it brings with it seven more evil spirits to inhabit that luring emptiness, and the state of that man is worse than in the beginning. Vig, who resumes drinking early Sunday morning, becomes obsessed with the passage: "I am emptiness, nothing. Am I not swept and garnished?" He is ready to succumb to the evil spirit. "No despair," says Kierkegaard, "is entirely without defiance," and in a powerfully compelling psychological and symbolic episode, Vig becomes possessed as he conducts the service. Perhaps the arrogance or the pride of emptiness possesses him, he reasons, but he feels himself in open conflict with the souls of the united congregation. Once again he is the outsider, this time a malignant one, who cannot belong and so will destroy. The spell which he exercises over those assembled is broken when Erik's widow (in response to his direct, cruelly cynical question, "Has the son of God helped you?") looks beyond him in her naive simplicity to the image of the crucifixion, mistakes his meaning, and re-affirms her faith in Christ. "When Christ drives out the evil spirit, the woodcock comes," an old superstitious believer had said the evening before, and Vig, either in reality or in the reality of imagination, hears the sound of the woodcock's flight as he sits alone in the sacristy after the service, shaken and still partially drunk. According to Kierkegaard, despair is a negativity through which one must pierce to reach truth. Momentarily, Vig has been lifted out of the grasp of demonic negation, but unfortunately the respite is only temporary.

When the ice is swept away, When Oluf arrives with the ship, he and Annemari conclusively end their engagement. Vig, who consciously has held back on principle, now rushes to Annemari to make his bid. He is too late, however. She had given him an opportunity to speak at the spring ball but in reaction against his ironic jesting had given herself that evening to the young engineer. Symbolically, Vig's defeat means that his sublimated desire to seek for meaning through the pursuit of happiness-pleasure is really an illusion for a man such as he.

That afternoon he rebounds into Rigmor's bed, where in anguished conversation they evaluate their situations. In the main, their attraction has previously been colored by the grayness of melancholy and submerged rebellious inclination. Speaking of his "possessed" extremity at the church service, Rigmor confesses that at the time she was "madly infatuated" with him; "Then the devil has sex," he replies. In coming to her now, he comes not simply to commit adultery with a friend's wife but, what is worse, "to do harm, to destroy." Their sexual liaison is thus nihilistic, a kingdom divided against itself.

By contrast, on the previous evening at the spring ball, in an atmosphere of elves, fairy queens, and pagan non-reality, Vig had opened to her his inner self and had touched a hopeful chord within her. He had made her feel genuinely needed, awakening for her suddenly the belief that her life could be meaningful. She had expected him to come from his rejection by Annemari, needing her as someone to share his grief. Instead, he comes as a wild and evil force, whose demonic negativity revives her old sense of life's futility: "How then can I believe in God?" she asks. "You must," is his considered reply. "For when you reach the limits of meaninglessness, you find that all is a battlefield where two forces fight, and there isn't any no man's land." The schoolmaster sees here perfectly well the necessity of the leap to faith; he knows that at the moment of crisis Kierkegaard's Knight of Faith must "plunge confidently into the absurd," into an absolute relation with the absolute. Alas, he can only fear and tremble on the brink, and at the same time he recognizes that the nihilism into which he has fallen endangers Rigmor's precariously awakened hope. If he cannot himself leap into the realm of faith, at least he will not stand in her way.

That afternoon he finds that the woodcock have come and brings Rigmor to search for them with him: "I'm becoming superstitious, I guess, but I think a great deal depends on getting one for you today," he says, and just at dusk he succeeds. It is a pact between them, a rebirth of her hope, a renunciation of his own consolation in her in order not to stifle the spark of her awakened humanity, what she calls her new beginning.

Vig has some compensatory developments in these three days of spiritual crisis. Two mystical moments, one in his schoolroom on Sunday afternoon, one on Western Hill Monday evening somewhat after the shooting of the woodcock, confirm in him a feeling that finally, at least, he belongs on the island. His classroom had "opened up" to him in such a way that, in spite of his keenly felt weaknesses, he realizes that the island and its people need his particular efforts as a teacher to preserve the traditions of Sandoe, to help those who are born there to a sense of their roots and identity. On the hill, near a stone resembling an altar, he is aware for the first time "that my fate was bound for always to this hill in the sea: not bound by a root as are those who are born here, but struck into the island like a spear that is thrown from afar." The place becomes holy for him, and he figuratively offers a part of himself as sacrifice on that altar.

Earlier Vig had spoken of "those lovely spruce trees that screen me from the ever present view of the monotonous island and the everlasting sea as I sit in my room." Those trees have now been felled by Anders on the morning that the boat came, opening up the schoolmaster's isolation, symbolically removing a barrier to his incorporation into the heart of the community. He finally is burning his boats like old Marie. Somewhat later, the dark, shading trees at the Headlands are also removed, suggesting that for Rigmor, too, the isolation from the rest of the island is breaking down.

The time structure of Vig's account allows us to see the outcome of these internal and external events thirteen months later. The bird dog, Pigro, Vig's most intimate companion, is dead; significantly, he becomes sick and must be shot soon after Vig's hope of happiness is gone. The dog's death and Vig's giving up the luxury of hunting are final renunciations of the

esthetic life. Instead, Vig is reconciled to "a more exacting principle, a sterner law" to live by, one which suggests the ethical stoic principle of old Marie yet is more complex. Sometimes, when he looks over toward the Headlands, the possible alternatives seem to be only twofold: "Either to go over there and take what some would call my right, or drink myself senseless. I do neither." Instead, he writes his natural and cultural history of Sandoe, leaves Rigmor to continue her fruitful new beginning, provides for the unwed Elna and her baby. The only way to endure, he realizes, is to persevere in one's duty as did the arctic explorer Bronlund, who when his legs would carry him no further through the icy waste, still lay writing information for polar explorers who would some day follow him.

"The paradox of faith is this," says Kierkegaard, ". . . that the individual determines his relation to the universal by his relation to the absolute, not his relation to the absolute by his relation to the universal." Johannes Vig's condition at the end of his confessions, notwithstanding his longing to believe, is that he can only reach out to God uncertainly from within the ethical principle. Still, he has gone beyond old Marie's simple stoicism by virtue of the extremity with which he has wrestled and which, in spite of all, still remains. He has made an uncertain truce with existence, and he maintains the status quo, feeling, in his desperate postulation of God, a lot like Job. "It is God's will," he concludes, "that however much I suffer his wrath and affliction in the night, my burden of loneliness is never lightened when I wake."

In this posture has not Vig become Kierkegaard's Knight of Infinite Resignation—living still within the ethical realm, at the threshold of faith, yet infinitely estranged? It is the ethical realm at its noblest extreme, where duty is fulfilled only at the cost of self-renunciation; it is a condition where peace and rest combine paradoxically with pain to reconcile one to existence. It is the condition of the tragic hero as Kierkegaard defines him, and Johannes Vig is, in a modest way, a hero. (pp. 53-64)

H. Wayne Schow, "Kierkegaardian Perspectives in Martin A. Hansen's 'The Liar'," in Critique: Studies in Modern Fiction, *Vol. XV, No. 3, 1974, pp. 53-65.*

NIELS INGWERSEN   (essay date 1974)

[*Ingwersen is a Danish critic and educator. In the following excerpt from the introduction to the English translation of* Lucky Kristoffer, *he explicates the meaning of the novel.*]

Lucky Kristoffer (Lykkelige Kristoffer) belongs to the middle period of Martin A. Hansen's all too short career as a creative writer. The book appeared in 1945, and together with **Jonathan's Journey (Jonathans Rejse)** from 1941, it exemplifies the author's attempt to utilize past forms of narrative fiction. While **Jonathan's Journey** is written in imitation—although as a very independent one—of the age-old chronicles of one man's wandering toward his goal, **Lucky Kristoffer** obviously harkens back to the magnificent work that some critics see as the first modern novel, *Don Quixote* by Miguel Cervantes. In this case, too, Hansen treats his model in a very independent fashion, for the knight of the sorrowful countenance, Kristoffer, the idealist, the searcher, the man with a quest, is pushed in the background in favor of a very sophisticated Sancho Panza, the wry clerk, Martin, who—and here is another departure from Cervantes— serves as the narrator of the story of the journey from Skrokhult through the strife-ridden countryside to the embattled city of Copenhagen.

These two novels mark Martin A. Hansen's actual breakthrough as a novelist in Danish letters. Earlier, in the bleak 1930s when Denmark, like most other Western nations, suffered under the Depression, Hansen had started his career as a creative writer by publishing two realistic novels that treated the decline of the old farming culture and which, quite in keeping with narrative practice during these years, substituted a milieu for the protagonist and debated Marxist solutions to the problems of society. Hansen, however, left this realm of social realism for a more imaginative approach to storytelling, and he never quite returned to straight realism. In fact, many of his works are experiments with narrative form, and in *The Thorn Bush (Tornebusken),* a book comprised of three long short stories, he reveals why he felt this need for experimentation. He demonstrates that the writer is a man beset by severe pangs of conscience: how can he know that what he produces is not a falsification of life, for the poet might very well be a liar, who distorts his readers' sense of reality. In *The Thorn Bush* he, therefore, moves story by story toward a less and less traditional form, an experimentation which mirrors his quest to be absolutely truthful toward his subject matter. Readers of *Lucky Kristoffer* will know that this problem of the writer is one which surely taxes our narrator, Martin, as he tries to recapture past events. This quest for truth, the necessity of facing the reality of one's situation, is a major theme in many of Hansen's short stories and in his novel *The Liar (Løgneren).* This novel, which seems to be extremely realistic on the surface, but which is narrated by a man who sees symbols everywhere and who understands life in terms of symbols, is Hansen's best-known work, and unfortunately, his last major piece of fiction. (pp. 5-6)

It has been intimated above that Martin A. Hansen suffered a premature death. This farm boy, who left his milieu to become a school teacher, lived to be only 46 years old. By his death in 1955 he had nevertheless established himself as being quite probably the most important writer of fiction in Denmark during the forties and fifties. The prominence of his achievement is evidenced by the interest which scholars take in his works; new analyses appear at a rate which makes it a taxing job to keep up with current views on Martin A. Hansen.

It should be mentioned that Martin A. Hansen played a major role as a cultural critic. He lived in difficult times during which cultural transitions created ideological bewilderment. Such transitions were often the topic of his historical writings, e.g., his account of the Nordic peoples' shift from paganism to Christianity in *Orm og Tyr,* a book presently being translated into English. Although Hansen often sought back to the past in his writings, he always did so with the present in mind. *Lucky Kristoffer* is a splendid example of this. On the surface this novel seems to be a historical novel, but the confusion and violence we witness is a mirror of the reality of the war years in occupied Denmark. While Hansen wrote, the Second World War was coming to a bloody end, and like old Martin, Martin A. Hansen might wonder whether he would be able to finish his book before the allied troops would invade Denmark.

In this context it ought to be added that Hansen was active in the Danish resistance movement. He had, in fact, written an article, published in the underground press, which advocated the killing of Nazi informers. This article was written with a heavy heart, and echoes of this dilemma can be detected in *Lucky Kristoffer.* The clerk Martin and Paulus Helie (Povl Helgesen), are both writers, not men of action, but they are both responsible for influencing other men to action.

These brief remarks should hopefully have shown that *Lucky Kristoffer* cannot be read exclusively as a novel about the civil war which tormented Denmark during the Reformation. In a sense, the novel treats a universal theme, the painful transition which occurs as old values are replaced by new ones. The men who find themselves caught in such a cultural upheaval are bound to be confused as they are forced to participate in events they hardly understand. They observe how old ideas which gave order to their lives are questioned and debased, and they witness how new ideas, which can hardly make their lives meaningful, take over.

This loss of harmony, the loss of the individual's feeling of living a meaningful life, is at the core of *Lucky Kristoffer.* It is quite clear that this novel, in part, renders the turbulent transition from the ordered medieval world to the modern age of scientific thought—not to say, of relativity. The dialogue between the captive Father Mattias and the scientist Master Thygonius is a clash between two world views: Thygonius advocates the validity of the Copernican view, which reduces God's heaven to mere emptiness and man to a well-functioning machine, and he clearly has reason on his side. The mild-mannered and tolerant old monk is quite intrigued by this new outlook, but does not for one moment allow reason to bring doubt into his mind. He has lived for—and eventually dies for—the old belief, Catholicism, which grants man a life of harmony even though his lot may be hard. Father Mattias is no mystic; rather, he is a practical man who serves as a teacher for and a competent consoler of his fellow human beings, and he foresees and predicts the grave results of Master Thygonius's insights: if Christianity is proven to be a lie, man will learn that he is a destitute, superfluous being.

The picture of Father Mattias is drawn with compassion by the narrator, a man who may realize that Thygonius makes sense, but who, deep within himself, feels attracted to the losers, and who, as an old man, lets himself be consoled by the Virgin Mary, *Maria, Mater amabilis.* Father Mattias is a loser, and his death as a martyr signals the end of an age and its belief. Another such loser is young Kristoffer. In a bewildered age, when shining white knights have been relegated to tales and when causes are no longer clear-cut, he confusedly searches for the cause for which he may give his life.

As an eminent critic of Martin A. Hansen, the poet Thorkild Bjørnvig, has pointed out, the passing of the Middle Ages—and its comparative simplicity—is represented by the death of two figures whom we associate with the days before modern insight shattered the belief that the earth was the center of the universe: *the monk* and *the knight.* Those who assume power are, in a sense, of lesser stature and have less to give to other men: they are the scientist and the materialist. Thygonius may offer men truths, but hardly meaning, and as we come to realize, the clerk who turned tradesman perceives of his subsequent life in terms of some kind of loss.

These remarks may lead one to believe that the author feels much more sympathy for the old world order than for the rising one. So he may, but Martin A. Hansen is no reactionary who only laments the passing of the long ago, and who overlooks the social inequities and misery of the age. Furthermore, he does not mold his characters as ideals, but endows them with many human frailties, and indeed, he can be highly critical of them. Kristoffer, for one, may seem slightly ridiculous in his quest, and his hardly unbroken gravity suggests a lack of humor and tolerance, which stands in contrast to Mattias's and Martin's attitudes. Whereas Father Mattias's death is surrounded by pathos, there may seem something arbitrary about Kristoffer's choice of bravely dying in defense of the scholar Paulus Helie. Bjørnvig comments that Kristoffer fails to find a just cause, and instead he lays down his life for a single man.

Another character, who is closely bound to the old world, and who has to meet death, is Paal, Kristoffer's guardian and enemy. While the monk and the knight may represent the latter part of the Middle Ages, this swearing, superstitious, obnoxious warrior harkens back to pagan times. His brutish behavior is in stark contrast to the idealism of his traveling companions, but the old heathen and Father Mattias get along curiously well together, and one feels that Paal definitely commands Martin's respect.

These three men, who meet their deaths in ways which rational minds might call unnecessary and foolish, if not meaningless—for none of these deaths will have any impact on the age which follows—have, thus, one thing in common: they do not allow reason or rationality to govern their minds, and their acts prove this abundantly. Another author—another choice of narrator—might have deprived Father Mattias of his saintliness, Kristoffer of his high idealism, and Paal of his ebullient stature, but Martin, who often opposes their lack of common sense, harbors a weakness for the grandeur and obstinacy with which these three men move toward their destinies. Martin is a rational man who will never allow himself to be caught in the impossible situations and fixes of the others—and if he gets caught, he is always able, through small compromises and deals, to save his own skin. He has an abundance of common sense, and yet, he who cleverly chooses to leave the life of a clerk behind and to become a tradesman, definitely feels—as he writes this chronicle—that his gain will not measure up to his loss.

It is, then, as an act of love and, maybe, of repentance that we shall understand the old, successful merchant's sitting down in his last days to write about the journey that took place some thirty years earlier. He knows that death is finally catching up with him, and as his last act he attempts to write the story of those who now are dead—and of himself as he was while he was with them. In spite of the title one must call Martin the protagonist of the novel. *Lucky Kristoffer* is his confession.

This choice of narrator gives the novel a unique quality. The above analysis may have suggested that *Lucky Kristoffer* is mainly an allegory, and surely it contains allegorical elements, but there is none of the dryness or bare-boned didacticism which so often characterizes this genre. Through the narrator the novel becomes an exciting, witty, chatty, realistic story with a universal perspective. It is a highly serious work, but wisely, Martin A. Hansen has allowed many situations initially to appeal to our sense of humor. One supreme, comic creation is Kristoffer's magnificent Rosinante, the monstrous and gallant horse, Rufulus. In fact, many scenes are structured in such a way that deep seriousness and comedy coexist in a delicate balance in which neither cancels the other out.

The story is told from Martin's point of view, and Martin possesses an ironic mind which allows him to see several aspects of each situation, its foolishness, its humor, and its pathos. This capacity, however, does not mean that he is possessed by the devil of irony which lets all values dissolve into mockery. Martin is definitely a man who can act and who can marshal a heroic or ethical response when such is called for; he is, however, a man who would rather not rise to such occasions. He often understates the danger of a situation in

favor of its humor, for he is keenly aware of its comical aspects which the others cannot perceive. On the first reading, this may allow us to be royally entertained and to laugh at many critical situations—just as Martin may have done; but beneath this shining surface of brilliant recollection and storytelling, Martin hints that he himself was profoundly influenced by the events which took place during the journey. So we must now turn to what is probably the most crucial question in the reader's mind: what happened to Martin during the journey? As a result of this quest he received a wife and a new vocation, but what do these outer indicators tell about the change in the man?

One might imagine that this question did not enter Martin's own mind until he started writing. Now, as he is approaching what very well may be a violent death, he focuses his attention on the most important part of his life, that which made him a tradesman. He seems to indicate that he was, at that time, a different man, for he does not employ the first person pronoun, *I*, as he tells his story, but objectifies himself with the term *Clerk*. This is reminiscent of Søren Kierkegaard's strategy of employing pseudonyms when dwelling on views which were not his own. This comparison, however, should not be carried too far, for Martin admits that he is the Clerk, but the distance between the man as he is now and as he was then is nevertheless telling: Martin was a changed man after the journey—or, rather, he was changed during the journey. He implies this much himself, for when his cherished manuscript on healing (and poisonous) herbs is lost he laconically states that this is why he became a tradesman.

This passage—this statement—requires interpretation, and the novel contains a number of clues which are helpful.

When we first meet the Clerk we realize that he is a man who is quite capable of managing for himself—and for others as well. He is a bit of a manipulator, but he is not marred with the coldness which we normally associate with this human species. He is quite capable of liking other people, although one may wonder just how much his easy conquests of women may mean to him. He is, surely, capable of using people, not really for the purpose of material gain or promotion but rather because he follows an irrational impulse in his own heart, one which starts the journey that we follow. It should be kept in mind that he has been Kristoffer's teacher; it is he who filled this boy with stories of great quests: and it is, after all, he who spurs Kristoffer on to leave Skrokhult. Martin is fascinated with—nearly in love with—the fantastic, that which is contrary to reason, otherwise he would not have agreed to be Kristoffer's scribe. His rationality is something which he may not be able to overcome when he orders his own life, but he may give his deepest inclinations free rein when it comes to those who are both willing to defy and capable of defying reason. His rationality is either more than a mask, or it is a mask which he is unable to doff, until he sits down to write his declaration of love for fools, those wholehearted idealists, whom he lived to see destroyed.

By now, this gradual characterization may have suggested that the light tone which Martin chooses for his story is another mask. The many admissions he makes as to his manipulative power must be seen as being indicative of the fact that he realizes his share of guilt in the deaths he is recording.

But let us retrace our steps to the beginning of the story. The young Martin—this circumspect man who has flirted seriously with Christianity, but settled for something else—finds himself at the pitiful place of Skrokhult in Halland (now a province of

Sweden), a clearing in the wilderness which has scarcely any contact with civilization. This aspect is worth considering if we are to understand this complicated man who seems more and more mysterious as we attempt to look behind his mask. Skrokhult is situated in the woods, in the midst of untouched nature; and it is, I suggest, in understanding his relationship to nature that we get closest to Martin himself. He is no romantic who has escaped from corrupt civilization to hide in unspoiled nature—he is, to be blunt, too corrupt to be such a man; but he is a man who is deeply fascinated with nature, because it has, as he says, a Janus head! This indicates that nature is both benevolent and cruel, both good and evil, and Martin is engrossed with both these aspects of it. Make note of the fact that in his small way he is a doctor, but one who concocts not only healing but poisonous brews as well. The admixture, the blend of attributes in nature, in life, fascinates him, and he may strike us, in turn, as being an image of nature himself, a man with a Janus head. By learning all that he possibly can, he achieves some understanding of nature; in a way he learns, or attempts, to control nature, just as he tries to manipulate and control other human beings. He is a man who wants knowledge and has much knowledge, both about nature and his fellow travelers. It is worth reading the passage following the battle in the forest carefully; as night falls and the wounded lie under a big spruce, Martin creeps into the minds of his companions, and this he can do because he has sized them up so accurately. But this man, who can so easily identify with others, avoids forcing his way into the mind of one single person, namely, Father Mattias. This pure spirit is not his ground; Mattias belongs in another realm to which mixed and mixed-up minds have no access. The Reverend Father and the Clerk, on this very night, are subtly posed as contrasts. This indicates that although it would be totally wrong to make Martin the devilish opposite of saintliness, he is a man who is somehow allied with that perverse instinct in man which creates havoc. The Warden, Father Mattias, is no manipulator; he is a leader who gives others the spiritual strength to endure hardships; he is overt in his influence on others, whereas Martin is exactly the opposite, exerting a secretive influence which may urge others on to grand deeds, but he cannot give them meaning in life or add to their spiritual strength. Father Mattias has a cause; Martin does not. The ancient and the modern man are juxtaposed, and through this comparison the modern man is judged. He can manipulate others, but he can scarcely give them the insights or the meaning which they strive for and need. He can only lead them to their destruction, but not make that destruction tragic in the sense that it is cathartic, i.e., necessary and meaningful.

All this, the old man writing must realize, but he does not state it; he only intimates it, and he does so very, very subtly. If we imagine his situation we may say that the insight he has gained, perhaps through his writing, is too harsh to be stated openly; moreover, if he had turned to a direct analysis of himself, he would be slighting the others—those who are, he realizes, so much more worthy than himself. In a sense, it may be taken as an act of humility that he does not write the story in the first person singular. By reducing himself to just another traveler he manages to force us closer to those long dead. Could this be why he eliminates himself in the title and lets the story be Kristoffer's?

We must, however, go back again. What happened to Martin? Once more the night under the big spruce may give us clues. As Martin stares into nature, he even identifies with the animals of the forest, and a careful reading suggests that he realizes that his attempt to control and understand nature has been in vain. That night he may be experiencing a fear of nature for the first time, and he may realize that his attempt to understand nature is indeed a dangerous one. His choice of becoming a tradesman, a materialist who only copes with matters that are extremely rational, may be caused by this fear. Throughout, his eyes have been open to the destructive, the tainted side of nature, and even though nature might contain much that is truly good, he has never been able to accept the dogma that divinely created nature is all good. This view, which suggests some kind of balance in nature (in life?), he now seems to spurn, and later—in the first passages of the chapter "The Forest Nymph"—he openly states that he never again *dared* to enter the forests.

When Martin finally finds himself to be alone, when all those who defied reason lay slain, he settles for a kind of life that somehow rejects the quest in which he had taken part. This would seem to be extremely sensible, but the old man in the besieged town lets us know that he now regrets that choice. His confession becomes an admission of defeat and of loss, and as he feverishly strives to end his account we become aware of his desperation and growing desolation. In the very end he seems utterly alone; nothing offers him consolation any longer: his jug of aqua vitae is empty; the fragrance of violets is replaced by the smell of the burning town; and the presence of the Virgin Mary is no longer sensed. He seems to feel that he is reaping the harvest of a futile life.

On these dark notes, although they are largely implicit, Martin finishes his account; but it would be wrong to assert that the novel ends in utter gloom, for there is an affirmation of life in the old man's final quest, his writing of this account. He has finally shunned the role of the tradesman and confronted himself with his past life, and it should be noted that he refuses to be rescued from the doomed town of Varberg. By writing about the past, about the others and himself, he supersedes mere storytelling, for his act of writing becomes a redeeming act of self-realization. If these papers are saved for the coming ages, the clerk-tradesman's life has, nevertheless, become meaningful.

One can view the act of writing this account as the old man's attempt to ally himself once more with those grand fools whose deeds he has been recording. His writing of *Lucky Kristoffer* can hardly be called reasonable or sensible, but by his doing so, life is finally becoming meaningful to Martin. He recaptures his old fascination with ambivalent nature and his sense of the beauty in life's irrationality. He dies as the others have done, and his death, too, may be called a folly, but his record may endow still others—the readers—with insight.

Writing, as indicated, was problematic to Martin A. Hansen, but the fact that his vocation became a problem to him demonstrates how seriously he looked upon his job. As the above analysis of *Lucky Kristoffer* has suggested, Martin A. Hansen's writing is much more than excellent storytelling; it contains the severe demand that man must search for an understanding of his times as well as of himself. *Lucky Kristoffer* is no treatise on how to go about this task; it is a quest for this understanding. (pp. 7-17)

Niels Ingwersen, in an introduction to Lucky Kristoffer *by Martin A. Hansen, translated by John Jepson Egglishaw, Twayne Publishers, Inc., 1974, pp. 5-22.*

FAITH INGWERSEN AND **NIELS INGWERSEN**   (essay date 1976)

[*Faith Ingwersen is an American critic and translator. In the following excerpt from their biographical and critical study of Hansen, the critics explore the major themes of Hansen's works.*]

[In the essay **"Legends in September"** (1947), as so often in Martin A. Hansen's writings, he] imaginatively travels back not only to the natural scenes of his childhood but also to its preindustrial culture, which had taken on mythical qualities for him and had provided his thinking and his artistic universe with a vital sense of values.

This essay contains a passage that sheds light on what Hansen perceived the storyteller's function to be. Legend and story-telling serve to consecrate the land:

> There is one who knows that scenery, landscape, land have not come "from Nature's hand" but are the fruits of culture, are spirit, something that the beliefs and gods of many generations have eventually given final form. The one who knows this is the Genius of Art. What man has experienced, believed, and thought—including the legend and the localized story—have not merely animated the landscape but have created it.

Art transforms nature into culture. This short and simple formula contains an important aspect of Hansen's view of the function of his own work. Although he may have often suspicioned his own vocation and regretted the price it exacted, he nevertheless considered his job as a writer to have a definite purpose. Like those who once plowed the land and like those who once told tales, he too was to serve culture, but by his pen. The obvious question that he inevitably had to ask himself—and one that his readers may repeat—was whether or not his authorship actually fulfilled its mission.

In order to consider this question and to ascertain more precisely the distinct character of Hansen's writing, one must delineate its major themes and value system—which make up a complex universe that is more generally suggested in the preceding biographical sketch. The passage quoted from **"Legends in September"** offers a fitting focal point for this consideration, since the opposition expressed between nature and culture is one that is made with telling frequency and consistency throughout his works. This opposition surfaces clearly in *Jonathan's Journey* and *Lucky Kristoffer* and asserts itself again in the desperate fervor of Hansen's very last writings. It thus seems valid to suggest that a thematic birds-eye view of his work can aptly be given from the vantage point of this opposition.

If one reads the body of Hansen's works consecutively and, preferably, chronologically, it becomes evident that what Hansen prizes is not nature as such, but the fields and meadows that have been formed by the peasants' age-old and work-worn tools. When Hansen is confronted with unspoiled nature, he may praise its beauty, but he will often hasten to add that it is foreign, and even threatening, to the spirit. Nature—whether it is the forest, the swamp, the stream, the mountains of Norway, the vast panoramas of Iceland, or even the ordinary landscape obscured by fog—gives him the feeling that he is in a region inimical to man, a region that suggests extinction.

The positive counterpart to nature, however, is not just civilization, for the modern technological world cannot furnish the meaning in life that the individual needs. This world may seem as indifferent to man's existential need for meaning as does unfeeling nature itself. The relativism of modern civilization provides no basis for making those moral choices that constitute a human being's identity. Hansen thus distinguishes between culture and civilization.

Culture, as has been previously suggested, must be broadly understood to be a mode of existence that, no matter how difficult may be the lot of the individual in any age, will grant him and his fellow human beings the assurance that they are leading purposeful lives. This definition may indeed seem vague and bordering on the cliché-ridden, but it reveals nevertheless the essential, positive credo to be found in Hansen's writings. Fairly early in his career (evidence is to be found even in *Now He Gives Up*), he felt that the old agrarian tradition offered the individual the sort of guidance through which he could cope with inevitably arising existential questions and by which he could thus live in close contact with nature without being overcome by its demonic aspects.

Hansen's concept of tradition, which was partially formed before he underwent his so-called "Cain's Altar" crisis, is at the core of what he calls culture. Tradition gives man the needed feeling of being a part of a whole and of working for that whole. The man who walked behind the plow and toiled for culture knew this intuitively, and it was Hansen's wistful hope that he who wielded a pen might also share in this spontaneous knowledge.

Perhaps the ultimate reward of a culture based upon a benevolent tradition is that life and, equally significantly, death seem meaningful to the human being who is firmly rooted in that culture. The cultural worker serves to uphold values, not only for the present day and his own sake but also for future generations. For such a man, the thought of extinction—a lot that is implied by both indifferent nature and nihilistic civilization—is nonexistent, for although he will die, his cultural effort endures. It would be a mistake to judge such a life to be idyllic, for the human lot is not easy and may entail much suffering; but such a life must still be called harmonious, for even if the individual were to make great sacrifices, he would find these sacrifices to be justified. He would live and die in accordance with the values of his tradition; thus, in spite of his personal fate, he would not be vulnerable to that nihilistic despair to which modern civilization would subject him.

One question is inevitable: how could Hansen be assured that his view of the old culture was correct? It was bound to be doubted by skeptics, who would find it to be a poetic fabrication. The answer lies less in the fact that Hansen conducted much painstaking historical research than in his conviction that, during his childhood on Stevns, he had experienced an essential harmony that had its origins far back in time. He came to believe that he could transcend both personal and familial memory and grasp the essence of that age-old tradition. Memory became *remembrance,* the supranatural recollection of times long past. Late in his life, in *Serpent and Bull,* he exercised with artistic mastery what he thought to be the faculty of remembrance and created his most concrete and comprehensive picture of the cultural tradition that had inspired him in his works.

It should be obvious that Hansen's view of the old culture deserves to be termed mythical. He allots to the past a sense of values that he elevates into guardian principles for his own age; in fact, he invokes the past to assume an existential function in the modern individual's life. The cultural tradition of the past becomes a state of consciousness that is promoted through art. Myth in this context shall be understood as a means by which the individual can confront and attempt to cope with his own and his age's spiritually crippling problems. Myths, which have put man in touch with the sustaining values of the past, have been expressed through tales told from generation to generation; and Hansen's narratives—as well as his contributions to cultural history—are written to serve the same mythical, therapeutic function. Skeptics, as mentioned, may balk at the *oeuvre's* myth about a meaningful life in the past, but it is important to grasp the fact that this very myth of a redeeming culture operates with a compelling power in Hansen's writing and constitutes the core of its value system. It was this myth that gave Hansen the spiritual strength to rise up against his age's moral confusion and to attempt to defy its destructive tendencies. The strength of the myth, as **Serpent and Bull** demonstrates, lies in its power to transform nature into culture and, thus, to exorcise nihilistic demons from the individual's life.

Although Hansen appears to be a guardian of the past, his work mainly depicts either the modern situation or a transition between the past and the present. Not unsurprisingly, the journey from the old into the new culture is deemed to be problematic: many of Hansen's travelers find themselves lost in an uncharted land. Whether this journey-motif is presented realistically or symbolically, the basic experience is the same: the travelers have left a world of order and now find themselves in an uncontrollable and chaotic world. Although the travelers may have once been cognizant of cultural values that could guide them, all their present knowledge is dissipated into a nothingness that leaves them without identity and in a limbo. Many facets of nihilism are presented in Hansen's writings, and it is revealing that he frequently chooses nature imagery to convey the destructiveness of this state of mind. He refers to the slimy depths of a swamp, to the bottom of a forest where plants rot away, to unfathomable waters into which one may sink and forget all human responsibility, or to dungheaps swarming with insects that follow only mindless instinct. Nihilism is clearly equated with nature or, rather, with all in nature that defies cultural endeavor.

This identification between nature and nihilistic culture may seem curious; but, as mentioned, they both are indifferent to cultural striving and to all human values, and ultimately they both offer man nothing but extinction. They also seem to signify a sense of man's beginning and ending and, thus, to form an ominous, fatalistic circle: culture originates in man's resistance to nature, but his emancipation and victory may be only temporary, for culture can degenerate into forms that deprive man of any sense of purpose. Hansen uses one particular setting, that of the dumping ground filled with civilization's debris and slowly being transformed into a jungle of tall weeds, strongly and symbolically to suggest this forbidding knowledge. The mind that has lost all cultural values finds itself once more in a demonic wilderness.

It is against such fatalism, which mocks all human striving, that Hansen posits his myth of the old cultural tradition. Culture and nature—which, with regard to the human being, are understood to be both external and internal phenomena—were posed as the positive and negative poles in works in which the author insisted on asserting the possibility of exorcising the demon of nihilism and establishing—or, rather, reestablishing—meaning.

The myth of the old culture served Hansen well. It gave him alternatives to what he viewed as being insufficient or dangerous solutions to the modern world's futility and, thus, provided him with the reassuring knowlege of his serving culture through writing. The typical structure of numerous of his narratives leads the bewildered protagonist through spiritual confusion and darkness, toward a resolution that promises rebirth, in the sense that the protagonist rediscovers an ethos and chooses to accept responsibility for himself and others. This may sound a bit didactic, not to say pat, and sometimes Hansen does approach sentimentality in his rendering of the past or postulates in his assertion of the rebirth theme; but often, within the given contexts, he convincingly depicts both the image of the old world and the spiritual transformations of his characters.

In part, the reason for Hansen's brilliant aesthetic accomplishment may be that, in spite of his sometimes quite didactic advocacy of fixed values, he refused to offer idyllic, simplistic solutions to the modern dilemma. In his works, rebirth does not denote the attainment of "happiness ever after," but merely a rejection of the temptation of nihilism in a determination to face an ambiguous and taxing world through repeated moral choices.

The above delineation of the value system inherent in Hansen's writings is—so to speak—the "official" one directly stated in many of Hansen's fictional and nonfictional works. The given characterization is however neither exhaustive nor sufficient, for it has hinted only very vaguely at the unrelieved tension that the authorship harbors. At times, a dark foreboding that nature or its spiritual twin, relativistic culture, will eventually negate all man's cultural striving seems to gain the upper hand.

It has been mentioned that the motif of a wandering or journey figures prominently in Hansen's *oeuvre;* and his writings may well be seen as stages in an unending quest for the sense of meaning that the past supposedly possessed. Like the author himself, the fictional wanderer who enters the modern world may be armed with the myth of the old culture, but numerous texts reveal that the strength of the myth is limited in the here and now. The myth casts a shining light over a culture that has disappeared, and although such a wanderer may hope that this sunken world will be spiritually resurrected, the rebirth theme is sometimes questioned through an undeniable ambiguity.

Hansen's use of symbolism underscores this tension in his work. He utilizes a symbolist technique that reinforces a mythical—or mythifying—perspective even in those works that on the surface seem realistic. Positive symbols are mainly taken from the cultural realm (the well-used tool, the tamed animal, the cultivated land, the instructively written page, the well-told tale, and the cultic site—such as mound or church), whereas those that are patently negative belong to nature (the fog, the swamp, the bottomless water, the barren land, the monstrous animal) or to the wasteland of culture (the dumping ground, the marl pit, the ravaged land). Such a clear-cut listing is nonetheless hazardous, for a great number of symbols are presented in an ambiguous light, and this ambiguity projects the confusion and mixed motives of the modern mind. Whether a symbolic element shall be judged to connote rebirth or spiritual extinction, or whether that element presents a fusion or—more precisely—even a confusion of these two concepts is an exasperating problem for any reader who penetrates into Hansen's complex, mythical universe.

For an author who was possessed by the idea of spiritual rebirth, Christianity was an obvious cultural source of symbols. Although the protagonist's situations and hopes are often conveyed through religious references, his alienation from Christian dogma is also felt. The use of the Christian frame of reference, which can be seen as an invocation of a waning tradition that once granted man harmony, shows an estrangement from, rather than a nearness to, God. It is as if Hansen's sufferers, born as they are into a world where old myths lose their strength, can well understand their plight in terms of Job's misery and lament, but rarely in terms of his vindication and restitution. Although Hansen wished to project a genesis through a spiritual renewal, the apocalyptic mood of his narratives is often so permeating that it actually subverts the theme of rebirth.

One feature, in particular, seems devastating to the hope vested in rebirth. At times, the nihilistic state becomes strangely and beautifully alluring and tempts the mind to forsake its cultural striving. Some characters trapped in this state either may voice a demonic delight in the destructive strength of the nihilistic mind or may yearn for release from the struggle for meaning and seek extinction. The seductive power of these nihilistic moments tends to overshadow any ensuing transformation that might vouch for their repudiation.

This fascination with what was destructive both to others and to the self was of course not in keeping with Hansen's values and, in fact, posed a threat to the therapeutic power of the myth of the old culture. The myth forced Hansen to write in a subtly didactic manner in order to advance his cultural mission, but in some texts Hansen seemed to be undertaking forays into regions—states of mind—over which the myth held no sway. These curious texts are filled with ambivalence, for they bear witness simultaneously to a revulsion from, and an attraction to, all that was forbidden by the myth. This peculiar feature implies that the myth restricted Hansen's *vision du monde* [''worldview''] and left him vulnerable to perplexities or paradoxes to which he could find no resolution.

In order to clarify what is meant with the restrictiveness of the myth, one concrete example, that of sexuality, should briefly be examined. It suggests that the ideological restriction in Hansen's thinking prohibits the realization of his ideal: the gap between the old and the new could not be bridged—at least not for an individual striving to be a bridge-builder through artistic means.

The relationship between the two sexes is at the core of many of Hansen's works, and the reader often encounters the existence of a polarity between an indulgence in ''loose'' sexual desire and the assumption of an ethical stance. Sexuality is judged according to what Hansen viewed the standards of the old culture to be; these standards were epitomized in the stories that the old ''epic women'' told. When they related tales of romance, they never indulged in teary, modern notions of the right of passion but cooly made it clear that unfettered sexual desires went against the unwritten social rules of the old culture. Inevitably, it seemed that such individualistic excesses in the name of love led to pitiful fates for those involved. Throughout Hansen's writings passion is suspect, and although a deeply felt passion may be described, it is usually shown to pose a threat to the culturally constructive. Quite significantly, passion is depicted in terms of destructive nature (as the lurid swamp, the dangerously fragrant flower, the swarming of insects, or the sabbat of soulless demons). The presence of a certain sexual ideology becomes particularly clear, since it is the woman who is associated with nature and, thus, with temptation and destruction. Although the male desires sexual pleasure, he is often ambivalent toward passion and may feel that he is being drawn down to his ruin by a temptress and by his own lust. The sexually attractive woman may thus be reluctantly rejected by a male who is himself in the grips of passion; in Hansen's work the male's rejection of the female would be interpreted as a cultural inclination.

The above characterization is admittedly a simplification, and one may argue that the woman often serves as an agent of culture and that she may warn the male that mere sensuality leads to alienation and meaninglessness. Often, however, such ethical women have left, or will leave, sexuality behind, a fact that, in itself, questions the value to be placed on sexuality. It is quite evident that, in the view of the male protagonist, woman assumes a place that is either above or below him in spiritual awareness. This inequality of the sexes excludes any actual communication between them and ensures a loneliness for both. It seems as if the spiritual transformation or rebirth that is valued so highly in Hansen's works entails a renunciation of intimacy between the sexes.

The way in which the value system inherent in Hansen's fictional universe affects sexuality should indicate the restrictiveness of the myth: sexuality is viewed to be one of nature's alluring traps, one that is detrimental to the individual's search for meaning and that, consequently, must be renounced. It should be obvious that Hansen's mythical approach to the cultural crisis of his age led him to judge the spiritual to be superior to the physical or material: the individual must choose the spiritual, for only by so doing does he ally himself with culture, and only then can he feel that he transcends death. Through this choice he becomes, so to speak, culture's protector, and, thereby, an integral part of mankind's cultural striving. Although his name may be forgotten, he will have generated a cultural significance that will ensure his being a spiritually constructive part of the future. It is in this frantic wish to reach an areligious concept of eternal life that the innermost drive of Hansen's creative quest as well as the core of the myth he consecrated are to be found. This concept is one that spiritualizes or ''mythicizes'' life to the point that the human being is forced to denounce much in his own nature.

Against this background, it is highly understandable that the protagonists who seem most surely to be made of flesh and blood find it extremely difficult to make the ''right'' choices and often make them only grudgingly and bitterly. They sense their loss of this life's possibilities, and their ethical resolutions to refrain from ''natural'' desires do not lead to any kind of spiritual bliss or religious joy, but rather to a gnashing of teeth and a loneliness of the soul. Hansen's dualism, which demanded a rigid choice of the spiritual over the material, could not help giving associations of death to life. This is not a judgment pronounced by the dissenting reader, but one that is voiced in various ways by many of the fictional characters, as well as by the narrator of their fates.

A cruel irony is obviously at play here, for the individual who, through difficult choices, wills his reintegration into a meaningful culture can achieve it only through an alienation both from other human beings and from a part of himself. This outcome is of course a far cry from that spontaneous existence posited by Hansen to have existed in the past. It seems consequently that, when Hansen used the myth—a static image of lost harmony—as a dynamic tool to recapture past harmony, the myth revealed its severe limitations. The myth of the past projected the ideal of a human being who was not haunted by an inner dichotomy, but the man who now attempts to realize the values of that very myth is made the victim of precisely such a dichotomy. The ironic paradox is that, whereas fulfillment in life supposedly was granted the human being of the past, fulfillment is now denied to modern man as if by a metaphysical law. This paradox is naturally of damning consequences, for the choice of the spiritual over the material signifies a disintegration within both the culture and the self, a disintegration that is thoroughly detrimental to the individual's sense of purpose in life and that, in fact, removes him further from his cultural ideal.

The tragic dilemma found in Hansen's writings arises, to put it simply, from the myth's failure to deliver what it promised. If the texts are studied carefully, they acknowledge the myth's inadequacy, but they do not do so in such a way that it seems possible to transcend it. The myth, which promised—and in some measure granted—spiritual liberation from the cultural crisis, became an ideological trap.

This characterization of Hansen's work may seem extreme, since it offers a number of examples of less tormented human destinies. It is however necessary to operate with a distinction between *the individual* and *the others*. The latter may be oblivious to, or victorious over, the inner tension that haunts the individual. He, in turn, must view his life as being dominated by that tension. He may cry out in anguish, but he persists nevertheless in deeming his sacrifices to be meaningful, for he knows—or frantically hopes—that others will benefit from them. Through these sacrifices, he realizes—or wants to realize—his dream of serving culture. Sadly enough, his situation is such that, although he may be the medium through whom harmony is granted to others, he cannot share in their spiritual renewal. Like a Moses, he may look into the promised land, but he himself cannot take part in the last phase of the exodus, the actual entry into that land; thus, he is brutally set apart from others.

Hansen's writings consistently reveal that the artist feels particularly caught in this trap. The tragic irony is that this cultural servant, who exerts himself to formulate and possibly resolve his age's existential problems, becomes an unwilling prisoner in the notorious ivory tower. As he works for his cause, he realizes that his very vocation estranges him from the kind of life he thinks ideal, and this desperate realization makes him prone both to an immense fatigue and to a feeling of having wasted his life. In such a moment he may want to throw all cultural aspirations overboard and may wish for the finality of death, but at the next moment he may shudder over his alienation, grope for new chances, and mourn life's pitiful brevity; thus, he fluctuates between an intense yearning for peace through death and an equally intense fear of death.

At last, in order to probe into the unresolved, paradoxical tension in Hansen's works, it is pertinent to return to the opposition between nature and culture and to arrive at a final modification of that opposition. The artist, Hansen, who produced a consummate, if mythical, picture of the old culture, sometimes admits that the absolute opposition between culture and nature is a fabrication. He knows that culture is not totally separate from nature, for when man emancipated himself from his so-called natural state, he did not reject nature, as such, but allied himself with its beneficial aspects and thus attempted to tame those sides of it that were inimical to his cultural striving. Although man had a healthy suspicion of nature and repudiated all notions of oneness with nature, he remained close to it and could see it for what it was. Man could then lead a meaningful life and perpetuate a harmonious culture. In such a world, as exemplified by the old agrarian tradition, the spiritual and the material, the reflective and the spontaneous were integrated; and much to the benefit of the human being, that detrimental opposition between culture and nature was neutralized. The man of that culture knew that nature bears a Janus head whose one face is benevolent and the other malevolent,

whereas modern man sees only the latter, demonic countenance of nature and becomes utterly alienated from it. Nature discloses to him only the fact that he stands apart from nature's cyclic promise of rebirth.

Driven by fear, modern man vehemently rejects nature and all that he feels it stands for, and he seeks refuge in what he views to be culture; thus, he makes a false opposition between the two absolute. He thereby demonizes nature and, in effect, transforms culture into nihilistic civilization. The result is that death and life become equally meaningless.

Although fear of nature is expressed with gloomy eloquence in Hansen's works, that fear did not eliminate his attation to nature's eternal and disturbing beauty. Hansen's ambivalence testifies to his entrapment in an insuperable emotional paradox.

Hansen's writing gradually became less abundantly humorous and more somber and searching. In spite of its constructive message, its explicit cultural mission, and the convincing ring with which its sense of values was offered, his work came to reveal an acknowledgement of its own profound and tortuous problem. This central feature of Hansen's *oeuvre* constitutes its complexity and limitation: its scope is determined by the fact that it contains its own contradiction and, intermittently, an authorial awareness of this contradiction.

If, finally, the question of whether Hansen's writing fulfilled its intended cultural mission is to be answered, the response must be a "both/and," for his work questions all the answers it gives. This may be why Hansen's works are so perplexing, so successful, and so compellingly fascinating and why they call forth so many readers and interpreters. (pp. 26-36)

Any reading of Martin A. Hansen's *oeuvre* that probes beneath the surface must be a study in human conflict. The texts depict a quest for meaning that proves to be illusive; thus, they suggest a very general resemblance to a number of prominent, albeit very different, novelists whose works Hansen knew: Hamsun, Proust, Kafka, Joyce, and Gide. It is important however to note that Hansen reacted against the open-ended fiction of those authors, for he refused to accept flux as the governing principle of life.

Hansen's quest for meaning led him to reject the religious, philosophical, and political solutions commonly offered to the cultural crisis. Like Kierkegaard, Hansen felt that such all-encompassing theories could have no significance for the single individual and would therefore leave him in moral chaos. Hansen attempted instead to bring the single individual into a relation to his past, to his forebears and their tradition, and thus to suggest purpose in a cultural fellowship: as upholders of a healthy tradition, the dead and the living would be united and, thereby, death would be transcended. That solution to an individualistic culture's crisis may be judged by some readers to be an intellectual fabrication, but it was proffered by Hansen as a very concrete historical reality: a state of consciousness that once had granted—and might again grant—the individual meaning in life and death. With that leap into the past for the sake of the present and the future, Hansen caused his thinking and writing to become suprapersonal and to assume mythical qualities.

The opposition between nature and culture was an integral part of that myth, for Hansen considered his writing to be a cultural defense against the encroachment of nature and of nature's spiritual twin, nihilistic civilization. An investigation of Hansen's work shows however that, ironically enough for its official program, nature also denoted many vital aspects of human existence, which, if denied, could trap the human being in a state of living death. As Hansen's portrayal of the past indicates, those vital aspects had once been a part of the individual's existence. Tragically, no such integration seemed possible to modern man, for whom the spiritual and the physical, the immaterial and the material emerge as irreconcilable opposites. Hansen, therefore, appears to have been both culture's insistent advocate and the modern divided world's restless prisoner.

That tragic irony is one that the most complex of Hansen's texts take cognizance of but cannot overcome; thus, they testify to an existing conflict and not to its impending resolution. The presence of this textual limitation may cause the reader to feel that Hansen's thought was molded by the dominant ideology of a specific age: the tendency to spiritualize all values and human relationships; the dependence upon vaguely, metaphorically stated concepts; the use of metaphysical terminology; and the expression of tortuous reasoning—all tie Hansen's works closely to the decades marked by World War II. It may also be that epochal limitation which accounts for the fact that Hansen's quite extensive impact on other authors has mostly resulted in a mannered and artificial imitation of his way of writing.

The restricted and restrictive scope of Hansen's work may seem obvious today, and it is quite clear that, if Hansen had allowed himself to be merely simplistically didactic and supportive of his quite conservative cultural ideal, his work would have seemed dated within a decade after his death. But only a few of his texts—the too philosophically twisted of his essays and the too sentimental of his works of fiction—have gathered dust. One reason that readers continue to be fascinated with Hansen's works, in spite of the passing of time, may well be that those ideologies that are reflected in his writings have remained a part of the readers' experience of existence. Such readers will still identify with Hansen's haunted and confused characters who long for rebirth and will still share those characters' paradoxical relationship to all that nature and culture may represent. If, however, the human being were to perceive itself differently in the future, Hansen's works would be of only historical interest.

Since the realm of conjecture has been entered, it may finally be in place to insert the subjective opinion that, although such a fate may lie in store for some of Hansen's texts, his best works will never share it. The reason, quite simply, is that Hansen—who was passionately intrigued by all that he rejected and who was ever subject to the artist in himself—in his most accomplished texts transcended his own official vision and, thus, the epochal limitations of his time in history. His readers must reach the consequent conclusion that Hansen's writings question the very answers they offer.

The readers' response may suggest both the failure of Hansen as a thinker who imbued his works with a cultural mission and the success of Hansen as an artist who deeply suspicioned his own vocation. It may be recalled that the protagonist of *The Liar,* in an oddly and rarely truthful moment, admits that "It is art . . . that I care about." In that context, as well as in Hansen's other works, art may not necessarily mean aestheticism but rather truthfulness; and it seems that, by giving in to the artistic inclination and by not adhering strictly to a self-imposed cultural mission, Hansen created a number of works that will continue to fascinate readers. In spite of Hansen's well-defined existential positions, his readers will not escape feeling that the life he depicts remains contradictory. Notwithstanding Hansen's ideological scope, he was a dialectical writer who will undoubtedly continue to appeal to any reader who admits to being caught up in the dialectical process of existence.

It seems fair to predict that the best of Hansen's works will continue to defamiliarize reality and, thus, to function existentially in the lives of its readers. (pp. 169-71)

> *Faith Ingwersen and Niels Ingwersen, in their* Martin A. Hansen, *Twayne Publishers, 1976, 197 p.*

ADDITIONAL BIBLIOGRAPHY

Christiansen, Eric. Introduction to *The Liar,* by Martin A. Hansen, pp. 11-17. London: Quartet Books, 1986.
> Describes Hansen's life and career and briefly examines *The Liar.*

Fleisher, Frederic. "Martin A. Hansen (1909-1955)." *Books Abroad* 30, No. 1 (Winter 1956): 35-6.
> Discusses Hansen's major works, calling him "one of Denmark's outstanding modern authors."

Printz-Påhlson, Göran. "*The Liar:* The Paradox of Fictional Communication in Martin A. Hansen." *Scandinavian Studies* 36, No. 4 (November 1964): 263-80.
> Discusses how the title of *The Liar* expresses the main character's, and Hansen's, mistrust of fiction.

Schow, H. Wayne. Introduction to *Against the Wind,* by Martin A. Hansen, pp. 1-12. New York: Frederick Ungar Publishing Co., 1979.
> Describes Hansen as "the greatest Danish author of his generation and among the foremost Danish writers of this century" and explains the reasons for his lasting appeal.

Thomas Hardy

1840-1928

English novelist, poet, dramatist, short story writer, and essayist.

The following entry presents criticism of Hardy's novel *The Mayor of Casterbridge: The Life and Death of a Man of Character* (1886). For a discussion of Hardy's complete career, see *TCLC*, Volumes 4 and 10; for a discussion of the novel *Tess of the d'Urbervilles*, see *TCLC*, Volume 18.

Hardy is considered one of the greatest novelists in English literature, and *The Mayor of Casterbridge* is consistently ranked as one of his best works. The novel develops the theme, common to much of Hardy's fiction, that "character is fate," implying that life is determined by internal compulsions of character beyond the individual's control. Hence, many commentators stress the significance of the subtitle "The Life and Death of a Man of Character." This appellation puzzled some early reviewers of the novel, who considered the protagonist, Michael Henchard, to be deficient in admirable traits. However, more recent critics have insisted upon a morally neutral interpretation of "character," and contend that the novel is most important as the psychological history of a complex individual.

Hardy was born and raised in the region of Dorsetshire, which he used as the basis for the fictional Wessex countryside of his novels, short stories, and poems. Over the course of his career he made Wessex a self-contained literary world, one of the most extensive and minutely developed in all of literature. Hardy was an established and successful novelist when *The Mayor of Casterbridge*, which shares the Wessex setting, began to appear serially in January of 1886. Serial publication demanded the inclusion of numerous incidents of plot, which Hardy felt marred his fiction, and his second wife wrote that *The Mayor of Casterbridge* "was a story which Hardy fancied he had damaged more recklessly as an artistic whole, in the interest of the newspaper in which it appeared serially, than perhaps any other of his novels, his aiming to get an incident into almost every week's part causing him in his own judgment to add events to the narrative somewhat too freely." As Hardy himself noted in his diary when the novel began to appear serially: "I fear it will not be so good as I meant, but after all, it is not improbabilities of incident but improbabilities of character that matter." However, Hardy had ample time to revise the novel before it was published in book form, and he made extensive textual changes, omitting some sensational elements and moderating others.

Like much of Hardy's fiction, *The Mayor of Casterbridge* features a dominant protagonist, complex human relationships, and an elaborate plot worked out against a background of social and economic changes taking place in the English countryside at a critical historical juncture—in this case, the mid to late nineteenth century, when mechanized agricultural methods were being introduced. *The Mayor of Casterbridge* opens with a prologue that imparts a fabular quality to the narrative. In these opening chapters the unemployed haytrusser Michael Henchard becomes drunk and, acting on a long-standing wish, sells his wife, Susan, and their baby daughter, Elizabeth-Jane, at a county fair, believing he will thrive once free of dependents.

The main action of the novel resumes after an interval of eighteen years. Henchard has prospered, becoming mayor of the agricultural center of Casterbridge as well as one of the town's wealthiest grain merchants. The novel depicts his gradual loss of wealth, social standing, and public office as the direct and indirect consequence of the selling of his wife and child.

The Mayor of Casterbridge is preeminently a character study of Michael Henchard. While commentators generally agree that Hardy excelled in presenting female protagonists, his male characters are considered far less successful. Henchard is recognized as Hardy's finest male characterization to that time and in interest and vitality is considered second only to Jude Fawley in *Jude the Obscure*. Albert Guerard has written that Henchard "stands at the very summit of his creator's achievement; his only tragic hero and one of the greatest tragic heroes in all fiction." According to Desmond Hawkins: "The portrayal of Henchard becomes a solo performance dwarfing everything else. . . . Henchard dominates *The Mayor* from the first page to the last. In all major respects he *is* the book." Indeed, Henchard dominates the narrative to such an extent that the other characters in the novel are all chiefly distinguished by their relationships to him.

Commentators often discuss *The Mayor of Casterbridge* as a tragedy in the classical tradition. John Paterson, for example, has found within the novel the assumption of a morally ordered universe, which is integral to classical tragedy. According to this interpretation, the moral order is so outraged by Henchard's perverse behavior that his consequent downfall is assured. The implication that Henchard's fate is inevitable has led many critics to compare Hardy's novel with the Oedipus plays of Sophocles: just as Oedipus's fate is predicted before the action of the play commences, so too is Henchard's fate sealed from the very first. A second critical approach to *The Mayor of Casterbridge* largely disregards its classical antecedents and views the novel as a masterful psychological study that is intensely modern in its in-depth characterization of an individual, with only incidental resemblance to classical tragedy. In this reading, Henchard's dehumanizing sale of his family does not violate a universal order; rather, it is indicative of a self-destructive tendency in Henchard that will ultimately lead him to embrace the means of his downfall. Principal among these means is Donald Farfrae, who, befriended by Henchard, eventually supplants him in business, in love relationships, and as the Mayor of Casterbridge.

Throughout the novel, Hardy vividly evoked the changes being wrought in the traditional culture of the English countryside by industrialized methods of planting and harvesting and by increasingly sophisticated methods of commerce. This historical perspective is a feature of most of Hardy's fiction, and in *The Mayor of Casterbridge* is made explicit, with Henchard embodying traditional agricultural methods and Farfrae representing the introduction of mechanized planting and harvesting techniques. It has been suggested that Hardy recognized the inevitability of the advances that were altering forever the culture of rural England, and so in *The Mayor of Casterbridge* the progressive Farfrae triumphs over the conservative Henchard. At the same time, some commentators maintain that Hardy's dislike of the introduction of modern methods can be inferred from his portrayal of Henchard as vastly more interesting and vital than Farfrae.

The Mayor of Casterbridge was well received by critics upon its appearance and has since been assessed as one of Hardy's finest novels. It has been heralded in particular as a turning point in Hardy's career, primarily for the unprecedented skill with which he presented a male protagonist. Frederick R. Karl has further pronounced *The Mayor of Casterbridge* "a major turning point in the development of the English novel. . . . No longer solely an important social document, [the novel] has become as well a significant psychological history."

(See also *Contemporary Authors*, Vol. 104 and *Dictionary of Literary Biography*, Vols. 18 and 19.)

R. H. HUTTON   (essay date 1886)

[*The following review of* The Mayor of Casterbridge *emphasizes Hardy's powers of characterization.*]

Mr. Hardy has not given us any more powerful study than that of Michael Henchard [in *The Mayor of Casterbridge*]. Why he should especially term his hero in his title-page a "man of character," we do not clearly understand. Properly speaking, character is the stamp graven on a man, and character therefore, like anything which can be graven, and which, when graven, remains, is a word much more applicable to that which has fixity and permanence, than to that which is fitful and changeful, and which impresses a totally different image of itself on the wax of plastic circumstance at one time, from that which it impresses on a similarly plastic surface at another time. To keep strictly to the associations from which the word "character" is derived, a man of character ought to suggest a man of steady and unvarying character, a man who conveys very much the same conception of his own qualities under one set of circumstances, which he conveys under another. This is true of many men, and they might be called men of character *par excellence*. But the essence of Michael Henchard is that he is a man of large nature and depth of passion, who is yet subject to the most fitful influences, who can do in one mood acts of which he will never cease to repent in almost all his other moods, whose temper of heart changes many times even during the execution of the same purpose, though the same ardour, the same pride, the same wrathful magnanimity, the same inability to carry out in cool blood the angry resolve of the mood of revenge or scorn, the same hasty unreasonableness, and the same disposition to swing back to an equally hasty reasonableness, distinguish him throughout. In one very good sense, the great deficiency of Michael Henchard might be said to be in "character." It might well be said that with a little *more* character, with a little more fixity of mind, with a little more power of recovering *himself* when he was losing his balance, his would have been a nature of gigantic mould; whereas, as Mr. Hardy's novel is meant to show, it was a nature which ran mostly to waste. But, of course, in the larger and wider sense of the word "character," that sense which has less reference to the permanent definition of the stamp, and more reference to the confidence with which the varying moods may be anticipated, it is not inadmissible to call Michael Henchard a "man of character." Still, the words on the title-page rather mislead. One looks for the picture of a man of much more constancy of purpose, and much less tragic mobility of mood, than Michael Henchard. None the less, the picture is a very vivid one, and almost magnificent in its fullness of expression. The largeness of his nature, the unreasonable generosity and suddenness of his friendships, the depth of his self-humiliation for what was evil in him, the eagerness of his craving for sympathy, the vehemence of his impulses both for good and evil, the curious dash of stoicism in a nature so eager for sympathy, and of fortitude in one so moody and restless,—all these are lineaments which, mingled together as Mr. Hardy has mingled them, produce a curiously strong impression of reality, as well as of homely grandeur.

Our only quarrel with Mr. Hardy is that while he draws a figure which, in spite of the melancholy nature of its career and the tragic close of that career, is certainly a noble one, and one, on the whole, *more* noble in its end than in its beginning, he intersperses throughout his story hints of the fashionable pessimism, a philosophy which seems to us to have little appropriateness to the homely scenery and characters which he portrays. For example, as Mr. Hardy approaches the end of his story, he says of his hero:—

> Externally there was nothing to hinder his making another start on the upward slope, and by his new lights achieving higher things than his soul in its half-formed state had been able to accomplish. But the ingenious machinery contrived by the gods for reducing human possibilities of amelioration to a min-

imum—which arranges that wisdom to do shall come *pari passu* with the departure of zest for doing—stood in the way of all that. He had no wish to make an arena a second time of a world that had become a mere painted scene to him.

To our minds, these very pagan reflections are as much out of place as they are intrinsically false. The natural and true reflection would have been that Michael Henchard, after his tragic career of passionate sin, bitter penitence, and rude reparation, having been brought to a better and humbler mind than that which had for the most part pervaded his life, the chief end of that life had been achieved, and that it mattered little in comparison whether he should or should not turn the wisdom he had acquired to the purpose of hewing out for himself a wiser and soberer career. Those who believe that the only ''human possibilities of amelioration'' of any intrinsic worth, are ameliorations of the spirit of human character, cannot for a moment admit that when that has been achieved, it can add much to such an amelioration, that it should receive the sanction of a little earthly success. If life be the school of character, and if the character, once fairly schooled into a nobler type, passes from this school to another and higher school, we have no reason to complain. What Mr. Hardy calls ''the ingenious machinery contrived by the gods for reducing human possibilities of amelioration to a minimum,'' appears to us to be the means taken by the moral wisdom which overrules our fate for showing us that the use of character is not to mould circumstance, but rather that it is the use of circumstance to chasten and purify character. Michael Henchard's proud and lonely death shows, indeed, that he had but half learned his lesson; but it certainly does not in any way show that the half-learned lesson had been wasted. There is a grandeur of conception about this shrewd, proud, illiterate, primitive nature, which, so far as we remember, surpasses anything which even Mr. Hardy has yet painted for us in that strong and nervous school of delineation in which he excels so much. Michael Henchard's figure should live with us as Scott's picture of Steenie Mucklebacket or David Deans lives with us. Indeed, Scott never gave to a figure of that kind so much study and such painstaking portraiture as Mr. Hardy has given to his Mayor of Casterbridge.

He has succeeded quite as well,—though the figure is not so interesting,—with the Mayor's step-daughter, Elizabeth Jane, a reticent and self-contained nature of singular gentleness and wisdom, cast in an altogether lower tone of vitality, though in a higher plane of self-restraint. There is much beauty and charm in the picture, though the carefully subdued tone of the character makes it seem a little tame, and we are not at all scandalised at the easy victory gained by the lively Jersey beauty over her sober-minded, un-self-asserting rival. This Jersey beauty is also admirably touched off; but as for the all-conquering Scotchman who fascinates everybody (except the reader) so easily, there must, we think, be some failure of art there. Mr. Hardy makes Farfrae vivid enough. We cannot complain of not seeing him exactly as he is represented. But we have, perhaps, a right to complain that he seems so very cold-blooded to us, so very inferior to the master whom he supplants, though to all Mr. Hardy's *dramatis personae,* Farfrae seemed so greatly the superior of Michael Henchard. Part of the reason is that Mr. Hardy paints the Scotchman from the outside, and the Southron from the inside, and that while we see the Southron as no one in the story sees him, unless it be himself, we only see the Scotchman as all the others see him. But though that explains why we like the Southron so much *better,* it hardly explains why we like the canny Scotchman, with all his imag-

inative sentiment, so little, though he wins so easy a victory over the hearts of the people of Casterbridge.

We will not select morsels for quotation from *The Mayor of Casterbridge,* for it is not a story which lends itself well to quotation. And though the scenery of Dorsetshire, and especially of Dorchester,—which is obviously enough the original of Casterbridge,—is admirably given, Mr. Hardy's art in describing the scenery of the South-West is too well known to need illustration. His impetuous and restless hero is really the centre of the story. Round him all its interest centres, and with him it ends. We cannot express too warmly our admiration for the art with which that stalwart and wayward nature has been delineated, and all the apparently self-contradictory subtleties of his moods have been portrayed. (pp. 752-53)

R. H. Hutton, in an unsigned review of ''The Mayor of Casterbridge,'' in The Spectator, *Vol. 59, No. 3023, June 5, 1886, pp. 752-53.*

[H. M. ALDEN]   (essay date 1886)

[*The following is a favorable review of* The Mayor of Casterbridge.]

In *The Mayor of Casterbridge* Mr. Hardy seems to have started with an intention of merely adventurous fiction, and to have found himself in possession of something so much more important that we could fancy him almost regretting the appeal first made to the reader's wonder. Henchard's sale of his wife is not without possibility, or even precedent; Mr. Hardy sufficiently establishes that; and yet when the grave, every-day problems resulting from that wild act began to grow under his hand, so fine an artist might well have wished them derived from some fact more commonly within the range of experience. After you have said this, however, you can have very little else to say against the story; and we are not strenuous that this is much against it. We suppose it is a condition of a novelist's acceptance by the criticism of a country now so notably behind the rest of Europe in fiction as England that he must seize the attention in an old-fashioned way; and we willingly concede to Mr. Hardy the use of the wife-sale for this purpose, though we are not sure that the non-professional readers of his book, even in England, would have exacted so much of him. The tangled web woven from Henchard's error is of the true modern design and honesty of material; and one forgets that he sold his wife in following all the consequences to his innocent and beneficent after-life, and to the good and guiltless lives of others. The wrong he has done cannot be repaired, because it cannot, to his mistaken thinking, be owned; and in the tragedy of its expiation your pity is more for him than for all the others. That wrong pursues him, it hunts him to death, with what natural reliefs and pauses the reader knows. Mr. Hardy has never achieved anything more skilful or valuable in its way than the recognition and development of these in his last story; we are not sure that he has not placed himself abreast of Tolstoï and the greatest of the Continental realists in their management.

Then the book is full of his proper and peculiar charm, which is for us always very great. It is a quality which, if he had no other great quality, would give him a claim upon his generation hardly less than that of any other contemporary novelist. It seems to exist apart from any beauty of style or felicity of phrase, and is like the grace of his women, which remains in your thought when you have ceased to think of their different pretty faces and variously alluring figures. It would be as hard to say what it is as to say what that grace is, and we can only suggest that it is a very frank and simple way of dealing with every kind of life, and of approaching men and women as directly as if they had never been written about before. In fact, thanks no doubt to his early training in another profession (Mr. Hardy was an architect), his first sense of people is apparently not a literary sense, but something very much more natural. He studies their exterior graphically, and deals with their souls as we do with those of our neighbors, only perhaps a little more mercifully. This absence of literosity, if we may coin a word as offensive as the thing, accounts for an occasional bluntness of phrase, which we have sometimes felt in Mr. Hardy's work, and for here and there an uncouthness of diction—or call it awkwardness; but we gain infinitely more than we lose by it. His natural method gives us in this story country folks as veritable as those in *Far from the Madding Crowd,* or *Under the Greenwood Tree,* never ironically or sentimentally handled, but left to make their own impression, among scenes and in surroundings portrayed as sympathetically and unconventionally as themselves. In fact, his landscapes are no more composed than his figures, and share evenly with them the charm of his treatment; no one except Tourguénief gives a fact or trait of nature with a more living freshness.

We should say that *The Mayor of Casterbridge* was not inferior to any other story of Mr. Hardy's in its grasp of character; and his humanity is so very pervasive that each of the leading personages has almost to the same degree that charm of his which we have not been very successful in defining. Henchard is brutal only in our first moments of him; his life, after these, is a willingness, if not an effort, to repair his wrong to his wife; and the heart aches with him through all his necessary ruin to the pitiable end of the old, broken, friendless man. Then that young Scot, Farfrae, gay, thrifty, and good, who supplants his benefactor in business, in love, and in public honors, without intending harm to Henchard, is one of the freshest and most clean-cut figures in recent fiction; if you have known any bright young Scotchman, this one will make you think of him. Henchard's wife is one of those women, single-minded, unknowing, upright, which Mr. Hardy has the secret of divining and presenting to us in all their probability; there is not much of her, but every word of that little seems true. There is not very much of Lucetta either, but she too is every word true; she is perhaps only too captivating in that combination of shrewdness and blind imprudence, of fickleness and tenderheartedness, of fascinating grace and helplessness. She is of the order of women whom Mr. Hardy is rather fond of drawing, like Bathsheba in *Far from the Madding Crowd,* like Fancy in *Under the Greenwood Tree,* like Elfride in *A Pair of Blue Eyes,* and some delicious young person in nearly every one of his books; the sort who guiltlessly compromise themselves by some love impulse, and then more or less amusingly, more or less distressingly, pay for it, but remain in the reader's mind an appealing, a distracting presence. Nothing is better in the book than Lucetta's dropping Henchard, and her conquest of the young Scotchman, whom she wins away from Henchard's putative daughter, Elizabeth Jane, such being the fond and foolish heart of man in the thriftiest and best of us. But Elizabeth Jane, with her unswerving right-mindedness and her never-failing self-discipline, is a very beautiful and noble figure; and Mr. Hardy has made her supremely interesting merely by letting us see into her pure soul. Hers is the final triumph, unmixed with remorse, because nothing but goodness like hers could come unscathed out of all that sorrow and trouble. The author who can discover such a type, on whom the reader's liking may wholesomely rest, has done his public a real favor. It is a very great thing to show goodness and justice and mercy like hers in their actual relation to other lives, and lovable; and it

is all the more useful to know Elizabeth Jane because her limitations are more than suggested, and she is not made St. Elizabeth Jane. (pp. 961-62)

[*H. M. Alden*], in a review of "The Mayor of Casterbridge," in Harper's New Monthly Magazine, Vol. LXXIII, No. 438, November, 1886, pp. 961-62.

ALBERT J. GUERARD   (essay date 1949)

[*Guerard, an American novelist and critic, has written extensively on Joseph Conrad and Thomas Hardy. In the following excerpt from his* Thomas Hardy: The Novels and Stories, *he praises the characterization of Michael Henchard and the nearly perfect structure of* The Mayor of Casterbridge.]

Hardy's men, prior to *The Mayor of Casterbridge,* are inadequate as human beings and even more inadequate as fictional creations. Hardy's great gift for conveying living personality reveals itself rather in his portraits of rustics and of women. It is perhaps significant that the women in particular are seen as objects—fascinating, incomprehensible, strange. (pp. 121-22)

None of Hardy's women are unalive, and very few of them are wholly uninteresting; even the innocent ingénues are capable of occasional violent flareups.... More importantly, Hardy's six greatest women characters differ radically among themselves: Elfride, nervous and evasive; Bathsheba, curiously masculine and feminine; the wild, proud, and unreconciled Eustacia; the tender and "pure" Tess; the tormented yet fun-loving Sue; and Arabella, the female animal. Against these six major characters and a host of convincing minor ones, Hardy offers only two men of more than average interest and vitality: Michael Henchard and Jude Fawley.

Henchard, who is Hardy's Lord Jim, stands at the very summit of his creator's achievement; his only tragic hero and one of the greatest tragic heroes in all fiction. He takes his place at once with certain towering and possessed figures of Melville, Hawthorne, and Dostoevsky: a man of character obsessed by guilt and so committed to his own destruction. He anticipates not merely Lord Jim and the Razumov of *Under Western Eyes* but also the Michel of André Gide's *L'Immoraliste.* Fifty years before Karl Menninger, Hardy recognized—as Shakespeare did three centuries before him—that the guilty not merely flagellate themselves but also thrust themselves in the way of bad luck; *create* what appear to be unlucky accidents. Henchard's decline in Casterbridge was no more fortuitous than Lord Jim's in Patusan. These two "men of character" pursued strikingly similar destinies: forceful, conscientious, and proud, alike outcasts thanks to the unaccountable flarings of a moment's fear and anger, dedicating their lives to an impossible rehabilitation and a distant ideal of honor. They are isolated and obsessed by guilt even in their fat years of power and prestige; they are determined to bear yet face down the past. Both are men of character in a strangely double sense. They want to atone for the past through self-punishment; yet they resist, humanly, merely compulsive self-punishment. In the end both are paralyzed by "chance" reminders from the past (Brown and the furmity-woman)—reminders which, in fact, they had never ceased to carry about with them. They achieve death in solitude, each having one dull-witted uncomprehending native who remains faithful to the last. Of the two Henchard, whose will was a final self-condemnation, may have shown more courage than Lord Jim, who turned to his executioners and to the world with a last look of proud defiance. Henchard was a "man of character"; Lord Jim was "one of us."

There was nothing in Hardy's earlier novels to suggest that he would some day produce such a figure; there is no series of links and experiments leading from Springrove or Manston to Henchard. Gabriel Oak, Diggory Venn, and many others seem to act perversely against their own interest, but this is owing to meditative impotence and a lack of normal aggressiveness. They are spectators rather than actors against themselves. Unlike them Henchard is a man of great force and destructive energy, which he turns outward occasionally but inward far more often. He has thus nothing in common with the irresponsible Wildeve, but a great deal in common with both Jude and Sue. There is little justification for the critic who sums up Henchard's tragic flaws as temper and addiction to drink; these were symptoms of the self-destructive impulse rather than its causes. Hardy himself was explicit enough:

> Thereupon promptly came to the surface that idiosyncrasy of Henchard's which had ruled his courses from the beginning, and had mainly made him what he was. Instead of thinking that a union between his cherished stepdaughter and the energetic thriving Donald was a thing to be desired for her good and his own, he hated the very possibility.

> Among the many hindrances to such a pleading, not the least was this, that he did not sufficiently value himself to lessen his sufferings by strenuous appeal or elaborate argument.

> He had not expressed to her any regrets or excuses for what he had done in the past; but it was a part of his nature to extenuate nothing and live on as one of his own worst accusers.

Henchard is simply incapable of acting consistently in his own interest. Captain Ahab, traveling the wide seas in pursuit of his own destruction, supposes cosmic hostilities in a whale. And so Henchard, earthbound in Casterbridge, comes at last to think "some sinister intelligence bent on punishing him." Had someone roasted a wax image of him? Was some power working against him? Unaware that the power was wholly inward, he "looked out at the night as at a fiend."

Thus Hardy, who had seldom troubled himself with crime and punishment, at last explored the great nineteenth-century myth of the isolated, damned, and self-destructive individualist— the more impressively because his Lara, Vautrin, Tito Melema, and Ahab was an ordinary Wessex farmer-merchant. The particular myth was conceived in terms as grand as the Wessex environment would allow—beginning with no less than the angry, drunken, and impulsive sale of a wife on the fairgrounds of Weydon Priors, to which Henchard would return a quarter of a century later in full circle. The tendency to paranoia and self-flagellation must have had its origin, like that of Sue Bridehead, in some part of an undisclosed childhood. At the very beginning Henchard has already the "instinct of a perverse character"; he drinks too much and thinks he has ruined his chances by marrying at eighteen. It is the crime of selling his wife which concentrates his energies, however; which both makes his character and destroys it. (Here too he is exactly like Lord Jim, who might have remained, in innocence, a fairly ordinary sea captain and trader.) Henchard looks in vain for his wife; swears an oath not to drink for twenty years; becomes mayor of Casterbridge, though equipped with little more than energy—becomes a man of character. When Susan finally reappears, he stolidly and conscientiously marries her; when Lucetta reappears, he acts honorably, though long tempted to revenge himself on Farfrae through her; when the furmity-woman reappears, he publicly acknowledges his guilt. He is fair in his savage fashion, and fights Farfrae with one hand tied behind his back. Ruined, he is the most conscientious of bankrupts.

The Mayor of Casterbridge is a novel of temperament in action, in minute action even; its distinction derives from a severe concentration on the self-destructive aspects of that temperament. The obligation to punish and degrade the self is at times fairly conscious. Thus Henchard marries Susan not merely to make amends to her and to provide Elizabeth-Jane with a home, but also "to castigate himself with the thorns which these restitutory acts brought in their train; among them the lowering of his dignity in public opinion by marrying so comparatively humble a woman." He licks his wounds by demanding that the journeyman sing the terrible One Hundred and Ninth Psalm; he goes to work for Farfrae wearing the rusty silk hat of his former dignity; he humbles himself unnecessarily before Lucetta; he lingers on the second stone bridge where the failures and drifters of the town gather. But Hardy recognized, intuitively at least, that the guilty may also punish themselves unconsciously and cause their own "bad luck." The man who repeatedly cuts and burns himself is no mere victim of absurd mischance; he is compelled to cut and burn himself, though he may not understand his compulsion. Freud has documented the hidden psychology of errors; Menninger the motives of chronic failures and of those who suffer repeated "accidents." Psychologists have proved that the unfortunate are more often than not the guilty, who must pay daily hostages to their fear.

Henchard is such a man, for whom everything "goes wrong" once he has begun to struggle with his guilt. So his elaborate public entertainment fails dismally while Farfrae's modest one succeeds. Rain does not fall at the beck of the accusing conscience, but Henchard's party is ruined by more than rain. "A man must be headstrong stunpoll to think folk would go up to that bleak place today." Later he gambles on disastrous rains to drive up the price of corn and is confirmed in his prophecy by the mysterious Mr. Fall; he buys enormous quantities of corn and is ruined by the blazing August weather. But the adverse force was his own lack of Wessex prudence. "He was reminded of what he had well known before, that a man might gamble upon the square green areas of fields as readily as upon those of a card-room . . . 'For you can never be sure of weather till 'tis past.'" Henchard's subconscious self-destructiveness shows itself far less equivocally at the time of the Royal Progress. He has a "passing fancy" to join in welcoming the royal visitor, though no longer a member of the town council. But what might have appeared a last conscious effort to reassert his dignity was in fact a half-conscious effort to degrade himself before the collected townfolk in the most humiliating way. "He was not only a journeyman, unable to appear as he formerly had appeared, but he disdained to appear as well as he might. Everybody else, from the Mayor to the washerwoman, shone in new vesture according to means; but Henchard had doggedly retained the fretted and weather-beaten garments of bygone years." And he was drunk. When he resumed drinking after twenty years, a short time before this, he had committed himself to focal suicide and certain self-punishment. Character is fate; and Newson and the furmity-woman, those symbolic reminders, were part of his character and fate. Henchard would have destroyed himself even had they not returned. As a man of character he was morally obligated to do so. Yet he was also obligated to resist mere compulsive self-destructiveness. Here too, in fighting his suicidal destiny, he was a man of character.

Thus grandly and minutely conceived, Henchard might yet have remained as wooden as Farmer Boldwood. But he is very nearly the most personalized of Hardy's men: a voice and an unforgettable massive presence, with his twitching mouth and distant gaze, his "vehement" gloominess, his severe friendliness, and his businesslike bluntness even when proposing marriage. No doubt it is as a well-meaning man isolated by guilt that he makes his strongest appeal to our sympathy. Loneliness as well as guilt prompts him to hire Farfrae impulsively and to pour out his confession at once. And guilt as well as loneliness attaches him to Elizabeth-Jane: "He had liked the look of her face as she answered him from the stairs. There had been affection in it, and above all things what he desired now was affection from anything that was good and pure." Finally, though his history is highly selective, we have the impression that we know Henchard's life in its every significant detail. The measure of the characterization's success is our unquestioning acceptance in its context of Henchard's stylized and symbolic will. It does not seem to us a gratuitous or merely ornamental offering of Hardy's pessimism, as a few of Jude Fawley's philosophical speeches do. Michael Henchard's excommunication of self is a reasoned one, for his life has actually so added up:

> That Elizabeth-Jane Farfrae be not told of my death,
> or made to grieve on account of me.
> & that I be not bury'd in consecrated ground.
> & that no sexton be asked to toll the bell.
> & that nobody is wished to see my dead body.
> & that no murners walk behind me at my funeral.
> & that no flours be planted on my grave.
> & and that no man remember me.
> To this I put my name.

"Let the day perish wherein I was born, and the night in which it was said, There is a manchild conceived"—Jude Fawley might have signed Henchard's will.

Jude is not, however, a tragic hero—if only because he is a "modern." Henchard's will is a final condemnation of self and of the "old mankind"; it is an achievement of the self-knowledge which tragedy compels. Jude's dying words are instead a condemnation of the cosmos in its dark and at last recognized absurdity. Not Jude but the cosmos is to blame. There are certain obvious links between the two characters: the common sensitiveness to music, the imprudent early marriages, the addiction to drink, the need to punish and degrade the self publicly. But the significant link occurs in the final paragraph of *The Mayor of Casterbridge;* in Elizabeth-Jane's observation "that neither she nor any human being deserved less than was given." The observation is pathetic and of course pessimistic in the commoner sense of that word. But it is not tragic, as all but the last pages of the novel are tragic. For the tragic attitude lays the blame not on the stars but on ourselves; it sees fate in character; its pessimism is grounded in the insufficiency of the human endowment; it insists, with Conrad's Marlow, that "nobody is good enough." (pp. 146-52)

Hardy was a great popular novelist and not a great deliberate artist. The rare popular novelist who also deserves our esteem is perhaps the most difficult one to account for and to analyze. We add up his distinguishable virtues patiently, only to arrive at an absurdly small sum. Dissatisfied with this sum, we posit still other virtues. This is what most of Hardy's critics have done. Starting from a wholly justified liking for the novels, they have gone on to discern the qualities which they assume a great novelist must show: profound thought, high unremittent seriousness of purpose, insight into social problems, excep-

tional psychological understanding, perfection of structure and style, realism and poetry. But we must look elsewhere than to Hardy for such qualities as these; we must look, for instance, to Conrad at his best. Hardy revealed repeatedly an initial sluggishness of mind, most often perhaps in his tendency to schematize and oversimplify dilemmas. His frank purpose through most of his career was to write books which would sell easily. Although he showed an aesthetic understanding of agricultural Dorset, he showed, prior to *Jude the Obscure,* little understanding of the moral and social condition of the late nineteenth century. His power to dramatize the personality and temperament of women was indeed extraordinary, but he presents fewer interesting men than almost any important novelist. And with the two exceptions of *The Mayor of Casterbridge* and *Under the Greenwood Tree,* his novels are radically imperfect in structure. His style conveys temperament but is abnormally relaxed and diffuse. And for realism and poetry his poems, not his novels, invite us.

His final and unmistakable appeal therefore rests on much less austere grounds than these: on the popular storytelling of a singularly uninhibited imagination, on an occasional mastery of atmosphere in relation to character, on a variety of manner and mood frankly modeled on Shakespeare's, on a fine purity of temperament—and, above all, on an incorrigible sympathy for all who are lonely and all who long for happiness. He understood the plight of ordinary, simple, and well-meaning persons, subjected to the extraordinary, complex, and seemingly malign circumstances of life. He could find a saving grace in all failure, while Conrad found evil in all success and behind every act of benevolence. Even the heroes of Conrad are subjected to pitiless analysis; the unworthy are looked upon with cold disdain. But which of Hardy's villains is irrevocably damned? And which . . . does not benefit at least briefly from this universal sympathy? Hardy's dark vision of the world compelled him, in compensatory fairness, to a certainly excessive charity. Good and evil seemed irrelevant in such an indifferent universe; he wanted people to be happy. He was not concerned with damnation and salvation—as Dostoevsky and Melville and the very greatest writers have been, as Conrad and Gide were to be.

The literary historian and the modern novelist alike can benefit from a study of Hardy's anti-realism and occasional symbolist experiments; they can discover in Hardy ways of escaping inanimate drabness. But it would be absurd to read into Hardy's anti-realism any profound metaphysical intentions, or into his symbolist experiments the complex aesthetic intentions of Conrad. For Hardy did not take his craft seriously in the way that James, Conrad, Proust, and Gide were to take it seriously; he did not conceive of fiction as a high art, at least not until very late; he rested on his poems all claims to uncompromising greatness. Was he finally persuaded by his admirers that novels too could be great works of art? In the end he did write, and seemingly with full consciousness of what he was doing, three very great novels: *Tess of the D'Urbervilles, The Mayor of Casterbridge,* and *Jude the Obscure.* But only two of these explore at all the great theme of nineteenth- and twentieth-century fiction: the myth of the morally isolated individualist lost in a world he never made; who searches for freedom, though bereft of faith, and who wills his own destruction. It would require Conrad, once thought a popular storyteller and historian of simple hearts, to explore the destructive element exhaustively. There will never be too many such exploring pessimists; there will never be too many Conrads. But in our darkening world there is also much to say for Hardy's purity of mind and antique simplicity of art. There may also be something to say for his charity. Less austere and less ambitious than Conrad, Hardy confined himself to our unregenerate longing for happiness and our common destiny of suffering. (pp. 157-59)

Albert J. Guerard, in his Thomas Hardy: The Novels and Stories, *Cambridge, Mass.: Harvard University Press, 1949, 177 p.*

D. A. DIKE　(essay date 1952)

[*In the following essay, Dike discusses the importance of the marketplace in* The Mayor of Casterbridge *in making the events and characters of the novel analogous to those of traditional tragedy.*]

Everyone, I suppose, would agree that Hardy's novel, **The Mayor of Casterbridge,** imitates a tragic action. Its form is unmistakably analogous to that of Greek drama, most notably *Oedipus Rex,* and to that of the folk ritual in which drama has its roots. Thus the career of Michael Henchard, upon whom has been visited the curse emblematic of the tragic hero, is so organized that the pursuit of his conscious purpose, to atone for the crime committed in the Prologue by sharing his wealth and prestige with his rediscovered family, reverses his fortune and prepares his downfall. Each of his groping endeavours to manipulate events favourably—as, for example, when he opens his wife's deathbed message to prove his paternity and thereby disproves it—contributes to the gradual and awful discovery that his expiation will consist not in action but in passion; suffering is apportioned him as the solitary means by which he, his family, and the community wherein he dwells can be cleansed of his guilt. The instrument of his suffering is, of course, his successor. The central *agon* of the novel, Henchard's struggle with Donald Farfrae, recalls the antagonism between Oedipus and Creon and also the sacred combat between the old god, priest, or father and the new, around which was constructed the primitive rite of the Seasonal King. As conclusion to that ceremonial combat, the rejected king was torn asunder and spread over the land. So Henchard, supplanted mayor, father, and corn merchant—for his profession is significant, reminding us of its religious antecedent—loses official authority, possessions, both wife and daughter, social function to his figurative son. He becomes a pariah, dies nearly anonymously, and is buried in unsanctified ground. But his suffering, which considered as a phase in the tragic pattern extends roughly from the marriage of Lucetta, his onetime mistress, to her death, wins him a rebirth, signalized by his response to the effigy in the dark pool, and a brief re-identification with life and nature. No longer able to preside over the autumnal harvest, he can, as petty retailer, at least distribute seeds for the spring planting. This rebirth and re-identification, although it occurs too late to save an inexorable situation, mitigates the effect of the final catastrophe. It is connected with the perceptive conclusion to the tragic action, with the general recognition which is the culmination of innumerable earlier but only partial discoveries and which is precipitated by the arrival of Newson, nineteenth-century equivalent of the inevitable Greek messenger. By the end of the novel the relations between the characters are precisely established and insight into the meaning of the drama they have enacted promises an escape from further calamity. This epiphany is the ground for an emotional reconciliation: not a literal one because Henchard, chastened by suffering, perceives that he must take himself off before the community can return to normal. Formerly its protector, he

now bears the load of its collective sins. His voluntary death is thus required as a sacrifice upon which will be based the *modus vivendi* of his survivors.

From the action briefly summarized, as from the parallel movement of *Oedipus,* it is possible to abstract an idea of Fate and the hypothesis of a Wheel of Fortune, though, as Francis Ferguson has suggested, for an analysis of Sophocles's play these concepts are mainly useful considered as metaphors, descriptions of a pattern, clues to a point of view, rather than as articles of belief. Hardy, aware not only of Greek drama but also of a theory of Greek drama and of what we have been led to believe was the official Greek position, seems to take Fate and the Wheel more literally. Or perhaps "literally" is too strong, for they stand in relation to the action of his novel as myth stands to ritual, symbolic explanation to imitation. Thus Henchard's Austerlitz, we are explicitly informed, occurs at the feast in his honour. He has reached the peak of his career and must necessarily begin to decline.

So too it is possible to abstract from the behaviour of the characters those generalized human qualities of which destiny is simply the temporal extension. Henchard's pride, jealousy, ambition, violent temper are the tragic vices associated with nobility; his sense of duty, like that of Oedipus, provokes disaster because, distorted by hubris, it is the reverse side of a profound irresponsibility. Susan and Elizabeth Jane are models of stoic virtue; Lucetta is a Jocasta who knows what she is about and must ultimately pay the extreme penalty for mismarriage. And Donald Farfrae, like Creon, is an opportunist, charming, efficient, a new man too occupied with his own success fully to recognize the extent of the tragedy in which he is involved.

But Hardy's success in this work is not effected by any mechanical manipulation of the forms and categories of classical drama. It rewards his having glimpsed these forms and categories in a raw subject-matter and realized them in a created situation derived from observation of the contemporary scene and informed by relevant attitudes towards that scene. In Greek drama the tragic pattern emerges from a coherent point of view or response to the serious business of living in the Greek world; to the extent that the details of the response are irrecoverable, we have difficulty appreciating the pattern's vital significance. So in Hardy's novel, the tragic pattern is not an abstraction, a literary convention imposed upon neutral subject-matter. Discerned in a living context, modified by the circumstances of nineteenth-century life, it is embodied in content, that is, in the array of motives and values which comprise Michael Henchard's world. Hence, working with and through the concrete particulars of experience, Hardy is both realist and symbolist, which is to say that by being intensely and imaginatively realistic, he passes beyond realism to discover the archetypal form, the timeless categories, implicit in an immediate context, a context which consequently becomes the symbolic utterance of a larger meaning. He isolates in the contemporary scene an area which is analogous to the matrix of classical drama and a characteristic action whose ideal form imitates the ritual mode of tragedy.

That area, which surveyed from Lucetta's window is a stage on which dramatic action occurs, is the Market of Casterbridge. It is figuratively bounded by three bridges, two of them representing suicidal opportunities for bankrupt members of the two main economic classes, the third a secret ingress to the town for thieves, and by three inns, whose degree of luxury further defines the varying financial status of Casterbridge's inhabitants. Henchard's career, after the Prologue, opens at the best of these inns, reserved for the patronage of property owners and employers and significantly named The King's Arms—significantly, in view of Henchard's last attempt to regain caste by greeting the Royal Visitor. After his fall he finds solace, not at the worst of the inns, for he retains some semblance of former dignity, but at that attended by employees, The Three Mariners, where his social degradation is signalized by the end of twenty years' abstinence from drink. His fall is thus from one class to another; it is the reverse of Farfrae's ascent. And the antagonism between classes is overtly asserted by the scene in Farfrae's barn, when Henchard bitterly reminds Lucetta of their relative social positions.

To the Market, a place of "individual unrestraint," come professions as distinctive as species, human shapes which specifically represent ready money. There come men who, whatever their expressions at home, wear market faces on the commercial stage: they wear the masks required by buying and selling. For throughout the novel we are reminded of the dangerous incongruity between Nature and Civilization, and Henchard's tragedy is of the kind wrought by Civilization, whose monstrous symbol the Market becomes.

But men not only do come to the Market, they *must* come to it. It compels their attendance and determines the course of their lives. "It's better to stay at home, and that's true," Donald Farfrae tells Lucetta, "but a man must live where his money is made." And several pages later, the Market "calls" him with an urgency which love cannot match. The scene of the action, in short, is also the essential motive for the action; the scene is both place-in-which and place-for-which. It organizes the desires of the characters, the values they respect, and the means of their interaction. As stage it literally supports what occurs upon it.

What occurs upon it is the genteel warfare of economic competition. This competition is dramatized as a mortal combat between two corn merchants: one relatively old, energetic, careless of details, committed to antiquated methods, generous, personally unpopular because of his prestige and the pride that accompanies office; the other young, systematic, scrupulous about details, an innovator of scientific techniques, a tightwad, popular because of his modesty and because he is the underdog. Their combat, which begins in a disagreement about how labour should be treated—Donald is more cordial to subordinates than Henchard but he pays lower wages—expands from rivalry in trade to rivalry in love, whose materialism is symbolized in the scene at Lucetta's mansion when the two suitors tug ridiculously at a single slice of bread. It ends in physical conflict, which because it is natural, uneconomic, uncivilized, outside the scope of the rules of the game, ends inconclusively. For though the survival of one contestant in the larger struggle depends upon the death of the other, the more powerful wrestler is too conditioned by the Market in which he has spent all his adult life to be nakedly Darwinian.

The object of competition, of course, is acquisition. The acquisitive impulse, engendered by the Market, reaches beyond the commodities of ordinary exchange and identifies people as property to be possessed or ignored, bought or sold. It invades and perverts the home, which ideally stands, as Farfrae's remark to Lucetta would indicate, in irreconcilable opposition to trade; it sets its stamp on the family, for whose institutional bourgeois form Hardy clearly has no use. Thus Henchard is anxious for Elizabeth Jane to take his name, the sign of his proprietary interest in her. When Susan dies, he announces

what he supposes to be his kinship to Elizabeth, openly asserts his ownership. The ownership ironically turns out to be illegal, whereupon Henchard, who seems to like only what he has or can buy, loses his affection for another man's daughter and encourages his enemy, to whom he has previously refused even a share, to court her—an obvious attempt to market worthless stock. He reinvests his surplus feelings in Lucetta, whose value has been enhanced by Donald's competition for her hand and by the fortune which she has inherited since her salad days. But such investments are unprofitable. Significantly, it is unwanted Elizabeth Jane who, because she does not abuse her unexpected opportunity as Henchard's daughter to buy all the luxuries she desires and restrains from competing with Lucetta for Donald Farfrae, receives both worldly goods and the man she loves at the end of the novel. Yet Elizabeth Jane unquestioningly acknowledges the conventional ethic. Her respect for paternal authority over her feelings is evinced by obedient discouragement of Farfrae early in the action and by her absolute rejection of Henchard and devoted allegiance to Newson once she is convinced to whom she belongs. While Henchard, having learned through deprivation that one can love what is not legally his, sadly recognizes that property rights force his withdrawal from the scene.

The Market coins the public values and legislates the means by which the citizens of Casterbridge seek to live. It encourages speculation: in Nature, as when Henchard stakes his wealth on a poor harvest; in humanity, when he wagers his last hope on Elizabeth's understanding. The merchant's career, an archetype, is a series of gambles. The Market poses an opposition between worldly success and marriage, introduced by the auction in the Prologue and reiterated by Henchard's bad luck after his family returns. It stimulates dissatisfaction with shared possessions, holds up sole proprietorship as an ideal, so that Henchard cannot countenance Elizabeth's division of her love between him and Farfrae, diplomatically and commercially useful as the alliance ensuing from this division would be.

But the most comprehensive effect of the Market is its subordination of instinctive feeling to the cash nexus. As I suggested earlier, the relations between characters in this novel are influenced by money. They take the active form of purchases and sales. While inferior horses are being auctioned off nearby, Henchard sells his wife for five guineas in what he later refers to as "the transaction of my early married life." That Susan should believe the transaction to be legally binding is more than proof of her ignorance; it is a bitter jibe at a society in which money can obtain anything and human beings are likely to be commodities. But this event, which names the crime to be expiated, is only the first in a series of commercial exchanges. Henchard buys Susan back for the original price; he substitutes generosity to his family for the genuine kindliness he is incapable of feeling; about to remarry Susan, he tries to settle with Lucetta by sending her money; he grants Elizabeth Jane an annuity to secure his own independence. These acts are useless as expiation because they repeat the initial offence. They are motivated by a sense of duty morally inadequate because at bottom no more than a conditioned dedication to the business ethic, an instance of the kind of honesty with which, we are told, the market place abounds. Old debts must be paid, creditors paid off. Whether the recipient be Susan, Elizabeth, Lucetta, or the tradesmen involved in his financial collapse, Henchard will meet his obligations to the last penny.

Henchard's moral limitations, of course, are not unique. They are forced upon him by the context in which he lives, by the

Market, which defines the character of his society. Even the chorus of old crones and derelicts, who provide an ironic commentary on the action of the drama, find the value of a man to be what he's worth financially, although they evince a sentimental preference for unsuccess, witness the general decline in sympathy for Farfrae once he acquires wealth and power. Wealth and power inspire civilized respect, not natural love; the claimant to the throne is always more popular before he ascends it.

Money, then, in one or another of its forms, is what Casterbridge primarily seeks. Secondary values, the ramifications of the social ethic, are scarcely disguised commodities. They are business assets, like honour, popularity, abstinence, frugality, or emblems of social distinction, badges of wealth and power. Thus Lucetta's chances of keeping her looks are coldly assessed in the light of her matrimonial intentions; her clothes are important because they will decide the exchange value of her personality; her marriage to Henchard is calculated to restore her social reputation. Elizabeth Jane is even more afraid of impropriety than Lucetta. "We must be respectable," she tells her mother as excuse for putting up at a better inn than they can afford, respectability being, of course, the passport to security. Meanwhile, Henchard is vastly annoyed by Elizabeth's provincialisms and by hearing that she has waited on customers in The Three Mariners; when she is about to leave him, he discovers in her room signs of cultivation which cause him to regret her departure. His snobbery is based on an appreciation of her quality as token of conspicuous consumption.

Indeed, the widely shared habit of estimating quality by public standards informs the novel with one of its major ironies: the temporary but crucial blindness of those concerned to the exact social value, status or reputation, of the persons whom they prize. Henchard believes for a time that Elizabeth is his own daughter; Donald Farfrae is not aware when he marries her that Lucetta is damaged goods; informed of the fact, he reconciles himself to her death with business-like acumen and casts about for a more acceptable substitute; the town of Casterbridge is ignorant of the shameful resourcefulness with which its mayor has traded in the past. These confusions, ultimate illumination, and consequent shock in each case sufficiently demonstrate, to the audience rather than the actors, that the social measuring rod is not only perilously insecure but itself a moral offence.

On the stage which I have described, and described at length because it motivates the action, a ritual drama is performed. One star declines, another rises. The older corn merchant, having achieved every eminence that his office can bestow, having reached the ambitious summit of Fortune's Wheel, must fall, significantly because of speculation, to be replaced by a younger rival. To his rival he loses wealth, power, prestige; even social reputation is stripped from him when the "transaction of his early married life" is disclosed—a penalty analogous to the revelation in *Oedipus Rex* that the king has slain his father and married his mother. Meanwhile, the fortune which is lost remains constant; it does not diminish with its maker. It is transferred, taken from the father and bestowed upon the son by the civilized, nineteenth-century equivalent of Fate, the inexorable laws of the Market, whose competitive structure and cyclical movement, beyond the control of men, decree that what one gains another forfeits and that success in gambling is followed by failure. Ironically, Henchard himself unwittingly appoints his heir, designates whose name shall be inscribed on the granary in place of his own. He rescues Farfrae from poverty, persuades him to stay in Casterbridge, gives him

a start: indiscretions summarized by his habit of throwing his arms around the shoulders of the newcomer, by the symbolic laying on of his hands.

But all bankruptcies are not tragic. Financial reverses are commonplace in a good deal of contemporary literature which, however disheartening, makes no pretence of being tragedy. What distinguishes Hardy's novel is the precise moment in the evolution of capitalism which he has selected for his scene. At this moment, the man of wealth is not a stockholder but an entrepreneur, whose ingenuity and hard work are indispensable to his success. At once owner and manager, he is an individual, not a board of directors or a corporation operating, perhaps, by remote control. Even more important, the entrepreneur is still invested, at least in a town like Casterbridge, with a degree of social responsibility, and it is this investment, together with the means he has of achieving position and losing it, which selects him for the role of tragic hero. For the tragic hero is at once individual and servant of the community; his difficulty is occasioned by his duality. So by Hardy's novel an ironic opposition is asserted between responsibility and private interest which is capable of disguising acquisitiveness as duty. The office of corn factor perverts a sanctified social function: to provide food for the city. Henchard, a buyer and seller whose calling is announced in the Prologue, inevitably assumes the office and, having served his community as well as he can— as well, that is, as the intention of personal aggrandizement enables—becomes the scapegoat for its organization. His death does not cure society but it temporarily takes the curse off the Market. When new difficulties arise, another sacrifice will be demanded and another Farfrae will providentially arrive.

The old difficulty, with which the action proper of the novel starts, is the blight that has afflicted the corn and rendered it inedible. This blight, a curse on Thebes, reminds us that Henchard's career is at its climax. By selling the wheat he has failed his obligation to the community and deserves dethronement; his inability to relieve the curse argues even more vigorously his incompetence. Donald Farfrae happens along, restores the grain, and a new order begins to replace the old. The break between Henchard and Farfrae is not so much between personalities as between methods, the capacities of different generations to meet changing needs. For Henchard's muscle, Farfrae substitutes brain, for energy system, for antiquated drudgery the efficiency of the machine. Thus Henchard's downfall is more than personal; like the downfall of the archetypal tragic hero it signifies the passing of an era, of ways which have outlived their purpose. By the end of the novel Henchard is one with the patriarchal shepherd who appears briefly in the market place to survey an alien world that has no use for him.

Alienation is the penalty for Henchard's sin. Separateness from society, particularly from the family he might have had, is a logical extension of the irresponsible economic individualism which has been his ruling principle. Dispossessed of his wealth and power and having no sympathies to sustain him, he becomes the Lonely Man, the Outcast. But his exile is both punishment and the means by which he achieves self-understanding. His illumination increases with his wretchedness: from the first insight, that Donald had married money and nothing more; to the contempt for human competition which ends his rivalry with Farfrae; to the perception that one can love what is not legally one's own; to the recognition that independence is less satisfying than dependence, to possess less gratifying than to belong. Even at the end of his career

Henchard cannot stomach Elizabeth's marriage to Donald Farfrae, but though he is unable to change his character, he has at least discovered how to control it. His wisdom is proportional to his nakedness. As he is stripped of the commodities which formerly reminded him of his importance, he at last understands that unloved he is worth nothing and learns to accept his nothingness. His will is a final comment on the fetishism of things; it is a final judgment on the Market and on himself.

The novel, as a whole, concurs in Henchard's judgment on the social values which have largely controlled his behaviour. And construed simply as behaviour, his career is pathetic rather than pitiable. But as Henchard is not, in D. H. Lawrence's phrase, the "dark villain" of Hardy's earlier work, not constitutionally dedicated to evil, neither is he the hapless victim of his cultural circumstance, index to that circumstance though he be. What saves him both from villainy and from futility is the extent of his involvement in the unconditioned ethics of his situation, in his proximity to its centre, where innocence and guilt converge. So that all his actions and feelings are morally significant, and his entire transaction with crime and punishment, with nature and society, represents for the reader a coherent and therefore responsible moral experience. The form of this transaction asserts the idea of the novel; it conveys a particular view of cultural depravity and a general view of human destiny, neither of which is, without the other, complete. (pp. 169-79)

D. A. Dike, "A Modern Oedipus: 'The Mayor of Casterbridge'," in Essays in Criticism, Vol. II, No. 2, April, 1952, pp. 169-79.

JOHN PATERSON (essay date 1959)

[Paterson was a Scottish educator and critic. In the following excerpt, he contends that The Mayor of Casterbridge is perhaps unique among modern novels as a tragedy founded upon a morally ordered universe, reflecting the premodern worldview of such authors as Sophocles and Shakespeare.]

As a man of his time and place, Thomas Hardy was ill-equipped to meet the challenge of tragedy in its traditional form. Although the romantic and scientific humanisms to which his expatriation in London had exposed him did not exclude a tragic vision of human experience, they were incompetent, by their denial of moral and religious universals, to provide that framework of theme and form which could alone make peace with a tragic vision. Hence the maimed achievements of The Return of the Native and Jude the Obscure. In the absence of a justice, an ethical substance, which is beyond man's power to shape or control but to which, at the same time, he is necessarily responsible, the disasters in which these works culminate are deprived of a moral and hence fully tragic significance. Celebrating the human at the expense of the superhuman, they cannot justify the ways of God to man.

Hardy was not, however, exclusively or even primarily a man of his century. As the citizen of a provincial Dorset which had had no news of Swinburne and Darwin, he inherited a traditional moral wisdom not yet damaged by the romantic and scientific inspirations which were everywhere shaking the confidence of the modern imagination. In Far From the Madding Crowd and The Woodlanders, for example, he could magnify not the romantic agonies of those condemned, like the Eustacias and the Judes, to live in a world without justice or dignity but the modest pieties of the Oaks and the Winterbornes, their decent adoration of a Nature that was still a mystery and a

miracle, still the earnest of a moral consciousness in the universe. Their diabolical antagonists, the Sergeant Troys and Dr. Fitzpiers, invite in fact not the fatuous indulgence of the romantic imagination but the horror and disgust of the medieval imagination in the presence of Dr. Faust. Even in The Return of the Native, the "tragic" apotheosis in death of the rebellious Eustacia Vye is criticized retroactively by the comic apotheosis in marriage of Diggory Venn and Thomasin Yeobright who have, like the Oaks and the Winterbornes, come to terms with central headquarters. As the beneficiary of a pre-nineteenth-century culture whose primitive decencies neither Swinburne nor Darwin had entirely confounded, Hardy's imagination could still be possessed, evidently, by what Keats has nostalgically called "our deep eternal theme," by "the fierce dispute, / Betwixt damnation and impassioned clay" that authorizes the form and substance of traditional tragedy.

Hence the lonely and peculiar significance in the literature of modern times of The Mayor of Casterbridge. Temporarily freed from the disabling humanistic biases of his age, exploiting a level of the mind to which his romantic sympathies and naturalistic assumptions could not penetrate, Hardy here assumes what the literature of tragedy after Shakespeare has not found it easy or possible to assume: the existence of a moral order, an ethical substance, a standard of justice and rectitude, in terms of which man's experience can be rendered as the drama of his salvation as well as the drama of his damnation. Reviving a body of beliefs about man and fate, nature and society, that were once the ordinary possession of the Western imagination, he exploits a wisdom that makes possible the achievement of tragedy in the heroical sense of a Sophocles or a Shakespeare.

The traditional basis of The Mayor of Casterbridge as tragedy emerges at once in the plainly fabulous or hyperbolical quality of its first episode. Discouraged by his failure to get on in the world and impatient of ordinary domestic restraints, Michael Henchard, the journeyman haytrusser, arrives at the fair at Weydon-Priors, steeps himself in the alcoholic brews of the furmity-woman, and in a drunken moment sells his wife to a sailor for five guineas. Clearly calculated to startle the imagination, to appeal to its sense for the grand and the heroic in human experience, Henchard's act of violence bears the same relation to the novel as the betrayal of Cordelia and the murder of Laius to Lear and Oedipus. Arousing such forces of retribution as will not be satisfied with less than the total humiliation of the offender and the ultimate restoration of the order offended, it will come to represent, like its counterpart in Lear and Oedipus, the violation of a moral scheme more than human in its implications.

That such is indeed its significance is underlined by its dramatic isolation in the structure of the novel, by the fact that twenty years intervene between the shocking event that commands the attention of the first two chapters and the events of the chapters that follow. For the primary effect of this structural peculiarity is to dramatize the causal relation between Henchard's crime and punishment. Recording the remorseless private and public deterioriation of the protagonist, the novel enacts the indignation of the moral order whose serenity his act of impiety has violently affronted. Forsaken by Farfrae, blasted by the disclosure that Elizabeth-Jane is not his daughter, and deprived of the love and loyalty of Lucetta; humiliated by the revelations of the furmity-woman and ruined in a trade war with his Scottish antagonist; crushed by his public rebuke on the occasion of the Royal Visit, rejected by the "daughter" whose affection had consoled him in defeat, and reduced in the end to the starkest of deaths, Henchard will be forced, like Oedipus and Faust and Lear, to rediscover in suffering and sorrow the actuality of the moral power he had so recklessly flouted.

The actuality of this power is otherwise expressed in the inexorability with which the guilty past asserts, as in *Hamlet* and *Oedipus*, its claim to recognition and atonement. The series of fatal reappearances that challenges and undermines Henchard's illegitimate power—i.e., Lucetta's, the furmity-woman's, Newson's as well, of course, as Susan Henchard's (''Mrs. Henchard was so pale that the boys called her 'The Ghost'' ')—schematizes the determined revenge of a supernatural authority for which a wrong left uncorrected and unpunished is intolerable. This sinister theme is early adumbrated in the mayor's proud refusal to make restitution for the damaged wheat he has sold to the community. ''But what are you going to do to repay us for the past?'' an indignant townsman challenges him from the street. ''If anybody will tell me how to turn grown wheat into wholesome wheat,'' the arrogant man replies with an irony of which he is, in the pride of his office, tragically unconscious, ''I'll take it back with pleasure. But it can't be done.'' Henchard thus defines in allegorical terms the conditions of his crime and punishment, his answer pointing up not only the irrevocability of that other and profounder crime buried in his past but also the uncanny pertinacity with which it will return, as the agent of a wounded moral intelligence, to haunt and destroy his life.

The authenticity of a moral intelligence beyond man's power to control is verified in the heroic imagination of Henchard himself. For it is the measure of his grandeur, the measure of his dissociation from such mere victims of naturalistic or unconscious force as Tess and Jude and Eustacia, that he should acknowledge from the very beginning the extra-human and specifically moral agency of the opposition that has set itself against him. On the morning after the sale of his wife, for example, he seeks as it were to propitiate the offended powers by presenting himself in the local church and swearing to give up drinking for twenty years. He will come to feel, as disaster overwhelms him, ''that some power [is] working against him,'' that he has fully deserved the opposition of a ''sinister intelligence bent on punishing him.'' His recognition of a justice beyond his power to control will be solemnized, finally, not only in the great words with which he leaves Casterbridge but also in the heroic self-condemnation of his last will and testament.

The universality of Henchard's experience is guaranteed by its reenactment in the story of Lucetta La Sueur. For one thing, she has sought, in the wilful and impious fashion of the mayor himself, to dissociate herself from the past: ''my ancestors in Jersey,'' she says defensively, ''were as good as anybody in England. . . . I went back and lived there after my father's death. But I don't value such past matters . . .''. More to the point, however, in having lived in sin with Henchard in Jersey, she too has been guilty of a moral indiscretion in the past. Indeed, in rejecting her old lover and electing to marry Farfrae, she has refused, once again like her more heroic male counterpart, to recognize and make restitution for her crime. ''I won't be a slave to the past—,'' she cries pathetically, when the demoniacal Henchard seeks forcibly to legalize their old association, ''I'll love where I choose!'' At the very moment, however, when her love-letters have been burned and she thinks herself free from the consequences of her delinquency, she hears the sounds of the skimmington ride which will publish her shame and eventually bring about her death. Her melodramatic and middle-class reenactment of Henchard's authentic

moral drama bears witness, like Gloucester's prose reenactment of Lear's crime and punishment, to the reality of an order whose indignation, once provoked, can neither be appeased nor controlled.

Henchard's terrible retrogression obeys, certainly, a law so distinct and irrefutable in its logic as to suggest an origin more supernatural than natural. Reduced to the humble trade with which he began, discarding the shabby-genteel suit of cloth and the rusty silk hat which had been the emblems of his illegitimate power, taking again to the drink he had twenty years before repudiated, leaving Casterbridge exactly as he had entered it, revisiting Weydon-Priors, the scene of the original crime, and dying at last, broken in body and spirit, on the barren wastes of Egdon Heath, Henchard travels with every stage of his decline and fall the long road by which he had come, embraces with every step the past he had denied, and rediscovers, like Lear, in the conditions of his going out the conditions of his setting forth. Having, as Tess and Jude have not, exchanged his humanity for worldly power and prestige, he is systematically deprived of that for which he had exchanged his humanity. Guilty, in a sense that Tess and Jude are not, of pride offensive to the gods, his suffering and death acquire a value to which theirs cannot quite lay claim. The fate that presides over Henchard's destruction as the witness of a moral intention in the universe is hardly interchangeable, indeed, with the vulgar and even brutish fate that presides, either as crass casualty or as unwitting opposition, over the destruction of the Tesses and the Judes and the Eustacias.

In its mysterious remoteness and refinement, fate in *The Mayor of Casterbridge* has much in common with Hegel's sublime and indestructible ''ethical substance.'' The conflict upon which the novel is founded does not suggest, after all, the grotesquely unequal contest between good and evil in which a malevolent ''superhumanity'' triumphs, as in *Tess of the d'Urbervilles* and *Jude* and to a certain extent in *The Return of the Native,* over an innocent and helpless humanity. It suggests, rather, the more equal, the more ambiguous, conflict that occurs when, to the discomfiture of a supernatural wisdom within whose bounds all merely natural oppositions are absorbed and reconciled, one great good is asserted at the expense of another. In this context, the conditions of Henchard's heroic grandeur—his pride, his passion, his ambition—are exactly the conditions of his downfall and destruction. They invite the correction of that absolute wisdom for which the more modest humanity of Elizabeth-Jane and Donald Farfrae is equally sympathetic.

Thus while Henchard stands for the grandeur of the human passions, for the heroism of spirit that prefers the dangerous satisfactions of the superhuman to the mild comforts of the merely human, Farfrae and Elizabeth stand for the claims of reason and thought, for the spirit of moderation that is prepared to come to terms with merely human possibilities. Elizabeth-Jane's Cordelia is said to feel ''none of those ups and downs of spirit which beset so many people without cause; . . . never a gloom in [her] soul but she well knew how it came there . . .''. Her would-be father, on the other hand, his morale destroyed by his crime, is victimized by mysterious and rebellious depressions which he can neither understand nor control. With her ''field-mouse fear of the coulter of destiny,'' Elizabeth declines to adorn herself in the pomp and pride of fine clothing: ''I won't be too gay on any account. It would be tempting Providence to hurl mother and me down . . .''. With his leonine pride and contempt of Fortune, on the other hand, Henchard makes love to his own destruction, affecting in his first appearance as chief magistrate "an old-fashioned evening suit, an expanse of frilled shirt . . . ; jewelled studs, and a heavy gold chain."

Again, if Henchard suggests the passionate extremities of King Oedipus, Farfrae suggests the less spectacular appeal to reason and compromise for which Creon stands. "In my business, 'tis true that strength and bustle build up a firm," says the mayor, unconsciously allegorizing the terms of their opposition as well as the basis of his own failure: "But judgment and knowledge are what keep it established. Unluckily, I am bad at science, Farfrae; bad at figures—a rule o' thumb sort of man. You are just the reverse . . .". The conflict between the passion of the one and the reason of the other is thus dramatized as a conflict between the rugged individualist and the organization man, between primitive and modern ways of doing business. In his victory over Henchard's gallant but corrupt and self-defeating Mark Antony, Farfrae in fact recalls, as much in his narrowness as in his shrewdness, the not altogether attractive figure of Octavius Caesar. He brings to the firm an order and regularity of which the owner is rendered, by the very largeness of his nature, mentally incapable: "the old crude *vivâ voce* system of Henchard, in which everything depended upon his memory, and bargains were made by the tongue alone, was swept away. Letters and ledgers took the place of 'I'll do't,' and 'you shall hae't' . . .". Later, identifying himself with the new mechanization, Farfrae will be responsible for introducing a modern sowing machine while Henchard, identifying himself with custom and tradition, will remain true to "the venerable seed-lip [which] was still used for sowing as in the days of the Heptarchy." Indeed, for all the irregularity of his behavior, the mayor is moved by profound emotions to which, in his rudimentary piety, he cannot or will not be unfaithful. As the Fortinbras, as the Octavius Caesar, of the drama, on the other hand, Farfrae is ready, not long after Lucetta's death, to dishonor the emotion to which he once had thrilled. "There are men," Hardy remarks, and he must have had Henchard in mind, "whose hearts insist upon a dogged fidelity to some image or cause . . . long after their judgment has pronounced it no rarity . . . and without them the band of the worthy is incomplete. But Farfrae was not of those. . . . He could not but perceive that by the death of Lucetta he had exchanged a looming misery for a simple sorrow."

The novel does not commemorate, then, as *Tess* and *Jude* commemorate, the total degradation of the good and the true. Henchard's defeat and Farfrae's accession to power simply reassert, however painfully, the necessary balance between two great values with equal claims to recognition and fulfilment: the grandeur that would transcend the limits of the human condition and the moderation that is satisfied to live within these limits. The fate that controls the world of *The Mayor of Casterbridge* resembles, to this extent, not the brutal and insentient force that presides over *Tess* and *Jude* but the ideal justice and wisdom that Hegel found presiding over the tragic drama of Sophocles and Shakespeare.

In the end, of course, Henchard carries within him, in the perverse instinct for betraying his own best interests, the seeds of his own downfall and disaster. *The Mayor of Casterbridge* is not, however, any more than *Lear* and *Oedipus,* a study in the impulse to self-destruction. Presupposing a concept of man as traditional as its concept of fate, the novel defines the disharmonies of Henchard's mind and imagination within an ethical and religious rather than a psychiatric or scientific frame of reference.

Founding itself upon an ancient psychology, *The Mayor of Casterbridge* celebrates, first of all, the subordination of the passions that link man with nature to the reason that unites him with God. It is Henchard's tragedy that, like Lear and Othello, he reverses and destroys this order. For when he sells his wife to a sailor for five guineas in violation of the profoundest moral tact, it is at a moment when, under the spell of the furmity-woman, he has allowed the passions to distort and deform the reason. Indeed, the surrender to passion responsible for the original crime will, in spite of his heroic resolution to give up drinking for twenty years, repeat itself in those sudden angers and indignations that alienate Farfrae, Elizabeth, and Lucetta, among others, and eventually deprive him of the ordinary consolations of love and friendship. The precarious balance between reason and passion will be reestablished only at the very end when, thoroughly scourged and chastised, all passion spent, Henchard is displaced by the Farfraes and Elizabeths in whose persons the claims of reason are piously acknowledged.

The novel rests, however, not only on the hierarchic psychology that enjoins the subordination of passion to reason but also on the hierarchic cosmology that enjoins the subordination of the human to the superhuman. Henchard's tragedy is that he has, in repudiating his solidarity with the human community, subverted the order that has placed man in the middleground between God and nature. Hence his explicit identification with Dr. Faustus, the archetypal representative of human rebellion: Henchard could be described, Hardy writes, "as Faust has been described—as a vehement gloomy being who had quitted the ways of vulgar men without light to guide him on a better way." Indeed, in selling his wife to a sailor who will later return to claim his due, in joining with Farfrae to make his damaged wheat whole again (that is, to manipulate and defraud nature), in approaching the conjuror Fall for illegitimate insights into the future course of the weather, Henchard is discovered in the attitude and situation made legendary in the story of the diabolical doctor.

Hence the traditional pattern of his decline and fall. In contriving to be more than human, Henchard inevitably becomes a great deal less than human. Arrogating powers and prerogatives that rightly belong to the gods, he forfeits, like Faust and Lear and Othello before him, his own humanity. This retrogression is first of all apparent in his brutal loneliness, in his increasing alienation from the human community. It is also apparent, however, though more indirectly, in the elemental or natural imagery with which he is persistently associated. Troubled by the presence of Elizabeth-Jane, he moves "like a great tree in a wind." After the cruel discovery that she is not after all his daughter, he greets her in a manner described as "dry and thunderous." His habit, after his estrangement from Farfrae, is to look "stormfully past him" and in their grim trial of strength in the loft, they rock and writhe "like trees in a gale."

At the very last, of course, the mayor is restored to the human community from which he has wilfully separated himself. In marching Abel Whittle off to work without his breeches and exposing him to public humiliation, Henchard had committed once more, at the level of the comic and pathetic, the startling crime at Weydon-Priors. Once again he had dishonored, as Cain to the Abel of his servant and factotum, the sacred bond that unites man with even the lowliest of his kind. For when the antiheroic terms of Abel's creation are granted, his nature is ironically revealed as essentially continuous with the mayor's: he is, in all but the pomp and pride of office, Michael Henchard's own brother.... Hence the significance of the novel's final episodes in which Henchard dies abandoned by all but his simple and stubbornly-loyal workman. He has rediscovered in the figure of a hapless and dim-witted laborer, as Lear has rediscovered in a fool and a madman, that brotherhood with all men to which he had in the pride of his nature and his office been unfaithful. The novel invokes, in short, as *The Return of the Native* and *Jude the Obscure* with their humanistic orientation do not, the traditional notion that man has been confined not unjustly to a fixed place in the hierarchy of being and is inspired to go his wilful way only at the risk of the direst penalties.

As the particular terms of Henchard's deterioration may already have suggested, the novel's concept of nature is in many respects as traditional as its concept of man and fate. Certainly, there is no equivalent in *The Mayor of Casterbridge* for the grotesque image of an Egdon Heath that dwarfs and ultimately overwhelms a helpless humankind. Where nature does enter the novel, it enters as a force obedient and instrumental to a moral order whose rights and claims take priority over man's. Like Oedipus in murdering his father and like Lear in denying his daughter, Henchard affronts, in casting off wife and child, a nature that antedates both Wordsworth and Darwin.

The barbarous violence of his deed and the Babylonian character of the fair that is appropriately its setting are opposed, for example, to a piety in nature that is a reflex of a piety in the universe:

> The difference between the peacefulness of inferior nature and the wilful hostilities of mankind was very apparent at this place. In contrast with the harshness of the act just ended within the tent was the sight of several horses crossing their necks and rubbing each other lovingly as they waited in patience to be harnessed for the homeward journey. Outside the fair, in the valleys and woods, all was quiet. The sun had recently set, and the west heaven was hung with rosy cloud....

The specifically moral agency of this nature becomes most obvious, however, in the catastrophic weather that eventually insures the defeat and humiliation of the hero. For if the rains and tempests that control the world of *The Mayor of Casterbridge* do not perform in the violent and dramatic terms of the storm in *Lear*, they bear in the end the same significance. They reflect, as the symptom of a demoralization in nature, the demoralization of the order that Henchard's unnatural act has, much in the manner of Lear's, produced. Insofar, too, as they confound his designs at the same time that they cooperate with Farfrae's, they reveal the extent to which he has lost the power to "sympathize" with, to intuit, its mysteries. Finally and more especially, they enforce, as the agents of the superhuman, the powerful claims which Henchard's guilty humanity has flouted and abrogated. (pp. 151-61)

The traditional basis of the novel is nowhere more distinct than in the anachronistic theory of society upon which it is predicated. Isolated and dissociated from a nineteenth century whose unity has been undermined by science, industry, and democracy, Casterbridge suggests, with its agrarian economy, with its merchant aristocracy and its rude population of mechanics, artisans, and laborers, a primitive hierarchic society. Thus Henchard resembles less the modern mayor than the tribal chieftain and is in fact displaced by Farfrae not in a democratic vote but, figuratively if not literally, in a rude trial of strength. His

status and stature as a tragic hero are not affected, certainly, by his membership, at the novel's most superficial level, in the anti-heroic middle-class. He is not after all the mayor of Dorchester, the provincial town whose reality is continuous with London and Liverpool and Manchester, but the mayor of Casterbridge, the provincial capital whose historical associations are more Roman and Hebraic than English. Hence, although he is greater in will and energy than the Christopher Coneys and Solomon Longways, he is at the same time, in his taciturnity, in his fatalism, in his grotesque and often brutal humor, their true apotheosis, their "hero" in the epic sense. In his physical resemblance to the town of Casterbridge itself—they are both described in terms of squares and rectangles, for example—he becomes the very symbol of the place, his leadership acquiring to this extent a supernaturalistic rather than a merely naturalistic sanction.

Hence the virtually religious interdependence of the man and the city. Participating, like nature, in a universal moral organization, society is demoralized, as Henchard himself has been demoralized, by the outrage for which no atonement has been made. In receiving and rewarding a man whose ancient crime has gone unacknowledged and uncorrected, Hardy's city has invited, like the Thebes of Sophocles and the Denmark of Shakespeare, the disapprobation of the gods—a plague, a profound social and political disturbance—from which it will not be released until the guilty party has been publicly identified and punished. (pp. 162-63)

It is therefore one aspect of the city's ordeal that its safety and stability are threatened throughout by serious internal conflicts. As in *Hamlet* and *Lear*, the disturbance of the moral order expresses itself in the disturbance of the social order. The discontinuity between the moral order that Henchard has insulted and the social order that has received and rewarded him is made evident almost at once. Twenty years after the original crime, Susan enters the provincial capital expecting with good reason to find the culprit occupying the stocks: she finds him instead presiding arrogantly over a civic banquet as the wealthiest and most powerful man in the community. Hence, while the mayor and the members of the local oligarchy hold court in the King's Arms for all the world like depraved Roman emperors, a surly populace . . . gathers in the outer darkness of the street on the point of revolt. "As we plainer fellows bain't invited," one citizen remarks in unconscious criticism of the insolence of high office, "they leave the winder-shutters open that we may get jist a sense o't out here." (p. 167)

The corruption of those in power will eventually be exposed, of course, with the re-appearance and trial of the furmity-woman, the agent of the mayor's original moral subversion. Charged with committing an outrage on the church wall, charged in effect with an irreligious act not different from that for which Henchard, her judge, has gone unpunished, she publicizes the crime he has concealed for twenty years and exposes therewith the discrepancy between the social order of which he is the head and the moral order to which he has done violence. She not only represents, then, the past's determined and inexorable reassertion of its rights and bears witness, in her own moral delinquency, to the brutalization of the lower classes already discoverable in Christopher Coney and the maimed citizens of Mixen Lane. She also expresses their revulsion against the social and political order whose mandate to rule and administer justice has, by the fact of its own moral disability, been rendered fraudulent. "It proves," says she, delivering the moral of the occasion, "that he's no better than I, and has no right to sit there in judgment upon me.'' The moral inadequacy of Henchard's society is in fact underlined by Hardy's farcical treatment of the whole episode. For if, in his tragic embarrassment, the mayor recalls the figure of Duke Angelo, the arresting constable Stubberd recalls, and indeed fulfills the same function as, Shakespeare's clownish constable Elbow. Regarding the furmity-woman "with a suppressed gaze of victorious rectitude," Stubberd reflects, in his physical decrepitude, in his ignorance and absurd self-righteousness, the moral impotence of the society whose law he has been hired to enforce.

The disharmony and confusion to which Henchard's original act of impiety has exposed the city becomes climacteric, finally, in the nearly-savage violence of the skimmington ride. For the hidden imposthume that silently undermines the moral stability of the town has not, in spite of Henchard's public degradation, been fully removed. In refusing like the mayor to acknowledge the crime in her past, in marrying the man who has supplanted him as the town's chief merchant and magistrate, Lucetta has in effect perpetuated the ancient wrong. Furthermore, in publicly repudiating the sadly-deteriorated Henchard on the occasion of the Royal Visit, Farfrae as well as Lucetta becomes guilty of the same pride, of the same offense against human solidarity, of which the fallen mayor himself had been found guilty.

In this light, the skimmington ride expresses the demoralization and confusion of a social order that has continued wilfully to dissociate itself from the moral order. If, as Farfrae not altogether wrongly suspects, the organizers of the barbaric rite have been inspired by "the tempting prospect of putting to the blush people who stand at the head of affairs," it is because their claims to rulership have been fraudulent and dishonest. Indeed, the moral incompetence of the society over which Farfrae and Lucetta prevail is dramatized, as in the episode of the furmity-woman's trial, by the comedy of its cowardly constabulary. Described as shrivelled men—"yet more shrivelled than usual, having some not ungrounded fears that they might be roughly handled if seen"—Stubberd and his crew conceal in a water-pipe the staves that are the instruments of their office and take refuge up an alley until the skimmington ride is over.

At the very last, of course, the agonies of this divided and demoralized society are permitted to subside. With the total eclipse of Henchard and Lucetta and the marriage of Farfrae and Elizabeth-Jane, the social order is brought once again into harmony with the moral order. In marrying Lucetta with her pride and her guilt and her fine clothing, Farfrae had compromised his right to rule, had aroused, like Henchard in his day, the animosity of his citizen-subjects. However, in uniting himself with Elizabeth-Jane who has declined, unlike Lucetta, to antagonize the superintending powers, Farfrae restores himself to the good graces of the folk and brings to an end the civil division that had registered the resentment of an affronted moral order. Hence, in the novel's final passages, the restoration of the society whose authority Henchard and Lucetta had jeopardized, the reconciliation of the classes whose mutual hostilty had threatened its total collapse, can be celebrated in the mild dominion of an Elizabeth-Jane who perceives "no great personal difference between being respected in the nether parts of Casterbridge and glorified at the uppermost end of the social world."

In the context of this novel, then, the social order acquires a virtually religious sanction of which it is almost wholly deprived in the naturalistic contexts of *Tess* and *Jude*. Michael Henchard is not, like the protagonists of the later novels, cru-cified by a brutal and depraved society. Disabled, on the contrary by *his* crime and guilt, society emerges not as the victimizer but as the victim. Its corruption and demoralization register, as in *Oedipus* and *Hamlet,* the corruption and demoralization of its chief magistrate. They register the disapprobation of a universal order whose morality the defection of the hero has profoundly disturbed. Like fate and nature, society here operates within a traditional moral frame. The sociology of the novel is as archaic as its psychology and cosmology.

To argue that *The Mayor of Casterbridge* observes the traditional norms of tragedy is not of course to argue that it has no realistic basis whatsoever. It would hardly be a novel if it did not admit something of the life of its particular time and place. The presence of the conjuror Fall and the incident of the skimmington ride bear witness to the amateur anthropologist's authentic interest in the folkways of a dying culture. Indeed, Hardy was himself to acknowledge in his preface that the story was specifically inspired by three events in the real history of the Dorchester locality: the sale of a wife, the uncertain harvests which preceded the repeal of the Corn Laws, and the visit of a member of the royal house. To describe the dominating motive of the novel as therefore realistic, however, would be not only to underestimate, but also to leave largely unexplained, the great vitality that it ultimately generates. It would be to ignore the fact that its realistic data are in the end assimilated and controlled by the tragic form, and that it is this form and not the content, not its fidelity to the data of social history, that finally accounts for its perennial power. Wife-sale may well have been a virtual commonplace in the rural England of the nineteenth century, and such magicians as the conjuror Fall may still have frequented the countryside of Wessex. But their appearance in *The Mayor of Casterbridge* as the *matériel* of two of its most crucial episodes is adequately explained less by their reference to aspects of contemporary reality than by their reference to the novel's artistic necessities, by their adaptation as stations in the tragic martyrdom of Michael Henchard. Again, Hardy may well have been concerned, as a social historian, with the new mechanization, with the decay of the primitive agriculture that had been practised since the days of the Heptarchy. Quite clearly, however, this conflict between the old method and the new is exploited not for the sake of history but for the sake of the novel: it defines and develops the tragic conflict between Henchard and Farfrae, between the old god and the new. The novel is not damaged as tragedy, in other words, as *Tess* and *Jude* were to be damaged, by a preoccupation with social history or social issues. Cut off from contemporary experience as the later novels are not, *The Mayor of Casterbridge* repudiates prose fiction's characteristic willingness to admit, more undiscriminatingly than is possible for epic and tragedy, the unblessed life of time and history. This is so much the case that, as has already been pointed out, the atmosphere of the novel is more Roman and Hebraic than English: it evokes not so much the world of London, Liverpool, and Manchester as the world of Thebes, Padan-Aram, and ancient Rome.

To argue, finally, that *The Mayor of Casterbridge* satisfies the traditional norms of tragedy is not to argue that the celebrant of nineteenth-century romantic and scientific doctrines is altogether suppressed. If the novel assumes, in its concepts of man and fate, nature and society, a traditional frame of reference tolerant of tragedy, there are inevitably occasions when the Swinburnian and Darwinian Hardy reasserts himself with results that make for a reduction of the tragic temperature. After he has identified an order in nature as the delicate reflex of a moral order in the universe, he must pay his respects to the contemporary scientific doctrine that has taken nature out of its traditional frame: "in presence of this scene after the other, there was a natural instinct to abjure man as the blot on an otherwise kindly universe; till it was remembered that . . . mankind might some night be innocently sleeping when these quiet objects were raging aloud." And having decided that the ugly weathers of the novel expressed the reaction of a just and morally-intelligent fate, he must temporarily reassert his humanistic allegiances and openly commiserate with a cruelly-persecuted humanity: the impulse of the peasantry, he remarks, "was well-nigh to prostrate themselves in lamentation before untimely rains and tempests, which came as the Alastor of those households whose crime it was to be poor."

Not even the traditional symbolism of Mixen Lane as the cancer that undermines the sanity and health of the Casterbridgean city-state is proof against an author tempted momentarily to humanistic apologetics: "yet amid so much that was bad needy respectability also found a home. Under some of the roofs abode pure and virtuous souls whose presence there was due to the iron hand of necessity, and to that alone." Most glaringly of all, perhaps, the balance between the heroic passion of Henchard, on the one hand, and the modesty of Farfrae and Elizabeth, on the other, is at times upset by the author's insurgent romantic sympathies. Rebelling against the traditional frame he has himself set up, rebelling against the moral dispensation that Henchard himself has been great enough to accept as right and just, Hardy will bitterly revile the mediocrities who have supplanted his doomed and suffering protagonist. Elizabeth's "craving for correctness" he denounces as "almost vicious"; Farfrae he mocks as celebrating the "dear native country that he loved so well as never to have revisited it."

The outrage and indignation of the nineteenth-century humanist in the presence of a suffering mankind, common enough in *Tess* and *Jude* and indeed the primary condition of their creation, are not, however, the predominating motives of *The Mayor of Casterbridge*. These emotions may flare momentarily at the surface of the novel; but they do not penetrate to or issue from its vital center. They appear after all only at the superficial level of authorial commentary and are contradicted and ultimately overwhelmed by the novel's fundamental assumptions, by the traditional moral or religious values rendered at the crucial level of character and action, form and structure. Hence the novel's emergence as one of the truly remarkable anachronisms in the history of English literature. Rejecting the disabling doctrine of the nineteenth century and exploiting the enabling doctrine of a time still capable of vibrating to the vision of a just and ordered universe, *The Mayor of Casterbridge* approximates, as perhaps no novel before or since has approximated, the experience of tragedy in its olden, in its Sophoclean or Shakespearean, sense. (pp. 167-72)

> *John Paterson, "'The Mayor of Casterbridge' as Tragedy," in* Victorian Studies, *Vol. III, No. 2, December, 1959, pp. 151-72.*

HARVEY CURTIS WEBSTER (essay date 1960)

[*Webster, an American educator and critic, is the author of* On a Darkling Plain: The Life and Thought of Thomas Hardy *(1947, rev. ed. 1964) and of the introduction to a 1948 edition of* The Mayor of Casterbridge. *In the following excerpt, he disagrees with John Paterson's assessment of* The Mayor of Casterbridge *(see excerpt above), and specifically rejects Paterson's interpretation of what constitutes traditional tragedy.*]

In many ways, John Paterson's "*The Mayor of Casterbridge* As Tragedy" deserves strong praise. Apart from Robert Stallman's "Hardy's Hour Glass Novel," it is the only extended close study of a Hardy novel I can remember. (Has Hardy's usual unevenness kept him from detailed examination by those who spend many pages on the more formally "correct" novels of Conrad, James, and Faulkner?) Mr. Paterson's careful examination of the parallels between *Lear* and *The Mayor of Casterbridge* is masterly. . . . Mr. Paterson's is a very good essay that should make any reader reconsider his interpretation of *The Mayor of Casterbridge* and other Hardy novels. It stimulates and illuminates whether in the end one agrees or disagrees.

His main argument is that *The Mayor of Casterbridge* answers to the norms of traditional tragedy which, he believes, justifies the ways of God to man by dramatizing what Keats called "our deep eternal theme . . . the fierce dispute / Betwixt damnation and impassioned clay." Unusual though he is, Henchard, like Oedipus and Lear, deserves and knows he deserves his fate because he acts on "the violation of a moral scheme more than human in its implications." He will not accept the middle ground between gods and beasts assigned him by "the presidency of a rational power in the universe." He affronts nature: hence the storms that assist his failure. His corruption affects and represents the degradation of Dorchester society as Claudius affects and represents the degradation of Elsinore. The nemesis of Susan's return and of the appearance of the furmity woman at just the right time to complete his destruction are actions of the absolute moral order Henchard has offended. Mr. Paterson's conclusion is that "*The Mayor of Casterbridge* approximates, as perhaps no novel before or since has approximated, the experience of tragedy in its older, in its Sophoclean or Shakespearean sense."

Although Mr. Paterson never says so explicitly, his interpretation of *The Mayor of Casterbridge* and the general tenor of his remarks make it clear that he accepts the "traditional" view of tragedy as the most tenable one. This may be so and, apart from some mistakes in interpretation, his essay is as sound as it is complimentary. But must we agree with Hegel, whom Mr. Paterson quotes approvingly, that "ideal justice and wisdom" preside "over the tragic drama of Sophocles and Shakespeare"? I am not at all sure that "ideal justice" presides over the plays of Sophocles; there is of course reconciliation to the universe as it appears in its "goodness" and "badness" and there is purgation through the terror and pity the audience or reader feels. But is it an ideal justice that causes the admittedly impulsive Oedipus to kill his father and marry his mother when he had never seen either of them in mature life? And is the suffering of Oedipus at Colonus ideal justice? I am even more doubtful that ideal justice presides over Shakespeare's plays. Does Lear's foolishness in dividing his kingdom and rejecting Cordelia justify the "divine wisdom" that brings on his madness? Is Hamlet's death an example of the operation of "ideal justice," or Othello's? Less of an apologist for the ideal than Hegel might blame a little the intervention of accident in *Romeo and Juliet*, not to mention the social condition of a world they never made. Possibly Lady Macbeth deserves some blame for fanning Macbeth's ambition; or is she an agent of ideal justice and wisdom who helps him to his deserved destruction? It is further true that no one has proved convincingly that Hardy was either influenced by Hegel (or Aristotle or St. Thomas).

I do not know whether Mr. Paterson is a follower of the New Critics or not, but I am sure that his over-rigid formulation of the nature of tragedy can claim at least cousinship. His contention that *The Mayor of Casterbridge* gives "the expression of tragedy, in its older, in its Sophoclean or Shakespearean, sense" as no novel before or since (he does insert a faint "perhaps" here) is manifestly absurd. It is absurd partly because he dogmatically asserts a dubious view of Sophoclean and Shakespearean tragedy and because he excludes more than a few novels that could be forced into even his categorical abstraction. Is it not possible, for instance, that a reasonable case could be made out for *Brideshead Revisited, Middlemarch, Crime and Punishment* and *Anna Karenina* according to his criteria? But I must admit that a quite different conception of tragedy would have to be used to fit *Tess of the D'Urbervilles, Jude the Obscure, The Woodlanders,* and *The Mayor of Casterbridge.* I would not try any more than he would to fit *The Return of the Native,* if one includes its reluctantly added last part, into any scheme of tragedy, though there are tragic elements in the characters of both Eustacia and Clym throughout most of the novel.

Let us try some other formulations of the nature of tragedy, particularly as they might apply to *Jude the Obscure, Tess of the D'Urbervilles,* and *The Mayor of Casterbridge.* Hardy's own definition (which admittedly he did not always apply) seems worth consideration—"the WORTHY encompassed by the INEVITABLE." Too brief though this is, it is not difficult to see how this might be applied to both Greek and Elizabethan tragedy. To expand somewhat, from other ideas Hardy often expressed and sometimes implied by his practice, the worthy are those of high moral stature (unlike Sophocles' and Shakespeare's tragic heroes they can come from any class of society). "The Inevitable is the nature of the universal," according to Marcus Aurelius' phrase that Hardy quotes frequently and with approval. Until about 1895 he did not develop his conception of the Immanent Will that is unconscious but may become conscious through its infection by the consciousness of good men, nor did he give it definitive expression until *The Dynasts* in the early years of our century. Until he was forty-five, Hardy believed that the Inevitable was a combination of natural law as Darwin formulated it, the occurrence of coincidence and accident that Darwin did not try to explain and that he could not, and the inevitable presence of flaws in man's finite character (Jude's naïve idealism leading him to drink when idealism failed; Eustacia's almost movie-queen imagination; Tess's sexuality—that was controlled except when she was tired; Henchard's impulsiveness). Though these elements were never fitted together with absolute cohesion in any of the novels (particularly since Hardy inconsistently added to these the belief that man, conditioned by nature and in turn conditioning society, could alter society towards the better), and though Hardy never regarded himself as a systematic philosopher and was always somewhat the agnostic who framed "weak phantasies" out of the finally incomprehensible nature of reality, they form an adequate basis for tragedy if one does not assume with Mr. Paterson that tragedy *must* "justify the ways of God to man." For certainly Hardy (in *Tess of the D'Urbervilles, Jude The Obscure, The Mayor of Casterbridge,* to a lesser extent in *The Woodlanders* and *The Return of the Native*) was always involved deeply with the most basic questions about life, as one can see as early as "Hap" and as late as his last poems published in 1928. The major characters in all these novels are as deeply (though dissimilarly) involved as Hardy was himself. Hardy and these characters are equally aware of the original terror; they would like to feel their universe secure but cannot. For them the struggle for existence, the ill-timed occurrence of accident and coincidence, their half-recognized inner flaws are always mysterious and a reason neither for complete op-

timism nor for complete despair. Hardy sees himself and his characters as questioners, naked and alone in confronting the mysterious. They live with unsolved questions and unresolved doubts. Neither Hardy nor his best characters are confirmed anything. Much of the time they are like the Zen master who when asked the meaning of the universe replied, "Yes"; they transcend a condition they cannot comprehend. Only at moments are they desolate as Hardy has sometimes been presumed to be. The "inherent will to enjoy" persists despite what seems the "circumstantial will against enjoyment." Tess, about to be executed, says "I am almost glad—yes glad. This happiness could not have lasted. I have had enough." On his deathbed Jude (though he does quote Job's agonized cry as well), says, "As for Sue and me, when we were at our best, long ago— when our minds were clear, and our love of truth fearless— the time was not right for us! Our ideas were fifty years too soon." Henchard, dying, says, "But my punishment is not greater than I can bear." None of them lived ignobly nor regretted their lives. They accepted the universe that often seemed malign and sinister, always essentially mysterious, never totally bad (as, Gad, they'd better, and we too). Like Hardy they realized that "if way to the better there be, it exacts a full look at the worst." In isolation and bravely, they transcend the worst, accept the incomprehensible, do not go to death sorry that they lived or unwise enough to protest against the mysterious inevitable. They arouse pity and terror, not hopelessness. One would rather be any one of them than the so moderate Farfrae, or the quiescent Elizabeth Jane, or the Sue who falls back to dogma, or the too careful Angel Clair, just as one would rather be Oedipus than Theseus, Lear than Edgar, Othello than Todovico, Quentin Compson than Flem Snopes.

I hope I have made my main point. I do not argue that any of these novels is a perfect example of even a more inclusive conception of tragedy than Mr. Paterson's. There is a little too much of the oppressiveness of Egdon Heath which reduces man's significance to a minimum in all of Hardy's tragedies (but not more than there is in *Lear* or *Hamlet*). All of the novels are flawed in one way or another: Death is the expense of life as failure is the expense of greatness, as R. P. Blackmur says. *Tess of the D'Urbervilles* is sometimes sentimental and I doubt that Henry James would have ended with "the President of the Immortals had finished his sport with Tess," an interpolation which, like many others Hardy made, is an aesthetic flaw. (Yet somehow, since it was written into the novel and all of us have sometimes felt just as unreasonably bitter, I like even this with the unobjective part of me.) Father Time travesties the bitter view Hardy often felt and spoils (for a while) the tragic vision the novel as a whole expresses (as little Nells spoil Dickens' novels, a pile-up of sensational incidents the work of Wilkie Collins, and sentimental moralizing a lot of Thackeray's good fiction). *The Mayor of Casterbridge* is marred by too many unhappily converging accidents, by too many explicit comments about the struggle for existence, by an excessive dragging-in of archeological and architectural details that stem, I believe, from Hardy's early interest in these subjects and are only sometimes as functional as Mr. Paterson finds them.

I must close, anti-climactically, with some specific comments about Mr. Paterson's interpretation of *The Mayor of Casterbridge.*

It is incredible that in *The Mayor of Casterbridge* alone Hardy's subconscious suddenly jumped back into the traditional frame of reference he accepted as he grew up in Bockhampton and Dorchester. There is, of course, the inexplicable force of Accident in all his novels and he is always well aware of the belief in a supernatural order in many of the people upon whom his characters were based. It might even be said that all Hardy's characters wished as Hardy himself did to believe in a supernatural order: "Oh, doth a bird deprived of wings / Go earth bound wilfully?" (**"An Impercipient at a Cathedral Service,"** *Collected Poems*). But, considering the novels that preceded and followed *The Mayor of Casterbridge* and the comments he made in his journal, the sudden, temporary emergence of a "traditional" view of tragedy that then disappears entirely is more incredible than the most arranged of Hardy's own coincidences. *Two on a Tower* (1882) is imbued thoroughly with what Mr. Paterson regards as the malignant influences of Darwin and Swinburne. So is *The Woodlanders* (1887). Only in *The Well-Beloved* (1892) is there anything in Hardy's fiction that could be misinterpreted as Christian supernaturalism (at the expense of a disregard for Hardy's conception of the Immanent Will). In his journal for 1884 Hardy speculates that events and tendencies are "in the main the outcome of *passivity*—acted upon by unconscious propensity." In one of his frequent notes looking forward to *The Dynasts,* Hardy says in 1886 that "the human race should be shown as one great network or tissue which quivers in every part when one point is shaken, like a spider's web if touched." Whatever Henchard believes at times (and it is fortunate aesthetically that few of Hardy's characters feel their actions totally determined), there is in these beliefs a widespread fluctuation among a just justice, a sinister force, and a mere something. It is clear from Hardy's interpolations and his management of events that it is a combination of "natural selection" (referred to explicitly and often), inexplicable accident and coincidence (more malign in appearance than unjust, as characteristically Hardyean as those in the novels that preceded), the innate impulsiveness of Henchard's character, and the cold indifference and hypocrisy of a society archaic in form but not in substance, that account for the tragedy. The novel does not justify God's way to man; if anything, it tries to explain God's apparent injustice so that man can accept, without docility, the look at the worst that may be followed by the discovery of the better.

Other details of misinterpretation I pass over quickly. Auctorial commentary is not contradicted "at the crucial level of character and action, form and structure" any more than it is in the novels of Jane Austen or Thackeray. Though I too prefer a minimum of commentary in a novel, commentary that helps us to understand the novel's flow has been a common element in works from *Don Quixote* to the work of Forster and Snow. To judge all novels by the accepted, sophisticated conception of James and the *Southern Review* seems too much like what was done with the baby when the bath was thrown out. None of Hardy's characters—Troy and Fitzpiers included—are diabolical as Mr. Paterson claims. The good and the true are *never* totally degraded in any novel of Hardy's. Humanism cannot justify the ways of God to man—here Mr. Paterson is correct. Nothing can. No philosophy or theology can do more than *present* the ways of God or Force (or the Zen Nothing) to man, however much it tries to justify. The infinite cannot be justified to the finite, though it can be represented with reverent wonder that quarrels lovingly with the world as man understands it. As long as there is pain, death, injustice, and human limitation, facts and humanism, psychiatry, science, and writing that is more than apologetics or propaganda, there is tragedy that may be feelingly presented in a magnificent variety of ways. Any valid work of tragedy, whether it is Cervantes' *Don Quixote,* Shakespeare's *Othello,* *Jude the Obscure,* Goethe's *Faust,* or Sophocles' *Oedipus,* purges and terrifies, for there, even with the grace of God, go we. Tragedy also makes us understand the noble finiteness of man that can endure the worst, remedy the inevitable, and say 'yes' to what cannot be altered or more than partially comprehended.

If Mr. Paterson uses his obvious talents in a less constricting frame of reference than he has employed in "*The Mayor of Casterbridge* as Tragedy," he should be able to produce close critical examinations of other novels that will, like tragedy, help us to adjust, with muted joy and incomplete comprehension, to the nature of the universe every good work of art helps us to understand and accept, with that mixture of joy and resentment that is as peculiar to man as his admirable, limited intelligence. (pp. 90-3)

> *Harvey Curtis Webster, in a review of "The Mayor of Casterbridge," in* Victorian Studies, *Vol. IV, No. 1, September, 1960, pp. 90-3.*

FREDERICK R. KARL   (essay date 1964)

[*Karl is an American critic who has written extensively on English literature and literary figures of the eighteenth, nineteenth, and twentieth centuries. He is particularly known for his studies of the life and works of Joseph Conrad. In the following excerpt, Karl examines* The Mayor of Casterbridge, *finding that Hardy's "peculiar kind of realism" marked a turning point in the development of the English novel.*]

Unless a novelist can raise drabness to metaphysical torment or the ordinary to cosmic hilarity, he is doomed to mediocrity. In *The Mayor of Casterbridge,* as well as in *Jude the Obscure, Tess of the D'Urbervilles,* and *The Return of the Native,* Thomas Hardy was able to transform insignificant details into cosmic importance, so that trivialities expand into great moments. Even though Hardy's prose rarely sparkles, part of his success lies, curiously, in his use of language. Its directness and sincerity, its sense of unwavering truth, its refusal to compromise with the vision it conveys all make it suggest more than at first seems possible. Hardy constructed a world in which universal unhappiness and despair appear to be the natural consequence of having been born.

If the above description seems to fit Kafka more than Hardy, that is the result of the latter's peculiar kind of realism. As he noted in 1880: "Romanticism will exist in human nature as long as human nature itself exists. The point is (in imaginative literature) to adopt that form of romanticism which is the mood of the age." Hardy's romanticism was not that of Stevenson or early Conrad, no more than his realism was that of Zola or Gissing. Although Hardy's roots, like Meredith's and George Eliot's, were solidly within a nineteenth-century intellectual framework—a pre-Freudian world of Darwin, Spencer, and Huxley—nevertheless, his characters and plots obviously move in a sphere unknown to his contemporaries, an area of personal anxiety and neurosis that no other Victorian, excepting Dickens in some aspects, had attempted to define. Hardy's mixture of romantic realism is peculiarly close to that of Flaubert in France; while both eschewed the strict realism of the naturalist, each skirted a sentimental or romantic conception of character and plot. What they cultivated instead was a kind of symbolic realism in which the actual fact exists prosaically but can nevertheless be projected far beyond the immediate historical situation.

When Hardy wrote in 1886 that his "art is to intensify the expression of things . . . so that the heart and inner meaning is made vividly visible," he foreshadowed Conrad's famous definition of realism: "by the power of the written word to make you hear, to make you feel—it is, before all, to make you *see.*'' This kind of realism entails, among other things, a new type of protagonist and a new way of developing scenes: one finds, for example, characters and scenes that relate to the narrative on both a nonrealistic and realistic basis, in the same way that some of the seemingly nonfunctional passages work in Conrad's major novels and in Lawrence's *The Rainbow* and *Women in Love.* To define Hardy's realism, particularly that of *The Mayor of Casterbridge,* is to reveal a major turning point in the development of the English novel: the novel is no longer solely an important social document but has become as well a significant psychological history.

Hardy once remarked that ''Coleridge says, aim at *illusion* in audience or readers—*i.e.,* the mental state when dreaming, intermediate between complete *delusion* (which thc French mistakenly aim at) and,a clear perception of falsity.'' In this ''suspension of disbelief,'' Hardy found a way both of raising the implausible to a philosophic system and demonstrating that art is a ''disproportioning'' of reality. As aware as George Eliot that the realism of the naturalist is not art, Hardy used chance as a way of infusing ''imaginative realism'' into his narratives, for chance not only suggested something supernatural, but it also fitted the terms of his own beliefs.

In *The Mayor of Casterbridge,* as well as in his other major novels, chance becomes a universal symbol of Hardy's personal philosophy; what he calls chance is everything over which man has no control. Although man's will is not nullified by chance, neither can will itself overcome chance; the latter is, in its functioning, the will of the universe, what Hardy, in his long narrative poem, *The Dynasts,* later called the Immanent Will. This force operates in the world without conscious design; even though it is not a controlling force, in that it does not direct man, it frequently seems to evoke more malignity than benevolence. Hardy's view evidently derived directly or indirectly from Schopenhauer's definition of will as ethically evil, the force that causes and sustains pain. For Schopenhauer as well as Hardy, life is made to seem futile, a period full of mere glimpses of happiness in an expanse of pain. There is no escape except through nullification of the will, for unfulfilled wishes cause pain, while attainment of desire brings disgust.

Hardy claimed, notwithstanding, that chance is not a sinister intelligence, that it can work either for good or evil. With Michael Henchard, chance seems more apparently sinister because he lacks proportion and balance, is himself *sinister* in the original sense of the word. That Henchard—and also Jude, Clym Yeobright, Tess and Eustacia Vye—happens to be constituted *this* way is, however, of no consequence to the principle of chance. Each may have been completely different, Hardy suggests, but, except for Tess, each would still have become a victim, because each is obsessed by inexplicable forces that waste his energies. As D. H. Lawrence, with some disappointment, noted, Hardy ''used'' chance as a way of punishing his social deviates, while at the same time claiming that chance is an indifferent force.

Lawrence, however, was really arguing for his own brand of rebellion and aggressiveness. Hardy's point is different, perhaps more complex, and certainly more consistent. His emphasis on chance and the Immanent Will places his characters in curiously existential situations that ring true on several levels. One of the results of a chance-filled universe is the creation of anxiety-ridden individuals who, futilely or not, must each seek his own identity in a maze of possibilities. *Identity* is the key word in *The Mayor;* who is the father? who is the daughter? what is the allegiance of each? who can rely on what forces?

Closely connected to the theme of identity in the novel is the pervasive theme of deception. Even if one intends good will (or *bonne foi,* as Sartre called it), it can easily be dissipated in a universe in which deception is a condition of existence. Under such circumstances, the will is made indifferent or neutral, even nullified.

In *The Mayor* nearly all human relationships are based on precisely such deceptions. Henchard is not Elizabeth-Jane's father, yet leads her to believe he is. Elizabeth-Jane is not his daughter, but thinks she is. Susan, although she knows differently, allows Henchard to believe that Elizabeth-Jane is his daughter. Lucetta deceives Farfrae about her past, as she deceives Henchard about her marriage. Henchard has deceived the townspeople about *his* past, as much as later he deceives Lucetta about his former relationship to Susan. In such relationships, the character's true identity cannot be clear to the reader, is often unclear to himself. Only Farfrae (his name implies his distance from the fray) is far from this deception, but even he is deceived by Lucetta. Only the fact that he does not think or probe too deeply saves him.

The possibility that something new may indifferently turn up to unbalance a seemingly stable situation is close to the absurd universe that the existentialists posit. The prime tenet of such a universe is that one may count on little, often on nothing. Anything is possible, plausible, probable. All those given, accepted facts one usually takes for granted are removed, or else become hostile in unfamiliar contexts. Each situation requires a new posture, a new response.

Thus, a good deal of Henchard's seemingly placid acceptance of his lot—strikingly close in this respect to the attitude of Camus' Meursault—is the consequence of the absurdity of his situation. If the existential absurd is broadly analogous to the Freudian unconscious, then we can see that Henchard can never consciously find or fix his bearings. If he seems to acquiesce too easily to his worsening situation, we remember that he is reacting to something absurd that drags him under, as if it were a pull from his unconscious. In a way, the absurd is both within and without; it is found in the Immanent Will of the universe and in the recessive depths of the individual.

As we shall see, the duplication of characters and situations that occurs so frequently complements the deceptive actions of the main characters. Deception of course entails a dual situation—the ostensible one and the underlying one; similarly, duplication entails a multiple play of action. In *The Mayor* the character-duplications are evident: Henchard's ''two daughters,'' Elizabeth-Jane's ''two fathers,'' Susan's ''two husbands,'' Lucetta's ''two lovers,'' Farfrae's ''two wives,'' Henchard's double past and his double life. The duplication of scenes is also ever-present: Henchard meets Lucetta where he met Susan, in the vast amphitheatre; he leaves Casterbridge as a trusser, as poor as he entered it; he arrives in Weydon-Priors twice; he faces the furmity woman twice, and each time is destructive to his fortunes. The possibilities for duplication are seemingly endless, as though Hardy were working with musical motifs which must reappear at the introduction of each theme. However, it becomes clear that the doubling elements are less musical than philosophical: that Hardy has used duplication, as before deception, as a whole mode of being for modern man. People reappear, situations recur, ideas duplicate themselves as a way of forcing the power of circumstance upon man. If as Hardy claimed character is fate, then man must reassert himself, events must recur, situations must be repeated. Man is never free of his past; the contemporary Fury is the individual's unconscious.

Thus, Hardy's "philosophy of chance"—if carried to this extent—evokes several modern responses. While its form is still Victorian, its point cuts deeply into post-Freudian ideas, and it shares many points in common with modern existential beliefs. While certainly neither original nor consistent, it did allow Hardy to move from the realistic-romantic nineteenth-century mold into his unique expression of changing values. Like any valid psychological or existential insight, it allows the formulation of a universal truth. Many of Hardy's readers are put off by his chance-filled universe; but on the contrary, it appears that a reliance on chance is a reliance on all those factors which the conscious self cannot control. Certainly now, seventy-five years after the publication of *The Mayor,* it is impossible to doubt Hardy's premise: that unseen, inexplicable forces operate which counter or obviate what the will commands. If Hardy learned anything from the classic Greek dramatists, he learned this.

In *The Mayor of Casterbridge,* the unreality, even the absurdity, of a chance-filled world is at once indicated in the fable-like beginning, with its simple evocation of distance and timelessness. Hardy writes:

> One evening of late summer, before the nineteenth century had reached one-third of its span, a young

Woodcut by Agnes Miller Parker illustrating the opening scene of The Mayor of Casterbridge.

man and woman, the latter carrying a child, were approaching the large village of Weydon-Priors, in Upper Wessex, on foot. They were plainly but not ill clad, though the thick hoar of dust which had accumulated on their shoes and garments from an obviously long journey lent a disadvantageous shabbiness to their appearance just now.

The straightforward, matter-of-fact style conveys both the immediate setting and the potential doom awaiting the couple. They walk along the road together, yet alone, and their isolation here foreshadows their inability to connect personally, even though later they do remarry. The fact is, Henchard must always be alone and isolated ("his taciturnity was unbroken, and the woman [Susan] enjoyed no society whatever from his presence"). She and he walk to the fair-grounds unknown and unknowingly, only to be separated even further there by his perverse act of selling her and the child. Later, the still isolated Henchard enters Casterbridge, painfully builds up a business alone, tries unsuccessfully to win a friend in Farfrae, unsuccessfuly woos Lucetta, then remarries Susan, who is dutiful but unloving, tries unsuccessfully to win Elizabeth-Jane as his daughter, and gradually loses each in turn, leaving Casterbridge as alone, stripped, and alienated as when he entered.

Henchard's rashness of temperament and lack of moderation, leading to bursts of anti-social behavior while he is drunk, do not by themselves adequately explain his character. In his bull-like strength (Hardy emphasizes his physical strength in the fight with Farfrae), in his inability to love (he offers marriage, but never love), in his need to humiliate himself (among other things, his marriage with Susan lowers him in public opinion), in his antiheroic tendencies (he rises in stature as, paradoxically, he demeans himself)—in all of these Henchard is more an inexplicable force than a frail human. Like Conrad's Lord Jim, he seems himself to choose the terms of his victimizing, and yet he is unable to help himself—the kinds of forces that will destroy him are, Freud indicated, too deep in the unconscious to manifest themselves in easily recognizable form. Henchard's quest is to pursue a course of action that will satisfy both his destructive drives and the overt desires of his social life. He is, Hardy suggests, a man obsessed by a single passion and, therefore, a man doomed in a world that rewards flexibility. Chance will always victimize him.

Farfrae's balance and flexibility are suggested not only by his name but by his musical ability; he is truly in harmony with the world and can make it bow to his tune. It is not fortuitous that at his first appearance in the Three Mariners he wins over the guests, who judge him a good fellow, albeit a foreigner. His songs indicate that he is the correct mixture of romanticism and realism: when necessary he can turn each on and off. While Henchard as it were sulks in his tent, Farfrae sings and dances. In his flexibility Farfrae is in tune with the music of the spheres, while in his alienation Henchard must remain discordant and gruff. Perhaps part of our distaste for Farfrae (which Hardy perhaps would not share) is based on his graceful ease in attuning himself to the tones of the world, whereas Henchard in his bear-like massiveness stumbles and flounders at every turn.

By moving at the extremes of behavior which he himself cannot understand, Henchard recalls in part, among Hardy's earlier contemporaries, Dickens's Steerforth (*David Copperfield*) and Bradley Headstone (*Our Mutual Friend*) and foreshadows Conrad's Lord Jim, Gide's Lafcadio and Michel, Camus' Meursault, and several of Mann's artists, each of whom is obsessed by demons that they fail to recognize, although all perceive that there is something within they must control. When control, nevertheless, becomes impossible, they commit acts which directly or indirectly injure others and which also lay the groundwork for their own destruction. Only Dickens among other major ninteteenth-century English novelists was aware of the self-destructive demons nourished within an otherwise respectable and controlled individual, although he, like Hardy after him, was unable to account for them.

Hardy's other immediate predecessors and contemporaries, Thackeray, George Eliot, and Meredith, were so far committed to a "normal" world that they avoided all extremes of social behavior; but Hardy, like Dickens in his later novels, attempted to create a society in which the extremist, what Dostoyevsky considered the criminal or underground man and later French novelists the rebel, clashed with the social norm. Hardy differed from Dickens, however, by concerning himself *primarily* with what happened to the radical who is the potential criminal and rebel: Henchard, Jude, Clym, Eustacia, and all those who are destroyed by their intransigence and/or their obsession with a single mode of behavior. Moreover, since they are unable to help themselves, Hardy's world seems excessively cruel, even antagonistic to individual needs, a world in which chance becomes a malevolent rather than an indifferent force. Yet the savagery of Hardy's world—in which continued cruelty, pain, and suffering become the norm for his heroes and heroines—is merely a reflection of man's insignificance when he attempts to exert more force than he has or tries to function without self-understanding. Hardy's protagonist usually means well and is, like Henchard, basically decent. But as Albert Guerard has pointed out, his obsessions are clearly uncontrollable—like Gide's and Malraux's protagonists, as well as Conrad's Jim and Kurtz, he must defy the restrictions placed upon him, and in his defiance lies the stuff of his self-destruction.

Henchard's fixed, linear behavior further strengthens the fable or fairy-tale atmosphere that surrounds the narrative, with its seeming simplification of character development, and also becomes the substance of Hardy's "symbolic realism." The Fair scene itself, with its readers of Fate, its games of chance, its auctions of animals, its waxworks and peep shows and conning medical men, with its hag-like furmity woman, who, like a *Macbeth* witch, stirs her large pot, is a timeless symbol of man's irrational quest for pleasure in a grim world of expedience. Moreover, at a Fair, anything goes; normal behavior is no longer adhered to, and eccentricity can itself become the norm. In Freudian terms, the id can here triumph over (or force out) the censorship of the superego, and man's ego, his ultimate behavior, is deflected into cruel acts both to his loved ones and to himself. Thus, the relatively simple act of auctioning horses at the Fair becomes an unambiguous foreshadowing of Henchard's sale of Susan, and the swallow circling through the tent trying to escape is an obvious reference to Henchard's desire to escape a marriage that he claims has bound him in penury. The Fair, then, assumes its traditional significance: a place where people are liberated from personal cares and freed from their daily burdens. Like the quickly curving swallow, Henchard is to fly from the tent alone.

Escape itself becomes, ironically, a form of isolation that Henchard can never avoid; and the sordid business at the Fair becomes the terms both of his freedom and his thralldom. When he sells Susan, that act is the only one in which *he* throws off another human being; the rest of the novel finds him "being sold" and thrown off. Hardy remarks: "Henchard's wife was dissevered from him by death; his friend and helper Farfrae by estrangement; Elizabeth-Jane by ignorance." Moreover, Lu-

cetta leaves him for marriage with Farfrae; the sailor Newson returns to claim Elizabeth-Jane; the town itself casts him out as Mayor. Further, one part of Henchard is dissociated from the other, so that his personality is split, a split manifest on the surface as the sober part and the drunken part, but of course the division goes far deeper. Hardy evidently lacked the psychological equipment to analyze the double role that grips Henchard, although his artistic suggestion of the type is psychologically true. Conrad, in *Lord Jim*, likewise lacked the analytical knowledge, but he was able to create a "true" type: in Jim, the split occurs between his romantic ideals and his realistic situations, and his tragedy is his inability to reconcile the two. Henchard's tragedy, similarly, is his inability to reconcile drunkenness (romance) and sobriety (realism). The self-destructive Henchard cannot perceive that the latter preserves while the former destroys.

Henchard's isolation from himself is given nearly exact definition in Hardy's use of several overlapping scenes that both indicate his alienation and emphasize the element of fable. Man is split and isolated, first, by his juxtaposition to surroundings that dwarf his stature and diminish his spirit. In Chapter 19, for example, Henchard gazes at the cliffs outside Casterbridge and his eyes alight on a square mass of buildings cut into the sky. Hardy describes the bulky monument as a pedestal missing its statue, the missing element significantly being a corpse; for the buildings were once the county jail, their base forming the gallows where crowds would gather to watch executions. This passage occurs soon after Henchard has read Susan's letter telling him that Elizabeth-Jane is not his daughter, Henchard having recently tried to convince the girl that she is his. Then, after Henchard learns the facts, Newson's daughter comes to him and says that she does accept him as her father. We recognize that the missing corpse is the doomed Henchard, trapped between uncontrollable forces, one part trying to gain love and life, the other, unable to effect an attachment, caught by death. Like the Captain in Strindberg's *The Father* (1887)—another man also snared in the tightening coils of wife and daughter—Henchard has to discover exactly what he is and what is his: who is the father? who is the daughter? His family unsettled, the Captain dies in madness, while Henchard expires abandoned to his masochism.

This powerful scene in which the split Henchard foresees his own doom recurs in a different context when, after the cruel mummery, the despondent and suicidal outcast thinks of drowning in the river as a solution to his misery. The sight, however, of his straw effigy floating in the water—the same effigy that had horrified Lucetta and caused her fit—suggests his own death, acts out, as it were, a substitute death, and dissuades him. "Not a man somewhat resembling him, but one in all respects his counterpart, his actual double, was floating as if dead in Ten Hatches Hole." The supernatural aspect of the sight impresses Henchard, and, ironically, the effigy, which in another way has helped destroy him, here saves his life. "That performance of theirs killed her [Lucetta], but kept me alive."

"Supernatural" aspects of the fable further appear when man is enclosed in a historical setting that indicates his fate. The Roman amphitheatre at Casterbridge serves the purpose of a meeting-ground and at the same time frames the puny dimensions of puppet-like man against a mighty historical past. Henchard, who has been heroic amidst the townspeople, is now diminished by the immensity of the amphitheatre where he meets Susan; and their immediate problems, when viewed against the melancholy background, seem petty indeed.

This kind of scene recurs in various forms: it appears, as we saw, when Henchard gazes at the Franciscan priory with its gallows and missing corpse; it reappears with intended irony near the end of the novel in the form of the pre-historic fort, Mai-Dun, where Henchard hides, telescope in hand, to spy on Farfrae and Elizabeth-Jane. The fort is described as "of huge dimensions and many ramparts, within or upon whose enclosures a human being, as seen from the road, was but an insignificant speck." Here, Henchard, already in decline because of his personal losses, squanders even his physical dimensions, dwarfed as he is by the fort and made to seem still smaller by the meanness of his objective—to scan the Roman *Via* for the two lovers. Then the amphitheatre itself recurs as a meeting-place for Henchard and Lucetta, the successor to Susan; within the huge enclosure, her pathetic figure revives in his soul "the memory of another ill-used woman who had stood there . . . [so that] he was unmanned." As they meet, the sun rests on the hill "like a drop of blood on an eyelid," a half-closed eyelid which sees reality only absently, masked as the latter is by personal ambition and willful revenge. His strength drained, the once heroic Henchard finds his revengeful feeling for the woman turning to pity and disdain amidst the hugeness of their overwhelming enclosure.

Not only is man insignificant and absurdly pathetic in relation to natural surroundings, Hardy suggests, but also in his contacts with uncontrollable human forces. The reappearance of the furmity woman, that Fate who reveals the iniquity of Henchard's past, indicates how limited his career can be once he has offended the order of the universe. He bends to his burden, and like Oedipus, he expands spiritually as he declines physically. Further, his reliance on the weather-prophet, a person deep within superstition, exemplifies Henchard's growing insecurity and also puts him at the mercy of a human interpretation of the uncertain elements. That Henchard should rely on a fabulous prophet, who, mysteriously, seems to be expecting him, demonstrates his recurring fears now that Farfrae opposes him. The "hero" can no longer rely on his own devices and by taking counsel from a false prophet wills a destiny that crushes him. The furmity woman and the weather-prophet "destroy" Henchard on the fable level as much as Farfrae, Lucetta, Elizabeth-Jane, Susan, and the town itself nullify him on the realistic level. Split by the two forces, Henchard is indeed trapped.

Hardy had the poetic ability, as Lawrence did after him, to suggest the whole in every part, to bring into each scene a miniature of the entire work. This is particularly evident in *The Mayor of Casterbridge,* where the structure is tight, the plot limited to essentials, and the main characters few. One recognizes the novel's stylization in the anti-realism of implausible events, in the evident symbolic patterns, and in the poetic evocation of characters and events. Albert Guerard has commented that at the poetic and imaginative level Hardy is capable of tragedy, although when he thinks philosophically he seems commonplace and his limitations become obvious. His finest scenes, frequently, are those in which "pure thought" does not dominate, scenes which remain close to a fable tradition and can be suggested poetically rather than realistically.

Unlike George Eliot and Thackeray, whose obvious forte was realism, Hardy, like Conrad and Lawrence, was more at home when he could avoid a head-on realistic scene and, instead, evoke the conflict obliquely. He could, so to speak, be true to human feeling but not to human truth. Lacking the philosophical orderliness of George Eliot and Thackeray's uniformity of

viewpoint, as well as the sheer vivacity of Dickens and Meredith, Hardy retreated to the oddities of life which determine man's frail existence. Thus, as we suggested above, his reliance on cosmic irony and the chance occurrences of implausible events bolstered his way of working; for a dependence on chance enabled him to touch his subject, as it were, from the side and gave philosophical substance to his oblique attacks upon complacency, deviation, and immoderation. Chance, in effect, was his weapon to strike through surface reality to areas where the poetry of men offers resistance to the drab starkness of a malevolent universe.

We can see, then, that certain short but powerful scenes fulfill Hardy's genius, although they may well seem peripheral or fanciful to the unsympathetic reader. In Chapter 29, for example, Lucetta and Elizabeth-Jane encounter a rambling bull, whose uncertainty seems to be theirs as well as Henchard's. The bull proves to be dangerous, an old cranky one, and uncontrollable except by an experienced hand. It begins to pursue the two women, the air from its nostrils blowing fear over them, until Henchard runs up, seizes the stick attached to the nose-ring, and subdues the frustrated animal. How ironical the scene becomes! for Henchard is recognizably the bull, or at least suggestive of the bull first in its brazen fierceness and then in its flinching half-paralysis once a stronger force masters it. Henchard is himself literally imprisoned by a nose-ring of events, and the two women whom he saves are, ironically, the Furies who will not give him rest.

This kind of intense scene, otherwise ordinary, joins with several others of the same type to comment indirectly upon the main characters and to create an atmosphere of lost opportunities and muddled human relationships. Earlier, upon recognizing that Lucetta and Farfrae are lovers, Henchard is offered an apple by the nervous Lucetta, which he rejects just as she has rejected his proposal: both offers are based on deceit and both are to bring unhappiness. Then, late in the novel, the dead body of the goldfinch in Henchard's gift to the Farfraes is a sentimentalized but effective symbol of the isolated Henchard, his life snuffed-out, forgotten, and alone in the darkness. The selling-scene itself, which runs like a leitmotif through the novel—for it becomes the basis both of Henchard's potential salvation and his real destruction—contains the grotesqueness and expediency that are essential to a world that pays only lip service to the amenities of life.

According to Ruth Firor (in *Folkways in Thomas Hardy*, 1931), wife-selling was common in rural England in the nineteenth century. No doubt such practices were the consequence of the tremendous changes occurring in rural areas, for agricultural England was beginning to be caught in the squeeze between the growing industrial urban centers and the decaying farm economy, particularly in the years preceding the repeal of the Corn Laws. Nevertheless, Hardy treats the episode less as a commonplace than as a sacramental crime. Like the Mariner's murder of the Albatross in Coleridge's poem, or Cain's murder of Abel, Henchard's sale of Susan is a universal crime from which there is no deliverance. The Mariner must eternally confess his crime, and Henchard must as well admit his. Since this stain on his past can never be effaced, such being the nature of the crime, he must reveal to the court the truth of the furmity woman's accusation.

Wife-selling is a sacramental crime even in a pagan society because it nullifies the choice and will of another being and it destroys the stability of what must be everlasting, no matter how unstable: the family. While it is true that Susan nominally agrees to the sale, she nonetheless does so only because Henchard is temporarily insane from drink. Further, the crime is universal because it derives not from reason, but from passion, the great motivator of all great crimes. Thus, when passions rule, man has damned himself and become a creature of insanity. For twenty-one years Henchard practices control and enjoys success, but a universal crime cannot be wiped away by repentance; like Oedipus, another criminal acting out of passion, Henchard must pay (with his entire being) for a sacramental crime. Confession does not lead to absolution; it leads only to further pressures, which must themselves be relieved by the destruction of the whole person. From that can be reborn something: a new being, perhaps; in some sense, an awareness, a feeling of humility, or simply an acceptance of one's frailty.

If Henchard's crime is indeed "sacramental" then Henchard could be seen to be a "wounded" king, a cousin of Jessie Weston's Fisher King. Henchard's "wound" is of course his irrational act committed while drunk; the wound is psychological: an act, a memory, a past. As long as the wound is hidden beneath other deeds, the King functions brilliantly. But the poisoned wound is ever there, ready to suppurate and fester. Only by squeezing out the pus, by bringing it to the surface, can the system be cleansed.

Such a wounded King chooses what Dostoyevsky called "exalted suffering" over cheap happiness. In some inexplicable way, like a shaman he takes upon himself the salvation of his people; his suffering, in fact, becomes a focal point for all their ills. That some wrong he has once committed is the reason for their bad fortune (drought, plague, flood) does not diminish the fact that it is only through him, their scapegoat, that balance can be reachieved. In contemporary fiction, such a scapegoat is the underground man, the isolato, the hopelessly alienated enemy, possibly the "schlemihl." He suffers so that other people can enjoy life or be oblivious of its pain. There is for all but the "schlemihl" no such thing as cheap happiness; the only joy offered him is the sense of power he has achieved in rejecting life, the very power which will cause him exalted pain. He is above the mass, for he has a Nietzschean strength of will. He measures his will, often, by the amount of pain and torment he can bear. Pain in itself becomes a good, not an evil, in this formulation, for pain elicits further strength of will. In one place Nietzsche indicates that he hopes that life will become more evil and more full of suffering, for then man's will may be further tested. At precisely this point of tension, the ruler experiences exalted suffering. Can anything equal the exquisite exultation Oedipus feels at the moment he gouges out his eyes?

Similar grotesque suffering recurs in Henchard's fight with Farfrae; the declining Mayor realizes that he cannot destroy his rival, for at the moment of triumph he is struck by the sadness of his inhuman act in the past, and to think of killing Farfrae is to relive his former shame at the Fair.

This scene is itself duplicated by one shortly after. As Farfrae is defeated by Henchard at the height of his good fortune (as, conversely, the Scotsman had triumphed over the Mayor), so too Lucetta, at her peak of assurance, is trapped by the satirical mummery, which causes her death. Everyone closely associated with Henchard's past is tainted by his misfortune. Only Farfrae and Elizabeth-Jane can escape because they are outside Henchard's range and remain flexible: they can move *with* chance and defy the Fates, although Farfrae escapes death or serious injury only because Henchard is guilt-ridden. The trag-

edy of Lucetta, on the other hand, is the tragedy of any Hardy woman who seeks a clear path to happiness without the perceptive awareness of potential evil, and who tries to defy the precepts of a malevolent universe that demands obedience to its strict terms of behavior.

Henchard himself, confused by the pressures of the outside world, declines rapidly once he forgoes his twenty-one-year penance and returns to drink, his position in the town having been exploded by the furmity woman. He celebrates the breaking of his oath, appropriately, with the recitation of verses from the 109th Psalm, to the effect that a wicked man shall lose his family, his riches, even all semblance of dignity; and, his name despised, he will be swiftly destroyed. Hardy evidently conceived of Henchard as an enduring Job, an inarticulate sufferer of destiny's wager, but one without the possibility of salvation through faith. Henchard, like Job, is caught amidst forces he cannot understand, caught among forces, however, created by the terms of his own character rather than those strictly imposed upon him. Therefore, Henchard's tragedy is potentially greater than Job's (he is closer to the Greeks than he is to the Hebrews), for his only salvation would be to transcend himself, an impossibility for one who is condemned to be destroyed.

All of Henchard's acts reveal a fatalism, as if he must drive himself until he falls. Thus, his seeming impetuosity in ignoring all advice is more than mere rashness or ill temper. It is the chief constituent of an innate need to debase himself, to act out a role that will ultimately diminish him. Nowhere more than in the scene when the obsessed ex-Mayor kneels to welcome the Royal Personage passing through Casterbridge is his growing insignificance stressed. Fortified by drink and carrying a small Union Jack, Henchard, wearing a brilliant rosette over his weatherbeaten journeyman garments, tries to regain some of his former glory without disguising his present misery. Advancing to the Personage, Henchard waves the flag and attempts to shake his hand, until, seized by Farfrae, he is removed forcibly. From the large-sized individual who struggled against powers he could not understand, Henchard here dwindles into the court fool, whose pathetic figure, however, causes not comedy but vexation and annoyance. Reduced from his former self and diminished by the blows of chance, Henchard allows his former employee to sweep him aside as a foolish meddler.

Nevertheless, Hardy's Henchard, although dwarfed by his natural surroundings, isolated by his townsmen, and made absurd by his grotesque acts, is still of heroic stature, evidently a nineteenth-century counterpart of an Aeschylean or Euripidean protagonist. Hardy had early recognized that Aristotle's definition of classical tragedy needed to be transformed or amended to suit present-day realities and wrote his own definition shortly after completing *The Mayor of Casterbridge*: "Tragedy. It may be put there in brief: a tragedy exhibits a state of things in the life of an individual which unavoidably causes some natural aim or desire of his to end in catastrophe when carried out." Thus defined, Henchard, as well as Clym, Jude, and several others of low birth, is a tragic hero, frustrated and hindered by the very things he hopes to attain and blinded by the obsessive nature of his quest. Clearly, Henchard's flaw is, as we suggested, more than a rash temper; his whole character, Hardy is careful to indicate in his definition, is his fate.

His character, like Lear's, is of heroic proportions, although so molded that the vast energies are dissipated in foolish acts of pride and vanity. As an outcast, Henchard gains identification with a whole host of alienated figures, Ishmael, Oedipus, the Ancient Mariner, Lear himself, but, most of all, with the Cain of the Bible, whom Hardy saw as the obvious prototype of all outcasts. Once fallen from his eminence, Henchard, now no different from the "naked" man who had entered Caster-bridge nearly a quarter of a century before, leaves the town: "'I—Cain—go alone as I deserve—an outcast and a vagabond. But my punishment is *not* greater than I can bear.'" Henchard's ordeal—all part of the universe's unconscious design—is a peculiarly nineteenth-century one even though Hardy carefully drew attention to its Greek and Biblical counterparts. True, Henchard is caught within the workings of a destiny he cannot understand, but he has committed the unnatural act of ridding himself of a family burden, and this while frenzied (drunk). Further, while his free will can work successfully within a certain sphere—only by sheer energy and drive has he become a leader, for he is a man of small ability—it nevertheless is restricted to a line of action in which the whole person is not engaged. Still further, while the novel is subtitled "A Story of a Man of Character," indicating that the emphasis is to be on man and on character, the definitive acts in the novel clearly derive from an area outside Henchard's control. A split indi-vidual, an absurd universe, a misdirected will—all these ele-ments help to define a new type of nineteenth-century man.

Henchard's display of will in the face of adversity, his pride that amounts to arrogance, his exhibition of physical strength—all these qualities place him close to Nietzsche's Noble Man. The Noble Man is an aristocrat of the spirit, one who refuses the normal weaknesses of the human race. The Noble Man does not give in to what Nietzsche considered to be Christian weaknesses. He tries to bend all to his will, which is the sole thing he can count upon. Essentially, his will is a will to power, although his struggle for power was to take many different forms in late nineteenth- and twentieth-century literature. Im-plied in this struggle, whether misdirected or not, is a mon-strous ego, the ego of the rebel, the stranger, the alienated fool. Dostoyevsky's Underground Man is first an egoist before he becomes a saint.

If we compare Henchard with George Eliot's Adam Bede, we can distinguish sharply between two kinds of lower-class pro-tagonists and show further how Hardy was moving from the traditional matter of the novel. Adam is in the line of somewhat prosaic young men whose aims are restricted to what they can possibly attain. Imperfect in certain ways, these characters do not set goals that are outside their reach, and they display relative equanimity in their quests. Adam himself is by no means perfect, but his imperfections are of a kind that will provide only disappointment, not nullification. Moreover, the terms of his desires are themselves small and always bounded by the explicable. There is little in the world that Adam could not understand, Geroge Eliot leads us to believe, provided he was mature and intelligent enough to extend himself. What is true of Adam is also true of Dickens's protagonists, Thack-eray's middle-class gentlemen, Jane Austen's genteel pro-vincials, and Meredith's romantic heroes: the world holds few secrets from those who would banish ego and vanity in favor of common sense. Henchard's world is obviously quite dif-ferent. While a simple frettish woman disappoints Adam, a whole series of reappearing women seem to doom Henchard, and each time he fails it is almost always over a woman or related to one. Moreover, while imperfections of character are merely a sign of immaturity in Adam, they *constitute* the char-acter of Henchard. While Adam has to go through an emotional ordeal in order to purge himself of his temper and gain insight into real love, the ordeal of Henchard is not a matter of de-

velopment but of life and death, the ordeal of the tragic hero set back by phenomena outside his control.

In addition, while Adam has to understand only visible things, Henchard must master invisible forces and obviously he cannot succeed, for he himself engenders several of the forces which help destroy him. Furthermore, Adam is the lower-class "hero" who is *like* everyone else despite low birth, while Henchard is *unlike* anyone else—he is marked, like Cain, almost from the beginning, and marked he goes through the novel, a gro-tesque figure of wasted energies and misdirected will. Adam was not intended to be, and cannot be, a tragic hero, while Henchard could not be the center of a conventional love story or the protagonist in a dramatic narrative lacking tragedy.

George Eliot was interested in presenting the detailed grandeur of passions that Wordsworth considered "incorporated with the beautiful and permanent forms of nature." Hardy, also, was interested in the "permanent forms of nature," though not as something necessarily ennobling; rather, as a background for human tragedy and as a silent force supposedly indifferent both to man and to its own powers. Nature, like society, gives Henchard something from which to be isolated and helps define the terms of his alienation, while in George Eliot it brings about attachment and purification. This distinction is impor-tant, for Hardy turned the Victorian lower-class "hero" into an unreasonable, guilt-stricken, and alienated figure who is denied even the saving powers of nature.

The seeming simplicity of Henchard's actions should not ob-scure Hardy's not-so-simple conception of his character. The grotesqueness and obsessiveness of Henchard's position—in several ways he is not unlike a muscular version of Kafka's K.—become more meaningful when we see that his tragedy, like K.'s, is played out against a relatively calm and imper-turbable background. The townspeople themselves are under no pall of tragedy; even Farfrae is untouched by the deeper aspects of Henchard's position, as is Elizabeth-Jane, whose relative insubstantiality precludes her suffering too much. Su-san, likewise, is too simple and flexible to suffer little more than shame at her position, and her early removal from Hen-chard would seem more a source of happiness than misery. Perhaps Lucetta suffers for a short time on a scale comparable to that of Henchard, but she, like Elizabeth-Jane and Susan, is not solid enough to transform suffering into tragic feeling. Only Henchard is tragic, only Henchard really suffers, and this emphasis helps convey his monumental anguish. His profile dominates Casterbridge, and even in decline he has size and scope.

Although Henchard is diminished by juxtaposition with the amphitheatre, as well as with the Roman road and the Chapel on the Cliff, he nevertheless gains identity from their massive impressiveness at the same time he is dwarfed by their gran-deur. One is reminded here of that great scene in *Tess of the D'Urbervilles* in which Tess lies immolated on the stone slab of Stonehenge, the pretty dairy girl identified with a vast history of martyrs and victims. So, too, Henchard gains in massiveness and substance through identification with his surroundings. Like many other Hardy heroes, Henchard cannot be separated from the earth, which denotes both defeat and life. The spirit of place remains close to him: he works in the earth before coming to Casterbridge and dies close to the earth after leaving. He places his trust in the earth, and when it, like everything else, fails him, he willingly forsakes life.

The outline of *The Mayor of Casterbridge,* as befitting a tragedy, is quite simple, despite the several new incidents occurring in each chapter. Hardy himself was afraid that the demands of weekly publication, with the need to force an incident into each installment, would strain the credulity of the reader of the novel as a whole; but while the play of intercrossing incidents—especially those concerning the returned sailor Newson—does seem overworked at times, the main profile is clear. Perhaps the very simplicity of the novel caused Henry James to call the author, "the good little T—— H——," a remark that caused Hardy considerable discomfort.

The important elements, however, do stand out boldly, so boldly that Joseph Warren Beach thought the spareness was more suitable to a motion-picture scenario than to a novel. Yet fullness of development could not have been Hardy's intention, certainly not the fullness of *Tess of the D'Urbervilles* or *The Return of the Native,* both of which are longer novels with fewer single incidents. What Hardy evidently intended was a Greek tragedy appropriate for his own time. Certainly the formal elements of the novel (although these elements are not necessarily its virtues) attempt the simple line of Greek tragedy, with the apparent rise and fall of incident leading to the hero's recognition of his situation. Even the moral alienation of Henchard, which places him close to a twentieth-century "hero," finds its source in the isolation of Aeschylus' and Euripides' protagonists. Consider, also, the leitmotif of the furmity woman, together with the recurrence of themes of isolation, the reappearance of key people, the use of the weather prophet, the prevalence of classical architecture, the starkness of the landscape, the morbidity of Henchard's "sickness," the victimizing of the hero by women, the use of folk customs like the skimmity ride, the presence of the townspeople as a chorus, the aura of fatalism cast over the main character because of events lying outside his control, the inability of the main character to find happiness as long as there is a taint on his conscience—all these are throwbacks to the chief elements of Greek tragedy now reproduced and brought to bear upon the novel, elements, moreover, that have become the common staple of the novel after Hardy.

Henchard is an Oedipus who instead of marrying his mother after twenty years remarries Susan after a similar lapse of time; in another way, he is an Orestes whose revenge is against himself, not his mother, for having killed a part of his own being. Henchard can never be free from himself, just as he can never be free from society. Often, the conflict in a Hardy protagonist is between social convention, which restricts, and the individual need to be free, which can never be fulfilled in the terms the individual expects. This conflict can take several forms, although rarely does Hardy shape it along the simple line of duty versus passion. Frequently, he complicates the terms of the inner conflict by showing that duty itself can be and often is degrading, while passion can as frequently lead to fear and insecurity as it does to personal happiness. Doubtless, Hardy changed the terms of the traditional conflict (especially strong in the Victorian novel) because they would, under certain conditions, lead to a qualified happiness and "heroization," both of which he felt falsified a tragic sense of life.

As several critics have remarked, criticism of Hardy during his novel-writing days was directed more toward his pessimism than toward the sexuality of his themes. Perhaps Hardy's readers would have more readily accepted Lucetta's happiness (after sufficient penance) than the cruel death that she must suffer. D. H. Lawrence, for instance, was outraged that Hardy killed off his "living" characters and let the prosaic ones escape,

and Lawrence's opinion was not far from the general public's dismay at Hardy's lack of optimism. Hardy himself wrote in 1886: "These venerable philosophers seem to start wrong; they cannot get away from a prepossession that the world must somehow have been made to be a comfortable place for man." Hardy suggests his own prepossession in the last line of *The Mayor:* "that happiness was but the occasional episode in a general drama of pain."

A frequent criticism of Hardy is that as a counter to mid-Victorian optimism (or what passed for it) he would not allow anyone to be happy who could feel deeply or think broadly. There is some truth to this stricture, for Hardy had been strongly influenced by Darwin's work during his maturing years prior to his first published novel in 1871. The battle between man and nature, manifest in the mysterious and even malevolent power that determines the process of natural selection, becomes translated into a cosmic pessimism in which man is countered at every turn by antagonistic forces. Because man can never be sure of himself—like the Greek hero, he can be struck down at the peak of his success—Hardy's novels seem cruel. Henchard undergoes rebuffs that seem in excess of what his original crime demands, and his punishment appears more than what a basically decent man deserves. That Hardy will not give him the chance to recover after penance, a kind of resurrection traditional in the nineteenth-century novel, is evident in his relationship with Elizabeth-Jane. During his decline, Henchard has hopes of living closer to the girl: "In truth, a great change had come over him with regard to her, and he was developing the dream of a future lit by her filial presence, as though that way alone could happiness lie." This passage is measured against a later one in which the girl, now married, rebuffs his attempt at reconciliation: "'Oh how can I love, or do anything more for, a man who has served us like this [deceived her about her real father].'" Thus, one of Henchard's few real acts of demonstrable affection is rejected out of hand, and rejected, moreover, by a girl now secure with a husband and a father. The cruelty here is unbearable for the reason that Henchard has been discarded by one who is solidly part of society, while, previously, his rejections had at least been at the hands of people equally insecure. Now, Elizabeth-Jane, respectable, cared-for, loved, confident, and youthful, strikes at Henchard's last vestige of dignity: he indeed becomes the dead goldfinch forgotten in the dark cage.

The cruelty of the main lines of the novel does help prevent a potentially sentimental tale from becoming mawkish. Like Conrad, Lawrence, Joyce, and Virginia Woolf after him, Hardy was clearly reacting to Victorian sentimentality, although he did not evade it on several occasions when he was sure his audience desired tears. However, by imposing the starkness of Greek classical tragedy on a late 1820's rural English setting, and intermixing that with a Darwinian cosmos, Hardy tried to avoid an excess of direct feeling. Nevertheless, he failed to recognize that Greek tragedy is not necessarily bleak and pessimistic but merely the working out of man's conflicts with himself or with his state and gods. He did recognize, though, that to approximate such tragedy he would have to manipulate many things artificially in order to make his philosophy—one necessarily alien to the surrounding culture—work out consistently. The Greek tragedian could write with his entire culture behind him, while Hardy was generally isolated from the practices of his literary contemporaries and certainly from the beliefs of a dominant part of his audience. Therefore, we sense the strain, the need to impose consistency even at the expense of art.

The cruelty of Hardy's pursuit of Henchard is mitigated, if only partially, by the latter's stubborn resistance to forces that would soon have defeated a man of lesser stature. The mere array òf circumstances aligned against Henchard—in this sense comparable to Job's ordeal—makes his struggle seem epical. Henchard's opposition to the onslaughts of chance incidents, each of which might demolish him, exemplifies his power of defiant endurance. When he declares scornfully, "'But my punishment is *not* greater than I can bear,'" he seems, in his Promethean strength, to become as large as the forces which are attempting to nullify him. The fact that Henchard *is* tragic— that despite several excessive circumstances, Hardy is still able to convey a tragic sense—gives him a power beyond that of a mere mortal, who would appear pathetic, not Promethean. When Henchard has been defeated, one has witnessed the conflict of a powerful will with an implacable force, and his dying wishes give him the unearthly power of a maddened Lear, whose defiant cry of "Ere they shall make us weep, we'll see 'em starved first" should be the epitaph for Casterbridge's former Mayor. Significantly, Hardy wrote in his diary just two days after finishing *The Mayor* his own epitaph for Henchard: "The business of the poet and novelist is to show the sorriness underlying the grandest things, and the grandeur underlying the sorriest things."

Henchard, we should remember, is a decent man whose early sins are not those of a cruel or ill-intentioned character, but rather the mistakes of a man carried away by a frenzy he finds impossible to control. In his dealings in Casterbridge, he is particularly fair and honest. He willingly destroys himself by admitting the furmity woman's accusation in court, and his action in remarrying Susan is an attempt to do what is right even though no love is involved. Although Henchard is a primitive in his inarticulateness, he recognizes the need for a softer side at the same time he is unable to summon these feelings. He agrees, out of duty, to take care of Susan, Elizabeth-Jane, Farfrae, and Lucetta, while feeling intimately only about Farfrae, who returns mere decency for the Mayor's compulsive need for companionship. Henchard, however, so dominates all relationships that he forbids any opposition; lacking love, which itself forces flexibility, he loses all hold upon humanity, including at times his own. His inability to love is equated to his self-destructive tendencies, and it is difficult to distinguish where each begins or ends. Consequently, Henchard often seems harsher than his character warrants simply because he smashes certain moral bonds by acting from duty rather than love. Moreover, Hardy appears to nullify him exactly as he, in turn, nullifies others by refusing them the deeper feelings that he himself is unable to summon. The disparity between Henchard's abortive attempts to be decent and the ill results of his efforts is the extent to which Hardy's philosophy precluded uncontested happiness.

The quality of one's happiness is determined by his flexibility and aims; if he can, like Farfrae and Elizabeth-Jane, remain outside any dominating obsession and live more by common sense than force of will, he will not be destroyed or even seriously injured. Hardy indicates that if one is an idealist— that is, one who tries to impose his will upon an antagonistic or indifferent world—then his exertions create a Promethean conflict leading to his destruction; if, however, one is a realist and does not attempt to change himself or the world, his chances of destruction are minimized. This pattern is not of course always true for Hardy's characters—Tess is an evident exception—but it does define the major figures of *The Mayor.*

Nevertheless, even to suggest that the other characters in the novel have individual lives is to see how far Henchard overshadows them and how much of *The Mayor* is his novel alone. To a much greater extent than either George Eliot, Thackeray, or Meredith, or the later Dickens, Hardy used a single character to dominate his narratives. Even Becky Sharp fails to predominate in *Vanity Fair* to the degree that Henchard controls Hardy's novel, and we must return to *Wuthering Heights* to find a comparable figure, that of the domineering Heathcliff. We recognize that for Hardy the domination of the central character, even though he be an anti-hero, was another carry-over from Greek tragedy, the nature of whose protagonist determined the nature of the drama. If the novel is, as Hardy believed, an outgrowth of events from a particular character who shapes them (except those things which chance controls), then the novel must be directed in its details by this single force. Thus, the events that help nullify Henchard are those that develop from his own character: he makes the world that first envelops and then squeezes him to death. The subtitle, we note again, is "A Story of a Man of Character."

Hardy's use of the town, similar to George Eliot's presentation of *Middlemarch* as a comment upon the main characters, creates a chorus that is as malevolent in its gossip as it is a form of social commentary. Hardy took the Greek chorus as both a representation of public opinion and a force for warning the protagonist of excesses and remolded it into an interfering group of townspeople who directly influence the protagonist's fortunes. Accordingly, the town is both public opinion and participant in the drama: its opinion is more than mere warning, it can force its way. George Eliot and Hardy realized that the town's opinion in a democratic age would entail more than mere commentary; with class mobility less restricted, the individual's business was no longer his sole concern: the individual now belonged to everyone. In *Middlemarch*, town gossip cuts through Bulstrode's hypocrisy and ruins his reputation, while in *The Mayor* the skimmity ride destroys Lucetta's hopes for happiness. In each, the town becomes a force for reliving the past, whose unwelcome recurrence is the basis for gossip and hearsay.

Both George Eliot and Hardy show a sharp awareness of social structure, recognizing that the mighty (Bulstrode) and the outsider (Lucetta and Henchard) can each be destroyed by a demonstration of majority opinion, whether it be justified or not. Further, both use country customs, implicit in the chorus, as a way of trapping the urbanized characters, and by so doing remove the country from mere picturesqueness and take the romance from the pastoral. This is not to claim that George Eliot and Hardy forsake the picturesque quality of rural life— one need think only of the Poysons in *Adam Bede* or of the dairy workers in *Tess*—but it is to suggest that in their later work they discount the pictorial quality in favor of a more individualized comment. The farmer and his wife are no longer merely decorative; they now have sentiments that must be heeded and values that can upset those whom they oppose. Thus, the chorus of townspeople and farmers has come full turn; in a democratic age, it loses its aloofness and sense of cosmic justice. Now, it too is involved, and no one can escape its approval, condemnation, or interference in his personal life. The chorus, as Kafka's K. was to learn, can impose its will regardless of the individual's rights, more often than not sending the alienated protagonist into exile. Hardy's Henchard, then, is in some ways the English prototype of the twentieth-century's isolated hero, the dominating figure in a world suddenly inexplicable to human reason.

Hardy is important, therefore, not only intrinsically but also historically. If we compare him again with Jane Austen, Thackeray, Dickens, Meredith, and George Eliot, and then with the nearest pivotal English novelist after him, Joseph Conrad, we can see how he has changed the nineteenth-century novel, although change in itself is of course no criterion of quality. The century that began with Jane Austen's well-balanced heroines of strong mind, who literally "will" themselves into normal behavior, rushes toward its end with the willful self-destructiveness of Hardy's heroines and heroes, who "will" themselves not into normality but into an obsession with guilt and penance. From the suave, unquestioned "inner-direction" of Darcy and Mr. Knightley, who live within an intensely realistic world of everyday fact to the "inner-direction" of Henchard, whose compulsive life is played out in an absurd puppet show that passes for the real world, is a far cry.

Granted, obviously, that Hardy's major predecessors and contemporaries had each brought individual genius to the novel, it is nevertheless in "the good little T—— H——" that we find the first sustained attempt to examine new aspects of late Victorian reality and to probe into areas barely suggested before in English fiction. In Hardy, almost for the first time, we have an author who is counter to the central tendencies of his age, the enemy personified; (we can only marginally claim this for Dickens and Meredith). Hardy recognized that idealism is a component of egoism, and that the true idealistic hero is not one who conquers or triumphs as Christ did, but one who can destroy himself in muddle and noncomprehension. Hardy was primarily concerned with the stranger whose attempts to get inside society are self-destructive. Already, we recognize a world that is somewhat subversive and antisocial; Greek tragedy serves modern sensibilities, and its external determinism is now internalized and seen as of man's own making. The stranger is indeed Promethean in his quest for a particular kind of truth, but the mere fact that he is a stranger is sufficient to doom him. In his perception of the great grotesque depths lying beneath conventional morality, Hardy in *The Mayor of Casterbridge* and his other major novels wrote a parable for our times. The lesson is that life itself destroys even when man is basically good. On this note, an age of fiction turns into a living nightmare. (pp. 295-322)

> *Frederick R. Karl, "Thomas Hardy's 'Mayor' and the Changing Novel," in his* An Age of Fiction: The Nineteenth Century British Novel, *Farrar, Straus and Giroux, 1964, pp. 295-322.*

ROBERT C. SCHWEIK   (essay date 1966)

[*In the following excerpt, Schweik maintains that conflicting interpretations of* The Mayor of Casterbridge *are due to fundamental inconsistencies within the novel.*]

Perhaps the most compelling evidence of really fundamental inconsistencies in *The Mayor of Casterbridge* is to be found, not in those analyses intended to show that the novel is seriously flawed, but in the startlingly divergent interpretations proposed by critics who have attempted to discover some underlying consistency in Hardy's treatment of the relationship of Henchard's character to his fate. Two recent discussions of *The Mayor of Casterbridge* exemplify the almost polar extremes to which this divergence can tend: as John Paterson has interpreted the novel, Henchard is a man guilty of having violated a moral order in the world and thus brings upon himself a retribution for his crime [see excerpt dated 1959]; but, on the other hand,

as *The Mayor of Casterbridge* has been explicated by Frederick Karl, Henchard is an essentially good man who is destroyed by the chance forces of a morally indifferent world upon which he has obsessively attempted to impose his will [see excerpt dated 1964]. The fact is that *The Mayor of Casterbridge* is capable of supporting a variety of such conflicting assessments both of Henchard's character and of the world he inhabits, and further discussion of the novel must proceed, I think, by giving this fact more serious attention. Hardy strenuously insisted that both as novelist and as poet he dealt with "impressions" and made no attempt at complete consistency; what is worth considering is whether or not Hardy put his inconsistency to any use and what, if any, advantage he may have gained by doing so.

The sacrifice of simple consistency in fiction can yield some important compensations, particularly in the freedom it allows a novelist to manipulate detail and aspect as a means of controlling and shifting reader attitude as the work progresses. It is possible to make a rhetorical use of elements whose implications will not add up to a logically consistent whole. Clearly such a rhetoric can serve the imaginative purpose of the novel if it is arranged to generate an initial image of life which is then altered by subsequent changes in the handling of character and event, and when the progress of the whole is such as to move the reader from one way of looking at things to another less immediately acceptable view of them. A novelist may meet his readers by providing a view of life which is socially orthodox, familiar, and comforting, then more or less deliberately shift his ground and, in effect, undertake to persuade his audience to adjust or abandon that view in order to accommodate some other less familiar or less comforting one. In such cases, it is not in the sum of its particulars but in the organization of their presentation that the novel will have its unity, and this, I believe, is true of the organization of *The Mayor of Casterbridge*.

The largest elements in *The Mayor of Casterbridge* are four relatively self-contained and structurally similar "movements" of progressively diminishing lengths, roughly comprising chapters i-xxxi, xxxi-xl, xli-xliii, and xliv-xlv. Each provides a variation on a common pattern: an initial situation which seems to offer some hope for Henchard is followed by events which create doubt, fear and anxious anticipation for an outcome that comes, finally, as a catastrophe. Furthermore, in each of these succeeding movements there is a reduction in the scope of Henchard's expectations and a corresponding increase in the emphasis which Hardy puts both upon Henchard's anxiety for success and upon the acuteness of his subsequent feeling of failure. Much of our response to Hardy's account of Henchard's final withdrawal and lonely death depends, certainly, upon the cumulative impact of these successively foreshortened and intensified movements from hope to catastrophe; but the particular tragic response which *The Mayor of Casterbridge* seems calculated to evoke is also the product of other adjustments in detail and emphasis from movement to movement which have the effect of repeatedly shifting our perception of Henchard's character, of the kind of world he inhabits, and of the meaning of the catastrophes which he suffers.

The first and by far the longest of these movements (slightly more than half of the novel) falls into two almost equal parts. The opening fourteen chapters of *The Mayor of Casterbridge* establish a situation which seems to offer hope for Henchard's success. Following the brief prefatory account of Henchard's economic and moral nadir at Weydon Priors and his resolution to make a "start in a new direction," Hardy abruptly bridges an intervening eighteen years to reveal the outcome of Henchard's vow; and not only does Henchard reappear transformed into a figure of affluence and social standing, but events now seem to augur his further financial and social success: he gains the commercial support and personal companionship of Farfrae, effects a reconciliation with his lost wife and child, and seems about to find a solution to the awkward aftermath of his affair with Lucetta. Hardy implies, certainly, that Henchard has undergone no equivalent moral transformation; we learn that he is conscientiously abstemious, but is otherwise simply "matured in shape, stiffened in line, exaggerated in traits; disciplined, thought-marked—in a word, older," and what details contribute to our first impression of the new Henchard—his aloofness, his harsh laugh, the hint of moral callousness in his stiff reply to complaints about his bad wheat—tend to support, as Hardy remarks,

> conjectures of a temperament which would have no pity for weakness, but would be ready to yield ungrudging admiration to greatness and strength. Its producer's personal goodness, if he had any, would be of a very fitful cast—an occasional almost oppressive generosity rather than a mild and constant kindness.

Yet, an examination of the following nine chapters will reveal that it is precisely Henchard's fitful personal goodness that Hardy does emphasize. Henchard's consistent if "rough benignity," his gruff friendliness and frankness with Farfrae, his concern for Lucetta, his efforts to make amends to Susan and Elizabeth Jane, his determination to "castigate himself with the thorns which these restitutory acts brought in their train," and his humanizing acknowledgments of his own loneliness and need for companionship—these are the most prominent signs of Henchard's character in chapters vi-xiv; they tend to minimize his earlier harshness, so that by chapter xiv, at the high-water mark of Henchard's apparent success, Hardy's bland comment that he was as kind to Susan as "man, mayor, and churchwarden could possibly be" squares so well with the repeated evidences of Henchard's gruff personal goodness in action that it carries little more than a muted suggestion of stiffness and social pride.

The remaining chapters of the first movement (xv-xxxi) then reverse the course of Henchard's fortunes, and as Hardy gradually increases the sharpness of Henchard's disappointments and anxieties, he also arranges the action so that Henchard's frustrated wrath is vented with increasing vehemence and with more obvious moral culpability on persons who appear to deserve it less and who suffer from it more intensely. In short, the "temperament which would have no pity for weakness" gradually re-emerges, and by the conclusion of the first movement it is again the dominant feature of Henchard's character. The first sign of this progressive deterioration in Henchard—his grotesque attempt to punish Abel Whittle—is almost immediately countered by a revelation of Henchard's previous charities to Whittle's mother and by the frankness he displays in his reconciliation with Farfrae. But as the action continues Hardy develops situations which manifest more and more clearly the vehemence and injustice of Henchard's conduct. A first petty annoyance at his loss of popularity turns gradually into the more clearly misplaced and unjustly envious anger which prompts Henchard to dismiss Farfrae and to regard him as an "enemy." It is in this context that Hardy supplies an often quoted authorial comment which broadly implies a connection between Henchard's moral stature and his fortune: "character is fate," Hardy reminds his readers, and he pointedly observes

that Farfrae prospers like Jacob in Padan-Aram as he blamelessly pursues his "praiseworthy course," while the gloomy and Faust-like Henchard has "quitted the ways of vulgar men without light to guide him on a better way."

The chapters which follow seem designed to illustrate this point, for as Henchard's harshness and pitilessness become more apparent, his fortunes decline. What begins in Henchard's impulsive desire for a "tussle . . . at fair buying and selling" develops into his more desperately planned and culpably savage effort to destroy Farfrae's career, "grind him into the ground," and "starve him out." Henchard's turning on Farfrae is followed by his more cruelly felt coldness to the unsuspecting Elizabeh Jane, who is the innocent victim of Henchard's anger over the ironic turn of events by which he has discovered the secret of her parentage. And, finally, in his last exasperated effort to best Farfrae, Henchard takes the still more obviously vicious course of wringing an unwilling promise of marriage from Lucetta by mercilessly threatening to reveal their former relations. At this point in the action, Hardy reintroduces the furmity woman, whose public exposure of Henchard's past wrong to his wife not only helps to bring abut Henchard's fall but also serves to reinforce momentarily the sinister aspect of his character which the previous chapters have made increasingly evident.

Thus, throughout the long first movement of *The Mayor of Casterbridge* Hardy uses both action and authorial comment to shift our impression of Henchard's moral stature in a curve which parallels his economic rise and fall. Nature and chance are repeatedly made to serve what seems to be a larger moral order in the world; Henchard himself comes to feel that some intelligent power is "bent on punishing him" and is "working against him"; and the course of Henchard's career might stand as testimony for the familiar and comforting belief that the wise and good shall prosper and the wicked and rash shall fail. Certainly there is almost a fable-like congruity in the sequence by which Hardy gradually brings Henchard back to something like his moral nadir at Weydon Priors just before public disgrace and bankruptcy come like a retribution and precipitate him to social and economic ruin. Hence, in spite of its really complex and ambiguous cause and effect relationships, the first movement of *The Mayor of Casterbridge* does seem to exemplify the dictum that "character is fate"; it does so largely because Hardy maintains a general correspondence between the changes in Henchard's apparent moral stature and the changes in his fortunes.

Henchard's fall marks, however, the beginning of another tragic cycle in the novel—a second movement which again opens on a note of rising hope that is followed by a reversal and a falling action which terminates in catastrophe. Hardy clearly intends to leave no doubt about Henchard's fate after the furmity woman has revealed his past: "On that day—almost at that minute—he passed the ridge of prosperity and honour, and began to descend rapidly on the other side." But having predicted the imminent collapse of Henchard's fortunes, Hardy once more shifts the aspect in which he presents Henchard's character and career; and out of his account of Henchard's failure he contrives to establish a situation which seems to offer renewed hope. Thus he makes the court incident an occasion for a comment which puts Henchard's career in a more favorable light:

> The amends he had made in after life were lost sight of in the dramatic glare of the original act. Had the incident been well-known of old and always, it might by this time have grown to be lightly regarded as the

rather tall wild oat, but well-nigh the single one, of a young man with whom the steady and mature (if somewhat headstrong) burgher of today had scarcely a point in common.

Thereafter, Hardy stresses Henchard's generosity and integrity. We learn that it was the failure of a debtor whom Henchard had "trusted generously" which brought about the final collapse of his fortunes, and the bankrupty proceedings themselves serve to dramatize Henchard's scrupulous integrity as well as the finer instinct for justice which prompts him to sell his watch in order to repay a needy cottager. In short, Henchard now begins to appear in a character which seems worthy of the general approval of his creditors and the renewed sympathies of his townsmen, who, we are told, come to regret his fall when they have perceived how "admirably" he had used his energy. These signs of a hopeful change in Henchard's public reputation are followed in the next chapter by indications of a corresponding change in his private attitudes. Hardy suggests, first, the possibility of Henchard's reconciliation with Farfrae by a scene in which the kindness of Farfrae prompts Henchard to admit, "I—sometimes think I've wronged 'ee!" and to depart, after shaking hands, "as if unwilling to betray himself further." This is followed by Henchard's reconciliation with Elizabeth Jane, who tends him through a brief illness; and the result, Hardy remarks, is a distinct alteration in Henchard's outlook:

> The effect, either of her ministrations or of her mere presence, was a rapid recovery . . . and now things seemed to wear a new colour in his eyes. He no longer thought of emigration, and thought more of Elizabeth. The having nothing to do made him more dreary than any other circumstance; and one day, with better views of Farfrae than he had held for some time, and a sense that honest work was not a thing to be ashamed of, he stoically went down to Farfrae's yard and asked to be taken on as a journeyman hay-trusser. He was engaged at once.

Through the space of two chapters, then, Hardy repeatedly presents Henchard in ways which not only emphasize his maturity, integrity, and good sense but also suggest the possibility that he may now successfully accommodate himself to his new situation.

But in the following chapters there is an abrupt reversal, a second descending action, and what at first appears to be a second corresponding degeneration of Henchard's character. In rapid succession we are told that Henchard has undergone a "moral change" and has returned to his "old view" of Farfrae as the "triumphant rival who rode rough-shod over him"; that Henchard's drinking has brought on a new "era of recklessness"; and that "his sinister qualities, formerly latent" have been "quickened into life by his buffetings." Certainly, the series of progressively heightened crises which follow depend upon and repeatedly dramatize Henchard's sinister potential for hatred and violence. But they do so with an important difference: previously Henchard's antagonisms have been checked by external forces; now Hardy emphasizes the internal compulsions toward decency and fairness which at critical moments in the action decisively frustrate Henchard's destructive intent. Thus the crisis which Henchard precipitates by reading Lucetta's letters to Farfrae comes to an unexpected conclusion:

> The truth was that, as may be divined, he had quite intended to effect a grand catastrophe at the end of this drama by reading out the name: he had come to the house with no other thought. But sitting here in

cold blood he could not do it. Such a wrecking of hearts appalled even him.

Twice more Henchard brings matters to the brink of violence, and in each case the crisis is resolved when he is prompted by some inner compulsion to desist. In his determination to defy Farfrae and personally greet the Royal Visitor, Henchard presses the issue to a point just short of violence, only to be moved by an "unaccountable impulse" to respect Farfrae's command and give way. This incident precipitates Henchard's attack on Farfrae in the hayloft; and once again, at the moment when Farfrae's life is in his hands, Henchard is so touched by Farfrae's reproachful accusation that he feels compelled to relent. Instead, he flings himself down on some sacks "in the abandonment of remorse" and takes "his full measure of shame and self reproach." What seems central to Hardy's characterization of Henchard throughout these crises then, is that incapacity for callous destructiveness which repeatedly frustrates his reckless antagonism. Then, as the action continues through the events which culminate in the death of Lucetta, it is the frustration of Henchard's attempt to redeem himself which brings about his personal catastrophe. For Henchard is "possessed by an overpowering wish . . . to attempt the well-nigh impossible task of winning pardon for his late mad attack"; he vainly attempts to save Lucetta's life, and finding himself unable to persuade Farfrae to return to his wife, he is brought, finally, to the point of despair:

> The gig and its driver lessened against the sky in Henchard's eyes; his exertions for Farfrae's good had been in vain. Over this repentant sinner, at least, there was to be no joy in heaven. He cursed himself like a less scrupulous Job, as a vehement man will do when he loses self-respect, the last prop under mental poverty.

When we attend closely to what Hardy has been doing with Henchard's character in chapters xxxiii-xl, it is apparent, then, that although he exploits situations which depend for their effects upon our awareness of Henchard's potential for reckless cruelty, he in fact uses those situations to gradually strip Henchard of the features which earlier in the novel gave rise to "conjectures of a temperament which would have no pity on weakness." But more is involved here than a change of the aspect in which Henchard's character appears; there is really a marked change in tragic mode as well—a shift from that fable-like correspondence of fate and character which earlier in the novel seemed to dramatize a connection between Henchard's moral offense and a just retribution which followed upon it. Now something less than an ideal justice seems to govern the grim irony of events, unknown to Henchard, through which his decent attempt to return Lucetta's letters is turned to her destruction by the viciousness of Jopp and his degenerate companions from Mixen Lane; and what Hardy repeatedly dramatizes is Henchard's frustrated incapacity to find either the will to destroy or the means to win pardon. It is, finally, the failure of his well-intentioned acts which brings about Henchard's second catastrophe—that loss of self-respect which verges on despair—and in his second fall he appears no longer as a Faust figure but rather, in Hardy's new image, as a "less scrupulous Job" and a self-tormented "repentant sinner" who curses himself for the failure of his own redemptive efforts.

The death of Lucetta marks another major turning point in the novel and the opening of a third cycle from hope to catastrophe for Henchard. Shorn of other interests, he now begins to feel his life centering on his stepdaughter and dreams of a "future lit by her filial presence." By one desperate and unthinking lie he turns away Newson and manages for a while to persevere in the hope that he can fulfill his dream. But just as the furmity woman returned to ruin Henchard by her exposure of his past, so Newson now returns to expose Henchard's lie and dash his hope. But the parallel serves mainly to emphasize a difference, for Henchard appears in a greatly altered character, and Hardy's account of his loss of Elizabeth Jane and his withdrawal from Casterbridge as a self-banished outcast is clearly intended to evoke quite another kind of tragic effect. Hardy now presents Henchard in a character so soberly chastened as to seem "de-naturalized." He is reduced to suicidal despair at the thought of losing Elizabeth Jane and to anxiously calculating what he says and does in an effort to avoid her displeasure—so much so, Hardy remarks, that "the sympathy of the girl seemed necessary to his very existence; and on her account pride itself wore the garments of humility." Hence, while he looks forward with dread to living with a "fangless lion" in the back rooms of his stepdaughter's house, Henchard comes to acknowledge that "for the girl's sake he might put up with anything; even from Farfrae; even snubbings and masterful tongue scourgings. The privilege of being in the house she occupied would almost outweigh the personal humiliation."

But it is not only Henchard's pathetic subjection to Elizabeth Jane which Hardy stresses; he now directs attention to Henchard's conscious moral struggles (as opposed to those "unaccountable" impulses which previously checked his drunken recklessness), and he makes increasingly clear that Henchard now thinks and acts with heightened conscientiousness. Thus, when Henchard is again prompted by his perverse instinct to oppose Farfrae, Hardy pointedly reminds his readers that in the past "such instinctive opposition would have taken shape in action" but that "he was not now the Henchard of former days." Instead, Hardy portrays Henchard's struggle against his instinct: Henchard vows not to interfere with Farfrae's courtship of Elizabeth Jane even though he is convinced that by their marriage he will be "doomed to be bereft of her," and when the impulse returns, he rejects it as a temptation, wondering, "Why should I still be subject to these visitations of the devil, when I try so hard to keep him away?" At the same time, Henchard now suffers through moments of self-doubt and agonized casuistry in which, after the lie to Newson, his "jealous soul speciously argued to excuse the separation of father and child." The problem, Hardy suggests, continues to trouble him:

> To satisfy his conscience somewhat, Henchard repeated to himself that the lie which had retained for him the coveted treasure had not been deliberately told to that end, but had come from him as the last defiant word of an irony which took no thought of consequences. Furthermore, he pleaded within himself that no Newson could love her as he loved her, nor would tend her to his life's extremity as he was prepared to do cheerfully.

And, finally, when Henchard leaves Casterbridge, Hardy makes clear that he goes as a self-condemned man, hoping that Elizabeth Jane will not forget him after she knows all his "sins" yet assenting both to the fact of his guilt and the appropriateness of his fate: "I—Cain—go alone as I deserve—an outcast and a vagabond. But my punishment is *not* greater than I can bear!"

In view of the crushed submissiveness, remorse, earnest casuistry and conscious moral effort which have come to figure so prominently in Henchard's character, this self-accusation and self-imposed exile is certainly designed to impress us as excessively harsh. But by having Henchard accept an excessive burden of guilt and determine to bear it, Hardy does enable him to achieve a kind of expiation; and although excessiveness is certainly a constant in Henchard, in his third catastrophe we are brought to see in him a kind of excess which makes claims upon our sympathy in a way that his earlier excesses of moral callousness, antagonism, drunkenness, and frustrated violence have not. In short, Henchard now appears to suffer disproportionately, and he has taken on qualities of character which serve to justify on the moral level the pity and sympathy for him which Hardy evokes in other ways by emphasizing his declining health, his morbid sensitivity, his fears of "friendless solitude," his character as an "old hand at bearing anguish in silence," and his lack of friends who will speak in his defense.

The final two chapters of *The Mayor of Casterbridge* form a short coda which, on a still lower level, again involves a movement from hope to catastrophe—from that slightest of hopes which prompts Henchard to consider that he need not be separated from Elizabeth Jane to the rebuke which leads to his second departure from Casterbridge and his lonely death. Despite its brevity, this fourth movement has the important function both of further shifting our perception of Henchard's character and situation and of establishing more explicitly the final meaning of his tragedy. Hardy describes Henchard's journey from Casterbridge to Weydon Priors as a kind of pilgrimage carried out "as an act of penance." There Henchard mentally relives his past and retraces the foiled course of his career; and from both Henchard's reflections and Hardy's authorial comment upon his situation there emerges a central point—that Henchard's present situation is a consequence of "Nature's jaunty readiness to support unorthodox social principles." For as Henchard grimly reflects on the "contrarious inconsistencies" of Nature which have nullified his recantation of ambition and foiled his attempts to replace ambition with love, Hardy comments on another of those contrarious inconsistencies—that Henchard, as a result of his suffering, has acquired "new lights," has become capable of "achieving higher things," and has found a "wisdom" to do them precisely when an almost malicious machination in things has caused him to lose his zest for doing. Henchard does make a final effort to return to Casterbridge and ask forgiveness of Elizabeth Jane, but now, in being condemned and rebuffed by her, it is he who is made to appear more sinned against than sinning. Even Farfrae, toward whom Hardy has been otherwise sympathetic or at least relatively neutral, is momentarily brought forward to contrast with Henchard's sincere repentance by being put in a hypocritical posture, "giving strong expression to a song of his dear native country, that he loved so well as never to have revisited it," and, most significantly, Elizabeth Jane comes to regret her own harshness and attempts too late to make amends.

It is in the last chapters of the novel, then, that Hardy emphasizes most strongly the disjunction between Henchard's moral stature and the circumstance which has blindly nullified his repentance, his recantation of ambition, and his new capacity for a higher kind of achievement; and in doing so Hardy seems intent on reversing the fable-like correspondence between character and fate which figures so conspicuously in the first half of the novel. If throughout the opening portion of *The Mayor of Casterbridge* both nature and the course of events seem joined in support of the reassuring belief that the good shall prosper and the wicked fail, the remainder of the novel seems designed to reveal with progressively greater clarity that the fable is false. At its conclusion we are told that Elizabeth Jane has learned the "secret . . . of making limited opportunities endurable" by "the cunning enlargement . . . of those minute forms of satisfaction that offer themselves to everybody not in positive pain.'' Henchard obviously has not learned that secret, and, by contrast, he remains characteristically excessive and tragically mistaken even in his last acts—in ''living on as one of his own worst accusers'' and in executing a will which bears testimony to his final acceptance of a terribly disproportionate burden of guilt. But at the same time, by having Henchard persist in these acts, Hardy continues to dramatize his acceptance of a moral responsibility which now tends to set him quite apart from—and above—the indifferent circumstance which has frustrated his effort and contributed to his defeat. It is appropriate, then, that *The Mayor of Casterbridge* should end with the reflections of Elizabeth Jane, who has found the cunning to make the most of limited opportunities, as she gravely ponders the mysterious ''persistence of the unforeseen'' in men's destinies and concludes that ''neither she nor any human being deserved less than was given'' while ''there were others receiving less who had deserved much more.'' Certainly that pointed distinction with which the novel closes—the distinction between what men deserve (which is a question of worth) and what men receive (which may be enlarged and made endurable by self-control, good sense, and cunning stratagems) is central to the final meaning which Hardy puts upon Henchard's tragedy; for although Hardy makes clear that Henchard fails ultimately because he lacks those qualities of character by which he might make the most of his opportunities, he clearly expects, at the same time, to have brought his readers to see that Henchard must finally be classed among those ''others receiving less who had deserved much more.''

There is, then, a marked contrast between that image of a morally ordered world projected by the long opening movement of *The Mayor of Casterbridge* and the more somber, disenchanted vision of man's predicament with which the novel closes; and what is suggested about the relationship of Henchard's character to his fate by the first part of the novel is clearly inconsistent with the implications of its conclusion. Yet, considered rhetorically, such an arrangement probably worked to Hardy's advantage, for it enabled him to avoid abruptly confronting many of his readers with a view of life which would have sharply conflicted with their own assumptions and attitudes. Instead, Hardy first met his audience on the more readily acceptable ground of the moral fable; only after he had worked out Henchard's rise and fall on this level did he undertake to bring his readers to face the much more grim image of the human condition with which the novel closes, and even then the change was effected gradually, almost imperceptibly, by those various adjustments in detail and emphasis from movement to movement which I have attempted to trace in the preceding pages.

But, however rhetorically advantageous such an arrangement might have been, it need not be assumed to have been the outcome of a deliberate and preconceived plan. I think it more likely, rather, that the progressive changes which I have noted in *The Mayor of Casterbridge* came about in the process of its composition and were the result of Hardy's effort to develop his subject and to work out its implications. There is nothing really surprising in the fact that Hardy began *The Mayor of Casterbridge* with an action which strongly implied a connection between Henchard's moral stature and his fate; for, although Hardy had intellectually rejected the traditional belief in an ethically ordered universe, that belief retained a strong and pervasive hold upon his mind at the level of imagination and feeling, and certainly it shaped some of his most deeply rooted and habitual attitudes toward life. But these attitudes

remained at variance with his intellectual commitments, and the gradual shift in aspect and emphasis which takes place throughout the second half of *The Mayor of Casterbridge* suggests that, as composition of the novel progressed, Hardy began to exhaust the line of development which stemmed from his more immediate imaginative grasp of his subject and that thereafter he tended to reflect more deliberately upon the implications of Henchard's fall and did so within the framework of his consciously considered views on man's place in a Darwinian world. Yet it is important to note that even then Hardy's treatment of Henchard's character implies his continued respect for an older, pre-scientific conception of man's dignity and worth as a moral agent, and the conclusion of the novel seems to be as much an affirmation of faith in the transcendent worth of the human person as it is an acknowledgment of man's precarious situation in a blind and uncertain universe. (pp. 249-62)

> *Robert C. Schweik, ''Character and Fate in Hardy's 'The Mayor of Casterbridge','' in* Nineteenth-Century Fiction, *Vol. 21, No. 3, December, 1966, pp. 249-62.*

IRVING HOWE (essay date 1966)

[*A longtime editor of the leftist magazine* Dissent *and a regular contributor to the* New Republic, *Howe is one of America's most highly respected literary critics and social historians. He has been a socialist since the 1930s, and his criticism is frequently informed by a liberal social viewpoint. Howe is widely praised for what F. R. Dulles has termed his ''knowledgeable understanding, critical acumen, and forthright candor.'' Howe has written: ''My work has fallen into two fields: social history and literary criticism. I have tried to strike a balance between the social and the literary: to fructify one with the other; yet not to confuse one with the other. Though I believe in the social approach to literature, it seems to me peculiarly open to misuse: it requires particular delicacy and care.'' In the following excerpt, Howe maintains that the ''complex of character traits'' evident in Henchard from the novel's opening make the inexorable downward course of his life and career inevitable.*]

To shake loose from one's wife; to discard that drooping rag of a woman, with her mute complaints and maddening passivity; to escape not by a slinking abandonment but through the public sale of her body to a stranger, as horses are sold at a fair; and thus to wrest, through sheer amoral willfulness, a second chance out of life—it is with this stroke, so insidiously attractive to male fantasy, that *The Mayor of Casterbridge* begins. In the entire history of European fiction there are few more brilliant openings.

When some of the reviewers complained that Michael Henchard's sale of his wife is incredible, Hardy hastened to defend himself with his customary appeal to history. Cases of wife-selling he noted, had been frequent in rural England and were still to be heard of during the mid-nineteenth century. Today this argument seems naive: we recognize that the historically possible or even the historically actual is not a sufficient basis for the imaginatively plausible. Still, Hardy's defense is not quite so irrelevant as recent criticism has made out, for in ways more complicated than Hardy could say, history does form a matrix of the literary imagination. Had he lived a few decades later than he did, Hardy might have argued that the opening scene of the novel, partly because it does rest on a firm historical foundation, embodies a mythic kind of truth. Speaking to the depths of common fantasy, it summons blocked desires and transforms us into secret sharers. No matter what judgments one may make of Henchard's conduct, it is hard, after the first chapter, simply to abandon him; for through his boldness we have been drawn into complicity with the forbidden.

The detached composure with which this first chapter is written Hardy would seldom equal again. Nothing is rushed, nothing overstated. There is almost no effort to fill out the characters of Henchard and Susan, since for the moment they matter as representative figures in outline, a farm laborer and his wife plodding along a country road in search of work. Nor is there any effort to set off a quick emotional vibration. What Henchard feels we barely know, and Susan, carrying her baby and trying—the phrase is subtly evocative—to keep "as close to his side as possible without actual contact," remains impassive in her distress. Hardy's intention here is not to penetrate the deeper feelings of his characters, but to set up a bare situation that will serve as the premise of their fate. This is a novel in which plot—the shaping of an action toward a disciplined implication—is to be central. And accordingly, the prose displays few signs of portentousness, strain or ornament. At least in this book, Hardy trusts the tale.

We encounter at the very outset Hardy's characteristic mixture of realism and grotesque, with the realism in the characterization and the grotesque in the event. The place is the familiar countryside of Wessex, and the figures are the familiar agents of its traditional life; but the action seems startling, extreme, and with an aura of the legendary. Details of conduct establish a context of verisimilitude: a farm laborer with the "measured" and "springless" walk of "the skilled countryman as distinct from the desultory shamble of the general laborer"; and then the two of them, husband and wife, sullen in their "atmosphere of stale familiarity." Each feels trapped, neither quite knows why. Through a few broad descriptive strokes, these barely articulate people are sketched in. Henchard and his wife are approaching the town of Weydon-Priors, in Upper Wessex, and it is a fair day. First the stress is placed upon the economics of trading and hiring, but then, a few paragraphs later, Hardy turns to the fair as a communal activity, with its slackening of moral standards and its echoes of old custom. "A haggish creature," the furmity woman sits in her tent and mixes her brew—she looks like one of the witches in *Macbeth* and is clearly meant to be more than realistic in reverberation. Henchard, grown "brilliantly quarrelsome" on drink, sells his wife for five pounds. That he does this through a travesty of an auction heightens the terribleness of his deed. For, with the spitefulness to which guilt can drive a man, he forces himself to prolong and brutally measure out what had begun as a whim.

The terms of the drama are now set: a violation of human dignity, by which an intimate relationship is made subject to the cash nexus. Yet it should be stressed that Henchard does this not out of greed but because he is supremely dissatisfied with the drabness of life and driven toward a gesture that will proclaim his defiance and disgust. What Henchard does now will later become a curse settling upon his life—Hardy might, with Hawthorne, have said, there will be blood to drink! The intended stroke of liberation proves to be a seal of enslavement; the seller, sold. And much of what follows in the novel consists of a series of variations upon Henchard's initial crime, with each variation crowding him further into aloneness. As a realistic portrait of social life, *The Mayor of Casterbridge* is by no means always credible or well drawn; but as a chain of consequences in which Henchard is trapped and from which he keeps struggling to break loose, it is severely appropriate. Here, as often in Hardy, verisimilitude is subordinated to internal pressures of theme and vision. To the ordinary program of literary realism Hardy cannot long be faithful.

At the same time, the sale of Henchard's wife constitutes a kind of fortunate fall. From this deed there follows whatever suffering and consciousness Henchard can reach—and it is one of Hardy's most remarkable achievements that, through incident and gesture, we are steadily made aware of how deeply Henchard suffers at being unable to declare in language the consciousness he has won. A major reason for Henchard's recurrent fits of temper is a rage over the inadequacy of his own tongue.

In the opening chapter, then, the dynamics of Henchard's psychology are set into motion. He is a man with energy in excess of his capacity for release. He is a blundering overreacher confined to a petty locale, so that he must try to impart some grandeur to a life of smallness even while dimly sensing the futility of his effort. He thrashes out at whatever comes within reach, sometimes with open hostility, sometimes with clumsy affection—but soon enough, with exhausted regret and self-contempt. He can neither contain his aggressions nor keep them going in cold blood. Everything he does comes from inner heat and ends with the clammy despair of contrition. He cannot draw a clear boundary between self and other, what is his and what is not. Having sold his wife, he is foolishly indignant that she keeps their child: "She'd no business to take the maid—'tis my maid." There is an element in human character which consists of primitive thrusting will and fiercely refuses social adjustment; it is particularly strong in Henchard.

Once he realizes what he has done, Henchard searches for months to find his wife and child, for he is now convinced that he must "put up with the shame as best he could. It was of his own making, and he ought to bear it." There is, as Hardy remarks, "something fetichistic in this man's beliefs." To give this observation its proper weight, a cannier novelist would have postponed it until later in the book, but even here, awkwardly placed, it has a strong impact. For Henchard is one of those unfortunate people whose burden it is that he responds with excessive force to both the demands of ego and the claims of moral commandment. He is "fetichistic" in that he lives by the persuasion that meaning does inhabit the universe, but a meaning that, somehow, maliciously eludes him. Bewildered, he must fall back upon curses, superstition and self-lacerating vows (he swears he will not touch liquor for twenty years).

Meanwhile, another motif is introduced in these early pages. Throughout Hardy's novels there keep appearing figures who need to confront life as if it were a dramatic performance being acted out on a cramped stage. Seldom conscious rebels yet refusing to accept their lot, they choose, at whatever cost, the roles of assertion and power. Is the world indifferent, dry and listless? Then they will impose themselves upon it. Is the universe drained of purpose and faith? All the more reason to impress upon one's time, with a kind of clenched prometheanism, the conquest of personality which a chosen act of drama can signify.

The impulse to create a drama of self-assertion is one of the main sources of "character" in Hardy's world, "character" here indicating energy and pride of personal being. (Not accidentally, there is at work in the novels a counter-principle to which Hardy is still more strongly attached: a wisdom of passivity that consists in accepting traditional roles and bearing inherited burdens.) In a world where the trees and the waters no longer speak of meaning or spirit, certain powerful figures can still slash their way to a marred identity. Their probable end is failure and pain, but struggle remains the substance of their experience. "My punishment," says Henchard at the end, "is *not* greater than I can bear."

It is this contrast between a setting of dusty indifference and figures both fierce and zestful in their performance that provides much of the drama in *The Mayor of Casterbridge*. The two are kept in a balance of tension, as if to satisfy Coleridge's description of the poet as one who achieves a "reconciliation of opposite or discordant qualities." Once the cast of the book is brought fully on stage, there follow a number of contests structured as a series of intensifying crises, and through these contests Henchard realizes himself to the full—that is, completes his own destruction.

Strong anticipations of this clash between listlessness and desire, the inert universe and driven men, appear in the first few chapters. The road upon which Henchard walks is "neither straight nor crooked, neither level nor hilly," just another nondescript and wearisome road such as men have climbed for centuries. The only sound breaking the silence is "the voice of a weak bird singing a trite old evening song that might have been heard on the hill at the same hour, with the self-same trills, quavers, and breves at any sunset of that season for centuries untold." And then comes Henchard's gesture of perverse self-definition—the humiliation of the human being closest to him—by means of which he seeks to release his grievance against the universe. Yet, no sooner does he leave the furmity woman's tent than things lapse back into their accustomed listlessness. The rural folk who have watched the sale of Susan now sink into a drunken stupor, and the only creatures witnessing Henchard's departure are a dog and a fly.

The irony here is both austere and wounding. Henchard's defiance of customary standards and the moral law has no importance to anyone but a handful of people; the world, barely noticing, continues with its customary drone. Henchard has strained past decorum and conscience to assert himself, but Hardy, watching, as it were, from a distant height, sees that in any larger scheme of things even the most extreme gesture is trivial and unavailing. Later—it is another superb touch— the furmity woman, who is to be Henchard's Nemesis, will barely be able to remember what happened in her tent. Fate itself seems absentminded.

The prologue is now complete. A period of twenty years is skipped over, years in which Henchard rises to mercantile prosperity and political prominence. This leap in time is strictly justifiable, once we have been persuaded by the opening chapters that, if Henchard can but hold his turbulence in check, he is a man vigorous and hard enough to succeed in the commerce of a country town. The way is thus open for the main action of the novel: Henchard's steady downward course in both personal life and social condition. And what sets this downward course into motion is precisely the complex of character traits that has been at work in his opening appearance. The spring of Henchard's decline is personal in nature—the return of his wife Susan and her daughter Elizabeth-Jane to Casterbridge, which makes impossible any further evasion of his youthful sin. The occasion for Henchard's decline is social in nature— a prolonged and doomed struggle with a new merchant, Donald Farfrae, who brings to Casterbridge methods of economy Henchard can neither understand nor compete with. And the plot of the novel, as it moves from Henchard's vulgar triumph as mayor to his lonely unregenerate death, is structured with the intent of making the consequences of Henchard's past seem organically related to the social struggle occupying the present.

As a maker of plots—I assume for a moment that this aspect of a novel can be conveniently isolated from the total act of composition—Hardy was never brilliantly successful. He came at a difficult moment in the history of English fiction: he could neither fully accept nor quite break away from the conventions of his Victorian predecessors. He felt obliged to use a variant of the overelaborate and synthetic plot that had become fixed in the Victorian novel, the kind of superstructure that, becoming an end in itself, could smother seriousness of thought and make impossible seriousness of characterization. And he kept using the Victorian plot not only because it satisfied the requirements of the serial form in which he first printed his fiction but also for a more important reason: he wanted plot to serve as a sign of philosophic intent and this seduced him into relying too heavily upon mechanical devices. Yet Hardy also came to look upon the Victorian plot as a rigid and repressive convention, from which in his final great novels he would slowly "liberate" himself. What he could not do, however, was either to employ a plot with the confidence of a Fielding that it would release his full vision, or work his way into a modern view of plot, according to which the action must be strictly adjusted to the psychological makeup of the characters. His novels are therefore likely to seem curiously uneven: the men and women he imagines are superbly vital, while the events he assigns to them are frequently beyond their bearing or our belief.

Hardy made excessive demands upon his plots. Just as certain writers of our day suppose that the color of a man's soul can be inferred from the way he holds a cigarette or bends the brim of his hat, so Hardy supposed that the motions of fate—which he declared to be ethically indifferent while often writing as if they were ethically malicious—could be revealed through the manipulation of plot. Whether operating as psychological claim or literary method, such assumptions are naive. They posit equations too neat for our sense of social reality or our sense of literary form.

Hardy hoped to endow the worn devices of Victorian plotting with nothing less than a metaphysical value: the plot of *The Mayor* is meant to serve as a kind of seismograph registering his vision of man's place in the universe. Where plot in Victorian fiction had often become little more than a means of providing a low order of suspense and complication, plot in Hardy's novels is supposed to signify, through its startling convolutions, a view of the human condition. But to succeed in such an aim, Hardy would have had to establish in his fiction an aura of the inevitable—and this was very difficult for a writer whose idea of fatality was itself pretty much of an improvisation. The aura of the inevitable was possible to classical tragedy, in which the gods were clearly apprehended and their desires, if not always their motives, were beyond question. It is also possible, I think, to modern fiction, in which the psychology of the characters controls the action. But it is virtually impossible for a novelist using the Victorian plot or something like it. Because Hardy remained enough of a Christian to believe that purpose courses through the universe but not enough of a Christian to believe that purpose is benevolent or the attribute of a particular Being, he had to make his plots convey the oppressiveness of fatality without positing an agency determining the course of fate. Why he should have boxed himself into this position is intellectually understandable but very hard to justify esthetically. The result was that he often seems to be coercing his plots, jostling them away from their own inner logic. And sometimes, in his passion to bend plot to purpose, he seems to be plotting against his own characters.

The plot of *The Mayor* suffers from most of Hardy's faults: coincidences which cannot be justified even in terms of his darkening view of life, transitions so awkwardly managed they cannot be excused by references to Hardy's kinship with the balladeers, improbabilities that threaten the suspension of disbelief he has himself induced. Yet the plot of *The Mayor* is probably the best that Hardy ever contrived, if only because its numerous flaws pertain to the things happening near and around Henchard but never seriously diminish his power at the center of the book. The thread of credence may be broken by certain turns of the action, such as the reappearance and withdrawal of the sailor who had bought Henchard's wife; such incidents are poorly managed, and it would be foolish to seek excuses, through vague invocations of Hardy's metaphysics, for what is mostly ineptitude and carelessness. But Henchard's own responses at such critical moments—his boiling self-incitements which start with a plunge into brutal aggression or oppressive affection and end with a dull and bewildered regret—are always credible. The accumulation of disasters with which he is afflicted must strike even the most indulgent reader as excessive; but the mixture of heroic force and sickening blindness with which he confronts these disasters is never in doubt. The plot may creak, but Henchard lives. And since he does emerge vivid and intact, it seems reasonable to conclude that the plot serves the rough but essential purpose of charting and enabling the curve of Henchard's fate. The plot fulfills the potential for dramatic gesture—or, if you prefer, self-destruction—which is Henchard's project in life. It does not do this smoothly, or without shocks of disbelief; it does not always persuade us that quite so overwhelming a concentration of troubles is really in the nature of things; but what it does succeed in doing is to persuade us that Henchard's personal struggle—the struggle of a splendid animal trying to escape a trap and thereby entangling itself all the more—is true. By the end of the story, there is nothing further for Henchard to do; he has exhausted himself as a man, he has exhausted himself as a character.

In its opening chapters *The Mayor of Casterbridge* reads like a fable, a story stripped to a line of essential happenings, but once Hardy leaps across two decades and shows Susan and Elizabeth-Jane returning to the town where Henchard is now a prosperous middle-aged merchant, the setting is thickened with social detail. Hardy portrays Casterbridge in its unsettled condition, which is somewhere between a small-scale market economy and the new impersonal commerce.

In these pages Hardy comes as close as he ever can to being a social novelist. It would be idle to look for the subtleties of observation we associate with a book like *Middlemarch,* that marvellous confrontation of social status and spiritual being. What Hardy does offer is an authoritative portrait of a country town as it begins to experience a social change it can neither control nor comprehend. He keeps observing the lag of consciousness behind events, both as a factor in historical development and a common fact of existence. Few people in Casterbridge try to grasp any meaning in their lives, few even suppose there is a need to. Most accept the lumpishness of daily routine. Henchard does not really care to understand what is happening to him; he merely wants, through will and magic, to coerce the direction of his personal fate and the turns of the impersonal market, which in his case are almost indistinguishable.

Slowly the isolation of Casterbridge is coming to an end; that mystery known as the market, beyond scrutiny or challenge, plays on every nerve; and soon machinery will transform and replace labor. Yet it is crucial to Hardy's theme that Casterbridge remains a town dependent on agriculture, "the complement of the rural life around, not its urban opposite."

Signs of class division are frequent, but not yet fixed into a rigid hierarchy. Hardy contrasts the mayor and his half-drunken merchant cronies at the banquet with the poor folk staring through the window; he quietly remarks upon the snobberies to which Susan and Elizabeth-Jane are subject when they come to town; and he soon brings into play the shabby "rustics" of Mixen Lane, who form a kind of *lumpen* mixture during the transition from country to town. Yet all of these people are bound together in a community of sorts—which is not to say that they live in harmonious bliss but that they do experience a sense of relationship with both one another and their common past. When Henchard's doting workman, Abel Whittle, cannot wake up early enough to begin a business journey, Henchard does not discharge him as an "enlightened" employer might. He does something better and worse. He rushes to Whittle's cottage, shakes him out of sleep and marches him through the town without his breeches—in order to teach him a lesson and get him on the job. It is an outrageous thing to do, but it is personal and direct.

Hardy is shrewd at juxtaposing old and new styles of economy:

> Here lived burgesses who daily walked the fallow; shepherds in an intra-mural squeeze. A street of farmers' homesteads—a street ruled by a mayor and corporation, yet echoing with the thump of the flail, the flutter of the winnowing fan, and the purr of milk into the pails. . .

The tone here, as throughout the book, is dispassionate and balanced. Hardy is not so foolish as to yield himself to an unqualified nostalgia for the agricultural past nor so heartless as simply to embrace the ways of the future. The social biases at work in both his earlier and later novels come together in *The Mayor* as an uneasy equilibrium, somewhat like that which forms the character of Henchard.

The portrait steadily built up of Casterbridge is never to be at the center of Hardy's concern, yet is essential to all that follows in the book. For without a full exposure to this social milieu, it would not be possible to register the significance of the struggle between Henchard and his young rival, the Scotchman Farfrae. First his friend and employee, then his competitor in business and love, and finally his employer and replacement as mayor, Farfrae comes—his name suggests it—as the stranger from afar.

At first their conflict is apprehended as a clash of temperaments, a contrast in kinds of character. So the absorbed reader is likely to regard the book, and so the scrutinizing critic ought finally to take it.

Henchard responds to his personal experience passionately, through volcanic upheavals; Farfrae sentimentally, through mild quaverings. Henchard wishes to wrench his environment; Farfrae to glide through it. Henchard can never adjust self to social role; Farfrae keeps self and social role harmonious, as partners in a busy enterprise. Henchard is rock; Farfrae smooth pebble. Their clash cannot be avoided, if only because Henchard keeps assaulting whatever equilibrium of personal and business relations they establish. Repeatedly Henchard provokes Farfrae to contests of manliness and guile, without realizing that the two are by no means the same. And the more Henchard emerges as a personal force, the less he survives as a social power.

Their conflict reflects, but is not reducible to, a shake-up within the dominant social class of Casterbridge, the merchants and traders. Men accustomed to a free-and-easy personal economy, in which arrangements are sealed by a word, will now be replaced by agents of an economy more precise and rational, in which social relationships must be mediated through paper. Henchard is "bad at figures," he keeps his money in an old safe, and

> His accounts were like bramblewood when Mr. Farfrae came. He used to reckon his sacks by chalk strokes all in a row like garden palings, measure his ricks by stretching with his arms, weigh his trusses by a lift, judge his hay by a chaw, and settle the price with a curse.

Henchard runs his affairs by hunches—which works well enough as long as he need only confront problems he can apprehend intuitively, as elements of an economy local and familiar. Toward the men who work for him Henchard is both generous and despotic, close and overbearing. He can be an autocrat, but never a hypocrite. He prepares the way for a triumph of bourgeois economy, but cannot live at ease with the style it brings. And he is not really able to distinguish between business and personal affairs, since for better or worse, he assumes that a man's life should be all of a piece. Will Farfrae be his manager? Then Farfrae must be his friend. And not only must Farfrae help with the books and the grain, he must eat heavy breakfasts with him and listen to the story of his life, as if to slake Henchard's thirst for relationship and impact.

Farfrae, says Hardy at one point, "is the reverse of Henchard." It is an important observation, and important, paradoxically, because of its generality. For what matters in the kind of social displacement Hardy is here portraying, is not so much the character of the newcomer, who must be something of a riddle precisely because he is new, as the ordeal of the old-timer, who forms part of a known and shared experience.

Farfrae bears the fruits of science; he introduces new machines to the farmers; he treats his men with "progressive" blandness, which at this point in history means neither to abuse nor pay them as much as Henchard. With Farfrae there comes to Casterbridge the rule of "functional rationality," what Karl Mannheim describes as "a series of actions . . . organized in such a way that it leads to a previously defined goal, every element in this series of actions receiving a functional position and role." This outlook is expressed by Farfrae with amusing precision when he explains the benefits of the new seed-drill:

> "It will revolutionize sowing hereabouts! No more sowers flinging their seed about broadcast, so that some falls by the wayside and some among thorns. . . . Each grain will go straight to its intended place, and nowhere else whatever."

Who, comparing the ways of Henchard and Farfrae, will easily choose between them? Certainly not Hardy. He is too canny, too reflective for an unambiguous stand, and his first loyalty is neither to Henchard nor Farfrae but the larger community of Wessex. Hardy's feelings may go out to Henchard but his mind is partly with Farfrae. He knows that in important respects the Scotchman will help bring a better life to Casterbridge, even if a life less vivid and integral. Yet he also recognizes that the narrowing of opportunity for men like Henchard represents a loss in social strength. In his own intuitive and "poetic" way Hardy works toward an attitude of mature complexity, registering gains and losses, transcending the fixed positions of "progress" and "tradition." Because he is so

entirely free of sentimental or ideological preconceptions in *The Mayor,* he achieves not only a more balanced view of the developments in Casterbridge than either Henchard or Farfrae can reach; his voice also emerges as that of a communal protector and spokesman.

Hardy's design requires that, to sharpen the contrast between looming protagonist and the secondary figures, Henchard be scaled as somewhat larger than life: that which is passing away seems larger than that which is yet to come. And in defeat men can grow into eloquence; they rant, they rave; sometimes they even discover their humanity. Farfrae, however, has no reason to cry out. He lives in modest harmony with the prevailing social trends, and need never call upon—need not even discover whether he has any—deeper emotional resources. Farfrae's feelings are always obedient to his will and are not, in any case, of a kind that could seriously interfere with his role as businessman. But Hardy also recognizes tacitly that a disagreeable role in society does not necessarily make for a disagreeable character, and he avoids the error of portraying Farfrae as a slick commercial schemer.

It has been customary among Hardy's critics and, I would guess, frequent among his readers to feel some dissatisfaction with Farfrae. He is said to be a figure too dim, never closely examined, more outline than substance. This kind of complaint rests, I think, upon a misunderstanding of both the book and the character. *The Mayor* is not a psychological novel in the sense that it provides, through a narrator's scrutiny, an intensive probing of psychic life. Henchard's psychology is, of course, extraordinarily interesting, but it is a psychology neither analyzed nor minutely examined: we must infer it from the unfolding of his behavior. Much the same, if on a smaller scale, holds true for Farfrae. And dramatically there is no reason why we should be allowed a fuller scrutiny of Farfrae's inner life. His function in this novel is to serve as "the reverse of Henchard," and if there is something a little shadowy about him, that is partly because he is a stranger bringing untested ways to a tested place.

In any case, Hardy maintains a finely balanced poise—it holds together wariness, irony and some respect—toward Farfrae. Clearly the Scotchman cannot engage Hardy as a Jude or even a Henchard can, yet he is conceived with clarity of outline and a modest quotient of sympathy. Farfrae wants no revenge upon Henchard and is quite ready to help him once everything has been lost; in fact, Farfrae wants nothing but quiet prosperity, domestic peace and modest preferment. As the victor, he is even ready to be tolerant toward Henchard's outbursts and provocations. That there must also be something intolerable in the tolerance of the victor, Hardy silently recognizes—it is the kind of recognition we expect from him. And it informs some of the most striking incidents in the novel, those showing Henchard, after his downfall, in the grip of a compulsive and self-lacerating pride. They are incidents that stay in one's memory as tokens of Hardy's intuitive craft: when Henchard comes to work as a day laborer for Farfrae, wearing the silk hat that is the single remnant of his lost prosperity; when he encounters Lucetta as the wife of his new employer and elaborately pretends to humble himself before her; and when he thrusts himself forward, as if from an inflamed will, during the visit of "the royal personage."

Shrewd as a Scotchman, Farfrae is sentimental as a Scotchman. At the Three Mariners tavern he delights the Casterbridge folk with his nostalgic song, *"It's hame, and it's hame, hame fane would I be."* Yet this is the same Farfrae whose first appearance in the novel comes as a man who has chosen to leave his old hame, like many Scotchmen of the nineteenth century who had drifted south in search of prosperity. As Hardy remarks in a quietly sardonic sentence, Farfrae is always "giving strong expression to a song of his dear native country that he loved so well as never to have revisited it." That anyone should manage as readily as Farfrae to compartmentalize his experience is a somewhat comic idea: the dry comedy of self-insulation.

Hardy marshals expertly the materials compelling us to see Henchard and Farfrae as representative men, each the agent for an embattled segment within the merchant class of Casterbridge; yet he also writes out of a fine realization that no human figure, unless meant as comic caricature, can be grasped entirely through his social function. Men like Henchard and Farfrae will release impulses and display characteristics that are not strictly harmonious—indeed, are likely to clash—with their social roles. Farfrae is indeed a new man of commerce, but also a stranger, a sentimentalist, a creature of milky mildness. Henchard does come out of the besieged old order, but also carries within himself some of the vices that will characterize the new. Among the most striking pages in *The Mayor* are those in which the private voice of one man is taken as public speech by another—as in the critical incident in which Henchard pleads with Farfrae to return to his sick wife and, because of the battle that has just occurred between the two men, is simply not believed.

I have spoken of Henchard's guilt and of his drive to impose significance upon his life through a dramatic overreaching of the will. Let us, for convenience, call these the personal themes of *The Mayor.* How then—the question must arise—do they relate to the social confrontation between Henchard and Farfrae, so clearly meant to have a large representative weight?

The first impulse of a critic facing this kind of question is usually to look for patterns of neat alignment, so that the different strands of action can be brought together and the novel declared to have a satisfactory structure. I wonder, however, at the value of such a procedure. Is it not a mistake to keep tidying up works of fiction, like compulsive housekeepers after a wild party? Is not one of the pleasures of the novel as a *genre*—and the novel more than any other *genre*—that within a structure of some comeliness and coherence there is likely to be a portion of that contingency, that vital disorder we know to be present in human existence? For a novel to emerge as a work of art, its materials must be shaped, selected, suppressed; for the form thereby achieved to persuade and move us, it must also create an illusion of the rich formlessness of reality.

Now what I have called the personal and the social themes of *The Mayor* do converge toward a significant interlocking. Henchard's personal qualities are distinctively his own, but they take on a resonance that would be quite impossible were they not rooted in a portion of Wessex history. The fortitude of character that renders him so notable a man is not merely an idiosyncratic trait; it has been nurtured and made possible by the society of old Wessex. A figure of potency and assurance in the Wessex that is dying, he is a mere foundering wreck in the Wessex that is coming to birth.

After the first few chapters we see that Hardy is weaving together an entanglement between the personal and public sides of Henchard's experience, the psychic turbulence that erupts within him and the social contests in which he finds himself caught up. This entanglement is tightened at a key point, when the old furmity woman comes before Henchard sitting as magistrate. She serves the plot as a kind of Nemesis, the voice of memory as it dredges up the mayor's shame. Thereby the theme first advanced in the opening chapter is brought to climax: Henchard cannot escape the consequences of his past. But reappearing at the moment she does, the furmity woman also hastens the collapse of Henchard as a social force in the world of Casterbridge.

That this connection is logically unassailable may surely be doubted. There is no necessary or sufficiently coercive reason why the consequences of a personal sin should coincide in time and impact with the climax of a socio-economic failure. Several things, to be sure, are working for Hardy which enable him to paper over the difficulty: first, that behind the two strands of action—Henchard's personal story and his social struggle—there operate the same turbulent elements of his character, so that we may thereby be induced to accept a similarity of effects; second, that we are emotionally persuaded to acquiesce in the notion that troubles run in packs, one kind precipitating another; and third, that by this point in the book Hardy is so involved in overplotting that the relentless accumulation of intrigue distracts us from the weakness of this major turning point in the plot. Yet, even if one makes all these allowances, it cannot be said that Hardy succeeds in establishing the aura of inexorability which both the logic of his story and the conception behind his protagonist require. The fault is a serious one, still another instance of the way Hardy's plots crumble beneath the thematic weight with which he burdens them.

Faults of this kind and magnitude can be found in all of Hardy's fiction, and it would be idle to deny that they are troublesome; yet they are not, either in *The Mayor* or Hardy's other major novels, finally decisive. They count for more in one's reflections upon Hardy's work than in one's actual experience of it. For the strongest impression created by a book like *The Mayor* is that of a unified tone, an integration of sensibility and effects. And if we do not claim for the book a tragic stature it neither invites nor requires, the impression of unity is particularly strong. It is an impression that depends upon specific compositional achievements. [In a footnote, Howe comments: "Apparently out of a wish to honor the novel, critics in recent years have spoken about *The Mayor* as a tragedy, with consequent comparisons between Henchard and Oedipus and Lear. I doubt that these help us in responding to the book Hardy actually wrote.]

Certain elements in *The Mayor* do bear a resemblance to a tragic action, but then so do elements in any serious work of fiction. What seems lacking in the story and character of Henchard, however, is that 'proper magnitude' of which Aristotle speaks. By this admittedly vague phrase I take Aristotle to mean a resonance of large philosophic and cultural issues: the destiny of a race, the fate of a people, the ordeal of a hero who embodies the strivings of a nation. Impressive as Henchard may be, he cannot be said to embody in his character or conduct issues of such magnitude. He is too clearly related to the particularities of a historical moment and a social contest; he is too clearly a character with only the most limited grasp, or growth, of consciousness; and he does not elicit, in my judgment, that blend of pity and terror amounting to awe which is characteristic of the tragic hero.

My own sense of Henchard would place him not in the line of tragedy but in the tradition of romanticism. He strikes me as a descendent of those stubborn figures in romantic poetry and fiction who refuse to submit to their own limitations and demand more from the world than it can give them.''']

The Mayor is a novel packed with incident, and if we examine closely some of the devices Hardy used to keep his serial exciting, we can charge him with overcrowding. Except, however, in the first few chapters, none of the incidents is developed at much length or with much fullness. Hardy continues—rightly enough, since this is where his greatness lies—to depend upon a series of intensely wrought and symbolically charged bits of action, scattered through the book and so brief in scope as to prevent us from thinking of them as dramatic scenes. These bits of action form the intermittent points of climax, transition and accumulation in the movement of the plot.

Another reason for the integration of effects is the way Hardy handles his ''rustics.'' In his earlier novels these figures weave in and out of the main action, serving mostly as comic relief or minor conveniences of plot, at best as a low-keyed chorus expressing a traditional wisdom in response to the deracination or defeat of the major characters. But in *The Mayor* they form a significant part of the story. It is they who precipitate the skimmity-ride which throws Lucetta into a fever and then death. The social transformation Hardy dramatizes through the clash between Henchard and Farfrae is sharply reflected in the life of the ''rustics,'' now ill at ease in the town, beginning to express a measure of social *ressentiment,* and clearly losing their cohesion as a group. Some of the usual tasks of the Hardyan chorus are still performed here, and very beautifully, as when Mother Cuxsom muses on the death of Susan:

> Well, poor soul; she's helpless to hinder that or anything now. . . . And all her shining keys will be took from her, and her cupboards opened; and little things a' didn't wish seen, anybody will see; and her wishes and ways will all be as nothing!

or when Abel Whittle recalls Henchard's end:

> We walked on like that all night; and in the blue o' the morning, when 'twas hardly day, I looked ahead o' me, and I zeed that he wambled, and could hardly drag along. By that time we had got past here . . . and I took down the boards from the windows, and helped him inside. ''What, Whittle,'' he said, ''and can ye really be such a poor fond fool as to care for such a wretch as I!''

But such passages, fewer here than in Hardy's earlier novels, are really no more than occasional grace notes. In the main, the rustics are viewed in a hard and realistic light; their moral seediness and decay reflect the social changes portrayed through the dominant line of plot. One could almost speak of the events at Mixen Lane as a sub-plot, the darkened reflection through plebeian grotesquerie of the main strand of action.

Yet it surely must be the common experience of Hardy's readers that in *The Mayor of Casterbridge* it is Henchard himself who is the unremittent center of interest. He is that rarity in modern fiction: an integral characterization, a figure shown not through a dimension of psychology or an aspect of conduct, but at a single stroke, in his full range of being. Henchard neither grows nor changes; and we do not really come to understand him any better as the novel progresses. We do not need to. For we know him immediately and completely, through an act of intuitive apprehension. He appears before us through those gestures of conduct and speech which realize his uniqueness: a man exemplifying the heroism and futility of the human will. For a novelist to have created this image of character is a very great

achievement—it adds to the stock of archetypal possibilities that inhabit our minds. (pp. 84-102)

> *Irving Howe, in his* Thomas Hardy, *The Macmillan Company, 1967, 206 p.*

JEAN R. BROOKS (essay date 1971)

[*In the following excerpt, Brooks explores the relationship between the setting of Casterbridge and the novel's characters.*]

The Mayor of Casterbridge, like *The Return of the Native,* is primarily a novel of environment in relation to character. But instead of the almost changeless face of Egdon heath, with its few scattered inhabitants, the factor that controls the action is the evolving social organism of Casterbridge the county town. The novel reflects the changes that were taking place in Casterbridge, and beyond, in the nineteenth century: the increasing mastery over environment, the advance of mechanization, the development of new business methods to keep pace, the importance of education for a rapidly changing world, the breaking down of social barriers, the spread of co-operative and humanitarian principles. The concept of a static world in which changes are only superficial was being replaced by the evolutionary concept of change as ultimate reality.

The plot, with its epic hero representing a whole culture and way of life, the characters, situations, and rhythms of narrative movement, are subtly balanced in relation to the Casterbridgean environment of space, time, and society, to form a poetic correlative of the inevitable on-going of the world. The two chief characters, Michael Henchard and Donald Farfrae, are engaged in a commercial struggle that brings in the new order to supersede the old.

The movement of the plot, divided clearly into a prologue and six acts, or the stanzaic steps of a ballad, is one of reversal that recalls Greek tragedy. It climbs upward through intensifying conflict and complication to a peak point—Henchard's bankruptcy, and the hag's disclosure—from which he falls and Farfrae rises. The movement is repeated, fugue-like, a little later in the fall of Lucetta and the rise of Elizabeth-Jane. The Prologue tells, in the simple rhythms of fable, of Henchard's sale of wife and daughter, the act to which all subsequent action looks back. The rest of the story plots his double pursuit of the affection he has sold to his ambition, and of the self-destruction he unconsciously invites to punish the guilt of self-assertion against the limitations of the human condition.

The twenty-year gap between prologue and the drama proper stresses the link between crime and punishment. The first act shows his wilful violation of human relationship apparently bearing fruit. He is rich, successful, and the Mayor of Casterbridge. But the seeds of his destruction are already there; in the corruption of bread, for which his ignorance is responsible (which, as a spoiling of nature, recalls the furmity hag's corruption of wholesome furmity and its consequences); in the return of Susan and her daughter, hand in hand—a detail that compels comparison with the isolation of Henchard from his wife at the beginning of the story—and in his appointment of the astute Farfrae as his manager. But the re-marriage of Susan and Henchard brings the act to a close on a note of apparent retrieval of past error.

The second act robs Henchard of affection—friend and manager Farfrae, wife, and child. Farfrae is lost to him through the possibilities of division that are present, together with the possibilities of creative partnership, in the new ideas of the

Map of Hardy's fictional Wessex.

man "frae far." Susan is lost through death, and Elizabeth-Jane through his disregard of Susan's instructions not to open, until the girl's wedding day, the letter which discloses that she is Newson's daughter. The irony of reversal operates again when Elizabeth-Jane's removal to the house of Lucetta, the lady whom Henchard "ought" to marry for conventional reasons, and Henchard's withdrawal of his objection to Farfrae's courtship of Elizabeth-Jane, results in Farfrae's attraction to Lucetta.

The third act graphs the competition in business and love between Henchard and Farfrae, and Henchard's failure in the ambition which he substituted for affection. In the conflict between old and progressive ideas, in the foresight and judgement needed to safeguard Casterbridge crops and Casterbridge entertainment from uncertain weather, Farfrae gains ground and Henchard's wrong-headed impulsiveness leads to bankruptcy. His social status receives "a startling fillip downwards" by the furmity hag's disclosure in court of his sale of Susan, which robs him of the moral right to lead the flourishing town. Reversal of roles with his rival is complete when Farfrae buys his house and business, employs him as workman, marries the woman he was going to marry and eventually Henchard's stepdaughter, and becomes Mayor of Casterbridge.

Act four charts the degradation and increasing isolation of the former Mayor. The close of his period of teetotalism marks

violations of human dignity that recall the beginning of the novel; the anathema on Farfrae, the fight in the loft, the self-humiliation at the Royal visit. Twenty-four hours sees violent reversals. The pomp of the Royal visit is parodied by the grotesque skimmity in the evening; Lucetta is dead in the dawn after her triumph; Henchard's murderous attack on Farfrae in the morning is balanced by his desperate attempt to warn Farfrae of Lucetta's illness in the evening. Finally, his new hope of affection from Elizabeth-Jane is qualified by the return of Newson, who brings with him, like Farfrae in act two, possibilities for good or ill, and is sent away with a lie.

The fifth stage is a period of regeneration for Henchard; of renewed contact with love through Elizabeth-Jane, and with the natural world untouched by big business through his little seedshop. He schools himself to accept Elizabeth-Jane's growing love for Farfrae, but the uneasy interval comes to an end with Newson's second return and Henchard's departure from Casterbridge, outwardly the hay-trusser who had entered it twenty years ago. The final act brings him to full stature as the tragic, isolated, self-alienated scapegoat, whose impulse to self-destruction sends him to die like an animal on the heath after Elizabeth-Jane's rebuff and his refusal "to endeavour strenuously to hold his own in her love."

Hardy's poetic readings of life, the stylized ironies of reversal and substitution, are evident in a mere recital of the events. . . .

The incidents that affect Henchard's life are like violent hammer blows set in motion by his first violent act. A chain of eventful arrivals which substitutes something else for the thing desired—Farfrae's friendship for wife and child, Susan and Elizabeth-Jane for Farfrae, Lucetta for the daughter lost in Elizabeth-Jane, and Farfrae for Henchard in Lucetta's affections—leads the mind back inevitably to the first link in the chain, the substitution of ambition for love. The crises are brought about by revelation of hidden acts: the sale of wife and child, Henchard's association with Lucetta, the secret of Elizabeth-Jane's birth. Accidents and coincidences add their effect to acts of human wilfulness. Some can hardly be called accidents; Henchard's impulse to self-punishment places him in the way of bad luck. Nothing else can account for his entrusting Lucetta's letters to his enemy Jopp, or his rashness in acting on the long-range forecast of the weather-prophet without waiting for the oracle's full development. The return of Susan, Newson, Lucetta, and the furmity hag (who appears in court on the one day when Henchard is sitting as substitute magistrate): the appearance of Farfrae at the very moment when Henchard needs his knowledge to get out of a difficulty; the bad weather that intensifies his failure by the failure of others involved in his speculations—stress the long arm of coincidence. But not all the coincidences are disastrous—Henchard's sight of his substitute self, the effigy, in the water saves him from suicide—and the poetic mood created by the stylized plot makes them credible as correlatives of the past and its claim to atonement.

The plot owes some of its emotional force to the feeling that it is archetypal. The myth of human responsibility and rebellion against the human condition is deep-seated. Henchard is overtly or implicitly compared with Achilles, Ajax, Oedipus, Orestes pursued by the Furies, Cain, Saul, Samson working in the mill of the Philistines after his fall, Job, Coriolanus, King Lear, and Faust. Farfrae can be regarded as the Creon to his Oedipus and David to his Saul; Elizabeth-Jane as the Cordelia to his Lear. The Abel to his Cain, and Fool to his Lear, is provided by Abel Whittle, who represents, at Henchard's first clash of principle with Farfrae and at Henchard's death, the brotherhood which the self-alienated man had rejected and finally embraced. His self-alienation and impulse to self-destruction recall more modern heroes: Emily Brontë's Heathcliff, Melville's Captain Ahab, Conrad's Lord Jim and Razumov, the ambiguous heroes of Gide and Dostoievsky, Camus' Meursault. Older than any literary manifestation is the seasonal rite of the corn-king supplanted, after ritual combat and supernatural agency (furmity hag and weather-prophet) by his adopted "son" in his role as virile leader of an agricultural community. The ancient myth of the scapegoat-king meets the modern saga of the nineteenth-century self-made man deposed by the new order of big business, in a penetrating study of the alienation from self and natural harmony that follows the guilt of wilfully imposing conscious desires on the human condition.

The alienation suffered by Henchard and his feminine counterpart, Lucetta (who suffers in a pathetic, not tragic, capacity) is expressed through scenes that function as dramatic metaphor. The scenes of civic ritual point to the gulf between appearance and reality that is a vital theme of the story. The bow window that separates the banqueters at the King's Arms from the "plainer fellows [that] bain't invited" also puts a stage-frame round the feast. The disharmony within, the distorted shapes of the diners, the straight-backed figure in the Mayoral chair, distance the scene to a mock representation of Mayoral responsibility. Elizabeth-Jane's relationship to the public im-age—"the natural elation she felt at discovering herself akin to a coach"—is later balanced by the bankrupt Henchard's sight, through the same window, of the reality of the love he has missed in Elizabeth-Jane. It is the public image which Henchard wishes to preserve. When he is superseded in his civic role, he crumbles to the nothingness implied by his will.

The high drama of the police court faces his public image with the reality of the past action his appearance has denied. The furmity hag is part of his past, and so part of the self he cannot escape. The power of that other self is one of the notes that creates the rich resonance of Chapter XLI, where Henchard gazes at his effigy-self in Ten Hatches Weir. The savage ritual of the skimmity which placed effigies of himself and Lucetta in positions of inverted honour, recalls the past of that other self and points to his future fate as scapegoat outcast for the sins of existence. Yet at this juncture the sense of a magical substitution saves the life of the man who cannot escape from himself. The phenomenon has a natural cause, yet the theatrical, hallucinatory effect of the scene becomes symbolic of a Dostoievskian ultimate reality of the divided self.

The skimmity ride is a caricature of the Royal visit, whose pomp has already been parodied within itself by the drunken Henchard, drawing down on his grotesque image of Mayoralty the degradation imposed by the real Mayor Farfrae. The maid's description of the effigies' dress—an effective adaptation of the Greek messenger technique—dramatically diminishes the civic importance of Henchard and Lucetta to a puppet show of hollow pomp and poses covering an inharmonious past.

> "The man has got on a blue coat and kerseymere leggings; he has black whiskers, and a reddish face. 'Tis a stuffed figure, with a falseface.... Her neck is uncovered, and her hair in bands, and her back-comb in place; she's got on a puce silk, and white stockings, and coloured shoes."

The market place, where many of the important scenes of the novel are enacted, takes on the character of a commercial stage. "The *carrefour* was like the regulation Open Place in spectacular dramas, where the incidents that occur always happen to bear on the lives of the adjoining residents." There, men assume the roles and "market-faces" required by buying and selling. Seen from Lucetta's window, they take on distortions ("men of extensive stomachs, sloping like mountain sides; men whose heads in walking swayed as the trees in November gales") that compel comparison with the dehumanizations of the banqueters: gigantic inflations caused by the ready money they represent to Casterbridge, which misshapes reality. Lucetta, who believes that she can remain in the wings as a mere spectator ("I look as at a picture merely") is forced onto the stage because her house is part of the *carrefour*. High Place Hall has a market face of Palladian reasonableness, counterpointed by the distorted mask, recalling the grotesque theatrical masks that hang over the proscenium arch, that marks a past of intrigue and violence. It is significant that Henchard chooses this entrance to make his renewed contact with Lucetta.

The commercial stage, viewed through Lucetta's window, defines her relationship with Farfrae. Their common sympathy for the predicament of the old shepherd and the courting couple, whose relationship is threatened by the commercial standards of the hiring fair, and its resolution by Farfrae's compassion, draw them together. The old shepherd remains in the memory as a poetic symbol of the human cost of the new market techniques introduced in the next scene. Lucetta is linked to the seed-drill by the assumption of a role that foreshadows, through the leitmotif of colour, both her triumph and tragedy. Her decision to be "the cherry-coloured person at all hazards" links her to the red machine, to the future of Farfrae and the commercial values of Casterbridge, and to the "puce silk" of her effigy that comments on the hollowness of her role. The artificial brightness of her appearance is suddenly placed by the reality of the sun, which is in harmonious relationship with the drill.

> The sun fell so flat on the houses and pavement opposite Lucetta's residence that they poured their brightness into her rooms. Suddenly, after a rumbling of wheels, there were added to this steady light a fantastic series of circling irradiations upon the ceiling, and the companions turned to the window. Immediately opposite a vehicle of strange description had come to a standstill, as if it had been placed there for exhibition.

The metaphor of the stage, in fact, is one which pervades the novel. The action grows out of dramatic conflict, and life is seen as a vast arena where the battle for survival takes place. The Ring has always been an arena for violent and tragic spectacle. Its ghosts and skeletons are a memorial to the military power of the Romans. Reverberations of gladiatorial combat, the law of force, add pathos to Henchard's furtive meetings there with Susan and Lucetta. As Henchard leaves Casterbridge, the metaphor sums up his experience. "He had no wish to make an arena a second time of a world that had become a mere painted scene to him." It recalls, with compassionate irony, Elizabeth-Jane's hopeful entry into Casterbridge, which was to her a romantic sunset backdrop of "towers, gables, chimneys, and casements"—romantic, but not insubstantial—and the earlier sunset backdrop that defines Henchard's act of human violation as part of a great cosmic drama.

> The sun had recently set, and the west heaven was hung with rosy cloud, which seemed permanent, yet slowly changed. To watch it was like looking at some grand feat of stagery from a darkened auditorium. In presence of this scene after the other there was a natural instinct to abjure man as the blot on an otherwise kindly universe; till it was remembered that all terrestrial conditions were intermittent, and that mankind might some night be innocently sleeping when these quiet objects were raging loud.

The prologue concentrates into a dramatic scene, which has the starkness of a ballad, the themes that operate in the wider world of Casterbridge to drive Michael Henchard to destruction. He enters the novel anonymously, as the "skilled countryman" defined by his clothes, his tools, and "measured, springless walk." The atmosphere of "stale familiarity" that surrounds him and Susan identifies him with the universal drabness of the human condition, embodied in the long dusty road,

> neither straight nor crooked, neither level nor hilly, bordered by hedges, trees, and other vegetation, which had entered the blackened-green stage of colour that the doomed leaves pass through on their way to dingy, and yellow, and red.

The "noises off" of Weydon Fair counterpoint the drabness with the search for gaiety that is another familiar Hardy image. Henchard's sale of his wife, to the background noises of 'the sale by auction of a few inferior animals, that could not otherwise be disposed of', in a blaze of narrative intensity, challenges human limitation with a self-assertive act that violates the deepest human, natural and moral instincts.

The swallow, seeking escape from the mercenary perversion of nature inside the tent, provides a moment of equilibrium, always present in Hardy's work, when human choice could give fate a different turn; and looks forward to the caged goldfinch of XLV, which symbolizes the consequences of the act that made Henchard unfree. But Henchard assumes his role and his destiny. The result is to turn a stage play into reality, with "the demand and response of real cash" which is to become a symbol of power in Casterbridge.

> The sight of real money in full amount, in answer to a challenge for the same till then deemed slightly hypothetical, had a great effect upon the spectators. Their eyes became riveted upon the faces of the chief actors, and then upon the notes as they lay, weighted by the shillings, on the table.

The meaning of the scene—Henchard's obsessive desire to sacrifice human relationships to the power of money—is pointed by the similarity of Susan's warning, "If you touch that money, I and this girl go with the man. Mind, it is a joke no longer," to Farfrae's, when he clashes with Henchard over respect for Abel Whittle.

> "I say this joke has been carried far enough."
>
> "And I say it hasn't! Get up in the waggon, Whittle."
>
> "Not if I am manager," said Farfrae. "He either goes home, or I march out of this yard for good."

The prologue ends with a return of leitmotifs. The morning after, the drabness of the cosmos is accentuated by the buzzing fly and the barking dog; Henchard's isolation by routine family matters proceeding at all levels: "He went on in silent thought, unheeding the yellowhammers which flitted about the hedges with straws in their bills." But the movement from lurid candlelight through darkness to the newly risen sun, from the temporary man-made structure of the tent and its man-made commercial atmosphere to the fresh September morning on the uplands "dotted with barrows, and trenched with the remains of prehistoric forts", to the church where Michael Henchard is defined for the first time by name and the conscious purpose of his oath, stresses the rhythm of defeat and regeneration, degradation and redefinition, that marks the life of Michael Henchard in Casterbridge. The whole movement, with its foreshadowing in stark dramatic terms of the delicate balance between human dignity and vaulting ambition, its market ethics, and its denial of nature and responsibilities formed in the past, ends with a widening out from the claustrophobic tent to the social world where the balance will be worked out.

> Next day he started, journeying south-westward, and did not pause, except for nights' lodgings, till he reached the town of Casterbridge, in a far distant part of Wessex.

The solidity of Hardy's evocation of Casterbridge, both concrete and poetic, vouches for its effect on the characters. The plane of myth and fable in the prologue modulates to the plane of physical reality as Elizabeth-Jane moves from the fairy-tale transformation of Henchard to the local voices and local issues of bad bread which prove the fairy-tale Mayor vulnerable. But continuity with the prologue is there, in the evocation of Casterbridge as a town in vital contact with the forces which Henchard's act had denied or embraced—nature, the past, and the values of the market.

The environment that changes lives is itself in a continuous process of change, without which there is no progress. The passing of time finds its correlative in the clocks, chimes, and curfews; the seasonal character of the shop-window display; references to Casterbridge features no longer in existence. And while Casterbridge is growing in stature by virtue of its size and favourable position, the three visits to Weydon stress that "pulling down is more the nater of Weydon," where "the new periodical great markets of neighbouring towns were beginning to interfere seriously with the trade carried on here for centuries." These cyclic rhythms of rise and fall, seen and heard through the observant senses of Elizabeth-Jane as she approaches the town, prepare us for their reenactment in the career of the man they are seeking. The squareness she notes in Casterbridge is repeated in the descriptions of the Mayor, its representative citizen; its conservative distrust, "huddled all together," in his inflexible attitude to new inventions.

The approach of the two women, downhill towards the town, is sensuously realized in a description that moves from the architect's plan ("to birds of the more soaring kind") to an elevation drawn in increasing detail as its features are encountered by "the level eye of humanity." Yet it is not a blueprint. The details are selected to form an impressionist picture of an interlocking "mosaic-work of subdued reds, browns, greys, and crystals" in vital pattern-relation to the "rectangular frame of deep green" and the "miles of rotund down and concave field" that held the individual pieces in shape. The architect's eye and the poet's selective detail provide a comment on the relationship of Casterbridge individuals to their surroundings. The weather- and time-nibbled church, the individual voices of curfew and clocks, add the dimension of time to Hardy's evocation of Casterbridge in space. The cumulative poetic effect is to make the entry of the two unassuming women into the boxed-in "snugness and comfort" of the town through the dark avenue of trees, an image of the tragic solitary human condition. Then, the individual sounds modulate into the communal brass band, and the still-life picture begins to move with the rhythms of vigorous natural life.

The physical position of Casterbridge, "a place deposited in the block upon a corn-field," without transitional mixture of town and down, is essential to its growth as a living organism. It retains a vital link with nature, which Henchard corrupts and Farfrae respects, in his treatment of the corrupted grain, his purchase of the seed-drill that takes the chance out of sowing, his creative use of the tree-lined walk for his entertainment, and his respect for human dignity. (pp. 196-206)

The link with nature in Casterbridge is often integrated with evidence of past layers of Casterbridge life. The wall of Henchard's house "was studded with rusty nails speaking of generations of fruit-trees that had been trained there," and the open doors of the houses passed by Elizabeth-Jane reveal a floral blaze "backed by crusted grey stone-work remaining from a yet remoter Casterbridge than the venerable one visible in the street."

The "past-marked prospect" of Casterbridge, dotted with tumuli, earth-forts, Roman remains, and evidence of violent blood sports and man's continuing inhumanity to man, is a physical reminder of the barbarity of a ruthless competitive battle for survival, still present (as in Mixen Lane) under the civilized front. Henchard is placed in a setting that speaks of the primitive past, which both diminishes and enhances his ephemeral dignity, whenever he tries to disown his own past. Significantly, it is from the massive prehistoric fort of Mai-Dun that he sees the past he tried to deny catching up on the present, in the figure of Newson striding relentlessly along "the original track laid out by the legions of the Empire," to claim his daughter.

Casterbridge as a market town has symbolic value. The market, as D. A. Dike points out [see essay dated 1952], organizes the values and desires of the citizens. The perennial problem of a market town is to preserve respect for the individuality of human beings who are cogs in a machine for making money. Henchard and Lucetta, who buy and sell human relationships, fail to keep the balance. Lucetta's offer of money to pay Henchard's debts on the day she had broken faith with him to marry his rival; Henchard's gift to her sent "as plaster to the wound"; the annuity he settles on Elizabeth-Jane to rid himself of her presence when the discovery of her parentage makes her worthless stock in his eyes; his gift of five guineas to buy Susan back again; his free entertainment; his reaction to Farfrae's disinterested help, "What shall I pay you for this knowledge?"; his insult to the self-respect of Jopp and Whittle when business cannot wait for their tardy arrival; all are repetitions of the original violation of love by measuring it in the commercial terms of the market place. Farfrae, on the other hand, manages to keep the delicate balance between humanity and business. It is in the market place, appropriately, that he shows respect for the family unit of the old shepherd as well as for the revolutionary seed-drill. Abel Whittle, another man who has cause to thank Farfrae's respect for human dignity, sums up the meaning of the change from Henchard's ownership of the corn business to Farfrae's.

> "Yaas, Miss Henchet," he said, "Mr. Farfrae have bought the concern and all of we work-folk with it; and 'tis better for us than 'twas—though I shouldn't say that to you as a daughter-law. We work harder, but we bain't made afeard now. It was fear made my few poor hairs so thin! No busting out, no slamming of doors, no meddling with yer eternal soul and all that; and though 'tis a shilling a week less I'm the richer man; for what's all the world if yer mind is always in a larry, Miss Henchet?"

Casterbridge is a more complex Egdon heath, in that it represents the given conditions of life which the characters variously adjust to or defy. Their responses to the values of nature, the past, and the market control the curves of their lives. Henchard's career, after the bid for freedom that enslaves his life and liberates his awareness, is a hard-won progress through rejection of market ethics to integration with the past and the family he had cast off, and finally to the realization that he can love what is beyond market price and not his own, in Elizabeth-Jane.

The primitive past and primitive nature operate in Michael Henchard's instinctive impulses, usually disastrous in a modern civilization that must progress morally. The elemental and animal imagery that defines him ("moving like a great tree in a wind," "leonine," "tigerish," "a bull breaking fence"); his energy and inarticulacy, his retrogression to brutal loneliness after his defiance of the moral order; his recourse to rivalry for love, territory, and possessions; his admiration for ruthless business methods in and out of the market; the touchstone of brute strength in all things which makes him despise Farfrae's slight physique while admiring his brains, and give himself a handicap before he fights Farfrae in the loft—are all traits that link Henchard to the pre-human world. The instructions he leaves for his burial are appropriate for an animal—one whose conscious self-assertion against nothingness has failed. When, stripped of everything that built up his public image as man and Mayor, he accepts the nothingness under the robes of office; a nothingness that is physically present in the mud hovel where he dies, scarcely distinguishable from the ancient natural world of Egdon Heath, and advances to the unselfish love which alone can make him significant, Henchard has risen, paradoxically, from the status of a magnificent animal to the nobility of man.

In Casterbridge Farfrae is faced with the same chances and conditions of success or failure. But his character and the needs of the time are on his side. In a social organism where further progress depends as much on co-operation as competition, Farfrae is the man whose chariot they will follow to the Capitol. No-one could be less of a gloomy being who had quitted the ways of vulgar men. While Henchard believes that superiority can only be maintained by standing aloof, Farfrae can be found dancing reels at his cooperative entertainment and singing songs at the Three Mariners, where, we remember, Henchard violated the social ritual of music by forcing the choir to sing an anathema on his rival. He has no past to hide, and no market face required by a role that is different from his reality. He provides the education, method, intelligence, foresight, drive, judgment, sympathy and respect for others, and swift adaptation to conditions of environment, which is lacking in Henchard's "introspective inflexibility." The reign of chance and rule of thumb comes to an end under Farfrae's leadership. The new seed drill is symbolic of man's increasing mastery of his environment: "Each grain will go straight to its intended place, and nowhere else whatever!" His ability to live with honour and dignity within human limitations balances the other great value of Henchard's defiance.

The relation of Henchard's other rival, Newson, to the market ethics of the place where he is an alien passing through (as his name suggests) is double-edged. He holds the rights of property, by which Henchard has lived, and which deal the last blow to his hopes of Elizabeth-Jane. His unpossessiveness is an effective foil to Henchard's possessiveness, yet it is a bitter irony that soon after the wedding he leaves his daughter. Henchard is not capable of the abnegation of identity by which Newson drops out of Susan's life, until the terrible negation of his Will. Yet Newson's too facile acceptance of another man's wife and contribution to the skimmity suggest that the character he negates is not deep. However, he is more socially acceptable to Casterbridge than the deeper-souled Henchard, because he never attempts to disguise his real character, slight as it is. Hence his closeness to the ballad stereotype of the genial, open-handed sailor is a merit rather than a defect in characterization.

Newson shares with Susan Henchard, that other lightly-sketched but convincing ghost from the past, a fidelity to the basic human loyalties expressed for her by the simple moral code of the unlettered peasant. It is founded on acceptance of cosmic injustices and the cyclic movement of lives and seasons. Market ethics is something Susan suffers from, as a woman dependent on a man, but does not subscribe to in her individual values. Her momentary flash of independence at Weydon Fair has the fatalistic assumption of property rights behind it—

> "Will anybody buy her?" said the man.
>
> "I wish somebody would," said she firmly. "Her present owner is not at all to her liking!"

—but her feeling for the continuity of past with present (it is fitting that she should be buried in the old Roman burial ground) and present with future, in her desire for a wider horizon for her daughter, liberates her from Lucetta's need to snatch feverishly at evanescent present pleasures.

Lucetta and Elizabeth-Jane compel comparison in their response to Casterbridge. The values of the market impel Lucetta's emotions and actions.

> "I was so desperate—so afraid of being forced to anything else—so afraid of revelations that would quench his love for me, that I resolved to do it offhand, come what might, and purchase a week of happiness at any cost!"

The commercial terms in which her confession of marriage to Farfrae is worded, her assessment and use of her ephemeral beauty as an asset of marketable worth, her treatment of Elizabeth-Jane as a counter in her pursuit of a man, now as bait for Henchard, now as "a watch-dog to keep her father off" when "a new man she liked better" appears, her concern for external appearance, suggest how thoroughly Lucetta has embraced market ethics. She has tried to repudiate her past in the change of environment from Jersey to Casterbridge, and the change of name from Le Sueur to Templeman "as a means of escape from mine, and its wrongs." She has also rejected the role she could have taken in Casterbridge. Ostensibly she is the stranger, like Farfrae, who brings new ideas into the town. Her furniture, contrasting with Henchard's old-fashioned, pretentious Spanish mahogany, is fifty years ahead of the Casterbridge times. Her ability to distinguish between true culture and false in Elizabeth-Jane, as Henchard cannot ("'What, not necessary to write ladies'-hand?' cried the joyous Elizabeth") provides an ironic comment on the gulf she makes in her own life between appearance and reality, past and present. What might have been remains in the mind as the external image she has built up crumbles under the skimmity ride's rude revelation of what lies underneath. It kills her, but keeps Henchard alive, because his will to defy circumstances makes him more than the puppet of his role.

It is fitting that Hardy draws Lucetta from the outside, while Elizabeth-Jane's thoughts and feelings guide the reader's emotions. She is trustworthy and balanced, because she does not admit any gulf between appearance and reality, past and present, nature and civilization. Consequently the values of the market cannot touch her. She can see nothing wrong in waiting on [customers] at the Three Mariners to pay her board, speaking dialect, or picking up coals for the servant—all "social catastrophes" to Henchard. She refuses to be treated as a chattel either by Henchard or Lucetta. The confusions that surround her name do not affect the intrinsic worth of her character, which Henchard comes to value. The social forms of a simple moral code are not artificial conventions to which she pays only lip-service, but expressive of her deepest convictions. However, there is a final appeal from them to the basic instinctive loyalties she inherits from her parents. It is the same woman who shares the adversity of the man she believes to be her father, and who would 'root out his image as that of an arch-deceiver' to return to a still deeper loyalty of the past, even though by current social standards recognition of Newson's paternity makes her illegitimate. The mood built up by Hardy's picture of Casterbridge in its natural setting, in Chapter XIV, leads to the poetic suggestion of her affinity with that world, when the wheat-husks on her clothes make the instinctive contact with Farfrae that her mother had desired. Her vision of the past as continuous with the present is reflected in her 'study of Latin, incited by the Roman characteristics of the town she lived in', in contrast to Lucetta's irreverent attitude.

Though she balances the enterprise of Farfrae by keeping 'in the rear of opportunity', her desire for knowledge, to make the furnishings of her mind match the furnishings of her beauty, faces her towards a future of complex change—the future of Tess and Jude—where the simple unquestioning values of the older generation will prove inadequate to human experience.

The meaning of those values, expressed through characters and action, is assessed by the Casterbridge people, who both suffer from change and have the elective power to bring it about. The Hardeian chorus is divided into one main and two subsidiary groups, whose social and moral status is marked by their inns. At the top and bottom of the social scale, the King's Arms and Peter's Finger groups are both deceived by appearances. The King's Arms, where Henchard is seen in his success, tests his worth by his actions. But the story reveals that the truth about the curse sung on Farfrae, the hag's disclosure, and Henchard's failure to preserve correspondence between bulk and sample, is more complex than their simple definitions of hatred, immorality, and dishonesty.

If the vision of the King's Arms is distorted by wealth and the power of the civic image, the grotesque effigy of vice created by Mixen Lane is just as far from the truth. Mixen Lane is a negative place, doomed to extinction. The negative way of life is threatened by the vitality of Henchard's bid to achieve meaning. (One can compare the situation in John Whiting's play, *The Devils*.) Reality for them is measured by the failings, not the virtues, of the more vital characters. Hardy's presentation of Mixen Lane makes it less of a place than a human problem correlative to the unlocalized guilt of godless man. (pp. 207-13)

The "philosophic party" of rustics who frequent the friendly, unpretentious Three Mariners provide the most realistic judgement on Casterbridge affairs. Their concern with the essentials of labouring and victualling, bringing up their children, and burying their dead leaves them little time to be influenced by appearances. The two-dimensional inn sign of traditional worthies symbolizes the values of their traditional community. There are no barriers at the Three Mariners. Even the horses stabled at the back mingle with the guests coming and going, and the inn has given hospitality to the Mayor and to members of the Peter's Finger group. The ale lives up to its promise, and no one sings out of tune until Henchard chooses the Three Mariners to break his vow and their traditional Sunday custom. Though they do not put too fine a point of honour ('why *should* death rob life of fourpence? I say there was no treason in it') they take a kindly interest in the careers of Farfrae and Elizabeth-Jane, and their judgement of Elizabeth-Jane severs her intrinsic worth from accidents of family connection and environment. Their response to Farfrae's mixture of common-sense and idealism (which does not preclude criticism of his musical sentiment, "What did ye come away from yer own country for, young maister, if ye be so wownded about it?") places the promise of the new age firmly in the commonalty of the Three Mariners.

Yet it is through the workfolk of Casterbridge that Hardy sounds the deep elegiac note for the passing of the old order, in the deaths of Susan and Michael Henchard. Direct death-bed scenes do not attract Hardy, for the meaning of a life that defies death is to be found in its effect on the survivors. The biblical and Shakespearean cadences of Mrs. Cuxsom's elegy on Susan join with homely Wessex idiom, and the refusal to be overawed by sentiment in contemplation of Coney's theft of the penny weights, to celebrate her patience and endurance, her closeness to the facts of the earth, and the necessity for preserving human dig-

nity in death, "that 'a minded every little thing that wanted tending."

The sublime tragic simplicity of Whittle's elegy on Henchard, with its physical details of his last hours offset by the bond of compassionate love ("'What, Whittle,' he said, 'And can ye really be such a poor fond fool as to care for such a wretch as I!'") which has become Henchard's ultimate value, defines the meaning of his life with a fierce affirmation of love and pain that makes the negations of his Will positive. The Biblical rhythms of deep emotion in the elegiac Wessex voice are the pervading rhythms of Hardy's poetic images of the human condition; of a lonely heroic man, outside the traditional rituals that celebrate the human dignity which his Will refuses, creating his own moral order and meaning.

> Then Henchard shaved for the first time during many days, and put on clean linen, and combed his hair; and was as a man resuscitated thenceforward.
>
> > (XLI)
>
> ". . . God is my witness that no man ever loved another as I did thee at one time. . . . And now— though I came here to kill 'ee, I cannot hurt thee!"
>
> > (XXXVIII)
>
> "If I had only got her with me—if I only had!" he said. "Hard work would be nothing to me then! But that was not to be. I—Cain—go alone as I deserve— an outcast and a vagabond. But my punishment is *not* greater than I can bear!"
>
> He sternly subdued his anguish, shouldered his basket, and went on.
>
> > (XLIII)

Henchard's tragic plight is threefold: cosmic (representative of man's predicament in an uncaring universe), social (showing the plight of a rural community when old methods are swept away by new) and personal. But it is intense poetic response to the personal tragedy that makes *The Mayor of Casterbridge* cosmic tragedy that will stand comparison with the Greeks and Shakespeare. (pp. 213-15)

> *Jean R. Brooks, in her* Thomas Hardy: The Poetic Structure, *Cornell University Press, 1971, 336 p.*

LAWRENCE J. STARZYK   (essay date 1972)

[*In the following essay, Starzyk contends that analogies between* The Mayor of Casterbridge *and Sophoclean or Shakespearean tragedy do not make Hardy's novel a traditional tragedy. Starzyk maintains that Hardy's novel is "a work modern in its orientation and defiantly alien to whatever is implied by 'the traditional basis of tragedy'."*]

It has been argued that the tragic significance of Hardy's *The Mayor of Casterbridge* is owing to the novel's reliance upon traditional notions of tragedy, particularly with respect to an inviolable moral order. An ethical standard necessarily supernatural or transcendent is invoked, according to the argument, in order to ensure and make intelligible the tragic consequences befalling anyone violating these moral universals. To celebrate the purely human or terrestrial at the expense of this superhuman system of values would preclude a justification of the ways of God to man. It would also preclude the possibility of repentance for that individual who sins against the powers that be. Therefore it is imperative that Hardy adhere in the *Mayor* to a traditional system of values, not only to guarantee a basis for sin and repentance, but also to ensure against the artistic failure of a novel like *The Return of the Native* in which the denial of an ethical power beyond man's control deprives the work of genuine tragic and moral significance.

Such an argument certainly justifies the conclusion that a work of art constructed in keeping with these criteria is fashioned after the traditional basis of tragedy as represented by Sophocles' *Oedipus* and Shakespeare's *Lear*. It would indeed be futile to deny that Hardy's *Mayor* approximates in many ways the characters of the classical or traditional tragedies named here. But because analogies exist between Henchard and Lear or Oedipus does not mean that the *Mayor* is a traditional tragedy. Nor does it justify the grand assumption that since a traditional or classical tragedy demands recognition of a moral power superior to man, the *Mayor,* as an example of traditional tragedy, testifies to the operation of some superhuman agency governing the destinies of mankind. Nothing, it seems to me, could·be farther from the truth of Hardy's novel than this refashioning of the text to fit a predetermined mold never intended for the work. Far from being a tragedy with a traditional basis, the *Mayor,* as I intend to show here, is clearly a work modern in its orientation and defiantly alien to whatever is implied by "the traditional basis of tragedy."

A decade after the *Mayor* began to be serialized in *Harper's Weekly* (1886), Hardy commented on how easily one could "call any force above or under the sky by the name of 'God'— and so pass as orthodox cheaply, and fill the pocket!" If we are to believe Florence Hardy, her husband never acted cheaply in this regard, although the impression of orthodoxy is certainly possible from reading even a work like *The Mayor of Casterbridge*. The truth is that in Hardy's world "neither Chance nor Purpose governs the universe, but Necessity." Two years before he actually began writing the *Mayor* (1884), Hardy records the following as a possible theme for a future work: "Write a history of human automatism, or impulsion—viz., an account of human action in spite of human knowledge, showing how very far conduct lags behind knowledge that should really guide it." The comment, we are told, refers to a project which from this time on increasingly consumed Hardy's energies and attention, namely *The Dynasts*. To suggest that the *Mayor* is a fictional exploration of the drama eventually written between 1903-1908 would demand a closer scrutiny than the scope of this paper allows. But I think it is safe to suggest that the notion of autonomous human action, impulsion, and particularly the idea of incongruity between knowledge and conduct certainly provides a valuable insight into the tragedy which befalls Henchard. It is also to suggest, in part, what Hardy means by Necessity governing the universe. Although it is inaccurate to state that in Hardy's universe every cause necessarily has an effect, and specifically a determined effect, it is correct to remark that in Henchard's case a particular act of his has certain consequences which form the major plot line of the novel. From a temporal perspective, this causal relationship can best be summed up by saying that Henchard's past cannot be denied. It necessarily returns, as is so dramatically evidenced by the eighteen-year separation between chapters two and three of the novel. There is simply no indication in the early stages of the novel's action to suggest that this interval of time argues the fact that some moral power beyond man's control is at last demanding retribution of the offender, Henchard. If anything, it suggests that terrifying incongruity between knowledge and conduct which characterizes Henchard's life at so many points.

Henchard's life has its beginnings, in the novel at least, with his marriage at eighteen. It is at this point that his past, his present, and his future have their genesis. Arriving at the tent of the furmity woman, disconsolate that a man of his talents has not made his mark on the world because of the encumbrance of a wife and child, Henchard complains that "I married at eighteen, like the fool that I was; and this is the consequence o't." An impulsive act, uninformed by sufficient thought as to its gravity and consequences, precipitates another foolish act, the selling of Susan and Elizabeth-Jane. To the man whose conduct is determined by prudent consideration of effects, control remains within his possession. Once having acted incongruously, that is, without thought, Necessity assumes governance over the individual.

The necessity for judgment is reinforced by the only other comment about Henchard's early life. Having met and engaged Farfrae, Henchard sits regarding the young Scot's face and recognizes there the features of his brother. What the Mayor's surrogate brother provides for Henchard's impulsive existence is precisely that balancing factor of judgment. "In my business," Henchard remarks, "'tis true that strength and bustle build up a firm. But judgment and knowledge are what keep it established." The significance of Henchard's statement is not that he fails to follow the advice implicit therein, as is evidenced by his random management of business affairs, nor that he seems incapable of heeding it, as is evidenced by his repeated precipitate actions throughout the novel. The statement's significance, rather, lies in the fact that it testifies to Henchard's recognition, momentary as it is, that conduct informed by wisdom provides an effective approach to a life characterized by incongruity.

Now the incongruity which Henchard's actions reveal is symptomatic of a much more deep-seated and pervasive incongruity characteristic of the universe generally. Far from being a realm of existence determined by law, order, or purpose, Casterbridge—in fact the entire universe—lacks any determination whatever. Its laws are tentative, its operations unpredictable, and its reality relative. It is a world, in short, devoid of any absolute values, moral or religious. As evidence of this incongruity is Hardy's description of the consequences of Henchard's impulsive selling of his wife. From the detached perspective of the narrator of the novel, Henchard appears after the sale to be a blight upon an otherwise harmoniously ordered world. In striking contrast to the cruelty of the man is the affection of nature and specifically of the horses "crossing their necks and rubbing each other lovingly." "In presence of this scene after the other there was a natural instinct to abjure man as the blot on an otherwise kindly universe; till it was remembered that all terrestrial conditions were intermittent, and that mankind might some night be innocently sleeping when these quiet objects were raging aloud." The indeterminacy of nature and of whatever powers may be said to operate through its agency is further illustrated as Hardy captures Henchard at the end of the novel musing over the fact that "It was an odd sequence that out of all this tampering with social law came that flower of Nature, Elizabeth. Part of his wish to wash his hands of life arose from his perception of its contrarious inconsistencies—of Nature's jaunty readiness to support unorthodox social principles." Henchard is quite frankly perplexed at the thought that nature operates randomly, absurdly in producing from a single act, if not actually, then symbolically, both tragedy and joy, both evil and good, both the alienated Cain and the reconciled Elizabeth. To infer from such a situation that a law, whatever its nature, exists is to argue "cheaply" for an orthodoxy that reason refuses to substantiate.

But if there is no predictable order or law according to which the universe operates and according to which man can reasonably expect his actions to be met with foreseeable consequences morally or religiously, then what is the origin of Henchard's guilt, of his crime? Immediately before pondering the universe's incongruity, life's "contrarious inconsistencies," Henchard recalls his tragic act: "Then I drank, and committed my crime." Traditionally crime implies an order or law violated and the necessity of some force of forgiveness external to man capable of relieving the sinner's guilt. That Henchard neither conceives his crime in this traditional framework nor seeks restitution or forgiveness from some power beyond his control is evident from his conception of "God" or Fate and from his understanding of his crime.

Now the immediate context in which Henchard, at the end of his life, regards his "crime" suggests that it constitutes less a violation of some superhuman power than it does a violation of some human power, specifically himself. In characteristic fashion, Henchard returns to the scene of his crime "as an act of penance," recalling the first act of penance he engaged in immediately after the sale of Susan when he visits a chapel to vow abstinence in reparation for his deed. Having departed Casterbridge for good because of the imminent return of Newson, Henchard is compelled to return. "He could not help thinking of Elizabeth," Hardy informs us, "and the quarter of the horizon in which she lived. Out of this it happened that the centrifugal tendency imparted by weariness of the world was counteracted by the centripetal influence of his love for his stepdaughter. As a consequence, instead of following a straight course yet further away from Casterbridge, Henchard gradually, almost unconsciously, deflected from that right line of his first intention; till, by degrees, his wandering, like that of the Canadian woodsman, became part of a circle of which Casterbridge formed the center." The centrifugal and centripetal tendencies described here are specifically defined when Hardy mentions that Henchard, sorrowing for his offense, attempted "to replace ambition by love," but was foiled in this attempt as he had been foiled in his ambitious business and political enterprises. The inference to be drawn from this is that any centripetal tendency, like ambition or even love, when unchecked by judgment, ends in tragedy and despair, ends in alienation from the center of the circle. Ironically for Henchard, the recognition that his driving ambition, which generates political, social, and economic alienation, is insufficient in such an impulsive man to bring him to the recognition that unchecked love produced the same and perhaps bitterer alienation. For in trying to keep Elizabeth to himself and away from her legitimate father, Newson, Henchard drives her away in the same fashion that he alienated Casterbridge from himself earlier. The tragedy, the centripetal tendency, however, clearly resides within Henchard himself. The force that impels him to make of his own ego the controlling center of the circle of his small universe, whether in business or in love, is his own character. If there is a necessary law in Hardy's universe, it is that he who seeks the vortex of life in an effort to control its "contrarious inconsistencies" by imposing his own will upon its random developments precipitates tragedy upon himself.

That Henchard is aware of this law is clearly evident in his conception of fate, or that power which is supposedly beyond man's control. Whenever Henchard speaks of fate or destiny, it is always tentatively and without real conviction. When he learns that Elizabeth-Jane is not his daughter, Henchard's first reaction is to regard this crushing fact as "the scheme of some sinister intelligence bent on punishing him." It is Henchard's fetishistic nature, however, which really disposes him to interpret the concatenation of events leading up to this knowledge as the workings of some malign power. And yet, he quickly recognizes and then disregards the superstitious element in his character once he understands that his own impulsiveness and disregard of Susan's injunction not to open the fateful letter regarding Elizabeth-Jane's identity precipitates the crushing revelation.

Similarly when Henchard, late in the novel, alienates himself from Farfrae by challenging the new mayor to a life and death struggle in the loft of Farfrae's barn and considers suicide as the only escape from his isolation, he is turned back from his resolve of plunging into the dangerous stream of Ten Hatches by the sudden appearance of his own effigy. "The sense of the supernatural was strong in this unhappy man," Hardy comments, "and he turned away as one might have done in the actual presence of an appalling miracle." Meeting Elizabeth-Jane shortly thereafter and inquiring of her whether miracles are possible, he learns from her that she does not believe in their possibility in modern times. Rhetorically, Henchard asks, "No interference in the case of desperate intentions, for instance?" In reply to his question, he answers, "Well, perhaps not, in a direct way." But Henchard's impulsiveness in this matter is sustained by the spectacular character of his recall back from death. And as the father leaves his "daughter," Elizabeth-Jane overhears Henchard say, "Who is such a reprobate as I! And yet it seems that even I be in Somebody's hand!"

Not only is this highly emotional and superstitious conviction temporary, as we see the notion of a controlling destiny quickly die out in Henchard's breast, it is also a superficial rather than an essential belief of the man. The tendency of Henchard to explain seemingly miraculous or disastrous situations by relying upon some supernatural force is simply one more evidence of the incongruity in the man, of the tendency for conduct to outrun knowledge. Once knowledge balances impulsion, once Henchard seriously meditates on his particular situation, the real attitude of his mind on the matter of supernatural power becomes evident. "His usual habit was not to consider whether destiny were hard upon him or not—the shape of his ideas in cases of affliction being simply a moody 'I am to suffer, I perceive'." When he suffers bankruptcy as the result of miscalculation and adverse weather, Henchard's response to his situation is the same. Hardy remarks that "The movement of his mind seemed to tend to the thought that some power was working against him." The important qualification here is the word "seemed." The reality of the situation, the real *perception* is not that some power beyond man's control (to whom man is responsible once he engages in "moral" acts) is accountable for the tragedy of life, but that man is, and more specifically, that existence itself is. When the I, free of impulsiveness and possessed of judgment, looks objectively at existence, there dawns only one realization: "I am to suffer."

It is interesting to note Hardy's description of Henchard at those moments when he is least possessed of such judgment and, for that matter, when he is most possessed of it. Having fallen out with Farfrae and determined to defeat the young Scot economically by monopolizing the market, and emotionally by denying him access to Elizabeth-Jane, Henchard is symbolically described as a blind man. According to Hardy, Henchard "might not inaptly be described as Faust has been described—as a vehement gloomy being who had quitted the ways of vulgar men without light to guide him on a better way." In one respect this is a curious analogue to use in describing Henchard, for he is not at all like Faust in the sense that in Goethe's character knowledge or wisdom outstrip the emotions and in Henchard the emotions outstrip wisdom or judgment. In either case, however, there results that incongruity which is so fatal to the finality both men seek. With Faust, as with Henchard ready to plunge into Blackmore, finality in a universe characterized by absurdity is attainable only in suicide. There is no light, it appears, to illumine the universe for a man whose response to the pervasive incongruity of existence is "defiant endurance of it." Here again impulsiveness ultimately outstrips wisdom for Henchard and for Faust in the early parts of both stories, for both men allow defiance to blind them to the reality of their situations. The light of the rising sun on Easter morning provides Faust with the perspective which, if only momentarily, reconciles him again to life. But not so with Henchard: there is no saving grace, no resurrected divinity to guide him, save his own tragic self. And this appears to be sufficient, for at the close of the novel, Hardy comments that "Externally there was nothing to hinder his making another start on the upward slope, and by his new *lights* achieving higher things" (italics mine).

Henchard's realization that his tragedy has provided him with "new lights," however, is qualified by Hardy; quite typically, the narrator remarks, as he does in so many of his other works (*Tess of the d'Urbervilles* and *Jude the Obscure* for example), that wisdom to begin anew has come too late. The manner in which Hardy registers this recognition is unusual because of the ambiguity or ambivalence characterizing the causal relationship involved between this failure to do and the reason(s) for it. "But the ingenious machinery contrived by the Gods for reducing human possibilities of amelioration to a minimum," Hardy adds after Henchard's realization of his "new lights," "—which arranges that wisdom to do shall come *pari passu* with the departure of zest for doing—stood in the way of all that. He had no wish to make an arena a second time of a world that had become a mere painted scene to him." What is the reason or cause of Henchard's inability or refusal to begin anew? Is it the gods who contrive events so that a second chance is not granted to an individual who has fumbled in his first effort at life? Or is it Henchard's perception of the world as "a mere painted scene"? The causes here appear to be distinct if not mutually exclusive. To believe that the gods have arranged for the incongruity in Henchard now between wisdom and zest for doing is to maintain that there does exist a law beyond man's control which determines guilt and punishment. But more significantly, such an understanding of his situation radically undermines the importance of Henchard's *perception* that he is ultimately responsible for viewing the world as a dumb show. In other words, the recognition of supernatural intervention undercuts human determination: the vision of the world's insignificance is a consequence of the peculiar workings of the ingenious machinery of the gods. To interpose between the power of making another start and the exercise or actual fulfillment of that power the insuperable objection of the gods is to argue that the insubstantiality of life, the illusory character of the world as an arena of achievement, is the result of some sinister intelligence.

In Hardy's universe, as detailed in the *Mayor,* nothing is further from the truth. What is insubstantial for Henchard by the close of the novel is the ingenious machinery of the gods, and the only substantial reality in a world of "contrarious inconsistencies" is human perception, the "I perceive." As Henchard is about to slip away silently from the festivities of Elizabeth-Jane's wedding, Hardy describes the outcast's movements: "He rose to his feet, and stood like a dark ruin, obscured by 'the

shade from his own soul upthrown'." The quotation Hardy introduces here to describe the ruined Mayor is from Shelley's *The Revolt of Islam,* in which the heroine is explaining her conception of the divinity to her captors. According to Shelley in the poem divinity is nothing more than "the shade from [man's] soul upthrown." The statement is consistent, of course, with another quotation introduced earlier in the novel from Novalis. "Character is Fate," Hardy concurs with the German writer. The implication of these two quotations is the admission of a supernatural force beyond man's control as nothing more than a figment of man's imagination, generated in that moment when impulse or emotion outstrip thought. More positively, the result is that the divinity is regarded as a manifestation of the individual's own identity, of his perception. Consequently, it is not the malicious machinations of forces extraneous to man that are responsible for tragedy and the consequent recognition of the world as a painted scene, but man himself.

The peculiar optics of the novel which explains tragedy and ultimately guilt as a myopia or blindness whereby the world's incongruity is inaccurately regarded as being intelligible through the imposition of the individual's will or vision of things also explains the success of those individuals in Hardy's world who escape tragedy and guilt. "To learn to take the universe seriously," Hardy remarks in discussing the vigil of Elizabeth-Jane at Susan's death-bed, "there is no quicker way than to watch—to be a 'waker,' as the country people call it." What is remarkable about the perception of a "waker" like Elizabeth-Jane is that she regards the world as a mere painted scene in which all objects in existence testify to the insubstantiality of life by virtue of their pervasive efforts to escape "terrestrial constraint." Henchard's recognition of the arena of life as nothing more than a prop motivates his own symbolic departure from terrestrial constraint at the end of the novel when he leaves Casterbridge and all he once possessed. Henchard's real tragedy, and in a very real sense his crime, results from his misconception of the arena of life as an area of activity and involvement instead of a mere painted scene. Instead of being the waker, he plays the role of an active participant in life. Elizabeth-Jane, on the other hand, "was awake, yet she was asleep." Her approach to existence, her perception of it, resembles that of a waker's, and more accurately that of a catatonic individual who recognizes simultaneously her own imprisonment by "terrestrial constraint" and the inadequacy of any human act to release her prematurely from such constraint. Instead of wanton defiance of such a condition, as Henchard exhibits in his actions, Elizabeth-Jane has learned to live "the lesson of renunciation."

Elizabeth-Jane's renunciatory philosophy, however, owes nothing to a particular ethical or religious frame of reference; rather it is dependent upon her perception of life as "a tragical rather than a comical thing." And the tragedy of life for Elizabeth-Jane is not, as it is for Henchard in his moment of impulse and emotion, the result of some sinister intelligence bent on destroying him but the corollary of the pervasive incongruity of life in general. The empirical basis of Elizabeth-Jane's renunciatory philosophy derives from her recognition that "what she had desired had not been granted her, and what had been granted her she had not desired." Her life, in short, "had consisted less in a series of disappointments than in a series of substitutions." Fortunately for Elizabeth-Jane, she had learned this philosophy early. Henchard, on the other hand, learns it too late. Bankrupt, Henchard comments in words reminiscent of Elizabeth-Jane's that "the bitter thing is, that when I was rich I didn't need what I could have, and now I be poor I can't have what I need.'' Completely alienated at the end of the novel, Henchard stands overlooking Casterbridge and in surveying mankind remarks an even more terrifying incongruity when he says, ''Here and everywhere be folk dying before their time like frosted leaves, though wanted by their families, the country, and the world; while I, an outcast, an encumberer of the ground, wanted by nobody, and despised by all, live on against my will.''

Henchard's comment here is crucial for a number of reasons, but primarily as indicative of the ''modern'' as opposed to the traditional basis of tragedy. It is crucial too, particularly as it is further developed in *Tess* and especially in *Jude,* in understanding how tragedy is the peculiar characteristic of life as Elizabeth-Jane views it. ''I suffer, I perceive'' is as accurate a statement of man's general condition in Hardy's world as it is of Henchard's plight. And the most painful thing that man can suffer is the incongruity between the consciousness of his own existence and the realization that he must live on against his will. In the last analysis, Henchard's tragedy, and ultimately his punishment, must be understood in light of this incongruity made even more acute by virtue of the man's repeated failures in life. It is almost as though Henchard had achieved a kind of immortality as the result of his impulsive and frustrating existence: he cannot die, at least not willingly. And this is his punishment. And this he deserves: ''I—Cain—go alone as I deserve—an outcast and a vagabond. But my punishment is *not* greater than I can bear.'' That punishment is, of course, life against one's will. Henchard would have his life end as quickly as possible in both the present and in the future, as his will dictates: he would have his memory completely blotted out from the record of mankind's history. But unfortunately this cannot be accomplished. The sense of guilt, of some controlling agency beyond man's comprehension which determines the duration of that punishment, all of these things give the reader and in a sense Henchard too the impression that an ethical standard does in fact exist over which man has no control.

The impression that continued life is a punishment for an offense against some superhuman agency is negated, however, by Elizabeth-Jane's feeling in this matter which closely parallels Henchard's. Elizabeth-Jane never implicates herself in life. And yet she asks, almost in the same vein that Henchard does at the end of the novel, ''why she was born.'' Sitting in the churchyard, she says aloud to herself, and to Lucetta who appears unnoticed on the scene, ''Oh, I wish I was dead with dear mother!'' The striking thing about Elizabeth-Jane's remarks is that she has no apparent reason for making them. The motivation which compels the ruined Henchard to repeat such sentiments on several occasions hardly seems appropriate to an understanding of Elizabeth-Jane's admissions. And yet the motives in the two cases are the same, for both Henchard and Elizabeth-Jane recognize life to be tragic because they first of all recognize it as a punishment. Henchard's ''crime'' of selling his wife and alienating all those he comes in contact with is ultimately insignificant in light of the far greater crime of having been born, of being imprisoned by ''terrestrial constraints'' against one's will. To come into existence is to begin to perceive. To perceive is to suffer. And the only way to cease suffering is not to perceive, not to be. There is nothing religious or ethical about this maddening syndrome. There is no evidence to conclude that the punishment of existence is consciously being levied by some sinister intelligence bent on destroying us. And if this is so, there can be no other evidence except our perception for the recognition of a certain act as being criminal or not. That life is destructive, that it is synonymous with suffering requires no moral foundation for its validity. It simply *is* that way.

The notion of life as destructive, the belief that existence is tragical not because of some moral basis but simply because it is perceived as such, is nowhere more convincingly demonstrated than in the theory of society illustrated by Casterbridge. It is incorrect to state that in accepting as one of its members a man who has committed a crime which has yet been unpunished, Casterbridge implicates itself in Henchard's wrong and thus brings upon itself the wrath of the sinister intelligence; that until Henchard is punished, Casterbridge will not be released from the decay which is so prevalent in the city isolated from industrialized society of the nineteenth century. Casterbridge has implicated itself in a ''crime'' long before Henchard ever arrives on the scene. And when Farfrae arrives, singing with pride of his fatherland, he is told by Christopher Coney that ''When you take away from among us the fools and the rogues, and the lammigers, and the wanton hussies, and the slatterns, and such like, there's cust few left to ornament a song with in Casterbridge, or the country round.'' What is said of Weydon-Priors literally at the beginning of the novel is figuratively true of Casterbridge: ''Pulling down is more the nater of Weydon.''

Historically, the most significant fact about Casterbridge is its first act of pulling down as it were, of rebellion against the Romans. ''Casterbridge is a old, hoary place o' wickedness, by all account,'' Buzzford tells Farfrae. '''Tis recorded in history that we rebelled against the King one or two hundred years ago, in the time of the Romans, and that lots of us was hanged on Gallows Hill, and quartered. . . .'' The act of rebellion seems to have had long-lasting consequences, to the point of determining the very fiber and character of the inhabitants. For as Coney adds, ''we be bruckle folk here—the best o' us hardly honest sometimes. . . . We don't think about flowers and fair faces, not we—except in the shape o' cauliflowers and pigs' chaps.'' Such descriptions of the past define the place as a lawless society. Having repudiated the Roman domination of the past, Coney's ancestors repudiate the laws which structure society. And as living testimony to the act which ushered in the reign of lawlessness stands the Roman amphitheater, which represents not so much the affirmation of Roman order as its denial even in the present. ''Apart from the sanguinary nature of the games originally played therein, such incidents attached to its past as these: that for scores of years the town-gallows had stood at one corner; that in 1705 a woman who had murdered her husband was half-strangled and then burnt there in the presence of ten thousand spectators. . . . In addition to these old tragedies, pugilistic encounters almost to the death had come off down to recent dates in that secluded arena.'' As the stage for public punishment, the Coliseum symbolizes not justice and lawful restitution but rather a brutal means of satisfaction as criminal as the acts of those prosecuted there. It is as though the ten thousand spectators of the wife's cruel execution implicated themselves willingly in a crime far more heinous than the killing of a man. But if there is a negative criminality about the amphitheater in this respect, there is also a positive aspect, for ''crimes might be perpetrated there unseen at mid-day.'' The Coliseum, thus, formerly representative of the Roman rule, is now symbolic of the new reign of lawlessness which allows crime to go unpunished if *unseen.*

This qualification is most important, for it is not until an individual's act is seen, literally or metaphorically, that he is punished, not by some superhuman power beyond man's control, but by the bruckle, dishonest society of Casterbridge that is intent upon pulling down what is exalted at the first opportunity. When, for instance, Lucetta's affair with Henchard becomes known at the Peter's Finger, the inhabitants of Mixen Lane determine upon the skimmity ride as a form of derisive punishment. Nance Mockridge's statement in this regard is characteristic of the thinking of a great deal of Casterbridgeans. Observing Lucetta, distinguished from the rest of the crowd by her finery on the day of the royal visitor's arrival, Nance tells Buzzford, ''I'd like to see the trimming pulled off such Christmas candles. I am quite unequal to the part of the villain myself, or I'd give all my silver to see the lady toppered. . . . And perhaps I shall soon.'' The problem with distinguishing oneself in Casterbridge, as Henchard does by his fancy clothes and as Elizabeth-Jane refuses to do in contrast, is that so many citizens are really equal to the villainy that Nance eventually engages in. Lawlessness prevails to such an extent that the police of the town, responsive to numbers, capitulate in the face of crime and conceal the very symbols of their office. It is not some violation of ethical or even social values which inspires Casterbridgeans to punish those who call attention to themselves but the basest of all passions or motives, vindictiveness, jealousy: ''The tempting prospect of putting to the blush people who stand at the head of affairs—that supreme and piquant enjoyment of those who writhe under the heel of the same—had alone animated them,'' Henchard thinks of the Casterbridgean rationale for the skimmity ride. The same rebelliousness which motivated the ancient people of Casterbridge to level all distinctions between themselves and their Roman masters through repudiation of Roman authority impels the people of Casterbridge in Henchard's time to resort to the same peculiar democratizing process. Equality before the law gives way to equality in degradation. There is no law, no moral or supernatural values to distinguish the criminal from the just man. In Casterbridge, in life ultimately, all men are criminals because they exist and perceive. Those who exalt themselves to a position where they are seemingly exempted from this burden are quickly brought back to the reality of life's criminal aspect by the rebellious spirit of society which just as easily levels the superiority of a powerful master like the Roman Empire as it does the superiority of a Henchard or a Lucetta.

The civil lawlessness of Casterbridge, however, is equaled only by its moral or religious lawlessness. In fact, the former aspect of the community is the most damning of all denials of the notion of some superhuman agency controlling the destiny of Casterbridge and its inhabitants. The strange transvaluation of values implicit in Hardy's description of a tavern as ''the church of Mixen Lane'' testifies to the general repudiation of any and all higher ethical values here. And so too does the furmity woman's crime. Stubberd reports to Henchard, the acting justice at the moment, that ''An old flagrant female'' had been apprehended ''swearing and committing a nuisance in a horrible profane manner against the church-wall, sir, as if 'twere no more than a pot-house.'' Stubberd's reference to the pot-house is indeed significant as indicating the corruption of the sacred into the profane. The church becomes the pot-house and the tavern becomes the church in the rebellious society of Casterbridge. It is interesting to note that the woman's offense is quickly forgotten in the excitement generated by her revelation of Henchard's crime. Standing before Henchard awaiting her judgment and sentence, the furmity woman questions Henchard's right to sit in judgment of her. ''He's no better than I,'' she tells the second magistrate, ''and has no right to sit there in judgment upon me.'' The furmity woman's observation

testifies to the pervasive confusion of values in Casterbridge between the civil or social norms and the religious or moral ones. It might be said that the equation of the one with the other is not merely a profanation of the spiritual norms but ultimately a denial of them. Just as the amphitheater stands as living proof of the rebelliousness of Casterbridge society to civil authority (of the community's repudiation of it, in fact), so too does the Franciscan priory stand as testimony of the city's denial of religious values. The notion of a superhuman power controlling man's destiny is a dead idea to Casterbridgeans who maintain the concept of a divinity only in their fetishistic moods, in those moments when emotion outruns knowledge. Religious values are no longer viable in this community; instead of life, the Church produces the means of death. ''Here were the ruins of a Franciscan priory, and a mill attached to the same, the water of which roared down a back-hatch like the voice of desolation.'' It is interesting to note that the waters here described as almost originating from the monastery are the very waters that Henchard contemplates as the means of ending his life; the very waters, it should be noted, where many before Henchard's time prematurely ended their lives. If ''In a block of cottages up an alley [in Mixen Lane] there might have been erected an altar to disease,'' the waters of the priory might be reconsecrated as the river of death not only for those actually taking their own lives but for all men who, with Elizabeth-Jane, wish they were dead. Just as there is no consolation for despairing man in the Church, there is no law to make intelligible the ''contrarious inconsistencies'' of existence or the criminal punishment of death all men suffer under the moment they begin to live, to perceive.

To argue that the *Mayor* is a ''remarkable anachronism'' satisfying the traditional norms of tragedy because it recognizes a moral law according to which man must regulate his actions, is to misread the peculiarly modern and heterodox character of the novel. For on so many significant levels—social, scientific, religious, and moral—the work represents the rebelliousness of man against all that is traditional. That man in his rebellion is at times seemingly ''punished'' by powers beyond his control is, in the novel, attributable either to superstition or to the natural concatenation of events. ''Henchard,'' as Hardy at one point comments in clear denial of the traditionalist position, ''like all his kind, was superstitious, and he could not help thinking that the concatenation of events . . . was the scheme of some sinister intelligence bent on punishing him. Yet they had developed naturally.'' It would be far more accurate to state that in Hardy's world, as it is developed in the tragic novels, there is no punishment, only crime, if only the primal crime of being born. The social rebellion of Casterbridge against the Romans, the scientific recognition of nature's ''contrarious inconsistencies,'' the religious repudiation of man represented by the ruined condition of the Church, and the realization of traditional ethical values as a superstitious figment, all of these facts argue not that Casterbridge and a man like Henchard deserve to be punished for some crime but rather that man suffers the moment he begins to perceive that no intelligible law exists which explains why he must suffer.

The real greatness of Henchard as a tragic figure is not that he recognizes in the end that the universe is ordered and just, that his suffering is deserved; it is rather that he has accepted his lot as something almost entirely of his own making and in part of the very essence of life. Unfortunately, he has recognized this too late. This in no way detracts from the stature of the man, however, nor does the fact that Elizabeth-Jane appears always to have recognized life as ineluctably tragic detract from her role as "heroine" of the novel. The means both characters employ in achieving similar insights are different; that Henchard is active to the point of impulsiveness, that Elizabeth-Jane is negative and resigned to the point of superhuman asceticism only reinforces what is so significant for Hardy in a world suffering from the dislocation consequent upon the loss of traditional values. The perception, in the final analysis, in other words, is all. And that perception, that vision which it is imperative to possess in a world condemned to unintelligible death, is most lucidly defined in the closing moments of the novel. The secret of life consisted, as Elizabeth-Jane had learned, in "making limited opportunities endurable." If happiness was unexpectedly afforded man, it was simply to be regarded not as a blessing from some superhuman power pleased with the actions of man but rather as "the occasional episode in a general drama of pain." (pp. 592-606)

> Lawrence J. Starzyk, "Hardy's 'Mayor': The Anti-traditional Basis of Tragedy," in Studies in the Novel, Vol. IV, No. 4, Winter, 1972, pp. 592-607.

IAN GREGOR   (essay date 1974)

[*In the following excerpt, Gregor discusses the themes and narrative structure of* The Mayor of Casterbridge.]

> While his eyes were bent on the water beneath there slowly became visible a something floating in the circular pool formed by the wash of centuries; the pool he was intending to make his death-bed. At first it was indistinct by reason of the shadow from the bank; but it emerged thence and took shape, which was that of a human body, lying stiff and stark upon the surface of the stream.
>
> In the circular current imparted by the central flow the form was brought forward, till it passed under his eyes; and then he perceived with a sense of horror that it was *himself*. Not a man somewhat resembling him, but one in all respects his counterpart, his actual double, was floating as if dead in Ten Hatches Hole.

In that memorable moment we find revealed an essential perspective for **The Mayor of Casterbridge.** No longer, as in **The Return of the Native,** is there "a dialogue of the mind with itself" expressed in diverse ways—the Heath, the acts of human desire, the self-conscious meditation on what the age demands—but rather a mute self-recognition, taking place within an individual consciousness fatally divided against itself. It was a shift which Hardy recognised in his Preface to the novel: "The story," he writes, "is more particularly of one man's deeds and character than, perhaps, any other of those included in my Exhibition of Wessex life." "One man's deeds" is a phrase which describes the great achievement—and the limitations—of the novel.

For Hardy, with **The Return of the Native** behind him, to be able to find in one man his governing interest suggests how richly he felt himself able to register a notion of "character," capable of containing within it all the essential interests so lavishly dispersed in the earlier novel. That is to say, we do not feel, as we move from one novel to the other, any narrowing of scope, any diminution in tragic scale. The title page defines the arena of dramatic interest—**The Life and Death of The Mayor of Casterbridge: A Story of a Man of Character.** In that tension between the public circumstances and the individual response, we have the dynamic of the novel. Continually, we are made aware of both elements operating throughout the novel, so that we cannot think of Henchard apart from his

work, his work apart from the town, the town apart from the age, whether it is the age which "bespoke the art of Rome, concealed dead men of Rome," or the age which finds the town still just beyond the outstretched arm of the railway. But no more can we think of Henchard without hearing "a laugh not encouraging to strangers," without seeing a man "reckon his sacks by chalk strokes . . . measure his ricks by stretching with his arms," without feeling "the blazing regard" he gave to those who won his feelings. If we were to try to characterise the distinctiveness of this 'one man' we might echo Kent's remark to Lear:

> "You have in your countenance that which I would fain call master."
>
> "What's that?"
>
> "Authority."

In describing Henchard in these terms I am thinking more of the decisive imaginative impact he makes on the reader, than of the detail of his own personality. When we reflect on the latter, we are faced with sustained ambivalence. The adjectives crowd in to make their rival claims—egotistic, rash, jealous, generous, self-critical, honourable. And these claims are pressed home with force and precision—there are no half-measures, no truce between them.

If, however, we ponder the force that is "Henchard," we cannot really say that it arises from the interplay, however vigorous, of these various elements. We cannot, in other words, feel that he inhabits Hardy's imagination, and in turn ours, as a complex psychological figure. For Hardy, the imaginative pressure at work in the creation of Henchard is not expressed in individual analysis, but in terms of a series of actions whose effects can be neither determined nor confined. "One man's deeds" in this novel can contain the exploration of a community, not in the sense of its detail, but in the contrast between the solidity of its present and the haunting power of its past.

It is Hardy's ability to find within Henchard a multidimensional perspective which prompts the word "epic" as an appropriate descriptive term. The force that he exerts, the authority with which he speaks, these belong to someone who can be titled, with propriety, "The Mayor of Casterbridge," and in that role he can add a footnote to history, and play a part in a tragedy. But within the Mayor is the hay-trusser, the man who sold his wife at a fair in a drunken stupor, who later deceived a father about the existence of his child so that "scarcely believing the evidence of his senses, (he) rose from his seat amazed at what he had done." For Hardy, then, to explore "the volcanic stuff beneath the rind" in Henchard, is to explore the whole area of conflict which so preoccupied him in **The Return of the Native**: the divisiveness of consciousness within man himself whereby his very energies become directed towards his self-destruction, and the relation of that consciousness to inevitable processes of change, whether these are seen in terms of society or in terms of nature. If we isolate any of these elements, so that we see Henchard as a psychological case study, or a tragic hero, or as the last representative in a changing agrarian order, we fail to do justice to Hardy's conception of character, to the fact that "one man's deeds" can serve as an "Exhibition of Wessex life," "Egdon," "Clym," "Eustacia"—all these elements are present in that confrontation Henchard has with "himself" in Ten Hatches Hole.

That Henchard should permit Hardy this inclusiveness of vision is certainly one of the triumphs of this novel; it is also its limitation. If we say that Henchard drains life out of the other characters, this is not to say that he is the only convincing character in the novel. Elizabeth-Jane, and certainly Farfrae, can be thought of as genuine presences. The way he affects the life of the other characters is in making us feel they are never allowed to live and breathe apart from him. At the level of plot, he systematically dismisses them from his life: Susan, Farfrae, Lucetta, Elizabeth—all are cut off from him as severely as he aims to cut himself off from the human community in the prescriptions of his Will.

In both Elizabeth and Farfrae we sense an intended elaboration of character which we can only observe through a glass darkly. Elizabeth's pursuit of learning is perfunctorily presented, her books become stage properties, her reunion with her father is hurriedly dismissed. Farfrae in his relationship with Henchard is skilfully presented; in his relationship with Lucetta and Elizabeth, he hardly exists. If it comes as a shock to read his reflection on Lucetta's death, "it was hard to believe that life with her would have been productive of further happiness," it is not so much because of its crude insensitivity, as because we realise that Farfrae's relationship with her has hardly been created for us at all. Newson only lives as a simple device of the plot, because for Henchard that is all he is. Susan's case is a particularly revealing one, as R. B. Heilman has pointed out in a shrewd essay on the novel [see 1962 Heilman entry in Additional Bibliography]. Heilman traces out her "career," that of one continuously presented as meek and barely competent; he concludes: "Hardy might well have told us about Susan's energy, spirit, inventiveness, native shrewdness amounting at times to foxiness, strategic sense and managerial skill little short of brilliant, and pointed out that she was one of the few women who get what they want." If Susan does not quite strike us in that way, Heilman's account makes us sharply aware how much we have become influenced by Henchard's reaction to her and how, indeed, he seems to have persuaded Hardy to connive in his account too. What all these incidents have in common is that all these characters draw their dramatic life directly from Henchard, and that once they become involved in scenes which do not concern him in any direct way, then they would seem to forfeit not only Henchard's interest but Hardy's also. It is wryly amusing to see that Henchard's power is such that it appears to cut the author off too, so that his occasional *obiter dicta* seem to italicise themselves awkwardly, and remain rather sour asides having little to do with the actual drama that is taking place.

It is, of course, the dominance of Henchard that causes Hardy to get into a great deal of trouble with his plotting in this novel; in order to keep it moving, he has to have recourse to letters which are not properly sealed, parcels which are badly packed, and conversations which are overheard. These always remain devices and have none of the resonance that so often accompanies Hardy's plotting. Hardy himself was very conscious of this defect in *The Mayor* and remarked that "it was a story which he had damaged more recklessly as an artistic whole . . . than perhaps any of his other novels." He attributes the damage to serial pressures, which had led him into over-plotting. This may have been the effect upon him, but the cause lay in the conception of a novel centred on "one man's deeds," which required leisurely development, careful distribution of interest, and a plot stripped of superfluous incident. (pp. 113-17)

The function of the opening two chapters [of *The Mayor of Casterbridge*] is to initiate the action and to serve as an overture to the novel as a whole. Their subject matter is the arrival of Henchard with his wife at the Fair in Weydon-Priors; the selling of Susan to the sailor in a mood of drunken frustration; Henchard's recognition, the following day, of the terrible deed he has done; his solemn vow never to touch alcohol for twenty-one years, "being a year for every year I have lived"; and his setting off alone to Casterbridge to look for work and to begin a new life.

> One evening of late summer, before the nineteenth century had reached one-third of its span, a young man and woman, the latter carrying a child, were approaching the large village of Weydon-Priors, in Upper Wessex, on foot. They were plainly but not ill clad, though the thick hoar of dust which had accumulated on their shoes and garments from an obviously long journey lent a disadvantageous shabbiness to their appearance just now.

The novel opens in these classical cadences of "once upon a time." At the centre, taking the attention, is Henchard, at first sour and indifferent, then made quarrelsome and pugnacious by drink, then bewildered but finally determined in his remorse. It is a kaleidoscope of moods all being lived out at the nerve's end, and fuelling them all, there is a deep and diffused sense of self-estrangement. Self-enclosed, his wife appears "to walk the highway alone, save for the child she bore." About the family there is an "atmosphere of stale familiarity," and in Nature too, life has faded, the leaves are "doomed" and "blackened green," the "grassy margins of the bank" are "powdered by dust." The mood is suggestive of that described by Donne in "The Nocturnall upon St. Lucie's Day":

> The world's whole sap is sunke:
> The generall balm the hydroptique earth hath drunk,
> Whither, as to the bed's-feet, life is shrunke.

That is the general mood of these opening pages; Henchard's particular mood is more difficult to define. We feel in it bafflement, frustration, a sense that life has possibilities which have been denied him. It is interesting that the very first words which are spoken in the novel, the first gesture towards self-fulfilment, takes the form of the question "Any trade doing here?" It is the sense of the centrality of work in finding fulfilment that is such a major preoccupation of this novel.

As soon as we put it that way we can see what a rare novel *The Mayor of Casterbridge* is in the history of English fiction, where the model of self-fulfilment is found, invariably, in personal relationships. If we think of Lawrence, a novelist who comes very close to Hardy in many ways, and think of the self-estrangement of Tom Brangwen and the self-estrangement of Henchard, the rarity of Hardy's position becomes plain. *The Mayor* is an intensely public novel in its drive; how public can be gauged from the fact that it must be one of the very few major novels—or for that matter, very few novels—where sexual relationships are not, in one way or another, the dominant element. That Hardy can write a novel which engages his full imaginative range without making us feel the relative absence of such relationships, suggests that it is not the individual human heart which beats at the centre of his fictional world.

The marriage that is broken at Weydon-Priors is not, so far as Hardy is concerned, an individual affair. In these opening chapters we move steadily away from the individual—we are never, at any point, taken "inside" Henchard—to the world in which he is finding it difficult to make a living, the world of houses being pulled down and people having nowhere to go. There is the voice of the auctioneer selling off the last of the horses and gradually insinuating into Henchard's mind a wish to start again, to shake himself free from all encumbrance, to sell his wife. Susan is sold at a strange dream-like auction in which there are no bidders, but the price goes up and up. I think it is possible to make too much of the particulars of this vivid and bizarre scene, so that the whole emphasis falls on the act of selling itself, the reduction of a person to a commodity. But Hardy's interests are not those, say, of James in *The Spoils of Poynton*. His eye is not so much on money, as on the notion of "freedom" it appears to offer, and which Henchard is so intent on grasping, "if I were a free man again I'd be worth a thousand pound before I'd done o't." That is the sentence which catches the undercurrent of meditation that runs persistently through the chapter, the keenly felt "if I were." It is that sentiment which is present in the visitation of the late swallow finding its way into the tent, like the men who watch it, "absently," a migrant, but unlike them free in a way they can never be. This meditative note is struck most firmly at the end of the chapter when we are taken outside the tent, and the sight of the horses "crossing their necks and rubbing each other lovingly" is set in contrast to the harsh act of humanity we have just witnessed. But, immediately, that note is played in a different key: we are asked to reflect on the occasions when humanity sleeps innocently while inanimate nature rages round him. And there at the end of the paragraph we find an unobtrusive phrase which gives us bearings on the whole scene—"all terrestrial conditions were intermittent." In other words those who seek to impress themselves on the universe, to lay violent hands on time, to forget that man is the slave of limit—such men can only succeed in destroying themselves. They will be extinguished as surely as the last candle is, when the furmity seller goes out to leave Henchard alone in the tent sunk in a drunken sleep.

But for Hardy flux is always followed by reflux, an essential element in his narrative compulsion, no less than in his metaphysical outlook. Chapter 1 then tells for Hardy precisely half of the human story; Chapter 2 reverses the emphasis and, in so doing, tells the other half.

Henchard is again at the centre, Henchard now waking to find "the morning sun" streaming through the crevices. Outside, "the freshness of the September morning inspired and braced him as he stood." He can see far across the valleys "dotted with barrows, and trenched with . . . prehistoric forts." *This* is a world upon which man has impressed himself, so that "The whole scene lay under the rays of a newly risen sun, which had not as yet dried a single blade of the heavily dewed grass." The voice of the weak bird of the previous night singing "a trite old evening song" gives way to "the yellowhammers which flitted about the hedges with straws in their bills." This vitality and purposiveness encompasses Henchard too.

The previous night he sought to set aside time, to disown his past; now he will bind himself to time, more, he will mortgage his future. He gave himself away in a drunken stupor in a furmity tent, now in re-collecting himself he swears his great vow on the clamped book which lies on the Communion table in a nearby village church. Instinctively, he seeks a ritual gesture, "a fit place and imagery," which will release him from the thraldom of the moment. "He shouldered his basket and moved on"—that is the driving sentiment of this second chapter. Purposeful and resilient, Henchard has now a full consciousness of his position. He tries, without success, to find his wife and family and then, learning of their emigration, "he said he would search no longer. . . . Next day he started, journeying southwestward, and did not pause, except for nights' lodgings, till he reached the town of Casterbridge, in a far distant part of Wessex." In that closing sentence of the chapter we hear the classical cadences of the archetypal story, present in the opening paragraph, announce themselves again. And it is to be there, in Casterbridge, that the complementary tensions so explicitly set up in these two opening chapters will be developed and pursued.

"A series of seemings"—the opening of *The Mayor of Casterbridge* reveals, in a remarkably pure way, the characteristic Hardy stance towards experience. Within each chapter a set of reverberations is released from a single violent act—the sale of the wife, Henchard's vow. A perspective on the human deed is established. The act of an individual person cannot be contained by that individual life; it leads persistently outwards to the whole social context, a context both personal and social, as the full title of the novel we are considering makes plain: *The Life and Death of the Mayor of Casterbridge.* The "seemings" are here, but in themselves they don't constitute the shape of a life. They are true to consciousness heightened in moments of vision; they fail to do justice to consciousness as continually present, continually altering. It is here that "series" has its part to play, with its emphasis on process and continuity.

In the aesthetic structure of a Hardy novel the tension between the terms is expressed in the dynamic interplay between plot and image, and encompassing both is the compassionate presence of the narrator, whose mediating consciousness is an integral part of the drama he is concerned to reveal. In the very elements which go to make up his fiction—the narrative trajectory, the sudden moment of symbolic concentration, the oscillations between story and commentary—in all of these elements, Hardy is acting out his own impression of life as a series of seemings, and the novelist's art is here not simply to reveal but to enact it. In particular terms, this is communicated most frequently in that air of ambivalence which hangs over so many incidents in the novel, an ambivalence which creates in the reader not so much an awareness of complexity as a desire to suspend judgement and to sense a more inclusive view.

It is an air which is strongly present in the presentation of Casterbridge itself. Our first glimpse of the town is in lamplight "through the engirdling trees, conveying a sense of great snugness and comfort inside. But to the eyes of the travelled, if inexperienced, Elizabeth-Jane it already seems "an old-fashioned place." Hardy holds a delicate balance in his initial presentation of Casterbridge between the warm nostalgia prompted by his boyhood memories of Dorchester in the 1840s and the reflections of an adult already aware of its remoteness, its inability to adapt itself to a changing world. "Country and town met at a mathematical line"—it is like a child's drawing, and like such a drawing exhibits its own charm, its own falsity. The town's band may be shaking the windows with "The Roast Beef of Old England," Henchard may be re-introduced to us through his laughter, but outside in the streets, the newly arrived wayfarers hear that he has over-reached himself: he has sold "blown wheat," and there has never been such "unprincipled bread in Casterbridge before." The adjective does more than catch the vivacity of dialect, it casts a sardonic eye on one aspect at least of the Mayor's rise to prosperity. To the wayfarers, Casterbridge offers "a sense of great snugness and comfort," but to Buzzford, the local dealer, it is "a old hoary place o' wickedness."

From the outset of the novel the reader is made quietly aware of ambivalence, and aware of it as arising from "the way things are'' rather than through the artifice of the novelist. Consider the relatively unobtrusive, but significant, play which is made of Farfrae's songs of home. The tone is lightly ironical at the expense of a man who looks back fondly on a country he has certainly no wish to return to; but at the same time, his sentiments are expressed in song, indicative of his resilience, his desire to travel, the ease he feels in company, and the unfeigned pleasure he gives to others. As the rivalry between Farfrae and Henchard builds up, we feel the same duality of feeling present, so that when Abel Whittle is reprimanded for his lateness at work, we feel Henchard's treatment is concerned, but humiliating, Farfrae's impersonal but just. In the rival entertainments they set up for the town, Henchard is bountiful but patronising, Farfrae cannily prudent, but infectiously ingenious.

The oscillation of sympathy is not confined to the main action. It is present in that fine town-pump chat which followed the death of Susan Henchard. ''She was as white as marble-stone,'' says Mrs. Cuxom with evident relish, as she proceeds to relay the details of Susan's preparations for her burial. ''Ah, poor heart!''—and a general sigh goes up. Then suddenly the tone changes from elegy to indignation. Christopher Coney has removed the pennies from the dead woman's eyes and spent them at The Three Mariners. '''Faith,' he said, 'why should death rob life o' fourpence . . . money is scarce and throats get dry.''' Beneath the humour a genuine point is being made. Just as

Hardy's sketch of the inn that served as the model for the inn described in The Mayor of Casterbridge.

suddenly the tone shifts back again, not to the gossipy note of concern with which the conversation began, but to an impersonal note of elegy, which both pays tribute to Susan and also recognises the substance in Coney's remark, though without approving his action:

> ''Well, poor soul; she's helpless to hinder that or anything now,'' answered Mother Cuxom. ''And all her shining keys will be took from her, and her cupboards opened; and little things a' didn't wish seen, anybody will see; and her wishes and ways will all be as nothing.''

It is a small incident, existing in the margin of the main action, but like Abel Whittle's speech about the death of Henchard in the last chapter, making the grain of the novel suddenly glow— the cadence may point to the inevitable obliterations of time, but there, in the centre, taking the eye, hard and personal, are Susan's ''shining keys.''

All this indicates something of the distinctive rhythm of the novel; but before looking at the resolutions towards which it moves, I would like to examine a chapter which exists almost at the very centre of the novel. I emphasise the word ''chapter'' here because it is the rhythm established by that aesthetic unit that I wish to draw attention to. It is Chapter 24 and the subject matter is simply told.

Lucetta, now a lady of means, and Elizabeth-Jane are regarding the affairs of the Casterbridge market-place. From Lucetta's window they can observe the varied activity, and one day they see the arrival of a new seed-drill. Going out into the market-place to satisfy their curiosity, they find its arrival due to Farfrae, who is busy examining and displaying it. Hesitantly, the two women meet Henchard, who is also looking at the machine, and there is a sardonic exchange about the latest innovation. Both women are made increasingly conscious of their emotional involvements. Elizabeth, isolated from her father, has a growing sense of Lucetta's fascination with Farfrae. Lucetta admits as much, and the episode closes with an oblique attempt on her part to seek Elizabeth's advice.

Even from such a summary as this it is clear that Hardy, in a sure and economical way, is securing the interpenetration of the public and private themes of the novel and bringing them into sharp focus, almost wittily, in Farfrae's singing his romantic song of exile from inside the new agricultural machine. As he sings about Kitty ''wi' a braw new gown,'' we remember that Lucetta is also wearing a new gown which alone rivalled the machine in colour. New machines, new London fashions: the complementary development is made. Lucetta looking at her gown spread out on the bed chooses ''to be the cherry-coloured person at all hazards'' as surely as Mixen Lane will choose that particular gown to identify her in the skimmity-ride. These are ironies of a now familiar kind, but what ought to take our attention in this chapter is not the oscillation of feeling, but a point of growth, a decisive move forward in the articulation of the novel.

The chapter opens with the phrase ''Poor Elizabeth-Jane,'' and it closes with the sentence ''For by the 'she' of Lucetta's story Elizabeth had not been beguiled.'' The decisive move in this chapter lies not in the scene contemplated from the window or in the market-place, sharp and vivacious as it is, but in Hardy's creation of ''a contemplative eye'' for Elizabeth. He is in the delicate process in this chapter of merging the authorial consciousness of the veiled narrator with that of Elizabeth. Hinted parallels between the artist's eye and Elizabeth's begin to be made. We are told that the market-place offers itself to the

House like a stage for a drama, and when Elizabeth reacts to the new seed-drill it is in a very literary manner. Responding to Farfrae's enthusiasm about its efficiency she says, "Then the romance of the sower is gone . . ." and then, more characteristically, "How things change!" It is worth observing the reactions of Farfrae and Lucetta to this. Farfrae says, "But the machines are already very common in the East and North of England." And Lucetta, whose acquaintance with Scripture is, as Hardy says, "somewhat limited," remarks admiringly and practically, "Is the machine yours?" It is a small exchange, but it neatly conveys a new authorial relationship to "poor Elizabeth-Jane." This, of course, is given a decisive orientation at the end of the chapter when Elizabeth is asked to respond to Lucetta's carefully contrived story of her past. She has no difficulty in interpreting its true meaning. Interpreting, but not condemning, this provides her initiation into sympathetic detachment, beginning paradoxically with her own increasing emotional involvement with Lucetta and with Farfrae. And in that paradox Elizabeth is revealing herself not simply as a companion for Lucetta, but as a companion for Hardy too. In Chapter 24 we have a decisive step in her education: she is to learn the distinction between the fictive world and the real one, Newson's daughter, not Henchard's.

The full importance of Elizabeth's role, which begins to appear in this chapter, becomes quite clear in the final chapters of the novel. Hardy is going to need her "quiet eye" less in the dramatic unfolding of the tale—though she has her small part to play here too—than as a way of enabling us to understand its resolution. It is a resolution which will involve the most dramatic nuancing of "the series of seemings," and which will incorporate the developed consciousness of Elizabeth-Jane as part of its meaning.

The last two chapters stand in the same dramatic relationship to the novel as the first two. The main action is completed and the centre of our attention is Henchard—once more a wayfarer and a hay-trusser. "He could not help thinking of Elizabeth"—that is the dominant mood of the penultimate chapter, everything else takes its bearings from that. But first Henchard must encounter his past again. He returns to the hill at Weydon-Priors where the furmity tent had stood twenty-five years previously, "Here we went in, and here we sat down." With absorbed intentness he recreates the scene of his crime and the authorial voice lends him support: "And thus Henchard found himself again on the precise standing which he had occupied a quarter of a century earlier. Externally there was nothing to hinder his making another start on the upward slope. . . ." But it is too late in the day for that. Haunted by thoughts of Elizabeth in Casterbridge, he hears that arrangements have been made for her wedding to Farfrae, and he resolves to return for the occasion. Delaying his arrival until the festivities are well under way, he makes himself known at the house, after unobtrusively leaving his gift in the garden—a caged goldfinch. It is the first time he has met Elizabeth since she discovered that Henchard had delayed Newson's return to her. Face to face now, he seeks forgiveness, but she rejects him, and without any further defence of his conduct he bids her a final farewell and goes out into the night.

It is interesting to recall that it was this chapter which Hardy decided to omit from the first edition of the novel, fearing that Henchard's return to Elizabeth would weaken the final effect of the tragedy. Hardy was prevailed upon to restore the chapter, and this was done for the 1895 edition. And rightly, because its inclusion gives the emphasis to two essential elements in the conclusion of the novel. The first is the force given to Henchard's isolation from the community, not simply by a kind of muted withdrawal, but by rejection. The second is the creation of a reverse effect. Elizabeth's life with Farfrae is, we must feel assured, to be one of happiness. Whatever happens to Henchard that relationship will prosper in its own quiet way. And so we find the chapter reaching out towards that balance of contraries so characteristic of the novel as a whole. And reaching out in a way that quite naturally will employ the rhetoric which conveys a classical ending to an archetypal story—the marriage and wedding feast on the one hand, the exclusion of the disruptive force on the other.

But Hardy distrusts this kind of finality, this confident distribution of sympathy. And so in his final chapter Hardy is concerned to de-individualise his novel, to distance its themes. There is a moment in the penultimate chapter where we can see the kind of temptation which hovered over the ending, a temptation to go for emotional "bravura." Henchard's wedding gift to Elizabeth, the caged goldfinch, remains an unfocused poignancy—the size of the gesture concealing its imprecision, so that if it is meant as some kind of symbolic expression about Henchard's fate, we remain uneasy as to whether the expression is Henchard's or Hardy's. I draw attention to the goldfinch only to show how sure Hardy's touch is in the remainder of the last chapter, where there is no forced symbolism of any kind, nothing mawkish in a situation where that tone is difficult to resist. And, when we consider that the chapter is written from the vantage point of a worried and remorseful daughter, the achievement becomes all the more remarkable.

It is the discovery of the bird-cage which sets Elizabeth and Farfrae off to look for Henchard. If it is Casterbridge and the wedding feast which set the mood for the preceding chapter, so now, in the last chapter, it is the heath and an isolated hut which "of humble dwellings was surely the humblest." Henchard has returned to a tract of land "whose surface never had been stirred to a finger's depth, save by the scratching of rabbits, since brushed by the feet of the earliest tribes." In this sense everything is to be stripped to essentials, the world which is to be seen by the travellers is a moral landscape as well as a natural one, and we are moved to see, in Wordsworth's phrase, into "the life of things." Characteristically, on this bedrock of human experience, Hardy continues his contraries.

The perspective the Heath offers is one of timeless change, the endless ebb and flow of human existence, stretching back to a limitless past, forward to a limitless future. At the centre, two wayfarers pursue a difficult search. The scene offers itself irresistibly as an image of our terrestrial condition. Then, suddenly, casually, a figure appears, Abel Whittle, whose only role in the novel so far has been to provide the first occasion when Henchard and Farfrae clashed. And now—like Mother Cuxom on the death of Susan—it is this marginal figure who is chosen to express, in one of the most moving passages of the novel, the contrary perspective to that proffered by the Heath. Comparison has sometimes been made between Whittle's role here and that of the Fool in *King Lear*. Like the larger comparison, the smaller is wide of the mark. The Fool proffers "wisdom," a self-conscious commentary on Lear's plight. Whittle offers the purest form of human gesture, the instinctual made sublime by its disinterestedness, "ye wer kind-like to mother if ye were rough to me, and I would fain be kind-like to you." It is "love thy neighbour as thyself," presented with total dramatic simplicity and conviction. It is the felicity of "kind-like" with all its overtures of kinship and kindred, that demands, in Hardy's eyes, no less recognition as part of any terrestrial condition than the humbling perspectives suggested by the Heath. In Henchard's Will we find the confluence of these views. There is the wish for annihilation in death, "that no man remember me"; there is also the unshakable belief in the personal rightness of the testimony, "To this I put my name—Michael Henchard," just as twenty-five years before, "Dropping his head upon the clamped book which lay on the Communion-table, he said aloud—'I, Michael Henchard, . . .'." It is a perspective which resists challenge and remains untouched by irony, Hardy's sense of "a man of character."

For Henchard life has been tragic, but never at any time has it lost dignity and it is this which Elizabeth responds to when she comes finally to mediate this experience for us. The Heath, Abel Whittle—the contraries caught here are too intense for the ebb and flow of ordinary lives. It is "the ordinary" Elizabeth offers. When she responds to Henchard's Will it is not to the prescriptions, but to the knowledge that "the man who wrote them meant what he said . . . (they) were not to be tampered with to give herself a mournful pleasure, or her husband credit for large-heartedness." She disclaims "mournful pleasures," and with Henchard's life now behind her she is given full liberty to reflect. It is a reflection which attempts to render continual justice to the contraries of existence, to the series of seemings, as these make themselves felt in the last, and much misunderstood, sentence of the novel:

> And in being forced to class herself among the fortunate she did not cease to wonder at the persistence of the unforeseen, when the one to whom such unbroken tranquillity had been accorded in the adult stage was she whose youth had seemed to teach that happiness was but the occasional episode in a general drama of pain.

How often the final phrase has been wrenched from its context and made to do duty for a view not only of this novel, but of the general tenor of Hardy's fiction. "The persistence of the unforeseen," it is this phrase which mobilises the paragraph, keeps the contraries open, and is as resistant to a view of life as "a general drama of pain" as it is to one of "unbroken tranquillity." Elizabeth's eye—and Hardy's too—is on the wonder of change here, on flux and reflux, putting her youth beside her "adult stage," not intent on finding in those phases prescriptions for life in general. It is not simply the unseen that keeps us alert to such change, but its *persistence:* it is this which becomes part of the fabric of everyday living. At times, Henchard had tried to separate out the unseen from that fabric and to live by it, and the past and the future devoured his present; at times, Farfrae was so totally absorbed by the fabric that being out on the heath was being "reduced," and staying overnight there a matter of making "a hole in a sovereign." Elizabeth, like Thomasin in *The Return of the Native,* accepts the Heath, and the drama it has witnessed, calmly, and for what it is, neither an implacable force nor a backdrop to man's desires.

If at the end of *The Mayor of Casterbridge* Elizabeth leaves us thinking about the relation of past to present, we are taken back to consider . . . Hardy's sense of man-in-history, and the way in which this is present in *The Mayor of Casterbridge.*

The Preface which Hardy wrote for the 1895 edition reminds us directly of this:

> The incidents narrated arise mainly out of three events, which chanced to range themselves in the order and at or about the intervals of time here given, in the real history of the town called Casterbridge. . . . They were the sale of a wife by her husband, the uncertain harvests which immediately preceded the repeal of the Corn Laws, and the visit of a Royal Personage to the aforesaid part of England.

Of these, the first and third have little literary-critical interest, though as always it is interesting to watch Hardy, particularly in the case of the wife-sale, feel the necessity of validating its inclusion by reference to factual circumstances. He would appear to have come across several instances in the pages of the *Dorset County Chronicle*, which he began to read in 1884 in preparation for his novel. Beginning with the issues of January 1826, he read through the files in a systematic way as far as late 1829 or early 1830. In the course of this reading he discovered no less than three instances of wife-selling, one of the most relevant of which reads:

> *Selling Wife:* At Buckland, nr. Frome, a labring (sic) man named Charles Pearce sold wife to shoemaker named Elton for £5 and delivered her in a halter in the public street. She seemed very willing. Bells rang.

It is an incident which Hardy's love of the factually bizarre would find highly congenial, but it was a remarkable sense of confidence that allowed him to open the novel with this incident, and give it the tragic, as distinct from the merely bizarre, resonance which he needed.

The appearance of the Royal Personage sits very lightly to Hardy's main interests in the novel. It would seem almost certain that the reference was to Prince Albert who passed through Dorchester in July 1849 on his way to Weymouth to lay the foundation stone of Portland Breakwater. The incident obviously provided Hardy with an opportunity for parodying pomp and circumstance, and, more to his interest, for showing the blight that ran throughout Casterbridge, so that the preparations being made in the Council Chamber for the Royal visit occur simultaneously with the preparations being made in Mixen Lane for the skimmity-ride. But this kind of social satire engages Hardy's attention only lightly, and it is difficult not to regard the whole episode as one of those which he felt had been forced upon him by the constant demand made by the serial form for continuous plotting.

The third factor which Hardy draws attention to in his Preface, the repeal of the Corn Laws, is very different in importance. Indeed, it has an importance which has influenced the way the novel, as a whole, has been read. It shapes, for instance, the kind of reading which Douglas Brown offers in his perceptive study of Hardy:

> *The Mayor of Casterbridge,* then, is the tale of the struggle between the native countryman and the alien invader; of the defeat of dull courage and traditional attitudes by insight, craft and the vicissitudes of nature; and of the persistence through that defeat of some deep layer of vitality in the country protagonist. . . . *The Mayor of Casterbridge* turns on the situation that led to the repeal of the Corn Laws. The consequences of that repeal to Victorian agricultural life are the centre of this book, provide the impulse that makes it what it is [see Brown entry in Additional Bibliography].

"The native countryman," "the alien invader"—this is the kind of polarity that a concentration on the phrase "the repeal of the Corn Laws'' can lead to, so that Brown can go on to say that the consequences of the repeal are ''the centre of the book.'' But, as Hardy's Preface makes clear, he is not talking about the repeal of the Corn Laws as such; his emphasis is on ''the uncertain harvests which immediately preceded their repeal,'' and his emphasis will not really encourage a reading of the novel which sees it in terms of a polarising conflict between ''the native countryman'' and ''the alien invader.''

If we look at ''the native countryman'' we find a good deal that is less flattering than ''dull courage''; he is tetchy, grasping, superstitious, and indifferent to any consequences beyond the immediate present. If we look at ''the alien invader'' we find that, so far from invading the community, he actually joins it (a point which Brown concedes in a later account of the novel without, however, feeling that this calls for an overall revision of his general reading), and indeed Farfrae goes on to give it whatever prosperity it can obtain. If we are concerned with the Corn Laws at all directly in this novel then, as J. C. Maxwell has pointed out, Hardy is going out of his way, in his remark about ''the uncertain harvests,'' to indicate that he is choosing ''the *latest* period at which the uncushioned dominance of price fluctuations depending on the home harvest . . . still persisted.'' In other words, far from presenting an innocent agrarian economy undermined by new grasping business methods, Hardy shows in Henchard (if we really want to talk in these terms) the last of the old profiteers, existing by courtesy of a closed system of economic protection. With the repeal of the Corn Laws, the local weather ceased to exert its tyranny on the market, and Farfrae certainly began to prosper by ''canny moderation''; but as Maxwell remarks, it is really Henchard's colleagues who are ''the lineal descendents of Shakespeare's farmer who hanged himself on the expectation of plenty.''

Clearly, it would be absurd to read the novel in such a way as to make it an indictment of Henchard and a vindication of Farfrae. I have put the counter-case simply to show that when concentration is made too directly on the historical implications of the novel, so that we see a precise agricultural crisis constituting its ''centre,'' then the move takes us further and further away from its imaginative life.

The sense in which history is deeply meaningful in *The Mayor of Casterbridge* can be suggested, I think, by looking at a passage which captures with some of the intensity of his lyric poetry a basic apprehension about the passage of time. Elizabeth has been sitting up through the night looking after her mother who is dying:

> the silence in Casterbridge—barring the rare sound of the watchman—was broken in Elizabeth's ear only by the time-piece in the bedroom ticking frantically against the clock on the stairs; ticking harder and harder till it seemed to clang like a gong; and all this while the subtle-souled girl asking herself why she was born, why sitting in a room, and blinking at the candle; why things around her had taken the shape they wore in preference to every other possible shape. Why they stared at her so helplessly, as if waiting for the touch of some wand that should release them from terrestrial constraint; what that chaos called consciousness, which spun in her at this moment like a top, tended to, and began in. Her eyes fell together; she was awake, yet she was asleep.

That is a moment of imaginative distillation in the novel. ''The subtle-souled girl'' has little reality for us; it is rather the author caught reflecting on the nature of the imagination itself. Elizabeth is caught suspended between two levels of reality, so that she becomes the subject and object of her own perceptions. Withdrawing from the particularities of the scene about her, the girl knows a moment of heightened consciousness, but the intensity brings with it its own chaos, and then it subsides into the forgetfulness of sleep. The paragraph links time with consciousness, and that link is built into the very shape the novel takes.

''What is your history?'', the question Lucetta puts to Elizabeth, is a question which Hardy puts to the reader, puts to himself, and puts to his characters. The way in which it is put to the reader is to be found in the opening paragraph of the Preface:

> Readers of the following story who have not yet arrived at middle age are asked to bear in mind that, in the days recalled by the tale, the home Corn Trade, on which so much of the action turns, had an importance that can hardly be realized by those accustomed to the sixpenny loaf of the present date, and to the present indifference of the public to harvest weather.

''The days recalled . . . the present date,'' the whole novel was coloured by that interplay for Hardy's readers and it gave depth to its meaning. With time's lengthening perspective *The Mayor of Casterbridge* takes its place as a Hardy novel of the mid 1880s, but we should remember that for Hardy and his readers this was 'a historical novel' about the 1840s, and more briefly, about the 1820s. We get something of the effect if we imagine ourselves reading in the 1970s a story set in the 1930s, whose opening lies in the years immediately preceding the First World War. It is the layering of time, the years between, that help to create the perspective within which we read, and extend the novelist's meaning. By the 1880s readers really *are* aware of the consequences of the repeal of the Corn Laws, the agricultural depression created by the importation of wheat from across the Atlantic really has affected the domestic market, and Farfrae's career for good or for ill can already be thought of as completed. But this is not a perspective which is sardonic. Hardy's eye, like Elizabeth's at the end of the novel, is on change, on flux and reflux; it is that idea that the dates are there to suggest, rather than any particular events with which they might be associated. Thus, the question ''What is your history?'' has a personal significance, as well as a public one. The author, in recalling the Dorchester of the 1840s, is recalling the period of his own boyhood, and the novel is as much concerned with recapturing the feeling of that period, as it is with charting social and economic change. Hence—we might go on to say—the deliberate blur that Hardy creates over a precise chronological scheme.

Implicit in memory for Hardy is tension, the inevitable tension between past and present; and this applies not only to the reader's experience of the novel and to the author's experience of writing it but also to the characters within it—most noticeably of course, to Henchard. Here again we have a history which is both public and private. It is public in the clash of interests between Henchard and Farfrae, a clash suitably described by the townspeople when they say of Henchard that ''His accounts were like a bramblewood when Mr. Farfrae came. He used to reckon his sacks by chalk strokes all in a row like garden-palings, measure his ricks by stretching with his arms, weigh his trusses by a lift, judge his hay by a chaw, and settle the price with a curse. But now this accomplished young man does it all by ciphering and mensuration.'' That is the notion of change which belongs to the public history of the nineteenth century.

But the notion of history has for Henchard another, more urgent aspect. Henchard is looking at his daughter asleep: "He steadfastly regarded her features. . . . In sleep there come to the surface buried genealogical facts, ancestral curves, dead men's traits, which the mobility of daytime animation screens and overwhelms. . . . He could not endure the sight of her and hastened away." It is the hunger of a father for a child which he wants to claim as his own. Henchard's feeling for Elizabeth moves from that moment of anger when Susan takes her away, "She'd no business to take the maid—'tis my maid," to that moment of renunciation when he leaves her to Farfrae and goes to make his Will. That is a moment which could find suitable expression in lines from Eliot's "Marina," even though the mood which prompts them is very different:

> This form, this face, this life
> Living to live in a world of time beyond me; let me
> Resign my life for this life . . .

This is a longing inseparable from the needs of the human heart and such a coming to terms with change constitutes, for Hardy, a profound wisdom.

As we ponder this sense of a public and a private history we become aware that the particular tension which this novel describes works to keep them distinct from one another. On the one side, there is the element of "work," on the other, the element of "love." What is absent is that sense of interrelatedness presented most clearly in sexual relationships. There is passion in *The Mayor of Casterbridge,* but it is the passion of individual assertion, a passion which finds an appropriate epigraph in the phrase "A Man and his History." (pp. 117-34)

> *Ian Gregor, in his* The Great Web: The Form of Hardy's Major Fiction, *Rowman and Littlefield, 1974, 236 p.*

W. EUGENE DAVIS (essay date 1985)

[*In the following excerpt, Davis explores the ways in which the past, both collective and personal, intrudes into the present in* The Mayor of Casterbridge *to profoundly affect the lives of the characters.*]

In no other novel was Hardy as concerned with Past and Present, that Victorian obsession, as in *The Mayor of Casterbridge.* Not only do most of the novel's major characters have "a past," even Casterbridge has one, as references to ancient customs and the Roman occupation prove. As earlier students of the novel have noted, moreover, the past refuses to stay in its place. As in a typical Victorian ghost story, the restive spirit (the past) must intrude itself into the consciousness of the new proprietors of the mansion (the present) to frighten and to appall (in a word, haunt). As mentioned earlier, however, a critical problem arises: what and how much to make of the impact of the past on the present. In large part the problem can be traced to the narrator, who is so emphatic and explicit as to invite a definite interpretation—but one which may not suit a larger understanding of the novel. One example concerns a group of interrelated symbols: skeletons, the past, and ghosts. In Chapter 20, when Elizabeth-Jane Newson went to visit her mother's grave in the "still-used burial-ground of the old Roman-British city," the narrator observes that "Mrs. Henchard's dust mingled with the dust of women who lay ornamented with glass hair-pins and amber necklaces, and men who held in their mouths coins of Hadrian, Posthumus, and the Constantines." It is as though the reposing bodies of Susan and the Romans belong to the past but, as suggested by the repetition of "dust,"

not to the same stratum of the past. Similarly, in Chapter 11, the narrator carefully distinguishes between certain properties of Roman skeletons and those of more recent time: "Imaginative inhabitants [of Casterbridge], who would have felt an unpleasantness at the discovery of a comparatively modern skeleton in their gardens, were quite unmoved by these hoary [Roman] shapes. They had lived so long ago, their time was so unlike the present, their hopes and motives were so widely removed from ours, that between them and the living *there seemed to stretch a gulf too wide for even a spirit to pass.*" How appropriate, then, that the Casterbridge boys should have called the living Susan "The Ghost"; after her death she certainly haunts her twice-taken husband, Michael Henchard. In Susan's case, no spirit-barring gulf of long time or indifference separates living from dead. Thus the narrator invites us to assemble clues into a pattern: while the living characters have nothing to fear from certain skeletons in the garden (those of long-dead Romans or, figuratively speaking, deeds from the remote past), they are likely to experience "unpleasantness" when others (deeds that took place in the recent past) are unearthed. Is this, then, the key to the novel: live to avoid scandal, or to avoid creating a skeleton for a closet (or garden), for it will return to haunt you? Surely not, and yet the haunting past, a concern shared by most of the characters, is an important issue. To interpret it correctly one must be open to ambiguities, even contradictions between certain obvious clues in the narrative and larger patterns of meaning.

Readers will recall several scenes in *The Mayor of Casterbridge* when the past returns to upset someone's well-laid plans. But by simply analyzing such moments as when Newson came searching for his daughter or when Mrs. Goodenough confronted Michael in the police-court, a reader cannot gauge what they "mean" any more than one can comprehend an iceberg by focusing binoculars on its tip. To see how the past came to have such power over the present we must trace backwards and downwards from effects to causes.

The events which characters think back on with mingled shame and regret in this novel are few and have remarkable similarities: Michael's sale of his wife and daughter; Newson's purchase of them and his exploitation of Susan's "meekness" by living with her as her husband; Michael's affair with Lucetta. All are social crimes, acts which violate society's laws governing love, marriage and parenthood. All, therefore, profoundly confuse the question of human relationships in *The Mayor of Casterbridge.* Michael Henchard is the father of Elizabeth, but he is not Elizabeth's father; Susan is Michael Henchard's wife—or is she Richard Newson's? Lucetta promises to marry Michael, her former love, but secretly marries Donald Farfrae—is she Donald's mate or Michael's? The point is, of course, that these spontaneous, forgivable errors, hardly crimes, have the power to haunt the later lives of Michael, Elizabeth, Susan, Newson and Lucetta. Why is this so? The answer is two-fold: the past haunts because of the special nature of life within the Henchard Circle in Casterbridge, and because most members of that circle choose to conceal, or attempt to escape, the past.

It is significant that Hardy, who so often dealt with natives in his novels, chose strangers for all the central characters of *The Mayor of Casterbridge.* Upon arriving in Casterbridge, not one has any family ties with the town, was born there or has any native Casterbridge friends. Paradoxically, however, most are not strangers to each other. Susan comes looking for her husband, Lucetta for a former lover, Newson for his daughter.

Only Michael and Donald arrive without friends or relations already there. Thus, Hardy creates a crucible-like situation by bringing together in rude, sequestered Casterbridge, this "old, hoary place o' wickedness," as Buzzford somewhat hyperbolically calls the town, six outsiders, five of whom are already related, whose private lives later become a tangled web of conflicting claims and relationships. All the late arrivals have business of one sort or another with the first, Michael Henchard, Casterbridge's mayor and a prominent citizen. Out of this springs the Henchard Circle. The main drive among its principals is establishment; each wants to find some basis for a secure, satisfying life. Michael and Donald work to succeed at business; Susan wants security, principally for her illegitimate daughter, Elizabeth; Lucetta comes to the town as a *nouveau riche* in search of social security and a husband.

To succeed in their various quests, most of the chief characters feel obliged, despite the promptings of their own consciences, and of certain confidants, to conceal certain chapters of their earlier lives. In Susan's case, the urgings of conscience are weaker than her conviction that telling Elizabeth how she came to live with Newson as his wife would cause the girl misery. As she nears Casterbridge on her quest to locate her husband, we learn that "A hundred times she had been upon the point of telling her daughter Elizabeth-Jane the true story of her life, the tragical crisis of which had been the transaction at Weydon Fair. . . . But she had refrained." Indeed, "The risk of endangering a child's strong affection by disturbing ideas which had grown with her growth was to Mrs. Henchard too fearful a thing to contemplate." Similarly, even Newson, the "genial sailor," could not bring himself to speak the truth to Susan and reveal that he had no legal right to her. As he explains to Michael, "Well, it was not in my heart to undeceive her when the deed was done" [their going away together after the fair]. "I never would have undeceived her till the day of her death."

Michael and Lucetta, on the other hand, seem to have no tuggings of conscience (of this kind, at least); rather, both share their pasts with confidants to whom they turn for advice. Within a day of meeting Donald, Michael confesses his past in detail to the young Scotsman and asks what to do about the dilemma the return of Susan and Elizabeth has caused him: should he honor his promise to marry Lucetta, or take back his wife? With no hesitation Michael accepts Donald's advice to honor the prior commitment and inform Lucetta that he cannot marry her. But when he asks whether or not to tell Elizabeth the truth, Donald's unequivocal response—"I think I'd run the risk, and tell her the truth. She'll forgive ye both"—only provokes a vehement "Never!" from Michael. Lucetta also turns to a younger person as confidante. Early in their relationship Lucetta tells Elizabeth much about her early life. Later, transparently veiling herself as "my poor friend," she tells her young friend of her dilemma: should she marry Michael, whom she loved long ago and whom she promised, or Donald, whom she loves. When she asks for advice, Elizabeth initially demurs: "I cannot answer. . . . It is so difficult. It wants a Pope to settle that!" Later, however, she pontifically lectures Lucetta, "I think when any one gets coupled up with a man in the past so unfortunately as you have done, she ought to become his wife if she can, even if she were not the sinning party." Lucetta must refuse this advice. By this point in the narrative she has already married Donald without, of course, revealing anything to her husband of her earlier relations with his chief business rival, Michael.

Thus the key points of a recurrent pattern are clear: someone makes a socio-sexual error, initially conceals it from those around him and later, even when prompted by conscience or confidant, prefers to hide the truth. As demonstrated by the several memorable epiphany scenes in which a ghost, a visitant from the past, unexpectedly arises to belie a character's present position, however, the past will out. Susan, "the Ghost," whispers to Michael from beyond the grave that Elizabeth is not his daughter; Lucetta's past, her affair with Michael, is paraded through the streets of Casterbridge in a skimmity ride whose central figures are effigies of Michael and Lucetta; Mrs. Goodenough reveals Michael's past in the police-court to escape punishment; the supposedly dead Newson returns twice to belie Michael's claim to be Elizabeth's father. Disasters follow all these grim epiphanies: Michael rejects his stepdaughter, Lucetta dies from the shock of the revelation; the disclosure of Michael's past marks the turning point of his fortunes; Newson's return causes Elizabeth's rejection of Michael and his own loss of hope and death.

Clearly, several characters in *The Mayor of Casterbridge* are haunted by their past but, as Hardy's Novalis quotation "Character is Fate" reminds us, no account of such a fate is possible without due regard being paid to the afflicted one's character. In this novel, one index of character is a person's willingness to "own" his past, to accept responsibility for that earlier edition of himself who committed certain indiscretions which the later, revised edition considers unfortunate. There is, for example, the possibility of reparation: an act which grows out of the acceptance of responsibility for some past wrong and is an attempt to compensate for it. Significantly, this theme is introduced by the chief topic of conversation the night Susan and her daughter first enter Casterbridge—the bad bread. As a bystander tells the two women, "There's less good bread than good beer in Casterbridge now. I've been a wife, and I've been a mother, and I never see such unprincipled bread in Casterbridge as this before." The key word here is "unprincipled," suggesting that a want of principles led to the preparing of flour from "grown" wheat. Soon after, the women learn that the fault is traceable to their relation, Michael Henchard, mayor and chief grain merchant. In a query aimed at Michael by "a baker or miller," one of the chief sufferers from the Mayor's oversight, we hear a question that reverberates through the novel: "But what are you going to do to repay us for the past? Will you replace the grown flour we've still got by sound grain?" The point, bluntly stated by the miller, is that some mistakes are reparable. Michael's response is to evade the question. In so doing he fails both to accept responsibility for the "unprincipled bread" and to offer reparations. Yet it would be wrong to conclude that this refusal was characteristic of him. After Donald showed him how by a simple treatment the grown grain could be restored, he shared that knowledge to help the millers and bakers. In several of his later speeches and deeds that same desire to make reparations stands out: setting up the returned Susan as a well-to-do-widow, courting and marrying her "would leave my shady, headstrong, disgraceful life as a young man absolutely unopened; the secret would be yours and mine only. . . ." After their marriage, "He was as kind to her as a man, mayor, and church-warden could possibly be." The reparations theme is even stronger in Michael's dealings with Lucetta. After Michael left Jersey, he confesses to Donald, Lucetta "suffered much on my account . . . till, latterly, I felt I owed her something, and thought that, as I had not heard of Susan for so long, I would make this other one the only return I could make, and ask her if she would . . . marry me, such as I was." Even though, as with the bad bread, in both these cases Michael acts reluctantly, they are genuine attempts at reparation, to repay someone for an earlier error.

Donald and Elizabeth contrast sharply with Michael and the other principals because their past is an open book and because they do not seem burdened by it. It is true that Donald's book of the past is virtually blank; he walks into Casterbridge an almost perfect *tabula rasa*. Except for a handful of general details about his Scots origin, we learn nothing about his past. Although Elizabeth's past might have led her to attempt to conceal her humble origins, she resembles Donald in her openness. At an appropriate time, she tells Lucetta "the tale of her life as she understood it." Both Donald and Elizabeth, meek, peace-loving souls, accept their past calmly; but then the choice of candor over concealment cannot have cost either of them much apprehension. Similarly, both have learned from the past and let experience guide present choice and actions. After Lucetta's death the narrator observes that "Time, 'in his own grey style', taught Farfrae how to estimate his experience of Lucetta. . . ." Elizabeth resolves not to spend money on clothes lavishly "because it was inconsistent with her past life to blossom gaudily the moment she had become possessed of money." From her "earthly career" she "had learnt the lesson of renunciation, and was . . . familiar with the wreck of each day's wishes. . . ."

The cases of Michael and Lucetta are very different. Faced with vivid memories of bold, iconoclastic acts—the sale of a wife and daughter, a scandalous affair—these two repeatedly choose concealment, but not in ignorance of other alternatives. As we saw, both do confess, at least in part, to their confidants. The narrator bluntly suggests that further confession might have spared them agony. Regarding the sensational disclosure about Michael's past Mrs. Goodenough makes, the narrator observes that even this "edge or turn in the incline of Henchard's fortunes" might have been made less traumatic through confession: "Had the incident been well known of old and always, it might by this time have grown to be lightly regarded as the rather tall wild oat, but well-nigh the single one, of a young man with whom the steady and mature (if somewhat headstrong) burgher of to-day had scarcely a point in common." In telling us about Lucetta's emotions and thoughts as she hears Michael reading aloud portions of her love-letters, the narrator seems to echo his observation about Michael's failure to confess earlier: "Had she confessed all to Donald in their early acquaintance he might possibly have got over it . . . but for her or any one else to tell him now would be fatal."

As the last quotation suggests, a person's late-dawning awareness that he or she should have owned or confessed his past sooner does not lead to a resolution to confess now rather than risk later and more serious consequences. Both Michael and Lucetta, it seems clear, prefer concealment, with all its hazards, to candor. After discovering her cooling ardor for Michael, Lucetta defiantly says, "I won't be a slave to the past—I'll love where I choose!" The pathos of Lucetta's situation after she marries Donald arises from a paradox: she has shown herself a free spirit, no "slave to the past," by marrying Donald, and yet she lives perilously by continuing to conceal it. Of course, she does finally confess to her husband. As she lies dying "she informed him of the bare facts of her peculiar intimacy" with Michael. Michael's actions parallel those of Lucetta. Late in the novel, after Michael sends Newson away by his unpremeditated lie that Elizabeth has died, the narrator gives a telling glimpse of Michael's mind in action: "instead of considering how best to right the wrong, and acquaint Eliz-

abeth's father with the truth at once, he bethought himself of ways to keep the position he had accidentally won." The odd double-reversal involving Elizabeth's parentage is another instance of Michael's characteristic way of thinking. At first, Michael disregards Donald's advice and conceals the story of his and Susan's folly from Elizabeth; then he confesses part of that story to win her acceptance of himself as her father; then he learns a crucial part of Susan's story when he reads in her "time capsule" that the girl's father is really Newson. Michael, of course, will not confess the truth to Elizabeth: "He was far too self-willed to recede from a position, especially as it would involve humiliation. His daughter he had asserted her to be, and his daughter she should always think herself, no matter what hypocrisy it involved."

Another, and perhaps more significant, difference between this pair and Elizabeth and Donald has nothing to do with confession, or overt honesty about the past; it concerns a person's private conception of himself—how what he is now relates to what he was before. The earlier point, that Hardy shows the younger pair capable of being instructed by experience, suggests an approach. Lucetta and Michael, when they become two sides of the love triangle that forms in High Place Hall, show little evidence that they will *allow* past experience to guide present actions. Lucetta tells Donald on his first visit that "Lovers ought not to be parted like that! O, if I had my wish, I'd let people live and love at their pleasure!" We are therefore not surprised to learn that she chooses the color red, which Hardy invests with so much passional significance in *Tess,* for her costume that spring; she resolved to "be the cherry-coloured person at all hazards." Even though the scandal her relations with Michael caused in Jersey might have taught a more ordinary woman that discretion is the better part of ardor, Lucetta, clearly no "slave to the past," cannot tame her desires. Michael is similar. A more ordinary man might have learned to bridle his passing fits of rage but Michael, as critics have noticed, is too bull-like for that. His obstinate rage is abundantly evident—the dismissal of Donald, his tyrannical forcing of Lucetta to accept his proposal, his near murder of Donald. It is first evident in an event that might have been powerfully instructive for a more ordinary man—the sale of Susan. But Michael learns little or nothing from it. Even his mighty oath covers only abstinence from drinking and only for a span of 21 years. Michael and Lucetta, whose defiance of the codes and shalt-nots gives their careers a cometlike brilliance, obviously learn little restraint from experience. With people of such extraordinary wills and appetites, the novel suggests, experience is no teacher at all.

There is, then, so much unheeded good advice of certain kinds in *The Mayor of Casterbridge* that one might suspect Hardy of intending to write a *roman à these* to illustrate a familiar aphorism: "Honesty is the Best Policy." It is, at least, tempting to infer such a moral from the narrator's position, hinted at in his aside about the unpleasantness felt at the discovery of a modern skeleton in one's garden, and made explicit in many places in the novel. The sale of Susan might, by the time of Mrs. Goodenough's disclosure, have been "lightly regarded" by the public as a single tall wild oat if the truth had been revealed earlier; had Lucetta told all early in her acquaintance with Donald, the skimmity ride might not have killed her. Those scenes in the novel in which a character moves toward the brink of confession but then steps back lead one to a similar inference. Michael might have confessed to Richard Newson when the latter came searching for his daughter; Michael or Lucetta might have told Donald the truth about their earlier relations after the love letters are read aloud; Michael might have revealed to Elizabeth, after reading her mother's letter, that he is not her father. In several of these scenes we are very conscious of the narrator, reminding us how differently things might have turned out—if a character had confessed, told the truth, done those things he or she ought to have done. But do we follow the narrator's lead? Or do we instead realize that circumstances may proscribe such virtuous behavior? To take but one instance, what would have happened if Michael had followed the explicit advice, not of the narrator but of a character who frequently seems to speak with his voice, Donald Farfrae? Donald counsels Michael that after being reunited with his wife and Susan should tell Elizabeth the truth about the real relations between Michael, Susan and Richard Newson. This may appear to be good advice, but the *novel will not allow that it be followed.* Such a disclosure would probably lead to the revelation of Elizabeth's parentage, for how would Susan explain to Elizabeth and Michael the time difference between the birth dates of the two Elizabeths?

Despite the clarity with which the narrator's position is presented, then, no such skeleton key can unlock the moral complexities of *The Mayor of Casterbridge.* Instead, Hardy creates combinations of character and situation in which candor does not exist as a viable possibility and, in so doing, undermines the moral asides of his narrator. Is it conceivable that Richard Newson could have told Susan he had no legal right to her and that their daughter was therefore illegitimate? Or that Susan might have told Michael in a less melodramatic, more direct way and risked Michael's rejection of Elizabeth? The alternatives seem no more reasonable or viable than concealment. In that scene of near-confession when Michael, within Lucetta's earshot, reads Donald portions of her old love letters, Michael could have confessed—although technically the secret is Lucetta's—but Hardy has made it dramatically right for Michael to acquiesce to Lucetta's desire to conceal the past. Despite powerful motivation to strike back at the woman and man he felt had wronged him, Michael was "appalled" by the prospect of revealing his and Lucetta's shared past and left without fulfilling his intention. While candor is a theoretical possibility here and at other points, extenuating circumstances, sometimes the psychic damage that might befall an innocent person, make it seem humanly right for characters to choose concealment.

The question of the degree of sympathy with which the characters of *The Mayor of Casterbridge,* especially Donald and Elizabeth, are presented has been much debated. To some it has seemed that Hardy half-heartedly rewarded the patient, dull Elizabeth by a marriage to the pushy, materialistic Donald; others have seen their marriage as befitting the participants' flexible, evolutionary approach to life. Critics seem divided on whether Hardy sympathizes primarily with the dynamic, iconoclastic Michael and Lucetta or with the more tradition-bound younger pair. In my view, authorial sympathies are apportioned about equally. Since Donald and Elizabeth were not shadowed by a scandalous past and seemed to welcome experience as a teacher, one might suppose that they would earn the narrator's unqualified sympathy. In two instances, however, Elizabeth falls from grace: her narrow, pietistic lecture to Lucetta and her rejection of her stepfather late in the novel. The narrator tells us that the past, from which Elizabeth had learned valuable lessons, had also tended to form a certain streak of prudishness in her: "Owing to her early troubles with regard to her mother a semblance of irregularity had terrors for her. . . ." Hence her advice to Lucetta, "You ought to marry Mr. Henchard or nobody—certainly not another man!"

seems narrow, inflexible and based on pure emotion. The tone of her interview with Michael on her wedding day is similar. Even after Henchard pleads that she not forget him she replies: "But how can I [love you] when I know you have deceived me so—so bitterly deceived me!" She concludes her outburst, "O how can I love as I once did a man who has served us like this!" Hardy, I think, conceived of Elizabeth as a young woman with real virtues and capacities, but one soon out of her moral depth when faced with the puzzles of human relationship with which this novel abounds. Readiness to learn from past experiences, the novel suggests, is no guarantee that one will behave virtuously.

In the eyes of Donald and Elizabeth (and the narrator), as we have seen, Lucetta and Michael repeatedly choose the wrong way to act; despite their younger confidants' counsel, they conceal their pasts from others and fail to own it to themselves. Yet it is undeniable that the novel is vitally sympathetic with and concerned about these "lost violent souls." Hardy helps us understand the radically different value systems of these two couples within the Henchard Circle by showing sharply different ways these strangers establish themselves after coming to Casterbridge: the apparently successful Donald and Elizabeth are clay in the hands of the potter Society, who shapes them in conformity to her ideals and values and so enables them to thrive. The unsuccessful Michael and Lucetta, on the other hand, only initially and superficially adopt those values and come, in time, to exist outside the bounds of society. In this extra-societal realm, ordinary middle-class values do not apply.

If this discussion yields no dictum to replace Miller's contention that *The Mayor of Casterbridge* is "a demonstration of the impossibility of escaping from the past" [see Additional Bibliography], it should nevertheless show that there is a steady, discernible tension, or a lack of congruence, between the narrator's view of past and present and the logic of the human drama Hardy creates in *The Mayor of Casterbridge.* This is not to argue that the novel is flawed, that such a tension should be read as a contradiction or as indication of uncertainty of purpose. Rather, a reader is induced to form his own views of character, event and meaning from the various, and conflicting, sources of testimony and evidence the novel provides. Doing so does not, I believe, involve choosing one view over another but, as Bayley counsels [in *An Essay on Hardy*], becoming aware of multiple points of view or, as Gregor suggested [in his introduction to the New Wessex edition of *The Mayor of Casterbridge*], suspending judgment, and sensing a more inclusive view. (pp. 109-19)

> *W. Eugene Davis, "Comparatively Modern Skeletons in the Garden: A Reconsideration of 'The Mayor of Casterbridge',"* in English Literature in Transition: 1880-1920, *Special Series, No. 3, 1985, pp. 108-20.*

JAGDISH CHANDRA DAVE (essay date 1985)

[*In the following excerpt from* The Human Predicament in Hardy's Novels, *Dave contends that the action of* The Mayor of Casterbridge *is characterized by "movement in mutually opposite directions"—Henchard toward destruction and Elizabeth-Jane toward fulfillment.*]

The movement in mutually opposed directions—one towards strife and extinction, the other towards peace and survival, one embodied in Henchard's career, the other in that of Elizabeth-Jane—are evident in [*The Mayor of Casterbridge*]. But if they are not so very well defined as in *The Return of the Native,* it is because Hardy, as stated in the preface to the [later] novel, is absorbed here in "a study of one man's deeds and character" almost exclusively. *The Mayor of Casterbridge* is more interesting as a narrative than as a clear exhibition of Hardy's philosophy of life.

"Casterbridge was the complement of the rural life around; not its urban opposite." That is the setting of the novel. The action is largely confined to the town, although the story starts and concludes a little beyond its bounds. It is Dorchester itself, rechristened in the Wessex world and realistically delineated. The language accordingly has the rhythm of prose. But when Hardy's history-consciousness carries us back to the town's Roman foundations, Casterbridge symbolically assumes the character of world arena.

> Casterbridge announced old Rome in every street, alley, and precinct. It looked Roman, bespoke the art of Rome, concealed dead men of Rome. It was impossible to dig more than a foot or two deep about the town fields and gardens without coming upon some tall soldier or other of the Empire, who had laid there in his silent unobtrusive rest for a space of fifteen hundred years.

The most conspicuous of all the Roman features of the town is its Amphitheatre, "Melancholy, impressive, lonely, yet accessible from every part of the town." Hardy himself describes the place as suggestive. Centuries roll by; new gladiators enter the lists as the older ones die defeated in shame or after a moment or two of victory; characters and chorus change; but the spectacle of man ranged in struggle against Nature, against fellow-creatures, ever persists.

Now, the hero in this arena is Michael Henchard, not a Roman, but martial still in physical build and temper. . . . He has achieved both wealth and status in keeping with his ambition. Yet at heart he is unsatisfied. Amid all his bursts of vitality he feels lonely and miserable. He is feared and honoured, but not loved. His "tigerish affection" needs an object. That is why he is drawn irresistibly towards Farfrae, Lucetta and Elizabeth-Jane by turns. For a brief spell when Susan returns to him after the reported death of Newson, the drift of events seems to converge in fulfilment towards his violent longing for love, and he is truly a happy man living with his wife, daughter and dearly loved friend Farfrae. But this happiness does not last. Death snatches Susan away. Elizabeth-Jane is discovered to be Newson's daugher. Farfrae's lovable qualities which win popular regard rouse his envy which estranges Farfrae. He loses even Lucetta, his betrothed before Susan's return, as she loves and marries Farfrae. Largely his own nature, though partly also the indifferent occurrence of events, make him lonely. His whole life reveals his strong urge for love at strife with his stubborn pride which builds walls around him. His tragedy is that he can relinquish neither. He is self-doomed to his fate.

As is usual in Hardy, the characters in a state of frustration turn heretic and invent a malicious cosmic Being, to lay on Him the blame for their misfortune. That is what Henchard does when rudely shocked at learning that Elizabeth is not his but Newson's daughter:

> He looked out at the night as at a fiend. Henchard, like all his kind, was superstitious, and he could not help thinking that the concatenation of events this evening had produced was the scheme of some sinister intelligence bent on punishing him. Yet they had developed naturally.

It was in a desperate desire to beat Farfrae in the trade-war that he consulted the weather prophet, staked his all on his forecast in purchasing grains and ruined himself. In the event of the fatal loss which made him a bankrupt "the movements of his mind seemed to tend to the thought that some power was working against him." "These isolated hours of superstition came to Henchard in time of moody depression, when all his practical largeness of view had oozed out of him." After his desperate attempt at suicide was thwarted strangely by the sight of his effigy whirling in the pool below, Henchard read in the incident Divine intervention to prevent his escape into peace. He says: "Who is such a reprobate as I! And yet it seems that even I be in Somebody's hand."

In tragic grandeur Henchard remains unparalleled among all Hardy's characters, and he is said to have his peers only in Shakespearian and Sophoclean tragedy. The events of his tumultuous life have chastened him at the end. His weary soul finds its last refuge in Elizabeth-Jane's affection. But with Newson's arrival this last refuge also lies demolished, and he banishes himself from Casterbridge. He is exhausted in his struggle against destiny which issues from his character.

> He had been sorry for all this long ago; but his attempts to replace ambition by love had been as fully foiled as his ambition itself.
>
> Externally there was nothing to hinder his making another start on the upward slope, and by his new lights achieving higher things than his soul in its half-formed state had been able to accomplish. But the ingenious machinery contrived by the Gods for reducing human possibilities of amelioration to a minimum—which arranges that wisdom to do shall come *pari passu* with the departure of zest for doing—stood in the way of all that. He had no wish to make an arena a second time of the world that had become a mere painted scene to him.
>
> Very often, as his hay-knife crunched down among the sweet-smelling grassy stems, he would survey mankind and say to himself: "Here and everywhere be folk dying before their time like frosted leaves, though wanted by their families, the country, and the world; while I, an outcast, an encumberer of the ground, wanted by nobody, and despised by all, live on against my will!"

He dies, ultimately, a broken man upon the Egdon wastes.

John Paterson reads in this novel "Hegel's sublime and indestructible 'ethical substance',", and regards it as a traditional tragedy justifying "the ways of God to man." Accordiing to him, Henchard, in selling his wife at the start of the novel, had violated the moral order of the universe, arousing thereby "such forces of retribution as will not be satisfied with less than the total humiliation of the offender and the ultimate restoration of the order offended" [see excerpt dated 1959]. But this interpretation appears forced. It is curious that Paterson fails to note that Henchard prospers rapidly after he has sold his wife, but suffers a steady deterioration more than twenty years later after he has made amends by remarrying Susan. The fact is that here as elsewhere in Hardy's novels the Fate that presides over the life of man is the same amorality of the world regarded mistakenly by Hardy's heretics as sinister Intelligence. There is none to punish Henchard. No supernatural Nemesis dogs his footsteps. The trouble is that the inertia of the amoral world-order is never roused to fury. It is utterly inviolable. But one who does not understand it as such, who is temperamentally a misfit in the web of social relationships, and has a highly demanding attitude to life, suffers and perishes. Henchard's own pride, a constant feature of his mind, thwarts his longing for love and estranges people from him. An isolated sin or incident does not matter. Even if he had not sold his wife at the beginning of his career, the story of his life would have been different only in detail, not in substance.

H. C. Webster reads in Henchard's stubborn endurance of his fate "the purgation of our emotions that tragedy produces":

> We may be struck by terror at his fate, but we are
> also aroused to admiration by his dogged courage.
> We feel that it is an honour to belong to the same
> race with a man who so courageously resists an implacable and sinister Fate [see excerpt dated 1960].

But Webster is mistaken if he thinks that this endurance in itself constitutes the affirmative note of Henchard's tragedy. Henchard looks resigned near the end of the novel. But his resignation, bitter and negative, is the outcome of the extremity of despair. Such loss of the will to live, when a little more acute, drives one to suicide. It is not the stoical resignation that tends towards "introvertive" mysticism. It shows how bravely Henchard died, but not how wisely he could have saved himself.

The corrective note of affirmative resignation comes here from Elizabeth-Jane. Her gift of calm thinking keeps her secure in a state of repose beyond the onslaughts of both happiness and sorrow. She is brought up in poverty and has passed through vicissitudes of fortune ordinarily difficult to endure. She loses her father first, and her mother soon afterwards. Henchard's affection is as moodily withdrawn as earlier it was lavished upon her. In Farfrae's marriage with Lucetta she loses not only her lover, but also the only home she then had under Lucetta's roof. All these events and the absolute loneliness of this quasi-orphan girl are more heart-breaking in the objective sense than those which Henchard suffered. Yet, while Henchard is broken, she lives, and not only lives, but "the solidity of her character" positively helps and consoles her better-placed friends—Henchard, Lucetta, Farfrae—in their troubles.

Very early in the novel Hardy reveals Elizabeth-Jane's thinking when she thinks about Farfrae's appearance at the Three Mariners where both she and he had put up on their first arrival in the town.

> She admired the serious light in which he looked at
> serious things. He had seen no jest in ambiguities
> and roguery, as the Casterbridge tosspots had done;
> and rightly not—there was none. She disliked those
> wretched humours of Christopher Coney and his tribe;
> and he did not appreciate them. He seemed to feel
> exactly as she felt about life and its surroundings—
> that they were a tragical rather than a comical thing;
> that though one could be gay on occasion, moments
> of gaiety were interludes, and no part of the actual
> drama.

Such were her own views, though there is nothing else in the novel to suggest that Farfrae shared them with her. They are only further consolidated in the light of her later experiences. This revelation of her mind on her first appearance in the novel, particularly the last sentence in the passage quoted above, agrees well with her conclusive feeling, much quoted to illustrate Hardy's thought, that happiness is an occasional episode in the general drama of pain. It reflects not pessimism, but affirmative resignation.

After Henchard's remarriage with Susan, when "The freedom she experienced, the indulgence with which she was treated, went beyond her expectations," she refused to be shaken from her equanimity. Her prettiness developed into beauty, and there was plenty to satisfy her every wish.

> Perhaps, too, her grey, thoughtful eyes revealed an
> arch gaiety sometimes; but this was infrequent; the
> sort of wisdom which looked from their pupils did
> not readily keep company with these lighter moods.
> Like all people who have known rough times, light-
> heartedness seemed to her too irrational and incon-
> sequent to be indulged in except as a reckless dram
> now and then; for she had been too early habituated
> to anxious reasoning to drop the habit suddenly. She
> felt none of those ups and downs of spirit which beset
> so many people without cause; never—to paraphrase
> a recent poet—never a gloom in Elizabeth-Jane's soul
> but she well knew how it came there; and her present
> cheerfulness was fairly proportionate to her solid
> guarantees for the same.

> Her triumph was tempered by circumspection; she
> had still that field-mouse fear of the coulter of destiny
> despite fair promise, which is common among the
> thoughtful who have suffered early from poverty and
> oppression.

> "I won't be too gay on any account," she would say
> to herself. "It would be tempting Providence to hurl
> mother and me down, and afflict us again as He used
> to do."

"Knowledge—the result of great natural insight—she did not lack; learning, accomplishments—those, alas, she had not. By knowledge Hardy means the awareness of the human situation and the wisdom to ease its rigours. To add learning to her knowledge she studies books of philosophy and becomes "a young perusing woman." Such habit of serious reading is a characteristic of most of Hardy's idealists. She does not simply cram information or amuse herself in the intellectual gymnasium of philosophy in the western academic sense. Hers is "adversity's sweet milk philosophy." She translates her thought into action and follows philosophy as a way of life. There can be no doubt that Hardy thinks through her. "To learn to take the universe seriously there is no quicker way than to watch— to be a 'waker,' as the country-people call it," writes Hardy, commenting on thought-obsessed Elizabeth tending night after night on her sick mother. It is the author's own observation in his third-person narrator's capacity. Watching means witnessing without emotional involvement. It amounts to becoming a disinterested spectator of all time and the universe. That is what Elizabeth-Jane has been doing.

Despair comes from repeated disappointment of strong desires. Renunciation of desires, therefore, is the surest way to avoid it. Hardy reflects on behalf of Elizabeth-Jane when Farfrae's attachment was shifted from her to Lucetta:

> She had learnt the lesson of renunciation, and was
> as familiar with the wreck of each day's wishes as
> with the diurnal setting of the sun. If her earthly
> career had taught her few book philosophies it had
> at least well practised her in this. Yet her experience
> had consisted less in a series of pure disappointments
> than in a series of substitutions. Continually it had
> happened that what she had desired had not been
> granted her, and that what had been granted her she
> had not desired. So she viewed with an approach to
> equanimity the now cancelled days when Donald had
> been her undeclared lover, and wondered what un-
> wished-for thing Heaven might send her in place of
> him.

After Newson's return, Henchard's death and her marriage with Farfrae, there ensues in her life a period of happiness. But she is not unaware of its episodic character. A brief interlude, whether painful or happy, cannot be held as the conclusion of life which continues to drift through indifferent weather. But the story has to end somewhere, and it is better for the novelist to stop at a happy moment which, after a series of sad occurrences might have a sound restitutive effect in keeping with the aesthetic demand of tragedy. So the novel ends with the wedding. The state of Elizabeth-Jane's mind at the conclusion of the novel is near Hardy's ideal. He writes:

> All was over at last, even her regrets for having misunderstood him [Henchard] on his last visit, for not having searched him out sooner, though these were deep and sharp for a good while. From this time forward Elizabeth-Jane found herself in a latitude of calm weather, kindly and grateful in itself, and doubly so after the Capharnaum in which some of her preceding years had been spent. As the lively and sparkling emotions of her early married life cohered into an equable serenity, the finer movements of her nature found scope in discovering to the narrow-lived ones around her the secret (as she had once learnt it) of making limited opportunities endurable; which she deemed to consist in the cunning enlargement, by a species of microscopic treatment, of those minute forms of satisfaction that offer themselves to everybody not in positive pain; which, thus handled, have much of the same inspiriting effect upon life as wider interests curiously embraced.
>
> Her position was, indeed, to a marked degree one that, in the common phrase, afforded much to be thankful for. That she was not demonstratively thankful was no fault of hers. Her experience had been of a kind to teach her, rightly or wrongly, that the doubtful honour of a brief transit through a sorry world hardly called for effusiveness, even when the path was suddenly irradiated at some half-way point by daybeams rich as hers.
>
> But her strong sense that neither she nor any human being deserved less than she was given, did not blind her to the fact that there were others receiving less who had deserved much more. And in being forced to class herself among the fortunate she did not cease to wonder at the persistence of the unforeseen, when the one to whom such unbroken tranquillity had been accorded in the adult stage was she whose youth had seemed to teach that happiness was but the occasional episode in a general drama of pain.

A mood of serene equanimity lifts her above the ups and downs of fortune. Her affirmative resignation has turned the absurd into harmony for herself. Her compassion for those who demand from life the sort of happiness they deserve but do not get, as well as her perception of the lack of wisdom in such a demand, is essentially Hardy's. Hardy himself admires the solidity of her character which she has built up by the exercise of understanding and will. But H. C. Webster, when he describes her as "too impersonally human to be vain, showy or coquettish," refuses to give her any credit for her stoical triumph against the outward situation and inward unruly impulses. If she does not break in consequence of a failure in love, it is because, he feels, "sexual impulses are not sufficiently strong" in her "to require much resisting." He thus displays the almost dogmatic psychological tendency of our times to treat every divergence from the normal pattern of human behaviour as abnormal or subnormal, ruling out the possibility of conscious, supernormal, will-based and wise divergence, and to dismiss

the obvious moral greatness of an individual as a limitation that could not be surmounted. (pp. 63-70)

> *Jagdish Chandra Dave, in his* The Human Predicament in Hardy's Novels, *The Macmillan Press Ltd., 1985, 216 p.*

ADDITIONAL BIBLIOGRAPHY

Abercrombie, Lascelles. "Dramatic Form." In his *Thomas Hardy: A Critical Study*, pp. 97-128. London: Martin Secker, 1912.
    Pronounces *The Mayor of Casterbridge* "a distinct change" for Hardy: "the tragedy of one man, not of a group."

Alexander, Anne. "Man and Society." In her *Thomas Hardy: The "Dream-Country" of His Fiction*, pp. 156-80. London: Vision, 1987.
    Examines ways that the physical and historical aspects of the setting of *The Mayor of Casterbridge* affect the novel's characterizations and plot.

Baker, James R. "Thematic Ambiguity in *The Mayor of Casterbridge*." *Twentieth Century Literature* 1, No. 1 (April 1955): 13-16.
    Considers *The Mayor of Casterbridge* ambiguous because Hardy never specifies if impersonal twists of fate or Henchard's moral flaws are responsible for his downfall.

Beach, Joseph Warren. "Movie." In his *The Technique of Thomas Hardy*, pp. 134-57. New York: Russell & Russell, 1962.
    Discusses the "succession of surprising turns" in an outline of the plot of *The Mayor of Casterbridge*, which Beach maintains resembles the incident-crammed outline of a motion picture scenario.

Brown, Douglas. "Novels of Character and Environment: *The Mayor of Casterbridge*." In his *Thomas Hardy*, pp. 63-70. London: Longmans, 1954.
    Maintains that *The Mayor of Casterbridge* dramatizes the struggle between the vanishing traditions of the rural order, symbolized by Henchard, and the growth of mechanization, symbolized by Farfrae.

————. *Thomas Hardy: The Mayor of Casterbridge*. London: Edward Arnold, 1962, 64 p.
    Examines some of the primary themes of *The Mayor of Casterbridge*, including those of cultural transition, commerce, and conflict between society and the individual.

Chase, Mary Ellen. "*The Mayor of Casterbridge*." In her *Thomas Hardy from Serial to Novel*, pp. 15-65. New York: Russell & Russell, 1964.
    Textual study of the differences between the serialized publication of *The Mayor of Casterbridge* in the *Graphic*, which concluded in May 1886, and the publication of the novel in book form later that year.

Cox, R. G., ed. "*The Mayor of Casterbridge* (1886)." In his *Thomas Hardy: The Critical Heritage*, pp. 133-40. New York: Barnes & Noble, 1970.
    Reprints early magazine reviews of *The Mayor of Casterbridge*.

Draper, R. P. "Hardy and Respectability." In *An English Miscellany: Presented to W. S. Mackie*, edited by Brian S. Lee, pp. 179-207. Capetown: Oxford University Press, 1977.
    Explores the theme of social respectability in *The Mayor of Casterbridge*.

————. "*The Mayor of Casterbridge*." *Critical Quarterly* 25, No. 1 (Spring 1983): 57-70.
    Notes that Hardy supplies *The Mayor of Casterbridge* with a broad historical perspective that leads moral judgments made within the narrative to transcend contemporary standards.

————, ed. *Hardy: The Tragic Novels*. London: The Macmillan Press, 1975, 256 p.

Collection of previously published essays on *The Return of the Native, The Mayor of Casterbridge, Tess of the d'Urbervilles,* and *Jude the Obscure,* including studies by John Paterson, Robert C. Schweik, J. C. Maxwell, Douglas Brown, and Ian Gregor.

Duffin, H. C. "The Novels." In his *Thomas Hardy: A Study of the Wessex Novels, the Poems, and The Dynasts,* pp. 1-257. Manchester: Manchester University Press, 1937.

Contains numerous scattered references to such elements as characterization, plot, and humor in *The Mayor of Casterbridge.*

Edmond, Roy. "'The Past-Marked Prospect': Reading *The Mayor of Casterbridge.*" In *Reading the Victorian Novel: Detail into Form,* edited by Ian Gregor, pp. 111-27. New York: Barnes & Noble, 1980.

Explores the ways in which the past, both collective and personal, is "brought into a complex relationship with the present" to give *The Mayor of Casterbridge* thematic and structural integrity unusual in Hardy's fiction.

Edwards, Duane D. "*The Mayor of Casterbridge* as Aeschylean Tragedy." *Studies in the Novel* 4, No. 4 (Winter 1972): 608-18.

Maintains that *The Mayor of Casterbridge* most closely resembles Aeschylean and not Sophoclean tragedy, because "whereas in fact the Sophoclean hero . . . wreaks his own destruction in the present . . . the Aeschylean hero is doomed in the present because of what he did in the past. There is, then, a relationship between the deeds of the Prologue . . . and the Mayor's eventual fate."

Epstein, Leonora. "Sale and Sacrament: The Wife Auction in *The Mayor of Casterbridge.*" *English Language Notes* XXIV, No. 4 (June 1987): 50-6.

Contends that, just as the fair at which Henchard sells his wife offers a distorted reflection of ordinary society, so the wife-selling itself distortedly mirrors the marriage ceremony.

Firor, Ruth A. *Folkways in Thomas Hardy.* Philadelphia: University of Pennsylvania Press, 1931, 357 p.

Discusses numerous legends, superstitions, and customs that appear in Hardy's novels, including the wife-selling and the skimmington or "skimmity-ride" that take place in *The Mayor of Casterbridge.*

Gardner, W. H. *Some Thoughts on "The Mayor of Casterbridge."* 1930. Reprint. Folcroft, Pa.: The Folcroft Press, 1969.

Personal response to *The Mayor of Casterbridge* considering it a well-written, interesting, and effective novel.

Giordano, Frank, Jr. "Michael Henchard: *Le misérable* of Casterbridge." In his *"I'd Have My Life Unbe": Thomas Hardy's Self-destructive Characters,* pp. 78-97. Tuscaloosa: The University of Alabama Press, 1984.

Considers the self-destructive nature of Michael Henchard central to the plot and action of *The Mayor of Casterbridge.*

Gregor, Ian. "What Kind of Fiction Did Hardy Write?" *Essays in Criticism* XVI, No. 3 (July 1966): 290-308.

Maintains that with *The Mayor of Casterbridge* Hardy overcame the shortcomings of his earlier novels and created a work with an integrated tragic structure.

———. Introduction to *The Life and Death of the Mayor of Casterbridge: A Story of a Man of Character,* by Thomas Hardy, pp. 13-31. London: Macmillan, 1974.

Examines the social conditions in *The Mayor of Casterbridge* under which private acts yield public consequences.

Grindle, Juliet M. "Compulsion and Choice in *The Mayor of Casterbridge.*" In *The Novels of Thomas Hardy,* edited by Anne Smith, pp. 91-106. New York: Barnes & Noble, 1979.

Discusses the complex web of relationships among the six main characters of *The Mayor of Casterbridge.*

Hawkins, Desmond. "The Professional Author, 1878-1885." In his *Hardy: Novelist and Poet,* pp. 79-102. London: David & Charles, 1976.

Comments on the innovative nature of Hardy's portrayal of a powerful and dominant male character in *The Mayor of Casterbridge.*

Heilman, Robert B. Introduction to *The Mayor of Casterbridge,* by Thomas Hardy, pp. v-xliv. Boston: Houghton Mifflin, 1962.

Lengthy consideration of plot, characterization, action, scene depiction, narration, and literary style of *The Mayor of Casterbridge.*

———. "Hardy's *Mayor* and the Problem of Intention." *Criticism* V, No. 3 (Summer 1963): 199-213.

Notes wide discrepancies between authorial description and narrative presentation of characters in *The Mayor of Casterbridge.*

———. "Hardy's *Mayor*: Notes on Style." *Nineteenth-Century Fiction* 18, No. 4 (March 1964): 307-29.

Offers an examination of Hardy's varying style, drawing examples from *The Mayor of Casterbridge* "because it is Hardy's best novel; hence the divergencies of style will stand out in most striking independence as habits of the writer rather than as accompaniments of other qualitative ups and downs."

Kramer, Dale. "Character and the Cycle of Change in *The Mayor of Casterbridge.*" *Tennessee Studies in Literature* XVI (1971): 111-20.

Examines the cyclical nature of events in the plot of *The Mayor of Casterbridge.*

Lerner, Laurence, and Holmstrom, John, eds. "*The Mayor of Casterbridge.*" In *Thomas Hardy and His Readers,* edited by Laurence Lerner and John Holmstrom, pp. 49-54. New York: Barnes & Noble, 1968.

Reprints contemporary reviews of *The Mayor of Casterbridge.*

Lucas, John. "Hardy's Women." In his *The Literature of Change: Studies in the Nineteenth-Century Provincial Novel,* pp. 119-91. Sussex: The Harvester Press, 1977.

Characterizes the three main female characters in *The Mayor of Casterbridge* as "victims of their menfolk" and devoid of choices as to how they will lead their lives.

Maxwell, J. C. "The 'Sociological' Approach to *The Mayor of Casterbridge.*" In *Imagined Worlds: Essays on Some English Novels and Novelists in Honour of John Butt,* edited by Maynard Mack and Ian Gregor, pp. 225-36. London: Methuen & Co., 1968.

Discusses the social history of Wessex and the gradual destruction of the agricultural way of life by encroaching industrialism.

Migdal, Seymour. "History and Archetype in *The Mayor of Casterbridge.*" *Studies in the Novel* III, No. 3 (Fall 1971): 284-92.

Maintains that in contrasting the two different characters of Henchard and Farfrae, Hardy in *The Mayor of Casterbridge* is not only tracing the demise of agrarianism and the rise of industrialism, but also indicating "the coming of a new society" in which a tragic sensibility such as Henchard's has no place.

Miller, J. Hillis. *Thomas Hardy: Distance and Desire.* Cambridge: The Belknap Press, 1970, 282 p.

Compares Hardy's poetry, novels, and nonfiction to identify underlying themes that unify all of his works and delineate Hardy's development as an author.

Millgate, Michael. "*The Mayor of Casterbridge.*" In his *Thomas Hardy: His Career as a Novelist,* pp. 221-34. New York: Random House, 1971.

Close study of *The Mayor of Casterbridge,* focusing on its place in Hardy's development as a novelist.

Moynahan, Julian. "*The Mayor of Casterbridge* and the Old Testament's First Book of Samuel: A Study of Some Literary Relationships." *PMLA* LXXI, No. 1 (March 1956): 118-30.

Compares the theme of generational conflict in *The Mayor of Casterbridge* with the Biblical story of Saul and David in Samuel I.

Payne, William Morton. "Recent Fiction." *The Dial* VII, No. 75 (July 1886): 65-70.

Favorable review of *The Mayor of Casterbridge.*

Rutland, William R. "The Novels, 1875-1891." In his *Thomas Hardy: A Study of His Writings and Their Background*, pp. 176-220. Oxford: Basil Blackwell, 1938.
>   Examines Hardy's philosophical outlook and provides biographical and literary background to his works.

Southerington, F. R. Chapter VI. In his *Hardy's Vision of Man*, pp. 96-105. New York: Barnes & Noble, 1971.
>   Examines the mythic bases of *The Mayor of Casterbridge*.

Weber, Carl J. "Portrait of a Man of Character." In his *Hardy of Wessex: His Life and Literary Career*, pp. 139-53. 1940. Rev. ed. New York: Columbia University Press, 1965.
>   Account of Hardy's life at the time he wrote *The Mayor of Casterbridge* and critical discussion of the novel.

Webster, Harvey Curtis. *On a Darkling Plain: The Art & Thought of Thomas Hardy*. Chicago: The University of Chicago Press, 1947, 240 p.

>   Contains numerous scattered references to plot, characterization, and underlying philosophy in *The Mayor of Casterbridge*.

Winner, Anthony. "Hardy's Moderns: The Ache of Uncertain Character." In his *Characters in the Twilight: Hardy, Zola, and Chekhov*, pp. 28-72. Charlottesville: University Press of Virginia, 1981.
>   Finds that Hardy's basic pessimism is clearly displayed in the character of Michael Henchard, whose essentially primitive and animalistic vitality renders him unsuited to respond to the demands of the modern world.

Woolf, Virginia. *A Writer's Diary*, edited by Leonard Woolf. London: The Hogarth Press, 1959, 372 p.
>   Contains scattered references to Thomas Hardy and his works. The entry for Sunday, July 25, 1926, recounts a visit with Hardy and his wife, during which Woolf mentioned her enjoyment of *The Mayor of Casterbridge*.

William James

1842-1910

American philosopher and psychologist.

For further discussion of James's career, see *TCLC*, Vol. 15.

One of the most influential figures in modern Western philosophy, James was the founder of Pragmatism as a philosophical school. The English philosopher Alfred North Whitehead called him "one of the greatest philosophic minds of all time," and despite formidable resistance to James's ideas during his lifetime, his works have become recognized as landmarks in the development of modern thought. In opposition to the tenets of scientific materialism and philosophic idealism, which had prevailed in Western philosophy throughout the eighteenth and nineteenth centuries, James attempted to comprehend and to describe human life as it is actually experienced, rather than formulating models of abstract reality far removed from the passion and pain of life. In James's philosophy of Pragmatism, the rationalist doubts of science as well as the nonrational certainties of mysticism are subordinated to the diverse moral and psychological needs of human beings.

Like psychologists Sigmund Freud and C. G. Jung and philosopher Henri Bergson, James was a highly original and often unorthodox thinker whose work has had an impact on various aspects of life and culture, including literature, religion, and psychology, as well as on philosophic movements that emerged later in the twentieth century. In particular, his thought is considered a forerunner of the phenomenological movement in philosophy and psychology for its emphasis on the role of individual consciousness in the active creation, as opposed to the passive perception, of reality and meaning. In his first major work, *The Principles of Psychology,* James proposed the view of human consciousness as an unbroken process, rather than as a series of isolated thoughts and perceptions, a concept that provided the term "stream-of-consciousness" for describing the narrative technique of such Modernist authors as James Joyce and Gertrude Stein. As a philosopher of religion, James offered an encyclopedia of spiritual beliefs in his *The Varieties of Religious Experience,* which argues for the acceptance of values derived from a stratum of human experience that is beyond rational discussion.

Among the best-known and most controversial examples of the tolerant and liberal spirit in James's work is "The Will to Believe." In this essay, as well as in his writings that expound the Pragmatic theory of truth, James attempted to resolve one of the oldest questions of philosophy—what can or cannot be known as "true"—by viewing any given truth as something that not only differs from person to person and is subject to change over a period of time, but also as something that may depend upon an individual's willing belief. This philosophy of the diversity and changeability of truths, which James later developed as the doctrine of "radical pluralism," stood in contrast to the monist absolutism of such thinkers of the time as F. H. Bradley, Charles Sanders Peirce, and Josiah Royce, who held that ultimate truth was unchanging and that reality was an immutable transcendent unity known as the absolute. These philosophers, who found James's view of the universe overly literal and materialistic, comprised one of two principal

groups that attacked James's ideas. The other group was made up of such figures as G. E. Moore and Bertrand Russell, strict materialists and logicians who saw James's Pragmatism as simply indefensible in rational terms. While it was the doctrines of this latter group that would dominate Anglo-American philosophy throughout the twentieth century, rather than those of either James himself or his most illustrious successor, John Dewey, as an individual thinker James continues to be regarded among the most important in Western intellectual history.

Born in New York City and raised in various cities throughout New England and Europe, James was the eldest in a wealthy family of five children that included the novelist Henry James, Jr. and diarist Alice James. James's father, Henry James, Sr., was a deeply religious man who was trained to enter the Presbyterian ministry; however, he became dissatisfied with the solutions of conventional religion to fundamental spiritual questions and eventually developed a system of beliefs based on the writings of the eighteenth-century Swedish mystic Emmanuel Swedenborg. Henry, Sr. believed that a divinity emanating from God was intrinsic to all human beings, and that conventions of society and organized religion largely served to blind individuals to their spiritual worth and to their absolute equality with one another. These beliefs were the source of his strong conviction that an individual should be allowed every opportunity to realize his or her personal qualities and abilities, a process that would ultimately result in a social utopia of diverse personalities unbent by the pressures of conformity, yet nonetheless capable of living together as equals. These principles were the basis for the culturally stimulating, liberal home environment in which William and his siblings were raised.

Because his father was as distrustful of educational institutions as he was of what he called "professional religion," James was educated at home in his early years, with sporadic attendance at various schools in England, France, Switzerland, and Germany. As a young student, he was divided between his strong attraction to the natural sciences and to art. In 1860 he made a decision to study painting with noted Pre-Raphaelite painter William H. Hunt, but a brief period of study revealed to James that painting was not his field, for his artistic talents were modest and did not develop significantly under Hunt's tutelage. Believing that to be a mediocre artist was a contemptible occupation, he abandoned art while still cultivating his sensitivity for the detail and abundance of the visible world. James next rediscovered his enthusiasm for natural science, entering the Lawrence Scientific School at Harvard in 1861. There he studied chemistry, anatomy, and physiology under such professors as Charles W. Eliot and Louis Agassiz, and in 1864 transferred to the Harvard Medical School. While in medical school, James traveled to Brazil as an assistant on the Thayer expedition, a mission of exploration and study led by Agassiz, which, he later wrote, taught him "the difference between all possible abstractionists and all livers in the light of the world's concrete fulness."

While he continued to study medicine during the years 1867 and 1868, both at Harvard and in Europe, James suffered from a variety of what are widely considered to have been psychosomatic ailments—ocular sensitivity, pain in the lower back, and generalized lassitude. Accompanying these physical symptoms were frequent considerations of suicide and the feelings of acute anxiety which he later described in *The Varieties of Religious Experience,* where he disguised one particularly harrowing episode of "panic fear" as the testimony of an anonymous Frenchman. James's account details an experience of "a horrible fear of [his] own existence," a seizure of panic which summons the mental image of an epileptic patient he had seen in an asylum, "a black-haired youth with greenish skin, entirely idiotic, who used to sit all day on one of the benches. . . . He sat there like a sort of sculptured Egyptian cat or Peruvian mummy, moving nothing but his black eyes and looking absolutely non-human." The combination of this frightful image with James's abnormal fear gave rise to a personal revelation: "*That shape am I,* I felt, potentially." Elsewhere in *The Varieties of Religious Experience,* James wrote: "We are all *potentially* such sick men. The sanest and best of us are of one clay with lunatics and prison-inmates." This conviction, while losing the pathological force of the moment, became significant to James's later philosophy, which found an affirmation of human life meaningless without a recognition of evil and accident in the universe.

Although James's emotional and physical frailty persisted, he managed to keep up a demanding course of readings, both in medicine and now as a serious student of philosophy and psychology, and in 1869 he received his medical degree from Harvard. In 1870, the severity of James's neurasthenia abated when he read *Essais de critique génerale* by the French philosopher Charles Renouvier, and he thereafter resolved to achieve a greater measure of physical health and mental balance. James

also credited Renouvier's philosophy of pluralism with freeing him of the "monistic superstition" of his earlier education and revealing to him that "the world may *compose* a whole without being determined by it . . . that unity should not predetermine the many." An opponent of scientific determinism and an advocate of the doctrine of free will, Renouvier provided a particular focus—that of morality—which James praised for leading him out of a "paralysis of action occasioned by a sense of moral impotence." Believing now in his own power to oppose the malady which, as a moral evil, afflicted him, James determined to attain a state of health. "I finished the first part of Renouvier's second *Essais,*" he wrote in 1870, "and see no reason why his definition of free will—'the sustaining of a thought *because I choose to* when I might have other thoughts'— need be the definition of an illusion. At any rate, I will assume for the present—until next year—that it is no illusion. My first act of free will shall be to believe in free will." This belief in the benefits of a "posited" free will became a component of James's later philosophy, particularly in the doctrine of "The Will to Believe," which offered scientific and philosophical support for what had begun as a personal need.

Nevertheless, James lived in a state of semi-invalidism until 1872, when he was appointed as an instructor at Harvard; his association with the university lasted until 1907. Noting that the first subject James taught at Harvard was physiology, scholars of his intellectual development often underline the significance of his background in the natural sciences for his later career as a psychologist. When he became an instructor in psychology in 1876, he treated this field of study not as a branch of philosophy, one especially laden with metaphysical speculation, but as a natural science subject to the rigors of laboratory experiment. James's desire to eliminate metaphysics from future studies in psychology, and to consider this discipline strictly as a natural science, resulted in the innovative perspective of his first major work, *The Principles of Psychology.* Commissioned in 1878 to complete a textbook on this subject by 1880, James ultimately took twelve years to produce a monumental consideration of all knowledge in the field. Upon its publication in 1890, *The Principles of Psychology* was recognized as a landmark work of its kind, and although some of its conceptions—such as the distinction between metaphysical psychology and psychology considered as a natural science— aroused controversy, this treatise was nevertheless respected for its encyclopedic scope and the stimulating originality of its insights. Both as a focus of controversy and a vitalizing intellectual force, James's work as a psychologist presaged his later work as a philosopher.

In 1878 James married Alice H. Gibbens. Beginning with his first years of marriage, he entered a period of prodigious activity which established his popular image as a robust, adventurous, and above all open-minded investigator of human life and philosophic truth. For much of the time he was working on *The Principles of Psychology,* James was already an instructor of philosophy, shifting his interests from scientific inquiries about human behavior to philosophic questions of moral values, free will, and the reality of a spiritual dimension to life. Fascinated by the possibility of life after death, James joined the Society for Psychic Research in 1882, later serving as its president for a brief time. Regarding religious belief, James's ability to maintain both the skepticism of a trained scientist and a sympathetic open-mindedness is reflected in such early collections as *The Will to Believe, and Other Essays in Popular Philosophy, Human Immortality: Two Supposed Objections to the Doctrine,* and *The Varieties of Religious*

Experience. With *The Will to Believe*, James began to establish himself as a philosophic iconoclast who presented a serious challenge to the prevailing schools of rationalism and absolutism, and eventually he attained the stature of the most important and most popular figure in American philosophy. Each new volume became an occasion for attacks from his critics and reaffirmed loyalty on the part of his supporters. However, among critics and supporters alike James was respected and admired, and his friendships included illustrious thinkers of diverse and often conflicting ideologies: Josiah Royce and F. C. S. Schiller, Charles Sanders Peirce and Henri Bergson, F. H. Bradley and Theodore Flournoy. He was widely regarded not only as a philosopher, but also as a poet, sage, and mystic whose works and personal presence were inspirational as well as intellectually enlightening.

In the last decade of his life, James suffered from a heart condition. Seeking rest and recovery, he traveled to Europe with his wife in 1910, visiting his brother Henry in London. Although biographers find there were basic frictions between the personalities of the two renowned brothers—which may be approximated by Henry's identification with an old, aristocratic Europe and William's with a new, populist America—they held each other, if not each other's works, in mutual respect and affection. In the summer of 1910, William returned to America and died not long after his arrival.

When *The Principles of Psychology* appeared in 1890 it was immediately recognized as a major effort to assemble a massive quantity of research from leading authorities of several nations, and this contribution alone would have established its importance. In addition, James also proposed a number of particular theories that have been received as pioneering concepts in the field. As a researcher, James created the first laboratory for psychological study in America, and his *Principles of Psychology* emphasizes the necessity for practical observation, rather than metaphysical speculation, in attempting to understand the workings of the mind and emotions. Advocating the abandonment of such concepts as "the soul, the transcendental ego, the fusion of ideas and particles of mind stuff, etc.," he pursued a definition and description of "mental states," considering the influence of the physical brain and of bodily experiences upon individual consciousness and emotions. Among the most renowned of his conceptions in this area is the controversial James-Lange theory of emotion, which James and Danish psychologist Carl George Lange developed independently of one another. This theory states that it is a person's reaction to a stimulus which causes an emotion rather than the emotion causing the reaction; that is, we feel afraid because we run, not run because we feel afraid. It was James's search for a material answer to the function of emotions, as much as the supportability of this particular theory, that was important for the history of psychological study. Perhaps James's most famous contribution to psychology was his view of consciousness as a physical process—a continuous flux of feelings, ideas, and sensations—and not as a static condition in which isolated thoughts and perceptions abruptly appear and disappear. The chapter "The Stream of Thought" in *The Principles of Psychology* revised traditional conceptions of human consciousness, particularly the idea that thought and feeling are separable experiences not affecting each other, just as James's opus in general undermined the view of psychology as the "philosophy of the soul." James wrote that "the kind of psychology which could cure a case of melancholy, or charm a chronic insane delusion away, ought certainly to be preferred to the most seraphic insights into the nature of the soul." While many of

James's ideas have been inevitably replaced by ones more sophisticated and advanced, *The Principles of Psychology* is still considered a masterpiece for its sensitive and inspired articulation of human experience.

James's first collection of philosophical writings was *The Will to Believe*, and the title essay of this volume elicited much of the controversy surrounding James's value as a thinker. The "belief" discussed by James is not specifically that of religion but rather any general belief which facilitates moral decisions. James contended that such beliefs, although without the support of logic or science, could ultimately make true what was at first merely believed to be true, as in the case of some task the successful performance of which requires a strong faith in the inevitability of success. Critics of this idea argue that, given James's own admission of the potential fallibility of a belief concerning the outcome of any action, there appears to be little justification for such a moral program, which is equated with wishful thinking or, in the sarcastic phrase of Dickinson S. Miller, "The Will to Make-Believe." Some critics have suggested that James should have termed his concept "The Right to Believe," especially as it applies to matters of religious faith. Considering James an essentially agnostic thinker, George Santayana wrote of him: "He did not really believe; he merely believed in the right of believing that you might be right if you believed." Defenders of "The Will to Believe," including F. C. S. Schiller and William Barrett, praise James for offering a liberating alternative to the restrictions placed upon human will by doctrines demanding logical support as a prerequisite for belief, doctrines that presuppose a deterministic, possibly nihilistic reality. As in all his works, however, James's intention in "The Will to Believe" was not to argue for the adoption of a specific dogma, not even his own, but to encourage the exercise of ways of thinking that he believed could improve human life. James's interest in various forms of belief is also reflected in his writings on parapsychology and his lectures on *Human Immortality*, reaching its culmination in one of his most celebrated works, *The Varieties of Religious Experience*.

Examining the sources and nature of religious belief, *The Varieties of Religious Experience* is considered the founding work in the psychology of religion. Although this study was the first to extensively document case histories of individual religious experiences, critics have primarily regarded James's work as more relevant to the philosophy of religion than to its psychological aspects. Recently, however, this view has been challenged by Gary T. Alexander, who finds that James significantly related his earlier study of psychology to his study of religion, lending psychological as well as philosophical dimension to the later work. Subtitled "A Study in Human Nature," *The Varieties of Religious Experience* has as its premise the idea that the persistence of religious feelings testifies to their value in human life and to their importance to any serious understanding of human behavior. This attitude was intended as a counterpoint to the prevalent scientific view of the time that strong religious feelings—such as those of spontaneous mystical experience or a sudden religious conversion—are pathological states meaningful only as they illuminate a subject's physical or psychological condition. After considering such manifestations of religious feeling as "'once born' and 'twice born' characters," the morbid hypersensitivity of the "sick soul," episodes of religious conversion, the lives of the saints, and overwhelming mystical experiences of "cosmic consciousness," James concludes that these phenomena indicate the existence of a real power or powers external to a particular subject. However, while recognizing the religious experience of individuals as the foundation of which the doctrines of organized religions are the superstructure, or "by-products" in the phrase of Jacques Barzun, James also concludes that no specific meaning can be attached to the varieties of religious experience that would uphold the dogma of any established religion. Summarizing his observations on religious experience, he stated: "The only thing that it unequivocally testifies to is that we can experience union with *something* larger than ourselves and in that union find our greatest peace." In the conclusion to the *Varieties,* as well as in the later work *A Pluralistic Universe,* James proposed the existence of a finite God or a plurality of gods. This being or these beings, while offering superhuman spiritual comfort, would not be vulnerable to the philosophic indictments against an all-loving, all powerful god who, paradoxically, lacks the power to abolish evil in the world or who, malevolently, is unwilling to do so. The concept of a limited, pluralistic deity synchronizes with James's opposition, in such later works as *Pragmatism* and *Radical Empiricism,* to any form of absolute, preferring the "risk" that common sense finds inherent in the universe. "Common sense," wrote James, "is less sweeping in its demands than philosophy or mysticism have wont to be, and can suffer the notion of this world being partly saved and partly lost. . . . No fact of human nature is more characteristic than its willingness to live on a chance."

The body of ideas most commonly associated with James are those of the philosophy known as Pragmatism, which was introduced in his 1898 lecture "Philosophical Conceptions." Critics have emphasized, however, that all of James's works are founded on the basic principles and attitudes of the Pragmatic philosophy. James's focus on concrete experience, rather than on abstract speculation, in *The Principles of Psychology,* his concern with the practical consequences of believing in *The Will to Believe,* and his refusal of absolutism in *The Varieties of Religious Experience* emerge as the major themes in the collection *Pragmatism: A New Name for Some Old Ways of Thinking.* While James traced the Pragmatic temperament— temperament being to James a major determinant of what ideas one will adopt and defend—back to Socrates, with Immanuel Kant, John Locke, and Francis Bacon among those included along the way, he acknowledged the immediate source of this philosophy to be C. S. Peirce's 1878 essay "How to Make Our Ideas Clear." Peirce was a colleague of James at Harvard and during the 1870s was a member, with James and others, of a philosophical society called the "Metaphysical Club." Peirce's essay outlined a method for determining solutions to philosophic and scientific questions through a systematic clarification of their meaning. He stated that "in order to ascertain the meaning of an intellectual conception one should consider what practical consequences might conceivably result by necessity from the truth of that conception; and the sum of these consequences will constitute the entire meaning of the conception." In his writings on Pragmatism, James extended Peirce's methodology beyond the original field of logical investigation it was intended to serve, developing it into a full-blown philosophy applicable to all areas of human experience, especially those outside the purview of logic and science, such as religious faith.

James asked: "What difference would it practically make to any one if this notion rather than that notion were true? If no practical difference whatever can be traced, then the alternatives mean practically the same thing, and all dispute is idle. Whenever a dispute is serious, we ought to be able to show some practical difference that must follow from one side or the other's being right." Implicit in this statement is James's intention that Pragmatism should serve as a program for human action, as opposed to a method for organizing abstract problems of logic. A given "truth" is thus determined not exclusively according to whether or not it can be proven in rational terms; whenever a question of truth cannot be resolved by logic or present scientific knowledge, this question may be resolved by considering the benefits to an individual or society and including this as a factor in the decision for or against its truth. Hence, a given truth may change in light of circumstances which alter its beneficial consequences. James also specified another very important factor in the Pragmatic theory of truth: that the question of something being true or not must be a serious one and its resolution one way or the other "momentous," as in matters of religion or morality. Critics of the Pragmatic theory of truth have attacked its logical weaknesses, as well as remarking on the difficulties in arriving at an objective determination of the benefits of upholding a particular truth. Defenders of James's theory point out that it was not designed to serve the ends of logic or contribute to objective knowledge but to aid individuals in their adaptation to a world of change, and that the theory's value lies entirely in the area of subjective decisions and the consequences which result from them.

Fundamental to Pragmatism is James's rejection of the concept of absolute truth and his belief that the universe is a pluralistic, not a monistic, reality. Nevertheless, he recognized the right of absolutists to believe in a unified reality in accordance with the needs of their temperament, which he called "tender-minded"—personalities who are "rationalistic (going by 'principles'), idealistic, optimistic, religious, free-willist, monistic, and dogmatical"—as opposed to "tough-minded" individuals, who tend to be "empiricist (going by 'facts'), materialistic, pessimistic, irreligious, fatalistic, pluralistic, and skeptical." James also recognized the difficulties of promoting during his lifetime—which was an era of idealism and rationalism—a philosophy of pluralism in which "there appears no universal element of which all things are made." Writing of the concept of the absolute in Eastern mysticism, James remarked: "As compared with it, pluralistic empiricism offers a sorry appearance. It is a turbid, muddled, gothic sort of affair, without a sweeping outline and with little pictorial nobility." For James it was precisely these qualities of formless diversity and risk-filled possibility that constituted the essence and much of the appeal of the human condition.

Toward the end of his life James had plans, which remained undeveloped, to organize the various themes and elements of his writings into a work of systematic philosophy, thereby clarifying many of the ambiguities and inconsistencies critics had found in his thought. He had often found it necessary in his works to address frequent and sometimes serious misunderstandings of his ideas on the part of his critics. In some cases his philosophical position was seen as the inverse of what he intended, as when Paul Elmer More found James's ideas to be those of a rationalist or F. H. Bradley described him as an idealist whose Pragmatism was "in harmony with views against which it is commonly understood to protest." The most common misconception about Pragmatism has been that it serves as a code, one nearly synonymous with America's capitalist system, that sanctions any method or behavior so long as it is efficient and profits the adherent. Such a misconception became outstandingly evident when Benito Mussolini credited James with teaching him the principles "to which Fascism owes a great deal of its success." Success divorced from a humanistic morality was in fact never a formula put forth by James, who coined the phrase "the bitch goddess, success" to castigate what he saw as a weakness among Americans for commercial advancement at the expense of moral integrity.

James's Pragmatism considered human emotions and subjective viewpoints as a necessary and much-neglected part of philosophy, and this perspective perhaps accounts for many of the problems early critics had in evaluating his works. The willingness to accept a philosophy in which feelings openly confront intellectual propositions has led to an increasing appreciation of James among later critics. In 1975 William Barrett, author of *Irrational Man*, a study of Existentialist philosophy, wrote of a James revival in his essay "Our Contemporary, William James." Studies by Jacques Barzun and Howard M. Feinstein are distinguished contributions to this revival and are among recent affirmations that James is the most important philosopher America has yet produced.

(See also *Contemporary Authors*, Vol. 109.)

PRINCIPAL WORKS

The Principles of Psychology. 2 vols.   (treatise)   1890
*The Will to Believe, and Other Essays in Popular
    Philosophy*   (essays)   1897
*Human Immortality: Two Supposed Objections to the
    Doctrine*   (lectures)   1898; enlarged edition, 1899
*Talks to Teachers on Psychology and to Students on Some of
    Life's Ideals*   (lectures)   1899
The Varieties of Religious Experience   (lectures)   1902
Pragmatism: A New Name for Some Old Ways of Thinking
    (lectures)   1907
The Meaning of Truth: A Sequel to "Pragmatism"   (essays)
    1909
A Pluralistic Universe   (lectures)   1909
Memories and Studies   (essays)   1911
*Some Problems of Philosophy: A Beginning of an
    Introduction to Philosophy*   (unfinished treatise)   1911
Essays in Radical Empiricism   (essays)   1912
Collected Essays and Reviews   (essays and criticism)   1920
The Letters of William James. 2 vols.   (letters)   1920

ELLWOOD JOHNSON   (essay date 1972)

[*In the following excerpt, Johnson examines the influence of James's psychological theories on the depiction of character in American fiction written between 1915 and 1945.*]

It is a truism that the most immediate influence on the literature of any period of history is the way in which the people of that period define the self and man's power and position in the universe. Whether the individual is seen as rational or irrational, divine, diabolical, or soulless, whether the universe is anthropocentric or man is meaningless in the chaos of the universe, may determine to a large extent the ways in which the fiction-writer presents character and incident. As an aside, one might remark that if our immediate posterity is to see mankind as Ray Bradbury has recently described it, as a "God awakening to the universe," we shall have a heroic literature in which science fiction has ceased to be either fantasy or satire and has become epocal and tragic—another Elizabethan "age of discovery." But my concern here is with the "modern"

period of American literature, 1915-1945, during which there was in one sense a "loss of the self," as Wylie Sypher has described it [in his *Loss of the Self in Modern Literature and Art*], and in another sense, an expansion of the self to the point where the subject and objects of experience are no longer distinguishable. I think it is not generally recognized that the most concrete and direct influence on this period was William James's speculations on human consciousness in his ***Principles of Psychology,*** in which he postulates that man has no soul in the traditional sense of the term, no epicenter of identity, for the very reason that the self exists "in time," in the flux of experience, and that volition and time, rather than soul, spirit, or reason, are the essences of human identity.

James's psychology marked a turning point in American literary history not only to the extent that it was a testing of the visionary ideas of American Transcendentalist individualism in a relatively scientific and empirical language but, most important for the American writer, it placed the self "in time," so to speak; it added a new dimension to the art of characterization in fiction. (p. 285)

The premise of James's psychology is that "thought is impulsive," that is, there is a selecting and attending principle at work in the "process" of consciousness which determines immediate action and behavior; and also, the impulsive, or volitional, nature of consciousness is the reason it is a continuum, or "stream." James premises his work on the "principle that *no actions but such as are done for an end, and show a choice of means, can be called indubitable expressions of Mind,*" and this principle becomes the "criterion by which to circumscribe the subject-matter of this work." Were it not for the continuous focusing and attending of thought, a better metaphor might be a "lake" or "field" of consciousness, as all elements of memory and experience would interact chaotically. So it is the volitional nature of human consciousness that makes it directional; we are constantly becoming rather than being.

Because it is directional and "impulsive," the events of consciousness are not separable.

> Consciousness, then, does not appear to itself chopped up in bits. Such words as "chain" or "train" do not describe it fitly as it presents itself in the first instance. It is nothing jointed; it flows. A "river" or a "stream" are the metaphors by which it is most naturally described. In talking of it hereafter, let us call it the stream of thought, of consciousness, or of subjective life.

He used the terms "continuum of thought," "stream of thought," and "stream of consciousness" to suggest the lack of the present in human life; we can no more stop the self to examine it than we can stop time in order to take a look at the present moment. Nor can we localize the immediately passing images and events for examination because our consciousness is composed of relationships and continuities rather than isolated particularities, "instants and moments." We perceive in memory, imagination, and in the passing moment things in continuity and in relationship to each other.

The expression "stream of impulsive thought" is the closest James came to a solid definition of the human self. There is, inherent in this expression, the principle that "will is identity." Whatever it is in consciousness that focuses, selects, attends is the individuality of the person. Consciousness tends to eliminate peripheral perceptions. As I write this page, my attention withdraws into my own thought and the page literally dims before my gaze and then becomes more vivid before me as my attention shifts to the mechanical process of writing: this act of focusing the continuum of my thought is the "I" of my reality. That my will is my identity is not evidence, however, that I have a "dreadful freedom"; my consciousness is "impulsive," "habitual," and "obsessional," to the extent that both my mental and physical behavior and even my perceptions can be explained in terms of habits of thought. (pp. 285-86)

We do not will ourselves to act; we will ourselves to think, or at least, to focus our consciousness, and this in turn *becomes* physical action. In whatever way we are inclined, or oriented, or focused, or attentive, we will move; and if I may take this one step further to form a basic pragmatic-transcendentalist principle, in such a way we form our entire lives—to the way we see and shape our environment, to the visions we create, religious and otherwise to the personal, physical, mental, and sexual power we develop.

Like Emerson, James believed in a "heroic" theory of history, although, if he had written a series of essays on great men as Emerson had, he probably would have chosen an entirely different set of heroes for consideration and would have emphasized much different characteristics in them. He had no illusions about the vital currents of being that energize great men; nor did he see very much difference in terms of psychological power between men of different ranks. In **"The Importance of Individuals,"** he tells us that the very slightest distinctions to be made between individuals are the most important and that the distinctions that are historically important are generally mere preferences. A Washington has slightly different preferences and interests from Jenkins, and on these slightly variant attitudes history is dependent. One can see a kind of Existential anti-heroism in this individualism. A great man is an "upsetter of unstable equilibria"; his actions unblock social-historical energy. His influences on history are, in a sense, volitional accidents; it is not his genius that affects posterity but his individuality, the leanings and tendencies of his character which cannot be explained deterministically but simply "appear." They appear, in fact, as "spontaneous variations" in the same way that variants appear in nature according to Darwin's theory. . . . The analogy with Darwinism continues in the principle that a change of "utter insignificance" in itself by a great-man variant may, and is apt to, have far-reaching extensions in history: ". . . the great man, whether he be an importation from without like Clive in India or Agassiz here, or whether he spring from the soil like Mahomet or Franklin, brings about a rearrangement, on a large or a small scale, of the pre-existing social relations." History is "due to the accumulated influences of individuals of their examples, their initiatives, and their decisions." It is not "due to the environment, to the circumstances, the physical geography, the ancestral conditions, the increasing experience of outer relations."

Individuals form society, then, rather than the other way around. . . . But even though society forms itself out of the accidental positioning of individuals, it also builds itself into the individuals of succeeding generations. There is something of the "central man" and also Emerson's ameliorative evolution in the idea of each man containing within himself all of the past: "A living being must always contain within itself the history, not merely of its own existence, but of all its ancestors." Society, then, forms limits to the possibilities of change. It selects individuals in the same way nature selects variant species, and the individuals brought to power form a selective influence on their posterity. There is in this historical process

as well as in natural evolution a tendency from chaos toward unity.

James conjectures that the entire universe, in fact, is moving from chaos toward stability and suggests the possibility that human will is a more regularizing influence in this evolution than we suspect, as the "aberrant and inconstant variations . . . wander off as unrelated variants," and nature adjusts itself to principles of balance forming within itself. Thus he can say that the universe can be described either in terms of its unity or its disconnection, but that "there appear to be actual forces at work which tend, as time goes on, to make the unity greater." (pp. 287-89)

The turning point in the history of Puritan literature may be the nearly worldwide acceptance of William James's description of the self as a continuum of experience; it is a "turning point," however, not because this history turned away from individualism and Victorian puritanism but because it brought all the solipsistic tendencies of American fiction into full focus.

A major difference between the old and the new art is suggested by the tendency of modern novelists to structure fiction from within character. In modern narratives, scene and plot are presented through the consciousnesses of characters so that the externalities, or reality, of a writer's fictional world become data of characterization. The Edwardian-Victorian novelist presented his characters usually from a distance, omnisciently, to give his reader a perspective on each character as an element in a scene; the tendency in the twentieth century has been to place the reader in the protagonist's mind, seeing his experiences and his scene through his senses. Dramatic tension usually occurs within the single character, and hence there has been an emphasis increasingly on subjective psychological problems as opposed to the relatively objective problems arising out of the opposition of the individual and society. Dramatic action in this fiction is set within the solitude of the self.

Another distinction is that the narrator using an exterior, omniscient viewpoint could stop the action to discuss character and situation or to editorialize; he was apt, in fact, to stop the action in order to talk about what was going on inside one of his characters; but the narrator using an interior viewpoint (interior monologue or a stream-of-consciousness technique) is always inside a character and must be "time-conscious": he works in a fictional world in which there is no present moment to stop; the consciousness through which he presents his fictional scene is continually becoming; the action continually ongoing.

The stream-of-consciousness technique, of course, is not an American innovation; it has, in fact, had very few American practitioners. There are important distinctions to be made between the techniques, on the one hand, of Dorothy Richardson, James Joyce, and Virginia Woolf, who were perhaps more directly influenced by the examples of Dujardin, Dostoyevsky, and Henry James than by William James's original theory, and, on the other hand, what Philip Rahv calls the "cult of experience" in American fiction. The former group experimented with structural and stylistic techniques; they were especially concerned with the ways in which the past and the becoming moment come together in consciousness. The latter group, which includes the major writers of the twenties and thirties, relate to William James in more subjective ways that are revealed through the content of their work, especially in the way they see the individual as a part of objective experience, and not so much by their technical, stylistic innovations. There seemed to be in their fiction a "loss of the self" as Wylie Sypher has described it, or "vanishing subject" as John Dewey had it, because the self was seen as William James had defined it, as a volitional focus in a continuum of experience. In theory, the new techniques of characterization were not revolutionary; they were the ultimate conceptions of identity toward which the whole Puritan tradition of letters was always tending. There was no stable, creative "Emersonian epicenter" in James's self, but in another sense, the self had been expanded to include the whole of an individual's subjective and objective identity.

The three terms of this psychology of modern fiction are time, volition, and experience. Of these, experience is the universal characteristic of modern American fiction. Writers have tended to equate self and experience and to present characters as patterns of experience. They have been perhaps too preoccupied with the act instead of the actor, or with sensation instead of idea. And experience has usually meant violence and abnormal sex for them. The values of immediate experience have replaced traditional values. In seeing the self as experience, the American writer treats experience as both means and end; there is no meaning to life beyond the experience of it.

Much of the complexity of contemporary literature results from the efforts of writers to turn things around and present environment as subject and self as object in a way that loses the self in experience. The expression "stream of consciousness" has been taken too literally as a psychological premise; a character in a modern novel is apt to appear as a point of focus between memory and immediate experience and at the same time as a nebulous totality of the "remembered" tradition and immediately experienced environment, just as Leopold Bloom combines ironically in his consciousness Odysseus setting out on his journeys and the toilet he is sitting on, also a part of his consciousness.

Leopold Bloom is the sum of the history of Western civilization, but the major characters in Hemingway, Steinbeck, and Wolfe are only the sums of their own experiences (we might say this also of their authors); there is implicit in much of American fiction the belief that the wider the range of experience a person has, the more person he will become. In *The Sun Also Rises,* for example, Count Mippopopolous can provide a lesson in modern values because, like Jake Barnes, he has "seen a lot," and his life is a search for experience. He has been in seven wars and four revolutions. Proud of his arrow wounds, he pulls up his shirt to show how they went "clean through."

> "Where did you get those?" I asked.

> "In Abyssinia. When I was twenty-one years old."

> "What were you doing?" asked Brett. "Were you in the army?"

> "I was on a business trip, my dear."

> "I told you he was one of us. Didn't I?" Brett turned to me.

The count goes on to explain that ". . . it is because I have lived very much that now I can enjoy everything so well," and "You must get to know the values," meaning the values of experiential living. Brett points out to him that he really has no values in a traditional sense; he and his values are dead. He and his values are obviously being made fun of but, in a broader sense, the entire novel is self-satirical; it is Hemingway's picture of himself and his own "lost" generation. That which is being satirized in the count is the given of Jake's life.

For the count there is no romantic ideal of love left in the world, there is only the experience of love, and one might as well have the experience with whomever happens to be available at the moment: "'I am always in love.'" So the word *values* has an ambiguous and ironic function in this passage. The old values are dead, and the values of experience have replaced them. "Food had an excellent place in the count's values. So did wine." Eating, drinking, fighting, and making love are valid in the experiential life; talking and thinking are not. "Talking's all bilge," Brett says; and Jake, later: "What a lot of bilge I could think up at night." In a world where values, identity, and experience are equated, life is lived, but not interpreted; experience is its own meaning and value. The code forbids sentiment, as well as horror, that which Jake might think up at night. (pp. 290-91)

As there was an increasing tendency in James's work subsequent to the publication of *Principles of Psychology* to merge subject and object, that is, to describe the self in terms of its objective experience and the data of the senses, so there has been also, a tendency for American writers to present fictional characters as kinds of experience. Characters in the experimental novels do not really have souls, nor values, therefore, that might be said to transcend the immediate experience of life, although they may have other things that for Hemingway, at least, are more important: they have style, grace, and irony, for examples, and these give a certain moral quality to experience and to their own identities. (p. 292)

> *Ellwood Johnson, "William James and the Art of Fiction," in* The Journal of Aesthetics and Art Criticism, *Vol. XXX, No. 3, Spring, 1972, pp. 285-96.*

HENRY SAMUEL LEVINSON   (essay date 1981)

[*Levinson is an American educator and author of works on religious and philosophical subjects. In the following excerpt, he considers the development of James's religious thought in the context of the changing attitudes toward religion during the late Victorian era.*]

Matthew Arnold spoke for a large class of Victorian Anglo-Saxon intellectuals when he wrote in 1875 that "at the present moment two things about the Christian religion must surely be clear to anybody with eyes in his head. One is, that men cannot do without it; the other, that they cannot do with it as it is." Even if James confided to friends from his twenties on that he could not be Christian because Christ played no crucial role in the process of salvation as he understood it, Arnold's formula caught the essence of James's religious situation. By the time James was twenty-eight years old he had tried to do without religion and he had failed.

During his teens and early twenties, he had dabbled with both Epicureanism and Stoicism, common adventures for wealthy, educated, transatlantic Anglo-Saxon gentlemen at the time. He found Epicurean aestheticism too loose and ultimately comical; Stoic moralism was suffocating and tragic. His inability to devote himself to either of those classical alternatives to Christianity probably contributed to his near-suicidal depression during 1868-72, a period marked by acute acedia and its arrest by religious consolation. In a memoir quoted anonymously as part of his Gifford Lectures in 1901, he made it clear that disgust with human existence and a carking question whether life was worth living led to his despond. Personally nearly disastrous, James's acedia was far from idiosyncratic. Sloth was a common response among intellectuals to their own sense of power. As

Robert Solomon has put it, in the post-Napoleonic period (and for Americans in the period immediately following the Civil War), "the Absurd was born, not of loss of religion, but of gains in humanism. The more we thought of ourselves, the less we thought of our Reality. There was no one else to blame." In a period when intellectuals entertained simultaneously the notions that humanity might be divine and that the difference between the savage and the civilized rested on a series of contingencies, there were grounds for life-arresting pessimism. In such a state, James

> went one evening into a dressing-room . . . when suddenly there fell upon me without any warning, just as if it came out of the darkness, a horrible fear of my own existence. Simultaneously there arose in my mind the image of an epileptic patient whom I had seen in the asylum. . . . He sat there like a sort of Egyptian cat or Peruvian mummy, moving nothing but his black eyes and looking absolutely non-human. This image and my fear entered into a species of combination with each other. *That shape am I*, I felt, potentially. Nothing that I possess can defend me against that fate, if the hour should strike for me as it struck for him.

Experiences like those led to a condition that, according to James, was the opposite of nightmare. "In nightmare," he said, "we have motives to act, but no power; here we have powers, but no motives." The total carelessness of the catatonic, together with James's own great powers, which came and went, haunted him and left him without self-esteem. "After this," James said, "I awoke morning after morning with a horrible dread at the pit of my stomach, and with a sense of the insecurity of life that I never felt before, and that I have never felt since." The fear was so revelatory that "if I had not clung to scripture texts like 'The eternal God is my refuge,' etc., 'Come unto me all ye that labor and are heavy laden,' etc., 'I am the resurrection and the life,' etc., I think I should have grown really insane."

Neither Epicureans nor Stoics could pray, but James could not help praying. Whether or not James ever prayed again is beside the point, but it is interesting to consider that while he told James Pratt on a public questionnaire that he always felt silly praying, he privately stopped by the church in Harvard Yard on his way to work every day. In any case, he came away from his experience of morbid despair believing that neither aestheticism nor moralism could sufficiently satisfy "the religious demand" that is felt by many people as inescapable. Even if he never prayed again, he was convinced that plenty of people had to and that their religious requirements had to be accounted for by philosophers concerned with characterizing human life.

It makes no sense to pin James's depression on any one cause or set of causes. In general, he suffered from what he called "philosophical melancholy" (in essays like **"Is Life Worth Living?"**) or *Grübelsucht*, the questioning mania. The new intellectual climate seemed to make all things possible, and the new materialism seemed to make them insignificant. Popular materialist tracts like Ludwig Büchner's *Kraft und Stoff* (1855), which James read thoroughly in 1862, persuaded him that existence obeyed mechanical laws inherent in "the things themselves"—laws that made both supernaturalism and idealism, or natural supernaturalism, superfluous. Büchner's deliberately shocking formula—"no force without matter; no matter without force"—haunted tough-minded students with any religious propensities during the 1860s and 1870s. James was no exception.

Caricature of James by G. K. Chesterton, 1908.

By comparison, Darwin's *Origin of Species* (1859) was a breath of fresh air, foisting history into the limelight, showing that if descent was actual, progress was possible, and demonstrating that fit results could be produced by chance events. But in the hands of popularizers like Huxley, Spencer, and Tyndall, Darwin's theory became a great leveler, reducing the quality of humanity to that of brutality and displacing all questions about personal and national destiny with the final solution of fatalism. James never held Darwin responsible for this pessimistic frame of mind, but it hung over his youthful intellectual crowd like a black cloud and seemed to be mirrored now and again in his own nation's emerging troubles. In an intellectual atmosphere in which self-esteem and national destiny meant just about everything, materialism challenged the very existence of a self to esteem and evolutionism, something James carefully distinguished from Darwinism, made destiny meaningless.

James delivered his lecture **"Is Life Worth Living?"** in 1895 before the Harvard YMCA, some twenty-five years after his own bout with psychotic melancholy. But it is an accurate narrative of James's own reflections on the period; more important, it shows that he was conscious, at least in retrospect, about how common his troubles were.

In this lecture, James attempted to show Christian students "the profounder bass-note of life." He noted that some people answer the question whether life is worth living with a temperamental optimism that makes them incapable of seriously believing that anything evil can exist. The young Rousseau was like this, as was America's own Walt Whitman. If everyone could live in such a mood, there would be no reason to ask the question. But universal optimism was a pipe dream. James said: "That life is *not* worth living the whole army of suicides declare—an army whose roll call, like the famous evening gun of the British army, follows the sun round the world and never terminates."

Even if a person never experienced an urge to commit suicide, James argued, "the plainest intellectual integrity—nay more, the simplest manliness and honor—forbid us to forget their case." The problem with life was not just abstract; it was not just that people might be governed by "kraft und stoff" or that destiny might be a sham. The problem was more tangible, accurately caught by John Ruskin when he reminded English ladies and gentlemen enraptured by the glamour of the Crystal Palace (the center of the first world's fair in 1851, and the first prefabricated public building in history, designed to demonstrate Britain's supremacy in manufacture and design) that a few feet of ground were "all that separate the merriment from the misery."

While the English gentry were dining in their townhouses, untold numbers of people in London were famished and miserable, "pale from death, horrible in destitution, broken by despair." The lives of the fortunate were built on the rubble heap of the human herd. Members of that herd were not reflective enough to consider suicide. If they killed themselves, they did so helplessly. Life was not pondered by the herd, but their misery was a problem for the fortunate who were "honorable" and "manly" enough to realize that they not only shared the globe with downtrodden humans but also could do nothing to ameliorate the situation. Human misery was symptomatic of "the hard facts of nature" to Victorian intellectual ways of thinking and, hence, intractable.

James asked his audience to suppose that they were dealing with a person whose only comfort lay in knowing he could commit suicide, a person suffering from the metaphysical *tedium vitae* peculiar to reflective men. What reasons could be given for living? Ultimately, James claimed, only religious ones. Pessimism was not a moral stance; it was a religious disease, contracted when a person made religious demands "to which there comes no religious reply." He said that there were both tough- and tender-minded people but that "minds of either class may be intensely religious." By "religious" he meant that they could "equally desire atonement and reconciliation, and crave acquiescence and communion with the total soul of things."

In a tough-minded person, one intellectually loyal to hard facts, like James himself, but also many of his Christian students, the disappointment of religious craving could lead to pessimism. The contradiction between the hard facts of nature and the heart's craving for divine harmony could result in a kind of inner discord. In the face of this trouble, one was left with two responses: one could cease "longing to read the facts religiously," or one could find that "supplementary facts may be discovered or believed in." These two ways of relief, James said, were really "two stages of recovery." Indeed, they were the stages of recovery that James had traversed himself during the preceding twenty-five years, and clarified both the sort of religion James could not live without as well as the sorts he could not live with.

James asserted that "natural religion" must inevitably lead to melancholy for intellectuals "of the nineteenth century, with our evolutionary theories and our mechanical philosophies." By natural religion he meant not only the deisms of Enlightenment philosophers but also the natural supernaturalisms of Romantics in his father's generation. Nineteenth-century intellectuals could no longer live with religions that construed nature as the adequate expression of spirit or divinity. They required as much emancipation from Romantic doxologies as their fathers had required escape from Calvinism, because they knew that "visible nature is all plasticity and indifference—a moral multiverse." Voices like Büchner's and Spencer's had made it plain to them that "if there be a divine Spirit of the universe, nature, such as we know her, cannot possibly be its *ultimate word* to man." Natural supernaturalists had been searching for divinity in the wrong book. "Either there is no spirit revealed in nature, or else it is inadequately revealed there; and (as all the higher religions have assumed) what we call visible nature, or *this* world, must be a veil and surface show whose full meaning resides in a supplementary unseen or *other* world."

The problem with natural supernaturalism was that the smallest unit it dealt with was "the world" or "the universe." Confronted with the actuality of human misery, students brought up under the "monistic superstition" had one plausible option. If "the world" was not good (because there was human misery) it must be evil. But, James suggested, denial of the idol of a substantially unitary world or universe was the first step of escape from philosophical melancholy. If a person owed no allegiance to "the world" then the thought of suicide was "no longer a guilty challenge or obsession." If the human misery that Ruskin spoke of was taken piecemeal and "the world" was classified as an intellectual's fiction, one could appeal to the reflective suicide "in the name of the very evils that make his heart sick there—to wait and see his part of the battle out." This, James suggested, was Carlyle's solution, the relief of melancholic pessimism through protest. Anyone with "a normally constituted heart" (that is, any genuine Victorian) was honorable enough to "take some suffering upon ourselves, to do some self-denying service with our lives, in return for all those lives upon which ours are built."

According to James, people had better live without natural supernaturalism, and they could, if only through Carlylean resistance. This recommendation recapitulated his own first curative step. Upon reading Charles Bernard Renouvier's second of the "Essais" in April 1870, James found himself maintaining the latter's notion of free will—"the sustaining of a thought *because I choose* to when I might have other thoughts." He said his first act of free will was to believe in free will and tried to discipline himself to "care little for speculation." In this mood, he asserted that

> not in maxims, not in *Anschauungen* ["perceptions"], but in accumulated *acts* of thought lies salvation. *Passer Outre.* Hitherto, when I have felt like taking a free initiative, like daring to act originally, without carefully waiting for contemplation of the external world to determine all for me, suicide seemed the only manly form to put my daring into; now, I will go a step further with my will, not only act with it, but believe as well; believe in my individual reality and creative power. My belief, to be sure, can't be optimistic—but I will posit life (the real, the good) in the self-governing *resistance* of the ego to the world. Life shall be . . . [MS doubtful] doing and suffering and creating.

In other words, as he put the case generally in 1895, James "cast away all metaphysics in order to get rid of hypochondria" but was "resolved to owe nothing as yet to religion and its more positive gifts."

But James went on to recommend religion as a second stage of cure for philosophical melancholy. He said he meant religion ''in the supernaturalist sense'' or ''faith in the existence of an unseen order of some kind in which the riddles of the natural order may be found explained.'' He argued that religion in this intellectualist sense was appropriate even if nothing positive was known of the unseen world, on the grounds that ''we are free to trust at our own risks anything that is not impossible, and that can bring analogies to bear in its behalf.'' ''Trusting'' did not carry with it any license to define in detail an unseen world or to anathematize and excommunicate those whose trust was different. This meant that no one who was ''honorable'' could live with any religion that exemplified the spirit of sectarianism.

The ''worshippers of science'' like Clifford and Huxley who tried to make life without faith respectable by insisting on ''the duty of neutrality'' simply lacked ''scientific imagination,'' according to James. They failed to realize the extent to which ''trusting'' played a role in scientific discovery and neglected the fact that science itself responded to ''an imperious inner demand on our part for ideal logical and mathematical harmonies.'' These were demands that scientists brought to data in order to wrest results from them.

Carlylean protest amounted to the courage to stake one's life on a possibility. Religious faith, according to James (echoing his brother-in-law, William Salter, spokesman for the Philadelphia Ethical Society), amounted to the belief that the possibility exists. James argued that ''all the converging multitude of arguments that make in favor of idealism tend to prove . . . that the world of physics is probably not absolute.''

He gave a curious analogy that clarified what he had in mind when he suggested that people could act as though an invisible world were real. The analogy carried through James's 1870 remark that his faith could not be optimistic. His image was startling: the physical world might lie soaking in a spiritual atmosphere in the same way that our domestic animals live in a human world that they cannot appreciate. People might be related to unseen spiritual reality the way ''a poor dog whom they are vivisecting in a laboratory'' is related to the intentions of the vivisector! ''He lies strapped on a board and shrieking at his executioners, and to his own dark consciousness is literally in a sort of hell. He cannot see a single redeeming ray in the whole business; and yet all these diabolical seeming events are often controlled by human intentions with which, if his poor benighted mind could only be made to catch a glimpse of them, all that is heroic in him would religiously acquiesce. . . . Lying on his back on the board there he may be performing a function incalculably higher than any that prosperous canine life admits of.''

Likewise, James suggested, the world may be ''still wider'' than the tragic one in which people live: ''For my own part, I do not know what the sweat and blood and tragedy of this life mean, if they mean anything short of this.'' Either the unseen order explained tangible misery as adequately as James had explained vivisection to himself when he was a medical student, or life was incredible and worth living only for the sake of the protest.

James, of course, did not go on to suggest that there *was* an unseen order to provide the requisite theodicy. Instead, he took a line of thought that he had developed in light of Renouvier's ''free-will'' in the early 1870s. He argued that ''*maybes* are the essence of the situation.'' He suggested that ''life *feels* like

a real fight—as if there were something really wild in the universe which we, with all our idealities and faithfulnesses, are needed to redeem; and first of all to redeem our own hearts from atheisms and fears.''

People had attempted to ''read'' nature for signs of divinity when their trust in the Gospel itself began to fail for various reasons. James suggested that his Christian students should keep reading, but in an unlikely set of ''books''—the passions of men according to men. Thus, he asked, ''If needs of ours outrun the visible universe, why may not that be a sign that an invisible universe is there?'' (pp. 25-32)

Henry Samuel Levinson, in his The Religious Investigations of William James, *The University of North Carolina Press, 1981, 311 p.*

CHARLENE HADDOCK SEIGFRIED   (essay date 1982)

[In the following excerpt, Seigfried discusses James's ''dramatic'' prose style as particularly suited to the dynamic quality of his thought.]

William James called his ''pluralistic empiricism . . . a turbid, muddled, gothic sore of an affair,'' bound to alienate philosophers, whose stock in trade is to substitute ''economical and orderly conceptions for the first sensible tangle.'' As glorified janitors ''cleaning up the litter with which the world apparently is filled,'' philosophers' characteristic failing for James is that, enchanted by our own ''esthetically pure and definite'' formulations, we ascribe ''to the world something clean and intellectual in the way of inner structure.'' Despite all the accusations of subjectivism hurled at James, he staunchly refused to confuse our need for order with the inner structure of the world. Since, for the pluralist, the ''crudity of experience'' is a permanent feature of reality, the aesthetic attractiveness of the clear and distinct ideas achievable in a closed system is offset by their falsification of the merely fortuitous character of much of our experience.

In *The Will to Believe,* James acknowledges that his views would appear irrational to other philosophers, but is not yet ready to attack rationalism as such, and so apologetically puts off until later a ''technical'' treatise, and continues putting it off. He characterizes *The Will to Believe* as consisting of ''illustrations of the radically empiricist attitude rather than as argumentations for its validity. . . . These essays seem to light up with a certain dramatic reality the attitude itself, and make it visible. . . .'' He is groping towards a defense of his literary style and philosophic method. He mastered the style long before he could defend it as legitimate, although he felt abashed to the very end before the members of his profession who set the standard for what strict argumentation in philosophy should be.

In reference to his acceptance of the Hibbert lectures, later published as *A Pluralistic Universe,* James wrote to F.C.S. Schiller on January 4, 1908: ''I actually *hate* lecturing; and this job condemns me to publish another book written in picturesque and popular style when I was settling down to something whose manner would be more 'strengwissenschaftlich' ['strictly scientific'], i.e., concise, dry, and impersonal.'' That he has in mind the professional ''gatekeepers,'' rather than the appropriateness of method and content, is explicitly said in the next sentence: ''My free and easy style in *Pragmatism* has made me so many enemies in academic & pedantic circles that I hate to go on increasing their number, and want to become tighter instead of looser.''

I would like to argue that James's "dramatic" rather than "systematic" style was not the failing he (in less self-confident moments) and others often took it to be, but was a fitting match of content and expression. A word frequently used by James in reference to style and method is "vague," and it is not always clear whether this is meant in praise or blame or what distinguishes the contradictory valuations. This is partly a reflection of his own ambivalence towards his style and partly due to the difficulty of revaluing values, in Nietzsche's sense. Vagueness has obvious affinities with another fecund but largely undeveloped notion of the "fringe." In a positive sense, it means fidelity to experience. Negatively, it refers to terms used so loosely that they can accommodate disparate facts and therefore have no predictive value. I will reconstruct the Jamesean texts on vagueness both to point out the coherency of outlook which becomes apparent when considering them in conjunction and to show explicitly that in such texts James was implicitly defending both his own style and crucial assumptions about experience.

We can adopt rationality to accomplish certain purposes, and the sciences are the most telling examples of the gains to be made by choosing this course. But it is tempting to argue from the fact that the world of our experiences *can* be organized according to a rational plan that the experienced world *is* rational. This move James denies through various strategies. One is to argue that no systematic interpretation of experience so far has succeeded in accounting for all of reality. Among his favorite examples of all encompassing systems which have failed to unify reality are those of Spencer and Hegel. No physical or biological science of his time even came close to competing in comprehensiveness with these. Since this could simply be due to the state of the art, which could conceivably be corrected in the future, by a unified field theory, for instance, this line of argumentation is not compelling. James also argues, though, that reality cannot be rational through and through, that is, correspond point by point, to any rational system, because a completely rational system is necessarily a closed system and the world is still in the making. "Radical empiricism allows that the absolute sum-total of things may never be actually experienced or realized in . . . [its absolute totality], and that a disseminated, distributed, or incompletely unified appearance is the only form that reality may yet have achieved." Furthermore, no single system can match the complexity of experiences which draw on different, sometimes mutually exclusive, expressions. The taste of chocolate cannot be correlated with Gucci's taste in clothes, nor with the chemistry of taste buds, nor with the taste which is a kind of narrow silk ribbon. To call words homonyms is to assume, in some sense, the non-reciprocity of systems.

I am not arguing that James advocated obscurantism and sloppiness in philosophical discourse, as if a study of mud had to be muddy. But he is eager to build into structured explanations of the world acknowledgement of the tentative and necessarily limited character of such projects. It is not merely accidental nor a psychological curiosity that adherence to a system of explanation that is believed to be true and unassailable, whether because certain protocols of empirical investigation have been adhered to or because cultural beliefs have rendered the system impregnable, has tended to promote smug self assurance which ignores alternative possibilities, some of which may turn out to be more viable, and some of which, if ignored, may even prove lethal. This is not a question of making theories less systematic or of countenancing wild speculation or ungrounded superstitions or unbridled relativism. This is a claim that even the best explanations we have, and less than the best should not be aimed for, are necessarily limited, and the best way to avoid being trapped in such limitations is to integrate methodologically an acknowledgement of other alternatives.

Like Nietzsche, James revalued values, and like Nietzsche, he continued to use both the original and the revalued terms, to the chagrin of later commentators. "Vagueness" is one of these terms used both negatively and positively by James. The distinction is clearest in some remarks on Herbert Spencer. Science, considered as a closed system, has adopted what James calls a "mechanical explanation of nature." Within this framework exactness and consistency are necessary in order for the system to work. Spencer is criticized because he aimed at such a mechanics of nature and yet "his terms are vagueness and ambiguity incarnate." This inconsistent use of terms, with ambiguously different meanings in different passages, giving the illusion of unification when only the word remains the same, is indefensible in a system valued for its reduction of configurations of matter and motion into univocal mathematical formulas. But on the level of living things, displaying the organic unity of interdependence, merely mechanical explanations are inadequate. Here, the human element intrudes and "we are frankly on teleological ground, and metaphor and vagueness are permissable."

One of the reasons James was so attracted to Darwinian evolutionary biology was that it combined a careful enumeration of disparate factual details with an open-ended theory. Like his friend, C. S. Peirce, he was fascinated by what has prosaically come to be called a "logic of discovery." As early as *The Principles of Psychology* he substitutes one theory for another because it "allows for zoological differences as we know them, and is vague and elastic enough to receive any number of future discoveries of detail." "Vagueness" sometimes means negatively an overarching system with terms so elastic they can accommodate all facts and thus recognize no anomalies and consequently betray the singularly compelling nature of quotidian facts. But vagueness can also be a positive value, since "at a certain stage in the development of every science a degree of vagueness is what best consists with fertility." It will take some care to distinguish when vagueness is merely sloppiness and disdain of factual detail and when it is conducive to highlighting the abundance and variety of the encountered world.

A fundamental strategy for James is to shift the locus of discourse from rationality versus irrationality to immediate experience and reflection on experience. From his earliest writings on psychology to his last published work he insisted that one's own experiences, in all their richness, should be the starting point for reflection and any attempt to reduce experience to a single explanation necessarily falsifies that experience to the degree that it leaves out some aspects of the experience. Part of what James means can be expressed as a tautology. Any explanation of experience necessarily leaves something out just because it is an explanation and not the living experience itself. Thus clarity, understood as absolute unity, is rejected by him, despite the fact that it has been the goal of most of Western philosophy, at least since Descartes. He asserts that "there still remains the opacity of the finite facts as merely given, with most of their peculiarities mutually unmediated and unexplained."

Clarity is a necessary but insufficient condition as a method of inquiry. We must be as clear as we can in explanations, but the goal should not be clarity at all costs. The blind support of absolute clarity will eventuate in an absolutely closed system, elegant in its simplicity. The univocal definition of terms will eliminate irrelevant connotations but it will also beg the whole question of the system's relevance to any particular experience or kinds of experience. In fact, the pursuit of clarity as a goal rather than a means will interfere with explicating some salient aspects of experience. As Martin Heidegger also says, "Exact thinking is never the strictest thinking, if the essence of strictness lies in the strenuousness with which knowledge keeps in touch with the essential features of what-is. 'Exact' thinking merely binds itself to the calculation of what-is and ministers to this alone."

Philosophers mediate facts through language, which never simply is "history or happenings displayed," as James rather surprisingly called perceiving, but a substitute for actual happenings. Although translation of fact into specific sentences and forms of language can be judged better or worse, clear or unclear, there is an impassible barrier which no amount of clarity can overcome, which is the fact that the translation never is the reality as occurring. In order for absolute clarity to exist the words would have to be absolutely transparent, and this is impossible. They are always to some extent opaque, i.e., by definition they are language and not what language is about.

Furthermore, it makes no sense to say that language in general displays reality in general, because it is the case that someone in some specific speaking situation communicates something about some aspect of reality. And therefore, the point of view of the speaker cannot be eliminated, and "what is inwardly clear from one point remains a bare externality and datum to the other." The clarity that my point of view alone allows me to experience is always, from your point of view, to that extent unclear. What can be included from one point of view cannot be included from all points of view nor from some meta-view. This necessarily limited character of all ways of reflecting on and communicating about the world is one way that vagueness is inexpugnable, even for those who take clarity as their goal. James calls this limitation of points of view, in that there is no absolute over-view, pluralism.

Part of James's search for striking phrases and colorful metaphors grows out of his dissatisfaction with the desiccated picture of life which emerges from scientific discourse, the more careful the discourse, the further away one gets from the vibrant sense of lived experience. I think this helps explain why James deliberately adopted a more poetic and less systematic mode of discourse. Although he frequently deprecated his own popular approach as less than "*strengwissenschaft-lich,*" one suspects that he did so out of his own deference to editorial arbiters of proper philosophical style and not out of conviction. It is clear that he thought that public lectures should catch the public imagination, not from a displaced desire to amuse, but because the truth of philosophical systems finally derives, not from the elegance of the arguments philosophers pride themselves on, but from their success in illuminating human life. As Peter Hare points out in his introduction to *Some Problems of Philosophy:* "No matter how impressive the technical achievement of a metaphysical system, such a system is ultimately pointless, James felt, if it does not express a *Weltanschauung,* an attitude toward life, a picture of the universe, whose practical implications can be emotionally as well as intellectually grasped by readers."

James thought it a necessary part of the justification of theories that they be efficacious in dealing with the relevant facts. Part of this testing was carried out in professional journals, books, and private correspondence, where he presented his position to other professionals and defended it from attacks. But the success of any theory was also dependent on its substantiation of human efficacy. And an equally important part of the testing involved engaging anyone who would give it a hearing in checking out whether his assertions significantly illuminated their experiences. Since James wanted to probe human experience and not just philosophers' experience, he deliberately addressed non-professional groups and challenged them to consult their own experiences as to whether he made sense or not. He wanted to confine himself in the *Principles,* for instance, "to what could be immediately verified by everyone's own consciousness" and to bring his reader "into direct concrete acquaintance" with "living reality" rather than invent an "artificial schematism." It cannot be reiterated too strongly that "experience" was not just a concept for James, but the actual lived situation.

In a series of lectures later published as *A Pluralistic Universe* James worried about the difficulty of putting an intricate argument into easily understandable language. His motivation for attempting to do so was his belief that "*technical* writing on *philosophical* subjects . . . is certainly a crime against the human race!" He concludes that the very seriousness with which the matter is pursued in professional circles, that is, the fact that a problem is considered important enough to be labored over at length is a token that it is worth opening up to a wider public. He indicates, furthermore, that the attempt to explain the problem in terms the audience will understand is integral to solving it. If he can bring the audience along with him, so that they recognize the dimensions of the problem and can find satisfaction with its resolution, as being meaningful in their own experience, then this can be counted as evidence that the explanation has arisen out of and provides a genuine solution to an aspect of experience which, though personal, is not thereby idiosyncratic.

It would be tempting to say that it was integral to his strategy to translate his technical philosophic discourse into ordinary language accessible to the non-professional listener. And this is true insofar as he made a deliberate effort to avoid technical jargon in his lectures. However, much of his philosophic writings were revised lectures, and even in his *Principles of Psychology,* metaphor and non-technical language abound. Plainly, James was most comfortable using language as a poet does, to create such a sense of some aspect of life that the reader can appropriate it as her own, rather than in using language as a logician does, to elaborate a consistent system and avoid errors of technique. Like Nietzsche and Wittgenstein James found the multi-faceted aspects of experience more clearly communicated in terms which were themselves multi-leveled. This is not an escape into ambiguity or mysticism, but a careful explication drawing on other uses of language than the strictly denotative. It is well known that James's philosophy was deeply influenced by Darwin, but not sufficiently realized how much the style as well as the substance of Darwin's position was assimilated by, or at least congenial to, James's own. In commenting on Darwin's use of metaphor Edward Manier, drawing on Mary Hesse's views, makes a point that applies equally to James's use of language: "In contrast with the so-called *comparison view* of metaphor, the interaction view *denies* that a metaphor can be replaced without remainder by an explicit literal statement of the similarities between the field to which the metaphor is extended (the primary system of the explanandum, or phenomenon requiring explanation) and the proper field of the metaphor itself (the secondary system, for Hesse).''

Different points of view disclose different aspects of reality. This is the reason that the sheer number and variety of texts assures the historian that she has more likely grasped a civilization or era than if she has only a few or of one genre only. But James also argues that some insights are better than others, that great statesmen, scientists, poets, and moral revolutionaries are great because of their creative restructuring of received opinion, changing the shape of the mental, political, artistic, or physical landscape for many others, who happily adopt the results. In addition to the richness and variety of individual voices James also advocates multiple formal structurings of reality, by which he means the varied systems of ethics, aesthetics, science, common sense, and philosophy, each of which discloses aspects of reality which would otherwise be missed.

It is a logical extension of this line of thought to argue that a use of language that is multi-leveled and ambivalent is likewise preferable to a univocal use of language. He says in *The Will to Believe,* for instance, that when we lack compelling evidence ''we are free to trust at our own risks anything that is not impossible, and that can bring analogies to bear in its behalf.'' This cryptic directive is less startling when understood in reference to the chapter on reasoning in the *Principles,* which was written at about the same time as *The Will to Believe.* It is there explained that association by similarity is the defining characteristic of rationality. Whether spontaneously or through the discipline of scientific investigation, analogous instances to some phenomenon are brought into consciousness at one time so that their similarities or differences can become apparent. Geniuses possess the ability to the highest degree, while animals probably lack it entirely, passing from one concrete object to its habitual successor and associating exclusively by contiguity. James cites J. S. Mill's *Logic* and his ''four methods of experimental inquiry,'' as expounding the analogical method. Thinking by the analogical method is one of the few fundamental means we use to organize experience. It is significant that it applies equally to artists, i.e., all who spontaneously collect analogous instances and to scientists, i.e., all who deliberately and methodically collect instances of analogous phenomena. James asserts that ''after the few most powerful practical and aesthetic interests, our chief help towards noticing those special characters of phenomena, which, when once possessed and named, are used as reasons, class names, essences, or middle terms, *is this association by similarity.*''

Because of the much-at-oneness of experience, in which no isolated monads exist but processive, temporal interrelated events, not simple but multifaceted explanations disclose more of reality. There is no such thing as a single true statement, just as there is no such thing as an isolated individual object. A world or context must be supplied. At least one is always operative but we too often selectively ignore it. ''There is never a proposition that does not require other propositions after it, to amplify it, restrict it, or in some way save it from the falsity by defect or excess which it contains. . . . Life, too, in one sense, stumbles over its own fact in a similar way; for its earlier moments plunge ceaselessly into later ones which reinterpret and correct them.''

But the tautology that language is not experience does not exhaust the meaning of the shift to experience as the beginning and test of reflection. Jamesean commentators are often puzzled whether his pragmatic maxim means that only tests resulting

in some specific sense data are legitimate or whether the results can be more broadly interpreted as changing a way of life or providing scope for more interesting experiments or instancing preferred values, such as pluralism rather than monism or freedom rather than constraint. One way out of the ambiguity is to resolutely separate the pragmatic, epistemological texts, such as *Pragmatism* and *The Meaning of Truth* from the metaphysical, such as *Essays in Radical Empiricism,* from the ethical, such as *The Will to Believe* and ''The Sentiment of Rationality.'' But this tearing apart of the fabric of James's writings into the strands of currently fashionable philosophic specialties distorts the texture of his thought. The problems James was puzzling out do not lie neatly within these artificial boundaries.

True enough, James says that ''the deeper features of reality are found only in perceptual experience.'' But it has to be pointed out that, although James grounds his explanation in perceptual experience, he is not dealing with percepts as understood by or which provide the subject matter of laboratory psychology, despite the fact that James wrote the classic nineteenth century text in psychology, nor that of traditional, or even current, philosophical empiricists or positivists, despite the fact that he works out of the Lockean, Humean, Berkeleyan tradition. As his list of ''the deeper features of reality . . . found only in perceptual experience'' clearly indicates, James is focusing on the person experiencing and not ''perceiving'' in its usual, narrow sense. The categories he picks out, such as continuity, activity in its various modes, novelty, tendency and freedom, are not derived from an analysis of perception as a limited cognitive process, but rather from the lived world of a person who is perceiving. In fact percepts have to be understood in the Jamesean vocabulary as a heuristic device, necessarily tied, in antithesis, to concepts. He uses perceptual language and analyses as deliberate contrasts to overly conceptualized theoretic systems not tied down to personal experience. It is actually the personal experience he is defending when he seems to be defending the traditional empiricist's more narrowly discriminated use of ''percept.''

James's philosophical contribution does not lie in any analytic refinement of the terms, ''percept'' and ''concept,'' which are parasitic on his larger and more promising project of reasserting the connection between philosophy and life. That his defense of percepts can sound naive to us today is a measure of the distance we have traveled in building formal systems about which supposedly neutral internal criticism is the only philosophically respectable stance to take. In this splendidly scholastic isolation of subject matter any connection with the person responsible for all or part of the system is considered to be a private, not a philosophic matter, and any larger connection with human or societal interests is so irrelevant as to demand a separate subject category, such as ''social and political'' philosophy or ''ethics.'' Thus if percepts, for instance, form an integral part of an epistemological system, they will not show up, except incidentally, in a theory of society.

Running counter to this trend is James's insistence that even seemingly neutral technical discussions of percepts and concepts involve commitments to larger world views and express irreducibly individual and human concerns. His defense of percepts is actually a defense of the empiricism which ''stays inside the flux of life expectantly.'' Again, empiricism is played off against rationalism by James as a means of reasserting the priority of lived experience. Although you will not find it in any philosophical text as a definition of empiricism, James's ''empiricism'' is a place holder for, among other things, claims that "reality is created temporally day by day," experience "is self-containing and leans on nothing" in that it is not reducible without remainder into organs, cells, atoms, or "mindstuff," and that verified knowledge is always limited and therefore totalizing claims are inherently suspicious.

Of course, philosophical empiricism cannot bear the burden James lays on it, but this is irrelevant in textual context. As a label it is helpful in deciphering James's interpretation of personal experience of the world as the prototype of all other systematic orderings of experience. James's own empiricism is more accurately called "radical empiricism," but confusion can arise because he often just calls it "empiricism" in an effort to reinvigorate the empirical tradition. The importance of James's reordering of philosophical priorities can be adumbrated in the observation that the level of experience in which a person feels herself both active in ordering experience and thus co-generator of the factual and responsible for her actions can provide a model for linking scientific, technological, philosophical and political products with human values, while no amount of internal development or criticism of these products or external imposition of abstract values can disclose the actual connections of society and individual, facts and values.

The "real" can be defined by James as "anything . . . which we find ourselves obliged to take account in any way" because that is the way reality impinges on each person. While never denying that the individual's necessarily limited view must be built out into more comprehensive views, taking the experience of others into account and using theoretical constructs, the original touchstone should never be superseded because then there is no way for the individual to assent to or dissent from the truth claims except on faith. The tie to the individual's experience is the silken thread which, once broken, allows systems, claims, and organizations to float away into unreality. This would allow, for instance, that the oppression that one experiences from a political system be dismissed publically and theoretically as a merely personal experience which does not disclose the reality, which is defined otherwise. It would allow, for instance, that an individual soldier's physical disabilities after exposure to Agent Orange defoliant could be "detached" from the defoliant as cause, since the producer's list of ingredients and studies of the effects of the chemical could stand for the reality of the product, or the strategic use of the chemical as a stratagem of war could stand for the reality of the defoliant, were we not obliged to take account of reports of individual experiences as no less real.

This is not to say that any and all individual experiences are definitive of reality as such, but they are certainly a significant part of reality. James, in his reconstruction of empiricism, has "reflectively justified our instinctive feeling about immediate experience." The definition, already alluded to, of perceptual reality as "history or happening displayed," as contrasted to the static coherency of the conceptual systems of mathematics, logic, aesthetics and ethics, is understandable as a description of individual experience as the locus of the human ordering of the world. What he attributes to empiricist philosophy is really his own contribution to it.

In contrast to our belief in "objective" time and space, according to which every event occupies a specified location, in our everyday experience we actually operate in a much less straightforward manner. "Everything that happens to us brings its own duration and extension, and both are vaguely surrounded by a marginal "more" that runs into the duration and extension of the next thing that comes." Instead of sharp breaks between yesterday and the day before yesterday and the actual map coordinates displaying a fixed distance between London and Moscow, the past as actually experienced is often "churned up together" and directions and distances are "vague, confused and mixed." This is not a contrast between an objectively existing univocal space and time and a limited psychological apprehension of reality, but a claim that the ideal exactness pictured in abstractly determined space and time coordinates is an instrumental tool, useful for certain purposes, but parasitic on the everyday apprehension of reality. Just as we organize the everyday world for practical and aesthetic reasons, drawing on the funded past, using common sense categories, so do we project an ideally simple, clear reality as existing behind or beyond the messy everyday world.

But the degree of exactness required is a function of our needs: one scale for mercator projection maps, another for airplane schedules, still another for rocket launchings. Our projections in turn restructure our needs. The quartz crystal accuracy so useful for scientific tests becomes the standard in watches for busy executives. The vague, marginal "more" is not eradicable because reality is not translatable without remainder into any linguistic construct. The indeterminacy of ordinary experiencing is not replaced by fine-tuned instrumental measuring devices. A pedometer, for instance, may measure the exact number of feet a runner travels but will not affect the runner's feeling that the distance traveled was "short and painless" or "long and painful." But, beyond what is too easily dismissed as a merely "psychological" as opposed to an "objective" assessment, the exactness of the pedometer would, in turn be wildly inaccurate to a nuclear physicist. Exactness, like clarity, is a function of the task at hand and the understanding that there is always more that is not captured in our schemes is a truer insight into our actual situation than the belief that we have exactly determined the gravitational pull of the moon on the tides and therefore have at last an absolutely clear grasp of the nature of the world.

In conclusion, James's "vagueness" is a result of his intent to stay "inside the flux of life expectantly." It is the opposite of clarity achievable only within an ordered, closed, system, but not of clarity understood as fidelity to experience. As usual, it is best expressed in James's own words, and as usual, what he gives us is not a definition but an insight.

> Something forever exceeds, escapes from statement, withdraws from definition, must be glimpsed and felt, not told. No one knows this like your genuine professor of philosophy. For what glimmers and twinkles like a bird's wing in the sunshine it is his business to snatch and fix. And every time he fires his volley of new vocables out of his philosophic shot-gun, whatever surface-flush of success he may feel, he secretly kens at the same time the finer hollowness and irrelevancy. . . .

(pp. 357-66)

Charlene Haddock Seigfried, "Vagueness and the Adequacy of Concepts," in Philosophy Today, *Vol. XXVI, No. 4, Winter, 1982, pp. 357-67.*

JAMES WILLIAM ANDERSON   (essay date 1982)

[*In the following excerpt, Anderson examines the influences of James's early psychological traumas on the development of his philosophical writings, especially* The Varieties of Religious Experience.]

William James's "spiritual crisis," which culminated in 1869, was a six-year period of intense emotional and physical distress. Feeling that his will was paralyzed, and frequently suffering from depression, James also had eye and back trouble, insomnia, gastro-intestinal disturbances, and periodic exhaustion. On several occasions, he was tempted to kill himself. As he later commented, "*I* was entirely broken down before I was thirty."

A nineteen-month trip to Europe in 1867-1868 had brought him no relief. Thus, when James reached his twenty-seventh birthday in January of 1869, he was living with his family in Cambridge, Massachusetts.

One reason James had abruptly terminated his trip to Germany and France was his belief that rest would lead to recovery, and that was more easily obtained on Quincy Street than in European boarding houses and spas. Several months after his return he was still clinging to this hope. He wrote to one of his friends, ". . . I have discovered that I must not only drop exercise, but also mental labor, as it immediately tells on my back." He added, "I have consequently made up my mind to lose at least a year now in vegetating and doing nothing but survive."

His mother believed in a different remedy—"moderate bodily activity." During one period in which physical activity and improved health coincided, she commented: "My theory about him (of which I said little) will I think be proved which is, that the complete rest which he kept up for so long was bad for him. . . ." But soon he had a relapse. Eventually, after claiming for so long that rest was the answer, James concluded that he got better "by going into town every day or paying a visit than by keeping [to] the house," but he added, "—not that *I improve* under it, but it's a less evil than the rest."

The medical profession was of no greater help. J.J.G. Wilkinson, a physician and close friend of James's father, visited the family during 1869 and made a thorough examination of the young invalid. James's mother reported Wilkinson's impressions: "He says the original strain is not now the trouble but the morbid condition of his whole system which is the result of it." This analysis, of course, explains nothing. Wilkinson prescribed medications, "high dilutions of Rhus and Nux Vomica."

In addition to Galvanism and hydrotherapy, another method of treatment involved chemically inducing boils on his back in an attempt to alleviate the pain. James tried, but failed, to find a correlation between any of these procedures and the state of his health. On one occasion he underwent a sudden relapse and thought the reason was that the efficacy of the boils had worn off. But then, "suddenly and without known cause," his health improved again. A few days later, he found that "the old weakness (equally without cause) has partially returned." On another occasion he noted that "there seem so many days now on which my state surprises me at not being as bad as I should from past experience have anticipated"; but he also found that interspersed with these days there "abound days of equally unexpected collapse."

James was probably expressing his bewilderment at the causes of his own relapses and recoveries when he commented, after hearing that his brother Henry had inexplicably found some relief from back trouble in a "lifting cure," "What a dark business it all is, don't you think?"

Although James was unable to make sense of his distressing condition, he made one statement which can help organize our investigation. He noted that during this period of his life he was in a "state of philosophic pessimism and general depression of spirits about my prospects." Although a medical student at Harvard, James had no intention of becoming a physician, and he also lacked any practicable alternatives. He did manage, however, to complete his medical degree during 1869, but the manner in which he did so illustrates his disinterest in medicine. To qualify for his degree, he had to write a thesis and pass an oral examination. Feeling listless, and plagued by numerous symptoms, he abandoned his hope of doing an original or challenging thesis. Instead he chose a safe, undemanding topic—the physiological effects of coldness—which he could write from secondary sources without doing any primary research.

The minimum standards for the examination were no more stringent than for the thesis. From the time of his return to Cambridge, James read medicine to prepare for the examination, but he did so, as he put it, "lazily," without concentrated study. As 21 June, the date of the examination, approached, he became so anxious that he could not study at all. He considered himself "totally unprepared," and he felt his brain was "worth no more than so much old hay." But he knew he was unlikely to fail, if only because a close family friend was among the examiners. Oliver Wendell Holmes, Sr., who was intimate with James's father and whose son was one of James's closest friends, was a professor at the medical school, and James realistically concluded that Holmes would be likely to "veto my being plucked no matter how bad my examination may be." As he had predicted, James passed the examination. Afterwards he said the examination was "trifling enough" but noted that his lack of preparation caused him "some embarrassment" in the part on midwifery.

During the first half of 1869, his chief concern was finishing his work in medicine. After receiving his degree, he had to confront the question of a career. While in Europe he had considered becoming involved in physiological research. But he had found that his various symptoms made it impossible for him to work in the laboratory. He had felt he needed a vocation which would provide meaning to his existence, and his conclusion had been that if he were to abandon permanently the possibility of becoming a scientist, he would feel "as if all value had departed from my life." Now he was flirting with the idea of studying psychology, no doubt because he thought the young science might provide insight into his non-organic problems. But he felt his condition prevented him even from reading seriously.

For years his father, Henry James, Sr., had been arguing that he ought to become a scientist. For example, when William James at the age of seventeen expressed an interest in art, his father wrote to a friend, "I had always counted upon a scientific career for Willy. . . ." But the elder James did not advocate this career because he thought it suited his son's abilities or because he expected his son to find it fulfilling. Rather, Henry James, Sr., had a more personal aim: he was distressed that his theological ideas had received so little attention, and he hoped that his son, as a respected scientist and a defender of those ideas, would be in a position to gain a hearing for them. But, in fact, the more exposure William James had to science, the harder it became for him to accept his father's theology.

Furthermore, the elder James, even while advocating a scientific career for his son, did not conceal his disdain for this field. For example, after writing an article on "Swedenborg's

Ontology'' and learning that his son had had difficulty with it, James, Sr., wrote: "It is very evident to me that your trouble in understanding it arises *mainly* from the purely scientific cast of your thought just at present, and the temporary blight exerted thence upon your metaphysic wit." He went on to talk abusively of people who are "dupes of scientific activity" and who have "puerile" minds because they believe that answers can be found in the natural world. And then, as if to make sure that his son realized he was speaking of him, he added, "Now here it seems to me is exactly where you are as yet intellectually: in this scientific or puerile stage of progress. . . ." To make matters even worse, William James's mother, Mary James, stood for a position—practical and down-to-earth— which clashed with his father's other-worldly emphasis.

James needed to look within himself and to select a vocation that stemmed from his sense of who he was, what he liked, and what his abilities were. But this was just what he was unable to do. Often when an individual is thrown into such confusion over his choice of career, it is because he does not have a fully consolidated self. Such an individual experiences life as if it were not real; he feels hollow; and he fears that the center of his personhood is in danger of giving way. Without a well-formed self, he lacks a foundation upon which to build a vocation.

Clearly, James's depression over his vocational prospects was closely related to his "state of philosophical pessimism." Indeed, Ralph Barton Perry, the scholar who first characterized this period of James's life as a "spiritual crisis," believed that James's problems were, at heart, philosophical. He saw James's spiritual crisis as "the ebbing of the will to live, for lack of philosophy to live by—a paralysis of action occasioned by a sense of moral impotence." There is no doubt that James, both in his comments at the time and in his later reconstructions, portrayed his crisis in philosophical terms, but Perry failed to notice that James also viewed his philosophical concerns as inextricably tied to psychological factors. James was well aware that in his case the one could not be considered without the other.

James described his basic difficulty as being his lack of will power; since the world appeared meaningless to him, he could not find a reason to act. In his diary he wrote that when the outer world "seems to me void or evil, my will is palsied. The difficulty: 'to act without hope,' must be solved." In his daily life in 1869, he not only found it hard to make long-range plans, he often could not bring himself to do anything but lie down. Even reading seemed too taxing. (pp. 369-74)

Because he was "swamped in an empirical philosophy," he felt as if he had no will and as if every decision he thought he was making were actually determined by forces outside his control. He wrote in a letter to his friend Thomas W. Ward, "I feel that we are Nature through and through, and that we are wholly conditioned, that not a wiggle of our will happens save as a result of physical laws. . . ."

His philosophical dilemma came out most clearly in a private note written during this period. He considered adopting the pursuit of truth as his purpose in life, but he felt this would lead to materialism. And materialism, he thought, failed to "supply any moral incentive" to a devotion to truth. Materialism, he went on, seemed to commend a "frivolous" instead of a "*serious* reaction towards the world"; in other words, materialism, in James's view, worked at cross-purposes to his attempt to find meaning in life.

Another alternative, he noted, might be to accept "superstition," by which he presumably meant an unquestioning religious faith. He concluded that "frivolity"—the consequence of materialism—and "a fool's paradise in superstition" were equally unacceptable to him.

Years later, in a transparently autobiographical essay, James cast light on his inability, in 1869, to sustain a belief in God, even though such a belief would have solved one of his most pressing problems by giving meaning to his life. He explored the origins of the "nightmare view of life," the view which led to a feeling of meaninglessness and pessimism and a temptation to commit suicide. Such a view, he suggested, was grounded in "the contradiction between the phenomena of nature and the craving of the heart to believe that behind nature there is a spirit looking at the outer world, he felt forced to conclude that it could not possibly be the expression of a divine spirit. The trouble for James was the existence of evil. As he wrote his brother, "I can't bring myself, as so many men seem able to do, to blink the evil out of sight and gloss it over. It's as real as the good, and if it is denied, good must be denied too." If a just God existed, James wondered, then how could there be so much evil in the world?

Seeking the answer, while in Europe, James had studied his father's ideas, only to conclude that they were not personally meaningful to him. The elder James, suffering as a young man from depression and fear not unlike what his son now faced, had found an answer in his personal version of Swedenborgianism. William James, seeing the comfort his father derived from his faith, probably still hoped his father's ideas would have a similar effect on him, for he turned to his father's philosophy again in 1869. Despite having found it wanting while in Europe, he read at least three of his father's books. He described his reactions in a letter to his brother Henry. James felt that he and his brother, with their serious health problems, were "victims" of the "evil in the world," but he could not understand "[f]or what purpose we are thus tormented." And, he went on, "I don't see that Father's philosophy explains it any more than anyone else's." He concluded that "many points which before were incomprehensible to me because doubtfully fallacious, I now definitely believe to be entirely fallacious." Once again, James had to admit that his father's theology simply could not work for him.

Although in 1869 James saw philosophical concerns as being at the root of his lack of will, years later he saw this same issue in psychological terms. The section entitled "The Obstructed Will" in *The Principles of Psychology* focused on what James called "abulia," that is, a lack of will power, the very problem that troubled him in 1869. James wrote that in a person suffering from abulia inner "ideas, objects, considerations" fail to "*get to* the will"—they "fail to draw blood"—and as a result they seem "distant and unreal." For some reason, which seemed inexplicable to James, a "pungent sense of effective reality" does not attach to the inner ideas of the individual with an obstructed will. For this person "moral knowledge" is "always there grumbling and rumbling in the background,—discerning, commenting, protesting, longing, half resolving." But this moral knowledge "never gets its voice out of the minor into the major key"; it "never takes the helm into its hands." The individual lives, according to James, with a "consciousness of inward hollowness" because of "habitually seeing the better only to do the worse," and this sense of hollowness "is one of the saddest feelings one can bear with him through this vale of tears."

James had himself in mind when he wrote about "the obstructed will." In one letter he described himself much as he depicted the individual suffering from abulia: "Two souls are in my breast; I see the better and in the very act of seeing I do the worse." In another letter he wrote, "I am a victim of neurasthenia, and of the sense of hollowness and unreality that goes with it."

As James's comments on "the obstructed will" illustrate, he realized that his abulia was not merely a philosophical phenomenon. The problem was not that he lacked ideas and morals; rather, it was that—for psychological reasons—he was not able to draw upon them, and they seemed "distant and unreal." Again, consideration of this theme leads to James's self. An individual whose self is not well developed finds, characteristically, that his inner goals are not strong enough to induce action because these goals do not feel as if they are deeply anchored. One psychoanalyst explains that such a person often feels impoverished because his self is thin, and the split-off parts of himself do not fuel his personality. The person is unable to forge a link between his inner motives and his actions; he feels hollow and suffers from something like what James called an obstructed will.

It would seem that James's philosophical concerns and the state of his self, interacting with each other, precipitated his abulia. If he had lived in an era during which belief was secure and duty was clear, he may not have felt that life had no meaning, even if he had had the same difficulties. But James was exposed to intellectual currents which challenged the settled religious assumptions of his father's generation. As James commented, the "times are past" when one could believe in the old-fashioned idea of a God who acts as a "Moral and Intelligent Contriver of the World"; "we of the nineteenth century, with our evolutionary theories and our mechanical philosophies," he went on, cannot accept such a God. On the other hand, if he had been faced with the same philosophical concerns but did not have an underlying sense of hollowness, he probably would not have found his will obstructed. James's friend, Oliver Wendell Holmes, Jr., shared his concerns about a world that seemed to have lost meaning, but these concerns did not substantially trouble the future jurist, who kept living and working as he always had. James could find meaning neither when looking at the outside world nor when looking inside himself. As a consequence, he fell prey to a feeling of emptiness so profound that he became like the person he described in a later essay "who is on such terms with life that the only comfort left him is to brood on the assurance, 'You may end it when you will.'"

James's crisis was deepened by his inability to sustain intimate relationships. He found himself feeling bitter towards his closest friends, Ward and Holmes. It was unusual for James to criticize anyone severely. But after Ward, who lived in New York City, had visited him in Cambridge, James described him as "unpleasantly egotistical and ostentatious of his eccentricity." And he wrote that "the noble qualities" of Holmes, whom he continued to see from time to time, are "poisoned" by "cold-blooded conscious egotism and conceit." He added, ". . . and friendly as I want to be towards him, as yet the good he has done me is more in presenting me something to kick away from or react against than to follow and embrace."

That James criticized both Ward and Holmes for egotism suggests that he was uncomfortable with them because of his own uncertain self-esteem. Their confidence made more acute his inner view of himself as a "low-lived wretch" (to use a self-

description which he one time offered in banter). He protected himself by viewing them as egotistical. Such an interpretation gains support from a comment James made to Holmes in a letter written from Germany. James candidly explained that Holmes had "a far more logical and orderly mode of thinking" than he did, and consequently "whenever we have been together I have somehow been conscious of a reaction against the ascendancy of this over my ruder processes. . . ." The reaction, he added, was "caused by some subtle deviltry of egotism and jealousy" in himself, and he found the source of these feelings "untraceable." As a result of them, he wrote, "I put myself involuntarily into a position of self-defense, as if you threatened to overrun my territory and injure my own proprietorship." In short, he concluded, his chief reason for being uncomfortable with Holmes was his own "meanness." James was thousands of miles from Holmes when he wrote this letter, and he hoped that when they were together again he would no longer feel so insecure with him. But, as we have seen, James found it just as difficult to be with Holmes after returning to Cambridge.

James fared no better in his relationships with young women than in his male friendships. Occasionally he spent time with Fanny Dixwell, an attractive and intelligent young woman who eventually married Holmes. But months would pass in which he failed to visit her. In the summer of 1869, while vacationing with his family in Pomfret, Connecticut, James passed many hours talking with Lizzie Boott, an artistic young woman who was also on a holiday in Pomfret. He experienced a temporary alleviation of his symptoms during the summer, and perhaps his flirtation with Lizzie was the chief reason. But he did not keep in touch with her after she left Pomfret. Another time of respite from depression was the week during which his "delightful" and "cheerful" cousin Mary ("Minny") Temple visited the James family. After her visit, he apologized to his brother for having previously criticized her and explained that "she is more devoid of 'meanness,' of anything petty in her character than anyone I know." But soon after her visit, Minny, who suffered from respiratory problems, left for California, and in March of 1870 she died of tuberculosis.

A decisive development also occurred during 1869 in the most significant romantic relationship James had in the years before he met his future wife. While in Europe, James had lived in Dresden in a boarding house run by a Frau Spangenberg, and for about three weeks an American woman named Kate Havens stayed in the boarding house too. James and Havens developed what Havens later described as "an intimate friendship." He considered her to be lovely; the "extraordinary musical talent" which she displayed at the piano impressed him; and he found her "hysterical, hypochondriac" tendencies intriguing. James and Havens had many thoughtful conversations in Dresden, and they often went on rides together. He wrote to Ward at the time that she "has stirred chords in this dessicated heart which I long thought had turned to dust."

On Christmas Day, 1868, and on 24 February 1869, James wrote long letters to Havens, who was still in Europe. In the second of these letters he hinted that he would like to see her:

> I often remember back to those peaceful old days at
> Grandmother Spangenberg's . . . , to our discussions
> on the back piazza in the balmy evenings, etc., and
> wonder whether anything similar can ever take place
> again.

He arranged to visit Havens in New York after her return, and Frau Spangenberg wrote him that Havens was "counting heavily'' on his visit. But the grandmotherly German woman advised him not to visit her if he wished that their relationship ''should remain only a friendship,'' because ''confidentially she wishes more than a friendship,'' and ''she would certainly become sick again'' if she were disappointed. Unfortunately, it is impossible to determine what occurred at this point. All we know is that Havens later wrote, ''It was owing to the continuance of my nervous weakness that I felt obliged to discontinue our correspondence from 1869 until 1872, when it resumed. . . .'' Apparently James was willing to risk having more than a friendship with Havens, but she abruptly terminated their correspondence. In any case, his experience with Havens in 1869 could only have aggravated his isolation.

He also was unable in 1869 to establish any satisfactory intimacy within his family. His relationship with his mother was particularly strained, although they did not express their hostility openly. She was aggravated by his ''morbidly hopeless'' temperament and his tendency to talk about his symptoms; he was angry about her lack of sympathy. He and his father kept their distance. James shared some affection with his sister, Alice, and often discussed his reading with her. But she had just undergone her first major breakdown in 1868; so, with the combination of her fragility and his, their closeness was severely limited. He and his brother Henry wrote to each other frequently and frankly, but Henry was in Europe, and both of them probably knew by this time that when they were together their respective symptoms worsened.

''[T]he distant, cynical isolation in which we live with our heart's best brothers,'' James remarked to Ward, ''sometimes comes over me with a deep bitterness. . . .'' He feared that some defect in himself made him unable to maintain an intimate relationship; in his diary he commented, ''Nature and life have unfitted me for any affectionate relations with other individuals.''

James wrote a long personal note in which he explored his concerns about his isolation. He commented that two basic approaches are possible for any individual. The terms we would use today for these approaches are isolation and intimacy. James called the first of these ''the centripetal, defensive'' tendency; it amounts to ''self-sufficingness,'' he wrote. He added that this is the approach which ''the theological view'' proposes. In it, ''sympathy''—which for James was an emotionally charged word meaning an empathetic feeling of closeness—is ''abridged.'' The disadvantage of this approach, he wrote, is that it requires ''self-sufficiency,'' that is, it excludes the possibility of true intimacy.

James called the second approach the ''expansive, embracing tendency'' and commented that ''sympathy'' is central to it. The disadvantage of this approach, he pointed out, is that ''sympathy gives pain.'' Still discussing the second approach, James continued, ''Should sympathy go so far as to dictate suicide? As when I [because I am] sick become but an eyesore and stumbling block to others. . . .'' Later in the note, he wrote more about the perils of closeness. He noted that before choosing closeness, he would have to determine three quantities. The first of these quantities is ''how much pain I'll stand.'' The second is ''how much other's pain I'll inflict (by existing).'' And the third is ''how much other's pain I'll 'accept,' without ceasing to take pleasure in their existence.''

During 1869, James found it increasingly difficult to make contact with others. As he stated so clearly in his personal note, he experienced intimacy as bitterly painful. Not only did he find himself suffering when others became close to him,

but he was tormented by the thought that his closeness to others caused them pain; in fact, this last thought was so disturbing to him that he even considered committing suicide in order to avoid inflicting pain on others. Whereas James might have, through the acceptance, support, and admiration of others, built up his self, with increasing isolation grew the risk that his self—already so fragile—would fragment.

James did, in fact, undergo a temporary fragmentation experience in 1869. We know about the experience because he described it, while disguising his identity, in *The Varieties of Religious Experience,* but he did eventually reveal that the narrative was actually about himself. James presented his experience in the context of a discussion of people whose confrontations with melancholy have sensitized them to the existence of evil. He introduced his account by calling it an ''excellent example'' of ''the worst kind of melancholy.''

One evening, probably in the autumn of 1869, James walked into his dressing-room, and ''suddenly,'' as he later wrote, ''there fell upon me without any warning, just as if it came out of the darkness, a horrible fear of my own existence.'' In talking of this fear he seems to be referring to the feeling of losing his sense of reality. This sense of annihilation is what, according to recent psychoanalytic writing, an individual experiences when his self gives way.

''Simultaneously,'' James continued, ''there arose in my mind the image of an epileptic patient whom I had seen in the asylum. . . .'' The patient had black hair and ''greenish'' skin, and he would sit all day ''moving nothing but his black eyes and looking absolutely non-human.'' . . . At that moment, James had a frightening thought: ''*That shape am I,* . . . potentially. Nothing that I possess can defend me against that fate, if the hour for it should strike for me as it struck for him.'' James apparently became aware of a primitive self image, deep within himself, which resembled the patient.

As a result of his ''horror'' of the patient and his realization of ''my own merely momentary discrepancy from him,'' James explained, ''it was as if something hitherto solid within my breast gave way entirely, and I became a mass of quivering fear.'' His image of something giving way within his breast is a particularly graphic metaphor for a self-fragmentation experience.

The ''panic fear'' which he felt at the moment receded. But ''morning after morning'' he awoke ''with a horrible dread at the pit of my stomach,'' and for months he was ''unable to go out into the dark alone.''

As 1869 drew to a close, he apologized to one of his friends for not having written to him. ''I have been a prey to such a disgust for life during the past three months as to make letter writing almost an impossibility.'' He added, ''My own condition, I am sorry to say, goes on pretty steadily deteriorating in all respects. . . .''

After the period of his ''spiritual crisis'' ended in the 1870s, he never again suffered from prolonged depression, the temptation to commit suicide, nor a chronic inability to work. But he continued for the rest of his life to struggle with psychological difficulties. In 1887, he wrote that he had a generally ''miserable nervous system,'' and in 1909, just a year before his death, he remarked that he had ''carried,'' throughout his life, ''neurasthenic fatigue.''

Although James in his late years was a changed man in comparison to the James of the ''spiritual crisis,'' his experience in 1869 was not merely an aberration which students of his life and thought may overlook. The year 1869 fundamentally shaped his interests and his world view, including his attitude toward religion. James himself specifically commented, "I have always thought that this experience of melancholia of mine had a religious bearing." Before his fragmentation experience, as we have seen, he was unable to sustain a belief in God. The only image he then had was of a masculine God, who was a rational "Contriver" of the universe. But during his fragmentation experience, James found himself relying on a maternal image of God, a God who protects and offers refuge to those who are in need. He wrote that during the experience he "clung to scripture-texts like 'The eternal God is my refuge,' etc., 'Come unto me, all ye that labor and are heavy-laden,' etc., 'I am the resurrection and the life,' etc." These thoughts, he believed, kept him from becoming "really insane." Later on in his life, although he never developed what he called "a living sense of commerce with a God," he retained a "germ" of belief, and he found that "there is *something in me* which *makes response*" when he heard others speak of their consciousness of God. Throughout *The Varieties of Religious Experience,* James maintained an appreciative, uncritical tone towards those with faith; his tone no doubt owes much to the solace he received when he thought about God during his fragmentation experience.

In addition, as James wrote in his account of that frightening evening in 1869, "the experience has made me sympathetic with the morbid feelings of others ever since." James went on to introduce the study of psychopathology into academic psychology. And he consistently avoided the denigrating attitude toward the mentally ill which was characteristic of many professionals in the field. Beginning with the 1893-94 academic year, he taught what was probably the first course at an American university on abnormal psychology. One student later recalled being impressed that James did not see those with "unhealthy" minds as being radically different from those with "healthy" minds. After taking the class on a visit to two insane asylums, James told his students, "President Eliot would not like to admit that no sharp line could be drawn between himself and the men we have just seen, but it is true." In 1896, James gave a series of lectures at the Lowell Institute in Boston on "Abnormal Mental States." A comment from the lectures suggests that he was still concerned, after all these years, about his fragmentation experience. He wrote in his lecture notes: "Now some minds get easily out of gear, & go to pieces, others keep together. Why? is the one great question in theoretic psychology." In addition, he was receptive, long before almost all other American psychologists, to the pioneering work of European psychiatrists such as Pierre Janet, Hippolyte Bernheim, and Sigmund Freud. He also took a central role in promoting the mental hygiene movement. In addition to public support, he made several generous donations to the movement and wished he could have done more. As he wrote to the movement's founder, Clifford W. Beers, "I have long thought if I were a millionaire, with money to leave for public purposes, I should endow 'insanity' exclusively."

But the most important consequence of his experience in 1869 was its influence on his basic view of the world. James argued that there are two fundamental stances which an individual may take. The "healthy-minded person" views life optimistically. By contrast, the "morbid-minded person" sees evil as being at life's essence. In an undated note which James probably wrote in the aftermath of his fragmentation experience, he commented:

To the man who has been insane and come back from it should not the tranquil confidence of most people in the absoluteness of their sane consciousness have an almost ghastly effect? It too is special, and as it were accidental, around it an ocean of undreamt of (or of only dreamed of) possibilities, whose imminence the crazy man realizes all the time. The sane are *blind* then.

James no doubt identified himself with the man who has returned from insanity. He did not have confidence in the "absoluteness" of his "sane consciousness." In his diary, three and a half years after his fragmentation experience, he noted his fear that "that dream-conception 'maya,' the abyss of horrors, would 'spite of everything grasp my imagination and imperil my reason." He accepted that the healthy-minded person might go through life satisfactorily. But healthy-mindedness, he concluded, "is inadequate as a philosophical doctrine, because the evil facts which it refuses positively to account for are a genuine portion of reality." What is more, he suggested that these evil facts "may after all be the best key to life's significance, and possibly the only openers of our eyes to the deepest levels of truth." In short, James, as a result of his experience in 1869, decisively cast his lot with the "morbid-minded" view of life. A comment he made late in his life succinctly summarized his position: "Melancholy! gives truer values." (pp. 374-86)

James William Anderson, "'The Worst Kind of Melancholy': William James in 1869," in Harvard Library Bulletin, *Vol. XXX, No. 4, October, 1982, pp. 369-86.*

MARCUS PETER FORD (essay date 1982)

[*In the following excerpt, Ford evaluates James's philosophical doctrines as presented in the essays collected in* The Will to Believe.]

The first four essays in *The Will to Believe and Other Essays* deal respectively with the relationship between emotion and understanding, the right to believe certain propositions under certain circumstances, and the relationship between belief and truth (or belief and verification); the fifth through eighth essays discuss the problems of moral and social philosophy; the ninth is a good-natured critique of Hegelian philosophy; and the tenth is James's appraisal of the accomplishments of psychical research and a comment on scientific mentality in general. The first eight of these essays, placed virtually in reverse chronological order, stand against the background of Darwin's theory of evolution and James's early attraction to Spencer's evolutionary philosophy. The ninth essay fits somewhat oddly among the others because it does not pertain to anything scientific, but it is related to the other essays insofar as it is concerned with the existence of God and the possibility of real freedom.

As a young man James was "carried away with enthusiasm" for Herbert Spencer's evolutionary materialism. In Spencer's schema, everything physical, biological, and social evolved or is evolving according to a single, fixed progressive pattern. James, however, was troubled by Spencer's failure to explain conscious experience and by his subsequent denial of free will. Although there were other problematic aspects of Spencer's philosophy (e.g., his epistemology), it was Spencer's failure to explain these two topics that troubled James most profoundly. For James, a philosophy that could not account for experience overlooks one of the most basic facts of human existence, if not *the* most basic fact—namely, that it is experiential—and a philosophy that denies free will could not support any ethical claims.

Simply to say that conscious experience evolved out of entities that lack experience does not explain *how* this is possible. Poking fun at Spencer, James writes: "Spencer seems to be entirely unaware of the importance of explaining consciousness. Where he wants consciousness, he simply says, 'A nascent consciousness arises.' . . . Notice the terms 'incipient' and 'nascent.' Spurious philosophers of evolution seem to think that things, after a fashion, as it were, kind of 'growed.'" To speak of "nascent" consciousness is to equivocate. For James a "not yet quite born" bit of awareness is equivalent to a "not yet experienced experience." An "experience" that is not experienced is no experience at all, and one is still left with the problem of experiential actualities evolving out of nonexperiential entities.

Without experience there can be no free will or self-determination, and without free will there can be no ethical requirements. Ethics presuppose free wills and free wills presuppose experience. In his lecture notes of 1876-1877 James links together what he judges to be Spencer's two major inadequacies:

> I now express my belief that we can give no clear scientific description of the facts of psychology . . . without resorting to the inner at every step, that *active originality and spontaneous productivity* which Spencer's law so entirely ignores. . . . His law leaves out an immense mass of *mental fact*. My objection to it is best expressed by saying that in psychology he repeats the defects of Darwin's predecessors. . . . Pre-Darwinians thought only of adaptation. They made organism plastic to its environment . . . Darwin almost wholly discards this. He never means that spontaneous variations are causeless; nor that they are not fatally implied in the environment, since they and it are both parts of the same natural whole. He means to emphasize the truth that the regulator or preserver of the variation, the environment, is a different part from its producer.

> Let me not be understood to undervalue the enormous part which direct adaptation, i.e., the teachings of experience, plays in mental evolution. The environment, meaning the sensible facts of our experience, is a vastly more potent agent in mental evolution than in physical. All the individual's acquisitions, properly so-called, come from it—and so, very likely, do many inheritances. . . . It is precisely because the action of the environment moulds the mind in so peculiar and distinct a way, that I object to allowing Spencer to say that it moulds it in every way.

What Spencer's law leaves out, according to James, is the "active originality and spontaneous productivity" otherwise known as "free will." In James's eyes Darwin's theory of evolution not only allows for the possibility of free wills, it requires them. Without the originality and spontaneous productivity introduced by free wills, evolution would proceed at too slow a pace. Natural selection alone would take far longer to produce organisms as complex as human beings than nineteenth-century geology could justify.

Two important facts that have bearing on *The Will to Believe* essays may be established from the preceding discussion. First, James's fundamental argument for free will is not scientific but moral. As a youth James was so impressed with the possibility that reality might be deterministic that for a time he was unable to do anything. It was only his belief that there may indeed be free will that saved him from his volitional paralysis. In his now-famous diary passage of April 30, 1870, James wrote: "I think that yesterday was a crisis in my life. I finished the first part of Renouvier's second *Essais* and see no reason why his definition of free will—'the sustaining of a thought because I choose to when I might have other thoughts'—need be the definition of an illusion. At any rate, I will assume for the present—until next year—that it is no illusion. My first act of free will shall be to believe in free will." If actions follow from thoughts, then the ability to sustain one thought when one might have other thoughts is all that is needed to put an end to determinism. The ability to sustain one thought when one might have others and to do one thing when one might have done another means that the future is open-ended, that it is being fashioned each moment, and that each individual is at least partially responsible for which future possibilities become actual. Twelve years later, in a letter to Charles Renouvier, James wrote: "I believe more and more that free will, if accepted at all, must be accepted as a postulate in justification of our moral judgment that certain things already done might have been better done." Without free will, regret and a sense of responsibility are illusory sensations. James believes that Darwin's theory of evolution provided scientific support for the reality of free will, but his major argument is that moral behavior presupposes the self-determination of free wills.

Second, James tends toward panpsychism as a way out of the difficulties he associated with materialism, especially Spencer's materialism. Convinced that Spencer's evolutionary materialism cannot account for the presence of experience (and that experience cannot be denied), James shifts towards panpsychism. Critiquing Spencer in *The Principles of Psychology*, he contends that "consciousness, however little, is an illegitimate birth in any philosophy that starts without it, and yet professes to explain all facts by continuous evolution. *If evolution is to work smoothly, consciousness in some shape must have been there at the very origin of things.*" More complex types of consciousness can evolve out of less complex types of consciousness but consciousness itself cannot evolve out of nonconscious entities. And in **"Reflex Action and Theism"** (1881), James cites idealism and panpsychism as examples of speculative philosophies that are congenial with his analysis of experience as purposive. "If anyone fears that in insisting so strongly that behavior is the aim and end of every sound philosophy I have curtailed the dignity and scope of the speculative function in us, I can only reply that in this ascertainment of the *character* of Being lies an almost infinite speculative task. Let the voluminous considerations by which all modern thought converges towards idealistic or pan-psychic conclusions speak for me."

Now the earliest essay in *The Will to Believe,* **"Great Men and Their Environment"** (1880), deals with the social implication of belief in the free will of individuals. James argues against Spencer's position that the course of history may be explained apart from the activities of individuals. James maintains that it is the individual, and especially the "great man," who makes history; without individuals there would be neither historical advances nor declines.

> Our problem is, What are the causes that make communities change from generation to generation? . . . I shall reply to this problem. The difference is due to the accumulated influences of individuals, of their examples, their initiatives, and their decisions. The spencerian school replies, The changes are irrespective of persons, and independent of individual control. They are due to the environment, to the circum-

stances, the physical geography, the ancestral conditions, the increasing experience of outer relations; to everything, in fact, except the Grants and the Bismarcks, the Joneses and the Smiths.

In James's estimation, the personal decisions of the Grants and the Bismarcks, the Joneses and the Smiths, determine the course of history.

Drawing on the Darwinian notions of "spontaneous variation" and "natural selection," James makes a distinction between the causes that *produce* novelty and the causes that *maintain* novelty after it is produced. He then uses this distinction on two levels: on the individual level it is free will that is the cause of novelty and the physical environment that either maintains or squelches it; on the societal level it is the "great men" who are the causes that produce novelty and the society that either supports it or fails to support it. In both cases, what is affirmed is the openness of the future. The future does not unfold according to a cosmic law but rather is made by individual men and women.

In **"The Dilemma of Determinism"** (1884), James openly links the possibility of freedom with morality. If reality consists of nothing but a plurality of actualities interacting in predetermined ways, then it is senseless to speak of the "moral life."

> For the only consistent way of representing a pluralism and a world whose parts may affect one another through their conduct being either good or bad is the indeterministic way. What interest, zest, or excitement can there be in achieving the right way, unless we are enabled to feel that the wrong way is also a possible and a natural way . . .? And what sense can there be in condemning ourselves for taking the wrong way, unless we need have done nothing of the sort, unless the right way was open to us as well? I cannot understand the willingness to act, no matter how we feel, without the belief that acts are really good and bad. I cannot understand the belief that an act is bad, without regret at its happening. I cannot understand regret without the admission of real, genuine possibilities in the world.

It makes no sense to speak of morality apart from a view of reality that is open-ended.

The "dilemma of determinism," as James defined it, is that between pessimism and what he calls "gnosticism" or "subjectivism." In his estimation, optimism is not a viable alternative for the determinist *if* the determinist admits to the existence of evil. To admit that there is real evil is to imply regret—for it means that things would have been better if the evil that is present did not exist—and, for the determinist, this cannot be. *If* there is evil, one cannot be both an optimist and determinist. The consistent determinist must be either a pessimist or a "gnostic." The pessimist admits to the existence of evil; the gnostic denies it. Both positions are compatible with determinism. Unlike the optimist, the pessimist is free from contradiction because he or she regrets the whole of history not just some particular "evils." The "gnostic" or the "subjectivist," on the other hand, denies evil altogether. For the gnostic there are neither goods nor evils but only knowledge—reality is ethically neutral. "The dilemma of this determinism is one whose left horn is pessimism and whose right horn is subjectivism. In other words, if determinism is to escape pessimism, it must leave off looking at the goods and ills of life in a simple objective way, and regard them as materials, *indifferent in themselves,* for the production of consciousness, scientific and ethical, in us."

The only escape from the dilemma of determinism, James maintains, is a belief in a world that is open-ended—a world in which the future is the result of free decisions in the present. James admits that pessimism and "gnosticism" are logically consistent alternatives, but in his opinion they are unsatisfactory because they violate his "moral demand." Any vision of the world that cannot satisfy this "moral demand" is unacceptable to James.

In the closing pages of **"The Dilemma of Determinism,"** James attempts to demonstrate that a conception of the world as openended is not necessarily antithetical to a belief in divine providence. "The belief in free will," James contends, "is not in the least incompatible with the belief in Providence, provided you do not restrict Providence to fulminating nothing but *fatal* decrees." Using the example of a chess master competing against a novice, James maintains that the final outcome of the game may be assured despite the fact that the actual moves are not themselves already determined. In this way, James suggests, there can be both real freedom and divine providence.

But here James clearly contradicts himself. What sense does it make to speak about real freedom within the context of a determined system? Keeping with James's conceit, why play the game if the winner is already assured? What difference does it make in the end if one gives careful consideration to each move or simply makes whatever move first pops into his or her head? Whatever his motivations for trying to reconcile the notion of providence with the view that the future is really open, the argument does not work. Unless the outcome of the game is actually dependent upon one's particular moves—unless the future is really open—moral life is undercut. Only if the outcome is really "up for grabs" does it make sense to regret making one move rather than another or to argue that one ought to make this move rather than that.

In the four will-to-believe essays, **"Reflex Action and Theism"** (1881), **"The Sentiment of Rationality"** (1896)—which is a slightly longer version of his essay **"Rationality, Activity, and Faith"** (1882), **"Is Life Worth Living?"** (1895), and **"The Will to Believe"** (1896), James explores the relationship between belief and understanding, the right to believe certain propositions under certain circumstances, and the relationship between belief and truth (or belief and verification). It is important to keep these three issues separate, even though James sometimes confuses them.

James's first point in these will-to-believe essays is that all experience is interpreted in light of some end. Because experience is teleological—because it is not simply passive but also active—no facet of human understanding is uncolored by beliefs and motives. This is as true of the scientific understanding of reality as it is of the religious understanding. James flatly rejects the notion that scientific knowledge is based solely on the facts. "As if the mind could, consistently with its definition, be a reactionless sheet at all," he exclaims. "As if conception could possibly occur except for a teleological purpose, except to show us the way from a state of things our senses cognize to another state of things our will desires! As if 'science' itself were anything else than such an end of desire, and a most peculiar one at that! And as if the 'truths' of bare physics in particular, which these sticklers for intellectual purity contend to be the only uncontaminated form, were not as great an alteration and falsification of the simply 'given' order of the world, into an order conceived solely for the mind's convenience and delight, as any theistic doctrine possibly can be!'' Apart from the scientific purpose and the belief that nature is uniform, science is impossible.

James's contention is not that all experience is *only* a manifestation of one's beliefs, although he has often been understood in this way, but rather that one's beliefs affect one's experience. Even the belief ''that one ought not to allow his or her beliefs to enter into one's experience'' is a belief that enters into one's experience. There is no escaping the teleological nature of experience.

James's second point in these essays grows out of his first point. If all experience is teleological, i.e., shaped by beliefs, one's beliefs are important. Moreover, because thoughts are at least partially self-determining, one is free to believe one thing rather than another (though one is not free not to believe anything). Under certain circumstances this freedom entails a responsibility and therefore it ought to be thought of as a ''right.'' The ''right to believe'' is a conscious decision to believe one proposition rather than another. Originally James refers to this as the ''duty to believe.'' After Chauncy Wright convinced him that this was a misuse of the term ''duty,'' James coins the phrases the ''will to believe'' and later the ''right to believe.'' The concept, however, remains the same. Under certain circumstances one is free to choose to hold one belief rather than another *and one is responsible for the decision that he or she makes.* In **''Is Life Worth Living?''** he writes, ''we are free to trust at our own risk anything that is not impossible, and that can bring analogies to bear in its behalf''; and in **''The Will to Believe''** he says, ''we have the right to believe at our own risk any hypothesis that is live enough to tempt our will.'' It is necessary *that* one believes something, but *what* one believes is determined, at least at certain times, by oneself and therefore one is responsible for one's beliefs.

The ''right to believe'' only pertains when a decision is ''forced'' and ''momentous'' and when it concerns ''live options.'' By ''live'' James means capable of being believed by the individual who is confronted with the decision. Decisions that are not forced need not be made, nor do forced decisions that are not momentous or whose options are not ''live.'' But when a decision is forced and momentous and presents live options, a conscious decision is required; for indecision amounts to a decision against the proposition.

James's primary example of the ''right to believe'' is in the choice between believing that God exists and therefore that there is a moral order in the universe or believing that no God exists and that the world is morally neutral. In **''The Will to Believe''** he argues that because God might exist and because God either exists or does not exist and because it would be of paramount importance if God did exist, one has the right to believe that God exists. In **''The Moral Philosopher and the Moral Life,''** James makes a similar case for the existence of a moral order, an order that presupposes God as the creator of that order. Of course one also has the right to believe that God does not exist and that morality is simply a human invention. Quoting Fitzjames Stephen, James says, ''If a man chooses to turn his back on God and the future, no one can prevent him; no one can show beyond reasonable doubt that he is mistaken. If a man thinks otherwise and acts as he thinks, I do not see that any one can prove that *he* is mistaken. Each must act as he thinks best; and if he is wrong, so much the worse for him.'' The right to believe allows for religious faith but it does not demand it.

James's third point in his will-to-believe essays is that in some cases one's beliefs may make something true that otherwise might not have become true. There is a certain class of truths, he contends, whose existence is contingent upon the beliefs and actions of human individuals. ''The desire for a certain kind of truth . . . brings about that special truth's existence. . . .'' At times James is quite clear about where belief in a fact may help create the fact believed in and where it cannot. ''In our dealings with objective nature we obviously are recorders, not makers, of truth. . . . Throughout the breadth of physical nature, facts are what they are quite independently of us.'' Outside of ''objective nature,'' however, one's beliefs may help create the fact believed in.

James gives two types of examples of belief that may create its own truth: matters concerning personal relations and matters concerning meaning or worth. The belief that someone will become a friend may be a crucial factor in that person's actually becoming a friend. Without the belief and the actions that follow from the belief, the friendship might not occur. Likewise, the belief that one will be successful in business or in sports may help bring about success. These are examples that James gives in **''The Will to Believe.''** In **''Is Life Worth Living?''** James suggests that the belief that one's life is worthwhile may actually make it worthwhile. ''Believe that life *is* worth living,'' he says, ''and your beliefs will create the fact.''

To maintain that *in some cases* the belief in a fact may help create the fact, or more exactly, that the actions that follow from a particular belief may help create the fact believed in, is not unusual. Many people have thought this. What would be unusual would be the contention that *in all cases* one's belief creates the fact believed in. Some individuals understood this to be James's position. In particular they thought that James was contending that if one believes that there is a moral order in the universe or if one believes that God exists, then there is in fact a moral order (or will be) and God exists. What James says, however, is this: ''I confess that I do not see why the very existence of an invisible world [a moral order] may not in part depend on the personal responses which any one of us may make to the religious appeal. God himself, in short, may draw vital strength and increase of very being from our fidelity. For my own part, I do not know what the sweat and blood and tragedy of this life mean, if they mean anything short of this.'' The existence of a moral order may ''in part'' depend on the beliefs of individuals and God might ''draw vital strength and *increase of very being*.'' To say that one's beliefs and actions might increase God's being is not to say that God's existence depends upon one's beliefs and activities. Indeed, it presupposes that God exists; if God did not exist it would be impossible for God to be increased by anything.

The matter of the moral order is exactly the same. In **''Moral Philosophy and the Moral Life,''** an essay that James considered to be very important, James concludes that it is necessary for the moral philosopher to postulate the existence of God.

> The stable and systematic moral universe for which the ethical philosopher asks is fully possible only in a world where there is a divine thinker with all-enveloping demands. If such a thinker existed, his way of subordinating the demands to one another would be the most appealing; his ideal universe would be the most inclusive realizable whole. If he now exists, then actualized in his thought already must be that ethical philosophy which we seek as the pattern which our own must evermore approach. In the interests of our own ideal of systematically unified moral truth, therefore, we, as would-be philosophers,

must postulate a divine thinker and pray for the victory of the religious cause.

If there is a moral order in the universe, it is the order that results from God's evaluation of the relative value of things. A moral order requires a divine perspective. According to this view, the *existence* of a moral order is not dependent upon the beliefs of individual human beings. If God exists, a moral order exists. However, insofar as God may draw strength and increase in being from the beliefs and actions of human individuals, the moral order may *in part* depend upon beliefs. To construe James as saying that the belief in God or the belief in a moral order in itself insures God's existence or the existence of a moral order is to misconstrue James in a very serious manner. He maintains that one has the right to believe that God exists and therefore that there is a moral perspective because it is possible and because it is a forced decision and because it is a momentous decision with "live options"; *and* in addition to this, he maintains that God might draw strength and increase in being when individuals believe that God exists and act accordingly. These are two separate contentions.

James's essay, **"What Psychical Research Has Accomplished"** (1890), is significant for a number of reasons: it restates his conviction expressed in his will-to-believe essays that all experience is interpreted, it presents another statement of his dissatisfaction with the traditional scientific view of the world and his own inclination toward panpsychism, and it contains his endorsement of unconscious experience. His major thesis is that traditional scientists ignore the facts that run counter to their beliefs whereas the psychical researchers, because of their beliefs, attend to all the facts. Traditional scientists would have one believe that they simply observe facts. Nothing could be further from the truth, according to James. Because they *believe* that paranormal experiences are impossible, traditional scientists do not consider the evidence. The disagreement between traditional scientists and psychical researchers is not a matter of different interpretations of the same facts, but rather a matter of different beliefs as to what are the facts to be interpreted. James is also concerned with pointing out the limitations of traditional scientific beliefs, but his major concern is with pointing out that science is based on beliefs.

James does not explicitly mention a panpsychic position in this essay, but he moves in that direction. "The only complete category of our thinking, our professors of philosophy tell us, is the category of personality, every other category being one of the abstract elements of that. And this systematic denial on science's part of personality as a condition of events, this rigorous belief that in its own essential and innermost nature our world is a strictly impersonal world, may, conceivably, as the whirligig of time goes round, prove to be the very defect that our descendents will be most surprised at in our own boasted science, the omission that to their eyes will most tend to make *it* look perspectiveless and short." He cautions against a wholly unchecked romanticism that might resemble "Central African Mumbo-jumboism" but he contends that some movement toward animism or panpsychism is desirable. The impersonal materialism of traditional science is simply not adequate.

It is also significant that he reverses his earlier judgment that all experience is conscious and endorses Frederic Myers's theory of unconscious experience. In James's opinion the vast array of data collected by psychical researchers is best explained by accepting the existence of unconscious experience. Each experience—and consequently each self—is more encompassing than that small bit that is conscious and the slightly larger portion that is marginally conscious. In *The Varieties of Religious Experience,* unconscious experience is viewed as central to his explanation of "religious experiences" and in *A Pluralistic Universe* it is unconscious experience that allows for the possibility that experiences that are consciously separate may in fact be together. In fact, unconscious experience is so crucial a concept in James's later works that it is easy to forget that he denied it in *The Principles of Psychology.*

The Will to Believe and Other Essays is a collection of essays written during and just after the writing of *The Principles of Psychology.* In these essays James focuses his attention on his wider concerns: the questions of free will, the existence of God, and the status of morality. These questions lead him into other questions, most notably, the relationship between belief and understanding, the right to believe certain propositions under certain circumstances, the relationship between belief and truth. He is also interested in the social implications of free will and in psychical research. At first glance it may seem that these issues are not closely related. In his preface to *The Will to Believe and Other Essays* he tries to relate the essays on the basis of "radical empiricism" (in this case meaning the position that reality is pluralistic and open-ended) and the legitimacy of religious faith. He might have been more specific in his preface. What he ought to have said is that individual experiences are partially determined and partially free—that is to say, partially self-determining—and that this fact relativizes all knowledge, makes the individual person at least partially responsible for his or her beliefs, and makes certain events in the future contingent upon the beliefs and actions of present individuals; and that therefore the truth about those events is contingent upon the beliefs and actions of present individuals. Each of the essays points to one or more of these three conclusions that result, at least partially, from the "freedom" of experience to determine itself.

James's critique of sociological determinism is predicated on his conviction that each individual is free. Historical events come about largely because certain individuals freely decide to do one thing rather than another. "Society" is a description of how various individuals have chosen to exercise their various degrees of self-determination. It is the individuals, especially the great individuals—the bright, the powerful, the learned—who determine society, not the reverse.

James's conviction that one can make one's life worthwhile by believing it is worthwhile or that one can help bring about success in business or sports by believing that one is or will be successful is simply a corollary to his conclusion that the future is open-ended. One's future self, the person that one will be at some time in the future, is not yet determined. In part, but only in part, what one does now determines what one will become. Because each experience is influenced (i.e., partially determined) by past experiences of the same self, one's present experience plays a role in determining who one will be in the future. Believing that one's life is worthwhile or believing that one will be successful affects who one will be in the future. It does not guarantee that in the future one's life will be worthwhile or that one will be successful, but it increases the likelihood.

James's critique of traditional science and his defense of religious beliefs stem from his conclusions that all knowledge is relative and that one is finally responsible for what one believes. Scientific knowledge is not knowledge without suppositions. It is not a mere reporting of objective facts. Scientists presume that nature is similar to a machine, that it follows certain fixed laws, and that what cannot be strictly quantified is meaningless. Scientists *believe* these things just as strongly as religious individuals *believe* that God exists, that there is an objective moral standard, and that salvation is possible (if not already assured). In James's words: "We all, scientists and non-scientists, live on some inclined plane of credulity. The plane tips one way in one man, another in another; and may he whose plane tips in no way be the first to cast a stone!" Not all beliefs are equally valid. Some beliefs are more correct than others. However, James's major point is not that religious beliefs are more correct than scientific beliefs; his point is rather that science does not exist apart from certain beliefs.

Freedom entails responsibility. Because science and religion offer competing beliefs and because an individual is free to decide what to believe, the individual is responsible for his or her beliefs. If one chooses to believe as a scientist believes, one is responsible for that decision. If one chooses to believe as a religious person believes, one is responsible for that decision. Responsibility cannot be avoided. One cannot escape being responsible for one's belief by choosing not to believe anything. Nonbelief is not an option. Choosing not to accept the religious beliefs is no different in its effects from choosing to accept scientific beliefs, and choosing not to accept scientific beliefs is no different in its effects from choosing to accept religious beliefs.

The fact that James fails to provide a clear framework within which to place each of the essays in *The Will to Believe and Other Essays* and the fact that he sometimes confuses logically separate issues do not invalidate his conclusions. If experience is partially self-determining—i.e., free from being completely determined by factors other than itself—then all knowledge is perspectival, individuals are at least partially responsible for their beliefs, and certain events in the future (and therefore the truth about those events) are contingent upon the beliefs and actions of present individuals. Unless one can refute the premise that experience is to some extent self-determining or free, one must accept James's conclusions. (pp. 25-38)

> *Marcus Peter Ford, in his* William James's Philosophy: A New Perspective, *The University of Massachusetts Press, 1982, 124 p.*

H. S. THAYER   (essay date 1983)

[*Thayer is an American educator and critic who has written extensively on the philosophical school of Pragmatism. In the following excerpt, Thayer explicates the philosophical doctrines James propounded in "The Will to Believe" as an empirical defense of religious belief.*]

The development of James's thought was to a considerable extent shaped as a critical alternative to the systems of absolute monistic idealism that dominated Anglo-American academic circles at the end of the nineteenth century. Pragmatism, radical empiricism, and pluralism were the forms in which he stated and advanced the critical and positive tenets of his outlook. It is to be noticed that in spite of major differences in orientation and doctrine, James viewed both agnostic empiricism and absolute idealism as alike in expressing an all-inclusive and abstract rendition of mind and nature, and in deprecating mutability, novelty, and unique forms of experience. The dilemma in philosophy, as he viewed it in 1907, was between "an empirical philosophy that is not religious enough, and a religious philosophy that is not empirical enough" for human needs and purposes. James was to assert that pragmatism supplied the method and mediating way of resolving this dilemma. But to accomplish this task required a new kind of empiricism, in which the emphasis was on the prospective consequences rather than the retrospective origins of thought and experience, and a significantly new conception of religious belief. It is to this last topic that we now turn.

James's famous essay **"The Will to Believe"** was published in 1896. In earlier writings, notably **"The Sentiment of Rationality"** (1879), **"The Dilemma of Determinism"** (1884), and *The Principles of Psychology* (1890), he had argued that sentiment and emotional interests and expectations play decisive roles in the selection and acceptance of philosophical, metaphysical, and religious beliefs. In a remarkable paper of 1878, he criticized Spencer's influential "empiricist" theory of the mind as an adaptive structure passively responding and adjusting to environing stimuli for purposes of survival; and he developed a richer, more comprehensive and accurate account of mental activity in which he was led to conclude:

> I, for my part, cannot escape the consideration . . . that the knower is not simply a mirror floating with no foot-hold anywhere, and passively reflecting an order that he comes upon and finds simply existing. The knower is an actor, and co-efficient of the truth on one side, whilst on the other he registers the truth which he helps to create. Mental interests, hypotheses, postulates, so far as they are bases for human action—action which to a great extent transforms the world—help to *make* the truth which they declare. In other words, there belongs to mind, from its birth upward, a spontaneity, a vote. It is in the game, and not a mere looker-on; and its judgments of the *should-be*, its ideals cannot be peeled off from the body of the *cogitandum* as if they were excrescences, or meant, at most, survival.

The mind is a teleological organization, James was to maintain, and "the conceiving or theorizing faculty . . . functions *exclusively for the sake of ends* that do not exist at all in the world of impressions we receive by way of our senses, but are set by our emotional and practical subjectivity altogether." If the formative and controlling conditions of thinking are *a priori*, as many philosophers have held, then "these interests are the real *a priori* element in cognition." A mind concerned with survival or prosperous continuance has instituted for itself a choice and selective ideal end of what *should be*. But there are any number of other kinds of interests that also might serve as conditions for action and for interpreting the world. Moreover, these ideal interests do not only precede action or the selection and interpretation of external facts; they have a part in determining the quality and eventuation of action and the character of what, accordingly, is regarded as externally real.

This form of voluntarism and pluralism advocated by James as essential to an account of "mental evolution," in which the mind is pictured less as a mirror than as a "luxuriant foliage of ideal interests," became the underlying theoretical basis for the argument of **"The Will to Believe."** But worked into this basis was also a phenomenon that James had recognized in his studies in medical physiology and abnormal psychology. As early as 1869 . . . James entered in one of his diaries some observations concerning a book on insanity he was reading. He cited the case of a man whose dreams were so "frequent and peculiar" that he ended by accepting them as "revelations" of reality. James then noted that

> insanity in its different forms was *literally* a dreaming. . . . Example of the determining influence which

the intellectual condition of a patient may have on the ulterior course of his disease.

The phenomena of belief as partially determinative of the ulterior course of a disease, now known as psychotherapeutics, keenly interested James. This was an empirical datum that empiricists had neglected or unjustly ignored in their accounts of mind. Not only was it a fact of personal experience for James, it was of particular importance in the analysis of the moral and religious function of belief.

The critical thrust of the argument in **"The Will to Believe"** was directed against the scientific agnosticism of Thomas Henry Huxley and especially of William Kingdon Clifford who held, as James says, that "it is wrong always, and everywhere, and for everyone, to believe anything on insufficient evidence." James's response was that not only do we sometimes believe on insufficient evidence but, under special circumstances, we may sometimes be justified in so doing. Essentially this was to argue that while sufficient evidence is one criterion for accepting one kind of belief, it is not adequate for assessing certain other kinds of beliefs (again, under certain circumstances—a qualification that leads into the substance of James's argument). And this is to say that there is no one criterion of acceptability for all kinds of belief. It is also to say that differing criteria for accepting beliefs are, like beliefs themselves, susceptible of different adjudications depending on differences among our purposes and needs.

James was interested in developing an empirical defense of religious belief. The way to impress empiricists is to argue on empiricist premises. Thus in the construction of his argument we can discern him applying a lesson from no less an empiricist than Hume. Hume had shown that some of our most fundamental and compelling beliefs, such as belief in the order of nature and of causal laws so basic to our understanding of how we know the world, are products neither of logical demonstration nor of evidence derived from facts. We believe that the sun will rise tomorrow for it has always done so in the past. But this belief, Hume showed in effect, is not defensible on a criterion of "sufficient evidence." For in this instance there is no sufficient evidence at all. The belief is a product neither of demonstrative reasoning or facts, but of custom or habit. Still Hume would not have recommended our abandoning the belief nor checking our more basic propensity to suppose that the future will resemble the past. We could feign to be skeptical about all our experiences and propensities to believe, but if we were to do so we should soon come to grief. As Hume says, in *An Enquiry Concerning Human Understanding,* if the principles of "excessive skepticism" were to prevail, human life would perish; but "nature is always too strong for principle."

So a Jamesian moral can be glimpsed in the consequences of Hume's argument: our belief in causal connections and the regularity of experience, while not *demonstrable,* is nonetheless rationally *defensible* as a condition of practical action. On such grounds excessive skepticism would be unreasonable and no more condoned by Hume than the sophistical attempts in divinity or metaphysics to furnish demonstrations. It was these latter, and not the practical and pragmatic defense of belief, that Hume enjoined his readers to commit to the flames.

There is also an echo of Hume in the very beginning of James's essay. His intention, he says, is not to offer a justification *by* faith but "*of* faith, a defense of our right to adopt a believing attitude in religious matters, in spite of the fact that our merely logical intellect may not have been coerced."

"The Will to Believe" is well known and does not require detailed exposition here. Its fame is perhaps exceeded only by the numerous criticisms and overly confident refutations it has occasioned. The gist of James's reasoning is to show that if we think of belief as a disposition and as "measured by action" and "willingness to act," we may regard any proposed subject of belief as a "hypothesis." The decision between two hypotheses is an "option." James then points out that options may sometimes be of great urgency and significance to us, and sometimes may not. Urgency and insignificance, or as James phrases it, "liveness" and "deadness" of hypotheses and options are not intrinsic properties; they are related to and dependent upon the individual thinker. Options that are *living, forced,* and *momentous*—where each of two alternative hypotheses is of great importance to us—are distinguished from cases where both alternatives are equally trivial or dead. A "genuine option" is of the living, forced, momentous kind. James's thesis is then stated:

> Our passional nature not only lawfully may, but must, decide an option between propositions, whenever it is a genuine option that cannot by its nature be decided on intellectual grounds.

For in such cases the decision not to choose at all but leave the question open "is itself a passional decision," and "is attended with the same risk of losing the truth."

The hypotheses for belief that interest James concern practical, moral, and religious issues. While it is, he says, a duty in all questions of opinion, first, to know the truth and, second, to avoid error, the two laws have different consequences. For some people, such as Clifford, the precept to shun error may be so paramount that no risk of believing, in the absence of sufficient evidence, is worth taking—even if the belief should happen to be true. For others, including James, the fear of possible error or of being duped is not so great; there may be beliefs which, when the evidence for or against is not decisive, may be worth adopting and may also be true.

It is to be stressed that James is considering only forced and momentous options. He is not concerned with the many possible instances in which it may be reasonable not to decide upon an option but to suspend judgment. He has been criticized for seeming to overlook occasions on which we might tentatively act on a hypothesis and occasions on which complete belief or disbelief are not the only alternatives open to us. But these objections miss the point. James's discussion, he says, is confined to "dogmatic ground" where systematic skepticism and indifference have no place. Here the hypothesis under consideration compels either belief or disbelief. But James also acknowledges that there may be people for whom no choice of hypotheses of a religious kind is a "genuine" option. For them, as he remarks, the argument will "go no farther." (In this, as I shall try to show, James was conceding more than was necessary, for his argument can be given an almost universal application when the "religious" aspect is reinterpreted.)

There is a further point to be noticed in James's discussion of belief. The kinds of belief with which his thesis is concerned are not only those of a practical moral, metaphysical, and religious nature and those over which genuine options are to be decided, they are also of a very special character. The truth of these beliefs is, in a subtle and complicated sense, "dependent on our personal action." As James says, there are cases where "faith in a fact can help create the fact," and "faith . . . creates its own verification." He gives examples of athletes and armies in which the belief in winning a contest contributes to the winning. The man who seeks promotion and who believes he will be promoted, and the man who believes that his destiny is to fail, will in each case increase the chances of the anticipated outcome. "How many women's hearts are vanquished by the mere sanguine insistence of some man that they *must* love him! He will not consent to the hypothesis that they cannot."

It will not do to hold that a belief creates its own truth (even if *truth* is defined pragmatically), though at times James's language misleadingly suggests such a view. It would be more correct to say that under certain conditions, certain beliefs contribute to their own realization or confirmation: What is believed truly about some event will indeed turn out to be true. But the truth of the belief does not make the event occur, for truth is not some causal property of beliefs, nor a causal property at all. However, it is entirely reasonable to maintain that certain beliefs in conjunction with other conditions of action and in appropriate circumstances, contribute to their projected outcomes. Such beliefs are partially self-fulfilling and play a role in the realization of their truth. It may have been cases in abnormal psychology and medicine that first drew James's attention to this phenomena; but, as he points out, it is familiar enough in ordinary experience.

For convenience, let us refer to beliefs that possess this character of being partially self-fulfillng as *projectively fulfilling*. One of James's negative conclusions is that a logical law that rules out all projectively fulfilling beliefs on grounds of insufficient evidence of their truth is irrational.

This brings me to the main theme and culmination of James's essay, namely, his "defense of our right to adopt a believing attitude in religious matters." While the ideas we have been considering hitherto have occasioned much criticism, so far as I know James's own application of his argument to religious belief has largely been ignored. He is repeatedly alleged to have endeavored to justify the belief in God or belief in religion. He does not, however, discuss the existence of God in **"The Will to Believe"** nor does he advocate belief in religion. For it is difficult to know what "belief in religion" is supposed to mean. It cannot mean belief in the existence of religions, for the truth of that historical fact does not require philosophic proof. But if it means *subscription* to a religion or creed, so that James could be regarded as hoping to persuade an audience whose sentiments are otherwise unsettled to join the devout legions of the chuches, it is altogether mistaken, as we shall see.

We must ask: What is the religious hypothesis that (for some persons) provides a genuine option for belief according to William James? His formulation of the hypothesis is surprising on two counts. First, it takes a wholly secular form divested of theological associations. Second, it is framed in such a way as to preclude, in part, issues of verification and testing. The main part of the hypothesis is given a moral and aesthetic content and might, until recently, have been condemned by scientifically minded philosophers of a logical positivist persuasion as "emotive" or cognitively meaningless or as a pseudostatement, by virtue of its untestability. However, philosophers are now less clear and confident as to what "meaninglessness" and "meaning" mean. And it should be added that part of the religious hypothesis is both practically and theoretically verifiable in James's account of it.

Religion affirms two things, James contends. "First . . . the best things are the more eternal things . . . 'Perfection is eter-

nal'—this phrase of Charles Secrétan seems a good way of putting this first affirmation." This, he remarks, is not subject to scientific verification. The second affirmation is that "we are better off even now if we believe [the] first affirmation to be true." There is a third affirmation following from these two: The more perfect aspect of the universe is represented as having a personal character, it "is no longer a mere *It* to us, but a *Thou*, if we are religious." This is as close as James comes in this essay to a notion of God.

A difficulty that immediately arises concerns the first affirmation. What are we affirming in the belief that "perfection is eternal"? James states his intention to keep the "religious question . . . generic and broad" and to avoid the differences and accidents that shape specific religious doctrines. His disinclination to sharpen or narrow the affirmation was not due to carelessness; it was, I believe, quite deliberate. The idea was to keep the object of belief as broad and unparochial as possible—almost to the dangerous point of being so broad as to be vacuous—so as to define a common religious attitude in which, despite other differences, all persons might share. Room remains for variety, therefore, even in the affirmation's specific applications and thus its particular meaning for an individual's conduct and experience. In a letter to his good friend John Jay Chapman, James commented that he was avoiding in this way those "full-blooded faiths" that "begin to cut each other's throats too soon."

The second affirmation is that we are "better off even now if we believe" the first affirmation to be true. In regard to this affirmation we must recall James's discussion of those special cases in which belief is projectively fulfilling, where "faith in a fact can help create the fact." The point is that in believing we are better off by affirming that perfection is eternal, we may indeed in some way become better off—that, to speculate, our lives and relations to other people and the world are felt to acquire richer worth and interest. The belief contributes to its confirmation. This second affirmation, it should be evident, is either true or false and is in principle verifiable. Thus in cases where individuals affirming the religious hypothesis are better off, the hypothesis is, *to this extent*, true. James, of course, wished to conclude something more than this. He argues that the religious hypothesis as a whole might be true and "taking the world religiously" might be right, because for some persons "religion is a live hypothesis which may be true." But it remains puzzling in what sense the first affirmation (perfection is eternal) is or could become true or false. It is especially noteworthy that James does not discuss the matter and that the emphasis of his argument is not on the truth of the affirmation but on the "vital good" that we may gain through religious belief and lose through skeptical disbelief.

But it begins to be clear, I think, that James's defense of the right to adopt a religious attitude is based upon a perception of the regenerative and healthy-minded quality of an essentially moral and aesthetic affirmation of the world. Thus "taking the world religiously" finds its justifiable truth, if at all, in the pathology and therapeutics of belief. The object of religious belief and reverence is for James, as it was for Plato, the vivid sense and appreciation of some aspect of beauty and excellence in the real world. The justification of such belief is in the progressive realization in one's self, and in sundry outer relations and attachments, of a strain and distributive presence of "the best things . . . the more eternal things." The belief is then projectively fulfilling.

The possibility remains that we might still err in this affirmation of belief. James maintains, however, that for some the belief is worth accepting and worth the risk. The unbeliever takes the other option and at another kind of risk. We continue to respect "one another's freedom," says James, and his spirit here is one of tolerance of "live and let live." The right to believe was not proposed as a universal command.

"The Will to Believe" has often been characterized as a defense of irrationality and egotism, a philosophic contribution to the madness of the modern world. James has been represented as holding that anyone has the privilege to believe what he will as long as he feels "better off" for so believing. If I believe that triangles have four sides or Santa Claus exists *and* believe I am better off for these beliefs, I may exercise my right to believe. But James had no intention of espousing irrationality or mere wishful thinking. There is no right to believe hypotheses known to be false or even improbable in the light of available evidence. He writes, "The freedom to believe can only cover living options which the intellect of the individual cannot by itself resolve."

We may observe, further, that responsibility does not cease with the acceptance of belief. Living options, once decided, determine consequences in continuing experience and action and thus affect other beliefs. The affirmation or denial of a hypothesis, however urgent the alternatives, is not an isolated or uniquely insular act. Choice is facilitated and managed by means of other already accepted beliefs and reliance on a prior body of more or less extensive knowledge of the world. James recognized the intersystematic form by which critical standards affect and guide the adoption of belief. In some important comments made on his views in 1907 and revealed in recently discovered letters, he says:

> The question whether we have a right to believe anything before verification concerns not the constitution of truth but the policy of belief. It is *usually* poor policy to believe what isn't verified, but sometimes the belief produces verification—as when it produces activity creative of the fact believed; and again, it may without altering given facts, be a belief in an altered meaning or value for them. In that case why isn't it "true," if it *fits* the facts perfectly?

As to the systematic organization of beliefs he wrote:

> The total goodness of a belief for the believer depends on his other beliefs and *their* goodness, and you can only call a single good belief true with the reservation "ceteris paribus." Those who defend the Kantian "as if," teleology, etc., mean that a view of the world's purposiveness that *combines with everything else we know* can pass for "true."

A further feature of James's argument deserves our notice. This concerns the third affirmation of the religious hypothesis about which, as we found earlier, James says, "The more perfect and eternal aspect of the universe is represented . . . as having a personal form. The universe is no longer a mere *It* to us, but a *Thou*."

The conceived quality of the universe is thus different in an especially significant way from the religious or the nonreligious outlook. And this is not simply a difference over the biblical conception of the universe as the product of God's creation and artistry. For James, the important point is rather that in religious belief the universe assumes a personal character; something of a self, some human trait is imputed to its depths and workings. He remarks that "any relation that may be pos-

sible from person to person might be possible here." He goes on to suggest that a kind of partial identity between ourselves and the universe is a part of the religious affirmation. For while we are in one respect merely "passive portions of the universe," in another we seem to be autonomous "small active centers on our own account." We are each, to follow James's suggestion (for he does not develop the idea at all), moral universes in a universe in some sense with affinities alive in us. And James's contention is that the religious hypothesis—if acted upon—is an invitation and resolution to engage the universe on these moral and personal terms: to respect and love it as we might a person, or as we might even respect and love ourselves.

It is noteworthy that in this essay on the right to religious belief James does not discuss the belief in God; indeed God is scarcely mentioned at all. In his conclusion, however, James does speak—not of God, but gods.

> This feeling, forced on us we know not whence, that by obstinately believing there are gods (although not to do so would be easy for our logic and our life) we are doing the universe the deepest service we can, seems part of the living essence of the religious hypothesis.

It will be worth our pausing for a moment to reflect on the foregoing account of the nature of religious belief. For what James says is exceptionally novel and not at all the religious attitude as it has been conceived historically or in orthodox circles. Indeed, the statements just adduced admit of a completely naturalistic interpretation. The colloquial and affable style conceals a radical recasting of the meaning of religious belief. To say, as James does, that through one's persevering in the belief that there are gods one is doing the deepest service to the universe, is to designate the central object of religious belief as neither gods, nor God, but the universe. The belief in gods is thus not itself an end but a means of expressing and consecrating that respect and service. Nor does the persuasion that the belief in gods performs such a service result from reasoning, for James says it is a *feeling*, "forced on us we know not whence." We are to feel that our believing there are gods is our way of doing deepest service to the universe. Moreover, we are to feel that this belief is maintained "obstinately," that is with a certain effort and intensity of conviction which is not the product of the more prudential or immediately practical concerns of, as he says, logic or life. But then it is possible that the gods so affirmed are not to be construed literally as the omnipotent deities of old, and it is difficult to think of James entertaining the religious hypothesis in traditional terms at all. His impatience with abstract dogmatic theology—whose conception of God's attributes is "only a set of dictionary-adjectives, mechanically deduced"—was emphatic. The "gods" are symbols whose role is to suggest and celebrate the ultimate object of religious belief; they are dramatic representations of certain forces and conditions in the universe that are friendly to our existence and whose presence and operations secure the continuance of life and our fortunes. Such ultimate life-giving and life-sustaining conditions, regarded literally and naturalistically, would be subjects of scientific observation and inquiry—and not gods, then, in any recognizable sense, although perhaps still commanding awe. But the moral implications of these same conditions in their bearing on vital human interests is the essence of their religious significance and of the allegiance, devotion, and reverence they might prompt in us. The underlying facts are not altered, but belief may institute, James says, "an altered meaning or value for them." The same conditions then pass from being matters of scientific investigation to becoming grounds of profound respect for the universe in which they are found: the universe that occasioned human life and that contains, therefore, in some of its germinal structures and maturations origins and traces of a human kind: a *Thou*.

It should be added, if only as a conjecture, that the *Thou* so interpreted represents not only the generative source of human reason and expression in the vast nature of things but also some eternal nourishing promise of the betterment of life. This would not be in itself a standard or ideal of excellence but rather the grounds and possibility of these; so that creatures naturally moved to live and think are also naturally moved to conceive and pursue, in differing forms and various ways, such perfections and beauty as are discernible and attainable to them. Perhaps this ground of possible excellence is what James meant when he found the first part of the religious belief to be that "perfection is eternal."

Our little gloss on James's text might be censured for departing considerably from what he actually said. But I do not think we have been unfair to the spirit of his argument or his intentions. His attempt to remain "generic and broad" on the subject, so as to avoid divisive partisan zeal and fanaticism, incurs the opposite danger of vagueness and elusive formulation; the treatment thus invites the interpretive effort. In any case, we can rejoin James by concluding with him that any "rule of thinking" that refused us the right to believe, in terms and along the lines just suggested, would indeed be an irrational rule. (pp. 92-103)

H. S. Thayer, "The Right to Believe: William James's Reinterpretation of the Function of Religious Belief," in The Kenyon Review, *n.s. Vol. V, No. 1, Winter, 1983, pp. 89-105.*

JACQUES BARZUN (essay date 1983)

[*Barzun is a French-born American man of letters whose wide range of learning has produced distinguished works in several fields, including history, culture, musicology, literary criticism, and biography. Barzun's contributions to these various disciplines are contained in such modern classics of scholarship and critical insight as* Darwin, Marx, Wagner *(1941),* Berlioz and the Romantic Century *(1950),* The House of the Intellect *(1959), and the critical biography* A Stroll with William James *(1983). Barzun's style, both literary and intellectual, has been praised as elegant and unpretentious. In the following excerpt, Barzun discusses James as a literary critic, focusing on his insights into the works of his brother, Henry James. (The material in this excerpt is incorporated in Barzun's* A Stroll with William James.*)*]

Throughout his life William James kept reading (sometimes reviewing) the new authors as well as returning to the old. His letters telling others what or whom he had just discovered tell us at the same time what he thought of Shaw's "exquisite" *Caesar and Cleopatra*, or Turgenev's or Hardy's or William Dean Howells' latest novel. He also succumbed, like the rest of the Western world, to the spell of the young Kipling ("Much of his present coarseness and jerkiness is youth only, divine youth"), though his admiration for some of the later works grew less.

Despite his disclaimer that he was deaf to poetry, James's prose is studded with quotations and allusions to the English poets from Crashaw to Francis Thompson, as well as to Dante, the Greek Anthology, and the great French and German writers. He felt the power and the vision in Zola's "truly magnificent"

Germinal, and in *Madame Bovary* "the persistent *euphony*, a rich river that never foamed or ran thin." As for Renan, then a demigod to the French, James quite early detected in him, behind the music of the prose, foppish vagueness, insincerity, and pretension.

He was moved by the "art and spirituality" of Baudelaire at a time when his brother Henry James found little in *Les fleurs du mal* but "weeds plucked from the swamps of evil." William knew his Walt Whitman thoroughly, taught his students to enjoy him, and quoted him repeatedly and at length in his philosophical essays, though rejecting his voracious Oneness that engulfed all concrete things. He perceived, moreover, the difference between that poetic transcendentalism and Ralph Waldo Emerson's. He enjoyed reading Shakespeare through in chronological order—not just reading about him—and the upshot was equal surprise at the playwright's power and the amount of ranting and bombast, due no doubt to his "intolerable fluency." Independently of Shaw and Tolstoy, who were no idolators of the Bard, William James like them was puzzled by Shakespeare's lack of moral, cosmic, or other convictions; for he was close reader enough to see that in a work of fiction without a perceptible tendency, the characters' utterances cancel each other out and produce a species of nihilism. These judgments, like his objection to the monotony of Palgrave's *Golden Treasury* ("too much of an aviary") were not the conventional ones acquired in college. William James had never gone to college; his humanistic education was foreign; and we may be sure that his opinions owed nothing to low, middle, or high fashion: they were his own, formed without aid from literary cliques.

For some students of James's life and work, the vital test of his critical taste is his attitude toward the novels and tales of his brother Henry James. There is no question that the Jameses— father, mother, sister and brothers—were an intensely affectionate and spiritually united family, what I have called elsewhere an erotic-intellectual commune. One proof of this polygamy of true minds is that they read one another's works. Reading the productions of one's family is extremely unusual. And they went on to discuss them with candour and delight. Accordingly, for many years William's appreciation of Henry's work was sincere and unbounded—until Henry began to develop his "late manner." At that point, some have thought that William's coarser being came into view. He lost his critical poise and literary judgment, and condemned what his sensibility was not fine enough to take in.

One need not go into the reasons given for this alleged fall— some have believed that it was jealousy; others have said that to Henry's civilised perceptions and delicate art William was opposing his crude and "typically American" outlook. The word "Pragmatism" is then brought out with an air of discovery, in ignorance or forgetfulness of Henry's enthusiastic adherence to that theory of truth, coupled with the declaration that for his own part he had been a pragmatist all his life—as indeed every artist, at least in his art, must inevitably be. What one should consider in place of these modern mumblings is the brothers' recorded views about literature and about each other's works.

Here is the critical part of the letter that William wrote to Henry about *The Golden Bowl* and *The Wings of the Dove*. It begins, let it be noted in passing, with a remark about *The American Scene*, which William says seems to him "in its peculiar way *supremely great*." He goes on:

You know how opposed your whole "third manner" of execution is to the literary ideals which animate my crude and Orson-like breast, mine being to say a thing in one sentence as straight and explicit as it can be made, and then to drop it forever; yours being to avoid naming it straight, but by dint of breathing and sighing all round and round it, to arouse in the reader who may have had a similar perception already (Heaven help him if he hasn't) the illusion of a solid object, made (like the "ghost" at the Polytechnic) wholly out of impalpable materials, air, and the prismatic interferences of light, ingeniously focused by mirrors upon empty space. But you *do* it, that's the queerness! and the complication of innuendo and associative reference on the enormous scale to which you give way to it does so *build out* the matter for the reader that the result is to solidify, by the mere bulk of the process, the like perception from which *he* has to start. As air, by dint of its volume, will weigh like a corporeal body; so his own poor little initial perception, swathed in this gigantic envelopment of suggestive atmosphere grows, like a germ into something vastly bigger and more substantial.

Now that is criticism of the rarest kind, which, while objecting to the manner or method or substance of a work of art, none the less describes these exactly, vividly, and appreciates the effect without relishing it. William James admired without enjoying and said so fairly—not a word here of sarcasm or denigration or belittlement, which indeed no student of William's character would think possible about *any* subject of discourse, much less the work of the *"Dearest Henry"*, *"Beloved H."*, whom he salutes at the head of every letter.

True, from the very intensity of that affection, and no doubt from habit as the elder and leader since boyhood, William goes on to warn, not hectoring, only pleading with the solicitude of love:

> But it's the rummest method for one to employ systematically as you do nowadays; and you employ it at your peril. In this crowded and hurried reading age, pages that require such close attention remain unread and neglected. You can't skip a word if you are to get the effect, and 19 out of 20 worthy readers grow intolerant. The method seems perverse: "Say it *out*, for God's sake," they cry, "and have done with it." And so I say now, give us *one* thing in your older, directer manner, just to show that, in spite of your paradoxical success in this unheard-of method, you *can* still write according to accepted canons.

The "paradoxical success" William refers to is that which he himself so fully perceives, not any success Henry had with readers and critics. Henry James in his final period lost them, bewildering them as he did *not* bewilder William. Except for a little band of faithful, it took some forty years for the third manner to justify itself and become fodder for academic dissertations. And to this day there are (and will continue to be) objectors, armed with tenable arguments against it. Those put by William James imply no obtuseness or philistinism:

> For gleams and innuendos and felicitous verbal insinuations, you are unapproachable, but the *core* of literature is solid. Give it to us *once* again!

In so urging, William James was inspired by unmixed devotion. He wanted for Henry the widest renown, the fulfilment of his manifest destiny as the greatest living American novelist. Henry was unmoved, quite properly. He had retorted in strong words to earlier hints of the same sort.

I mean (in response to what you write me of your having read the *Golden B.*) to try to produce some uncanny form of thing, in fiction, that will gratify you, as Brother—but let me say, dear William, that I shall be greatly humiliated if you *do* like it, and thereby lump it, in your affection, with things of the current age, that I have heard you express admiration for and that I would sooner descend to a dishonored grave than have written.

The brothers knew how to take each other better than their biographers do: "your last was your delightful reply to my remarks about your 'third manner', wherein you said you would consider your bald head dishonored if you ever came to pleasing *me* by what you wrote, so shocking was my taste. Well! write only *for* me, and leave the question of pleasing open!" And William reiterates his clear perception of Henry's achievement: "I have to admit that in *The Golden Bowl* and *The Wings of the Dove* you have *succeeded in getting there* after a fashion, in spite of the perversity of the method and its *longness*." And after the critiques comes a due disclaimer of their authority: "For God's sake don't *answer* these remarks, which (as Uncle Howard used to say of Father's writings) are but the peristaltic belchings of my own crabbed organism."

These brotherly exchanges are exemplary. It is remarkable that literary artists—for William is, in his own genre, a literary master too—possessed of radically different aims should so far sympathise with each other's productions.

William James saw his own task as discerning, transfixing, and reproducing in concrete language the multiplicities of experience, in order to have it seen as the fundamental reality that we take in endless ways for as many purposes. Henry James, out to slay the *very same* conventions of life and thought, wanted to go beneath them into the ramifications of feeling, fantasy, and will concealed from ordinary sight. So his exhibiting could not be done through direct exposition like William's, but only through the presentation of the stuff itself: he must not tell, but show—and hence their divergent methods.

That both writers acquired from their father and the James home circle a comparable gift of language, a genius for imagery and similitudes, and the power to disentangle and describe the motions of the human mind, is what inspired the anonymous epigram that Henry wrote novels like a psychologist and William wrote psychology like a novelist. But the range of their tastes was not the same, as we just saw, and the "contemporary productions" that William admired and Henry dismissed show William—the sampling above is proof enough—as the more inclusive appreciator.

There is no need to set the two geniuses up against each other, like prizefighters to be rooted for by hostile groups of fans. Each perfectly fulfilled his creative destiny in literature. Each was also a literary critic, Henry in the full-fledged way as author of many superb essays and prefaces; William reflectively, as reader, and also casually, in talk and correspondence. Both had extraordinary scope. But the one had the advantage of sorting out his views in formal exposition; the other had the advantage of being himself a creator of fiction, and produced only for his own art the theory of its making. We know where to find Henry James's critical thought. William James's is scattered, abundantly, throughout his writings, which is but one more good reason for going back to them. (pp. 41-4)

Jacques Barzun, "The Philosopher as Literary Critic," in Encounter, *Vol. LX, No. 1, January, 1983, pp. 41-4.*

GEORGE COTKIN (essay date 1985)

[*In the following excerpt, Cotkin examines James's use of the "cash-value" metaphor in developing the philosophical doctrines of Pragmatism.*]

The cash-value metaphor, which figures so prominently in William James's writings on pragmatism, has long been a source of controversy among philosophers. To many the metaphor was typical of James's highly colloquial style of exposition. While the cash-value metaphor, remarked a writer in the British paper the *Spectator,* might be useful as a "good rough-and-ready test for the ordinary dogmas of the marketplace," it clearly had no proper standing within philosophical discourse. Marxist critics would come to fixate upon the metaphor as indicative of James's supposed celebration of the crass values of the marketplace or as proof positive that Jamesian pragmatism was the philosophical expression of American capitalism. No contemporary reviewer singled out the cash-value metaphor as a particularly convincing or helpful trope. To the contrary, many critics latched onto the term as paradigmatic of pragmatism's problems, both of style and content. For instance, Paul Carus, the influential editor of the *Monist,* and Princeton University philosopher John Grier Hibben analyzed the term and found it wanting. To Hibben it suggested, in the end, something akin to the "kiting of checks" while Carus was convinced that the metaphor ill suited the essence of pragmatism. More recent philosophers have remained perplexed by the term. A. J. Ayer has called the cash-value metaphor "more vivid than precise," or, quite simply, "not clear."

Although James was painfully aware that his metaphor troubled many, he persisted in using it. In fact, the cash-value metaphor is ubiquitous in the Jamesian corpus, appearing in his popular works quite as much as in those intended for a more philosophically sophisticated audience. The metaphor was first introduced, and remained employed in similar fashion in later works, in James's important address of 1898 to the Berkeley Philosophical Union on **"Philosophical Conceptions and Practical Results,"** the precursor to the pragmatic doctrines published in *Pragmatism.* In the Berkeley address, after agreeing with the English empiricists and Charles Peirce that concepts must be rigorously investigated and defined, James then offered a series of rhetorical questions concerning any concept. "What is its *cash-value,* in terms of particular experience?" In essence, what practical difference to an individual would a conception make be it true or false? Further on in the paragraph, James again invoked the metaphor in his discussion of Locke and Berkeley on matter. The discussion of matter is cleared up, that is rendered concrete, James declared, only when "the cash-value of matter is our physical sensations." This is how we verify matter, in fact, this constitutes "the whole meaning of the word 'matter'."

While the Berkeley address and its conceptions of the pragmatic method would be substantially expanded and revised as James presented them in a series of public lectures to audiences at Chicago, the Lowell Institute in Boston, and Columbia University before finally committing them to print and the history of philosophy in *Pragmatism,* the usage of the cash-value metaphor remained consistent and constant. In *Pragmatism* James employed the metaphor to demonstrate how concepts or substances such as matter or chalk must be judged only according to their "sole cash-value for our actual experience." In that volume's crucial and controversial chapter, **"Pragmatism's Conception of Truth,"** James echoed his Berkeley address when he asked what, in short, is a "truth's cash-value in ex-periential terms?" James considered this passage especially significant; he quoted it as effectively summing up the essentials of pragmatism in his defense of the doctrine in the collection of essays, *The Meaning of Truth.*

It was in *The Meaning of Truth* that James attempted to explicitly defend his cash-value metaphor against the charges that it was inappropriate for philosophical discourse and too weak a metaphor upon which to determine value. In the essay, **"The Pragmatist Account of Truth and Its Misunderstanders,"** (1908) James especially sought to dispel the notion that pragmatism meant only action, that ideas were true only when they were capable of "enabling us to make money or gain some 'practical' advantage." That concepts or ideas sometimes worked in such a fashion James could not and would not deny, but he strongly maintained that this narrow application of pragmatic ideas did not constitute the wide range of an idea's cash-value or utility. While admitting that many unfortunately sought to reduce pragmatism to "some sort of a rough and ready *weltanschauung,*" James contended that the cash-value of a concept, its experiential worth, could be variable when applied in a purely theoretic sense, one without apparent "practical" bearings. To the critic who implored James to cast out the cash-value metaphor from his writings because of its pecuniary connotations, James responded explicitly only by reiterating the theoretic no less than the utilitarian usefulness of his pragmatic method and implicitly by retaining the metaphor throughout *The Meaning of Truth.*

Nowhere, then, did James really offer either his critics or his supporters any explanation as to why he considered the cash-value metaphor particularly effective in conveying the spirit and meaning of pragmatism. In sum, one might inquire as to why then did James continue to use such a problematic and unpopular metaphor to explain his pragmatic notion of truth?

In evaluating the cash-value metaphor, William James might well have asked whether it worked, assimilated new knowledge into one's previous stock of truths, and satisfied our desire for intellectual clarity, simplicity, and beauty. In spite of some trenchant criticisms of the term, especially with regard to its lack of clarity and inability to work on any level other than the mundane "rough and ready" world, . . . the metaphor was quite appropriate within the context of James's theory of pragmatism. While certainly typical of the colloquial language that James loved to playfully employ, the cash-value metaphor figured centrally because it worked, the *sine qua non* of the pragmatic temper. . . . [This metaphor also] had a deep, personal resonance to James. It served to link his personal financial problems with the cash realities inherent in the format of lecturing that he used to test and present his ideas as well as to help support himself and his family.

At first glance, James's explanation of the meaning of truth with the metaphorical structure of cash-value appears, as his critics claimed, to be grievous error, especially when evaluated within the stock of values associated with the term from American thought. The views of American intellectuals towards the marketplace and its values were, at best, redolent with ambivalence. When Emerson spoke of commerce, for example, he sometimes celebrated it as a kind of transnational experience, in which barriers were knocked down and the world brought closer together. At the same time Emerson, while admitting that the wings of commerce gave to all nations and individuals a common language, a new argot, to his mind, the business enterprise was sullied with the stench of materialism and lowly desires for gain. Emerson commonly invoked terms such as market-value in a pejorative or satirical sense, once going so far as to write that "Commerce is a varioloid of Cannibalism." For Emerson, no less than for Henry David Thoreau and especially for Herman Melville in *The Confidence Man,* the marketplace was hardly the site where cash-value for one's wares could be easily secured or worth established on a firm foundation. Cash-values were illusions, part of the shady dominion of the confidence man who figured so prominently in American thought and literature in this period.

James thus appears, on the surface, to have used a term that had a long association with deceit, masquerades, and falsity; he seemingly based his system for the verification and validation of concepts upon a metaphorical tradition which was, to say the least, shaky. Moreover, James was a political mugwump, someone who personally disdained the values of modern capitalist culture and who certainly placed little faith in the market economy. But, as Karen Halttunen has indicated, this pejorative tradition was on the wane by the last third of the nineteenth century, the contrast between character and capitalism with its attendant anguish and uncertainty had passed. In its stead was another image for the marketplace and capitalism. In the cult of the self-made man, or the popularity of Andrew Carnegie as a cultural figure, the capitalist-as-hero inhabited a ground that while still saturated with the tricks of the confidence man now also appeared to be someone who had built an empire based upon substantial foundations, putting his product up against the wares of others in the changing conditions of the market, and finally by producing a good that "paid" in a cash-value economy. Thus may one surmise that at the time James was employing his cash-value metaphor the term was suspended in two worlds of meaning, one suggesting an ephemeracy of value, the other pointing towards a durability and real worth. For James, a master ironist, the dual connotations of cash-value would prove both aesthetically appealing and useful in the elucidation of pragmatic assumptions.

The tension inherent in the cash-value metaphor by the turn of the century was well suited to James's pragmatic maxims, although his critics failed to realize it. With cash-value, James had a metaphor that did not suggest something with immutable value, inherent worth; yet, at the same time, the term was never devoid of value; every concept or idea had a theoretical worth until put to the test, and in a specified situation. James's chief antagonists over the metaphor, Hibben and Carus, were incapable of discerning the double-edge of truth, of accepting that the metaphor allowed James to emphasize that ideas and concepts did not have truth within them as an innate quality of being. The worth or cash-value of any concept, as James often times repeated, was in how the concept helped the individual to cope, how it aided the individual in his or her actual, practical, and concrete experiences. In one sense, then, the cash-value of any concept was computed or validated according to the personal financial system of the individual. As a philosophical position, this of course drew the fire of many who could not see or did not want to see truths as individually validated without any other criteria for value; nonetheless, the metaphor did effectively serve to illustrate James's meaning of truth. In a second sense, however, James contended that this personal experience, its pay-off, was also a social or community experience. Again, since the cash-value of any concept or idea did not solely reside in any innate qualities of the entity nor in the simple subjective currency of the individual, it also had to answer to the marketplace of ideas, the larger network of financial transactions and obligations. To be sure, the marketplace remained a denizen for deceit, but it was also an arena where buyers and sellers spoke a similar language, and where the testing out of hypotheses and their evaluation and revision occurred. In this sense, the cash-value of any concept or idea became part of a social experience—though James did not emphasize community verification as strongly as Charles Peirce—where the cash-value of the individual's perceptions became a worthy figure for negotiation. Through such negotiations one could live up to their general obligation to seek truth, not only for some abstract satisfaction, but because true ideas would bring payments, whereas false ideas would, in the end, register only in debits. To add to our certainty concerning the truth value of our concepts, James regularly connected the cash-value or expediency and utility of his own concepts to what he referred to as the "marketplace." James presented his ideas and concepts, whose cash-value was real to him, in the marketplace not only as a gift or offering, but also for the very real returns that he would gain from the criticism and debate.

The metaphor of cash-value also proved useful, as Jacques Barzun has recently demonstrated, when James sought to identify the use of an idea with the nature of a loan, or promissory note. The note is worthless when it cannot be converted into cash, no value inheres in the note as such. So too with James's emphasis on cash-value "to express," as Barzun phrases it, "the fact that an idea is worthless if it cannot sooner or later be converted into the concreteness aimed at." Truth in his view was something that only became apparent as the intellectual coin of the realm was placed into circulation. While this concept troubled Carus and thus initiated his attack upon the metaphor, the cash-value trope did express, in accessible terms, two crucial concepts of the pragmatic method and meaning of truth: that qualities were not abstract or innate and that the determination of worth was measured in terms of experiences and practical application.

The cash-value metaphor worked because it captured the tension and duality upon which James sought to base his theory of truth. From a pragmatic perspective, however, an additional consideration might be evaluated: to what needs and desires within James did the metaphor satisfy or respond to? The answer to this question may lie in the nexus of James's personal life and the demands that he encountered as a professional lecturer who was paid for his labors.

Throughout the period when James was lecturing on pragmatism, he was troubled by financial problems, in part because of his growing family, generosity with money, and frequent sojourns in Europe. To supplement his professorial income from Harvard and his meagre trust funds, James was forced to take his philosophy on the road, not only delivering his *Talks to Teachers* and other occasional pieces for pay, but accepting, at times, payment for lectures on pragmatism. The production and presentation of pragmatism was inexorably linked to the marketplace of ideas, the arena where James the seller literally presented his intellectual wares. Thus when James invokes the term cash-value within his discourse, it appears to come from the heart and is, in some respects perhaps, a psychic cry of despair emanating from a proud man who faced each public lecture with anguish and dread. To view William James and the production and presentation of pragmatism as connected to the marketplace and intimately linked to cash-value should in no way denigrate the achievement, nor sully the value and purity of the philosophy produced. What it may do is explain James's recourse to the cash-value metaphor just as Leon Edel has helped to construct Henry James's life and literary production by demonstrating how the writer was forced to practice his craft for a living.

A biographer of William James has written that the philosopher had the dream of becoming some day a gentleman farmer, free from financial obligations and the rigors of teaching, but that financial exigency prevented the realization of this desire. James was not poorly paid as a Harvard professor, but the funds were inadequate for him and his family. By the 1880s he had discovered additional sources of income, sending off chapters of the long-in-preparation *Principles of Psychology* to paying journals and composing a shorter, better selling version of the monumental volume. In the 1890s when James's reputation had flowered, he found himself in constant demand as a public lecturer. Armed with a series of lectures—sometimes his *Talks to Teachers,* at other times enticing lectures on exceptional mental phenomena or pragmatism—James crisscrossed the country gathering in money, estimating the size of his audiences, and evaluating the quality and reception of his lectures.

Public lectures attested to the cash-value of James's ideas; they brought into the family bank account impressive and needed sums of money. The allure of the revenues was sometimes so great as to force James to give up his much loved summer vacations at Chocorua to make money, as he put it, by lecturing to boring high school teachers on psychology. James hated the public lecture forum—although it must be admitted that in the last few years of his life he felt more confident about his lecturing abilities, greater rapport with audiences, and began to enjoy basking in the sunshine of their adulation for him— to the point of referring to lecturing as "a sort of prostitution." He was selling his ideas for money and in a way chasing after the hated "bitch-goddess success." Moreover, the time he spent in the preparation and presentation of these public lectures as well as the interminable social gatherings connected with them led to great frustration for James; lecturing for money was "a bad way of expending energy," especially when he felt that he could better spend his time working on his long-delayed philosophical opus. After the completion of each lecture series James would explain, and his avowals lasted for a period of nearly ten years, that he was forsaking the public lecture podium once and for all. Thus in 1898 he wrote to his wife, "I am *never* going to lecture again outside. That decision is a fixed point; and we shall shape our expenses accordingly." Five years later he swore to his wife, that there would be "no more miscellaneous lectures for me; thank you." Finally, in remarking on his Columbia University lectures on pragmatism in 1907, James wrote to his son that he would risk the strain of delivering his addresses only because they represented "the last lecture engagement of my life."

The summer of 1898 saw William James in California delivering his *Talks to Teachers* in Oakland, after presenting them first in Salt Lake City, and his **"Philosophical Conceptions and Practical Results"** to the Philosophical Union at Berkeley. James had long wanted to visit the West Coast but he could not readily afford the trip. In a correspondence with George Holmes Howison, philosophy professor at Berkeley, that continued for two years, James negotiated and bargained over fees, arrangements, and dates for the public lectures that would finance the excursion. In no uncertain terms he wrote Howison, "As for our 'business,' 1000 dollars for sixteen lectures at the U. of Cal/ two courses of eight, one on Psychology for Teachers and on Exceptional Mental Phenomena will cover all my demands, both for cash and for work." But James made clear to Howison that he lectured only for the money and gave only as many addresses as necessary: "I hate lecturing, on the whole." Subsequent letters to Howison read like advertisements as James sets out his terms, describes the contents of the lectures, and specifies the attractiveness of each lecture series for particular audiences. While always seeking to limit his lecturing, James nonetheless let it be known that if Berkeley would pay him fifty dollars apiece for each lecture, "of course I should not refuse more if it were urged upon."

"Philosophical Conceptions and Practical Results," where James first employed cash-value as the metaphor which served as the foundation for the pragmatic method was thus inexorably connected with the reality of fees and public lectures. That James sought to divorce the two, his "pure" philosophy of pragmatism and his "cash" philosophy contained in the *Talks to Teachers,* was apparent as he sternly informed Howison that he would give the talk on the pragmatic method to the Union only as a "free gift." After completing his paid lectures, giving a free lecture on pragmatism, and receiving strenuous criticism from Howison and his students, James asked only that his "remains . . . be gathered up and sent home by freight to my wife with what money remains—my pocket from the experience." Short would be the verbal distance traveled from this humorous epithet to James's asking in his first sustained analysis of the pragmatic method that one should know a conception's "*cash-value,* in terms of particular experience."

The cash-value metaphor remained in successive drafts of *Pragmatism* and became etched forever in the printed volume. During the years of *Pragmatism*'s final elucidation, 1906-1907, James delivered lectures on the subject, sometimes for excellent fees, at Glenmore, Chicago, the Lowell Institute, and Columbia University. The cash-value of these lectures on pragmatism was never, therefore, distant from James's mind. By this time, the Jamesian refrain was old but still genuine—the frustrations of public lectures and the glare cast upon the philosopher as paid lecturer. The feelings must have been mixed, somewhat like the metaphor itself, as James sat at his desk and wrote out checks covering his accumulated bills from the fees he had received from the Lowell Institute lectures which had come to "a prosperous end" the previous evening. As always, though the cash was deeply appreciated, James was "glad they're over." Especially important to James was that they might now be collected into a volume that would make "a solid and original little chunk of truth when written out & published." Not only would they, as James correctly anticipated, create a rumble in the philosophical world, but their publication would free him from once again delivering them as lectures. The cash-value of the lectures had been long established and their delivery brought only cash-returns, not personal satisfaction. The cash-value of his pragmatism lectures would now have to be worked out in the marketplace of ideas.

The cash-value metaphor, then, in spite of all the controversy it engendered, retained a tenacious hold upon the consciousness of William James. It captured certain ambiguities in James's pragmatic method that he did not wish to be ignored or simplified. It also had the kind of stylistic exuberance, the colloquial currency that James favored throughout his writings. Lastly, the term had cash-value within James's personal experiences, a close connection with the production and presentation of pragmatism. All of these explanations conspired to make James unwilling to drop the metaphor in the face of sustained and harsh criticism. The style, no less than the metaphor, in this case, was the same as William James. (pp. 37-44)

George Cotkin, "William James and the Cash-Value Metaphor," in ETC.: A Review of General Semantics, *Vol. 42, No. 1, Spring, 1985, pp. 37-46.*

ANDREW J. RECK (essay date 1986)

[*Reck is an American educator and author of numerous studies devoted to philosophical subjects. In the following excerpt, he considers the importance of James's* Principles of Psychology *to American philosophy.*]

The publication of James's *Principles* marked a watershed in American psychology, so much so that Jay Wharton Fay, *the* historian and apologist for earlier American psychologies, has entitled his work, *American Psychology before William James*. In an address delivered in 1898 the psychologist J. M. Cattel asserted, ''the history of psychology here prior to 1880 could be set forth as briefly as the alleged chapter on snakes in a certain natural history of Iceland—'There are no snakes in Iceland.''' While Cattell's remark should be put down as a mere witticism, as Fay's study reveals, it is minimally true if the term ''psychology'' be restricted to psychology as a natural (or experimental) science.

Following the lead of the German practitioners of experimental psychology, and with a background in medicine and physiology, James pioneered scientific psychology in America. As early as 1875 he wrote his friend, Thomas Ward, from Berlin: ''It seems to me that the time has come for psychology to be a science. . . .'' In 1867 he offered a graduate course on ''The Relations between Physiology and Psychology,'' and in connection with this course he and his students conducted experiments in a specified place, *having* then, if not *founding*, the first psychological laboratory in America. Although James championed the experimental method in psychology, he often expressed his personal distaste for it, as when he facetiously remarked:

> This method taxes patience to the utmost, and could hardly have arisen in a country whose natives could be bored. Such Germans as Weber, Fechner, Vierordt, and Wundt obviously cannot.

Nevertheless, James occasionally experimented in psychology, taught others to do so, and consequently advanced the adoption of the method of experimentation in psychology. The Preface to the *Principles* may be read, indeed, as the charter for the establishment of psychology as a natural (or experimental) science. As James wrote:

> I have kept close to the point of view of natural science throughout the book. . . . This book assuming that thoughts and feelings exist and are vehicles of knowledge, thereupon contends that psychology when she has ascertained the empirical correlation of the various sorts of thought or feeling with definite conditions of the brain, can go no farther—can go no farther, that is, as a natural science. If she goes farther, she becomes metaphysical. . . . In this strictly positivistic point of view consists the only feature of it for which I feel tempted to claim originality.
>
> (pp. 2-3)

Over half a century ago Dewey pointed out that there are two strains in James's *Principles,* one defined by the traditional method of introspection in psychology, the other by the experimental method. Of course he favored the experimental method, for it opened the way for the exploration of psychology and behavior, crucial to the development of psychology into a science. Yet each of these methods bore fruit in James's employment, affecting the subsequent courses of philosophies. It is beyond my compass here and now to touch on all the topics James explored by these methods—habit, instinct, emotion, to mention but a few, which I shall pass by; yet surely it is worthy of mention that often James's treatments were received appreciatively not only in academic halls but in the general culture outside.

Whereas the method of introspection, having served the advocates of the associationist psychology of traditional British empiricism for so long so well, yielded for James the doctrine of the stream of consciousness, with which he demolished associationism, it was the new experimental method that reached behind consciousness, uncovered the physiological basis of mind in the brain and other bodily activities of the muscles and nerves, and further illuminated the expression of mind in behavior. The experimental method ushered in psychology as a natural science, first functionalist, then behaviorist, and now, as if returning to James, functionalist again in the revival of the study of physiology for psychology and in the emergence of cognitive science.

The separation of psychology as a science from philosophy rests upon the assumptions which only metaphysics, not science, can explain and justify. In recognizing the difference between psychology as a science and metaphysics, James engaged in a kind of inquiry that is neither science nor metaphysics; it is what I have elsewhere called *philosophical psychology*. Philosophical psychology analyzes and defines the fundamental concepts of psychology. It examines the methods of psychology. It circumscribes the field of psychology, and lays bare its basic assumptions. It scrutinizes the intrusions of metaphysics into psychology and halting it from distorting the procedures or the results of science, it even expels metaphysics from psychology, as James sought to do in his critiques of the automaton theory with its doctrine of epiphenomenalism, of the mind-stuff theory, of the material-monad theory, and of the soul theory. In addition, philosophical psychology detects themes that stretch beyond the limits of psychology as a science and that invite metaphysical speculation and moral reflection. (pp. 4-5)

The assumptions upon which James contended psychology as a natural science rests were explicitly formulated in the Preface to the *Principles.*

> Psychology, the science of finite individual minds, assumes as its data (1) *thoughts and feelings,* and (2) a physical world in time and space with which they coexist and which (3) *they know* . . . [P]sychology when she has ascertained the empirical correlation of the various sorts of thought and feeling with the definite conditions of the brain, can go no farther. . . .

So in the *Principles* James professed dualism in a twofold sense: the psychophysical dualism of mind (or consciousness) and body (or brain), and the epistemological dualism of thoughts and feelings in the mind correlated with external objects in the world.

It may be pertinent to recall that the golden age of American philosophy in which James was the preeminent figure was marked, as one of our leading historians has put it, by ''the damnation of Descartes.'' To James belongs credit for making the dualistic assumptions explicit, and ultimately for participating in the philosophical enterprise of overhauling and overcoming them. Elsewhere I have suggested that the presence of these dualistic assumptions in the *Principles* is evidence of just how entrenched dualism was at the beginning of the era in philosophy that A. O. Lovejoy dubbed ''the revolt against dualism.'' When James formulated dualism as assumptions that, in spite of being required by science in its present state, call ultimately for metaphysical justification, he exposed it to the philosophical critique and reconstruction that followed, and to which he himself contributed grandly in his works on pragmatism, radical empiricism, and pluralism.

James described the relations of mind and body, or of consciousness and brain, as "the ultimate of ultimate problems." In the *Principles* he posited a variety of empirical parallelism that correlates states of consciousness with physical events in the body. Further, he affirmed a form of causal interaction, so that consciousness can perform for the brain the role of a regulator harnessing an unstable machine in the service of ends. In the first chapter of the *Principles* James defined psychology and mind; in the second chapter he discussed the functions of the brain.

A doctor of medicine and a physiologist, James approached the philosophy of mind from biology. An adherent of the evolutionary biology of Charles Darwin, he applied the scientific theory of evolution to psychology. Here, indeed, is a major trait of the revolution in psychology and philosophy that he wrought. He defined mind or consciousness in terms of purposiveness, locating its mark or criterion in "the pursuance of future ends and the choice of means for their attainment." And he traced the development and function of mind in organisms. Thus he fathered functionalism in psychology although the term was invented and the movement arose later.

James began with the fundamental situation in which an organism interacts with its environment; he sketched the reflex arc, which was to win Dewey so much of his early fame. Further, James distinguished within an organism its mind (or consciousness) from its body (including especially the brain). Drawing upon the most advanced empirical research of his time to illuminate the foundation of mind (or consciousness) in the brain, he acknowledged the relevance of physiology for psychology and advanced a line of inquiry that, despite its interruption for several decades after his death, has recently been resumed.

At the same time James retained mind (or consciousness), ascribing to it an essential function in the lives of organisms with highly developed cerebrums. Thus he viewed mind (or consciousness) as a kind of instrument that works in the interval between stimulus and response, particularly when action is blocked. Mind not only effectuates the adjustment of the organism to its environment but also guides the choice of means, altering the environment, in order that the organism may better attain its own ends. Consciousness is, in James's words, a *"fighter for ends."*

While working within a dualistic framework, then, James began the movement to overcome psychophysical dualism. In stressing the biological basis of mind, James initiated a revolution that was to continue in later American pragmatism and instrumentalism and that, when allied with social science, was to shape the thought of John Dewey and George Herbert Mead. For in the *Principles* James demonstrated that mind (or consciousness), instead of dwelling in a separate domain, is intimately connected with its natural environment. Interests rooted in biology and becoming conscious as ends direct all human mental processes and activities, influencing reasoning, knowing, and believing. While bridging the gulf between mind and body in a natural environment, James also broke down the traditional faculty psychology that had long segregated emotion, will, and cognition. He advanced the recognition, in Dewey's words, "that experience is an intimate union of emotion and knowledge."

Application of the method of introspection in James's hands had borne the influential doctrine of the stream of consciousness, a doctrine with a decisive impact on our general culture. This doctrine, anticipated by the British philosopher, Shadworth Hodgson, whom James studied, admired, and cited, is presented in Chapter 9 of the *Principles,* reprinted in part from an article **"On Some Omissions of Introspective Psychology,"** which originally appeared in *Mind* in January 1884. James portrayed consciousness as a stream: personal, always changing, sensibly continuous, dealing with objects other than itself, and choosing among them. By means of an appeal to direct experience, by introspection, James reported that he found consciousness to be a moving multiplicity of objects and relations from which so called sensations are produced by discriminative attention, and so he undermined the traditional empiricist concept of consciousness. In brief, for the picture of consciousness as a static mosaic he substituted the picture of consciousness as a stream.

In the picture of consciousness as a stream James found relations to be as immediate as the qualities they relate. As James said, "We ought to say a feeling of *and,* and a feeling of *if,* a feeling of *but,* and a feeling of *by,* quite as readily as we say a feeling of *blue* and a feeling of *cold.*" So he anticipated a cardinal tenet of his later radical empiricism, although, as Professor Seigfried has demonstrated in the first chapter of her probing study of William James, *Chaos and Context,* the theory of relations in the *Principles* needed further reworking. In addition to the felt relations within the objective field of consciousness, James found felt connections between the transitive states of consciousness, upon which he rested the sense of personal self-identity. Further, in his discussion of how the images or data of consciousness relate to others not present, he introduced the terminology of "halo," "fringe," "horizon," "topic of thought," and "object of thought," which caught on in subsequent phenomenological analyses.

In the picture of consciousness as a stream, James also considered consciousness as dealing with objects; he therefore found intentionality to be a mark of consciousness. Intentionality in James is twofold: cognitive and volitional. In cognition consciousness refers to objects that exist independently of it. Moreover, the objects with which it deals depend, in part, on its own selection; they are the objects to which it attends, and attention is a volitional act.

Here in the juxtaposition of consciousness and its objects is the fundamental epistemological dualism of Subject and Object that psychology allegedly assumes. Toward epistemology James's attitude in the *Principles* was ambivalent, as he searched for a coherent theory of knowledge that embraces themes from empiricism and rationalism. On the one hand, James dismissed *Erkenntnistheorie,* the critique of the faculty of knowledge as practiced by the post-Kantians, on the grounds that it is vacuous inquiry into the possibility of knowledge in general for the sake of establishing absolute foundations. On the other hand, he proposed the criticism of knowledge on the part of psychology. For assuming the existence of knowledge, psychology criticizes and explains "the knowledge of particular men about particular things that surround them." In effect, James prepared the way for the major revolution in Anglo-American philosophy in the 20th century; he transferred epistemology from metaphysics to scientific psychology, and within epistemology he brought into question and transcended foundationalism.

On the topic of epistemological foundations James vacillated. Often he intimated that knowledge rests on secure empirical foundations, as when he wrote: "Sensations are the stable rock, the *terminus a quo* and the *terminus ad quem* of thought." But on the whole, James passed beyond empirical foundationalism, because he held that sensations themselves are the products of discrimination in experience. Indeed, I would argue that James was a contextualist. Epistemologically, contextualism holds that knowledge is bound to the context in which it is achieved, so that what is basic to knowledge is context-dependent. As there is a shift in contexts, the basis of knowledge may be sensations or it may be conceptual meanings. Since, moreover, context is a matter of choice, it depends upon the selective interest of the knowing organism.

Throughout the *Principles,* therefore, the seeds of James's later pragmatism are strewn. Interests guide the cognitive activities of the conscious organism. Reasoning, general idea, definition, classification are construed to be teleological; they are tools of the conscious, interested organism as it copes with its environment to further its ends. James was the first to name and discard the spectator theory of knowledge, and to portray knowledge as instrumental to the active organism. James, however, extended his theory to the way knowledge and action, cognition and emotion, fact and value, are fused, to the point that practicality is not for him the primary mark of reality. For he held that interest determines belief in reality and moulds the sense of reality. Chapter XXI of the *Principles,* entitled "Perception and Reality," is, with revisions and additions, the reprint of an article that James published in *Mind* in 1889 under the title of **"The Psychology of Belief."** Anticipating theories of the *Lebenswelt* espoused in later phenomenology and social psychology, James sketched seven belief systems, each correlated with a distinctive world invested with reality, from the universe revealed in common sense experience to the wildest constructions of madness. As James maintained:

> [R]eality means simply relation to our emotional and active life.... In this sense, whatever excites and stimulates our interest is real.

Yet in the concluding chapter of the *Principles* James espoused a complex theory of necessary truth. Long before W. V. Quine and Morton White, he denied the analytic-synthetic distinction. But he upheld a theory of the *a priori* and even argued that some *a priori* propositions are true. *A priori* propositions, he contended, arise not from experience but from the native structure of the human mind, and to some extent his theory foreshadows the conceptual pragmatism of C. I. Lewis. Always a physiologist, however, he grounded the *a priori* not in the social structures of communication—language—but in the human brain.

In the picture of consciousness as a stream James accentuated the characteristics of the personal. That every thought is a part of personal consciousness meant for James that a thought always belongs to an individual personal consciousness, and to that consciousness exclusively. "Absolute insulation, irreducible pluralism," he asserted, "is the law." Add to this his argument against the theory of compound consciousness— namely, that any combination of units of consciousness is *known* only as effects upon some consciousness not included in the compound. The upshot was that later when in his radical empiricism James held that the same part of pure experience could be contained in more than one context,—say, a fire as imagined in a mind, and the same fire causally effective in a physical fireplace—he found himself in difficulty. Sensitive to this contradiction in his thought, James wrestled with it in his pluralistic metaphysics near the end of his life.

From the survey of personal consciousness James took up the issue of the consciousness of self. He steered a course midway between the empiricist conception of the self as a bundle of perceptions and the spiritualist conception of the self as a substantial soul. He rejected both conceptions: the empiricist because it failed to do justice to the unity of personal consciousness; and the spiritualist because it never could be verified in experience. More pertinently, he transformed the issue from a metaphysical question concerning the nature of the self into a psychological question concerning the sense of the self in consciousness, the sense of personal identity, self-consciousness. His stress on the personal was to feed into the mainstream of American personalistic idealism, particularly through the work of his student, Mary Whiton Calkins. His conception of the social self and his distinction between the "I" and the "me" as functional aspects of personal consciousness were adopted and transmuted in the social psychology of George Herbert Mead. His account of the thinker as the passing thought, accompanied by an undeveloped theory of appropriation, anticipated Whiteheadian doctrines of prehension, subjective form, and concrescence.

Consciousness, according to James, flows in pulses, each of which appropriates past thoughts and is in turn appropriated by succeeding thoughts so long as its personal form survives. Each pulse of consciousness is what he called "the passing thought." It is "a vehicle of choice as well as cognition: among the choices it makes are these appropriations, or repudiations of its 'own.' But the Thought never is an object in its own hands, it never appropriates or disowns itself." Feelings of warmth and intimacy accompany those mental states each of us individually recognizes as his own, and these feelings cluster about one's own body. The centrality of the body in the sense of the self, the import of bodily feelings, seems extraordinarily contemporary, and startling in a writer of the Victorian age. The appropriations of the thought, James continued, "are therefore less to *itself* than to the most intimately felt *part of its present Object, the body, and the central adjustments,* which accompany the act of thinking, in the head. *These are the real nucleus of our personal identity."* And James concluded, "The passing thought then seems to be the Thinker...."

Later in his 1904 article, **"Does 'Consciousness' Exist?"** James was to raise a question in the title and offer an answer in the text which have stimulated considerable commentary and controversy. In the aftermath John Dewey and Milic Capek, to mention two, have participated on opposite sides. In either case, the intellectual provocation of James's treatment of the consciousness of self is undeniable.

In spite of James's disclaimer, metaphysics keeps bursting out of the pages of the *Principles,* whether it be in his treatment of time with the notion of the "specious present" or the theory of conception with the realist-nominalist controversy resolved or in numerous other passages. For James, however, the "pivotal question of metaphysics" is whether or not there is freedom.

Central to James's psychology is volition or will. It is operative in attention and, further, in the effort of attention. Attention is the mental act of concentrating, intending one part of the flowing field of consciousness. What attention selects becomes an idea, and, on James's account, ideas lead directly to overt action unless inhibited by other ideas or obstructed by factors either in the body or in the external environment. Hence to attend, to have an idea is normally to act it out. The issue of human freedom then hinges on the question of whether the effort to attend is the effect of events transpiring in the brain according to mechanical laws or the expression of spontaneous, spiritual agency. Although science inclines toward the mechanistic hypothesis, James insisted that our feeling of reality, the sting and excitement of life, favored the theory of spiritual agency. However, he also insisted that psychology as a natural science could not resolve the issue.

In post-Kantian fashion James framed the question of determinism vs. freedom as a manifestation of the dualism of science and morality. Opposed to the scientific postulate that the universe is regulated by mechanical causal laws is the moral postulate that "what ought to be can be, and that bad acts cannot be fated, but that good ones must be possible in their place." As for James's own position on the issue, he wrote in the *Principles:*

> Psychology will be Psychology, and Science Science, as much as ever (as much and no more) in this world whether free-will be true of it or not. Science, however, must be constantly reminded that her purposes are not the only purposes, and that the order of uniform causation which she has use for, and is therefore right in postulating, may be enveloped in a wider order, on which she has no claims at all.

What the wider order might be challenged James's speculative powers to the end of his life, and it provoked the philosophical energies of numerous American thinkers, especially John Dewey, who strove so valiantly to overcome the dualisms James so neatly defined. As for the lineaments of this wider order adumbrated in the *Principles,* the scholars disagree, some affirming naturalism, others idealism. But in consideration of the influence of James on our general culture what has proved to be most original in the *Principles* and to have had the greatest and longest lasting impact on the public is not James's metaphysical speculations, nor even his hope for a scientific psychology. Rather it is his discovery and employment of the psychological point of view. From the psychological point of view questions concerning philosophy, morality, religion, and science are construed to be, not about objective topics as traditionally understood, but about the psychological processes of our feelings, attitudes, and beliefs toward these topics. The dominance of the psychological point of view in our popular, if not our academic, philosophy is in the contemporary American style, permissive, egalitarian, and affluent. It may well be the ultimate legacy of James's *Principles of Psychology* to American thought and culture.

Still we are philosophers, or at least students of philosophy, and James was one of us. In regard to philosophical enigmas, no matter how much they troubled him, he sought and offered no easy salving formulas. After all, in his day he had encountered quite a few such formulas—the Unknowable of Herbert Spencer and the higher synthesis of the Absolute idealists, to mention two he repudiated. What he said of them may reveal why to the end of his life he pondered the ultimate metaphysical problems —shifting back and forth, no doubt, but always within the early 20th century *Weltanschauung* of process and experience that he had helped to birth. Let me then conclude with a quotation from James. It may also serve as an exhortation to all young thinkers who, unlike James, would resort to formulas that excuse them from taking further thought.

> It may be a constitutional infirmity, but I can take no comfort in such devices for making a luxury of intellectual defeat. They are but spiritual chloroform. Better live on the ragged edge, better gnaw the file forever!

(pp. 5-13)

Andrew J. Reck, "The Place of William James's 'Principles of Psychology' in American Philosophy," in The Philosophical Psychology of William James, edited by Michael H. DeArmey and Stephen Skousgaard, Center for Advanced Research in Phenomenology & University Press of America, 1986, pp. 1-16.

JAMES C. S. WERNHAM   (essay date 1987)

[*In the following excerpt, Wernham provides a reevaluation of James's concept of the "will to believe."*]

Without an orthodoxy there can be no heresies, and it is arguable that there is no received view of James's will-to-believe doctrine. In the secondary literature, one finds a rich diversity of interpretations, even if one limits the survey to fairly recent discussions of it and ignores differences that are differences in detail only. There *is*, nevertheless, an orthodox view of the doctrine and it was blessed by James himself. That view is that the doctrine is a right-to-believe one, that it is about a right, therefore, and that it is about belief. It has much to commend it. Not only does it have James's endorsement, but it makes best sense of the well-advertised opposition of James to Huxley and Clifford. Theirs was an *ethics* of belief, a duty-not-to-believe doctrine. To be opposed, James's had to be an ethics of belief too, had to be either a duty-to-believe or a moral right-to-believe doctrine. Orthodoxy holds that it started as the former and quickly became the latter. A recent postscript to orthodoxy holds that it is not one but two right-to-believe doctrines, one a more and the other a less liberal one. The more liberal of the two is a right-either-to-believe-or-not-to-believe doctrine. The less liberal one is a right-only-to-believe doctrine. [In a footnote the critic adds: "Madden's claim is mistaken. It depends on a failure to recognize that James is sometimes talking prudence and sometimes ethics. The complaint that 'James had the unfortunate habit of alternating between his weaker and stronger versions in a confusing way in response to criticisms' and that he 'was one of those people who try to please everybody and thereby please nobody' is an unprovoked piece of character assassination. There is nothing either evasive or vacillating in claiming, as James did, that it is foolish not to believe, but not immoral."] . . . [My thesis] is that orthodoxy, with or without that addendum, is mistaken in all of its essential ingredients. . . . James's doctrine is essentially one of "obligation," not just one of "right," and that the obligation is prudential, not moral. If it is about belief at all, it is, then, what Price has called an "*economics* of belief," not an "ethics of belief." The second part of the thesis is that the doctrine, though nominally about belief, is in fact about one or other of the several things which James, demonstrably, failed to distinguish from belief.

By "James's will-to-believe doctrine," I mean the doctrine expressed in his essay **"The Will to Believe"** and elsewhere. It is a doctrine which appears at least as early as 1875, and reappears at intervals throughout the roughly twenty-year period following. (pp. 3-4)

[James] wrote once that he had been "in much hot water lately" over his will-to-believe doctrine. The heat came from different quarters. Some complained that his defence of faith was a defence of something so thin and tepid as not to deserve to be called faith. "Damned if I call it faith!" [wrote John J. Chapman]. "Damme if I call that faith, either," James replied, adding that his own faith was robuster than any variety of it that could be successfully adapted to the conditions of academe.

His usual response, however, was to cry "Foul," to claim misrepresentation. For that, he sometimes blamed his title. Had he not labelled his article **"The Will to Believe,"** one critic "would have been without a pretext for most of what he says." As it was, the criticism was wholly off target. "It is a complete *ignoratio elenchi,* and leaves untouched *all* my contentions." When the title was not made the culprit, his response stayed otherwise the same. Another critic was chided for substituting "*a travesty* for which I defy any candid reader to find a single justification in my text." But, if that account of him was bad enough, it was, apparently, not yet as bad as could be, for still another one was "vastly worse," a "really farcical interpretation of my **'Will to Believe'**." It was a situation that prompted prayer: "and I cry to Heaven to tell me of what insane root my 'leading contemporaries' have eaten, that they are so smitten with blindness as to the meaning of printed texts."

In the main, that response was right; there was misreading and misrepresentation. Still, his rhetoric was a bit excessive. The fault, moreover, was not all on the other side. His statements of his position are often less clear than they needed to be, and his position itself is less clear than he thought it was. Today, he is still in much hot water over his will-to-believe doctrine. The sad thing is that his characteristic response is now no less in order than it was then. There is still occasion to cry "Foul," and to wonder what is "the virus, the insane root, the screw loose (or what), that condemns these fellows to judicial blindness in their reading." (p. 5)

James called his lecture "an essay in justification *of* faith, a defence of our right to adopt a believing attitude in religious matters." He was right; what it argued for was faith, religious belief; what it argued against was the veto on faith urged by public relations men for science like Huxley and Clifford.... James's topic was faith, religious belief. The trouble is that he was never clear what faith is, never clear what he was defending. At times, but not consistently, he identified faith with "working hypothesis." That is what gives a toe-hold grip on reality to descriptions of the essay as a showcase for science. (pp. 5-6)

It is as an argument for belief that James's case has been widely understood and widely criticized. Russell made the main point as well as anyone. At a fork in the road, I must take one way or the other to have any chance of reaching my destination. I cannot afford just to sit there: I am faced with a forced option. Suppose no signs are posted. In that case, I act on one or other of the two possible hypotheses, but I do not believe either that the way I have chosen leads to my destination or that it does not. The option, as Russell put it, is forced "from the point of view of action." It is not forced from the point of view of belief. Although I cannot afford to suspend action, I can well afford to suspend belief. So, if James's argument is to be one for believing theism, he will have to argue that the option posed by theism is forced, and momentous too, from the point of view of belief. He gives no such argument. He claims that we do best to make willing advances towards theism, to meet it half-way. It is a recommendation to take theism as a working hypothesis. The reason is that only if we do so, do we have a chance of getting the evidence which will enable us, sometime, to decide about theism on intellectual grounds. That claim does nothing at all to support the conclusion that we do best to believe theism unless, of course, it is one and the same thing to believe theism and to take it as an hypothesis; and these, manifestly, are not the same thing.

The argument fares hardly better as an argument for taking theism as an hypothesis. An hypothesis is a tool of inquiry. As such, it is useful if it advances the inquiry of which it is a part. In order to do that, it must satisfy two conditions. We must be able to say what else will be true, if theism is true. We must also have some way of telling whether that something else is true or not. Much that James writes implies that theism as an hypothesis fails that second test. We cannot tell, for example, how the world is to end, safely at journey's end, or in shipwreck. But just that, he suggests sometimes, is what we must know to know if theism is true or not. Nor can we tell what will be the experience and collective verdict upon it of all who agree to allow their willing nature into the game. But that, his other suggestion is, is what we have to know to determine if theism is true or not.

If I am right, it is as an argument for gambling on theism that James's argument fares best. So understood, it runs like this. Whether theism is true, or atheism, is something we cannot now decide on intellectual grounds; so the wise thing is to suspend belief, to believe neither. If we can suspend belief, however, we cannot suspend action; we have to decide how to live our lives. We can live as if theism were true, or as if atheism were true, or on neither of these principles. Any choice we make is pure gamble. Nevertheless it is foolish not to gamble on theism. That is because an "immediate reward," as Ducasse put it, attaches to the act itself of betting on that side. That reward James called "the strenuous mood." The capacity for it could be activated, he thought, by postulating theism, not just by believing it; and the strenuous life was the best life whether or not it was also the right life.

It will be objected that that account of James's argument makes it say both more than the original does, and also less. Both claims are true. The original does not say that, because the religious option is now intellectually undecidable, we ought to suspend judgment about it; and there is much that it does say that is relevant only to a different argument, one for taking theism as an hypothesis. If the match is imperfect, however, between James's text and the account of it given here, the reason has already been made clear. It is that the original fails to distinguish things which are clearly different and, impossibly, offers itself simultaneously as an argument for believing theism, for taking it as an hypothesis, and for gambling on it. In short, the facts objected are admitted, but the fault is traced to the original, where it belongs.

If I am right about that, then, James's doctrine is neither a duty-to-believe one, nor a right-to-believe one, nor a foolish-not-to-believe one. It is a foolish-not-to-gamble one. If that gives an answer to the exegetical question, however, it simply raises another, no less important one, the question whether an argument for gambling on God is "a justification of faith."... [The] remarks that follow sketch only an approach to an answer.

1. Gambling is different from guessing. I can guess at the number that will win the raffle, but I do not gamble unless I buy a ticket. I gamble only if there is something that I put at risk, something that I stand to lose if I am wrong. Gambling, in short, is necessarily connected with acting, with doing something. Guessing is not; nor is believing. It is said that faith without works is dead, is not faith. If that is right, if faith is necessarily connected with action, that will be some reason for thinking that faith is gamble rather than belief.

2. Gambling excludes knowing. If I know the race is fixed, I do not gamble on Aristotle even if I put my money on him.

If I do not know the race is fixed and put my money on him, I gamble even if the race is fixed. That is why I can gamble on something that is already decided. What is necessary is that I should not know how the matter turned out. Some define faith as knowledge of God. If it is that, it follows at once that it is not gamble. More commonly, it is defined as belief, not knowledge. That is how James's schoolboy defined it; and most will agree that he had got something wrong. But what he had got wrong, they will also say, was not the "believing" but only the place of the "not." The smiles of amusement would be smiles of approval on most faces if the order were changed to "believing what you *don't know* is true."

3. Gambling does not exclude believing. Having studied his track record, I may believe that Aristotle will win, and back him to win. I may also back him to win without believing that he will. In that way, gambling is like hoping. Just as I can both hope and believe that p, I can both gamble and believe that p. As I can hope that p without believing it, I can also gamble that p without believing it. If faith is gamble, then, the religious person is not as such a believer, but he may be also a believer. Even if he is not a believer, he will be widely *called* a believer, for most are persuaded that "actions speak louder than words," so that if someone acts on a proposition—as the gambler does—ipso facto he believes it.

4. We call some things "a big gamble," others "not much of a gamble." The distinction turns on two things. If I gamble that p, the gamble is bigger or smaller depending on the probability that p. If it is very probable that p, that makes it less of a gamble than it would otherwise be. If it is very improbable that p, that makes it more of a gamble than it would otherwise be. The size of the gamble depends also on the size of the stake, on the value of what I stand to lose if I am wrong. If it is only a trifle, it is not a big gamble even if the probability that p is very low. If I am putting my life at risk, it is a big gamble, even if the chances are good that I shall come out of it without a scratch. Faith, if it is gamble at all, is a big gamble. That is not because the probability is low that God exists. The problem, there, is to establish what the probability is. Some estimate it so low as to be negligible. Others estimate it so high that they speak of faith as knowledge and certainty; and neither side is much moved by the considerations brought forward by the other. What makes faith a big gamble is the size of the stake. "Go sell your possessions and give to the poor." That was the price to the rich man of the ticket of admission to the game. Staking everything they possess; that was Pascal's description of the mature in faith. No doubt one can quibble over whether it is "gambling with one's life"; but there is no question that, as described, it is definitely a high-stakes game.

5. Whether something is called a gamble or not a gamble, a big gamble or not much of a gamble depends on the *speaker's* estimate of the stake and of the probabilities. So an agent and an observer may well differ on the size of a gamble, and even on whether it is a gamble at all. Typically, that happens over faith. For the unbeliever, it is too much of a gamble: that game, he says, is not worth the candle. For the believer, it is no gamble at all. He calls it a "sure thing." It does not follow that he is right about that. So called "sure things" can be anything but sure. He may also come to call it no gamble at all because he no longer values the stake the way he did. From saying, "If I lose, I lose all," he now says, "If I lose, I lose nothing."

"Damned if I call that faith." Perhaps that is the right response if James's case is for gambling on God, not for believing. It isn't obvious, however, so it needs argument; and such argument as I have found is impressive only in its weakness. Faith cannot be gamble, it runs, because it is knowledge. Or, faith cannot be gamble because it is belief. Or, faith cannot be gamble because faith is serious. The first two of these simply beg the question. They "prove" that faith is not gamble by assuming that it is something else. The assumption is less plausible in the first case, more plausible in the second. The third assumes that gambling is a frivolity, a pastime only. Sometimes it is, sometimes not. It depends on what one is gambling with. And if faith is gambling with one's life, there is nothing frivolous about it at all. Superficially at least, the case looks better on the other side. Abraham is known as the father of faith. That is because, as Hebrews puts it, "he went out not knowing whither he went." For all the world, it looks like gambling. (pp. 102-05)

> *James C. S. Wernham, in his* James's Will-to-Believe Doctrine: A Heretical View, *McGill-Queen's University Press, 1987, 130 p.*

ADDITIONAL BIBLIOGRAPHY

Allen, Gay Wilson. *William James: A Biography.* New York: Viking Press, 1967, 556 p.
> Most complete biography of James, making use of materials unavailable to Ralph Barton Perry (see Additional Bibliography entry below) which enabled a fuller portrait of James's wife. Jacques Barzun, author of the critical study *A Stroll with William James* (1983) calls Allen James's "best biographer."

Blanshard, Brand, and Schneider, Herbert W., eds. *In Commemoration of William James, 1842-1942.* New York: Columbia University Press, 1942, 234 p.
> Collection containing essays on various aspects of James's life and works. Critics included in this volume are Dickinson S. Miller, John Dewey, Julius Bixler, Ralph Barton Perry, and Charles Morris.

Boutroux, Emile. *William James.* Translated by Archibald Henderson and Barbara Henderson. New York and London: Longmans, Green, & Co., 1912, 126 p.
> Highly laudatory study divided into sections that examine James's psychology, religious psychology, Pragmatism, metaphysical views, and philosophy of education. The general basis of Boutroux's admiration for his subject is that James "thought that philosophy, even in its boldest speculations, should maintain its bond with the soul of the thinker if it is not to degenerate into an empty assemblage of words and of concepts, devoid of all real content."

Brennan, Bernard P. *The Ethics of William James.* New York: Bookman Associates, 1961, 183 p.
> Study intended to answer the challenge that by definition Pragmatism is not concerned with ethics but only with expediency. Brennan finds that "morality plays a major role in the pragmatism of William James," and that although James did recognize an absolute moral code, in his ethical philosophy moral ideals have an objective validity "lodged in the *de facto* constitution of some existing consciousness."

———. *William James.* New York: Twayne Publishers, 1968, 176 p.
> Useful introductory study.

Browning, Don. "William James's Philosophy of Mysticism." *The Journal of Religion* 59, No. 1 (January 1979): 56-70.
> Questions whether or not James viewed mysticism as a support to moral action. Browning concludes that, as an experience that effaces individuality and pluralism, mysticism in James's philosophy eliminated the possibility of moral action on the part of individuals or groups.

Bruns, Gerald L. "Loose Talk about Religion from William James." *Critical Inquiry* 11, No. 2 (December 1984): 299-316.

Examines the language James used in *The Varieties of Religious Experience* to discuss phenomena that have a doubtful status in the material world.

Compton, Charles H., ed. *William James: Philosopher and Man.* New York: Scarecrow Press, 1957, 229 p.

Compilation of quotes and references from a variety of sources. Part One consists of quotations concerning James, many of them passing references made by such figures as Oliver Wendell Holmes, Theodore Roosevelt, and Adlai E. Stevenson. Part Two consists of references to James in 652 books by 344 authors.

Dittes, James E. "Beyond William James." In *Beyond the Classics? Essays in the Scientific Study of Religion,* edited by Charles Y. Glock and Phillip E. Hammond, pp. 291-354. New York: Harper & Row, 1973.

Discussion of James's influence on the field of the psychology of religion. Dittes states that "James can be appropriately regarded as the founder of American psychology of religion not for the psychological theories or psychological data or psychological method he offered, but for his philosophical position or perhaps more accurately, philosophical temper or outlook."

Dooley, Patrick Kiaran. *Pragmatism as Humanism: The Philosophy of William James.* Chicago: Nelson-Hall, 1974, 220 p.

Critic states that he has "attempted to articulate and defend the unity and coherence of James' philosophical vision," and finds that the philosophy of humanism is the binding theme of James's works.

Feinstein, Howard M. *Becoming William James.* Ithaca, N.Y.: Cornell University Press, 1984, 377 p.

Psychoanalytic biography of James up to the age of thirty, with particular emphasis on his relationship with his father.

Fontinell, Eugene. *Self, God, and Immortality: A Jamesian Investigation.* Philadelphia: Temple University Press, 1986, 320 p.

Employs the central doctrines of James's thought to explore the question: "Can we who have been touched by the intellectual experiential revolutions of the contemporary world still believe with any degree of coherence and consistency that we as individual persons are immortal?"

Gavin, William J. "The 'Will to Believe' in Science and Religion." *International Journal for Philosophy and Religion* 15, No. 3 (1984): 139-48.

Illuminates James's ideas concerning when the "will to believe" should or should not be exercised.

Hocks, Richard A. *Henry James and Pragmatistic Thought: A Study in the Relationship between the Philosophy of William James and the Literary Art of Henry James.* Chapel Hill: University of North Carolina Press, 1974, 258 p.

Critic states that "the key which the thesis of this entire book turns on is above all else our grasping and understanding William's thought through Henry's own eyes." Hocks finds that Henry James had "an extraordinarily good grasp" of William James's philosophic thought and that in his later fiction he "actualized" the doctrine of Pragmatism.

Lentricchia, Frank. "The Return of William James." *Cultural Critique* 4 (Fall 1986): 5-31.

Observes a recent intellectual trend of a "new pragmatism" which opposes abstract thought that is divorced from action.

Levinson, Henry S. *Science, Metaphysics, and the Chance of Salvation: An Interpretation of the Thought of William James.* Missoula, Mont.: Scholars Press, 1978, 258 p.

General study which, rather than concerning itself with "*how* James asks and answers questions of philosophical import," centers its "arguments and claims about James either on *what* questions James asked or on what James construed to be the sorts of circumstances and conditions that generate those questions."

Linschoten, Hans. *On the Way toward a Phenomenological Psychology: The Psychology of William James.* Edited by Amedeo Giorgi. Pittsburgh: Duquesne University Press, 1968, 319 p.

Study of James's psychological theory based on the viewpoint that *The Principles of Psychology* "presupposes" concepts of the phenomenological school of psychology, specifically the idea that experience does not exist apart from a particular "experience-of-something."

MacLeod, Robert B., ed. *William James: Unfinished Business.* Washington, D.C.: American Psychological Association, 1969, 106 p.

Collection of essays on James's psychological theories, including "William James's Humanism and the Problem of Free Will" by psychologist Rollo May.

Moore, Edward C. *William James.* New York: Washington Square Press, 1966, 194 p.

Introductory study designed for the general reader. Moore considers the full range of James's thought in order to avoid what he believes has been an undue emphasis placed on the essay "The Will to Believe" and the Pragmatic theory of truth.

Morris, Lloyd. *William James: The Message of a Modern Mind.* New York: Charles Scribner's Sons, 1950, 98 p.

Introductory study designed for the general reader. Separate chapters describe and discuss James's central philosophical doctrines, including "The Pragmatic Method," "The Nature of Truth," and "A World of Pure Experience," while a closing chapter considers "The Influence of William James."

Myers, Gerald E. *William James: His Life and Thought.* New Haven and London: Yale University Press, 1986, 628 p.

Primarily devoted to the comprehensive analysis of James's "writings on the nature of consciousness, the mind-body complex, space and time, memory, attention and will, emotion, thought, knowledge, pragmatism, reality, self, psychical research, morality, and religion."

Otto, Max, and others. *William James: The Man and the Thinker.* Madison: University of Wisconsin Press, 1942, 147 p.

Centenary collection of essays which includes contributions by Dickinson S. Miller, John Dewey, and Julius Seelye Bixler.

Perry, Ralph Barton. *The Thought and Character of William James.* 2 vols. Boston: Little, Brown, and Co., 1935.

The first extensive biography of James, including many useful excerpts from letters and unpublished manuscripts.

Roth, John K. *Freedom and the Moral Life.* Philadelphia: Westminster Press, 1969, 157 p.

Studies the development throughout James's writings of the belief that individuals have the power and freedom to change themselves and their environment. In light of this freedom, Roth asks, what moral and ethical values would James advise adopting? Roth concludes that James's moral philosophy "stresses the pursuit of meaning through the extension of the values of freedom and unity," values which promote "an ordered existence and a sense of meaning that will not cease to grow."

Seigfried, Charlene Haddock. *Chaos and Context: A Study in William James.* Athens: Ohio University Press, 1978, 137 p.

Studies James's doctrine of relations, his idea that "the relations between things, conjunctive as well as disjunctive, are just as much matters of direct particular experience, neither more so nor less, than the things themselves." This direction of inquiry is accompanied by a consideration of James's doctrine of experience, which states that experience is never abstract but is always an experience of something particular, just as consciousness, in James's view, is always consciousness of somethng particular. Seigfried states in her conclusion that "the quasi-chaos of pure experience [Seigfried's modification of the "ordinary absolute chaos" posited by James] allows for tendencies and resistances which can be ignored only at our peril, since the flux of sensation has its own continuity, movement, and sense of direction. These experience tendencies are the basis for James's claim that relations are really experienced."

Skrupskelis, Ignas K. *William James: A Reference Guide*. Boston: G. K. Hall, 1977, 250 p.
> Annotated bibliography of critical writings on James through 1974.

Smith, John E. "William James's Account of Mysticism: A Critical Appraisal." In *Mysticism and Religious Traditions,* edited by Steven T. Katz, pp. 247-79. Oxford: Oxford University Press, 1983.
> Analysis of *The Varieties of Religious Experience,* particularly as James's theories in this study pertain to the relationship between mysticism and conventional religious institutions.

Spears, Monroe K. "William James as a Culture Hero." In his *American Ambitions: Selected Essays on Literary and Cultural Themes,* pp. 10-25. Baltimore and London: The Johns Hopkins University Press, 1987.
> Comparison of James's life, character, and writings with those of Samuel Johnson.

Taylor, Eugene. *William James on Exceptional Mental States: The 1896 Lowell Lectures*. New York: Charles Scribner's Sons, 1982, 222 p.
> Reconstructs from James's notes eight lectures on such subjects as dreams, hypnotism, multiple personality, demoniacal possession, witchcraft, and genius.

Thayer, H. S. "The Right to Believe: William James's Reinterpretation of the Function of Religious Belief." *The Kenyon Review* n.s. V, No. 1 (Winter 1983): 89-105.
> Defense of James's concept of the will to believe.

Vanden Burgt, Robert J. *The Religious Philosophy of William James*. Chicago: Nelson Hall, 1981, 167 p.
> Study of James's views on the relationship between God and humanity.

Wild, John. *The Radical Empiricism of William James*. Garden City, N.Y.: Doubleday & Co., 1969, 430 p.
> Treats James as "an early member of that significant group of thinkers, scattered widely over the Western world, who became dissatisfied with the artificial abstractness of traditional systems of thought." Wild finds that James's later philosophic attitude of radical empiricism also informs the direction of his early works, most prominently *The Principles of Psychology*. This view accounts for James's avoidance of abstract systems of philosophical terminology, an intellectual policy which enabled him "to keep his thought in line with structures that could be found in the brute facts of existence." As such, James's thought anticipates the later school of phenomenological philosophy, which sought "not to construct but rather to find patterns in existence."

A(ndrew) B(arton) Paterson

1864-1941

(Also wrote under the pseudonym The Banjo) Australian poet, short story writer, novelist, journalist, and essayist.

A popular poet at the turn of the century, Paterson is known for his romantic and humorous portrayal of the Australian bush, or inland wilderness. Unlike his contemporary Henry Lawson, with whom he is often compared, Paterson did not emphasize the harsh conditions of bush life, but rather wrote of its beauty and the fortitude of those who lived there. Paterson is also the reputed author of the lyrics for "Waltzing Matilda," a popular song that has become Australia's unofficial national anthem. Although his authorship of these lyrics has been questioned, Paterson is nonetheless celebrated for his important role in the development of a sense of national identity among Australians.

Paterson was born into a sheep-ranching family in Narrambla, New South Wales. He attended grammar school in Sydney, living with his grandmother, who was a poet and member of the city's literary circle. During vacations Paterson returned to his father's ranch, where he developed a love for the outback. At the age of sixteen he entered Sydney University to study law, and upon graduation set up a legal practice in the city. In the late 1880s he began submitting verses to the Sydney *Bulletin*, the leading publication for Australian writers of the time, under a pseudonym, "The Banjo," that he had taken from the name of a racehorse. In 1892 Paterson engaged in a verse debate in the *Bulletin* with several other poets, most prominently Henry Lawson, over the advantages and disadvantages of life in the bush. Lawson considered Paterson's bush ballads to be romantic and sentimental, while Paterson considered Lawson's emphasis on hardship and human suffering to be unnecessarily bleak and an expression of Lawson's own temperament rather than a true description of bush life. Although some maintain that this controversy was begun by Lawson and Paterson to provoke interest in their work, the debate grew more heated as it developed, until Paterson wrote a conciliatory poem to settle the matter in October 1892.

Paterson's popularity grew for the next three years, and in 1895 his first collection, *The Man from Snowy River, and Other Verses*, was a great success. During the same year, Paterson is said to have written the lyrics of "Waltzing Matilda" to the tune of an old English march. The piece was not published in any of Paterson's collections until in 1917 it appeared in *Saltbush Bill, J.P., and Other Verses*. Paterson's authorship of the verse has been questioned by critics who claim that "Waltzing Matilda" was a folk song which Paterson may have altered but did not originate. These critics cite the testimony of people who claimed to have known the work before 1895, the length of time that elapsed between the composition and publication of the lyric, and differences between Paterson's published version and the popular one most commonly sung in Australia. Other critics, notably Frederick T. Macartney, have vigorously defended Paterson's authorship, claiming that Paterson, a man of undisputed integrity, would not have claimed the song as his own had he not written it. They further contend that recollections of the song many years after its popularization may

be faulty, and that other versions of the song are inferior variants of Paterson's original.

In 1899 Paterson left his legal practice to become a correspondent in the Boer War. After the war he continued to work as a journalist for several years and during this time edited a Sydney newspaper. In 1908 he bought some grazing property, left journalism, and lived an outdoor life for the following six years, until he enlisted for service in World War I. Paterson returned to Australia after the war and continued to write until his death in 1941.

Paterson approached writing as a hobby rather than as a vocation, and his verse was intended primarily as a source of entertainment. His poems are simple in both form and subject, facilitating their widespread and enduring appeal. Among the inhabitants of the Australian outback during Paterson's lifetime, his works were preferred to those of the more cynical Lawson. Such ballads as "Clancy of the Overflow" and "The Man from Snowy River," which have passed into Australia's folk tradition, evoke a romantic image of carefree and adventurous life in the bush. Throughout his works, Paterson captured the spirit of early-twentieth-century Australia with the warmth, humor, and affection displayed in his bush ballads. His enduring popularity and the esteem in which Australians hold his verse are testimonies to his success at portraying a positive vision of Australia's bush frontier.

PRINCIPAL WORKS

The Man from Snowy River, and Other Verses (poetry) 1895
Rio Grande's Last Race, and Other Verses (poetry) 1902
An Outback Marriage (novel) 1906
Saltbush Bill, J. P., and Other Verses (poetry) 1917
Three Elephant Power, and Other Stories (short stories) 1917
The Collected Verse of A. B. Paterson (poetry) 1921
The Animals Noah Forgot (poetry) 1933
Happy Dispatches (sketches) 1934
The Shearer's Colt (novel) 1936

FREDERICK T. MACARTNEY (essay date 1921)

[*In the following excerpt, Macartney discusses the subjects and style of Paterson's poetry.*]

Paterson's poetry has a special connexion with the time when it was written. The Sydney *Bulletin* had been founded in 1880, and, by encouraging Australians to write about life outback, it set bushmen rhyming. This was not entirely new. There were already some bush songs, sung around camp-fires, in huts and shearing-sheds, and on the track. The tunes were mainly those of oversea songs. The words, of unknown authorship, were often similarly imitative, but with more originality because of the Australian themes. It was a local folklore so far as this was possible in a land with so short a history as that of the white man in Australia. The verse of the *Bulletin* bards had a similar but wider significance in a multitude of rhymes of droving and boundary riding and shearing and other station activities, of bushrangers, life on farms and in remote townships, with horse racing and other diversions, often alcoholic. Of the many who wrote them, a score are represented by collections in book form, but the two outstanding names are Paterson and Henry Lawson.

They had different points of view which they aired in the *Bulletin* in a kind of verse debate. A poem like Paterson's "**Clancy of the Overflow**" was to Lawson a false idealization of bush life, which he accordingly attacked in "Up the Country"; Paterson's reply, "**In Defence of the Bush,**" was just as forceful; Lawson then satirized Paterson as "The City Bushman" in a poem with that title; and Paterson dealt with Lawson and other detractors of the bush in "**An Answer to Various Bards.**" The question of their respective merits as poets does not arise here, and Lawson certainly wrote some excellent bush ballads; but his unfortunate personal experience led him to stress unduly the harsh aspects of the outback, and a corollary of this was the recurring note of social protest in his verse. Neither of these traits, though both had foundation enough, was typical of bush life, with its acceptance of the bad with the good, often sardonic, but not much concerned with any social problems involved. Thus Paterson's simple approach is truer, and his range makes him, as compared with the others besides Lawson, pre-eminent among the balladists.

Allowing for the difference of time, his verses are like the ballads which chronicled common life and doughty deeds in medieval times, and which are now enhanced by the romantic atmosphere of a distant past and its archaic manner. Oral transmission through generations obscured their origin and, in the best of them, distilled the diction finely. More generally, faults are not hard to find, but are accepted as having the common tang of the time. It is somewhat the same with the verbal defects in Paterson's verse. His work has enough quality and resource to show that he could have overcome them, but they are often so much the natural expression of the life he writes about that they help to reveal it, almost as if he were its passive instrument. The gleams of authentic poetry—say, for instance, the opening of "**The Travelling Post Office**" or passages in "**The Man from Snowy River**"—occur as casually as the lapses. The worst of these consist of sentimentality in a few detached instances like "**Only a Jockey**" and "**A Bunch of Roses,**" or when though rarely, as in "**Lost,**" a bush poem emphasizes a sentiment disproportionately. The comic element, on the other hand, is wholesome, and Paterson revels in it. Sometimes it helps to typify a place, as with the two "Dandaloo" poems and "**Hay and Hell and Booligal**"; or it gives colour to a character such as "Saltbush Bill" or "The Man from Ironbark"; or it may divert incredibility, as in "**Father Riley's Horse**" and "**The City of Dreadful Thirst,**" with their approach to the supernatural or eerie—for this is perhaps the only phase of balladry that Paterson fails to make convincing, even when he is wholly serious about it in "**Rio Grande's Last Race.**" His comic ballads are outright fun, but they nevertheless vitalize the circumstances and people portrayed.

His verse belongs to the true ballad tradition of tales musically told and heightened with simple glamour. This may consist of some special prowess, as of "**The Man from Snowy River**"; or heroism like that of the bushranger giving his life to save a comrade in "**How Gilbert Died**"; or even the exploit of a less romanticized outlaw as in "**Conroy's Gap**"; or the outcome of a horse race in more than a dozen of Paterson's poems; or it may be concerned with bush life apart from any special event, as in "**Clancy of the Overflow**" and "**A Bushman's Song**"; but always there is the tone of period and place and the manner of the people in the telling. He writes as bush folk themselves would if they were able, and it is this that has made his poetry popular with them and with city people to whom it is on that account just as interesting. It is not likely to be less so. Time, with the changes of a mechanical age, has already given a legendary attraction to some of the old bush ways. When the future looks back to the past as we look back to the middle ages, Paterson's poetry will probably have the aura of old minstrelsy. He best of all has sung the action of bush life in that natural music of rhythm and rhyme which has a perpetual general appeal. (pp. vii-ix)

> *Frederick T. Macartney, in an introduction to* The Collected Verse of A. B. Paterson, *1921. Reprint by Angus & Robertson Publishers, 1982, pp. v-ix.*

ARCHIE JAMES COOMBES (essay date 1938)

[*In the following excerpt, Coombes praises Paterson's bush ballads for their faithfulness to the spirit of the Australian outback.*]

Paterson's most characteristic work is that in which he pictures life in "the West." He enters with confidence into his "land of lots of time," and mingles memories, observations, sentiments, and impressions, in verses that ring between jingle and tune. In "**Clancy of the Overflow**" he conveys something of the spaciousness and freedom of the drover's life, together with the simple yet exhilarating pleasures springing from nature's direct contact with his bushman's heart.

> And the bush hath friends to meet him, and their kindly voices
>   greet him
>   In the murmur of the breezes and the river on its bars,
> And he sees the vision splendid of the sunlit plains extended,
>   And at night the wondrous glory of the everlasting stars.

It will be observed that Paterson makes no attempt to present Clancy directly to the reader's eye. He furnishes no details as to his personal appearance, but prefers to allow the reader's imagination to shape him as it will under the direction of certain of his acts or thoughts or preferences, in conjunction with— and this is indispensable—an environment with which he is in perfect harmony. The poet creates the atmosphere, and the atmosphere creates Clancy. He becomes a personality not necessarily seen, but certainly felt; a type rather than an individual. In general, Paterson adheres to this method.

Again in **"In the Droving Days"** the theme imperfectly glanced at in **"Clancy of the Overflow"** is reverted to. Here Paterson essays with greater detail and in a more direct manner to find the key to the abiding exhilaration which the West is able to impart. He finds it inherent in immediate intimacy with "nature's ways," the impulse to express it taking a physical outlet in the dashing moments of the drover's life. However, he makes no attempt to philosophize his experience. He records his sense perceptions quite simply, and yet the reader feels an emotional effect imparted which succeeds in elevating the verses above the level of mere chronicle.

His debt to the distinctive atmosphere of the West Paterson nowhere makes more clear than in **"The Daylight Is Dying,"** a poem of genuine lyrical value. It is a pleasing thing in itself to encounter the quiet sincerity of tone that dwells in this little piece. The poet writes with just that touch of wonder that twilight and silence and a sense of infinite space beneath and beyond the stars can impart. While falling darkness diminishes the interpretive function of the eye, the power to feel oneself into intelligent community with nature is sensitively quickened. This it is which weaves the bushman's heart irrevocably, although it may be unconsciously, into the pattern of his environment. The thousand impulses from nature, falling like language upon his feelings, shape the current of thought within his mind to an identity with the flow of her moods without it. Paterson has recognized this as an universal principle working among the simple experiences which he relates, and he therefore gives expression to a truth of emotional perception that is real, even if it be intangible—that is, until a poet passes by.

It has been objected against Paterson that his bushmen and his bush are fictions; that his observations of country life and interests are superficial and misleading; that his experiences are those of an amateur on holiday, and are not such as fall to the normal lot of folk beyond the "Divide"; and that he gives little or no record of having seen what any man intimately acquainted with the West must inevitably have seen.

However, it still holds good that "Love looks not with the eyes, but with the mind," and that nevertheless many writers look with their eyes, relying upon the ordinary rule of reasoning that "seeing is believing." Peter Bell saw primroses "by the river's brim" year in, year out; and Wordsworth who cites him, saw them with a difference. And so, in respect of our outback life, the genuine realities are not solely those sordid and obvious banalities which are familiar to every Peter Bell of the plains. In the lives of our western folk cheerfulness and resource and buoyant independence are more in evidence than their opposites. The genuine westerner ignores or is quite unconscious of many an accident of geography which writers have discovered and dressed up as really portentous bogies. The terror of circumstance has been overcoloured and overdrawn by our publicists, especially by those tigers for truth whose fangs must ever be blooding in realist impressions.

Perhaps the most remarkable reality of the West lies, not in its heat or drought or dust or flies or thirst or profanity, but in its wonderful power of recovery. It is that which breeds in its people the long hope. But, while inextinguishable, it is also an untheatrical vitality. The true significance of the "land of lots of time" is not to be caught in a moment of dramatic accident. Paterson senses the vitality of his environment. His Clancy is a type of those whose soul's compass points true north in all weathers, in every season. Circumstances do not dominate him, rendering him peevish or melancholy or bitter. He has that simple serenity of heart that can sing in solitude, work unwatched, or laugh because a touch of the infinite exhilarates him with a natural joy. Clancy is not the fiction of an idealist. He is a permanent reality of western life; and part of Paterson's popularity is due to his having discovered him to the multitude.

In the early nineties Paterson engaged in a controversy, chiefly with [Henry] Lawson, in regard to his view of the West. He resented the inaccuracy of accurate impressionistic pictures, as his **"In Defence of the Bush"** may indicate:

> Yet, perchance, if you should journey down the very track you
>   went
> In a month or two at furthest, you would wonder what it
>   meant;
> Where the sunbaked earth was gasping like a creature in its
>   pain
> You would find the waving grasses like a field of summer
>   grain,
> And the miles of thirsty gutters, blocked with sand and choked
>   with mud,
> You would find them mighty rivers with a turbid, sweeping
>   flood.
> For the rain and drought and sunshine make no changes in the
>   street,
> In the sullen line of buildings and the ceaseless tramp of feet;
> But the bush hath moods and changes, as the seasons rise and
>   fall,
> And the men who know the bush-land—they are loyal through
>   it all.

Paterson's contention is just. His view is not so much that the facts have been distorted or are untrue, but rather that the minds applied to the facts have been unequal to interpret them; and have tended rather to hug the fallacy that the part is equal to the whole; to represent the experience of a moment as the truth of a lifetime; to read into the West the imperfections of their own imperfect sympathies, damning the interior of Australia "on internal evidence," as Quiller-Couch would say, "that is, on the evidence of their own internals." Hence the appositeness of Paterson's prescription:

> So before they curse the bushland, they should let their fancies
>   range,
> And take something for their liver, and be cheerful for a
>   change.

To Paterson's credit be it recorded that he felt the permanent and universal element of his environment, and did not permit his vision to be short-circuited by any temporary circumstance, however violent. It is that which gives him his poise, his sincerity, his sense of proportion, and his humour. In his serious moods he does not handle extravagances. His course is laid among normal conditions as affecting normal people. He makes no effort to intensify the abnormal and present it as the typical reality. Sensationalism and realism in its stark sense are as foreign to his nature and his treatment of the West as they are to the daily lives of the people dwelling there. The secret of the happy heart was the most memorable thing that the bush taught him, and it was his sincere and cheerful endeavour as a poet to impart again to his readers, however artlessly, the simple charm of what he had learned. To those who by experience or from a sympathetic imagination can sense his "atmosphere" there lingers in Paterson's outback verses a quiet pleasure that is akin to the pleasure of possession. It is the pleasure of a non-professional patriotism. (pp. 80-5)

Within the limits of the ballad . . . Paterson is quite at his ease. He handles his themes lightly and naturally and his gift of graphic phrasing enables him to present an action and its setting with an air of simple and spirited reality. He can tell a story well where the story is, as it were, a single thread, though he gives no evidence in his verse of possessing sufficient dramatic sense to deal with a complicated action.

For the purposes of simple narrative and description his metrical skill is adequate. It is light and easy, very seldom wholly commonplace, and very seldom sufficiently striking to attract especial attention to itself. Judged by the world's standard of poets, Paterson does not rank very high. The greater portion of what he has written is verse rather than poetry, and is restricted in its appeal to an Australian public. But the march of time has not diminished the esteem in which his verse is held among the people whom it was designed to interest and amuse. (p. 86)

Archie James Coombes, "A. B. Paterson," in his Some Australian Poets, *1938. Reprint by Books for Libraries Press, 1970, pp. 77-86.*

VANCE PALMER (essay date 1954)

[*In the following excerpt, Palmer discusses the folk origin of Paterson's ballads.*]

In the literature of the nineties two figures stand out distinctly in the popular mind, those of Lawson and Paterson. They appeared almost at the same time in the columns of the *Bulletin*, both writing verse, Paterson over the nom-de-plume of "The Banjo," and Lawson over his own name: immediately they attracted attention. Here, it was felt, was the voice of the country, speaking through two different men, but with the one recognizable accent. Plainly Paterson had seen life from the pastoralist's angle and Lawson had not; yet, though a savage conflict was being waged on the Western plains between squatters and shearers there was a region, or so it seemed, where the thought and feeling of the station was identical with that of the shed. (p. 109)

[In] spite of Paterson's polo-playing and fashionable success, he had, in fact, more of the folk-impulse in his ballads than Lawson had. They were not merely racing rhymes and light jingles, these ballads; they really sprang from the life of the community. All its vigour, fantasy, and sardonic humour found expression in them; essentially they were one with the early anonymous songs, though shaped with greater skill. Even if Paterson invented his incidents and heroes they did not seem like inventions: they seemed like legends that had had their origin in the popular mind.

And, as a balladist, Paterson accepted the general ideas of his day. Unionism was the symbol of a man's loyalty to his mates,

and the most dangerous threat to it came from the Asiatic. In one of his best songs we find the rouseabout turning contemptuously from the cockie-farmer who had offered him a job.

"We shear non-union here," says he. "I call it scab," says I,
I looked along the shearing-board afore I turned to go,
There was eight or ten dashed Chinamen a-shearing in a row.

Alternatively, the intruder was the alien Englishman, trying to keep Saltbush Bill's starving sheep from his grass, seizing on the homely Kiley's Run and turning it into Chandos Park Estate, a pretentious place past which the lonely traveller must hump his swag, knowing that he is not likely to find a camp there or free rations at the store.

In all this, Paterson kept faithfully to the values of the people for whom he was writing. He even was a little troubled by his small experience of working-class conditions and, like an earnest young man in a nineteenth-century novel, sought to remedy this by going to live for a while in a slum. His first pamphlet was *Australia for the Australians,* an argument for land reform. . . . (pp. 110-11)

But this was hardly more than a mechanical response to the ideas in the air around him: Paterson was not, like many of his contemporaries, carried away by visions of a paradisal future. On the contrary, he went back to an idyllic past, to the "droving days," before railways had begun to throw a web over the country, when all cattle had to travel by hoof and the stock-routes were filled with large mobs moving to the coast. A happy period, with drovers raising up "Willie Riley" by the campfire's cheery blaze, Clancy riding singing behind his mob as it picked its way along the grassy stretches of the Cooper, and station-owners, like Kiley, working in hearty comradeship with their men. It was a fresh, inspiriting world, and the only trouble was that it had vanished; new men, who knew a racehorse from a cow but nothing else of stock, were taking over the stations. There was not a good time coming, as the Ballarat miners had sung: the good time lay behind.

The idea of a golden age that had existed in his boyhood was strong in Paterson, and came to the surface whenever his personal feelings were uncovered. In what is usually (but quite wrongly) considered his most poetic piece, **"Black Swans,"** he pictures himself lying on his back in a city park and watching the birds fly west toward the country of his dreams. But it is to a day that is dead they are returning. Apparently the strongest emotion felt by this vigorous young man in his twenties was a nostalgic hankering for the way of life he had known in his youth, now gone forever.

But it was not in the expression of feeling that Paterson's strength lay: when he attempted it he always hovered on the brink of sentimentality, sometimes slipping over the edge. He was only really at home in the robust, masculine world of action, where men played uproarious practical jokes, or raced heroically down the perilous mountainside after brumbies, or walked out to face the troopers, like Gilbert, so that their mates might escape into the night. For his brief dramas he created a background that was a little romanticized, but recognizable— not the drought-stricken nightmare country of the realists, nor the anglicized landscape of Kendall, with its dells and forests, but a sunny country of well-grassed plains and flowing rivers. It was his vision of the bush that was new and stimulating.

What distinguished Paterson's verse, however, was a touch of the folk-element. It is hard to analyse, this sense of a voice rising out of the anonymous mass, but it lifts his work above that of Ogilvie and other more skilful balladists, and preserves its original freshness. In later life, when his writing had become more commonplace and mechanical, he could still find words, in **"Waltzing Matilda,"** to make an old tune sing itself into the heart of the country. (pp. 111-12)

> Vance Palmer, *"Literature Emerges,"* in his The Legend of the Nineties, *Melbourne University Press, 1954, pp. 109-30.*

H. M. GREEN (essay date 1961)

[*An Australian poet and critic, Green is the author of the comprehensive critical study* A History of Australian Literature: Pure and Applied. *In the following excerpt from that work, he praises Paterson for his contribution to Australian poetry.*]

Paterson more than any other balladist, more indeed than any other Australian writer of verse, conveys to us the atmosphere of the Australian countryside and its inhabitants. Country conditions have changed since Paterson's day, and in a time to come the appearance of bush life may be such that he would scarcely recognize it if he were born again; but the nature of the seasons and the broad shape of the land remain, and the temperaments and types that have developed under their influence are not likely to alter much. There will always be

> . . . waving grass and forest trees
> On sunlit plains as wide as seas,

and the man that rides across them, whatever he rides and whatever he rides for, will always be

> A speck upon the waste of plain;

there will always be

> A scent of eucalyptus trees in honey-laden bloom,

and

> A dry sweet scent on the saltbush plain;

there will always be "The roving breezes" that "come and go," "the sleepy river" that "murmurs low, and loiters on its way," the "land of lots o' time"; there will always be

> . . . rocky range, and rugged spur, and river running clear
> That swings around the sudden bends with swirl of snow-white foam.

There will always be a **"Man from Snowy River,"** even if he no longer races his horse downhill among the flying flint-stones; and there will always, as far as one can look ahead, be the wheat country, in which

> When the burning harvest sun sinks low,
> And shadows stretch on the plain,
> The roaring strippers come and go
> Like ships on a sea of grain;

there will always be picnic and other outback races, even if the racers ride metal instead of horseflesh; and amateur riders, and queer decisions, and the contrast between country and city; and bush christenings, and boring for artesian water, and even, in a different guise no doubt, a **"Man from Ironbark"**; and droving in one form or another and cattle-duffing and the roving and independent bushman and the lonely camp-fire. All these aspects and instances of the bush and its life Paterson has caught and fixed for us, and if his word-pictures are in detail true only to the bush life of his own day, in substance they are true to the bush life of our day also, and seem likely to remain true to outback life as far as we can look ahead. Paterson has caught

and fixed something that is essentially enduring and Australian; has translated into words certain rhythms of the national life and temperament; he has conveyed to us a

> . . . vision splendid of the sunlit plains extended,

and of the men who move about them, as no one else has done, or perhaps is ever likely to do, at least in verse. It is true that this vision is of a countryside, a country life that is idealized, brightened, as they appear to those who are fondest of them, and above all to light-hearted and adventurous youth; but it was the spirit and outlook of such youth that ruled that age; there were many older men and women then (and indeed there are not a few even nowadays) among whom that youthful spirit and outlook was not strange. And at his best Paterson conveys them in the manner in which one feels that they ought to be conveyed. It is a curious fact that though, as has been said, the aim and method of the balladist differ essentially from those of the poet, and though Paterson is a balladist of balladists, the quality that in the end he stands by is after all a poetic quality, in that he has expressed something that is essential, in words sometimes so suitable that here and there matter and manner are scarcely to be separated. He has been accused of throwing away the lyre for the banjo, but this is doubly wrong, for in the first place the lyre as an instrument would not have suited Paterson at all; and in the second place he is at his best in glimpses that are lyrical, by whatever means he managed to attain them. It is true that there is a great deal of chaff among his wheat. He can be, though he is not often, melodramatic or sentimental; his work is almost always careless and often clumsy or marred by forced rhymes or journalistic clichés or patches of sheer doggerel, and at times he pads out lines, fumbles his rhymes and muddles his rhythms, though he has sufficient craftsmanship when he takes the trouble to use it. (pp. 364-65)

Paterson has been called the balladist of station life; he was that, but he was also much more. The station, and the horse, with which the station is so closely associated, were the centre of his field, but it extended to every type of bush life with which any aspect of station activity came into touch. It was the "in station" however, the kind that is in comparatively close contact with civilization, rather than the "out station," with its isolation and monotony and vast distances: Paterson's terrain is therefore the centre of a community, however scattered and small in number, not an outpost in the hot, arid solitudes. In Paterson democracy and Australianism had advanced a long stride. . .: Paterson's conception of the ideal station-owner was of a man who worked with his men on the run, paid high wages, and sympathized with unionism; who was generous to the passing swagman and just to the drover with his hungry mob. . . . He was for the countryman as against the "cuff and collar brigade," though for the greater part of his life he belonged to that brigade himself: he knew the wheat-grower as well as the sheep or cattle man; he knew trooper and sheep-stealer, bush pub and small township, country races and their trickeries and excitements, car and bicycle as well as horse and bullock. As a balladist he made occasional excursions north to the Gulf, west to Coolgardie and east to the cities; and his **"Ballad of the Calliope"** is among the finest of Australian patriotic ballads. Paterson is also among the best of Australian verse-humorists. . . . Paterson's humour is of the soil and vital; it is that of the outback anecdote: dry and ironic, as in **"Been There Before,"** or **"The Man Who Was Away"**; a little more lively, as in **"An Idyll of Dandaloo,"**

> A township where life's total sum
> Is sleep, diversified with rum,

or **"Father Riley's Horse"**; or boisterous, as in **"A Bush Christening"** or **"The Man from Ironbark."** Here the descriptions of the barber and of the

> . . . gilded youths that sat along the barber's wall,
> Their eyes were dull, their heads were flat, they had no brains
>   at all

are even better than the action. Only once Paterson's humour is fantastic, in **"Waltzing Matilda"**; but that stands out in the company of anything of its kind. All the sources of the Australian ballad are visible in Paterson, but they are absorbed in his extremely individual style. [Adam Lindsay] Gordon's influence is most evident in Paterson's racing ballads, taking the word "racing" in the widest possible sense, to which Gordon contributes not only an initial impetus but something in their general manner. Yet the characteristic rhythms of Paterson's racing ballads are different from those of Gordon. He took from Gordon the easy, loping rhythm of "The Sick Stockrider"—

> 'Twas merry 'mid the blackwoods, when we spied the station
>   roofs,

and used it in **"The Man from Snowy River"**:

> There was movement at the station, for the word had passed
>   around,

and in several other racing ballads. But Gordon preferred as a rule a brisker rhythm, that of "Young Lochinvar"; still with four beats only, but without the extra syllables that slow down "The Man from Snowy River," as in "How We Beat the Favourite,"

> "Aye, squire," said Stevens, "they back him at evens,"

or in **"From the Wreck,"**

> There was bridling with hurry, and saddling with haste.

Paterson uses this metre in **"How the Favourite Beat Us,"** which contains an element of parody; but he uses also a longer, six-beat line, as in **"The Amateur Rider,"**

> Ride! Don't tell *me* he can ride. With his pants just as loose as
>   balloons;

and he used the same line, split in two, in **"Old Pardon, the Son of Reprieve,"** in which form Gordon also had used it. In Gordon's racing ballads there is deeper feeling than in Paterson's and more imaginative vision: but about Paterson's there is a dry, up-country colloquial tang that stamps them as Australian, which Gordon's are not: **"The Man from Snowy River,"** for instance, is a new thing, which has nothing except the metre in common with "The Sick Stockrider," even though in this Gordon was at his most Australian. Kipling's influence was slight; good in so far as it also encouraged Paterson to write ballads, but not when it led, as it sometimes did, to downright imitation: in Paterson's South African War verses and in his patriotic verses generally he tried to assume a kind of lofty rhetoric that is often bad enough in Kipling and that in Paterson is also quite out of character; and elsewhere there are occasional borrowed mannerisms; for example in **"Saltbush Bill"** a good Australian ballad is handicapped by the cheap Kiplingese of the introductory line,

> Now this is the law of the Overland that all in the West obey,

and by several similar excrescences.

Paterson may have derived something directly from the oversea folk-ballad; he was certainly a reader of the Scottish folk-ballads, as may be seen from **"Santa Claus in the Bush,"**

which parodies some of their mannerisms. And he skimmed off the cream of the Old Bush Song, and whipped it up in his own way; but it is not always easy to say where he drew from these songs and where he and they drew from similar sources; for Paterson was the first verse-maker, or the first of any ability, to breathe the same air as the Old Bush Song-makers, to sympathize with their point of view, and like them he lived, in spirit at least, close to the soil. So that the plain-spoken directness of "The Old Bark Hut" and "The Stringy Bark Cockatoo," the sardonic air of "The New England Cocky," the happy-go-lucky feeling of "The Mustering Song" and "My Four Little Johnny Cakes" may have influenced Paterson directly or may have merely reinforced something that he possessed already; but there seems no doubt about the direct influence of such songs as "The Murrumbidgee Shearer," "On the Way to Gundagai" and "Flash Jack from Gundagai." In these, which are close to the heart of the Old Bush Song, Paterson found no doubt qualities of independence, of careless adventure, with which he could thoroughly sympathize; but in them also, and more particularly in "Flash Jack," are to be recognized not only the feeling and outlook of the most representative of Paterson's ballads, but something even of the texture of for example, **"A Bushman's Song."** It is in such ballads as these, rather than in any of his racing ballads, that Paterson is at his best: in **"The Travelling Post Office,"** which breathes the very essence of the central western plains, and perhaps also in the other Clancy ballad; in **"The Man from Snowy River,"** which embodies the spirit of daring outback horse-loving youth; in **"The Two Devines,"** in which two brothers, summoned to their father's death-bed, ride back at once, seeing that he is "as good as dead," to "tackle the ewes" that they have yet to finish shearing; in **"Waltzing Matilda,"** which deserves all the praise it has received; in the **"Song of the Artesian Water,"** which is almost as much a classic of its kind; and perhaps in one or two of the humorous ballads. But on the whole, the ballad of Paterson's that is the most characteristic of the outback Australia of his day, and in particular of the young, devil-may-care station-hand who rode within its centre; a ballad that is also among Paterson's best, and therefore among the best of Australian ballads, is **"A Bushman's Song."** . . . Paterson's ballads carry with them something of the bush and the outback which, though it is not the whole truth, is true in itself and deeply true: they are the more important in that they represent an attitude which was that, on the whole, of the Australian community in Paterson's day, and which is still, and will probably long remain, even where it is unacknowledged, at the back of the mind of very many Australians. Paterson had also something new to say, both for himself and for his country, and nobody else has been able to give it so fresh and appropriate an expression. These things give his work a degree of importance that it would not otherwise possess: his contribution, more than that of any other individual, has given the Australian ballad its not unimportant place in the history of modern balladry. (pp. 366-70)

> *H. M. Green, "Third Period, 1890-1923: Self-Conscious Nationalism," in his* A History of Australian Literature, Pure and Applied: 1789-1923, *Vol. I, Angus and Robertson, 1961, pp. 347-842.*

H. P. HESELTINE   (essay date 1964)

[In the following excerpt, Heseltine views Paterson as a poet in the pastoral tradition.]

There is at least one quality which unites both [Paterson] and [his] verse, and intimately joins them both to the Australian ethos: the quality of adventurousness. P. R. Stephensen puts the point with his customary candour. "The basic element in the Australian mystique," he writes, "is the spirit of adventure." . . . The proposition has, I think, a good deal to recommend it. Certainly, it was adventure as much as politics which took Paterson off to the Boer War and the Great War, and which, at home, sustained his love of the racecourse. The same unadulterated love of physical excitement provides the material of many of his best known poems: **"The Man from Snowy River,"** for instance, or **"Conroy's Gap,"** or **"Old Pardon, the Son of Reprieve."** Further, the human attitudes which are presented concurrently with the action of such poems are those which have traditionally recommended themselves to Australians—admiration for physical prowess, loyalty to a mate, and, not infrequently, contempt for the law or any kind of constituted authority.

In **"The Man from Snowy River"** the adventure is brought to a successful conclusion. In **"Rio Grande's Last Race"** it has all the trappings of the ghost story. In **"With French to Kimberley"** it is accomplished to the clamour of imperialist trumpet and drum. But when the simple thrill of action for its own sake is not deemed sufficient to sustain the verse, its most usual support is comedy. The comic plots of Paterson's verse come in a number of versions, but the basic formulae are few. There is for instance that familiar Australian figure, the smart operator—always ready with the sharp retort whether he is on the racecourse or carrying a stone in his pocket all the way to Walgett. Sometimes the smart operator outsmarts himself—as, for example, when he takes on the Man from Ironbark. But even that heroic countryman pales beside the achievements of Saltbush Bill. Bill, it seems to me, is Paterson's most considerable comic creation. Whether he's playing a newchum for a sucker or cleaning up in a cockfight with his own genuine Australian bird (an emu), Saltbush Bill exhibits a fertility in crime, an energy and largeness of behaviour which suggest that, for once, something more than the hobbyist's interest inspired Paterson's pen. The reason for this raising of imaginative pressure is not far to seek. Paterson concluded a letter to a Mr. Thomas Whitley of Blackheath, written on July 27, 1896, with these words:

> While living in the bush I used to hear a great lot of bush songs, "The Wild Colonial Boy" "Dunn Gilbert and Ben Hall" "The Squatter's Man" "The Old Bark Hut" and so forth—I would like to find out something about these and get the words.

Perhaps there can be detected in that brief comment the genesis of Paterson's *Old Bush Songs,* published by Angus and Robertson nearly a decade later, in 1905. Paterson certainly seems to have had an enduring interest in the anonymous folk culture of the bush. My point, then, is simply this: he wrote much of his best work when he was dealing with situations which approximated the material of bush yarns or when he could draw directly on the material of folk culture. Saltbush Bill is the nearest he came to creating an authentic folk hero; he is cast in the legendary mould of a Paul Bunyan or a Davy Crockett.

Granted his personal background, his interest in the old bush songs, the general circumstances of life in Australia during his formative years, it is not surprising that Paterson usually asserts the virtues of the country at the expense of life in the city. The distinction, implicit through much of his work, is made explicit in one of his best known pieces, **"Clancy of the Overflow"**:

> I am sitting in my dingy little office, where a stingy
>   Ray of sunlight struggles feebly down between the houses tall,
> And the foetid air and gritty of the dusty, dirty city,
>   Through the open window floating, spreads its foulness over all.
>
> And in place of lowing cattle, I can hear the fiendish rattle
>   Of the tramways and the buses making hurry down the street;
> And the language uninviting of the gutter children fighting
>   Comes fitfully and faintly through the ceaseless tramp of feet.
>
> And the hurrying people daunt me, and their pallid faces haunt me
>   As they shoulder one another in their rush and nervous haste,
> With their eager eyes and greedy, and their stunted forms and weedy,
>   For townsfolk have no time to grow, they have no time to waste.
>
> And I somehow rather fancy that I'd like to change with Clancy,
>   Like to take a turn at droving where the seasons come and go,
> While he faced the round eternal of the cash-book and the journal—
>   But I doubt he'd suit the office, Clancy, of The Overflow.

The creator of a body of verse founded on adventure, affiliated with folklore, and committed to the country, Paterson, it might well seem, could properly be described as a balladist—as indeed he often has been described. The description, however, seems to me an unfortunate one. It has been responsible for much of the unfavourable criticism which Paterson has had to suffer. If we think of him as a balladist and compare him (as the label invites us to) with the Scots border balladists, Paterson is going to be adjudged a poor second. He does not really possess those qualities of mind and expression which make for the genuine balladist. He does not claim, does not even aspire to, the spare dramatic realism, the intensely realised emotion, the compassionate simplicity which are the peculiar glories of, say, "Sir Patrick Spens" or "Lord Randal." Paterson's bush is not the landscape of balladry. It is, rather, never-never land; the country, in his own phrase, of "Come-by-Chance":

> All the happy times entrancing, days of sport and nights of dancing,
> Moonlit rides and stolen kisses, pouting lips and loving glance:
> When you think of these be certain you have looked behind the curtain,
> You have had the luck to linger just a while in "Come-by-Chance."

The desire to push experience into an idealised land-that-never-was that is evident in this stanza, plays in and about practically every good line Paterson ever wrote. He did not, in effect, write about the Australian bush; he re-created Arcadia "down under." The boundaries of his antipodean pastoral realm are clearly drawn. It occupies a boomerang shaped segment of New South Wales. It starts up Walgett way, broadens out towards Hay and Hell and Booligal, encompasses Conroy's Gap and Kiley's Run, and turns upon the axis of the Monaro region, whose clear mountain air can always be relied upon to produce the finest men in Paterson country. Then it swings north and east, narrowing through Goulburn and Grabben Gullen, and terminating somewhere near the eastern limits of Royal Randwick. Other territories or provinces are from time to time annexed, but that is the extent of the Home Counties.

Arcadia, however, does not grow simply (or even mainly) out of a subject matter. It is fundamentally the product of certain conventions and techniques. And herein lies the crux of my argument. It is Paterson's special use of the Arcadian conventions rather than his basic material which is responsible for his continuing vitality in our popular literature. If all we wanted was a poet of outback action, of horses, sheep, and cattle, a dozen of Paterson's contemporaries could supply the need just as well as he. It is to the *quality* of Paterson's poems that we must look if we are to judge their status aright; and that quality will most completely reveal itself within the context of Arcadia.

It was, indeed, what I shall describe as the Arcadian elements in Paterson's verse which inspired the title I have appended to these remarks ["'Banjo' Paterson: A Poet Nearly Anonymous"]. I wished in part, of course, to indicate the significance of the obscurity which shrouds Paterson's biography. Even more, I wished to invoke a famous essay by the American poet and critic, John Crowe Ransom: "A Poem Nearly Anonymous." This essay is a subtle and compelling study of Milton's "Lycidas" and of the literary conventions which allow that work to become a great poem. The relationship between Paterson and Milton may seem so remote as to be non-existent; and I would no more want to claim parity for Paterson with the author of *Paradise Lost* than I would want to elevate him to equality with Shakespeare. But on at least one point there is a close and pertinent relationship: "Lycidas" is not merely a great poem, it is a great pastoral poem. Much of Ransom's essay is given over to investigating the conditions which make possible great poems in this mode. What Ransom can tell us, therefore, about the conventions which operate greatly in "Lycidas" will be of real assistance in establishing the nature and value of Paterson's versions of pastoral.

Ransom begins from the notion that any worthwhile poem must, in a sense, be anonymous. "Anonymity, of some real if not literal sort," he writes, "is a condition of poetry. A good poem, even if it is signed with a full and well-known name, intends as a work of art to lose the identity of the author. . . ." In other words, it is the responsibility of the poet—whether he be Paterson or Milton—to make his ideas and emotions so effective in the verse that embodies them that they can stand alone without appealing to their author for sanction. There is a number of ways in which such an independence can be achieved for verse. One of them is the use of craft skill so competent and polished that the poem becomes artificial, an artifact. This is one of the major devices of "Lycidas." Ransom is blunt on the point. "'Lycidas' is a literary exercise; and so is almost any other poem earlier than the eighteenth century; the craftsmanship, the formal quality which is written on it, is meant to have a high visibility." In addition to the exercise of a perfect technique, a poet may also choose one of a number of poetic conventions. Milton in "Lycidas" chose the pastoral convention, that of dramatising one's themes through the discourse of classical shepherds in a formalised landscape. "The point of view of Greek shepherds," Ransom maintains, "as romantic innocents and rustics, is excellent and offers a wide range of poetic discourse. . . ." But "it is important mostly that the poet know his part and speak it fluently."

If the poet is a good craftsman and thoroughly understands his chosen conventions, he stands a good chance of writing competent poetry. To write great poetry he must possess a fine and subtle imagination (which Milton had); and he must satisfy a further condition (which Milton could). He must have an audience thoroughly acquainted with the conventions he is using.

"Probably the sad truth is that a subtle art is unlikely in the first place, whose artist does not reckon upon the background of a severe technical tradition, and the prospect of a substantial body of public appreciation." All the circumstances of Milton's time and place encouraged him to create in "Lycidas" a great, anonymous pastoral elegy. He almost succeeded in doing so, but marred the classic finish of his creation in a curious way. On this point it is worth quoting Ransom at some length:

> It is not merely easy for a technician to write in smooth metres; it is perhaps easier than to write in rough ones, after he has once started; but when he has written smoothly, and contemplates his work, he is capable actually, if he is a modern poet, of going over it laboriously and roughening it. I venture to think that just such a practice, speaking very broadly, obtained in the composition of "Lycidas": that it was written smooth and rewritten rough. . . .

After, that is to say, he had written his perfect and perfectly anonymous poem, Milton was at pains to impress the stamp of his own personality on it. In turning "Lycidas" into a poem *nearly* anonymous, he recorded the beginnings of the modern poetic mind. "In the irregular stanzas and the rhymeless lines is registered the ravage of his modernity."

Ransom's analysis of Milton's traffic with the pastoral mode encourages me to attempt a similar comment on Paterson's verse. Of the anonymity of Paterson's work there cannot, it seems to me, be any question. It is just as difficult to construct an imagined personality from the evidence of his poetry as it is to construct an image of the man himself from the biographical evidence he left behind. With remarkable completeness, Paterson's poetry is a poetry devoid of sensibility. What it offers, as literature, is absolute artificiality experienced for its own sake. The craftsmanship of Paterson's poems is so singularly apparent that, almost, it blots out the possibility of any other quality being exhibited.

The primacy of Paterson's technique begins, of course, with his metres, which are sloggingly unvarying within each poem and insistent throughout the whole body of his writing. It is almost impossible to speak of the rhythm of Paterson's writing, for rhythm implies some adjustment of metre to the inner movement of poetry. Such an adjustment never takes place in Paterson. Up hill and down dale, fresh or fatigued, the Man from Snowy River always rides to the same unvaried gait. The result, quite simply, is that there is no inner movement in a representative Paterson poem. As an aesthetic stimulus, all it presents is the impressive artificiality of its technique. It can be no accident that in **"Come-by-Chance"** Paterson reduplicated the metre of one of the most obstinately artificial poems in the English language, Edgar Allan Poe's "The Raven." Nor can it be entirely a matter of chance that in many of his four-line stanzas Paterson adopts the same metric pattern as one of the most famous artificial versifiers of our own time—Noel Coward.

Paterson's artificiality is not limited to his metres. It extends through his rhythms, through the formidable caesuras of his long lines, through a syntax wrenched into forms which Paterson probably construed as "poetic," into his very vocabulary. In one or two extreme instances (usually humorous) Paterson's delight in what he is writing is focussed on the mere sound and shape of words at the expense of any meaning they may be capable of carrying. The sound of aboriginal place names is the sufficient cause of **"Those Names,"** for instance;

or **"Tar and Feathers"** displays a brand of humour whose basis is the delighted manipulation of metre and rhyme:

> Oh! the circus swooped down
> On the Narrabri town,
> For the Narrabri populace moneyed are;
> And the showman he smiled
> At the folk he beguiled
> To come all the distance from Gunnedah.

The tale which follows this opening stanza is entertaining enough, but its chief attraction for Paterson was the chance it gave him to show off as a rhymester.

The effect of such obtrusive, such unvarying craftsmanship on the characteristically excited material of Paterson's verse is indisputable. It is to push it into so remotely stylised a region of the mind that it becomes eternally and universally available as the dreamland of the Australian fancy; a land where violence loses its terror and immorality its guilt, a land where all that is potentially disturbing is tamed by its settled air of Arcadian inconsequentiality.

In a poetry which freezes even the most excited activity into idealised gestures, it is not surprising that some of Paterson's most genuine imaginative successes are to be found in verse whose subject, from the beginning, is static. It is perhaps in pieces like **"The Travelling Post Office"** that Paterson comes closest to pushing his work away from the artificiality of craft skill to the anonymity of poetic insight. In that poem he can use to their full effect the conventionally descriptive epithets which are part of his Arcadian machinery—the swaying reedbeds, the gently blowing breezes, the turning seasons, the rushing streams, the slowly moving sheep. He can impose on the Australian land the timelessness not of pre-history but of European pastoral. In the more obviously lyric aspect of the pastoral mode, one of Paterson's most complete successes is **"The Road to Gundagai,"** whose couplets present a young Australian man and woman under the aspect of Arcadia:

> The mountain road goes up and down
> From Gundagai to Tumut Town.
>
> And, branching off, there runs a track
> Across the foothills grim and black,
>
> Across the plains and ranges grey
> To Sydney city far away.
>
>   •   •   •
>
> It came by chance one day that I
> From Tumut rode to Gundagai,
>
> And reached about the evening tide
> The crossing where the roads divide;
>
> And, waiting at the crossing place,
> I saw a maiden fair of face,
>
> With eyes of deepest violet blue,
> And cheeks to match the rose in hue—
>
> The fairest maids Australia knows
> Are bred among the mountain snows.
>
> Then, fearing I might go astray,
> I asked if she could show the way.
>
> Her voice might well a man bewitch—
> Its tones so supple, deep, and rich.
>
> "The tracks are clear," she made reply,
> "And this goes down to Sydney town,
> And that one goes to Gundagai."

> Then slowly, looking coyly back,
> She went along the Sydney track
>
> And I for one was well content
> To go the road the lady went;
>
> But round the turn a swain she met—
> The kiss she gave him haunts me yet!
>
>   •   •   •
>
> I turned and travelled with a sigh
> The lonely road to Gundagai.

The poem's success is due, I suspect, to the fact that it deals with a favourite theme of Paterson's when he forsook physical action or natural description—romantic nostalgia for what might have been. But in **"The Road to Gundagai"** he avoids the sentimentality which usually afflicted his treatment of this theme by uttering it in a dramatic voice wholly appropriate to the emotions and the circumstances—that of the rejected swain. In other exercises in first person statement, however, Paterson was nowhere near so happy in his effects. In **"The First Surveyor"** the task of assuming the identity of the widow of an early pioneer proves quite beyond him. There is equally little sense of a dramatised personality in **"The Flying Gang,"** spoken by an ex-member of an emergency railway repair team. For the most part Paterson solved the problem of finding a suitable dramatic voice for stating his themes by ignoring it; his lines are characteristically inscribed in the third person singular.

The achievement of an appropriate dramatic voice was one of Ransom's criteria for successful pastoral poetry, above and beyond the exercise of a proper craft skill. Paterson's failure to do so is, to that extent, a gauge of his limitations. It is also a gauge of his special historical difficulties. If, as Ransom maintains, the existence of a critically alert audience, sophisticated and well schooled in literary tradition and convention, is necessary for a great and subtle poetry, then, it may be, Paterson was condemned from the start to the simplistic manner he adopted. He certainly commanded a widely appreciative audience; but that they could not respond with the awareness and rigour of Milton's readers is suggested by the very conduct of Paterson's verse. From time to time there enters into his writing a note of dis-ease, even of desperation, which, it may not be too fanciful to argue, is the sign that Paterson recognised the impossibility of his cultural situation: in order to release his limited imaginative talents into their fullest expression rather than continue as "The Banjo," the popular versifier, he needed a kind of audience which simply did not exist in the Australia he was writing for. The signs of strain in his verse are, I would suggest, the symptoms of a half-hearted attempt to create the kind of audience he needed or (more likely) the rueful acknowledgement of defeat.

The unsatisfactory relation between Paterson and his audience is registered in a number of ways; in, for instance, the latinisms he used from time to time. These lines, from **"Old Pardon, The Son of Reprieve,"** are typical:

> Experience *docet*, they tell us,
> At least so I've frequently heard;
> But, "dosing" or "stuffing," these fellows
> Were up to each move on the board.

Or these, from **"Our New Horse"**:

> And one said, "I move that instanter
> We sell out our horses and quit;
> The brutes ought to win in a canter,
> Such trials they do when they're fit."

Or these, from **"A Voice from the Town"**:

> Their watchword is *nil admirari*,
> They are bored from the days of their birth.

Such tags bear no more than a philological resemblance to the latinity of "Lycidas." In Milton's work the classical allusions are confident appeals to a still living culture fully shared and understood by both poet and audience. Paterson's latinisms are no more than humorously remembered scraps from an inert lump of learning he had brushed against in pursuit of the pound. Still, for all their actual inadequacies in his verse, they were the relics of that rich cultural matrix which might have given his work a more ample life. In the same way, I think it fair to assert that the embarrassingly "poetic" diction and syntax which Paterson was prone to insert into even his most rollicking narratives are further signs of his search for a common ground wherein he and his audience might meet and more deeply understand each other. And perhaps it was his realization that these "poetical devices" had failed to achieve anything like what he had hoped for that led him, from time to time, to base his humour on the parody of poetic models. The self-derision, the jeering at the outward forms of poetry cannot be missed in a number of Paterson's works. They can be detected, starting with the title, in a piece like **"An Idyll of Dandaloo."** The first stanza is sufficient to indicate the parody of what with Paterson probably passed for the grand style:

> On Western plains, where shade is not,
> 'Neath summer skies of cloudless blue,
> Where all is dry and all is hot,
> There stands the town of Dandaloo—
> A township where life's total sum
> Is sleep, diversified with rum.

Yet even in his moments of self deflation and literary parody, Paterson was never moved to inject into his verse that peculiar quality which Ransom ascribes to "Lycidas": the roughness of conduct which mars the poem's anonymity and is the sign of Milton's modernity. Even in parody, the total artificiality which is the mark of Paterson's minor anonymity is never once shattered by the submission of craft to personal consciousness. Never do his lines, by the admission of irregular metres or imperfect rhymes, register the ravage of modernity.

That is to say, the formal elements of Paterson's work corroborate certain conclusions about the nature of his total achievement which other aspects of his life and art strongly suggest. The kind of poet that the evidence, both biographical and textual, commands us to see in Andrew Barton Paterson can be described more or less like this: Here was an aristocratic amateur with a limited talent for poetry, a considerable if narrow proficiency in the mechanics of his craft, an unwearying devotion to the formal properties of verse, a love of adventure, and some uneasiness about his relation to his admiring public. It is tempting to speculate under what circumstances that uneasiness might have been allayed, and Paterson's other qualities thus released into their fullest expression. The answer, I think, is plain enough: Paterson would have enjoyed his fullest personal success in literature had he been a minor Elizabethan pastoral poet of the 1580s. That, however, he was not. Starting to write in Australia and in the late nineteenth-century, the Minor Pastoral Poet was destined to become the National Literary Figure, and it is as such that we must come to terms with him.

Historically, the achievements of the National Literary Figure admit of little dispute. He wrote a considerable body of unpretentious poetry, which by virtue of its gusto and the con-

ditions of the times was experienced as popular verse among a wide audience. Thanks to the authority he enjoyed as a successful writer, he helped to transmit a certain kind of material (the physical adventures of bushmen) into the stream of our popular culture. Nevertheless, if we feel inclined to blame Paterson for such debased performances as **"The Pub with No Beer,"** we can also be grateful to him. In attempting the hopelessly anachronistic convention of the pastoral, he helped to acclimatise conventions of any sort in our literature, and so cleared the way for some of our most distinguished contemporary poets. It is not Paterson as Artist or Paterson as Historical Monument who is yet to be seen plain and evaluated; it is Paterson as Culture Hero. For his writing is still held to maintain a living relation to our popular culture. And here, it seems to me, our last and greatest difficulty lies. By what right does a poet whose achievement, in literary terms, is distinctly minor, whose subject matter and ethos are grounded in a fast disappearing set of circumstances—by what right does such a poet continue to hold the place of esteem that he does?

I hope that the answer to this last question will have begun to emerge from the main course of my argument. Paterson's may be a minor poetry, but it is a special kind of minor poetry—an Arcadian poetry. It removes its material and attitudes to the realm of myth, and in so doing makes them permanently available to later readers. The myth of behaviour that Paterson has bequeathed us is not a profound or disturbing one; above all it enshrines the simple, rational virtues, the qualities by which Australians have learnt to keep the surface of their lives intact. It is good that we should have such a figure in our cultural pantheon, but it is not good that he should be alone. Not content to remember Paterson for what he was and did, we have transformed his life and work to our own uses. To that extent we stand in his debt. We can most fittingly pay that debt by supplying what Paterson most acutely lacked: a public widely responsive to and thoroughly schooled in high art. Then perhaps we will be blessed with another popular poet; a poet who can do for the deepest reaches of our national existence what Paterson did for its simplest needs. (pp. 392-402)

> *H. P. Heseltine, "'Banjo' Paterson: A Poet Nearly Anonymous," in* Meanjin, *Vol. XXIII, No. 4, December, 1964, pp. 386-402.*

CLEMENT SEMMLER　(essay date 1967)

[Semmler is a prominent Australian short story writer, essayist, and critic and the editor of The World of "Banjo" Paterson *(1967). In the following excerpt, he compares Paterson's verse with that of Rudyard Kipling.]*

Both [Kipling and Paterson] in their verses succeeded where so many more sophisticated writers before and since them had failed: they recovered in their verses the qualities of the traditional ballad, and they accomplished this because they sought to convey no more to their audiences than could be taken in by them in a simple reading or hearing. With this simplicity of purpose went a gift of word, phrase and rhythm, all constituting an artistry of expression in a sort of material commonly given mediocre utterance by bush rhymsters. Kipling's "Overland Mail"

> From aloe to rose-oak, from rose-oak to fir,
> From level to upland, from upland to crest,
> From rice-field to rock-ridge, from rock-ridge to spur,

Fly the soft-sandalled feet, strains the brown naked chest.
From rail to ravine—to the peak from the vale—
Up, up through the night goes the Overland Mail.

is an almost uncanny duplication in subject and action, set only against a different terrain, of Paterson's **"The Travelling Post Office"**:

And now by coach and mailman's bag it goes from town to
town,
And Conroy's Gap and Conroy's Creek have marked it
"Further Down."
Beneath a sky of deepest blue, where never cloud abides,
A speck upon the waste of plain the lonely mailman rides. . . .

The vision of the mail-carrier as a dot, a speck, against a vast panorama of plain and mountain is common to both, for in another stanza Kipling writes "There's a speck on the hillside, a dot on the road . . .".

But then these coincidences occur repeatedly when one looks at the life and work of these two men who were at their creative best in the 1890's when Victoria was still on the throne. They were born within a year of each other (Paterson in 1864, Kipling in 1865) and died within 5 years of each other (Kipling in 1936, Paterson in 1941). Each became a journalist (and I use the phrase to include newspaperman) at an early age and turned out a fantastic amount of material in the way of newspaper articles and reports. Paterson's dispatches as a war correspondent from South Africa ran into many hundreds of column inches. Each through his life was poised between two worlds. Kipling's position was between a world in which literature and the arts were regarded as among the most serious things in life (his mother's family included a sister who married Edward Burne-Jones and another who married Edward Poynter, a painter who became President of the Royal Academy), and a world of soldiers and administrators—men of action prone to regard artists and writers as unreliable characters. Paterson, from his boyhood, and by strong inclination a lover of the Australian outback and its people, whose poet he became, was nevertheless for most of his life anchored in the city, first as a lawyer, later as a newspaper editor and man-about-town and clubman. But even from these dilemmas came forth much fruit.

For the first time in British history, Kipling through his ballads made the figure of the private soldier vivid and sympathetic. And Paterson for his part established for all time the place of the bushman—the jackaroo, the shearer, the station-hand, the drover—in our Australian legend.

In these processes both were myth-makers. The poems that made up Kipling's *Departmental Ditties* were personal and topical in their origin and gained tenfold in force for readers who could supply the names and places. Just as many people claimed that they knew "Jack Barrett" of "The Story of Uriah," as claimed they knew, or indeed were, **"The Man from Snowy River."** Indeed, at least one mountain man of the Snowy has a plaque on his grave to that effect, despite Paterson's repeated statements during his life that he had no particular person in mind. Gunga Din, like Paterson's Mulga Bill and Saltbush Bill, has gone into legend too. It has always seemed to me perfectly appropriate that Kipling composed "On the Road to Mandalay" with the air of a popular waltz in his head, for did not Paterson compose **"Waltzing Matilda"** to a tune which he heard his friend Christina McPherson humming to herself up at Dagworth Station and which haunted him for days until he got the ballad off his chest? And now both **"Waltzing Matilda"** and "The Road to Mandalay," neither the best work of each balladist, are perhaps the best known of their verses, and have

become the words of songs that are and will continue to be sung wherever there are music and voices. In a sense this leads to the controversy about whether Kipling and Paterson wrote "poetry." I have no doubt that they did, for at times their ballads and popular verses break into poetry. T. S. Eliot once wrote that Kipling's best work was "great verse" rather than poetry. The phrase has been characterized as a blurring of issues (we would say, in the popular idiom, that Eliot was "having two bob each way")—but at least it suggests a quality of Kipling's (and Paterson's for that matter) poetry that it is hard to deny, that earlier than most both men learned what they could do as poets, or if you like, versifiers, and from that point on avoided what they thought they could not do. And this I think is the reason why *Departmental Ditties* and *Barrack Room Ballads* in their day enjoyed such a phenomenal publishing success, and why to this day, *The Man from Snowy River and Other Verses* has for nearly 75 years outsold the work of every other Australian poet.

Kipling's vision of India and Paterson's of Australia differed somewhat. Kipling's experience of Indian life led him to concern himself with the top and bottom of Indian society, and though at both ends he found ideals and values he was prepared to admire, he saw an India that was traditional in social structure, and he accepted the virtues he saw in a quasi-feudal society. Paterson on the other hand, though born into the squattocracy and station manager scheme of things, came to love the people at the lower end of the bush scale, the "battlers," from drovers and shearers and teamsters to the "hands" and rouseabouts, and thus, like Lawson, was an architect of Australian egalitarianism. But when it came to a vision of Empire, both men drew much more closely together. To Kipling the British Empire was various things, foremost a moral idea, and then an enormous and exciting storehouse of material for his writing. Paterson was hardly as jingoistic as Kipling, but as his record in two Wars shows his patriotism was just as strongly underlined; as for the storehouse he too loved to visit it. He was able to travel only a fraction of the amount that Kipling did—one visit to South Africa, one to the China Seas, one to London. But remote parts of Australia and the islands to the North were the microcosm of Empire. These places he visited often and enthused and wrote at length about them. He applied a romantic imagination to the Australian outback in precisely the same way as Kipling did to the Empire at large. And just as Paterson has left in his writing an idealized vision of the bush and its courageous, philosophical and independent people as the popular imagination would have it fixed for all time, so too Kipling left for succeeding generations a vision of Empire that is very much more than a memory of red patches proliferating on a map, or a mighty complex of commercial development. Rather it is a saga of intrepidity and men pushing onwards into an unknown; of dedicated proconsuls and administrators and soldiers of the Queen and thin, red lines; and of the endless, colourful pageant of nations in the diversity of their creeds and societies united in a concept of imperialism more magnificent and more benevolent than any Empire, even the Roman Empire, before it. (pp. 75-8)

Clement Semmler, "Kipling and A. B. Paterson: Men of Empire and Action," in The Australian Quarterly, Vol. XXXIX, No. 2, June, 1967, pp. 71-8.

FREDERICK T. MACARTNEY (essay date 1967)

[*In the following essay, Macartney defends Paterson's reputed authorship of "Waltzing Matilda," disputing Oscar Mendelsohn's assertion to the contrary (see Additional Bibliography).*]

Discussion of the origin of **"Waltzing Matilda"** has become the Australian equivalent, in its tinpot way, of the Shakespeare-Bacon controversy, now fortunately exhausted by its own vacuity. Our little local puddle could be left to evaporate in the same way but for being stirred up by Oscar Mendelsohn's *A Waltz with Matilda*, which is a compendium of pretty well everything that can be imagined to Paterson's discredit as supposedly guilty of an imposture in cribbing an old ballad and passing it off as his own. The adherents of this myth are not deterred by its basic defect in that nobody has produced the old ballad, and obviously anything of the kind that might now be preferred could not be accepted as genuine unless proved to have been written down before Paterson wrote his **"Waltzing Matilda"** verses in 1895. So, if only in the interests of reputable research, it is necessary to examine the speculations relied on.

First, however, there is a new aspect of the matter to consider. *A Waltz with Matilda* ascribes the music of the song, tune and all, to a Toowoomba musician named Harry A. Nathan and reproduces a photograph of his manuscript. On the cover-sheet is written, "**'Waltzing Matilda,'** words by A. B. Paterson," followed by the statement, "This composition of music entirely by Harry A. Nathan," but he wrote at the end of the manuscript on the third page the words, "Harmonised by Harry A. Nathan." The plain dictionary meaning of this term is "to add notes to a melody to form chords," a quite different thing from "entire" composition of the music. Mr Mendelsohn describes this glaring contradiction as "unequivocally claiming to be composer of the music," and his "guess" concerning the reference to harmonization is that "Nathan could have wished to emphasize that he was not in the category of those amateur song composers who invent a melody and rely upon some more sophisticated musician to harmonise it"; but this shallow pretext of Mr Mendelsohn's is cancelled elsewhere by his assertion that "The manuscript shows that Nathan was a trained musician."

Since we have only guesses to go on, I offer a more plausible one. The unfortunate Nathan, within seven months of the last date on "this copy," as he calls the manuscript, died a chronic alcoholic at the age of forty in an institute for inebriates. The jumble of inscriptions on the manuscript could hardly be the product of normal mentality and they indicate he was tinkering with it toward the fatal end of his addiction. His use of the emphatic word "entirely," probably without precedent in musical history, far from sustaining his full claim, shows it was open to dispute. He acknowledged Paterson as author of the words, which for five years had been spread around by the tune without either being transcribed, so that they would have reached him together, and the kindest view is that in a sober mood he corrected the outcome of a fuddled one in a last note on his manuscript saying he had merely harmonized the tune, which he no doubt did, without subsequent publication.

To deal with the origin of the words of the song . . . , a bare synopsis of the necessary data will do, as follows. Miss Christina McPherson memorized and played at her Melbourne home a catchy tune she had heard a band play in 1894 at a race meeting at Warrnambool, Victoria. Late in the following year she visited Dagworth Station in the Winton district of Queensland. A. B. Paterson also was there and heard her humming the tune about the house. She played it for him and he wrote the **"Waltzing Matilda"** words to fit it. They took it to another station and, with a group around the piano, she improvised an accompaniment for it, not, however, transcribed. The party went on to Winton for the annual races and sang it there; it caught on at the local hotel, and people who had come in for

the meeting took it home with them, some of them with copies of the words, and it spread through central Queensland and even beyond. Paterson sold the words cheaply to a publisher; a tea firm bought the right to use them for a song; Marie Cowan composed a setting for the tune; the song was printed and distributed as an advertisement; and subsequent publications stimulated and were stimulated by its popularity. The tune was afterwards supposed to be that of a march, "Craigielea," derived from a song about that Scottish region.

Those are the facts which, forty-six years after Paterson had written the verses, Sydney May collected for his book, *The Story of Waltzing Matilda*. When he began his inquiries Paterson and the Dagworth McPhersons were no longer living, but the Paterson family confirmed his results as being what Paterson told them, and he obtained information from people who were more or less on the spot at the time of the incidents described. Though it shows differences of detail such as usually occur in evidence by different people about the same events, especially when they are elderly and after such a lapse of time, it corroborates the essentials. As for subsequent recollections of a supposed older ballad, these come within Mr Mendelsohn's rejection of testimony by "elderly persons who, under jogging, remember having heard a song sixty or seventy years ago," so we need not bother about some instances of the kind; but he puts forward two notable figures, E. J. Brady and M. H. Ellis. Brady, whom he describes as "an accurate reporter," wrote, he says, to him and to Dr Russel Ward, "to emphasize that he had heard '**Waltzing Matilda**' before Paterson was born." All that need be said about Brady's accuracy as an informant is that Paterson was born (in 1864) before Brady (born in 1869). Mr Ellis is quoted as saying he was born in the Winton district and learnt in early boyhood the tune of an old marching song (about which more later) with **"Waltzing Matilda"** words, which were not given. He was four years of age when Paterson wrote his song, which soon became known in that region, so the only reasonable conclusion is that what Mr Ellis heard was Paterson's song or perhaps some garbled version of it.

It would take another book to deal with Iago-like accumulation of assumptions and innuendoes in *A Waltz with Matilda*, but one or two specimens are necessary to typify what I mean. Mr Mendelsohn imagines a scene in which Paterson ("this modest young man," as J. F. Archibald called him) is showing off with his new ballad to impress "young women of the squattocracy" at Dagworth, and he "accepts their plaudits without finding it necessary to enter into an explanation that only this line or that phrase was his"—this concerning a poet who, lionised in Sydney for the enormous success of his first book some months earlier, had gone to Queensland "to get away from the fuss," as one of his friends put it in a letter to me, and as Clement Semmler also indicates in his recent biography of Paterson. Mr Mendelsohn quotes Dr Russel Ward with his permission as saying that, when Paterson first included **"Waltzing Matilda"** in one of his books "he possibly took steps to see that it was in a form as different as possible from what he by then remembered of the folk ballad," which, do not forget, is not known to have ever existed. Could anything more contemptible be imputed to Paterson than this deceit to hide a deceit? Yet Dr Ward naïvely adds, "I hope this hypothetical story will not be construed as adverse criticism of Paterson." There is nothing to show that Paterson himself had anything to do with changes of either words or music of the song inevitably occurring in the course of its wide and long diffusion.

Next take Mr Mendelsohn's suggestion that Paterson became evasive about the verses (a falsification of his well-known reticence about himself and his writings) "because he found himself caught in a trap the existence of which he could not possibly have suspected," or, in plain words, that he was a sneak who would not have done what he is imagined doing if he thought he would be found out. This is an absurdity, anyhow, for if the supposed old ballad had really existed, he would have had gumption enough to realize that others would know it.

Mr Mendelsohn supports an opinion that Paterson could not have been the author of **"Waltzing Matilda"** because it is so different from his other verses. "I challenge anybody," he says, "to point to a ballad by Paterson in the same *genre.*" I would go further and challenge anybody to point to any bush ballad in the same *genre.* Why? Because **"Waltzing Matilda"** has nothing in common with the structure of any of our ballads through its having been written to the tune of a quick march, not merely adapted to one, which can be easily done with many verses not written to a marching stride.

This takes us back to the very beginning. Mr Mendelsohn peremptorily rejects the evidence of Christina McPherson's visit to Warrnambool, or "that she ever heard the local band play 'Craigielea,' or even that the band itself performed the tune"; but in the Latrobe Library at Melbourne the *Warrnambool Standard* of 25 and 27 April 1894 has a full account of the two-day race meeting and the items played by the band, which for the first day, including "March, Craigielea," is exactly as in Sydney May's *The Story of Waltzing Matilda.* Is it necessary to say that the events at Dagworth as I have summarized them at the outset fall into line? The alternative of dismissing them as a concoction is too silly to be even entertained.

A Waltz with Matilda, besides giving contradictory dates likely to seem adapted to suit its particular slant, confuses the song "Thou Bonnie Wood of Craigielea" with the "Craigielea" march. The march was published but I have not seen it though I have the song, of which the march is apparently a transcription; but the song is so different from the tune of **"Waltzing Matilda"** that I cannot believe the transcription is the music that caught the fancy of Christina McPherson and Paterson. I am not aware that she ever gave it a name but she said it came from an old Scottish song, and that may have led to it being afterwards referred to as the "Craigielea" march. The tune she memorized must therefore have been something else programmed, for, besides seven other marches, there was an item, "Scottish Songs." Whatever it was, there is evidence, including some given to me personally which I feel compelled to accept, that it was the tune of an old marching song, "The Bold Fusilier," which could have been played by the band under another name. It is the song which Mr Ellis mentions, and its tune was possibly learnt by English soldiers from continental troops alongside whom they served in Marlbrough's time. Some efforts I made to trace scores of the music played at Warrnambool were unsuccessful, but I am not much concerned with origins except for the purpose of defending Paterson's reputation—although I realize that he himself would not have condescended to do so, as when, insolently asked whether he really did write **"Waltzing Matilda,"** he disdained to reply.

The persistent smirching of Paterson which I have here typified is incongruously accompanied by references to him as of such "general loftiness of character" (Mr Mendelson's words) that "all who knew him agreed that he was a man of exceptional

integrity" (Dr Ward's words). Yet details which are not now capable of absolute proof one way or the other are distorted in fictitious incidents or interpreted with determinedly unfavourable bias as to the doings of "so upright a man" (Mr Mendelsohn's words), in flagrant disregard of the fundamental principle of justice which always gives the benefit of any doubt even to an accused person of the very lowest kind. (pp. 211-15)

> *Frederick T. Macartney, "The Matilda Muddle," in* Meanjin, *Vol. XXVI, No. 2, June, 1967, pp. 211-15.*

CLEMENT SEMMLER (essay date 1967)

[*In the following excerpt, Semmler examines Paterson's prose works.*]

A. B. Paterson's first prose piece, **"How I Shot a Policeman,"** appeared in the *Bulletin* of 4th January 1890, some four years after his first verses were published in that journal. Admittedly he had written a polemical tract on the plight of small landholders a year or two before this; it was entitled **Australia for the Australians—A Political Pamphlet Showing the Necessity for Land Reform Combined with Protection,** and in it he bitterly assailed the system of granting land away in fee simple. But he very soon regretted it: he blamed it on a young man's infatuation with the teachings of Henry George; and his fear that its effect might prejudice his career as a writer was perhaps the principal reason why he began writing his verse under the pen-name of "The Banjo."

But we have to thank Edward Dyson for the fact that Paterson *did* decide to try his hand at prose sketches. For in the *Bulletin* of 21st December 1889 there had appeared "The Tiredest Man," wherein Dyson humorously described a policeman of his acquaintance who for twenty years had

> fluttered feebly about his beat, dragging his feet after him with a painful effort, lurking in the shadows hooked to convenient projections, sleeping in unfrequented places, leaning hopelessly in out of the way corners and hanging dejectedly over railings and horsetroughs, and growing more and more fatigued as the years rolled by. . . .

Paterson's piece began:

> He was a short, fat, squat, baldheaded officer with a keen instinct for whisky, and an unlimited capacity for taking things easy; he would have been a tall man had Providence not turned round so much of his legs to make his feet. He used to mooch about the village at night. . . .

and it is clear that having read Dyson's piece he decided he could write about a policeman too, and this was the stimulus he needed. And even here we can observe Paterson's journalistic flair for getting into his subject quickly; the quick, neat brush of the bit of detail here and there is noticeable; and as it turned out the sketch was much more effective than Dyson's even though only half as long.

So Paterson was launched as a prose-writer, and J. F. Archibald of the *Bulletin* urged him to write especially of his experiences and knowledge of the bush and its characters. With increased assurance Paterson wrote some magnificently authentic pieces in the next year or so: **"His Masterpiece"** (about the classic bush liar); **"The Cast-Iron Canvasser"** (exploiting his larger-than-life, Mulga Bill technique); **"The Downfall of Mulligan's"**; and, especially, his comically grim account in the epistolary manner (**"The History of a Jackaroo in Five Let-**

ters'') of an English remittance man sent out to Australia as a jackaroo. He was quick to realize that the world of the outback, ''the land of lots o' time'' as he described it in one of his ballads, offered wider and more rewarding scope for his shrewd observations and for his sense of kinship with the bush folk. Nor was it merely the fact of a subject-matter at hand. Paterson's own writing style was developing—a journalistic style it is true, but attractive, immensely readable, and always colloquially literate. He displayed quite early in his writing career the capacity to salt description with details of human interest. Reporting after all, as A. J. Liebling once said, is being interested in everyone you meet; the most casual meetings can turn up fascinating material, the off-beat events can create curiosity about people.

As early as 1892 Paterson had described for the *Bulletin* a tug-of-war event, held at Darlinghurst Hall, Sydney.... [Any] present-day sporting journalist would be proud to sign his name to it; it is actuality reporting at its best, rich in atmosphere and with a rare touch of style—as in, ''a batch of broad, soft buttery brogue'' and ''one enormous drayhorse drag.''

Seven or eight years later Paterson got his chance to further develop his reporting instincts when he went off to the Boer War as a war correspondent for the *Sydney Morning Herald*.... [His dispatches from the South African campaign] are some of the most graphic and interesting examples of all Paterson's prose writing, illustrating his flair for quick-moving narrative, for relating the terrain and environment in which he moved to his own country, and his ability to pass on to his readers an abiding impression of the personalities and celebrities he met (as in the case of Rudyard Kipling and Olive Schreiner). Paterson earned a high journalistic reputation for his war-reporting and the international news agency, Reuter's, made him a correspondent for its own organization. The dispatches make an extraordinarily vivid picture of the Australians (and the New Zealanders) at war in South Africa. (pp. v-vii)

Happy Dispatches, which Paterson published in 1934 after repeated exhortations from his friends, including Norman Lindsay, to set down some record of his experiences and travels, is a valuable repository of Paterson's best prose pieces. His modest foreword described himself as a looker-on seeing most of the game, a ''not very proficient'' writer in the game able to say something about the players. The game had ranged from the Boer War (where he culled extracts from his own dispatches) to his Eastern travels and his experiences in the Great War. His bushman's eye for the tell-tale detail gave particular sharpness to his thumbnail sketches of many great men whom he met, as he put it, ''stripped of their official panoply, and sitting as one might say, in their pyjamas''; certainly his portraits have stood the test of over thirty years and by present-day journalistic standards, when the cult of the personality has been so zealously and indeed ruthlessly exploited, they read entertainingly and vividly in their own right. Kipling, ''Chinese'' Morrison, Allenby—his descriptions are all vignettes, their etching the more remarkable since they were by an easy-natured and unassuming colonial who had ''started on his travels unencumbered by any knowledge of the world other than what could be gleaned from life in the Australian bush and in a solicitor's office in Sydney.'' Yet in these pieces there are flashes of quite unusual insight as well as epigrammatic assessments that convey more than long passages of descriptive prose—as in his observation of Lord Derby, ''a man who stood four-square in a world peopled largely by weathercocks''; of a local Sussex magnate whom he met on his ramblings with Kipling, ''as

stodgy as a bale of hay''; and of Captain Towse, V.C., as one of those men who ''in a regiment, a ship, or a shearing shed . . . unobtrusively exerts the same sort of influence that lubricating oil exerts in a motor-car.'' Then again there was Paterson's skill—that of a first-class journalist—in recording items of memorable detail: the Chinese trader in his tiny little shop in a Manila bazaar with a gamecock tied by the leg to a counter, watching for an opponent to come along; a little brown Malay, carrying a sword, trotting behind a corpulent Dutchman with spectacles and silk umbrella in a small port in the Celebes. Quite apart from its wealth of biographical detail about Paterson himself, *Happy Dispatches* can be read with much pleasure for Paterson's prose style at its casual and unpretentious best. . . .

Indeed, it was this happy combination of colloquial ease and enthusiasm for his subject that made Paterson successful as a broadcaster for the A.B.C. in the 1930s. . . . Similarly because he loved racehorses and racing (he was editor of the Sydney *Sportsman* for many years, and a racing journalist for *Truth*) he applied the same directness of style and expression to his writing about the Turf. . . . And, because of his unequalled knowledge of the race-course and its denizens, his short story ''The Oracle'' deserves to be regarded, along with Cecil Mann's ''Stiff Luck for the Colonel,'' as a classic of its type in our literature. It also serves to demonstrate that the abiding characteristic of most of Paterson's prose, as it is of his ballads, is his humour—laconic, tinged with the sardonic; as Brian Elliott once said in this context, ''Every nation has its own characteristic humour, may be this is ours.''

For the essence of Paterson's humour lies not in contrived situations, nor in any form of wit, but simply and purely in the everyday occurrences and manifestations of the environment that he frequented. It was often near-the-knuckle humour as in his essay on ''The Merino Sheep.'' But then, Paterson had studied animals as closely as he had human beings; he wrote of their individual idiosyncrasies just as knowledgeably (as in ''The Bullock''); and a dog is the central character in one of his most farcical stories, ''Hughey's Dog.'' Nevertheless his finest achievement in the rollicking comedy of the absurd is ''The Cast-Iron Canvasser'' about a firm of publishers and printers of dubious reputation who sold books on time payment through the agency of door-to-door salesmen, and hired an inventor to make them ''a patent cast-iron canvasser—a figure which when wound up would walk, talk, collect orders, and stand any amount of ill usage and wear and tear.'' From then on the story develops to an almost unbelievable point of hilariousness. The remarkable thing is that the story stands up just as well in 1967 as it did in 1897—the term ''robot'' had not been invented then, and the high pressure door-to-door book salesman, though Paterson no doubt had something pretty definite in mind, seems a phenomenon of the mid-twentieth century. (pp. vii-viii)

Undoubtedly Paterson's wide reading as a youth and young man gave poise and gloss to his prose style. In a stimulating study of Paterson's verse, H. P. Heseltine [see excerpt dated 1964] has referred to Paterson's latinisms as they occur in his ballads as ''no more than humorously remembered scraps from an inert lump of learning he had brushed against in pursuit of the pound. . . . They were the relics of that rich cultural matrix which might have given his work a more ample life.'' I would suggest that this matrix did just that in the case of Paterson's prose, where literary allusions fall sweetly into place and give, sometimes because of their very unexpectedness, a freshness to his writing. ''Virtue herself 'scapes not calumnious strokes'' he quoted in his racing manuscript when writing of the race-horse owner whose horses, sent out as favourites, were beaten; and he used a line from *Hamlet,* "I speak by the card," as the heading for his chapter on bookmakers. A punter, like the witness in Dickens, he wrote, had to be "prepared in a general way for anythink"; often his lot in the end was that of "Marius sitting among the ruins of Carthage." In his general writing he drew often on Byron and Swinburne. "Had Kipling been a spectacular person like Gabriel d'Annunzio," he wrote in *Happy Dispatches,* "he might have led a great Imperialist movement." He compared Kipling, in another passage, to Goethe's hero who "toiled without haste and without rest." He referred back to Carlyle's *Sartor Resartus* for the word "hinterschlag" in describing his school-days. Often in his prose sketches he quoted from Tennyson, Swift, or Shakespeare, and he showed that his reading had ranged from Horace to Conan Doyle. ("Cras ingens iterabimus aequor," he wrote at the beginning of his "Overland to Melbourne" reports; "Tomorrow we start on a reliability trial, as our old friend Horace used to say.") Yet there was never a suspicion of conscious literariness in his work: on the contrary his idiom in general was that of the bush-workers and "battlers" he wrote about.

Most of the characteristics of his prose style can be found in his novels *An Outback Marriage* and *The Shearer's Colt.* The latter is limited in plot and atmosphere because it deals entirely with horse-racing. *An Outback Marriage* allows Paterson much more scope: he is able to roam through the Australia he knew: to draw on the characters he met and on his most memorable experiences. . . . Yet Paterson as a prose writer was much better served by his short pieces than by his novels—he did not have the patience to develop his characterization; and, while the shorter sketch came as naturally to him as the writing of a ballad, he had not studied sufficiently the form and structure of the novel to master it effectively. It is all the more credit to him then that those parts of his novel where he was on his most familiar ground, the mountain country and the plains of the outback, remain in the memory, and the people he writes about there are eminently recognizable as bush types. Thus for instance there is depth and understanding when he writes of the bushman:

> The eyes were . . . very keen and piercing . . . deep-set in the head; even when he was looking straight at anyone he seemed to be peering into endless space through the man in front of him. Such eyes men get from many years of staring over great stretches of sunlit plain where no colour relieves the blinding glare—nothing but dull grey clumps of saltbush and the dull green Mitchell grass. . . . When he spoke he used the curious nasal drawl of the far-out bushman, the slow deliberate speech that comes to men who are used to passing months with the same companions in the unhurried Australian bush. Occasionally he lapsed into reveries, out of which he would come with a start and break in on other people's conversation, talking them down with a serene indifference to their feelings.

And nothing is so true of the manner of news dissemination in the bush as in those memorable lines in *An Outback Marriage* when Mary Grant, the station owner's daughter returning to her father's property at Kuryong, introduces herself to the garrulous hotel-owner, Mrs. Connellan; the latter immediately tells the cook, who tells the landlord's son:

> Dan told the station-master when he went back for the next load, and when he had finished carting the luggage he got on a horse and went round telling everybody in the little town. The station-master told the ganger of the four navvies who went by on their trolly down the line to work. At the end of their four-mile length they told the ration-carrier of Eubindal station, who happened to call in at their camp for a drink of tea. He hurried off to the head-station with the news, and on his way told three teamsters, an inspector of selections, and a black boy belonging to Mylong station, whom he happened to meet on the road. Each of them told everybody that they met, pulling up and standing in their stirrups to discuss the matter in all its bearings, in the leisurely style of the bush.

Of those who have written on Paterson only Brian Elliott has most effectively made the point of the wider aspects of Paterson's talents shown in his prose, and that here "out of his singing robes, he appears in strength," most himself, as it were, and "best of all in short passages of digressive reflection." This combined with his humour made him, as Elliott describes him "tantalizingly Australian," because no matter how or what he wrote his style was always Australian, made up of a sort of indolent cynicism and above all of his intimate knowledge of his country and his people and of the moods of which they were blended. This "happy intimacy with all sort of queer people," as Elliott notes too, gave him an unrivalled capacity to translate Australian dialogue to the printed word. Indeed I think this was the strongest, and, as in the case of the Steele Rudd, likely to be the most enduring quality of Paterson's prose—reflected not so much in "queer" characters as in outback characters, in the articles of mateship, in bush talk and incident:

> Just as the coach was about to start a drover came out of the bar of the hotel, wiping his lips with the back of his hand. He stared vacantly about him, first up the street and then down, looked hard at a post in front of the hotel, then stared up and down the street again. At last he walked over, and, addressing the passengers in a body, said, "Did any of yous see e'er a horse anywheres? I left my prad here, and he's gorn."
>
> A bystander, languidly cutting up a pipeful of tobacco, jerked his elbow down the road.
>
> "That old bloke took 'im," he said. "Old bloke that come in the coach. While yous was all talking in the pub, he sneaks out here and nabs that 'orse, and away like a rabbit. See that dust on the plain? That's 'im!"
>
> The drover looked helplessly out over the stretch of plain. He seemed quite incapable of grappling with the problem.
>
> "Took my horse, did he? Well, I'm blowed! By Cripes!"
>
> He had another good stare over the plain, and back at the party.
>
> "My oath!" he added.
>
> Then the natural stoicism of the bushman came to his aid, and he said, in a resigned tone,
>
> "Oh, well, anyways, I s'pose—s'pose he must have been in a hurry to go somewheres. I s'pose he'll fetch him back some time or other."

(pp. x-xii)

Clement Semmler, in an introduction to The World of "Banjo" Paterson: His Stories, Travels, War Reports, and Advice to Racegoers *by A. B. Paterson, edited by Clement Semmler, Angus and Robertson, 1967, pp. v-xii.*

ADDITIONAL BIBLIOGRAPHY

Driscoll, Judith. "A Thaw on Snowy River." *Australian Literary Studies* 5, No. 2 (October 1971): 190-95.
> Analyzes the popular appeal of Paterson's poem "The Man from Snowy River."

Franklin, Miles. "The Nineties and the *Bulletin*." In her *Laughter, Not for a Cage: Notes on Australian Writing, with Biographical Emphasis on the Struggles, Function, and Achievements of the Novel in Three Half-Centuries*, pp. 96-118. Sydney: Angus and Robertson, 1956.
> Includes a brief discussion of Paterson.

Green, H. M. "'Banjo' Paterson." In his *Fourteen Minutes: Short Sketches of Australian Poets and Their Works from Harpur to the Present Day*. Revised by Dorothy Green, pp. 34-40. Sydney: Angus and Robertson, 1950.
> Categorizes Paterson as a balladist rather than a poet and reprints some of his verses.

Lindsay, Norman. "'Banjo' Paterson." In his *Bohemians of the Bulletin*, pp. 77-83. Sydney: Angus and Robertson, 1965.
> Biographical sketch by an acquaintance.

Long, Gavin. "Young Paterson and Young Lawson." *Meanjin Quarterly* XXIII, No. 4 (December 1964): 403-13.
> Compares verses by Paterson and Lawson that appeared in the *Bulletin* during the 1880s and early 1890s.

Macartney, Frederick T. "Jostling Matilda." *Meanjin Quarterly* XXIV, No. 3 (Spring 1965): 359-63.
> Defends Paterson's reputed authorship of "Waltzing Matilda."

Mendelsohn, Oscar. "'Banjo' Paterson." In his *A Waltz with Matilda: On the Trail of a Song*, pp. 69-83. Melbourne: Lansdowne Press, 1966.
> Argues that Paterson did not write the Australian anthem attributed to him. For a refutation of this position, see the essay by Frederick T. Macartney dated 1967.

Miller, E. Morris. "Poets and Poetry: New South Wales." In his *Australian Literature from Its Beginnings to 1935, Volume I*, pp. 18-102. Melbourne: Melbourne University Press, 1940.
> Sketch of Paterson's life and work.

Pearce, Harry Hastings. *On the Origins of Waltzing Matilda*. Melbourne: The Hawthorn Press, 1971, 145 p.
> Presents evidence that Paterson's poem "Waltzing Matilda" is a version of an earlier bush lyric that in turn had sources in European folklore and popular song.

Arthur Wing Pinero

1855-1934

English dramatist.

Pinero was the most popular and prolific English dramatist of his time, dominating the London stage throughout the late nineteenth and early twentieth centuries. His early works display the artificial plots and tight structure of the French *pièce bien faite*, or well-made play, while his later works additionally exhibit the realism and social awareness promulgated by the dramas of Norwegian playwright Henrik Ibsen. Because his works reflected continental techniques and trends during an especially stagnant period in the history of the English stage, Pinero has frequently been credited with the revitalization of the English drama. His works are also regarded as significant in marking the transition in England from traditional theater to modern theater.

Pinero was born in suburban London to a wealthy family of Portuguese descent. His father and grandfather were solicitors, and it was assumed that Pinero would also practice law; toward that end, he was obliged to work in his father's office from the age of ten. However, Pinero found the law unendurably dull and aspired to an acting career, leaving home at the age of nineteen to join a theater company in Edinburgh. Although his involvement in the Edinburgh company was limited to a series of nonspeaking parts, he soon graduated to more substantial roles on the London stage, including an appearance in the 1876 dramatization of Wilkie Collins's popular novel, *Armadale*. Pinero's performance in *Armadale* attracted the attention of Henry Irving, the most influential of London's many actor-managers, and Irving subsequently offered the young actor a permanent position at the renowned *Lyceum* theater.

During his acting apprenticeship, Pinero began to write one-act plays, known as "curtain-raisers," and the first of these, *Two Hundred a Year*, was produced on 6 October 1877 by one of Pinero's former employers, R. C. Carton. Irving, impressed with this work, agreed to produce Pinero's second play, *Daisy's Escape*. Over the next four years Irving accepted several more of Pinero's curtain-raisers, often casting Pinero in the central roles. In 1881, the young playwright achieved popular success with his first full-length comedy, *The Squire*, and one year later he retired from acting in order to devote his full attention to writing. During the remainder of the 1880s, Pinero wrote a series of increasingly well-received farces and sentimental comedies, most notably *The Magistrate, The Schoolmistress, Dandy Dick,* and *Sweet Lavender*.

Having achieved popularity and wealth with his comedies, Pinero turned to serious drama in 1889, hoping, in his own words, "to write great plays, regardless of the predilections of the public." His first attempt at tragedy, *The Profligate*, which portrayed the downfall and demise of an immoral man, was neither a popular nor a critical success. However, his second attempt resulted in one of his most highly regarded dramas, *The Second Mrs. Tanqueray*. Described by Denzil England as "nothing less than the most important serious play in the English language for two hundred years," *The Second Mrs. Tanqueray* was a huge success, running for 225 performances and bringing fame to Mrs. Patrick Campbell, the ac-

tress who first played the eponymous heroine. Pinero continued to write serious dramas for the next twenty years, and he frequently directed performances of his plays. In 1909, at the peak of his popularity, he was honored with a knighthood for his accomplishments in the theater.

During the latter portion of his career, Pinero experimented with various dramatic styles, producing a propaganda play for the English government during World War I, a fantasy entitled *The Enchanted Cottage*, a pantomime, and several social satires. However, these plays were artistically and commercially unsuccessful, and Wilbur Dunkel has suggested that, despite Pinero's attempts to modernize his art after 1910, he "failed utterly to live in the new social order brought on by the World War." Nevertheless, continuing productions of his earlier plays maintained Pinero's popularity throughout this period, and, ignoring repeated failures, he continued to write new plays until shortly before his death in 1934.

Critics frequently cite Pinero's skillful exploitation of the major theatrical trends and techniques of his time as his greatest achievement. The most important and enduring influence on his work was the French well-made play, a genre characterized by intricate, carefully developed plots and most commonly used as a vehicle for comedy. However, critics contend that in creating his early works, which were predominantly comedies of the well-made type, Pinero improved significantly upon the conventions of the genre as practiced by mid-nineteenth-century French dramatists by substituting believable, well-defined individuals for such stock characters as the jealous husband, the miser, and the buffoon. This focus on characterization reflects one of Pinero's primary artistic aims, which was to portray the action of his plays not as a series of episodes contrived to advance a comic plot, but as the natural result of the personal qualities of his characters. In *Dandy Dick*, for example, the events of the play are initiated by the naivete of a highly respected cleric, who allows himself to be drawn into the morally ambiguous world of horse racing and thus triggers a series of calamities that threaten his reputation. Pinero used this formula consistently throughout his comedies, leading Walter Lazenby to describe the characters in these works as "possible people doing improbable things."

In his later works, Pinero continued to utilize the form of the well-made play, while transferring its conventions from the realm of comedy to that of tragedy. Beginning with *The Profligate*, Pinero's works also reflect the influence of the dramatic realism that had been introduced to a limited extent into English drama during the latter half of the nineteenth century and had been exploited on the European continent with some success by Gerhart Hauptmann, Maurice Maeterlinck, and Ibsen. Pinero denied the influence of Ibsen, but he freely acknowledged his debt to the mid-nineteenth-century English playwright Tom Robertson, who had called for the use of more realistic sets and had rejected conventions such as the soliloquy and the aside. Pinero added to Robertson's innovations by having characters speak in a colloquial manner and by creating an even greater sense of realism in his staging effects. Despite Pinero's assertions to the contrary, critics find the influence of Ibsen in the subject matter of his tragedies, which were often called "problem plays" or "social dramas" because they consistently dealt with social concerns of the day. The problem most commonly addressed in Pinero's tragedies is that of the moral double standard implicit in Victorian society, which demanded sexual propriety from women but not from men; this topic is central to *The Second Mrs. Tanqueray, The Notorious Mrs. Ebbsmith, Iris, Letty,* and *His House in Order,* all of which feature female protagonists whose moral conduct was considered scandalous by Victorian audiences. Yet, while Pinero's audiences found his frank treatment of such concerns daring and controversial, some critics, most notably Bernard Shaw and Max Beerbohm, argued that Pinero failed to exonerate his heroines from blame, thereby implicitly subscribing to the very standards he ostensibly condemned.

Although critics were nearly unanimous in their praise for Pinero's comedies, his attempts at serious drama drew a mixed response. With the enormous success of *The Second Mrs. Tanqueray,* a number of commentators hailed Pinero as the greatest English dramatist since the Restoration period of the seventeenth century. Recent commentators, acknowledging that Pinero was clearly a skilled dramaturgist, argue that his serious plays lack intellectual depth and generally agree with John Russell Taylor's suggestion that Pinero had "no 'philosophy of life,' no message that he was burning to deliver to the public, no deep-rooted personal obsessions." Nevertheless, Pinero's social dramas are considered significant in advancing the trend toward dramatic realism, and several critics have noted that, while Pinero clearly lacked the iconoclastic vigor of Ibsen and Bernard Shaw, he did display great intellectual courage in his sympathetic portrayals of female characters whose behavior departed radically from Victorian standards. Moreover, Pinero

remains celebrated as the creator of well-crafted, highly entertaining comedies, several of which remain an integral part of the modern repertoire.

(See also *Contemporary Authors*, Vol. 110 and *Dictionary of Literary Biography*, Vol. 10.)

PRINCIPAL WORKS

Two Hundred a Year　(drama)　1877
Daisy's Escape　(drama)　1879
Bygones　(drama)　1880
Hester's Mystery　(drama)　1880
The Money Spinner　(drama)　1880
Imprudence　(drama)　1881
The Squire　(drama)　1881
Lords and Commons　(drama)　1883
The Rocket　(drama)　1883
In Chancery　(drama)　1884
The Magistrate　(drama)　1885
The Hobby Horse　(drama)　1886
The Schoolmistress　(drama)　1886
Dandy Dick　(drama)　1887
Sweet Lavender　(drama)　1888
The Profligate　(drama)　1889
The Weaker Sex　(drama)　1889
The Cabinet Minister　(drama)　1890
Lady Bountiful　(drama)　1891
The Times　(drama)　1891
The Amazons　(drama)　1893
The Second Mrs. Tanqueray　(drama)　1893
The Benefit of the Doubt　(drama)　1895
The Notorious Mrs. Ebbsmith　(drama)　1895
The Princess and the Butterfly　(drama)　1897
Trelawney of the "Wells"　(drama)　1898
The Gay Lord Quex　(drama)　1899
Iris　(drama)　1901
Letty　(drama)　1903
A Wife without a Smile　(drama)　1904
His House in Order　(drama)　1906
The Thunderbolt　(drama)　1908
Mid-Channel　(drama)　1909
Preserving Mr. Panmure　(drama)　1911
The "Mind the Paint" Girl　(drama)　1912
Playgoers　(drama)　1913
The Big Drum　(drama)　1915
Mr. Livermore's Dream　(drama)　1917
The Freaks　(drama)　1918
Quick Work　(drama)　1919
The Enchanted Cottage　(drama)　1922
A Seat in the Park　(drama)　1922
A Private Room　(drama)　1928
Dr. Harmer's Holidays　(drama)　1931
A Cold June　(drama)　1932

BERNARD SHAW (essay date 1895)

[*Shaw is generally considered the greatest and best-known dramatist to write in the English language since Shakespeare. Following the example of Henrik Ibsen, he succeeded in revolutionizing the English stage, disposing of the romantic conventions and devices of the "well-made play," and instituting the theater of ideas, grounded in realism. During the late nineteenth century, Shaw was also a prominent literary, art, and music critic. In 1895 he became the drama critic for the* Saturday Review, *and his reviews therein became known for their biting wit and brilliance. During his three years at the* Saturday Review, *Shaw determined that the theater was meant to be a "moral institution" and "elucidator of social conduct." The standards he applied to drama were quite simple: Is the play like real life? Does it convey sensible, socially progressive ideas? Because most of the drama produced during the 1890s failed to approach these ideals, Shaw usually assumed a severely critical and satirical attitude toward his subjects. Although he later wrote criticism of poetry and fiction—much of it collected in* Pen Portraits and Reviews *(1932)— Shaw was out of sympathy with both of these genres. He had little use for poetry, believing it poorly suited for the expression of ideas, and in his criticism of fiction he rarely got beyond the search for ideology. As Samuel Hynes has noted, Shaw was driven by a rage to better the world. A Fabian socialist, he wrote criticism that was often concerned with the humanitarian and political intent of the work under discussion. In the following excerpt from his 1895 review of* The Second Mrs. Tanqueray, *Shaw contends that the play fails to achieve greatness because of its concessions to conventional morality.*]

I am indebted to Mr. Heinemann for a copy of **The Second Mrs. Tanqueray,** which he has just published. . . . Those who did not see the play at the St. James's Theatre can now examine the literary basis of the work that so immoderately fascinated playgoing London in 1893. But they must not expect the play to be as imposing in the library as it was on the stage. Its merit there was relative to the culture of the playgoing public. Paula Tanqueray is an astonishingly well-drawn figure as stage figures go nowadays, even allowing for the fact that there is no cheaper subject for the character draughtsman than the ill-tempered sensual woman seen from the point of view of the conventional man. But off the stage her distinction vanishes. The novels of Anthony Trollope, Charles Lever, Bulwer Lytton, Charles Reade, and many other novelists, whom nobody praised thirty years ago in the terms in which Mr. Pinero is praised now, are full of feats of character drawing in no way inferior—to say the least—to Mr. Pinero's. The theatre was not ready for that class of work then: it is now; and accordingly Mr. Pinero, who in literature is a humble and somewhat belated follower of the novelists of the middle of the nineteenth century, and who has never written a line from which it could be guessed that he is a contemporary of Ibsen, Tolstoi, Meredith, or Sarah Grand, finds himself at the dawn of the twentieth hailed as a man of new ideas, of daring originality, of supreme literary distinction, and even—which is perhaps oddest—of consummate stage craft. Stage craft, after all, is very narrowly limited by the physical conditions of stage representation; but when one turns over the pages of **The Second Mrs. Tanqueray,** and notes the naïve machinery of the exposition in the first act, in which two whole actors are wasted on sham parts, and the hero, at his own dinner party, is compelled to get up and go ignominiously into the next room "to write some letters" when something has to be said behind his back; when one follows Cayley Drummle, the confidant to whom both Paula and her husband explain themselves for the benefit of the audience; when one counts the number of doors which Mr. Pinero needs to get his characters on and off the stage, and how they have finally to be supplemented by the inevitable "French windows" (two of them); and when the activity of the postman is taken into consideration, it is impossible to avoid the conclusion that what most of our critics mean by mastery of stage craft is recklessness in the substitution of dead machinery and lay figures for vital action and real characters. I do not deny that an author may be driven by his own limitations to inge-

nuities which Shakespeare had no occasion to cultivate, just as a painter without hands or feet learns to surpass Michael Angelo in the art of drawing with the brush held in the mouth; but I regard such ingenuity as an extremity to be deplored, not as an art to be admired. In **The Second Mrs. Tanqueray** I find little except a scaffold for the situation of a step-daughter and a step-mother finding themselves in the positions respectively of affianced wife and discarded mistress to the same man. Obviously, the only necessary conditions of this situation are that the persons concerned shall be respectable enough to be shocked by it, and that the step-mother shall be an improper person. Mr. Pinero has not got above this minimum. He is, of course, sufficiently skilled in fiction to give Ellean, Mrs. Cortelyon, Ardale, Tanqueray, and Cayley Drummle a passable air of being human beings. He has even touched up Cayley into a Thackerayan flaneur in order to secure toleration of his intrusiveness. But who will pretend that any of these figures are more than the barest accessories to the main situation? To compare them with the characters in Robertson's *Caste* would be almost as ridiculous as to compare *Caste* with *A Doll's House.* The two vulgar characters produce the requisite jar— a pitilessly disagreeable jar—and that is all. Still, all the seven seem good as far as they go; and that very little way may suggest that Mr. Pinero might have done good creative work if he had carried them further. Unfortunately for this surmise, he has carried Paula further; and with what result? The moment the point is reached at which the comparatively common gift of "an eye for character" has to be supplemented by the higher dramatic gift of sympathy with character—of the power of seeing the world from the point of view of others instead of merely describing or judging them from one's own point of view in terms of the conventional systems of morals, Mr. Pinero breaks down. I remember that when I saw the play acted I sat up very attentively when Tanqueray said to Paula, "I know what you were at Ellean's age. You hadn't a thought that wasn't a wholesome one; you hadn't an impulse that didn't tend towards good; you never harbored a notion you couldn't have gossiped about to a parcel of children. And this was a very few years back," etc., etc. On the reply to that fatuous but not unnatural speech depended the whole question of Mr. Pinero's rank as a dramatist. One can imagine how, in a play by a master-hand, Paula's reply would have opened Tanqueray's foolish eyes to the fact that a woman of that sort is already the same at three as she is at thirty-three, and that however she may have found by experience that her nature is in conflict with the ideals of differently constituted people, she remains perfectly valid to herself, and despises herself, if she sincerely does so at all, for the hypocrisy that the world forces on her instead of for being what she is. What reply does Mr. Pinero put into her mouth? Here it is, with the stage directions: "A few—years ago! (*She walks slowly towards the door, then suddenly drops upon the ottoman in a paroxysm of weeping.*) O God! A few years ago!" That is to say, she makes her reply from the Tanqueray-Ellean-Pinero point of view, and thus betrays the fact that she is a work of prejudiced observation instead of comprehension, and that the other characters only owe their faint humanity to the fact that they are projections of Mr. Pinero's own personal amiabilities and beliefs and conventions. Mr. Pinero, then, is no interpreter of character, but simply an adroit describer of people as the ordinary man sees and judges them. Add to this a clear head, a love of the stage, and a fair talent for fiction, all highly cultivated by hard and honorable work as a writer of effective stage plays for the modern commercial theatre: and you have him on his real level. On that level he is entitled to all the praise **The Second Mrs.**

Tanqueray has won him; and I very heartily regret that the glamor which Mrs. Patrick Campbell cast round the play has forced me to examine pretensions which Mr. Pinero himself never put forward rather than to acknowledge the merits with which his work is so concisely packed. (pp. 36-40)

Bernard Shaw, "An Old New Play and a New Old One," in his Dramatic Opinions and Essays, Vol. 1, Brentano's, 1906, pp. 32-40.

BERNARD SHAW (essay date 1895)

[*In the following excerpt from his 1895 review of* The Notorious Mrs. Ebbsmith, *Shaw suggests that the play fails because of Pinero's lack of knowledge about the kind of woman he is attempting to portray.*]

Mr. Pinero's [*The Notorious Mrs. Ebbsmith*] is an attempt to reproduce that peculiar stage effect of intellectual drama, of social problem, of subtle psychological study of character, in short, of a great play, with which he was so successful in *The Profligate* and *The Second Mrs. Tanqueray*. In the two earlier plays, it will be remembered, he was careful to support this stage effect with a substantial basis of ordinary dramatic material, consisting of a well worked-up and well worn situation which would have secured the success of a conventional Adelphi piece. In this way he conquered the public by the exquisite flattery of giving them plays that they really liked, whilst persuading them that such appreciation was only possible from persons of great culture and intellectual acuteness. The vogue of *The Second Mrs. Tanqueray* was due to the fact that the commonplace playgoer, as he admired Mrs. Patrick Campbell, and was moved for the twentieth time by the conventional wicked woman with a past, consumed with remorse at the recollection of her innocent girlhood, and unable to look her pure step-daughter (from a convent) in the face, believed that he was one of the select few for whom "the literary drama" exists, and thus combined the delights of an evening at a play which would not have puzzled Madame Celeste with a sense of being immensely in the modern movement. Mr. Pinero, in effect, invented a new sort of play by taking the ordinary article and giving it an air of novel, profound, and original thought. This he was able to do because he was an inveterate "character actor" (a technical term denoting a clever stage performer who cannot act, and therefore makes an elaborate study of the disguises and stage tricks by which acting can be grotesquely simulated) as well as a competent dramatist on customary lines. His performance as a thinker and social philosopher is simply character acting in the domain of authorship, and can impose only on those who are taken in by character acting on the stage. It is only the make-up of an actor who does not understand his part, but who knows—because he shares—the popular notion of its externals. As such, it can never be the governing factor in his success, which must always depend on the commonplace but real substratum of ordinary drama in his works. Thus his power to provide Mrs. Tanqueray with equally popular successors depends on his freedom from the illusion he has himself created as to his real strength lying in his acuteness as a critic of life. Given a good play, the stage effect of philosophy will pass with those who are no better philosophers than he; but when the play is bad, the air of philosophy can only add to its insufferableness. In the case of *The Notorious Mrs. Ebbsmith*, the play is bad. But one of its defects: to wit, the unreality of the chief female character, who is fully as artificial as Mrs. Tanqueray herself, has the lucky effect of setting Mrs. Patrick Campbell free to do as she pleases in it, the result being an

irresistible projection of that lady's personal genius, a projection which sweeps the play aside and imperiously becomes the play itself. Mrs. Patrick Campbell, in fact, pulls her author through by playing him clean off the stage. She creates all sorts of illusions, and gives one all sorts of searching sensations. It is impossible not to feel that those haunting eyes are brooding on a momentous past, and the parted lips anticipating a thrilling imminent future, whilst some enigmatic present must no less surely be working underneath all that subtle play of limb and stealthy intensity of tone. Clearly there must be a great tragedy somewhere in the immediate neighborhood; and most of my colleagues will no doubt tell us that this imaginary masterpiece is Mr. Pinero's *Notorious Mrs. Ebbsmith*. But Mr. Pinero has hardly anything to do with it. When the curtain comes down, you are compelled to admit that, after all, nothing has come of it except your conviction that Mrs. Patrick Campbell is a wonderful woman. Let us put her out of the question for a moment and take a look at Mrs. Ebbsmith.

To begin with, she is what has been called "a platform woman." She is the daughter of a Secularist agitator—say a minor Bradlaugh. After eight years of married life, during which she was for one year her husband's sultana, and for the other seven his housekeeper, she has emerged into widowhood and an active career as an agitator, speaking from the platforms formerly occupied by her father. Although educated, well conducted, beautiful, and a sufficiently powerful speaker to produce a great effect in Trafalgar Square, she loses her voice from starvation, and has to fall back on nursing—a piece of fiction which shows that Mr. Pinero has not the faintest idea of what such a woman's career is in reality. He may take my word for it that a lady with such qualifications would be very much better off than a nurse; and that the plinth of the Nelson column, the "pitch" in the park, and the little meeting halls in poor parishes, all of which he speaks of with such an exquisitely suburban sense of their being the dark places of the earth, enter nowadays very largely into the political education of almost all publicly active men and women; so that the Duke of St. Olpherts, when he went to that iron building in St. Luke's, and saw "Mad Agnes" on the platform, might much more probably have found there a future Cabinet Minister, a lady of his own ducal family, or even a dramatic critic. However, the mistakes into which Mr. Pinero has been led by his want of practical acquaintance with the business of political agitation are of no great dramatic moment. We may forgive a modern British dramatist for supposing that Mrs. Besant, for example, was an outcast on the brink of starvation in the days when she graduated on the platform, although we should certainly not tolerate such nonsense from any intellectually responsible person. But Mr. Pinero has made a deeper mistake. He has fallen into the common error of supposing that the woman who speaks in public and takes an interest in wider concerns than those of her own household is a special variety of the human species; that she "Trafalgar Squares" aristocratic visitors in her drawing-room; and that there is something dramatic in her discovery that she has the common passions of humanity.

Mrs. Ebbsmith, in the course of her nursing, finds a patient who falls in love with her. He is married to a shrew; and he proposes to spend the rest of his life with his nurse, preaching the horrors of marriage. Off the stage it is not customary for a man and woman to assume that they cannot co-operate in bringing about social reform without living together as man and wife: on the stage, this is considered inevitable. Mrs. Ebbsmith rebels against the stage so far as to propose that they shall prove their disinterestedness by making the partnership a friendly business one only. She then finds out that he does not really care a rap about her ideas, and that his attachment to her is simply sexual. Here we start with a dramatic theme capable of interesting development. Mr. Pinero, unable to develop it, lets it slip through his fingers after one feeble clutch at it, and proceeds to degrade his drama below the ordinary level by making the woman declare that her discovery of the nature of the man's feelings puts within her reach "the only one hour in a woman's life," in pursuance of which detestable view she puts on an indecent dress and utterly abandons herself to him. A clergyman appears at this crisis, and offers her a Bible. She promptly pitches it into the stove; and a thrill of horror runs through the audience as they see, in imagination, the whole Christian Church tottering before their eyes. Suddenly, with a wild scream, she plunges her hand into the glowing stove and pulls out the Bible again. The Church is saved; and the curtain descends amid thunders of applause. In that applause I hope I need not say I did not join. A less sensible and less courageous stage effect I have never witnessed. If Mr. Pinero had created for us a woman whose childhood had been made miserable by the gloomy terrorism which vulgar, fanatical parents extract from the Bible, then he might fitly have given some of the public a very wholesome lesson by making the woman thrust the Bible into the stove and leave it there. Many of the most devoted clergymen of the Church of England would, I can assure him, have publicly thanked him for such a lesson. But to introduce a woman as to whom we are carefully assured that she was educated as a secularist, and whose one misfortune—her unhappy marriage—can hardly by any stretch of casuistry be laid to the charge of St. Paul's teaching; to make this woman senselessly say that all her misfortunes are due to the Bible; to make her throw it into the stove, and then injure herself horribly in pulling it out again: this, I submit, is a piece of claptrap so gross that it absolves me from all obligation to treat Mr. Pinero's art as anything higher than the barest art of the theatrical sensation. As in *The Profligate,* as in *The Second Mrs. Tanqueray,* he has had no idea beyond that of doing something daring and bringing down the house by running away from the consequences.

I must confess that I have no criticism for all this stuff. Mr. Pinero is quite right to try his hand at the higher drama; only he will never succeed on his present method of trusting to his imagination, which seems to me to have been fed originally on the novels and American humor of forty years ago, and of late to have been entirely starved. I strongly recommend him to air his ideas a little in Hyde Park or "the Iron Hall, St. Luke's," before he writes his next play. I shall be happy to take the chair for him. (pp. 40-5)

> *Bernard Shaw, "Mr. Pinero's New Play," in his* Dramatic Opinions and Essays, Vol. 1, Brentano's, *1906, pp. 40-7.*

W. KINGSLEY TARPEY   (essay date 1900)

[*In the following excerpt, Tarpey discusses Pinero's work to 1900, noting his achievements and his failures.*]

Alike in popular favor and in critical estimation, Mr. Pinero stands foremost among living English dramatists. For close on twenty years he has been our most prolific and notable author; and during that time has essayed, with the exception of melodrama, plays of every class; while it may almost be said of him that "he has touched nothing that he has not adorned." After a few lesser experiments, and those in somewhat well-worn paths, he established his claim to strength and originality by *The Money Spinner....* In the career of success thus inaugurated he has never really faltered, though of course he has had his failures. But his failures were only in the beginning of his day; and since the date of his brilliant series of successful farces at the Court Theatre he has produced no work that has not been awarded at least the respect of an adequate hearing, due to one established in public opinion as a master of his craft. For it is as a master of his craft, above all things else, that we think of Mr. Pinero. Others of our playwrights may be more keenly on the alert for the dramatic story, others (though I doubt it) may be more subtle delineators of character, others more profound thinkers; but not one has an equal mastery of stagecraft, or so nice a sense of the adaptation of dramatic means to dramatic ends. It cannot but be felt that in the drama Mr. Pinero has found his appropriate medium of expression; it may well be, his only medium. Facts favor the latter supposition; for with a restraint, equally rare and commendable in these days of multifarious and incongruous self-advertisement, he has devoted himself singly to the stage. His excursions into other paths have been few indeed; as a story writer, an essayist, a lecturer, he is all but unknown.

To make a complete survey of the varied field of Mr. Pinero's work were impossible, within these limits; enough if I indicate where, in my opinion, he has superlatively succeeded, where he has partially failed. If not his most distinguished, certainly his most distinguishing, achievement has been in the domain of farcical comedy. The famous Court farces mark, in their way, an era in the history of our stage. Mr. Pinero has rendered to English farce a service analogous to that rendered by Mr. Gilbert to comic opera; and, like Mr. Gilbert, he has as yet found no adequate competitor. The salient quality, I shall call it the salient merit, of these plays is that, full of incident, and genuinely amusing incident, as they are, their mainspring is character. The delights of a play that depends merely on its incidents are generally exhausted at one hearing; once we know the story, our interest is discounted. Plays that have character for basis may be lingered over, and listened to again and again with recurrent and enhanced enjoyment; while to the lover of good acting, repeated hearings cannot cause the fountain to run dry. Nay, the very recollection is a perennial joy.... A single method ran through these pieces, for the most part: the placing of a character, generally a dignified and serious character, in an incongruous and irrelevant situation, and the working out of the consequences with relentless logic. The magistrate is entrapped into breaches of the law that lead direct to his own court; the portly, solemn, pompous dean is suddenly involved in horse-racing, and innocently mixed up with the practices of the lowest criminals of the turf; the cabinet minister of blameless, even humdrum, character finds himself guilty of selling the secrets of his cabinet. To take an absurd situation, and treat it seriously, is provocative of more genuine and more enduring mirth than can be extracted from the absurd treatment of a serious situation. Nothing has ever more clearly demonstrated this truth than the plays of Mr. Pinero. And here, again, comes in an analogy to Mr. Gilbert, and his well-known topsy-turvy-dom; though the advantage lies with Mr. Pinero, in that his postulates are more easily granted, and never seem to outrage probability. So consummate is the art, that at no point in these plays do we find ourselves able to say: "This is incredible. It could not possibly happen." (pp. 117-20)

Besides these, Mr. Pinero, in his earlier days, wrote one or two adaptations from the French, some dramas that had just a flavor of French influence, comedies, farces, and eccentric plays difficult to classify. A special word must not be denied to the idyl of *Sweet Lavender,* strung on the slender strand of one of the oldest stories in the world, enriched to overflowing with humor, pathos, and tender and loving studies of character. In all these works, certain merits stood out plainly: dialogue unprecedentedly witty and humorous, character-drawing clear and firm, and well-nigh perfect stagecraft. Of the merits of his dialogue it is difficult to speak too highly. To be so constantly humorous, yet so seldom, if ever, to write dialogue out of harmony with the character, is a talent given to few. As to character, I know no better draughtsman, nor any who can get his effects with fewer strokes of the brush. Stagecraft is the dramatist's technique; it is, essentially, a combination of the subtle dramatic instinct and the capacity to take infinite pains. Both the instinct and the pains-taking are Mr. Pinero's in a high degree.

In the year 1889 came a turning-point in Mr. Pinero's career. It was about that time that the work of Ibsen was brought to the notice of the English play-goer. It is dangerous to assign influences, to point to possible sources of inspiration and incentive, to indicate cause and effect, when nothing more than coincidence may have been at work. It may or may not have been that the example of Ibsen fired Mr. Pinero with the laudable ambition to enroll his name among playwrights of European reputation. Certain it is that whereas his earlier work had been, on the whole, the reverse of serious, and quite conspicuously marked by a leaving alone of all vexed moral and social questions, he now suddenly began to devote himself, with remarkable vigor, to the production of the "problem play." In a few years he produced *The Profligate, The Second Mrs. Tanqueray, The Notorious Mrs. Ebbsmith,* and *The Benefit of the Doubt.* Let it be said at once that these plays showed no falling off in the kind of excellence that had characterized his earlier work, and that, mooreover, they gave evidence of a degree of strength hitherto unsuspected. Also, they were good acting plays; that they provided, for the actor, opportunities of the highest kind, Mr. Forbes Robertson, Miss Kate Rorke, Mrs. Patrick Campbell, and Miss Winifred Emery, among others, have abundantly proved to us. But when Mr. Pinero essayed to write plays such as these, dealing with the deepest problems of life, he challenged comparison not merely with the world of dramatists, but with the world of thinkers. And it is in this respect that he must be held to have failed. He has been at the pains to deal with difficult problems, only to prove to us that he has but little light to throw upon them. His setting forth of the problem is in almost every case quite masterly; his solutions are in the last degree inadequate. In *The Profligate* (I take the version originally written, and afterwards chosen by him for publication), he declines to unravel the knot, he cuts it by the cheap expedient of suicide, and this, moreover, an accidental suicide, for had Mrs. Renshaw entered the room two minutes earlier the catastrophe would have been averted. Precisely similar is the ending of *The Second Mrs. Tanqueray.* In *The Notorious Mrs. Ebbsmith,* the woman of socialistic and agnostic views, inherited and matured, incredibly turns her back upon the whole tenor and purpose of her life in a moment, at the bidding of a narrow-minded and particularly ill-bred curate. In *The Benefit of the Doubt,* the tortured wife, who has been goaded to recklessness, whose every fibre is quivering with the intensity of her moral struggle, is bidden to find comfort in an assured social position, under guardianship of such respectability that, whatever people may be pleased to think, no tongue shall dare to wag. A pistol to the head, a phial of poison, Bible classes in a quiet English village, social rehabilitation under the ægis of a bishop and his wife—these are

all the answers Mr. Pinero has to make to the agonized cries of the beings he has created, the deep and intimate struggles of whose souls he has depicted for us with surpassing force and vividness.

The Benefit of the Doubt stands in a quite special position. I mean, the first two acts of the play; for so overweighted was the author by the task of solving the problem he himself had stated, that in the third act his hand shook, and, for once, even his stagecraft forsook him. The first two acts of this play, to my thinking, are Mr. Pinero's dramatic high-water mark. No element of excellence is wanting. Dialogue, character, stagecraft, intense and thrilling dramatic movement and situation, all are there to perfection. I venture to predict that this splendid fragment will stand out for many a year at once the admiration and the despair of the aspiring playwright.

After this period of storm and stress, Mr. Pinero seemed for a while to be resting on his oars, breathing gently, humming pretty, delicate, soothing airs such as *The Princess and the Butterfly,* and *Trelawney of the "Wells."* Then came his latest work, *The Gay Lord Quex,* the success of which was immediate and undeniable, and, to a certain extent, deserved. For this play is, in parts, perhaps more brilliant than anything he has previously done. Yet it has essential defects. The dramatist would seem to have expended all his stagecraft upon one scene of the play, all his power of characterization upon the drawing of a single character. These, indeed, are masterly; but one result of their outstanding excellence is to convey a sense of inequality, and lack of balance, in the work as a whole. In the case of Mr. Pinero, criticism must needs be fastidious, for he himself has taught us confidently to look for something only very little less than the best. The generation he has delighted and interested awaits his progress with no ordinary expectation. And for the future, I think it is safe to say that, to what extent soever ours may be adjudged to have been an imperfect and transitional era, no review of the English stage will ever be just or complete that shall not assign a share, and a very large share, of the contribution to its improvement to Arthur Wing Pinero. (pp. 120-23)

W. Kingsley Tarpey, "English Dramatists of To-Day," in The Critic, *New York, Vol. XXXVII, No. 2, August, 1900, pp. 117-31.*

MAX BEERBOHM (essay date 1901)

[*Although he lived until 1956, Beerbohm is chiefly associated with the fin-de-siècle period in English literature, more specifically with its lighter phases of witty sophistication and mannered elegance. His temperament was urbane and satirical, and he excelled in both literary and artistic caricatures of his contemporaries. "Entertaining" in the most complimentary sense of the word, Beerbohm's criticism for the* Saturday Review—*where he was a long-time drama critic—everywhere indicates his scrupulously developed taste and unpretentious, fair-minded response to literature. In the following excerpt from a review of* Iris *that appeared in the* Saturday Review *on 28 September, 1901, Beerbohm notes that while Pinero is clearly a skilled playwright, he does not possess genius.*]

According to Mr. [William] Archer, any one who denies to Mr. Pinero "the quality of genius" must be "the victim of a paralysing prejudice." If that is true, mine is a clear case of paralysis. But possibly my reluctance to hail Mr. Pinero as a genius may be due to a laudably nice sense of words—a sense which is not to be deflected by the electric atmosphere of a successful first-night. If Mr. Pinero is a genius, what are we to call Ibsen, for example? "Genius" seems to me a term which must be reserved for men who are distinguished by some great force of originality, men who bring into the world, out of their own souls, something that the world has not known before. Such a definition of genius may be faulty. Genius is a thing that can hardly be summed up in words. But, even as Mr. John Morley knows a Jingo when he sees one, so do I know a man of genius. I never read or saw any one of Ibsen's plays without feeling that Ibsen was a genius (however limited and unlovely his genius may have appeared to me). I never read or saw a play of Mr. Pinero's without admiring his skill; but genius I never scented there. Ibsen I scented there, and Tom Robertson and Thackeray and many other influences; but Mr. Pinero himself never leapt forth to impress me. He ever seemed to me a catholic adapter of other men's discoveries; one who sympathetically observed life through other men's eyes, and told us very cleverly as much as he dared tell us of what he had seen. That he is a born playwright I have never denied. But artistry, though it is essential, is not all-sufficient in art. It is but the means of expression. One is concerned also with the quality of what is expressed. What did Mr. Pinero express in *Mrs. Tanqueray, Mrs. Ebbsmith* and his other serious plays? Nothing that other men had not expressed before him. He went nearer to seriousnesss than any other Englishman had gone in writing for the stage. That was all. And when you penetrated beneath the superficial boldness you found a timid conventionality; beneath the superficial sincerity, cunning substitutions of stage-tricks for human character. Those plays were little more, really, than good entertainments. Like them, *Iris* is a thoroughly good entertainment. You may always rely on Mr. Pinero to hold your attention, to keep you excited in his story. You may rely, in fact, on good craftsmanship. What you cannot rely on is intellectual honesty, intellectual originality. (pp. 163-64)

Drama of the best type is that in which the situations are evolved from, not imposed on, the conflicting characters. *Iris* answers to this test much more nearly than any previous play of Mr. Pinero. The characters have been well realised from the outset, and are, except at certain points, allowed to act consistently with themselves. Their inconsistencies are of that consistent kind which . . . no! I will spare the overdone reference. I hope that by laying stress on the few points at which Mr. Pinero, in my opinion, has strayed into theatricalism, I shall not incur the charge of "paralysing prejudice." My motive is merely to spur Mr. Pinero to still deeper self-respect in his future work. The first point at which he yields to temptation is when Iris refuses to go with Laurence Trenwith to the colonies. The antecedent circumstances are these. Iris is a rich widow who must sacrifice her fortune if she marry again. She loathes the idea of poverty as deeply as she loves Trenwith. Therefore Trenwith must go and make money before she will join him. On the eve of his departure she learns that all her money has been embezzled and that she is as poor as her lover. Trenwith urges her to come and be poor with him. "No," she says, "I must stay behind. I must go through a period of probation." She has a long and ingenious series of arguments to prove that she must not accompany him. But we know that in real life she would not have used them, would have merely told her maid to pack her boxes. We know that she is only repeating, like a parrot, what Mr. Pinero has taught her to say. If she did not stay behind, poor Mr. Pinero would have to sacrifice practically the whole of his play. So here she remains, fallen far in our estimation of her as a human being. Again, (limited space, or laziness, compels me to write on the assumption that my readers know the outlines of the play) she would not have

accepted the millionaire's cheque-book with such alacrity after her lover's departure. In course of time, no doubt, she would have drifted into that acceptance. Mr. Pinero should have given her a respite. His introduction of a young girl whom Iris is eager to help out of financial difficulties is ingenious, but it is not convincing. Even if Iris, in real life, would have used the cheque-book for that girl's sake, we know that in real life that girl would not have entered thus in the nick of time. Her entry is a stage-trick, unworthy of the play. Again, consider the conduct of Trenwith when, returning love-sick from the colonies and finding Iris under the protection of the millionaire, he refuses to take her away with him. In real life, Trenwith would either have forgotten Iris after his three years' absence, and would not have returned to claim her, or, coming back and finding her, he would have forgiven her everything. That he loved her, and that she loved him, and that she was unhappy, would have been (unless he was a hopeless prig, as Mr. Pinero does not suggest) the only considerations to sway him. Here Mr. Pinero has made a concession of truth to conventional morality. He did not dare to let an "erring" woman end happily. The stalls, even the pit, might have forgiven him, but the dress-circle never. There is another point at which I suspect Mr. Pinero of inartistic timidity. I mean the scene of the first parting between Iris and Trenwith. As written, it is quite otiose. It takes place in Iris' room, where the lovers have been sitting up throughout the night to see the last of each other. The dawn breaks, the moment comes for Trenwith's departure. Certainly the scene is a beautiful one; very true and pathetic is the way in which, at the last moment, the two lovers stand making little feeble jokes, awkwardly, unable to find words for grief. But the scene is not necessary to the play, develops nothing, reveals nothing essential. Mr. Pinero is too sound a craftsman, surely, to have conceived it thus. If the lovers had been behaving more in the manner of Romeo and Juliet, it would have point. It would materially increase the poignancy of the subsequent drama. And I suggest that Mr. Pinero must have conceived it thus, but then had not the courage to execute it. However, this is merely speculation from internal evidence, and it is the last of the objections I have to make to Mr. Pinero's drama as drama.

The rest of my strictures are but against the actual writing of the play. It seems to me the worst-written of all Mr. Pinero's plays. In an unlucky moment, years ago, some rash creature hazarded the opinion that Mr. Pinero wrote well. Since that time, the dramatic critics (who, as a class, have as little sense for literature as is possible in human bipeds) have with one accord been prating of Mr. Pinero's "polished diction" and his "literary flavour" and so forth. The consequence is that Mr. Pinero, elated, has been going from bad to worse, using longer and longer words, and more and more stilted constructions, under the impression that he was becoming more and more literary. In *Iris* he has horribly surpassed himself. Not one of his characters but talks as a leader-writer for a small provincial newspaper writes. When the millionaire in the play makes a speech in honour of Trenwith's departure, one or two of the other characters object to the pomposity of his language. Why? They themselves use exactly the same vocabulary even in ordinary converse—nay! sometimes even in moments of utmost agitation. Trenwith himself, bidding farewell to a friend of his *fiancée*, exclaims "I shall always think of you—it will be a consolation for me to do so—as being at Iris' side." Iris dilates gaily on the advantage of having "a fashionable solicitor—*one whose practice is rooted in the gay parterres of Society*"! The *ingénue*, glad to have been asked to a dinner-party, murmurs "It was so sweet of you to *include* me!"

Looking at the view from a window, she exclaims, "Oh, I could gaze at this *prospect* for ever, Aunt!" "Shall I *assist* you?" says a smart woman to a man who is taking off his overcoat. "You *resemble* the pictures of angels," cries Trenwith gazing into the eyes of his beloved. "*I fear*" and "*I surmise*" are frequently placed (between commas, too) in the mouths of Mr. Pinero's unhappy interpreters. I do solemnly assure Mr. Pinero that these tricks are not "literary." Even if they were, they would be inappropriate to a modern realistic play. By all means let us have literary graces (if we can get any playwright to supply them) in artificial comedy or in romance. But in modern realism the only proper "style" is that which catches the manner of modern human beings in conversation. If that style is beyond Mr. Pinero's range, he ought to have his future MSS. completely rewritten by some one within whose range it happens to be.

After all, though, how the characters in a play talk is much less important than how they feel and act. In *Iris,* I repeat, Mr. Pinero has made his characters feel and act more convincingly than in any other of his plays. When all has been said, *Iris* remains a fine play, a work worthy of its author's great talent for play-writing. Mr. Pinero has progressed. And (though Mr. Archer may not believe me) I am glad accordingly. (pp. 164-67)

> *Max Beerbohm, "Mr. Pinero Progresses," in his* Around Theatres, *revised edition, Simon and Schuster, 1954, pp. 162-67.*

FRANK WADLEIGH CHANDLER (essay date 1914)

[*In the following excerpt from his essay "Wayward Woman," Chandler discusses examples of this character type in Pinero's plays.*]

Pinero is a master analyst of the feminine heart. Three of Pinero's heroines, in particular, may here be taken as types of the wayward,—Mrs. Ebbsmith, Mrs. Tanqueray, and Iris.

Iris is weakest of the three, a lover of pleasure, without moral fibre. In the play that bears her name, she is shown alternating between two men, one for whom she cares, and the other, who, by means of his wealth, finally conquers her. Trenwith she would have married except that he is poor, and the terms of her dead husband's will require her to forfeit an estate in case of remarriage. Although she cannot bring herself to accompany Trenwith to his ranch in British Columbia, she promises to wait for him to make his way there. When he is gone, and she has been left in poverty by an embezzlement, the other man supplies her with funds, and ultimately ruins her. Then Trenwith returns, prepared to make good his promise of marriage. But when she tells him the truth, he leaves her; and the brute, who from hiding has watched her meeting with his rival and found his suspicions of her love for the other man confirmed, turns her out of his rooms, and in fury smashes the furniture.

Iris is a new Manon Lescaut. She knows her own weakness. "Poor, weak, sordid Iris," she calls herself, "who must lie in the sun in summer, before the fire in winter, who must wear the choicest laces, the richest furs, whose eyes must never encounter any but the most beautiful objects,—languid, slothful, nerveless, incapable almost of effort." She knows that she needs either recklessness or self-denial; and, lacking both, she temporizes with Trenwith. Though she cannot marry him without losing her property, she is willing to support him and let tongues wag as they may. When he plucks up courage and goes forth to the wilderness alone, she quickly succumbs to his wealthy rival. But on Trenwith's return, she begs to be taken back, alleging that it is the good in her that has proved her downfall, that her scruples lest she be a burden to him in the New World have exposed her to temptations greater than she could bear. In other words, she excuses her conduct, whereas the spectator of the play must condemn it as far from inevitable.

In *Letty,* Pinero has drawn a heroine tempted, like Iris, to follow the line of least resistance, but gathering her forces to oppose elopement with a married man of superior class, and justified in the end by the happiness she achieves as wife of a little photographer of her own world. Letty is a clerk in a bucket-shop. Her employer offers her marriage. He is well-to-do but rough-and-ready. She cares nothing for him, yet is attracted by the thought of the comforts that he can give her. In the meantime, she has been fascinated by Nevil Letchmere, a customer of the firm, who wishes to save her from her employer. Nevil has a wife with whom he does not live. He cannot marry Letty, but he will take her abroad. She has about surrendered to his proposal, and has come at midnight to his rooms to perfect the plans of their journey, when word is brought that Nevil's sister, herself mismated, has eloped to the Continent with an admirer. The brother is shocked; he feels that, in his own philandering, he has failed to watch over his sister as he should. Moreover, both he and Letty recognize in Mrs. Ivor Crosbie's mistake a forecast and analogue of their own proposed action. The good in Letty recoils. She begs Letchmere to save her as the only reparation he can make for having neglected to save his sister; and the duty thus imposed upon him he accepts.

No novel idea is developed by the piece. It merely reaffirms the worldly wise maxim that it doesn't pay to fly in the face of convention, or to scorn the lines of class-cleavage. The play exists, however, less to enunciate this commonplace doctrine than to tell a story and to set forth a group of characters with fidelity to life. The hero talks too much in the stilted and sententious vein dear to the younger Pinero but Letty is quite natural—a well-meaning, weak, affectionate, vacillating creature, who by a narrow chance avoids the shoals and rocks that threaten her, and slips into the smooth waters of a bourgeois marriage.

Letty escapes waywardness by virtue of witnessing it in another. As soon as she is forced to think, she is saved; at heart she is a conservative. Iris, however, is neither conservative nor radical. She never thinks; she merely feels, and her waywardness is a matter of weakness. The heroine of Pinero's *The Notorious Mrs. Ebbsmith* differs from these other two women in that she is always a thinker, a rational radical, whose waywardness—if you call it such—is due to her strength. Agnes Ebbsmith is a good woman of revolutionary ideas, caught from her father, and deepened by her own unhappy experience of wedded life. She is an advocate of spiritual free love. As a nurse, she has fallen enamored of her patient, Lucas Cleeve. He, too, has been unhappy in marriage, and fancies himself ready to accept all her theories. So, they have formed a union designed to be ideal. But Pinero's play—*The Notorious Mrs. Ebbsmith*—exhibits the failure of this union, a failure due to the character of the man in the case and to the nature of love in general.

Lucas is a sensitive egoist wrapt up in his career. He has self-esteem without self-confidence. As soon as his friends begin to deplore his departure from convention, he is done for. Already he has feared that each success he achieved might be his last. Now he suffers agonies at being ridiculed by the worldly.

He realizes that he is unfitted to shine as a social reformer; he knows that it is passion, not principle, that has bound him to Agnes, and ultimately he decides to renounce her. The steps in his falling away are carefully indicated. First, he recants faith in their dream of marital reform. Then, he resolves to win back respectability by marrying Agnes when possible. And, next, he considers returning to his wife, at least in appearance. Up to this point, Agnes has consented to follow him. Her earlier fear had been lest she find herself "loving Lucas in the helpless, common way of women." But, bit by bit, she has come so to love him, complacently donning the beautiful dress he has bought for her, and yielding to his every whim, since, in fighting his uncle, the Duke of St. Olpherts, for mastery over Lucas, she has needed to draw upon every physical charm in her armory,—weapons hitherto disdained.

But when Lucas, for the sake of quieting all scandal, would return to his wife, although still maintaining in secret his relations with Agnes, the latter rebels, and prepares to seek refuge with friends. At this juncture, the wife comes in person to beg the woman she has deemed a Circe to continue exerting her spell over Lucas until he can be lured back to his former associates and ambitions. This suggestion is both an insult and a confession; yet Agnes, who learns for the first time what the wife, too, has suffered from the meanness and vanity of Lucas, consents. But the wife, now stung with self-shame at having asked of her rival this wretched service, rejects it. Then, when Lucas pleads with Agnes to rejoin him, she grows firm in refusal, for at last she sees him truly and sees herself.

Yet she promises, when she has again learned how to pray, to remember him in her prayers. He stares at her, incredulous. "Pray!—You!" he exclaims; and his words are proof that he never has fathomed the depths of her nature.

Agnes Ebbsmith has learned the futility of defying a social institution. She has learned the weakness of human nature that renders such institutions essential. And Pinero, in his masterpiece—*The Second Mrs. Tanqueray*—, again lays stress on the same general moral. The question here proposed is not, May marriage be dispensed with? but rather, Can marriage clothe with respectability the woman who has earlier sinned? Aubrey Tanqueray believes that it can, and to prove his contention, marries, with eyes open, the lovely yet once disreputable Mrs. Jarman. But only misery results. Aubrey's daughter by his first marriage is as cold as her mother had been. She feels an instinctive aversion to Paula. Society will have nothing to do with the second Mrs. Tanqueray, and the only woman who calls comes, after months of neglect, merely to rescue Ellean from her influence.

Paula herself is bored, yet hungering for love and sympathy. Try as she will, she cannot shake off the ideals and the habits of thought of her earlier life. Angry that Ellean has been so anxious to leave her, and that Aubrey has been so willing to let the girl go, Paula insists upon bringing as guests to the house two of her quondam friends—the déclassé Mabel Hervey and her tippling husband, Sir George. But these people whom once she could have liked, distress and disgust her, and she yearns to be rid of them. Then Ellean, who in Paris has fallen in love with an English officer, comes home, transformed from her colder self. She even embraces Paula as she tells how her lover is waiting there in the garden. Paula, delighted at Ellean's first confidence, begs her to bring him in. But, as Paula turns to receive him, the past, which she had thought forever banished, confronts her. For Ellean's Captain Ardale, the hero of India, is her own unheroic first lover. Of their past alliance

Tanqueray is in ignorance, and Ardale wishes him kept so. But Paula refuses.

Ardale storms and pleads, bullies and begs, and then weakly withdraws. For the loss of her lover, Ellean blames Paula. "Why, after all, what can *you* know?" she asks. But the truth dawns upon her, and Paula's protestations are in vain.

"It's a lie!" cries Paula, forcing the girl to her knees. "You shall beg my pardon for it. Ellean, I'm a good woman! I swear I am! I've always been a good woman!"

Yet, after this outburst Paula grows hopelessly calm. The patient Tanqueray tries to encourage her. They will begin life afresh somewhere else. But Paula is now convinced that they cannot outlive the past. "I believe the future is only the past again," she tells him, "entered through another gate. . . . Tonight proves it." Then she pictures for him the future, when her beauty shall have faded. "You'll see me then at last with other people's eyes," she tells him; "you'll see me just as your daughter does now, as all wholesome folks see women like me. And I shall have no weapon to fight with—not one serviceable little bit of prettiness left to defend myself with! A worn out creature . . . my hair bright, my eyes dull, my cheeks raddled and ruddled—a ghost, a wreck, a caricature, a candle that gutters, call such an end what you like! Oh, Aubrey, what shall I be able to say to you then? And this is the future you talk about!" In her speech, Paula misses the moral view, the conception of growing old nobly, of rising through a conquest of character to higher levels with the passage of the years. But the speech is in keeping with her own nature. She has scarcely made it and gone out, when Ellean comes running in

Pinero at the height of his popularity.

to announce that Paula has killed herself. "I helped to kill her! If I'd only been merciful!"

Few plays of the modern stage can compare with this in power,—a power due less to the plot and the moral, than to the dramatist's accurate characterization and his technical skill. Like all great art, *The Second Mrs. Tanqueray* seems perfectly simple. It relies upon action, gesture, and facial expression rather than rhetoric. The most impressive scenes are those in which the words are in themselves least noticeable. When Paula, all happiness, springs upon the sofa to be sure, by catching a glimpse of herself in the mirror, that she is looking her best before Ellean's lover is brought in, there is a moment of silent suspense more telling than any verbal eloquence. The most affecting dialogue is almost monosyllabic. As Wordsworth advised with regard to poetry, so here, it is the feeling that gives importance to the words, and not the words that give importance to the feeling. (pp. 139-45)

> Frank Wadleigh Chandler, "Wayward Woman," in his Aspects of Modern Drama, *The Macmillan Company, 1914, pp. 120-45.*

LUDWIG LEWISOHN (essay date 1915)

[*A German-born American novelist and critic, Lewisohn was considered an authority on German literature, and his translations of Gerhart Hauptmann, Rainer Maria Rilke, and Jakob Wassermann are widely respected. In 1919 he became the drama critic for the* Nation, *serving as its associate editor until 1924, when he joined a group of expatriates in Paris. After his return to the United States in 1934, Lewisohn became a prominent sympathizer with the Zionist movement, and served as editor of the Jewish magazine* New Palestine *for five years. Many of his later works reflect his humanistic concern for the plight of the Jewish people. In the following excerpt, Lewisohn provides an overview of Pinero's career.*]

[Arthur Wing Pinero's] very early plays are harmless and negligible: *The Magistrate* (1885) is amusing enough; *Sweet Lavender* (1888) is a sentimental hodge-podge in which the poor working-girl turns out to be the rich man's daughter. One would not dream of discussing work of this quality in any art except the art of the English drama. No history of English literature is likely to discuss the novels of "The Duchess." But Mr. John Hare's production of *The Profligate* (1889) at the New Garrick Theatre with Mr. Forbes Robertson in the title role has been said to mark an epoch in the history of the modern drama. *The Profligate,* however, is really a more lamentable because a more pretentious play than the early farces and melodramas. It is the old-fashioned story of betrayal with all its false and foolish moral arrogance, with the phantastic insistence on sex instinct as the exclusive property of one sex and as being, in that sex, a monstrous perversity which slays its shuddering and unwilling victims. The technique of the play represents the long arm of coincidence as the arm of a skilled prestidigitator. It must be an extraordinarily primitive audience that is taken in by the various reappearances of Janet Preece and the discovery of the real culprit in the third act.

At the end of four years, however, years marked by the introduction of Ibsen into England, by the founding of the *Independent Theatre* and by the appearance of Mr. Shaw, Pinero produced *The Second Mrs. Tanqueray.* The absolute value of that play is, clearly, not of the highest. The catastrophe which inheres so closely in the characters is brought about by an unlikely and violent coincidence. And that coincidence is effected because Pinero had not the fine artistic courage to leave

Aubrey and Paula Tanqueray merely with a recognition of their real tragedy—the irrevocableness of the past. But intellectually *The Second Mrs. Tanqueray* is in a different world from that of *The Profligate.* The outlook upon life is true and fearless within the given limits of merely social morality; a free and human justice is dealt out in the characterisation of Paula Tanqueray herself.

The Notorious Mrs. Ebbsmith (1894) though less effective as a whole marks a still further advance in artistic and intellectual sincerity. The situation of that deadly compromise which Lucas Cleeve hesitates to reject, and which would have reduced Agnes Ebbsmith from a free personality in a free union to a common wanton—that situation is finely conceived and embodied without cheap concessions to the mechanism of intrigue. Equally sound is the plea of Sybil Cleeve in the last act and her immediate repudiation of its disgrace. Indeed Pinero's progress in the projection of character was very notable during these years and approved itself especially in the relations between John and Olive Allingham in his next play: *The Benefit of the Doubt* (1895). It is unfortunate that the whole action of this interesting work hinges upon a conversation overheard through an elaborate bit of technical trickery.

The level of these three plays Pinero was unable to sustain. By perceptible gradations from play to play he sank once more to the shoddy and external intrigue of *The Gay Lord Quex* (1899). Then, gathering his powers with an almost visible effort, he produced his most elaborate and ambitious drama in *Iris* (1901). The merits of that piece are solid and obvious. Iris, as a character, is incontestably alive and permanent; the portrait of Maldonado is earnestly attempted and vividly elaborated; the last interview between Lawrence Trenwith and Iris is not without true pathos; the ending is, for once, unafraid of its own inherent necessities. But the base of all this excellent structure is built on stubble. For the drama is that art in which men shall go through the recognisable gestures of their mortal fate driven by an inner impulse, not by the tug and thrust of the deviser's clever mechanism. Now the action of *Iris* is wholly conditioned on two external accidents and one piece of shameless trickery. The impetus that starts the play is the unusual will left by Iris' husband; the turning point of the action comes fortuitously from without, through the absconding of Archibald Kane; to force the catastrophe Iris must write a letter, tear it up, scatter the fragments on the floor, and fail to observe Maldonado gather them in her very presence. Thus only does he learn of her apparent treachery and returns to drive her out into the streets.

Iris was again followed by a rapid decline in Pinero's work. In 1904 appeared *Letty,* mawkish, melodramatic and unreal; in 1905 *A Wife without a Smile* which is farce at its most trivial. But the best quality in Pinero is his ever resurgent ambition which wrung from him a new group of serious attempts at the art and not at the trade of the drama. He reaches his highest point in *The Thunderbolt* (1909). It is still, to be sure, the old Pinero. The action of the play is still based on the destruction of a will. But at last the exposition in the excellent first act is of character rather than of incident, the several members of the Mortimore family are not only well observed but projected without caricature; the confession of James Mortimore in the closing act is a dramatic solution for once conditioned in the uncontorted nature of men and things.

But is this the real Pinero? Or is it the creator of Lavender, of Letty, of Lily Parradell in *The "Mind the Paint" Girl* (1912)? Is it possible to take quite seriously the analysis of Paula Tanqueray, the defence of Agnes Ebbsmith, the judgment upon Iris Bellamy, since Pinero returns unceasingly to a flattery of the coarsest delusions and the most worthless tastes? No one doubts that there are decent girls in the chorus, girls with their own proper notions of honesty and self-respect. But is it not pandering to the vainest of romantic follies to base a play upon the promise of married happiness between a high-minded and sensitive gentleman and a girl whose social instincts would have driven him to desperation, the very thought of whose mother would have driven him to drink? I can but point once more to Mr. Galsworthy's treatment of the same theme in *The Eldest Son* (1909). Before the plain nobility of truth Pinero's devices shrink aside and lie prone with the other lumber of the green-room and the property man.

In reality it is not difficult to sum up Pinero's character as a dramatic artist. His is a conventional mind under the impact of a world in the throes of moral protest and readjustment; his, a conventional technique under the impact of a nobler and a plainer art. In the direction of that finer art his progress has been less than moderate. With the intellectual dilemma he has dealt by pleading for certain exemptions from the full rigour of the social law. Except in *Iris* he has always treated the problem of sex as one of social, rather than of personal reality and conflict. In that emphasis upon the external social order his art is akin to the art of the French stage, but he lacks the latter's passion, its keen intelligence, its conviction and its style. The extraordinarily high position which he holds in the world of the English drama is sure to decline rapidly with the introduction of such critical standards as are unhesitatingly applied in every other department of imaginative literature. (pp. 183-89)

> *Ludwig Lewisohn, "The Renaissance of the English Drama," in his* The Modern Drama: An Essay in Interpretation, *B. W. Huebsch, Inc., 1915, pp. 166-219.*

WILBUR DWIGHT DUNKEL   (essay date 1941)

[*In the following excerpt, Dunkel discusses the philosophy underlying Pinero's plays.*]

The prevalent notion that Pinero was Victorian in his philosophy is utterly false. He had nothing whatsoever to do with Browning's declaration of the Christian faith; nor was he racked with doubt, as were Tennyson and Matthew Arnold. Though he posed not at all as a philosopher, he had a fixed point of view on life, scientific in its emphasis upon cause and effect, strikingly advanced for his time. But Shaw represented himself as a thinker, a creative evolutionist, a prophet in the wilderness, and wrote long prefaces and essays expounding his views. And [Henry Arthur] Jones, too, wrote essays but floundered in his thinking between the dictates of his Puritan conscience and his disillusionment over hypocrisy within the church.

In what kind of world do Pinero's characters live? This question is fundamental to the understanding of the plays, indicating after production in the theater is past what the reader may hope to gain from them. For the reader is not carried away by the illusion created on the stage; he must buid in his mind that illusion. And the playwright's philosophy thus becomes of primary concern. What forces shape the characters? How do the characters face the struggle of life? For if the drama depends upon conflict between characters or between the leading character and his environment, then the points of view on these conflicts hold significance.

Pinero took himself seriously. He did not depend upon the fortuitous development of circumstances; he struggled to prepare himself and make his own future. Everything that he did seemed to him to lead to something else, to be indicative of the future. For his time he was downright materialistic; the spiritual goal was secondary, if not neglected. The Cinderella theme could not appeal to him. Luck, good fortune, benevolent influences, were all beyond his reckoning.

Even in his early farce comedies his characters fail to attain their objectives because of some mistake earlier in their lives. Though they have hopes and sentiments, their judgment, physical condition, and limitations of environment eventually bring about frustration, since they are the kind of people they are. Stated in philosophical terms this is determinism. The psychological and physiological factors in their personalities make them thus and so; not fate, not the conjunction of their stars, not the wrath of God.

Pinero's simplest comedies are strikingly based on the sentiments of his characters rather than plot, however weak at times appear the characters. They make their own mistakes leading to frustration, exposure, and the peculiar embarrassment fundamental to Pinero's theory of comedy. Though in his ironic comedies and tragedies he permits the audience to sympathize with the plights of his characters so that the audience will not laugh at them but feel with them the absolute futility of striving for happiness, his characters recognize that happiness cannot be based upon a miserable foundation; that the future is only the past, no matter how an individual may strive to atone for past errors and struggle to redeem himself.

For Pinero's early contemporaries this cold, dispassionate, irreligious point of view was distinctly unpleasant, but he maintained it, and finally it became fashionable. But by that time Pinero's plays had lost favor, and many critics wrote of Pinero's lack of a settled philosophy.

Pinero was neither a fatalist nor a predestinarian; nor exterior force molds the destiny of his characters. They all find, as later did Barrie's characters in *Dear Brutus,* that a second choice would not be different from the original, being the kind of persons they are. But Barrie invariably postulated the belief that the spirit could dominate the physical; that, in the words of Milton, the mind could make a heaven of hell, a hell of heaven. Barrie's greatest comedies are based on the premise that the world is as the characters would like to have it. For example, *Quality Street* represents the dream-come-true type of world; *Alice-Sit-by-the-Fire* reveals adults willing to accept the point of view of adolescence; *The Admirable Crichton,* for half its action, takes place amid a social cataclysm; and *Mary Rose* and *Peter Pan* exist in the illusions of childhood. But Pinero's comedies have no philosophy of escape.

The philosophy at the turn of the century most popular to Englishmen involved religious controversy. But only in *The Notorious Mrs. Ebbsmith* did Pinero discuss religion. And there he did so because the chief character was formerly a street preacher in London and represented an unorthodox attitude. When she meets the Reverend Amos Winterfield of the Church of England, she is disillusioned. The clergyman explains that his sister was saved by the mercy of heaven from leaving her husband. But Agnes, whose lover is about to desert her, cries out in anguish that if that miracle should happen to her, she would lose the last sustaining comfort to be got from life. Here is the universal cry of humanity for what it wants but cannot have.

In the end, however, Agnes sends her lover back to his wife, promising to pray for him when she has again learned how. Does Pinero suggest in this poignant scene that Agnes's contrition, necessary for prayer, will enable her to forgive Lucas for leaving her? I think not. Here is the basic principle of Pinero's philosophy: the utter hopelessness of the individual to change. Agnes' love for Lucas was predicated on her being a particular person. Through separation and suffering she may hope to, but never will, find solace in prayer. Someone else might, but not Agnes.

The Notorious Mrs. Ebbsmith created a furor among churchmen because, in the midst of Agnes' conversation with the clergyman, she hurls the Bible he has given her into the fire. This action was strictly in character, revealing the impulsiveness of her character. But Bibles are not burned on the stage. Even though she did thrust her hand into the stove to retrieve the Bible, its charred pages were symbolic of her sacrifice of every convention for personal happiness.

Clergymen appear in *The Hobby-Horse* and *Dandy Dick,* but they do not engage in religious debates. On the other hand, Jones wrote two of his most successful plays, *Saints and Sinners* and *Michael and His Lost Angel,* around religious controversies. And Shaw presented satirical sketches of orthodox religion in *Androcles and the Lion* and in *Back to Methuselah.* In particular, however, in *Candida* the clergyman with social welfare at heart is presented as weaker than a maladjusted poet. But Shaw himself informed me that *Saint Joan* was merely the biography of a real girl, thus dismissing the religious implications.

In pursuing this relentless philosophy of cause and effect, Pinero created characters who do not moan to high heaven or curse their fate. They seem to think for themselves, to realize and to perceive why things happen to them. Thus they become self-reliant though disillusioned. Confronted with choice, they invariably take the cash and let the credit go. They are not and cannot be idealists in the sense that they choose the hard way, sacrificing present pleasure for future happiness. For this reason the Victorian critics found Pinero without a philosophy. The truth is, these critics simply disliked what they found.

In the present scientific era, however, the simplest of men plant hybrid seeds and ignore the almanac of their fathers. If the seed is right and the conditions controlled, the plant will be determined, quite independent of fate or choice. Chemical and physical reactions which were miracles or the results of chance can now be predicted. And so to human beings comes the realization that experience cultivates the individual within the limits of his capacity. But the human factor of will-power, which Pinero strangely ignored, remains the great undeterminate.

Pinero's philosophy consequently seems more negative than it is because he selected people for his plays who lacked strength of will. His characters invariably fail to meet their responsibilities. That is his chief weakness as a philosopher. For in actual life he himself illustrated the principle that a man willing to sacrifice everything for a single objective can achieve success far beyond any prediction based upon his talent and education could hold for him.

Had Pinero created strong characters, his plays would have been inspirational rather than depressing. But he did not seek out the exceptional men and women; his characters are not heroic, except in their ability to suffer defeat unmitigated with hope. His view of man was cynical and bitter, based on the assumption of the prevailing weakness of man. And for this reason, more than any other, audiences and readers alike turned from the ideas in his plays to the stagecraft; from the unpleasant to the amusing.

If and as Pinero's plays come to be more widely read, his philosophy of cause and effect, determinism, and cynical rationalism will receive recognition for its clarity, firmness, and forthrightness, despite the limitations he imposed upon it through the selection of characters without will-power.

The *raisonneurs,* those understanding gentlemen who present to the perplexed characters the author's point of view, represent Pinero's philosophy. These omniscient fellows, like Cayley Drummle, Hilary Jesson, and Peter Mottram, look beyond the present to the future and in their expression of the long view emphasize Pinero's philosophy of conduct with an eye to the future. It is a practical matter, like honesty is the best policy. This materialistic attitude hardly spins itself into a theory, but it is a fixed view of life, a philosophy, whether admirable or not.

In *The Second Mrs. Tanqueray,* for example, Tanqueray objects to Cayley's suggesting the similarity between the reputations, the past lives of the new Lady Orreyed and Paula Ray; then Cayley says that he himself is only a spectator, like a man in the theater, but he wants to see certain persons happy in the end. It is Cayley, furthermore, who advises Tanqueray to permit Ellean to travel and to hope that in so doing she will find someone who will complete her life with happiness.

In *His House in Order,* Hilary Jesson reminds his brother that it is wrong to expect the special qualities of one woman in another—those of Annabel in Nina. And he suggests that the difficulty with marriage is that the husband wants his wife to accommodate herself to his interests, whereas he fails to adapt himself to hers. And, finally, it is Hilary who urges Nina to give up using her discovery about Annabel as a means of avenging herself on her husband and on Annabel's family. People who use power uncharitably, says Hilary, are never happy. But the people who conquer that temptation and sacrifice themselves find happiness in the end.

In *Mid-Channel* Peter argues with Zoe and Theodore to be patient with each other. He describes the middle years of marriage as similar to a rough crossing of the English Channel. Halfway across, the shoal causes the swift current to become excessively rough and unpleasant, but once the other side is reached the water is serene.

All three of these bachelors offer to their married friends sound, practical advice. Their advice, however, may be so obvious that it is not appreciated. Indeed, Pinero's philosophy lacks pretentiousness and deals with realities rather than ideals; certainly it is as usable today as when he set it down on the manuscript of his play. (pp. 103-08)

> *Wilbur Dwight Dunkel, "Pinero's Philosophy," in his* Sir Arthur Pinero: A Critical Biography with Letters, *1941. Reprint by Kennikat Press, Inc., 1967, pp. 103-08.*

CECIL W. DAVIES   (essay date 1962)

[*In the following excerpt, Davies views Pinero's plays as examples of the "drama of reputation."*]

Hamlet told the players that the purpose of playing is, among other things, to show "the very age and body of the time his form and pressure." Drama is to be a critique of society. Not only is it to appeal to the individual—showing virtue her own feature, scorn her own image—but to a social group, a section or cross-section of society united at a certain level by the theatrical experience and situation. And if the dramatist follows Hamlet's advice closely, he will pay particular attention to the patterns and stresses (the form and pressure) of *contemporary* society. Such a dramatist is Pinero.

By 1885 the thirty-year-old playwright had won popularity and had himself made "money-spinners" of his brilliant, cynical comedies; but he was not satisfied. He knew that he had neither discovered his own true strength, nor assessed clearly the kind of drama society wanted. Pausing in his headlong career—he had written nine full-length plays in five years—he took stock and decided that the temper of contemporary society was fundamentally sentimental, and that the kind of comedy he had been writing, an echo of the harsh clarity of the Restoration, was not what his audience really desired. They wished to "sport with human follies, not with crimes." With this idea in mind he wrote the series of highly successful plays we know as the Court Farces—notably *The Magistrate, The Schoolmistress,* and *Dandy Dick.* In these plays the greatest wickedness is the butler's attempt to poison a horse with strychnine. The scrapes from which Mr. Posket the Magistrate, Miss Dyott the Schoolmistress, and The Very Rev. Augustin Jedd the Dean extricate themselves involve nothing worse than offences against licensing hours, taking part in comic opera, and having a flutter on the local races. *But* the comedy arises because of the respectability of these three worthies, and the importance attached to their reputation; not one dare "shake hands with Reputation."

As long as there has been human society men and women have placed a value upon their reputation, and presumably always will; but never has reputation (as distinct from intrinsic merit) been so important to the individual as in the latter years of the nineteenth and the early years of the twentieth century. Similarly the idea of Reputation, as the phrase from Webster reminds us, has always played some part in drama, especially in comedy, but between about 1885 and 1914 the Drama of Reputation became almost a genre in its own right. More than anyone else Pinero was responsible for originating and developing this genre. All his great plays, comic and tragic, belong to the Drama of Reputation.

That a Mr. Posket should find himself after hours on licensed premises is nothing: that a magistrate should so find himself is everything. ("What a weak, double-faced creature to be a magistrate! I really ought to get some member of Parliament to ask a question about me in the House.") That a woman should take part in comic opera in order to support a foolish husband is not particularly funny unless the woman is Principal of a girls' school and must be concerned for her reputation. ("Think of the people who believe in the rigid austerity of Caroline Dyott, Principal of Volumnia College. Think of the precious confidence reposed in me by the parents and relations of twenty-seven innocent pupils.") So too, *Dandy Dick* depends for its comedy on the fact that the punter is a dean. Arrested for an offence he has not committed, he dare not send word home:

> Because it would involve revelations of my temporary moral aberration. . . . Because I should return to the Deanery with my dignity—that priceless possession of man's middle age!—with my dignity seriously impaired. . . . How could I face my simple children who have hitherto, not unreasonably, regarded me as faultless? How could I again walk erect in the streets of St. Marvell's with my name blazoned

on the records of a police station of the very humblest description?

Reputation is the pivot upon which later comedies of Pinero also turn. The Gay Lord Quex, with a bad reputation, proves himself a gentleman, while the wonderful reputation of Annabel for keeping *His House in Order* proves posthumously to have been most ill founded. ("This immaculate lady; the sainted Annabel—your stained-glass-window sister-in-law . . . she was nothing but Maurewarde's—woman.") Though technically a comedy, *His House in Order* is a serious play. Even more serious is the comedy *The Benefit of the Doubt.* As the title implies, the basis of this play is uncertain reputation, the benefit of the doubt given by the judge to Theophila Fraser.

If, however, it were only comedies (even serious ones) that Pinero had based upon the question, "What will people say?", his claim to originality would be less than it is. It is probably fair to say, nevertheless, that no other dramatist has placed the question so centrally in his comedies. In doing so he learned the way to his own greatness—his sombre and impressive Tragedies and Dramas of Reputation. No dramatist before Pinero found the key of his dramaturgy here. His characters (primarily his heroines) suffer not because of what they are or what they have done, but because of the attitude of society to them and their actions. The tragedy of *The Second Mrs. Tanqueray* is that of a woman with a past. Aubrey Tanqueray believes that he and his new wife can live down the conventions of society: "And in a few years, Cayley, if you've not quite forsaken me, I'll prove to you that it's possible to rear a life of happiness, of good repute, on a miserable foundation." He fails. Paula finds that "the future is only the past again, entered through another gate." A few minutes before she kills herself she tells Aubrey, 'You must see now that, do what we will, go where we will, you'll be continually reminded of—what I was.' Reputation is stronger than reformation.

A similar conflict between reality and reputation provides the dynamic for *The Notorious Mrs. Ebbsmith.* "She moves firmly, but noiselessly—a placid woman, with a sweet, low voice. Her dress is plain to the verge of coarseness; her face, which has little colour, is at first glance almost wholly unattractive." Of her Gertrude Thorpe says:

> If I were a man searching for a wife, I should be inclined to base my idea upon Mrs. Cleeve (i.e. Mrs. Ebbsmith). . . . I don't share all Mrs. Cleeve's views, or sympathise with them, of course. But they succeed only in making me sad and sorry. Mrs. Cleeve's opinions don't stop me from loving the gentle, sweet woman; admiring her for her patient absorbing devotion to her husband; wondering at the beautiful stillness with which she seems to glide through life. . .!

Because of her own unhappy background, and as a matter of principle, she disbelieves in marriage and lives with Lucas Cleeve on a basis of mutual respect and intellectual communion.

> We agree to go through the world together, preaching the lessons taught us by our experiences. We cry out to all people, "Look at us! Man and woman who are in the bondage of neither law nor ritual! Linked simply by mutual trust! Man and wife, but something better than man and wife! Friends, but even something better than friends!" I say there is that which is noble, finely defiant, in the future we have mapped out for ourselves—if only it could be free from passion.

But this George Eliot is compelled to disguise herself physically and spiritually in the current conception of a mistress. Having thus far surrendered her ideals, she learns through bitter experience the way society and man treat a woman of no reputation. This, indeed, is the aspect of reputation that dominates Pinero's plays. The Gay Lord Quex at forty-eight may prove himself a gentleman at heart and marry the fair lady; but Paula Tanqueray may never leave her past behind her. And although in comedy Pinero may imply that the reformed rake in his forties is a better bridegroom than Captain Bastling, an unreformed one in his twenties, in his serious plays we are never far from his indignation at the double standard of morality.

That indignation is nowhere more clearly seen than in *The Profligate*. While still enjoying the success of the Court Farces, Pinero wrote this play, a tragedy in its original form, as a devastatingly direct indictment of the double standard. He wrote without a particular cast or theatre in mind: he wrote it because it was in him and had to be written. The very urgency has resulted in the play's being almost crude, compared with his later dramas on the same theme. Dunstan Renshaw, the Profligate, marries Leslie, an orphan. She and her brother Wilfred befriend Janet Preece, a victim of Dunstan's premarital escapades. The truth about his character emerges, and the marriage breaks up. Hugh Murray, a Scots laywer, who had foreseen some such outcome, tries to bring the couple together; but just before Leslie arrives for a reconciliation scene, Dunstan drinks poison.

When John Hare, hoping for another "Court" farce, asked Pinero for a play to open W. S. Gilbert's new Garrick Theatre, this is what he was offered. Such was Pinero's reputation that he accepted it, though he did persuade the playwright to soften the ending by allowing Leslie to arrive in time to prevent Dunstan from taking the poison. In this way, through a reputation founded on farce, Pinero was given the opportunity to establish himself as a serious dramatist.

An epitome of Pinero's treatment of this theme in his plays can be found in the ending of Act II of *Mid-Channel*. Theodore and Zoe Blundell fall foul of the shoals in "mid-channel"— that is, the middle of married life. They part for a time. During that time he takes a mistress, she a lover. But they want to be reconciled. A friend, Peter Mottram, brings them together. Theodore confesses his affair with Mrs. Annerly, asks for, and receives, forgiveness. He then starts questioning Zoe's relationship with Leonard Ferris, driving her farther and farther, until at last she says: "Theo—I've forgiven you; forgive me." This however, he cannot do. ("I must have some advice about this.") He says it is impossible for them ever to live under the same roof again under any conditions. ("The cases are as far apart as the poles.") So Zoe, like Paula Tanqueray, is driven to suicide, not because of what she has done (for Theodore has done the same), but because of the attitude of others to it. This is the Tragedy of Reputation, in the acute case of the Double Standard. Here Pinero shows "the very age and body of the time his form and pressure."

In this core of his strength lies a principal reason for Pinero's present neglect. Despite the implications of, for example, the deodorant and furniture polish advertisers, we today care far less "what people will say" than did our fathers and grandfathers, and most of us fully share Pinero's abhorrence of a social ethos which offers forgiveness to man and not to woman for the same offence. The society in which and for which he wrote did not share his view, and his plays thus not only reflected, but criticized the society which constituted his audience.

> When he (the playwright) can stab people to the heart
> by shewing them the meanness or cruelty of some-

thing they did yesterday and intend to do tomorrow, all the old tricks to catch and hold their attention become the silliest of superfluities. . . . When you despise something you ought to take off your hat to, or admire and imitate something you ought to loathe, you cannot resist the dramatist who knows how to touch these morbid spots in you and make you see that they are morbid. The dramatist knows that as long as he is teaching and saving his audience, he is as sure of their strained attention as a dentist is, or the Angel of the Annunciation. . . . It is the technique of playing upon the human conscience; and it has been practised by the playwright whenever the playwright has been capable of it.

Thus Shaw upon Ibsen. Equally well it might have been upon Pinero. The first editor of *The Profligate* reminds us that when that play was written, "Ibsen was still, as far as England was concerned, an exotic of the library." Pinero was not just another Ibsenite. Shaw, with his blinkered, *Doll's House*, thesis of the Quintessence of Ibsenism, admired Ibsen for qualities he could equally well have found in Pinero.

Pinero, like Ibsen, "showed us ourselves in our own situations." Neither does so today, and we must look for other qualities to account for Ibsen's perennial popularity and universality—qualities of "poetry in the language of everyday life," of imaginative depth, of symbolism growing organically out of the soil of naturalism. These qualities were lacking in Pinero. He was a conscious artist, never, it would seem, possessed by his unconscious. His wonderful control of language was limited to naturalistic dialogue: he never even mastered the art of writing readable stage-directions, and consequently his reputation suffered from book publication of plays. His finest character creations, even the fascinating heroines of his latest great plays, *Letty, Iris,* Helen in *The Thunderbolt*—are individuals, firmly rooted in their own times and ways, and lack the universal qualities which enable Mrs. Alving, and even Hedda Gabler, to remain alive for us in a changed society.

Pinero moreover deliberately limited the imaginative interpretation of his plays by the use of the *raisonneur*. The *raisonneurs* (Peter Mottram in *Mid-Channel*, Cayley Drummle in *The Second Mrs. Tanqueray*, Hugh Murray in *The Profligate*, and many others) speak for the author, steer us through the plays underlining his intention, determining our viewpoint, and limiting the meaning to that which the author consciously intended. We find no *raisonneurs* in Ibsen: any character who appears to be one soon turns out to be something altogether different.

Because of his peculiar contribution to drama, Pinero is also a distinct influence upon the dramatists who were his younger contemporaries, and many plays commonly regarded as Ibsenite can more properly be seen as deriving from Pinero and his Drama of Reputation. Among these are Granville-Barker's *Waste* and some of Galsworthy's (e.g. *Loyalties*): indeed, even when they deal with other themes, Galsworthy's plays often, in structure and method, owe more to Pinero than to Ibsen. The Drama of Reputation did not survive the Great War, and Pinero's subsequent work did nothing to enhance his name; the genre he had virtually created had ceased to be relevant to the "age and body" of the new times. But now that the society in which he wrote is two world wars away from us, remote enough to be not merely old-fashioned, the time has come for a revival of his great grim dramas, which reflect with some nobility an age that has gone, and offer the theatre some of the most rewarding parts ever written for women. (pp. 14-17)

Cecil W. Davies, "Pinero: The Drama of Reputation," in English, Vol. XIV, No. 79, Spring, 1962, pp. 13-17.

WALTER LAZENBY (essay date 1972)

[*In the following excerpt, Lazenby examines Pinero's theory and practice of stagecraft and his critical reputation.*]

Recognizing the desire of predominantly middle-class audiences to see themselves and their values reflected in plays, Pinero evolved a theory of playwriting to satisfy this "intellectual and spiritual" need, as he called it. In some other age, he acknowledged, this need might not prevail, and his form would not be right. He posited a moral function for the playwright and thought that, in his own age, his finest task was to give "back to the multitude their own conceptions illuminated, enlarged, and, if needful, purged, perfected, transfigured." "Multitude" implies the broadly constituted late-Victorian audiences, including aristocrats and commoners; but, as Pinero's practice shows, he did not mean merely to defend the idols of the tribe. The words "illuminated, enlarged" imply the heightening of effect which is necessary even in the most Realistic plays. The significant phrase "purged, perfected, transfigured" shows that by 1895 Pinero had embraced the moral aim—a "modernist" one—of exposing the souls of playgoers, leading them to self-evaluation and bringing them, in Shaw's later words, to a "conviction of sin." Unlike Shaw, Pinero did not characteristically polemicize or propagandize; he was content to "give back." Shaw spoke scornfully of *belles-lettres* and addressed his plays to a pit of philosophers; Pinero called what he practiced "Dramatic Art" and aimed at a much more inclusive public.

Granted that Pinero wanted to interest a great number of people and, in a sense, to provide what was demanded, he thought that the drama ought to be as artistic as possible. It had legitimate ways of arousing interest that were distinct from those of the novel. In this connection, in his essay on Robert Louis Stevenson, he made a distinction between *dramatic* and *theatrical* talent. The first, as he defined it, is a general ability to "project characters, and to cause them to tell an interesting story" in dialogue, but tell it in such skillfully-devised form and order as shall, within the limits of an ordinary theatrical representation, give rise to the greatest possible amount of that peculiar kind of emotional effect, the production of which is the one great function of the theatre."

Pinero also distinguished between the two parts of technique, *strategy* and *tactics*. The first is the more general laying out of the story; the second is "the art of getting . . . characters on and off the stage, of conveying information to the audience. . . ." The strategy employed by the dramatist is to some extent shared with the novelist, but the tactics belong to the art of the theater alone. Attacking Stevenson for thinking that tactics necessarily falsify life, he defined the modern dramatist's problem as "nothing else than to achieve the *compression* of life which the stage undoubtedly demands *without* falsification. . . . It is the height of the author's art, according to the old maxim, that the ordinary spectator should never be clearly conscious of the skill and travail that have gone to the making of the finished product." He knew well that contrivance was a necessity and that, like acting, the playwright's art could imitate but not reproduce life.

He further elaborated his version of the Realist's credo in specifying that the ideal play should be "closely observant in its portrayal of character," but he turned away from extreme Naturalistic effects by stipulating that it be "stirring in its development" and "dignified in expression." On the whole, it should convince the spectator (presumably through settings as well) that the events are not beyond his possible experience of life.

This theory effectively accounts for Pinero's practice in all the genres. As a strategist, he always tried to give his plots stirring development. He recognized his audiences preoccupation with reputation and with the mating game, and he therefore made these the cornerstones of many plays. The climaxes in *The Notorious Mrs. Ebbsmith, The Benefit of the Doubt,* and *The Gay Lord Quex* were so strong that the plays could be identified for a time by reference to the Bible-burning scene, the listening scene, and the bedroom scene. He relied heavily on the reversal (peripety) to stir spectators, not always one major reversal but often a series of smaller ones. In his best plays, these reversals grow out of and express the characters' oppressive inner struggles and establish the logic of events. Like Ibsen, he transcended the scheme of the "well-made" play by mastering it and then by rendering its superficialities obsolete.

Independently, Pinero worked out variations of a three-track plot scheme which did workmanlike service, hardly more, except in two plays. In *The Second Mrs. Tanqueray* and *The Notorious Mrs. Ebbsmith,* the triplicity of the stories broadens the applicability of the themes, almost allegorically repeating the frustration and unhappiness in marriage. Later, he fashioned more classically simple plots for *His House in Order, The Thunderbolt,* and *Mid-Channel;* and he used seemingly insignificant actions and objects symbolically with quiet effectiveness and economy. But many of the plays begin better than they end, giving rise to the quip that the maxim *respice finem* ["look to (consider) the end"] applies to Pinero in a new way.

In tactics, Pinero gradually gained competence to produce naturalness. One can trace with delight these steps forward in Act One of *The Squire,* the opening of *The Weaker Sex, The Magistrate,* Act Two of *The Profligate,* and Act One of *Lady Bountiful.* By 1892, he was a master at arousing interest and in foreshadowing. And, though he expended vast ingenuity and cleverness on exposition in his mature plays, he said, ". . . when an exposition cannot be thoroughly dramatized . . . it may best be dismissed, rapidly and even conventionally, by any not too improbable device . . ." as in *Mid-Channel.*

In the service of naturalness, Pinero gradually worked away from conventional techniques, making a major contribution to modern English drama when he discarded the old-fashioned soliloquy and aside. To maneuver his characters into place, he tactically relied on the assumption that a table was always laid in the next room; his characters characteristically enter from a meal or exit to consume one; and, like Chekhov's, they often "sit down to supper" on the stage. This technique is more than a logical way of motivating entrances and exits; for it accords with Pinero's linking eating with frustration and disappointment of hopes, which describe the condition of man; and it occasions quiet, natural talk and action, rather than catastrophes. His early experiments with mistaken identity and disguise (in *The Hobby Horse* and *Lords and Commons*) led finally to subtly elaborated presentation of role-playing as it disguises one's instinctual life or serves a code in such plays as *The Schoolmistress, The Amazons, The Princess and the Butterfly,* and *Trelawney of the "Wells."*

His settings also remind spectators that it is their world which they see behind the proscenium. A true Realist, he referred to actual streets and areas of London; and he reflected myriad aspects of modern life through his choice of settings. His actions take place in a variety of locales: a gymnasium, a manicurist's parlor, a boat-house, a photographer's studio, a boudoir in an aged country house, a gentleman's study with a shaving closet, restaurants, the theater itself, and others. Some of these settings, notably Letty's boardinghouse rooftop and Overcote Park, are tinged with "fancy and romance," which Pinero thought had "immortal rights" in the drama. Interior sets are always arranged with regard to architectural logic, and in *Letty* Pinero put almost a whole apartment onto the stage. This practice necessitates detailed stage directions; and many of them call for carefully controlled lighting effects—those of midday, late afternoon, or sunrise.

In drawing characters, Pinero followed his own dictum and was "closely observant." He modestly attributed his success to his "small powers of observation." When he first drew characters who were not immediately recognizable as entirely good, he was regarded as a cynic; but he persisted in observing human nature and in reporting what he saw. Perhaps he agreed with the French curate in his early play *La Comète* who said, "We can learn more from the erring than from the circumspect." He wanted to "paint man man, whatever the issue," as Browning had wanted to do; and he said, ". . . from the truths of life as they appear to my eyes I have never wavered in any degree." In the drama prior to his time, characters had too often shown little motivation and insufficient relation to each other. Pinero gave his characters minds of their own, and he made them listen and react to each other.

Even in forgivably repeating certain types of characters (in the process of writing fifty-seven plays), Pinero provided them with fresh differentiae. Beginning with stereotyped "low" characters, he moved to more honestly circumstantial portraits; but he retained the traditional device of personanyms, partly to avoid libel suits. One recurring type is the sophisticate, frequently identifiable as the ineffectual *raisonneur*. Another is the woman with endangered or lost reputation, often too idealistic in her outlook on the world, in her disregard for society's strictures, or in her hopes of starting a new life. His young men are mostly *roués*, his clerics are by no means stodgy or unbending, his youngsters are fresh and engaging. On the whole, he effectively presents a wide variety of characters reflecting various occupations and levels: doctors, lawyers, rectors, government officials, painters, novelists, dramatists, journalists, (one) photographer, manicurists, shop girls, and housekeepers.

As an apologist for women and as a student of their psychology, Pinero is at his best. Most of the titles indicate the prominence of women in the plays, even in *The Money-Spinner, The Squire,* and *A Cold June.* His women are usually comfort-loving and desirous of personal happiness, they seem always ready to act on impulse and to break away from rigid codes, and they frequently try to avoid hurting others. Lacking grand passions, however, they find the choice of a mate a hard one. They make their choices on the basis of money, manners, reputation, escape from boredom or middle age, or their illusions about these. Some are capable of unselfish renunciation.

Because Pinero wrote "dignified" dialogue, some have regarded it as too literary; because it contains slang and topicality, others have considered it unliterary. Neither assumption is warrantable. He sensibly realized that fine speeches alone do not make a good play: "The literature of a play I understand to be contained in the development of character and the suggestion of the unwritten portions—those which, by stimulating the imagination, suggest all that the novelist would describe. Really literary dialogue, if you must use the word, is that in which the right word always appears in its right place, and conveys its exact meaning with reference to the evolution of the dramatic idea." By his own standard, then, much of his dialogue has a distinguished literary quality; but, when he was asked once whether he thought that his plays were literary, he replied, "Heaven forbid! More dramatic authors have died from literature than from any other cause." His practice reveals that he recognized the subsidiary and integral role of diction in creating character, that it must be in keeping with the data regarding the character who speaks. He would have faulted Wilde for his excrescences of wit that are not integral to consistent character development. There is engaging wit in Pinero's plays, but it is never allowed to take on unnatural brilliance or to supersede character delineation.

Doomed to near oblivion in recent years, Pinero may some day receive a fair judgment of his place in English literature. By then, thorough studies of more of his contemporaries and standard histories of the period will have been written; and more of his best plays may have been brought back to theater repertories. Some sixty years after the onset of his obscurity and nearly forty years after his death, revaluation of his accomplishment seems overdue; and there are a few signs that it will be forthcoming: the appearance of some doctoral dissertations on Pinero; recent revivals of several of his plays in England, especially at the Chichester Festival; successful revival of *Trelawney of the "Wells"* in New York (1970); and reissue of Hamilton's standard four-volume collection of eight of the plays (1967). At present, only a tentative assessment of his enduring qualities may be possible.

It cannot be doubted that he did much in his time for the theater, its personnel, and its status. Building on Robertson's reforms, he cultivated a full-blown Realism beyond which none of his important contemporaries went, except perhaps Galsworthy. At the very least, this aspect of his work did away with the old unrealities of the mid-Victorian stage. For actors and managers, Pinero brought good fortune in the form of challenging and interesting roles and successful productions. Mrs. Patrick Campbell and Irene Vanbrugh had their initial acting successes in his women's roles, and John Hare and George Alexander became identified with typical Pinero parts. And Eleonora Duse and Sarah Bernhardt, the greatest actresses of the time, won acclaim as Paula Tanqueray. Pinero practically sustained the Court Theatre with his farces and the St. James's through thirty-five years and two managements; and his productions of *Sweet Lavender* at Terry's and of *The Profligate* at Hare's Garrick were landmarks, not to mention the production of *The Second Mrs. Tanqueray* at the St. James's. As one writer too slightingly put it, he "kept the theatres open."

He participated in the emergence of the modern director by staging his own plays; and, in doing so, he jealously guarded the prerogatives of the author. Thus he enhanced the status of his calling. According to Hamilton, before Pinero's time audiences went to the theater to see great actors; after his time, they went to see good plays.

Pinero was the leading figure in what Jones has called the Renaissance of English drama after 1890; and, according to Harley Granville-Barker, he did most to make the theater of the 1890s. Without Pinero's groundwork, it is doubtful that Wilde would have had a form into which he could readily pour his brilliant wit. Though audiences were ready to accept sophisticated comedies, Pinero recognized their readiness before Jones, who, also starting in the theater in the late 1870s, wrote melodramas until about 1890.

Aside from Pinero's importance in his own era, he must in the long run be recognized as having attained high artistry in a variety of genres. He unabashedly wrote pure farce, thereby purging it of the tendency to disguise itself in sentiment; and he also strengthened the old form through his genuine concern for character delineation. He cannot be outranked as a farceur by any other English writer; not even Shakespeare consistently expended on this form the care and art which went into the Court Theatre farces or achieved such thoroughly satisfying results. Separately, Pinero embraced the comedy of delicate sentiment, well before Barrie did; but he also broadened its form to admit a subtle irony. His *Trelawney of the "Wells"* will likely be revived no longer than T. W. Robertson's plays, which it gently mocks. Pinero wrote sentimentalized comedies of manners before Wilde did, but he later turned to a more rarefied style which deemphasized the sentiment lingering from the eighteenth century. As a sophisticated comedist, he may be found to rank near the top. Divorcing seriousness from melodramatic sensationalism and sentimentality, Pinero pioneered in the form of the modern problem play, in which naturalness and objectivity made his seriousness all the more convincing. Among the problem plays, *The Thunderbolt, Mid-Channel,* and the perennial *The Second Mrs. Tanqueray* can be favorably compared with some of the best modern plays. Pinero was the first Englishman to attempt modern prose tragedy—a genre which Shaw did not undertake. Of course his critical fortune will rise and fall, in some measure, with that of Realism, the mode to which he committed himself.

Undoubtedly, Pinero lacked Shaw's intellectuality, Wilde's vivacity, Galsworthy's broader social concerns, and Jones's evangelism in the cause of a new drama. But he also surpassed Wilde and Jones in breadth and flexibility; and, unlike Galsworthy, he avoided the practice of dealing with specific abuses in contemporary society—a practice which almost always guarantees obsolescence as soon as the abuses are corrected. At their best, his plays reward study and deserve to be revived; they contain near-perfect craftsmanship of a dedicated artist, give insight into an attractive era as social history, hold the interest of persons who are remote from it, and express a view of life at least as sound as that of most Realists. After readng them, one hopes that Boas's statement [see Additional Bibliography] concerning Pinero will hold true: "Fashions change in the theatre, but the work of a single-minded master-builder can never become wholly obsolete." (pp. 149-56)

> *Walter Lazenby, in his* Arthur Wing Pinero, *Twayne Publishers, Inc., 1972, 173 p.*

EDMUND J. MINER (essay date 1976)

[*In the following essay, Miner discusses Pinero's use of the conventions of Naturalism in his dramas.*]

When the name of Sir Arthur Pinero arises in discussion today, one thinks of this or that recent revival of *The Magistrate* or *Trelawny of the "Wells,"* that charming little period piece which captures so well the language and spirit of the London stage in Tom Robertson's pioneer days. Pinero's triumphs of his major period (1893-1909), his "daring" forays into the new territory of naturalistic domestic drama, are all but forgotten. It is to be hoped that one day television will be the vehicle by which the better of these plays—*The Thunderbolt, Iris, His*

House in Order, for example—will be resurrected for devotees of the Victorian theatre. Certainly it is regrettable that Pinero revivals are invariably confined to such "safe" but innocuous offerings as the first of his Royal Court farces and the sentimental story of Rose Trelawny.

Anyone who has read extensively in this dramatist cannot have failed, however, to observe the importance of the Court farces in his work as a whole. One rather remarkable feature of Pinero's more mature work is its peculiar basis in the original formula he adopted for the farces which started him on his way to commercial success and contemporary critical acclaim. For whether we consider his initial radical departure from farce-comedy to have been *The Profligate* or *The Second Mrs. Tanqueray,* the fact remains that Pinero never really abandoned his formula of "possible people doing improbable things." As the years passed, his formula became more consciously an expression of what might be called "conventional people doing unconventional things." Most of his people, despite their many serious defects of character, observe those particular conventions which ensure their social acceptance. At some crucial moment in their lives, though, they engage in activities which, considering the conditions of their environment, are unconventional, and hence "improbable" for people in their position.

Together with this evolving farce formula, certain other elements—all associated with the power exercised over the individual by the conventions of society—are enduring characteristics of his work: the preoccupation of the individual with preserving her reputation; her inevitable failure to protect or enhance it, that is, to maintain the appearance of respectability; and the realization of the futility of struggling further against the stern moral code in control of her destiny. The first of these is undoubtedly the dominant theme of Pinero's drama; the second reflects the dramatist's cause-and-effect pattern, for the failure to preserve one's reputation is usually the direct consequence of erroneous decisions and flaws of character; the third element is an expression of Pinero's own deterministic outlook on life. If one fact emerges clearly from his plays as a whole, it is that of the futility of striving to overcome the prejudices and taboos prevailing in society.

There is no doubt that Pinero's view of life tends to be realistic rather than romantic or idealistic. He stresses the unpleasant aspects of existence, though without falling into the error of thinking that life offers man no compensations along the way. Nevertheless, it is a very limited happiness which the more fortunate of his characters achieve. Three protagonists, in fact, commit suicide out of frustration, and a fourth dies shortly after marrying the man she loves. Agnes Ebbsmith has her idealistic dreams shattered without even the satisfaction of seeing the woman she has wronged reconciled with her husband. Helen Thornhill in *The Thunderbolt* is forced to leave her favourite branch of the Mortimore family in an atmosphere of strained relations. Letty Shell finds a certain contentment in marriage with someone from her own station in life, but she can never forget her idyllic romance with Nevill Letchmere. In *The Enchanted Cottage,* Pinero's major excursion into fantasy, Oliver Bashforth escapes his intolerable relatives, and finds love and understanding in Laura Pennington, but he must suffer the disappointment of learning that he and Laura have not really been miraculously transformed in appearance. In *The Benefit of the Doubt* Jack and Olive Allingham are reunited—unfortunately—while Theophila retreats to the Cloys' residence to begin her long journey back into "respectable" society and a dubious happiness with Fraser of Locheen. Most of the central figures experience frustrating disillusionment because of the discrepancy they observe between their aims and their achievements, whether as a result of their own mistakes and imperfections or of the social pressures of their environment. Agnes Ebbsmith, for example, is deluded into hoping that she and Lucas can achieve an idyllic union free of physical love, that society will not intrude upon their peace, that at the moment of decision Lucas will choose to stay with her rather than agree to a hypocritical reconciliation with his wife. In the end, Agnes arrives at a better understanding of herself, Lucas, and the society in which she lives, but the experience is a painful one. In the final analysis, Agnes is thwarted by her social environment, for the Duke of St. Olpherts' strategy is the determining factor in her ultimate fate, and he more than anyone else in Pinero's drama personifies late Victorian society with all its outward respectability and moral rectitude, and all its inner hypocrisy and ruthlessness.

The determinants customarily found in naturalistic drama are of many kinds, but perhaps the chief are heredity, environment, biological urges, psychological needs, or conditioned reflexes. Naturalists see man's fate as determined by such factors, either individually or in combination, although they vary in their assessment of the extent of man's freedom of choice. Even in naturalistic drama the failure of a character to gain control over the conditions affecting his life may be due to errors of judgement and his own personal imperfections.

Arthur Pinero can best be described as a limited naturalist, not only because some of the qualities that make for a realistic portrayal of life are not found consistently in his work, but also because in his philosophic determinism he emphasizes one specific influence, the social environment—and that in an uncommonly narrow sense—almost to the exclusion of all others. For Pinero, the individual in late Victorian society is at the mercy of those self-appointed moral guardians who formulate the rules of conduct and impose sanctions upon those who violate them. A psychological or emotional imbalance has driven a woman like Paula Ray (the future second Mrs. Tanqueray) to promiscuity, but in her efforts to reform she encounters greater obstacles in society than in her own disordered nature. In Pinero, the conventions are stronger than any individual, and, indeed, stronger than any other force operating upon him.

There are, it is true, several instances in Pinero's plays of other determinants associated with naturalistic drama. Leslie Brudenell's violent reaction to Dunstan's exposure in *The Profligate* is one example of that conditioned response we should expect to find among the members of the middle class. Women like Zoe Blundell and Theophila Fraser (in *Mid-Channel* and *The Benefit of the Doubt* respectively), because of their failure to find companionship in marriage, appear to have some psychological need to seek compensation in the constant attendance of unattached males—a need urgent enough to warrant risking their reputations. In *Iris* there is even the suggestion of an unnatural affection tying Fanny Sylvain to the heroine; she confesses to Croker Harrington: "Listen to that silly bird. It's the same with me—always has been; my heart thumps—thumps—thumps—whenever she approaches. . . ." This questionable emotional attachment, unconscious though Fanny may be of its true nature, serves to explain her excessive concern over Iris's friendship with Laurence Trenwith. In the same play, Croker Harrington's insane devotion to a woman who has made so little return for all his good offices represents an emotional need to create a relationship with Iris that will fill the void left by her refusal to marry him. And Aubrey Tanqueray's morbid and irrational obsession with his daughter's virtue is a determining factor in the failure of his second marriage, for his compulsion to overcompensate Ellean for Paula's deficiencies arouses his wife's jealousy. His state of mind is clearly evident in a conversation with Cayley Drummle:

> Ellean! What is to be her future? It is in my hands. What am I to do? Cayley, when I remember how Ellean comes to me, from another world I always think,—when I realize the charge that's laid on me, I find myself wishing in a sort of terror, that my child were safe under the ground!

There are instances, too, among the male characters in Pinero's drama—Walter Harmer, Theodore Blundell, Nevill Letchmere, for example—of biological urges propelling them to actions beyond their powers at times to resist.

Occasionally there are lines of dialogue, too, which express more directly Pinero's awareness of naturalistic determinants other than one's social environment. In *Iris,* Archie Kane assures the heroine that he has no intention of scolding her for extravagance since she was "sent into the world so constituted," and Iris seizes upon this remark to excuse her worldliness and moral cowardice: ". . . one is sent into the world shaped this way or that." Such instances of attributing moral lapses or defects to the influence of heredity or some form of predestination are relatively infrequent, and nowhere do we find a character who consistently espouses this naturalistic doctrine. Like expressions recur in much Victorian drama and obviously reflect a current fashion; even Lady Windermere on one occasion proclaims, "Life is terrible. It rules us, we do not rule it."

Regardless of the influence exercised from time to time by these other determinants, however, the overriding cause of man's frustration, in Pinero's view, is the inhibiting force of society's sanctions and restrictions. Throughout the dramatist's major period (1893-1909), there is scarcely an exception to the rule that a character's failure to control the circumstances of his life or to achieve an adequate self-fulfillment is due ultimately to some form of social pressure. Such pressure may be an impalpable force of opinion as in *The Second Mrs. Tanqueray,* or it may be embodied in a single individual like the Duke of St. Olpherts in *The Notorious Mrs. Ebbsmith.*

While there is no character who speaks out for or against the naturalist position as such, there are individuals who dispute Archie Kane's implication in *Iris* that the individual in society has little freedom of choice or decision. The majority of the heroines, in fact, would tend rather to agree with Bernard Shaw's Vivie Warren:

> Everybody has some choice, mother. The poorest girl alive may not be able to choose between being Queen of England or Principal of Newnham; but she can choose between ragpicking and flower-selling, according to her taste. People are always blaming their circumstances for what they are. I don't believe in circumstances. The people who get on in this world are the people who get up and look for the circumstances they want, and, if they can't find them, make them.

Obviously Zoe Blundell (*Mid-Channel*) feels that she and her husband have failed to make their own circumstances for a happy marriage, and she blames one early decision in particular—their agreement to have no children until they were financially sound—for the deterioration of their relationship.

Mrs. Patrick Campbell and George Alexander in the first production of The Second Mrs. Tanqueray, *1893.*

Similarly, Phyllis Mortimore (*The Thunderbolt*), despite the temptation to fall back upon the excuse of environmental pressures, is unwilling to take anything less than full responsibility for her criminal action.

Nonetheless, if Pinero's characters are often conscious of some degree of independence in their choices and decisions, it is still made clear through the development of the action that they are never completely free from the coercion of others and the influence of the world about them. Even Jack Allingham (*The Benefit of the Doubt*), who has little regard for the conventions or opinions of other people, succumbs to his wife's pressure sufficiently to destroy his chances of clearing Theophila's name once for all. Frazer's initial decision to forgo the London season is an obvious case of considering society's feelings ahead of his wife's; and his change of heart, far from being a fully independent choice, represents an attempt to placate his wife following her unexpected behaviour in Allingham's cottage at Epsom. Few characters in Pinero are heroic enough to withstand tears and recriminations, but fewer still have the moral courage to make decisions and stand by them in the face of the opposition mounted by those who represent the cult of respectability and a narrowly ethical code.

There is something defective about the personalities or characters of nearly all the major figures which disposes them to become involved in situations they are peculiarly unable to control: they do not venture into them merely by accident or for the sake of thrills and novelty. Pinero's characters fall under the power of that amorphous and hostile force known as Society. Once trapped, they further complicate their lives by committing errors of judgement, and their weakness of character becomes apparent in their tendency to despair. This is an understandable reaction, of course, in view of the irreversible nature of their decisions and the reluctance of society to forgive and forget. But the heroines in particular are so taken up with the importance of social esteem that there is nothing else worth living for once they have lost their reputations. Iris Bellamy surrenders to despair even when Maldonado offers to make some sort of amends by marrying her: "It's too late, I tell you, I'm down, beyond recovery. I've lost heart. I no longer care." Iris makes one last desperate attempt, however, to salvage something of her past relationship with Laurence Trenwith; but this, like Zoe Blundell's abortive effort to rekindle Leonard Ferris's romantic interest in *Mid-Channel,* only renders her spiritual fatigue more pronounced. The character of such a woman continues, meanwhile, to degenerate: even if most of the heroines revert to an outwardly respectable life, they are not better human beings for their experience. This fact, coupled with their sense of futility, underscores Pinero's pessimistic attitude towards his society.

Almost all of his heroines in the domestic problem plays show some such pattern as this. Paula Tanqueray, Agnes Ebbsmith, Iris Bellamy, Zoe Blundell, and Theophila Fraser reveal a deterioration at the close of their dramas, though in most instances the potentialities for unconventional or even immoral conduct have been clearly evident from the beginning. Zoe Blundell progresses from marital dissatisfaction and indiscretions through estrangement and adultery to suicide. Theo Fraser ends where Zoe began; fortunately for her, she is rescued in time, and Olive Allingham, her antagonist, is the instrument of her "salvation." Iris ends where Paula began—in prostitution. And in her disillusioning contest with Lucas Cleeve's family, Agnes Ebbsmith comes to the realization herself that the association with Lucas has had a pernicious effect upon her character.

Dr. Harmer's Holidays illustrates, on the male side and from Pinero's declining years, the same pattern of degeneration in a more pronounced form. Walter Harmer, a bachelor, is beset with serious personal problems arising from his maladjusted sex life: though admired by all who know him professionally, he appears to be incapable of eliciting any emotional response in the other sex. Torn between two determining forces in his life—the psychological need to establish a normal relationship with a woman, and the necessity of conforming to the rules of respectable society—he becomes increasingly sensible of his inadequacy as a human being.

As a result of his problems, Harmer develops a strong tendency to involve himself emotionally with his patients. Not satisfied with trying to cure Elsie Speed's chronic ailment, he makes an ill-considered decision to propose to her, partly out of pity for her situation after her fiancé breaks his engagement, and partly because he hopes through marriage to overcome his debasing habit of seeking out prostitutes. He wrecks his chances with Elsie by adopting too possessive an attitude and discouraging her from enjoying normal relationships outside. In his despondency, he loses all hope of curing his disorder and gives himself up to what proves to be his final bout of debauchery.

Modern psychology would probably find nothing implausible about a self-depreciating individual seeking fulfillment and approval through social action and occasionally straying away from his duties to satisfy his baser instincts. It is perhaps a measure of Pinero's intuitive grasp of human nature that such a discrepancy between a man's image and his real self—and the inner conflict that results from his attempts to reconcile them—should be more easily understood today than in the year of the play's first production.

It is quite evident that the individual's dominant virtue or defect has an important bearing in these plays on the extent to which he will use his already limited freedom of choice and on the nature of his decisions. There is some substance to the notion of several early reviewers that Pinero's plays illustrate the idea that character is destiny. Even in the sentimental *Lady Bountiful* it is Dennis Heron's independence of spirit which leads him to improve his prospects and become a suitable candidate for the hand of Camilla Brent. Helen Thornhill's magnanimity in *The Thunderbolt* induces her to surrender most of her rightful inheritance. Lucas Cleeve's weak resolve disqualifies him from devoting his life to popularizing liberal tendencies in *The Notorious Mrs. Ebbsmith*. And the shameful Mr. Panmure comes to grief because his sense of morality is not based upon any deep convictions. But the expression "character is destiny" must be interpreted with some degree of latitude in a discussion of Pinero's drama. Theophila Fraser tells Jack Allingham that

her "character's gone," and she adds: "And yours has gone too, Jack; only a man gets on comfortably without one." The word "character" is often used in Pinero, as in many other playwrights of the time, for "reputation"; and for Theophila, as for Paula and Zoe, reputation is destiny. Weaknesses of character may account for some of the unhappiness experienced by these women, but society passes sentence upon them without regard for their characters as such.

Pinero's point of view in his serious drama is more consistent than has often been credited. As Dunkel has said, it is "scientific in its emphasis upon cause and effect." In addition to reiterating in play after play that the individual's capacity for change is limited, that there is no escape for him in such a restrictive society, Pinero also emphasizes the fact that someone must pay for human errors. In *The Benefit of the Doubt,* Jack Allingham's conscience troubles him when he reflects upon Theophila's wretched state following the embarrassing interview at Epsom:

> And so, you see, after all, we've had our fun, and enjoyed it, and yet pay nothing for it! But, at the same time, we mustn't forget that in this world everything has to be paid for by somebody.

Jack, of course, has paid something: for one thing, he has lost Theo's respect. But Theo herself undoubtedly bears the chief burden of the debt. In *The Second Mrs. Tanqueray* everyone concerned pays dearly for his mistakes—Paula pays for hers in full—and much of the sympathetic response of audiences in this century has been due to the recognition that the payment seems to be exorbitant. But Pinero will not have it any other way: in this kind of society, sins against the moral and social proprieties come rather high.

Pinero's must be considered a limited naturalism for reasons other than his preoccupation with a narrowly interpreted social environment as the overriding determinant of an individual's destiny in Victorian London. Such reasons have to do with his use of those features, shared by naturalists and realists alike, which in combination result in a more authentic depiction of life as it is. Briefly, it may be said that Pinero displays certain limitations in his efforts to present the norm of experience from his own personal observations and with some degree of objectivity.

Sometimes he relies upon experience which he has not closely observed: Brian and Betty Gillbanks in *Child Man* leave one with the impression that he has derived his only knowledge of children from occasionally overhearing the prattle of some child brought to rehearsal by its actress-mother. In this instance, as is often the case with Pinero, it is the dialogue which betrays his unfamiliarity with his subject and weakens his claim to consideration as a realist of the first order.

The whole question of Pinero's dialogue is pertinent to any discussion of his realistic or naturalistic qualities, but it requires a much more thorough treatment than can be given here. What must surprise anyone who has read extensively in his drama is the critical disagreement over the merits of his dialogue. Perhaps the more hostile critics—F. S. Boas and George Rowell readily come to mind—find too literary a flavour in it; certainly, they do not consider it realistic. Fyfe, Ernest Reynolds, and Cecil Davies, on the other hand, are among those who find it commendable; and many actors, including Arliss, Maude, and Denys Blakelock, have spoken highly of it from personal experience. On the printed page, its quality varies from the unnatural, inflated style of *The Notorious Mrs. Ebb-*

smith to the more natural one of *The Benefit of the Doubt* and the best of the Court Farces.

In his study of Ibsen and Strindberg, Maurice Valency comments upon the difficulty writers have always encountered in selecting an authentic language for naturalistic drama:

> It would have seemed ludicrous in the theatre of 1875 to hear laborers and shopkeepers speak in the literary style of the salon drama, and revolting to have them speak the idiom of the street. In France, naturalistic dialogue was, accordingly, a literary compromise, a version of common speech tempered to the tastes of a polite audience. It was the Russian and German dramatists who first made a point of approximating the speech of real people in all of its non-syntactical splendor, yet neither Tolstoi nor Gorki, nor Holz, Schlaf, nor Hauptmann really went so far as to make actors talk or think quite like people.

It should not surprise one, then, to find Pinero, writing for a Victorian audience, resorting to a literary compromise. Unfortunately, he compromises too much, and his dialogue is undeniably too refined and syntactical. This cannot be fully excused on the grounds that Pinero, unlike most writers with naturalistic tendencies, chose to dramatize his conflicts in the drawing-rooms of comfortable homes. In fact, the conversation of his characters in polite society is at times less natural than that of his middle-class figures, especially in moments of high emotion.

There is, for example, a curious absence of passion in the domestic quarrel scenes of his major plays. For a dramatist who claims that "the emotions are stronger than the intellect," there is little evidence on such occasions that he has fully shaken off the influences of Second Empire writers like Augier and Dumas fils. If at times the exchanges are sharp, they are invariably polite. There seems to be a reserve which must spring either from an intellectual self-control or from long practice in the observance of the proprieties. Probably he was most concerned about the sensibilities of his audiences, as well as about their sense of decorum. Modern audiences, after an evening with Albee's George and Martha, would find the quarrelling of Theo and Zoe Blundell unbelievably restrained, although Pinero succeeds rather well in creating the atmosphere of tension which attends domestic bickering. The Victorian stage would not, of course, have been ready for anything like a George-and-Martha dialogue, and Pinero made use of the little freedom permitted him to suggest rather than show the bitterness of domestic squabbles. Even Maldonado in his violent tirade towards the close of *Iris* remains impeccably correct in his language. It is true he calls Iris a "rag of a woman," "a double-faced trull," and a "liar," in an unusually strong burst of vituperation, but on the whole he dismisses her into the street in a manner befitting a gentleman whose social position demands a nice regard for the proprieties.

It is difficult, too, in some respects to accept Pinero's characters as representative of the norm of experience. As a case in point, there is no character in the entire Pinero canon (apart, perhaps, from Georgiana Tidman in *Dandy Dick*) with anything approaching a genuine sense of humour. This is a strange omission for a writer of farces, especially in view of Pinero's own quiet reputable sense of humour, but the point surely is that he has failed to depict his society in its fullness.

A more important instance of this limitation is his tendency, as he descends the social scale, to treat his characters romantically, in a manner reminiscent of those early sentimental novelists who associated poverty and the simple life with innocence and virtue. When he introduces the lower classes, it is usually for the sake of novelty or contrast—for he obviously recognizes that they have a certain colour and picturesqueness lacking in the more genteel classes—or merely because they have become associated in his mind with the trend to greater realism. It is only rarely that he achieves any pronounced success in portraying the lower classes: his scenes in Lilian Dipple's room (*Dr. Harmer's Holidays*) are his best, largely because the dialect is more truly reproduced here than anywhere else in his work. In his handling of the poorer classes he does not focus attention upon their problems or injustices as the social realist does, nor does he dwell upon the real conditions in which they live. Instead, he obtains considerable sentimental mileage out of such characters as Lavender Rolt, her hardworking mother, and the improvident Richard Phenyl (*Sweet Lavender*); the destitute clergyman Noel Brice (*The Hobby Horse*); the good-hearted Veales (*Lady Bountiful*); Letty Shell's rooming-house friends; and the struggling actors and actresses of the Bagnigge Wells Theatre. Most of these, of course, actually belong to the lower middle class: Pinero almost never ventures into the regions of the desperately poor. But it is evident that in his portrayal of characters below the level of the upper bourgeoisie, his realism is in general not well sustained; this is the case, in fact, whenever Pinero attempts people or situations beyond his range of experience.

Pinero never portrays the sordid aspects of life with the unremitting fervour of a dedicated naturalist. But there are situations and motives which reveal a constant awareness of the meaner attributes of human existence. Always he tries to treat the matter with some degree of restraint, for it must be remembered that he depended largely upon the middle classes for his audiences, and these were the most intolerant of breaches of propriety in the theatres. Often he suggests more than he actually shows, as we see in his handling of Rippingill's erotic dancing doll in *A Wife without a Smile,* the adulterous affair of Zoe Blundell and Leonard Ferris, or Iris Bellamy's questionable relationship with Laurence Trenwith at Lake Como. He can afford to be less reserved in his portrayal of the Mortimores' greed, Roderick Heron's selfishness and ill-treatment of an amiable family (*Lady Bountiful*), and Mrs. Gaylustre's blackmail efforts to gain social prestige (*The Cabinet Minister*). But persons guilty of sexual irregularities, especially if they belong to London society, must be packed off to some European hotel, and their sins are merely alluded to on stage.

By 1924, though, when the conventions had been noticeably relaxed, Pinero cast aside some of his usual reserve. In *Dr. Harmer's Holidays,* with its Jekyll and Hyde motif, we encounter his only genuine excursion into the region of the sordid. Even here he stops short of exhibiting brutality or depravity. Despite the surprising innovation (for him) of presenting a scene showing the drunken doctor in bed with a prostitute, his treatment of their relationship does not go beyond the limits of suggestion. Such restraint is maintained throughout the play. The brutal murder of the doctor by the prostitute's associates is relegated to an episode off stage; as the killers enter the room the curtain falls, and the ninth scene is a brief tableau showing the room in disorder and "lying stark and stiff among the wreckage, with arms outspread and eyes staring upward, is Harmer's body." *Dr. Harmer's Holidays* comes closer than any of his other plays to the naturalists' ideal of drama as a kind of clinical case history. In the scenes involving Lilian Dipple and her friend Florence Portch, together with the underworld characters Crickmay, Kelk, and Alf Gorham, Pinero's objectivity and detachment are unusually well sustained. Moreover, he captures with considerable fidelity the feelings of repulsion and self-disgust which overwhelm Harmer when he sobers up and prepares to return to his medical practice.

Although as a realist Pinero understandably strives for some measure of objectivity, it is not surprising that as a naturalist he will betray at times his disapproval of those elements in society which have such a determining influence upon man's fate. It is clear, after all, that it is more difficult to remain objective when the determinant is social environment than it is when the determinant is some biological impulse or psychological need. Hence, in *Mid-Channel* Pinero is merely the observer when Theodore and Zoe Blundell go their separate ways to indulge in extramarital relationships; but he quickly becomes a critic of the existing social system when the double standard of morality places the burden of guilt on the shoulders of the woman and excuses the man altogether. Moreover, Pinero possesses satirical qualities as well as realistic ones, and the objects of his satire—usually the conventional upper middle-class and the aspiring commercial class—are responsible for most of the restrictions and taboos which oppress his individuals (especially his women) in society.

Pinero shares with most naturalistic writers a bias against middle-class manners and morals. Such plays as *The Times, Letty, Iris,* and *The Thunderbolt* show a decisive rejection of many of the material values of a commercial middle-class society, especially in their satirical treatment of the ineffectual attempts of social upstarts to "crash" higher society. Maldonado, the most successful financier in all of Pinero, rises above such parvenus as Egerton-Bompas and Mandeville only through his superior culture and his realistic appraisal of the defects of the English nation as a whole. He still retains enough middle-class values, however, to merit Pinero's disapproval before the drama closes. The practice of self-advertisement, which the dramatist found particularly reprehensible in the literary and theatrical circles he frequented, is satirized in *The Big Drum, The Times, His House in Order,* and *Child Man.* The cult of respectability is still a target for his scorn as late as *The Freaks* and *Dr. Harmer's Holidays,* both written in the 1920's. In such plays as *The Cabinet Minister, The Times,* and *The Notorious Mrs. Ebbsmith,* political expediency is found to be as common in the middle classes as in the upper—and generally more obnoxious. Intellectual poverty is evident everywhere, from the exclusive social gatherings of *The Weaker Sex* and *The Princess and the Butterfly* to the back-stage chitchat of grasping actresses in *The "Mind the Paint" Girl.* These and many other censurable features of English society receive his attention over a period of several years, but his sharpest satire is reserved for the social ambitions and shallow morality of the commercial middle class.

In *The Second Mrs. Tanqueray,* Aubrey does not repudiate his society's moral prejudice against a *femme déclassée* like his wife. And Cayley Drummle even advises him to launch his daughter in the same society for its advantages: "the opportunity of gaining friends, experience, ordinary knowledge of the world." It is always the victim of society who cries out against it—a Paula or a Jack Allingham. The observers of society, like Drummel or Croker Harrington, who as "raisonneurs" are thought by some to speak for Pinero, uphold the status quo. This circumstance might suggest that Pinero is a faithful supporter of the conventions of late Victorian society. But, although there are certain passages in which men like Hilary Jesson or Peter Mottram most certainly express some of Pinero's sentiments, it cannot be said definitely that any one character speaks consistently for him.

In *The Benefit of the Doubt* Pinero satirizes the very society which Cayley Drummle and Aubrey Tanqueray recommend for Ellean. In more than one ironic passage, Theophila's mother bemoans the unfortunate consequences of the lawsuit for the family's social prestige. Weeping, Mrs. Emptage warns: "Oh, oh, oh! how glad our friends will be!. . . Here's a triumph for our friends!" Her son thinks the world a "hideous mockery," and Jack Allingham regards it as a "damnable world." Fraser of Locheen, meanwhile, realistic as usual, tells his wife that her prized society is merely a "shabby little circle." There is considerable evidence that Jack Allingham reflects Pinero's views of society more accurately than any of the so-called "raisonneurs," and the reiteration of his sentiments by other characters in the play reinforces the conviction that Pinero is not always so objective and unconcerned about the ills of society as he has often been considered.

In *Iris,* for example, it is quite probable that Maldonado speaks for Pinero when he lashes out at English society as a "paradise only for the puritan and the hypocrite," a land of "money-worship, of cant and pharasaism, of false sentiment and namby-pamby ideals. . . ." Elsewhere in the play, so far as the dialogue is concerned, Pinero remains an observer of society rather than an outspoken critic: if there is any "raisonneur" element in Croker Harrington it appears to be somewhat muted. But for all that, the play contains more implied criticism than any other drama of Pinero's major period. [In his study *The New Drama* (1963)] Carl M. Selle has suggested that this play "raises the issue of whether Pinero, beneath his acceptance of the social establishment, was not aware that English aristocracy and upper bourgeoisie needed partial reform as national institutions." In *Iris,* to be sure, Pinero moves closer to the naturalists' position by criticizing the existing order more severely than usual. But he does more than this. With the fall of Iris he registers a serious indictment of a society which judges a woman's worth solely on the basis of her wealth and the superficial qualities which accompany it. And he rejects, more forthrightly than he does in either *The Second Mrs. Tanqueray* or *The Notorious Mrs. Ebbsmith,* a social establishment which sacrifices the welfare and happiness of the individual to preserve its own arbitrary rules and conventions. (pp. 147-59)

> *Edmund J. Miner, "The Limited Naturalism of Arthur Pinero," in* Modern Drama, *Vol. XIX, No. 2, June, 1976, pp. 147-59.*

ROBERT RONNING   (essay date 1977)

[*In the following essay, Ronning discusses Pinero's contributions to the development of English comedy.*]

Sir Arthur Pinero has long been considered by many critics as the premier realist of the modern English drama, that, having written *The Second Mrs. Tanqueray,* he was chiefly responsible for initiating a new form in England. But then, so goes the argument, he was passed by and rendered outdated as other English dramatists such as Shaw, Jones, and Galsworthy followed the realistic movement begun by Ibsen. This line of thinking, as I will try to suggest, has been misleading, for it places Pinero at the center of the avant garde while most evidence (his life, plays, and philosophy) points to the contrary. Pinero's most lasting contributions are in the development of native English comedy and the perfection of the English eccentric character for dramatic comedy. Pinero will probably be most remembered for his eccentric comedy and as the playwright who perfected this older but popular dramatic form which was the culminating step in a type of mass entertainment excellently suited to the Victorian stage. Most of his life was devoted to writing one or another form of native-born English comedy, a form he repeatedly developed through the creation of the English eccentric in comic farce—a curious and rather timeless type of character who had appeared and reappeared, even before Dickens on the stage, and in the literature of England for many years. With the eccentric as the centerpiece of his comic farce, Pinero's humor was indigenously English and his form distinctively original; in a similar achievement to Gilbert in light opera, Pinero's master of a form led the way—if not backward to an English comedy of manners—to a modern form of farce and, perhaps, a kind of twentieth-century English comedy of manners. In a sense, I am suggesting that Pinero is a father not of the serious drama of Shaw, Galsworthy, and Granville-Barker, but a father to the modern English comedy of Wilde, Maugham, and Coward.

Pinero was to shape and perfect the form, and, in effect, it marked the transition from Victorian to twentieth-century English comedy. The development of what I am calling English comic farce was an evolution of a popular and original comic form: it had its roots in Robertson's early comedies of plain domestic life, in Gilbert's farces depicting a world of cynicism and fantasy, and to a lesser extent in the French well-made play. Pinero developed the form and made it wholly and peculiarly English by the time he had completed the Court farces: *The Magistrate, The Schoolmistress, Dandy Dick, The Cabinet Minister,* and *The Amazons.* The first three are the best; in each the form is embodied in a most amusing and original central character. His comic farce draws its vitality from the peculiar or eccentric qualities of the principal character—an elaborately drawn, very English-type character—who finds himself caught up in most unusual circumstances. Pinero's eccentrics, paradoxically, are drawn from conventional Victorian society. It is Pinero's magic that he transforms an English magistrate, an impoverished aristocrat, and a village clergyman—types normally regarded as conventional, rather dull personages—into finely drawn and unusual comic creations. These droll characters are, debatably, at a level with the best in the tradition of English stage comedy. While eccentric comedy was prevalent throughout the nineteenth century, the traits of Pinero's eccentrics are a throwback to characters in the comedy of manners. Such characters as Lord Ogleby in *The Clandestine Marriage,* Mr. Hardcastle in *She Stoops to Conquer,* Sir Peter Teazle in *The School For Scandal* incline toward certain quirks of behavior—self-deception, playful deceit, role-playing, and self-dramatization. But they are peripheral characters in those plays, while Pinero's characters are at the center of his plots. Pinero uses these character quirks as earlier writers had, but whereas English comedy of manners reflected an age which, at its very least, leaned toward the decadent and amoral, the Victorian stage comedy projected, if not reflected, a world of duty, respectability, compromise, and good sense. Since the slightest misbehavior could undermine the image of the Victorian, Pinero uses his eccentric characters to invert the traditional forms of duty, respectability, and compromise which were the code words of the Victorians. Their misdeeds are minor, usually harmless, but the effect of such a rigid code of conduct on Pinero's eccentrics is nearly traumatic and the plot consequences are far reaching.

The pattern is repetitive but very effective in each of the Court farces. The touchstone is a seemingly conventional character who gets caught up in circumstances which result in his becoming a compulsive character. Critics have said that Pinero's farce characters are conventional people who do improbable things, and this is superficially the case. But this pattern or formula misses the point—the character, especially the eccentric, has little chance to act predictably or conventionally because he is carried away by his self-deceptions and role-playing within what he considers a very topsy-turvy world. In Pinero's comic farce, the recurring pattern shows a character—a magistrate, a dean, or a cabinet minister—who applies a steadfast logic to a very "human" situation, a situation which by its nature is open to moderation and compromise. But the eccentric character defies or ignores the human element and refuses to compromise; he continues a course, a collision course, that while it may be absurd and destructive, appears "logical" and consistent from the eccentric's point of view.

In the most notable examples of comic farce, the central characters are drawn into a predicament—the venerable Aeneas Posket in *The Magistrate,* the impoverished but snobbish Hon. Vere Queckett in *The Schoolmistress,* and The Very Reverend Augustin Jedd, D.D. in *Dandy Dick*—and from the inciting moments of the plays they proceed into a web of harmless deceptions and playful intrigue; they resist disagreeable circumstances with a dogged determination which surely would be unbecoming in ordinary, placid individuals. Mr. Posket might have chalked up as bitter experience his minor indiscretion with his stepson at the Hotel des Princes, cut his losses by giving himself up when the police raided the hotel suite, and salvaged his dignity after only minimal embarrassment. The Hon. Vere Queckett might have begun with less secrecy, might have been honest with his friends and less pretentious about concealing his poverty behind his wife's support; instead Queckett continues an elaborate charade as a means of preserving a pride and dignity which later he realizes he never possessed. Rev. Augustin Jedd might have settled on a compromise instead of foolishly agreeing to match donations of the church restoration fund, and might have checked his priggish concerns about the Deanery becoming tainted after the arrival of his sister and his old Oxford schoolmate, who stables his racehorse, "Dandy Dick," at the Deanery; but he continues a course of pompous self-deception in which he, hypocritically, tries to save the church fund by secretly betting on the racehorse—ending in jail.

While neither Posket, Queckett, nor Jedd's situation is ordinary, their curious reactions to it are partly a result of being innocent victims of chance and coincidence, and partly due to their own compulsive needs to follow things through, come what may. Their course has a kind of inner logic but its resolution is impractical and even asinine—and funny to us. They are perpetrators as well as victims of their actions. Posket assures his wife Agatha while they are hiding under the table at the hotel in Act I, that he is "entirely the victim of circumstances," and in the cheery dénouement, Posket makes his position quite clear when he tells Agatha that her boy "has been my evil genius!" In his defense he explains to his friends "when you have heard my story you will pity me," and find "your old friend a man, a martyr, and a magistrate!" Similarly, Queckett reaches a point in Act II of *The Schoolmistress,* when the combination of his friends' suspicions, the anger of the guests and the utter shambles of the dinner party, makes Queckett enter at one point with "his hair disarranged, his appearance generally wild," and conclude: "I can't help it! I am in the hands of fate. Arrange the table. I cannot help it!." As a snob as well as a bit of a dandy, Queckett is less repentant than either Posket or Jedd in the end, but for a time he believes that unless there is a solution to the flurry of mischief he and the girls of Volumnia College have caused—all on the premises of his wife, Miss Dyott's "seminary for young ladies"—that he "shall become a gibbering idiot!" While Posket's final blow is self-inflicted, Queckett is abused by an outraged father and by his own wife, both of whom attempt to assault him, the former physically and the latter verbally. The pattern of victimization and self-victimization is repeated with regard to Rev. Jedd, and though the dean is prone to overstatement, one of his first remarks from his cell in a country police station in Act III—that he is "the victim of a misfortune only partially merited"—is certainly justified, after having placed himself "in an equivocal position." Mistakenly arrested for arson and for poisoning "Dandy Dick," he sees his case thus: "In the eyes of that majestic but imperfect instrument, the law, I am an innocent if not an injured man." The point is that in order to clear himself of his alleged crime, Dean Jedd would have to reveal his "temporary moral aberration!", involving his dealings with the racehorse; he would return to the Deanery with his "dignity seriously impaired!" So unwilling is he to compromise his dignity—the dean refers to it as "that priceless possession of man's middle age!"—so shameful is his present condition, as he sees it, that a plan is contrived for his escape. Reason, judgment, moderation, and good sense are thrown to the wind—the dean is beset by a moment of irrationality. He is willing to compromise himself further in order not to be caught in a "compromising" situation. He is a compulsive character, compelled by an inverted Victorian code of conduct.

Pinero's magistrate, dandy, and dean get trapped in situations from which they "reason" they cannot escape without injury to their dignity and sense of decorum. Facing the predicament more or less head on, they tangle themselves into such knots that there is a temporary loss of ability to compromise as sensible, Victorian gentlemen—and compromise was a golden rule for a respectable Victorian.

The eccentric character enriches humor and this is a principal delight in Pinero's comic farce. Delight in the eccentric accounts for much of the pleasure to be found in earlier as well as later English comedy, and in order to appreciate the originality of Pinero's characters, it will help to look briefly at the state of characters in Victorian comedy prior to his time. In his early comedies W. S. Gilbert, among others, had used eccentrics and the device of inverting values was employed with very amusing results. Gilbert's comedy, *Topsyturvydom,* as the title suggests, dealt with turning around or inverting the standard codes of conduct so that vice becomes virtue, beauty becomes ugliness, and so on. In *Engaged,* Gilbert's sardonic characters engage solely in the pursuit of money, raise hypocrisy to the level of an art, and by their rather delicate cynicism and inversion of those same Victorian codes of duty and respectability, they too resemble the early comedy of manners. "This point of view and this dramatic material," Michael R. Booth says of Gilbert, "is embodied in a deeply ironic, graceful, and witty comedy" which had an influence not only on Pinero, but on the comedies of Jones, Shaw, and Wilde as well. Ten years later Pinero's development of this eccentric strain in nineteenth-century comedy shows more subtlety and believability, when his eccentric is set in a more respectable, middle-class scene. In such a scene Pinero's eccentrics become conspicuous in their inverting of values because the society the plays reflect was so acutely conventional ("Mrs. Grundyism" and the appearance of straightlaced conduct was the accepted rule), so the slightest deviations were noted, were often amusingly approved, or were just as often condemned. "The aesthetic conventions of the well-made play," John Russell Taylor

points out, "depended on the moral conventions of the society it was written about and for." And so too did comic farce, as a well-made play, grow out of eccentric conduct which depended on and was the result of a break in a stable, highly ordered and disciplined society. Eccentrics, by definition, depart from the norm; Pinero's eccentrics find themselves placed in compromising situations in which they swerve in off-beat, erratic movements away from the conventional and predictable.

If one searches the Victorian theater for comparable English comic farce and eccentric humor, one is hard put to find such consummate handling and skillful mingling of the comic and the eccentric as in Pinero's. Consider, for example, the famous and immortal *Charlie's Aunt* (1892), in which the humor of Lord Babberly's predicaments relies mainly on mistaken identity, chasing and hiding behind bushes, broadly defined character types, and the general knockabout of farce—in short, the hundred and one devices of claptrap common throughout the nineteenth-century theater. These were mostly the French devices of farce tidied up for an English setting (and audience); comic wit and repartee, not to mention development of character, eccentric or otherwise, were the exception. Thus it comes as no surprise to find William Archer referring to "that gross supersaturation which we find in the lower order of farce— plays of the type of *Charlie's Aunt* or *Niobe.*" Pinero's best comic farces seldom depend upon the more obvious gimmicks such as changes and disguises in clothing, physical ridiculousness, outrageous byplay, or silly and improbable dialogue. Posket, Queckett, and Jedd may become soiled and a bit dishevelled, but they continue to wear the same suit of clothing— they do not exchange it for a clown's.

But if Brandon Thomas' *Charlie's Aunt* seemed like hack work compared to Pinero's, other of Pinero's contemporaries used a pattern of eccentric comedy, at least in part, and with varying degrees of skill. So that we find Wilde, Shaw, and Henry Arthur Jones creating unconventional character types by dint of the peculiar circumstances in which they find themselves. While Jones moved primarily along the line of melodrama, Wilde and Shaw delighted in devising comic as well as dramatic situations in which characters invert the standard codes of Victorian and Edwardian society. Yet, Wilde and Shaw may bear similarity to Pinero in form and technique, but their natures and intentions were so fundamentally dissimilar to Pinero that they could hardly be claimed his successors. They poked ingenious fun at the stuffiness and peculiarities of English temper—indeed, Wilde's *The Importance of Being Earnest* (1895), a trivial comedy (for serious people), in many ways not only succeeds but overshadows Pinero's comic farce—but both Wilde and Shaw were moving in another direction, Wilde in writing elegant society dramas and comedies, and Shaw in writing clever thesis comedies and dramas; Pinero's eccentric comic farce and manners comedy tradition would be continued by later, so-called "light" comedy playwrights.

Pinero's immediate successor was W. Somerset Maugham who had written *Loaves and Fishes* (c. 1907), an early work in which a clergyman—in the best Pinero tradition of eccentric conduct—is the object of comedy. Maugham's affinity to Pinero was not only apparent in subject matter, but also in his rather brittle tone, unusual characterizations, and deft, often witty, dialogue; and especially in his successful manners comedies of the 1920's—beginning with the light and trivial *Home and Beauty* (1919) and the elegant manners tone of *The Circle* (1919)—he showed a debt to Pinero and the tradition of English eccentricity. Perhaps Maugham's comment on his series of brilliant manners comedies, those showing conventional characters who become outrageous or who say outrageous things, will clarify the kind of comic sensibility which Pinero and his successors seemed to be developing. Maugham states that most of these plays were comedies:

> They are written in the tradition which flourished so brightly in the Restoration Period, which was carried on by Goldsmith and Sheridan, and which, since it has had so long a vogue, may be supposed to have something in it that peculiarly appeals to the English temper. The people who do not like it describe it as artificial comedy and by the epithet foolishly think they condemn it. It is drama not of action, but of conversation. It treats with indulgent cynicism the humours, follies and vices of the world of fashion. It is urbane, sentimental at times, for that is in the English character, and a trifle unreal.

Maugham recognized in his comedies the peculiar appeal to the English temper, and in referring to their indulgent cynicism he is acknowledging a trait of which Pinero had been accused very early in his career. Clement Scott had scolded Pinero in his early farces for writing such cynical pieces, all in an age which the critic confidently asserted was one of sentiment and ought to be reflected as such in the drama. Thus it makes sense that Maugham calls his comedies at once urbane and sentimental, for both qualities were firmly entrenched as part of the English character.

While Pinero and Maugham were mixing sentiment and cynicism in their work through a kind of controlling sensibility of the eccentric character, Pinero's view was essentially Victorian—a farcical tone results when his stuffy magistrates and deans attempt to extricate themselves from compromising situations—whereas Maugham's view was Edwardian and essentially modern—a manners comedy emerges as the characters reflect a freer, more brittle and urbane wartime and postwar culture. Neither resort to French bedroom farce, for that would go against the grain of the English comic temper. But they each show a difference and reveal the changing nature of English humor: Pinero's silly Mr. Posket struggles to preserve his respect and decorum in *The Magistrate* while Maugham's Freddy and Bill in *Home and Beauty,* for example, are rather earthy types who attempt to free themselves from the gentle clutches of the callous but amusing Victoria, to whom they are quite by misfortune both married. In such plays the tone is cynical and the characters alternate between quaint sentiments and drollery, and a series of boldface hypocrisies and indiscretions. Maugham rightly claims that his comedy is not one of action, but of conversation, and in spite of certain indelicacies of farce, Pinero's works are primarily literate, conversational pieces as well. In essence, both Pinero and Maugham's comedies show far greater similarities, including eccentric characterization, than cultural changes and theory might allow.

Pinero's next major successor, Noel Coward, shows a rather similar point of view, and Coward himself points to his own early plays and the influence of Pinero in the former's *Easy Virtue* (1924). Citing the plays of Pinero and Maugham in particular, Coward says of the earlier age: "This world was snobbish, conventional, polite, and limited by its own codes and rules of behavior and it was the contravention of these codes and rules—to our eyes so foolish and old-fashioned—that supplied the dramatic content of most of the plays that I have mentioned. . . . The narrow-mindedness, the moral righteousness and the over-rigid social codes have disappeared but with them has gone much that was graceful, well-behaved and

endearing." Coward respected such conventions; indeed, his dependence on them for scandalous and shocking effects in his own comedies and dramas was as intense as, though different from, earlier masters. In Coward's comedies we also see the same play of conversation rather than of action, the urbane, indulgent cynicism of sophisticated characters who are capable of flights of sentimentality as well. In *Private Lives* (1930), Elyot and Amanda embody those very contradictions which Maugham in his comedies had claimed as essentially English in character. Such works as Coward's *Private Lives* and *Hay Fever* are clearly connected to the line of Maugham's comedy of manners or "high" comedy, but not so apparent is the fact that Pinero's eccentric comic farce has also reappeared: the brawl at the end of Act II between Elyot and Amanda is only one of many instances in which Coward uses blatant farce. It is the equivalent of Pinero's venerable but dithering eccentrics committing minor outrages against good sense and decorum in a Victorian drawing room.

I have avoided trying to show that a strict continuity exists between Pinero, Wilde, Maugham, Coward, and other English comic writers such as Ben Travers—most of whom have written far and wide in various forms—but I have attempted to suggest that a common point of view and comic sensibility are present in their plays. Each accepts the world as it is—conventional and conservative, rather restricted and more than a trifle stuffy—and each proceeds to subvert that world by creating an ironic, urbane tone, and by introducing conventional characters who act as eccentrics and who commit little outrages in word or deed. This subverting of the system, this inverting of the conventions of polite society, has always been a purpose of humor and its peculiar manner in these comedies is very English. Indeed, Pinero's eccentric tone and its variation in his successors begins to take on dimensions of a national comic expression. This very point was examined in Hamilton Fyfe's 1902 study of Pinero, in which he discusses the extent to which Pinero's dramatic art was "essentially English in character," Fyfe claiming that the Victorians "have evolved, during the past generation, two art-forms which are distinctively English—the Savoy opera and Mr. Pinero's farces of character." In fact, the comic often does reflect the character of a nation as effectively (or at least differently) as the serious drama.

The implication is that Pinero's comic farce reflects an eccentric quality that is, in part, a feature of the national English identity; or, put another way, if humor teaches tolerance, then at the very least tolerance for diversity has been a traditional English sentiment, a condition often reflected in their drama. There appears to be, in effect, an eccentric sensibility that has grown out of timeless English eccentric—including Pinero's embodiment of the type—and this has given us a rich affinity in English comedy and a mirror of the manners and habits of an age. (pp. 51-8)

> *Robert Ronning, "The Eccentric: The English Comic Farce of Sir Arthur Pinero," in* The Quarterly Journal of Speech, *Vol. LXIII, No. 1, February, 1977, pp. 51-8.*

JOHAN R. HENDRICKX (essay date 1983)

[*In the following essay, Hendrickx offers a reevaluation of* The Magistrate, The Schoolmistress, *and* Dandy Dick, *noting that because the farce form afforded Pinero greater freedom to criticize Victorian morality, these works are more readily accepted by contemporary audiences than are his serious dramas.*]

Before he devoted himself exclusively to dramas treating women with a past, Sir Arthur Wing Pinero was a successful *farceur*. Unfortunately, his farces have been critically neglected in favour of such problem plays as *The Second Mrs. Tanqueray* or *The Notorious Mrs. Ebbsmith,* two dramas prominent in the history of the British stage because they offered the English audience a first glimpse of the "new" play of ideas in the Ibsen mould. Time has shown that *The Second Mrs. Tanqueray* owes nothing to Ibsen and everything to melodrama; Pinero was not a daring revolutionary, but a clever adapter of what was tried and true according to contemporary Edwardian taste. Consequently, these problem plays are now dated and of little interest to the modern reader. Yet Pinero's Court farces were until recently dismissed as mere theatrical exercises in preparation for the later problem plays. In this vein, Allardyce Nicoll's assessment can hardly be accepted today:

> The value of these farces for the development of Pinero's art rests in the experience they gave him in the building of plot and the requirements of stage speech. That they make no pretence to mirroring life naturalistically matters not at all; their importance is definitely theatrical. Through them Pinero learned the use of his chosen instrument.

Apart from the sentimental comedy *Trelawny of the "Wells",* the farces are in fact Pinero's only dramatic works to survive in the modern repertoire, and not without good reason. Pinero was the only English *farceur* to invent "a new formula for farce based on showing possible people doing improbable things" [Walter Lazenby, *Arthur Wing Pinero* (1972)]. He pushed aside the stock characters of the older farce, introducing recognizable figures of flesh and blood into the genre. Bringing out the inherent cruelty of farce, his dramatis personae are more than mere automata puppeteered by the playwright into a contrived situation. They remain believable people, not deposited but constrained by circumstances in an outrageous position.

Pinero knew the limitations of the old stereotyped farces of James Kenney and John Maddison Morton, and he burlesqued them successfully in his earliest farces, *The Rocket* and *In Chancery*. Unusual in Victorian farce, both plays contain references to contemporary events. In addition, the character of McCafferty, the stage Irishman, is almost ridiculed to death in *In Chancery*. All in all, however, these plays are slight, and it is only with his following play, *The Magistrate,* that Pinero reached his prime after nearly ten years of writing. *The Magistrate* was Pinero's first great success with audience and critics alike, as more than three hundred performances help to testify; it had been written at the request of John Clayton and Arthur Cecil, managers of the Court Theatre, who wanted something light to fit the bill.

This first success has all the smoothness of French farce, but not its immorality. With *The Magistrate,* Pinero brings "back to life the farce of character, the farce based upon incongruity, the farce which shows us in the most light-hearted and entertaining fashion, possible people doing improbable things." "[P]ossible people doing improbable things" is Pinero's credo for farce, and in the characters of Mr. Posket and the other members of his household, he fully realizes his ideal. One may question Posket's ready acceptance of his wife's story, in which she slices five years from her son's age; but Posket is presented from the beginning as a bumbling, good-hearted man who has trouble even condemning criminals in his police court—so why should he not believe his Agatha's tale? His soft-heartedness increases his agony when he has to condemn his wife and his sister-in-law to jail.

The Magistrate is not inhabited by lower-class people of early Victorian farce; rather, it is occupied by solid upper-middle-class citizens who fall lower, their tribulations provoking more mirth than the shenanigans of a mere cobbler. These upright characters are bound to the decorum which rules their class: all the troubles in *The Magistrate* stem from the characters' desire to uphold appearances of being moral. Posket accompanies his stepson, Cis Farrington, to the dubious Hôtel des Princes out of a desire to protect the "youngster"; Agatha Posket goes to the restaurant to save her marriage and takes her sister along to keep up appearances. In a perfectly logical avalanche of plot complications, all characters finally meet in the same room. Posket is a moral man caught in the semblance of indecorum, and to keep moral decorum intact, the poor magistrate, symbol of righteousness, must flee the wrath of his own police court. The characters suffer the indignities imposed on them by malicious circumstances: they are struggling with a too restrictive sense of class decorum.

The plot is built along conventional lines. The first act therefore introduces the dramatis personae and plants the situations which will eventually detonate in act two. In the second act, the private dining-room of a hotel serves as the locus where all the characters who should not meet bump into each other. The police raid at the end of the act causes a chain reaction that will force Posket to condemn his own kin to jail in the final act. The third act, featuring Posket's actions in the police court, is no mere unravelling of the plot, because new complications are added to the general confusion.

With its farce mechanism that mows down just and unjust alike, the construction of the play is French in origin, but it does not admit the cheerful amorality of the French farces: Posket does not want to deceive his wife; Charlotte is not unfaithful to her fiancé, Captain Vale. In a contemporary French play, the action of the second act would be set in a bedroom of the "dubious" hotel, not in a dining-room, and unclad characters would pop in and out of multiple doors. But the whole tone of *The Magistrate* is innocent, appropriate to the general domesticity of Victorian drama. Charlotte's unfaithfulness to Captain Vale consists in giving a pair of worked slippers to another man three days after her engagement; naturally, the domestic objects were given in all innocence.

Posket is the ideal victim of farce and that fickle goddess, Fate; he is hurled from his respected position into the abyss of humiliation and defeat through no fault of his own. In his fall, Posket drags with him his entire household: Agatha Posket has to pay a high price for her little deceit, and Charlotte suffers similarly because of the worked slippers. The physical beatings Posket undergoes are not gratuitous to the action, like comparable punishments in Charles Hawtrey's *The Private Secretary;* rather, they objectify Posket's mental agony and mortification. Yet it is Posket who introduces a sour note near the end of the play, when he acts the god of revenge and banishes his stepson to Canada. Nevertheless, the gloom is relieved: Cis does not mind too terribly because he will take his beloved Beatie with him. In short, Pinero's treatment of Posket's humiliation is one of the most finely balanced executions of farce in the nineteenth century.

Pinero's next success at the Court Theatre was *The Schoolmistress,* in which the author "portrayed another title figure symbolic of Victorian propriety and developed more fully the idea of people in real life playing roles, their true selves disguised." Miss Constance Dyott, the principal of Volumnia College for Daughters of Gentlemen, feels the strain of the age's rigid code of conduct. As a respectable woman, she cannot earn enough money to keep in fashion her penniless husband, Vere Queckett, a gentleman of total leisure. Because of the stern social code, she cannot even make her marriage public and has to forgo her rightful name, Mrs. Queckett. She is not the only one to suffer from the harsh Victorian conventions. Dinah Rankling, a pupil at Miss Dyott's school, must marry Reginald Paulover behind her parents' backs. Vere Queckett is a victim, too: as a gentleman he may not earn money, may only spend it, and is consequently always without it. When Miss Dyott sees a chance to make enough money to keep her fidgety husband happy, she takes on yet another name and identity. As Constance Delaporte, she will play the role of Queen Honorine in a new comic opera. In consequence of the Victorian code of conduct, she has three alternative identities: Miss Dyott, the respectable schoolmistress; Mrs. Vere Queckett, the dutiful wife; and Miss Constance Delaporte, the *opera buffa* queen. Only when she rejects the Victorian conventions does she integrate these three identities into one.

Miss Dyott's absence from the school to star at the theatre sets the farce mechanism going. By the end of the evening everyone's nerves are in shreds, and in the banquet scene of the second act Vere Queckett becomes the quintessential victim of farce: he is degraded by the pupil's blackmail from an elegant man of leisure to something of a pimp at Dinah's wedding-party. The party is the culmination of a general revolt by all the participants against the suffocating conventions of the time: Dinah opposes her father, Admiral Rankling, who does not even know what his own daughter looks like; the pupils revolt against the authority of Miss Dyott; and Vere reacts against the too dominating financial position assumed by his wife. When the school is accidentally set on fire, this revolt is forced into the open. Here Pinero creates one of the most striking images of farce literature, as Miss Dyott in full costume as Queen Honorine comes to the rescue of her tiny husband, Vere, and carries him bodily through the window down the ladder. With this image, the absurd is rendered plausible—the ultimate in the achievement of farce.

In *The Schoolmistress,* Pinero strikes a more bitter tone than he had in *The Magistrate.* Though the unravelling of the plot is traditional in that everyone is happily paired off, Miss Dyott strikes a blow for freedom by putting the schoolmistress to rest and continuing her lucrative role as Constance Delaporte: the Victorian figure of the stern schoolmistress has disappeared, the *opera buffa* queen reigns. Moreover, a cynical spirit pervades the play. It appears through Vere Queckett, who is quite happy to forgo his dignity as a gentleman for the extra money provided by the "fast" Miss Delaporte; and through the young girls of Volumnia College, who are not the innocent lasses of earlier farces, but already know about the lobster salad and pink champagne without ever having stepped out into the wicked world. In addition, the precocious marriage between Dinah Rankling and Reginald Paulover (just this side of puberty himself) is not the idealistic love to be found in earlier farce such as James Kenney's *Raising the Wind;* these two youngsters are spoilt children playing at being in love. However, Dinah's parents are in no position to lecture the couple, since the Ranklings have a loveless and shaky marriage.

The Schoolmistress thus makes a stronger indictment of the Victorian preoccupation with decorum than Pinero's more "serious" problem plays, presenting an almost Pirandellian concept of people wearing masks behind masks. But it would be reductive to notice only the darker sides of this farce, since the play is also a high-spirited romp at the expense of the pet peeves of Victorian England. Though the comedy is again French in origin, it is completely English in execution. The schoolmistress's direct address to the audience at the conclusion belongs to the native comic tradition, and both Admiral Rankling and Reginald Paulover are humour characters in the Jonsonian mould. Further, while the play can be interpreted as an attack on the Victorian worship of decorum instead of true morality, which Pinero does not really challenge, the unravelling of the final scene is a confirmation of the *status quo:* Admiral Rankling is quite happy to continue his unhappy marriage; the four girls are happily paired off into domestic bliss; and Miss Dyott herself is still saddled with her parasite, the gentleman Vere Queckett.

The successor of *The Schoolmistress* at the Court Theatre was *Dandy Dick.* Like its two prototypes, this play focuses on an embodiment of Victorian propriety brought to the edge of ruin through no fault of his own: the victim is the Very Reverend Augustin Jedd, Dean of St. Marvells Church. This righteous man is saddled with two undeanlike daughters, Salome and Sheba, who are more interested in fashion than in the states of their immortal souls. The girls, though apparently demure, go to some lengths to sneak off to a fancy dress-ball and bring disgrace to their "saintly" father. The dean himself, who does not allow card-playing in his house, is forced by capricious fate to place a bet on the horse Dandy Dick, partially owned by his "horsy" sister Georgina Tidman, known on the track as George Tidd. When the Reverend Augustin Jedd wants to give the ailing horse a bolus, he is arrested for attempted poisoning. Like his spiritual kin Posket, Jedd has to flee the revenging police, whose authority he himself upholds as a member of the establishment. Jedd is a man who has stifled within himself the sportsman of his Oxford days and allowed the rigidness of a dean to dominate his life instead. Much of the humour of the play arises from this dichotomy within the Dean's character.

As in *The Schoolmistress,* all the characters in *Dandy Dick* wear masks and pay lip-service to a code of social conduct in which they do not really believe. This glaring contradiction appears in the open at the beginning of Act Two, when the Dean's family lounge after a boring dinner. Everything seems at ease, but in revealing asides the family members betray their true thoughts: the Dean is thinking about his financial difficulties; the two girls are dreaming about the forbidden but alluring fancy ball; and the girls' suitors are nursing their hatred for each other. Only Georgina is lucid enough to observe the dichotomy between behaviour and thought, as she remarks cynically "(*after a few bars—looking round quietly*) Well, after all, George, my boy, you're not stabled in such a bad box! Here is a regular pure, simple, English Evening at Home!" Though Georgina is the one honest person in the play, she has to shed some of her personality in order to be accepted by the racing crowd as George Tidd: she must submerge her femininity to be taken seriously at the track; and yet when she finally breaks down and cries over Dandy Dick's burnt tail, paradoxically she finds love in the person of Sir Tristram Mardon, the co-owner of the horse.

The same hypocrisy is a feature of the minor characters as well. Blore, the perfect butler, is not beyond blackmailing his own employer; and Hannah Topping, though reassuring her husband, the Constable, that she is on his side, lets the Dean escape from jail. By means of these characters, Pinero shows his wit and inventiveness: the actions of the minor dramatis personae are far removed from the physical business and comic antics of the low comedian of earlier farces:

> To sum up in a few words, the qualities that give these [Court] farces their special merit are the substantial reality of the character-drawing—not of the central figures alone, but many of the subordinate characters as well; the natural manner in which the plot and situations arise out of the idiosyncrasies of the people; the easy humour and wit of the dialogue.

The language of the play sparkles like champagne and overflows with good-natured wit. All the characters use lingoes of their own, sometimes to hilarious effect. As a result, Pinero burlesques the use of contemporary language: Dean Jedd speaks inflated patter faintly echoing the pulpit; and Georgina joyfully expresses herself in the vernacular of the track to the consternation of her stuffy brother and fussy nieces. Yet finally, like all good farces *Dandy Dick* has a menacing and sometimes evil overtone. The Dean is quite happy to see his troublesome daughters married, though the girls' suitors are pompous asses and a far cry from the dashing gallants of an earlier decade: Lieutenant Darbey represents all the defects of the British Army which led to such catastrophes as the Charge of the Light Brigade; and Major Tarver lacks part of his liver, this deficiency effectively intensifying an already gloomy disposition.

With *The Magistrate, The Schoolmistress* and *Dandy Dick*, Pinero achieved the zenith of British farce during the nineteenth century. In these three plays:

> the characters for the first time have enough credibility to seem to resist the plot maneuvers. They have a past and a future; they have plausible motives; they exist in recognizable contemporary settings. Thus tension develops between plot and character, and the inevitable outcome seems more credible and logical. By imbuing the characters with some reality, Pinero reflected, but theatrically stylized, the actual life and manners of his time.

Pinero borrowed the machinery of French farce and transformed it with home-grown conventions:

> In a series of growing crises Pinero carries us onward from one ridiculous situation to another, indulging in the impossible certainly—for such is the way of farce—but retaining always a lively sense of theatrical values.

Pinero's other farces, composed in respites from his problem plays, do not belong in the same class with his three exceptional farces. *The Cabinet Minister* lacks a hounded victim of farce, the title character being a secondary figure; instead, this play gives us an ironic view of London society and its season. But the air is stale, and the work lacks the driving madness and whirlwind events of the previous farces. Pinero wrote his final farce for the Court Theatre, *The Amazons,* while relaxing from the agonies of *The Second Mrs. Tanqueray.* Labelled "A Farcical Romance" by the author, the play offers no novelty, especially in the tiresome humour characters of the sickly Earl of Tweenwayes and the Count de Grival, an unrelenting stage Frenchman. *A Wife without a Smile, Preserving Mr. Panmure* and *Child Man,* called a "Sedate Farce" *(sic),* are too slight to warrant any examination.

The Court farces deal with respectable people struggling in vain with restrictive social conventions. In Pinero's later drawing-room dramas, the same conflict results in tragedy for the principal characters. Pinero's attack on Victorian hypocrisy in his problem plays seems puerile, because he had to avoid giving

offence to the public opinion of his time: so the atheistic heroine of *The Notorious Mrs. Ebbsmith* embraces religion near the end of the play and thus expiates her "social" sins. Because farce with its apparently frivolous guise offers wider scope, Pinero was able to make a fuller statement about Victorian morality in his Court farces. The problem plays which deal with the inflexibility of the Victorian and Edwardian moral code and social decorum no longer hold our attention because, treated seriously, these conventions look childish: Paula Tanqueray's dilemma can no longer be taken seriously by the modern theatre-goer. In the farces, however, where the same conventions are ridiculed or exposed as silly, the conflict remains interesting to the modern viewer: Victorian propriety is treated as puerile. Consequently, the Court farces bear and deserve revival, whereas Pinero's more "serious" plays are confined to the theatre library. In the former, we find something almost equivalent to the finest French farces of Labiche and Feydeau; and among the private secretaries and the Brazilian aunts of his English contemporaries, Pinero's creations are giants among pygmies. (pp. 54-60)

> *Johan R. Hendrickx, "Pinero's Court Farces: A Revaluation," in* Modern Drama, *Vol. XXVI, No. 1, March, 1983, pp. 54-61.*

GEORGE ROWELL   (essay date 1986)

[*Rowell is an English critic and theater historian. In the following essay, he traces Pinero's development as a dramatist.*]

In most theatrical records the two suitors who woke the Sleeping Beauty of Victorian drama from a century's slumber were Wilde and Shaw, and the popularity of their plays in the modern repertory supports this view. But a dramatic critic assessing the state of the English stage in 1899 would have formed a very different opinion. Wilde's career as a playwright in effect lasted four years, during which he produced three diverting but flawed "dramas of modern life" and one comedy for all time, but his trial and imprisonment then banished his plays from the stage. By 1899 Shaw had written ten plays, of which only one had received a public performance in London. Had his cycling accident near Edgware in 1897 proved fatal, he would now appear in English theatre history as a successful critic and failed playwright. Both the press and the public at the end of Victoria's reign named as the leading English dramatist Arthur Wing Pinero, whose range and output placed him well ahead of his nearest rival, Henry Arthur Jones. Devotees of Hilaire Belloc's *Cautionary Tales* will recall the fate of that untruthful miss, Matilda, and may remember that the treat her aunt denied her was "to see that interesting play, *The Second Mrs. Tanqueray* / . . . A deprivation just and wise, / To punish her for telling lies."

Pinero's reputation as the masterbuilder of the new English drama was built on stout and substantial foundations. Born in 1855 into a London family of Portuguese origin (the name had been anglicised from Pinheiro), he followed his father into a solicitor's office but at eighteen threw up the law for the stage. Valuable experience in leading "stock" companies, notably the Theatre Royal, Edinburgh, and the Alexandra, Liverpool, led to his engagement at the Lyceum with Irving in 1876. It may be deduced that, like Shakespeare or his cherished Tom Robertson, Pinero was never greatly gifted as an actor. His most responsible assignment at the Lyceum seems to have been Roderigo, and though his Desdemona, Ellen Terry, observed loyally: "He was always good in the 'silly ass' type of part, and no one could say of him he was playing himself,'' it is not a leading role. Later at the Haymarket, Squire and Marie Bancroft entrusted him with Sir Anthony Absolute in their production of *The Rivals,* but his performance was generally judged to be ineffective, and this reaction may have contributed to his decision to give up acting (at the age of twenty-nine) in favour of full-time writing. The following year he wrote *The Magistrate* and achieved widespread recognition, both at home and abroad.

What his acting experience, first in the provinces and then in London's two leading playhouses, did provide was a command of the needs and scope of stage performance which was to distinguish all his best work for the next forty years. Though the standing of that work has varied, with once ''major'' achievements like *The Notorious Mrs. Ebbsmith* or *The Gay Lord Quex* suffering eclipse, and ''minor'' pieces such as the Court farces or *Trelawny of the "Wells"* growing in stature, that respect for the theatre which Pinero learnt under Irving and the Bancrofts has earned him a solid, even formidable, reputation ever since. Moreover it was the Lyceum under Irving and the Haymarket under the Bancrofts that helped to train him as a playwright as well as an actor. *Two Can Play at That Game, Daisy's Escape* and *Bygones* were three of his earliest pieces with which Irving filled out the Lyceum bill, and *Lords and Commons,* produced at the Haymarket while he was associated with the Bancrofts, one of his first full-length serious plays. Many actors aspire to write for the stage, some achieve a certan success, and a handful have confirmed that success. Pinero's particular achievement was to attain in his writing a human insight which as an actor he could not command but knew was lacking in the drama of the day.

While playing at the Lyceum and Haymarket he was also busy writing for other theatres and companies, notably two light-hearted pieces, *Hester's Mystery* and *Girls and Boys,* for the veteran farceur J. L. Toole, and another, *In Chancery,* for the popular comedian Edward Terry. But more significant was his work for the increasingly fashionable St James's (with which Pinero was to be associated throughout his career). Some of this work was routine adaptation from the French, but two early contributions caught the public's and critics' attention, not least for the opportunities offered to the redoubtable Madge Kendal. In *The Money-Spinner* she portrayed a wife prepared to cheat at cards to save her husband from bankruptcy, and in *The Squire* another wife concealing her marriage (and risking scandal) for her husband's sake. Both pieces are tentative and often trite, but the resolve to extend the range of character-drawing is apparent and points forwards.

Pinero's decision in 1884 to devote himself to writing produced handsome rewards over the next three years in the shape of his three major farces for the Court Theatre. *The Magistrate, The Schoolmistress* and *Dandy Dick* are distinguishable not only from other farces of the period but also from Pinero's own later work in this vein, like *A Wife without a Smile* or *Preserving Mr. Panmure,* even when designed for the same address and much the same company as were *The Cabinet Minister* and *The Amazons.* The first three Court farces have a lightness of touch and a respect for good intentions which is endearing as well as richly entertaining. Their humanity and warmth are especially apparent when they are compared with other favourite farces of the period. Adaptation from the French was the standby of most Victorian playwrights, from Nicholas Nickleby onwards, *Pink Dominos,* taken by James Albery from *Les Dominos Roses* by Hénnequin and Delacour, typifies the ''sophis-ticated'' article discreetly diluted for English consumption. Both *Pink Dominos* and *The Magistrate* propel married couples to clandestine assignments in a dubious restaurant, but Albery's farce aspires no higher than titillation, whereas Aeneas and Agatha Poskett in *The Magistrate* visit the Hôtel des Princes to save their nearest and dearest from distress.

Charley's Aunt, which like *The Schoolmistress,* focuses on an educational establishment, is energetically English, but if Brandon Thomas's work is all his own and clean as a whistle, it is equally shrill, which perhaps accounts for the public's readiness to hear it. *The Schoolmistress,* on the other hand, is the most delicate of Pinero's farces. While *The Magistrate* and *Dandy Dick* trace their situations within the framework of the majestic, essentially male, world of the Law and the Church, it is set inside the petticoat principality of Volumnia College, and much of the humour derives from the struggles of the menfolk to throw off their silken chains. The outbreak of the fire provides the male sex with a momentary advantage, but in the end feminine enterprise triumphs. Even the Admiral's wife mutinies, and whereas Poskett and Dean Judd are content to hush up their adventures and stuff the family skeleton back in the cupboard, Miss Dyott renounces pedagogy and glories in the disclosure that she is Queen of the Opera Bouffe. *The Schoolmistress* is also notable for letting youth call the tune. Although Miss Dyott gives her name to the play, she is absent for most of the crucial second act and the controlling force is really Peggy Hesslerigge, so that an apter title might be *The Pupil Teacher.* Pinero's manuscript reveals that Peggy even claimed the curtain speech but Mrs. John Wood, the Court's leading lady, evidently objected and could not be denied.

It is customary to hail Pinero's precision engineering in his farces and contrast its comic impact with the calculation and contrivance of the social dramas. Of course sound construction is essential if a farce is not to collapse from overloaded incident, but at their best Pinero's farces offer more than technical excellence. The range of their characterisation has already been stressed and the affection with which the characters are presented distinguished Pinero not only from Gilbert or Brandon Thomas but also from Labiche and Feydeau. The dialogue too has a quaint formality which contrasts eloquently with the familiar, functional note of earlier Victorian farce. In later, more oracular plays this note was to earn him charges of pompousness and artificiality, but here it counterpoints the development of the action. Even in emergencies the characters are never lost for words. When the guests in *The Schoolmistress* decline to listen to the Fire Brigade's *raconteur* while awaiting rescue by ladder, only Pinero could have provided the superintendent's protest: ''Really gentlemen, I must say I've never heard Mr. Goff treated so hasty at any conflagration,'' with its firm avowal of professional and personal loyalty.

Between his first major success with *The Magistrate* and his recognition as the leading dramatist of the day with *The Second Mrs. Tanqueray,* Pinero experimented widely. Since he lacked the gift of satire his essays in this vein (*The Hobby Horse, The Weaker Sex, The Times*) were always laboured and usually spoilt by sentiment. He was in fact much more successful with undiluted sentimentality, as in the modest but greatly loved *Sweet Lavender,* a tale of romance, past and present, and barristers, broken or beginning. Nevertheless an insistent call to attempt serious drama of social significance is detectable in the plays of this period. The time and temper of the theatre fostered such a call. Though Pinero claimed: ''When I wrote *The Profligate* [produced 1889] I had no knowledge of Ibsen, nor have I, I believe, been influenced in the smallest degree by his works,'' he could not continue unaware of the strength of feeling English performances of Ibsen provoked in the early 1890s, and must have been considerably impressed to tell William Archer: ''I went down on my knees to Irving, begging him to do *Hedda Gabler* at the Lyceum with himself and Ellen Terry as Lövborg and Hedda'' (an odd suggestion—Ellen Terry was in her mid-forties by 1891 when Archer's translation was published, and Irving nine years older).

Whether conceived as an English response to Ibsen or not, Pinero's social dramas of the 1890s took up the serious note of *The Squire* or *Lady Bountiful* and modulated it towards unity of tone and tragic resolution. This end he felt to be only attainable in terms of high society. In an interview with William Archer in 1901 he claimed ''not only that wealth and leisure are more productive of dramatic complications than poverty and hard work, but that if you want a certain order of ideas expressed or questions discussed you must go pretty well up the social scale.'' His first fully articulate demonstration of this belief was *The Profligate,* and his first *raisonneur* or spokesman for the establishment Lord Dangars in that play. Its impact has been weakened by other plays (including some of Pinero's) on the theme of the philanderer whose past interposes to ruin his happiness just as he grasps it, but the manager, John Hare, took fright at its tragic conclusion, with the young husband drinking poison, and forced a conventional curtain achieved by the wife's forgiveness. Pinero's acquiescence nevertheless stiffened his resolve to pursue the theme to its logical end in *The Second Mrs. Tanqueray,* with the ''other woman'' moved to the centre of the story and the profligate a late though fatal intruder.

This centrality followed logically from Pinero's earlier essays in a serious vein. *The Squire, The Money-Spinner, The Hobby Horse, Lady Bountiful* all pivot on the dilemma in which the heroine finds herself, and may have been a conscious reaction against the conventions of melodrama, which was essentially a man's world with the heroine kept waiting in the wings to be rescued from starvation or seduction. But the emphasis placed on the *woman* with a past was also a concession to the taste of the fashionable element in the late Victorian audience. The stalls patrons at the St James's and other smart houses could recognise the authenticity with which the stage mirrored their drawing-rooms, but looked to the playwright to introduce a character they would never willingly admit to their own homes, the mysterious female without a pedigree whose efforts to ''acquire some relations as soon as possible,'' in Lady Bracknell's words, provided the plot of so much Society drama of this period. Doubtless the notoriety attaching at this time to certain of Ibsen's heroines, particularly Rebecca West and Hedda Gabler, added a savour to the audience's taste, though Shaw contemptuously dismissed the English playwrights' response: ''It seemed to them that most of Ibsen's heroines were naughty ladies. And they tried to produce Ibsen plays by making their heroines naughty. But they took great care to make them pretty and expensively dressed.''

Pinero's portrait of Paula Tanqueray is better assessed by comparing her with the ''naughty ladies'' of his British colleagues Wilde and Henry Arthur Jones than with Ibsen's. Mrs. Erlynne in *Lady Windermere's Fan* and Mrs. Cheveley in *An Ideal Husband* are flamboyant and entertaining figures but their situations do not demand serious consideration, while Mrs. Arbuthnot in *A Woman of No Importance,* though wholly serious, is neither flamboyant nor entertaining. Jones's cautious han-

dling in *The Case of Rebellious Susan* and *The Liars* of a wife tempted by her husband's callousness to pay him out in kind stops short of real candour and therefore lasting comedy, while Mrs. Dane is ultimately dismissed as a woman more sinning than sinned against. Uniquely in the Society dramas of this period, Paula is presented as a human being compounded of strength and weakness, charm and coarseness. She has been exploited and discarded by her ''protectors,'' but her own caprice and shallowness contribute to her ruin. It was the subtlety with which the virtually unknown Mrs. Patrick Campbell realised this complex character that ensured the play's original impact. Later productions have had to contend with its legendary reputation and appeal to mature actresses (including Mrs. Campbell, who went on playing Paula in her fifties), but the National Theatre revival of 1981, by casting the *gamine* but incisive Felicity Kendal, showed convincingly how the woman her husband calls ''dear baby'' could nevertheless be driven to suicide.

The play took risks. John Hare turned it down as ''immoral'' and George Alexander originally proposed it for matinées only. But there were other grounds on which the St. James's audience might have taken offence. Pinero had reduced the profligate's part, yet he was increasingly severe on the profligate's behaviour. Aubrey Tanqueray condemns not only Hugh Ardale and such unseen ''protectors'' of Paula as Selwyn Ethurst and Peter Jarman, but also himself for leading what many of Pinero's public accepted as ''a man's life.'' In the original text even Cayley Drummle, the acknowledged *raisonneur,* pleaded guilty to this charge, and the play finished with his General Confession:

> And I—I've been hard on this woman! Good God,
> men are hard on all women!

Evidently Pinero found this overemphatic and reverted to the purely visual—Ellean ''beats her breast'' and ''faints upon the ottoman''—for the final tableau. A modern playgoer does not need the dual moral code of Victorian Society spelled out, but the play's boldness calls for acknowledgement.

The success of *Mrs. Tanqueray* confirmed Pinero's pre-eminence not only as a dramatist but as a director of his own work. Possibly as a reaction to his treatment over *The Profligate,* he took a firm hold of rehearsals and continued master of any stage on which his work was being prepared. Frequent accounts (not always appreciative) by actors whom he rehearsed are confirmed by the meticulously detailed promptbooks he kept and by the texts of his plays published from 1891 onwards. This insistence on controlling the performance and publication of his work constituted Pinero's stand against actor—managerial exploitation, which in preceding decades had treated the writer's word as a draft scenario on which to enlarge, and was a crucial step in establishing the self-sufficiency of English drama. It aligned him with Robertson and Gilbert as a dramatist-director, and prepared the ground for Shaw to rule over his rehearsals. Robertson and Gilbert, however, had worked with semi-permanent ensembles offering a clearly established genre. Pinero brought his work to life at different theatres with companies specially assembled, and evidently felt the need for an even stricter discipline.

Greatly as this discipline raised the standards of performance, it tended to codify what is essentially a spontaneous and shared process, and to confer on some of his more delicate pieces (*The Princess and the Butterfly, The ''Mind-the-Paint'' Girl*) an impression of love's labours lost. It is understandable that an author directing his own play should want to impose on the cast his own interpretation and should view unsolicited suggestions as unwelcome (Noel Coward is a more recent example of this approach). But a logical development from the dramatist-director was the independent director, and it is not surprising that the younger Dion ("Dot") Boucicault, who created Sir William Gower for Pinero and married his Rose Trelawny, Irene Vanbrugh, should emerge as the first major independent director in the English theatre. Marie Tempest, herself not the most malleable of material, declared of Boucicault: "I was a blank page on which he was able to write at will, and if he ever created anything, Dion Boucicault created me as an actress." But such uncompromising methods inevitably provoked a reaction. The call for imagination and insight from the actors themselves, voiced by Granville Barker and the intellectual movement in the theatre, was in some sense a protest against the dramatist-director as formidably personified by Pinero.

After *The Second Mrs. Tanqueray* the struggle of an intelligent woman to achieve independence in a society that allowed her only one career—as wife and mother—increasingly obsessed Pinero. Agnes in *The Notorious Mrs. Ebbsmith* is the child of one unhappy marriage and the survivor of another who has turned to political agitation and atheism until called on to nurse a rising politician separated from his wife. The two became lovers, but while Agnes dreams of sharing his study rather than his bed, Lucas Cleeve drifts towards the compromise his worldly brother-in-law, the Duke of St. Olpherts, puts forward, in which an apparent reconciliation allows him to return to political life while establishing Agnes as his mistress. From this point the play suffers a terminal decline into theatrical gesture (Agnes discards her sexless black dress in favour of a concubine's finery, then hurls into the fire a bible offered her by a well-meaning clergyman, only to burn herself in retrieving it) and anti-climax: Cleeve's wife appeals successfully to her to forgo her claims and thus reactivate his career. The weakness of the conclusion is underlined by the strength of the exposition.

Unquestionably the seriousness of Pinero's intentions in examining these heroines is blunted by the assumption that they cannot support themselves and by the enervating affluence in which they live. In *Iris* a young widow who will lose her fortune on remarriage turns down the honourable advances of a young admirer about to make his way to Canada. When her wealth vanishes with her financial adviser, she accepts the dishonourable proposals of a ruthless "protector." The return of her suitor, now able to support her, leads to rejection by both men and humiliation (apparently) on the streets. In *His House in Order* (which achieved Pinero's longest London run amongst his social dramas) a governess finds herself married to a humourless widower and harried by his disdainful in-laws. Chance places in her hands evidence that the first wife was unfaithful and her child illegitimate, yet the *raisonneur* persuades her to "wear a halo" and give up her revenge. An audience is likely to be less forgiving. Zoe Blundell in *Mid-Channel* suggests a more sensitive cousin to H. A. Jones's rebellious Lady Susan or flirtatious Lady Jessica. Like them she has been neglected by a brutish and inconstant husband and turns for consolation to a series of admirers, the last of whom proves all too accommodating. When the husband finds out, Pinero engineers her suicide, whereas a modern observer wishes so intelligent a woman would take a tip from an exact contemporary, Kate in Barrie's *The Twelve Pound Look*, and go in search of typing lessons.

Pinero is far happier in the theatrical world of *Trelawny of the "Wells,"* or more accurately its two theatrical worlds, those of Sadler's Wells after the departure of Phelps (his local playhouse as a child in Islington) and of the Prince of Wales's in the time of Robertson (whose triumphs he witnessed as a boy). Pinero seems disposed to make light of this piece, describing it as "a comedietta" on the title-page and "this little play" in an author's note. It was written at the summit of his success as a "modern" playwright and perhaps viewed as an exercise in nostalgia. Irene Vanbrugh, who played the heroine, recalled "that first night each individual entrance was hailed with a good deal of laughter," presumably on the grounds that last year's fashions are always funnier than last century's. But it is neither simple to stage nor slight in content. The theatrical types are exaggerated but never ridiculous. The aspiring playwright, Tom Wrench, is not only recognisable as Robertson-in-the-making (Pinero's notes for the play reveal that he first used the name Tom Robinson); he is also touching in his devotion to Rose Trelawny, the young actress who outgrows the fustian of *The Pedlar of Marseilles* and is ready for what Robertson's critics called "cup-and-saucer comedy," but perhaps could be termed "ball-of-wool-gathering" in *Life*, as Tom Wrench conceives it.

Moreover it is not just contrast in theatrical convention that distinguishes the play. The rigidity of the Cavendish Square household in which Rose's engagement to Arthur Gower enmeshes her is sketched with insight and wit. Above all, Sir William Gower, its tyrant, grows in understanding and humanity as the play develops. Unlike the lordly Dangars, St. Olpherts and Quex, he comes to appreciate Rose's predicament and waives his own "rules" to assist her. Their discovery of a mutual bond in Edmund Kean, "the splendid gipsy," adds a third theatrical perspective, and the conclusion—with Arthur, Rose and Tom about to challenge fortune—is far more stirring than the contrived endings of so many plays of the period. *Trelawny of the "Wells"* is not only Pinero's happiest inspiration but a key-document in Victorian drama.

The intrusion of a working girl (again played by Irene Vanbrugh) into the boudoirs of high society is a feature of his next two comedies. In *The Gay Lord Quex* Sophie Fullgarney is the efficient manageress of a manicurists' salon, skilfully presented, but her involvement in the private lives of the Marquis of Quex and the Duchess of Strood is only brought about by the unlikely device of making her a foster-sister to the play's nominal heroine. It was a considerable success, owing to the elaborate (though wholly decorous) bedroom-scene, but Sophie's persistence in arranging her protégée's future grows increasingly obtrusive. *Letty* is an equally careful portrait of three City girls and their followers, with meticulous accounts of a rooftop reception and a restaurant supper-party, though the heroine is anaemic in every sense and neither her difficulty in deciding between the coarse but legitimate proposal of her employer and the illicit luxury offered by a married admirer, nor her ultimate destiny as a suburban wife and mother, fires the imagination.

By 1908 the theatrical climate had undergone notable change. Shaw's position as a challenging if controversial playwright was assured by the *réclame* of the Court Theatre seasons, and his lead was being taken up not only in London but in Manchester, where at the Gaiety Miss Horniman was brewing provincial repertory with her inheritance from the family tea business. It is tempting to see *The Thunderbolt* as Pinero's response to these developments. Its setting and background (Midland

and middle class) seems a deliberate break with the West End / East End contrasts of the plays that preceded it. The stage directions themselves suggest a closer familiarity with the lives of the author's fellow men than his society dramas convey. "The room and everything in the room are eloquent of narrow means, if not of actual poverty"; "The architecture, decorations, and furniture are pseudo-artistic and vulgar"; "The whole suggests the home of a common person of moderate means who has built himself a 'fine house'"—these are three such directions, and they contrast strongly with "A rich and tastefully decorated room"; "Everything to suggest wealth and refinement"; "Everything charming and tasteful" (comparable directions from *The Second Mrs. Tanqueray*). In moving away from Mayfair Pinero's dialogue acquires a sharper edge, as does the crowded but compact gallery of family portraits. Clayton Hamilton, the American editor of Pinero's *Social Plays*, recorded with some surprise the author's insistence that he "loved" the Mortimores. No doubt that surprise sprang from a comparison with the engaging company at Volumnia College or Sadler's Wells Theatre. But presumably Pinero's comment implied that he loved what he had achieved in drawing the Mortimores—imperfect beings, but recognisably human despite (or rather because of) their failings and follies.

Technically, too, the play exhibits an economy and discipline not always apparent in the relaxed and almost invertebrate structure of (say) *The Princess and the Butterfly*. One feature often commended by critics is the "overlap" between the Second and Third Acts: the latter starts at a point preceding that reached by the end of Act Two and "catches up" with Thaddeus' arrival at the family conclave. More integral to the play's taut design is the almost total absence of sub-plot or side-issue. Except for the (merely touched on) romantic attachment of young Trist to Helen Thornhill, the entire business of the play concerns itself with the disposal of Edward Mortimore's estate. Even the obtrusive (to modern taste) figures of Thaddeus' children are part and parcel of this design, since their future is involved and their mother's action undertaken for their sake. It is this solidity of structure, as opposed to the sometimes overwrought fabric of the Society plays, that gives *The Thunderbolt* its special strength. There is a momentum to the story which is all the more remarkable since the "mystery" is exploded early by Phyllis's confession to her husband before the play is half over.

If it is tempting to see *The Thunderbolt* as Pinero's recognition of a new horizon opened up in English drama by the repertory movement, it is also tempting to compare the play with one of Granville Barker's contributions to the Court Theatre programme, *The Voysey Inheritance*. The background here is suburban and professional, not provincial and commercial, but the display of family ties shattered and family expectations dashed by a skeleton in the cupboard and unsuspected death duties is common to the two plays. Pinero shows his more traditional training by employing the materials of the well-made play (a missing will, an illegitimate child), whereas Barker's method is shaped by specialist legal processes. There are traces too of the coy humour of Pinero's early work in the comic curate and precocious children. But the overall tone is clear and compelling, and the story maintains its grip to the "open" end. Since he stood for the theatrical establishment against which the Court enterprise and the repertory movement had issued their challenge, it was predictable that he should offer the play to the St James's, whose audience found the setting drab and the

casting of George Alexander as a run-down music-teacher unacceptable. It might have earned a very different response played by Manchester's skilled ensemble with authentic accents. Because of this initial rejection *The Thunderbolt* has made very little impression on the English stage; it deserves another chance to strike home.

Between the muted impact of *The Thunderbolt* and the deep waters of *Mid-Channel* Pinero followed Gilbert as the second dramatist to be knighted for services to the theatre. (Forerunners had been honoured for their services to literature, an achievement open to question in the case of F. C. Burnand.) There was aptness, if also foreboding, about the timing in Edward VII's last Birthday Honours. Pinero continued to write almost until his death in 1934 but found himself increasingly disregarded. His attempt to present a Rose Trelawny of the musical comedy stage in *The "Mind-the-Paint" Girl* struck few chords; his last piece for the St. James's, *The Big Drum*, failed to divert a wartime audience, and *The Enchanted Cottage* tackled a theme more suited to Barrie. His was too oracular a voice for a generation attuned to the staccato tones and scepticism of Maugham, Lonsdale and Coward. While his new work withered in performance, revivals of some of his successes were welcomed as period pieces, notably *Trelawny of the "Wells,"* at the Old Vic in 1925—in a revised text positively identifying Rose's training-ground as Sadler's Wells, to whose rebuilding the production was dedicated. This objective was achieved in 1931, three years before the playwright's death.

Pinero's plays reflect a leisurely age: his characters travel by carriage or train, communicate by letter, have time to converse in complete sentences, or even whole paragraphs. His tempo therefore seemed over-deliberate and his tone too measured for playgoers who drove fast cars, depended on the telephone and talked in broken phrases spiced with slang. But his best work was inspired by love of the theatre and theatrical method, and marked by respect for his public's judgment. Respect usually begets respect, and Pinero has retained critical regard for his craftsmanship. Love on the other hand does not necessarily engender love in return, so that the theatre fifty years after his death favours Wilde's glittering epigrams and Shaw's thrusting argument before his solid worth. But there will always be admiration for the proud workmanship of his writing and deep affection for the warm humanity of his people. (pp. 1-10)

> *George Rowell, in an introduction to* Plays by A. W. Pinero, *edited by George Rowell, Cambridge University Press, 1986, pp. 1-11.*

ADDITIONAL BIBLIOGRAPHY

Armstrong, Cecil Ferard. "Arthur Wing Pinero." In his *Shakespeare to Shaw*, pp. 206-45. 1913. Reprint. Freeport, N.Y.: Books for Libraries, 1968.
> Survey of Pinero's plays to 1911. Armstrong concludes that Pinero "occupied the difficult but important position of a bridge between the old order and the new."

Boas, Frederick. "Sir Arthur Pinero: Dramatist and Stage-Chronicler." In his *From Richardson to Pinero*, pp. 250-80. New York: Columbia University Press, 1937.
Discussion of Pinero's career.

Burns, Winifred. "Certain Women Characters in Pinero's Serious Drama." *Poet Lore* 54, No. 3 (Autumn 1948): 195-219.
Examines Pinero's portrayals of "the new woman in England at the close of the [nineteenth] century," focusing on the characters Paula Tanqueray, Iris Bellamy, Agnes Ebbsmith, and Zoe Blundell as representative examples.

Collins, J. P. "The Plays of Sir Arthur Pinero." *Quarterly Review* 254, No. 504 (April 1930): 292-310.
Positive assessment of Pinero's work.

Dickinson, Thomas H. "Arthur Wing Pinero." In his *The Contemporary Drama of England*, pp. 108-32. Boston: Little, Brown, 1917.
Compares Pinero's comedies with his serious plays, finding the former superior.

England, Denzil. "Pinero: A Centenary." *Contemporary Review* 187 (May 1955): 313-18.
Brief survey of Pinero's career in which England applauds the playwright's attempt to bring dramatic realism to the English stage.

Fyfe, H. Hamilton. *Arthur Wing Pinero*. London: Greening, 1902, 250 p.
Critical biography.

———. *Sir Arthur Pinero's Plays and Players*. London: Ernest Benn, 1930, 311 p.
Study of Pinero's plays which includes discussion of plots, casting, and staging, as well as anecdotes concerning various productions.

Hale, Edward Everett, Jr. "Pinero." In his *Dramatists of Today*, pp. 91-111. New York: Henry Holt, 1911.
Brief survey of Pinero's plays.

Hamilton, Clayton. Introduction to *The Social Plays of Arthur Wing Pinero*, vol. 1, pp. 3-33. 1917. Reprint. New York: AMS Press, 1967.
Provides biographical and background information concerning Pinero's social dramas.

Howells, W. D. "Three Differently Interesting Plays." *Harper's Weekly* 50, No. 2605 (24 November 1906): 1682-83.
Negative review of *His House in Order*. Howells objects in particular to the seemingly artificial device by which the heroine of the play is rescued from an unpleasant fate.

Jameson, Storm. "While Ibsen Came." In her *Modern Drama in Europe*, pp. 110-35. London: W. Collins Sons, 1920.
Discusses the influence of Ibsen in Pinero's work.

Kaplan, Joel H. "'Have We No Chairs?': Pinero's Trelawney and the Myth of Tom Robertson." *Essays in Theater* 4, No. 2 (May 1986): 119-33.
Interprets *Trelawney of the "Wells"* as Pinero's homage to the mid-nineteenth-century playwright Tom Robertson. Kaplan suggests that Pinero exaggerated the extent of Robertson's commitment to dramatic realism.

Krutch, Joseph Wood. "Pinero the Timid." *Nation* 119, No. 3098 (19 November 1924): 551-52.
Review of *The Second Mrs. Tanqueray*. Krutch finds the play simplistic and concludes that "Pinero's view of the demi-mondaine is sentimental and outmoded."

Leggatt, Alexander. "Pinero: From Farce to Social Drama." *Modern Drama* 17, No. 3 (September 1974): 329-44.
Suggests that Pinero's farces and social dramas are alike in dealing with the subject of threatened respectability.

Mais, S.P.B. "Arthur Pinero." In his *Some Modern Authors*, pp. 303-10. New York: Dodd, Mead, 1923.
Discusses *The Second Mrs. Tanqueray* and *Iris*, noting: "The difficulty with both *Iris* and *Mrs. Tanqueray* is that we simply do not believe in the things that people in their day believed."

Massee, Will W. "Arthur Wing Pinero." In *Living Dramatists: Pinero, Ibsen, D'Annunzio*, edited by Oscar Herrmann, pp. 3-62. New York: Brentano's, 1905.
Survey of Pinero's plays to 1901. Massee contends that "Pinero's greatest serious play is *Mrs. Tanqueray;* his greatest comedy, *The Magistrate*."

Miner, Edmund J. "The Theme of Disillusionment in the Drama of Arthur Pinero." *Contemporary Review* 226, No. 1311 (April 1975): 184-90.
Examines the element of self-deception in Pinero's depiction of interpersonal relations.

———. "The Novelty of Arthur Pinero's Court Farces." *English Literature in Transition, 1880-1920*, 19, No. 4 (1976): 299-304.
Identifies the three sources of humor in Pinero's court farces as eccentric characters, incongruous situations, and social satire.

Morgan, A. E. "Pinero." In his *Modern English Drama*, pp. 35-41. New York: Charles Scribner's Sons, 1924.
Brief discussion of Pinero's serious plays. Morgan suggests that "the fundamental failing in Sir Arthur Pinero's tragic art is that it is made of human stuff which is too mean."

Nathan, George Jean. "Attitude toward the Drama." In his *Autobiography of an Attitude*, pp. 200-34. New York: Alfred A. Knopf, 1925.
Discusses *The Second Mrs. Tanqueray* as a typical example of Pinero's work, finding it "pathetically feeble."

Nicoll, Allardyce. "Sir Arthur Pinero." In his *History of Late Nineteenth Century Drama, 1850-1900*, vol. I, pp. 173-82. Cambridge: Cambridge University Press, 1946.
Positive appraisal of Pinero's work.

Phelps, William Lyon. "Sir Arthur Pinero." *Bookman* (New York) 47, No. 2 (April 1918): 212-14.
Review of the 1917 Dutton edition of Pinero's serious plays. Phelps concludes that Pinero's plays are too neatly constructed to rival the works of the great dramatists, which raise complex and ultimately unanswerable questions.

Rowell, George. "Arthur Wing Pinero." In his *The Victorian Theater: A Survey*, pp. 112-18. London: Oxford University Press, 1956.
Discusses the development of Pinero's dramatic art.

Short, Ernest. "The British Drama Grows Up." *Quarterly Review* 295 (April 1957): 216-28.
Stresses Pinero's importance in revitalizing the English theater during the late Victorian and early Edwardian periods.

Stoakes, James Paul. "The Reception of *The Second Mrs. Tanqueray*." *Florida State University Studies*, No. 11 (1953): 89-95.
Discusses the critical history of *The Second Mrs. Tanqueray*.

Taylor, John Russell. "Arthur Wing Pinero." In his *The Rise and Fall of the Well-Made Play*, pp. 146-60. London: Methuen, 1967.
Survey of Pinero's works in which Taylor stresses Pinero's skillful utilization of and effective departures from the conventions of the well-made play.

Walkley, A. B. "*Letty*" and "*His House in Order*." In his *Drama and Life*, pp. 170-93. New York: Brentano's, 1908.
Reviews of *Letty* and *His House in Order*. While he objects to the way the characters speak in *Letty*, Walkley praises *His House in Order* as "the high water mark of theatrical enjoyment."

Wearing, J. P. "Two Early Absurd Plays in England." *Modern Drama* 16, Nos. 3 & 4 (December 1973): 259-64.

Contends that the one-act plays *Playgoers* and *A Seat in the Park* ''are remarkable for the traits they exhibit of what is now widely called the Theater of the Absurd.''

Wellwarth, George E. ''The Career of Sir Arthur Wing Pinero: A Study in Theatrical Taste.'' *Southern Speech Journal* 26, No. 1 (Fall 1960): 45-58.
     Attempts to explain the decline in Pinero's popularity, suggesting that his serious plays relied too heavily on transitory topical concerns to endure.

Wimmer, Uta. ''A Structural Analysis of A. W. Pinero's Problem Plays.'' *Studies in Nineteenth Century Literature* 87, No. 2 (1980): 109-44.
     Discusses *The Second Mrs. Tanqueray, The Notorious Mrs. Ebbsmith, Iris,* and *Mid-Channel* as outstanding examples of the well-made play.

Graciliano Ramos

1892-1953

Brazilian novelist, short story writer, autobiographer, essayist, and nonfiction writer.

Regarded as one of the most important Brazilian novelists of the twentieth century, Ramos was associated with the Generation of 1930, a group of Brazilian writers whose works focused on the social, economic, and political problems of the impoverished and culturally backward northeastern region of their country. At the same time there are features of Ramos's work that distinguish him from this group. Ramos's contemporaries were largely concerned with using fiction as a means for social change; their works are less devoted to artistic than political ends and are inherently optimistic with respect to the betterment of Brazilian society. In contrast, Ramos's works display a conspicuous artistry in their prose style and narrative structure, while their underlying philosophy is clearly one of pessimism regarding the human condition in general as represented by the grim destinies of his Brazilian protagonists. In addition, Ramos's novels have a psychological depth unparalleled in the more sociologically oriented works of his contemporaries.

Ramos was born in Alagoas in northeastern Brazil. His father, a merchant who became a cattle rancher, was nearly ruined financially when a severe drought caused this venture to fail. In the following years, Ramos's father worked at various occupations, necessitating several relocations for his growing family. Throughout his childhood, Ramos experienced first-hand the harsh realities of life in the sertão ("backlands") of Brazil. Although Ramos attended both primary and secondary schools, he strongly disliked formal schooling and was largely self-educated. Ramos's father introduced him to literature, and at an early age he began reading Brazilian and European novelists, among them Eça de Queiroz and Fyodor Dostoevsky. This concern for Ramos's education was uncharacteristic of his father, who is portrayed in Ramos's childhood memoirs, *Infância* (*Childhood*), as stern, authoritarian, and uncommunicative, and who, along with Ramos's ill-tempered mother, mistreated Ramos. A generally unhappy childhood, marked by alienation from his parents and the hardships of the sertão, is considered the probable origin of the misanthropy and pessimism expressed in Ramos's writing.

When he was twenty-one, Ramos moved to Rio de Janeiro, where he had a brief, unsuccessful career as a journalist and began writing short stories. In 1915 he moved to Palmeira dos Indios and opened a dry goods shop. During the next fifteen years, he edited the town newspaper, wrote his first novel, *Caetés,* and was elected mayor. Ramos's mayoral report to the state government concerning social and political problems in Palmeira dos Indios greatly impressed the Alagoas authorities with its honesty, nonbureaucratic style, and simple, precise Portuguese. This report was published in national newspapers and came to the attention of Augusto Frederico Schmidt, a prominent poet and publisher. Schmidt learned that Ramos was the author of an unpublished novel, and under his auspices *Caetés* appeared in 1933. During the 1930s Ramos published three more novels—*São Bernardo, Angústia* (*Anguish*) and *Vidas sêcas* (*Barren Lives*)—and associated with a small group of northeastern Brazilian novelists whose writing realistically portrayed Brazilian life and reflected the rise of a nationalist movement in Brazil. In addition, he held public service positions, among them Director of Public Instruction in Alagoas. It was while serving in this capacity in 1936 that he was imprisoned during a political upheaval. The dictatorship in power regarded Ramos as a communist and his books as subversive; although the reasons for his incarceration are unknown, this official view of Ramos has been considered a probable cause. Upon his release from prison, he returned to Rio de Janeiro and in 1938 was appointed to another public service position. In the following years, he produced works in several genres, the most notable of which are his autobiography *Childhood* and his prison memoirs, *Memórias do cárcere. Childhood* is considered especially important as a rare personal account of life in a remote area of Brazil in the late nineteenth and early twentieth centuries, as a memoir of Ramos's gradual awakening to his artistic vocation, and as a work of verbal artistry. Serving as president of the Brazilian Writers Union, Ramos attended a literary congress in Moscow near the end of his life, and an unfinished essay about his trip, *Viagem,* was published posthumously. He died in Rio de Janeiro in 1953.

Largely episodic in structure, Ramos's novels have a psychological emphasis uncommon in other Brazilian works of the same period, subordinating plot to character studies of individuals struggling in hostile natural environments and unjust societies. In *Caetés*—a novel which examines self-interest as the determinant of ethical values—the adulterous affair of João Valério, a clerk, with his employer's wife leads to the suicide of his employer. Valério is also an aspiring novelist who has abandoned his historical novel about a local cannibalistic tribe, the Caeté Indians, when he concludes that he cannot fathom the mind of a cannibal, yet ultimately he recognizes the same savagery in himself and in his society. Similarly, Paulo Honório in *São Bernardo* is forced to confront his life in which he ruthlessly ascended from fieldhand to landowner and caused the suicide of his wife by falsely accusing her of infidelity. *Anguish* takes place in the tormented mind of Luís da Silva, who is trapped by painful childhood memories and by the hopeless circumstances of his adult life: his meager existence, lack of purpose, and sense of failure and frustration. *Barren Lives* is the story of Fabiano and his backlander family, victims of poverty and the periodic drought, who suffer and survive many trials and humiliations. Critics have noted that despite the extreme adversity and degradation experienced by Fabiano, a sense of dignity and of hope for the future somewhat distinguishes him from the other protagonists who, in the words of Russell G. Hamilton, "live either in a desolate present or a ruinous past.

In addition to creating characters of psychological depth and complexity, Ramos revealed himself to be a skillful prose stylist, and critics have praised him for avoiding both the stilted, formal Portuguese traditional in Brazilian literature as well as the ungrammatical Portuguese of his contemporaries. While his novels are all distinguished by the same artistic prose style, each exhibits a different narrative approach. *Caetés* has been compared with the well-made novel of the nineteenth century, following the formalistic tradition of Gustave Flaubert and de Queiroz, while *São Bernardo* is written in a more vernacular style popular in the 1930s. *Anguish,* a work in which Ramos employed stream of consciousness technique, is a fragmented, chaotic confession notable for its eerie, dreamlike quality. *Barren Lives* is composed of disconnected sketches, each of which focuses more on character than action. Reflecting on the variety of styles and techniques in Ramos's novels, Fred P. Ellison has observed, "Using language perfectly in accord with the theme, the characters, and the locale, Ramos achieves an artistic form which is incomparable in its sobriety, elegance, and refinement."

While Ramos's novels derive their subject matter from Brazilian life, these works nonetheless attain a universality that has made Ramos one of the few Brazilian authors of his time to achieve and sustain international recognition. As Ralph Edward Dimmick has stated: "By reason of the keenness of his psychological insight, of his deep feeling for the vernacular, of his unfailing sense of proportion, of his skilled craftsmanship in construction, Ramos has been able to fashion from the simplest and most unpromising of materials works which stand among the most impressive creations of modern Brazilian literature."

PRINCIPAL WORKS

Caetés (novel) 1933
São Bernardo (novel) 1934
  [*São Bernardo,* 1975]
Angústia (novel) 1936
  [*Anguish,* 1946]
Vidas sêcas (novel) 1936
  [*Barren Lives,* 1965]
Infância (autobiography) 1945
  [*Childhood,* 1979]
Insônia (short stories) 1947
Memórias do cárcere (autobiography) 1953
Viagem (nonfiction) 1954
Obras completas. 6 vols. (novels, short stories, nonfiction, and autobiography) 1961

MORTON DAUWEN ZABEL (essay date 1946)

[*Zabel was an American poet, critic, and prominent scholar who was influential in increasing the study of North American literature in South America. During the mid-1940s he held the only official professorship in North American literature in Latin America, and wrote two widely used American literary studies in Portuguese and Spanish. In the following excerpt from his review of* Anguish, *Zabel discusses the general qualities of Ramos's works.*]

Graciliano Ramos is notable among contemporary Brazilian writers for a severity of style, an accuracy of social and moral observation, and an intensity of tragic sensibility which derive as much from a scrupulous fidelity to native experience as from the stylists—Proust, Joyce, and, more relevantly, Céline—whom his American publisher mentions as his models. These qualities, already evident in his books *São Bernardo, Angústia,* and *Vidas Sêcas,* were reaffirmed last year in the first part of his personal memoirs, *Infância,* one of the best intimate records yet achieved by a modern Brazilian writer. His talent, with its combination of irony and pathos, anguish and lyricism, may

perhaps be compared with that of the poet Carlos Drummond de Andrade. There is no lack of social purpose or physical realism among the better of Ramos's fiction-writing contemporaries—Jorge Amado, Aníbal Machado, Raquel de Queiroz, Marques Rebello, Monteiro Lobato, or the Steinbeckian José Lins do Rego, chronicler of the sugar workers of the northeastern states—but Ramos exceeds these in tragic sympathy, controlled violence, and an independent method of achieving his effects. *Angústia,* now translated as *Anguish* by L. C. Kaplan thus introduces one of the most considerable figures in Latin American and Brazilian fiction to American readers.

Whether its harsh record of the moral frustration and psychic disintegration of Luis da Silva, a struggling nobody caught in a small government clerkship and a corrupt journalistic world, finally to end in crime, break-up, and insanity as a result of the personal odds and social depravity set against him, will appeal to American readers is a question, but it should be noted that Ramos controls and usually masters the methods—subjective tenuity, irresponsible surrealist fantasies, mass accumulation of physical detail—which beset and vitiate the efforts of his more facile contemporaries. . . . Of South American novels brought to American notice during the past five years, this is easily one of the most distinguished. It introduces a writer of stamina and profundity. It may send the reader and the publisher to others of Ramos's books; notably *Vidas Sêcas* and *Infância,* and so to an acquaintance with one of the best efforts and results in Brazil's current literary ambitions. (pp. 482-83)

> *Morton Dauwen Zabel, "A Brazilian Tragedy," in* The Nation, *New York, Vol. 162, No. 16, April 20, 1946, pp. 482-83.*

H. R. HAYS (essay date 1946)

[*Hays is an American novelist, critic, and playwright with an interest in Latin-American literature and culture. In the following review of* Anguish, *Hays provides a character study of the protagonist, commends the realism and style of the novel, and discusses its importance as a representation of the political situation in Brazil and as a reflection of the universal anguish of modern humanity.*]

It is a rather terrifying fact that, currently, the fiction which moves us most is concerned with man self-destroyed or man desperately attempting to establish his own sanity. This accounts, perhaps, for the particularly disturbing quality of Graciliano Ramos' novel, *Anguish.* For, although this is a tale of an obscure clerk and journalist in a provincial Brazilian town, the soul state so vividly dramatized is something we all feel to a greater or lesser degree: it is the utter alienation of modern man from fundamental values, the "angoisse" of the existentialists, a choking rage at the dirty joke which the creature that used to be called "the lord of creation" has played on himself.

Ramos' hero, Luis da Silva, typifies specifically the frustrated Latin American intellectual. Author of two hundred unpublished sonnets, he dreams continually of the books he will never write and, instead, turns out articles for a corrupt press, articles defending or praising crooked politicians. He is always hard up, always bitter at the fat capitalists who plunder the country, yet he does nothing about it except chat with the revolutionaries in the café. He dreams of marrying the sensual little gold-digger, Marina, who lives next door, but loses her when she is made pregnant by a wealthy playboy.

Now it is a fact that the middle class in the Latin American republics is too small to support its intelligentsia. Even the most important writers cannot live from their books and, unless they are translated and published in other countries, they scarcely feel they are being read at all. The typical intellectual is therefore compelled, like da Silva, to make up to the party in power in order to obtain some small sinecure and, since this is never enough to live on, he must also dissipate himself in meretricious journalism. He lives in a limited, provincial atmosphere and his familiarity with European culture only intensifies his dissatisfaction with his poverty-stricken environment. When one adds to this the fact that Brazil has been controlled by a repressive dictatorship for years, it is easy to see why the weak and embittered intellectual of the novel feels precisely like a cornered rat.

Da Silva tells his own story backward. In the beginning he informs us that it is only a month since he got out of bed, and by a kind of thematic repetition, plunging each time a little deeper into the action, he carries us back into the tightening net of hysteria and nervous exacerbation which results in his breakdown. The affair with Marina was simply the immediate cause. There is a kind of perversion, a figurative impotence, running through his relationship with her and his attempts to sleep with her while they are engaged. When Juliano Tavares seduces Marina and leaves her, Luis' resentment acquires symbolical quality. He does not hate Tavares because he has harmed Marina (love has already turned to sadistic dislike) but because Tavares' success is an affront to himself, underlining the impotence and insignificance of his whole life, symbolizing what the world has done to him. Thus it is, as his world grows more distorted, that a fixation upon Tavares develops which ends in a meaningless murder and a descent into real madness.

Ramos' style and method are original. There is a hypersensitivity to detail which creates a sense of distance and fantasy within reality. "His voice made me shudder; it reminded me of something fat, white and spongy, like raw pork." The musical repetition of certain images from his childhood accentuates the meanness of the present, for da Silva is descended from the rancher, Trajano, a lusty frontiersman to whom life did not present the same problems it does to his grandson. It is also made clear that Luis suffers from a traumatic hatred for his father. As his spirit engages in a shadowy battle with perception, its evasions and compensations grow more and more symbolical, and, as the details of his daily life, the familiar inhabitants of his street hem him in, they acquire a mysterious menace.

In other words, something of what Kafka achieves by subtly altering life into a fantastic dream, Ramos manages to suggest by exaggerations of reality just as a microscope, by revealing invisible textures, turns the housefly into a monster and woolen thread into a forest.

The average writer who attempts to tell a story by piling up sensory material achieves only triviality; it takes a poet to create an effect of lyrical terror from the rubbish accumulated by the trash basket of the human mind. In the last analysis Ramos is a poet and this is why his book achieves importance through intensity and—although the details of the hero's life are alien to us—we cannot remain unmoved by his desperation.

Hitherto we have had no fiction from Brazil which reflected the contemporary political situation, even though that country was one of the earliest to adopt some form of totalitarianism. Señor Ramos' book suggests that stagnation rather than successful regimentation has resulted. By indirect ideological allusion and by means of a single limited character he has written an agonized indictment of life in his own country and at the same time he has created a work of literature which reflects the anguish of the entire world.

> H. R. Hays, "The World's Sorrow," in The New Republic, *Vol. 114, No. 24, June 17, 1946, p. 876.*

FRED P. ELLISON (essay date 1954)

[*In the following excerpt, Ellison surveys Ramos's novels, focusing on their artistry and underlying philosophy.*]

[Although] there is much implicit social criticism, nothing in Ramos' work would serve directly as political propaganda. Presumably, he was dedicated to some sort of reorganization of society. Yet he seems to imply in his writings that attempts at improvement are futile and that happiness for man is an impossibility. The social reformers, the humanitarians, come to naught in their efforts: one of them is forced to commit suicide; others are made to appear ridiculous. In the opinion of several discerning critics, it is extremely difficult to reconcile the distinctly unhumanitarian philosophy of Ramos with his radical political beliefs.

Floriano Gonçalves, a well-informed critic of the novelist, finds the key to Ramos' social thinking in the "terrible determinism" that rules the lives of his characters. The novelist's pessimism, he believes, is not extended to all men but solely to the individual of the society and economic situation of the Northeast. The nordestino is condemned to suffer as long as the bases of society remain as they are. Says Gonçalves: "Only a change in the framework of forces which surround him and crush him will be able to transform the Caeté, the brute, José Bahia, and Fabiano. In this respect the art of Graciliano Ramos is the most intensely revolutionary of any of living Brazilian writers. His thoughts have a logical end, and revolution is an essential necessity within the social setting which he paints." This "logical end" of the novelist's thinking must be supplied by the speculative critic. However, Gonçalves' interpretation deals squarely with the attitude of Ramos toward society and is probably the most convincing. He takes into account the author's constant preoccupation with the nature of society and its pressures acting upon his characters. From this obvious fact as well as from Ramos' known political radicalism, Gonçalves draws his conclusion that the novelist is a revolutionary writer. Yet such works as **Anguish** and **St. Bernard** are in no sense propaganda—their meaning is too cryptic to have doctrinary value. Furthermore, Ramos is too innately a literary artist to create a novel for any political end.

An entirely different interpretation of Ramos' inner meaning is that of the European critic Otto Maria Carpeaux, who holds that the novelist's attitude toward social change is one of irony. Carpeaux says that Ramos is aware of the ridiculousness of attempting to change the social structure through revolution.

> I am sufficiently well acquainted with his convictions to be convinced, for my own part, that they represent merely the surface of his thought. They are not transformable into art; and this is significant. Luis Padilha and the Jew Moisés [a minor figure of **Anguish**] are not revolutionary heroes. Every time the novelist gives in to the temptation to formulate programs of social reform—the schoolteacher Magdalena talks in these terms—he falls right into the trap of his most detested

enemy: the commonplace; in this case, the humanitarian commonplace concerning "generosity."

"Merely the surface of his thought," then, is Ramos' personal political belief, and his work is far from having a revolutionary meaning. Carpeaux offers an ingenious interpretation of the novels in relation to the personality of their creator: they are seen as subconscious attempts to destroy the agonizing world of the author's memories, the city, civilization,—the pitfalls of his characters—in order to return to the relatively tranquil world of the sertão from which he, like his characters, has come.

Although provocative, Carpeaux's thesis leaves out of account the sociological groundwork on which all the novels, after *Caetés,* rest. Ramos' comparison of the relative purity of sertanejo society with the corrupt environment of the littoral, a fundamental social theme, is not subconsciously introduced, but is a basic idea. Simply because the theme is given an unprecedented artistic form, so that it is always on a secondary plane, we cannot dismiss Ramos as a social thinker. This is not to detract from his work as a psychological novelist, but to affirm his significance as a sociological novelist as well.

The personality of the novelist constitutes another puzzle. The phrase "cultured sertanejo" seems to sum up best his contradictions and conflicts. As a literary man, Ramos had to make his mark in the comparatively brilliant and refined society of the coastal cities, but, despite the critical acclaim given him as one of the foremost writers of Brazil, he appeared unable to accept the civilization of the capital. To those who knew him best, he remained the unvarnished sertanejo, or country "hick." A pose? Modesty? In all likelihood neither. Through his resistance to the comforts and adornments of civilization, through his sharp criticism of the men and institutions of the littoral, he probably was expressing the vaunted individualism of the dweller of the backlands, particularly of the sertanejo frustrated in his desire to return to the sertão. Always at odds with the civilization to which he owed his renown, he seems to have been a tragic misfit in society.

As Alvaro Lins has said, "The question of whether or not one accepts the entire conception of life which arises out of the novels of Graciliano Ramos should not prevent anyone from admiring the artist who upholds it." Ramos has come to grips with the major theme of his time, that of social man against the land. To give it intensity and clarity, he has presented it in the minds of individual men. And to make it permanently endure, he has cast the whole—four short novels—into the time-resistant shape of great art.

According to Osório Borba, a shrewd Brazilian observer, we must go to the novels themselves in search of Graciliano Ramos.

> I know of no work [*St. Bernard*] that better portrays its author, not that it is completely and rigorously autobiographical. But in the person of the author one cannot help seeing the physical appearance of Paulo Honório, a demoralized and brutalized senhor de engenho, his fifty years spent in useless endeavor, and persisting in perpetuating the memory of a stupid and sterile existence because of a literary whim late in life. People often call Graciliano "Fabiano." Paulo Honório, Fabiano, Luis Silva, Seu Tomás, Padilha, a gallery of restless failures, victims of one knows not what inner maladjustments, of a conflict between ambition and weakness, concocting evil thoughts, in a constant fermentation of dissatisfaction toward life, muttering obscenities against humanity and against

themselves. . . . In each of these figures, a bit of self-portraiture.

Only a novel like *Dom Casmurro* of Machado de Assis could stand comparison with the modern-day achievements of Graciliano Ramos in the realm of the psychological novel. Like Machado, Ramos was an acute student of character who saw life with irony and pessimism. He is distinguished from his predecessor by his insistence upon the social theme, and from his fellow nordestinos by his greater interest in character. In the last quarter of a century, he has been the outstanding psychological novelist of Brazil, and his tormented protagonists are frequently compared with Dostoevski's creations. In the depressing, inwardly seething mental world he portrays, his heroes carry heavy mental burdens, and their terrible thoughts are systematically explored. [As stated by Ramos in his *São Bernardo,* the] soul's "highest aspirations to love, to sincerity, to beauty, to piety, struggle violently in the clutches of barbarous instinct, of animal cruelty, of the eternal denial of beliefs and sentiments that are seemingly the most sincere." To Ramos men are simply animals, complicated animals, to be sure, who are subject only to the conditioning of their physical and social environment, who fight to survive in hostile surroundings, and who are wretched creatures deprived of the possibility of happiness. Rats, dogs, pigs, beasts—these are often the symbols for man in the pages of his novels.

Ramos' first novel is the least inclined toward psychological exploration. In *Caetés,* however, the characters fit into the author's pessimistic scheme of things. In this novel he showed that man's notions of right and wrong, indeed of all ethical values, are determined by nothing but self-interest.

The novel's ironic title *Caetés,* which relates to the question of the relativity of moral values, comes from the name of a cannibalistic Indian tribe inhabiting the Northeast at the time of the conquest. João Valério, as the story opens, is writing a novel about them, but advances no farther than the second chapter, for, as he says, "I have no way of knowing what goes on in the mind of a cannibal." In the course of Ramos' often wryly humorous novel, the reader begins to perceive, along with João Valério, that the youth has much in common with the cannibal Caetés: "What am I if not a savage, lightly polished, with a tenuous coat of varnish on the outside? Four hundred years of civilization, different races, different customs. And I said I did not know what happened in the mind of a Caeté! Probably what happens in my own, with a few differences."

The setting is Palmeira dos Indios, a quiet, dusty backlands town where life is monotonous. João Valério falls in love with the wife of his employer and benefactor, Adrião Teixeira. No sooner does the affair reach the adulterous stage than Adrião is informed of it. João Valério manages to convince his friend of his "innocence," whereupon Adrião remorsefully commits suicide for having doubted his wife's fidelity. Later, the lovers discover that their love has withered.

João Valério's seduction of the wife of a friend, his denial of the affair to Adrião, his callous acceptance of the man's deathbed apology, and his solicitude in seeing that the suicide is buried with appropriate lamentations, all run counter to established social ethics. Valério's behavior is motivated by immediate self-interest. And nowhere does he show remorse. "The recollection of Adrião's death little by little vanished from my mind. After all, I need not trouble myself over something which I could not help. My guilt is not great, for there are numerous men who have been bothered by unfaithful wives.

I am unable to suffer for long." Adrião's wife Luisa, despite the admirable moral qualities attributed to her by João Valério, despite her conjugal dignity and her generous sentiments for the poor, is at length seen to be a "Caeté" herself, "a sensitive creature who, needing to love someone, had preferred me to Dr. Liberato or Pinheiro, the young men who frequented her house." João Valério's conclusion concerning his relationship with Luisa is simply that he has discovered "a law of nature." As Ramos sees it, all human activity and especially all ethical, religious, and social values are subordinate to this "law."

The underlying materialistic philosophy of *Caetés* links it with the rest of the novels. However, though published in 1933, it had lain in a drawer since 1926. This time factor in a period of literary evolution is important for *Caetés* and explains why it is so different from the rest of Ramos' works. *Caetés* is a novel in the nineteenth-century tradition of a Flaubert or an Eça de Queiroz. There is no sustained interest in the socio-logical, and the language still retains a certain refinement that was to be discarded when the novelists of the early 'thirties embraced the vernacular. In its structure *Caetés* points to an earlier day than the 'thirties, when it actually appeared. The critic Floriano Gonçalves assigns to Eça de Queiroz the major influence shaping the novel: "In his initial work it was Eça de Queiroz who gave it the structure of the French novel, with well-balanced chapters, much movement, and a great deal of dialogue. From Eça, above all, comes his taste for delineating his figures in caricature." Gonçalves points out the absence of monologues (despite the book's being related in the first person) that were to make possible the introspection of *St. Bernard* and *Anguish*.

Although Ramos' first novel is his least impressive accomplishment, it does succeed in reconstructing the oppressive and tedious atmosphere of a Northeastern small town, where men and women of superficial culture and civilization are provoked to act like the primitive Indians who occupied the land before them. A remarkable feature is the treatment of minor characters, who, in their movement and sharp delineation, recall the villagers of *Madame Bovary*. Furthermore, *Caetés* is commendably broad in its scope. Ramos' study of the bases of social ethics is applied to an insignificant person of the Brazilian Northeast, but his conclusions have applications everywhere. There is little attempt to invoke the regional or socio-logical background in order to explain João Valério. In the mid-twenties, when the book was conceived, character evidently did not have the fascination it was to have for Ramos in the early 'thirties, when the sociological novel appeared.

In *Caetés* his preoccupation with the nature of the novel is shown, exaggerated, of course, in the character of João Valério. Satirically the novelist conveys his aversion for the so-called regional novel, with its obscure vocabulary of native terms ("My aim was in reality to employ a tremendously effective word: *tibicoara*"), its picturesque figures (various Caeté types), and its melodramatic action (the cooking of the human victim, the recipe for which João Valério, substituting goat for human flesh, obtains from his landlady).

For Ramos the novel must deal with human life here and now. Regional and sociological elements must be integrated with the characters themselves. A passage from *Caetés* exemplifies the manner in which a description of nature is used to delineate character.

> Mountains to the left, near, green; mountains to the right, distant, blue; mountains in the background, very distant, white, almost invisible, in the direction

of the São Francisco River. I lit a cigarette. And dejectedly I mused that there was in me something of that landscape: a vast plain surrounded by mountains. . . . Hopes and fears that devour me are easily exhausted in brief journeys in this flat and bare expanse which is my life.

In *St. Bernard* (*São Bernardo*) the Brazilian novel attains its most dignified and artistic form. Although presented in miniature, the elements making up the society of the cane-growing littoral of Alagoas are as carefully handled as in the best of José Lins do Rego's sociological novels. The ways of agricultural life, the cotton fields, the ginning, the cattle grazing, are integral parts of the story. And the human types are familiar to anyone who knows the Northeast: the cabras, the sertanejo overseer, the declining rural aristocracy, and Ramos' specialties—the small-town newspaper editor, the parish priest, the lawyer, and the politician, urban types well set off against the rural. More important, the sociological theme remains secondary. The reader is aware of it only as background and is likely to consider *St. Bernard* primarily a psychological novel.

In this second novel by Ramos, the method used is the first-person narrative of a man who reviews his past actions in a state of mental turmoil. Paulo Honório, conditioned by his physical, social, and psychological environment, has risen from obscure parentage. As a boy he led a blind beggar and was later "mothered" by a Negress candy-seller, old Margarida. He is driven by relentless ambition to become the master of the fazenda St. Bernard, where he once did the brutalizing work of a hired hand. Paulo Honório's is a success story based upon shameless methods of advancement, from petty cheating and political opportunism to murder. This heartless backlands *arriviste* marries a young schoolteacher; the result is a violent conflict between man and wife as well as within the man himself. The presence of young Padilha, the penniless but educated *doutor* whom Paulo has bilked out of his ancestral estate, provides a powerful irritant to Paulo's egoism: jealousy. Life on the plantation is made unbearable for Magdalena, who, although innocent of infidelity, poisons herself. Her husband afterward learns that part of a letter from Magdalena he had found and assumed to be destined for another was in reality his wife's suicide note to him.

Paulo is telling his story as a distraction, after Magdalena's death. He feels old, and life has no meaning for him. "How many useless hours! For a person to consume his entire life without knowing for what reasons! Eating and sleeping like a pig. Like a pig! Getting up early every morning to run out and look for food! And then stocking food for one's children, for one's grandchildren, for many generations. What stupidity! How revolting! Would it not be better for the devil to come and take all?" Men are animals. Some, like his friends the priest and the lawyer, are domesticated; others, like Casimiro Lopes, the sertanejo overseer, are in the wild state. And Paulo Honório, despite his ability to read and his interest in writing these memoirs, places himself in a category little if any higher. Happiness for him is an impossibility; he does, however, muse: "If I had kept on scouring old Margarida's copper pan, she and I would have had a quiet existence. We would have spoken little, thought little, and at night, after coffee and sugar, we would have prayed, on the mat, our African prayers, in the grace of God." The memory of Magdalena torments him, reminding him of the ruin of his own life as well as hers. But, "if it were possible to start all over again, exactly the same thing would happen. I cannot change myself, and that is what disturbs me."

Graciliano Ramos' hard-hearted philosophy of man is recapitulated in the words "brutality" and "egoism" as Paulo Honório applies them to himself. His is the law of the herd, of every man for himself, of the survival of the fittest. Thus oriented, Paulo remains in a state of shock when confronted by those who have more civilized ideals. Thus he comes to view Magdalena, with her ideas of social betterment, as a Communist who poses a threat to himself. Although the thought is in nowise offered as a thesis, the author's meaning is clear: Paulo Honório is neither admirable nor despicable; he is simply the product of the cruel social and economic realities of the Northeast. Paulo places the blame not on himself but on the world of the Northeast: "It was this way of life that made me worthless." We are reminded of the violence of Viçosa, the "hardhearted landholders," and the severity of Ramos' own father as factors that helped to form Paulo Honório.

Descriptions of nature are sparingly used: the hostile landscape limits and blights the lives of the characters, and has no other meaning. Paulo Honório appreciates its beauty only because the cotton fields, the red-backed cattle, and the green forests are his property. Only the sight of the land can stir a spark of aesthetic appreciation in him; then he can declare, "I became convinced that this is not a bad world."

In *St. Bernard* Graciliano Ramos most directly enunciates his aesthetic views, based on absolute honesty in communicating thought and feeling. Though satirically expressed, a central opinion is well shown in the scene which takes place after Paulo has decided to write a novel in collaboration with his friends the priest, the lawyer, and the newspaperman.

> The result was disaster. Two weeks after our first meeting, the editor of the *Cruzeiro* presented me with two typewritten chapters, so full of stupidities that I got mad:
>
> "Go to hell, Gondim. You fouled up everything. This is too high-falutin', it's awful, it's idiotic. Nobody in God's world talks like that!"
>
> Azevedo Gondim extinguished his smile, gulped, picked up the pieces of his small vanity, and replied with vexation that an artist cannot write as he talks.
>
> "He can't?" I asked in amazement. "Why not?"
>
> Azevedo Gondim replied that he cannot because he cannot.
>
> "That's why it's written as it is. Literature is literature, Seu Paulo. People discuss, quarrel, conduct business naturally, but putting words down on paper is something else again. If I set out to write as I speak, no one would read me."

Paulo Honório will not write that kind of novel. He abandons his collaborators and begins his book with the request, "Those who read me will please be kind enough . . . to translate this into literary language, if they care to."

With *Anguish* (*Angústia*) Ramos carries the Brazilian novel to a stage beyond that reached by Machado de Assis. In his effort to capture as much of the human essence as possible, Ramos adapts the so-called interior monologue to the study of an individual Northeasterner, Luis Silva, whose existence is endowed with sociological as well as psychological meaning. The full impact of the social criticism in *Anguish* is felt only after a second or third reading. Lest it be forgotten, this is the novel that Ramos wrote during the period of his political persecution and imprisonment.

Anguish is the history of the mind of Luis Silva, which has been scarred by depressing childhood experiences; which has registered impressions, sometimes vague, of thirst in the sertão, of a brave and respected grandfather whose fazenda had gradually gone to ruin, of a father who died when Luis was a boy and whose death cannot be forgotten; and which can call up the image of Seu Evaristo, after he hanged himself, or of the amiable José Bahia, his grandfather's bodyguard hired on occasion to do murder. Luis Silva's mind has recorded more—his life at school as a small boy in a backlands town, his education in Maceió, his "gypsy's life" as a poor schoolteacher, moving on when he had taught all that he himself had been taught, his rounds as a beggar, a "hitch" in the army, and a period in jail for his political beliefs. After the collapse of his grandfather's holdings in the sertão, Luis Silva painfully attempts to eke out an existence in the society of the littoral. Overcome by misery and frustration, he ends in a dingy little room in Maceió, where, as a petty bureaucrat, he writes "what he is told to write." Ungovernable forces of sex complete the destruction.

The harried Luis Silva has never known real love, although he has purchased its facsimile, until he glimpses Marina, the girl next door on a shabby street in Maceió. At first promising to marry him, she leaves him because he is poor, and transfers her affections to a well-to-do young lawyer of the upper class, Julião Tavares. Tavares seduces the girl and abandons her when she becomes pregnant. Luis Silva's jealousy now turns to rage. In this crisis, the past, the figure of his proud and dignified old grandfather, the image of men violently dying in the sertão, of the killer José Bahia, of a snake coiled around a man's neck, of the swelling abdomen of Marina, of a rope—the ineluctable past merges in the unbearable present. His mind unhinged, Luis Silva strangles Julião Tavares, and the final pages of the novel, reminiscent of Molly Bloom's soliloquy, reveal the nature of Luis Silva's madness.

Only after the novel is finished does the reader realize that the entire story has been related by a man out of his mind. There are two levels of action: in one, Luis Silva narrates the love affair with Marina; in the other, past and present, memories, fears, and speculations are interwoven and at last chaotically confused. The account thus gains the eerie quality of a dream, or of delirium, which is unparalleled in the Brazilian novel.

The anguish of Luis Silva is the result of his thwarted sexual desire for Marina. This is made clear in page after page of morbid eroticism, in which the man's instinctive urges are shown compressed within him like a spring. His crime against Tavares was motivated by defeated love and by accompanying jealousy and wrath. However, Luis Silva's mind was already in a precarious state, weakened by years of privation and despair.

Another sharper kind of anguish in the novel is that of Graciliano Ramos himself, surveying the unfortunate and apparently irremediable social and economic conditions of his Northeast. The novel's high social sense is found in its representation of the degrading conditions of life of the masses—the Marinas and the Luis Silvas, victims of an unjust organization of society, scourged from the sertão, like Luis Silva, to be crushed by civilization, to be coerced, like Marina, by a wealthy Julião Tavares, or to be reduced, like Dona Adélia, the pathetic mother of Marina, to "a piece of filthy rag." None of these characters is shown as courageous or virtuous, as might be the heroes of a Jorge Amado. Curiously, not even Julião Tavares is blackened. "Marina was an instrument and deserved compassion. Julião Tavares was also an instrument, but I did not feel sorry for him. I felt the same hatred, now increased, that he has always inspired in me.''

Does the author mean to equate the oppressed and the oppressor? Jorge Amado would have made it clear that Marina was a victim and that Tavares was a culprit. Does Ramos, seeing farther than Amado, find them both innocent? Or both guilty? Or is he indifferent to their fate? Is something called "civilization" responsible for their misery? The novelist never made clear his attitude toward society and its organization. It is as if this aspect of his writing had purposely been obscured.

Ever since *St. Bernard* this much, at least, of the novelist's meaning has been clear: the struggle for existence in the littoral is so desperate that the individual must, as did Paulo Honório, sell his soul in order to survive. In Luis Silva, Álvaro Lins sees a character who, "in a certain sense, represents the other side of Paulo Honório." Paulo Honório has conquered his environment; Luis Silva has succumbed to his. To Ramos, life in the agricultural and relatively Europeanized belt of the coastland is untempered hell, whether one prospers, as does Paulo Honório, or perishes, as does Luis Silva.

Throughout his works, with the exception of the somewhat unrepresentative *Caetés,* the novelist juxtaposes "sertão" and "civilization" in a remarkable way. We are reminded of Euclydes da Cunha, who called attention to the chasm between sertanejo society and the European-type communities of the littoral.

The one character who is unsoiled by contact with the coastal society is the cowherd Fabiano of *Parched Lives* (*Vidas Sêcas*). It is meaningful that Fabiano, because he has remained apart from civilization, is the purest and most tranquil of the novelist's creatures. Through Fabiano, Victória, and the boys—not to mention the dog Baleia—the author of *Parched Lives* has translated into human terms the tragedy of life as it must be lived in the sertão, the skills of the vaqueiro upon which livelihood depends, the physical conditions of existence under the threat of the great climatic monster at whose whim all live, flee, or die—the periodic seca. Spare in action, the novel concentrates upon Fabiano and his family, who, scourged by the drought, take refuge in an abandoned ranch house, and at last are saved by the rains. Later the deadly seca again sets them loose on the barren sertão.

Fabiano is wise in the ways of taming wild horses, of tracking cattle in the underbrush of the spiny caatinga, of curing their diseases. He knows how to survive and to take care of his wife Sinha Victória and the two boys. His ignorance is that of the man raised in the wilderness.

> He lived far from men and got along well only with animals. His hard feet broke thorns and did not feel the heat of the ground. When mounted, he became one with his horse, glued to him. He spoke a sing-song language, a monosyllabic and guttural language that his companion understood. On foot, he had trouble walking. He leaned first to one side, then to the other, clumsy, stooped, and ugly. At times, in his relations with people, he used the same language which he would address to the animals—exclamations, onomatopoeias. In truth he spoke little. He admired the long and difficult words of city people, tried in vain to reproduce some of them, but he knew they were useless and perhaps dangerous.

Civilization is represented by the distant town to which Fabiano made infrequent trips—to church once a year because he "had religion"; to the business office of the fazendeiro to settle accounts and perhaps be cheated because he could not read or add; to the store where he procured supplies. In town the risks that lay in wait for him were the saloon, with its rum and gambling, and the "yellow soldier" (yellow, presumably from worms or malaria), who, representing the abstraction "government," teased him and stepped on his sandaled toes with heavy boots.

Fabiano is not ambitious for himself. His aim is to teach his boys to be like him, as he is like his own father and grandfather before him. He knows he must work for others and, like a cabra, "keep his place."

> All right. He was born with his destiny, no one was to blame for his having been born with an evil destiny. What could he do? Could he change fate? If someone had told him he could improve his situation, he would have been amazed. He had come into this world to break animals, cure their sores with prayers, mend fences from wet season to dry. . . . He accepted it, he didn't ask for anything more. If they gave him what was his, it was fine. They didn't. He was out of luck, he was like a dog, he got only the bones. Why was it that rich men still kept taking some of the bones away from him? It even made you sick at your stomach the way important people bothered about such trifles.

Significant are the closing words of *Parched Lives,* for they explain much not only about Paulo Honório and Luis Silva but also about Ramos himself. As Fabiano and Victória are forced from the backlands and head for the coast, their thoughts and fresh hopes turn to the *mata,* the well-watered farming belt, where lie the possibilities of improving the sertanejo's hard lot. "The children in schools, learning difficult and necessary matters. They themselves, two little old people, finishing up like dogs . . . What could they do? Fearfully, they slowed their pace. They would reach an unknown, civilized land and would be held fast in it. And the sertão would continue to send people there. The sertão would send to the city strong, brutish men like Fabiano, Sinha Victória and the two boys.''

Structurally, *Parched Lives* differs from the well-made nineteenth-century novel typified by *Caetés*; from the autobiographical novel represented by *St. Bernard*; and from *Anguish,* which in form derives from modern stream-of-consciousness writing. Ramos' last novel is related entirely in the third person. There is scarcely a word of dialogue, and Fabiano and Sinha Victória are brought to life through the narration of an artist who appears to be endowed with the same temperament as his characters. Thus is created the impression of the novelist's profound understanding of sertanejo psychology.

Parched Lives is made up of disconnected scenes. Each chapter (some examples are "Moving," "Baleia," "The Jail," "Fabiano," "Holiday," "Flight") has its own unity, its own near-independence, and might be said to constitute a short story, in which action is less important than the study of the psychological make-up of the character, even though it be the dog Baleia, whose death is described in one of the most moving chapters in all of modern Brazilian literature. The novelist himself has said that *Parched Lives* grew out of a short story, **"Baleia,"** based upon the death of a pet dog that he had seen his grandfather kill. The story was published and well received, and he later returned to the subject of Fabiano and elaborated it into a novel. We may speculate that Ramos found in the short-story form the literary vehicle that best suited him. All his writings since *Anguish* have taken that form—even his autobiography *Childhood,* certain chapters of which have been published separately. In less than two hundred pages, *Parched Lives* reveals more about life in the sertão than several thousand pages of sociological treatises could reveal. This book, which is both regional and universal, equals Ramos' earlier masterpieces *St. Bernard* and *Anguish.*

Rich in psychological revelations of the human soul and in sociological meaning, the novels of Ramos are esteemed also for their literary style. As Osório Borba has described it, Ramos writes as he talks, "an erudite version of the countryman's dialect of the Northeast, regionalism in classic form, slang of the zone and plebeian 'cuss words' carefully set down in the purest of Portuguese, with pronouns rigorously placed and exact grammatical usage." Using language perfectly in accord with the theme, the characters, and the locale, Ramos achieves an artistic form which is incomparable in its sobriety, elegance, and refinement. And although his language is not notable for poetic effect, it has what might be called a Parnassian beauty. Strange that it has also been called "uncouth," "arid," "dry," "barren," and even "too highly refined." But as Guilherme de Figueiredo has said: "The constant polishing of his style, so far from robbing it of its effects, lends astounding force to a mere sentence, to a mere word. He writes almost mathematically: his expressions are immutable within their framework." With Ramos, language is a precision tool with which effects hitherto unrecorded in Brazilian literature have been made possible.

That his style and, indeed, every detail of the novel are the result of continual purification is illustrated by the fact that *St. Bernard* was thrice written before its final form was attained. We have reason to suspect that the choice of an adjective may have caused Ramos "to sweat in agony," as has been said of Flaubert. The purifying process accounts for the fact that Ramos' novels and short stories are few in number and contain such richness within reduced dimensions. The four slender volumes of prose may prove to be the most solid achievement in the field of the modern Brazilian novel. (pp. 116-32)

> Fred P. Ellison, "Graciliano Ramos," in his Brazil's New Novel: Four Northeastern Masters, *University of California Press, 1954, pp. 111-32.*

RALPH EDWARD DIMMICK   (essay date 1965)

[*In the following excerpt, Dimmick surveys Ramos's major writings, focusing on the characterization, style, and individuality of each of Ramos's novels.*]

While not worthy to stand beside his later novels, *Caetés* is nevertheless a very respectable example of the masterwork of an apprentice—the proof that he has absorbed the lesson of his elders and is ready to strike out on his own. It falls clearly within the current of post-Naturalism, showing great concern with the establishment of a milieu in all its details, dwelling on events of the most ordinary nature, presenting a slice of life in small-town northeastern Brazil. The chief influence to be noted is that of Eça de Queiroz, whose use of a similar device in his *A Ilustre Casa de Ramires* (*The Illustrious House of Ramires*) may have inspired Ramos to assign the writing of a historical novel as a pastime for his protagonist-narrator, João Valério. This undertaking, concerned with the Caeté Indians who once inhabited Alagoas—and whose chief recorded exploit seems to have been the cannibalizing of the first bishop of Brazil—not only provides the title of the novel but also gives rise to passages in which Ramos reveals something of his approach to the literary process. Here João Valério has been trying

to describe the shipwreck which caused the ill-starred bishop to fall into the hands—and stomachs—of the savages:

> With a hesitant pen I meditated a long while on the floating wreckage. I had counted on that shipwreck; I had imagined an impressive description full of vivid adjectives. And there I had only a colorless, insignificant account of a second-rate disaster. It was short too: written in a large hand, and with some words crossed out, it ran to only eighteen lines. Putting a sinking ship in my book—what foolishness! When had I ever seen a galleon? Besides it may have been a caravel. Or a barkentine.

Like João Valério, Ramos, from the beginning, found himself incapable not only of high-flown language but of drawing episodes out beyond the essential. He was also incapable, or felt himself to be so, of describing that with which he did not have firsthand experience.

The plot of *Caetés* is a simple one. João Valério, a store clerk, nourishes an adulterous desire for Luísa, his employer's wife. She yields to him during an absence of her husband. The latter, informed of her infidelity, commits suicide. Though now free to marry, João Valério and Luísa go their separate ways, their passion dead.

About these central figures revolves a host of minor ones—politicians, boardinghouse keepers, clergy, merchants—occupied with the petty intrigues and gossip of small-town existence. They are singularly lifelike. A number of Ramos' acquaintances claimed to recognize their portraits and accused him of writing a *roman à clef,* a charge that greatly annoyed him. He himself says, regarding the genesis of his characters, "One thing surprised me: my personages began to talk. Previously my wretched, abandoned, incomplete creatures had been all but mute, perhaps because they had tried to express themselves in an overly correct Portuguese, altogether impossible in Brazil. My book turned out to be full of dialog; it reads like a play."

Indeed, it is largely through dialog that the characters reveal themselves, bit by bit. The resulting psychological portraits are doubtless superficial, for people are not wont to bare their souls in casual dinner-table conversations. The abundant dialog also offers another advantage: by its liveliness it causes the reader to all but overlook the paucity of narrative element.

In *Caetés,* as in his later novels, Ramos is concerned much less with telling a story than with studying an individual in a particular situation. The critic Antônio Cândido penetratingly observes: "Without recourse to introspection, inner life is described through the *situation* of a character within a context of actions and events. A double perspective results, for, if the character is revealed by the events, these present themselves in the light of the problems affecting him." Ramos' preoccupation with the case of the individual, with his particular view of ambient reality, is emphasized by the fact that each of his first three novels is related by the protagonist, an arrangement which of necessity results in subordinating all events and characters to his private angle of vision. (Indeed, save for the short stories and *Barren Lives,* virtually the whole of Ramos' writing is in the first person, the author speaking either directly for himself, as in the case of the autobiographical works, or through the mouth of a fictional creation.)

Although not only this approach to the novel but also a number of Ramos' other characteristics—the spareness and precision of his vocabulary, the brevity of his periods, his disillusioned view of life, his wry humor—are to be found in *Caetés,* that book by no means prepares the reader for the novels that were to follow, all of which show a mastery of style and technique that assign Graciliano Ramos a place apart in Brazilian letters. They are remarkably different one from another, and each has found critics to support it as the author's masterpiece.

"Stark" is perhaps the adjective which best befits *São Bernardo,* by reason of the obduracy of the protagonist, the harshness of the book's atmosphere, the bareness of the narrative, and the strength of the work as a literary creation.

If in *Caetés* Ramos described the society surrounding him in Palmeira dos Indios, for *São Bernardo* he went back to an earlier period in his existence, situating the action in the district of Viçosa. This was a region of both farmers and stock raisers, whose mutually repellent interests led to what at one time was said to be the highest homicide rate in any municipality in Brazil. Small property owners, particularly crop raisers, were systematically eliminated—with a rifle or through economic and political pressure—by the larger proprietors, usually cattlemen. Only the strongest and most ruthless survived.

The story Ramos tells is well suited to so harsh a background. The protagonist-narrator, Paulo Honório, is a self-made man. A foundling, he has forged ahead in life by hook, by crook, by indomitable will, and by endless energy. At the age of forty-five he has achieved the goal of his existence: he is the owner of the property which gives the book its name, a rural estate on which he had once been a field laborer; the ne'er-do-well son of the former proprietor is now in his employ. With a view to begetting an heir, he takes a wife, Madalena, a woman of great goodness and compassion for all. Her charity and sensitivity are totally incompatible with Paulo Honório's brutal, possessive nature. He cannot conceive of Madalena as other than an item of his property, and she, weary of an unending struggle against cruelty, misunderstanding, and jealousy, commits suicide. Paulo Honório realizes at last that he had, in his own way, truly loved his wife, that everything else has no real meaning for him. To fill the empty hours, to unburden the soul he had been unable to reveal even to Madalena, he undertakes to set their story down on paper.

Unlike the protagonist of *Caetés,* Paulo Honório is not a function of his environment; on the contrary the environment is entirely subordinated to his own compelling personality. Paulo Honório embodies the instinct of ownership. It is not a question of avarice; for Paulo Honório all humanity is divided into two classes—men of property and those who work for them. All his efforts have been bent to achieving entrance into the former class. The consequences of his single-mindedness he recognizes in a final summing up:

> I do not think I was always selfish and brutal. My calling made me so. . . . This way of life destroyed me. I am a cripple. I must have a very small heart, blank spots in my brain, nerves different from those of other men.

Hypertrophied though he may be, he is not, however, all of a piece. He still possesses human feelings, and it is the inner conflict to which they give rise that makes of him a dramatic personality, that leaves him in the end not one of life's victors but one of life's vanquished.

It would be difficult to imagine a work more thoroughly reduced to essentials than *São Bernardo.* Paulo Honório's early career is related in a dozen short, but extraordinarily vivid, paragraphs. There is not a single description for its own sake.

The phrases that evoke the property of São Bernardo are of the briefest and are always introduced to further in some way the development of events. Here, for example, is the opening of the scene in which Paulo Honório proposes to take over the estate from Luís Padilha, the ne'er-do-well into whose hands it has fallen by inheritance:

> I rode toward the plantation house, which looked even older and in worse need of repair under the pouring rain. The spiderflowers had not been cut. I jumped off the horse and walked in, stamping my feet, my spurs clinking. Luís Padilha was asleep in the main room, stretched out in a filthy hammock, oblivious to the rain that beat at the windows and the leaks from the roof which were flooding the floor.

Everything needed to explain Padilha's subsequent acquiescence is here suggested to the reader—his indolence, the neglect into which he has let his property fall, the domineering manner in which Paulo Honório approaches him, stamping, and entering without so much as a by-your-leave.

While the conversations are fully as natural as those of *Caetés,* Ramos has limited them, like all else, to the significant. The sharpness of the interchanges gives them often an air of verbal duels between the characters.

Ramos, speaking through his protagonist-narrator, describes the reduction to essentials quite simply: "The process I have adopted is this: I extract a few elements from an event, and reject the rest as waste."

Stylistically, *São Bernardo* is a tour de force. The short, abrupt sentences, with their energetic vocabulary, are thoroughly expressive of the personality of the narrator. The writing has the ease and naturalness of popular speech, without recourse to dialect, looseness of construction, imprecision in choice of words, or syntactical error.

It would be hard to conceive of a work more different in overall effect from *São Bernardo* than the novel which followed, *Angústia* [*Anguish*]. Once again the story is told in retrospect by the protagonist, but whereas Paulo Honório is a man strong of body and purpose, who has battled his way from field laborer to landed proprietor, the Luís da Silva of *Anguish* is the abulic final off-shoot of a decadent family of plantation owners, reduced to a meager existence as a petty clerk in a government office. While *São Bernardo* has an out-of-doors atmosphere of space and light, the drama of *Anguish* unfolds in the dark, tortuous recesses of the protagonist's mind. Dialog, so brilliantly handled in the preceding novels, is abandoned for an all-but-uninterrupted inner monolog. Straightforward narrative is replaced by a fragmented confession, in which events are presented in a complex interplay of objective reality, memory, and speculation. The view of persons and events is not merely one-sided; it is deformed by the distorted vision of the protagonist.

The new manner is suggested by this passage from the beginning of the novel:

> If I could, I would give up everything and resume my travels. This monotonous existence, chained to a desk from nine to twelve and from two to five, is stupefying. I might as well be a clam. Stupefying. When they close the office, I drag myself over to the clock tower and take the first streetcar to Land's End.
>
> What can Marina be doing? I try to get her out of my mind. I could take a trip, get drunk, commit suicide.

I can see my dead body, thin as a rail, my teeth showing in a grin, my eyes like a pair of peeled grapes, my hands with their tobacco-stained fingers crossed on my hollow chest. . . .

I shake off these depressing thoughts. They come and go shamelessly, and with them the recollection of Julião Tavares. Unbearable. I try to get my mind off these things. I'm not a rat, I don't want to be a rat. I seek distraction looking at the street. . . .

Fifteen years ago it was different. You couldn't hear the church bell for the noise of the streetcars. My room, on the second floor, was as hot as hell. So at the hour the other boarders were leaving for medical school, I would go over to the public park and read the crime reports in the shade of the trees. Of course the boardinghouse has been closed and Miss Aurora, who was old even then, has died.

If Paulo Honório personifies the instinct of ownership, Luís da Silva is the embodiment of frustration. The thought of his family reminds him how far he has come down in the world; his bureaucratic routine gives him no sense of purpose in life; an overdeveloped critical faculty makes him keenly aware not only of the lack of merit of those more favored by fortune but also of his own shortcomings. He had once written a collection of poems; unable to pay for their publication under his own name, he has sold them one by one to others who wished to figure as possessors of literary talents.

Timid in his personal relations, particularly with women ("sex for me was always something painful, complicated, and incomplete"), he is ensnared into an engagement by Marina, the idle daughter of a neighbor family. She spends on a trousseau what he has saved and borrowed for household goods. At this point a man appears who is the exact opposite of Luís da Silva. Julião Tavares, the son of a merchant, has money, social position, women, self-confidence, and an untroubled conscience. Taking a passing fancy to Marina, he seduces and abandons her. All of Luís' pent-up frustration finds its object in his triumphant rival. So obsessed with him does he become that at last he is led to action. One night, as Julião returns from a visit to his latest conquest, Luís strangles him. He tells his story upon recovery from the extended period of nervous prostration that ensued.

Though attention centers on the personality of Luís da Silva, the novel offers a varied gallery of vivid portraits. Particularly striking is the servant woman Vitória, who buries her savings in the back yard only to dig them up for constant recounting, and who is deeply perturbed when, without her knowledge, Luís borrows from the hoard and makes restitution in coins of different denomination.

Despite the nightmare air of the book, many of the characters are drawn from life. Luís da Silva's grandfather, for example, is patterned on Ramos' own; the latter's henchman José Baía appears under his own name. The original of Moisés, the Jewish revolutionary, was a source of concern to Ramos at the time of his incarceration.

It is curious that this somber story, with its prison-like atmosphere, should have appeared precisely at that darkest period in the author's life—curious because no relation of cause and effect exists between the two facts. The book had been finished prior to Ramos' arrest; one of his many worries in jail was how it might fare in the hands of the publisher. Persecution of the author did, however, contribute to the success with which the novel met on its appearance. It was greeted as a masterpiece;

the author was hailed as a Brazilian Dostoevsky. Somewhat more reserved views are expressed today. Antônio Cândido, while paying due tribute to *Anguish*, as a tour de force, finds it "overdone." The work is still, however, the one regarded by a majority of critics as Ramos' best.

The genesis of his next and final novel, *Barren Lives*, Graciliano Ramos describes thus:

In 1937 I wrote some lines on the death of a dog, an animal that turned out overly intelligent to my way of thinking, and for this reason somewhat different from my bipeds. Afterwards I did a few pages on the dog's owners. These pieces were sold, one by one, to newspapers and magazines. When [the publisher] José Olímpio asked me for a book at the beginning of last year, I invented a few more narratives which could just as easily be short stories as chapters of a novel. Thus there came into being Fabiano, his wife, their two boys, and the dog, the last creatures I have put in circulation.

It is interesting to note that all of Ramos' novels, by his own account, began as short stories. *São Bernardo* and *Anguish* were sketched in embryonic form before he took up the theme of *Caetés*; in this last case "the short story grew all too long and deteriorated into a novel." *Caetés* having been accepted for publication, Ramos returned to his earlier sketches, developing them too into novels.

Barren Lives is a compromise between genres. The book possesses unity: it presents a cycle in the life of a herdsman and his family, from their arrival at a ranch as refugees from one drought to their departure in flight from another. Yet the individual chapters are relatively independent entities; their order could be altered in various ways without detriment to the whole. Not only were the first parts written for separate publication as short stories, but Ramos himself included three chapters ("Jail," "Feast Day," "The Dog") with other selected short narratives in a volume he published in 1946 under the title of *Histórias Incompletas* (*Incomplete Stories*).

The title, as Antônio Cândido shrewdly notes, is perhaps more significant than Ramos intended, for it well indicates the deficiency that marks his work as a short story writer. None of his compositions in this genre forms a satisfying narrative unit. Each seems but a sketch for, or fragment of, a larger work. In *Barren Lives*, however, the recurrence of the same figures in varying situations gradually produces that sense of wholeness requisite to the self-sufficiency of a work of art.

Of all his output, *Barren Lives* is the work in which Ramos is most concerned with narration, with telling a story, tenuous though it may be. As in the case of his short stories, he here abandons the use of the first person for the third. This technique does not result in any sense of detachment, however, for he still writes at all times from the viewpoint of one of the characters. Five of the chapters in fact are named for the personage whose vision of events colors their presentation. In four more Fabiano reappears as the dominant figure. In the remaining chapters the viewpoint shifts from character to character. Only in the closing sentence of the books does Ramos, perhaps regrettably, speak from a standpoint foreign to his characters.

One can hardly speak of psychological analysis in the case of Fabiano and his family; they are not so much simple as elementary. Their actions are guided by instinct rather than thought; Fabiano's attempt to understand how he comes to be in jail, for instance, suggests that ratiocination is beyond his capabilities. Ramos can therefore treat the dog on very much the same level as her masters, as a member of the family.

Dialog, of which Ramos had made such skillful use in earlier works, is here almost totally missing. Having a minimum of ideas to convey to one another, the members of the family are generally silent, to such an extent that the parrot they once owned never learned to talk. A gesture or an interjection serves for a large part of the communication among them.

The personages of *Barren Lives* are admirably studied in regard to their surroundings. This is, in fact, of all Ramos' works the one in which the relation between man and his milieu is most clearly developed. In *Caetés* the characters are distinctly small-town products, but the town might have been any one of countless others in Brazil rather than Palmeira dos Indios. The action of *São Bernardo* is set in the district of Viçosa and that of *Anguish* presumably in Maceió, but the locale is of little importance to the development of personalities and events.

Barren Lives, however, could take place nowhere save in the drought-ridden interior of northeastern Brazil. (The literal meaning of the Portuguese title, *Vidas Sêcas,* "Dry Lives," reflects both the parched atmosphere of the region and the desiccating effect it has on the existence of its inhabitants.) It is the work which identifies Ramos with the so-called novel of the Northeast, one of the most fertile veins in Brazilian literature since 1930. Its practitioners have dealt with varying aspects of the region—José Lins do Rêgo with the sugar plantations of coastal Pernambuco and Paraíba, Jorge Amado with the street urchins of Salvador and the cacao wars of southern Bahia, for example. No aspect of the area has attracted greater attention, doubtless by reason of the dramatic effects it offers, than the terrible droughts that periodically visit the backlands. Only a hardy breed could survive such trials, especially when prospects of reward are so few.

Fabiano and his family own little more than the clothes on their backs. Their few belongings are easily contained in a tin trunk which Vitória balances on her head when they set off on one of their forced treks. Their pleasures are small ones—an occasional swig of rum for Fabiano, a pair of high-heeled shoes for Vitória, a trip to town for all at the time of the Christmas festivities. Fabiano is a good herdsman, and the ranch prospers under his management as long as the rains come. He gets no thanks from the proprietor, however, whose conversation with his employee usually takes the form of a dressing-down. By a skillful system of advances of money and overcharges for interest, the proprietor sees, moreover, that little or nothing in the form of wages comes into Fabiano's hands at the end of the year. Tradesmen cheat the ranch hand, townspeople scorn him as a bumpkin, a policeman avenges his ill luck at cards by throwing him into jail. Yet Fabiano accepts all this abuse as his natural lot; so was his father used before him, and he has only vague illusions that his sons may know a better life. The height of his wife's ambition is ownership of a single piece of furniture, a comfortable bed.

It is to be remarked that Ramos has no recourse to the more dramatic aspects of life in the backlands—banditry and religious fanaticism—which crop up frequently in other novels of the region. His very descriptions of the drought are sober; he suggests by details, such as the vultures circling in to peck out the eyes of moribund animals, in preference to painting a large-scale picture of natural catastrophe. One might recall in this regard João Valério, whose attempt at a grandiose depiction of shipwreck resulted in a "colorless, insignificant account of

a second-rate disaster." Unlike João Valério, who had never seen a galleon, Graciliano Ramos had experienced drought from his earliest years. The restraint of his treatment reflects his austere temperament rather than any insufficiency of knowledge.

It is difficult to say why Ramos to all intents and purposes turned his back on fiction after the publication of *Barren Lives.* Perhaps he felt he had exhausted the varieties of approach open to a writer of his particular abilities and preferred to avoid any air of repeating himself. Again it may have been a desire to comment still more directly upon the world of his experience that led him to abandon fictional mouthpieces and to devote the major literary efforts of his last years to autobiography.

Infância (*Childhood*), in its poetic presentation of distant figures and events, preserves something of the atmosphere of fiction. Ramos in a sense was still writing from a viewpoint external to himself—that of the boy he had been half a century earlier, a boy who had left a few traces of his existence in *Anguish* and *Barren Lives.* The distinguished critic Álvaro Lins holds *Childhood* to be the best-written of all Ramos' works, and indeed it is one of great distinction and charm. It possesses full literary autonomy; while of much interest for the light it throws on the man and his fictional compositions, it can be read and enjoyed for itself alone, as a story or collection of stories.

The *Prison Memoirs,* on the other hand, constitute a spiritual diary of a period much nearer at hand, which had left an indelible impression on Ramos' mind. One cannot but wonder at the wealth of its recorded detail, even if, as the author admits, it may not be accurate in all particulars, for it is in its entirety a reconstruction from memory. (Ramos took extended notes during the first part of his imprisonment, but these were later lost.) Highly uneven—pedestrian passages being interspersed with pages of great power—the *Memoirs* would undoubtedly have benefited from tightening and revision had not death overtaken the author as he was approaching the end of his chronicle.

Ramos once wrote that in his view the principal deficiency from which Brazilian fiction of his day suffered was "lack of careful observation of the facts that are to enter into the composition of the work of art," adding that, "in an undertaking so complex as the novel, ignorance of those facts is detrimental to characterization and results in a lack of verisimilitude in the narrative." He himself was constant in writing only of that with which he had firsthand acquaintance and a feeling of intimacy. In an interview given a year before his death he declared:

> I could never conceive an abstract novel, a work of escape literature. My novels are all concerned with the Northeast, because it was there that I spent my youth; it is what I really know and feel. I have lived in Rio for twenty years [sic], but I could never succeed in writing a novel about Rio, because I do not know the city.

Ramos did not, however, feel any scruple about rearranging facts to suit artistic purpose. In *São Bernardo,* Paulo Honório describes the process which we may assume was Ramos' own:

> This conversation, obviously, did not proceed exactly as I have set it down on paper. There were pauses, repetitions, misunderstandings, and contradictions, all quite natural when people speak without thinking of the record. I reproduce what I consider interesting. I suppressed a number of passages and altered others. . . . For example, when I dragged Costa Brito

over to the clock, I told him what I thought of him in four or five indecent terms. This abuse, unnecessary since it neither added to nor detracted from the effect of the whiplashes I gave him, has gone by the board as you will note if you reread the scene of the attack. That scene, expurgated of obscenities, is described with relative sobriety.

Sobriety is indeed one of the key characteristics of Ramos' manner. It has been noted in the discussion of *Barren Lives,* for example, that the author avoids the more melodramatic aspects of life in the backlands and that in picturing the catastrophic effects of the drought he exercises great restraint. Even Luís da Silva's murder of Julião Tavares, the most violent scene in all Ramos' writing, admirable as a revelation of the workings of the narrator's tortured mind, is related with great simplicity of terms.

Ramos' constant aim was to obtain maximum effect from minimum resources. What he has to say he says in relatively few words. Save for the *Prison Memoirs,* none of his works can be described as long. As novels, *São Bernardo* and *Barren Lives* are decidedly short. Ramos' sentences too are for the most part brief; at times they seem almost curt. Descriptive adjectives and adverbs are held to a minimum: a sample six-page chapter of *São Bernardo* exhibits but two of the latter and two dozen of the former.

Ramos was greatly concerned with what he considered acceptable standards of literary expression. Up to the third decade of the present century, Brazilian authors tended to take the usage of Portugal as their model, without regard for the transformations which time, geographical separation, and the introduction of new ethnic elements had of necessity wrought in Portuguese as spoken in Brazil. The Modernist movement of the 1920's revolted against this practice of "speaking one language and writing another," and advocated vernacular usage as the basis of literary style. The inevitable question, of course, was what level of usage was to be taken as standard. If turns of popular speech often brought savoriness and spontaneity to literature, excessive reliance on the model provided by the man in the street, or in the field, resulted in what Ramos characterized as "the intentional mistakes of certain citizens who systematically write things the wrong way." Such writers, he continued, "are purists who have gone astray, seeking to create an artificial language of halting effect." Recognizing, on the other hand, that an "overly correct Portuguese" was "altogether impossible in Brazil," he sought to steer a middle course, avoiding both the stilted and the incorrect. He succeeded admirably. One might well apply to Ramos what he said of one of his contemporaries: "He expresses himself correctly and without floweriness; this gives his prose an air of naturalness which deceives the unwary reader. We do not perceive the artifice; we have the impression that the effect is altogether spontaneous, obtained without effort of any kind."

Álvaro Lins, for his part, describes Ramos' style thus:

> Graciliano Ramos' prose is modern by reason of its leanness, the vocabulary it employs, and the taste it exhibits in the use of words and syntactical constructions. It is classic in its correctness and in the tone of what one might term Biblical dignity that marks the sentences. Its distinction derives not from sensual beauty but from precision—from a capacity for transmitting sensations and impressions with a minimum of metaphors and images, simply through the skillful interplay of words.

Both for the transparency of his writing and for the pessimistic view he takes of life, Ramos has been compared to the greatest of his Brazilian predecessors, Machado de Assis. The aristocratically disillusioned prose of the latter, most often manifested in ironic wit, contrasts with a more profoundly fatalistic attitude on the part of Ramos. It is well exemplified by the passage setting forth Fabiano's feelings following his settling of accounts with the ranch owner:

> Couldn't they see he was a man of flesh and blood? It was his duty to work for others, naturally. He knew his place. That was all right. He was born to this lot; it was nobody's fault that it was a hard one. What could he do? Could he change fate? If anyone were to tell him it was possible to better one's lot, he would be amazed. He had come into the world to break untamed horses, cure cattle ailments by prayer, and fix fences from winter to summer. It was fate. His father had lived like that, his grandfather too. . . . He accepted the situation; he did not ask for more. If only they gave him what was coming to him, it was all right. But they didn't. He was a poor devil; like a dog, all he got was bones. Why then did rich people go and take part of the bones?

Life is essentially unjust, and there is nothing anyone can do about it: this is Ramos' view. Other writers of his generation, particularly those from his own Northeast, likewise saw the injustice; they, however, felt that something could and should be done about it. Several took an active part in left-wing politics, and in their works there breathes a conviction that sooner or later a new day must dawn for the disinherited of the earth. Not so Ramos. He admitted of changes in individual situations: a Paulo Honório could rise, a Luís Padilha could sink. There will always, however, be oppressed and oppressors. Toward both he took an equally cold, one might say clinical, attitude. Suffering he treats with dignity but without compassion.

Though Ramos seems to have taken human pettiness and meanness for granted, human generosity caused him surprise. Gratuitous acts of kindness of which he was the object during prison days were a source of unresolved wonder to him. Is it coincidence that the work which followed upon that period of his existence was not the somber *Anguish* but *Barren Lives,* relatively speaking the most optimistic—or perhaps one should say least pessimistic—of his creations? Despite the natural disasters and human injustices which overtake them, Fabiano and his family breathe an elemental heroism; they bear witness to the unconquerable spirit that bids man carry on, whatever adversity he may be called to face.

By reason of the keenness of his psychological insight, of his deep feeling for the vernacular, of his unfailing sense of proportion, of his skilled craftsmanship in construction, Ramos has been able to fashion from the simplest and most unpromising of materials works which stand among the most impressive creations of modern Brazilian literature. Commonplace incidents, related with that apparent artlessness which is one of the highest forms of art, acquire a depth of meaning far surpassing that of the spectacular shipwrecks to which the João Valérios of the literary world turn for effect. The backlander Fabiano, humble and inarticulate though he may be, takes on a stature and a dignity approaching that of figures of classic tragedy.

"Less is more," Mies van der Rohe has proclaimed. The power of Graciliano Ramos' austere creations well betokens the truth of that dictum. (pp. xiv-xxxiv)

Ralph Edward Dimmick, in an introduction to Barren Lives (Vidas sêcas) *by Graciliano Ramos, translated by Ralph Edward Dimmick, University of Texas Press, 1965, pp. vii-xxxiv.*

RUSSELL G. HAMILTON   (essay date 1968)

[*Hamilton is an American critic and educator specializing in Portuguese language and literature. In the following excerpt, he argues that the characterization, tone, and intent of* Vidas sêcas *set it apart from Ramos's other novels.*]

When critics of contemporary Brazilian literature write and speak of Graciliano Ramos, they often use such terms as "introspective," "somber view of the world," and "pessimistic." Certainly when we consider Ramos' first three novels, *Caetés, São Bernardo,* and *Angústia,* these terms all seem to apply. So great has become Graciliano Ramos' reputation as a writer who viewed life with acrimony that even *Vidas Sêcas* has been called a story of hopelessness and despair. The title, in both its literal and figurative meanings, contributes of course to the general belief that this last of Ramos' novels, perhaps his masterpiece, contains the despondency of the first three works. And one can hardly deny the circumstances of drought and social and economic adversity that plague the small family group throughout *Vidas Sêcas'* thirteen chapters. But if we classify the illiterate cowboy Fabiano with the pusilanimous clerk of *Caetés,* or the nihilistic anti-hero of *Angústia,* or even *São Bernardo's* self-defeated protagonist, we ignore a definite change of tone and intent in *Vidas Sêcas.*

In *Caetés* João Valério fails to rise above his petty bourgeois existence; Paulo Honório, the owner of the plantation São Bernardo, attempts to reconstruct his emotionally barren life; and Luís da Silva seeks to affirm himself through a desperate act. All three of these negative characters live either in a desolate present or a ruinous past. With Fabiano and his family, on the other hand, we encounter characters with a germ of hope, and the author explicitly expresses this sense of hope through the ideas that the ignorant cowboy, his wife, and their two sons possess.

Vidas Sêcas obviously differs from the three earlier novels in its purely technical features: the story is narrated in the third rather than the first person, and the episodic chapters bear a title instead of merely a number. The presence of the *sertão* with descriptions of the landscape, and more significantly, tone and the treatment of character truly set *Vidas Sêcas* apart from the others.

In the Generation of 1930 Graciliano Ramos emerged as an often caustic commentator on the foibles of the small town bourgeoisie of his Northeast region. Thus, João Valério and Luís da Silva are products, or better, victims, of this ambience to which they acquiesce or by which they are crushed. Even Paulo Honório, the self-sufficient plantation owner, gravitates toward the small provincial town in his desire for social ascension and materialistic gain. Fabiano and sinhá Vitória, however, are untrammeled by petty, middle-class morality, and although Graciliano Ramos displays the degradation of their dry lives, he also demonstrates unprecedented sympathy for his main characters, a sympathy which derives from his belief in the *sertanejo* as the archetypal northeasterner whose very brutishness and resignation appear as positive values. *Vidas Sêcas* does not concern the psychological drama of one character, but deals rather with a type, the *sertanejo:* "O sertão

mandaria para·a cidade homens, fortes, brutos como Fabiano, sinhá Vitória e os dois filhos."

This positive, sympathetic attitude often approaches heroic grandeur, and for the first time in any of his works Graciliano Ramos employs the theme of man against nature. He takes advantage of this *sertão* setting to recreate the drama of people eking out a living in a land flagellated by natural calamities. The humans belong to this harsh land, and in the following passages the onomatopoeic word *chapechape* serves as a stylistic term of identification with the earth: "Chapechape. Os três pares de alpercatas batiam na lama rachada, sêca e branca por cima, preta e mole por baixo. A lama de beira do rio, calcada pelas alpercatas, balançava." The family, like the hardy *sertão* vegetation, resists the ravages of climate, and Fabiano, in exaltation, "olhou as quipás, os mandacarus e os xique-xiques. Era mais forte que tudo isso, era como as catinguerias e as baraúnas. Êle, sinhá Vitória, os dois filhos e a cachorra Baleia estavam agarrados à terra." (pp. 86-7)

Vidas Sêcas, unlike those northeastern novels that recreate the plight of hundreds of refugees fleeing the drought, synthesizes the pathos of the *sertão* drama with an intimate view of the inner as well as outer struggle of a small group of backlanders. Graciliano Ramos tells the story of Fabiano, Vitória, the two boys, and Baleia with a sentimentality absent in his three previous novels. Far from being a pessimistic novel, *Vidas Sêcas* presents a measure of the romanticism seen in the works of other members of the Generation of 1930, and Ramos certainly identifies with the *sertanejo* on an emotional level. The crux of the novel's social message, if one cares to see such a message, lies in the family's ideas, all of which contain, to a greater or lesser degree, a note of protest or at least a desire for change. . . . (p. 92)

Russell G. Hamilton, "Character and Idea in Ramos' 'Vidas Sêcas'," in Luso-Brazilian Review, *Vol. V, No. 1, June, 1968, pp. 86-92.*

MARIE F. SOVEREIGN   (essay date 1970)

[*In the following excerpt, Sovereign examines the pessimistic philosophy expressed in Ramos's works.*]

Pessimism lends its note of despair to many modern novels. Few authors, however, have more consistently portrayed a defeatist philosophy of life than the Brazilian Graciliano Ramos. Without exception, his works express the feelings of futility and despair which often characterize existential pessimism. Typical of this attitude is an expression found in *Vidas Sêcas,* where Ramos places in the mind of Fabiano, his main character, this thought: "Se ao menos pudesse recordar-se de fatos agradáveis, a vida não seria inteiramente má." The frequent recurrence of such bitter remarks leads one to believe that the author himself has no pleasant recollections.

Born and reared in the hinterland of northeastern Brazil, Graciliano Ramos emerged to take his place as a writer in the civilized jungle of Rio de Janeiro. Not surprisingly, therefore, his works reveal the tension he must have experienced between urban and rural existence. Both surroundings serve as a backdrop for the hopelessness and cynicism with which he regarded the human condition. The character of his writings is eminently psychological. Each of his novels and short stories takes place mainly in the interior world of thoughts and feelings. In contrast to his first novel, which develops primarily through dialogue, Ramos achieves the almost complete absence of any spoken words in his final work. Exterior circumstances or events serve only to stimulate the continual flow of pessimistic reactions. Clearly, the author has made his works the vehicle for expounding his own subjective view of life. All but the last of his novels are written, as one would expect, in the first person. Moreover, several of his heroes possess individual traits, such as the urge for creative writing, which can be closely identified with those of the author himself. (pp. 57-8)

The explanation for Ramos' profoundly negative view of life is not hard to discover. Describing his own childhood in *Infância,* he states that fear was the dominant emotion he experienced in his early years. It becomes apparent that he never received the tender affection most children take for granted. When he refers to his mother, it is always to describe her as impatient, angry, or moody, with a face devoid of kindness. (p. 58)

The recurring themes of Ramos' novels elaborate upon the perversion and hypocrisy inherent in human nature. Underlying these outward symptoms or manifestations of human behavior is a basic cruelty which, thinly camouflaged by polite conventions, erupts repeatedly in scenes of unmitigated ugliness. In Ramos' first novel, *Caetés,* even the title suggests that barbarian instinct which the would-be writer, João Valério, satisfies by describing violent scenes of savagery and cannibalism; in this way, the hero "acts out" mentally the personal vengeance which he cannot express acceptably in society. In *São Bernardo,* brutality is openly expressed by Paulo Honório toward Magdalena, his wife, to the point where, at her suicide, it is clear that her husband was as guilty of murder as if he had handed her the fatal poison. Cruelty is present also in *Angústia,* though in the form of circumstances which torture the individual, forcing him to perpetrate a murder. Cruelty in *Vidas Sêcas* is personified in nature and in society, with man as the helpless victim.

Unfaithfulness in marriage, as in the works of Machado de Assis, is a favorite theme in Ramos' novels. In *Caetés,* the adultery is real, though the infatuation proves shortlived. When the husband conveniently dies, having shot himself due to lingering illness and the shock of suspecting his wife's infidelity, the lovers realize that their love has evaporated completely, bearing out the suspicion that their relationship was nothing more than primitive savagery all along, a perverted kind of cruelty masked as affection.

In *São Bernardo,* the adultery is all in the husband's imagination. Haunted by his own infidelity and deep feelings of inferiority, Paulo Honório cannot believe that Magdalena married him with the best of intentions or that she is trying desperately to perform the impossible task of pleasing him. Gazing intently at his infant son's face, he tries in vain to find his own or another man's likeness. With the tenacity of paranoia, he tries to force his wife to admit her guilt and treats her as if she were in fact an adulteress.

Closely related to the author's skepticism regarding matrimony is his thinly veiled but distinctly uncharitable opinion of women in general. It is quite possible that Ramos' mother may have been to some degree responsible. In *São Bernardo,* Paulo Honório reflects that, since he wanted an heir, a wife was the obvious necessity. He confesses matter-of-factly: "Amanheci um dia pensando em casar. Foi uma idéia que me veio sem que nenhum rabo de saia a provocasse. Não me occupo com amores, devem ter notado, e sempre me pareceu que mulher é um bicho exquisito, difficil de governar." His courtship

proceeds on a purely materialistic basis, his secure financial status being the decisive factor for all concerned. His wife turns out to have some intellectual ability and interest, whereupon he remarks caustically, "Não gosto de mulheres sabidas. Chamam-se intellectuaes e são horríveis."

Luisa in *Caetés* has no qualities to recommend her. Weak and dishonest, she does nothing to elevate woman's reputation. Like most of Ramos' heroines, she causes only grief and disillusionment to the men in her life. Marina is the incarnation of stupidity, greed, and fickleness in woman. Far from redeeming her sex, she is one of its least attractive representatives. She, more than any other, is responsible for the bitter agony of Luiz da Silva in *Angústia.*

Curiously, Sinhá Vitória is an exception to the list of unsavory feminine characters in Ramos' books. Patient through want and privation, she excites compassion with her wistful longing for a decent bed to sleep in. More skilled in arithmetic than Fabiano, she is also intuitively wise, with almost prophetic insight. During the last pages of *Vidas Sêcas,* she timidly voices the hope that her boys may go to school and have a better life than she and her husbnd. In this, among Ramos' last published words, a tiny ray of optimism or the final irony, since so many flock to the cities hoping in vain?

Most significant is the portrayal of the female dog, Baleia, who emerges as perhaps the outstanding heroine of Ramos' novels. Gifted with human qualities of unselfishness and patient endurance, Baleia mutely reveals an ideal of womanhood not found among Ramos' human heroines. The contrast is painfully evident, a pathetic witness to the author's lack of faith in women.

Basic to the many ills that plague the characters in Ramos' novels and short stories is the complete lack of understanding among persons. The most shocking failure to communicate is that already mentioned between Paulo Honório and his ill-fated wife, Magdalena.

The short stories of *Insônia* likewise graphically illustrate various individuals' inability to relate to others. The self-torture described in "Insônia" is the result of extreme loneliness and insecurity—in short, failure to relate comfortably to society. "O relógio do hospital" describes a typical patient who, before and after surgery, imagines the worst and misinterprets or exaggerates what he sees and hears due to utter loneliness, again resulting from lack of communication, relatedness, or trust in others. "Luciana" and "Minsk" portray a little girl's loneliness due to being constantly misunderstood and persecuted by adults. The little girl's only true friend is a pet bird she inadvertently kills. She frequently escapes from reality by imagining herself a sophisticated lady. "Dois Dedos" is the poignant recollection by a modest physician of his childhood friend, now a governor, before whom he cowers awkwardly, not daring even to mention their former intimacy. One could enumerate each story from this collection, showing how it vividly develops the situation of aloneness and consequent maladjustment to society.

One of Ramos' best characterizations is Fabiano, who escapes loneliness because he has Sinhá Vitória, his sons, and his faithful Baleia, but who, nevertheless, is a complete misfit in society. He is deeply suspicious of every stranger he meets and imagines that everyone will do him harm if given the chance. When in town, he is constantly on guard, even miserable with apprehension. His sentiments are described thus:

Olhou as caras em redor. Evidentemente as criaturas que se juntavam ali não o viam, mas Fabiano sentia-se rodeado de inimigos, temia envolver-se em questões e acabar mal a noite . . .

Comparando-se aos tipos da cidade, Fabiano reconhecia-se inferior. Por isso desconfiava que os outros mangavam dêle. Fazia-se carrancudo e evitava conversas. Só lhe falavam com o fim de tirarlhe qualquer coisa.

Given the absence of relatedness between human beings, it is not surprising to observe a similar lack of relatedness to any divine being or to a secure, well-ordered universe. The separateness of persons not only impedes normal social relationships but consists of, or springs from, a deeper, cosmic loneliness. Religion, far from supplying meaning to existence or offering solutions to its problems, is considered basically irrelevant. References to it are few but significant. Paulo Honório muses laconically:

A verdade é que não me preocupo muito com o outro mundo. Admitto Deus, pagador celeste dos meus trabalhadores, mal remunerados cá na terra, e admitto o diabo . . . Tenho, portanto, um pouco de religião, embora julgue que, em parte, ela é dispensavel num homem. Mas mulher sem religião é horrivel.

The speaker's character, however, demonstrates clearly that a man without faith is just as pitiable as a woman without religion. Significantly, Paulo Honório felt no moral obligation to pay his workers a better wage, having concluded that deity would compensate them. It is also interesting to note that he uses the same phraseology here with respect to religion, "não me preocupo muito," which he used with respect to love of women. Two aspects of life, which many people regard as decisively important, Paulo Honório has seen fit to neglect. There could very well be a causal relationship between this fact and his sense of futility.

Fabiano likewise found no comfort or moral guidance in religion. We are told that, "Como tinha religião, entrava na igreja uma vez por ano." "Having religion" is about as meaningful, apparently, as a doubtful pedigree. The ritual he observed in the cathedral had no meaning for Fabiano or his children, who were more conscious of their physical discomfort in unaccustomed clothing and the crowded conditions of worship than of any pious sentiment. There is no hint that religion might offer the believer a sense of belonging in the universe, a perspective of the fatherhood of God or the brotherhood of man, forgiveness to alleviate guilt, or dynamics for right conduct among men. Any suggestions of this nature are conspicuously absent from Ramos' writings.

Other predominant themes in his works are despair and frustrated ambitions. Paulo Honório reflects bitterly after completing fifty years of apparently meaningless existence:

Cincoenta annos! Quantas horas inuteis! Consumir-se uma pessoa a vida inteira sem saber para que! Comer e dormir como um porco! Levantar-se cedo tôdas as manhãs e sahir correndo procurando comida! E depois guardar comida para os filhos, para os netos, para muitas geracões. Que estupidez! Que porcaria! Não é bom vir o diabo levar tudo?

To sum up all human aspiration in such a negative manner reveals a dearth of insight. However, for one to whom life on this planet is reduced completely to such a primitive process, despair is indeed a fitting conclusion.

Luiz da Silva in *Angústia* echoes the same note of hopelessness. In his sad stream of consciousness, he thinks of himself not as a pig but as a rat. He tries to persuade himself that he is not a rat, that he does not want to be one. Living with sordidness, in degrading intimacy with neighbors of doubtful reputation, he finds nobody who cares about him. Marina, the girl next door, becomes engaged to him only for what she can get out of him to supply her hope chest. At thirty-five years of age, his most heroic act, committed in panic and blind revenge, is to murder Marina's seducer. In such a world, there is clearly no satisfaction possible since there is no true affection, no mutual trust between persons, no home for the weary spirit.

Vidas Sêcas points up society's devaluation of the underprivileged, symbolized in the person of Fabiano. This dispossessed refugee does not have even the dignity of a pig or a rat. He feels like a tough, wild animal.

Não queria morrer. Estava escondido no mato como tatu. Duro, lerdo como tatu. Mas um dia sairia da toca, andaria com a cabeça levantada, seri homem.

On another occasion, he feels like a dog.

Er um desgraçado, era como um cachorro, só recebia ossos. Porque seria que os homens ricos ainda lhe tomavam parte dos ossos?

One might readily develop a thesis concerning animalism in Ramos. He saw all kinds of men in the context of animal nature and seemed to envision little for them on a higher plane.

As for Fabiano, one is led to believe that his station in life is irremediable. "Quem é do chão não se trepa." "Que fazer? Podia mudar a sorte?" "Que remedio? . . . Podia reagir? Não podia. Um cabra." "Tinha o direito de saber? Tinha? Não tinha." "Tinha culpa de ser bruto? Quem tinha culpa?"

Through such rhetorical questions, Graciliano Ramos wrestled over the miserable fate of his heroes, trying to discover some explanation, some justification for their unrelieved woe. One is not surprised to find that he was consciously expressing his own self through these characters. On one occasion [in *São Bernardo*], he plainly confessed:

Fabiano procede nas páginas do livro como eu procederia na vida se estivesse no seu lugar, pois êle e outras personagens são no fundo frações psicológicas de mim mesmo.

This, then, is the secret of Ramos' greatness as a writer and of his success in communicating his attitudes toward life. He has so identified himself with the underdog in human existence that he has been able poignantly to reveal the loneliness, the misunderstanding, the frustration, and the meaninglessness which is commonly shared, to a greater or lesser degree, by all men. In so doing, he challenged his own loneliness by saying, in effect, "This is the way I see it. Have you, the reader, not had such an experience?" At least, in the act of reaching out to unburden his own soul, Ramos eloquently speaks to ours about certain aspects of human reality. (pp. 58-63)

Marie F. Sovereign, "Pessimism in Graciliano Ramos," in Luso-Brazilian Review, *Vol. VII, No. 1, Summer, 1970, pp. 57-63.*

WILSON MARTINS   (essay date 1970)

[*Martins is a Brazilian educator and literary critic who has written extensively on Brazilian literature and society. Jack E. Tomlins,*

the English translator of Martins's O Modernismo (The Modernist
Idea), has stated that a "combination of historical accuracy, a
sense of history, keen literary discernment, and unfailing wit
readily identifies the lively critical personality of Wilson Martins
to a generation of Brazilianists." In the following excerpt from
The Modernist Idea, Martins provides an overview of Ramos's
literary career.]

Graciliano Ramos was the writer of the political revolution of
1930 rather than of the literary revolution of 1922. More than
that, his Northeast (speaking in terms of literature) was not the
Northeast of José Lins do Rêgo or Jorge Amado. I mean that
although in the history of Brazilian publishing he belonged to
the same famous generation that produced the so-called Northeastern literature of the thirties (an expression which is only
geographical by extension, contrary to the opinion of certain
participants of the Congresso de Crítica de Assis), he was truly
the great loner and eccentric.

In the bookish and abbreviated retrospect with which we usually perceive literary history, attracted merely by an irresistible
temptation to classify, we forget that Graciliano Ramos was
born in 1892 and that he was thirty years old at the time of
the Week of Modern Art. At that moment he no doubt took
no cognizance at all of the great literary event. It is also quite
likely that he had heard nothing at all of that other "regional"
modernism of 1926, even more limited to Recife than the
Modernism of 1922 had been concerned in its first stages with
the city of São Paulo. In the twenties Graciliano Ramos was
a man of considerable culture, who on his own had undertaken
more serious literary and linguistic studies than most of his
contemporaries. It appears, however, that he in no way seemed
destined for a career as a professional writer, for the national
fame as a novelist which came to be his. Moreover, in no way
whatsoever did he possess the "Modernist spirit" nor even the
modern spirit in the name of which the literary generation of
the thirties built their work.

His contemporaries, and in particular the more or less numerous
groups of frivolous souls who, in all periods, constitute what
we might call "literary circles" and thus influence—indirectly
but vigorously—the establishment of critical perspectives, always viewed the grumpy and pessimistic nature of "old Graça"
as if it constituted a particular kind of worldly attitude all his
own. An unprejudiced reading of his work, and notably of his
spontaneous and occasional pages, demonstrates that he was
above all a marginal personage in the literature of the day, just
as he was a marginal character in the reigning political system
and, in a quite obvious way, a marginal personage among the
social groups in which he lived. All of this marginalism was
conscious and, at the same time, responsible for his remorse
and pride: hence the reason for the singular stratification of his
character as man and writer in a paradoxical mixture of pessimism and idealism, of the lure of creativity and the disdain
for literature. (pp. 300-01)

The understanding of the kind of bad literary and political
conscience that identified him (ambivalent bad conscience, because it embraced at one and the same time his options and
his rejections) depends on knowledge of some of the details
of his life . . . and an objective attitude toward those details.
Among these, that of his spiritual development has obviously
still not been sufficiently clarified. All that we possess in that
regard is the invaluable volume of the *Homenagem*, published
on the occasion of his fiftieth birthday in 1943. There we read
the well-known story of the "discovery" of Graciliano Ramos
by Augusto Frederico Schmidt through the reading of the *Re-*

latório, now famous, which as mayor of Palmeira dos Índios
he had sent in 1929 to the governor of the state of Alagoas.
And we also know that when the publisher asked the mayor
for a novel, because it seemed to him that the official possessed
exceptional writing ability, that novel had already been written
in 1926, and it was *Caetés*. More than that: Nineteen chapters
of *São Bernardo* had been written in the province, in the "dusty
little town," the novelist says, where he might have continued
"to play chess and backgammon, attending to my petty chores,
listening to the endless arguments on the sidewalks, taking
refuge in the afternoon in the hulking cathedral." These qualities, if not of the writer at least of the intellectual, were not
recognized by Augusto Frederico Schmidt alone; the governor
of Alagoas seems to have recognized them as early as 1930
when after the second—and somewhat unconventional—report, he brought Graciliano Ramos to the directorship of the
State Press. The "redemptive Revolution" did not cut short
his bureaucratic career because from 1933 to 1936 he was still
director of public education in his native state. Thus the future
revolutionary adjusted to both the Old Republic and the New
Republic. At the same time, after 1933, with the publication
of *Caetés,* he enrolled in that Northeastern literature which was,
without his knowing it, the novel of São Paulo Modernism.
Simultaneously the winds of revolution blew him to Rio de
Janeiro, where he established permanent residence in 1936.

Nonetheless in that literature Graciliano Ramos was a writer
apart, beginning with his language, as is well known. It is no
secret that he repudiated *Caetés*—he repudiated it but continued
to republish it. That contradiction, better than any other, serves
to substantiate the ambivalences to which I referred. That and
the articles collected in *Viventes das Alagoas*. We are in the
presence of a man who prepared himself to be a classical and
traditional writer, a respecter of the Portuguese language, read
of course in the non-conformist text of Eça de Queiroz and
who, as he said in his expression of gratitude for the *Homenagem*, "was forced by events to undergo unforeseen dis-
placements." Without expecting it, he was thrown into a career
of professional writing; without expecting and without wishing
it, he became a "Modernist" writer because in the thirties one
tried to be a Modernist or died. If the older Alcântara Machado
spoke of Gonçalves de Magalhães as the "repentent Romantic," with regard to Graciliano Ramos, it would be proper to
speak of the Modernist *malgré lui*, the Modernist of ill will.
In many of his articles, even in the forties, he betrays his disgust
in the face of linguistic error and carelessness; in the 1929
Relatório (the one in which he mentions the episode of D.
Pedro Sardinha "devoured" in the sixteenth century by wild
Indians, this with regard to the economics of telegraph ex-
penditures), the erudite placement of objective pronouns betrays the man's cultivated literary taste: "I intend to lengthen
it [the Palmeiras de Fora road] to the boundary of Sant'Ana
do Ipanema, not in its present condition, because the income
from the county would not allow me to undertake a job of that
magnitude." This anti-Modernist correctness he retained to the
end of his days, just as he practiced to the end a type of prose
fiction which bore little substantial resemblance to Northeastern
fiction. The basic novelist of this period was, to be sure, José
Lins do Rêgo; beside him Jorge Amado represents the second
generation, the generation which neither had nor wished to
have any connection with literary history prior to 1922. Within
the "sociological novel" of the thirties, Graciliano Ramos
wrote the "psychological novel": the prestige of ready-made
ideas and simplistic views was so great that at the time no one
noticed such scandalous behavior. On the other hand, there
was no one more alien to "socialist realism" than this Com-

munist writer: even in this regard, Jorge Amado achieved what José Lins do Rêgo and Graciliano Ramos "ought" to have achieved. The latter's "socialist realism" found an outlet in his travel-book, precisely and paradoxically in his least realistic book, and also in the *Memórias do Cárcere,* which are his "notes from underground"—what we might call reality seen through the telescope of a novelist.

None of this escaped the experienced eye of Otto Maria Carpeaux, who wrote one of the most stimulating studies in the *Homenagem.* He justly regards the novelist as a classic, but

> an experimental classic. His extremely tardy appearance as a writer, when he was past forty, ought to have been preceded by the slow preparation of an experimentalist, for even afterward he always continued to experiment. Our friend in common, Aurélio Buarque de Holanda, called my attention to the fact that every one of Graciliano Ramos's works is a different type of novel. In effect: *Caetés* is the product of an Anatole or a Brazilian Eça; *São Bernardo* is worthy of Balzac; *Angústia* has something of Marcel Jouhandeau in it; and *Vidas Sêcas* reminds me of recent North American short story writers.

Otto Maria Carpeaux reminds us that it is not a question of comparison nor even, I would add, of exacting literary assimilation. But these names have the value of a suggestive indication; they bring Graciliano Ramos close to the universal novel in the same measure that they remove him from the "Northeastern literature" of the thirties. I would compare those prestigious allusions to Balzac and Eça de Queiroz to the chess and backgammon which Graciliano Ramos, even if it was only in his imagination, played in Palmeira dos Índios or in Maceió. Actually no Brazilian Modernist of the first decade would admit to a knowledge of backgammon; not one of them was or could be a chess player. If in intellectual life everything responds and corresponds, then one can assert that Northeastern literature was born of minds that no rule of chess ever entered, nor the spiritual conformity which those rules presuppose. By the same token, the chess expert would never have written novels like those of our thirties. Graciliano Ramos was in literature a Northeasterner and a Modernist of *that decade* (be sure to stress those words!); that is, he was gradually and inevitably influenced by the literature which was being produced all around him. It is easy to see that his "experimentalism" has an unconscious meaning and direction. If *Caetés* never was more than a truly literal echo of Eça de Queiroz, *São Bernardo* is then the Northeast seen through the eyes of a Balzac, but a primitive Balzac; *Angústia* is an attempt to surpass the two limitations implicit in these literary coordinates, and it all adds up in my opinion to obvious failure. *Vidas Sêcas* demonstrates a desire for integration into the Northeastern group; it reveals that José Lins do Rêgo's laurels robbed Graciliano of his sleep from time to time.

The inadmissable, shocking, unacceptable, and inevitable conclusion is that Graciliano Ramos's career, after all is said and done, adds up to a frustration, not over what it was but over what it ought to have been. He could not withstand the pressures of his literary milieu and abruptly altered the direction of his work, attempted to conquer his original propensities and the very nature of his mind. *Caetés* is the novel most deserving of criticism of all those which he published (if we take into account that *Vidas Sêcas* is not, properly speaking, a novel), but at the same time it does represent that which he possessed that was truly genuine. Let us be satisfied to say that Graciliano Ramos might have been not our Balzac but our Jean Giono or,

at the other extreme, our Caldwell. Literary "events" led him to be a novelist divided between a vocation that opposed dominant currents and a work that sought to reconcile those antagonisms.

Let us add that his Queirozian or Balzaquian side suffered from an obvious weakness: Graciliano Ramos lacked imagination and notably social imagination (which would be inexplicable in a militant Communist if his adherence to Communism had not stemmed from the same kind of misunderstandings as his adherence to literary Modernism). All of his novels begin and end with the individual; they are "stories" of the Northeast composed more or less on the same plane employed by the regional story tellers. In that regard nothing is more typical than the conversations of Alexandre and Cesária; they reveal certain of the novelist's limitations, just as they reveal the effort which was, after all was said and done, his novelesque work and what came from it.

That work was a victory over himself in every sense of the word. It is not by accident that in the **"Pequena História da República"** he refers to José da Alencar as a "splendid novelist": in the history of the Modernist novel we still have not studied the schizophrenic presence of the writer from Ceará. The subject is too vast to be undertaken at this point. Let us only say that the theoretical fate of Graciliano Ramos, if the direction suggested by *Caetés* had not undergone the abrupt change which the sudden entrance into the world of literary professionalism imposed upon him, would have been that of a modern José de Alencar (much more than an Eça de Queiroz or a Balzac). He took from Alencar the idealizing vision and the sense of the uniqueness of the character. Both understood literature as a linguistic creation and as a national creation; both saw the novel as an essentially epic form of literature. It simply happens that José de Alencar was able to reach fulfillment and become a "splendid novelist," while Graciliano Ramos stifled his native tendencies and took his place in a literary picture which opposed them. At last it was all resolved for the best, since he was warmly and sincerely applauded for being what he was not. But he himself, I hold, was aware of so many confounding errors which, it seemed, could be righted through revolution, a revolution which would destroy the society which opposed him and, with a shining miracle, would restore to him his rightful unity. Graciliano Ramos's revolution was also Alencar's: a romantic revolution. At heart his disturbed and disturbing life could have been the great novel which lay in his power to create and which he almost wrote in the *Memórias do Cárcere.* (pp. 302-06)

> *Wilson Martins, "Graciliano Ramos," in his* The Modernist Idea: A Critical Survey of Brazilian Writing in the Twentieth Century, *translated by Jack E. Tomlins, 1970. Reprint by Greenwood Press, 1979, pp. 300-06.*

RICHARD A. MAZZARA (essay date 1974)

[*Mazzara is an American educator specializing in Romance languages and literature. In the following excerpt from his* Graciliano Ramos, *the only book-length biographical and critical study of Ramos in English, Mazzara discusses Ramos's place among his contemporaries and the autobiographical nature of Ramos's fiction.*]

Graciliano Ramos was outstanding among Brazilian writers engaged in a new cultural mission starting in the 1930's. Somewhat apart from the mainstreams of Modernism and Regionalism because of its author's age, location, and temperament, his work reveals from the beginning a happy blend of regional and universal elements. Graciliano, unlike many of his fellow Northeasterners and other compatriots, always favored celebrated European novelists of the Realist and Naturalist movements as models. It was in these largely traditional molds that he poured his own very personal materials, often autobiographical in whole or in part. Nor should the great Brazilian novelist Machado de Assis be overlooked as an important model, although contrasts between the two writers are as significant as comparisons.

Consequently, Graciliano escapes both the picturesque excesses typical of regionalists of all ages and the linguistic eccentricity that characterizes Modernists. His work develops subjects and themes on the individual as well as on the collective levels, in forms that are classical in the best sense of the word. Graciliano has left a faithful portrait of modern Brazilian life with all its problems. Meticulous and vigorous in his art, he re-creates the human scene more than the physical landscape, sometimes showing the influence of the latter on the former, sometimes the interpretation by the human of the physical surroundings. Like other modern and contemporary writers, Graciliano depicts the decadence of a ruling class, in particular that of his native *sertão* (drought-ridden backlands), but avoids the trivial of so much Regionalistic literature. Above all, he emphasizes the result on individuals of the contrasts and conflicts of Brazilian life in his time, very much including himself both as author and actor.

Ironically, the "discovery" of Graciliano Ramos and the publication of *Caetés* in 1933 made him a Modernist. He seems to have felt obliged to adhere somewhat to the artistic and political tenets of the movement. Having been drawn out of his relative isolation, Graciliano produced his best novels, although not necessarily his most significant or authentic work. He was not comfortable with the Modernists' sometimes studied negligence in linguistic matters, nor with "Socialist Realism." His use of down to earth language is always appropriate and formally correct. Although it is as valid to interpret Graciliano's works "sociologically" as it is to so interpret those of his fellow Northeasterners, his writings are better classified as "psychological" whether they are autobiographical or not. The realism of the best of them results from artistic distillation rather than from any doctrinaire attitude. (pp. 7-8)

Significantly, Graciliano's first three novels are written in the first person. *Vidas Sêcas* is not, but the writer has penetrated his characters so thoroughly that, despite the use of the third person, the reader scarcely notices that it is not the first person. In *Infância* and *Memórias do Cárcere* Graciliano resumes the use of the first person—to be sure, the first work has many autobiographical elements and the second is pure autobiography. Seldom can an author disengage himself from one of his leading characters, and, as he himself seems to have realized, Graciliano less than most.

One always assumes that the writer is hiding behind the narrator-character, although this device does not necessarily serve as a mask. In Graciliano's case the assumption is quite correct, especially as regards the identity of philosophies of life and art between characters and author, and their awareness of them. Graciliano's world is seemingly one in which Naturalistic determinism reigns largely unopposed, and in which people suffer with few amenities or poetry of any sort. Like their author, his characters are, however, very conscious and critical of themselves. Their surroundings tend to be accessory, other people secondary, and any effort at satisfaction or a higher

emotion illusory. It is as though man wished to be nature's accomplice, but ennobling himself through consciousness as he is destroyed. Thus, Graciliano's style is quite different from that of Machado de Assis, whose narrator, Dom Casmurro, uses precise composition and language in an attempt to deceive himself and his reader. Graciliano's narrators are careful with language, sometimes to the point of contradicting their station in life thereby, but in the interest of revealing the truth about themselves and their fellows as directly as possible. Like their creator, they employ honest, earthy language when required by the subject. In a sense they are "cultivated backlanders," to use the epithet that came to be applied to Graciliano both as a writer and as a man. The semi-legendary figure thus described becomes all the more vivid when concrete comparisons are made between him and his chief characters. Whether or not they are autobiographical, whether or not Graciliano was proud of his work, they reveal their creator's personality. Their world, although it reflects his faithfully, is one in which Graciliano could accommodate himself better than in his own. (pp. 26-7)

[The] study of literature and writing became a refuge early in the life of Graciliano Ramos. His background and environment prepared him to be not only withdrawn bùt misanthropic. Although he had written and published poetry, Graciliano's most important works exhibit little that is normally thought of as poetic imagination, aesthetic beauty, or gentle emotion. These seem to have slight place in the grimly realistic world of the author and the man.

João Valério, the protagonist of *Caetés,* seeks to forget his humdrum existence, including what turns out to be a petty love affair, in the novel that he vainly attempts to compose. Paulo Honório and Luís da Silva wish to re-create and understand their tragic lives. *São Bernardo* is Paulo Honório's memoirs and *Angústia* the narrative of Luís da Silva's derangement. As João Valério observes and meditates more than he acts, he realizes that true life closely resembles the book on the life of cannibals that he is trying to create with such difficulty, so much so that he no longer feels the need to write it. *Caetés* is that book. Paulo Honório sets out consciously and conscientiously to order what remains of his life by ordering and setting down his recollections of what has happened. Emotion seems occasionally to impede his efforts, and he fuses periods in time and events. Luís da Silva's unbalanced mind interferes constantly with his narration. The author and reader collaborate with each other and with the characters to establish the necessary relationships and draw conclusions. Reality is thus transformed into art, which gives form and meaning to life. What makes the process unique in Graciliano's novels, as well as in the autobiographical writing, is his deliberateness and the degree to which the results are personal.

Apparently quite different from other works because of its division into units resembling short stories more than the chapters of a novel, the use of the third person, and the more humble station of its principal characters, *Vidas Sêcas* is as representative of Graciliano as an artist and a man as his other writings. Although not his most successful genre, the short story was practiced by Graciliano to a considerable degree. Apart from collections of writings designated as short stories, there is evidence of his inclination toward the genre in the structure of *Infância* and *Memórias do Cárcere* as well as in *Vidas Sêcas*. As to the third person, it has already been noted that this device does not prevent the reader from imagining often that the characters, who address themselves in the third person, are in fact using the first. The supposedly objective device was no doubt required because of the extremely primitive nature in every respect of Fabiano, his family, and their dog. Yet these *sertanejos* are types with whom Graciliano was most familiar and could identify; they represent him especially well when they reveal surprising depths of intellect and emotion, despite their seeming incapacity to communicate verbally.

A Modernist in spite of himself, Graciliano, whether he makes use of a narrator or not, or narrates in his own first person, plunges the reader into the matter of his work. There is generally no pretense of having planned the book in advance; on the contrary, more often there is a protest against such planning or a complaint of inability to plan. Largely memoirs and episodic in character, Graciliano's works have less obvious need of structure than other forms of literature. Paulo Honório had engaged *littérateurs* of his acquaintance to write his story, but soon became disgusted with their artifices. These were no doubt attributable as much to their traditionalist rhetoric as to the composite nature of the project. (Incidentally, it is interesting that Graciliano should later have collaborated with several Northeastern colleagues in a similar venture or misadventure.) Paulo Honório chooses to tell his own tale forthrightly, with a minimum of false literature. It will be recalled that João Valério concludes that the book he has been struggling to produce is vain compared with life as he observes it and meditates upon it. Luís da Silva, despite apparent good taste and a keen critical faculty, is a hack writer who thinks vaguely of composing a great work one day. Much like João Valério's description and commentary, Luís' narrative of his background and recent tragic events turns out to be the book that he would probably never have written. *Vidas Sêcas* is a similar record of the innermost thoughts and feelings of Fabiano and those close to him, kept by Graciliano without benefit of a narrator. He had always dealt quite faithfully in real life, if not precisely in autobiography, and did not therefore need the intermediary of a narrator-character to lend plausibility to his work. The autobiographies do not, of course, require this particular literary device either, although they are not lacking in others.

As long as he wrote about the kind of people he knew intimately (and chiefly about himself), the lives they led, the problems they faced, great or small, and the setting in which they resolved them, Graciliano seems to have felt that his stories should for the most part tell themselves. There was much less laissez-faire, however, in his attitude regarding content and style. His function was to provide the knowledge necessary to the reader and to analyze it, sometimes openly, sometimes more discreetly, but always in language that was as pure, clear, and honest as he could make it. Graciliano and his characters, whether they write or not, are sociologists and psychologists in their fields, and both realists and classicists, if not with respect to overall form, certainly in regard to particulars. Theirs are reactions and accommodations to the life of their day and art, past and present, as well as reflections of personal temperament. Purity and clarity of style were difficult to find in most traditional and contemporary Brazilian literature, and Modernist honesty seemed of little value to Graciliano if expressed in gross, obscure language. If others had been able to add color and relevance for their times to classical forms, so could he, and *le mot juste* could be a well-placed regionalism or earthy expression and remain respectable. Graciliano disciplined himself to these ends.

As to the gentler emotions, their background and temperament tend to make Graciliano and his protagonists repress them. The misanthropes among them resemble other misanthropes, however, and the rougher types are no more of one piece than they. Both kinds of characters require and respond to love, although their awareness of this need may become clear only after they have been subjected to and purged by more violent emotions. (pp. 27-30)

All of Graciliano's work is a repetition with variants of his whole existence. As he constantly revised a given work because of dissatisfaction and the desire to be perfect, so from work to work he reevaluated his life and career from fresh, complementary points of view.

In *Memórias do Cárcere* Graciliano Ramos reveals the worst and the best of his experience as an adult. He has been forced almost without respite to come to grips with all forms of humanity while in prison. Like his protagonists, he has been unable frequently to escape mental and physical anguish except through the most primitive forms of sedation and apathy. His attitudes toward his fellows and the human condition are reinforced, to be sure, and, on those occasions when he is able to work, he is more than normally convinced of the futility of writing. Yet Graciliano is sometimes surprised, perhaps all the more so at the time of composition, after a lapse of some years, to observe the kindness of individuals and solidarity of certain groups of his recent acquaintance.

It is almost as though the note of hope to be found in earlier works were wishful thinking on his part, now realized in fact as he recollects, and doubtless reinterprets, life in prison after the fact. Graciliano wonders if his memory fails him and if the reader will believe what he writes of good works performed under abnormal conditions. Accustomed as he is to contrary actions and to considering these universal, he further wonders if he is capable of being less hostile, more outgoing, and truly generous. Much like Paulo Honório, Graciliano finds it hard to believe people completely selfless. Like Paulo Honório, too, he regrets his objectivity and consequent pessimism. This regret, plus some good deeds, save him and his protagonists after João Valério from the cynicism and pettiness of Machado de Assis' narrators. One admires Graciliano for his powers of observation and urgent need for the most part to record what he sees and thinks as impartially as possible. Again resembling his protagonists, the novelist-memorialist considers the material, psychological, and moral problems of life chiefly from his own experience, leaving little to the imagination either in the realm of nonfiction or fiction. (pp. 31-2)

From the purely human point of view, Graciliano seems closest to Fabiano of all his fictional protagonists. Fabiano's usual lack of sophistication and apparent inability to articulate, however, make him Graciliano's spokesman in a literary sense as well. The resemblance is particularly noticeable when Fabiano's reactions and mental processes occasionally become superior to what one comes to expect of him. I have pointed out how, in addition to the content of some chapters, the perspective and organization of *Infância* remind the reader especially of *Vidas Sêcas*. The themes and structures of the *Memórias* reveal further the closeness of Graciliano to Fabiano in many episodes that tell of the incredible humiliation endured by the author and his fellows in prison. The pain of this experience echoes that of Graciliano's childhood, recorded with his conclusions in *Infância* and prolonged throughout his life and other works. Graciliano and his protagonists isolate and insulate themselves against others, yet they do not like being ''strangers'' and must break into the outer world in one way or another.

Despite great culture, which he manifests often enough, Graciliano's *sertanejo* characteristics again identify him most closely with Fabiano. He is by nature and conditioning somewhat rough, and it suits him to be so both in life and art. Believing life generally empty of real poetry, Graciliano mistrusts poetic literature and claims to be ignorant of it. It is known that he wrote and published verse, however, and he gives evidence of being a fine judge of poetry. Having experienced little of the gentler emotions, he feared superficial sentimentality. For all their repression and restraint, Graciliano and his protagonists can be tender as well as explosively passionate. Paulo Honório cares for his old foster mother and his son. Fabiano loves his family, however crudely, and Graciliano's style in *Vidas Sêcas,* e.g., his discreet use of diminutives, reveals affection for Fabiano's sons. In the *Memórias* Graciliano repeatedly shows a certain fondness and concern for his own wife and children; if he is grouchy or apathetic on occasion, circumstances as much as temperament are responsible.

The rude terms employed by the "cultivated backlander" are well known through his narrators in works of fiction and autobiography alike. Like other forms of disparagement, they are directed against the self as much as against others. More than masochistic or misanthropic, Graciliano's sufferings made him wish to be honest with everyone. If others are "burros," so is he at times, and he can send his own work to the devil as well as another's. Indeed, he is his own severest critic so that he can be severe with others. The situation at the conclusion of *Vidas Sêcas* seems to be repeated when Graciliano tells the reader that he will never return to Alagoas. He now realizes that his troubles have been the fault of a naïve presumption in thinking his efforts of any consequence. Fabiano's hope of a better life elsewhere, however, is absent in his creator, whose bitter irony in *Vidas Sêcas* is made evident from the *Memórias.* Finding no persons guilty, Graciliano nonetheless cannot absolve the dirty business in which all have become enmeshed. His proposed educational reforms would render too many incompetents unhappy. It is better that they continue to teach patriotic songs and otherwise make dolts of the children. Like Fabiano and others who suffer in Graciliano's books, the memorialist blames the system rather than the individuals who are its instruments. Nevertheless, his reactions must inevitably be directed against concrete persons. Resolutely negative concerning society, normally reserved with individuals even when he admires them, Graciliano seems most enthusiastic about humanity. In any case, the future Communist continues to care, which is to hope, and therefore to write, much as Fabiano sets out to seek a better life.

In the *Memórias,* then, as in all of Graciliano Ramos' career, there are two fundamental, contradictory tendencies. Graciliano the man, the several protagonists through whom he projects himself, and sometimes secondary characters too, are subject to many chaotic impulses. These are usually triggered from outside the individual. Sometimes actively, sometimes passively, he exercises his will against them. Paulo Honório's negativism is seen in his ruthless climb to wealth and power. Luís da Silva is antisocial in a passive way until he murders Julião Tavares and enters his delirium. Graciliano reacts much like the narrator of *Angústia,* rejecting his environment psychosomatically to the point of terminating many vital bodily functions. Graciliano the thinker and artist strives to dominate the confusion through clarity and harmony, and he imposes these controls on his creatures. The struggle between the two opposing currents is the basic theme of Graciliano's work and determines its structures. A simple, terse, clear style is the chief instrument employed by Graciliano to bring order out of chaos. If he does not succeed in every instance, it is because Graciliano's re-creation, like life, does not always succeed. If his characters do not triumph, or triumph only in a limited or ambiguous sense, it is because Graciliano's work must reflect life. Their efforts to succeed, largely through the medium placed at their disposal by the author, reflect life also. The struggle through a prolonged, highly tense period leads, however, from one extreme to its antithesis, as in classical drama. (pp. 69-71)

> *Richard A. Mazzara, in his* Graciliano Ramos, *Twayne Publishers, Inc., 1974, 123 p.*

ASHLEY BROWN   (essay date 1979)

[*Brown is an American educator and critic. In the following excerpt, he elaborates on the relationship between subject and form in Ramos's novels, observing that Ramos's development of form distinguishes him from other Brazilian writers whose work is flawed by their emphasis on sociological and didactic matters at the expense of artistry.*]

Since about 1930 a group of novelists in the North-east, including José Lins do Rêgo, Rachel de Queiroz, and Jorge Amado, as well as Graciliano Ramos, have been important.

This is the part of Brazil which most resembles the South in the United States—say the coastal plantations of Mississippi and Louisiana falling away towards the dry lands of Texas and Oklahoma. Salvador, the old colonial capital, recalls New Orleans in various ways (cooking, architecture, popular culture), and nothing reminds you more of Louisiana than the oil-drilling operations along the Bahían coast. In the North-east the plantation economy has been slowly deteriorating for several generations now, and the "new men" have challenged the power of the old patriarchs and their system without necessarily improving things. In short, we have a situation similar to that in the American South during the 1930s, the Agrarian decade, when novelists as different as Faulkner and Erskine Caldwell and Caroline Gordon dramatized the regional crisis.

In 1954 an American scholar, Fred P. Ellison, published a very useful study of the literary *nordestinos* in *Brazil's New Novel* [see excerpt dated 1954]. Professor Ellison is perhaps too generous in his praise of this regional movement. He has a way of separating the "sociology" from the "psychology" which is not altogether convincing. A novel of permanent value should never have to be justified according to its documentation, and I think it likely, according to Professor Ellison's own account, that many of the novels of the North-east have only this interest—they are "about" a certain phase of Brazilian history. Critics and readers in Rio and Sao Paulo were, as they should have been, shocked by the revelations of social failure—starvation, brutality, and ignorance on every hand. But the sociological (not to say the didactic) intentions of some of these writers often flaw their work. I should exempt Graciliano Ramos entirely from this criticism.

His four novels exhibit a masterly development of form; one might say that in each case the subject is discovered *through* the form. In *Caetés* the narrator, Joao Valério, is writing a historical novel about the Caeté Indians, who lived in Alagoas at the time of the Portuguese conquest; cannibals, they were said to have devoured the first bishop of Brazil. (Ralph Edward Dimmick, the translator of *Barren Lives,* notes that Graciliano Ramos may have borrowed the device of the historical novel from Eça de Queiroz [see excerpt dated 1965].) But Joao Valério abandons his work; he rightly claims that he cannot fathom the savage mind. And as the novel proceeds, he thinks that *he* is a savage. Graciliano Ramos actually sets his story in Palmeira dos Indios. The action has Joao Valério, a clerk in a store, starting an affair with Luisa, the wife of his employer and friend Adriao Teixeira. During her husband's absence she gives herself to Joao. When the husband is informed of this he commits suicide. The unscrupulous Joao and Luisa, however, discover that they no longer have any use for each other and they part. To mention Eça de Queiroz is perhaps to think of his master Flaubert, and indeed this novel is a kind of *Madame Bovary,* if one could imagine the story told from the point of view of one of Emma's lovers. It is, in the last analysis, the drama of a mind, and the perspective afforded by the abandoned historical novel gives us just the ironic complication that we need to see the savagery that cuts across civilized values. Technically, at least, this is as advanced as Conrad; certainly it is no mean achievement for a first novel, and it will not quite do to say, with Professor Ellison, that "There is no sustained interest in the sociological."

São Bernardo also has a strong-minded narrator, Paulo Honório, a poor youth who aspires to become the owner of Sao Bernardo, the plantation where he was once a labourer. He achieves his end through the most extreme methods, including murder. (The novel is set near Viçosa, whose brutality is sardonically described in *Childhood.*) The complication here comes with his marriage to a young schoolteacher, Madalena, a woman quite unlike himself. Eventually his cruel and jealous nature proves too much for her (he imagines that she, in her despair, is betraying him with the former owner of Sao Bernardo), and she poisons herself. The novel is really about his attempt to come to terms with his life, which he tries to put down in a narrative. Unlike the protagonist of *Caetés,* he has no historical imagination; he has to face himself with the utmost candour.

If this novel is more characteristic of Graciliano Ramos, that may be because the style is closer to the vernacular. I have heard Brazilians describe him as *sêco,* which means not "dry" or "barren" in this case but something like "laconic." The language is pruned away sometimes to bare utterance, dialogue is gradually abandoned (in *Childhood* it hardly appears), the sentences are often remarkably short for Portuguese. Certainly by the time he wrote *São Bernardo* Ramos had taken the language of prose fiction some distance from the ironic inflections of Machado de Assis, and perhaps his importance for the Brazilian novel was that he showed how it could proceed without being dependent on the stylistic devices of the late nineteenth century. In this respect he resembles Hemingway.

The most extraordinary of the novels, and the masterpiece in my opinion, is *Anguish* (*Angústia*). Here Graciliano Ramos shows himself to be the Brazilian writer who has most successfully absorbed certain technical devices of the modern European novel, for instance the "interior monologue." But he must also be indebted to Machado de Assis (especially in *Dom Casmurro*), who, by concentrating on a single consciousness and its shifting contradictory moods, brings us to the centre of a psychological drama. (The difference between them, however, is that Machado de Assis, like many great comic writers, plays a game with the reader about the illusion of his art.) Thus *Anguish* is not only the story of Luís da Silva, it is the projection of his paranoia as it draws him towards insanity. His early experience, involving the ruin of a way of life on the family plantation, has scarred him, and he obsessively rehearses the painful images of his childhood. Again we have the story told

by the protagonist, this time a petty bureaucrat with literary ambitions, reduced to near-poverty in Maceió. Again we have the jealousy that destroys. Luís da Silva is undone by his thwarted desire for the faithless girl next door, Marina, and his jealousy of the rival Juliao Tavares. He eventually murders Juliao. Three of Graciliano Ramos' novels, then, turn on much the same action, but here it has been carried forward to an excruciating pitch.

Although the story is not in itself remarkable, its mode of rendition is, with the past erupting into the present in a kind of continuum as the narrator broods over his wrongs:

> I enter the room and seek a refuge in the past. But I cannot hide myself completely in it. In the first place, I am no longer what I was then. I lack the tranquillity, the innocence; I have become a rag that the city has worn out and defiled.

Much of the narration occurs in the present tense, as we follow Luís da Silva out of his dark room with its view of a garbage heap, on his futile streetcar ride to the seaside (symbolically, his only attempt to escape the self-centred existence of his room). We listen with him to the noises of a sexual encounter through the wall which separates him from the adjoining house. We feel his humiliation at the hands of Marina, who spends his money on her "trousseau." And we follow him on the night when he strangles the odious Juliao. The final paragraph, ten pages long, is a crescendo of madness. Lurking in the background is the old servant Vitória, burying her savings in the yard and digging them up to count them: a passive counterpart to the death-in-life which has its chief focus in Luís da Silva.

In *Anguish* Graciliano Ramos has more boldly than before used characters and scenes from his own life, and many of these appear later in *Childhood*: Amaro the cowboy and José Baia, Antônio Justino and his school, Father Inácio berating his parishioners, André Laerte the barber, Sergeant José da Luz in his uniform, the frogs on the Penha dam, the noise of the cotton gin in the Cavalo-Morto, and the terrible droughts of the *sertao*. His protagonist here, unlike those in the earlier novels, has nothing to look forward to; he is imprisoned by the past. The close "existential" observation of psychic life is a nightmare.

I use the term "existential" deliberately. *Anguish* resembles in certain ways another novel of the 1930s, Jean-Paul Sartre's *Nausea,* and I mention this in order to indicate how far Graciliano Ramos has come into the mainstream of modern fiction. . . . There can be no possibility of Sartre's having influenced Ramos, whose novel was published two years earlier. In each case we have the distraught narrator viewing the world from his room in a provincial seaport (Sartre's Bouville is Le Havre). We have the constant eruption of the past, the presentation of events as if they were happening now, the acute feeling that civilized life has broken down. Both narrators look upon the townspeople with amused contempt if not loathing. Neither has any connection with family or colleagues (who in fact don't exist in the foreground). The effect of this odd kind of restricted vision is to make us see things as though for the first time; it is the perception, not the action, that counts.

Nausea, which is Sartre's chief contribution to modern fiction, is important, but I regard Graciliano Ramos' novel as the more powerful. It has a completed action, it doesn't draw back from the horrific implications of the situation. At the end of *Nausea* we find Roquentin attaining a rather dubious salvation through hearing for the last time an American song, "Some of These

Days,'' which purifies his existence. We are even led to believe that he will write a novel: "It would be beautiful and hard as steel and make people ashamed of their existence.'' The nightmare of *Anguish* never relents.

How did Ramos in Maceió and Sartre in Le Havre write novels so similar in technique and theme? The explanation is that both of them are descended from Dostoevsky, and specifically *Notes from Underground*. Ramos and Sartre don't have the apocalyptic tone of their great forerunner—indeed Sartre can be almost comic—but the Dostoevsky strategy should be clear. (pp. 9-13)

With *Barren Lives* (*Vidas Sêcas*) Graciliano Ramos turns to the enclosed world of the poor inhabitants of the *sertao*, somewhat like Faulkner in moving from Quentin Compson in *The Sound and the Fury* to the Bundrens in *As I Lay Dying*. The technique of this novel is not as original as Faulkner's, but the problem is much the same: how to give dignity to a family who can scarcely articulate themselves. It is the mark of a superior writer, I think, to be able to deal with such a subject without being patronizing. That is where Faulkner and Ramos succeed and Steinbeck in *The Grapes of Wrath* fails. Faulkner solves the problem in part by contriving an intricate point of view that allows the narration to pass rapidly from one member of the family to another. (p. 13)

Ramos solves the problem, to begin with, by working without a narrator for the first time in his novel-writing career. The author hovers, as it were, over the action and follows events with a movie camera. This is a strikingly visual book in which very little lies outside the pictorial framework:

> The jujube trees spread in two green stains across the reddish plain. The drought victims had been walking all day; they were tired and hungry. Generally they did not get very far, but after a long rest on the sands of the riverbed they had gone a good three leagues. For hours now they had been looking for some sign of shade. The foliage of the jujubes loomed in the distance, through the bare twigs of the sparse brush.

So the novel begins.... A great deal follows from this first paragraph, and when Nelson Pereira dos Santos made his beautiful film of *Barren Lives,* his camera angles were already set up by the author. This is not to say that Ramos is completely external to the psychology of his characters—we see what they see—but we infer the complications of mind from the small events that compose the book—things as poignant as the death of the family dog. The human lives are simply part of the events.

The family who are the subject of the novel have no name: they are simply Fabiano the herdsman, his wife Vitória, and two young sons. They come out of nowhere, driven across the *sertao* by the drought, settle for a time on an abandoned ranch, survive various disasters and humiliations, and at the end they are ruined once more by the drought and start out on another journey. The book thus has a simple cyclical form. The author perhaps "forces" his last sentence out of the pictorial framework: "And to the city from the backland would come ever more and more of its sons, a never-ending stream of strong, strapping brutes like Fabiano, Vitória, and the two boys.'' But this is the generalization which the informed reader—at least in Brazil—would draw from the events. In recent years a popular singer, Maria Bethania, has made a great success of a song called "Carcará,'' the Brazilian name for a vulture-like hawk, a symbol of the social distress of the North-east. In

Graciliano Ramos' book (which is not a "protest" work like the song) the vultures are very real and fearful as the wretched farm animals die slowly under the heat. It is a graphic and substantial little novel.

The world of *Childhood* (*Infância*) is Brazil not long after the end of the Empire in 1889. (Unlike other South American countries, Brazil, after its independence in 1822, maintained a monarchy.) In 1891, the year before Graciliano Ramos was born, Marshal Deodoro da Fonseca became the first president of the Republic, but he assumed dictatorial powers and was forced to resign. In *Childhood* he and other political figures of the 1890s are occasionally mentioned in the conversation of the older generation, but we feel that the North-east is far from the centre of revolt and power in Rio de Janeiro. The other great event of the period was the abolition of slavery (by an edict issued by Princess Isabel), which occurred in 1888 and in fact brought down the Empire. This had a drastic effect on the great landowners of the North-east. Although the ethos of the slavery era lingered on in Graciliano Ramos' boyhood, racial attitudes are not easy to assess by his account of them. Antagonism undoubtedly existed, but the overt racialism that developed in the United States during the late nineteenth century was not a feature of Brazilian public life. I suspect that miscegenation had already gone too far for that to happen.

But public events are only the enveloping action of the book. This is the story of a child's finding his vocation as a writer: a theme which is familiar in the fiction of Europe and the United States. To some North Americans and Europeans Brazil is an oral culture where people are always in groups, always talking, gossiping, arguing. Life is spent out of doors in this fashion much of the time, and I have often observed that the printed word does not count so much for even educated Brazilians, who can be very sophisticated indeed. It is significant that Graciliano Ramos as a child is always *hearing* the letters of the alphabet or the snatches of poetry and song that are his introduction to the literary art. (pp. 13-15)

Childhood is, among other things, the best account that we have of the North-east of Brazil in the 1890s. (The only comparable book is *The Diary of "Helena Morley"* that Elizabeth Bishop introduced to American readers in 1957: the diary kept by a young girl in a remote part of Minas Gerais during the same period.) But we get into the life of the family and community only gradually, as the adult Ramos attempts to penetrate the infant's clouded vision:

> A new interruption. The shadows enveloped me, almost impenetrable, broken by vague flashes of light: the earrings and the dark complexion of Miss Leopoldina, the leather jacket of Amaro the cowboy, the white teeth of José Baía, a face of a pretty girl (my natural sister), harsh voices, the bellowing of animals almost like human speech. The rascal José still hadn't made himself known. My father and mother remained large, fearful, unknown. I see again only fragments of them, wrinkles, angry eyes, irritated mouths without lips, hands—some hard and calloused, others fine and gentle, transparent. I hear knocks, shots, curses, and jingling of spurs, the stamping of shoes on worn bricks. Shreds of cloth and sounds were scattered about. Fear. It was fear that guided me through my first years, real terror.

Out of this welter of sensations some human images emerge which endure through a lifetime. There is the ranch hand José

Baía, his first friend, who sings the slightly tall tale about his origins:

> I was born in seven months,
> I was raised but never weaned.
> I drank milk from a hundred cows
> At the gate of our corral.

There is "the rascal José," the small black boy who has a chapter to himself later on—a rather painful lesson for Graciliano. There are the grandfathers, especially the maternal one, a strong figure who stands out against the *sertao*:

> His gestures were slow. A man of immense vigour, he survived the dry seasons, sometimes in prosperity, sometimes in despair, courageously reconstructing the fortune that generally didn't materialize. He listened peacefully to conversation, his red handkerchief on his shoulder or knees, his blue eyes lost in the familiar rough land covered by a second growth of trees, perceiving signs unfamiliar to the common observer.

Most of all there are the parents, the father unpredictable and stern, the mother neurotic and sometimes violent. It is not the happiest childhood, at least in its human aspects, but even at the beginning there is a kind of celebration of living that I think of as typically Brazilian. The glazed china vase filled with pitomba fruit, the dam that blocked "the great expanse of water where ducks and teals were swimming, the incredible plague of pumpkins, "looking like a beautiful shifting pavement"—these images from the first chapter alone build up the sense of a natural world that sustains the spirit through the most painful human encounters.

The human encounters, however, are the substance of the book, and after the first few chapters the narrative is less of a prose-poem. Ramos' relationship with his father is difficult. This handsome man, so authoritative, on horseback "very swanky, as though he were riding in a joust, executing his part according to the rules," can sink into total despondency and then lash out in a single-minded anger. The incident of the broad belt is painful enough—"the first contact that I had with justice." Then there is the occasion when "the rascal José" is beaten and Graciliano intervenes—this ends with Gracilian receiving the punishment. But at an important moment the father, no doubt ashamed because his son is almost illiterate at the age of nine, commands him to fetch a book and open it. The boy reads it aloud in his painful way, "moaning, like a car on a road filled with holes."

> Perhaps the businessman had collected some lost debt: in the middle of the chapter he started talking to me; he asked me if I understood what I had read. He explained that this was a story, a novel; he demanded attention and summarized the part already read. A couple with children walked through a forest on a winter night, pursued by wolves and wild dogs. After much running, these creatures arrived at the shack of a woodsman. Was it or wasn't it? He translated for me in kitchen talk several literary expressions. I was encouraged to chat. Yes, there really was something in the book, but it was difficult to know everything.

This is his effective entrance into the world of printed pages; it is a difficult process. But his mind is taken over by a book for the first time, and soon he works his way through the ridiculous Samuel Smiles to better things. Within three years he is a contributor to a little magazine called *Dawn* in Maceió; his literary career is under way.

Childhood is in my opinion the most attractive of Ramos' books. Always extremely honest as a writer, Ramos has, as I have suggested, drawn directly on his own experience for his fiction. ***Childhood*** is a memoir written like a novel, episodic in structure but beautiful in its cumulative force and "felt life," and perhaps he has here the form most congenial to his nature. Few writers have told us so acutely what it means to grow up, to find one's "identity." (pp. 15-17)

> *Ashley Brown, "Graciliano Ramos: An Introduction," in* Childhood *by Graciliano Ramos, translated by Celso de Oliveira, Peter Owen Limited, London, 1979, pp. 7-17.*

ADDITIONAL BIBLIOGRAPHY

Aiex, Nola Kortner. "From Rural to Urban: A Painful Transition." *Proceedings: Pacific Northwest Council on Foreign Languages* XXX, Parts 1 and 2 (19-21 April 1979): 106-08.
> Compares Ramos's *Anguish* with Ciro dos Anjos's *O Amanuense Belmiro*, novels published within a year of each other which represent two different treatments of "the urbanization of the traditional rural families of the Brazilian interior." According to Aiex, although both novels present pessimistic visions of their worlds, the tone of *O Amanuense Belmiro* is gentle and sensitive, and the tone of *Anguish* violent, cruel, and frightening.

Burgum, Edwin Berry. "Luiz da Silva of Brazil." *The New York Times Book Review* (31 March 1946): 10.
> Review of *Anguish*, discussing the atmosphere of moral discontent in this novel, which Burgum considers "a psychological study of a grotesque and fearful kind of perversion."

De Oliveira, Celso. "Graciliano Ramos's Memoirs." *Arizona Quarterly* XLII, No. 1 (Spring 1986): 17-30.
> Examines *Childhood* as a memoir of Ramos's boyhood, an account of Brazilian life in the late nineteenth and early twentieth centuries, and a revelation of Ramos's early awakening to his artistic vocation. Ramos's life and career, including an overview of Brazilian literary culture and Ramos's association with a small group of novelists from northeast Brazil, are also discussed in this essay. De Oliveira compares Ramos's technique in *Childhood* with the techniques of Proust and Joyce, and he recommends *Childhood* as a literary work in its own right.

Fernández, Oscar. Review of *Barren Lives*, by Graciliano Ramos. *The Modern Language Journal* LI, No. 2 (February 1967): 119-20.
> Considers *Barren Lives* to be Ramos's most representative work, identifying the psychological interest, sympathetic character portrayal, pessimistic tone, and terse, economic style as the distinguishing traits of this novel. Fernández states that Ramos "sketched his portrayals with introspective illumination, with a psychological insight and intensity not generally found in other works of the same period in his country."

Harmon, Ronald M. "Time Planes and the Gaining of Conscience in Graciliano Ramos' *São Bernardo*." *Proceedings: Pacific Northwest Council on Foreign Languages* XXVIII, Part 1 (21-23 April 1977): 88-91.
> Analyzes Ramos's use of past and present tense in the narration of *São Bernardo*, arguing that "the spiritual and psychological lesions in Paulo Honório are most evident" when these two time planes "fuse to form a new, confused plane of reality." According

to Harmon, "the interplay of time planes, during which the catharsis of recounting the past develops a call to conscience in the narrator's present, is an important element in the structural vehicle by which Graciliano Ramos conveys his indictment of a malefic society."

Mazzara, Richard A. "New Perspectives on Graciliano Ramos." *Luso-Brazilian Review* V, No. 1 (June 1968): 93-100.
Discusses the circular structure of Ramos's *São Bernardo, Anguish,* and *Barren Lives,* and identifies a generally overlooked note of hope in the lives of Ramos's characters.

Parker, John. "A Self-Made Man." *The Times Literary Supplement* No. 3851 (2 January 1976): 17.
Reviews *São Bernardo* and compares Ramos with his contemporaries from northeastern Brazil. Parker commends the structure, style, and characterization of Ramos's four novels, discussing the narrator-protagonist of *São Bernardo* in particular.

Tavares de Sá, Hernane. "A Major Brazilian Novel." *The Saturday Review of Literature* XXIX, No. 15 (13 April 1946): 76.
Describes *Anguish* as "a major novel of the contemporary literary movement of Latin America," and Ramos as "one of Brazil's leading writers." According to Tavares de Sá, "what gives [*Anguish*] its power and its grip on the reader is the accumulation of vivid details, the artful repetition of incidents that builds it into an almost unbearable intensity, and above all the matter-of-fact, driving, almost casual style."

Viera, David J. "Wastelands and Backlands: John Dos Passos' *Manhattan Transfer* and Graciliano Ramos' *Angústia.*" *Hispania* LXVII, No. 3 (September 1984): 377-82.
Identifies "differences of technique, point of view, the use of time, and to some extent style" in these two novels while pointing out parallels in their "themes, motivation, conception of main characters, ideologies, imagery, and symbols."

Acknowledgments

The following is a listing of the copyright holders who have granted us permission to reprint material in this volume of *TCLC*. Every effort has been made to trace copyright, but if omissions have been made, please let us know.

THE COPYRIGHTED EXCERPTS IN TCLC, VOLUME 32, WERE REPRINTED FROM THE FOLLOWING PERIODICALS:

American Literature, v. XXXIV, January, 1963. Copyright © 1963 Duke University Press, Durham, NC. Reprinted by permission of the publisher.

The American Scholar, v. 47, Spring, 1978 for "J. G. Frazer Revisited" by Robert Ackerman. Copyright © 1978 by the author. Reprinted by permission of the publishers.

The Antigonish Review, nos. 69 & 70, 1987 for "Finding D'Sonoqua's Child: Myth, Truth and Lies in the Prose of Emily Carr" by Peter Sanger. Copyright 1987 by the author. Reprinted by permission of the publisher and the author.

The Australian Quarterly, v. XXXIX, June, 1967 for "Kipling and A. B. Paterson: Men of Empire and Action" by Clement Semmler. Copyright by the author. Reprinted by permission of the publisher and the author.

Canadian Literature, n. 33, Summer, 1967 for "Quite a Girl" by David Watmough. Reprinted by permission of the author.

Critique: Studies in Modern Fiction, v. XV, 1974. Copyright © 1974 Helen Dwight Reid Educational Foundation. Reprinted with permission of the Helen Dwight Reid Educational Foundation, published by Heldref Publications, 4000 Albemarle Street, N. W., Washington, DC 20016.

The Dalhousie Review, v. 56, Spring, 1976 for "Rereading 'Tarzan of the Apes'; or 'What Is It,' Lady Alice Whispered, 'A Man?' " by John Hollow. Reprinted by permission of the publisher and the author.

Encounter, v. XXV, November, 1965; v. XXVI, April, 1966. © 1965, 1966 by Encounter Ltd. Both reprinted by permission of the publisher.

English, v. XIV, Spring, 1962. © The English Association 1962. Reprinted by permission of the publisher.

English Literature in Transition: 1880-1920, special series, n. 3, 1985 for "Comparatively Modern Skeletons in the Garden: A Reconsideration of 'The Mayor of Casterbridge'" by W. Eugene Davis. Copyright © 1985 *English Literature in Transition: 1880-1920.* Reprinted by permission of the publisher and the author.

Essays on Canadian Writing, n. 29, Summer, 1984. © 1984 Essays on Canadian Writing Ltd. Reprinted by permission of the publisher.

ETC.: A Review of General Semantics, v. 42, Spring, 1985. Copyright © 1985 by the International Society for General Semantics. Reprinted by permission of the publisher.

Extrapolation, v. 27, Fall, 1986. Copyright 1986 by The Kent State University Press. Reprinted by permission of the publisher.

Harvard Library Bulletin, v. XXX, October, 1982 for " 'The Worst Kind of Melancholy': William James in 1869" by James William Anderson. Copyright 1982 by the President and Fellows of Harvard College. Reprinted by permission of the publisher and the author.

The Journal of Aesthetics and Art Criticism, v. XXX, Spring, 1972. Copyright © 1972 by The American Society for Aesthetics. Reprinted by permission of the publisher.

The Journal of General Education, published by The Pennsylvania State University Press, University Park, PA, v. XXVIII, Spring, 1976. Copyright 1976 by The Pennsylvania State University Press. Reprinted by permission of the publisher.

The Kenyon Review, n.s. v. V, Winter, 1983 for "The Right to Believe: William James's Reinterpretation of the Function of Religious Belief" by H. S. Thayer. Copyright 1983 by Kenyon College. All rights reserved. Reprinted by permission of the author.

Luso-Brazilian Review, v. V, June, 1968; v. VII, Summer, 1970. Copyright © 1968, 1970 by the Board of Regents of the University of Wisconsin System. Both reprinted by permission of The University of Wisconsin Press.

Meanjin, v. XXIII, December, 1964 for " 'Banjo' Paterson: A Poet Nearly Anonymous" by H. P. Heseltine. Reprinted by permission of the author./ v. XXVI, June, 1967. Reprinted by permission of the publisher.

Modern Drama, v. XIX, June, 1976; v. XXVI, March, 1983. Copyright 1976, 1983 *Modern Drama,* University of Toronto. Both reprinted by permission of the publisher.

The New York Times Book Review, June 7, 1942. Copyright 1942 by The New York Times Company. Reprinted by permission of the publisher.

Nineteenth-Century Fiction, v. 21, December, 1966 for "Character and Fate in Hardy's 'The Mayor of Casterbridge' " by Robert C. Schweik. © 1966 by The Regents of the University of California. Reprinted by permission of The Regents and the author.

Philosophy Today, v. XXVI, Winter, 1982. Copyright 1982 by the Messenger Press. Reprinted by permission of the Messenger Press, Carthagena Station, Celina, OH 45822.

The Quarterly Journal of Speech, v. LXIII, February, 1977. Copyright 1977 by the Speech Communication Association. Reprinted by permission of the publisher.

Saturday Night, v. 81, November, 1966 for "Emily Carr's Journals" by David P. Silcox. Copyright © 1966 by *Saturday Night.* Reprinted by permission of the author.

South Atlantic Quarterly, v. LXVI, Spring, 1967; v. 84, Summer, 1985. Copyright © 1967, 1985 by Duke University Press, Durham, NC. Both reprinted by permission of the publisher.

Studies in the Novel, v. IV, Winter, 1972; v. X, Spring, 1978. Copyright 1972, 1978 by North Texas State University. Both reprinted by permission of the publisher.

Victorian Studies, v. IV, September, 1960 for a review of "The Mayor of Casterbridge" by Harvey Curtis Webster. Reprinted by permission of the Trustees of Indiana University and the Literary Estate of Henry Curtis Webster.

THE COPYRIGHTED EXCERPTS IN TCLC, VOLUME 32, WERE REPRINTED FROM THE FOLLOWING BOOKS:

Aldiss, Brian W. From *Trillion Year Spree: The History of Science Fiction*. Atheneum Publishers, 1986, Victor Gollancz, 1986. Copyright © 1973, 1986 Brian W. Aldiss. Reprinted with the permission of Atheneum Publishers, an imprint of Macmillan Publishing Company. In Canada by Victor Gollancz Ltd.

Attebery, Brian. From *The Fantasy Tradition in American Literature: From Irving to Le Guin*. Indiana University Press, 1980. Copyright © 1980 by Brian Attebery. All rights reserved. Reprinted by permission of the publisher.

Barzun, Jacques. From *A Stroll with William James*. Harper & Row, 1983. Copyright © 1983 by Jacques Barzun. All rights reserved. Reprinted by permission of Harper & Row, Publishers, Inc.

Bredsdorff, Elias. From an introduction to *The Liar*. By Martin A. Hansen. Translated by John Jepson Egglishaw. Twayne, 1969. Copyright 1969 by Twayne Publishers. Reprinted with the permission of Twayne Publishers, Inc., a division of G. K. Hall & Co., Boston.

Brooks, Jean R. From *Thomas Hardy: The Poetic Structure*. Elek, 1971. © 1971 Jean R. Brooks. All rights reserved. Reprinted by permisison of Grafton Books, a division of the Collins Publishing Group.

Brown, Ashley. From "Graciliano Ramos: An Introduction," in *Childhood*. By Graciliano Ramos, translated by Celso de Oliveira. Peter Owen Limited, London, 1979. English translation © Peter Owen Ltd. 1979. All rights reserved. Reprinted by permission of the publisher.

Chandler, Frank Wadleigh. From *Aspects of Modern Drama*. The Macmillan Company, 1914. Copyright, 1914 by Macmillan Publishing Company. Renewed 1942 by F. W. Chandler.

Crane, Stephen. From *Stephen Crane: Letters*. Edited by R. W. Stallman and Lillian Gilkes. New York University Press, 1960. © 1960 by New York University. Reprinted by permission of the publisher.

Dave, Jagdish Chandra. From *The Human Predicament in Hardy's Novels*. The Humanities Press, 1985, The Macmillan Press Ltd., 1985. © Jagdish Chandra Vallabhram Dave 1985. All rights reserved. Reprinted by permission of Humanities Press International, Inc., Atlantic Highlands, NJ 07716. In Canada by Macmillan, London and Basingstoke.

Dimmick, Ralph Edward. From an introduction to *Barren Lives (Vidas Secas)*. By Graciliano Ramos, translated by Ralph Edward Dimmick. University of Texas Press, 1965. Copyright © 1965 by Heloisa de Medeiros Ramos. All rights reserved. Reprinted by permission of the publisher and Ralph Edward Dimmick.

Dunkel, Wilbur Dwight. From *Sir Arthur Pinero: A Critical Biography with Letters*. University of Chicago Press, 1941. Copyright 1941 by the University of Chicago. Renewed 1968 by Wilbur Dwight Dunkel. Reprinted by permission of the publisher.

Dziemianowicz, Stefan R. From an introduction to *Tarzan of the Apes: Four Volumes in One*. By Edgar Rice Burroughs, edited by Claire Booss. Avenel Books, 1988. Copyright © 1988 by OBC, Inc. All rights reserved. Used by permission of Avenel Books.

Ellison, Fred P. From *Brazil's New Novel: Four Northeastern Masters*. University of California Press, 1954. Copyright 1954 by The Regents of the University of California. Renewed 1982 by Fred Pittman Ellison. Reprinted by permission of the publisher.

Ford, Marcus Peter. From *William James's Philosophy: A New Perspective*. University of Massachusetts Press, 1982. Copyright © 1982 by The University of Massachusetts Press. All rights reserved. Reprinted by permission of the publisher.

Gallagher, Idella J. From *Morality in Evolution: The Moral Philosophy of Henri Bergson*. Nijhoff, 1970. © 1970 by Martinus Nijhoff. All rights reserved. Reprinted by permission of the publisher.

Geismar, Maxwell. From *Rebels and Ancestors: The American Novel, 1890-1915*. Houghton Mifflin, 1953. Copyright, 1953, by Maxwell Geismar. Renewed 1981 by Anne Geismar. All rights reserved. Reprinted by permission of Houghton Mifflin Company.

Gibson, Donald B. From *The Fiction of Stephen Crane*. Southern Illinois University Press, 1968. Copyright © 1968 by Southern Illinois University Press. All rights reserved. Reprinted by permission of the publisher.

Green, H. M. From *A History of Australian Literature, Pure and Applied: 1789-1923, Vol. I*. Angus and Robertson, 1961. © Dorothy Green, 1962, 1984. Reprinted by permission of Angus & Robertson Publishers.

Gregor, Ian. From *The Great Web: The Form of Hardy's Major Fiction*. Rowman and Littlefield, 1974, Faber, 1974. © 1974 by Ian Gregor. All rights reserved. Reprinted by permission of Rowman and Littlefield. In Canada by Faber & Faber Ltd.

Guerard, Albert J. From *Thomas Hardy: The Novels and Stories*. Cambridge, Mass.: Harvard University Press, 1949. Copyright 1949 by the President and Fellows of Harvard College. Renewed 1977 by Albert Joseph Guerard. Excerpted by permission of the publishers.

Hergesheimer, Joseph. From "Introduction: 'The Red Badge of Courage', 1895-1924," in *The Work of Stephen Crane, Vol. I*. Edited by Wilson Follett. Knopf, 1925. Copyright 1925, renewed 1953 by Alfred A. Knopf, Inc. Reprinted by permission of the Literary Estate of Joseph Hergesheimer.

Hesse, Hermann. From *My Belief: Essays on Life and Art*. Edited by Theodore Ziolkowski, translated by Denver Lindley. Farrar, Straus and Giroux, 1974. Translation copyright © 1974 by Farrar, Straus and Giroux, Inc. All rights reserved. Reprinted by permission of Farrar, Straus and Giroux, Inc.

Hoffman, Michael J. From *The Subversive Vision: American Romanticism in Literature*. Kennikat Press, 1972. Copyright © 1972 by Michael J. Hoffman. All rights reserved. Reprinted by permission of the author.

Howe, Irving. From *Thomas Hardy*. The Macmillan Company, 1967. Copyright © 1967 by Macmillan Publishing Company. Copyright © 1966 Irving Howe. All rights reserved. Reprinted with permission of the publisher.

Hyman, Stanley Edgar. From *The Tangled Bank: Darwin, Marx, Frazer and Freud as Imaginative Writers*. Atheneum, 1962. Copyright © 1959, 1960, 1961, 1962 by Stanley Edgar Hyman. All rights reserved. Reprinted with the permission of Atheneum Publishers, an imprint of Macmillan Publishing Company.

Ingwersen, Faith and Niels Ingwersen. From *Martin A. Hansen*. Twayne, 1976. Copyright 1976 by Twayne Publishers. All rights reserved. Reprinted with the permission of Twayne Publishers, a division of G. K. Hall & Co., Boston.

Ingwersen, Niels. From an introduction to *Lucky Kristoffer*. By Martin A. Hansen. Translated by John Jepson Egglishaw. Twayne, 1974. Copyright 1974 by Twayne Publishers. Reprinted with the permission of Twayne Publishers, Inc., a division of G. K. Hall & Co., Boston.

Jarvie, I. C. From *The Revolution in Anthropology*. Routledge & Kegan Paul Ltd, 1964. © I.C. Jarvie 1964. Reprinted by permission of the publisher.

Karl, Frederick R. From *An Age of Fiction: The Nineteenth Century British Novel*. Farrar, Straus and Giroux, 1964. Copyright © 1964 by Frederick R. Karl. Reprinted by permission of Farrar, Straus and Giroux, Inc.

LaFrance, Marston. From *A Reading of Stephen Crane*. Oxford at the Clarendon Press, 1971. © Oxford University Press, 1971. Reprinted by permission of Oxford University Press.

Lazenby, Walter. From *Arthur Wing Pinero*. Twayne, 1972. Copyright 1972 by Twayne Publishers. All rights reserved. Reprinted with the permission of Twayne Publishers, Inc., a division of G. K. Hall & Co., Boston.

Levinson, Henry Samuel. From *The Religious Investigations of William James*. University of North Carolina Press, 1981. © 1981 The University of North Carolina Press. All rights reserved. Reprinted by permission of the publisher.

Lewis, Wyndham. From *Time and Western Man*. Harcourt, Brace and Company, 1928. Copyright, 1928, by Harcourt, Brace and Company, Inc. Renewed 1955 by Wyndham Lewis. Reprinted by permission of the Literary Estate of Wyndham Lewis.

Lewisohn, Ludwig. From *The Modern Drama: An Essay in Interpretation*. Huebsch, 1915. Copyright 1915 by B. W. Huebsch. Renewed 1942 by Ludwig Lewisohn. Reprinted by permission of Viking Penguin, a division of Penguin Books USA, Inc.

Malinowski, Bronislaw. From *A Scientific Theory of Culture and Other Essays*. University of North Carolina Press, 1944. Copyright, renewed 1972 by The University of North Carolina Press. Reprinted by permission of the publisher.

Maritain, Jacques. From *Ransoming the Time*. Translated by Harry Lorin Binsse. Charles Scribner's Sons, 1941. Copyright 1941 Charles Scribner's Sons. Copyright renewed © 1969 by Jacques Maritain. Reprinted with the permission of Charles Scriber's Sons, an imprint of Macmillan Publishing Company.

Martins, Wilson. From *The Modernist Idea: A Critical Survey of Brazilian Writing in the Twentieth Century*. Translated by Jack E. Tomlins. New York University Press, 1970. Copyright ©, 1971 by New York University. Reprinted by permission of the publisher.

Maurois, André. From "Henri Bergson," translated by Carl Morse, in *From Proust to Camus: Profiles of Modern French Writers*. By André Maurois, translated by Carl Morse and Renaud Bruce. Doubleday & Company, 1966. Copyright © 1966 André Maurois. Reprinted by permission of the Literary Estate of André Maurois and the author's agents, Scott Meredith Literary Agency, Inc., 845 Third Avenue, New York, NY 10022.

Mazzara, Richard A. From *Graciliano Ramos*. Twayne, 1974. Copyright 1974 by Twayne Publishers. All rights reserved. Reprinted with the permission of Twayne Publishers, Inc., a division of G. K. Hall & Co., Boston.

Moskowitz, Sam. From *Explorers of the Infinite: Shapers of Science Fiction*. World Publishing Co., 1963. Copyright © 1963, 1959, 1958, 1957 by Sam Moskowitz. Copyright © 1960 by Ziff-Davis Publishing Co. Reprinted by permission of the author.

Perella, Nicolas J. From *Midday in Italian Literature: Variations on an Archetypal Theme*. Princeton University Press, 1979. Copyright © 1979 by Princeton University Press. All rights reserved. Reprinted with permission of the publisher.

Reck, Andrew J. From "The Place of William James's 'Principles of Psychology' in American Philosophy," in *The Philosophical Psychology of William James*. Edited by Michael H. DeArmey and Stephen Skousgaard. Center for Advanced Research in Phenomenology & University Press of America, 1986. Copyright © 1986 by The Center for Advanced Research in Phenomenology, Inc. University Press of America,® Inc. All rights reserved. Reprinted by permission of The Center.

Rowell, George. From an introduction to *Plays by A. W. Pinero*. Edited by George Rowell. Cambridge University Press, 1986. © Cambridge University Press 1986. Reprinted with the permission of the publishers and the author.

Russell, Bertrand. From *A History of Western Philosophy, and Its Connection with Political and Social Circumstances from the Earliest Times to the Present Day*. G. Allen and Unwin Ltd., 1946. Copyright 1945, renewed 1972 by Bertrand Russell. All rights reserved. Reprinted by permission of Unwin Hyman Ltd.

Semmler, Clement. From an introduction to *The World of "Banjo" Paterson: His Stories, Travels, War Reports, and Advice to Racegoers.* By A. B. Paterson, edited by Clement Semmler. Angus and Robertson, 1967. © Retusa Pty. Limited. Reprinted by permission of Angus & Robertson Publishers.

Siegel, Sandra. From "Literature and Degeneration: The Representation of 'Decadence'," in *Degeneration: The Dark Side of Progress.* Edited by J. Edward Chamberlin and Sander L. Gilman. Columbia University Press, 1985. Copyright © 1985 Columbia University Press. All rights reserved. Used by permission of the publisher.

Starkie, Enid. From "Bergson and Literature," in *The Bergsonian Heritage.* Edited by Thomas Hanna. Columbia University Press, 1962. Copyright © 1962 Columbia University Press. Used by permission of the publisher.

Vickery, John B. From *The Literary Impact of "The Golden Bough."* Princeton University Press, 1973. Copyright © 1973 by Princeton University Press. All rights reserved. Reprinted with permission of the publisher.

Weisinger, Herbert. From *The Agony and the Triumph: Papers on the Use and Abuse of Myth.* Michigan State University Press, 1964. Copyright © 1964 Michigan State University Press. Reprinted by permission of the publisher.

Wernham, James C. S. From *James's Will-to-Believe Doctrine: A Heretical View.* McGill-Queen's University Press, 1987. © McGill-Queen's University Press 1987. Reprinted by permission of the publisher.

Wilkins, Ernest Hatch. From *A History of Italian Literature.* Cambridge Mass.: Harvard University Press, 1954. Copyright 1954 by the President and Fellows of Harvard College. Renewed 1982 by Robert H. Wilkins. Excerpted by permission of the publishers.

Wolford, Chester L. From *The Anger of Stephen Crane: Fiction and the Epic Tradition.* University of Nebraska Press, 1983. Copyright 1983 by the University of Nebraska Press. All rights reserved. Reprinted by permission of the publisher.

PERMISSION TO REPRINT PHOTOGRAPHS APPEARING IN *TCLC*, VOLUME 32, WAS RECEIVED FROM THE FOLLOWING SOURCES:

Fonds Doucet (Seuil): pp. 1, 18

Photograph by Dangereux: p. 33

Copyright © 1975 Edgar Rice Burroughs, Inc.: p. 54

Photograph by W. E. Lake: p. 191

T. & R. Annan & Sons Ltd., Glasgow (Scotland): p. 228

Copyright Royal Danish Ministry of Foreign Affairs: p. 247

The Granger Collection, New York: p. 328

The Australian Club, Sydney, for the illustration from *A. B. (Banjo) Paterson,* by Clement Semmler, Lansdowne Press, 1965: p. 368